Psychiatry in Law/
Law in Psychiatry

Psychiatry in Law/
Law in Psychiatry

Psychiatry in Law

RALPH SLOVENKO

Brunner-Routledge
New York • London

Published in 2002 by
Brunner-Routledge
29 West 35th Street
New York, NY 10001

Published in Great Britain by
Brunner-Routledge
27 Church Road
Hove, East Sussex, BN3 2FA

Brunner-Routledge is an imprint of the Taylor & Francis Group.

Printed in the United States of America on acid-free paper.

10 9 8 7 6 5 4 3 2 1

Library of Congress Cataloging-in-Publication Data

Slovenko, Ralph.
   Psychiatry in law/law in psychiatry / Ralph Slovenko.
      p.   cm.
   Includes bibliographical references and indexes.
   ISBN 0-415-93365-X (set)—ISBN 0-415-93363-3 (vol. 1)—
   ISBN 0-415-93364-1 (vol. 2)
   1. Forensic psychiatry—United States.   2. Psychiatrists—Legal status,
laws, etc.—United States.   I. Title.

KF8965 .S59 2002
614'.1—dc21
                                                    2002018494

To the memory
of
Dr. James A. Knight
Beloved friend, colleague, and teacher

Contents

Preface

The interplay of law and psychiatry has changed markedly during the twentieth century. Before World War II the interplay was mainly the penetration by psychiatry into law, but after the war it has been primarily the other way. The practice of psychiatry is no longer unfettered as it once was. In both the case of the penetration by psychiatry into law or the penetration by law into psychiatry, there are swings of the pendulum, but whatever the vagaries of the day, there is one constant. The state—through elected officials, judges, legislators, and administrators—determines when, where, and why psychiatry and law interact.

Psychiatry in law, commonly called *forensic psychiatry*, is the application of psychiatry to legal issues for legal ends. During the nineteenth century the focus was on criminal responsibility. In the early part of the twentieth century, with the advent of Freudian psychiatric ideology, psychological principles emphasizing motivation and determinism challenged and influenced society's views toward deviant behavior. Many crimes were redefined as mental health problems. The use or abuse of alcohol or drugs was labeled a disease, like asthma or diabetes. Sex offenders came to be known as *sexual psychopaths* and were confined in special institutions. Juvenile misbehavior was classified as a problem of delinquency or neglect and received the special attention of a juvenile court. Prevailing psychological notions of child development infiltrated child custody cases. The language of psychiatry became a part of the common language of the age, so much so that the country began to sound like a giant psychiatric clinic.

In the latter part of the twentieth century, a strong backlash occurred as the states moved to demedicalize or recriminalize certain acts against society that were previously defined as mental health problems. Michigan, the first state to enact sexual psychopath legislation in 1935, repealed it in 1968, and other states followed suit. In recent years, over the objection of psychiatrists, various states have enacted *sexually violent predator* laws that target sex offenders who have a "volitional impairment" making them "dangerous beyond their control." In another development, changes in both procedural and substantive law brought about a restructuring of juvenile court processes. Juveniles are increasingly being transferred to the criminal courts to be tried as adults. There is more and more open questioning of what psychiatry can and cannot do in regard both diagnosis and treatment.

From the dawn of civilization deviant behavior has been explained in one of three ways: stupidity, sin, and sickness—with various disciplines (educators, clergy, lawyers and judges, and physicians) each using its own techniques of persuading, preaching, punishing, and prescribing. The decline in the influence of family and religion has led to a more prominent role of law and medicine, especially psychiatry, in the resolution of human conflict and controversy. Psychiatry has increasingly replaced the church as the refuge of the troubled. (Psychiatrists are called the new secular priests.) The conversion of major church buildings into law offices and centers of psychotherapy—as seen in many places—is a visible answer to Dr. Karl Menninger's question, "Whatever became of sin?" In the book by that title, Dr. Menninger pointed out that some behavior both popularly and professionally viewed as sickness is old-fashioned conscious wrongdoing or, bluntly, sin. What was formerly considered a sin is now a crime or a symptom or collective irresponsibility.

Most notably, there has been a lawyerization, as well as psychiatrization, of the country since the early 1960s. The interplay of law and psychiatry has prompted mental health professionals to become aware of legal issues and the legal profession to become aware of psychiatric issues, so much so that at times the mental health professional sounds like a lawyer and the lawyer sounds like a mental health professional.

As a discipline, the law is divided into a number of categories, including crimes, torts, contracts, property, and domestic relations. Psychiatry plays a role in all of these categories. In criminal law, mens rea, that is, a guilty mind, is an essential element. Much of the law of torts rests upon the negligence of the individual sought to be found liable. Under the law of contracts the contracting parties must have a "meeting of the minds." The validity of testamentary disposition of property is largely based on the mental competency of the testator at the time the will is formulated.

The infiltration of psychiatry into law may be broadly cataloged into matters of credibility, culpability, competency, compensation, and custody. In other words, the intermix of psychiatry in law includes problems of a witness's credibility, a defendant's competency to stand trial, the culpability of the accused, the imposition and carrying out of the death penalty, the individual's competency to make a will or contract or to take care of oneself or one's property, the compensation of injured persons, and the custody of children. Although the interplay of psychiatry in law is not limited to those areas, they constitute a major part of forensic work.

Conversely, law has played a role in the practice of psychiatry. The growing intervention of law in psychiatry has been fueled by criticism of psychiatry from both inside and outside the profession. According to civil libertarians, the primary reason underlying the recent movement to restrict coercive psychiatry is that the benevolent motive—to help the disturbed who are in distress—is not achieved by mental hospitalization, major tranquilizers, electroshock therapy, behavior modification, or psychosurgery. They put forward two additional arguments against involuntary hospitalization: (1) that the mental health system, like other social service systems, has an inherent conflict of interest, as it is responsive to those it employs as well as to its consumers; and (2), that there is no moral basis to deprive a harmless disturbed person of physical freedom for the sake of unwanted treatment by substituting a psychiatrist's decision for that of the disturbed person. As a result of these criticisms, criminal justice procedures and standards, as opposed to psychiatric professional standards, are now applied in civil commitment procedures.

Some say that physicians no longer have the best interest of patients at heart. Since 1960, civil libertarians have been challenging benevolence as a mask for intrusion and have been establishing legal rights for their clients. Legislation has been enacted—some say to enlarge the market for lawyers—that provides for the establishment of legal services for the mentally ill and developmentally disabled persons and for residents in private and public mental hospitals and in community facilities. Even more upsetting to the psychiatric profession is a sudden shift of emphasis away from self-regulation toward external governmental control. Psychiatry is now called, in the words of Dr. Jonas Rappeport, the "belegaled profession."

The most frequently law-related issues raised by psychiatrists fall into three major areas: (1) malpractice (risks of particular drugs or other forms of therapy, commitment and voluntary hospitalization, liability for acts of others, treatment without informed consent, insurance coverage, suicide, and duty to warn); (2) business-related matters; and (3) confidentiality and privilege.

The interplay of psychiatry and law was once an arcane subject matter, but since about 1960 has emerged from an elective seminar to a topic of national prominence. There has been a substantial increase in lawyer involvement and litigation in this area, essentially due to the financial support by public, private, and charitable organizations. Perhaps indicative of this relatively recently developed interest of the legal profession in problems of law as related to mental disorder is the inclusion for the first time of a special topic, *Mental Health*, in the *Sixth Decennial Digest*, the digest of court cases. A monthly summary of reported state and federal court decisions relating to mental health, *Mental Health Court Digest*, is prepared especially for mental health agencies and personnel. Beginning in 1963, the American Bar Association has published a bimonthly, *Mental & Physical Disability Law Reporter*.

During the past half-century a substantial body of literature as well as case law on psychiatry and law has developed. In particular, the decisions of Chief Justice Warren Burger of the U.S. Supreme Court and Chief Judge David L. Bazelon of the District of Columbia Circuit Court of Appeals, which figure prominently in any collection of cases, and the publications of Dr. Karl A. Menninger and of Dr. Thomas S. Szasz have stimulated discussion regarding the role of the psychiatrist in the legal process. Their untraditional and pioneering views are provocative and have reached a wide audience, including television viewers. For many students, it is Dr. Szasz's writings that prompt registration in law-psychiatry courses. One might take issue with these writings, but they will certainly be found interesting.

Also during the past half-century a number of extended programs of study and research and a number of professional organizations in law and the behavioral sciences have developed. Paralleling the broadening of the scope of psychiatric residency training programs to include community problems, concern about curriculum relevance has prompted law schools to seek breadth and depth in legal education. Foundations have made substantial grants to a number of law schools to establish interdisciplinary teaching and research in law and the behavioral sciences. The American Academy of Psychiatry and the Law (AAPL), founded in 1969, and the American Psychology-Law Society (AP-LS), founded in 1968, have rapidly grown in membership. Then, too, there are the American College of Forensic Psychiatry, American College of Forensic Psychology, and the International Academy of Law and Mental Health. The American Academy of Forensic Sciences has a section on forensic psychiatry. These associations publish specialized journals on law and psychiatry or psychology. They include the *Journal of the American Academy of Psychiatry and the Law, International Journal of Law and Psychiatry, Journal of Forensic Sciences*, and *Law and Human Behavior*. Then, too, there are *American Journal of Forensic Psychiatry, Behavioral Sciences and the Law, Journal of Psychiatry and Law*, and *Psychology, Public Policy, and Law*, and the *Hastings Center Report*. In addition, many law reviews published by law schools present symposia or feature articles on law and psychiatry. Several casebooks on law and psychiatry have been published for law school use. As a by-product, they stir up wide interest. The MacArthur Foundation has given multimillion-dollar support for research on mental health and the law.

This two-volume publication—*Psychiatry in Law/Law in Psychiatry*—is designed to serve three principal purposes. First, it is intended to serve as a course textbook for psychiatric residents and law students, and as a basic reference source for the psychiatrist or lawyer who is only occasionally confronted with problems in law and psychiatry. Secondly, it is designed to assist those practitioners who regularly work in this area by suggesting new approaches and by providing material to assist them in preparing and documenting their cases. Thirdly, it is intended to provide a critical exposition of many of the practices and basic premises of the terrain of law and psychiatry.

Acknowledgments

This work has its roots in my book *Psychiatry and Law* published in 1973 by Little, Brown. I am grateful for the reception given that book. It received the Manfred Guttmacher Award of the American Psychiatric Association and it was a selection of the Behavioral Science Book Club, and later Lederle Pharmaceuticals distributed over eight thousand copies as four paperbacks. The book was used in many training programs. Little, Brown asked that I do a second edition, but I dallied until such time that Little, Brown no longer published law or medical books. Herb Reich, then senior editor at Wiley, heard of it and persuaded me to go forward on a second edition. Many readers also from time to time asked that I do a second edition. Given the many years that have elapsed and new developments in the field, this publication is more than a second edition, hence a new title, *Psychiatry in Law/Law in Psychiatry*.

As with two other of my books, Dr. Abraham L. Halpern carefully studied the entire manuscript and provided helpful suggestions. Dr. Halpern was always encouraging, and I am most grateful to him. Dr. Halpern's impulse is always to assist and inspire. He is a friend to all who meet him. Dr. Cathy Frank and Dr. Nada Milosavljevic also read the entire manuscript and provided suggestions. Dr. Alan Felthous and Dr. Jonas Rappeport provided comments on psychiatric court clinics, and Dr. Harold I. Lief on regulation of psychotherapy. I want also to take the opportunity to thank the many people for interesting discussions over the years. I can mention only a few: Dr. Abraham L. Halpern, Dr. Harold I. Lief, Dr. Elliott Luby, Dr. George Mendelson, Dr. C. B. Scrignar, Dr. Daniel Sprehe, Dr. Emanuel Tanay, Dr. Gene L. Usdin, and Dr. Tuviah Zabow, and the late Dr. Maurice Grossman, Dr.

James A. Knight, and Dr. Karl A. Menninger. The meetings of the American Academy of Psychiatry and the Law provided nurturance and I am grateful to AAPL. I thank Matthew Lager, class of 2000 of the Wayne State University Law School, for his research assistance, Lois Cowan for her secretarial assistance, and Georgia Clark of the Wayne State University Law Library for her assistance in obtaining materials. To one and all, thank you.

Prologue

The Sporting Theory of Justice

At first sight, few things seem farther apart than the domains of law and games, for one seems solemn and the other playful, but they share many elements. The Greek word *agonia* referred to any kind of contest or conflict, and also it meant mental anguish. In considerable measure, the adversarial judicial process with its rules of evidence finds explanation in the theory of games that people play. Many of the rules are based on "the sporting theory of justice," prompting Abraham Goldstein, then dean of the Yale Law School, to observe, "Anyone familiar with games theory and with the growing literature on role playing will readily see their analogue in the adversary system."[1]

In *Homo Ludens*, a groundbreaking book published in 1944, Dutch historian Johan Huizinga described the play element in culture and pointed out the affinity between law and play. Huizinga held that play was a font for most forms of human culture, and play can have its darker side, giving rise to such phrases as *playing with people's lives, mind games, war games, sex games,* or *playing for keeps*.[2] Twenty years later, in *Games People Play*, Dr. Eric Berne described as a game the commonplace interpersonal pattern or social disturbance created to gain some secret relief or satisfaction. Berne pointed out that people tend to live their lives by consistently playing out certain games in their interpersonal relationships, which they play for a variety of reasons: to avoid confronting reality, to deal with helplessness, to conceal ulterior motives, to rationalize their activities, or to avoid actual participation. These games—if they are not destructive—are both desirable and necessary. The "courtroom game" in its everyday form, Berne says, is easily observed among children as a three-handed game between two siblings and a parent:

"Mommie, she took my candy away."
"Yes, but he took my doll, and before that he was hitting me, and anyway we both promised to share our candy."

In his thesaurus of games, Berne offers examples that strike a familiar chord.[3] The childhood prototype of cops and robbers is hide-and-seek, in which the essential element is the chagrin at being found. (The game is now called "cops and robbers and lawyers and Supreme Court.") Among older children, one who finds an insoluble hiding place, thereby spoiling the game, is regarded as not being a good sport. It is also deemed unsportsmanlike conduct for the police to hide behind plain clothes or to entrap suspects. In childhood, deception is aggravating.

The adversary method of trial, or gamesmanship under the gavel, is well suited to the popular Anglo-American conditioning to games. The phrase *sporting theory of justice* is an apt description of the Anglo-American judicial process. It is considered, for example, unsporting to try a person who is unable to comprehend the proceedings. Learned Hand, one of the leading judges in American jurisprudence, observed, "The requirement of due process is merely the embodiment of the English sporting theory of fair play."[4] The concept is not popular everywhere; the games that people play depend upon their families and society as a whole. Consider, for example, the observation of Luigi Barzini, who is responsible for the following: "Many rules of 'fair play' appear to the Italians as a joke. Such as the English formula, 'Do not hit a fallen enemy'! . . . When would it be better and more advantageous to hit him?"[5]

While the idea of the trial as a game—a sporting event, a form of play—is commonplace in the Anglo-American (or common-law) world, it is less certain (as Huizinga recognized) that the same idea holds in other countries where a trial is largely conducted by the presiding judge rather than by lawyers for opposing parties. In any event, if lawyers and judges in the non-common-law world are playing a game, it is a different game than that played in the common-law world. The play-forms evident in a particular country are socially determined—contiguous with other elements in that country's culture. Still, it may not be possible in any kind of trial to be completely "serious." If one tried to make the common-law trial less of a sporting event, the play element would simply reassert itself in another form.

Mastery over Helplessness

Through play a child achieves mastery over helplessness. Play is the child's work; recreation is indeed re-creation. By re-creating a traumatic event, children assume an active role turning passive experiences in which they have been a victim into ones in which they are in charge. A child who experienced a frightening event at the dentist may want to do dental work on his pet.[6] A child who has been in the hospital may want to play with bandaged dolls, miniature intravenous poles, and toy beds. Assuming the active role, the child is able to master the experience psychically. Another illustration is ring-around-the-rosy, a game of joining hands, forming a circle of life, which began in medieval Europe to mock the peril of the black death.[7]

The same psychodynamic prevails in adults. Friedrich Nietzsche observed that hidden in every man is a child who wants to play. Freud showed in detail the ways in which the infantile past survives in the adult. Berne in his work on Transactional Analysis stated that every person is actually three persons—child, adult, and parent. At any given time, a person's ego state may be that of a child, adult, or parent. Adults are driven by essentially the same forces as children, and the way that adults deal with these forces is permeated and affected by their childhood experiences. "Monopoly," a popular board game in which real estate and properties are bought and traded for large sums of money, was created by an unemployed salesman during the economic depression of the 1930s. Active mastery of the reality of economic helplessness was not possible for most people during this period, but passive mastery through the game fantasy of enormous compensatory wealth and power was possible. The game struck a responsive chord in the universal anxiety of the times.

A recurrence of childlike magic is to be expected in conditions of intense anxiety or preoccupation with a particular desire. To say that an adult is acting childishly has the flavor of an insult, but to behave in a childlike manner in certain adult contexts may be the very best way of coping with a situation.

Like the individual, society sutures itself by re-creating in a trial an event that has disturbed its peace. In doing so, society asserts its mastery. A trial resolves conflict and serves to educate, as does play. As in play, adherence to the rules set out in law contributes to the formation of individual conscience. The judicial process was initially a contest and has always been subject to restrictive rules that set the lawsuit squarely in the domain of orderly play. Pronouncement of justice takes place in a court, in a kind of sacred circle, a place set off from the ordinary world. The ambience of the theater envelops the proceeding. Like show business, the law makes use of certain properties. Judges don robes and sometimes wigs. Scenery, too, is as important to a legal drama as it is to the theatrical play. The courtroom production begins with the court crier's "Oyez," announcing the coming of the judge.

Trial as Drama

When the judge tours or plays in the provinces, he is said to go on *circuit.* In former times, when the judge came to town, on his circuit, the cry went out, "Here comes the judge!" and people all assembled. Apart from going to church, attending a trial was formerly the big event in people's lives.

Traditionally, a trial has been regarded as a type of drama and is preeminently a theatrical form. The trial, like the classical form of the drama, is always a contest between protagonist and antagonist, the resolution of the play being comparable to the verdict on the action. A very early historical account of a trial comes from the drama the *Eumenides,* of Aeschylus' trilogy, the *Oresteia.* Like the old morality play, the trial presents in dramatic fashion the conflicting moral values of the community. Thurman Arnold says that both civil and criminal trials perform this function, but since the criminal law is the buttress of morality, the criminal process has more important emotional impact upon society.[8] Thus, like the morality play, the criminal trial seeks to vindicate moral values. The struggle features the universal agony of morality or the passionate tension between good and evil.[9]

The art of acting is as necessary in a trial as in a play. Advocates like Clarence

Darrow are regarded by the public with much the same affection as that extended to athletes and actors. Advocates have always trained themselves to give histrionic displays in the legal drama in which they were engaged. Cicero studied the performances of Aesopus and Roscius, the theatrical stars of his day. In Athens every man acted as his own lawyer, but the profession of speech writer developed to help those who were inept. The Ionian Sophists, who hired philosophers to defend disputes in court and engaged in spectacular exercises of logic, were ridiculed by Socrates, who (through Plato) made out of his trial a very entertaining play.

The importance of advocacy is exemplified in the lifetime record of Texas attorney Percy Foreman—seven hundred wins against one loss. It was clearly not the rightness of the client's case that won all these decisions in his favor. Rather, this score resulted from Foreman's ability to make black look white. (In one case, he threatened to reveal the truth if his fee was not paid.) One columnist put it thus: "Foreman, like most successful trial lawyers, often plays the ham, diverting the minds of the jury from whatever the prosecution may be trying to prove."[10]

In a unique but winning style, Gerry Spence wears a cowboy-style fringed jacket (attorneys usually wear a medium-to-dark blue suit) and he is a master at melodrama. Then too, Richard "Racehorse" Haynes gained fame by winning cases that seemed impossible. He summed up his defense strategy at an American Bar Association (ABA) seminar: "Say you sue me because you say my dog bit you. Well, now this is my defense—my dog doesn't bite. And second, in the alternative, my dog was tied up that night. And third, I don't believe you really got bit. And fourth, I don't have a dog."[11]

Much so-called truth is accepted through faith. Without denying or affirming its validity, there is the belief of a virgin birth and of heaven and hell. The phrase "seeing is believing" may be turned around—"believing is seeing." Psychological testing—for example, Rorschach's ink-blot test and Murray's thematic apperception test—recognizes that the individual projects himself into what is seen. And Freud pointed out how much we shape our thoughts and ideas to suit our moods and needs.

A person would rather have one good soul-satisfying emotion than a dozen facts. "Reason against passion!" Albert Einstein wrote. "The latter always wins if there's any struggle at all. . . ."[12] The solemn ceremony of the trial, the prescribed formalities, the stereotyped patterns of speech, and the long deliberations and sifting of evidence are designed to control emotions and to allow "sovereign reason" to prevail. They form a protective screen, much like the compulsive ceremonials of a neurotic individual, in trying to keep emotions under control. An emotion, which is a passion, ceases to be a passion, Baruch Spinoza said, when we form a clear and distinct idea of it. Although the trial lawyer relies on histrionics, the judge or jury often sense that exclamatory words—"This is outrageous," "I could not object more"—do not really reflect underlying feelings. In any event, the thespian activities of the advocates aside, the judicial process aims to control emotion. The relationship of judge or jury and litigant is institutionalized in an attempt to exclude the many irrelevancies that play upon human frailty.

Establishing Truth at Trial

Many people expect a trial to establish the truth and to explain an event. A common assumption is that a trial, if fairly conducted, will provide complete information about an event to the public. After all, a witness does swear "to tell the truth, the whole truth, and nothing but the truth." Thus, when James Earl Ray entered a plea of guilty to the murder of Martin Luther King Jr., there was an outcry in the press that the public was being denied the facts of the assassination. One news editor complained, "Too many questions remain unanswered . . . the court did not seek the answers. It was no search for truth. It was no search at all."[13] People unhappy with the verdict in the O. J. Simpson case felt unsettled, as though they might never, now, know the truth, although, of course, they already knew most of the relevant facts.

A trial, however, is not an investigative but essentially a demonstrative proceeding, which, according to predetermined norms and a particular mode of proof, evaluates only the evidence brought forth by the parties. It is not anticipated that a trial, however fair, will produce all the evidence that exists. Moreover, however important its public function, a trial is not obligatory; the guilty plea, or plea bargaining, is a legal prerogative of the accused. Quite often, both society and the defendant are better served by the less expensive, expeditious plea-bargaining process than they are by a trial.[14]

The law's method of inquiry attempts to be dispassionate, but it differs substantially from a scientific inquiry. The functions and aims of the two, after all, are quite different. There are differences between law and science in intellectual objectives as well as emotional and attitudinal differences. The fundamental aim of law is justice while that of science is knowledge or truth. Results in law are primarily practical, and only secondarily theoretical.[15]

The researcher in experimental work sets up a number of competing hypotheses to be tested one by one. A legal decision maker may do this to a certain point but ultimately must decide in favor of a single version. Victory (winning as the lawyers put it) is for one party or the other, as on the playing field; and the outcome of a case is often unpredictable. The chancery court is commonly referred to as the "chances court."

There are many areas in which the legal and the scientific inquiries can be compared and differences noted. Some are included here.

1. A lawsuit is not an abstract search for truth, but a proceeding to settle a controversy between two or more persons without physical conflict. The primary purpose of each case is to resolve a controversy rather than to contribute to the development of a general theory. The court does not entertain moot controversies. The work of science, on the other hand, is a cooperative effort that attempts to ascertain empirical relationships through the examination of repeated instances and has for its purpose the growth of a body of general principles.[16]

2. The fact-finding processes of science and of law differ in methods used to secure and test data. The scientist selects facts with a view to supporting or testing hypotheses. In law, evidence is gathered by antagonistic parties. The lawyers are involved as partisans interested in the outcome of the case. Loyalty to client comes before loyalty to truth. In the adversary process the court, which undertakes no investigation, adjudicates or decides between the competing claims, with each side attempting to develop the evidence that is helpful to its side and to play down or exclude evidence harmful to it. The law has policy reasons for this practice, which do not concern the scientist. As in any debate, out of the friction a type of truth may emerge.

3. The legal system's method of screening data—the rules of evidence—was

developed and persists for reasons that pertain uniquely to the legal craft. Under the adversary system the trial judge considers only those objections that the attorneys urge; the judge is not required to search for other objections that the attorneys have not asserted. The rules of admission and exclusion of evidence are not self-operative. If an objection is not urged, evidence is admitted for whatever effect it may have in the solution of the fact issues.

4. Much evidence may be rejected in a court of law, even though in other disciplines it is considered substantial enough from which to draw inferences. The law may suppress evidence even when such evidence clearly establishes an accused's guilt, as when, for example, an overzealous law-enforcement officer fails to comply with the technical requirements for a search warrant. The objective is to educate police officers to respect the rights of a suspect although as a by-product such restraint sometimes allows guilty persons to go free. Further, on the basis of evidentiary rules, information may be withheld on the grounds of privileged communication. Science is not bound by such considerations and may utilize evidence from any source, however indirect.

5. The court is hampered by limitations of time and place. The court must be expedient in resolving a dispute, whereas scientists have the luxury of seeking truth unconstrained by the demands of court dockets. In law, a decision based on incomplete information is often better than no decision at all.[17] The courts say that a defendant is entitled to a fair trial but not a perfect one. Aristotle said centuries ago: "We must not look for the same degree of accuracy in all subjects; we must be content in each class of subjects with accuracy of such kind as the subject matter allows."[18] Law Dean John Wigmore observed, "A scientist can wait till he finds the data he wants; and he can use past, present, and future data; and he can go anywhere to get them. . . . But a judicial trial must be held at a fixed time and place, and the decision must be then made, once for all."[19]

6. The law's method of arriving at a result is often purposely nonscientific or dependent upon a nonprofessional assessment. However able judges may be, they are usually not experts on the subject matter before them. Frequently, the results or verdicts are announced as the general, flat, unexplained decision of untrained minds—the jury—purposely selected for their lack of training. In its earliest form, the jury, drawn from the local community, relied on its own knowledge of the facts, however obtained. Witnesses as we know them today were rarely called; the jurors themselves were both witnesses and judge. In slow steps evolved the present but totally different method of trial by jury, which well may be less effective as a fact finder.

7. Science is not concerned with values, but only with formal relationships between observable events. Results in science are based on measurement and are obtained mathematically. Results in law, on the other hand, are influenced but not ruled by hard data or hard facts. Scientific evidence, no matter how reliable, is not conclusive and binding on the court. Justice incorporates social needs as well as scientific accuracy, but neither to the exclusion of the other. In the case most often cited by those who advocate taking away from the jury the right to reject scientific evidence, Charlie Chaplin was held to be the father of Joan Berry's child, notwithstanding blood-grouping tests excluding him. In paternity cases generally, a desire to legitimize the child or to find a financially responsible person to care for the child has more meaning for the court than a factually determinative blood test. In the Chaplin case, moral considerations were also present. Other evidence showed

that Chaplin and Berry had been living together in an illicit relationship. Although his sperm did not happen to meet with her egg, the jury in its concern for the welfare of the child felt that he should bear the responsibility. (Another jury shortly before, notwithstanding the cold war climate of the time, acquitted Chaplin of a criminal charge under the Mann Act, which prohibits the transporting of women from one state to another for prostitution.)

8. The element of subjectivity is vastly greater in law or psychiatry than in the natural sciences. This is not to say that fantasies do not play a role in science, as may be illustrated by the theories of scientists inspired by their dreams. In evaluating human behavior, though, one must constantly make inferences, and it is precisely in making these inferences that judge or jury or psychiatrist can go astray.

9. Procedure—basically a form of etiquette—is more important in law than in science. The content or substantive issues of the law are often resolved indirectly via questions of procedure. The name of the game, lawyers say, is *procedure.* To spit against the wind is to spit in one's own face, and to approach the real issue directly in law is to do just about the same. In the nineteenth century most cases never did get to trial on the merits, as the procedural rules were so complicated.

10. Law and psychiatry may be called sciences of human behavior, but the practice of lawyering or psychotherapy is an art. Percy Foreman's score has already been mentioned. To achieve justice in the form of a favorable decision, attorneys resort to various tactics to overcome the element of chance. Sporting theory or no, there is something of Machiavelli in it. Like the play of bridge hands, what may be good tactics in one case may be quite unsuitable in another. One tactic that is followed consistently, however, concerns the dialogue of a trial, technically called "evidence." Like the dialogue of a play, it is rarely a matter of improvisation. Attorneys, although they do not write parts for their witnesses, rehearse them carefully to see that they are letter perfect. Like Hamlet, the attorney strongly urges them to "speak no more than is set down for them." One golden rule of advocacy is, "Never ask a question unless you know the answer." Sometimes, however, due to the pressure of work, the attorney is forced to go to a trial unprepared, a practice called "shooting from the hip," which often will result in improvised evidence.

11. A trial is basically a tribal ceremony. Julian Barry's Broadway play *Lenny,* based on the prosecution of Lenny Bruce for obscenity, depicted the trial as a tribal development, complete with drums, chants, and a ritual of sacrifice. The costumes, though they seemed to imply a sort of semicaveman-tribal situation, were of no specific region. Like any trial, the play raised issues of the uses of authority, the "hypocrisy of standards," the survival of individuality, and the relations in life between self and others.

12. The law, unlike science, requires a "yes" or "no" answer. One court observed, "[T]o the psychiatrist mental cases are a series of imperceptible gradations from the mild psychopath to the extreme psychotic, whereas criminal law allows for no gradations. It requires a final decisive moral judgement of the culpability of the accused. For purposes of conviction there is no twilight zone between abnormality and insanity. An offender is wholly sane or wholly insane."[20]

The Morality Play in Various Forms

In its rulings the Supreme Court has tried to reinforce the importance of a trial, but the proceedings of the courtroom, except in notorious or well-publicized cases, are soporific. In the majority of cases, the court proceeding is not a great public ceremony or a morality play, and so in the usual situation (except on television) a trial has fallen into disuse. The development of the pretrial conference in civil cases (actually a trial in chambers) and plea bargaining in criminal cases are indicative of the decline of the public-trial process. In so-called minor offenses the offender frequently pays a fine through the mail, giving rise to the barb that the court is nothing more than a revenue court. In cases when a trial does occur, the courtroom is usually empty, although spectators are occasionally drawn from clearly definable segments of the population.

In modern times, the use of the theater itself as a forum for public, moral judgment has declined in importance and has become rather a place in which private quarrels and agonies are staged. The verdict that events render upon characters in most modern plays often has no relevance beyond the play itself. The function of the old morality play is now essentially presented in other forms. In some fine arts, the central purpose is to instruct or tell the truth. Poet Josef Brodsky, émigré from the Soviet Union, pointed out that in Russia the church, the system of justice, and several other social institutions have always been in extremely unsatisfactory condition and have not managed to discharge their duties. It happened, he said, that literature was forced to assume many of these functions. "Literature took upon itself the 'instructive' role," he wrote. "It became the focus of a people's spiritual life, the arbiter of its moral character."[21]

In sports, wrestling has been a popular substitute for the morality play. The wrestling match is for some people what the soap opera is for others—the clearly defined characters develop and interact with other characters, and their good-to-evil ratio is constantly shifting to keep the fan intrigued. A beer drinker who was observed watching a wrestling match on television slammed his fist on the bar and shouted, "I don't give a damn if it is a fake! Kill the S.O.B." Although he seemed aware that the match was staged, the fan was caught up in the heat of the performance—the struggle between beauty and ugliness, between good and evil. He was crying for blood, or more mildly, to see justice done.[22]

The role of the criminal trial as morality play was emphasized by the late Philip Q. Roche, a psychiatrist who was also a lifelong student of criminal law. He wrote:

> The criminal trial is an operation having a religious meaning essential as a public exercise in which the prevailing moral ideals are dramatized and reaffirmed. The religious meaning is the adjusting of tensional moral conflict within the law-abiding. The conflict is materialized in the actions of the criminal and dissipated in the ritual of guilt fastening, condemnation, and punishment. The ritual is the homologue of the child-parent interaction containing the same motivational mechanisms and rationalizations. In this view, the criminal trial has the function of public edification rather than that of welfare of the individual wrong-doers who pass over its stage in an endless process. In fixed formula and procedure, the trial reiterates the moral parables of our child-rearing and, in the person of the judge, brings to the transgressor a power and punitive enforcement once exercised by the parent. Both judge and parent act as agents of an order defined by the prevailing ethical system.[23]

By and large, the press, television, and radio now function as our public forums and trials are acted out on television (for example, Judge Judy),[24] although the courthouse remains to some extent a public forum, and a trial takes the form of a debate of a public issue.[25] Notable examples, past and present, include Dred Scott and the issue of slavery, Oscar Wilde and the issue of homosexuality; Aaron Burr and the power of the presidency; John Scopes and evolution; the Soviet trials of the thirties and party loyalty; the Nuremberg trials and war morality; Adolf Eichmann and genocide; Brother Daniel Rufeisen and Jewish identity; Lieutenant William Calley and the inhumanity of My Lai; Daniel Ellsberg and Anthony Russo and government control over information. In the United States, the court has also moved into such general areas as desegregation, reapportionment, and the right to medical treatment, assuming the task neglected by other institutions. While the usual run-of-the-mill court trial, like the theater itself, no longer serves as a morality play, the constitutional right to a fair trial and due process continues to serve as a kind of tranquilizer.

The Search for Justice

Seething passions are unleashed by a wrong, be it real or fancied, and some means are needed to channel and control them. The law, of course, is one of the major institutions designed by man to control his impulses. The disturbing disequilibrium provoked by the commission of a crime demands a response, if the fabric of society is not to be rent. Disequilibrium is quelled by the knowledge that the offender has been identified, apprehended, usually tried and convicted. There is a compelling need for the imposition of punishment, either when there is a strong reason to believe that the behavior in question can be deterred or when noncompliance with a particular norm is generally felt to be so serious that doing nothing will be unacceptable to individuals or groups in the society.[26] To illustrate, murder is considered to be one of the crimes least capable of being deterred, since it is more impulsive than planned, but members of society would not likely tolerate nothing being done about it. Mario Puzo's popular novel *The Godfather* opens with Amerigo Bonasera looking to the law, losing faith in it, and then going on his knees to Don Corleone for justice.

Seeking a definition of *justice* brings to mind a colloquy between an examiner and a law school graduate seeking admission to the bar. To the question, "What is justice?" the applicant said, after a bit of pondering, "I once knew, but now I've forgotten." "What a great loss for jurisprudence!" bemoaned the examiner. "The first person to know, and he's forgotten!" Recognizing Socrates' contribution, the late Mark Van Doren noted that the word *ius* in Latin meant *justice* and *juice,* two apparently unrelated things, and he suggested that they are related in that they both provide a good taste.

In early childhood we complain that things are unfair, and from the way that mother resolves the complaint our concepts of justice begin to formulate. Later on, the guarantee of a fair trial assures us that we will receive fair treatment. Man seems impelled to expect justice, despite, or perhaps out of, his continuing experience of injustice. John F. Kennedy, assassinated at the peak of his life, at one time had said, "All of life is unfair." Jesus was crucified, yet he had lived the holy life. We all suffer "the slings and arrows of outrageous fortune," but we have, echoing Job, a deep expectation that someone should appoint us a time to secure justice.

At various times and places, the manner of resolution of disputes has differed widely. The development of the judicial process reflects the ontogeny of a ritual, which is based on sanctified agreement rather than on passing outrage or personal revenge. The earlier modes of trial—by ordeal or battle—could be described as then socially acceptable but purely ritualistic procedures for preserving the peace by terminating disputes. They could be regarded as methods of determining the truth only on the theory that divine interpretation and intervention brought about the success of the party whose cause was right. But in common estimation the current mode of trial involves, like science, a search for objective truth. Procedures in early history were entirely formulary, not evidentiary. The oath at one time was the primary mode of proof, its value varying according to a man's rank in society; thus, the oath of a thegn was equal to the oaths of six ceorls. The individual disqualified from taking the oath was put through one of the forms of ordeal, which was an appeal to God to show where the guilt lay. Quite likely, in the Anglo-Saxon age, there were few guilty men who would refuse to confess their guilt when the alternative appeared to be a direct challenge to God. The stress now is on evidentiary substance, but it is tied in with the old stress on evidentiary procedure.

To the extent that the court does not have all the relevant evidence, its decision, which nonetheless may be a proper one, will be based on a distorted or lopsided presentation of the case, and it would not even give the appearance of having administered justice fairly. In a political sense, every man is said to have a right to his opinion, but in a court of law neither judge nor jury theoretically have the right to form an opinion in favor of the party having the burden of proof unless he has met this burden with good evidence. Only the appellate court judge is obliged to set out reasons for a decision.

In an opening provision of the Federal Rules of Evidence (and its counterpart in state rules of evidence), it is stated, "These rules shall be construed to secure fairness in administration, elimination of unjustifiable expense and delay, and promotion of growth and development of the law of evidence to the end that the truth may be ascertained and proceedings justly determined."[27] Too often, however, trials have been turned into circuses, notably the O. J. Simpson trial. To avoid that, military tribunals have been designated for the trial of foreign terrorist suspects. That designation has shaken confidence in the rules that define our culture.

Notes

For nonlawyer readers: The reports of cases, scarcely read by the general public, have a technical and uninteresting look about them, but each is a tale of a human tragedy, strange or commonplace. The decisions of the court are called *opinions;* each is a statement by the court of the facts and its ruling, with reasons. The case is recorded under the names of the plaintiff and the defendant, however humble or illustrious they may be. A person sometimes gains immortality from the novelty of the circumstances or the novelty of principle on which the claim was decided. The decisions of the court are published in books called *reports* or *reporters,* and are cited in this manner: Pavlicic v. Vogtsberger, 390 Pa. 502, 136 A.2d 127 (1957). Pavlicic and Vogtsberger are the names of the parties involved in the litigation. The initial number refers to the volume and the latter number to the page in the reporter, followed within parentheses by the year in which the decision was rendered. 2d indicates that the reporter is in a second series. Thus, in the example, the case appears in volume 390 at page 502 of the state reporter (Pennsylvania) and also in volume 136 at page 127 of the second series of the Atlantic regional reports.

The court does not entertain moot or theoretical issues. A party must have standing to bring an action; that is, he must allege such "a personal stake in the outcome of the controversy as to assure that concrete adverseness which sharpens the presentation of issues upon which the court so largely depends for illumination of difficult questions." Baker v. Carr, 369 U.S. 186 (1962).

1. See D. G. Baird, *Game Theory and the Law* (Cambridge: Harvard University Press, 1995); K. G. Binmore, *Game Theory and the Social Contract* (Cambridge: MIT Press, 1994).

2. In biological terms, man is usually called *Homo sapiens:* "man [genus] the intelligent [species]," a singularly unconvincing description. Man is also called *Homo faber*, meaning "man the tool-maker and -user." Huizinga suggested that man might be called *Homo ludens*, "the human being who plays." (*Homo ludens* means literally "man while he is [for a little time] playing"; the term actually needed is *Homo lusor*, "man as a sportsman, a lover of play [permanently]".) *Ludo, ergo sum;* I play, therefore I am. The truly *ludic* is play that brings about autonomous discipline; the *ludicrous* is games-playing social behavior that is obedient to a narrow set of rules. J. Huizinga, *Homo Ludens: A Study of the Play Element in Culture* (Boston: Beacon Press, 1955) (German edition published in Switzerland in 1944). See also L. Terr, *Beyond Love and Work: Why Adults Need to Play* (New York: Scribner, 1999).

3. Who has not played "WAHM" (Why Does This Always Happen to Me), or "SWYMD" (See What You Made Me Do), and its counterpart "UGMIT" (You Got Me Into This), a game played to perfection by Laurel and Hardy? Marital games include "Harried," "Look How Hard I've Tried," and "If It Weren't for You" (popular with both spouses). See E. Berne, *Games People Play* (New York: Grove Press, 1964). See also A. H. Chapman, *Put-Offs and Come-Ons* (New York: Putnam, 1969).

4. Quoted in Dodge v. Detroit Trust Co., 300 Mich. 575, 2 N.W.2d 509 (1942).

5. L. Barzini, *The Italians* (New York: Simon & Schuster, 1977).

6. Although the use of forms of *his* as universal reverberates with a not-so-subtle glorification of the male and a dismissal of the female, I want to assure that is not intended. Writing *his or her* is cumbersome, so in this book I simply use *his*.

7. See S. H. Fraiberg, *The Magic Years* (New York: Simon & Schuster, 1959).

8. T. Arnold, "The Criminal Trial as a Symbol of Public Morality," in A. E. Howard (ed.), *Criminal Justice in Our Time* (Charlottesville: University of Virginia, 1965), p. 39.

9. Sir Edward A. Parry some years ago wrote: "[F]rom the earliest dawn of civilization we find that justice has seen fit to cast her manifestations in a dramatic form. Even today when we think of a trial or a lawsuit we picture it to ourselves in terms of drama, applauding the hero or heroine, execrating the villain of the piece. . . . And as we read the report of a law case we recall the familiar scenery of a court house, the traditional costumes of the characters and that dramatic setting which we inwardly approve of as essential to the administration of justice." E. A. Parry, *The Drama of the Law* (New York: Unwin, 1924), pp. 7–8.

10. M. Smith, "Attorney Percy Foreman Wins Another Big Case," *Life*, Apr. 1, 1966, p. 92. "The 'art' of the advocate," says Cyril Harvey in his book *The Advocate's Devil*, "might be defined as 'the art of misleading an audience without actually telling lies.'" C. P. Harvey, *The Advocate's Devil* (London: Stevens & Sons, 1958), p. 2. There is a saying among lawyers that if the law is against you, pound the evidence; if the evidence is against you, pound the law; if both are against you, pound the table.

11. B. Nissen, "Texas Attorney Gains Fame Winning Cases That Seem Impossible," *Wall Street Journal*, Oct. 31, 1978, p. 1.

12. F. Stern, *Einstein's German World* (Princeton: Princeton University Press, 1999), p. 265.

13. J. Seigenthaler, *A Search for Justice* (Nashville: Aurora, 1971), p. 202. In a passage in Henry Cecil's novel *Friends at Court*, a client thanks his attorney for his help. "But what a lot of time and money," he said, "it has cost to arrive at the truth." "The truth?" said the attorney. "No one said anything about arriving at the truth." The late Professor Edmund M. Morgan of the Harvard Law School used to say that truth is only an ingredient of justice, which is something larger than truth and far more difficult to attain.

14. J. Epstein, "Truth in the Courtroom," *Commentary*, Aug. 1969, p. 50. The public has a right to demand only fairness in the procedure, and when a party has had the opportunity of a day in court, the community thenceforth in good conscience can ignore his complaint. The judicial process is a way of resolving conflicting claims that would otherwise disrupt society by self-help or private feud. The process, acceptable to the community, is called *justice*. H. B. Steinberg, Book Review, *Harv. L. Rev.* 80 (1966): 477.

15. V. Aubert, "The Structure of Legal Thinking," in *Legal Essays [Festskrift til Frede Castberg]* (Oslo: Universitetsforlaget, 1963).

16. T. Cowan, "Jurisprudence in the Teaching of Torts," *J. Legal Ed.* 9 (1957): 444, 455.

17. R. G. Collingwood put it thus: "The methods of criminal detection are not at every point identical with those of scientific history, because their ultimate purpose is not the same. A criminal court has in its hands the life and liberty of a citizen, and in a country where the Citizen is regarded as having rights the court is therefore bound to do something and do it quickly. The time taken to arrive at a decision is a factor in the value (that is, the justice) of the decision itself. If any juror says: 'I feel certain that a year hence, when we have all reflected on the evidence at leisure, we shall be in a better position to see what it means,' the reply will be: 'There is something in what you say; but what you propose is impossible. Your business is not just to give a verdict; it is to give a verdict now; and here you stay until you do it.' This is why a jury has to content itself with something less than scientific (historical) proof, namely with that degree of assurance or belief which would satisfy it in any of the practical affairs of daily life." R. G. Collingwood, *The Idea of History* (New York: Oxford University Press, 1956), p. 268.

18. *The Complete Works of Aristotle*, ed. & trans. J. Barnes (Princeton, N.J.: Princeton University Press, 1984).

19. J. Wigmore, *A Student's Textbook of the Law of Evidence* (Chicago: Foundation Press, 1935), pp. 10–11. See also D. L. Faigman, *Legal Alchemy: The Use and Misuse of Science in the Law* (New York: W. H. Freeman, 1999).

20. Holloway v. United States, 148 F.2d 665 (D.C. App. 1945).

21. *New York Times Magazine*, Oct. 1, 1972, p. 11. Brodsky was convicted of "parasitism" and sentenced to five years hard labor. The judge said, "Who said you're a poet? Who included you among the ranks of poets?"

22. G. P. Stone & R. A. Oldenberg, "Wrestling," in R. Slovenko & J. A. Knight (eds.), *Motivations in Play, Games and Sports* (Springfield, Ill.: Thomas, 1967), pp. 503–32.

23. P. Q. Roche, *The Criminal Mind* (New York: Farrar, Straus & Cudahy, 1958), p. 245.

24. Judge Sheindlin and her husband left the bench and became judges of cases on television, and Ed Koch went on television as a judge following his tenure as mayor of New York. Judy Sheindlin (Judge Judy) is described as having "the fastest, funniest mouth on TV." J. Jerome, "Chamber Mode," *People*, Sept. 27, 1999, p. 132.

25. See P. Irons, *The Courage of Their Convictions* (New York: Free Press, 1988).

26. J. C. Oates, "The Mystery of JonBenet Ramsey," *New York Review of Books*, June 24, 1999, p. 31.

27. Federal Rules of Evidence, Rule 102.

PART I

The
Psychiatrist
as
Expert
Witness

1

The
Use
of Experts
in the
Adversary
System

The adversary system is the distinguishing characteristic of Anglo-American justice, along with the importance attached to formal rules of evidence. The continental legal procedure, on the other hand, is without the formalism found in the Anglo-American system. Objections such as "inadmissible evidence," "hearsay," "opinion," or "leading question," customary in an Anglo-American trial, are unknown in a continental trial. In Anglo-American law, the key to a fair trial is not only the presentation of evidence according to formal rules of evidence but also the opportunity to use cross-examination, rebuttal evidence, and argument to meet adverse evidence. A cross-examining procedure, guaranteed by the confrontation clause of the Sixth Amendment to the U.S. Constitution, is at the very heart of the adversary system.

The adversary proceeding, in an impartial and public forum, provides a mechanism by which differences can be settled in a decision-making process that people generally trust. It provides a means of making even big government and big business accountable. The ability to assert a legal right in a proceeding where an individual has reasonable equality with his opponent buttresses self-image and sense of worth. It is the modern-day scene where David may defeat Goliath. To be sure, there are critics, particularly among losers. Charlie Chaplin in his autobiography said of the paternity suit in which the jury ruled against him, "Listening to the legal abracadabra of both attorneys, it seemed to me a game they were playing and that I had little to do with it."[1]

Under the adversary system the judge acts as arbiter to assure conformity to the rules of fair play that have evolved over time. The jury then decides the issues on the basis of those facts that the judge as a gatekeeper permits them to hear. Simply put, the adversary system is a process of contention in which the role of the lawyer is to initiate suit following the dispute, raise the issues, and propel the controversy. The judge does not venture forth like a Don Quixote seeking justice as he does under the inquisitorial system which prevails in most countries. The inquisitorial judge has the responsibility to arrive at the truth by his own exertions in conjunction with those of the official prosecutor. Experimental studies lend support to the claim that an adversary form of presentation, in contrast to an inquisitorial presentation, counteracts bias in decision makers.

The physical setting of the courtroom reflects the system of justice. Under the adversary system, in civil and criminal cases, the chairs of the parties in the courtroom are situated on the same level, without benefit of elevation above the floor, and are equidistant from the judge. The parallel location of the parties is designed to indicate to judge and jury that the word of one counsel—*prosecutor* (plaintiff in civil cases) or *defense counsel*—carries no more weight than that of the other. The scales of justice are thus held evenly. In countries employing the inquisitorial system, the prosecutor has a place well above that of the defense counsel, and he carries by virtue of that location a certain majesty, hardly distinguishable from that of the judge. In all systems, a judge sits elevated, a position communicating dominance or superiority, representative of his symbolic authority and the finality of judgment under law.

In the Anglo-American adversary proceeding, the rules governing the action are as formal and ritualistic as those of an ancient tournament or a game of chess. Each side is charged with presenting the strongest possible case on its own behalf and expects to be countered with the strongest possible case by the adversary, creating conditions like those of an ancient tournament. The adversary proceeding requires that lawyers, like gladiators, carry out their task in a fair or sporting manner.

The adversary system is based on the theory that truth (or viewpoints) emerges best out of the open combat over ideas. While physicians are trained to discover medical truth, lawyers are trained in representing any point of view. The theory of the adversary system, as Professor Edmund Morgan once put it, is that "each litigant is most interested and will be most effective in seeking, discovering, and presenting the materials which will reveal the strength of his own case and the weakness of his adversary's case, so that the truth will emerge to the impartial tribunal that makes the decision."[2] Richard A. Posner, the venerable chief judge of the U.S. Court of Appeals for the Seventh Circuit, views the adversary system as relatively efficient—not ideal by any means, but better for Americans than feasible alternatives. In general, Judge Posner likes its competitiveness and the incentives it provides, and he supports the lay jury.[3]

The adversary system is also employed in nonlaw forums. The American Psychiatric Association (APA) at its annual meetings uses an adversary system to debate topics such as whether depressive personality is a useful construct that should be included in the *Diagnostic and Statistical Manual of Mental Disorders* (*DSM*). In the Roman Catholic Church, a *postulator*—a priest assigned to investigate the possibility that someone is a saint—goes before a church tribunal to argue the case for sainthood against another priest whose job is popularly known as "the devil's advocate."

The Widening Use of Expert Testimony

The potential use of expert testimony expands with wider knowledge of the world and as the world becomes more complicated. In the film *Bananas,* Woody Allen is a products-tester trying out electrically heated toilet seats and coffins with piped-in music. As the modern age continues to become more complex, it is not surprising that modern litigation requires more expert opinion evidence than ever before. Not only is reliance on expert witnesses increasing, but new types of experts are developing.

At a time when trial by jury was not much developed, only two modes of using expert knowledge existed: first, to select as jurymen such persons as were especially fitted by experience to know the class of facts that were before them; and second, to call to the aid of the court skilled persons whose opinions it might adopt. The existence of the judge's power to call witnesses generally included the power to call expert witnesses who were regarded originally as *amici curiae* (friends of the court).

Technological advances along with the liberalization of the rules of evidence have prompted the use of a wider range of experts than ever. In complex and technical cases the expert is often crucial because the evidence is beyond the ken of the jury, but even in a single slip-and-fall case an expert may be used to establish the way the premises are usually maintained. As recently as 1970 nearly all tort cases were very simple. There were virtually no medical malpractice and mass injury cases, which today constitute 40 percent of cases. New technologies have created high-stakes litigation calling for expert testimony. As a consequence, the use of expert witnesses in recent years has been growing rapidly, but their use in courts is far from new. A seventeenth-century treatise numbered as experts only five: locksmiths, cutlers, peruke-makers, washerwomen, and ropemakers.[4] Earlier courts called on physicians to help determine whether a defendant was "bewitched."

The concept of *expert* in litigation, however, does not necessarily mean being at the top in one's field. It includes anyone whose knowledge of a subject extends beyond that of the average juror. By legal definition, an expert is almost anybody who can reasonably be expected to know more about a given subject than the average person. As Rule 702 of the Federal Rules of Evidence puts it, anyone with "knowledge, skill, experience, training, or education" who can assist the trier of fact may qualify as an expert. Sometimes the choice of an expert may seem bizarre—a narcotics user has testified as an expert to the identification of a drug;[5] an "expert burglar" has qualified as an expert witness.[6]

Along with the growing complexity of life, the liberalization of expert testimony rules in the last decade has had a prolific effect on the use of experts. Unlike an ordinary witness, an expert may now not only testify in the form of an opinion or otherwise, but, in forming an opinion, may rely on inadmissible evidence, such as hearsay, if "reasonably relied upon by experts in the particular field."[7] Evidence, though relevant, may be excluded, however, if it is likely to be confusing or misleading. The test, under Rule 403, is whether the probative value of the evidence is substantially outweighed by the danger of "confusion of the issues or misleading the jury."

A number of critics have charged that psychiatrists (and psychologists) have no useful place in the courtroom. These critics say that psychiatrists cannot answer forensic questions with reasonable accuracy, and they cannot help the fact finder reach more accurate conclusions than would otherwise be available. In fact, they claim, the involvement of psychiatrists as expert witnesses is not only not helpful but actually harmful, as they mislead by testimony that has little scientific underpinning.[8]

In criminal trials, where so much controversy surrounds psychiatric testimony, we must recall that a trial is very much a morality play. A trial without a psychiatrist is usually dull—indeed, without psychiatric testimony, jurors tend to go to sleep. Psychiatric testimony makes headlines. The public wants some understanding of why the accused acted as he did. Without psychiatric testimony trials are not very interesting or satisfying. Indeed, the press even insists on obtaining and printing off-the-cuff comments by psychiatrists on any and all facets of life and behavior.

The "battle of the experts," as it is called, heightens tension, prompting the trier of fact to pay attention. It stimulates thought; it enhances the deliberations. The evidence can serve as a guideline that the jurors can integrate with their own moral, social, philosophical, and religious backgrounds to arrive at an appropriate decision.[9]

Psychiatric testimony, whether or not accepted, opens options to judge and jury. It brings flexibility and an element of humanity into the law. The jury, following their conviction of Jean Harris for the killing of the so-called Scarsdale diet doctor, Dr. Herman Tarnower, wondered why no psychiatric testimony was presented. The jury wanted some excusing evidence, although it may have been conflicting, but got none. Whether in a given case judge or jury accepts or declines evidence is for them to decide—but without some testimony they may not be able to rationalize a decision they would like to return. The scale is the symbol of justice, but measurement alone would subvert the nature of a trial as a morality play. A trial, of course, has more to do with justice than show business, but a trial (especially a criminal trial) is, in large measure, a morality play.

The Doctrine of Judicial Notice

While the parties, and not the court, are responsible under the adversary system for gathering and presenting facts, there are many facts that need to be supplemented or cannot be established by formal proof. The doctrine of *judicial notice* recognizes the right or the necessity of the judge to notice evidence outside the record that is "a matter of general knowledge." The judicial notice apparatus, however, does not work well unless it is fed with information. Judge Frank of the Second Circuit once observed that judicial notice often amounts to nothing more than "cocktail-hour knowledge." He suggested that "competently to inform ourselves, we should have a staff of investigators like those supplied to administrative agencies."[10]

Almost any case can be used to illustrate the need for, and the propriety of, supplying the court with information. The usual method of establishing adjudicative facts—the facts of the particular case—is through the introduction of evidence, ordinarily consisting of the testimony of witnesses, whereas judicial notice is the usual method of finding those facts having relevance to legal reasoning and the lawmaking process.

In judicial lawmaking a prominent illustration is *Durham v. United States*,[11] a decision subsequently cast aside, where Judge Bazelon, without support in the evidence developed at the trial, declared: "Medico-legal writers in large numbers . . . present convincing evidence that the right-and-wrong test is 'based on an entirely obsolete and misleading conception of the nature of insanity.'" The court had no hesitation in using this "convincing evidence" even though it was not in the record. According to the grapevine, two prominent forensic psychiatrists assisted Judge Bazelon in writing the opinion in *Durham*. In the landmark case of *Wolf v. Colorado*,[12] Supreme Court Justice Murphy wrote to district attorneys of various cities to learn of police practices in their cities and obtained from their replies information that he used to confront the issue of illegally obtained evidence at trial. In the historic case in 1954 of *Brown v. Board of Education of Topeka*,[13] the Court cited the writings of Kenneth B. Clark and Gunnar Myrdal on the adverse effect of school racial segregation on personality development. Sociological and psychological theories also controlled the Court's separate-but-equal decision in 1896 in *Plessy v. Ferguson*, even though these theories were neither formally presented to the Court nor given formal recognition. In *Powell v. Texas*,[14] the Supreme Court resorted to various extrarecord facts to determine the prevailing view of the medical profession concerning whether alcoholism is a disease.

Participation as Amicus Curiae

The role of the professional expert as amicus curiae is an important function in providing the court with information. Apart from testifying, professionals in a pertinent field can offer invaluable suggestions to an attorney preparing an amicus curiae brief on a point of law or of fact for the information of the judge. In recent decades, the role of the amicus curiae brief has expanded, and it is quite common now to see an organizational presentation of a brief. It constitutes a modification of the adversary system that provides a form of information-gathering that is the judicial counterpart of lobbying and congressional hearing in the legislative process. Fairly speaking, it is often a "political statement" or "lobbying before the court."[15]

Should it be allowed? Permission to participate as a friend of the court is and has always been a matter of grace rather than of right. The theory of trial by duel between two contestants precludes an unlimited right of third persons to intervene or file a brief. As one court observed, the fundamental principle underlying legal procedure deems that parties involved in a controversy have the right to litigate without the interference of strangers. The late Chief Justice Burger as well as many other judges have been of the view that the role of the court is not to decide broad social issues, but rather to decide a contest between two litigants—and "friends" should remain outside the courtroom.

On the other hand, access to the judicial process on the part of third-party individuals or organizations is an extension of the view that the law is a process of social choice and policymaking. The outcome of litigation indirectly affects interests other than those formally represented. Groups organized to promote altruistic goals are likely, as amici, to represent important widespread public interests. Organizational participation in the judicial process focuses public attention on the judge's decision, and as a consequence, he is particularly cautious and deliberate in these cases. The National Association for the Advancement of Colored People (NAACP), almost from its inception, has participated as amicus curiae in litigation. The American Civil Liberties Union (ACLU) also found early on that the amicus curiae brief is a useful instrument in drawing widespread attention to its causes. The American Jewish Congress over the past years is one of the most active filers of amicus curiae briefs.

The American Medical Association (AMA), American Psychiatric Association, American Psychological Association, and American Orthopsychiatric Association (Ortho) at one time or another have participated as amici on various mental health issues. These associations, however, have no rational scheme for submitting amici briefs or instituting suit but do so when their attention is called by their attorneys, staffs, or interested members to a particular case considered to be directly relevant to their field, and if there are sufficient time and money. One or another of these associations—in a happenstance, often fortuitous manner—has submitted briefs on issues of criminal responsibility, competency to stand trial, admissibility of expert testimony by psychologists, psychological test validity in assessing employment placement, privileged confidential communication, services to the mentally retarded, adequacy of treatment in mental hospitals and institutions for individuals with mental retardation, peonage in mental institutions, psychosurgery, capital punishment, unusual punishment in solitary confinement, denial of admission of a candidate to medical school because of a prior mental hospital stay, imprisonment for possession of marijuana, and abortion. In addition, these associations on occasion have offered sundry proposals for model legislation.

The Supreme Court's 1972 rulings on competency to stand trial in *Jackson v. Indiana* and the death penalty in *Furman v. Georgia* drew heavily on the issues formulated and researched in the amicus briefs. In fact, most of the issues discussed by the Court in *Jackson* were not touched on by attorneys for the state or for the defendant but were raised only in Ortho's amicus brief. The brief called the Court's attention to the broad implications of the procedure used in commitment for incompetency to stand trial, and the Court, although it did not permit filing of the brief, responded by addressing itself to these issues.

While it may encumber the judicial process, many courts are grateful for the participation of amicus curiae. A court's opinion often incorporates verbatim the amicus brief, which has come to represent the intersection of scholarship and advocacy. An amicus may enter at the trial or appellate level although rarely is afforded the opportunity to participate at the trial level, as it did in *Wyatt v. Stickney*, the right-to-treatment case, where amici was actively engaged in the proceeding presenting numerous witnesses on all aspects of the case. In helping to formulate minimum medical and constitutional standards in hospital treatment, the court expressed gratitude for exemplary service to Ortho, ACLU, American Psychological Association, and American Association on Mental Deficiency.

Today, individuals look to their organizations to represent and further their professional interests and concerns. As individuals, they have neither the time nor the inclination to pursue a matter that does not directly and immediately impact their pocketbooks, and they have come to expect organizational representation in the courts on general professional matters. While there has been much criticism of the role of mental health professionals as expert witnesses in the adversary system, it is at the same time recognized that in some way their viewpoint should enter the judicial process.[16]

As an avenue of publicity, amici briefs are often published in the *Congressional Record*—any congressman can put anything in the *Record*, and on request he will usually do so. The *Record* makes it possible to publish at a low printing price (the cost is absorbed by the public). Each day, within thirteen hours of the close of debate, congressional presses turn out 49,000 copies of another thick edition of the *Record*. While production may be impressive, content unfortunately is not. In effect, the *Record* is a subsidiary xeroxing service for congressmen, producing by the thousands whatever item they choose. Nader's Study Group, which calls the *Record* a big charade, says that shrewd doctors soon will learn to stock their waiting rooms with copies of the *Record*. In any event, the *Record* is a means to heighten visibility and citizen consciousness of an issue, which is also the goal of much litigation.

Mass Litigation (Class Actions)

Organizational activity in the legal process has found a broad new field with the recent development of mass litigation (class actions), which allows representation of everyone in a similar position.[17] Since about 1990, mass litigation has become increasingly common in the areas of personal injury, product liability, and workplace discrimination. In the area of law and psychiatry, class action suits have notably been brought in regard the right to treatment and the right to refuse treatment. They have been instrumental in prison reform.[18]

Mass litigation is sometimes called *public interest* litigation. Today, entire industries—cigarette producers, gun makers, lead paint manufacturers, and health maintenance organizations (HMOs)—are struggling to protect their profits, or even their survival, in the face of new, outsized forms of litigation. The courts are increasingly being called upon to make public policy in areas vacated by politicians (such as gun violence, smoking, and HMO reform). In the lawsuits against gun makers, the tobacco industry, and health care industries, contentious economic, social, or political matter has been transformed into an ostensibly legal issue. The lawsuits have been prompted by the general feeling of the public that legislative policies were hamstrung and that these industries needed to be curbed. Of course, at the same time, there are outbursts against overly zealous lawyers, silly lawsuits, and outrageous fees. Turning difficult political choices into legal issues (disputes that can be litigated) usually involves a narrowing process that excludes important social considerations. In any event, the pace of legal change has suddenly accelerated as the third branch of government, the judiciary, assumes responsibilities from the other two branches, resulting in judicial regulation of whole segments of the country's industry.

The growth of mass litigation, and especially the newest kind of big lawsuit—civil suits brought by government to fight social problems such as smoking and gun violence—raise vexing questions about the role of law in U.S. society: Can mass justice be done without jeopardizing individual rights? Does the sheer size of these lawsuits exert undue pressure on defendants to settle? Are these lawsuits good for society—or just good for lawyers? In mass cases the lawyers do not maintain meaningful one-to-one contact with their clients, nor can they represent these people as individuals, each with his or her own needs and interests.

Up to a point, litigation has been "good for America," as Professor Alan Dershowitz put it. It provided something of a social safety net, in a country without a national health scheme and with only limited disability insurance. It helped to level the playing field between private citizens and large corporations. But is all the vast litigation still worth the price? Judge Jack Weinstein, of the U.S. District Court in New York, concedes the costs but stresses the benefits: "It has defects, and it has undoubtedly to some extent discouraged innovation and put economic pressure on some industries, perhaps unnecessarily. But in general it has fulfilled an equalizing function. This is a justice system open to everybody."[19]

Participation as Partisan Expert

While the amicus role is significant, partisan experts called by the contesting parties remain the familiar source of expert testimony. The appointment of experts by the court is expressly allowed under the rules of evidence but it is rare in the United States because it is viewed as an undesirable departure from the dueling nature of the adversary system. In the United States, experts are usually called by the parties. This is contrary to most countries, where the court itself appoints expert witnesses allegedly to ensure scientific objectivity. The advocates of party selection of expert witnesses maintain that the impartial witness is a myth and empowering the parties to choose the witnesses in judicial proceedings gives them some effective control over the proceedings and thereby vindicates democratic values.[20] To most observers of court proceedings, the concept of an "impartial expert" echoes hollowly.[21]

In procuring the assistance of an expert, the attorney typically talks in terms of "if"—"if you take the stand," reviewing the topics and the facts of the case. Once the expert agrees to serve, the attorney expects the expert to take on the role, in effect, of an advocate. That is, to make the best case he can for the lawyer's client. The expert is expected to carry out an evaluation and then if he feels he can be helpful, testify for the party, and do all that is possible for the party without fabrication. The witnesses and not only immediate parties to a legal action are adversaries: they are labeled as witnesses *for* the plaintiff or *for* the defendant. The adversarial process might be likened to a multilane highway, with several lanes going in one direction and several lanes in the opposite direction. The witness, like the traveler, must go one way or the other. To use another metaphor, the witness cannot be like a Roman candle, shooting sparks in every direction without aim.

Because each side is allowed to present its best version of the contested issue, the adversarial system insures that both sides will be aired. Yet, to make out its case, lawyers crudely say, quite often, that they "buy" experts. They call them "hired guns." In a sense, they are right, but it is not unethical so long as they do not ask the expert to fabricate or falsify their opinion. Who can say that the opinion of the so-called impartial expert, the expert called by the court, is less biased or more truthful and objective than that of the adversary witness? The partiality of the impartial expert is masked as impartiality, more or less deceiving the fact finder. The traditional adversary system of calling witnesses for each side and then examining witnesses by direct and cross-examination has evolved specifically for the purpose of exposing shortcomings and biases, of probing the accuracy and veracity of the opposition witnesses' testimony.[22]

Experience reveals that there is almost no subject that cannot be viewed in at least two ways. The adversary system, the battle of the experts that it entails, and the frequent reversals on appeal may all reflect the natural working of the human mind. In the very nature of things, every event has different versions. The famous Japanese film *Rashomon* is a dramatization of the classic enigma of truth, a metaphor of life reminding us that there is no one truth, that there are many truths, some valid for one, some for another. Events are seen in different ways. Freud has shown that ambivalence is the normal manner of human thought. The "adversary rumination" keeps the law in correspondence with human nature. Erik Erikson observed, "The conflicting evidence which parades past the paternal (or parental) judge, the fraternal jury, and the chorus of the public, matches the unceasing inner rumination with which we watch ourselves."[23]

To be sure, there are at least two sides to every story. Life is Janus-faced. In every war there have been virtuous and reasonable people earnestly fighting on both sides. Socrates would allow an adversary to pick any side of an argument. In the same spirit, Ralph Waldo Emerson would give a lecture on one side of a subject, then on the other side.[24]

Types of Expert Testimony

The role of the expert may be to reconstruct the past, analyze the present, or predict the future. In doing this, the expert may offer testimony of two general kinds: testimony as to facts and opinion testimony. The admissibility of each rests upon different theories. Expert testimony as to facts is admissible because special skill and experience are needed for the understanding of certain matters. For example, any person of ordinary understanding can testify as to whether a man had a cut or to the color of stains that may have appeared on his clothes. It requires special experience and knowledge, however, to say what arteries, nerves, or bones were injured and to determine whether the stains, if yellow, were due to urine or semen, or if brown, were human blood. Because the ordinary witness is not capable of making the determination, an expert is needed.

Unlike expert witnesses, lay witnesses are not allowed to give opinion testimony. Hence, the lay witness may not give a retrospective judgment or make a prediction. The lay witness is restricted to a presentation of facts with the judge or jury drawing the inferences or conclusions from such facts. In an amendment to the Federal Rules of Evidence (effective December 1, 2000), a lay witness may not give testimony in the form of opinions or inferences based on scientific, technical, or other specialized knowledge.[25] The amendment is designed to eliminate the risk that the reliability requirements for expert testimony would be evaded through the simple expedient of proffering an expert in lay witness clothing (but it also results in the added cost of expert fees). Under the amendment, a witness's testimony must be scrutinized under the rules regulating expert opinion to the extent that the witness is providing testimony based on scientific, technical, or other specialized knowledge. The amendment does not distinguish between expert and lay *witnesses*, but rather between expert and lay *testimony*. Certainly it is possible for the same witness to provide both lay and expert opinion testimony in a single case, as for example, a law enforcement agent could testify that the defendant was acting suspiciously, without being qualified as an expert, but the rules on experts would be applicable where the agent testified on the basis of extensive experience that the defendant was using code words to refer to drug quantities and prices.[26] Similarly, a therapist testifying about his patient may be providing both expert and lay testimony.

In many instances, the court, judge or jury, is not able to reach an intelligent decision because of the difficulty of the question involved, and the opinion of those skilled in the particular subject at issue may be obtained for assistance. Here the function of the expert's testimony is advising the jury by giving an opinion rather than proving facts. For example, the jury would be incapable of determining whether death resulted from a particular cut, even though it had before it a description of the wound; hence the opinion of a medical person is of assistance to the jury. However, when experts disagree, as they do more often than not, one may wonder how a jury composed of lay persons can fairly render a decision. For example, how can a jury decide whether an individual suffered from repressed memory syndrome if even the professional organizations point out that it is very difficult for an expert to determine this?[27] The answer may be in credibility. Simply, some experts are more convincing than others. Jurors may also decide on the basis of their own personal view of things.[28]

The problem of expert testimony, particularly that of a psychiatric character, whether as to facts or opinion, is somewhat different in criminal than in civil cases because of certain constitutional privileges of the accused. Because of the defendant's privilege against self-incrimination, the expert witness for the state in a criminal prosecution is much more restricted when the defendant's mental, rather than physical, condition is in issue. The accused may be compelled to submit to a physical examination by the medical witness for the prosecution since this does not involve testimonial compulsion.[29] The accused cannot be compelled to answer any questions asked by the expert in a mental examination, however, because this would violate his privilege against self-incrimination.[30] A proviso: a defendant who pleads insanity must submit to a psychiatric examination, and if he refuses he forfeits the right to present psychiatric testimony; the psychiatrist may testify only on the issue of mental status and may not reveal any statement made to him as to the commission of the offense.

Helpfulness as the Touchstone of Expert Testimony

The touchstone on the role of the forensic expert is *helpfulness*. It is on this basis, for pretrial or trial purposes, that a lawyer engages an expert. The expert may be engaged to serve as a consultant or as a witness at trial, or both. Even before filing a complaint, the lawyer might use an expert to develop knowledge about a technical area and to help him frame the complaint and understand relevant issues. The lawyer's familiarity with the subject matter will determine the need of assistance. Once the complaint is filed, the expert can be of assistance with discovery of facts or identification of documents. The expert can also be helpful in preparing for depositions, whether of lay or expert witnesses, or in identifying licensing agencies, and, sometimes, specific persons within agencies with whom the lawyer may find communication helpful.[31]

Experts often play a pivotal role in the settlement of a case, thereby avoiding a trial. More than 95 percent of tort cases are resolved without a trial. The expert's deposition or report is most important in determining whether to go to trial or in determining the settlement amount. Insurance companies can be persuaded by the expert's report or by the reputation of the expert.

At trial, the use of expert testimony poses two interrelated but separate questions: first, whether the subject matter of the litigation is such that the trier of fact (judge or jury) may appropriately receive assistance in the form of specialized knowledge; and second, whether the witness at hand is qualified to render the assistance. In resolving the first question, the test, under Rule 702 of the Federal Rules of Evidence and its state counterparts, is whether the testimony of the expert "will assist the trier of fact to understand the evidence or to determine a fact in issue." The helpfulness requirement means that experts may testify not only on subjects beyond the ken of lay juries (as common law courts often held) but also to aid the jury to understand even familiar matters, by virtue of experience or training that provides a more thorough or refined understanding than ordinary experience provides.[32]

Once at trial, the first step is to qualify the witness as an expert, not only to satisfy fundamental evidentiary and procedural rules but also to inform the jury about the expert's credentials. The better the credentials, the greater the witness's credibility, and the more weight the jury will give the testimony. It is apparently best that an expert be neither "virgin" nor "prostitute"—an expert who has never testified may have difficulty in getting qualified, while one who testifies often is discredited as a hired gun.[33]

Distressed by the testimony of forensic experts, especially the traveling expert, neurosurgeons and obstetricians from Florida urged the American Medical Association to address the matter. In response, the AMA in 1998 passed a resolution stating that "expert testimony is the practice of medicine."[34] The AMA also passed a Report of the Board of Trustees, *Expert Witness Testimony*, which discusses: (1) the importance and role of physicians, medical societies, and licensing boards in maintaining the integrity of physicians who provide expert witness testimony; (2) some of the inherent difficulties, both conceptual and practical, in conducting peer review of such physicians; (3) existing peer review programs within organized medicine; and (4) a possible role for licensing boards in this arena.[35] Given the concern over the traveling expert, these issues may become more prominent, and psychiatrists have been advised to review the problem of licensure with the out-of-state attorney at the time of retention. Professional liability insurance covers the individual only where he is licensed to practice.[36]

Notes

1. The 1944 verdict forcing Charlie Chaplin to pay child support for a child that blood testing had conclusively shown was not his outraged him. The trial judge allowed the case to go to the jury on the basis of the mother's "equally persuasive" testimony that Chaplin was the only man with whom she had had sexual intercourse at the appropriate times. The jury found the mother more credible than the scientific evidence. A New Jersey case six years later had the same result. J. A. Gold, "Science Tests Now Get Their Day in Court" (ltr.), *New York Times*, Jan. 23, 1992, p. 14. see C. Chaplin, *My Life in Pictures* (London: Bodley Head, 1974); L. G. Chaplin, *My Life with Charlie Chaplin* (New York: Bernard Geis, 1966). That the jury was permitted to consider the scientific evidence and decide against it was the heart of the issue. Is it nullification of the facts? Should a jury be allowed to go against the scientific evidence and rule on the basis of other evidence (namely, that Chaplin was living with the child's mother)? The notion that a scientific test may be so conclusive as to dispose of a case without jury deliberation has been difficult for courts to accept. Should DNA evidence be "Do Not Argue"? See B. Scheck, P. Neufeld, & J. Dwyer, *Actual Innocence* (New York: Doubleday, 2000); see also D. L. Faigman, *Legal Alchemy : The Use and Misuse of Science in the Law* (New York: W. H. Freeman, 1999).

Fred Trost, the well-known host of public television's *The Practical Sportsman*, had many reasons to rail against the justice system. Hit with a libel lawsuit, poorly defended by his attorneys, and devastated by a $4 million judgment against him, he experienced subsequent bankruptcy. An investigative report he aired on truth in advertising, exposing a manufacturer's fraudulent claims, started the legal nightmare in 1990 that dogged him for several years. The experience generated angst and soul-searching but led him down another road to explore justice—through law school. His thought was, "If I were an attorney, I wouldn't be in this jam, because I would have seen what was coming up and done what was necessary to protect myself." So, he enrolled in law school, and he said, "When I went into law, I was very mad. I was mad at the system. I was mad at everybody. But I found out that the law professors weren't there to teach people how to be snakes and to be deceptive. This was a totally up and up study of law. It changed my attitude towards the system. . . . I think it's too bad that everybody can't go to law school." Quoted in N. Stecker, "An Outdoorsman and the Law," *Mich. Bar J.* 80 (Dec. 2001): 40.

2. See E. M. Morgan, *Basic Problems of Evidence* (Philadelphia: American Law Institute, 1954), p. 60.

3. R. A. Posner, "An Economic Approach to the Law of Evidence," *Stan. L. Rev.* 51 (1999): 1477. On the other hand, in the book *The Argument Culture* (New York: Random House, 1998), Deborah Tannen criticizes the adversarial system. Polarized arguments, she contends, leave us without the facts we need to make up our minds. To avoid needless squabbling, Tannen recommends mediation or adoption of the French system, in which cases are decided not by a jury but by the *conviction intime de juge*—the judge's private belief. What Tannen is missing is the drama of conflict and the importance of a trial as a morality play.

4. *Causes Celebres* 3: 309, quoted in J. Bentham, *Rationale of Judicial Evidence* (London: Hunt & Clarke, 1827), pp. 37–38.

5. United States v. Johnson, 575 F.2d 1347 (5th Cir. 1978); People v. Boyd, 65 Mich. App. 11, 236 N.W.2d 744 (1975); Annot., 95 A.L.R.3d 978 (1979).

6. State v. Briner, 198 Neb. 766, 255 N.W.2d 422 (1977).

7. Federal Rules of Evidence, Rule 703.

8. See, e.g., D. Faust & J. Ziskin, "The Expert Witness in Psychology and Psychiatry," *Science*, July 1, 1988, p. 31; discussed in D. Goleman, "Psychologists' Expert Testimony Called Unscientific," *New York Times*, Oct. 11, 1988, p. 19.

9. James McElhaney, professor of trial advocacy, writes: "Within the limits of relevance and the constraints of ethics, the lawyer as playwright decides whether and how the trial will be a fascinating experience that will keep the judge and the jury on the edge of their seats, or a turgid, stultifying affair that will leave everyone in a stupor." J. McElhaney, "Creating Tension," *A.B.A.J.*, June 1, 1988, p. 84.

10. Triangle Publication v. Rohrlich, 167 F.2d 969 (2d Cir. 1945).

11. 214 F.2d 862 (D.C. Cir. 1954).

12. 338 U.S. 25 (1949).

13. 347 U.S. 483 (1954).

14. 392 U.S. 514 (1968).

15. E. R. Beckwith & R. Soberheim, "Amicus Curiae—Minister of Justice," *Fordham L. Rev.* 17 (1946): 38; F. V. Harper & E. D. Etherington, "Lobbyists before the Court," *U. Pa. L. Rev.* 101 (1953): 1172; S. Krislov, "The Amicus Curiae Brief: From Friendship to Advocacy," *Yale L.J.* 72 (1963): 694.

16. With the exception of governmental units, which can file amicus briefs as a matter of right, an individual or group desiring to file must obtain the consent of all parties or file a motion describing their interest in the case and showing that the brief will cover matter not presented or inadequately presented by the parties. 28 U.S.C., sec. 1706. Under the regulations of the Internal Revenue Service, sec. 1.501(c)(3), the status of contributions as gifts and the charitable classification of an association would not be jeopardized by involvement in court proceedings, either on its own behalf or as amicus curiae. There are, though, other limitations placed upon an organization as a nonprofit, tax-exempt organization that should be noted. The organization may not use any "substantial portion of its resources" in attempting to influence the legislative process. It may produce educational and informational materials, but it may not lead crusades or propaganda campaigns. It may respond to requests to testify before legislative hearings, and members of the staff may voluntarily appear, but only as

individuals and not representing the organization. If these restrictions are too confining, an organization could establish a coordinate activity organization, which would not be tax-exempt, and thus could become involved in political, propaganda, or legislative campaigns. Thus the ACLU and the NAACP are, respectively, the activist organizations of the ACLU Foundation and the NAACP Legal Defense Fund.

17. The *class action* is a device by which one or more representatives of a group of people affected by a particular defendant's actions can file suit and press claims on behalf of the entire group of similarly situated individuals. Class actions are often used when individual actions would be impractical because of the low value of the claims involved, such as in an action by consumers against a drug company for overcharges on medicine. On occasion the class action device is resorted to in mass tort cases involving personal injuries to a number of people, but in most such cases personal injury plaintiffs prefer to assert their claims as individuals. To certify a class, the judge must find that the named or representative plaintiff will adequately represent the interests of the class of persons on whose behalf suit is brought. Notice must generally be provided when money damages are sought to allow class members to opt out of the class and file their own suit if they choose. All settlements must be approved by the judge after notice to the class at a fairness hearing. See H. B. Newberg, *Newberg on Class Actions: A Manual for Group Litigation at Federal and State Levels* (New York: McGraw Hill, 1977); Jenkins v. Raymark Industries, 782 F.2d 468 (5th Cir. 1986).

18. See. S. P. Sturm, "The Legacy and Future of the Corrections Litigation," *U. Pa. L. Rev.* 142 (1993): 639. Class-action lawsuits over Ritalin were filed (without success) against the American Psychiatric Association and various pharmaceutical companies, alleging that they conspired to create the diagnosis of attention-deficit disorder and attention-deficit hyperactivity disorder as a way to reap pharmacological profits. D. Fulton, "Class Action Suits over Ritalin Filed against APA," *Clinical Psychiatry News,* Oct. 2000, p. 1; K. P. O'Meara, "Writing May Be on Wall for Ritalin," *Insight,* Oct. 16, 2000, p. 16.

19. J. B. Weinstein, *Individual Justice in Mass Tort Litigation* (Evanston, Ill.: Northwestern University Press, 1995). See also P. M. Barrett, "Why Americans Look to the Courts to Cure the Nation's Social Ills," *Wall Street Journal,* Jan. 4, 2000, p. 1; P. Waldmeir, "Legal Eagles Rule the Roost," *Financial Times,* Dec. 11–12, 1999, p. 1.

20. See Federal Rules of Evidence, Rule 706; E. J. Imwinkelried, "The Court Appointment of Expert Witnesses in the United States: A Failed Experiment," *Medicine & Law* 8 (1989): 601.

21. Dr. Bernard Diamond debunked the idea of an impartial expert in a classic article, "The Fallacy of the Impartial Expert," *Arch. Crim. Psychodynamics* 3 (1959): 221, and together with Professor David W. Louisell in another article, "The Psychiatrist as an Expert Witness: Some Ruminations and Speculations," *Mich L. Rev.* 63 (1965): 1335. See also N. Miltenberg, "Myths about 'Neutral' Scientific Experts," *Trial,* Jan. 2000, p. 62.

22. R. L. Goldstein, "Psychiatrists in the Hot Seat: Discrediting Doctors by Impeachment of Their Credibility," *Bull. Am. Acad. Psychiatry & Law* 16 (1988): 225. In a Louisiana case, the expert had just expressed his opinion that the claimant was not suffering from post-traumatic neurosis but was, instead, a malingerer. The attorney asked: "Is that your conclusion that this man is a malingerer?" To which the expert replied, "I wouldn't be testifying if I didn't think so, unless I was on the other side, then it would be a post-traumatic condition." Ladner v. Higgins, 71 So.2d 242, 244 (La. App. 1954).

23. E. Erikson, "The Ontogeny of Ritualization," presented in June 1965 to the Royal Society as a contribution to a symposium on "Ritualization in Animals and in Man." In a well-known joke about a couple who come to a rabbi, the husband gives his side of the story, and the rabbi says, "You're right." Then the wife gives her side of the story, and the rabbi says, "You're right." Then the husband says, "But, Rabbi, how can we both be right? She's right, and I'm right?" The rabbi says, "You're right."

24. Apparently every proverb—that pithy summary of popular wisdom—can be matched by another that contradicts it flatly, as for instance, "a rolling stone gathers no moss," as against "the traveling bee gets the honey"; or "look before you leap," as against "he who hesitates is lost"; "The Lord loveth a cheerful giver," but "fools and their money are soon parted"; "absence makes the heart grow fonder," but "out of sight, out of mind." R. Slovenko, "Mixed Messages in Proverbs," *J. Psychiatry & Law* 21 (1993): 405.

25. Federal Rules of Evidence, Rule 701.

26. See United States v. Figueroa-Lopez, 125 F.3d 1241 (9th Cir. 1997). The amendment

incorporates the distinctions set forth in State v. Brown, 836 S.W.2d 530 (Tenn. 1992), where the court noted that a lay witness would have to qualify as an expert before he could testify that bruising around the eyes is indicative of skull trauma.

27. In Bertram v. Poole, 597 N.W.2d 309 (Minn. App. 1999), the experts disagreed whether there is any scientific basis for repressed memory or whether the individuals involved in the case suffered from repressed memory syndrome.

28. "Where expert witnesses offer conflicting opinions, it is for the jury, as the ultimate trier of fact, to consider their qualifications and determine the weight to be given their opinions." McKay's Family Dodge v. Hardrives, 480 N.W.2d 141, 146 (Minn. App. 1992).

29. In the leading case of Schmerber v. California, 384 U.S. 757 (1966), the defendant was compelled to get a blood test against his will in a drunk-driving prosecution. Tracing the development of the law, the Supreme Court held that this did not violate the defendant's constitutional rights, noting, "The distinction which has emerged, often expressed in different ways, is that the privilege [against self-incrimination] is a bar against compelling 'communications' or 'testimony,' but that compulsion which makes a suspect or an accused the source of 'real or physical evidence' does not violate it." Thus, the privilege is no bar to compelling the defendant to submit to such tests as fingerprinting, photographing, or urine analysis. State v. Tarrance, 252 La. 396, 211 So.2d 304 (1968) (defendant compelled to give a handwriting sample).

30. People v. Stevens, 386 Mich. 579, 194 N.W.2d 370 (1972). The U.S. Supreme Court in its controversial decision in *Miranda* in 1966 ruled that persons suspected of crime must be advised of their rights before interrogation, or their confessions may not be used in court. See H. A. Davidson, "Psychiatric Examination and Civil Rights," in R. Slovenko (ed.), *Crime, Law and Corrections* (Springfield, Ill.: Thomas, 1966), p. 459; Comment, "Pretrial Psychiatric Examination and the Privilege against Self-Incrimination," *J. Ill. L. For.* 1971: 232.

31. R. E. Brooks, "Expert Witness, Used Properly, Can Expedite Fact-Finding Process," *National Law Journal*, Sept. 5, 1988, p. 20.

32. In re Japanese Elect. Prods. Antitrust Litig., 723 F.2d 238 (3d Cir. 1983); Garbincius v. Boston Edison Co., 621 F.2d 1171 (1st Cir. 1980).

33. I owe this observation to Dr. Emanuel Tanay.

34. Policy II-265.993, AMA Policy Compendium 1998. Dr. Larry Faulkner, dean of the School of Medicine at the University of South Carolina, urged in his presidential address at the 1999 annual meeting of the American Academy of Psychiatry and Law that forensic psychiatry be considered a medical specialty. L. R. Faulkner, "Ensuring That Forensic Psychiatry Thrives as a Medical Specialty in the 21st Century," *J. Am. Acad. Psychiatry & Law* 28 (2000): 14. Dr. Faulkner added (personal communication, Oct. 19, 1999):

> I do believe that forensic psychiatry is indeed medical practice, and I have no problem with licensing boards placing practical and reasonable "restrictions" on conducting "examinations on the road." We can't have it both ways. If we do not consider forensic psychiatry to be medical practice, then we have to also accept the proposition that anybody can do it. I would rather put up with the inconvenience of responding to the "restrictions" of licensing boards.

Approximately eleven states now require local licensing, and seven states require local licensing unless the out-of-state psychiatrist is a consultant for a state-licensed one. One state allows out-of-state psychiatrists to provide testimony a limited number of times without a local license. J. Arehart-Treichel, "Crossing State Line May Put Expert Witnesses in Jeopardy," *Psychiatric News*, Dec. 1, 2000, p. 10. The same licensing or certification issue arises in regard to "examinations on the road" by psychologists. See E. Y. Drogin, "Prophets in Another Land: Utilizing Psychological Expertise from Foreign Jurisdictions," *MPDLR* 23 (Sept./Oct. 1999):767.

35. Board of Trustees Report 18-1-98. The issue of peer review opens up questions: Who are the peers? Will transcripts of testimony be available? Will the peer reviewers enjoy immunity from suit?

36. R. I. Simon & D. W. Shuman, "Conducting Forensic Examinations on the Road: Are You Practicing Your Profession without a License?," *J. Am. Acad. Psychiatry & Law* 27 (1999): 75. Actually, the attorney general is not likely to proceed against the forensic expert on the ground that he is practicing medicine without a license, but a disgruntled litigant may create problems for the expert with the medical board. Indeed, should a forensic examination, as

suggested, be considered the practice of medicine? In an oft-quoted statement, Dr. Seymour Pollack described the field of psychiatry and law as one in which "psychiatric theories, concepts, principles, and practice are applied or related to any and all legal matters." The current definition of forensic psychiatry, adopted by the American Board of Forensic Psychiatry and the American Academy of Psychiatry and the Law, states, "Forensic psychiatry is a subspeciality of psychiatry, in which scientific and clinical expertise is applied to legal issues in legal contexts, embracing civil, criminal, correctional, or legislative matters; forensic psychiatry should be practiced in accordance with guidelines and ethical principles enunciated by the profession of psychiatry."

The forensic expert usually serves as an agent of the attorney, and the expert making an assessment is not in a physician-patient relationship with the examinee. Indeed, the forensic expert makes a point of advising the examinee that the examination is not for the purpose of treatment.

2

Boundaries of Legal and Ethical Forensic Practice

Mental health professionals express concern about potential ethical conflicts when serving as expert witnesses. With frequency, questions arise regarding the obligations and responsibilities of lawyers in their interaction with forensic experts. In this chapter we discuss the necessity at trial of expert testimony, selection of the expert, the underlying data of the expert opinion, fabrication and providing and withholding data, mode of presentation, sequestering witnesses, compelling expert testimony, depositions, discovery of expert opinions and reports, limitation of opinion on the ultimate issue, instructions to the jury, and the fee arrangement.

Necessity of Expert Testimony

The underlying theory of the adversary system is that each side presents its best version of the case, without perjury or manufactured evidence, subject to cross-examination and rebuttal by the adversary.[1] The lawyer is not free, as he might like to be, in the representation of a client. In many cases expert testimony is helpful and would be permitted as proof but at other times it is absolutely essential and required as a matter of law. Without expert testimony, in these cases, the court will not entertain the litigation. The testimony of lay witnesses in these cases would be insufficient as a matter of law. As a consequence, the lawyer is at the mercy of experts—he *must* find and engage one.

That is the situation in a professional negligence (malpractice) case, where the standard of care is that degree of skill and learning which is ordinarily possessed and exercised by members of the profession in good standing. The plaintiff must, as a matter of law, produce an expert to establish that standard and that there was a deviation from it (unless the negligence is sufficiently obvious as to lie within common knowledge, as where a foreign object, such as a sponge or needle, is left within the body of the patient).[2] In rendering professional services, a practitioner is held, with few exceptions, to a provider-defined standard of care. To put it differently, the law allows the profession to establish its own liability standards. On the other hand, in the ordinary negligence action (e.g., a collision case), the standard of care to which the defendant must conform is that degree of care which, in the jury's view, a reasonable person of ordinary prudence would have exercised in the defendant's place in the same or similar circumstances.[3]

In a medical malpractice case based on negligent nondisclosure, expert testimony is necessary to establish that a risk from the procedure exists, that it is accepted medical practice to know that risk, and that it is more probable than not that the undisclosed risk materialized in harm. (Informed consent is the theoretical construct but, needless to say, both physician and patient are beholden to the auditor and policymaker.) Nationwide, as a rule, the action for failure to disclose risks is deemed one of malpractice, requiring expert testimony.[4]

Is expert testimony necessary when the propriety of seclusion or restraint is question? In *Reifschneider v. Nebraska Methodist Hospital*,[5] it was argued unsuccessfully that the question of restraint is custodial or nonmedical and within the grasp or knowledge of ordinary laymen, and, therefore, no expert testimony as to the defendant's duty to restrain is necessary. In line with other decisions, the Nebraska Supreme Court required expert testimony to establish a duty of the defendant to restrain a patient. Assessing the status of a patient and determining whether restraints are needed are matters calling for expert testimony, the court said.[6]

One small but important and much-publicized area of the law of medical malpractice involves duties or standard of care mandated by the legislature or the courts. One illustration is the Washington Supreme Court's requirement of glaucoma tests not apparently required by the medical profession (or by legislation) as a matter of routine for patients under forty years of age.[7] Another illustration is the decision that outraged nearly all psychiatrists—the *Tarasoff* case in California,[8] and progeny in other states, calling upon psychotherapists to protect potential victims from the acts of a patient. The court in *Tarasoff* characterized the case as one of professional negligence, calling for expert testimony. The question whether a patient poses a serious danger of violence to others is measured, the court said, by whether the "therapist does in fact determine, or under applicable professional standards reasonably should have determined" the danger.[9] The court, while imposing the duty, deferred to the profession in assessing the danger though, in fact, the profession has no standards on the prediction of dangerousness.[10]

On the other hand, expert testimony was not mandated on the propriety of the course of behavior taken in view of the danger. The court in *Tarasoff* said that "the adequacy of the therapist's conduct must be measured against the traditional negligence standard of the rendition of reasonable care under the circumstances."[11] The court pointed out, "The discharge of this duty may require the therapist to take one or more of various steps, depending upon the nature of the case. Thus it may call for him to warn the intended victim or others likely to apprise the victim of the danger, to notify the police, or to take whatever other steps are reasonably necessary under the circumstances."[12] Placing an advertisement in the newspaper would likely not be found reasonable. It would be a jury question not necessarily aided by expert testimony.[13]

In criminal cases, failure to engage an expert may constitute ineffective assistance of counsel warranting reversal of a conviction. That is the implication of *Ake v. Oklahoma*,[14] a murder case, where no psychiatrist was called to testify although the only issue was insanity. In this case the U.S. Supreme Court overturned the conviction on the ground that the defendant, an indigent, should have access to psychiatric assistance in preparing an insanity defense.[15]

In some cases the courts want psychiatric testimony as window dressing. Decisions on civil commitment, child custody, and also on criminal responsibility are difficult and uncomfortable to make. Such decisions, however, have to be made, and the courts, mindful of public opinion, often abdicate their decision-making responsibility to psychiatrists or want to decorate their decision with psychiatric testimony. It's passing the buck, so to speak. It may give the impression of undue power of experts in the judicial process, but that is more appearance than reality. Taking it at face value, however, Dr. Jonas Robitscher in *The Powers of Psychiatry* concluded, "The psychiatrist is the most important non-governmental decision maker in modern life."[16]

In still other cases an attorney may engage an expert in order to have a report that will provide leverage in bargaining, rather than to assist in the quest for truth. In many cases, civil or criminal, the report may lead to a settlement without having been tested by cross-examination. Insurance companies in settling a case place great reliance, by and large, on the expert's report. Of course, the expert is subject to the time-honored crucible of cross-examination at trial—provided the case goes to trial. Most divorce cases (including those involving distribution of assets) are not tried; they are settled after the experts' reports are received. In domestic litigation it may well be that, as time goes on, the role of the parties or lay witnesses may be relatively minor compared to that of the experts.

Selecting the Expert

Under the rules of evidence the lawyer has wide discretion in selecting an expert. The task of qualifying a witness as an expert is not a major obstacle, though it is becoming more difficult as the result of widespread complaints about so-called junk science in the courtroom. The door to Plato's Academy, in Athens, bore the forbidding inscription, "Let no one enter who is not a mathematician." Webster's dictionary defines an expert as "a person who is very skillful, or highly trained and informed in some special field." The temple of justice, however, is not nearly so exacting. The expert need not have "special" or "complete" knowledge of his field of expertise[17]—the testimony, as we have noted, need be merely "helpful" to the court.[18] In medical malpractice cases, what the lawyer wants in an expert medical witness, of course, are the looks of Robert Redford, the knowledge of Michael DeBakey, and the presence of Ronald Reagan, but alas, not many doctors can fill that prescription.[19]

Sometimes in serving as an expert, the expert may have unfavorable information about a colleague on the other side of the case. There is divided opinion whether the expert should relate that information to the attorney retaining him. Is it within the proper scope of the expert's role in the case? Dr. Paul Appelbaum is of the opinion (not widely held) that it is not the role of the expert to help the attorney who has hired him to win the case but rather to provide honest and accurate testimony about the person who has been evaluated. He suggests that one goes beyond that role when one provides not generally known information regarding an expert. By and large, experts are of the opinion that if it is a matter of public record, such as the board of medicine having censured the expert for alcoholism or for being dishonest in court, it should be pointed out to the attorney as it may be useful in cross-examination or qualification as an expert.

Of special concern in the administration of justice are the conflicts arising out of the need to present expert testimony and the willingness of experts to say whatever is needed to prevail in a case. Unquestionably, there are experts who have no business being in a courtroom much less in their profession. Lawyers say, "Some experts are willing, upon request, to find a muscle spasm in a statue."[20] Lawyers too, it must be noted, are often willing to say anything to advance their cause. The prominent attorney F. Lee Bailey is also known as "F. Lie Bailey."

The courts traditionally deferred to the profession to set out the standard of care in malpractice cases, and in doing so they adopted a *school* method for qualifying expert witnesses. This method of qualifying allowed as an expert one who either practices in or is familiar with the particular school of the practitioner on trial. Thus, as familiarity was sufficient, a surgeon or a nurse could testify against a podiatrist as long as they were knowledgeable about podiatrists' standard of care.[21] Under this rule, it was not very difficult to obtain an expert to testify against the defendant. In recent years, however, at the behest of medical societies, various states have required that the testifying expert not simply be familiar with the practice of the defendant but that they be of the same specialty.[22]

In a suit in California for wrongful death, arising out of a suicide, against a church and its pastors, an order was initially entered forbidding testimony of a psychiatrist,[23] but the order was subsequently withdrawn, the court saying that the action was not one of malpractice (professional negligence), calling for expert testimony, but one of intentional infliction of mental distress, which requires no expert testimony.[24] The court thus avoided the issue whether a psychiatrist may testify in a clergy malpractice case. "We need not decide," the court said, "whether [the pastor] had a duty to refer [the individual] to a psychiatrist or other mental health professional or whether [the pastor] or the church had a duty to adequately train the pastors in methods of psychological counseling."[25]

In psychiatric malpractice cases, the plethora of therapeutic techniques and the eclectic nature of much psychiatric practice inevitably results in a blurring of school boundaries. This fact, together with the dogmatism of many practitioners, makes it likely that experts, though familiar with a school, will disagree as to the standard of care for that school. Indeed, the principal controversy in mental health care is over the development of standards of treatment.[26] Frederic Worden, a noted psychoanalyst and brain researcher, once observed that, unlike violinists, who all play violins and know what one looks like, psychiatrists "are not all playing the same instrument"; indeed, he said, "some are playing instruments that others disapprove of or disbelieve in or even, in some cases, instruments whose very existence is unknown to others in the group."[27] Following Illinois, a New York court ruled that psychologists are not qualified to testify as expert witnesses in malpractice suits against psychiatrists or the hospitals with which the psychiatrists are affiliated.[28]

The *locality* rule at one time was generally followed along with the school rule in regard to the medical profession but usually not in regard to other professions. The rule further constricted the pool of professionals qualified to testify as to the relevant standard of care. The expert testifying in a medical malpractice case had to be one who could testify as to the standard of knowledge and skill in terms of the practitioner in good standing for the community in which he practices or a similar one. The definition of *community* was a narrow one. Under the rule, to show what is the standard of learning or the customary practice in a small town, the only expert is a doctor who knows about this (or a similar) small town. Conjoined with the protective, provider-defined standard of care, the rule served to insulate the medical profession from liability. Current efforts to hold expert testimony by physicians as the practice of medicine is another attempt to curtail experts coming from a different state.

The locality rule arose in the days when medical education was not standardized and there was a wide variance in the knowledge and skill of doctors in different areas of the country. As this situation has changed, the courts have held that there is a minimum national standard especially for specialists. As a consequence, experts may come from places other than the locality of the practitioner on trial, subject to the school rule. This is evident in journals for lawyers, which are now replete with advertisements of experts offering their services nationwide. The use of experts has become so common that thriving businesses have been formed to serve as clearinghouses for witnesses. The lawyer looking for a medical expert, or other expert, can also search by computer for an expert by state or specialty. Trial attorney associations (plaintiffs' or defendants') maintain a regularly updated index of experts ranging from accidentalists to zoologists. In short, the lawyer, for a fee, now has a cornucopia of available services. Most law firms maintain a list, or "stable," of experts whom they call upon as needed.[29] However, in child custody litigation, some experts lose credibility the more they appear as a witness for a given lawyer, as these cases are tried before judges alone and they get to know the credibility of the witness.

In criminal cases, in order to avoid reversible error, trial judges tend to be more liberal in accepting the qualifications of a witness when tendered by the defense as an expert and in admitting the evidence as probative (thus the trial court allowed the defense to introduce as evidence the CAT scans of John Hinckley Jr.'s slightly shrunken brain).

The Underlying Data of the Expert Opinion under the Federal Rules of Evidence

The question is presented: Given that the polygraph or hypnosis itself is deemed so untrustworthy that it may not be admitted in evidence, may an expert rely on the results of the polygraph or hypnosis in forming an opinion? May an expert rely on inadmissible hearsay? On a criminal record in assessing a party? Rule 703 of the Federal Rules of Evidence, adopted in 1975, allows experts to rely on sources of information that are not admissible in their own right. Hence, the lawyer, by using an expert, would have passage around the exclusionary rules of evidence, and that may prompt the use of an expert. Rule 703 provides that an expert may base an opinion on facts or data "if of a type reasonably relied upon by experts in the particular field . . . the facts or data need not be admissible in evidence." The focus of the rule is not on the admissibility of the underlying data of the expert's opinion but on its validity and reliability as measured by the practice of experts when not in court. Thus, under it, a doctor as an expert witness may relate hearsay statements of other doctors or investigators in explaining the basis for his opinion.[30]

Take the case of *United States v. Madrid*,[31] as an example of expert testimony based, in part, on the criminal record of the accused. Ordinarily, testimony as to past crimes, standing alone, is excludable as impermissible character evidence.[32] However, in *Madrid*, involving a defense of insanity, the state's psychiatrist was allowed to testify that the defendant was sane, an opinion based, in part, on the fact that the accused "had committed armed robberies of stores prior to the offense in question in order to support a heroin addiction."[33]

Indeed, under the Federal Rules of Evidence, the lawyer in offering an expert need not even present the data underlying an opinion, unless the court requires otherwise. Under the Rules, it is left to the cross-examiner to attack the opinion and to ferret out its basis, if any. As a matter of trial tactics, however, the expert on direct presents the data for the opinion, otherwise it would not be persuasive. The examination of the expert may begin thus:

> "Doctor, do you have an opinion whether stress had a bearing on the defen-
> dant's conduct?"
> "Yes."
> "What is that opinion?"
> "It caused the defendant to act involuntarily."
> "Doctor, would you tell the court the basis for your opinion?"

The Treating Therapist as Expert

The Ethical Guidelines for the Practice of Forensic Psychiatry, which appear in volume 2, appendix 2, point to the problems related to a treating therapist serving as an expert witness. The relevant guideline states: "Treating psychiatrists should generally avoid agreeing to be an expert witness or to perform evaluations of their patients for legal purposes because a forensic evaluation usually requires that other people be interviewed and testimony may adversely affect the therapeutic and forensic relationship." Engaging in conflicting therapeutic and forensic relationships exacerbates the risk that experts will be more concerned with case outcome than the accuracy of their testimony. Moreover, it is often claimed that testifying as an expert on behalf of the patient jeopardizes the therapeutic relationship, but apparently there is no empirical evidence to support the claim. In any event, attorneys and juries tend to give more credibility to the testimony of a therapist than to a forensic expert. In a recent case in Michigan for breach of an insurance contract, where the jury awarded over a million dollars to the patient, the attorney who represented the patient said the key to winning the case was *not* hiring expert witnesses to explain the plaintiff's condition. Rather, he relied exclusively on the testimony of the plaintiff's treating doctors. Moreover, he indicated, "We never hired an expert psychiatrist. We relied exclusively on the treaters. If you've got good treaters and they are credible, that goes a long, long way with a jury as opposed to what any expert might say."[34]

When testifying in legal proceedings, some treating therapists seek to avoid dual-relationship problems by confining their testimony to fact issues. In these circumstances, treating therapists typically report their diagnostic findings, explain their patient's clinical condition, and detail the course of treatment. While limiting themselves to fact testimony, these therapists avoid expressing any opinions regarding the issues before the court (such as causation or responsibility), and they do not get an expert fee. The critics of therapists even serving as fact witnesses claim that such testimony can misinform and mislead in a legal proceeding.

Fabrication and Providing and Withholding Data

"Just remember that lying can get you into a lot of trouble if not done properly," says a lawyer to a witness in a cartoon, but many would say it is true to life.[35] Professional regulations define the duties of the lawyer to the court, to the client, to the profession, and to the public. It is the duty of the lawyer "to employ, for the purpose of maintaining the causes confided to them, such means only as are consistent with truth and never to seek to mislead the judge or juries by any artifice or false statement of the law."[36] To put it simply, the lawyer is ethically bound not to fabricate evidence. Preparation of a witness is good lawyering, but coaching of a witness is ground for reversal.

In the situation involving client-intended perjury, it may be noted, the well-defined duty to preserve client confidences conflicts with the lawyer's duty of candor and honesty toward the court. Disciplinary standards prohibit a lawyer in the course of representation from (1) knowingly using perjured testimony or false evidence, (2) participating in the creation or preservation of evidence when he knows or it is obvious that the evidence is false, or (3) counseling or assisting his client in conduct that the lawyer knows to be illegal or fraudulent. In a recent decision, the Supreme Court imposed an additional, judicially created duty on lawyers when it held that "it is the special duty of an attorney to prevent and disclose fraud upon the court."[37]

As an expert may express an opinion, for this reason as well, lawyers engage an expert. An opinion, unlike a statement of fact, is not subject to perjury. "That's my opinion," says the expert. In *United States v. Roark*,[38] a psychologist was permitted to testify that the defendant's confession was voluntary. And the opinion, as we shall discuss, may go to the "ultimate issue." Thus, in *People v. Whitfield*,[39] a physician was allowed to give an opinion as to whether the victim's injuries were caused by sexual assault.

An expert may base an opinion on facts about which the expert has personal or firsthand knowledge—doctors usually base their opinions in part on conditions and symptoms they personally observed during an examination of the patient—or the expert may rely on reports from third parties (as long as it is customary practice in the specialty to consider that kind of data). The expert may also express an opinion in response to a hypothetical question. In the hypothetical, the lawyer specifies the facts that the expert is to assume. Dr. Jonas Rappeport enters a criticism: "Often such [hypothetical] questions do not actually contain the full information necessary to enable a professional opinion to be reached. This is a serious defect with hypothetical questions and arises unless the expert helps to prepare or actually prepares the question."[40] In all cases, whether or not based on a hypothetical question, the expert must be willing to testify that he has formed his opinion to a reasonable medical or scientific certainty or probability.[41]

The Federal Rules of Evidence and their counterparts in the various states entitle the adversary to inspect any notes that a witness uses to refresh recollection at trial or prior to testifying.[42] The adversary has a right to use the notes on cross-examination. The witness is obliged to bring to court any notes which were viewed in preparation for trial. However, any list of questions prepared by the witness and given to the lawyer engaging him as an aid in asking questions is considered work product, protected from inspection by the adversary, if not reviewed by the witness to refresh recollection and intended solely as a trial aid for the attorney.

Lawyers vary in their ability, of course, in using expert witnesses (as in other matters). Some lawyers, although famous and successful—among them F. Lee Bailey and Melvin Belli—did not use experts well (say the experts). These lawyers wanted to be center stage, taking the limelight away from the expert. One may recall the song, "Oh Lord, It's Hard to Be Humble." Still, others use too many experts. Too many experts on a side tend to dilute the transference (to use psychiatric language) with the jury, and differences get exaggerated. Court rules generally limit the number of experts to three on an issue unless special circumstances can be shown. Within a time period as set out in the court rules, the attorneys must exchange lists of all witnesses to be called at trial. No witness, lay or expert, may be called at trial of the case unless listed, except by leave granted upon a showing of good cause.[43]

To maintain relevancy, the lawyer in preparing a case with an expert will quite frequently discuss the report that the expert is planning to write, or will go over a draft of the report and edit it. Litigation manuals instruct the lawyer: "An expert should never write a report until he has first discussed his conclusions with you orally."[44] Properly done, the lawyer provides useful guidance so that the report will focus on the key issues in the case. The process becomes improper, however, when misleading or manufactured statements are put into the report. At trial, the lawyer who withholds potentially damaging information from the expert may find, on cross-examination, that it has proven counterproductive. In many cases, experts have been forced to change their conclusion when, on cross-examination, they are confronted with additional or different data. This occurs, for example, when an expert is provided with only parts of hospital records or an incomplete history.

Forensic experts, with experience, usually advise the lawyer that they want to see everything that is available and they caution that, if information is withheld, it will likely boomerang at trial. The forensic expert wants all the information that is available in order to base his opinion on the best possible rather than on a limited amount of information. There are times, however, when lawyers tell the expert that they are not going to provide everything because they choose not to (as, for example, when they have information that they do not wish to make available to the opposing attorney) and that the expert should form his opinion on the information given and not to worry about the rest.

Generally speaking, experts are provided all the information that is available and relevant, but is it unethical for a lawyer to withhold information from an expert? As the ethics of the attorney are to provide the best possible defense for a client, this may include not showing certain materials to the expert at the risk of having that backfire in court. That is a legal judgment call, the lawyer's prerogative as part of his decision making or strategy. When an expert is on the witness stand, it is left to the lawyer to bring out what he wants and to deal with what he may not like in his own way.[45] That is his job under the adversary system; the job of the expert is to present his findings or opinion as clearly and honestly as the system will allow.

Mode of Presentation

The task of the expert witness, in sum and substance, is to educate judge or jury about issues that are beyond their knowledge. The use of expert testimony is determined, under the rules of evidence, on the basis of assisting the trier. To that end, may the expert present a lecture? May the expert (or other witness) testify in the form of a free narrative, or must he respond to specific questions? The narrative form is usually favored by the proponent of the evidence, especially when the witness is experienced in testifying—it tends (especially with the use of blackboard or other aids) to make a more effective presentation. The most helpful and informative kind of testimony can be elicited in the narrative form, particularly if the expert can feel that he is being a teacher, which many experts are by nature and preference.[46]

An adversary, by objections, may attempt to break up the continuity of a narration. The adversary complains that the narrative form makes the interposing of objections very difficult if not impossible. Rules of evidence require diligence of counsel in asserting objections; an objection is waived if counsel does not act with diligence. Once testimony is given and heard, a motion to *strike* (an after-objection) may not be effective as a practical matter. The jury has heard the testimony. The adversary is not entitled as a matter of right to demand the Q & A form of presentation. Usually, judges allow the expert to continue, but compel more questions from the proponent. The rules of evidence provide that the court shall exercise reasonable control over the mode of interrogating witnesses so as to make the interrogation and presentation effective for the ascertainment of the truth, and to avoid the needless consumption of time.[47]

Sequestering Witnesses

The trial judge's power to control a witness has traditionally included a broad power to sequester witnesses before, during, and after their testimony. The U.S. Supreme Court has pointed out that the aim of imposing the *rule of witnesses*, as the practice of sequestering witnesses is sometimes called, is twofold: (1) it exercises a restraint on witnesses tailoring their testimony to that of earlier witnesses, and (2) it aids in detecting testimony that is less than candid.[48] Rule 615 of the Federal Rules of Evidence provides that at the request of a party the court "shall" order witnesses excluded so that they cannot hear the testimony of other witnesses. In view of the use of the word *shall*, the Rule makes exclusion of witnesses mandatory at the request of a party.[49]

Rule 615 contains exceptions. One exception, most frequently invoked in the case of expert witnesses, exempts a person whose presence is shown by a party to be essential to the presentation of his cause.[50] It has been held that where a party seeks to except an expert witness from exclusion under the Rule on the basis that he needs to hear firsthand the testimony of the other witnesses, the decision whether to permit him to remain is within the trial judge's discretion, but where a fair showing has been made that the expert witness is required for the management of the case, the trial court must accept any reasonable representation to this effect by counsel.[51]

To form an opinion, the expert may wish to hear the testimony of the witnesses at trial.[52] An expert opinion may be based on testimony heard during the trial. Questions arise: Did the expert hear all of the evidence? On what aspects of the witnesses did the expert rely? On demeanor? In the much publicized trial of Alger Hiss, accused by Whittaker Chambers of passing secrets to Communists, Dr. Carl Binger testified that Chambers was a "psychopath with a tendency toward making false accusations." Binger testified that his opinion was based, in part, on personal observation of Mr. Chambers at trial.[53] The cross-examination of Dr. Binger is widely regarded as the single most devastating cross-examination of an expert ever conducted.[54]

Prosecutors have generally been permitted to have an investigative agent or expert at counsel table throughout the trial although the agent or expert may be a witness. The investigative agent's or expert's presence may be extremely important to counsel, especially when the case is complex or involves some specialized subject matter. The agent, too, having lived with the case for a long time, may be able to assist in meeting trial surprises where the best-prepared counsel would otherwise have difficulty. It could be dangerous to use the agent as a witness as early in the case as possible, so that he might then help counsel as a nonwitness, since the agent's testimony could be needed in rebuttal.[55] Most of the cases have involved allowing a police officer who has been in charge of an investigation to remain in court despite the fact that he will be a witness.[56] In Canada, the parties are not concerned about the costs of the experts, as they are paid by the Crown, and both sides tend to agree to allowing their experts sit throughout the trial.

Rule 615 does not resolve the debate over whether sequestration includes limitations on conduct outside of trial—for example, limitations on counsel in informing witnesses of other testimony, on witnesses' reading of transcripts, and on witnesses' presence at depositions. In doubt, counsel requests the court to acknowledge that the sequestering order prohibits counsel from informing sequestered witnesses as to what happened in court before the witnesses testify. In holding that providing a witness daily transcript copy constitutes a violation of Rule 615, one court stated: "The opportunity to shape testimony is as great with a witness who reads trial testimony as with one who hears the testimony in open court. The harm may be even more pronounced with a witness who reads trial transcript than with one who hears the testimony in open court, because the former need not rely on his memory of the testimony but can thoroughly review and study the transcript in formulating his own testimony."[57] As a sanction, the court may hold the witness in contempt or exclude him from testifying.[58]

Compelling Expert Testimony

May an expert be compelled to give testimony at trial (or in pretrial discovery)? A lawyer looks for a willing expert since one willing is more likely to be helpful than one who is not, but there are times when a willing expert is unavailable, and compelling an unwilling expert may be the only way to establish a case. As we have noted, there are areas of the law where it is absolutely essential to have expert testimony. In compelling testimony, the lawyer is not asking the expert to make any special preparation. It is agreed that an expert cannot be compelled to prepare for his testimony because this would be in the nature of involuntary servitude. However, when a lawyer is convinced that a particular expert's testimony will be of benefit, the testimony will be sought without regard to the expert's willingness to testify or familiarity with the particular facts of the case. The lawyer may feel the expert will be helpful by virtue of a publication, lecture, or testimony in a prior trial of a related matter, or simply because the expert's knowledge derived from his training and experience would make his testimony helpful.[59]

In many cases of medical malpractice, the lawyer is often faced with summoning a treating physician who is reluctant to testify against a doctor, the defendant, who previously treated and allegedly harmed the patient. The treating physician, should he testify, would make a more convincing witness against the defendant doctor than one called in merely as an examiner, but more often than not, he will not testify willingly. He could be called as a fact witness, if not as an expert witness.

Is an expert who is called upon to answer a hypothetical question or to set out a standard of care being required to do merely that which every good citizen is required to do on behalf of public order? The answer is apparently yes, but abuse of the expert must somehow be curtailed. Would a famous surgeon, for example, be compellable to testify in every malpractice case involving a unique operating procedure? The danger is that he might end up spending more time in the courtroom than in the operating room. Society would hardly benefit. In this age of litigation, involving sundry matters, unwilling experts could be made subject to the beck and call of attorneys. In a democracy, should not the expert be allowed the freedom to choose the best use of his time and who is to receive his labor and service? Compensating the expert is not an adequate remedy.

Is there a rational basis for applying different rules to witnesses furnishing scientific, as opposed to observed, facts? Certainly, one is the product of the witness's learning and experience, the other of direct perception, but, if the purpose of witness evidence is to assist the trier of fact, what is the functional difference? The arguments raised by experts as to why they should not be compelled to testify can be made as well by the nonexpert. Reliance on whether the proposed evidence is fact or opinion is not realistic, as these terms themselves escape workable definition. Further difficulty results when the litigants seeking to compel expert testimony must show that other qualified witnesses are unavailable. Who is qualified and what makes a witness unavailable? Is an expert available if he lives in another part of the country?

Is there not inequity in forcing an expert to go to the expense of hiring a lawyer to vindicate his position? How much must the judge decide in advance of trial whether to require the expert to appear? Must the judge determine how much time the expert will spend in the courtroom? Should the judge require a statement by counsel of what testimony he seeks to elicit from the expert before allowing such a subpoena to be deemed properly issued? Can the matter be decided on paper rather than on oral testimony? Must such a subpoena be served sufficiently in advance of trial to permit its resolution before trial begins?[60]

In contrast to factual witnesses, who possess knowledge that is unique and often irreplaceable, expert testimony is not based on any singular personal knowledge of the disputed events. Rather it depends upon specialized training or other acquired knowledge that allows the expert to draw conclusions or to set out a standard of practice. In most areas of expertise, since many individuals possess the necessary qualifications to render expert opinions, this kind of testimony is not unique, and a litigant will not usually be deprived of critical evidence if he cannot have the expert of his choice.

The courts in the United States are not in agreement as to when experts can be compelled to testify. The cases concerning the compulsion of expert testimony vary greatly depending on the factual situations and legal approach taken.[61] The commentators in law journals are also in disagreement.[62] The only reference in the Federal Rules of Evidence to the need of consent by an expert is in Rule 706(a), dealing with court-appointed experts. This provides in part that "an expert witness shall not be appointed by the court unless he consents to act."[63] The situation of the court-appointed expert who is expected to explore the problem and arrive at an informed and unbiased opinion differs markedly, however, from that of an expert called by a party to state the facts as he knows them and what opinion he may have formed on the basis without being asked to make any further investigation. If any inference is to be drawn from the Federal Rules of Evidence, it is against the claim of privilege by an expert, not for it.

In a noted case, *Kaufman v. Edelstein*,[64] the U.S. Court of Appeals for the Second Circuit held that the trial court did not abuse its discretion in allowing the government in its antitrust action against IBM to compel testimony from two individuals with considerable expertise in the computer industry. Specifically, the government wanted these witnesses "to explain the nature of their duties as computer systems consultants and especially to recount advice they gave to various users and potential users of computer systems." Significantly, the government was not asking for an expert evaluation of their evidence in the IBM case but instead stated that the witnesses' testimony would be confined to events which occurred between 1960 and 1972. In a concurring opinion, Judge Gurfein noted that these experts differed from the ordinary expert who has no personal relationship with the subject matter of the litigation. Indeed, they were intimately involved as observers of and participants in the growth and development of the electronic data processing market. The author of the majority opinion, Judge Friendly, indicated that a substantial part of the testimony sought by the government could only be given by these particular experts. They possessed unique information unavailable from any other source, though most of the testimony sought in the *Kaufman* case was factual rather than opinion.

In a case less known, *Wright v. Jeep Corp.*,[65] the defendant in a personal injury action, Jeep Corporation, sought discovery of a crash vehicle researcher who had published an adverse report on the safety of certain vehicles manufactured by the defendant. The information desired by Jeep concerned all research data and memoranda pertaining to a study of highway safety in which the researcher had participated and out of which grew the adverse report. Jeep was interested in the factual basis underlying the researcher's conclusion because it felt the study might be used against it at trial. Although the researcher objected to discovery, on the basis that, among other things, he was an expert and could not be compelled to testify, the court held otherwise. In its ruling, the court noted that the researcher was not being required to assist in explaining technical matters but rather was simply being required to disclose the underlying factual basis for his conclusions so that the parties and the court could judge their validity. As in *Kaufman,* the particular information sought from the experts was not readily available from other sources. Moreover, while the factual observation sought in discovery may have involved some of the expertise and experience of the expert, neither the court nor the litigant in *Wright* was seeking an expert opinion per se from the researcher. Thus, although both *Wright* and *Kaufman* affirm the general principle that an unwilling expert is not immune from compulsory process merely because he is an expert, they do not support the contention that the party has an unlimited right to compel the expert of his choice to provide opinion testimony. The decisions in these cases were based, in large part, on the peculiar need of the compelling party for the information sought and its unavailability from other sources.

Can we adhere to a rule that an expert may not be compelled to give testimony? Were this the rule, it would lie within the discretion of the expert to prevent some cases from being tried, and the lawyer or court would be powerless to provide the jury with any sort of basis for a decision. It would be, in a manner of speaking, an obstruction of justice. In *Kaufman,* the question was whether IBM had monopoly power. The experts on the subject were so uncommon that, were they to decline to testify, the court would be without crucial evidence.[66] In professional malpractice cases, as noted, the plaintiff is obliged to produce an expert to establish the proper standard and that there was a deviation from it. The use of learned treatises is not a happy substitute. As the law defers to the profession on standard of care, it behooves the profession to provide testimony on that standard of care. According to a number of reports, however, experts in the medical field are threatened by their insurers with a loss of insurance coverage or increase in premium rates should they testify in a malpractice case.

Wigmore, the leading authority on evidence, once wrote: "The giving of . . . testimony may be a sacrifice of time and labor, and thus of ease, of profits, of livelihood. This contribution is not to be regarded as a gratuity, or a courtesy, or an ill-required favor. It is a duty not to be grudged or evaded. Whoever is impelled to evade or to resent it should retire from society of organized and civilized communities, and become a hermit. He who will live by society must let society live by him, when it requires to." And he added, "All privileges of exemption from his duty (of giving testimony) are exceptional, and are therefore to be discountenanced. There must be good reason, plainly shown, for their existence."[67]

Depositions

Depositions are taken in order to preserve testimony, to make discovery, or for cross-examination (to impeach the credibility of the witness). Originally, depositions were done solely for the purpose of preserving testimony for trial. A relic of this historic root is that depositions for preservation of testimony were once required to be specifically noticed as *de bene esse* depositions, but now any deposition not specifically limited (as for example, for discovery only) may be used for preservation of testimony for use at trial. Of course, if a witness dies or is, for some reason, unavailable at trial, what the lawyer thought originally was not to be a deposition seeking to preserve testimony may turn out to function as the trial testimony of the deponent. As there is the opportunity to cross-examine at the time of the taking of the deposition, it is admissible at trial (where it may be read by anyone of the attorney's choice). In a discovery deposition, designed to gather information prior to trial, almost all the questions are asked by opposing counsel. Depositions take place in an office with attorneys for both sides and a court reporter present. Despite the informal setting, the deponent is under oath, and what is said can be brought up at trial, notably in cross-examination, and it can be the basis for a charge of perjury if deliberately inaccurate.

It is generally required that oral testimony from live witnesses be presented in any trial proceeding.[68] Exceptions permit the use of depositions for witnesses who are dead, witnesses who are at an inconvenient distance from the forum, the elderly, sick, insane, infirm, and the imprisoned who are not subject to subpoena. Such unavailability is required before a lay witness's deposition may be admitted. The deposition of an expert witness, however, may be used by any party for any purpose.

Experts' depositions are often *de bene esse* depositions, usually taken by videotape. At any time before trial a party may depose a witness expected to be called as an expert at trial.[69] In some instances, a witness will make a better appearance on videotape and will be more believable than if presented to a jury in person. The deposition is usually taken in the expert's office or where the demonstrative evidence of his profession (diplomas, etc.) can be seen, as this lends authority and credibility to his testimony. The deposition of a physician or physical therapist demonstrating an injured plaintiff's physical limitations often is better than an in-court demonstration, which can sometimes be distasteful to a jury.

In preparing the expert for a deposition, the attorney will use some or all of the techniques that he uses in preparing a client for a deposition, except that he will adapt them to the expert and take some special precautions. The expert is expected to review the materials that he has been furnished. The expert should understand that his file, minus any privileged materials, is open to the opposing lawyer. Usually that would be the entire file except for those materials giving the attorney's thoughts and impressions of the case, which are privileged under the attorney-client work-product rule. The attorney should learn beforehand, where possible, what the expert may have testified to in similar cases. The attorney should obtain beforehand, through discovery, other information the expert believes is necessary to formulate an opinion in the case; and (if he knows) he should familiarize the expert with such terms as *cause, reasonable degree of medical certainty,* and other key phrases as they are defined in law and which may be important to the case. A legitimate technique of preparation of a witness, particularly a client or an expert witness, is to practice with that witness, but the danger is that the witness may later try to remember the "right" answers to questions, or will relax too much or give testimony at trial that sounds stale.

Most cases are settled without trial; the depositions play an important role in this settlement. Throughout the preparation for a deposition, the lawyer keeps in mind its context in the case—that is, its relationship to settlement negotiation, its use for preparation of mediation summaries, and its potential use at trial. Before the deposition, the lawyer considers what facts can be developed in the deposition that will assist him in presenting his theory of the case to the other lawyer, to the mediators, to the judge, and to the jury. Some lawyers will try to talk to the opponent's expert, particularly in cases such as medical malpractice cases, where they believe they can influence the expert. The expert ought to be advised not to talk to anyone concerning the case prior to the deposition. When the expert is deposed by the adversary, the fee is owed by that party (and it is a good idea to be paid in advance). The high cost of litigation is due, in large measure, to the taking of depositions and other discovery.

Discovery of Expert Opinions and Reports

Rules on discovery are designed to avoid unfair surprise at trial and at the same time to protect the work product of the lawyer. The expert consulted is, in effect, an extension of the attorney's law firm and is bound by the obligation of confidentiality covering all of the lawyer's staff, including secretaries, investigators, and accountants, whether employees or independent contractors. The expert, for whatever reason, may not switch over to the side of the adversary.

Experts may be classified into three categories, with varying limits on discovery of their opinions and reports.[70] The lawyer must make an early decision when consulting an expert whether to use him as a trial witness. Consulting opinions and reports are placed at the risk of discovery when the expert crosses over the line and becomes a trial witness. The three categories of experts are as follows:

1. *Experts expected to be used at trial.* The opponent may learn by interrogatories the names of these trial witnesses and the substance of their testimony, but further discovery concerning them can be had only on motion and court order. By local rule or the practice of individual judges, a date is set in advance of trial for the declaration of experts. Failure to declare will preclude using the expert at trial.
2. *Experts retained or specially employed in anticipation of litigation or preparation for trial but not expected to be used at trial.* Except in the case of an examining physician, the facts and opinions of experts in this category can be discovered only on a showing of exceptional circumstances that make it impractical for the party seeking discovery to obtain the information by other means. The party seeking disclosure "carries a heavy burden."[71] Invoking the attorney work-product privilege to shield a consulting expert is an election not to use that expert at trial.[72]
3. *Experts informally consulted in preparation for trial but not retained for service in the litigation.* In the majority of jurisdictions, no discovery may be had of the names or views of these experts.[73] Problems arise in drawing a line between informally consulted experts and experts retained in anticipation of litigation. The determination is made on an ad hoc basis, depending on the manner in which the consultation was initiated; the nature, type, and extent of information or material provided to, or determined by, the expert in connection with his review; the duration and intensity of the consultative relationship; and the terms of consultation, if any.

Limitation of Opinion on Ultimate Issue

The basic approach to opinion testimony under prevailing rules of evidence is to admit it when helpful to the trier of fact. To allay any doubt on the subject, the Federal Rules of Evidence as adopted in 1975 specifically abolished the so-called *ultimate issue* rule.[74] The old stricture was designed to prevent "usurping the province of the jury," but it was unduly restrictive, difficult in application, and generally served only to deprive the jury of useful information. It led to odd verbal circumlocutions that were said not to violate the rule. Thus a witness could express his estimate of the criminal responsibility of the accused in terms of sanity or insanity, but not in terms of ability to tell right from wrong or other standards of criminal responsibility.[75]

The abolition of the ultimate issue rule does not result in admitting all opinions since the opinions must be "helpful" to the trier of fact. It would bar the admission of opinions that would merely tell the jury how to decide the case.[76] It would also exclude opinions phrased in terms of inadequately explored legal criteria. Thus the question, "Did the testator have capacity to make a will?" would be excluded, while the question, "Did the testator have sufficient capacity to know the nature and extent of his property and the natural objects of his bounty and to formulate a rational scheme of distribution?" would be allowed.[77]

With the abolition of the ultimate issue rule, physicians may testify as to cause of injury or death.[78] In product liability cases, the expert may give opinion testimony as to whether the product, at the time it left the hands of the manufacturer, was in a defective condition or was unreasonably dangerous to the user or consumer. Usually he is not required to state his definition of *defect, unreasonable danger,* or *reasonable safety.* The cross-examiner may question the standard of reasonableness or defect being applied by the expert.[79]

Among the legislative changes prompted by the trial of John W. Hinckley Jr., the would-be assassin of President Reagan, was an amendment, in 1984, to the Federal Rules of Evidence, which provides: "No expert witness testifying with respect to the mental state or condition of a defendant in a criminal case may state an opinion or inference as to whether the defendant did or did not have the mental state or condition constituting an element of the crime charged or of a defense thereto. Such ultimate issues are matters for the trier of fact alone."[80] Thus, while the Federal Rules generally abrogate the ultimate issue rule, a special exception applies in cases in which a criminal defendant's mental condition is in issue, as when insanity is raised as a defense. It brought back old circumlocutions, but not all states have adopted the exception. Psychological assessments often are made to approximate legal conclusions. It is found that ultimate issue testimony by experts does not affect jury verdicts in not guilty by reason of insanity (NGRI) defenses.[81]

Instruction to Jury

Out of concern that the expert will be unduly persuasive or will usurp the province of the jury, the adversary may request the judge to instruct the jury on the expert's testimony. The jury is told that it is not bound to accept the testimony. On this, a typical instruction provides:

> Certain witnesses have been called who testified as expert witnesses. You are not required to take the opinions of experts as binding upon you, but they are to be used to aid you in coming to a proper conclusion. Their testimony is received as that of persons who are learned by reason of special investigation, study, or experience along lines not of general knowledge, and the conclusion of such persons may be of value. You may adopt, or not, their conclusions, according to your own best judgment, giving in each instance such weight as you think should be given under all the facts and circumstances of the case.

In determining the weight to be given such testimony you should consider, among other things:

1. The education, training, experience and knowledge of the expert with respect to the matters about which he testified.
2. The reasons given for his opinion.
3. The sources of his information.[82]

There is little, however, to warrant the concern over usurpation of the jury by expert testimony. Actually, studies tend to show that in the majority of cases juries develop a strong leaning or make up their minds on the basis of the opening statements and closing arguments of the lawyer (though technically not evidence) and the demeanor of the parties (the court may specifically instruct the jury that demeanor is evidence).[83] In the *Hinckley* trial, the jury looked at the accused during the course of the trial, saw his bizarre behavior (chewing on his tie, for example), and concluded that he was not guilty by reason of insanity. The conflicting testimony tends to wash out, as lawyers say.

The Fee Arrangement

The expert, at times, may be a hired gun, but, quite often, he may need a gun to get paid. Who has the obligation to pay? Who has the ability to pay? The alternative arrangements for compensation of an expert include litigant-paid fees, attorney-advanced or promised fees, and fees taxed as costs or paid out of public funds as in the case of a court-appointed expert. The litigant may be unable or undisposed to pay the fee, especially when the outcome of the case is unfavorable. In cases handled by the lawyer on a contingency fee basis, the fee of the expert is taken as one of his expenses. He may, or may not, pay. In a number of situations, experts have turned to litigation to collect their fees. Hence, requesting payment up front is the recommended advice commonly given to those who would serve as experts. Failing that, the expert is advised to serve only on the condition that the attorney assume full responsibility for payment of all services in connection with the case. Court approval must be obtained for the payment of expert witness fees.[84] Attorneys paid on a contingency basis are more likely to advance expert fees.

The contingency fee—either a percentage or fixed amount conditioned on recovery of a judgment or settlement—is an option not available to an expert witness, on the theory that it would unduly intensify the expert's interest in the outcome of the case and would undermine the credibility of his testimony. That it would degrade testimonial reliability beyond present practices may be exaggerated, however.[85] Still others argue that the ban on expert contingency fees deprives litigants in many cases of the services of an expert.[86] Legislation enacted in Michigan in 1986 makes testifying on a contingency fee basis a misdemeanor.[87] An expert retained on a contingency basis violates ethical guidelines, and so any member of the profession learning of it has an obligation to report it to the board of medicine.

The adversary has the right to challenge all credentials, including fee arrangements. On cross-examination the expert is likely asked, "How much are you being *paid* for your testimony?" (The reply ought to be, "I am not being paid for my testimony. I am being paid for my time, like the other professional people in the courtroom.")[88] Fees for forensic services are usually higher than fees for treatment. The California Law Revision Commission of its rules of evidence states in a comment: "The jury can better appraise the extent to which bias may have influenced an expert's opinion if it is informed of the amount of his fee—and hence, the extent of his possible feeling of obligation to the party calling him."[89] Fiscal practicality aside, issues of credibility and ethics suggest that the expert be paid before providing an opinion or testimony, otherwise the expert may be challenged, "So, Doctor, you're testifying with a big bag of money hanging over your head, and your client may not be pleased if you answer the wrong way?"

A lawyer strategy of portraying a witness as a "professional expert" whose testimony has been purchased may be deemed so prejudicial as to require a new trial. In one case, the Michigan Supreme Court said, "We do not view . . . remarks concerning plaintiffs' experts as being merely 'breaches of good manners'; we perceive a studied purpose to prejudice the jury and divert the jurors' attention from the merits of the case . . . [W]e cannot believe that plaintiffs had a fair trial where defendants' counsel succeeded in characterizing plaintiffs' witnesses as 'professional experts' who made their living traveling around the country as a trio providing 'bought' testimony."[90]

In another malpractice case, the Michigan Supreme Court said, "Fairness to physicians requires the rule requiring expert testimony, but fairness to injured persons requires the plaintiff's expert witnesses not be impugned simply because they have testified for plaintiffs in other cases. . . . To allow the defendant to challenge a plaintiff's expert witness simply because he testifies for plaintiffs with some frequency is to permit the defendant to exploit unfairly the rule requiring, for defendant's protection, expert testimony, and the reluctance of physicians to testify against another member of their profession."[91] In a criminal case the Michigan Supreme Court, reversing a conviction, found that the prosecutor argued matters not in evidence in saying (in closing argument) that the defense expert on insanity had testified in the manner he did only because he was paid to do so.[92]

Invariably, in what may be described as a catch-22, the witness proffered as an expert who is a "virgin" in testifying is attacked as unqualified to testify while, on the other hand, the witness who testifies frequently as an expert is disparaged as a "whore."[93] One judge said to an expert witness, "Aren' you ashamed to be seen here in court so often?" to which the expert replied, "Why no, Your Honor, I always thought it was a very respectable place!"[94]

To enhance one's credibility as an expert witness, psychologist Stanley Brodsky recommends measuring devices suggested by Edward Colbach: a contrary quotient (CQ) and perhaps also a validity quotient (VQ). The CQ could calculate how many times the expert's opinion was or was not that desired by retaining counsel, and that, of course, he was called only when his opinion fitted with the case of the retaining attorney. The VQ would calculate the number of court decisions that were in accord with the expert's opinion, but this quotient is based on the assumption that the validity of the expert opinion is affirmed by legal standards as demonstrated by the court decisions.[95] Time and again, it has been shown that experience, by itself, is unrelated to the accuracy of clinical assessments.[96]

Notes

1. The proposition—that the task of each side under the adversary system is to put forward its best case—is not without criticism. Judge Harry T. Edwards of the U.S. Court of Appeals for the District of Columbia says, "As a judge, I see far too many examples of abusive

litigation tactics, such as the withholding of critical information from the court." H. T. Edwards, "Do Lawyers Still Make a Difference?" *Wayne L. Rev.* 32 (1986): 201, 206. Putting one's best foot forward, keeping silent on the negative, is not unique to the adversary system, of course. In one of Luigi Pirandello's short stories, "Moon Sickness," a husband tells his bride shortly after their marriage that he becomes like a werewolf at a full moon. "Why didn't you tell me before our marriage?" she asks.

2. See Koeller v. Reynolds, 344 N.W.2d 556 (Iowa App. 1983) (attorney malpractice); Annot., "Necessity of Expert Testimony to Show Malpractice of Architect," 3 A.L.R.4th 1023 (1981). In medical malpractice actions, a plaintiff must establish through expert medical opinion (1) the standard of care in the locality where treatment occurred, (2) that defendant breached that standard of care, and (3) that the breach of the standard of care was the proximate cause of injury. Gibson v. D'Amico, 97 A.D.2d 905, 470 N.Y.S.2d 739 (3d Dept. 1983); Bivins v. Detroit Osteopathic Hospital, 258 N.W.2d 527 (Mich. App. 1977).

3. W. Prosser & W. P. Keeton, *The Law of Torts* (St. Paul, Minn.: West, 5th ed. 1984). Expert testimony is sometimes required in breach-of-contract cases just as in malpractice cases. See, e.g., Steinmetz v. Lowry, 17 Ohio App.3d 116, 477 N.E.2d 671 (1984). In Blatz v. Allina Health System, 622 N.W.2d. 376 (Minn. 2001), the court held that the appropriate standard of care for paramedics in attempting to locate the home of a patient was that of an ordinary person, and therefore expert testimony was not required to establish standard of care.

4. See volume 2, chapter 7, on informed consent.

5. 387 N.W.2d 486 (Neb. 1986).

6. 387 N.W.2d at 489.

7. Helling v. Carey, 83 Wash.2d 514, 519 P.2d 981 (1974).

8. Tarasoff v. Regents of the University of California, 13 Cal.3d 177, 529 P.2d 553, 118 Cal. Rptr. 129 (1974), *vacated*, 17 Cal.3d 425, 551 P.2d 334, 131 Cal. Rptr. 14 (1976).

9. 551 P.2d at 345, 131 Cal. Rptr. at 25. In Louisiana, a *Tarasoff*-type case is called one of ordinary negligence, not malpractice, as the plaintiff is not a patient but a third party. As a result, the therapist is exposed to personal liability. Hutchinson v. Patel, 637 So.2d 415 (La. 1994). See volume 2, chapter 11, on duty to third parties.

10. A proposal of the APA Council of Psychiatry and the Law on the "Duty to Protect" states that "there are no accepted professional standards for the prediction of dangerousness" (p. 23), but a few pages later it says, "There will always be cases in which the patient's potential for violence seems so clear . . . that a clinician's failure to recognize it falls far short of professional standards" (p. 26).

The notion that mental health professionals have expertise in predicting dangerousness of individuals is based, in part, on the fact that they are recognized as specialists in human behavior and that, for years, they have been certifying individuals for commitment on the ground of dangerousness. Following *Tarasoff*, however, a volume of literature appeared disclaiming the ability of mental health professionals to predict dangerous behavior beyond the level of chance. See, e.g., J. Monahan, "The Prediction of Violent Behavior: Toward a Second Generation of Theory and Policy," *Am. J. Psychiatry* 141 (1984): 10; H. Steadman, "The Right Not to Be a False Positive: Problems in the Application of the Dangerousness Standard," *Psychiatric Q.* 52 (1980): 84. See the discussion in volume 2, chapter 11, on duty to third parties.

11. 551 P.2d at 345, 131 Cal. Rptr. at 25.

12. 551 P.2d at 340.

13. See J. C. Beck, "Violent Patients and the *Tarasoff* Duty in Private Psychiatric Cases," *J. Psychiatry & Law* 13 (1985): 361.

14. 105 S. Ct. 1087 (1985).

15. 105 S. Ct. at 1092. See the discussion in chapter 17, on psychiatric assistance for the indigent defendant.

16. J. Robitscher, *The Powers of Psychiatry* (Boston: Houghton Mifflin, 1980), p. xiii.

17. Rule 702 of the Federal Rules of Evidence in an earlier version called for "special" knowledge, but the qualification was omitted in the final version.

18. Rule 701, Federal Rules of Evidence. See the discussion in chapter 3, on *Frye* and *Daubert*.

19. For psychiatric testimony, Terence F. MacCarthy, the federal public defender in Chicago, said he would "get someone with a foreign accent and Freud as his middle name."

Quoted in S. Taylor, "Hinckley Trial: $2 Million So Far in Case Where Experts Plus Time Equal Money," *New York Times*, June 14, 1982, p. 16.

20. Comment by Sheldon Miller, well-known Detroit trial lawyer, in address on January 8, 1986, at Wayne State University School of Law. But who is the blameworthy party—the buyer or seller, or both? In the case of controlled substances (narcotics) both buyer and seller are condemned, while in prostitution only the seller.

21. Thus, in Miller v. Silver, 181 Cal. App. 652, 226 Cal. Rptr. 479 (1986), the court ruled that a psychiatrist could testify in a malpractice action regarding the standard of postoperative care that should have been afforded a patient receiving breast implants. The court acknowledged that the psychiatrist lacked the necessary credentials to give expert testimony concerning the surgical technique of plastic surgeons. However, the court found that the psychiatrist, by virtue of his medical education and internship training, possessed "the ability to research the role prophylactic antibiotics play in implant patients who have experienced life-threatening complications from recent surgery." Where the allegations of negligence concern matters within the knowledge and observation of every physician and surgeon and not a special course of treatment to be tested by the teachings and doctrines of a particular school, the testimony of a nonspecialist physician can still aid the trier of fact in its search for the truth, the court said.

22. See Mich. H.B. 5154; P.A. 178 of 1986, sec. 2192(d)(e); Dolan v. Galluzzo, 77 Ill.2d 279, 396 N.E.2d 13 (1979). See volume 2, chapter 4, on malpractice.

23. Nally v. Grace Community Church of the Valley, Civ. No. 67200 (not published but available through Westlaw or Lexis database services).

24. Nally v. Grace Community Church of the Valley, 157 Cal. App.3d 912, 204 Cal. Rptr. 303 (Cal. App. 1984). Following several years of coverage in newspapers and magazines (e.g., *National Law Journal*, July 16, 1984, p. 6), the case was featured on NBC's *20/20*, Apr. 6, 1986. See M. A. Weitz, *Clergy Malpractice in America* (Lawrence: University Press of Kansas, 2001); E. Barker, "Clergy Malpractice," *Trial*, July 1986, p. 58.

25. 204 Cal. Rptr. at 309. The California Supreme Court granted review and entered judgment dismissing the action. It granted review to address: "(i) whether we should impose a duty on defendants and other 'nontherapist counselors' (i.e., persons other than licensed psychotherapists, who counsel others concerning their emotional and spiritual problems) to refer persons to licensed mental health professionals once suicide becomes a foreseeable risk, and (ii) whether the evidence presented at trial supports plaintiffs' cause of action for wrongful death based on defendants' alleged 'intentional infliction of emotional distress' on Nally." The court rejected the proposition that the defendants have a duty to advise potentially suicidal counselees to seek competent medical care. It noted, "[T]he Legislature has exempted the clergy from the licensing requirements applicable to marriage, family, child and domestic counselors and from the operation of statutes regulating psychologists. In so doing, the Legislature has recognized that access to the clergy for counseling should be free from state counseling standards, and 'the secular state is not equipped to ascertain the competence of counseling when performed by those affiliated with religious organizations,'" quoting S. E. Ericsson, "Clergyman Malpractice: Ramifications of a New Theory," *Val. U. L. Rev.* 16 (1981): 163, 176. The court said that its opinion does not purport to "foreclose imposing liability on nontherapist counselors, who hold themselves out as professionals, for injuries related to their counseling activities." Nally v. Grace Community Church of the Valley, 47 Cal.3d 278, 253 Cal. Rptr. 97, 763 P.2d 948 (1988). It is well established that persons who hold themselves out as mental health professionals, even though they are not licensed, are generally held to the standard of care of the profession that they are purporting to practice. See, e.g., Corgan v. Muehling, 167 Ill. App.3d 1093, 118 Ill. Dec. 698, 522 N.E.2d 153 (Ill. App. 1988).

Suppose the pastoral counselors use corporal punishment as part of their counseling, claiming that the punishment is part of the treatment by "spiritual means" that they administer. In McCullum v. Faith Mission Home, 237 Va. 473, 379 S.E.2d 445 (1989), a state agency sought an injunction to prohibit a religiously run home for retarded children and adults from administering corporal punishment as spiritual means. The home claimed that, in accordance with the religious precepts of the church, it used "physical punishment under controlled conditions in limited situations to discipline residents for maladaptive behavior. The punishment takes the form of slapping the hand several times or spanking the buttocks a maximum of four strokes with the hand or a 'simple light paddle.'" The Virginia Supreme Court recited the arguments on both sides but ultimately concluded that the home was exempt from licensing requirements.

Following *Nally*, there has been extensive legal literature on the topic of clergy malpractice. It is suggested that once the particular counseling activity is defined as predominantly secular, the clergy who undertake that activity should be held to a duty of care commensurate with that applied to licensed practitioners who undertake such activities in nonreligious settings. See, e.g., R. J. Basil, "Clergy Malpractice: Taking Spiritual Counseling Conflicts beyond Intentional Tort Analysis," *Rutgers L.J.* 19 (1988): 419; P. Reidinger, "Puncturing the Faith Defense," *A.B.A.J.*, Feb. 1989, p. 89.

Too, in the aftermath of *Nally*, although the court did not impose liability, insurance companies promoted clergy malpractice insurance. With the availability of insurance, should that make a difference in law whether to recognize liability on the basis of clergy malpractice? Would insurance companies be collecting premiums without having any risk (other than to provide legal representation)? Lawyers tend to file a lawsuit only when the potential defendant has a deep pocket or has insurance, otherwise there would be no point to it. In one way or another, lawyers seek to circumvent rulings on nonresponsibility of the clergy. Would spiritual counseling, as a result, become so expensive that many would be forced to abandon the practice, thereby removing societal benefits provided by approachable, inexpensive, and familiar counselors? Despite the broad immunity given to clergy in cases such as *Nally*, it is reported that churches are abandoning counseling because they fear suit. In the 1990s, the clergy faced dozens of suits, and although they won almost all of them, they are dissuaded from counseling out of the fear of a lawsuit. L. Miller, "Surge in Malpractice Suits Leads Pastors to Offer Less Counseling to Parishioners," *Wall Street Journal*, Feb. 5, 1998, p. B-1. See volume 2, chapter 12, on regulation of psychotherapy.

Litigation was designed to replace dueling or physical assaults, and when litigation is precluded, there tends to be a return to assaults. A study by academics at London University's Royal Holloway College, compiled from responses by 1,300 clergy in five Church of England dioceses, reports the rising number of attacks on clergy stemming out of disputes over weddings and christenings. In some dioceses training, including self-defense classes, is being provided to help clergy to deal with violent parishioners. M. Bentham, "Clergy Threatened by 'Violent' Middle Classes," *Sunday Telegraph*, Nov. 18, 2001, p. 15.

26. R. O. Pasnau, "Response to the Presidential Address; Health Care Crisis: A Campaign for Action," *Am. J. Psychiatry* 143 (1986): 955.

27. Quoted in R. M. Restak, "Psychiatry in America," *Wilson Q.* 7 (1983): 95.

28. McDonnell v. County of Nassau, 492 N.Y.S.2d 699 (Sup. 1985). In Taormina v. Goodman, 63 A.D.2d 1018, 406 N.Y.S.2d 350 (2d Dept. 1978), a medical doctor was not allowed to testify to the alleged malpractice of a chiropractor.

29. In a bit of satire, humorist Art Buchwald has a lawyer saying: "We have lists of shrinks who believe anyone who commits a major crime is crazy, just as the government has lists of doctors who are willing to testify that anyone involved in one was sane. We don't use their lists and they don't use ours." Syndicated column, May 11, 1982.

30. O'Gee v. Dobbs Houses, 570 F.2d 1084 (2d Cir. 1978): Hernandez v. Faker, 137 Ariz. 449, 671 P.2d 427 (1983); Ballenger v. Burris Industries, 311 S.E.2d 881 (N.C. App. 1984). See D. W. Shuman, *Psychiatric and Psychological Evidence* (Colorado Springs: Shepard's/McGraw-Hill, 1986). For a discussion of the amendment in 2000 modifying Rule 703, see chapter 3, on *Frye* and *Daubert*.

31. 673 F.2d 1114 (10th Cir. 1982).

32. See Federal Rules of Evidence, Rules 403 and 404(b).

33. 673 F.2d at 1122.

34. Joseph Bird, attorney, quoted in *Michigan Lawyers Weekly* 15 (Sept. 10, 2001): 1362.

35. "Pepper and Salt," *Wall Street Journal*, Sept. 4, 1986, p. 23.

36. Ga. O.C.G.A. 15-19-14.

37. Nix v. Whiteside, 106 S. Ct. 988, 995 (1986).

38. 753 F.2d 991 (11th Cir. 1985).

39. 388 N.W.2d 206 (Mich. 1986).

40. J. R. Rappeport, "Ethical Issues in Forensic Psychiatry," in A. Carmi, S. Schneider, & A. Hefez (eds.), *Psychiatry—Law and Ethics* (New York: Springer-Verlag, 1986), p. 308. A typical instruction to the jury on expert opinion based upon a hypothetical question is as follows:

"An expert witness answering a hypothetical question assumes as true every material act stated in the question. The value of his opinion is dependent upon, and is no stronger than, the material facts upon which it is based. Therefore, the opinion of the expert should be disregarded by you, unless you find the material facts stated in the question are true." Nebraska Jury Instruction 1.43. This instruction is based on the general principle that "the premise being false, the conclusion based thereon cannot be accepted as true." Williams v. Watson Bros. Transp. Co., 145 Neb. 466, 16 N.W.2d 199 (1945).

41. J. R. Rappeport, "Reasonable Medical Certainty," *Bull. Amer. Acad. Psychiatry & Law* 13 (1985): 5.

42. Congress amended the Rules of Evidence to provide that a writing used to refresh the memory of a witness *before* he testifies need be produced only if the court in its discretion determines it is necessary in the interest of justice. A writing used *while* testifying must be shown to the adversary on request. Federal Rules of Evidence, Rule 612.

43. Thus, in Davis v. Lhim, 124 Mich. App. 291 (1983), involving a psychiatrist's duty to protect a third person endangered by a patient, defense counsel was not allowed to present expert witnesses, as they were not timely listed. Query: Should Dr. Lhim, found liable, have sued his lawyer for legal malpractice? As a state hospital employee, he was represented by the state attorney, who enjoys immunity.

44. P. I. Ostroff, "Experts: A Few Fundamentals," in *The Litigation Manual: A Primer for Trial Lawyers* (Chicago: American Bar Association, 1983), p. 84.

45. Humorist Art Buchwald has written (syndicated column, May 11, 1982):

I asked a defense attorney . . . "suppose you hire a psychiatrist to examine your client and he decides the person was sane at the time he committed the crime."

"I'd fire him. . . . I've had cases where five shrinks have examined my client before I could get one to say he was crazy."

"And that was the one you called to the stand?"

"If I called the other four, I could have been sued for malpractice."

46. However, when the witness has a tendency to ramble, as some do, the proponent of the witness would want to structure the testimony by Q & A (question and answer). In one case, where the expert often rambled in his testimony, the defense attorney, the proponent of the expert, was exasperated and said at one point, "Perhaps you'd let me ask you a few questions along the way." During cross-examination, some courtroom spectators applauded when the prosecutor made a sarcastic comment about the psychiatrist. The judge was obliged to intervene when the prosecutor and psychiatrist were speaking at the same time. "Doctor, would you listen to the question?" the judge said. When the psychiatrist began to interrupt, the judge said, "Would you fall silent for a moment and just listen to me? Answer the specific question, please." J. Kesnak, "Bailey Says He Knew Killing Boy Was Wrong," *Detroit Free Press*, Sept. 25, 1986, p. 1.

47. Federal Rules of Evidence, Rule 611.

48. Geders v. United States, 425 U.S. 80 (1976). And as the court in Miller v. Universal City Studios, 650 F.2d 1365 (5th Cir. 1981), put it: "The purpose of the sequestration rule is to prevent the shaping of testimony by one witness to match that of another, and to discourage fabrication and collusion."

49. Hollman v. Dale Electronic, 752 F.2d 311 (8th Cir. 1985).

50. Federal Rules of Evidence, Rule 615(3). Other exemptions from sequestration are the litigants, as is a person designated to represent a corporate or similar party. Federal Rules of Evidence, Rule 615(1), (2).

51. Hampton v. Kroger Co., 618 F.2d 498 (8th Cir. 1980); Morvant v. Construction Aggregates Corp. 570 F.2d 626 (6th Cir. 1978), *cert. denied*, 439 U.S. 801 (1978). In *Morvant*, the court stated it could "perceive little, if any, reason for sequestering a witness who is to testify in an expert capacity only and not to the facts of the case." 570 F.2d at 629. The court in *Morvant* further held, however, that Rule 703, providing wide bases of opinion testimony,

does not furnish an automatic ground for exempting an expert from sequestration under Rule 615. 570 F.2d at 630.

52. In United States v. Burgess, 691 F.2d 1146 (4th Cir. 1982), the court permitted psychiatric experts for both sides on the defense of post-traumatic stress disorder to remain in court throughout the proceedings, where written reports from the experts were delayed to the point where they were forthcoming from the defense only two days before trial and from the government on the second and last day of trial.

53. United States v. Hiss, 88 F.Supp. 559 (S.D. N.Y. 1950). See the discussion in chapter 5, on witnesses and the credibility of testimony.

54. The transcript of the cross-examination by prosecutor Thomas Murphy of Dr. Binger is used in trial tactics courses as illustrative of effective cross-examination. Transcript available from Professional Education Group in Hopkins, Minn.

55. Report of Senate Committee on the Judiciary on Rule 615, Federal Rules of Evidence.

56. United States v. Alvarez, 755 F.2d 830 (11th Cir. 1985).

57. Miller v. Universal City Studios, 650 F.2d 1365, at 1373 (5th Cir. 1981).

58. The remedy for sequestration violation is at the discretion of the trial judge. United States v. Oropeza, 564 F.2d 316 (9th Cir. 1977), *cert. denied,* 434 U.S. 1080 (1978).

59. D. W. Shuman, "Testimonial Compulsion: The Involuntary Medical Expert Witness," *J. Legal Med.* 4 (1983): 419.

60. In Karp v. Cooley, 493 F.2d 408, 424–25 (5th Cir. 1984), Dr. Michael DeBakey refused to answer whether it was bad medical practice in 1969 to put a mechanical heart in a human being. Vindicating his position was no easy task.

61. In People v. Barnes, 11 Cal. App. 605, 295 Pac. 1045 (1931), a handwriting expert was asked for an impromptu opinion on the stand as to the possibly identical authorship of several specimens of handwriting, some of which he had never seen before. It was held he did not have to express an opinion. See also Mason v. Robinson, 340 N.W.2d 236 (Iowa 1983); Commonwealth v. Vitello, 367 Mass. 224, 327 N.E.2d 819 (1975).

62. See P. L. Porterfield, "The Right to Subpoena Expert Testimony and the Fees Required to Be Paid Therefore," *Hastings L.J.* 5 (1953): 50; Comment, "Requiring Experts to Testify in Maine," *U. Me. L. Rev.* 20 (1968): 297; Comment, "Compelling Experts to Testify: A Proposal," *U. Chi. L. Rev.* 44 (1977): 851.

63. This language is taken verbatim from former Federal Rules of Criminal Procedure, Rule 28.

64. 539 F.2d 811 (2d Cir. 1976).

65. 547 F.Supp. 871 (E.D.Mich. 1982).

66. I. Younger, "On Technology and the Law of Evidence," *U. Colo. L. Rev.* 49 (1977): 1.

67. J. Wigmore, *Evidence,* rev. J. McNaughton (Boston: Little, Brown, 1961), vol. 8, sec. 1292.

68. Fed. Civ. P. 32(A); Mich. Court Rules 2.308.

69. Mich. Court Rules 2.302(B)(4)(d).

70. For a detailed discussion, see C. A. Wright & A. R. Miller, *Federal Practices and Procedure* (St. Paul, Minn.: West, 1970 and supp.), vol. 8, sec. 2029.

71. Ager v. Stormont Hospital & Training School for Nurses, 622 F.2d 496, 503 (10th Cir. 1980).

72. Garrett v. Coast Federal Savings & Loan Assn., 136 Cal. App.3d 266, 186 Cal. Rptr. 178 (1982).

73. Federal Rules of Civil Procedure; Annot., "Pretrial Discovery of Facts Known and Opinions Held by Opponents' Expert Under Rule 26(b)(4) of Federal Rules of Civil Procedure," 33 A.L.R. Fed. 403 (1977).

74. Rule 704.

75. Advisory Committee's Note, Rule 704.

76. People v. Robinson, 309 N.W.2d 624 (Mich. App. 1981). The expert may not give an opinion that the defendant committed "malpractice." Bender v. Dingwerth, 425 F.2d 378 (5th Cir. 1970). An arson investigator in a much-publicized case in New York was not allowed to testify whether he thought the fire was accidental because "that is an invasion of the jury's province." J. Feron, "Stouffer Case Built on Speculation, Judge Says," *New York Times,* Mar. 31, 1982, p. 1.

77. Advisory Committee's Note, Rule 704.

78. People v. Whitfield, 388 N.W.2d 206 (Mich. 1986); State v. Langley, 354 N.W.2d 389 (Minn. 1984).

79. D. Patterson, "Products Liability Litigation: The Rule-Making Power of Expert Witnesses," *For the Defense,* Oct. 1981, p. 10.

80. 98 Stat. 2064, amending Rule 704.

81. See S. Fulero & N. Finkel, "Barring Ultimate Issue Testimony: An 'Insane' Rule?" *Law & Human Behavior* 15 (1991): 495.

82. Nebraska Jury Instruction 1.42.

83. Under this view, the actual evidence presented at trial may be said to be merely supportive of the arguments (just as in olden times the oath was decisive and the evidence was merely supportive of it rather than the converse). See H. Silving, "The Oath," *Yale L.J.* 68 (1959): 1329.

84. See, e.g., M.C.L.A. (Mich.) 600.2164 (expert witness fee statute); Spearman v. Barron, 351 So.2d 856 (La. App. 1977). To avoid hiring an expert yet to utilize his name and reputation, there is the occasional (unethical) attorney practice of designating experts without notifying them. Most cases are settled, with insurers prompted to settle on seeing particular experts listed to testify. The expert is unaware that this has occurred. The practice of listing experts without their knowledge appears to run a gamut of scenarios of deceptiveness, from the more benign to clearly malignant. T. G. Gutheil, R. I. Simon, & J. T. Hilliard, "The Phantom Expert: Unconsented Use of an Expert's Name and/or Testimony, as a Legal Strategy," *J. Amer. Acad. Psychiatry & Law* 29 (2001): 313.

85. Note, "Contingent Fees for Expert Witnesses in Civil Litigation," *Yale L.J.* 86 (1977): 1680.

86. Argued in Person v. Assn. of Bar of City of New York, 554 F.2d 534 (2d Cir. 1977).

87. Mich. P.A. 178 of 1986.

88. P. J. Resnick, "The Psychiatrist in Court," in J. O. Cavenar (ed.), *Psychiatry* (Philadelphia: Lippincott, 1986), vol. 3, ch. 37, p. 8.

89. *California Law Revision Commission Reports* 7 (1965): 1. See also J. H. Friedenthal, "Discovery and Use of an Adverse Party's Expert Information," *Stan. L. Rev.* 14 (1962): 455.

90. Kern v. St. Luke's Hospital Ass'n. of Saginaw, 404 Mich. 339, 273 N.W.2d 75 (1978). The conduct of defense counsel was perceived as "a studied purpose to prejudice the jury."

91. Wilson v. Stilwill, 309 N.W.2d 898 (Mich. 1981).

92. People v. Tyson, 423 Mich. 357, 377 N.W.2d 738 (1985).

93. In one case involving an expert who testified frequently on product safety, it was noted on cross-examination that he had literally criticized products "from A to Z." The cross-examiner began writing items down on a large pad, starting with automatic garage door openers. He did fine up to J: "Jumping on a trampoline." "I think that should be under T," quipped the other attorney. The cross-examiner kept up through W, with wood preservatives, then petered out altogether, admitting, "I couldn't find X, Y, Z." C. Guyette, "Anatomy of a Verdict," *(Detroit) Metro Times,* May 17–23, 2000, p. 12.

94. Reported in E. Tanay, "Money and the Expert Witness: An Ethical Dilemma," *J. Forensic Sci.* 21 (1976): 769.

95. S. L. Brodsky, *The Expert Expert Witness* (Washington, D.C.: American Psychological Association, 1999), pp. 75–79; E. M. Colbach, "Integrity Checks on the Witness Stand," *Bull. Am. Acad. Psychiatry & Law* 9 (1981): 285. See also B. D. Sales & D. W. Shuman, "Reclaiming the Integrity of Science in Expert Witnessing," *Ethics & Behavior* 3 (1993): 223.

96. See D. Faust, "Are There Sufficient Foundations for Mental Health Experts to Testify in Court? No," in S. A. Kirk & S. D. Einbinder (eds.), *Controversial Issues in Mental Health* (Boston: Allyn & Bacon, 1994), pp. 196–201; H. N. Garb, "Clinical Judgment, Clinical Training, and Professional Experience," *Psychological Bull.* 105 (1989): 387.

3

From
Frye to
Daubert
and
Beyond

"It is time to take hold of expert testimony," said a prominent judge in 1986.[1] Before and since then much has been said and written about "junk science" in the courtroom.[2] During the 1992 election campaign Vice President Dan Quayle called for wide-ranging reform of expert witness practice in the federal courts.[3] Junk science in the courtroom was to end, mused many commentators, under the U.S. Supreme Court's celebrated decision in 1993 in *Daubert v. Merrell Dow Pharmaceuticals*.[4] The case involved expert testimony concerning the teratogenic effect of the antinausea drug Bendectin.

Before *Daubert*, for almost three-quarters of a century, the *Frye* test, from *Frye v. United States*,[5] reigned as the standard governing admissibility of scientific testimony. In 1923 the D.C. Circuit Court wrote,

> Just when a scientific principle or discovery crosses the line between experimental and demonstrable stages is difficult to define. Somewhere in this twilight zone the evidential force of the principle must be recognized, and while the courts will go a long way in admitting expert testimony deduced from a well-recognized scientific principle or discovery, the thing from which the deduction is made must be sufficiently established to have general acceptance in the particular field in which it belongs.[6]

In *Frye*, the defendant sought to utilize the testimony of an expert who would opine, on basis of blood pressure readings, that the defendant was telling the truth when he denied having committed the alleged offense. The D.C. Court of Appeals rejected the evidence on the ground that it was the product of a scientific theory that was not yet generally accepted within the relevant professional community.

Under *Daubert*, in implementing Rule 702 of the Federal Rules of Evidence (adopted in 1975) that allows "scientific, technical, or other specialized knowledge [that] will assist the trier of fact to understand the evidence or to determine a fact," the Supreme Court called upon trial judges to be active gatekeepers to insure that "any and all scientific testimony or evidence admitted is not only relevant but reliable." In less than a decade there have been nearly two thousand appeals based on the issue of science in the courtroom that make reference to *Daubert;* hundreds of these appeals related to the testimony of mental health experts.

Admissibility of testimony rests on two prongs: (1) the messenger, and (2) the message. The first prong requires the judge to decide whether the individual whose testimony is being proffered is an expert in a particular scientific field. A witness must be qualified as an expert in order to give testimony based on scientific, technical, or other specialized knowledge. The second prong requires the judge to make an inquiry into whether the evidence will be of genuine aid to the trier. The helpfulness standard under the rules of evidence requires "a valid scientific connection to the pertinent inquiry as a precondition to admissibility." At a hearing (which has come to be known as a *Daubert* hearing) the parties, or amici curiae, make their claims about the validity of the evidence. The effective application of *Daubert* would require the trial judge to learn about the scientific notion or technique in question.[7] The judge is not bound by a scientific "party line," as required under *Frye*, and allows researchers using new techniques in the vanguard of scientific knowledge to bring their knowledge to court.

Under *Daubert*, general acceptance within the relevant field of science is but one consideration in ascertaining reliability (or validity). *Daubert* did not eliminate the *general acceptance* test, but incorporated it as one of the indicia to be considered in determining whether to admit scientific evidence. The judge is to consider: Is the theory or technique testable, and has it been tested? Has the theory or technique been subjected to peer review and publication? What is the known or potential error rate for the technique? And is the expert's field a "well-accepted body of learning" with reasonably well-defined standards?

In *Daubert*, on remand, Judge Alex Kozinski of the U.S. Court of Appeals for the Ninth Circuit noted that under the Supreme Court's decision, while judges are largely untrained in science and no match for any of the witnesses whose testimony they are reviewing, "it is our responsibility to determine whether those experts' proposed testimony amounts to 'scientific knowledge,' constitutes 'good science,' and was 'derived by the scientific method.'"[8] He went on to raise the question:

> How do we figure out whether scientists have derived their findings through the scientific method or whether their testimony is based on scientifically valid principles? One very significant fact to be considered is whether the experts are proposing to testify about matters growing naturally and directly out of research they have conducted independent of the litigation, or whether they have developed their opinions expressly for purposes of testifying. That an expert testifies for money does not neces-

sarily cast doubt on the reliability of his testimony, as few experts appear in court merely as an eleemosynary gesture. But in determining whether proposed expert testimony amounts to good science, we may not ignore the fact that a scientist's normal workplace is the lab or the field, not the courtroom or the lawyer's office.[9]

Acceptance by the scientific community as the litmus test for admissibility under *Frye* did not keep out junk science. What about under *Daubert*, with its several criteria? Has it managed to keep out junk science? With expert testimony ranging from alloys to zygotes, can a judge evaluate under the *Daubert* criteria?

Many courts have interpreted the criteria set out in *Daubert* not in the conjunctive, as might have been expected, but in the disjunctive. In a post-*Daubert* decision, where the criteria were applied in the disjunctive, the U.S. Ninth Circuit Court of Appeals set aside the long-established per se rule under *Frye* that unstipulated polygraph evidence is inadmissible in civil or criminal trials.[10] The Ninth Circuit reasoned that the rule is inconsistent with the "flexible inquiry" posed by *Daubert*. The court nonetheless made clear that "we are not expressing new enthusiasm for admission of unstipulated polygraph evidence," but stated it would leave the question of admissibility to the trial judge.

Similarly, the Fifth Circuit stated that "the rationale underlying this circuit's *per se* rule against polygraph evidence did not survive *Daubert*."[11] The court went on to comment that "[t]here can be no doubt that tremendous advances have been made in polygraph instrumentation and technique in the years since *Frye*. . . . Current research indicates that, when given under controlled conditions, the polygraph technique accurately predicts truth or deception between seventy and ninety percent of the time."[12] The court, however, limited its ruling, commenting that: "[W]e do not now hold that polygraph examinations are scientifically valid or that they will always assist the trier of fact. . . . We merely remove the obstacle of the *per se* rule against admissibility, which was based on antiquated concepts about the technical ability of the polygraph and legal precepts that have been expressly overruled by the Supreme Court."[13] In sum and substance, under *Frye*, polygraph evidence was barred; now under *Daubert*, a *Daubert* hearing is held, taking time and expense, and then such evidence is excluded; the same occurs with other proffered evidence.[14]

In one way or another, the lower federal courts have resisted a literal application of *Daubert*. By and large, judges do not want to be thrust into the role of scientific arbiter. In 1995, in *McCullock v. H. B. Fuller Co.*,[15] Federal Court of Appeals Judge Joseph McLaughlin wrote that while trial judges must exercise sound discretion as gatekeepers of expert testimony under *Daubert*, they are not "St. Peter at the gates of heaven, performing a searching inquiry into the depth of an expert witness' soul—separating the saved from damned. Such an inquiry would inexorably lead to evaluating witness credibility and weight of the evidence, the ageless role of the jury."[16]

In the same year, in 1995, shortly after rendering a decision involving *Daubert*, Judge Gerald Rosen of the federal district court in Michigan explained in a conference at the Wayne State University Law School that trial judges are not in a position to carry out the mandate of the *Daubert* decision as originally envisioned, and as a consequence more evidence would be found admissible than under *Frye* where the judge would defer to the scientific community. The case, *Isley v. Capuchin*

Providence,[17] involved an alleged period of sexual abuse while the plaintiff attended a seminary. Judge Rosen allowed an individual who had a doctorate in psychiatric nursing to testify as to her theories and opinions concerning post-traumatic stress disorder (PTSD) and repressed memory, and she also was permitted to testify as to whether the alleged victim's behavior was consistent with someone who is suffering PTSD or repressed memory.[18] Judge Rosen might have avoided a *Daubert* hearing under the view as later developed of the flexible approach accorded the so-called soft sciences.

Apart from the way that *Daubert* criteria are applied, be it in the disjunctive or conjunctive, there is the question of the scope of their applicability. Do they apply to any type of science and do they apply to areas outside of science? Rule 702 speaks about "scientific," "technical," or "other specialized knowledge." Are the terms synonymous? Are they to be distinguished under the law on expert testimony? Psychiatry or psychology may be categorized as "other specialized knowledge," or "soft science," and it is often described as more art than science. Generally speaking, fields of knowledge are put in one camp or the other (hard versus soft) rather than on a continuum. The hard sciences could include neuropsychology, given its reliance on quantitative measurement.

Daubert clearly involved hard science. What about the distinction traditionally drawn between hard science, which deals with measurable facts, and soft science, which defies accurate measurement? UCLA Professor James Q. Wilson writes,

> I am an unashamed social scientist, but I would be the first to admit that though social scientists often know things about human behavior that ordinary folks do not, we also are aware that the human being defies accurate measurement in much of its important behavior; that even when measured, many people behave differently from what the theory predicts; and that some theories, when known to people, lead them to change their behavior in ways that confound the theory.[19]

More than anything, science at its foundation is an attitude that demands proof resulting from the empirical testing of hypotheses through controlled and carefully defined experiments. In addition, it demands replication of experiments so that results can be confirmed by other scientists. In other words, science requires that explanatory principles be testable. Anything that cannot be tested is not within the realm of science.[20]

In *Daubert*, Justice Blackmun, author of the Court's opinion, interpreted Rule 702 to require that the content of the expert's testimony be "scientific" in the sense that it be "ground[ed] in the methods and procedures of science." Justice Blackmun understood science to be a method or a procedure rather than simply a body of facts. Upon his death, in a memorial to him, it was stated that his discussion of the factors that make knowledge scientific—falsifiability, peer review, error rates, and general acceptance within the relevant scientific community—reflected his "longstanding receptivity to scientific ways in understanding complex events."[21]

Significant as to what is science is the decision of the federal district court in 1995 in *United States v. Starzecpyzel.*[22] In this case, the district court was asked to pass on the admissibility of testimony by questioned-document examiners. The court concluded that questioned-document testimony is not scientific knowledge under *Daubert* because there is a lack of systematic empirical validation for many of the assumptions in questioned-document examination. The court noted that *Daubert* was restricted to "scientific evidence."

In 1996 in *Compton v. Subaru of America*,[23] the Tenth Circuit stated, "[A]pplication of the *Daubert* factors is unwarranted in cases where expert testimony is based solely upon experience or training." The court went on to quote the *Daubert* ruling in saying:

> [I]n such cases, Rule 702 merely requires the trial court to make a preliminary finding that proffered expert testimony is both relevant and reliable while taking into account "[t]he inquiry envisioned by Rule 702 is . . . a flexible one." Subsequent to *Daubert*, we have continued to apply essentially the same Rule 702 analysis except in cases involving unique, untested, or controversial methodologies or techniques.[24]

For the soft sciences, the opinion of the courts on the application of *Daubert* has been somewhat divided. The majority of courts have held that the *Frye* or *Daubert* tests alike do not apply, and they apply a conventional analysis, while a minority has held that *Frye* or *Daubert* does apply, or give only lip service to *Frye* or *Daubert*.[25] The Eighth Circuit observed, "There is some question as to whether the *Daubert* analysis should be applied at all to 'soft' sciences such as psychology."[26] In Michigan, where the *Frye* test is the standard, the Michigan Supreme Court said:

> Psychologists, when called as experts, do not talk about things or objects; they talk about people. They do not dehumanize people with whom they deal by treating them as objects composed of interacting biological systems. Rather, they speak of the whole person. Thus, it is difficult to fit the behavioral professions within the application and definition of *Frye*.[27]

Unaffected by *Daubert* is the ruling of 1983 in *Barefoot v. Estelle*,[28] where at a death-penalty sentencing hearing, the state's psychiatric expert predicted that the defendant was likely to engage in dangerous behavior. In response to the argument that the weight of empirical studies did not support a claim of psychiatric expertise in predicting future dangerousness, the U.S. Supreme Court assumed that "all of these professional doubts about the usefulness of psychiatric predictions can be called to the attention of the jury." The Court did not subject the testimony to the standard of general acceptance within the relevant scientific community or to independent judicial scrutiny of the science underlying the opinion. It went on the assumption that the jury could understand and assess the evidence and thus it merely applied the standards of relevance that govern all evidence.[29]

Some courts have even used *Daubert* to broaden admissibility of expert opinion in the soft sciences. The traditional rule has been that the opinion of a psychiatrist or psychologist that a witness is lying or telling the truth is ordinarily inadmissible because the opinion exceeds the scope of the expert's specialized knowledge and that credibility is a matter that a jury can decide without the aid of expert testimony. That rule has been bent in the post-*Daubert* era to allow that kind of testimony.

In 1995, in *United States v. Shay*,[30] the First Circuit reversed the trial court's exclusion of psychiatric testimony that the defendant's inculpatory statements were caused by *pseudologia fantastica*, a mental disorder rendering the person a pathological liar, one who makes false statements without regard to their consequences. The First Circuit said that the evidence goes to character and that under the rules of evidence truthful or untruthful character may be proven by expert testimony.[31] Citing *Daubert*, the court assumed the reliability of expert testimony on character.

Similarly, in 1996, in *United States v. Hall*,[32] the Seventh Circuit ruled that the trial court erred when it excluded testimony on false confessions. In denying the use of proffered expert testimony to that effect, the trial judge had said that the jury needed no help in assessing the suggestiveness of the interrogator's techniques. Reversing, the Seventh Circuit noted that the trial judge had failed to comply with or even mention *Daubert*, and found that his conclusions were based on a misunderstanding of the helpfulness required of expert testimony. The Seventh Circuit noted that the Supreme Court in *Daubert* disclaimed "any intention of creating a rigid or exclusive list" for admission of expert testimony.[33]

On the other hand, just as prior to *Daubert*, a number of federal courts have applied *Daubert* to exclude certain psychological expert testimony. In 1995, in *Gier v. Educational Service Unit No. 16*,[34] the Eighth Circuit held that the use of psychological evaluations of alleged child abuse must conform to the standards set forth in *Daubert*. The evaluations in question consisted of (1) reviewing a Child Behavior Checklist completed by parents, (2) clinical interviews involving role playing with anatomically correct dolls, and (3) interviewing the plaintiff's parents. The court distinguished between a methodology reliable enough to determine a course of therapy and a methodology reliable enough to support factual or investigative conclusions in a legal proceeding. The court held, as it would have under *Frye*, that the *Daubert* standard of reliability was not met.

In another 1995 case, *Borawick v. Shay*,[35] involving repressed memory, the plaintiff, after hypnotherapy, claimed to recall that her aunt and uncle had sexually abused her when she was ages four and seven. She had no memory of the abuse for twenty years. The Second Circuit ruled the repressed-memory evidence inadmissible. The court conceded: "We do not believe that *Daubert* is directly applicable to the issue here since *Daubert* concerns the admissibility of data derived from scientific techniques or expert opinions." Nevertheless, "[e]ven though *Daubert* does not provide direct guidance, our decision today is informed by the principles underlying the Supreme Court's holding."[36]

In *United States v. Powers*,[37] the Fourth Circuit, also in 1995, ruled that the use of the penile plethysmograph as a method to measure sexual arousal failed *Daubert*. The court said:

> The evidence produced at trial clearly showed that [the *Daubert*] factors weighed against the admission of the penile plethysmograph test results. First, the Government proffered evidence that the scientific literature addressing penile plethysmography does not regard the test as a valid diagnostic tool because, although useful for treatment of sex offenders, it has no accepted standards in the scientific community. Second, the government also introduced evidence before the judge that a vast majority of incest offenders who do not admit their guilt, such as Powers, show a normal reaction to the test.[38]

Again in 1995, in *United States v. Brien,*[39] psychological evidence was excluded on the ground that reliability was lacking. In this case the testimony of an eyewitness expert was proffered on memory, image retention, and retrieval. The First Circuit determined that the failure of the defense to provide adequate data or literature underlying the expert's assumptions and conclusions failed to satisfy *Daubert.*[40] In 1994, in *United States v. Rincon,*[41] the Ninth Circuit, citing *Daubert,* excluded expert testimony on the fallibility of eyewitness identification. It upheld the trial court's exclusion of the evidence, saying that (1) it does not assist the trier of fact, (2) no showing was made that the testimony relates to an area that is recognized as a science, and (3) the testimony is likely to confuse the jury. In 1999, in *United States v. Hall,*[42] the Seventh Circuit ruled similarly. The court noted that under the Supreme Court's rulings, a trial court has broad discretion to admit or exclude expert testimony, and its decision is reviewed only for an abuse of discretion.[43]

In a sequela to its 1993 decision in *Daubert,* in *Kumho Tire Co. v. Carmichael,*[44] the U.S. Supreme Court in 1999 ruled that trial judges are to play the same gatekeeping role when it comes to technical or other specialized knowledge as for scientific knowledge. Nineteen amicus curiae briefs were filed. Writing for a unanimous Court, Justice Stephen Breyer said, "[I]t would prove difficult, if not impossible, for judges to administer evidentiary rules under which a gatekeeping obligation depended upon a distinction between 'scientific' knowledge and 'technical' or 'other specialized' knowledge." Technical knowledge (about a tire) was involved in *Kumho.* At the same time, Judge Breyer said that in fulfilling their gatekeeping obligation, judges should take a flexible approach tailored to the potential witness's experience and field of expertise, be it engineering, economics, handwriting analysis, or any of numerous other subjects.

"The Supreme Court, wisely, waffled." That is the apt evaluation of the decision by Professor James Starrs, who publishes *Scientific Sleuthing Review.*[45] On the one hand, the Court said that the testimony of nonscientific experts must satisfy the reliability requirements of *Daubert,* but, on the other hand, it said that the four factors described in *Daubert* as guidelines are advisory only, rather than mandatory, with the trial court at liberty to apply one or more, or none, under the particular circumstances of the particular case at issue.

Together with its decision in 1997 in *General Electric Co. v. Joiner,*[46] the *Kumho Tire* decision means less chance of reversal of a trial court's ruling on appeal. In *Joiner,* the Supreme Court affirmed that on appellate review of a trial court's decision to admit or to exclude expert testimony, it would not do a complete reevaluation of the factual basis for the trial court's decision. Instead, appellate courts were adjured to give great deference to a trial court's admissibility decision unless it was provably an abuse of discretion.

In *Kumho Tire,* Justice Breyer's oft-repeated refrain was that admissibility questions in the case of the many and diverse fields of expert testimony must be resolved through the application of "flexible" standards, in the best judgment of trial judges. Thus, in some instances, all of the four *Daubert* factors may be employed while in others a lesser number or even different factors may be called into action by a trial judge. This approach makes the admissibility of expert testimony a very case-specific matter, and problematical.[47]

Whatever the competency of the testimony under *Frye* or *Daubert,* there are other reasons why the testimony may be excluded. Testimony may be excluded because of issues of relevancy; if its probative value is substantially outweighed by the danger of unfair prejudice, confusion of the issues, or misleading the jury; or by considerations of undue delay, waste of time, or needless presentation of cumulative evidence. More often than not, psychiatric testimony is excluded on one of these grounds, not on a question of whether the evidence meets the *Daubert* criteria.

State Law

Daubert is based on an interpretation of the Federal Rules of Evidence, a federal statute; hence, as a statutory rather than a constitutional case, *Daubert* is not binding on the states, even in the forty jurisdictions with evidence codes modeled on the Federal Rules of Evidence. In declining to follow *Daubert,* the Arizona Supreme Court noted that it was "not bound by the United States Supreme Court's non-constitutional construction of the Federal Rules of Evidence when we construe the Arizona Rules of Evidence."[48] *Daubert* has not been widely adopted by the various states but it is problematical whether it would make any difference as its reception in the federal courts would attest.

California follows a modified version of *Frye,* known as the *Kelly-Frye* test, under which reliability of expert testimony is required for "new scientific techniques."[49] The test, it is said, is intended "to forestall the jury's uncritical acceptance of scientific evidence or technology that is so foreign to everyday experience as to be unusually difficult for laypersons to evaluate. In most other instances, the jurors are permitted to rely on their own common sense and good judgment in evaluating the weight of the evidence presented to them."[50]

One such instance is illustrated in the case of *People v. Ward,*[51] where the California Court of Appeals ruled that psychiatric and psychological testimony relating to the defendant's propensity to repeat his sexually violent behavior is not subject to *Kelly-Frye*. In deciding that it was not, the court said, "California distinguishes between expert medical opinion and scientific evidence. . . . *Kelly-Frye* applies to cases involving novel devices or processes, not to expert medical testimony, such as a psychiatrist's prediction of future dangerousness or a diagnosis of mental illness. Similarly, the testimony of a psychologist who assesses whether a criminal defendant displays signs of deviance or abnormality is not subject to *Kelly-Frye*."[52]

Accordingly, in *Wilson v. Phillips,*[53] the California Court of Appeals, finding that a psychologist's testimony about the phenomenon of repressed memory in childhood sexual abuse cases was based on her personal observations, not on a new scientific technique, it was not subject to the requirement of proof or reliability prior to admission. The expert testified that the manner in which the plaintiffs recalled being molested was consistent with other individuals who had repressed their memories of childhood sexual abuse. The court said that the expert formulated her opinion based on her personal evaluation of the plaintiffs, and her findings amounted "to little more than a run-of-the-mill expert medical opinion."[54]

In *People v. McDonald,*[55] the California Supreme Court explained the distinction between expert medical testimony and evidence derived from a new scientific device or procedure:

> When a witness gives his personal opinion on the stand—even if he qualifies as an expert—the jurors may temper their acceptance of his testimony

with a healthy skepticism born of their knowledge that all human beings are fallible. But the opposite may be true when the evidence is produced by a machine: like many laypersons, jurors tend to ascribe an inordinately high degree of certainty to proof derived from an apparently "scientific" mechanism, instrument, or procedure. Yet the aura of infallibility that often surrounds such evidence may well conceal the fact that it remains experimental and tentative.

The decision in *McDonald* is best known for allowing the use of expert testimony on the psychological factors relating to the reliability of eyewitness identification. Rejecting the notion a jury would be inclined to give undue credence to such testimony, the court observed, "We have never applied the *Kelly-Frye* rule to expert medical testimony, even when the witness is a psychiatrist and the subject matter is as esoteric as the reconstitution of a past state of mind or the prediction of future dangerousness, or even the diagnosis of an unusual form of mental illness."[56]

Thus, it is held that *Daubert* does not govern the admissibility of a physician's expert opinion about informed consent. In *Gilkey v. Schweitzer*,[57] the Montana Supreme Court held that a physician's expert opinion that an anesthesiologist cannot obtain a patient's informed consent to the insertion of a thoracic spinal epidural catheter without first advising the patient that the procedure is riskier when the patient is asleep required only the specialized knowledge of a medical professional, not novel scientific evidence. Thus, the court ruled, its admissibility was not subject to the *Daubert* foundational requirements for admitting expert testimony.[58]

In a post-*Kumho Tire* decision, *Brooks v. People*,[59] the defendant in a criminal case in Colorado argued that a dog handler's theory that bloodhounds may follow a scent trail of shed skin cells should have been scrutinized under either *Frye*'s general acceptance standard or the criteria set out in *Daubert.* However, the Colorado Supreme Court held that *Frye* and *Daubert* apply only to scientific evidence. The court stated that the expert testimony at issue was "experience-based" specialized knowledge, not scientific knowledge, and called for a straightforward application of the standards for nonscientific expert testimony (that is, whether the proffered expert testimony would be helpful to the trier of fact and whether the witness has the qualifications to offer the opinion). The court noted that its conclusion "is not altered" by *Kumho Tire,* which only holds that federal courts "may" consider *Daubert* factors.

In another post-*Kumho Tire* decision, *Leaf v. Goodyear Tire & Rubber Co.*,[60] the Iowa Supreme Court adopted a limited application of the *Daubert* evidentiary standards, ruling that trial courts "may, in their discretion," consider the gatekeeping guidelines set out in *Daubert.* The court stated, "Rule 702 and our cases applying it have served us well, and we see no need to replace them in favor of a mandatory application of the *Daubert* test, whether the evidence is scientific or technical in nature." Nevertheless, the court also stated that the "observations" in *Daubert* would be helpful to a court in assessing reliability of evidence in "complex cases." The court reiterated that it is "committed to a liberal view on the admissibility of expert testimony" and "will not reverse the trial court's receipt absent a manifest abuse of the discretion to the prejudice of the complaining party."

What of expert testimony as to what went on in an individual's mind? As the Michigan Supreme Court pointed out, people are not like other phenomena in the world that make up hard-core empirical science.[61] Psychiatry and psychology involve interpretations of verbal and physical behavior, and, of course, uncertainty as to what truly went on in an individual's mind. Must an expert's opinion about an individual's state of mind be based on an examination of the individual? In this regard, by way of illustration, the discussion in a Minnesota case is interesting.[62] The issue in the case was whether the exclusion of coverage in a homeowner's liability policy of "bodily injury . . . which is expected or intended by the insured" applied to the insured who, allegedly because of mental illness, lacked the capacity to form the intent to injure. The insurer argued there was no liability under the policy for injuries suffered by the victim who was shot by the insured who in turn killed himself. Testifying in response to a hypothetical question based on the shooting and the insured's unusual behavior days before, a psychiatrist opined that at the time of the shooting the insured had "a deranged mental intellect which did deprive him of the capacity to govern his conduct in accordance with reason." The trial court rejected this opinion as lacking foundation, stating:

> [I]t is this court's opinion that there was insufficient foundation for the tender of the [psychiatrist's] opinion. [The psychiatrist] did not ever interview [the insured] nor did he ever treat him for any problem, either physical or mental, nor did he review any medical records of [the insured]. There was no evidence of [the insured] being treated for any psychiatric problems. . . . [T]he psychiatrist's opinion is perhaps best described as "informed speculation," not the type of certainty courts require of most opinion evidence. It is apparent that the American Psychiatric Association's standards for rendering an opinion were not met here. The association's standards set forth that one should not testify regarding anyone's mental capacity without directly knowing that person.

Portraying this ruling as one questioning "whether [the psychiatrist's] opinion would be helpful to the trier of fact because of his lack of personal contact with [the insured]," the intermediate court of appeals held the trial court abused its discretion in excluding the psychiatrist's testimony because of there having been no personal contact with the insured.[63] The Minnesota Supreme Court agreed with the result reached by the intermediate appellate court, but for a different reason. It said:

> [T]he trial court questioned whether the hypothetical question itself presented sufficient facts to support [the psychiatrist's] opinion, not whether [the psychiatrist] was qualified or his opinion helpful. The foundational sufficiency of a hypothetical question, however, is judged by the contents of the question itself and not by whether the witness has ever examined the person, place or thing in question. . . . So long as the expert witness is qualified and the question contains sufficient facts to permit that witness to give a reasonable opinion based not on mere speculation or conjecture, the opinion of an expert witness may be adequately obtained upon hypothetical data alone.[64]

Thus, a *psychological autopsy*—whether a death was a homicide, suicide, or accident—may be rendered without meeting the *Daubert* or *Frye* test. Likewise, there may be an evaluation of "dangerousness" without an actual examination of the individual and without violating the *Daubert* or *Frye* test.

Workers' Compensation Cases

In workers' compensation cases, we may note, a claimant is not required to prove that a treating physician's opinions, diagnosis, or treatment satisfies either the *Daubert* or *Frye* test.[65] The Kansas Court of Appeals reasoned:

> A claimant's burden of proof in a workers' compensation case is to prove that it is more probably true than not true that he or she suffers from a disabling physical condition which is the result of his or her work. To require a claimant to also prove that a diagnosis is one universally recognized by and agreed upon in the medical community is above and beyond the scope and nature of the Workers' Compensation Act. To apply the *Daubert* or *Frye* standard to a workers' compensation case . . . would require us to apply our rules of evidence to those proceedings, and those rules of evidence have been held specifically not applicable."[66]

The Evolving Law on the Basis of an Expert's Opinion

The Federal Rules of Evidence that were adopted in 1975 (and their counterparts in the various states) made major changes in the law on expert testimony. Under Rule 703, experts may base their opinion upon facts received at or before the trial. Moreover, under Rule 703, it is provided that if experts in the particular field regularly rely on such data, the expert's foundation need not be admissible in evidence.[67] Rule 703, prior to amendment in 2000, provided:

> The facts or data in the particular case upon which an expert bases an opinion or inference may be those perceived by or made known to the expert at or before the hearing. If of a type reasonably relied upon by experts in the particular field in forming opinions or inferences upon the subject, the facts or data need not be admissible in evidence.

Rule 703 markedly widened the basis on which experts could rest their opinions. At common law the basis of the opinion would have to be in evidence. By allowing experts to rely on sources of information that may not be admissible in their own right, Rule 703 provides a way to bypass rules of evidence. The focus of Rule 703 is not on the admissibility of the underlying data of the expert's opinion but on its validity and reliability as measured by the practice of experts when not in court, now subject to *Daubert* and its sequela, as discussed, which call upon the trial judge to be a gatekeeper to ensure that there is a reliable basis for the expert's testimony.

The provision in Rule 703 allowing facts or data to be made known to the expert at the hearing permits having the expert attend the trial and hear the testimony setting out the facts, or permits the familiar hypothetical question. Generally, a hypothetical question would assume all facts disclosed by the evidence material to the theory of the case as viewed from the side propounding the question. Presumably, with the adoption of Rules 703 and 705, a trial judge, in his discretion, may require use of a hypothetical question, but at least one state (North Carolina), in its version of Rule 705, provides that the trial judge cannot require its use.

Prior to 1975, the hypothetical question was the vehicle for eliciting the expert's opinion upon facts as to which the expert had no personal knowledge—it was designed to reveal all the pertinent facts in the most logical order to support the expert opinion, but its objectives were never realized. Wigmore described its defects:

> In the first place, it has artificially clamped the mouth of the expert witness, so that his answer to a complex question may not express his actual opinion on the actual case. . . . In the second place, it has tended to mislead the jury as to the purport of actual expert opinion. . . . In the third place, it has tended to confuse the jury, so that its employment becomes a near waste of time and futile obstruction.[68]

Theoretically, under Rule 705, an opinion may be given without presenting its basis. Under the Rule it is the opponent of the expert who must fight the battle of what is reasonably relied upon by the experts in the field, since it is the opponent who might have to bring out the underlying data. Rule 705 provides,

> The expert may testify in terms of opinion or inference and gives reasons therefore without first testifying to the underlying facts or data, unless the court requires otherwise. The expert may in any event be required to disclose the underlying facts or data on cross-examination.

Of course, in practice, an opinion is more convincing when given with underlying data. Under Rule 705, the expert may be examined fully both on direct and cross-examination concerning the bases of his opinion.

There are a multitude of cases involving the provision in Rule 703 that the basis of the opinion may rest on facts or data reasonably relied upon by experts in the particular field (and the facts or data need not be admissible in evidence). The expert may support his opinion with testimony of discussions with others. Thus, in a case concerning the cause of an explosion, it was held error not to permit the expert to disclose that his opinion was based, in part, upon discussions with another expert. The disclosure of consultation with other experts would add to the credibility of the expert's opinion, and the court ruled that the expert had the right to buttress its opinion in this way. The court based its decision on the ground that an expert may reasonably base his opinion upon discussions with other experts.[69]

Data reasonably relied upon by an expert may come in many forms. A physician as an expert witness may rely on statements or opinions of other doctors, nurses, and technicians and on hospital records. The physician makes treatment decisions upon this type of information, so it can be used as the basis of testimony. The psychiatrist uses test results provided by a psychologist as well as other data not in evidence.

In making an evaluation, psychiatrists typically consider the criminal record of an individual. Hence, under Rule 703, expert testimony may be based, in part, on the criminal record of the accused although, ordinarily, testimony as to past crimes is excluded as impermissible character evidence. Thus, in a case involving a defense of insanity, the psychiatrist may include the accused's criminal record in support of his opinion. Accordingly, in line with the jurisprudence, the Tenth Circuit allowed the state's psychiatrist to testify that the defendant was sane, based, in part, on the fact that the accused had committed armed robberies prior to the offense in question in order to support a heroin addiction.[70]

In another of the many cases allowing an expert to give an opinion based on facts not in evidence, an expert in an aviation products liability case gave an opinion, based upon interviews with decedent's associates and friends that the plaintiff's decedent was under stress. The Third Circuit allowed the testimony because, the court found, such interviews are normally relied upon by experts when evaluating a pilot's fitness.[71]

In an oft-noted case, *Lilley v. Dow Chemical Co.,*[72] Judge Jack Weinstein provided a useful example of hearsay that was considered not to be the type of evidence on which an expert could reasonably rely under Rule 703. In this case the plaintiff's decedent had allegedly contracted cancer as a result of his contact with Agent Orange in Vietnam. On a motion for summary judgment, the defendants claimed that there was insufficient evidence of causation to create a genuine issue of material fact. The plaintiff produced the affidavit of a qualified medical expert who concluded that the decedent's illness and death had been caused by contact with Agent Orange. The expert had based his opinion partly upon conversations with family members, whose information in turn came mainly from the decedent. They reported to the expert that decedent had been in contact with Agent Orange and not with other chemicals.

Judge Weinstein granted the motion for summary judgment, noting that the expert's opinion would not be admissible at trial. The expert's facts about the decedent's symptoms, habits, and background were based almost exclusively on hearsay that was not the type of hearsay on which physicians customarily rely in diagnosing illness. The wife's statements to the expert, for example, were not "the kind of reliable statements about direct observation of actions, contemporaneous statements and symptoms usually related by a spouse." Instead, she had "little or no contact with her husband for long periods of time and made no direct observations about his work or its effects upon him." Judge Weinstein's opinion indicates that in some cases statements by a spouse might properly be considered by a medical expert in forming an opinion, as the Advisory Committee's Note to Rule 703 indicates.[73] Here, however, the spouse's reports, themselves confused and based on hearsay, were simply not sufficiently reliable.[74]

In *United States v. Lundy,*[75] a prosecution for arson, the opinion of the prosecution's expert that arson was the cause of the fire was based, in part, upon interviews with witnesses at the scene. The defense argued on appeal that the expert's testimony was inadmissible because it was based on hearsay statements and third-party observations. The Seventh Circuit agreed that it would be impermissible for the expert simply to summarize and testify to statements by third parties that the defendant was the person that torched the building. However, in this case, the court noted, the expert based his opinion upon observations and statements of witnesses that would reasonably be relied upon by experts. The court said that the expert "presented uncontroverted evidence that interviews with many witnesses to a fire are a standard investigatory technique in cause and origin [of fire] inquiries." The court highlighted the significance between an expert who merely recites hearsay and the expert who actually bases his opinion upon hearsay.

While a testifying expert may express an opinion based on consultation with others who are not witnesses, the expert cannot be a mere conduit for their opinion. Sometimes, the distinction is opaque. In a Florida case, Jessica Schwarz was charged with second-degree murder, as well as child abuse and other offenses, after her ten-year-old stepson was found dead in the family pool. The Florida Court of Appeals was faced with the issue: Was it proper for a pathologist who testified about the cause of death to testify on direct examination that he had consulted with other pathologists about the cause of death? The state's expert forensic pathologist testified that "there's a medical certainty that this is not suicide." He testified that when he gets involved in an unusual case he does not rely solely on his own opinion, but regularly consults two pathologists on his staff, and three others from different states, and he so testified over the defendant's objection. The defendant also objected to the expert's comment that one of the experts he consulted was "probably the best forensic pathologist that I have known and I think that he's the best that there probably has ever been." The Florida Court of Appeals ruled that the expert should not have been permitted to testify in the way that he did. The court said, "[W]hile there was nothing improper about [the expert] consulting with other experts in his field, he should not have been allowed to testify that he did so on direct examination. . . . Such expert omission improperly permits one expert to become a conduit for the opinion of another who is not subject to cross-examination."[76]

When is an expert acting simply as a conduit for another's opinion? In a Vermont case, a psychiatrist, who gave his opinion that the defendant was not mentally ill, testified that he had consulted with Dr. Richard Rada, who "of all the people in the United States . . . knows most about this stuff," and that "Dr. Rada is in concurrence with my opinion in this case." Holding it error, the Vermont Supreme Court said that the expert was not relying on facts or data provided by Dr. Rada, but was rather acting merely as a conduit for the other doctor's opinion.[77]

That too is the way the expert testified in the aforementioned Florida case involving Jessica Schwarz.[78] Consulting with other experts in forming one's opinion is distinguished from merely serving as a conduit for the opinion of another expert who is not subject to cross-examination. To be sure, the dividing line is not sharp, but there is a dividing line. Moreover, it is error to testify about the credibility of other experts. Both are improper attempts to bolster one's own opinion.[79]

What about a defendant's right of confrontation? Does an expert's reliance on hearsay violate that right? That issue was raised in *United States v. Lawson*.[80] In this case Darrell Lawson was accused of extortion and assault, and he pleaded insanity. Prior to trial he was examined for three months at a federal medical center where Dr. Robert Sheldon was chief of psychiatry. At trial Dr. Sheldon testified that in his opinion Lawson was sane at the time he committed the alleged offenses. His personal observation of Lawson consisted of informal conversations and participation at two staff interviews; he did not otherwise examine Lawson. In forming his opinion, he also relied upon several other sources, none of which were introduced in evidence. The district court admitted the opinion pursuant to Rule 703, and the Seventh Circuit affirmed. The court held that an expert's testimony based solely on hearsay reports would violate a defendant's right of confrontation, but that right was not violated in this case because "Dr. Sheldon had had at least *some* contact with Lawson himself."[81] Furthermore, the court said, effective cross-examination of Dr. Sheldon was assured because the defendant was given access in advance of trial to the hearsay information that Dr. Sheldon relied upon.[82]

Criticism of Psychiatric Testimony

Psychiatric testimony often embarrasses the profession in the public eye, not only when such testimony is made without examination but even when an examination is made. The criticisms include: psychiatrists excuse sin; psychiatrists disagree or say anything; psychiatrists give confusing, subjective, unhelpful, jargon-ridden testimony; and psychiatrists give conclusory opinions.[83] Thomas Sowell is one of many who asks, "Why do we keep taking shrinks seriously?"[84] A devastating assessment, if agreed to. Much quoted in the law reviews is the statement of Bruce Ennis, then of the American Civil Liberties Union, that a psychiatrist's prediction is as accurate as the flip of a coin, and he argued that, being so unreliable, psychiatric testimony ought to be excluded as nonprobative or incompetent.[85] The APA actually itself cited the article in its amicus brief in *Barefoot v. Estelle*,[86] where psychiatrists testified in a capital penalty hearing about the dangerousness of a criminal offender. The major work used by attorneys in challenging psychiatric evidence is the three-volume *Coping with Psychiatric and Psychological Testimony* by Jay Ziskin, a clinical psychologist and lawyer,[87] and it has given rise to the expression, "Ziskinizing the expert."[88]

In a case appealed to the Seventh Circuit,[89] the petitioner in a capital murder case claimed ineffective assistance of counsel because counsel failed at the sentencing hearing to utilize a report of a psychiatrist who had examined him on death row. No harm was done, said the Seventh Circuit. Ridiculing the psychiatric testimony, the court said, "The psychiatrist's uncritical dependence on the murderer's uncorroborated self-exculpatory statement, along with the psychiatrist's effort to blame [the petitioner's] behavior on an 'oedipal situation,' would have exposed the psychiatrist to lacerating cross-examination had he testified at the sentencing hearing."[90]

Various psychiatric opinions were given of John Hinckley Jr., the would-be assassin of President Reagan, though all were based on an examination. The experts could not even agree as to whether Hinckley was psychotic, much less as to the impact of his mental condition on cognition or control of his behavior. Experts for the defense said that Hinckley "was in a psychotic state at the time he performed the act."[91] In contrast, the opinions of a four-member team of experts retained by the prosecution said that Hinckley was not psychotic but that he met the criteria for *dysthymic disorder* ("sad mood disorder"), *narcissistic personality disorder* ("self-centered or self-absorbed personality disorder"), and *schizoid personality disorder* (lack of friends and emotional coldness or aloofness). Another prosecution expert, Dr. Sally Johnson, psychiatrist at the Federal Correctional Institute in Butner, North Carolina, where Hinckley was sent after his arrest, gave "narcissistic personality disorder" as the primary diagnosis.[92] Following the public outcry over the verdict finding Hinckley not guilty by reason of insanity, the APA along with the American Bar Association issued statements calling for a change in the law. The various opinions given by the psychiatrists about Hinckley as well as the law on criminal responsibility were ridiculed in the media.[93]

New Changes in the Rules of Evidence

Given the widespread criticism of expert testimony, not only of psychiatric testimony, the innovations adopted in 1975 in the Federal Rules of Evidence (and their counterparts in state laws) have recently been changed, as of December 1, 2000.

The amendments do not distinguish between scientific and other forms of expert testimony.

As amended (alterations in italic), Rule 702, on testimony by experts, provides:

> If scientific, technical, or other specialized knowledge will assist the trier of fact to understand the evidence or to determine a fact in issue, a witness qualified as an expert by knowledge, skill, experience, training, or education, may testify thereto in the form of an opinion or otherwise, *if (1) the testimony is based upon sufficient facts or data, (2) the testimony is the product of reliable principles and methods, and (3) the witness has applied the principles and methods reliably to the facts of the case.*

As amended (alterations in italic), Rule 703, on the basis of opinion testimony by experts, provides:

> The facts or data in the particular case upon which an expert bases an opinion or inference may be those perceived by or made known to the expert at or before the hearing. If of a type reasonably relied upon in the particular field in forming opinions or inferences upon the subject, the facts or data need not be admissible in evidence *in order for the opinion or inference to be admitted. Facts or data that are otherwise inadmissible shall not be disclosed to the jury by the proponent of the opinion or inference unless the court determines that their probative value in assisting the jury to evaluate the expert's opinion substantially outweighs their prejudicial effect.*

Undoubtedly, these revised rules will be the subject of much litigation, just as the replaced rules were in their time. The amended Rule 702 is seen by some legal commentators as merely a codification of the Supreme Court's rulings in *Daubert, Joiner,* and *Kumho,* but others think differently, saying that the new rule muddies the waters. Under 702(1), what criteria will be utilized to decide whether the "facts or data" underlying the expert's opinion are "sufficient" to authorize its admission into evidence? The same question can be asked of 702(3), namely, what standards will determine whether "reliable principles and methods" under 702(2) have been "reliably" applied to the facts of the case?

Amended Rule 703 is designed to prevent lawyers from getting inadmissible evidence, usually hearsay, before the jury by using the expert's including as the basis for his opinion the results or findings of other nontestifying experts. The amendment draws a fine, if not tenuous, line between the ability of the expert to rely on inadmissible evidence and the opportunity for the proponent of the testimony to bring it before the jury as additional evidence in support of the proponent's position. And, indeed, the amendment permits the trial judge to engage in a balancing approach for the purpose of admitting the otherwise inadmissible evidence in order to assist "the jury to evaluate the expert's opinion" when that need "substantially outweighs their prejudicial effect." Professor Starrs predicts "with uncompromising, even apodictic, certainty that the changes to Rules 702 and 703 will leave much room for judicial creativity in implementing them."[94]

To Sum Up

Psychiatric testimony, of all expert testimony, is the most lampooned.[95] At the same time, it is usually the most interesting and captivating of testimony presented at trials. That is why it makes the news, yet the ridicule embarrasses many psychiatrists. The ridicule is not a result of opinions made without examination, or by a cursory examination; it is a result of the nature of the opinion whether or not it is based on examination.[96]

Has *Daubert*, by and large, come to naught in excluding junk science? Now that a number of years have passed since the Court's decision, it can be asked: Has it been a turning point on expert testimony? *Daubert* hearings, as they are known, are held, raising the cost of litigation, but do they make much of a difference in outcome, if any? For behavioral and social science evidence, the answer is that since *Daubert*, evidence that would have been admitted prior to *Daubert* has been excluded only in isolated cases. Overall, *Daubert* has not resulted in changes in the admissibility of that kind of evidence.[97]

With the possible exception of product liability cases, the great expectation that D*aubert* would bring an end to junk science in the courtroom has not materialized. A review of the case law after *Daubert* shows that the rejection of expert testimony is the exception rather than the rule. As one court put it, "*Daubert* did not work a sea change over federal evidence law. . . . The trial court's role as gatekeeper is not intended as a replacement for the adversary system."[98] *Trial* magazine, which is published by the Association of Trial Lawyers of America, is still replete with advertisements of available experts. Referral firms continue to do a lively business.

Was it realistic to expect judges to apply the *Daubert* criteria as initially conceived? Arizona Supreme Court Chief Justice Thomas Zlaket jests that he chose law to escape from science and math.[99] Judge Pamela Ann Rymer of the U.S. Court of Appeals for the Ninth Circuit says, "I'm scientifically illiterate."[100] Judges are lawyers, not scientists, and they have neither the competency nor the time to scrutinize the various types of evidence that come before the courts as *Daubert* envisioned. As a consequence, the *Daubert* criteria have been interpreted in the disjunctive rather than the conjunctive, its scope of applicability has been limited, or it has been given lip service, and it has not been adopted by many states. As generally interpreted, *Daubert* provides for a "liberal" and "fluid" standard of admissibility, and the trial court's decision is rarely to be second-guessed by an appellate court. Quite likely, the publicity about junk science has had more to do with controlling expert testimony than has *Daubert*.

Notes

1. Judge Patrick Higginbotham in In re Air Crash Disaster at New Orleans, Louisiana, 795 F.2d 1230 at 1234 (5th Cir. 1986).

2. See, e.g., D. L. Faigman, *Legal Alchemy: The Use and Misuse of Science in the Law* (New York: W. H. Freeman, 1999); P. W. Huber, *Galileo's Revenge: Junk Science in the Courtroom* (New York: Basic Books, 1991).

3. D. Quayle, "Civil Justice Reform," *Am. U.L. Rev.* 41 (1992): 559.

4. 509 U.S. 579 (1993); Symposium, "Behavioral Science Evidence in the Wake of *Daubert*," *Behavioral Sciences & Law* 13 (1995): 127.

5. 293 Fed. 1013 (D.C. Cir. 1923).

6. Ibid.

7. E. J. Imwinkelried, "The Next Step in Conceptualizing the Presentation of Expert Evidence as Education: The Case for Didactic Trial Procedures," *Int. J. Evidence & Proof* 1 (1997): 128; P. S. Miller, B. W. Rein, & E. O. Bailey, "*Daubert* and the Need for Judicial Scientific Literacy," *Judicature* 77 (1994): 254.

8. Daubert v. Merrell Dow Pharmaceuticals, 43 F.3d 1311 (9th Cir. 1995).

9. In a footnote, Judge Kozinski noted: "There are, of course, exceptions. Fingerprint analysis, voice recognition, DNA and a variety of other scientific endeavors closely tied to law enforcement may indeed have the courtroom as a principal theatre of operations. . . . As to such disciplines, the fact that the expert has developed his expertise principally for purposes of litigation will obviously not be a substantial consideration." 43 F.3d at 1317 n. 5.

10. United States v. Cordoba, 1997 WL 3317 (9th Cir. 1997).

11. United States v. Posado, 57 F.3d 428 (5th Cir. 1995). The Tenth Circuit adopted the same position. United States v. Call, 129 F.3d 1402 (10th Cir. 1997).

12. 57 F.3d at 434.

13. Ibid.

14. In State v. Porter, 698 A.2d 739 (Conn. 1997), the Connecticut Supreme Court, after deciding to adopt *Daubert,* reviewed the scientific status of polygraph exams. While not deciding definitively whether the polygraph met the *Daubert* standard, it held that the probative value of the test results was so low that the value of the test was outweighed by its prejudice. Therefore, it reaffirmed Connecticut's per se rule against the use of polygraph evidence. See L. Saxe & G. Ben-Shahkar, "Admissibility of Polygraph Tests: The Application of Scientific Standards Post-*Daubert,*" *Psychology, Public Policy & Law* 5 (1999): 203. Military Rule of Evidence 707 expressly excludes from evidence the results of a polygraph examination, the opinion of a polygraph examiner, or any reference to an offer to take, failure to take, or taking of a polygraph examination. See United States v. Scheffer, 523 U.S. 303 (1998).

By and large, the same material that is admissible or inadmissible under *Frye* is held admissible or inadmissible under *Daubert.* In Gier v. Educational Service Unit No. 16, 66 F.3d 940 (8th Cir. 1995), a Child Behavior Checklist and testimony based on it were ruled inadmissible on an issue of whether mentally retarded clients at a state school had been sexually abused. The trial court ruled the checklist and related testimony inadmissible under the *Daubert* criteria. 845 F.Supp. 1342 (D.Neb. 1994). The Eighth Circuit commended the trial court, noting that the analysis conducted by the trial court "is precisely the type of analysis the decision in Daubert would appear to contemplate." 66 F.3d at 994. The same testimony would have been ruled inadmissible under *Frye* because such testimony would not reach general acceptance in the scientific community. The checklist was not normed or standardized on sexually abused children and, therefore, could not be used to answer this question.

Recently there have been a number of *Frye* or *Daubert* motion hearings in several states to bar use of "actuarial instruments" in the implementation of Sexually Violent Predator (SVP) laws. The courts, by and large, tend to oblige the defendant—better to hold a hearing, which amounts to nothing in these cases, so as to avoid reversible error. In SVP hearings, actuarial evidence is admitted, with the courts ruling that it passes muster under *Frye* or *Daubert.* Given the public outrage over sex offenses, an offender who has been convicted of a sex offense is likely to be committed following his incarceration under the SVP law. For a critique of the evidence, see T. W. Campbell, "Sexual Predator Evaluations and Phrenology: Considering Issues of Evidentiary Reliability," *Behav. Sci. & Law* 18 (2000): 111. In a departure from long-established doctrine, the rules of evidence have been amended to allow evidence of other acts of sexual assault, apart as a basis of expert testimony, to establish propensity to commit another sexual assault. Rules 413–415, Federal Rules of Evidence, enacted in 1994. See chapter 6, on propensity evidence, and chapter 18, on sex offender legislation.

15. 61 F.3d 1038 (2d Cir. 1995).

16. 61 F.3d at 1045. See E. J. Imwinkelreid, "Trial Judges—Gatekeepers or Usurpers? Can the Trial Judge Critically Assess the Admissibility of Expert Testimony without Invading the Jury's Province to Evaluate the Credibility and Weight of the Testimony?" *Marq. L. Rev.* 84 (2000): 1.

17. 877 F.Supp. 1055 (E.D.Mich. 1995).

18. In accord is Shahzade v. Gregory, 923 F.Supp. 286, 930 F.Supp. 673 (D.Mass. 1996).

19. J. Q. Wilson, "Trial by Expert," *National Review,* Mar. 10, 1997, p. 38.

20. J. F. Fielder, "'Daubert' Can Undermine Psychiatric Testimony," *National Law Journal,* Sept. 22, 1997, p. B-14. In a 27-page amicus curiae brief filed with the U.S. Supreme Court in 1986 in *Edwards v. Aguillard,* 482 U.S. 578 (1987), a case out of Louisiana concerning the constitutionality of teaching "creation science," it was argued that science, in essence, is defined by a certain attitude toward knowledge. The Arizona Supreme Court said that testimony about the phenomenon of repressed memory is not about science, and therefore neither *Frye* nor *Daubert* apply. Logerquist v. McVey, 1 P.3d 113 (Ariz. 2000).

21. Resolution in the U.S. Supreme Court in Tribute to Justice Harry A. Blackmun, Oct. 27, 1999.

22. 880 F.Supp. 1027 (S.D. N.Y. 1995).

23. 82 F.3d 1513 (10th Cir. 1996).

24. 82 F.3d at 1519.

25. In a study of hearings involving "battered woman syndrome" and "rape trauma syndrome" defenses, expert testimony was admitted in fifty-one of the cases and rejected in seventeen, largely on the basis of the credentials of the expert. In none did the judges refer to any scientific analysis. The issue that was examined by the judge was the relevance of the expert testimony to the case. Reported in S. L. Brodsky, *The Expert Witness* (Washington, D.C.: American Psychological Association, 1999), p. 34. An illustration of the minority view is Elcock v. K-Mart Corp., 233 F.3d 734 (3d Cir. 2000), where the appellate court held that the district court was required to hold a *Daubert* hearing to determine the reliability of the testimony of a psychologist who sought to testify as a vocational rehabilitation expert in a slip-and-fall action.

26. Jenson v. Eveleth Taconite Co., 130 F.3d 1287, 1297 (8th Cir. 1997). See Symposium, "*Daubert*'s Meanings for the Admissibility of Behavioral and Social Science Evidence," *Psychology, Public Policy & Law* 5 (1999): 1–242; T. G. Gutheil & M. D. Stein, "*Daubert*-Based Gatekeeping and Psychiatric/Psychological Testimony in Court: Review and Proposal," *J. Psychiatry & Law* 28 (2000): 235.

27. People v. Beckley, 434 Mich. 691, 456 N.W.2d 391 (1990).

28. 463 U.S. 880 (1983).

29. Federal Rules of Evidence, Rules 401–403.

30. 57 F.3d 126 (1st Cir. 1995).

31. Federal Rules of Evidence, Rules 405(a) and 608(a).

32. 93 F.3d 1337 (7th Cir. 1996).

33. 93 F.3d at 1341. In State v. Shuck, 953 S.W.2d 662 (Tenn. 1997), the Tennessee Supreme Court reached a similar result. The court ruled admissible a neuropsychologist's testimony concerning a defendant's acute susceptibility to inducement in support of an entrapment defense.

34. 66 F.3d 940 (8th Cir. 1995), cited supra note 14.

35. 68 F.3d 597 (2d Cir. 1995).

36. 68 F.3d at 610.

37. 59 F.3d 1460 (4th Cir. 1995).

38. 59 F.3d at 1471.

39. 59 F.3d 274 (1st Cir. 1995).

40. See J. Goodman-Delahunty, "Forensic Psychological Expertise in the Wake of *Daubert*," *Law & Human Behavior* 21 (1997): 121.

41. 28 F.3d 921 (9th Cir. 1994).

42. 165 F.3d 1095 (7th Cir. 1999).

43. 165 F.3d at 1101.

44. 119 S. Ct. 1167 (1999).

45. J. E. Starrs, "The Admissibility Factor," *Scientific Sleuthing* 23 (Fall 1999): 14. See also P. Giannelli & E. Imwinkelried, "Scientific Evidence: The Fallout from Supreme Court's Decision in *Kumho Tire*," *Criminal Justice* 14 (Winter 2000): 12.

46. 522 U.S. 136 (1997).

47. In the wake of *Kumho Tire,* and citing it, the Tenth Circuit in United States v. Charley, 176 F.3d 1265, 1278 (10th Cir. 1999), excluded an expert's testimony that a child's symptoms were more consistent with the symptoms of children who have been sexually abused than with the symptoms of children who witness physical abuse of their mother. The court found

that no sufficient foundation was laid for this kind of expert analysis, and no reliability inquiry was undertaken. 176 F.3d at 1278.

48. State v. Bible, 858 P.2d 1152, 1183 (Ariz. 1993). In Logerquist v. McVey, 1 P.3d 113 (Ariz. 2000), the plaintiff alleged that she had been sexually abused by the defendant, her pediatrician, and that she had repressed these recollections for almost twenty years until her memory was triggered by a television commercial featuring a pediatrician. She sought to introduce expert testimony at trial to support her contention that such memories can be repressed for years but can be recalled with accuracy once triggered by some external event. Applying the traditional approach articulated in *Frye*, the trial judge determined that the theories advanced by the plaintiff's experts were not generally accepted among trauma memory researchers. Both parties urged the state supreme court to adopt the standard set out by the U.S. Supreme Court in *Daubert*.

The court said that *Daubert* and its progeny force the trial judge to cross the line between the legal task of ruling on the foundation and relevance of evidence—which is a judge's traditional role—and the jury's task of determining whom to believe and why, whose testimony to accept, and on what basis. Reviewing the cases decided under the *Frye* standard in Arizona state courts, the court concluded that trial judges have had sufficient latitude to reject truly questionable expert testimony while retaining the ability to admit principles and techniques that will aid the jury in its resolution of the case. The court added that it would not adopt the *Daubert* approach even if it could be shown that trial judges do a better job than juries of weeding out unreliable expert witnesses. It noted that the state constitution preserves each litigant's right to have the jury pass upon questions of fact by determining the credibility of witnesses and the weight of conflicting evidence. In fact, the court said, judges are prohibited from even commenting on the credibility of the evidence, which would seem to preclude granting them the broader power of excluding proffered relevant evidence entirely. Returning to the plaintiff's claim, the court held that the expert testimony she had sought to introduce was not sufficiently novel to require application of the *Frye* standard, and directed that the plaintiff's expert witnesses be permitted to testify. See, in general, T. L. Bohan & E. J. Heels, "The Case against *Daubert:* The New Scientific Evidence 'Standard' and the Standards of the Several States," *J. For. Sci.* 40 (1995): 1030.

49. To satisfy this requirement, the proponent of the testimony must show: (1) the technique has gained general acceptance in the particular field to which it belongs, (2) any witness testifying on general acceptance is properly qualified as an expert on the subject, and (3) correct scientific procedures were used in the particular case. People v. Kelly, 17 Cal.3d 24, 130 Cal. Rptr. 144, 549 P.2d 1240 (1976).

50. People v. Venegas, 18 Cal.4th 47, 74 Cal. Rptr.2d 262, 54 P.2d 525 (1998).

51. 71 Cal. App.4th 368, 83 Cal. Rptr.2d 838 (1999).

52. 71 Cal. App.4th at 373.

53. 86 Cal. Rptr.2d 204 (Cal. App. 1999).

54. 86 Cal. Rptr.2d at 208.

55. 37 Cal.3d 351, 208 Cal. Rptr. 236, 690 P.2d 709 (1984).

56. 37 Cal.3d at 373.

57. 983 P.2d 869 (Mont. 1999).

58. The Montana Supreme Court rejected the defendant's argument that the plaintiff was presenting a novel theory that required her to show that the expert's opinion was reached by reliable scientific methods or that it was supported by the medical literature or other objective evidence. The court said that the expert's testimony required the specialized knowledge of a medical professional but did not involve novel scientific evidence. Consequently, the testimony was not subject to the *Daubert* requirements.

Likewise, in Waitek v. Dalkon Shield Claimants Trust, 934 F.Supp. 1068 (N.D.Iowa 1996), a federal district court held that *Daubert* did not apply to a gynecologist's expert testimony because his opinions "were not based on a novel scientific test or a unique, controversial methodology or technique; rather, he based his opinions on his experience and training as both a gynecologist and as a doctor experienced in the use of and medical problems associated with the Dalkon Shield."

59. 975 P.2d 1105 (Colo. 1999).

60. 590 N.W.2d 525 (Iowa 1999).

61. Supra note 27.

62. State Farm Fire & Cas. Co. v. Wicka, 474 N.W.2d 324 (Minn. 1991).

63. 461 N.W.2d 236, 241 (1990). See R. Slovenko, "Psychiatric Opinion without Examination," *J. Psychiatry & Law* 28 (2000): 103.

64. 474 N.W.2d at 332.

65. Sheridan v. Catering Management, 5 Neb. App. 305, 558 N.W.2d 319 (1997).

66. Armstrong v. City of Wichita, 21 Kan. App.2d 750, 907 P.2d 923 (1995), quoted in Sheridan v. Catering Management, 558 N.W.2d at 327.

67. Federal Rules of Evidence, Rule 703. The Michigan rule differs as follows: "The court may require that underlying facts or data essential to an opinion or inference be in evidence." Michigan Rules of Evidence, Rule 703.

68. J. Wigmore, *Evidence* (Boston: Little, Brown, 3d ed. 1940), sec. 686.

69. Lewis v. Rego Co., 757 F.2d 66, 74 (3d Cir. 1985).

70. United States v. Madrid, 673 F.2d 1114 (10th Cir. 1982).

71. Stevens v. Cessna Aircraft Co., 634 F.Supp. 137 (E.D.Pa. 1986), *aff'd*, 806 F.2d 254 (3d Cir. 1986).

72. 611 F.Supp 1267 (E.D. N.Y. 1985).

73. The Advisory Committee stated, "[Rule 703] is designed to broaden the basis for expert opinions beyond that current in many jurisdictions and to bring judicial practice into line with the practice of the experts themselves when not in court. Thus a physician in his own practice bases his diagnosis on information from numerous sources and of considerable variety, including statements by patients and relatives, reports and opinions from nurses, technicians and other doctors, hospital records, and X rays." Advisory Committee's Note, Rule 703 of Federal Rules of Evidence.

74. See J. R. Waltz & R. C. Park, *Evidence: Cases and Materials* (New York: Foundation Press, 9th ed. 1999), p. 800.

75. 809 F.2d 392 (7th Cir. 1987).

76. Schwarz v. State, 695 So.2d 452, 455 (Fla. App. 1997).

77. State v. Towne, 142 Vt. 241, 453 A.2d 1133, 1135 (1982).

78. Schwarz v. State, supra note 76. Likewise, in State v. Bradford, 618 N.W.2d 782 (Minn. 2000), it was held error for a medical examiner to testify that two other nontestifying experts agreed with him that a death was a homicide.

79. See United States v. Tran Trong Cuong, 18 F.3d 1132 (4th Cir. 1994).

80. 653 F.2d 299 (7th Cir. 1981), *cert. denied*, 454 U.S. 1150 (1982).

81. Ibid. at 303 (emphasis in original).

82. Ibid. at 302–3.

83. See R. Slovenko, *Psychiatry and Criminal Culpability* (New York: Wiley, 1995), pp. 225–37. In a dissenting opinion, Chief Justice Warren Burger, then sitting on the U.S. Court of Appeals for the District of Columbia Circuit, observed, "The jury wants and needs help from the expert, but it does not help a jury of [laypersons] to be told of a diagnosis limited to the esoteric and swiftly changing vocabulary of psychiatry. Every technical description ought to be 'translated' in terms of 'what I mean by this,' followed by a down-to-earth concrete explanation in terms which convey meaning to [laypersons]. A psychiatrist who gives a jury a diagnosis, for example, of 'psychoneurotic reaction, obsessive compulsive type' and fails to explain fully what this means, would contribute more to society if he were permitted to stay at his hospital post taking care of patients." Campbell v. United States, 113 U.S. App. D.C. 260, 307 F.2d 597, 614 (D.C. Cir. 1962).

84. T. Sowell, "Will Farce of Gun Control Follow Littleton Tragedy?" (syndicated column), *Detroit News*, May 2, 1999, p. B-7.

85. B. J. Ennis & T. R. Litwack, "Psychiatry and the Presumption of Expertise: Flipping Coins in the Courtroom," *Cal. L. Rev.* 62 (1974): 693.

86. 463 U.S. 880 (1983).

87. J. Ziskin, *Coping with Psychiatric and Psychological Testimony* (Marina del Rey, Cal.: Law and Psychology Press, 4th ed. 1988). For practical and entertaining discussion on serving as an expert, see S. L. Brodsky, *Testifying in Court: Guidelines and Maxims for the Expert Witness* (Washington, D.C.: American Psychological Association, 1991) and his *The Expert Expert Witness: More Maxims and Guidelines for Testifying in Court* (Washington, D.C.: American Psychological Association, 1999); see also T. G. Gutheil, *The Psychiatrist as Expert Witness* (Washington, D.C.: American Psychiatric Press, 1998).

88. Psychologist Terrence W. Campbell of Sterling Heights, Michigan, from time to time holds seminars for attorneys on how to discredit the testimony of psychiatrists and psychologists.

89. Thomas v. Gilmore, 144 F.3d 513 (7th Cir. 1998).

90. 144 F.3d at 517.

91. R. J. Bonnie, J. C. Jeffries, & P. W. Low, *A Case Study in the Insanity Defense: The Trial of John W. Hinckley, Jr.* (New York: Foundation Press, 2d ed. 2000) p. 23.

92. See R. J. Bonnie, J. C. Jeffries, & P. W. Low, *The Trial of John W. Hinckley, Jr.: A Case Study in the Insanity Defense* (New York: Foundation Press, 2d ed. 2000).

93. Both sides agreed that the best evidence of Hinckley's mental condition and state of mind when he fired at President Reagan was the letter he had written to Jodie Foster less than two hours before, but they reached different conclusions as to whether he understood what he was about to do, or the consequences for himself and others. He wrote, in part:

> Jodie, I would abandon this idea of getting Reagan in a second if I could only win your heart and live out the rest of my life with you, whether it be in total obscurity or whatever.
>
> I will admit to you that the reason I'm going ahead with this attempt now is because I just cannot wait any longer to impress you. I've got to do something now to make you understand, in no uncertain terms, that I am doing all of this for your sake! By sacrificing my freedom and possibly my life, I hope to change your mind about me. This letter is being written only an hour before I leave for the Hilton Hotel. Jodie, I'm asking you to please look into your heart and at least give me the chance, with this historical deed, to gain your respect and love.

94. J. E. Starrs, "Out with the Old—In with the New," *Scientific Sleuthing Review,* Spring 2000, p. 1.

95. Jokes abound about psychiatric testimony. It is quipped that if jumping to a conclusion were an Olympic event, then the psychiatrist would be the champion. In New Mexico in 1995 Senator Richard Romero offered the following oft-quoted proposal (Senate Bill 459 (1996 N.M. S.B. 459)):

> When a psychologist or psychiatrist testifies during a defendant's competency hearing, the psychologist or psychiatrist shall wear a cone-shaped hat that is not less than two feet tall. The surface of the hat shall be imprinted with stars and lightning bolts. Additionally, a psychologist or psychiatrist shall be required to don a white beard that is not less than eighteen inches in length, and shall punctuate crucial elements of his testimony by stabbing the air with a wand. Whenever a psychologist or psychiatrist provides expert testimony regarding the defendant's competency, the bailiff shall contemporaneously dim the courtroom lights and administer two strikes to a Chinese gong.

After the proposal passed the Senate by voice vote and the House by a vote of 46–14, Governor Gary Johnson vetoed it. *San Francisco Chronicle,* Jan. 31, 1996, p. E-8. Obviously the proponents of the legislation did not have a high regard for psychiatric testimony. In a presentation at a bar meeting, Federal District Court Judge Gerald Rosen recited the anecdote and the audience laughed heartily, but he admitted "revival of memory" testimony in the *Isley* case. See supra notes 17–18.

96. See B. Bursten, *Beyond Psychiatric Expertise* (Springfield, Ill.: Thomas, 1984).

97. D. W. Shuman & B. D. Sales, "The Impact of *Daubert* and Its Progeny on the Admissibility of Behavioral and Social Science Evidence," *Psychology, Public Policy & Law* 5 (1999): 3.

98. United States v. 14.38 Acres of Land Situated in Leflore County, Mississippi, 80 F.3d 1074 (5th Cir. 1996).

99. Quoted in S. Stern, "Science-Savvy Judges in Short Supply," *Christian Science Monitor,* Dec. 21, 2000, p. 17.

100. Ibid.

PART II
Evidentiary
Issues

4

Testimonial
Privilege

At common law (the *common law* is a phrase for court precedent rather than statutory law), the physician had no legal right or privilege to
remain silent when called as a witness. The only two relationships given a testimonial privilege at common law were the attorney-client and husband-wife relationship. In the United States the medical privilege was a statutory innovation
originating in New York in 1828, a time when a person sedulously wanted to conceal from the community the fact that he was the victim of some "dreadful" disease
that was rampant at the time. In the years following, legislatures of most other
states enacted some form of medical privilege, protecting communications revealed by permitted examination or by word of mouth.

From the viewpoint of litigation, the medical privilege was of comparatively
little importance when most of these statutes were enacted. At the turn of the
twentieth century, however, the development of life and accident insurance, workers' compensation, and liability of common carriers rapidly expanded the role of
the medical privilege. Personal injury litigation came to represent approximately
90 percent of all litigated cases, and the medical privilege penetrated these cases.

As a consequence, insurance interests came into conflict with the privilege, or
shield law, as it is otherwise known. Furthermore, strong antipathetic comment on
the part of authorities in the law of evidence contributed to the privilege's unpop-

ularity at law. Numerous exceptions were made by the courts to the privilege, to the extent that little remained of it. Surveys of decisions of appellate courts revealed that, for one reason or another, the privilege was held not to shield the physician-patient communication.[1] The Iowa Supreme Court in 1942 put it thus: "[There has been] considerable criticism of physician-patient privilege statutes in recent years, on the ground that such statutes [have] but little justification for their existence and that they [are] often prejudicial to the cause of justice by the suppression of useful truth, the disclosure of which ordinarily [can] harm no one."[2]

Litigants claiming personal injury while trying to conceal their medical history brought disrepute to the medical privilege. Charles McCormick, a leading authority in evidence, wrote in 1954: "More than a century of experience with the [medical privilege] statutes has demonstrated that the privilege in the main operates not as a shield of privacy but as the protection of fraud. Consequently the abandonment of the privilege seems the best solution."[3] Earlier, in 1938, the American Bar Association's Committee on Improvements in the Law of Evidence made a recommendation that was conciliatory in nature. It stated:

> The amount of truth that has been suppressed by this statutory rule must be extensive. We believe that the time has come to consider the situation. We do not here recommend the abolition of the privilege, but we do make the following recommendation: the North Carolina statute allows a wholesome flexibility. Its concluding paragraph reads: "Provided that the presiding judge of a superior court may compel such a disclosure if in his opinion the same is necessary to the proper administration of justice." This statute has needed but rare interpretation. It enables the privilege to be suspended when suppression of a fraud might otherwise be aided.[4]

The National Conference of Commissioners on Uniform State Laws, which seeks to promote uniform legislation throughout the country, voted in 1950 that the physician-patient privilege should not be recognized. However, in 1953 the conference reversed its previous action and by a close vote decided to recommend the privilege as optional. The recommendation contained so many exceptions that it would be difficult to imagine a case in which it might be applied.

The medical privilege over the years has been invoked most often in three areas, to wit: contested will cases where the testamentary capacity of the patient is under inquiry, actions for bodily injuries where the plaintiff's prior physical condition is at issue, and actions on life and accident insurance policies where misrepresentations of the insured as to state of personal health are at issue. In all of these situations, in one way or another, the privilege was circumvented by an exception or waiver.

In many jurisdictions, death of the patient terminated the privilege, so a legatee to a will in testamentary actions or a beneficiary of a life insurance policy could not claim the privilege of the deceased patient (except perhaps when it may be regarded in the interest of the patient, as when the disclosure is designed to protect the estate of the deceased).

In suits for personal injuries, the privilege was considered waived by the patient by instituting litigation. In an oft-quoted expression, the patient cannot make the medical statute both a sword and a shield. A good-faith claimant suing for personal injuries presumably would not object to the testimony of any physician who examined or treated him, but rather would want the physician to testify. The defendant is entitled to learn whether the injury being complained about predated the alleged incident. Individuals who file a lawsuit and resist the release of their medical record can forget about their case—it would be presumed that the evidence is unfavorable or it would have been produced.

In actions on life and accident insurance policies wherein the truth of the insured's representations as to his health are vital, the insurer may desire to introduce testimony of the insured's physician to show fraud on the part of the insured in making his application. The medical privilege may be circumvented quite easily by the insurer by inserting a provision in the application whereby the insured waives the right to the privilege, both for himself and his beneficiary. The same procedure is often followed in employment applications, and also for disability benefits, pensions, and compensation claims. Such a waiver by contract is generally upheld. For large life insurance policies, the insured is required to undergo a medical examination by the company's physician. As a result, most undesirable risks are eliminated and the problem of the medical privilege is diminished in importance.

Psychiatrists came to find that the medical privilege enacted in the various states was so riddled with exceptions that they sought a special psychiatrist-patient privilege. The Group for the Advancement of Psychiatry (GAP), an organization of some two hundred psychiatrists, in 1960 urged enactment of legislation granting a privilege to psychiatrist-patient communication that would parallel the attorney-client privilege. It issued a 24-page report on the need of privilege to protect confidentiality in the practice of psychiatry.

Shortly thereafter, at the suggestion of law professor Joseph Goldstein and Dr. Jay Katz of Yale University, GAP revised its proposal, realizing that privilege by analogy would be unworkable, and it urged the enactment of a psychotherapist-patient privilege similar to that enacted in 1961 in Connecticut (Goldstein and Katz were members of the committee that prepared the Connecticut bill).[5] The Connecticut law was the model of the statute subsequently adopted by the various states and proposed for the Federal Rules of Evidence of 1975. All fifty states have now adopted varying forms of the psychotherapist-patient privilege. Here is a typical statute:

(a) *Definitions*
   (1) A "patient" is a person who consults or is examined or interviewed by a psychotherapist.
   (2) A "psychotherapist" is
      (A) a person authorized to practice medicine in any state or nation, or reasonably believed by the patient so to be, while engaged in the diagnosis or treatment of a mental or emotional condition, including drug addiction, or
      (B) a person licensed or certified as a psychologist under the laws of any state or nation, while similarly engaged.
   (3) A communication is "confidential'" if not intended to be disclosed to third persons other than those present to further the interest of the patient in the consultation, examination, or interview, or persons reasonably necessary for the transmission of the communication, or per-

sons who are participating in the diagnosis and treatment under the direction of the psychotherapist, including members of the patient's family.

(b) *General rule of privilege.* A patient has a privilege to refuse to disclose and to prevent any other person from disclosing confidential communications, made for the purposes of diagnosis or treatment of his mental or emotional condition, including drug addiction, among himself, his psychotherapist, or persons who are participating in the diagnosis or treatment under the direction of the psychotherapist, including members of the patient's family.

(c) *Who may claim the privilege.* The privilege may be claimed by the patient, by his guardian or conservator, or by the personal representative of a deceased patient. The person who was the psychotherapist may claim the privilege but only on behalf of the patient. His authority to do so is presumed in the absence of evidence to the contrary.

(d) *Exceptions*

(1) *Proceedings for hospitalization.* There is no privilege under this rule for communications relevant to an issue in proceedings to hospitalize the patient for mental illness, if the psychotherapist in the course of diagnosis or treatment has determined that the patient is in need of hospitalization.

(2) *Examination by order of judge.* If the judge orders an examination of the mental or emotional condition of the patient, communications made in the course thereof are not privileged under this rule with respect to the particular purpose for which the examination is ordered unless the judge orders otherwise.

(3) *Condition an element of claim or defense.* There is no privilege under this rule as to communications relevant to an issue of the mental or emotional condition of the patient in any proceeding in which he relies upon the condition as an element of his claim or defense, or after the patient's death, in any proceeding in which any party relies upon the condition as an element of his claim or defense.[6]

History has a way of repeating itself. The psychotherapist-patient privilege, like the medical privilege, is a form of zero-sum game. What it gives with one hand it takes away with the other. Virtually nothing of relevance in litigation is shielded by the shield. In every jurisdiction, the exceptions make it difficult to imagine a case in which the privilege applies.

First of all, as the term *testimonial privilege* would indicate, it concerns a privilege not to provide *testimony*. Of course, outside the judicial process, society has a strong interest in protecting confidentiality, but that is protected not by privilege but possibly by a tort action for infliction of mental distress, invasion of privacy, defamation, a breach of the fiduciary duty of confidentiality, or a disciplinary sanction. Whether testimony may be barred in a judicial (or administrative) proceeding as a consequence of a privilege does not control the issue of liability for unauthorized extrajudicial disclosures. In *State v. Beatty,*[7] an impoverished mental patient confided to her psychiatrist that she committed a robbery to pay for food for herself and a sick friend. The psychiatrist called Crime Stoppers and provided enough information to allow the police to obtain a search warrant, which was challenged as "a gross violation of defendant's rights under the doctor-client privilege and use of that information, and its subsequent use in the search warrant, was a violation of defendant's constitutional rights." As ought to be expected, the Missouri Court of Appeals held that the testimonial privilege was not involved because the telephone call did not constitute "testimony." As generally understood, the court explained that the only prohibition dictated by a privilege statute is to bar testifying in a court proceeding. The court left for another day the question of whether the revelation of the type made by the psychiatrist was an ethical violation or whether there is a cause of action in tort law for the breach of confidentiality. That question was not before the court.

Then, too, testimonial privileges are narrowly interpreted because they work against a fair trial. Evidence is the basis of justice—the very essence of a fair trial. Having all the facts helps judges and juries to make better decisions. When a privilege keeps out relevant evidence, the goal of a fair trial is less attainable. Testimonial privileges are usually the result of political lobbying. The word *privilege* stems from the Latin *privata lex*, a prerogative given to a person or to a class of persons—the word is a composite derived from the words *privus* and *lex*. Because a privilege is contrary to general law, it is strictly construed. Of course, as one might expect, the attorney-client privilege fares best of all. The determination of whether an individual or communication in a particular case falls under an enacted privilege depends upon its scope, as interpreted by the court. The traditional judicial preference is for the "truth" (i.e., determining historical facts accurately) rather than the protection of confidentiality of a given relationship, but other goals may also be claimed: protecting the sanctity of the individual (e.g., the Fifth Amendment) or providing disincentives for governmental abuses (e.g., Fourth Amendment exclusionary rule). The sporting theory of justice may call for the exclusion of probative as well as nonprobative or prejudicial evidence.

It is to be noted, however, that when an attorney refers a client to a physician for examination, the attorney-client privilege protects a report made by the physician to the attorney. This is especially important in jurisdictions where there is no medical privilege. In cases of referral for examination, the physician acts as the agent of the attorney. In this situation, the physician is serving as an examining physician, rather than as a treating physician, and is performing the examination on behalf of the attorney in the preparation of a case. The physician, as an agent of the attorney, comes under the umbrella of the attorney-client privilege.[8] The attorney will call upon the physician to testify if the physician's opinion is favorable to the attorney's theory of the case, but if the opinion is unfavorable, the attorney will discharge him and seek another expert or will drop the case.[9]

The essence of any testimonial privilege is that it may be waived or terminated by the person who enjoys it. The confidential communication is protected from disclosure at the instance of the person who owns the privilege (or one acting on his behalf). The medical or psychotherapy privilege belongs to the patient, not to the physician, just as the attorney-client privilege belongs to the client. The privilege is for the benefit of the patient or client. Thus, patients have the option to require either silence or testimony from their physician (under ordinary process of summoning witnesses) on any communication made on the basis of the professional relationship that existed between them.

Since the privilege is the patient's, the physician or psychiatrist can be compelled to testify when the patient or ex-patient so desires. The patient is given legal control over his destiny, irrespective of other factors. The patient may believe, quite unrealistically, that testimony by his therapist may aid his legal position. A patient's waiver of the privilege may conceivably be a self-destructive technique, it may be an expression of hostility toward the therapist, or it may be an attempted repetition of a power struggle that occurred early in the patient's life. Even an attempt to clarify to a patient why it would be inadvisable to call upon the therapist to testify can be markedly prejudicial to effective therapy, especially when it comes at an inappropriate stage in treatment.

It has been argued that privilege in the psychiatrist-patient relationship should belong to the psychiatrist as well as, or rather than, to the patient. When an individual waives a privilege such as the attorney-client privilege, or the privilege against self-incrimination, the decision is made with awareness of what will be disclosed. However, in psychotherapy it may be detrimental for patients to see, for example, the report of projective tests that they have taken. When patients waive the psychotherapy privilege, they do not know what they are waiving. It may be harmful to reveal to patients that they have been labeled schizophrenic (whatever that might mean). Should the law allow an individual to make an irrational or irresponsible decision? Should the privilege be waivable? Privacy of the unconscious or of one's fantasy life is a requisite of man's dignity; no one, it is said, can remain dignified when the contents of his unconscious are disclosed.

Dr. Joseph Lifschutz of California, among others, has argued for a right of privacy separate from that of any individual patient, a right derived from what he sees as a duty not to a particular patient alone but to all patients. He argued that the disclosure of one patient's confidential communications causes damage to all the therapist's other patients.[10] That argument is echoed in the book *The New Informants* by Christopher Bollas and David Sundelson.[11] It is to be noted that a priest must keep absolutely secret anything told to him in a confession, even when the penitent (confessor) requests that the priest divulge what was communicated. The Episcopal Church's *Reconciliation* states: "The secrecy of a confession is morally absolute . . . and must under no circumstances be broken."[12] Be that as it may, the professional's urging of confidentiality allegedly on behalf of patients is often a facade to serve self-interest. The privilege is designed to protect the privacy of the patient, not that of the therapist; it is not to serve as a fig leaf to cover up incompetency or wrongdoing.[13]

Tort Cases

As in the case of the medical privilege, the most common form of waiver of the psychotherapist-patient privilege is the one when the patient injects his condition in tort litigation, as when his condition is an element of claim or defense. In this vein, no-fault automobile insurance legislation expressly and completely eliminates the statutory physician-patient privilege.

California's psychotherapist-patient privilege, a copy of the Connecticut statute and a model for the proposed Rule 504 of the Federal Rules of Evidence, was tested shortly after its enactment in 1965 in the much publicized case involving Dr. Joseph Lifschutz.[14] The case was featured in national news weeklies, and was reported at numerous meetings of psychiatric societies and in psychiatric and psychoanalytic bulletins and newsletters. The Northern California Psychiatric Society made a nationwide appeal to psychiatrists for contributions to cover legal expenses.

The American Psychoanalytic Association and the National Association for Mental Health filed amicus curiae briefs. Although great effort was exerted on behalf of privilege, the case illustrates the irrelevancy of privilege law (as well as the irrelevancy of much psychiatric testimony at trial).

Joseph Housek, a high school teacher, brought a damage suit against John Arabian, a student, alleging an assault that caused "physical injuries, pain, suffering, and severe mental and emotional distress." During a deposition taken by defense counsel, Housek stated that he had received psychiatric treatment ten years earlier from Dr. Lifschutz over a six-month period. The defendant then sought Housek's psychiatric records from Dr. Lifschutz. Dr. Lifschutz refused to produce any of his records, assuming there were any, and also declined to disclose whether or not Housek had consulted him or had been his patient.

Thereupon defendant Arabian sought a court order to compel Dr. Lifschutz to answer questions on deposition and to produce the subpoenaed records. The court determined that the plaintiff had put his mental and emotional condition in issue by instituting the pending litigation, so privilege was waived. To no avail, Dr. Lifschutz argued a right of privacy separate from that of any individual patient, a right derived from what he saw as a duty not to Housek alone but to all his patients— that the disclosure of one patient's confidential communications causes damage to all of the therapist's other patients. He argued that compelling him to testify unconstitutionally impairs the practice of his profession. The court was unpersuaded. It said: "[W]e cannot blind ourselves to the fact that the practice of psychotherapy has grown, indeed flourished, in an environment of a non-absolute privilege."[15]

Since the privilege is intended as a shield and not a sword, it is considered waived by the patient when he makes a legal issue of his physical or mental condition. Thus, when plaintiff Housek claimed that he had suffered emotional distress as a result of the injuries he had suffered, the privileged status of his communications with his psychiatrist was waived, said the trial court. However, on appeal, the California Supreme Court doubted that "the 10-year-old therapeutic treatment sought to be discovered from Dr. Lifschutz would be sufficiently relevant to a typical claim of 'mental distress' to bring it within the exception."

Thus the real test in protecting patient confidentiality is one of relevancy or materiality (which arises regarding all evidence in every trial), so it must be asked: What are the material issues, and what is relevant or competent to establish them? In other words, does the item of evidence tend to prove that precise contention or fact that is sought to be proved? In every case where the testimony or records of a physician or psychotherapist have been required by a court, it was because the evidence was deemed relevant or material to an issue in the case. As a consequence, in the last analysis, the confidentiality of a physician-patient or psychotherapist-patient communication is protected from disclosure in a courtroom only by a showing that the communication could have no relevance or materiality to the issues in the case.

A motion to quash a subpoena is in order when other evidence more relevant and material is available, or would be less intrusive to obtain. Such a procedure might even protect a patient from having to state in discovery processes whether or not he ever saw a psychiatrist. Quite often, mental health professionals and others automatically give up records simply because a subpoena has arrived in the mail, without realizing that a subpoena is not a court order, or they believe that it would be futile to challenge a subpoena, but the attorney who is representing the patient can be called upon to seek a quashing of the subpoena.

It is often contended that a forensic examiner can ascertain whether an injury predated the alleged complaint just as well as the patient's therapist, if not more accurately, but that may not always be the case. In his book *The New Psychiatry*,[16] Dr. Jack Gorman of Columbia University gives a vivid example from his practice of a case justifying discovery of records:

> Once I received a request from a patient's attorney to produce my office notes about [a patient]. She was apparently suing a driver following an automobile accident in which she claimed she had injured her back. The problem was that when I first saw the patient she had told me that she had suffered from back trouble for many years preceding the car accident. I had written that down. My records would obviously reveal that the patient was lying about the car accident; in fact, it hadn't hurt her back at all. When I told her what was in my records she was forced to amend her lawsuit.[17]

Privilege is also waived in a wrongful death action in which a party relies on the deceased's condition as an element of his claim or defense. In this type of action, the patient is not a party litigant, but rather the subject of the litigation. The defendant is entitled to discover evidence, including the testimony of a treating psychiatrist, to establish that the patient died, not as a result of any wrongful act on the part of the defendant but, on the contrary, as a suicide.[18]

It is held that the patient-litigant exception applies whenever either party, plaintiff or defendant, relies on the condition of a patient as part of that party's claim or defense, even when the patient does not personally place the condition at issue. Such a case is one in Texas, a personal injury action brought against a stepparent by a stepdaughter for allegedly sexually assaulting her, and also against a counselor for negligence in counseling.[19] The Texas Court of Appeals held that the counselor was not entitled to exercise the psychotherapist-patient privilege to protect treatment records. The court's order to turn over the mental health records was based on the exception to privilege for disclosure of records when "relevant to an issue of the physical, mental or emotional condition of a patient in any proceeding in which any party relies upon the condition as a part of the party's claim or defense." The court also rejected the defendant's argument that his right against self-incrimination precluded discovery of the records (on the ground that he would not lose any privilege against self-incrimination because the disclosure would not be voluntary.)[20]

What about privilege in lawsuits where the patient is not a litigant but where a third party sues the therapist? Unlike when a patient sues a therapist, a third party suing a therapist on account of harm inflicted by the patient faces obstacles in obtaining information as to what occurred in therapy. There may have been a duty to warn or protect, and in that event the dangerous patient exception to the therapist-patient privilege would come into play. The privilege is not applicable when the therapist has reasonable cause to believe that the patient was dangerous. A duty to report a patient who poses a danger to others, whether or not a report is made, may undercut any privilege, obliging the therapist to testify or provide information, as in the trial of the Menendez brothers.[21]

Certainly, a therapist's duty to third parties would have little meaning if third-party plaintiffs were not able to procure the information needed to vindicate their claims. In the usual case when a third party (family members) sues a therapist in the case of revival of memory of childhood sexual abuse, the patient has retracted the allegation and joins the parents in a lawsuit against the therapist, or when the patient sues the parents, the parents implead the therapist. In these situations, by filing a lawsuit, the patient waives the privilege. In any event, privilege can be overcome by joining the patient along with the therapist as a party defendant.[22]

In a variation of the theme where the record of a patient may be relevant to a resolution of a lawsuit yet the patient is not a party to the litigation are cases where third parties file a lawsuit against a pharmaceutical company claiming that its product had a disinhibiting effect on the patient and resulted in injury or death to third parties. In a much-publicized case, Joseph Wesbecker at the Standard Gravure printing plant in Louisville killed or wounded twenty people, with an AK-47 assault rifle, then turned the gun on himself. He had been on disability leave from Standard Gravure for a year, reeling from setbacks in his personal life and on the job. Suffering from severe depression, he was given Prozac, the popular antidepressant. The survivors and victims' families sued its maker, Eli Lily and Company. Both sides to the litigation had an interest in disclosing Wesbecker's psychiatric history, so no objection to disclosure of records was made. In the defense of Prozac, it was argued, "Joseph Wesbecker's attack on Standard Gravure on September 14, 1989, was not the act of a man suddenly turned mad by Prozac. . . . It was the final chapter in a very complex life, filled with hostility, fueled by job stress. It grew out of a life twisted by insidious mental illness. It was generated out of a lifetime of estrangements and isolation, and hostile withdrawals from spouses, parents, children, friends, co-workers and bosses." In any event, Wesbecker's family brought a wrongful death action against his psychiatrist, Dr. Lee Coleman, and as a consequence, privilege was waived.[23]

The question has arisen as to a waiver of the privilege shielding the health records of the plaintiff's family in a lawsuit involving a condition that is arguably genetic. Since the privilege belongs to the patient and is waivable only by the patient, as by filing a lawsuit, the privilege is not waived as to the records of other members of the family. Upholding the privilege as to other members of the plaintiff's family may make it impossible for the defendant to explore the cause of the condition. The issue thus becomes under what circumstances, if any, the defendant may gain access to the medical records of the plaintiff's family members in order to show genetic causation.[24]

Criminal Cases

Criminal cases, of course, as other cases, may involve a treating or examining psychiatrist. The shield law is applicable, at best, only to a treating psychiatrist and not to an examining one. In the examining situation, the relationship is likely to be one entered into at arm's length (the person examined is called an *examinee* or *evaluee*, not a *patient*). In criminal cases, however, even in the treating situation, there is in many jurisdictions no medical or psychotherapist privilege whatsoever.[25] In all states, by statute or case law, the medical privilege or the psychotherapist-patient privilege is inoperative when a defendant raises an insanity defense or a mental disability defense.[26] By and large, the courts hold that raising the insanity defense does not, by itself, waive the attorney-client privilege for retained, nontestifying experts.[27]

In the case of a defendant who asserts a defense of insanity (or other diminished capacity defense), the prevailing law is that he cannot claim possible self-incrimination with respect to psychiatric evidence, be it by a treating or examining psychiatrist. If the defendant does not cooperate with the court's or prosecutor's psychiatrist, he is deemed to have waived his insanity defense, or is denied the right to present expert testimony on his behalf. By pleading and offering evidence of insanity, the accused puts his mental state in issue, and thus waives any psychotherapist-patient privilege; his medical or psychiatric history is open to the prosecution, as occurred for example in the trial of John Hinckley Jr., the would-be assassin of President Reagan.[28] The very nature of an insanity defense is premised on a broad inquiry into every aspect of the defendant's life. As a matter of practice, the fact of treatment is often brought up by defense counsel in plea bargaining to demonstrate an interest in rehabilitation.

The Illinois psychiatrist-patient privilege expressly states that it does not apply in criminal proceedings in which the mental condition of the defendant is introduced by him as an element of defense.[29] Indiana and Wisconsin have similar statutory provisions.[30] Nebraska states that "[t]here is no privilege . . . in any judicial proceedings . . . regarding injuries to children, incompetents, or disabled persons or in any criminal prosecution involving injury to any such person or the willful failure to report any such injuries."[31] New Jersey's privilege does not cover cases of driving while under the influence of alcohol.[32] And as a general rule, the privilege is inapplicable when the "services of the therapist were sought, obtained, or used to enable or aid anyone to commit or plan a crime or fraud or to escape detection or apprehension after the commission of a crime or fraud."[33]

The privilege, moreover, does not cover communications involving fraud in receiving Social Security benefits.[34] Various states exclude the privilege in any judicial proceeding involving narcotics or to communications made to procure narcotics unlawfully.[35] And therapists have a duty to reveal information about the contemplation of a crime or harmful act.[36]

The various rules that have been developed to restrict the role of an examining psychiatrist in criminal cases are rooted in constitutional principles against self-incrimination and coerced confession, not the shield law. It is well established that a psychiatric examination does not violate the constitutional rights of the accused. As one court put it, "Even a cat can look at a queen."[37] However, the psychiatrist may testify only as to his evaluation of the defendant (although in reaching this evaluation inferences are made from the facts of the crime or other crimes). Under the law of the various states, he may not reveal admissions made to him by the defendant in the instant proceeding or in another proceeding.[38]

In the case of a defendant in a criminal case who seeks discovery regarding the alleged victim, there comes into play the right under the Constitution to summon witnesses and to obtain evidence to establish innocence. The U.S. Supreme Court has recognized on a number of occasions that a state's interest as expressed in its evidentiary laws are secondary to the constitutional considerations of fully confronting witnesses who testify against the defendant and of fairness to a defendant seeking to defend against criminal charges.[39] It is prevailing law that a criminal defendant is entitled to review the psychiatric records of a prosecuting witness but only after a judge has determined there is good cause for disclosure and that the material will in some way be relevant to the defense.[40]

This principle applies when an accused seeks evidence from a victim treatment or rape crisis center. An individual who claims to have been raped, for example, and having identified the defendant as the rapist, may confess in therapy that she had in fact consented to the sexual activity.[41] This behavior ought to be regarded as criminal as crimes committed by a patient in the course of therapy. The psychiatrist's response should give precedential concern to the protection of society. The victim treatment center or rape crisis center may or may not have evidence that would be important in a criminal proceeding.[42] Alan Dershowitz posed the legal and ethical issues in his novel *The Advocate's Devil*.[43]

In an Alaska case, a young woman whose records in a rape counseling center were sought by defense protested strenuously, "[The defense] thinks there's something big in the records, but there's not. That's the funny thing. There's stuff in there I haven't even told my parents. There's stuff in there I don't want to review. There's stuff I just wanted to get off my chest and never think about again. . . . [T]here written down [are] all my humiliating moments, my happy moments and my sad moments. They might as well strip me naked and make me walk in front of everybody naked. I'll tell you, it would be easier."[44]

In dealing with any privilege, the courts have recognized that before a judge can determine whether communications are to be protected, the judge should conduct an in camera inspection in order to determine whether the requirements of the privilege are met.[45] Accordingly, when a psychotherapist-patient or sexual assault counselor-victim privilege is asserted, the trial judge under proper circumstances should conduct an in camera inspection. The court must determine whether there are statements of the victim that may relate to important issues, such as identity of the assailant or consent. Due process and confrontation does not require disclosure of all the victim's statements; only those that are relevant to the preparation and presentation of the defense.[46]

A refusal by the alleged victim to release her psychological records for in camera review will result in the exclusion of her testimony at trial. An in camera review is not granted based solely on a defendant's request. There must be a threshold showing by the defendant that the records may reasonably be expected to provide information material to the defense. A general assertion that inspection of the records is needed for a possible attack on the victim's credibility is insufficient to meet this threshold showing.[47]

To avoid involvement in the criminal justice system, counseling centers over the years announced that they do not keep records, and make no evaluation or diagnosis. Failure to keep records, however, has generally lost its immunizing value. The fact that most psychiatrists or other therapists give reports to third parties for various purposes tends to cast doubt on not keeping records. In the current malpractice climate, the best defenses are records that detail the clinical factors that determine the judgment of the therapist to hospitalize or not to hospitalize in situations where hospitalization might be considered, or not to report behavior patterns that might be questioned in the future, where an infinite number of ambivalent situations requiring hairline judgments might be made. And, of course, third-party payers nowadays require the keeping of records, and without them, therapists will not be compensated for their services. Certainly, one must be circumspect about what is included in a record since the current vogue of getting search warrants easily is a threat to every record.

Military

Until recently, no privilege whatever was recognized in military law for the physician-patient or psychotherapist-patient relationship, regardless of whether the physician or therapist is military or civilian. The basis for not extending privilege to the relationship is that the harm done to the relationship by disclosure is considered of less seriousness than the harm done by nondisclosure to the securing of military order and justice. Then, in late 1999, President Clinton signed an executive order extending a psychotherapist-patient privilege to court-martial proceedings. The definition of a *psychotherapist* in the amended Military Code of Justice encompasses psychiatrists, clinical psychologist, clinical social workers, and assistants to a psychotherapist (assistants are people whom the psychotherapist assigns to provide professional service to a patient).

This addition to the Uniform Code of Military Justice, known as Rule 513, does not extend the shield to any aspects of military life other than court-martials. In disciplinary or administrative proceedings that do not come to trial, such as those involving dismissal of service members because they are gay, psychiatrists and other mental health professionals may still be subject to orders to provide information on a soldier's sexuality. The privilege, moreover, does not hold when the patient is dead, even if his family wants the confidentiality maintained. Military personnel also lose the privilege when any communication with their therapist contains evidence of spouse or child abuse or when federal, state, or military law specifically exempts such abuse allegations from confidentiality protection. Additional exclusions allowed under the new rule occur in cases in which a therapist believes that a patient's mental status makes him a danger to self or others, when the patient communicates intent to commit "fraud or crime," and when the information is "necessary to ensure the safety and security of military personnel, military dependents, military property, classified information, or the accomplishment of a military mission." The specific interpretation of the limits of these exclusions is left to the discretion of military judges who can thus choose to view them broadly or narrowly on a case-by-case basis. In sum and substance, the exceptions eviscerate the privilege.

Proceedings to Hospitalize

In proceedings to involuntarily hospitalize a patient, there is no privilege for communications relevant to the issue when the doctor has determined during the course of diagnosis or treatment that the patient is in need of such care. The Advisory Committee to the Federal Rules of Evidence commented, "The interests of both patient and public call for a departure from confidentiality in commitment proceedings. Since disclosure is authorized only when the doctor determines that hospitalization is needed, control over disclosure is placed largely in the hands of a person in whom the patient has already manifested confidence."[48] And as one court put it, "The evidence is not used against the individual but to aid the court in evaluating alternate treatment plans. Involuntary commitment proceedings are not penal in nature but humanitarian."[49]

The hospitalization exception does not mention guardianship but the justification for the exception would seem to apply as well to guardianship. Under the law, there are provisions for appointment of a guardian of one's person (e.g., with authority over health care decisions) and a guardian of one's estate (e.g., with authority over the making of contracts to sell one's property). In some jurisdictions, a guardian might be appointed for the specific purpose of consent to psychiatric hospitalization.[50] In a number of states, guardianship and civil commitment of a "gravely disabled person" takes place through a conservatorship proceeding (a guardian of one's estate is often called a *conservator* or *committee*).[51] In most cases where a psychiatrist is involved in giving testimony in a guardianship proceeding, it is as an examining rather than as a treating psychiatrist.

The intent of the hospitalization exception in the typical psychotherapist-patient privilege is for the treating psychiatrist to play a key role in commitment proceedings (and presumably in guardianship proceedings). In nearly all jurisdictions, as a matter of law, no warning as to privilege against self-incrimination or right to silence need be given prior to examination or treatment.[52] Michigan is apparently exceptional. Michigan's Mental Health Code (applicable to the public sector and agencies or clinics under contract with the state to provide services) sets out a requirement of notice. It states that privileged communications shall be disclosed "[w]hen the privileged communication is relevant to a matter under consideration in a proceeding to determine the legal competence of the patient or the patient's need for a guardian but only if the patient was informed that any communications made could be used in such a proceeding."[53]

A patient opposed to hospitalization, however, may be angered by the breach of confidentiality. The issue of whether disclosures by a therapist to a court-appointed examiner are reasonably necessary to protect the interests of the patient or others is one for the jury, said the Michigan Court of Appeals; hence the therapist is not entitled to summary disposition.[54] This ruling came out of a case where the patient's estranged wife (they later divorced) petitioned for the patient's commitment. The patient and his wife quarreled over finances and he contended that she wanted to "put him away." The psychiatrist who was appointed to undertake an examination consulted with the treating psychiatrist.

In a lawsuit called unprecedented, the patient sued the treating psychiatrist for breach of confidentiality. The trial court held that the defendant was entitled to judgment on motion for summary disposition, but the Michigan Court of Appeals held that the issue of whether the disclosures were reasonably necessary to protect the interests of the patient or others was one for the jury, since the facts of the case were such that reasonable minds could differ. The appellate court rendered that decision although the psychiatrist was in private practice and hence not governed by the Michigan Mental Health Code, which provides that a patient must be informed that communication may be used in a hospitalization (or guardianship) proceeding.[55] In Australia, among other countries, the treating psychiatrist must have the consent of the patient as a requisite for discussions with an examiner.

Child Custody

In a dispute between parents over the custody of a child, the best interest of the child sets the standard for decision making. That standard opens the door to a wide range of evidence pertaining not only to the fitness of the parents but also to the environment in which the child will be raised. As a general principle, the best interest standard overrides any psychotherapist-patient privilege, thereby allowing access to therapy records and to compelling the testimony of the therapist. The statutory law mandates that the court consider, among other factors, the mental and physical health of the parties.[56]

In contentious proceedings, attorneys search for data that will support their case. The case law reveals that the privilege provides some but uncertain protection of confidentiality. The majority of courts say, under the mandate of the statutory law, or otherwise, that the privilege yields automatically in child custody or related matters.[57] Other courts order disclosure only when health is in issue or when the circumstances indicate abuse or neglect. According to these decisions, the question is whether there is a compelling need to have past psychiatric records to evaluate the capacity of the parent with respect to current parenting abilities.[58] Various legislation provides that there is no privilege concerning matters of adoption, adult abuse, child abuse, child neglect, or other matters pertaining to the welfare of children or any dependent person, or from seeking collaboration or consultation with professional colleagues or administrative supervisors on behalf of the client.[59]

As one court stated, in custody proceedings and proceedings for the modification of custody decrees, the mental and physical health of the child as well as the parents is of great concern and importance. The court later said that in custodial disputes over infants, the parties seeking custodial authority open themselves to scrutiny of all factors relevant to the permanent and proper award of custody. The mental and physical health of all of the parties is taken into consideration, as is the determination of whether the child will be in an environment likely to endanger his physical, mental, moral, or emotional health. As another court put it, "The paramount consideration in a child custody matter is the child's best interest. . . . A court cannot determine the best interests of the child without considering whether [the parent] is physically, financially, or mentally able to care for the child.[60]

Quite often, the testimony as well as the records of the treating therapist are demanded. To quote an attorney, who has been involved in considerable child custody litigation, in an address to a law group: "The more I know about a parent the better. I would depose the treating doctor. The record standing alone is not sufficient."[61] Moreover, as a matter of routine, court-appointed or lawyer-appointed evaluators ask for the psychiatric records of the parents or child, and they usually get them. An evaluator would be remiss in not obtaining these records, for on cross-examination, the evaluator would likely be asked about matters revealed there, and legitimately so. Typical questions: "Didn't you know that she (or he) was diagnosed as schizophrenic?" "Didn't you know that she (or he) threatened the life of the child?" Even if the expert may not need the records to carry out an evaluation, the expert will want them to defuse a cross-examination, and also to confirm the evaluation, thereby enhancing the probative value of the report. This is all the more true where a party resists production of the records. When a party refuses a request, suspicion arises that the party is hiding something, and the records gain even more importance. Moreover, refusing to disclose psychiatric records is usually an expensive and time-consuming exercise in futility as the trial judge will likely order disclosure, but disclosure without court order may result in liability for breach of confidentiality.

There may be circumstances when the confidentiality of reports will be protected, particularly if it can be shown that the best interest of the child is advanced by confidentiality rather than disclosure. In some cases, disclosure of statements of the parents or the child could harm the parent-child relationship. In the process of evaluation, children may make statements that may result in a vendetta against the child. The evaluator is in a dilemma—how to inform the court and at the same time protect the child? A youngster says, "I hate my father." The data, put in a report in raw form, will expose the child negatively. In this type of situation, the trial judge might very well shield these communications. Disclosure may then be limited to communications relevant to fitness, or to the interaction and interrelationship of the child with the parent.[62]

It is argued that the best interest of the child is enhanced by confidentiality of parental psychotherapy records, by encouraging parents to obtain treatment that might otherwise not be sought. Discouraging people from consulting a psychotherapist, out of fear that confidences will be used against them in later court appearances, does not inure to the welfare of the child. The protection of confidentiality, with its attendant encouragement to seek help, may better serve the child. As one Florida Court of Appeal observed, successful therapy can be dependent upon the psychiatrist's ability to assure confidentiality.[63]

Records of treatment of a parent or child occurring years ago might be protected on relevancy grounds. A Michigan Court of Appeals said:

> [W]e do not find relevant to a party's present condition the testimony of a physician who has not treated the party for years. . . . Moreover, the . . . court was able, with the [party's] participation, to gather information with regard to her mental condition. . . . We also reject as meritless defendant's argument that by virtue of submitting to a court appointed psychological examination and introduction of the psychologist's testimony, plaintiff waived her medical privilege.[64]

Privilege claims aside, judges must decide the relevancy of all proffered evidence, and must also consider whether there is less intrusive but equally probative evidence available. In any kind of case, when the psychotherapist-patient privilege is raised, the guideline on the admissibility of evidence is relevancy, not privilege.

Group Therapy

With the increasing number of psychotherapy groups, questions have frequently arisen (mainly in nonlegal circles) regarding privileged communication in that type of therapy. While there has been some litigation involving confidentiality of joint marital counseling and family therapy, there is little involving group therapy, notwithstanding its wide use. Is, then, the prevailing concern warranted?

Various medical and psychiatric societies have sought to organize therapy or support groups for members who are facing a malpractice lawsuit. During this time, while these individuals may have the support of an attorney, they feel under stress and they feel isolated during the years awaiting the outcome of the litigation. In general, lawyers advise their clients not to talk to anyone about the litigation and this increases their sense of isolation. Many hesitate to enter a therapy or support group, it is said, out of concerns about confidentiality.

More commonly than medical or psychiatric societies, bar associations in various states have sponsored therapy groups for their members who have a problem with alcoholism. While their competency to practice law may be questionable, they usually are not facing a malpractice suit as are the members of medical and psychiatric societies who have been sued and enter a therapy group. Anyhow, "if criminals can be rehabilitated, then why not lawyers?"—said a Michigan lawyer about a proposal to permanently disbar lawyers for misconduct.[65]

Nationwide, group therapists express different views about the concern of group members about confidentiality. In an article in the *American Journal of Psychiatry*,[66] Dr. Howard Roback and colleagues surveyed fifty-one therapists who led psychotherapy for physicians recovering from substance abuse, and they report that concern about confidentiality was a significant factor in the group members' willingness to share secrets. Of those group therapists surveyed, 49 percent rated physician group members as exhibiting a moderate amount or a great deal of concern over potential confidentiality infractions. Moreover, they report, 27 percent of group therapists who treat impaired physicians have been subpoenaed at some time in the past to testify about physician members. Some states require physicians to report impairment of other physicians. They suggest that group therapy would provide a safer milieu for patients to share highly personal information if the members themselves could be held liable for violating confidentiality. They recommend legislation making group members liable for violating confidentiality.

To survey the concern, if any, of group members about confidentiality, I interviewed several group therapists and members of a group. In my survey, I discovered that therapists are far more concerned about confidentiality than members of the group. Some group therapists say that a person involved in litigation should not be in group therapy for his or her own protection. I am told by group therapists, novice and veteran alike, that while they have many times discussed the problem of confidentiality with colleagues and students, they know of no actual instance where there has been any serious problem in connection with lack of confidentiality. For example, Dr. Joseph J. Geller, who had been doing group therapy for many years, said:

> Over all the years, with many people becoming privy to a wealth of personal details about others, there seems to have been very little harmful use of the material. This is true of my own practice as well as the experiences of others. Each of us, having this rather uneventful experience, assumed it was unusual, but without comparing notes with others, we learned that it is fairly generally true.[67]

The executive director of the National Commission on Confidentiality of Health Records, advised that no incidents of group therapy breaches of confidentiality have been reported to the commission.[68] In any event, as a shield against a demand for disclosure in legal proceedings, the enactment of a legal privilege that would excuse testimony from a group member or therapist has often been suggested. The American Group Psychotherapy Association, desiring greater protection for group therapy, recommended the enactment of a specific privilege to cover group therapy. The history of privilege, however, reveals that it has not been very much of a shield. When push has come to shove, the privilege had ended up not shielding very much, if anything. It is like the warranty where the bold print giveth, and the fine print taketh away.

A rule of privilege law which is of particular significance in group therapy is that a communication loses any privileged status it may have had if it takes place in the presence of a third party. The privileges are formulated with the dyadic relationship in mind (attorney-client, physician-patient, accountant-client), and the presence of a third party is said to pollute confidentiality. The law equates disclosure to a third person with a general publication to the world. The rationale is: "The world knows about it, why not the court?" Will group members (and the insurance company) be considered a third party, polluting privilege, or will they be considered as agents taking part in the therapy process?[69] It may be noted that following adoption of the medical privilege in the early nineteenth century, a number of courts ruled that a nurse does not come under its umbrella, and because of this, later statutes on the medical privilege specifically include nurses and other attendants within the scope of the privilege (for whatever the privilege may be worth).

The prominent legal commentator Charles McCormick discussed the issue of whether the presence of third parties renders a statement to a physician nonprivileged, and he argued that the court should analyze the problem in terms of whether the third persons are necessary and customary participants in the consultation or treatment and whether the communications were confidential for the purpose of aiding in diagnosis and treatment.[70] In a Minnesota case,[71] where the defendant was charged with criminal sexual conduct, the prosecutor sought the records of group psychotherapy sessions in which the defendant participated. The Minnesota Supreme Court applied McCormick's approach and upheld privilege:

> Under [McCormick's] approach, we conclude that the medical privilege must be construed to encompass statements made in group psychotherapy. The participants in group psychotherapy sessions are not casual third persons who are strangers to the psychiatrist/psychologist/nurse-patient relationship. Rather, every participant has such a relationship with the attending professional, and, in the group therapy setting, the participants actually become part of the diagnostic and therapeutic process for co-participants.[72]

Likewise, in a California case, an appellate court held that disclosing information in the presence of members of a therapy group does not defeat the privilege.[73] The court said:

> Communications made by patients to persons who are present to further the interests of the patient comes within the privilege. "Group therapy" is designed to provide comfort and revelation to the patient who shares similar experiences and/or difficulties with other like persons within the group. The presence of each person is for the benefit of the others, including the witness/patient, and is designed to facilitate the patient's treatment. Communications such as these, when made in confidence, should not operate to destroy the privilege.[74]

In a Connecticut case,[75] the Connecticut Court of Appeals remanded for a determination of whether a murder suspect's alcohol treatment facility records were protected by the psychiatrist-patient privilege. In this case, Michael Skakel, the scion of Greenwich wealth, completed a required alcohol treatment program at Elan, a licensed treatment facility, after he was convicted of driving while intoxicated. Pursuant to a murder investigation, the state moved to compel the person who owned the facility to testify and produce records regarding Skakel's treatment. Skakel applied for an injunction on the grounds that the information was privileged under the psychiatrist-patient privilege. The trial judge denied the motion, because Skakel failed to (1) establish that Elan was a "mental health facility" within the meaning of the statute, and (2) demonstrate that the communications and records related to the diagnosis or treatment of a "medical condition" within the meaning of the statute. The appellate court said that interpreting "mental condition" in the statute to include alcohol-related disorders would effectuate the legislature's objective by providing individuals who have such disorders with an incentive to seek treatment and make a full disclosure to a psychiatrist. Because the trial court did not determine whether any of the communications and records sought by the state were related "to diagnosis or treatment" of the plaintiff's alcohol-related condition, the appeals court remanded.[76]

By and large, it appears that group therapists are more concerned than members of the group about confidentiality issues and testimonial privilege. In or out of court, group members assume confidentiality, though increasingly the assumption is being made explicit, sometimes in a contractual agreement. Be that as it may, therapists fear that one celebrated case, should it arise, would create a great deal of anxiety about group therapy. In fact, the likelihood of assault by subpoena is slight, but should it come, there are circumstances that tilt toward the maintenance of confidentiality.

Identity of Patient

Whether the identity of a patient is discoverable is problematical. In its formulation, a testimonial privilege covers only the content of communications and not the fact of a relationship. For a person to seek to invoke the privilege, there must be an initial showing, by affidavit or otherwise, that the person is one covered by the privilege. It is necessary to set out the existence of a therapist-patient relationship—the privilege does not cover communications between social guests.

While sometimes acknowledging that the identity of a psychiatric patient must be protected to maintain the purpose of the privilege, many courts nonetheless adhere to the formula and hold that the identity of patients, the dates on which they were treated, and the length of treatment on each date do not fall within the scope of the privilege.[77] Other courts, however, say that when disclosure of the fact of consultation also of necessity discloses the nature of the condition for which the patient sought treatment, then the fact of disclosure also becomes privileged.[78]

Given the context, disclosure of even a name may reveal much about the person. A story tells about a young man who goes to confession: "Forgive me, Father," he murmurs, "for I have sinned. I have sinned the cardinal sin with one of the female members of the congregation." "Who was it?" asks the priest. "Oh, I cannot betray that confidence," the young man says, but the priest is persistent. "Was it, by any chance, the lovely Mrs. Callahan?" The young man shakes his head. "Was it, then, the vivacious Miss O'Malley?" He shakes his head again. "Well, was it Michael's beautiful daughter?" He still refuses to answer. On leaving the church, he meets a friend outside. "Did the priest give you absolution?" "No," says the sinner. "But he did give me three good leads."

"Clearly," it is argued by commentators, "the idea of confidential communication must encompass the identity of the patient as well."[79] Illinois expressly includes the fact of psychotherapeutic treatment within the privilege.[80] Federal law prohibits the use or disclosure of "patient identifying information" concerning anyone diagnosed or treated for substance abuse at facilities receiving federal funds.[81] The principles of ethics of the profession declare, "The identification of a person as a patient must be protected with extreme care."[82]

In a discovery proceeding, individuals are asked whether they have ever been in treatment and, if so, where, when, and by whom. In a *Tarasoff*-type case, should the therapist have given a warning about the patient? In an assault case, the fact of psychiatric care might suggest that the patient was the aggressor in the fray. However, there is no justification in asking the question unless there is some basis in fact that would raise a legitimate question concerning the individual's condition.

In a malpractice action, a plaintiff may attempt to discover the names and addresses and, sometimes, the case histories of other people who have been treated by the defendant-physician. The attorney for the complainant wants the opportunity to talk to other patients of the physician in order to establish a pattern that would give credence to the complaint.[83] For example, a claim that the physician sexually exploited the plaintiff is more credible when supported by testimony of similar incidents with other patients. As a rule, discovery is disallowed on the ground of privilege or relevancy.[84]

In an article in *Trial*,[85] Linda Jorgenson, Pamela Sutherland, and Steven Bisbing cite research suggesting that "up to 80 percent of therapists who have had sexual contact with one patient, had sexual contact with other patients" (a debatable statistic), and they recommend the admission of evidence of these other acts to prove a case against an alleged abusing therapist. But how is evidence of these other acts to be obtained? Newspaper publicity of a lawsuit against a therapist for undue familiarity may bring forth other patients who have been violated, as occurred in *Roy v. Hartogs*.[86] But in lieu of that, is an attorney to be allowed to discover the names of all the therapist's patients, and then is the attorney to be allowed to contact the patients and ask them whether they have been sexually involved with their therapist? What will these patients think of the invasion of their privacy? What will they think of their therapist? What will it do to the therapeutic relationship with their therapist?

Demands for patient identification abound. A physician or a hospital who are defendants in a malpractice action urge that a discovery order for information about patients not privy to the lawsuit be set aside on the ground that it violates the physician-patient privilege. The physician or hospital may claim the privilege on behalf of a patient not privy to the action. In a California case,[87] the plaintiff sought to recover damages from a physician and hospital for injuries allegedly arising out of various tests performed on him. The plaintiff sought disclosure of the names and addresses of other patients to whom the defendants had given the same (angiographic) tests. The purpose of this information was to enable investigators to seek out and interrogate these patients and attempt to persuade them to discuss their experiences regarding the tests. The California Court of Appeals barred discovery—it concluded that disclosure of identity of patients receiving such tests would necessarily be revealing confidential information.[88]

In a Michigan case, *Dorris v. Detroit Osteopathic Hosp.*,[89] the plaintiff, Deborah Dorris, claimed that she was given the medication Compazine intravenously even though she tried to refuse that medication and asked for another. The medication allegedly triggered an abrupt drop in her blood pressure. The doctor who treated her denied giving her the medication against her wishes, but she insisted that a patient who shared her room heard the dispute and she sought a court order requiring the hospital to disclose the patient's name. Reluctantly, the Michigan Court of Appeals declined to order disclosure of the patient's name, feeling bound by the precedent of a 32-year-old ruling of the Michigan Supreme Court in *Schechet v. Kesten*,[90] where it was held that the privilege "prohibits the physician from disclosing, in the course of any action wherein his patient or patients are not involved and do not consent, even the names of such noninvolved patients." The Michigan Supreme Court in *Schechet* held that the identity of noninvolved patients was privileged. However, a few years before *Dorris*, in *Porter v. Michigan Osteopathic Hosp. Assn.*,[91] the Michigan Court of Appeals, over a strong dissent, allowed discovery in a case where the plaintiff was allegedly raped in a hospital of the names and addresses and the room assignments of any and all suspected assailants and also the name of a patient who may or may not have overheard a conversation between the plaintiff and medical personnel. Distinguishing *Porter*, the Michigan Court of Appeals in *Dorris* said that *Porter* presented stronger policy reasons than *Dorris* for disclosure. The Michigan Supreme Court affirmed *Dorris*, that had disallowed discovery, and it overruled *Porter*, that had allowed discovery.[92] The Michigan Legislature also amended the psychiatrist-patient privilege by including an express identity privilege.

In a case featured in the American Psychiatric Association's *Psychiatric News*, someone scratched graffiti on a bathroom wall in a building housing the offices of Maryland psychiatrist David Irwin. The police looked upon it as a hate crime because of its messages and ordered the psychiatrist to turn over the names, addresses, phone numbers, and appointment history of patients he had seen the day of the crime. The police suspected, with no supporting evidence, that one of his patients might have been responsible for the crime. The psychiatrist refused to comply with the police order and soon was served with a subpoena ordering him to appear in court to explain why he was not complying. None of the other professionals with offices on the same floor, including a dentist and two chiropractors, were ordered to turn over patient lists. The court ruled that the data the police wanted were not protected by psychiatrist-patient privilege or by the state's medical record confidentiality law and ordered the psychiatrist to provide the police with the information they sought. He appealed, and the appeals court affirmed that psychiatrist-patient privilege does not apply, but disagreed with the lower court's order that the state confidential law mandates that patient records are subject to release in a situation such as this. That law states that law enforcement and prosecution agencies must have written procedures in place describing how they will protect the confidentiality of the medical records they obtain during a criminal investigation. The appeals court said since the record of the case provided no indication that such written procedures do exist, the lower court, on account of this technicality, erred in ordering the psychiatrist to turn over the patient data to the police.[93]

Parents in Mississippi brought a negligence action against a hospital that mistakenly placed their infant with an unidentified female patient, who breast-fed the infant. Subsequently, the infant's health deteriorated. In response to the parents' request for discovery of the patient's identity, the hospital asserted the patient's privilege of confidentiality. Reasoning that the patient was a potential witness to the alleged negligence, the Mississippi Supreme Court ordered disclosure of her identity. The court said that the privilege "must give way where it conflicts with the sensible administration of the law and policy."[94]

Death of Patient

It is not uncommon for therapists to receive requests after the death of a patient for disclosure of confidential information. Such requests may be by relatives contesting the patient's will, police or life insurance companies investigating the cause of death, or bereaved family members attempting to deal with their own guilt or emotional distress.[95] The therapist is bound, both ethically and legally, to maintain confidentiality to the same extent after death of the patient as before, unless the law otherwise authorizes disclosure. The great weight of authority is that the right to waive the privilege extends to the patient's legal representatives after the patient's death. [96] (The writing of articles or books about a deceased patient occurs in an extrajudicial context and therefore raises issues of confidentiality, not privilege.)

In will contest cases, where the testamentary capacity of the testator is often under inquiry, there may be an attempt to overthrow a will through proof of the mental capacity of the testator at the time of the making of the will.[97] As a general rule, the courts say that those who stand in the place of the patient (the owner of the privilege) may waive the privilege. This is generally held to include the heirs of the deceased as well as the executor or administrator of the estate. The reason given is that the heir or personal representative will be as concerned with the preservation of the decedent's reputation and estate as was the decedent.

The majority of courts hold that a person having the right of waiver may exercise it as either a proponent or contestant of the will. The purpose of contesting the will is to determine whether the purported testament is, in fact, that of the decedent, or whether it is void as a result of the decedent's mental incapacity at the time of its making. Thus, in a Minnesota case, the court decided that the beneficiary of an insurance policy, the husband of the deceased, could waive the privilege, and implied that any personal representative or heir claiming an interest would be allowed to do the same.[98] A New York statute limits the right of waiver of the deceased patient's representative to those communications that are not confidential and that do not tend to disgrace the memory of the decedent. In a case that generated considerable critical comment in the law reviews, the physician was not allowed to answer questions concerning the effect of arteriosclerosis on the individual's mental capacity in writing a will.[99] The heir's waiver of the privilege permitted the doctor to testify only as to matters a layman could notice and describe, namely, that the patient had arteriosclerosis. The physician could not testify, however, as to information derived by reason of treating the patient.

There is, however, no restriction in most other states in a waiver provision excluding confidential communications. A few courts suggest that disclosures that would tend to disgrace the decedent's memory should be barred. The Connecticut statute on the psychiatrist-patient privilege provides that when a deceased patient's mental condition is introduced by any party claiming or defending through or as a beneficiary of the patient, there is no privilege if the judge finds "that it is more important to the interests of justice that the communication be disclosed than that the relationship between patient and psychiatrist be protected."[100]

The Self-Defense Exception

Any professional who is bound by confidentiality has the right of *self-defense.* The self-defense exception is justified on the well-established theory that a patient or client implicitly waives the privilege by making allegations against the professional. As the Advisory Committee to the Federal Rules of Evidence put it: "The exception is required by considerations of fairness and policy when questions arise out of dealings between attorney and client, as in cases of controversy over attorney's fees, claims of inadequacy of representation, or charges of professional misconduct."[101] Wigmore in his classic treatise on evidence likewise stated, "When the client alleges a breach of duty to him by the attorney, the privilege is waived as to all communications relevant to that issue."[102] This applies to other professionals as well as attorneys; hence, a therapist may disclose privileged information to defend against malpractice action.[103]

For waiver, it is not necessary for the client or patient to bring formal charges or proceedings against the professional. In the attorney-client context, the self-defense exception arises most frequently in posttrial assertions of a convicted defendant that put in issue the legitimacy of advice provided by the attorney, the effectiveness of the attorney's representation, or the attorney's competence.

Thus, as one court said, "It is well established that if a client assails his attorney's conduct of the case, or if a patient attacks his physician's treatment, the privilege as to confidential communications is waived, since the attorney or physician has a right to defend himself under the circumstances."[104] And in another case, the court said, "While the rule with respect to privileged communication between attorney and client should be zealously guarded, yet this privilege may be destroyed by the acts of the client in attacking the attorney on a charge of dereliction of duty.[105]

James Earl Ray, the assassin of Rev. Martin Luther King Jr., claimed that he was "coerced" by his attorney, Percy Foreman, to enter a plea of guilty so as to avoid a trial that might have implicated high-level accomplices. In response, Foreman said that he never recommended that Ray plead guilty to the murder of King, but advised Ray that "there is a little more than a 99 percent chance of your receiving a death penalty" if the case went to trial. Foreman displayed a letter he wrote to Ray. Foreman also disclosed that interviews with Ray convinced him that Ray alone assassinated King in the hope of becoming a hero to white people.[106]

The media, in the early 1990s, carried numerous articles describing the alleged misconduct of Harvard psychiatrist Margaret Bean-Bayog, whose patient, Paul Lozano, a medical student at Harvard, had committed suicide after being treated by her. These accounts were based on three thousand pages of documents filed in court by the lawyer for the deceased patient's family. They included allegations that the psychiatrist had fallen in love with her patient, had seduced him into a sexual relationship, and had regressed him to a stage where he believed she was his mother. Lozano killed himself about a year after Bean-Bayog stopped treating him.

The patient's family settled out of court for $1 million but with the stipulation that the settlement contain no admission of liability on the part of the psychiatrist.

Bean-Bayog also resigned her license rather than face a televised hearing before the Massachusetts Board of Registration in Medicine, which alleged that she provided substandard care, causing harm to her patient. Then came a report from the Committee on Therapy of the Group for the Advancement of Psychiatry that said:

> An immediate consequence that emerges from the Bean-Bayog case is that since a practitioner must adhere to the rules of confidentiality he or she cannot respond, without risk of a lawsuit, against charges of a patient or patient's family, regardless of how unfounded those charges may be. If a celebrity such as Michael Jackson or Woody Allen is accused of misconduct, he or she is free to call a press conference and openly refute the charges, revealing any information to strengthen his or her defense. This is not the case for physicians or other mental health therapists, who are required to keep the details of their patients' treatment confidential.[107]

In a press interview, Bean-Bayog stated, "It is important for a psychiatric audience to understand that if anything like this ever happened to them, they will not be able to say anything because of patient-therapist confidentiality."[108] "As the law now stands," the GAP committee said, "any accused therapist must bear all such accusations in silence."[109] Not so. While the privilege of confidentiality belongs to the patient (or the representatives of the patient in the event of the death of the patient), it is waived when the patient charges the practitioner with misconduct or malpractice.

Federal Law on Privilege

What about psychotherapist-patient testimonial privilege in federal courts? The Federal Rules of Evidence, when adopted in 1975, omitted a medical privilege, given the numerous exceptions that had been made to it. Its advisory committee, however, recommended a psychotherapist-patient privilege, modeled on the Connecticut law, but the proposal, along with several others, evoked considerable criticism. Two committees of the American Bar Association recommended to the ABA House of Delegates "the complete abolition of any and all privilege in the physician-patient area including the proposed 'psychotherapist-patient privilege.'"[110] The Committee on the Judiciary of the House of Representatives, after extensive hearings, recommended and the House approved the scrapping of all the proposed rules on privileges and left federal law of privileges unchanged, to wit, that the federal courts are to apply the state's privilege law in actions founded upon a state-created right or defense, while in other civil cases and in criminal cases, according to Rule 501 of the Federal Rules of Evidence, the principles of the common law, as interpreted by the federal courts in "the light of reason and experience," would be applied. In subsequent years the federal courts, in the light of reason and experience, adopted only an attorney-client privilege and a marital privilege, though by legislation all fifty states and the District of Columbia adopted some form of psychotherapist privilege. For long, privileges were said to arise only by statute, not common law, but Rule 501 provides that the law of privileges in the federal courts shall be determined by principles of federal common law, as developed in light of reason and experience.

After the adoption of Rule 501, the U.S. Second, Sixth, and Seventh Circuit Courts of Appeals have held in recent years that "reason and experience" compel the recognition of the psychotherapist-patient privilege in both civil and criminal cases. In contrast, the Fifth, Ninth, and Eleventh Circuits rejected the privilege. Given the conflict among the circuits, the U.S. Supreme Court granted certiorari in *Jaffee v. Redmond*.[111] In this civil rights case, coming out of the Seventh Circuit, surviving family members of a man who was shot and killed by a police officer sought the therapy records of the officer. Dr. Lifschutz filed an amicus curiae brief.

Mary Lu Redmond, a police officer in an Illinois town, fatally shot Ricky Allen after responding to a report of a disturbance at an apartment complex. She said she shot Allen because he was holding a butcher knife and was about to stab another man, but Allen's mother and other relatives alleged that he was unarmed. Redmond had undergone counseling with a licensed clinical social worker after the shooting, and Allen's relatives sought to have communications between Redmond and the social worker divulged. Both Redmond and the social worker refused, and the trial judge told jurors they could presume the information would be unfavorable to both Redmond and the town. The Seventh Circuit ordered a new trial. It upheld privilege under Rule 501 because "key to successful treatment lies in the ability of patients to communicate freely without fear of public disclosure."

The Seventh Circuit said that the privilege was not absolute and should be determined by balancing the interests protected by shielding the evidence sought with those advanced by disclosure. In this case the court found favor of applying the privilege, noting the strong interest in encouraging officers who are frequently forced to experience traumatic events by the nature of their work to seek qualified professional help. At the same time, the court noted that there were many witnesses to the shooting, and the plaintiffs' need for the officer's personal innermost thoughts about the shooting were cumulative at best, compared to the substantial nature of the officer's privacy interest. So, once again, privilege or no privilege, the outcome depended essentially on relevancy or materiality.

In oral argument before the U.S. Supreme Court, these issues were raised: (1) Do the Federal Rules of Civil Procedure provide trial judges with adequate tools to protect privacy interests involved in confidential communications with a psychotherapist without creation of new evidentiary psychotherapist-patient privilege under the Federal Rules of Evidence? (2) Should any privilege for psychotherapist-patient communications be extended to social workers, rather than being limited to psychiatrists and clinical psychologists? (3) Should a psychotherapist-patient privilege be recognized, and, if so, what would be the scope of the privilege?

In the course of oral argument Justice Scalia asked: "If somebody comes up to me and, let's say, my nephew comes up to me and says, 'You know, Unc, I want to tell you something in strictest confidence,' and I say, 'Yes, you tell me that, I promise you I won't tell this to anybody.' Is that enough that I've undertaken a duty of confidentiality to justify the creation of a privilege?" And Justice Breyer asked, "Why in logic or policy distinguish between physicians who treat physical problems and psychotherapists? Is there any reason in logic or policy, is there any reason, other than what the courts have held? I'm not interested, for this question, what courts have held in the past. I'm interested in whether there is a reason in logic or policy for drawing the line that I just referred to."

In its decision the Supreme Court declared the privilege to be absolute, or so it said, concluding that anything else would be worthless. "Making the promise of confidentiality contingent upon a trial judge's later evaluation of the relative importance of the patient's interest in privacy and the evidentiary need for disclosure would eviscerate the effectiveness of the privilege," Justice Stevens wrote for the majority. The decision went further than the appellate decision that it affirmed. The Seventh Circuit had created not an absolute privilege but a qualified one, to be balanced in appropriate cases by the "evidentiary need for disclosure."[112]

Although the ruling applies generally to federal litigation, the Court found the law enforcement context of the case to be particularly persuasive. "The entire community may suffer if police officers are not able to receive effective counseling and treatment after traumatic incidents," Justice Stevens said, "either because trained officers leave the profession prematurely or because those in need of treatment remain on the job." Two law enforcement organizations, the International Union of Police Associations and the National Association of Police Organizations, joined numerous organizations of mental health professionals in urging the Court to adopt the privilege. Given that all of the states and several circuits had adopted the privilege, it was justified in federal law, Justice Stevens wrote, in "the light of reason and experience."

Under the ambit of the privilege the Supreme Court included social workers who provide counseling. The Court noted that when Americans turn to psychotherapy, it is often provided by social workers who generally are less expensive than psychiatrists or psychologists. "Their clients often include the poor and those of modest means who could not afford the assistance of a psychiatrist or psychologist," Justice Stevens wrote.[113]

Justice Scalia wrote one of his fiery dissents, suggesting that people would be better advised to seek advice from their mothers than from psychiatrists, yet there is no mother-child privilege. Justice Scalia wrote:

> When is it, one must wonder, that the psychotherapist came to play such an indispensable role in the maintenance of the citizenry's mental health? For most of history, men and women have worked out their difficulties by talking to, inter alios, parents, siblings, best friends and bartenders—none of whom was awarded a privilege against testifying in court. Ask the average citizen: Would your mental health be more significantly impaired by preventing you from seeing a psychotherapist, or by preventing you from getting advice from your mom? I have little doubt what the answer would be. Yet there is no mother-child privilege.[114]

Justice Scalia's suggestion that people would be better advised to seek advice from their mothers rather than from psychiatrists prompted a comment in a letter to the *New York Times:* "Apparently he has never heard the old story of the mother who boasted about the devotion of her son: 'Not only did he buy me a condo, a Cadillac and a mink coat, but he also pays a psychiatrist $250 for a visit every week and all he talks about is me.'"[115]

Justice Scalia in his dissent argued that the privilege would interfere with the truth-finding function of the courts and cause the courts "to become themselves the instruments of wrong." He wrote:

Even where it is certain that absence of the psychotherapist privilege will inhibit disclosure of the information, it is not clear to me that that is an unacceptable state of affairs. Let us assume the very worst in the circumstances of the present case: that to be trustful about what was troubling her, the police officer who sought counseling would have to confess that she shot without reason, and wounded an innocent man. If (again to assume the worst) such an act constituted the crime of negligent wounding under Illinois law, the officer would of course have the absolute right not to admit that she shot without reason in criminal court. But I see no reason why she should be enabled *both* not to admit it in criminal court (as a good citizen should), *and* to get the benefits of psychotherapy by admitting it to a therapist who cannot tell anyone else. And even less reason why she should be enabled to *deny* her guilt in the criminal trial—or in a civil trial for negligence—while yet obtaining the benefits of psychotherapy by confessing fault to a social worker who cannot testify. It seems to me entirely fair to say that if she wishes the benefits of telling the truth she must also accept the adverse consequences. To be sure, in most cases the statements to the psychotherapist will be only marginally relevant, and one of the purposes of the privilege (though not one relied upon by the Court) may be simply to spare patients needless intrusion upon their privacy, and to spare psychotherapists needless expenditure of their time in deposition and trial. But surely this can be achieved by means short of excluding even evidence that is of the most direct and conclusive effect.[116]

What about Common Sense?

An individual who shoots and kills another as in *Jaffee* may feel guilty about it whether or not it was done in lawful self-defense or defense of others. Expressing such feelings in the course of therapy, however, may appear as a confession of wrongdoing when it is used in a legal proceeding. But absolute confidentiality is not acceptable to common sense, as illustrated by a recent Michigan case involving the murder of Dr. Deborah Iverson, an ophthalmologist.

In this case, as in all cases, trust meshed with common sense—not *absolute* confidentiality—has to be the measure of confidentiality. Every Thursday morning for several years Dr. Iverson would drive to see her psychiatrist, Dr. Lionel Finkelstein, and would park in an adjoining area. One Thursday morning she disappeared after leaving his office and was found strangled a distance away the next day in the backseat of her car. As the media reported, law-enforcement officials questioned Dr. Finkelstein for possible clues. Was the patient threatened? Did she fear someone? Apparently unsatisfied with their interview, the law-enforcement officials obtained a search warrant and seized the patient's file. It will be recalled that privilege is no bar to a search warrant.

Confidentiality cannot be turned into a holy grail without concern for good judgment in these matters. From the file on Dr. Iverson the law-enforcement officials learned that she was having problems with hospital coworkers and also "troubles or conflicts" with some relatives. Using that information, detectives focused much of their probe on relatives and coworkers, but it shed no light on the killing. Assuredly, the patient or the patient's family would want law enforcement to be informed about any fear that the patient may have had of an attack.[117]

Exceptions to the Federal Privilege

In a footnote to the majority opinion in *Jaffee*, Justice Stevens, while calling the privilege absolute, wrote, "Although it would be premature to speculate about most future developments in the federal psychotherapist privilege, we do not doubt that there are situations in which the privilege must give way, for example, if a serious threat of harm to the patient or to others can be averted only by means of a disclosure by the therapist." Justice Stevens also said, "Because this is the first case in which we have recognized a psychotherapist privilege, it is neither necessary nor feasible to delineate its full contours in a way that would govern all conceivable future questions in this area." The court did not base its decision on some notion of privacy grounded in the Constitution; rather, the decision was an interpretation of the Federal Rules of Evidence that apply in federal cases.

In the wake of *Jaffee*, no time was lost in the setting out of exceptions. Does the privilege cover unlicensed therapists? In *United States v. Schwensow*,[118] the defendant claimed the psychotherapist privilege recognized in *Jaffee* protected statements made to Alcoholics Anonymous (AA) volunteers. The government argued that the volunteers were not licensed counselors nor was the relationship justifying confidentiality present. The district court noted that the Supreme Court failed to designate who was considered a *psychotherapist* for purposes of the privilege. It then stated that lower courts would determine such details on a case-by-case basis. Ultimately, the district court held that the two volunteers were not "psychotherapists."[119] In *United States v. Lowe*,[120] the district court stated, "*Jaffee* does not control a determination of whether the federal privilege extends to communications with a rape crisis center employee or volunteer who is not a licensed social worker or psychotherapist." The court concluded that the policies of *Jaffee* call for some form of the psychotherapist privilege to be applied to communications with a rape crisis counselor.[121]

The First Circuit in 1999 held that the nascent psychotherapist-patient federal privilege encompasses a crime-fraud exemption similar to that of the established attorney-client privilege.[122] The decision arose out of subpoenas issued to two psychiatrists in the course of a grand jury investigation. It was alleged that the accused trumped up an array of disabilities, which he communicated to selected health care providers, who in turn provided the information to insurance carriers that had underwritten credit disability policies, thus fraudulently inducing payments. As with the attorney-client privilege, the exception applies even when the psychiatrist is an unknowing pawn of the patient.

Inevitably other exceptions will follow (and have followed), as in the case of the state-adopted privilege.[123] As I have noted, when push comes to shove, the principle of relevancy or materiality rather than privilege provides the protection of confidentiality. And, as I would emphasize, because these are elastic terms, given to interpretation, the therapist should withhold information until the patient consents or the court orders disclosure (and, of course, a subpoena is not a court order). The courts tend to find communications in therapy irrelevant, immaterial, or prejudicial, and do not call for their production.

In any event, psychotherapists have been enthused by the news of the Supreme Court's decision in *Jaffee*—at least it did not deflate the myth in the public mind and in the mind of therapists that the privilege is a solid shield.[124] Given the extensive publicity of decisions of the Supreme Court, a decision against privilege would have punctured the myth of privilege, though in practice, privilege or no privilege, the outcome is usually the same.[125]

Notes

1. See United States *ex rel.* Edney v. Smith, 425 F.Supp. 1038 (E.D. N.Y. 1976); C. DeWitt, *Privileged Communications between Physician and Patient* (Springfield, Ill.: Thomas, 1958).

2. Boyles v. Cora, 232 Iowa 822, 6 N.W.2d 401, 414 (1942).

3. C. McCormick, *Handbook of the Law of Evidence* (St. Paul, Minn.: West, 1954), p. 224.

4. American Law Institute (ALI), *Model Code of Evidence*, Rules 220–223 (1942).

5. J. Goldstein & J. Katz, "Psychiatrist-Patient Privilege: The GAP Proposal and the Connecticut Statute," *Conn. B.J.* 36 (1962): 175.

6. Nebraska Rules of Evidence, Rule 504.

7. 770 S.W.2d 387 (Mo. 1989).

8. It is to be noted that an attorney may but is not obliged to report a client who poses a danger, unlike a therapist who is obliged to report under the *Tarasoff* doctrine. A psychiatrist examining a litigant at the request of an attorney would fall under the attorney-client privilege and thus would not be obliged to report under *Tarasoff*. See United States v. Glass, 133 F.3d 1356 (10th Cir. 1998); Antrade v. Superior Court of Los Angeles County, 54 Cal. Rptr.2d 504 (Cal. App. 1996); see S. Saltzburg, "Privileges and Professionals: Lawyers and Psychiatrists," *Va. L. Rev.* 66 (1980): 597; Comment, "Function Overlap between the Lawyer and Other Professionals: Its Implications for the Privileged Communication Doctrine," *Yale L.J.* 71 (1962): 1266. It has occasionally been held, however, that the interests of public safety may outweigh the attorney-client privilege, calling for divulgence of the intention of a client to commit crimes in the future. Smith v. Jones, Vancouver Reg. C8876491 (Dec. 18, 1997); discussed in R. J. O'Shaughnessy, G. D. Glancy, & J. M. Bradford, "Canadian Landmark Case, *Smith v. Jones,* Supreme Court of Canada: Confidentiality and Privilege Suffer Another Blow," *J. Am. Acad. Psychiatry & Law* 27 (1999): 614.

9. In United States v. Talley, 790 F.2d 1468 (9th Cir. 1986), the court held that the government should not have been allowed to call as a rebuttal witness a psychiatrist, appointed for the defendant's benefit, but who was not called as a witness by the defendant. In White v. State, 1999 W.L. 124310 (Okla. Crim. App.), the prosecutor called as a witness a psychiatrist appointed by the trial court to aid the defense in presenting an insanity defense. The defense had elected not to call the psychiatrist as a witness on its behalf because, in reporting to the court, the psychiatrist had apparently found the defendant not to have been insane at the time of the commission of the crime. The prosecution summoned the psychiatrist, the defense expert, to give testimony to rebut the claim of insanity. The Oklahoma Court of Criminal Appeals ruled that the attorney-client privilege protected the findings of the psychiatrist from disclosure to or use by the prosecution. The defense's raising the issue of insanity was not considered a waiver of the protection of the privilege. See T. G. Gutheil & R. I. Simon, "Attorneys' Pressures on the Expert Witness: Early Warning Signs of Endangered Honesty, Objectivity, and Fair Compensation," *J. Am. Acad. Psychiatry & Law* 27 (1999): 546.

10. Matter of Lifschutz, 2 Cal.3d 415, 85 Cal. Rptr. 829, 467 P.2d 557 (1970). As pointed out in the case, a large segment of the psychiatric profession concurs in Dr. Lifschutz's strongly held belief that an absolute privilege of confidentiality is essential to the effective practice of psychotherapy. Cf. Annot., 20 A.L.R.3d 1109, 1112. An oft-cited study found in a survey of a group of lay people that "93% of those surveyed 'would have sought help for serious emotional problems' without the privilege and 74% 'did not know whether there was a privilege statute or guessed incorrectly that there was no privilege statute.'" D. Shuman & M. Weiner, "The Privilege Study: An Empirical Examination of the Psychotherapist-Patient Privilege," *No. Car. L. Rev.* 60 (1982): 893; expanded version, *The Psychotherapist-Patient Privilege* (Springfield, Ill.: Thomas, 1987).

11. Northvale, N.J.: Jason Aronson, 1995; reviewed in D. J. Kevles, "The Suspect on the Couch," *New York Times Book Review*, Dec. 31, 1995, p. 9.

12. *Reconciliation*, p. 446.

13. In the course of investigating a psychiatrist for fraudulent billing of his patients' insurance companies, a grand jury subpoenas his records identifying his patients' names, the

period of treatment, and their billings. The psychiatrist may not successfully assert privilege to avoid compliance. In re Zuniga, 714 F.2d 632 (6th Cir. 1983).

14. Matter of Lifschutz, supra note 10.

15. 2 Cal.3d at 426.

16. New York: St. Martin's Press, 1996.

17. P. 353.

18. Annot., 25 A.L.R.3d 1401.

19. In this case a mother alleged that a counselor was negligent in his diagnosis of the stepfather and in representing to her that his condition was no threat to their daughter. The mother claimed that, during their marriage, the stepfather sexually assaulted the daughter. The mother, on behalf of the daughter, a minor, brought suit against the stepfather for assault and against the counselor for negligence in diagnosis. The court noted that the condition of the stepfather would necessarily have to be determined in order to decide if the counselor was negligent. Easter v. McDonald, 903 S.W.2d 887 (Tex. App. 1995).

20. The court noted that Texas Rule of Evidence Rule 510 provides for exceptions to nondisclosure, including those communications and records "relevant to an issue of the physical, mental or emotional condition of a patient in any proceeding in which any party relies upon the condition as a part of the party's claim or defense." The court noted that the exception "represents a significant departure from the historical scope of the patient-litigant exception." The court noted, "The exception now terminates the confidentiality privilege whenever any party relies on the condition of a patient as part of that party's claim or defense, even when the patient does not personally place the condition at issue or is not a party." 903 S.W.2d at 890. However, in Reaves v. Bergsrud, 982 P.2d 497 (N.M. App. 1999), the New Mexico Court of Appeals in a malpractice action declined to allow the plaintiff to discover the physician's history of mental health treatment on the basis of the psychotherapist-patient privilege. Actually, the information would be irrelevant as it was not alleged that the physician's mental health was the cause of the plaintiff's postoperative problems. See the discussion in volume 2, chapter 7, on informed consent. See also Jaffee v. Redmond, 518 U.S. 1 (1996), discussed hereinafter.

21. People v. Hopkins, 119 Cal. Rptr. 61 (Cal. App. 1975). See also San Diego Trolley v. Superior Court of San Diego Cty, 105 Cal. Rptr.2d 476 (Cal. App. 2001); United States v. Glass, 133 F.3d 1356 (10th Cir. 1998). In contrast, in a 2–1 ruling, in United States v. Hayes, 227 F.3d 578 (6th Cir. 2000), the U.S. Court of Appeals, Sixth Circuit, ruled that issuing a *Tarasoff* warning does not abrogate the testimonial privilege. The court stated that such an exception would negatively affect the "atmosphere of confidence and trust" in the psychotherapist-patient relationship. Second, the court stated that although allowing a psychotherapist to testify against his patient in a criminal prosecution about statements made for treatment purposes may serve a public end, this end does not justify the means. And third, the court stated that the absence of the state's adoption of a dangerous patient exception support rejecting such an exception. In writing the opinion for the majority, Judge James Ryan reasoned that issuing a warning would not disrupt therapy as would testifying against the patient. In *Tarasoff*, however, the patient quit therapy when his therapist reported him to the police, then he killed Tatiana Tarasoff. Judge Ryan commented, "There is no question that the issue addressed in the *Hayes* case is difficult and that the resolution the court reached is subject to disagreement among reasonable people. We did what we thought was right and we recognized that the rule laid down in the case would not appeal to everyone." Personal communication (Dec. 19, 2000). Law Professor Vincent Johnson writes: "Students may be interested to learn that not all patients would be upset by learning that their therapists intend to divulge their threats to the intended victims. Indeed, [I have] a friend who works at the Counseling Service of Addison County. That doctor routinely tells any patient who makes a threat that the doctor intends to relay the threat to the intended victim. The doctor says that most patients are pleased to learn that the threat will be communicated because it gives them a sense of power." V. R. Johnson & A. Gunn, *Teaching Torts: A Teacher's Guide* (Durham: Carolina Academic Press, 1995), p. 167.

A decision in New York also ruled that issuing a warning does not result in having to testify at trial. State of New York v. Bierenbaum, No. 8295/99, discussed in "*Tarasoff* Warning Does Not Waive Psychotherapy Privilege, Judge Rules," *Psychiatric News*, Oct. 20, 2000, p. 2. In this case, Robert Bierenbaum, a plastic surgeon, discussed his serious marital problems with a psychiatrist who was alarmed by threats of violence he made against his wife. He carried out his *Tarasoff* duty by alerting Bierenbaum's wife, an action to which Bierenbaum assented. Two years later, the wife disappeared; her body was never found. Some fifteen years later, without the psychiatrist testifying at trial, Bierenbaum was convicted of killing his wife. He was suspected of dismembering her and dumping her into the ocean. P. Rogers et al., "Judgment Day," *People,* Nov. 6, 2000, p. 15. See R. Weinstock, G. B. Leong, & J. A. Silva, "Potential Erosion of the Psychotherapist-Patient Privilege beyond California: Dangers of 'Criminalizing' *Tarasoff,*" *Behav. Sci. & Law* 19 (2001): 437.

Section 1024 of the California Evidence Code codifies a *Tarasoff*-exception to the psychotherapist privilege. In People v. Clark, 50 Cal.3d 583 (1990), the California Supreme Court reaffirmed the difference between the psychotherapist-patient privilege and the attorney-client privilege. No exception exists within the attorney-client privilege that allows for the disclosure of confidential threats to harm third persons, so an expert hired by the attorney would come under the attorney-client privilege.

22. See also Easter v. McDonald, 903 S.W.2d 887 (Tex. App. 1995), discussed supra notes 19–20. In Johnson v. Rogers Memorial Hosp., 238 Wis.2d 227, 616 N.W.2d 903 (2000), the Wisconsin Supreme Court stated that lack of therapy records is not sufficient to dismiss a third-party case. In other cases, if the parents did not have access to therapy records, the case did not go forward.

23. Fentress v. Shea Communications, Jefferson Circuit Court, Louisville, Ky., case no. 90-CI-06033; see P. R. Breggin, *Brain-Disabling Treatments in Psychiatry: Drugs, Electroshock, and the Role of the FDA* (New York: Springer, 1997); J. Cornwall, *The Power to Harm* (New York: Viking, 1996); M. L. Harris," Problems with Prozac: Defective Product Responsible for Criminal Behavior?" *J. Contemp. Legal Issues* 10 (1999): 359; "Colorado Psychiatrists Fight Propaganda about Psychiatric Meds," *Psychiatric News,* Feb. 4, 2000, p. 8. See also M. J. Grinfeld, "Litigation Raises New Questions about Safety and Effectiveness of Depression Treatment," *Psychiatric Times,* Aug. 2001, p. 18.

24. In Palay v. Superior Court, 22 Cal. Rptr.2d 839 (Cal. App. 1993), the California Court of Appeals held that a mother's records relating to her prenatal care were discoverable and not protected by physician-patient privilege in a medical malpractice case she brought on behalf of her 16-month-old son. In Jones v. Superior Court, 119 Cal. App.3d 534, 174 Cal. Rptr. 148 (1981), an adult plaintiff instituted a product liability action for injuries allegedly sustained due to her mother's ingestion of a drug while pregnant with the plaintiff. The defendants sought to secure records of the mother's ingestion of the drug and of her physical condition during her pregnancy. The court held that although the mother may still have had the right to assert the privilege to protect that information after the plaintiff instituted the action, she waived the right by her subsequent deposition disclosures, which revealed the circumstances of her drug ingestion and the related communications with her physician. See L. O. Gostin, "Genetic Privacy," *J. of Law, Medicine & Ethics* 23 (1995): 320; L. B. Wright, "Genetic Causation and the Physician-Patient Privilege in Michigan: Shield or Sword?" *Wayne L. Rev.* 36 (1989): 189.

In Baker v. Oakwood Hosp. Corp., 239 Mich. App. 461, 608 N.W.2d 833 (2000), the plaintiff, a research nurse coordinator for a doctor, was allegedly fired after confronting the doctor about reportedly illegal and unethical conduct on his part. She subsequently filed suit against the doctor and hospital, alleging, among other claims, wrongful discharge. During discovery, the plaintiff requested patient records related to the research she worked on during her employment. Because none of the patients whose records were sought by the plaintiff had waived the physician-patient privilege, the Michigan Court of Appeals concluded that the records were protected from disclosure, even though patients' names would be redacted from the records.

25. The statutes are set out in R. Slovenko, *Psychotherapy and Confidentiality* (Springfield, Ill.: Thomas, 1998), pp. 150–85. In Peto v. Texas, 2001 WL 423286 (Tex. Ct. App. 2001), the Texas Court of Appeals ruled that the trial court did not err when it permitted the state at a sentencing hearing to cross-examine a psychiatrist about his letter of recommendation for the defendant, who pleaded guilty to felony theft, because there is no psychiatrist-patient privilege in Texas in criminal proceedings. In the District of Columbia, there is no medical privilege in criminal cases where "the accused is charged with causing the death of, or causing injuries upon, a human being, and the disclosure is required in the interests of public justice."

D.C. Code Ann., sec. 14-307. In jurisdictions where a psychotherapy or medical privilege applies in criminal cases, the question arises whether it is applicable in the emergency treatment of an unconscious patient. In People v. Childs, 243 Mich. App. 360, 622 N.W.2d 90 (2000), the defendant was charged with having started a fire while intoxicated. The defendant was unconscious when taken to the hospital, where blood was drawn and tested for alcohol content. The Michigan Court of Appeals affirmed the trial court's decision precluding the admission of the blood test results under the state's physician-patient privilege. It rejected the prosecutor's argument that the privilege should not apply to an unconscious patient on the ground that the privilege was designed only to protect and encourage communication between a patient and a physician. The court held that the plain language of the state's privilege statute provides that the privilege applies to "information" acquired in attending to a patient if the information is necessary to treat the patient. Thus, the court held that the statute applies to any information acquired, including blood test results, and is not limited to information acquired through communication with the patient.

26. Mark David Chapman, who shot and killed John Lennon, a former member of the Beatles, pleaded guilty to the crime, but if he had asked for a trial and raised an insanity defense, his prior visits to a psychotherapist would have been subject to discovery by the prosecution because his claim of insanity created an implied waiver of the psychotherapist-patient privilege. See, e.g., Ariz. Rev. Stat. Ann., sec. 13-3933.

27. See, e.g., Smith v. McCormick, 914 F.2d 1153 (9th Cir. 1990); Miller v. District Court, 737 P.2d 834 (Colo. 1987); People v. Hilliker, 185 N.W.2d 831 (Mich. App. 1971). But see Lange v. Young, 869 F.2d 1008 (7th Cir. 1989); Haynes v. State, 739 P.2d 497 (Nev. 1987).

28. United States v. Hinckley, 525 F.Supp. 1342 (D.C. 1981).

29. Ill. Stat. Ann., ch. 740, sec. 110/10.

30. Ind. Code Ann., sec. 25-33-1-17; Wis. Stat. Ann., sec. 905.04(4)(d).

31. Neb. Rev. Stat., sec. 27-504.

32. State v. Schreiber, 122 N.J. 579, 585 A.2d 945 (1991).

33. See, e.g., Alaska R. Evid. 504(d)(2). In In re Grand Jury Proceedings of Violette, 183 F.3d 71 (1st Cir. 1999), Gregory Violette was under a grand jury investigation for allegedly making false statements to financial institutions for the purpose of obtaining loans and credit disability insurance and fabricating disabilities in his communications to his health care providers. He was alleged to have prompted the communications of these falsehoods to the companies that underwrote the credit disability policies. The United States subpoenaed two psychiatrists who had seen Violette to appear before the grand jury. The crime-fraud exception to privilege allowed the inquiry.

34. D.C. Code Ann. 4-307(b)(4).

35. See, e.g., Neb. Rev. Stat., sec. 27-504.

36. See, e.g., Ill. Stat. Ann., ch. 740, sec. 110/10.

37. McDonough v. Director of Patuxent Institution, 183 A.2d 368 (Md. 1962).

38. See People v. Stevens, 386 Mich. 579, 194 N.W.2d 370 (1972).

39. The U.S. Supreme Court addressed the issue over a decade ago in State of Pennsylvania v. Ritchie, 480 U.S. 39 (1987). In this case the accused was charged with the sexual assault of his daughter, a minor, whereupon the matter was referred to the Pennsylvania Children and Youth Services Agency (CYS) for investigation and treatment. The accused sought production and disclosure of the agency's confidential records on the basis of the Sixth Amendment of the Constitution. The Court held that information "material" to the defense of the accused must be disclosed. The Court said, "[The accused] is entitled to know whether the CYS file contains information that may have changed the outcome of his trial had it been disclosed. . . . We disagree with the decision of the Pennsylvania Supreme Court to the extent that it allows defense counsel access to the CYS file. An in camera review by the trial court will serve [the accused's] interest without destroying the Commonwealth's need to protect the confidentiality of those involved in child-abuse investigations." 480 U.S. at 61.

The threshold test is not construed too strictly, so as to avoid placing the accused in a catch-22 situation. It is designed to prevent speculative or frivolous applications only. In Commonwealth of Massachusetts v. Bishop, 617 N.E.2d 990 (Mass. 1993), the defendant was accused of sexually assaulting members of his Boy Scout Troop. After the alleged incidents, two victims were treated by a psychologist. The accused sought pretrial production of the psychologist's records pursuant to his right to a fair trial. The court held that confidential documents were to be produced to the court where the accused demonstrated "a likelihood that the records contain[ed] relevant evidence." The accused was not required to demonstrate the actual existence of relevant evidence, only some factual basis indicating how the impugned records were likely to be relevant. A low threshold was preferred, because the court did not want to leave the accused in the catch-22 situation or interfere with his right to present a full answer and defense. The court expressed the opinion that the stated threshold was sufficient to prevent the accused from merely grasping at straws. 617 N.E.2d at 1000.

40. Shartzer v. Israels, 51 Cal. App.4th 641, 59 Cal. Rptr.2d 296 (1996).

41. Although I recognize that sexual assault is perpetrated against males as well as females, because it is much more common for the victim to be female, I employ forms of *she* in these contexts.

42. A. Meisel, "Confidentiality and Rape Counseling," *Hastings Center Report* 11 (1981): 5.

43. New York: Warner Books, 1994. The Canadian Supreme Court upheld the constitutionality of a law that prevents psychiatric records from being disclosed routinely in sexual assault cases. In a 7–2 ruling, the court upheld a 1997 law that requires trial judges to decide whether a request to examine psychiatric records is relevant to the case. R. v. Mills, No. 26358 (Nov. 25, 1999), reported in "CPA Helps Win Victory for Patient Confidentiality," *Psychiatric News*, Feb. 4, 2000, p. 2.

44. Quoted in E. J. Pollock, "Mother Fights to Keep Daughter's Records in Rape Case Secret," *Wall Street Journal*, Aug. 22, 1996, p. 1.

45. See United States v. Nixon, 418 U.S. 683 (1974).

46. West Virginia v. Roy, 460 S.E.2d 277 (W. Va. 1995).

47. State v. Cisneros, 535 N.W.2d 703 (Neb. 1995). In a prosecution in California for forcible sex offenses, Farrell L. v. Superior Court, 203 Cal. App.3d 521, 250 Cal. Rptr. 25 (1988), the defendant sought to cross-examine the victim, his minor daughter, regarding persons in her therapy group at a state hospital to whom she had revealed details of the offenses allegedly perpetrated against her. The victim declined to provide the names of the persons in her therapy group on the ground of confidentiality. After a hearing in chambers in which the victim's counselor at the state hospital testified, the trial court refused to allow defense counsel such line of cross-examination on the basis that it fell within the psychotherapist-patient privilege. The California Court of Appeals denied the petition. It held that the identification of persons in the victim's group counseling could only have been relevant in a subsequent attempt to impeach her testimony at trial and that the exclusion of the cross-examination did not deny the defendant a fair hearing. 203 Cal. App.3d at 528.

48. Federal Rules of Evidence, Rule 504 (as proposed).

49. Matter of Winstead, 67 Ohio App.2d 111, 425 N.E.2d 943 (1980).

50. Some twenty states have statutory provisions that allow commitment by guardians. See D. M. English, "The Authority of a Guardian to Commit an Adult Ward," *Mental & Physical Disability Law Reporter* 20 (1996): 584.

51. Cal. Welf. Inst. Code, secs. 5350–5371.

52. Matter of Farrow, 41 N.C. App. 680, 255 S.E.2d 777 (1979).

53. MCL 330.1750.

54. Saur v. Probes, 190 Mich. App. 636 (1991).

55. MCL 330.1750.

56. See, e.g., Ala. Code 26-18-7(a)(2).

57. See, e.g., Matter of A.J.S., 630 P.2d 217 (Mont. 1981). See also United States v. Burtrum, 17 F.3d 1299 (10th Cir. 1994) (criminal child sexual abuse context).

58. Laznovsky v. Laznovsky, 745 A.2d 1054 (Md. 2000). See C. P. Malmquist, "Psychiatric Confidentiality in Child Custody Disputes," *J. Am. Acad. Child Adolesc. Psychiat.* 33 (1994): 158.

59. Mo. Rev. Stat. 17:337.639.

60. Matter of von Goyt, 461 So.2d 821, at 823 (Ala. Civ. App. 1984).

61. Address by Marianne Battani on Apr. 30, 1991, at Michigan's Institute of Continuing Legal Education, Troy, Michigan.

62. Critchlow v. Critchlow, 347 So.2d 453 (Fla. App. 3d Dist. 1977).

63. Roper v. Roper, 336 So.2d 654, at 656 (Fla. App. 4th Dist. 1976).

64. Navarre v. Navarre, 191 Mich. App. 395, 479 N.W.2d 357 (1991).

65. Comment by East Lansing attorney Steven A. Mitchell, quoted in Editorial, *Detroit News*, Jan. 22, 2000, p. C-7.

66. H. B. Roback, R. F. Moore, G. J. Waterhouse, & P. R. Martin, "Confidentiality Dilemmas in Group Psychotherapy with Substance-Dependent Physicians," *Am. J. Psychiatry* 153 (1996): 10.

67. Personal communication.

68. Personal communication.

69. In Blue Cross v. Superior Court & Blair, Super. Ct. No. 32612 (Sept. 10, 1976), it being agreed that the patient's name and ailments were disclosed to Blue Cross for the purpose of paying the doctor's fees, the court held that confidentiality was not lost and the privilege was not waived.

70. McCormick's *Handbook of the Law of Evidence* (St. Paul, Minn.: West, 5th ed. 1999). This point is more fully developed in W. Cross, "Privileged Communications between Participants in Group Psychotherapy," *L. & Soc. Order* 1970: 191.

71. State v. Andring, 342 N.W.2d 128 (Minn. 1984); see P. S. Appelbaum & A. Greer, "Confidentiality in Group Therapy," *Hosp. & Community Psychiatry* 44 (1993): 311.

72. 342 N.W.2d at 133.

73. Farrell L. v. Superior Court, 203 Cal. App.3d 521, 250 Cal. Rptr. 25 (1988); discussed supra note 47.

74. 203 Cal. App.3d at 527.

75. Skakel v. Benedict, 738 A.2d 170 (Conn. App. 1999).

76. See T. Scheffey, "Beyond Rich Man's Justice," *Conn. Law Tribune,* Aug. 16, 1999, p. 1. In a New York case, Paul Cox, who broke into his boyhood home in Larchmont and fatally stabbed the husband and wife doctors who lived there, was arrested four years later, when seven AA members told the police about the killings. He was then linked to the crime by fingerprints at the victims' house. The defense contended that Cox was drunk and temporarily insane and thought he was killing his parents. He was convicted of manslaughter rather than murder under the theory that he suffered from extreme emotional disturbance. Associated Press news release, "Lawyer Says AA Testimony Should Have Been Barred in Cox Case," June 18, 1999.

77. In re Zuniga, 714 F.2d 632 (6th Cir. 1983); Ley v. Dall, 150 Vt. 383, 553 A.3d 562 (1988).

78. City of Alhambra v. Superior Court, 110 Cal. App.3d 513, 168 Cal. Rptr. 49 (1980).

79. D. Louisell & C. Mueller, *Federal Evidence* (Rochester, N.Y.: Lawyer's Co-operative, rev. ed. 1985), vol. 2, sec. 216, p. 857. See also E. S. Soffin, "The Case for a Federal Psychotherapist-Patient Privilege that Protects Patient Identity," *Duke L.J.* 1985: 1217. Some state statutes specifically protect the identity of a patient. For example, Rule 510 of the Texas Rules of Evidence provides that records of the identity, diagnosis, evaluation, or treatment of a patient shall not be disclosed (subject to the exceptions to nondisclosure).

80. 740 Ill. Comp. Stat. Ann. 110/2 (Supp. 1995).

81. 42 C.F.R., secs. 2.11, 2.12.

82. American Psychiatric Association, "The Principles of Medical Ethics with Annotations Especially Applicable to Psychiatry" (Washington, D.C.: Author, 1995 ed.); P. B. Gruenberg, "Some Thoughts on Confidentiality," *So. Calif. Psychiatrist* (Newsletter), Sept. 1996, p. 4.

83. Annot., "Discovery in Medical Malpractice Action, of Names of Other Patients to Whom Defendant Has Given Treatment Similar to that Allegedly Injuring Plaintiff," 74 A.L.R.3d 1055. In N.O. v. Callahan, 110 F.R.D. 637 (D.Mass. 1986), an action by inmates at a state mental health facility alleging systematic failures to provide adequate medical care, the plaintiffs sought medical records of nonparty patients. Although the court found that such records are privileged under state law, it held that a strong showing of need had been made and that the records could be discovered. The court required deletion of the names of the patients and limited disclosure of the records to counsel, clerical assistants, and experts.

84. Ex parte Abell, 613 S.W.2d 255 (Tex. 1981); see also Ltrs., "Ethics of Contacting Past Patients of Alleged Molester," *Clinical Psychiatry News,* Feb. 1989, p. 9.

85. "Evidence of Multiple Victims in Therapist Sexual Misconduct Cases," *Trial,* May 1995, p. 30.

86. 381 N.Y.S.2d 587 (1976).

87. Marcus v. Superior Court of Los Angeles County, 18 Cal. App.3d 22, 95 Cal. Rptr. 535 (1971).

88. In a commentary, law professors Jon R. Waltz and Roger C. Park say: "One would think that the information was much more important to the plaintiff than it would be to the

patient enquired about and, that in justice, the plaintiff should get the information. Certainly the physician defendant has no interest in keeping the information confidential except insofar as it shields him from liability for malpractice. It would seem that it should be privileged if this were a test for a sexually transmitted disease or various other things in which the other patients of the physician had a real privacy interest. Here it is hard to think that the third party interest is very strong. One is tempted to hold that a patient's angiogram is not a communication, but the problem is that it is clear that the patient would have had to make certain communications before the doctor would do an angiogram upon her, so the privilege is not non-existent on that account." J. R. Waltz & R. C. Park, *Evidence* (New York: Foundation Press, 9th ed. 1999), p. 607. See also Smith v. Superior Court, 118 Cal. App.3d 136, 173 Cal. Rptr. 145 (1981) (income of psychiatrist in action for spousal support could be learned in other ways); Costa v. Regents of the University of California, 116 Cal. App.2d 445, 254 P.2d 85 (1953); Boddy v. Parker, 45 App. Div.2d 1000, 358 N.Y.S. 218 (1974).

89. 220 Mich. App. 248, 559 N.W.2d 76 (1996).

90. 372 Mich. 346, 126 N.W.2d 718 (1964).

91. 170 Mich. App. 619, 428 N.W.2d 719 (1988).

92. Dorris v. Detroit Osteopathic Hosp., 460 Mich. 26, 594 N.W.2d 455 (1999).

93. Shady Grove Psychiatric Group v. State of Maryland, 128 Md. App. 163, 736 A.2d 1168 (1999); "Psychiatrist Wins Refusal to Release Patient Names," *Psychiatric News*, Nov. 5, 1999, p. 2. See, in general, W. Winslade, "Confidentiality of Medical Records," *J. Legal Medicine* 3 (1982): 497; see also J. B. Sloan & B. Hall, "Confidentiality of Psychotherapeutic Records," *J. Legal Medicine* 5 (1984): 435.

94. As for the production of medical records, the court noted both the parents' need for the medical history information from the unidentified patient to protect their infant's health and the unidentified patient's privacy interest in nondisclosure of her identity and medical records. The court ruled that the woman's medical records would have to be produced in camera for review to determine whether the infant's health was at risk. Baptist Memorial Hosp. v. Johnson, 2000 WL 5424 (Miss. Jan. 6, 2000).

95. R. L. Goldstein, "Psychiatric Poetic License? Post-Mortem Disclosure of Confidential Information in the Anne Sexton Case," *Psychiatric Annals* 22 (1992): 341; J. N. Onek, "Legal Issues in the Orne/Sexton Case," *J. Am Acad. Psychoanal.* 20 (1992): 655.

96. The son of a decedent requested to see his father's hospital records in Emmett v. Eastern Dispensary & Cas. Hosp., 396 F.2d 931 (D.C. Cir. 1967). The court recognized the duty of physicians to protect the interests of their patients under the privilege, but it also said there was a duty to reveal what the patient should know. "This duty of disclosure," the court said, "extends after the patient's death to the next of kin." In Drouillard v. Metropolitan Life Ins. Co., 107 Mich. App. 608, 310 N.W.2d 15 (1981), it was held that an insurance beneficiary or personal representative may waive a physician-patient privilege that had existed between a physician and the deceased insured. See also Scott v. Henry Ford Hosp., 199 Mich. App. 241, 501 N.W.2d 259 (1993).

97. G. L. Usdin, "The Psychiatrist and Testamentary Capacity," *Tul. L. Rev.* 32 (1957): 89; see generally H. Weihofen, "Guardianship and Other Protective Services for the Mentally Incompetent," *Am. J. Psychiatry* 121 (1965): 970.

98. Olson v. Court of Honor, 100 Minn. 117, 110 N.W. 734 (1907).

99. Matter of Coddington, 307 N.Y. 181, 120 N.E.2d 777 (1954); noted in *Cornell L.Q.* 40 (1954): 148; *Minn. L. Rev.* 39 (1955): 800; *N.Y.U.L. Rev.* 30 (1955): 202; *Syr. L. Rev.* 6 (1954): 213.

100. Conn. Gen. Stat., secs. 17-183, 17-206d. In Swidler & Berlin v. United States, 118 S. Ct. 2081 (1998), the U.S. Supreme Court held the attorney-client privilege prevents disclosure of confidential communications after a client has died even where the information is relevant to a criminal proceeding. The case involved notes taken by a Washington lawyer whom Vincent Foster, then White House deputy counsel, consulted about a week before his suicide. Independent counsel Kenneth Starr contended he needed the notes as part of his inquiry into whether administration officials lied in order to conceal first lady Hillary Rodham Clinton's alleged role in the 1993 firing of employees in the White House travel office.

101. Advisory Committee's Note, Rule 503 of Federal Rules of Evidence.

102. The courts have also permitted an attorney to disclose client confidences when a third party alleges wrongdoing. The Model Rules of Professional Conduct, Rule 8.3(a), provides, "A lawyer having knowledge that another lawyer has committed a violation of the Rules

of Professional Conduct that raises a substantial question as to that lawyer's honesty, trustworthiness or fitness as a lawyer in other respects, shall inform the appropriate professional authority." To defend against such an allegation, the attorney may disclose client confidences. See Application of Friend, 411 F.Supp. 776 (S.D. N.Y. 1975).

103. Ill. Comp. Stat., ch. 735, sec. 5/8-802; M. Graham, *Handbook of Illinois Evidence* (St. Paul, Minn.: West, 6th ed. 1994), pp. 279–80.

104. Pruitt v. Payton, 243 F.Supp. 907, 909 (E.D.Va. 1965).

105. United States v. Butler, 167 F.Supp. 102 (E.D.Va. 1957).

106. Associated Press news release, "Lawyer Denies He Advised Ray to Admit Killing King," *Detroit Free Press*, Nov. 14, 1978, p. D-3.

107. For the GAP report, see "Aftermath: Repercussions of the Bean-Bayog Case," *Psychiatric Times*, Feb. 1995, p. 7.

108. "Aftermath: Repercussions of the Bean-Bayog Case," *Psychiatric Times*, Feb. 1995, p. 7.

109. Ibid.

110. Notes to Proposed Rule 504, Federal Rules of Evidence.

111. The decision in the case was rendered in 1996. The case citation is 518 U.S. 1 (1996). The oral arguments and decision appear in R. Slovenko, *Psychotherapy and Confidentiality* (Springfield, Ill.: Thomas, 1998), pp. 565–602.

112. See E. Inwinkelried, "The Rivalry between Truth and Privilege: The Weakness of the Supreme Court's Instrumental Reasoning in *Jaffee v. Redmond*," *Hastings L.J.* 49 (1998): 969; C. B. Mueller, "The Federal Psychotherapist-Patient Privilege after *Jaffee:* Truth and Other Values in a Therapeutic Age," id. 49 (1998): 999.

113. See M. S. Raeder, "The Social Worker's Privilege, Victim's Rights, and Contextualized Truth," *Hastings L.J.* 49 (1998): 991. In Henry v. Kernan, 177 F.3d 1152 (9th Cir. 1999), the defendant believed that a medical doctor whom he consulted was a psychotherapist and, therefore, that his communications should not be discoverable. The court said, "There can be no psychotherapist-patient privilege . . . if there is no psychotherapist." 177 F.3d at 1159.

114. 518 U.S. at 18.

115. E. Muravchik, ltr., *New York Times*, June 19, 1986, p. 14.

116. 518 U.S. at 18.

117. J. Martin, "Slain Doctor Talked of Conflicts," *Detroit Free Press*, June 20, 1996, p. B-1.

118. 942 F.Supp. 402 (E.D.Wis. 1996).

119. 942 F.Supp. at 406–8.

120. 948 F.Supp. 97 (D.Mass. 1996).

121. 948 F.Supp. at 98–100.

122. In re Grand Jury Proceedings of Violette, 183 F.3d 71 (1st Cir. 1999), discussed at supra note 33. See D. W. Shuman & W. Foote, "*Jaffee v. Redmond*'s Impact: Life after the Supreme Court's Recognition of a Psychotherapist-Patient Privilege," *Professional Psychology, Research and Practice* 30 (1999): 479.

123. United States v. Glass, 133 F.3d 1356 (10th Cir. 1998), the Tenth Circuit held that the privilege does not extend to a criminal case in which the confidential communication constituted the sole basis for the government's prosecution and conviction for threatening the life of the president (the case was remanded to determine whether the threat was serious when it was uttered and whether its disclosure was the only means of averting harm to the president when the disclosure was made).

124. It was headline news on page one of the *New York Times*. L. Greenhouse, "Justices Uphold Psychotherapy Privacy Rights," *New York Times*, June 4, 1996, p. 1. APA President Allan Tasman wrote that the decision provides "additional needed protections for the psychotherapist-patient relationship." A. Tasman, "APA Fighting Hard for Better Medical-Record Privacy Rights," *Psychiatric News*, Dec. 3, 1999, p. 3. In the first-ever mental health report released by a surgeon general, David Satcher asserted that the decision "leaves little doubt that there is broad legal protection for the principle of confidentiality." The full report, "Mental Health: A Report of the Surgeon General," is available on the Web. "Satcher Focuses National Spotlight on Mental Illness," *Psychiatric News*, Jan. 7, 2000, p. 1. *www.psych.org* (Nov. 30, 2001).

125. For extended discussion of testimonial privilege, see R. Slovenko, *Psychotherapy and Confidentiality* (Springfield, Ill.: Thomas, 1998).

5

Witnesses and the Credibility of Testimony

The early method of settling disputes was by fist or club. Gradually, the concept of a trial evolved with its concomitant rules regarding the competency of witnesses and the admissibility of evidence. The early method of deciding disputes, however, has influenced the development of the rules of procedure; within this evolving framework various psychological notions are used to assess the credibility of testimony.

Historically, litigation is a substitute for trial by ordeal or by battle. During the feudal period, the issue in important cases, such as a disputed claim to land or an accusation of unjustifiable homicide, was generally determined by judicial combat between the principals or their legally appointed champions rather than in a courtroom. In knightly array, the two fought it out and the vanquished, if still alive, suffered whatever penalty the law prescribed.[1]

Around A.D. 1100, ambitious princes took heed of the political systems of Athens and republican Rome and adopted many of the same concepts in order to support and expand their jurisdiction. The function of the jury at this time was to give support to the king's administrative officials and, later, to his traveling justices in their efforts to extend the jurisdiction of the king's courts throughout England. The strong men of the locality were drawn to the aid of the judges and, as the jury, were not only witnesses but a determining body. These functions were not split as they are today between our modern jury and witnesses; rather these men had, or were supposed to have had, information regarding the matters in issue.[2] It is interesting to note that the original meaning of the word *juror* is one who took an oath and swore to declare truly what he knew or believed in a given case. There were no rules concerning the way in which the jurors acquired their knowledge.[3] During this period the independent witness was thought of as a meddler and, if he intervened, was in peril of being held guilty of maintenance.

The advent of the modern witness took place in the sixteenth century, the time of the end of the feudal order. Disputes were no longer provincial matters, and the jury gained in importance, becoming a symbol of political freedom. The Elizabethan Act of 1562, which created the statutory offense of perjury and provided for compulsory attendance of witnesses, initiated a new epoch in the law of evidence. Thereafter, the facts of the case were presented by outside witnesses and not by members of the jury. Previously the jurors were to know everything about the case, now they were to know nothing. The tabula rasa dictum, soon to be current in philosophy, found judicial application.

Initially, however, these outside witnesses were received with some circumspection as possible perjurers, and if there was any reason to suspect that a witness might be inclined to lie, he was considered incompetent to testify.[4] The common law borrowed heavily from the canon law in designating certain persons as incompetent to serve as witnesses. In his *History of English Law*, Holdsworth points out:

> The canon law rejected the testimony of all males under fourteen and females under twelve, of the blind and the deaf and the dumb, of slaves, of infamous persons, and those convicted of crime, of excommunicated persons, of poor persons, and of women in criminal cases, of persons connected with either party by consanguinity and affinity, or belonging to the household of either party, of the enemies of either party, and of Jews, heretics, and pagans.[5]

The grounds of incompetency, as developed through the centuries, may be broadly categorized under five I's:

1. *Interest:* A witness, whether or not a party to the controversy, if pecuniarily interested in the outcome of the cause, was not allowed to testify because of the temptation to falsify.
2. *Insanity:* A person considered insane was thought not to have the mental capacity to testify.
3. *Infancy:* A child was considered incompetent to understand the nature of an oath or to narrate with understanding the facts of what he had seen.
4. *Infidelity:* A person who did not believe in a Supreme Being who was a rewarder of truth and an avenger of falsehood was deemed incapable of taking an oath and therefore of testifying.
5. *Infamy:* Part of the punishment for crime in early common law was to render the guilty person infamous and, among other sanctions, he lost the right to testify in a court of law. In addition, a wife was not permitted to testify for or against her husband because in theory husband and wife were one (and that one was the husband).

A number of general basic reforms in trial procedure were accomplished during the seventeenth century, and major reforms also occurred during the nineteenth century, in a large measure stimulated by the writings of Charles Dickens. Today the rules on competency of witnesses have been replaced with the general principle that any person of "proper understanding" is a competent witness. The rules on competency have been converted into rules of credibility whereby nearly every proposed witness is allowed to testify, but on cross-examination his credibility may be impeached.[6] The question of competency, when raised, is a preliminary matter for the trial judge, whereas, once the witness is allowed to testify, his credibility is a question for the jury.

Cross-examination includes the right, as the courts say, "to place the witness in his proper setting and put the weight of his testimony and his credibility to a test, without which the jury cannot fairly appraise them."[7] The credibility of the witness is always relevant in the search for truth. Unquestionably, judges or juries are swayed by the relative attractiveness or unattractiveness of the parties or of the witnesses. As a consequence, cross-examination sometimes ends up being a smearing rather than a discrediting process.

The main lines of attack upon the credibility of a witness are: (1) showing that the witness on a previous occasion has made statements inconsistent with his present testimony; (2) specific contradiction, proving that some statement of fact made by the witness is in fact otherwise; (3) showing that the witness is biased by reason of such influences as kinship with one party or hostility to another, or motives of pecuniary interest, legitimate or corrupt; (4) showing a defect of capacity in the witness to observe, remember, or recount the matters testified about; (5) attacking the character of the witness; and (6) showing that the witness lacks the religious belief that would give the fullest traditional sanction to his obligation to speak the truth (now obsolete).

Under the rules of evidence, evidence of traits of the character of the witness other than honesty or veracity, or their opposites, is inadmissible to attack or support the credibility of the witness. Other character traits are not deemed sufficiently probative of a witness' honesty or veracity to warrant their consideration on the issue of credibility. Evidence of specific instances of a witness's conduct is inadmissible to prove a trait of character for the purpose of attacking or supporting credibility, with the exception that certain kinds of criminal convictions may be used, and specific instances indicating bias may be shown. Character evidence in support of credibility is admissible only after the witness's character has first been attacked, it being presumed that the witness is credible. The law of evidence on character for credibility of a witness is different than that on propensity to commit an act, which is discussed in chapter 6, on propensity.

The rules of evidence, including the method of challenging credibility, may appear to be an affront to common sense, but, as Chief Justice Vanderbilt once remarked, "The entire history of the law of evidence has been marked by a continuous search for more rational rules, first as to competency of witnesses, and then as to the admissibility of evidence."[8] The courts frequently point out that the rules of evidence are designed to obtain the truth by excluding unreliable testimony, such as hearsay, lay opinion, and biased testimony.

The concept of the Anglo-American system is that truth is best discerned by application of the rules of evidence in an adversarial proceeding, a procedure well suited to the popular American conditioning to games. The witness may feel that he goes through an ordeal just as harrowing as the ancient ordeal by battle. In various ways the witness is placed under stress, as it is believed that this will aid in the ascertainment of truth, whether the witness be shy or bold. The unfamiliar courtroom procedure and legal language are built-in stress factors. At one time, and still in most countries, the witness had to stand (from which derives the term *witness stand*), which increased his anxiety. The witness must swear to tell the truth, and he may be subjected to a vigorous cross-examination,[9] which lawyers say is "one of the principal and most efficacious tests which the law has devised for the discovery of truth."[10]

To be sure, there is need for a better test in the search for truth than the notion expressed by one trial judge—"wiping hands during testimony is almost always an indication of lying."[11]

The Rules of Evidence on Supporting or Challenging Credibility and the Role of Psychiatry

Testimony to support (as distinguished from challenging) the credibility or trustworthiness of a witness, *vouching* or *bolstering testimony* as it is sometimes called, is not permitted before the witness's credibility is attacked. Thus, a psychiatrist or other witness may not testify to support the believability of the complainant's or other witness's testimony before any attack has taken place on the witness's credibility.[12] To allow it would reconstruct the oath-helpers of the old common law (*oath-helpers* were usually relatives or close friends brought along by the parties to testify to their veracity rather than to the occurrence of facts). The decisions are beyond count that an expert or other witness (or prosecutor) may not render an opinion as to the veracity of a witness whose credibility has not been attacked.[13] Thus, in that type of case, the Oregon Supreme Court said in no uncertain terms, "We have said before, and we will say it again, but this time with emphasis—we really mean it—*no psychotherapist may render an opinion on whether a witness is credible in any trial conducted in this state.*"[14] The case involved a charge of attempted rape and attempted sexual abuse in which a psychotherapist was offered at the outset of the case by the prosecution to support the credibility of the victim, who had severe mental retardation. In oft-quoted words, as another court put it, credibility is an assessment to be made by the jury: "Credibility . . . is for the jury—the jury is the lie detector in the courtroom."[15]

What then about an attack on credibility? A witness may not be willing or may not be able to be truthful? What about ability to be credible? The late Dr. Henry Davidson, the well-known forensic psychiatrist, observed that the major clinical conditions affecting testimonial capacity are psychosis, mental deficiency, drug addiction, alcoholism, personality disorders, certain organic involvements of the brain, and sometimes certain forms of psychoneurosis. The person with schizophrenia, he claimed, can report an event with carbon-paper fidelity but may make an unreliable witness because of defective observation, distorted memory processes, or paranoid ideas. A senile psychotic person is unreliable as a witness because of frequent delusions of infidelity, impairment of memory, and delusions of ingratitude. The hypomanic witness is dangerous because his speech is plausible and positive; but the things he says can be the stuff of which dreams are made. A person with a drug addiction may not be a good witness because he may be under the toxic influence of a drug, or his testimony may not be reliable because the issue happens to concern his source of supply. An individual with a mental defect may make an adequate witness if the event is one that can be described simply, but since most events are complex, involving many subtle details, such a person would make a poor witness because of his deficient powers of observation and his inability to paint a vivid verbal picture. An alcoholic individual is often at the mercy of mixed and unpredictable emotions; the memory defects of chronic alcoholics are well known to psychiatrists. A psychopathic individual will twist his tongue to say anything. Among psychoneurotic people, recessional states or obsessional reactions may result in distorted interpretations of events.[16]

A paranoid patient, if not deteriorated, may appear to talk sense, but his testimony may be part of the delusional network. The late Ralph S. Banay, psychiatrist, said:

> The problem of the paranoid personality offers an illustrative example of the usefulness of psychiatric testimony, especially in civil cases. Paranoids who have a marked proclivity for getting into legal difficulties, often make a favorable appearance in court when not crossed or agitated, and they may impress the untrained observer as rational and sincere. They could conceivably mislead a judge, an attorney, or a jury into the sincerity of their claim but they would less likely deceive a clinically experienced psychiatrist. Similarly, in many borderline cases or in maladies of obscure manifestation, the root of the trouble may be discernible to the clinician although it is hidden from other observers.[17]

The Influence of Sigmund Freud

In the years preceding World War I, there was considerable interest in Europe, especially in Germany, in the psychology of testimony. Sigmund Freud in 1906 delivered a lecture to a law class at the University of Vienna entitled "Psychoanalysis and the Ascertaining of Truth in Courts of Law," in which he said:

> There is a growing recognition of the untrustworthiness of statements made by witnesses, at present the basis of so many judgments in Courts of Law; and this has quickened in all of you, who are to become judges and advocates, an interest in a new method of investigation, the purpose of which is to lead the accused person to establish his own guilt or innocence objectively. This method is of a psychological and experimental character and is based upon psychological research; it is closely connected with certain views which have only recently been propounded in medical psychology.[18]

The task of the therapist, Freud said, is the same as the task of the judge: he must discover the hidden psychic material. "To do this," Freud said, "we have invented various methods of detection, some of which lawyers are now going to imitate." However, Freud cautioned: "It is necessary to consider [the] points of difference in the psychological situation in the two cases."[19]

Was Freud, while cautious, naive in his assumption that psychoanalysis has something to offer in ascertaining truth in courts?[20] Although Freud failed his examination in medical jurisprudence—his only academic failure—he was a genius and generally was not naive about the law. At one time he seriously considered the study of law instead of medicine, perhaps because of the discrimination and persecution that he himself endured. When, in 1938, he was exiled from his country, he carried a manuscript on Moses, the supreme lawgiver of the Jewish people. He was intensely interested in law and criminal behavior, but apart from his lecture on psychoanalysis and the ascertainment of truth, he was exceedingly pessimistic about the possible application of psychoanalysis to the legal process.[21]

Shortly after Freud's lecture, in 1908, Hugo Munsterberg, professor of psychology at Harvard, in a book titled *On the Witness Stand,* suggested that prospective witnesses should be tested for reliability in experimental situations before their testimony be accepted in court. He severely criticized the legal profession for its failure to apply psychological principles to the evaluation of testimony.[22]

Dean John Wigmore, whose name is synonymous with the law of evidence, quickly took Munsterberg to task. In an article satirically cast in the form of a lawsuit against Munsterberg for defamation of the legal profession, Wigmore asked: "[W]here are the exact and precise experimental and psychological methods of ascertaining and measuring the testimonial certitude of witnesses and the guilty consciousness of accused persons?" Tell us, Wigmore urged, about the methods that might be applicable to judicial practice. Wigmore pleaded ignorance to the exactness and practical utility of these wonderful methods, which the legal profession had persisted in rejecting or ignoring.[23]

The *Hiss* Trial

Not until the spectacular *Hiss* trial of the early 1950s did the issue of psychiatric evaluation of a witness again attract much attention.[24] Alger Hiss, chairman of the Carnegie Foundation for Peace and the fair-haired boy of the Democratic party, was accused by Whittaker Chambers of passing secrets to Communists in the 1930s. The fate of the Democratic party was at stake, Senator Joe McCarthy having charged it with twenty years of treason. The defense offered psychiatric testimony designed to impeach the credibility of the government witness, Whittaker Chambers. In general, more leeway is given to the defense than to the prosecutor on the proffer of evidence. In this spirit, Judge Goddard ruled the psychiatric testimony admissible, saying:

> It is apparent that the outcome of this trial is dependent, to a great extent, upon the testimony of one man—Whittaker Chambers. Mr. Chambers' credibility is one of the major issues upon which the jury must pass. The opinion of the jury—formed upon their evaluation of all the evidence laid before them—is the decisive authority on this question, as on all questions of fact. The existence of insanity or mental derangement is admissible for the purpose of discrediting a witness. Evidence of insanity is not merely for the judge on the preliminary question of competency but goes to the jury to affect credibility.

Dr. Carl Binger, a renowned Harvard psychiatrist, testified that Chambers was a "psychopath with a tendency toward making false accusations." Binger testified that his opinion was based on "personal observation of Mr. Chambers at the first trial for five days and one day at this trial" and that "he had read plays, poems, articles, and book reviews by Mr. Chambers and books he had translated from German." Until the end of 1958, Chambers was senior editor of *Time*, but his family had no social or community ties—his grandmother, who went around the house brandishing a carving knife, was put in an asylum; his grandfather was an alcoholic; his father was unfaithful to his mother; his brother committed suicide; and Chambers himself made an unsuccessful attempt at "self-execution" (his own label) prior to the first *Hiss* trial. Binger gave his opinion after listening to a seventy-minute hypothetical question that accentuated unpalatable aspects of Chambers's life.

Binger was the author of what the Hiss defense called the "theory of unconscious motivation." He claimed that Chambers's accusations were rooted in an obsession with Hiss that began in the mid-1930s, when the two men had briefly known each other. At that time Chambers had developed feelings of love and admiration for the charming New Dealer, but when Hiss had cut off the friendship, the obsession allegedly metamorphosed into its opposite, an irrational hatred and rage that had set Chambers upon his vengeful course. That theory was also set out by psychoanalyst Meyer A. Zeligs in a 476-page book, *Friendship and Fratricide: An Analysis of Whittaker Chambers and Alger Hiss*.[25]

On cross-examination, Binger's testimony that Chambers was a "psychopathic liar" was discredited, and to this day that cross-examination, a high point of the *Hiss* trial, is used as a model at trial advocacy programs. On direct examination he had pointed out Chambers's untidiness, and on cross-examination he was made to acknowledge that the trait was found in many famous people. He testified that Chambers habitually gazed at the ceiling while testifying and seemed to have no direct relation with his examiner. The prosecutor in a turnabout told him: "We have made a count of the number of times you looked at the ceiling. . . . We counted a total of 59 times that you looked at the ceiling in 50 minutes. Now I was wondering whether that was any symptom of a psychopathic personality?" Shifting uneasily, Binger replied, "Not alone." He had testified that stealing was a psychopathic symptom and the prosecutor asked him, "Did you ever take a hotel towel or Pullman towel?" He replied, "I can't swear whether I did or not, I don't think so." The prosecutor thereupon asked, "And if any member of this jury had stolen a towel, would that be evidence of a psychopathic personality?"[26] The jury believed Whittaker Chambers, and a number of recent studies have vindicated Chambers.[27]

Assessing Credibility by Proof of Character

Historically, the most widely used method of attacking a witness as lacking veracity was by the personal opinion of those acquainted with him. Gradually, evidence of reputation in the community in regard to veracity replaced personal opinion.[28] In judicial opinions, the terms *reputation* and *character* in regard to veracity were (and are) often used interchangeably.[29]

The Federal Rules of Evidence and their counterparts in various states now allow not only reputation evidence but also opinion evidence as to the character of a witness (or in regard to truthfulness of an accused who testifies). This rule makes it clear that the belief of a character witness whose conclusion as to a witness's character is based upon personal acquaintance rather than on reputation will not be excluded. Rule 608(a) provides:

The credibility of a witness may be attacked or supported by evidence in the form of opinion or reputation, but subject to these limitations: (1) the evidence may refer only to character for truthfulness or untruthfulness, and (2) evidence of truthful character is admissible only after the character of the witness for truthfulness has been attacked by opinion or reputation evidence or otherwise.

With the change allowing opinion evidence, the question was raised: Should evidence in assessing credibility pass from the "crucible of the community" to the "couch of the psychiatrist"?[30] What is "character for truthfulness"? In the *Hiss* case, Dr. Binger looked at the character of Chambers in assessing his credibility. The question today is most frequently raised in sex-offense cases where the credibility of the accused or the prosecuting witness is in question. The victim frequently is a child of such early age that the report often cannot be considered reliable.

Is psychiatry capable of devising a test that can measure character for truthfulness? Test results of so-called lie detectors, truth serum, we may note, are uniformly rejected by the courts.[31] What about the psychiatrist as a walking lie detector? Davidson asserted that psychiatrists can play a major role in the administration of justice by appraising the credibility of witnesses.[32] There is a strong emotional component in the motivation and memory of witnesses, Davidson said, and thus credibility represents an area that should fall within the special field of the psychiatrist. Observation is selective and in large part dependent upon the condition of the observer as well as upon inner motivations. To give effective and accurate testimony, a witness must observe intelligently, remember clearly, speak coherently, and be free of any emotional drive to distort the truth. According to Davidson, the analysis of these traits should be a job for the psychiatrist.

Impeachment by use of medical records or other evidence indicating treatment for psychiatric problems, however, raises concerns over the personal privacy of the witness. The attack may be demeaning and unfair and would be precluded if the problems did not relate in important ways to capacity to observe or communicate.[33] In any event, suggestions are made that psychiatric diagnosis, whether based on clinical examination or courtroom observation alone, should be admitted whenever it is offered to show the unreliability of a witness. They would have the psychiatrist sit with a cross-examining attorney, at the counsel table, and thus "direct the cross-examination, thereby approximating a personal interview with the witness."[34]

In the courtroom the psychiatrist may observe the witness's mood, pressure of talk, stream of thought, brightness, content of thinking, and memory. But in the courtroom, where nobody believes anybody, the aura of cross-examination, with its concomitant implication of hostility and adversity of interest, provides an emotional climate far different from that of the ideal psychiatric interview. The witness feels attacked and abused, which immediately elicits defense mechanisms that can only shut out or distort pertinent psychiatric material.[35]

In the often-cited 1921 case, *State v. Driver,*[36] a twelve-year-old girl, upon whom an attempted rape was allegedly committed, was called as a witness. The defendant offered to show by the testimony of a psychiatrist that the girl was a "moral pervert" and not trustworthy. On the basis of courtroom observation, the expert was prepared to testify that he would classify the girl as a "lying moron" and unworthy of belief. The evidence was designed to be an attack upon her truthfulness, aimed at her credibility; and the inference to be drawn from the testimony, if it had been permitted, would have been that she was a habitual and confirmed liar because of her mental defectiveness. The court refused to hear the proffered evidence and said: "It is yet to be demonstrated that psychological and medical tests are practical and will detect a lie on the witness stand."

To vary the facts in *Driver,* consider the case of a woman in her late twenties who had a very poor childhood relationship with her father. She rarely dates. She meets a man at a social gathering, and following some pleasant conversation, he offers to take her home. She accepts, but he drives to a secluded spot. She reports that her memory was a "complete blank" from that time until she recalls finding herself in his arms. Let us assume that she regularly sees a psychiatrist and on the day following the alleged incident, she sees him and, still in a very anxious and overwrought condition, she tells him that she was raped. If this event becomes the subject of prosecution, does the psychiatrist have probative evidence to offer unavailable to others? The psychiatrist may know her to be hysterical, one who regularly mixes fact with fantasy, and he is also aware, we must assume, that hysterical women are not immune from rape.[37]

According to a number of decisions, testimony may be offered by a mental health professional as to whether the emotional or mental condition of the witness affected his *ability* to accurately perceive, recollect, or communicate information.[38] Testifying on the ability or capacity of a witness is a way to sidestep the rule against testifying on a witness's credibility. This tactic has passed muster in a number of cases. In *People v. Francis,*[39] the California Court of Appeals stated, "[The trial judge] did not understand the purpose of a psychiatric examination in the premises is not to determine whether, in the opinion of the psychiatrist, the witness is telling the truth in the case at bench but to determine whether or not the emotional or mental condition of the witness may affect his ability to tell the truth." In *United States v. Lindstrom,*[40] a decision that appears in a number of law school casebooks, the Eleventh Circuit observed,

> Although the debate over the proper legal role of mental health professionals continues to rage, even those who would limit the availability of psychiatric evidence acknowledge that many types of "emotional or mental defect may materially affect the accuracy of testimony; a conservative list of such defects would have to include the psychoses, most or all the neuroses, defects in the structure of the nervous system, mental deficiency, alcoholism, drug addiction and psychopathic personality."[41]

The court, reversing a conviction, said, "The jury was denied any evidence on whether [the] key witness was a schizophrenic, what schizophrenia means and whether it affects one's perceptions of external reality. The jury was denied any evidence of whether the witness was capable of distinguishing reality from hallucinations."[42]

Then too, the North Carolina Supreme Court said: "What could be more effective for the purpose than to impeach the mentality or the intellectual grasp of the witness? If his interest, bias, indelicate way of life, insobriety and general bad reputation in the community may be shown as bearing upon his unworthiness of belief, why not his imbecility, want of understanding, or moronic comprehension, which go more directly to the point?"[43]

Logically, an individual who does not have the ability to tell the truth ought not be allowed to testify. On taking the oath, the rules of evidence provide: "before testifying, every witness shall be required to declare that he will testify truthfully, by oath or affirmation administered in a form calculated to awaken his conscience and impress his mind with his duty to do so."[44] The witness swears that he will tell "the truth, the whole truth, and nothing but the truth." In early history, the oath was the factor that decided the issue, and it rendered a judicial decision unnecessary. Operating as proof, it was absolute proof. Originally, the oath was not incidental to testimonial evidence; rather the reverse was the case—witnesses supported the oath. Through the centuries, variations in oath formulae record the transition from proof by oath to testimonial proof.[45] Nowadays, just about anyone is competent to take the oath and testify, but the credibility or competency of the testimony is subject to attack.[46]

At trial in *United States v. Shay*,[47] the defense introduced psychiatric evidence to establish that the defendant was not capable of telling the truth. The defendant's confession to aiding and abetting an attempt to blow up his father's car was impugned. Psychiatrist Robert Phillips testified that the defendant suffered from "pseudologia fantastica," a condition that caused him "to spin out webs of lies which are ordinarily self-aggrandizing and serve to place him in the center of attention." The First Circuit noted that the cases excluding testimony on credibility involved "the more limited proposition that an expert's opinion that another witness is lying or telling the truth . . . exceeds the scope of the expert's specialized knowledge and therefore merely informs the jury that it should reach a particular conclusion," but the testimony in this case "would be beneficially informative to the jury." The court, after an examination of the law and the psychiatric literature, concluded that factitious disorders are an appropriate topic for expert testimony.[48]

In *United States v. Gonzalez-Maldonado*,[49] the government's case in regard to money laundering was heavily dependent on the taped conversations of one Julio Robles-Torres, and hence, in these unusual circumstances, the testimony of a psychiatrist that he had a mental illness that led to "verbosity," "grandeza," and exaggeration was admissible, as "an untrained layman would not be qualified to determine intelligently, and to the best degree the weight to place on the [defendant's] recorded statements without enlightenment from [the psychiatrist]."

Quite often, as a review of the cases would reveal, the admissibility of the expert's opinion depends on *doublespeak*, where one testifies about credibility in a roundabout way, and quite often, the defense is allowed to offer testimony that would be precluded if offered by the prosecution. Some examples may be noted. In an Oregon case, *State v. Gherasim*,[50] it was ruled that the trial court committed reversible error when it excluded a psychiatrist's testimony opining that a sexual assault victim had dissociative amnesia affecting her credibility to recall what took place. In this case the defendant, charged with attempted rape, asserted that he had not been the attacker, but had tried to help the victim when he found her on the side of the road. At trial, he sought to have a psychiatrist testify that inconsistencies in the victim's descriptions of what took place indicated she had developed dissociative amnesia, a condition that impairs one's ability to remember traumatic experiences.[51] The trial court, in excluding the testimony, said that it was a comment on credibility and that it was so within the common experience of jurors that it would not assist the fact-finding process. The defendant was convicted.

The Oregon Court of Appeals reversed, saying it was not a direct comment on the witness's credibility, and it concluded, "[T]he psychiatrist's testimony was no different from that of an ophthalmologist who testifies that an eyewitness has impaired vision or that of a psychologist who testifies that a witness suffers from dementia."[52] The Oregon Supreme Court (the same court that a decade earlier had exhorted against psychiatric opinion on credibility) affirmed, holding that the psychiatrist's testimony was admissible because it would be helpful to the trier of fact's understanding of the issue. No one witnessed the crime, so the jury could find the defendant guilty only if it considered the victim's version of events more credible than his. The defendant was entitled to present the testimony as evidence that would help the jury assess the victim's credibility, the court ruled, and it added that even though the psychiatrist did not give a detailed explanation of his diagnosis, this did not make it unhelpful to the jury.[53]

In *Westcott v. Crinklaw,*[54] a tort action brought under the civil rights law, it was claimed that the defendant, a police officer, was not justified in shooting the deceased. After the shooting, police officers questioned the defendant about the shooting at which time he said he "didn't know" if he was "in fear," and that he "did not know" if the deceased had a gun in his hand. At trial, to defuse these statements, a psychiatrist testified that the defendant suffered from post-traumatic stress syndrome after the shooting, and that it may cause a person to make inaccurate, unreliable, and incomplete statements. It was permissible for the expert to testify that the defendant suffered post-traumatic stress, but it was error, the Eighth Circuit ruled, for the expert to testify as to the reliability of the statements, as that was a credibility issue that should have been left in the exclusive province of the jury. The following is the testimony:

Q. Just focus upon the physiological, emotional and psychological reactions that the officer has afterwards in dealing with [a situation such as a shooting]?

A. Usually the heart is racing, adrenaline's flowing. Many officers report a numbness, an unrealness, difficulty making sense, an immediate attempt to try to reconstruct the events that have happened. Oftentimes incomplete, inaccurate or in some cases even total memory lapses of what's occurred.

Q. Is there a name applied in the psychological profession for this reaction that you're talking about?

A. Posttraumatic stress.

Q. Could you focus on how posttraumatic stress and these symptoms that you have listed would affect the police officer's ability to write reports and give oral accounts of what had happened.

A. Officers in this type of situation very frequently, in fact as a standard rule, give varying accounts . . . basically the ability to accurately report immediately following a situation's [*sic*] seriously impaired.

Q. Was Joseph Crinklaw exhibiting the symptoms of posttraumatic stress syndrome?

A. Yes, he was.[55]

In a similar holding in *Schutz v. State*,[56] which involved a charge against the defendant of aggravated sexual assault of his six-year-old child, the Texas Court of Appeals noted that the general capacity for truthfulness evidence admissible in a criminal proceeding includes evidence as to whether the person can distinguish between reality and fantasy or whether the person's physical or mental condition adversely affects that person's ability to accurately perceive or relate events, but the expert may not testify that the complainant's allegations "were not the result of fantasy," as that would constitute a direct comment upon the truth of the complainant's allegations. In a concurring opinion, Judge Womack questioned the drawing of the line:

> The Court's rule is [that] it is not error to admit testimony of the major premise of a syllogism (children who are fantasizing or being manipulated behave in certain ways) and the minor premise (this child did not behave in those ways), but it is error to admit testimony of the inevitable conclusion (this child was not fantasizing or being manipulated). Could jurors, who have heard the expert's opinion on the major premise and the minor premise, not be aware that the expert must hold the inevitable opinion about the conclusion? The conclusion is ineluctable after the premises have been admitted. It would be more natural and straightforward to admit the expert's opinion on the conclusion.[57]

Confirmation Hearings of Clarence Thomas

At the confirmation hearings of Clarence Thomas for the U.S. Supreme Court, psychiatric language abounded and there was much psychologizing about Thomas and Anita Hill. As everyone knows, Anita Hill accused Thomas of sexually harassing her in the early 1980s when Thomas was her superior at the Education Department and Equal Employment Opportunity Commission. According to the news reports, Senator John Danforth, who was Thomas's chief sponsor, called on Dr. Park Dietz, a leading forensic psychiatrist, for an opinion. Not having examined the parties, he declined to offer a diagnosis, but he provided a description of the disorder known as "erotomania," in which "the delusion is that another person, usually of a higher status, has romantic interest in the subject."[58]

Other psychiatrists were more willing to render a diagnosis without examination of the subject, though it may violate a dubious professional ethic. The Senate offices were inundated with calls, faxes, and letters from psychiatrists offering theories about Thomas and Hill, and both camps had psychiatrists prepared to take the stand.

A number of forensic psychiatrists at the annual meeting that year of the American Academy of Psychiatry and the Law privately expressed the opinion that Hill fits the diagnosis of erotomania. At the meeting, Dietz insisted that he did not pin a diagnosis on Hill but only provided "general information" about diagnostic categories. Another psychiatrist at the meeting expressed the opinion that Hill was lying, because, in this person's opinion, a woman traumatized as she allegedly was, despite the passage of ten years, would not testify in a dispassionate manner. Another found it surprising how she seemed to stick to a kind of script, and there was so little variation. To this psychiatrist, Thomas's anguish seemed honest and believable.

But there surely was no consensus among the psychiatrists offering an opinion in the corridors at the meeting. One psychiatrist, a renowned expert in the detection of deception, concluded that Thomas was lying, because an innocent person would have listened to Hill's testimony. Another psychiatrist noted Thomas's slip of the tongue, "I want to say *uncategorically* that I deny every allegation."

The opinions of these psychiatrists were as divided as lay opinion. Richard Starr, deputy managing editor of *Insight*, was not at the meeting, but he wrote, "The profession has reason to be thankful that the struggle to enlist psychiatry in the Hill-Thomas controversy remained mostly behind the scenes. Had the psychiatrists taken the stand for the two sides, the public indeed would have been educated—not about sexual harassment but about the limits of psychiatric expertise."[59]

Be that as it may, Harvard law professor Alan Dershowitz, in a luncheon address at the meeting, wondered about the character of Hill—using Thomas to advance herself over a period of ten years, and then turning on him. Character, after all, goes to credibility; she wanted to torpedo him, in secret no less, like an enemy submarine. Like Munsterberg years earlier, Dershowitz beseeched the psychiatrists to bring to bear their knowledge of human behavior to assist in the ascertainment of truth.

Is a psychiatrist better able to assess credibility when the witness has talked over the matter with him in psychotherapy? Theodor Reik, in his book *The Unknown Murderer*,[60] says that psychoanalysis has no contribution to make to evidence of guilt, as it is concerned with mental (inner) reality rather than material (outer) reality. A therapist does not ordinarily check on material reality. He is ordinarily concerned with the patient's view of the world rather than with what the world actually is. He does not cross-question the patient. Some therapists say that outside information about the patient interferes with their clinical work, and they prefer to close their eyes to it. They know the situation only through the eyes of the patient. Something more, then, is needed to test veracity. By and large, credibility is accorded witnesses who testify with confidence or certainty. The witness who testifies in that way is considered more likely to be accurate than the less positive witness. Intuitively, credibility is related to the confidence of the witness.

Reliability of Eyewitness Identification

The standard jury instruction on eyewitness identification states, in part: "Think about . . . how sure the witness was about the identification."[61] It also instructs: "How did the witness look and act while testifying?"[62] Jurors tend to assume that a witness who is nervous is lying. Witnesses who appear anxious tend not to be believed. Wiping one's hands while testifying is taken almost always as an indication of lying.[63]

Experiments, however, show that witnesses who say that they are 100 percent certain that the accused is the culprit are just as likely to be wrong as witnesses who are vague or ambivalent about their identification. Dr. Daniel L. Schacter, chairman of the psychology department of Harvard University, writes: "Even though juries believe confident witnesses more than uncertain ones, eyewitness confidence bears at best a tenuous link to eyewitness accuracy: witnesses who are highly confident are frequently no more accurate than witnesses who express less confidence. To make matters worse, eyewitness confidence can be inflated when a witness is told that another witness identified the same suspect, or when witnesses rehearse their testimony repeatedly during trial preparations. Clearly, eyewitness confidence is not set in stone at the time an event occurs."[64] The study of eyewitness identification by psychologists has a long history, particularly in the United States and England, going back at least to the early influential work of Hugo Munsterberg around the turn of the century.[65]

Can expert testimony be used to show that credibility is not related to the confidence of the witness? Since it is counterintuitive, as a witness who speaks with confidence is taken as trustworthy, expert testimony may be helpful to the jury. Testifying with confidence, albeit inaccurately, may stem out of various considerations. For example: A victim wanting revenge testifies with confidence. Witnesses who feel a social role in seeking justice help out by testifying with confidence. Witnesses who have been hypnotized testify with confidence. The delusional paranoid person has immutable beliefs even when they are contradicted by every shred of physical evidence. Then too there is the psychopath, or con artist, who is very convincing.[66]

When the expert testimony is about witnesses generally, however, the courtroom is turned into a classroom. And because the experts would be called in by the defense, they would tend to emphasize those experiments that would undermine any eyewitness's testimony.[67] In a civil case the burden of proof is a preponderance of the evidence, but in a criminal case the State has the burden of proving the case beyond a reasonable doubt, and as a consequence, testimony on eyewitness testimony, though of a general nature, can inject a reasonable doubt.

Psychologists, when allowed to offer expert testimony on eyewitness identification, trace the process of eyewitness observation and testimony from the initial acquisition phase (the initial observations of the event), the retention phase (when these observations are organized and stored in memory), the retrieval phase (when the eyewitness, on interrogation, reports on the observations as modified and then retrieved from memory). There follows the stage of matching and recognition, during which the images of the persons involved in the crime, retrieved from memory, are matched against a show-up, a photo lineup, or a live lineup. Then there is the formation of opinions and judgment by the eyewitness, and further identification and testimony in the courtroom.[68]

Psychologists claim that the rate of mistaken identification is significantly higher than most people tend to believe. They point out that witnesses have particular difficulty in making an accurate identification in cross-ethnic identification. By and large, the trial courts are left to decide whether they will allow expert testimony on the fallibility of eyewitness testimony (appellate courts usually defer to their judgment). The trial courts mostly rule against admissibility.[69] In a conference dealing with eyewitness testimony, Michigan trial judge Donald Shelton stated that he would be "reluctant to allow expert testimony on the credibility of eyewitnesses generally, but would allow it, of course, about a particular witness" (e.g., to show that the witness had poor eyesight).[70]

While usually deferring to the ruling of the trial court, the appellate court decisions nationwide reveal increasingly divided opinion. In *United States v. Hall*, the Seventh Circuit cited a long line of cases excluding expert testimony on eyewitness identification.[71] In *United States v. Rincon*,[72] the Ninth Circuit suggested educating jurors through cautionary instructions on eyewitness identification rather than by expert testimony. It would be less costly, said the court, and unlike expert testimony, it would not confuse or mislead the jury.[73]

In *United States v. Amaral*,[74] defense counsel sought to introduce the expert testimony of Bertram Raven, a social psychologist, on the effect of stress on perception and, more generally, on the unreliability of eyewitness identification. The trial court considered this a novel question and, in view of the prosecutor's opposition, requested both sides to submit authorities supporting their respective contentions. No appellate or trial court decision was cited by either counsel. The trial court excluded the proffered testimony on the ground that "it would not be appropriate to take from the jury their own determination as to what weight or effect to give to the evidence of the eyewitness and identifying witnesses and to have that determination put before them on the basis of the expert witness testimony as proffered."[75] The Ninth Circuit Court of Appeals, in an opinion of 1973, ruled that the trial court did not err in excluding the testimony. Six years later a trial judge allowed Dr. Raven's testimony, and he thereafter similarly testified a number of times, as have several other social psychologists.[76]

In *United States v. Fosher*,[77] the First Circuit in 1979 upheld a trial court's exclusion of such expert testimony on the ground that "the average lay juror, on the basis of his own life experiences and common sense, can make an informed evaluation of eyewitness testimony without the assistance of a psychologist, particularly when the jurors are aided by professional argument and skilled cross-examination."

The Arizona Supreme Court in 1983 took a different position in *State v. Chapple*,[78] the first appellate decision in the United States to rule that a judge abused his discretion in excluding expert testimony concerning eyewitness reliability. In this case, a murder prosecution in which the only issue was accuracy of eyewitness identification, the court held it error to exclude expert testimony offered by the defendant regarding factors relevant to identification accuracy: the effect of stress on perception, the rate of forgetting, *transference* (the tendency to believe a person was seen at a certain time and place when the person was actually seen at that place at a different time or at another place), and the tendency of witnesses who have talked together to reinforce one another's identifications. The court said, "Depriving [the] jurors of the benefit of scientific research on eyewitness testimony force[d] them to search for the truth without full knowledge and opportunity to evaluate the strength of the evidence. In short, this deprivation prevent[ed] [the] jurors from having 'the best possible degree' of 'understanding the subject' toward which the law of evidence strives."

A number of federal circuits have joined the ranks of *Chapple*. In *United States v. Downing*,[79] the Third Circuit in 1985 held that excluding expert testimony of the accuracy of eyewitness testimony is inconsistent with the liberal standard of admissibility under the Federal Rules of Evidence adopted in 1975. In this case, the defendant sought to adduce, from an expert in the field of human perception and memory, testimony concerning reliability of eyewitness identifications. The trial court refused to admit the testimony, apparently because it believed such testimony can never meet the helpfulness standard under the rules of evidence. The Third Circuit, holding error by the trial court, said that admission of such testimony is conditional, not automatic.[80]

The Fifth Circuit in 1986 concluded, "Expert testimony on eyewitness reliability is not simply a recitation of facts available through common knowledge. Indeed, the conclusions of the psychological studies are largely counterintuitive, and serve to 'explode common myths about an individual's capacity for perception.'"[81]

A number of state appellate courts have also joined the ranks of *Chapple*. In 1984 the California Supreme Court held that when an eyewitness identification "is a key element of the prosecution's case but is not substantially corroborated by evidence giving it independent reliability, and the defendant offers qualified expert testimony on specific psychological factors shown by the record that could have affected the accuracy of the identification but are not likely to be fully known to or understood by the jury, it will ordinarily be error to exclude that testimony."[82]

In 1988 in New York, a professor of psychology, an expert in the field of memory and perception, was permitted to testify at trial, on behalf of the defendant, as to the effect of stress on identification, the psychological effect of delay between the criminal event and subsequent identification, and the lack of correlation between a prospective witness's confidence and accuracy of recollection.[83] Then, in 2001, New York State's highest court ruled that expert testimony on the reliability of eyewitnesses could be admitted at trial. The court ruled such testimony "is not inadmissible per se" and warned judges not to exclude it solely on the grounds that jurors are already equipped to make an informed judgment.[84]

In 1991 the South Carolina Supreme Court, reversing a conviction, ruled it prejudicial error to exclude a psychologist's testimony on the unreliability of eyewitness identifications by white victims of black defendants.[85] The New Jersey Supreme Court, taking judicial notice of studies on the inaccuracy of cross-racial recognition, ruled in 1999 in a cross-racial rape case that even without expert testimony the jury should be told that cross-racial identifications may be less reliable than same-race ones.[86] The court urged caution:

> [W]e recognize that unrestricted use of cross-racial identification instructions could be counter-productive. Consequently, care must be taken to insulate criminal trials from base appeals to racial prejudice. An appropriate jury instruction should carefully delineate the context in which the jury is permitted to consider racial differences. The simple fact pattern of a white victim of a violent crime at the hands of a black assailant would not automatically give rise to the need for a cross-racial identification charge. More is required.[87]

There's a Russian saying: "He lies like an eyewitness." In sum and substance, expert testimony on eyewitness identification in general invariably puts into question its accuracy. It makes jurors wary of all eyewitness testimony. Therefore, the prevailing view would have it, as set out by Michigan Judge Donald Shelton, the appropriate role of the expert is to assist the attorney in attacking the credibility of a particular witness, not to discuss as in a classroom the credibility of eyewitnesses generally.

When testifying generally about eyewitness testimony, the expert may have no particular reason to challenge the witness. A cigar may be a cigar, as Freud said; in this case, an accurate witness. Ann Wollner, associate editor of the *Fulton County Daily Report*, writes: "The point is not to blunt the effect of all eyewitness identifications. The point is to inform juries when to be wary of them, when to look harder for corroborating evidence, when to remind themselves that just because the witness is certain doesn't mean the witness is right."[88]

Reliability of Messenger and Message

Who are unreliable as witnesses? Children are not very reliable. Individuals with a mental defect are unreliable. People with organic brain disease are unreliable. Psychotic individuals are unreliable. Psychopathic individuals are liars. Obsessive-compulsive people deny various things and obviously cannot be reliable about these things. The law is replacing the old categories whereby large groups of people were excluded as incompetent (those involved in the five I's of interest, insanity, infancy, infidelity, and infamy) with psychiatric categories. Popular disapproval of drug addiction and chronic alcoholism is so strong that it would be imprudent to introduce an addict as a witness. The courts say: "The habitual use of opium is known to utterly deprave the victim of its use and render him unworthy of belief."[89] "We believe it will be admitted that habitual users of opium, or other like narcotics, become notorious liars. The habit of lying comes doubtless from the fact that these narcotics users pass the greater part of their life in an unreal world, and thus become unable to distinguish between images and facts, between illusion and realities."[90]

A minority of courts take the position that addicts per se are predilected toward untruthfulness and, by so holding, the court takes away the jury's prerogative to assess credibility. In an old parallel, St. Thomas maintained with the authority of St. Chrysostom, *Daemoni, etiam vera dicenti, non est credendum* (the devil is not to be believed, even when he tells the truth). In the absence of other proofs, it was said, one must not proceed against those who are accused by devils. Christ imposed silence on the demons when they spoke the truth.

Obviously, though, no one can judge the reliability of a group of people as a class. It may be expeditious, but a great error, to generalize. For example, it is sometimes said that a person is alcoholic and then his testimony is excluded on the ground that alcoholics are not reliable witnesses. However, many persons are alcoholic (or have an alcoholic problem) even if they have not drunk any alcohol in a year or more. Many who have an alcoholic problem hold most responsible positions and are reliable when not drinking to excess. If all people who are addicted to alcohol were disqualified as reliable observers, we should disqualify many judges, lawyers, psychiatrists, and clergy. But suppose, instead of deciding on the basis of class, we consider each individual as an individual, try to understand his reactions to various situations, and examine the reliability of his stories under various circumstances. Would that be of any help in resolving disputes?

To estimate one's reliability presumably calls for knowing something of his unconscious motivation. Lawyers are specialists in verbal communication and usually deal with conscious motivation, but psychiatrists, specialized in listening with the third ear, are concerned about unconscious motivation and nonverbal communication. Of course, lawyers such as Perry Mason read between the lines, understanding unconscious motivation although not identifying it as such. Research has found, however, that even those allegedly skilled at lie detection, such as Jo-Ellan Dimitrius or police and customs officers, are no better than the general public at successfully detecting deception.[91] The only professional group found by psychologists to be consistently better than the general public at detecting deception were secret service agents selected for bodyguard duty, but their advantage appears to lie in the fact that they do not trust anyone.[92]

On a practical and personal level we all have known friends who are not alcoholic or addictive or psychopathic, but when they make out their federal income tax return, it becomes very questionable how far they are reliable. There may be times when perhaps no one is reliable. On the other hand, there are individuals who list every conceivable item on their tax return. They are scrupulously honest. We might say that they are reliably honest people. But the psychiatrist looks behind the scene and asks, "Why does this person have to be so honest?" Hamlet, looking behind his mother's pretenses, said: "The lady doth protest too much, me thinks."[93] When somebody is too scrupulously honest, he may be worried about his dishonest tendencies and distrustful of himself. An individual may be very compulsive, a perfectionist, always being sure that he is clean, et cetera, but when we look carefully at him, we may find that underneath his clean shirt, he has not bathed or wears dirty underwear.

What Is the Relationship of Man to His Message?

Philosophy traditionally has taught that words lead a life independent of the messenger. Under the correspondence theory of truth, the relation studied is strictly that between the statement and the world. Personalizing is ruled out under the well-known *ad hominem* objection. But, we may ask, does the ad hominem (or ad feminam) objection need reevaluation? What is the relationship between ideas, mentation, and biography? A person gains in understanding his own philosophy and ideas by examination and analysis of his mental processes and motivations, as psychoanalysis may attest. Do we likewise, in examining the philosophy or message of another person, add a dimension to it by understanding his personality? Man's message reveals the man; does man reveal the message?

Freud, although never concealing his identity as a Jew, often worried about protecting his new science from a closeness with the personality of its creator. Notwithstanding, psychoanalysis is often called a "Jewish science." David Bakan, in his book *Freud and the Jewish Mystical Tradition,* says that Freudianism is a laical transformation of the Jewish mystique. Bakan shows the decisive importance of Freud's Jewishness in the formulation of his work and the need to be aware of this fact for the best interpretation of his work.

That Immanuel Kant's neighbors set their clocks by his routine is not surprising to one having knowledge of his obsessive behavior. Arthur Schopenhauer too is known to have had obsessional neurotic personality. Jean-Jacques Rousseau's noble savage and state-of-nature philosophy may be linked with his psychosexual infantilism, which expressed itself also in exhibitionism, narcissism, and homosexual trends. Bishop George Berkeley's idealism and denial of reality may be tied in with his attitudes regarding excretion. Friedrich Nietzsche's mother was considered to be hereditarily tainted. G. W. Hegel's philosophical system begins where repression is involved, where thesis turns into antithesis. Albert Deutsch, in his book *The Mentally Ill in America,*[94] raises the issue of the credibility of Mrs. E. P. W. Packard, the famous crusader for the enactment of commitment laws, pointing to her psychiatric history.

Is such biography helpful to a study of a message? The roots of psychohistory, as it is called, may go back to Freud's *Leonardo da Vinci: A Study in Psychosexuality,* published in 1916, which analyzed the Renaissance genius on the basis of his work and from available records, and to his work, in 1939, *Moses and Monotheism,* which attempted to discover in Moses' life the origins of Christianity. Historian Robert G. L. Waite, in an afterword to Dr. Walter Langer's *The Mind of Adolf Hitler,*[95] praises

Langer's use of psychoanalytic principles in his secret wartime report to explore Hitler's psyche. The technique, he says, led not only to predictions of uncanny accuracy but to insights never provided by historians relying on traditional research methods.

It is necessary, it seems, to distinguish the various functions of language—informative, expressive, directive—that is, to transmit information, to express mood, and to promote action. Different criteria are relevant in evaluating each function: truth and falsehood for the informative; sincerity or insincerity, valuable or otherwise, for the expressive; and proper or improper, right or wrong, for the directive. Of all disciplines, there is the fullest exploitation of the genetic dimension in psychoanalysis; psychoanalysis links the present with genesis, but that is for the purpose of treatment. Genesis or biography has little relevance to a person's message if the message is to be evaluated in terms of truth and falsehood. The fact that Kant's neighbors set their clocks by his afternoon walks has no logical bearing upon the truth or informative significance of his philosophy. From his character we may surmise that he would ponder his statements at length, but the psychological origin of a belief, the motive for holding it, and the condition that leads to its acceptance are all irrelevant to its truth or falsehood. The chemist who formulated the benzene ring dreamed the night before of a snake with its tail in its mouth, but the theory of benzene rings is not to be equated with a dream about a snake. Freud's explanation of how belief in God is born need not be inconsistent with that belief. A message is substantiated by the available evidence, not by its genesis.

If the function of a message, however, is expressive and directive as well as informative (and usually all three functions are included), then, since criteria other than truth and falsehood are involved in its evaluation, biography should be not only helpful but essential to an evaluation and understanding of the message.

The court is essentially concerned with the informative function of a message; the fact that an individual may be an unreliable witness does not imply that he will be unreliable. No witness is completely unreliable at all times, just as the sky in Texas is not cloudy all the time. The courtroom process is a practical one, however, and when testimony conflicts and the evidence of a witness is crucial, the ad hominem approach may be practically, but not theoretically, justified. There are posters in some libraries that say, "If it is the truth, what does it matter who said it?" but in the mundane world, it is not only what a witness says but how he says it and who he is that is important. This is not epistemology. To look at a man, including his sacroiliac, is justified in terms of convenience and public policy, resulting in a rough sense of justice. It is a question of fair judgment; and it is thought that psychiatry may lend a hand in reaching that judgment. Yet, as pointed out, a number of factors in the legal setting make it difficult, perhaps impossible, to obtain a reliable psychiatric evaluation. A psychiatric evaluation usually rests on the complete trust between the patient and psychiatrist. This trust implies that the psychiatrist is totally on the patient's side, will not reveal information the patient has confided, and will be primarily concerned with the patient's welfare rather than that of society.

Psychiatrist as Detective

Freud in his lecture pointed out that a psychiatrist with a patient is different from a lawyer with a witness. A psychiatrist can allow himself to be hoodwinked, because if the psychiatrist does not show his belief in the patient, he will not be able to establish a successful relationship with him. The patient does not hurt the psychiatrist in hoodwinking him. Rather he is hurting himself. On the witness stand, however, in an attempt to hoodwink, the witness seeks to protect rather than to hurt himself.

A sharp poker player probably knows better than a psychiatrist whether a person is lying or, as the legal test puts it, whether the emotional or mental condition of the witness may affect his ability to tell the truth. A psychiatrist is a doctor, not a lie detector. A lawyer, too, has his shortcomings as an investigator. Although Perry Mason solves cases on the stand (he also solves cases out of court), skillful interrogation and evaluation can more readily take place in the police station than in the courtroom. Such a procedure, however, is against our tradition of law enforcement. In *Leyra v. Denno*,[96] working in a room that was wired, rather than rendering medical aid that the accused was expecting, the psychiatrist "by subtle and suggestive questions simply continued the police effort" to obtain a confession. The Supreme Court invalidated the confession and denounced the admission of statements made to the psychiatrist as "so clearly the product of mental coercion that their use as evidence is inconsistent with due process."

Refusal by a trial court to order a psychiatric examination of a witness has almost always been held not to be an abuse of discretion. When the court does order such examinations, what sanctions does it have available to compel compliance? Rule 35 of the Federal Rules of Civil Procedure and similar state statutes authorize trial courts to order a physical or mental examination of a party when his physical or mental condition is in controversy, that is, to determine injury sustained by a party in a personal injury suit. The rule probably does not include psychiatric examination as to credibility, especially of an ordinary witness, as credibility is not a matter directly in controversy. The power to order a psychiatric examination, although not provided by statute, may be said to be part of inherent or implied judicial power,[97] but even in rape cases some courts have been hesitant to order psychiatric examination of the complainant.[98]

Hypnosis is accepted by the American Medical Association as a valid medical technique. It is accepted by both the American Medical Association and the American Psychological Association as a legitimate psychiatric method of inquiry, but its use in the legal process at the pretrial or trial stage is highly dubious. The use of hypnosis or sodium amytal (truth serum) by District Attorney Jim Garrison on his star witness in the alleged investigation of President Kennedy's assassination was a national scandal; the defense was unaware that the witness had been hypnotized prior to this testimony. Not long before, Dr. Joseph Satten, then of the Menninger Foundation, at the behest of defense counsel, made a videotape of a sodium amytal interview of a person accused of murdering his wife. Its use was allowed at trial, resulting in the exculpation of the accused and was announced in television newscasts as a breakthrough in the search for truth.

An Ohio case is one of the few examples of in-court hypnosis (the subject in this case being the defendant).[99] On examination the hypnotist in the case contended that the subject had very little conscious control and would therefore be unable to lie in response to questions asked by the hypnotist. He testified that the statements made by a person under hypnosis would, with "reasonable medical certainty," be truthful and correct. He further stated that, except in the case of certain mental disorders, the use of hypnosis would find the facts. In this case, the court allowed the hypnotist to ask questions whenever it appeared that the defendant was having difficulty understanding the attorney's questions. The procedure has been criticized as inherently suggestive.

Whether hypnosis is done for forensic or clinical purposes, the individual who has been hypnotized may be precluded from testifying. A number of courts have ruled that witnesses who have undergone hypnosis cannot be allowed to testify because of the possibility of the pollution of their testimony or because they cannot be properly subjected to cross-examination. Based on a ruling by the California Supreme Court in *People v. Shirley*,[100] and followed by a number of other jurisdictions,[101] even a rape victim would not be allowed to testify about the rape if she had undergone hypnosis for any reason.[102] In so holding, these courts have restricted the use of hypnosis as an investigative device.[103] These rulings, however, do not preclude a defendant from giving testimony even though he has been hypnotized. With four justices dissenting, the U.S. Supreme Court held that a state may not bar the testimony of the accused. The majority opinion was "bottomed" on recognition of an accused's "constitutional right to testify in [his] own defense." It said: "A State's legitimate interest in barring unreliable evidence does not extend to *per se* exclusions that may be reliable in an individual case. Wholesale inadmissibility of a defendant's testimony is an arbitrary restriction on the right to testify in the absence of clear evidence by the State repudiating the validity of all post-hypnosis recollections."[104] In 1989, California joined the many other jurisdictions refusing to apply the exclusionary rule as to any witness to testimony about events recalled and recorded prior to the hypnotic session.[105]

Conclusion

To obtain an ideal climate for an effective psychiatric evaluation of a witness, a number of legal reforms would be necessary that might be unwise from either a social or legal point of view. If this is the case, then psychiatrists and jurists should realize the limitations that the legal procedure places on the accuracy and effectiveness of the psychiatric examination and, in turn, on the psychiatric opinion. But is psychiatry here being used more for its prestige value than for its probative value? And who is the reliable witness? Just thou and me, and I am not so sure about thee and thou is not so sure about me.

Notes

1. An early and graphic illustration is provided by the Song of Roland—the duel between Thierry and Pinabel to decide the fate of Ganelon. See C. Stephenson, *Mediaeval Feudalism* (Ithaca, N.Y.: Cornell University Press, 1942), p. 34.

2. L. Green, "Jury Trial and Mr. Justice Black," *Yale L.J.* 65 (1965): 482.

3. A. Goodhart, "A Changing Approach to the Law of Evidence," *Va. L. Rev.* 51 (1965): 759, 761.

4. S. Rowley, "The Competency of Witnesses," *Iowa L. Rev.* 24 (1939): 482, 491–92.

5. W. S. Holdsworth, *History of English Law* (London: Methuen, 3d ed. 1927).

6. It is unusual for a proposed witness today to be ruled incompetent and disqualified, except possibly in the case of the very young or the very old. That it does occur occasionally, however, is illustrated by the criminal case of People v. McCaughan, 49 Cal.2d 409, 317 P.2d 974 (1957), which involved the prosecution of a psychiatric aide at a state mental hospital charged with the involuntary manslaughter of one of the patients resulting from use of ex-

cessive force in spoon feeding. The patient, a seventy-year-old woman, had refused to eat, believing that the food was poisoned. The prosecutor offered, as witnesses against the accused, other patients at the hospital. Perhaps seeking to protect the aide from criminal conviction, the California Supreme Court ruled that the court below had committed error because these witnesses had a history of insane delusions regarding the same matter as did the deceased. The decision is criticized in Note, *So. Cal. L. Rev.* 32 (1957): 65.

In another criminal case, People v. Lapsley, 26 Mich. App. 424, 182 N.W.2d 601 (1970), patients in a state mental home were allowed to testify against the defendant for torturing another patient, a fourteen-year-old girl. The witnesses, all minors with mental problems, were examined by the judge prior to their testimony and deemed to be mentally competent for testimonial purposes.

7. J. W. Strong (ed.), *McCormick on Evidence* (St. Paul, Minn.: West, 4th ed. 1992), p. 77.

8. Robertson v. Hackensack Trust Co., 11 N.J. 304, 317, 63 A.2d 515, 521 (1949) (concurring opinion).

9. The chapter titles in one book on cross-examination include "Break Your Witness," "Step by Step Attack," "Witness on the Run," "The Kill," and "Shock Treatment." Chapter titles of another book include "The Deposition Game," "Hold the Eye of the Witness," "Roll with the Punch," "Don't Beat a Dead Horse," "When Should Mud Be Thrown?" "Making Speeches while Objecting," "Endure the Torment," "Indirectly Depreciating the Witness," "How about Sarcasm?" "Hot on the Trial," "Stay in Command," "Don't Telegraph Your Punch," "Preserve the Damaging Answer," and "You Are Awfully Expensive, Doctor." See J. A. Appleman, *Cross-Examination* (Fairfax, Va.: Coiner Publications, 1963).

10. C. B. Mueller & L. C. Kirkpatrick, *Evidence* (New York: Aspen, 2d ed. 1999), p. 1080. Here is what famed attorney Louis Nizer says of the efficacy of cross-examination in eliciting the truth:

> Cross-examination elicits the truth in innumerable ways: by forcing the witness to abandon his prepared positions and improvise under circumstances of stress; by inducing the witness to elaborate his inventions, by striking down the inventions and leaving the witness exposed, so that the truth is his only available alternative. The resourceful techniques for dislodging a lie are as many as an agile mind can devise. Cross-examination is the only scalpel that can enter the hidden recesses of a man's mind and root out a fraudulent resolve. Psychiatry and drugs may have given us new insights into motivation, but the classic Anglo-Saxon method of cross-examination is still the best means of coping with deception, of dragging the truth out of a reluctant witness, and assuring the triumph of justice over venality.

L. Nizer, *My Life in Court* (New York: Doubleday, 1961), p. 366.

11. Reversed in Quercia v. United States, 289 U.S. 466, 471–72 (1933). See also NLRB v. Universal Camera Corp., 190 F.2d 429, 430 (2d Cir. 1951). See the discussion in chapter 7, on body language.

12. In United States v. Azure, 801 F.2d 336 (8th Cir. 1986), the Eighth Circuit held that the trial court's admission of a pediatrician's testimony that an alleged victim of childhood sexual abuse "was believable" and that he could "see no reason why she would not be telling the truth in this matter" constituted reversible error. The court reasoned that, although some expert testimony may be helpful in child sexual abuse cases, "putting an impressively qualified expert's stamp of truthfulness on a witness' story goes too far." 801 F.2d at 339–40. But when the credibility of a witness has been attacked, an expert may bolster the credibility of the witness. Thus, in Schutz v. State, 957 S.W.2d 52 (Tex. App. 1997), where the defendant was accused of sexually assaulting his young daughter and argued that the charges were fabricated and a product of a bitter divorce, the state was allowed to call an expert to testify that the child's testimony was most likely not the product of manipulation or fantasy. The court held that the introduction of defense expert testimony that the child was coached opened the door to testimony by the state's expert that the child was not coached.

13. "It is well settled that an expert witness may not render an opinion as to a complainant's veracity. . . . Matters of credibility are to be determined by the trier of fact." People v. Miller, 418 N.W.2d 668 (Mich. App. 1987). In State v. Heath, 341 S.E.2d 565 (N.C. 1986), the North Carolina Supreme Court overruled a lower court decision allowing a psychologist to

state about a witness that there was "nothing in the record or current behavior to indicate that she has a record of lying." The appellate court held that the expert had gone beyond the scope of her expertise and had testified to the victim's credibility or record for truth or veracity, a matter upon which the jury was as qualified as the witness to decide.

14. State v. Milbradt, 756 P.2d 620, 624 (Ore. 1988) (emphasis by court).

15. United States v. Barnard, 490 F.2d 907, 912 (9th Cir. 1973), *cert. denied*, 416 U.S. 959 (1974). In United States v. Martinez, 253 F.3d 251 (6th Cir. 2001), the court held that a narcotics officer's testimony that a key informant-witness had always been accurate and truthful in prior instances constituted improper bolstering of the witness's testimony even though it did not amount to vouching for the witness's credibility. The court, quoting from United States v. Francis, 170 F.3d 546 (6th Cir. 1999), said, "[B]olstering occurs when the prosecutor implies that the witness's testimony is corroborated by evidence known to the government but not the jury." In People v. Farrar, 36 Mich. App. 294 (1971), the prosecutor in closing argument vouched for the credibility of police officers who had testified in the case. The prosecutor stated, "[Policemen] don't bring these things into court unless they really happened. . . . [T]he reason why the [defendant is] here is this actually happened as the officers testified that it happened." It was held error, but not reversible error in this case.

Supporting or bolstering the statements of a witness, however, passes muster when an expert makes use of the testimony in explaining an illness or causation. A physician may express an opinion about a patient's condition based, at least in part, upon belief in the credibility of the patient. Under Rule 703 of the Federal Rules of Evidence, a physician may base an opinion partly upon the "statements by patients and relatives," which means that the physician can believe the patient and base a diagnosis on that positive assessment of credibility. The only way to avoid having an expert rely on credibility is to ask the expert a hypothetical question specifying that certain facts must be assumed to be true—but the rules of evidence have done away with the need for hypothetical questions. Rule 702 uses a standard of helpfulness as the measure of admissibility, not whether the issue is beyond the ken of the jury. As will be noted, a number of courts have received testimony about the believability of child abuse victims, both in direct and indirect form. See M. A. Berger, "*United States v. Scop:* The Common-Law Approach to an Expert's Opinion about a Witness's Credibility Still Does Not Work," *Brooklyn L. Rev.* 55 (1989): 559.

16. H. Davidson, "Appraisal of the Witness," *Am. J. Psychiatry* 110 (1954): 481; see also his classic book *Forensic Psychiatry* (New York: Ronald Press, 1952).

17. R. Banay, "The Psychiatrist in Court," in R. Slovenko (ed.), *Crime, Law and Corrections* (Springfield, Ill.: Thomas, 1966), p. 433.

18. S. Freud, "Psycho-analysis and the Ascertaining of Truth in Courts of Law" (1906), in *Collected Papers*, vol. 2 (London: Hogarth Press, 1955), pp. 13–24.

19. Gandhi's observation is oft-quoted: "You can wake up a man who is asleep, but if he is merely pretending to be asleep, your efforts will have no effect upon him." K. Kripani (ed.), *All Men Are Brothers: Life and Thoughts of Mahatma Gandhi as Told in His Own Words* (New York: Columbia University Press, 1972).

20. Dr. Bernard Diamond interprets Freud's essay as saying that the use of psychoanalysis for obtaining legal evidence is of a highly experimental nature, that it should be utilized only in the spirit of research, and that the results should never be allowed to influence the verdict of the court. B. Diamond, "Criminal Responsibility of the Mentally Ill," *Stan. L. Rev.* 14 (1961): 59. That is not, however, my appreciation of Freud's essay.

21. In 1924, Colonel R. R. McCormick of the *Chicago Tribune* offered Freud $25,000, or anything he would name, to come to America to psychoanalyze Nathan Leopold Jr. and Richard Loeb, presumably to demonstrate that they should not be executed. Hearing that Freud was ill, William Randolph Hearst was prepared to charter a special liner so that Freud could travel undisturbed by other company. Freud declined both offers. Freud said, "I would say that I cannot be supposed to be prepared to provide an expert opinion about persons and a deed when I have only newspaper reports to go on and have no opportunity to make a personal examination." E. Jones, *The Life and Work of Sigmund Freud*, vol. 3 (New York: Basic Books, 1957), p. 103. See the discussion of the Bullitt-Freud book on Woodrow Wilson in P. Gay, *Freud: A Life for Our Time* (New York: Doubleday, 1989), pp. 560–62.

On another occasion, in a letter of November 4, 1920, from Vienna, to Dr. Emil Oberholzer, Freud said: "My appearance as expert witness in the litigation concerning [not against]

Wagner Jauregg didn't exactly mean the beginning of a new p[sycho]a[nalytic] era for Vienna. On the first day of the litigation, while I was present, the learned counsel behaved ever so sweetly. They used my absence the next day in order to bring out all the old, poisonous lies against p[sycho]a[nalysis]. I neither reacted myself, nor did I admit any reaction from another source. . . ." (Letter on file in the Menninger Museum, Topeka, Kans.).

22. H. Munsterberg, *On the Witness Stand* (New York: Clark Boardman, 1923).

23. J. Wigmore, "Professor Munsterberg and the Psychology of Testimony," *Ill. L. Rev.* 3 (1909): 999.

24. United States v. Hiss, 88 F.Supp. 559 (S.D. N.Y. 1950).

25. New York: Viking, 1967.

26. Fifteen years later, Dr. Binger, reflecting on the *Hiss* case, had this to say:

My opinion of Chambers and the Hiss trial was based almost entirely on the seven volumes of sworn testimony which he deposed in Baltimore before the trial. This was an exposition of a life so irregular and so delinquent that one could only interpret it as the story of a psychopath. Many of my psychiatric friends agreed with me in this decision, but were less willing to expose themselves to ridicule and contumely than I was. Perhaps they were wiser. But I never regretted my stand nor had I any serious doubts about Hiss's innocence. I did suspect some hidden, unconscious relationship with Chambers, of which I believe Hiss was unaware, and that this led him into an involvement which might well have looked like a conspiracy. He certainly never gave signed state documents to Chambers. . . . The prosecutor, Mr. Murphy, who looked like a dumb cop, turned out to be highly astute and tricky. He resorted to all kinds of subterfuges to trip me up. He tried to turn words around in my mouth and forced me to answer "yes" and "no" to questions framed by him in such a manner that the answers did not convey the meaning that I wished to present. I know that this is all part of the game, but it seemed to me shocking and preposterous. I had only one wish and that was to tell the truth and not lose my temper. I think I did both. Mr. Murphy, on the other hand, was determined to try to have me lose my temper and to distort the truth.

Correspondence of November 23, 1965, to Ralph Slovenko from Dr. Carl Binger, quoted with permission. See W. P. Hill, "The Use and Abuse of Cross-Examination in Relation to Expert Testimony: The Second Alger Hiss Trial," *Ohio St. L.J.* 15 (1954): 458.

27. See S. Tanenhaus, *Whittaker Chambers: A Biography* (New York: Random House, 1997); A. Weinstein, *Perjury: The Hiss-Chambers Case* (New York: Random House, 1978).

28. M. Ladd, "Techniques and Theory of Character Testimony," *Iowa L. Rev.* 24 (1939): 498.

29. See, e.g., Knode v. Williamson, 17 Wall. 586 (U.S. 1873).

30. These phrases are used in the state's "Supplemental Memorandum" to People v. Jones, 42 Cal.2d 219, 266 P.2d 38 (1954), a pioneering case in which the court said that if the crime on charge involved a trait indicating "a tendency toward sexual perversion," the accused may adduce expert psychiatric testimony that he is not sexually deviant. The case is critically examined in J. F. Falknor & D. T. Steffen, "Evidence of Character: From the 'Crucible of the Community' to the 'Couch of the Psychiatrist.'" *U. Pa. L. Rev.* 102 (1954): 980; but it is viewed with favor in W. Curran, "Expert Psychiatric Evidence of Personality Traits," *U. Pa. L. Rev.* 103 (1955): 999.

In Hopkins v. State, 480 S.W.2d 212 (Tex. Crim. App. 1972), the court said that the divergence of psychiatric opinion and its frequent inexactness render its value minimal in enabling the jury to decide the issue of credibility. In fact, the court said, the jury after being subjected to several conflicting, equivocating, and highly technical psychiatric opinions may actually be more confused than before. Another court failed to perceive the benefit to be gained from "an amateur's voyage on the fog-enshrouded sea of psychiatry." See Note, *St. Mary's L. Rev.* 4 (1972): 460.

31. See, e.g., Barrel of Fun v. State Farm Fire & Cas. Co., 739 F.2d 1028 (5th Cir. 1984); D. T. Lykken, *A Tremor in the Blood: Uses and Abuses of the Lie Detector* (New York: Plenum, 1998).

32. H. Davidson, "Appraisal of the Witness," *Am. J. Psychiatry* 110 (1954): 481. See also

H. B. Dearman, "Psychiatric Examination of the Client," *Tenn. L. Rev.* 32 (1965): 592; E. H. Moore, "Elements of Error in Testimony," *Ore. L. Rev.* 28 (1949): 293. See generally P. H. Hoch & J. Zubin, (eds.), *Psychopathology of Perception* (New York: Grune & Stratton, 1965); D. L. Schacter, *The Seven Sins of Memory* (New York: Houghton Mifflin, 2001); A. A. Smirnov, *Problems of the Psychology of Memory* (New York: Plenum Press, 1973).

33. In United States v. Butler, 481 F.2d 531 (D.C. App. 1973), the court said, "The question of when a trial judge should order a physical and psychiatric examination of a prosecution witness was directly considered by this court in United States v. Benn & Hunt. . . . We therefore explained that such an examination 'may seriously impinge on a witness's right to privacy; . . . the examination itself could serve as a tool of harassment;' and the likelihood of an examination could deter witnesses from coming forward . . . The resultant presumption against ordering an examination must be overcome by a showing of need." Quoting United States v. Benn & Hunt, 476 F.2d 1127 (D.C. App. 1973).

In People v. Carter, 128 Mich. App. 541, 341 N.W.2d 128 (1983), *rev'd on other grounds,* 42 Mich. 941, 369 N.W.2d 842 (1985), the Michigan Court of Appeals held that the trial court did not abuse its discretion on grounds of relevancy in precluding the defense from impeaching the complainant with evidence of her alleged drug use and psychiatric problems. A witness's history of prostitution was excluded in People v. Chaplin, 412 Mich. 219, 313 N.W.2d 899 (1981); the Michigan Supreme Court ruled that prior acts of prostitution have no relation to veracity. See C. B. Mueller & L.C. Kirkpatrick, *Evidence* (New York: Aspen, 2d ed. 1999), p. 541.

34. Comment, "Psychiatric Evaluation of the Mentally Abnormal Witness," *Yale L.J.* 59 (1950): 1324.

35. R. Monroe, "The Psychiatric Examination," in R. Slovenko (ed.), *Crime, Law and Corrections* (Springfield, Ill.: Thomas, 1966), p. 439.

36. 88 W. Va. 479, 107 S.E. 189 (1921).

37. In sex cases, less so today than previously, considerable latitude in cross-examination of witnesses is permitted, on the theory the accusation is easily made and difficult to disprove. The courts have permitted psychiatrists to expose mental defects, hysteria, and pathological lying of alleged victims of sex offenses. See, e.g., People v. Rainford, 58 Ill. App.2d 312, 208 N.E.2d 314 (1965); see S. Estrich, *Real Rape* (Cambridge: Harvard University Press, 1987); A. E. Taslitz, *Rape and the Culture of the Courtroom* (New York: New York University Press, 1997); M. G. Blinder, "The Hysterical Personality," *Psychiatry* 29 (1966): 227; R. Cavallaro, "A Big Mistake: Eroding the Defense of Mistake of Fact about Consent in Rape," *J. Crim. L. & Criminology* 86 (1996): 815; S. Estrich, "Rape," *Yale L.J.* 95 (1986): 1087; D. N. Husak & G. C. Thomas, "Date Rape, Social Convention, and Reasonable Mistakes," *Law & Phil.* 11 (1992): 95; C. L. Muehlenhard & L. C. Hollabaugh, "Do Women Sometimes Say No When They Mean Yes? The Prevalence and Correlates of Women's Token Resistance to Sex," *J. Personality & Soc. Psychol.* 54 (1988): 872.

38. Evidence Code, sec. 780(c) provides a specific basis for introducing evidence of mental illness on grounds that it affects the witness's "capacity to perceive, to recollect, or to communicate." In United States v. Partin, 493 F.2d 750 (5th Cir. 1974), it was held reversible error to refuse to admit evidence concerning the witness's mental condition and treatment where the witness entered a mental hospital five months before events to which he testified occurred, complaining of auditory hallucinations and belief that he was some other person. Impeachment with evidence of mental health problems is subject to the standard considerations of Rule 403, such as prejudice or confusion of the issues. United States v. Lopez, 611 F.2d 44 (4th Cir. 1979). Considerations of embarrassing the witness are not often mentioned, but undoubtedly are also taken into consideration. Some conditions, such as schizophrenia, have more probative value in showing that the witness's testimony may have been deluded than do others.

39. 5 Cal. App.3d 414, 85 Cal. Rptr. 61, 64 (1970).

40. 698 F.2d 1154 (11th Cir. 1983).

41. Quoting M. Juviler, "Psychiatric Opinions as to Credibility of Witnesses: A Suggested Approach," *Cal. L. Rev.* 48 (1960): 648.

42. 698 F.2d at 1168. In United States v. Barnard, 490 F.2d 907 (9th Cir. 1973), a case that is often cited in support of the inadmissibility of psychiatric and psychological testimony on challenging credibility, the court used a helpfulness approach in reaching its conclusion,

thereby anticipating the soon-to-be-enacted Federal Rules of Evidence. In *Barnard*, the defendant sought to impeach a codefendant, Dillon, who had testified for the government. The defendant called a psychiatrist and a psychologist, each of whom was prepared to testify that Dillon was a sociopath "who would lie when it was to his advantage to do so." The trial court's exclusion of the proffered expert testimony was affirmed. The appellate court looked at the specific facts of the case and found the probative value of the proffered evidence to be quite low: "The experts' knowledge about Dillon was limited, to say the least." The case is often cited, however, as though it stands for an absolute prohibition of expert testimony on credibility. For example, the court in United States v. Cecil, 836 F.2d 1431 (4th Cir. 1988) quotes extensively from *Barnard* as leading to the conclusion that "an opinion on the credibility of a witness by a psychiatrist is not allowable." 836 F.2d at 1442.

43. State v. Armstrong, 232 N.C. 727, 62 S.E.2d 50 (1950). In People v. Schuemann, 190 Colo. 474, 548 P.2d 911 (1976), the Colorado Supreme Court held it error to exclude psychiatric testimony that the prosecution witness was a delusional paranoid schizophrenic. In Mosley v. Commonwealth, 420 S.W.2d 679 (Ky. 1967), a rape case, the Kentucky Supreme Court held it error to exclude testimony of a psychologist that the complaining witness, who had been in a mental institution, was schizophrenic and had certain sex fantasies.

Yet taking a different view, the Oregon Supreme Court declined to overturn a trial court's refusal to order the complainant in a rape case to submit to psychiatric examination, saying: "It has not been demonstrated that the art of psychiatry has yet developed into a science so exact as to warrant such a basic intrusion into the jury process." State v. Walgraeve, 243 Ore. 328, 413 P.2d 6095 (1966). See R. J. O'Neale, "Court Ordered Psychiatric Examination of a Rape Victim in a Criminal Rape Prosecution—Or How Many Times Must a Woman Be Raped?" *Santa Clara L. Rev.* 18 (1978): 119.

44. Rule 603, Federal Rules of Evidence.

45. See H. Silving, "The Oath," *Yale L. J.* 68 (1959): 1328.

46. Rule 601, Federal Rules of Evidence.

47. 57 F.3d 126 (1st Cir. 1995).

48. The case is discussed in A. W. Scheflin & D. Brown, "The False Litigant Syndrome: 'Nobody Would Say That Unless It Was the Truth,'" *J. Psychiatry & Law* 27 (1999): 649.

49. 115 F.3d 9 (1st Cir. 1997).

50. 153 Or. App. 313, 956 P.2d 1054 (1998), *aff'd*, 329 Or. 188, 985 P.2d 1267 (1999).

51. Note that statements made by a declarant under hypnosis are not simply attacked for credibility but are excluded as incompetent evidence, yet statements made by a declarant who is suffering multiple personality disorder or is in a dissociative state are not excluded. See Dorsey v. State, 206 Ga. App. 709, 426 S.E.2d 224 (1992).

52. 956 P.2d at 1058.

53. The psychiatrist's proffered testimony was as follows:

Q. Doctor, have you had a chance to review a transcript of the testimony of [the victim] and the police reports in this case?

A. Yes.

Q. After reviewing the police reports, do you have an opinion with respect to [the victim], as to whether or not she suffered from any disorders as a result of the incident?

A. Yes, I do.

Q. Would you please tell us that opinion.

A. My opinion, from looking at this material, is that she suffers from a dissociative amnesic disorder.

Q. Why?

A. The information would seem to indicate a degree of amnesia or lack of memory of what went on, conflicting kinds of responses to what went on at that incident. She admits in her testimony, on a number of occasions, that she was very nervous, very frightened, that her mind wasn't functioning on what was going on, which is not uncommon after a traumatic incident of this nature, with normal people.

Q. Under our legal standards, the law does not permit a witness to testify with respect to the credibility or truthfulness of a particular witness. Are you testifying to that effect here?

A. No. I think that the transcript and the written statement of the victim, there is no question as to her, in my opinion, conscious intent at truthfulness. I think that the inconsistencies that appear in the police reports and in her own words, saying "I don't remember," validate my conclusion in terms of the diagnosis. I think she's credible in terms of her efforts to do the best she can. It's not a question of truthfulness. It's a question of her mental ability to perform, having experienced what would appear to be a traumatic encounter.

Q. If a group of individuals had suffered a traumatic encounter, such as being kidnaped and being sexually assaulted, would a person that had been subjected to that kind of an assault have emotional factors that would influence their ability to remember the events with precision?

A. Yes.

Q. And would this hold true with respect to a group of people, as opposed to a particular individual?

A. Yes.

The state's cross-examination included the following:

Q. Would you repeat for me the words of what you called the disorder—

A. Dissociative amnesia.

Q. Is it a condition or a disorder?

A. A condition.

Q. A condition. So when you say "dissociative amnesia," is that a diagnosis?

A. Yes.

Q. A medical diagnosis?

A. Yes.

Q. Are you making a medical diagnosis in this case?

A. It's a medical opinion.

Q. Can you tell the jury that you are diagnosing [the victim] with dissociative amnesia?

A. I can tell the jury that from the information available to me, it would appear that the condition pertains to the situation.

Q. But you can't tell them that you are diagnosing her as suffering from that?

A. Well, "suffering" is an ongoing term. It is related to this incident and her recall of the incident, it would seem, by virtue of my looking at her written information, the police information, and the transcripts of her testimony.

Q. So you are giving an opinion about her mental ability to perform when she is reporting the crime, her mental ability to—

A. Her recall of the incident.

Q. —to recall.

A. Memory.

Q. So you're saying that she cannot recall the incident?

A. Yes.

Q. And, in your opinion, she's confused about what she's saying?

A. It's my opinion she's confusing the events.

Q. The events? Which events?

A. The activities of the defendant here and the activities wherein she was assaulted.

Q. Well, where do you find the information on the police reports or her transcript that there were two separate events?

A. She describes different information than would apparently pertain to the arrest of the defendant.

Q. I'm sorry. I don't understand what you mean.

A. For instance, she doesn't describe a colored shirt, and defendant was apparently wearing one. She doesn't describe the seat belt in his car. There is quite a bit of questioning about a seat belt situation, and she says that the only type of seat belt she knows is one that goes around your waist. And then it looks like she's sort of led in questioning, one way or another. It would be my opinion that she's combining two incidents—one of a rescue situation, one of an attack situation—in her mind, retrospectively. It seems as though she's confused the two together.

Q. So the bottom line is that you don't believe the story she's telling?

A. I believe she believes what she's saying.

Q. But you believe that's not the truth?

A. I didn't say anything about truth. I believe she's telling the truth as she knows it.

Q. But you believe that it isn't the truth.

A. No. I believe that she has confused a situation because of an amnesic problem.

Q. You believe that there are other facts that she's not talking about?

A. No. I don't think she's doing anything volitionally.

Q. You believe that there are other facts that she is not able to talk about?

A. I think there are other facts that she doesn't remember.

On redirect examination, the defense asked the expert:

Q. Do you believe that [the victim's] conduct, as it relates to having this dissociative amnesia, compares with similarly situated people who have been subjected to violent attacks?

A. Yes.

985 P.2d at 1269–70.

54. 68 F.3d 1073 (8th Cir. 1995).

55. 68 F.3d at 1076.

56. 957 S.W.2d 52 (Tex. Cr. App. 1997).

57. 957 S.W.2d at 78. See chapter 7, on syndrome evidence.

58. A. P. Thomas, *Clarence Thomas: A Biography* (San Francisco: Encounter Books, 2001), p. 442.

59. R. Starr, "Psychiatrists Take Note: Sometimes Silence is Golden," *Insight,* Nov. 18, 1991, p. 40.

60. Reprinted in Reik's *The Compulsion to Confess* (New York: Farrar, Straus & Cudahy, 1959).

61. Michigan CJI 2d 7.8.

62. Michigan CJI 2d 3.6.

63. See NLRB v. Universal Camera Corp., 190 F.2d 429, 430 (2d Cir. 1951). See chapter 7, on body language.

64. D. L. Schacter, *The Seven Sins of Memory* (New York: Houghton Mifflin, 2001), p. 116.

65. H. Munsterberg, *On the Witness Stand* (New York: Clark Boardman, 1923).

66. In United States v. Pacelli, 521 F.2d 135 (2d Cir. 1975), *cert. denied,* 424 U.S. 911 (1976), the court refused to permit a psychiatrist to testify that the major prosecution witness was psychopathic and incapable of telling the truth. See G. L. Wells & E. Loftus (eds.), *Eyewitness Testimony: Psychological Perspectives* (Cambridge: Cambridge University Press, 1984).

In Farrell v. The Queen, [1998] 155 A.L.R. 652, the High Court of Australia in a 3–2 opinion held that the evidence of a psychiatrist about a complainant in a (homosexual) rape, aggravated sexual assault, and assault case should have been admitted and considered by the jury. The expert evidence, based on hospital and medical records (the psychiatrist did not personally examine the complainant), was that the complainant was suffering from "alcohol dependence and polysubstance abuse" as well as "personality disorder." The personality disorders referred to by the psychiatrist were antisocial personality disorder and borderline personality disorder. The most important aspect of the expert testimony was that persons with an antisocial personality disorder "are inherently less truthful than the average person." See I. Freckleton & T. Henning, "Lies, Personality Disorders and Expert Evidence: New Developments in the Law," *Psychiatry, Psychology and Law* 5 (1998): 271.

67. J. E. Bishop, "Memory on Trial: Witnesses of Crimes Are Being Challenged as Frequently Fallible," *Wall Street Journal,* Mar. 2, 1988, p. 1; see E. Loftus & K. Ketcham, *Witness for the Defense: The Accused, the Eyewitness, and the Expert Who Puts Memory on Trial* (New York: St. Martin's Press, 1991).

68. See G. L. Wells & E. F. Loftus (eds.), *Eyewitness Testimony: Psychological Perspectives* (Cambridge: Cambridge University Press, 1984); E. F. Loftus, *Eyewitness Testimony* (Cambridge: Harvard University Press, 1979); R. Buckhout, "Eyewitness Testimony," *Scientific American* 321 (1974): 23.

69. In United States v. Smith, 122 F.3d 1355 (11th Cir. 1997), the court said, "[W]e have

found only once case where a district court was reversed for excluding expert testimony regarding eyewitness reliability," and it cited United States v. Stevens, 935 F.3d 1380 (3d Cir. 1991). In *Stevens*, the trial court had admitted some of the expert's testimony, but the Third Circuit reversed because it had not admitted all of the relevant expert testimony. 935 F.2d at 1400. In *Smith*, a robbery case, an expert in eyewitness identification proposed to testify that eyewitness identification could be unreliable in the circumstances of the case: disguise, cross-racial identification, weapon focus, presentation bias in law enforcement lineup, delay between the event and the time of identification, stress, and eyewitness certainty as a predictor of accurate identification. The trial court excluded the proposed testimony in its entirety, holding that although the proposed testimony was relevant, it would not assist the trier of fact. Alternatively, the trial court held that the probative value of the testimony was outweighed by the possible danger of misleading or confusing the jury. The Eleventh Circuit affirmed. Some courts have held that such evidence would be admissible under "narrow" or "certain" circumstances. United States v. Harris, 995 F.2d 532, 535 (4th Cir. 1993).

70. Conference, "Dealing with Eyewitness Testimony," on Apr. 3, 1998, at the University of Michigan; reported in B. K. Hutson, "Eyewitness Testimony: Reliable or Misleading?" *Michigan Lawyers Weekly*, May 4, 1998, p. 1. In Michigan in 1978 in People v. Hill, 84 Mich. App. 90, 269 N.W.2d 492 (1978), the Michigan Court of Appeals concluded that the trial court had not committed reversible error in excluding expert testimony regarding the process by which people perceive and remember events, and in 1996, in People v. Carson, 217 Mich. App. 801 (1996), the Michigan Court of Appeals reaffirmed its decision in *Hill*.

71. 165 F.3d 1095 (7th Cir. 1999). In another line of cases, the Seventh Circuit finessed the issue by concluding that a trial judge has discretion to assess the utility of the evidence. United States v. Hall, 165 F.3d 1095 (7th Cir. 1999). In Carroll v. Otis Elevator Co. 896 F.2d 210 (7th Cir. 1990), the Seventh Circuit held it proper to admit the testimony of a psychologist about how colors influence children's behavior. In Krist v. Eli Lilly & Co., 897 F.2d 293 (7th Cir. 1990), the Seventh Circuit said, "An important body of psychological research undermines the lay intuition that confident memories of salient experiences . . . are accurate and do not fade with time unless a person's memory has some pathological impairment. . . . The basic problem about testimony from memory is that most of our recollections are not verifiable."

72. 28 F.3d 921 (9th Cir. 1994).

73. 28 F.3d at 925.

74. 488 F.2d 1148 (9th Cir. 1973).

75. 488 F.2d at 1153.

76. B. H. Raven, "Social Psychological Factors in Eyewitness Testimony," presentation at the conference on International Perspectives on Crime, Justice, and the Public Order, in St. Petersburg, Russia, June 21–27, 1992, sponsored by St. Petersburg University and John Jay College of Criminal Justice.

77. 590 F.2d 381 (1st Cir. 1979).

78. 660 P.2d 1208 (Ariz. 1983).

79. 753 F.2d 1224 (3d Cir. 1985).

80. See also United States v. Smith, 736 F.2d 1103 (6th Cir. 1984).

81. United States v. Moore, 786 F.2d 1308 (5th Cir. 1986).

82. People v. McDonald, 37 Cal.3d 351, 208 Cal. Rptr. 236, 690 P.2d 709 (1984); see B. Scheck, P. Neufeld, & J. Dwyer, *Actual Innocence* (New York: Signet, 2001); C. W. Walters, "Admission of Expert Testimony on Eyewitness Identification," *Cal. L. Rev.* 73 (1985): 1402.

83. People v. Beckford, 532 N.Y.S.2d 462 (N.Y. Sup. 1988). In another New York case, where it was alleged that the accused was a victim of mistaken identity, Dr. Elizabeth Loftus testified about academic studies on possible weaknesses in the way crime witnesses identify suspects. She reported that many studies show that when a weapon is visible, the eyes of a witness can focus more intently on it than on the criminal's face; that the memory of a witness can be corrupted by seeing files of police photos or new accounts of the crimes; and that witnesses tend to make more mistakes in identifying suspects whose racial identity is different from their own. C. Drew, "Conflicting Testimony on Identifying Assailant in Brick-Attack Trial," *New York Times*, Nov. 25, 2000, p. B-15.

84. People v. Lee, 2001 N.Y. Lexis 1061; reported in J. C. McKinley, "Court Opens Door to Data on Eyewitness Fallibility," *New York Times*, May 9, 2001, p. 27.

85. State v. Whaley, 305 S.C. 138, 406 S.E.2d 369 (1991).

86. State v. Cromedy, 158 N.J. 112, 727 A.2d 457 (1999).

87. 727 A.2d at 497.

88. A. Wollner, "Courts Eye the Problems of Eyewitness Identifications," *USA Today*, Sept. 29, 1999, p. 15. See also J. Gibeaut, "'Yes, I'm Sure That's Him,'" *ABAJ*, Oct. 1999, p. 26. The expert testifying skeptically about eyewitness testimony no matter what is really believed by the expert brings to mind Freud's skeptical-Jewish joke: Two Jews met in a railway station in Galicia. "Where are you going?" asked one. "To Cracow," was the answer. "What a liar you are!" replied the other. "If you say you are going to Cracow, you want me to believe you're going to Lemberg. But I know that in fact you're going to Cracow. So why are you lying to me?" S. Freud, *Jokes and Their Relation to the Unconscious*, trans. J. Strachey (New York: W. W. Norton), pp. 137–38.

89. State v. Concannon, 25 Wash. 237, 65 Pac. 534, 537 (1901). In drug cases, the truth is often battered, ignored, or shaded. From the sworn affidavit of police seeking a search warrant to a defendant's court testimony, what is said under oath often falls short of the promise to speak the whole truth and nothing but the truth. Indeed, in all criminal trials, drug cases or otherwise, lying is commonplace. As a rule, alcoholism or drug addiction are not deemed to be character traits that bear on truthfulness, but courts often admit such proof on the issue of capacity, that is, impairment of sensory and mental faculties. See United States v. Van Meerbeke, 548 F.2d 415 (2d Cir. 1976).

90. State v. Fog Loon, 29 Idaho 248, 158 Pac. 233, 236 (1916). The record in Irwin v. Ashurst, 158 Ore. 61, 74 P.2d 1127 (1938), discloses the following questions and answers:

> Q. As much as I hate to I am going to have to ask you a personal question. Do you use narcotics?
> A. No, sir, not now.
> Q. You don't use any at all?
> A. I was ill for ten years and the doctor gave me morphine at the time I had operations.
> Q. You don't use them at all any more?
> A. No.

During closing argument to the jury counsel said the following concerning the witness:

> Did you watch her? Did you see how she acted? The mind of a dope fiend, she was full of it, she was full of it when she testified; she showed she was an addict; why, she's a lunatic, she's a crazy lunatic; she's a dope fiend; how nervous she was all through her testimony; she's a hop head; her whole testimony is imagination and delusion from taking dope; all through her testimony she showed it; she testified she had taken dope for ten years, and you may well know that she is still taking it; you know when a person has taken dope for ten years, they never stop it; she's a dope fiend; she is lower than a rattlesnake; a rattlesnake gives you warning before it strikes, but this woman gives no warning; she is under a delusion from taking narcotics as long as she has; on account of her being an addict, I wouldn't believe a word she said.

91. See J. Dimitrius & M. Mazzarella, *Reading People* (New York: Ballantine, 1999).

92. R. Persaud, "Fifty Ways to Suspect Your Lover," *Financial Times*, Dec. 11, 1999, p. III.

93. Act 3, scene 2.

94. New York: Columbia University Press, 1949.

95. W. C. Langer, *The Mind of Adolf Hitler: The Secret Wartime Report* (New York: Basic Books, 1972), p. 217. Waite is the author of *The Psychopathic God: Adolf Hitler* (New York: Basic Books, 1977).

96. 347 U.S. 556 (1954).

97. State v. Butler, 27 N.J. 560, 143 A.2d 530 (1958).

98. The Indiana Supreme Court and the California Court of Appeals have ruled that in sex-offender cases, when there is reason to doubt the truth of the accuser's allegations, a psychiatric examination should be made of the accuser to ascertain his or her mental and emotional condition and whether they have bearing on the accuser's credibility. The rulings

stressed that the purpose of a psychiatric examination is "not to determine whether the witness is telling the truth, but to determine whether the emotional or mental condition of the witness may affect his or her ability to tell the truth." Easterday v. Indiana, 256 N.E.2d 901 (Ind. 1970); California v. Francis, 5 Cal. App.3d 414, 85 Cal. Rptr. 61 (1970). However, in Ballard v. Superior Court, 64 Cal.2d 159, 49 Cal. Rptr. 302, 410 P.2d 838 (1966), a physician who was charged with the rape of a patient to whom he allegedly administered an intoxicating narcotic or anesthetic substance in order to prevent resistance could not obtain an order requiring the complaining witness to undergo a psychiatric examination for the purpose of determining whether her mental or emotional condition had affected her veracity. The trial judge rejected the request, under the power of discretion invested in him whether or not to order such an examination. A failure to order an examination is rarely held to be an abuse of discretion. See M. Juviler, "Psychiatric Opinions as to Credibility of Witnesses: A Suggested Approach," *Calif. L. Rev.* 48 (1960): 648.

99. State v. Nebb, No. 39540, Ohio C.P., Franklin Co., June 8, 1962; discussed in Note, "Hypnosis in Court: A Memory Aid for Witnesses," *Ga. L. Rev.* 1 (1976): 269.

100. 31 Cal.3d 18, 181 Cal. Rptr. 243, 641 P.2d 775, *cert. denied*, 103 S. Ct. 13 (1982). The California Supreme Court was influenced by the testimony of Dr. Bernard Diamond. See B. Diamond, "Inherent Problems in the Use of Pretrial Hypnosis on a Prospective Witness," *Cal. L. Rev.* 68 (1980): 313. See also A. W. Newman & J. W. Thompson, "The Rise and Fall of Forensic Hypnosis in Criminal Investigation," *J. Am. Acad. Psychiatry & Law* 29 (2001): 75.

101. By a 4–3 decision, the Michigan Supreme Court held that the testimony of a hypnotized witness is inadmissible, absent proof by clear and convincing evidence that the testimony being offered was based on facts recalled and related before hypnosis. People v. Lee, 450 N.W.2d 883 (Mich. 1990). See also People v. Gonzales, 310 N.W.2d 306 (Mich. App. 1981). The North Dakota Supreme Court has ruled that a complaining witness whose memory is enhanced through hypnosis is not incompetent to testify, but rather, hypnosis affects the credibility of the testimony. State v. Brown, 337 N.W.2d 138 (N.D. 1983).

102. J. Swickard, "Woman Can't Testify in Sex Case," *Detroit Free Press*, Nov. 9, 1984, p. B-1; see also "The Trials of Hypnosis," *Newsweek*, Oct. 19, 1981, p. 96. In a prosecution in Cincinnati of Joseph Howard on a sexual battery charge, it was argued that "multiple personality people are notorious for faulty memory and are not credible." Associated Press news release, Oct. 10, 1994. In Dorsey v. State, 206 Ga. App. 709, 425 S.E.2d 224 (1992), the court held that the bar on statements in a hypnotic state does not apply to testimony of a victim in a dissociative state. The court said, "We believe the nonvolitional nature of a dissociative state itself makes statements made while in such a state inherently more reliable than statements made in a hypnotic trance." That view was rejected in Wall v. Fairview Hosp. & Health Care Services, 584 N.W.2d 395 (Minn. 1998).

The denial of the right of confrontation is also urged in cases of dissociative testimony. In the *Dorsey* case, a habeas corpus appeal was denied in a 2–1 decision in the Eleventh Circuit Court of Appeals. The court-appointed counsel for Dorsey argued without success that confrontation was denied because two personalities whom the victim, psychiatrist, and prosecutor acknowledged knew what occurred were not called, even though there was evidence that they had a different view of the situation. Is it possible to satisfy the Sixth Amendment right of confrontation without eliciting all known personalities? At one time there was a *res gestae* rule, requiring the prosecutor to call all known witnesses to the event. Dorsey v. Chapman, 262 F.3d 1181 (11th Cir. 2001). In Loeblein v. Dormire, 229 F.3d 724 (8th Cir. 2000), where the alleged sexual assault victim had been diagnosed with a multiple personality disorder (MPD), the court held that allowing one personality to testify to the abuse suffered by another did not violate the defendant's right of confrontation, though an expert witness testified that the various personalities of persons with MPD often do not have the same personal knowledge of what happened to the person. The court concluded that none of the victim's testimony indicated that she did not have firsthand knowledge of everything to which she testified, hence trial counsel was able to conduct a full cross-examination. See M. A. Miller, "The Unreliability of Testimony from a Witness with Multiple Personality Disorder (MPD): Why Courts Must Acknowledge the Connection between Hypnosis and MPD and Adopt a 'Per Se' Rule of Exclusion for MPD Testimony," *Pepperdine L. Rev.* 27 (2000): 193. Induction of a dissociative state followed by suggestion during interrogation caused a suspect to develop pseudomemories of raping his daughters and of participating in a baby-murdering Satanic cult. See R. J. Ofshe, "Inadvertent Hypnosis during Interrogation: False Confession Due to Dissociative State; Mis-Identified Multiple Personality and the Satanic Cult Hypothesis," *Int'l J. Clin. & Experimental Hypnosis* 40 (1992): 125.

103. K. M. McConkey & P. W. Sheehan, *Hypnosis, Memory, and Behavior in Criminal Investigation* (New York: Guilford, 1995); see A. W. Scheflin & J. L. Shapiro, *Trance on Trial* (New York: Guilford, 1989); A. W. Scheflin, H. Spiegel & D. Spiegel, "Forensic Uses of Hypnosis," in A. K. Hess & I. B. Weiner (eds.), *Handbook of Forensic Psychology* (New York: Wiley, 2d ed. 1999); M. T. Orne, "The Use and Misuse of Hypnosis in Court," *Int'l J. Clin. Exp. Hypnosis* 27 (1979): 311.

104. Rock v. Arkansas, 483 U.S. 44 (1987).

105. People v. Hayes, 49 Cal.3d 1260, 265 Cal. Rptr. 132, 783 P.2d 719 (1989). If the proponent of a witness who has been hypnotized is permitted to introduce untainted, pre-hypnotic memories, proof that these memories existed prior to hypnosis should go beyond a subject's posthypnotic recollections of the timing of his memories, since such posthypnotic recollections may not be accurate. Contreras v. State, 718 P.2d 129 (Alaska 1986).

6

Propensity
and
Other
Acts
Evidence

The characteristics of people, we know, make them more or less likely to respond in particular ways to events or circumstances. There is usually regularity of behavior and a link between personality and behavior. Thus, an introverted individual is unlikely (unless under the influence of drugs or alcohol) to tell loud jokes and become the center of attention at a gathering, but this behavior would not be unusual for a histrionic extrovert.

The law, however, on the admissibility of character evidence, otherwise known as *propensity* evidence, is bewildering, even to the most experienced trial lawyer, and that results from the conflict between the sporting theory of justice, calling for the exclusion of propensity evidence, and the reality of the probative value of the evidence, calling for its admissibility. In excluding such evidence, the rule contradicts everyday experience—for example, employers routinely ask people furnishing references to discuss the applicant's character and prior behavior—but out of a sporting theory of justice, evidence of the accused's character is not admissible to show propensity. However, the option is given to the accused to open the door to that kind of evidence about himself and also about the victim.

In any event, either party can offer evidence of *habit* to show propensity or lack thereof, or evidence of other crimes, wrongs, or acts, not to show propensity but to establish motive, opportunity, intent, preparation, plan, knowledge, identity, or absence of mistake or accident.

All in all, to be sure, this body of laws is bewildering. Their meaning is frequently the topic of litigation and of proposals for change. Supreme Court Justice Robert Jackson once described it as a "grotesque structure"—"archaic, paradoxical and full of compromises and compensations by which an irrational advantage to one side is offset by a poorly reasoned counter-privilege to the other."[1]

Of course, even without the formal introduction of character evidence, the focus on propensity (or credibility) by way of character takes place at the very outset of a trial. In ordinary thinking, character is judged by appearance, so defense attorneys go to great length to make their clients attractive and presentable. In defending the Menendez brothers, who brutally killed their parents, Leslie Abramson called them "my boys" and dressed them in Oxford shirts. Numerous studies have pointed out that attractive individuals are found guilty less often and sentenced less harshly. Similarly, individuals who appear "loving and warm" or show remorse are treated more leniently than those who seem "cold and unapproachable."[2] People are categorized and judged by characteristics such as social class, race, gender, education, empathy, marriage, parenthood, religion, political ideology, profession, physical stature, or affiliations with various groups. Fairly or unfairly, consciously or unconsciously, people are judged by these characteristics.[3]

Then too, apart from appearance, an indictment, which is read to the jury, may name the accused by an alias or nickname (such as "Sammy the Bull" or "Jimmy the Weasel"). References to character are made during closing argument, which, though not evidence, tends to be persuasive. Time and again, during closing argument, the prosecutor resorts to name-calling that implies propensity, such as referring to the accused as an animal, beast, snake, cunning rascal, or filthy pervert, or by referring to the accused by his nickname. Name-calling may result in reversible error.[4]

The basic principle of law, as a matter of policy, is that evidence of character is irrelevant in judging the merits of a case. In oft-quoted language: "The business of the court is to try the case and not the man; and a very bad man may have a very righteous case."[5] The rationale is that, in the ordinary case, be it civil or criminal, character evidence has a remote bearing as proof regarding whether the act in question has or has not been committed. In a criminal case, the accused is put on trial for a specific deed; he need not defend an entire life history. Character evidence is usually laden with prejudice, distraction, time expenditure, and surprise, although it may have some value as circumstantial evidence.

That having been said, the rule is then swallowed up by exceptions. Lady Justice's blindfold has as many holes as a poor man's stockings. Character evidence is admissible not only when character is in issue (as in cases of defamation, a fit parent for child custody, or entrustment of a vehicle to an incompetent driver) but also, at the option of the accused, for the purpose of suggesting an inference about the commission of the criminal act. An accused claiming mistaken identity may offer evidence of *inconsistent personality*, that is, that he is not the type of person who would or could commit the charged crime. In the event that the accused initiates the use of character evidence, the prosecutor may then rebut it.

In the penalty phase of a capital case, assessment of dangerousness is a factor in the imposition of the penalty (discussed in chapter 15, on the death penalty). Psychopathy (also known as *sociopathy* or *antisocial personality*) is highly correlated with violence proneness. Some research suggests that the diagnosis has no predictive power independent of that provided by the number and types of past antisocial acts committed by the individual. The evidence is about character in issue, so other acts may be shown, but in any event, the rules of evidence are not applicable in sentencing.

Pertinent Trait of Character

At trial, on character or propensity evidence, the rules of evidence provide: "Evidence of a person's character or a trait of character is not admissible for the purpose of proving action in conformity therewith on a particular occasion, except: . . . Evidence of a *pertinent trait* of character offered by an accused, or by the prosecution to rebut the same" (emphasis added).[6] What is a "pertinent" character trait depends largely on the nature of the charges. In a battery prosecution, a court would likely exclude evidence that the accused is "honest" but admit proof that he is "peaceable" or "nonviolent." The cases generally hold that "law-abidingness" is a trait of character and is pertinent to any criminal accusation (as distinguished from good character generally).[7]

Joseph Brill, whose colorful style and record of success made him one of New York's eminent criminal lawyers, would—with a straight face—portray his racketeer clients as being "pure as snow." In the civil wrongful-death trial, O. J. Simpson took the stand and, gently nudged along by his attorneys, painted a version of himself as a loving husband, father, and all-round good guy who could not have fatally slashed his former wife, Nicole Brown Simpson, and her friend Ronald Goldman.[8]

How limiting is evidence of pertinent trait of character? In *Shelton v. State*,[9] a murder case, the Arkansas Supreme Court set out a summary of the law:

> The prevailing view limits pertinent traits to those involved in the offense charged—proof of honesty in a theft charge or peacefulness in a murder charge. . . . However, it is necessary to allow evidence of defendant's character, as testimony that the general estimate of his character may be so favorable the jury could infer he would not be likely to commit the offense charged. . . . [In this case,] the defense proffered opinion evidence that Shelton was not a discipline problem and had an aversion to violence. Both of these traits—probative of law-abiding and nonviolent nature—have been traditionally admissible in a murder case and should have been admitted.

Upon a defendant's introduction of character evidence, the question arises whether the defendant is entitled to an instruction that positive character evidence, standing alone, can be sufficient to create a reasonable doubt. On this score, the courts are in dispute. Some courts have held that such an instruction is never necessary and often, if not always, is improper because it misleads the jury. As the Seventh Circuit put it:

> The "standing alone" instruction conveys to the jury the sense that even if it thinks the prosecution's case compelling, even if it thinks that defendant is a liar, if it also concludes that he has a good reputation this may

be the "reasonable doubt" of which other instructions speak. A "standing alone" instruction invites attention to a single bit of evidence and suggests to jurors that they analyze this evidence all by itself. No instruction flags any other evidence for this analysis—not eyewitness evidence, not physical evidence, not even confessions. There is no good reason to consider *any* evidence "standing alone."[10]

Other courts, however, have stated that a standing alone instruction is required where the defendant has presented character evidence.[11] Most courts, though, have held that while a defendant is not entitled to a standing alone instruction, it is ordinarily not an abuse of discretion to give one.[12]

Following discussion of evidence of habit and evidence of other crimes or wrongdoing, we will discuss character evidence of inconsistent personality.

Evidence of Habit

Evidence of the habit of a person is relevant to prove that the conduct of the person on a particular occasion was in conformity with the habit. It is propensity evidence. Unlike evidence of character, which is admissible only at the option of the accused, evidence of habit, under Rule 406 of the Federal Rules of Evidence and its counterpart in state rules, may be offered initially by either the prosecutor or the accused. In this context, *habit* refers to the type of nonvolitional activity that occurs with invariable regularity. Habit, a consistent method or manner of responding to a particular stimulus, has a reflexive, almost instinctive quality. In an oft-quoted statement, Diogenes (412–323 B.C.) said, "Habit is second nature."[13] Put another way, habit is a "trait jacket," but it does not have to amount to what is clinically known as a *compulsion* (an act that unless performed causes anxiety).

The commentary of the advisory committee in the Federal Rules of Evidence, quoting from McCormick's textbook on evidence, contrasts habit with character:

> Character and habit are close akin. Character is a generalized description of one's disposition, or of one's disposition in respect to a general trait, such as honesty, temperance, or peacefulness. "Habit," in modern usage, both lay and psychological, is more specific. It describes one's regular response to a repeated specific situation. If we speak of character for care, we think of the person's tendency to act prudently in all the varying situations of life, in handling automobiles and in walking across the street. A habit, on the other hand, is the person's regular practice of meeting a particular kind of situation with a specific type of conduct, such as the habit of going down a particular stairway two stairs at a time, or of giving the hand-signal for a left turn, or of alighting from railway cars while they are moving. The doing of the habitual acts may become semi-automatic.[14]

The courts give contrasting interpretations of habit. The character versus habit categories may lead to controversy because the categorization of the evidence determines its admissibility. A person who wakes up regularly at 6 A.M. can be described as an early riser or the person can be said to have a habit of getting up early. A person may be described as having a lustful inclination or as having a habit of sexually molesting children. Specificity provides the key: if specific conduct usually results from specific stimuli, the conduct is called a habit.

Habit is said to deal with the regularity of certain behavior whereas character is said to deal with inner nature. In *Perrin v. Anderson*,[15] the U.S. Tenth Circuit Court of Appeals held that five instances of violent encounters with the police are sufficient to establish habit of reacting violently to uniformed police officers. In the matter of informed consent, physicians have established it by evidence of habit of "routinely and regularly" informing patients of certain risks involved in a therapy.[16] In *Weil v. Seltzer*,[17] however, the U.S. Court of Appeals for the District of Columbia required that the conduct be "nonvolitional" to qualify as habit. In this case, testimony that a doctor had the habit of prescribing steroids to allergy patients was rejected. Likewise, the District of Columbia court held testimony concerning religious practices not admissible because "the very volitional basis of the activity raises serious questions as to its invariable nature, and hence its probative value." In *Levin v. United States*,[18] the court excluded a rabbi's testimony as to the defendant's habit of being home on the Orthodox Jewish Sabbath; the crime was committed on a Sabbath. In a South Carolina case, evidence that a motorist was involved in numerous collisions during a three-year period and is "an habitually reckless driver" was held not admissible as habit evidence.[19] A pattern of intemperate drinking is usually inadmissible to prove drunkenness on a specific occasion, but distinctive drinking practices that are routinely followed may qualify as a habit.[20]

Evidence of Other Crimes or Wrongdoing

As a general principle, under Rule 404(b) of the Federal Rules of Evidence and its counterpart in state rules, evidence of other crimes or wrongdoing may not be used to show propensity, but may be used to establish motive, opportunity, intent, preparations, plan, knowledge, identity, or absence of mistake or accident. The defendant has no option in excluding evidence of other crimes or wrongdoing when offered to establish one or other of these purposes, just as the defendant has no option in excluding evidence of habit. Thus, in the case of William K. Smith of the Kennedy family, who was charged with rape, the court excluded the testimony of three women who would testify that Smith sexually attacked them years ago. The other alleged acts would have been to show propensity and did not fall under one of the exceptions in Rule 404(b) for the admission of evidence of other wrongdoing.[21] Likewise, in a medical malpractice case, reference to other acts of malpractice may not be made unless designed to establish one of the exceptions.[22]

In recent years, a preponderance of the courts have sustained the admissibility of testimony as to prior or subsequent similar crimes, wrongs, or acts in cases involving sexual offenses such as incest and statutory rape. Among the grounds relied on for the admissibility of such evidence is that it is admissible to show motive or to show plan, with various phrases being used by the courts to describe those concepts. Motive may be inferred from previous occurrences having reference to and connection with the commission of the offense. Thus, in *People v. McConnell*,[23] the Michigan Court of Appeals said that when addiction is offered as the motive for robbery, past drug convictions may be used to show that the defendant is an addict. Motive, if established, would tend to rebut a contention that the defendant was at home and knew nothing of the crime charged against him. In *Elliot v. State*,[24] the Wyoming Supreme Court held that one who has committed acts of pedophilia could well be recognized as having a motive to commit such acts as are complained of by a victim.

Given the concern over sexual assault and child molestation, the U.S. Congress in 1994 enacted Rules 413–415 in the Federal Rules of Evidence, effective 1995, that marked a significant change in the long-established doctrine restricting evidence of other crimes or wrongdoing as propensity evidence against a defendant in a criminal case. Under Rule 413, to show propensity, evidence of the defendant's commission of another offense of sexual assault is now admissible in a criminal case where the defendant is accused of sexual assault. Rule 414 similarly allows evidence of the defendant's commission of a prior offense of child molestation in a case where the defendant is accused of child molestation. Rule 415 provides that such evidence is also admissible in civil cases "for damages or other relief" predicated on a party's commission of an offense of sexual assault or child molestation. To date, only a few states have enacted provisions similar to Rules 413–415.[25] As the Wyoming decision in *Elliot* would indicate, Rule 404(b) already provides an adequate basis for admitting prior crimes evidence in those cases where it is most needed, such as to establish motive, intent, preparation, plan, absence of mistake, and similar points.[26]

In a justification of the adoption of Rules 413–415, Chief Judge Richard Posner of the Seventh Circuit wrote:

> Most people do not have a desire to sexually molest children. Between two suspects, only one of whom has a history of such molestation, the history establishes a motive that enables the two suspects to be distinguished; prior-crimes evidence is admissible to prove motive. Unlike a molester, a thief, unless he is a kleptomaniac, does not have an overwhelming desire to steal. Theft is merely instrumental to his desire for money, and there are many substitute instruments. Committing a prior theft does not show that a defendant "likes" theft and so does not furnish a motive for his committing theft with which he is charged.[27]

On another occasion, Judge Posner noted that the principle under discussion is not limited to sex crimes. He wrote:

> A "firebug"—one who commits arson not for insurance proceeds or revenge or to eliminate a competitor, but for the sheer joy of watching a fire—is, like the sex criminal, a person whose motive to commit the crime with which he is charged is revealed by his past commission of the same crime. . . . No special rule analogous to Rules 413 through 415 is necessary to make the evidence of the earlier crimes admissible, because 404(b) expressly allows evidence of prior wrongful acts to establish motive. The greater the overlap between propensity and motive, the more careful the district judge must be about admitting under the rubric of motive evidence that the jury is likely to use instead as a basis for inferring the defendant's propensity, his habitual criminality, even if instructed not to.[28]

The exceptions in the Rules of Evidence allowing evidence of other crimes, wrongs, or acts that tend to establish motive, opportunity, intent, preparation, plan, knowledge, identity, or absence of mistake or accident can, like an accordion, be contracted or expanded. When expanded, the exceptions swallow the rule and, in effect, allow other acts to show propensity. Consider, for example, the decision by the Michigan Court of Appeals in *People v. Hoffman*,[29] on the admissibility of other acts to show motive. To establish that the defendant's actions were motivated by his misogyny (hatred of women), the prosecutor was allowed to present the testimony of two of the defendant's former girlfriends that the defendant had beaten and threatened them. One of the witnesses testified that the defendant told her that "women are all sluts and bitches and deserve to die." Writing the opinion, Judge Griffin turned to *Black's Law Dictionary* for a definition of motive: "Cause or reason that moves the will and induces action. An inducement, or that which leads or tempts the mind to indulge a criminal act." Judge Griffin noted that "the distinction between admissible evidence of motive and inadmissible evidence of character of propensity is often subtle." He offered the following hypothetical to clarify the distinction:

> In mid-afternoon, on the outskirts of a rural Michigan village, an African-American man is savagely assaulted and battered by a white assailant. The assailant neither demands nor takes any money or property. The assailant is a total stranger to the victim. The defendant is later apprehended and charged with the attack. After the arrest, the prosecutor discovers that the defendant had been involved in several other violent episodes in the past, including bar fights, an assault on a police officer, and a violent confrontation with a former neighbor.

Under this scenario, "[a]bsent a proper purpose (such as to prove a common plan, scheme, or other exception), these other acts evidence would be inadmissible on the basis that its only relevance is to establish the defendant's violent character or propensity towards violence," Judge Griffin wrote, and he went on to say:

> However, if we were to add to this scenario that all of the defendant's prior victims were African-American and that defendant had previously expressed his hatred toward blacks, then the evidence of defendant's prior assaults would be admissible to prove defendant's motive for his conduct. By establishing that the defendant harbors a strong animus against people of the victim's race, the other acts evidence goes beyond establishing a propensity toward violence and tends to show why the defendant perpetrated a seemingly random and inexplicable attack.

Judge Griffin then turned to a New Jersey decision in support of the hypothetical. In *New Jersey v. Crumb*,[30] the defendant was charged with hitting an elderly black man in the head and kicking and stomping on his face and chest. The defendant allegedly told a friend that he had beaten "an old black bum . . . just because he was there." The victim was not robbed. At trial, the prosecutor sought to introduce letters, verse, and drawings found in the defendant's apartment containing language that showed that defendant was a racist. In overruling the trial court's ruling excluding the evidence, the New Jersey Superior Court said that "some of the written material directly expresses defendant's hostility toward and hatred of black people and his concomitant desire to see them dead. This material is compellingly powerful evidence of a motive which helps to explain an otherwise inexplicable act of random violence." The New Jersey court also noted that, without the evidence of the defendant's bigotry, "a jury would not know the context [of the victim's] death and might be resistant to the idea that a young man purposely would inflict deadly harm on an elderly stranger without any apparent reason such as theft or substantial provocation."

Judge Griffin agreed with the analysis in *Crumb* and "adopt[ed] it as our own." Accordingly, he wrote:

> [W]e hold that in the present case the trial court did not abuse its discretion by admitting the other acts evidence for the purpose of establishing defendant's motive. Similar to the evidence of racism in *Crumb*, evidence that defendant hates women and had previously acted on such hostility establishes more than character or propensity. Here, the other acts evidence was relevant and material to defendant's motive for his unprovoked, cruel, and sexually-demeaning attack on his victim. . . . Absent the other acts evidence establishing motive, the jurors may have found it difficult to believe the victim's testimony that defendant committed the depraved and otherwise inexplicable actions.

Inconsistent Personality Evidence

What about inconsistent personality evidence? When opening the door to character evidence, the accused seeks to establish innocence by evidence of no propensity to commit the crime. His personality, it is argued, is inconsistent with the crime, but just how probative to an issue is inconsistent personality evidence?[31] It is a common mode of thinking.[32]

Not surprisingly, however, the use of expert psychological testimony to establish innocence by evidence of an inconsistent personality is controversial. There is considerable but conflicting jurisprudence as to whether an expert may be asked, "Doctor, do you have an opinion with a reasonable degree of psychological certainty whether or not the defendant has personality characteristics that would make it impossible for him to have committed the criminal act?"[33] The evidence is pertinent, as required under the rules of evidence, but is it probative?

The Third Circuit, in a narcotics case where the defense was entrapment, held it error to exclude testimony of a psychologist that the defendant had a unique susceptibility to inducement.[34] In a prosecution for pointing a gun at an officer who had been trying to arrest the defendant, the Seventh Circuit held it error to exclude testimony of a psychiatrist that the defendant was more likely to injure himself than to direct his aggression at others.[35] In a prosecution for statutory rape and contributing to the delinquency of a minor, the Alaska Supreme Court allowed psychiatric testimony that in view of defendant's personality it was improbable that he committed the offenses charged.[36]

The Arizona Supreme Court, in a murder prosecution, held it error to exclude, as bearing on premeditation, the testimony of a psychologist that the defendant had difficulty dealing with stress and that in a stressful situation his reaction would be more reflexive than reflective.[37] The Iowa Supreme Court allowed psychiatric evidence that one of the participants in a murder was a passive-dependent individual who would allow others to assume responsibility.[38] In a Wisconsin case where the defendant was charged with first-degree murder and first-degree sexual assault, the defendant contended that a conviction for a sexual assault requires the victim to have been alive during the alleged intercourse and that there was inadequate evidence to support a finding that the victim was alive if and when the intercourse occurred. Testimony was allowed that an assailant without necrophilic tendencies could have intercourse with his victim without realizing that she was dead.[39]

On the basis of a psychiatric report that the accused was a nonviolent man who found sexual satisfaction in consensual relationships, a Canadian judge was convinced that the accused did not rape his former girlfriend.[40] Then, too, many believed that Supreme Court nominee Clarence Thomas was "not capable" of the sexual harassment claimed by Anita Hill.[41] Woody Allen, confronted with an allegation by Mia Farrow that he sexually molested their adopted seven-year-old daughter, Dylan, in the attic of her summer home, said, "I have never been in an attic. I'm a famous claustrophobic; wild horses couldn't get me into an attic."[42]

The common-law rule that proof of the defendant's character is allowed only by evidence of reputation in the community, and not by opinion evidence, was first abandoned when the California Supreme Court in 1954, in *People v. Jones*,[43] allowed the defense to submit expert psychiatric opinion evidence of the personality traits of the defendant as bearing on the unlikelihood that he had committed the crime of sexual abuse of a nine-year-old child. This was also one of the first cases in which a psychiatrist was allowed to testify to an opinion based in part on a narcoanalysis interview with the defendant. The evidence submitted by the defendant was a negative diagnosis, that is, that he was *not* a sex deviate or sexual psychopath.[44]

In *People v. Stoll*,[45] a California child sexual abuse case, the trial court excluded a psychologist's opinion that the defendant had a normal personality function, with a low indication of antisocial or aggressive behavior, thus making it unlikely that he would commit the charged acts. The opinion was based on a combination of personality tests, interviews with the defendant, and the psychologist's professional experience. Moreover, the psychologist testified on voir dire as to the statistical accuracy of the personality tests used, but he noted that the tests were not the sole determinant of his opinion. He pointed out that the MMPI (Minnesota Multiphasic Personality Inventory)—the primary test—is "always" used by psychiatrists and psychologists to diagnose patients at various stages of clinical treatment, and it also is "frequently" given in "employment and re-employment situations in conjunction with a polygraph," and in "promotion studies in the industry," as well as to inmates and job applicants in correctional facilities. The trial court's exclusion of the evidence was appealed to the state supreme court.

On appeal, the prosecutor argued that the testimony should be admitted only if valid empirical evidence supported both the existence of a rapist profile and that the defendant did not fit that profile. In reversing the trial court, the state supreme court held that there was no need to subject the testimony to the kinds of tests *(Frye* and *Daubert)* applied to screening scientific or technical evidence. As a rule, empirical or statistical evidence is not a prerequisite or helpful in the determination of the admissibility of expert testimony in the soft sciences. The court said, "No precise legal rules dictate the proper basis for an expert's journey into [an individual's] mind to make judgments about his behavior."[46]

Opposition to Psychiatric Testimony on Inconsistent Personality

In the face of some support for allowing psychiatric testimony on inconsistent personality, there is at the same time substantial opposition to it. Illustrative is the New Jersey case, *State v. Cavallo*,[47] where the defendant, charged with rape, sought to introduce expert psychiatric testimony that he did not have psychological traits common to rapists. In rejecting the proposed testimony, the court said: "The danger of prejudice through introduction of unreliable expert testimony is clear. While juries would not always accord excessive weight to unreliable expert testimony, there is substantial danger that they would do so, precisely because the evidence is labeled 'scientific' and 'expert.'" The court noted that the testimony was based on two unproven and unreliable premises: (1) rapists have particular mental characteristics, and (2) psychiatrists can, by examination, determine the presence or absence of these characteristics.[48]

The U.S. Second Circuit excluded expert psychiatric testimony, that the defendant suffered from "dependent personality disorder," that was offered to show that the defendant did not know that certain property was stolen. It was excluded as unhelpful and as an opinion on the ultimate issue of mental state. The court, in a 2–1 decision, said that "the imprimatur of a clinical label was neither necessary nor helpful for the jury to make an assessment of [the defendant's] mind." In a lengthy dissent, the senior judge on the court argued that the proffered expert testimony should have been allowed.[49]

The U.S. First Circuit rejected a defendant's offer of psychological testimony in a fraud case that he was "too naive to know" as not being "character evidence" within the meaning of the rules of evidence.[50] In a prosecution for shooting at a helicopter, the Fifth Circuit held it not error to exclude testimony of defense witnesses that, based on psychological tests, the defendant was nonviolent and not likely to shoot at a helicopter. "This character trait was as plainly within the 'ken of lay jurors,' . . . as it was a proper subject for lay testimony."[51] The Tenth Circuit also said that generalized testimony about the influence of personality traits is excludable as within the common knowledge and experience of lay jurors.[52]

In *United States v. MacDonald*,[53] the defendant, Captain Jeffrey MacDonald, a physician, was on trial for the murders of his wife and daughters. The trial judge excluded psychiatric testimony that the defendant's "personality/emotional configuration" was inconsistent with violent crime as confusing and misleading. The defense sought to offer the testimony of leading forensic psychiatrists who contended that MacDonald's personality was inconsistent with the crime. Dr. Seymour Halleck said at the end of a 24-page report, "On the basis of my clinical experience as a psychiatrist and criminologist and on the basis of my knowledge of theories and research into the area of violence, I would conclude that there is only an extremely remote possibility that a person of his type would commit a crime of this type. Certainly, no one with Dr. MacDonald's personality organization has ever been known to commit such a crime." Dr. Robert Sadoff, who examined Dr. MacDonald in 1970, 1975, and 1979, says he would say again what he said before: "Dr. MacDonald's personality is not consistent with the type of personality likely to commit this crime. I think that it is very unlikely that he could have done this. I base this statement today, not only upon my previous examination of him, but upon his total actions and behaviors over the 13 years since the murder." A prosecution psychologist, Hirsch Lazaar Silverman, disagreed, "This man is a pathological narcissist. His personality is such that under certain pressures he would revert to violence."[54]

Profiles

"Round up the usual suspects," said the police chief in the film *Casablanca*. The suspects had a profile of criminality. Generally speaking, the term *profile* describes observable behavior patterns as distinguished from physical or psychological characteristics known as *syndrome evidence* that we discuss in chapter 7. Put briefly, *syndrome* means a group of symptoms or signs typical of an underlying cause or disease.

The term *profile* is loosely used not only as to its meaning but also as to its application. The process of inferring distinctive personality characteristics of individuals responsible for committing criminal acts had commonly been referred to as *criminal profiling*, but it has also been referred to, among other less common terms, as *behavior profiling, crime-scene profiling, criminal-personality profiling, offender profiling,* and *psychological profiling*. A distinction must be drawn as to the purpose for which the profile is used (as a basis to justify a search and seizure or as evidence at trial to establish guilt or innocence). The use of race as an indicia of suspicion, which has been called *racial profiling* (or "driving while black"), is to be distinguished from profiling that looks at the specifics of a particular crime in order to draw a portrait of the culprit.

In one use of the term, a profile is a list of characteristics compiled by a law enforcement agency, which have been found through experience to be common characteristics of those engaged in a certain type of criminal activity. The most common example is a drug courier profile, but officers also employ other profiles for specific criminal activity.[55] The primary use of profiles is in police investigation, where they are a tool for identifying crime suspects.[56] The Immigration and Naturalization Service also uses profiles of illegal immigrants.[57]

What about the use of profiles to establish guilt or innocence at trial where the rules of evidence apply? Larry King invited experts to discuss whether O. J. Simpson fits the profile of a stalking spousal killer, and Simpson's prosecutors did the same. In the 1980s, many therapists adopted the view that child molesters often have a psychiatric condition called *paraphilia*. They also established a battering parent profile (a "battering parent" frequently exhibits low empathy, short temper, and lack of self-esteem). At times, profiles have been admitted as evidence.[58] A number of courts have allowed testimony that the accused does or does not share the characteristics of individuals who typically abuse children.[59] In a case where medical testimony regarding the battering parent profile as well as the battered child profile was admitted at trial, the Minnesota Supreme Court said:

> We hold that the establishment of the existence of a battered child, together with the reasonable inference of a battering parent, is sufficient to convict defendant herein in light of the other circumstantial evidence presented by the prosecution. It is very difficult in these prosecutions for injuries and death to minor children to establish the guilt of a defendant other than by circumstantial evidence. Normally, as was the case here, there are no eyewitnesses. . . . The prosecution properly presented to the jury the psychological framework which constitutes a battering parent. It

did not attempt to point the finger of accusation at defendant as a battering parent by its medical testimony. Rather, it presented sufficient evidence from which the jury could reasonably conclude that defendant fit one of the psychological patterns of a battering parent.[60]

Three years later, the Minnesota Supreme Court determined that battering parent evidence was not an indispensable element of the state's case in a child abuse prosecution but held it was not reversible error to receive it into evidence.[61] Then, five years later, the same court ruled that the prosecution is not permitted to introduce evidence of a battering parent profile or to establish the character of the defendant as a battering parent unless the defendant first raises that issue.[62] The court stated, "We feel this finding is required until further evidence of the scientific accuracy and reliability of syndrome or profile diagnoses can be established."[63] In sum and substance, we would say: many people fit a profile, but few act accordingly. As evidence, it would be misleading as there would be too many false positives.

In *undue familiarity* cases the psychiatrist (or other defendant) may seek to offer evidence that he is not the type of person who would engage in that type of behavior. In his experience of evaluating, treating, and consulting on many cases of physician sexual misconduct, Dr. Glen Gabbard, then of the Menninger Foundation, found that the vast majority of the physicians involved fall into four psychodynamically based categories: (1) lovesickness, (2) masochistic surrender, (3) predatory psychopathy and paraphilias, and (4) psychotic disorders.[64] There is no way, however, to establish the known or potential rate of error in the classifications used to establish profile evidence, therefore this evidence would be excluded at trial. Exploiting therapists cover a wide range of people from the very good to the very bad, as Gabbard's findings indicate, hence profile evidence does not offer much to the jury in a particular case.[65]

Even assuming scientific reliability of character evidence, in a criminal case the accused may keep the evidence out by not introducing evidence of character (or by not pleading not guilty by reason of insanity). Once the defendant introduces evidence of good character, however, as noted, the prosecution then may rebut it with evidence of bad character.[66] The defendant, however, has no option in excluding evidence of habit or evidence of other crimes, wrongs or acts that tend to establish motive, opportunity, intent, preparation, plan, knowledge, identity, or absence of mistake or accident.[67]

Evidence of the Victim's Character

A defendant in a criminal case who alleges a defense that rests upon the conduct of the victim may offer evidence of the victim's character to prove that conduct. Under the rules of evidence, evidence of a pertinent character trait of the victim is admissible when it is offered by the accused to prove that the victim acted in conformity to his or her character.[68] Thus, when a defendant alleges self-defense, evidence of the victim's character trait of violence may be admissible for one or two purposes. First, the evidence may be offered on the issue of who was the aggressor. As John Wigmore, the leading authority on the law of evidence, put it, "One's persuasion will be more or less affected by the character of the deceased; it may throw much light on the probabilities of the deceased's actions."[69] The second purpose is to prove that the accused was apprehensive of the victim and that his defensive measures were reasonable. For the admission of evidence for this purpose, it must first be established that the accused knew of the victim's acts of violence or aggression. In this situation, the evidence is offered to prove apprehension or state of mind rather than to prove that the person actually was the first aggressor.[70]

It is an old trial strategy to blame or taint the victim—sometimes rightly, sometimes wrongly. Who has not heard it said that women who dress provocatively invite a rape?[71] And who has not heard the old Western saying that the first thing to do in a murder case is determine whether or not the victim deserved to die? "It ain't wrong to kill a S.O.B." It was that philosophy that led a Wyoming jury to free a law official in a killing. Ed Cantrell, a former public safety director in Wyoming, shot his own undercover agent between the eyes in front of two other policemen. He was found not guilty. The tactic of the defense attorney, the famed Gerry Spence, was to try the agent who was killed. He was made out to be a violent, unstable man who used and dealt in drugs.[72]

Jack Litman became famous as a defense attorney by blaming the victim. He used this tactic on behalf of Yale student Richard Herrin, who not only admitted to killing Bonnie Garland—he told police her head "split like a watermelon"—but testified that when he entered her room with a hammer, he intended to kill her. Litman's defense sympathetically portrayed Herrin as a love-struck young man driven temporarily insane by a manipulative and unfaithful girlfriend. Herrin was convicted of manslaughter rather than murder.[73] In another much-publicized case, Litman portrayed Jennifer Levin as sexually aggressive when Robert Chambers choked her one night in Central Park. A mistrial resulted, and as Chambers would be tried again, he entered a plea and got off with a few years of imprisonment.[74]

In the trial of Lyle and Erik Menendez, attorney Leslie Abramson portrayed the parents who were killed as abusive. With a shotgun, they blasted their parents, who were watching television, as "a pre-emptive strike in self-defense." In the first of two trials, blaming the victim succeeded as a defense.[75] It was one of many cases where the "abuse excuse" is offered as a defense.[76] In recent years, women who have been prosecuted for killing their partners have sought exculpation by asserting the defense of self-defense. In some of the cases, the "battered woman" killed the victim while he was asleep or during a significant lull in the violence. The battered woman introduces evidence of the decedent's violent nature in support of her claim of self-defense.

And then there is the case of *State v. Clark*,[77] involving a defendant who killed his estranged wife and the man she was living with. At the time of the homicide he had been separated from his wife for less than a week under a domestic violence protective order. He shot them when he found them in the home he himself had shared with her. At trial he sought to introduce in evidence the fact that his wife had a prior criminal record, used drugs during the marriage, had extramarital affairs, and had a baby by another man during her marriage to him. The court excluded the evidence on the grounds that the character of a victim is relevant only in cases of self-defense, not diminished capacity as was urged in this case. In oral argument, on appeal, one of the judges analogized the defendant's position to that of a battered spouse, but the court nonetheless ruled against the admission of the evidence. To no avail, his attorney argued that the defendant was traumatized by his wife and thus suffered diminished capacity. He was convicted of first-degree murder. Quite likely, had he been represented by Gerry Spence or Jack Litman, the outcome would have been different.[78]

Notes

1. Michelson v. United States, 335 U.S. 469, 486 (1948).

2. The emotional display of the defendant associated with his statements effect the character assessment of the defendant and the recommended sentence. *Affect control theory* explains sentencing through the relations between emotions, identities, and behaviors. If an offender displays unconcern after an offense, the emotion confirms a negative identity, perhaps that the individual typically engages in negative behaviors. If the offender displays sadness or remorse after the offense, the emotion disconfirms the negative identity. When a victim displays sadness after the offense, the decision maker may perceive the victim as undeserving of the offense, in other words, a positive identity. When a victim displays unconcern, the decision maker may perceive the victim as perhaps deserving of the offense, thus, a more negative identity. In turn, the victim's identity may influence perceptions of the offender and the offense. See D. R. Heise, "Effects of Emotion Displays on the Assessment of Character," *Social Psychology Q.* 52 (1989): 10; D. Landy & E. Aronson, "The Influence of the Character of the Criminal and His Victim on the Decisions of Simulated Jurors," *J. Experimental Social Psychology* 5 (1969): 141.

In a Florida death penalty case, Judge Edward Cowart wrote in his opinion, "This court has observed the demeanor and the action of the defendant throughout this entire trial and has not observed one scintilla of remorse displayed, indicating full well to this court that the death penalty is the proper selection of the punishment to be imposed in this particular case." State of Florida v. Robert Austin Sullivan, Circuit Court of 11th Judicial Circuit, Dade County, Fla., case no. 73–3236A. See S. E. Sundby, "The Capital Jury Absolution: The Intersection of Trial Strategy, Remorse, and the Death Penalty," *Cornell L. Rev.* 83 (1998): 1557.

3. See S. Deitz & L. Byrnes, "Attribution of Responsibility for Sexual Assaults: The Influence of Observer Empathy and Defendant Occupation and Attractiveness," *J. Psychology* 108 (1981): 17; M. J. Saks & R. Hastie, *Social Psychology in Court* (New York: Van Nostrand Reinhold, 1978), pp. 156–60. Many people concluded that Ted Bundy, because he was so photogenic and so articulate, could not have committed the crimes for which he had been convicted, but he was sadistic. R. K. Ressler & T. Shachtman, *Whoever Fights Monsters* (New York: St. Martin's Press, 1992), p. 72.

4. In United States v. Williams, 739 F.2d 297 (7th Cir. 1984), a police detective, in the course of his testimony, stated that he knew the defendant by the sobriquet "Fast Eddie." The court of appeals found that this testimony constituted reversible error, because it was an impermissible reference to the defendant's character. The court rejected the argument that "Fast Eddie" was a neutral name, concluding that it would "suggest to the jury that the defendant had some sort of history or reputation for unsavory activity." The court recognized that other cases had permitted evidence of a defendant's alias or nickname if it "aids in the identification of the defendant or in some other way directly relates to the proof of the acts charged in the indictment." However, in this case, "the detective's testimony about the defendant's nickname was completely unrelated to any of the other proof against the defendant." 739 F.2d at 300. See A. N. Bishop, "Name Calling: Defendant Nomenclature in Criminal Trials," *Ohio Northern U. L. Rev.* 4 (1977): 38.

5. Michelson v. United States, 335 U.S. 469 (1948).

6. Federal Rules of Evidence, Rule 404(a)(1). In the trial of 76-year-old A. Alfred Taubman, majority owner of Sotheby's auction house, who was charged with price-fixing, a defense witness testified that Taubman is "the kind of executive who is more interested in what type of lunch will be served at board meetings than in the financial matters being discussed." In closing arguments, chief prosecutor John Greene ridiculed that characterization. "The defense gave the dumb and hungry Taubman story," he told the jurors to laughter in the courtroom. "This is a man who served on the boards of Macy's and Chase Manhattan. If he was a do-nothing, would they have allowed him to stay on the boards?" K. Kranhold, "Taubman Trial Summations Offer Different Views," *Wall Street Journal*, Dec. 4, 2001, p. B-6. The jury found him guilty. R. Blumenthal & C. Vogel, "Ex-Chief of Sotheby's Is Convicted of Price

Fixing," *New York Times*, Dec. 6, 2001, p. 1. One columnist wrote, "We almost wish chief defense attorney Robert Fiske Jr. had been able to muster some kind of rebuttal based on facts—an attempt at alibi. Then we wouldn't have been forced to hear a laundry list of human failings, designed to appeal to the human sensibilities of the jury, in someone who has always been publicly portrayed for us in ideal terms." J. V. Higgins, "To Its Credit, Taubman Defense Team Didn't Play the Wealth Card," *Detroit News*, Dec. 6, 2001, p. 10. On the advice of defense counsel, Taubman's young wife, a former Israeli beauty queen, did not attend the trial, because she represents the stereotype of the blond "trophy wife." K. Kranhold, "Sotheby's Chief Is Convicted of Price-Fixing," *Wall Street Journal*, Dec. 6, 2001, p. B-1. The prosecutor highlighted the playboy side of Taubman's lifestyle—private jets, regular massage and pedicure appointments, and dinners with Palm Beach socialites—for a jury made up of lift operators and letter carriers. The foreman of the jury was a postman clad in T-shirt and jeans and whose biceps bore a tattoo of a scull pierced by a knife. In closing argument, the prosecutor cited a passage from Adam Smith's 1776 magnum opus, *The Wealth of Nations:* "People in the same trade seldom meet together even for merriment and diversion, but a conversation ends in a conspiracy against the public or in some contrivance to raise prices." J. Chaffin, "Sotheby's—A Bargain That Bit Back," *Financial Times*, Dec. 8–9, 2001, p. 12. The columnist Taki Theodoracopulos is critical of the prosecution, in no uncertain terms:

> A. Alfred Taubman, or Big Al, as his buddies call him, is among the very few very rich men who also happen to be very, very nice. . . . Details of Taubman's five "homes," his Gulfstream jet, and a staff of up to seven personal assistants were read out in court by the prosecution as if they constituted crimes. Now, I ask you, what's wrong with having five houses and a private jet? What could possibly be wrong with hiring more and more people? Taubman is a self-made man, and came up the hard way. Why should he suffer from any guilt? . . . Big Al is a philanthropist extraordinaire, which is much more than I can say for the rats who are singing trying to save their skin. Dee Dee Brooks, posing as a Wasp patrician, turned stool pigeon, and it makes my blood boil. Her so-called snobbery . . . was nothing but bad manners trying to pass itself off as good taste. . . . What bugs me is the unfairness of it all. Taubman has employed thousands, helped the poor and the handicapped, and was always nice when on top. . . . The man is innocent and the government should be ashamed of itself.

Taki, "Class Warfare," *Spectator*, Nov. 24, 2001, p. 69. Law professors would agree with the observation: "Mr. Taubman must have had thin hopes going into trial. His lawyers mounted a defense based on making the 76-year-old nondope look like a dope. . . . [The lawyers painted the participants] as upper-class twits of the year in hopes of appealing to the alleged prejudices of the alleged proles on the jury." H. W. Jenkins, "Silly Trial, Silly Law," *Wall Street Journal*, Dec. 12, 2001, p. 19.

7. United States v. Angelini, 678 F.2d 380 (1st Cir. 1982). The government has often argued that "being prone to law-abiding conduct" is not an actual character trait but is rather a conclusion that must be drawn from other character traits such as honesty, reliability, and rectitude. However, the courts have generally held that "character traits admissible under Rule 404(a)(1) need not constitute specific traits of character but may include general traits such as lawfulness and law-abidingness." Indeed, the defendant in the landmark case, Michelson v. United States, 335 U.S. 469 (1948), was permitted to prove his law-abiding character trait, and the Supreme Court held that a defendant may introduce favorable testimony concerning "the general estimate of his character."

This does not mean, however, that the defendant has unlimited freedom to define a character trait. For example, in United States v. Diaz, 961 F.2d 1417 (9th Cir. 1992), the defendant was charged with possession with intent to distribute more than five hundred grams of cocaine. Defense counsel sought to ask a defense witness whether the defendant had a "character trait for being prone to large-scale drug dealing." The Ninth Circuit found no error in excluding this testimony because a defendant propensity (or lack thereof) to engage in large-scale drug dealing "is not an admissible character trait." The proposed testimony was not the same as testimony that the defendant was law-abiding, because it was in effect too specific. The court reasoned that an inquiry into a propensity to engage in large-scale drug-dealing "would be misleading if addressed to a defendant with a record of criminal offenses other than drug dealing: If answered in the negative [as the defendant, of course, anticipated] the impression may be given that the defendant is a law-abiding person although he has a record of other crimes." 961 F.2d at 1419. See S. A. Saltzburg, M. M. Martin, & D. J. Capra, *Federal Rules of Evidence Manual* (Charlottesville, Va.: Michie, 6th ed. 1994), vol. 1, p. 317.

8. B. D. Ayres, "Simpson Testifies, Portraying Himself as a Loving Husband," *New York Times,* Jan. 11, 1997, p. 6. Psychologist Linda N. Edelstein sets out character traits including profiles of human behaviors and personality types in her book *The Writer's Guide to Character Traits* (Cincinnati: Writer's Digest Books, 1999).

9. 287 Ark. 322, 699 S.W.2d 728 (1985).

10. United States v. Burke, 781 F.2d 1234, 1239 (7th Cir. 1985).

11. See e.g., United States v. Lewis, 482 F.2d 632 (D.C. Cir. 1973).

12. See, e.g., United States v. Pujana-Mena, 949 F.2d 24 (2d Cir. 1991).

13. E. C. Brewer, *Dictionary of Phrase and Fable* (Philadelphia: Henry Altemus, 1898).

14. The quote appears in the commentary to Rule 406 of the Federal Rules of Evidence and in subsequent editions of *McCormick on Evidence.* See J. W. Strong et al., *McCormick on Evidence* (St. Paul, Minn.: West, 5th ed. 1999), sec. 195.

15. 784 F.2d 1040 (10th Cir. 1986).

16. See, e.g., Meyer v. United States, 464 F.Supp. 317 (D.Colo. 1979), *aff'd,* 638 F.2d 155 (10th Cir. 1980); Reaves v. Mandell, 209 N.J. Super. 465, 507 A.2d 807 (1986).

17. 873 F.2d 1453 (D.C. Cir. 1989).

18. 338 F.2d 265 (D.C. Cir. 1964).

19. Williams v. Johnson, 244 S.C. 406, 137 S.E.2d 410 (1964).

20. In Loughan v. Firestone Tire & Rubber Co., 749 F.2d (5th Cir. 1979), the court admitted as habit evidence testimony that a certain employee "routinely carried a cooler of beer on his truck," "was in the habit of drinking on the job," and "normally had something to drink in the early morning hours." In Keltner v. Ford Motor Co., 748 F.2d 1265 (8th Cir. 1984), the court admitted evidence of habit of drinking a six-pack of beer four nights a week.

21. D. Margolick, "3 Women's Testimony on Smith Is Barred," *New York Times,* Dec. 3, 1991, p. 9. The writer Dominick Dunne in his book *Justice* (New York: Crown, 2001) expresses outrage that evidence of a defendant's past offenses are kept from the jury. Moreover, in the trial of his daughter's killer, the defendant was "costumed" like a sacristan in a Catholic seminary and carried a Bible, which he read throughout the trial in a pious fashion (p. xi). The law of evidence on character of a person is distinguished from character of a place. Evidence of other wrongdoing is restricted in establishing an individual's propensity, but evidence of other events is admissible to establish character of a place, such as evidence of a number of accidents at an intersection to establish a dangerous intersection. See, e.g., Simon v. Kennebunkport, 417 A.2d 982 (Me. 1980).

22. Thus, in Persichini v. Beaumont Hosp., 238 Mich. App. 626, 607 N.W.3d 100 (1999), a question on cross-examination of the defendant physician with respect to the number of times he was sued for malpractice was deemed improper and highly prejudicial, warranting the grant of a mistrial.

23. 124 Mich. App. 672, 335 N.W.2d 226 (1983).

24. 600 P.2d 1044 (Wyo. 1979).

25. L. S. Eads, D. W. Shuman, & J. M. DeLipsey, "Getting It Right: The Trial of Sexual Assault and Child Molestation Cases under Federal Rules of Evidence 413–415," *Behavioral Sci. & Law* 18 (2000): 169.

26. C. B. Mueller & L. C. Kirkpatrick, *Evidence* (New York: Aspen, 2d ed. 1999), p. 309. For a criticism of Rules 413–415, see L. M. Natali & R. S. Stigall, "How Sexual Propensity Evidence Violates the Due Process Clause," *Champion,* Sept./Oct. 1997, p. 24.

27. R. A. Posner, "An Economic Approach to the Law of Evidence," *Stanford L. Rev.* 51 (1999): 1477, 1525–26.

28. United States v. Cunningham, 103 F.3d 553 (7th Cir. 1996).

29. 1997 WL 476532 (Mich. App. 1997).

30. 277 N.J. Super. 311, 649 A.2d 879 (App. Div. 1994).

31. M. A. Mendez, "The Law of Evidence and the Search for a Stable Personality," *Emory L. J.* 45 (1996): 221.

32. In a blurb on the dust jacket of Tony Hiss's book, *The View from Alger's Window: A Son's Memoir* (New York: Knopf, 1999), Lawrence Weschler (fellow *New Yorker* writer) wrote:

Tony Hiss's book about his father, Alger—remarkable on its own terms (warm, loving, nuanced, and revelatory)—is likely to have a profound effect on the ongoing debate over Alger's character and culpability. Hiss's detractors will now have to square their version of the man with the person who comes shining through Tony's narrative, based largely on a never previously published trove of intimate family papers, especially Alger's letters home from prison. How could a man capable of penning such letters ever have behaved in the manner they persist in alleging?

33. See S. Roll & W. E. Foote, "The Inconsistent Personality Defense," in D. J. Muller, D. E. Blackman, & A. J. Chapman (eds.), *Psychology and Law* (New York: Wiley, 1984), pp. 125–32; R. H. Woody & J. M. Shade, "Psychological Testimony on the Propensity for Sexual Child Abuse," *Michigan Psychologist*, Mar.–Apr. 1989, p. 12.

34. United States v. Hill, 655 F.2d 512 (3d Cir. 1981).

35. United States v. Staggs, 553 F.2d 1073 (7th Cir. 1977).

36. Freeman v. State, 486 P.2d 967 (Alaska 1971).

37. State v. Christensen, 129 Ariz. 32, 628 P.2d 580 (1981).

38. In State v. Wood, 346 N.W.2d 481 (Iowa 1984), the defendant introduced expert testimony evaluating her as a "passive-dependent personality." The expert testified that a passive-dependent individual will allow others to assume responsibility and will act in a manner to maintain such a dependent relationship. The defendant was allowed to offer this testimony to negate evidence that she had the requisite intent to kill her husband. The state law required the prosecutor to prove, on a first-degree murder charge, that the defendant "willfully, deliberately, and with premeditation kills another person." Iowa Code, sec. 707.2(1). In substance, she sought to show it was unlikely she would commit such an act.

39. State v. Holt, 382 N.W.2d 679 (Wis. App. 1985).

40. Canadian Press, "Man Gets Day's Probation in Rape of Ex-Girlfriend," *Globe & Mail*, June 21, 1990, p. 1.

41. Ltr., "Hill vs. Thomas," *Commentary*, May 1992, p. 10.

42. J. Adler, "Unhappily Every After," *Newsweek*, Aug. 31, 1992, p. 40.

43. 42 Cal.2d 219, 266 P.2d 38 (1954).

44. The case is discussed in W. J. Curran, "Expert Psychiatric Evidence of Personality Traits," *U. Pa. L. Rev.* 103 (1955): 999.

45. 265 Cal. Rptr. 111, 783 P.2d 698 (1989).

46. 783 P.2d at 709. The case is criticized in J. E. B. Myers, *Legal Issues in Child Abuse and Neglect* (Newbury Park, Cal.: Sage, 1992). In State v. Richard A.P., 223 Wis.2d 777, 589 N.W.2d 674 (Wis. App. 1998), the court held that a defendant may present expert psychological testimony as to his character for sexual deviance in order to show the defendant lacks the psychological profile of a sex offender and is therefore unlikely to have committed the crime. In State v. Davis, 2001 WI App. 210, 634 N.W.2d 922 (Wis. App. 2001), the same court held that a defendant who presents such expert testimony puts his mental status in issue and thereby waives the right against self-incrimination. The defendant may be ordered to submit to a psychiatric evaluation by an expert chosen by the state. In People v. Spigno, 156 Cal. App.2d 279, 319 P.2d 458 (1957), the California Court of Appeals held that there was no scientific recognition of a psychologist's ability to determine propensity for child molestation. See A. E. Taslitz, "Myself Alone: Individualizing Justice through Psychological Character Evidence," *Md. L. Rev.* 52 (1993): 1.

47. 88 N.J. 508, 443 A.2d 1020 (1982), noted in 42 A.L.R.4th 919 (1985).

48. Annot., "Admissibility of Expert Testimony as to Criminal Defendant's Propensity toward Sexual Deviation," 42 A.L.R.4th 937 (1985).

49. United States v. DiDomenico, 985 F.2d 1159 (2d Cir. 1993).

50. United States v. Kepreos, 759 F.2d 961 (1st Cir. 1985).

51. United States v. Webb, 625 F.2d 709 (5th Cir. 1980).

52. United States v. Esch, 832 F.2d 531 (10th Cir. 1987).

53. 485 F.Supp. 1087 (E.D. N.C. 1979), 688 F.2d 224 (4th Cir. 1982), *cert. denied*, 459 U.S. 1103 (1983).

54. Quoted in D. L. Breo, *Extraordinary Care* (Chicago: Chicago Review Press, 1986), pp. 140–41. Joe McGinniss in a best-selling book devotes 663 pages to building a case that Captain MacDonald committed the crime. J. McGinniss, *Fatal Vision* (New York: Putnam, 1983).

55. The profile of a pimp: track suit, Adidas sneakers, gold chain, sleeves short enough

to reveal the bulge of his muscles. R. Cohen, "The Oldest Profession Seeks New Market in West Europe," *New York Times*, Sept. 19, 2000, p. 1. In the wake of September 11, 2001, Attorney General John Ashcroft focused attention on nonimmigrants from the Middle East, and the concept of profiling sprang immediately to mind. See, e.g., W. H. Dance, "The Question of Aliens and the Possibility of Profiling," *Detroit Legal News*, Dec. 3, 2001, p. 32. See also D. Pryce-Jones, "Islam in Action," *National Review*, Dec. 3, 2001, p. 20. The internment of Japanese Americans during World War II was not all negative. See G. Robinson, *By Order of the President: FDR and the Internment of Japanese Americans* (Cambridge: Harvard University Press, 2001); S. Schwartz, "The Right Way to Lock Up Aliens," *Weekly Standard*, Dec. 10, 2001, p. 12. On racial profiling in regard African Americans, see R. Kennedy, *Race, Crime, and the Law* (New York: Pantheon Books, 1997), pp. 136–67.

56. The use of drug courier profiles is discussed extensively in United States v. Berry, 670 F.2d 583 (5th Cir. 1982). See also United States v. Malone, 886 F.2d 1162 (9th Cir. 1989) (the defendant was stopped by the police on the basis of a gang member profile). In an Oregon case, a profile of a serial killer was the basis for a search warrant that resulted in discovery of body parts in the suspect's residence. See R. Turco, *Closely Watched Shadows: Profile of the Hunter and the Hunted* (Wilsonville, Ore.: BookPartners, 1999). Dr. Philip Resnick provided a profile of a person who would kidnap a pregnant woman, perform a C-section, and steal the baby. A. Garrett, "4 Other Babies Stolen by C-Section," *Plain Dealer*, Oct. 4, 2000, p.1. The practitioner of criminal profiling looks at the specifics of a crime—the scene, the facts about the victim, the evidence, and the act itself—and extrapolates a portrait of the culprit. See J. Douglas & M. Olshaker, *The Cases That Haunt Us* (New York: Scribner, 2000); R. K. Kessler & T. Shachtman, *Whoever Fights Monsters* (New York: St. Martin's 1992); M. G. McGrath, "Criminal Profiling: Is There a Role for the Forensic Psychiatrist?" *J. Am. Acad. Psychiatry & Law* 28 (2000): 315. The criminal profiling program of the FBI's behavioral science unit is described in J. Douglas & M. Olshaker, *Mind Hunter* (New York: Simon & Schuster, 1995). Profiles of various types of offenders are described in B. Danto, *Dangerous and Mentally Disordered Offenders* (Laguna Hills, Cal.: Eagle Books, 1985). See also P. C. Ellsworth & R. Mauro, "Psychology and Law," in D. T. Gilbert, S. T. Fiske, & G. Lindzey (eds.), *The Handbook of Social Psychology* (New York: McGraw-Hill, 4th ed. 1998), pp. 684–732; B. Turvey, *Criminal Profiling* (San Diego: Academic Press, 1999); M. Higgins, "Looking the Part," *ABAJ*, Nov. 1997, p. 48. Objections to profiling are countered by a reductio ad absurdum: "If a tiger springs out of the bush and bites you on the rear end, and you give chase, you hunt for a tiger and not a hippo." J. Munna, "Crouching Tiger" (ltr.), *Wall Street Journal*, Nov. 12, 2001, p. 23.

Profiling has found a role in screening in the employment context as well as in police investigation. Psychiatrist Martin Blinder has constructed a profile "by which management can identify well in advance those employees most likely to engage in lethal acts of revenge." He postulates that there are 18 traits conducive to lethality and that a person exhibiting "any 10 or more" should give rise to concern. M. Blinder, "Profile of a Workplace Killer," *Wall Street Journal*, Feb. 10, 1997, p. 18.

In a cartoon in the *New Yorker*, a CEO notifies his deputy of a downsizing, "We've got to get rid of some people," and he asks the deputy, "Who are the least likely to come back and shoot us?" For a critical view of the utility of profiling in the workplace, see M. Braverman, *Preventing Workplace Violence* (Thousand Oaks, Cal.: Sage, 1999); R. V. Deneberg & M. Braverman, *The Violence-Prone Workplace* (Ithaca, N.Y.: Cornell University Press, 1999). In a spoof of profiling, a police chief in a film by Rainer Werner Fassbinder shows a threatening letter to a psychiatrist and asks for a profile. The psychiatrist looks over the letter and muses, "It could have been written by a man. It could have been written by a woman. It could have been written by a group."

57. S. H. Verhovek, "Besmirched 'Deportland' Wrestles with the I.N.S.," *New York Times*, Aug. 31, 2000, p. 12.

58. Prosecutors routinely offer drug courier profile testimony as the basis of expert opinion of law enforcement witnesses to bolster circumstantially substantive proof of guilt at trial. The fact that an individual matched a drug courier profile may be admitted as evidence to prove that the individual must have known that he was carrying drugs, and, consequently, that he intended to distribute them. See, e.g., United States v. Jackson, 51 F.3d 646 (7th Cir. 1995). See M. Kadish, "The Drug Courier Profile: In Planes, Trains, and Automobiles; and Now in the Jury Box," *Am. U. L. Rev.* 46 (1997): 747. In Iseley v. Capuchin Province, 877 F.Supp.

1055 (E.D.Mich. 1955), testimony that a defendant did not fit a sex offender profile was held inadmissible as a defense against a sexual assault claim. While PTSD testimony may be offered to show that a victim has symptoms that are consistent with sexual abuse, PTSD testimony is inadmissible to identify the perpetrator of the alleged sexual abuse. See State v. Alberico, 116 N.M. 156, 861 P.2d 192 (1993).

59. Reports are not infrequent about mothers who deliberately induce illnesses in their children in order to elicit sympathy or to play the role of heroic caregiver. Dr. Roy Meadow, chairman of pediatrics at the University of Leeds in England, observed parents simulating and producing dramatic illness in their children, and in a 1977 article he described the syndrome as Munchausen Syndrome by Proxy (MSBP). (The term *by proxy* means that instead of inducing illness in oneself, the person with the disorder creates illness in another person, almost exclusively a child.) It has also been called Meadow's Syndrome. See R. Meadow, "Munchausen Syndrome by Proxy—The Hinterland of Child Abuse," *Lancet* 2 (1977): 343. See also D. B. Allison & M. S. Roberts, *Disordered Mother or Disordered Diagnosis?: Munchausen by Proxy Syndrome* (Hillsdale, N.J.: Analytic Press, 1998); M. M. Brady, "Munchausen Syndrome by Proxy: How Should We Weigh Our Opinions?" *Law & Psychology Rev.* 18 (1994): 361; T. Vollaro, "Munchausen Syndrome by Proxy and Its Evidentiary Problems," *Hofstra L. Rev.* 22 (1993): 495; B. C. Yorker & B. Kahan, "The Munchausen Syndrome by Proxy Variant of Child Abuse in the Family Courts," *Juvenile & Family Court J.* 42 (1991): 51; B. Kahan & B. C. Yorker, "The Munchausen Syndrome by Proxy: Clinical Review and Legal Issues," *Behavioral Sciences & Law* 9 (1991): 73.

In People v. Phillips, 122 Cal. App.3d 69, 175 Cal. Rptr. 703 (1981), the defendant was convicted by a jury of murdering one of her two adopted children and willfully endangering the life or health of the other by adding a sodium compound to their food. In order to suggest a motive for the defendant's conduct, the prosecution, over objection, presented evidence by a psychiatrist of MSBP. The appellate court held that because the conduct ascribed to the defendant was incongruous and apparently inexplicable, the psychiatric evidence was relevant to show a possible motive. The court further held that the psychiatric evidence was not rendered inadmissible by the defendant's failure to make her mental state an issue. A significant aspect of the case was that the court allowed the use of psychiatric expert testimony to describe the phenomenon of MSBP and to give an opinion that the defendant mother fit the profile of a perpetrator, notwithstanding the rule that character evidence is admissible only at the option of the accused. Arguably, the evidence is admissible under Rule 404(b), which allows a series of acts to establish motive.

60. State v. Loss, 295 Minn. 271, 204 N.W.2d 404 (1973).

61. State v. Goblirsch, 309 Minn. 401, 246 N.W.2d 12 (1976).

62. State v. Loebach, 310 N.W.2d 58 (Minn. 1981). The rules of evidence specifically provide, as we have noted, that the accused must initiate the use of character evidence before the prosecutor may offer character evidence of a negative type. Rule 404(a), Federal Rules of Evidence. For discussions of the psychological profile of the batterer, see D. Dutton, *The Batterer: A Psychological Profile* (New York: Basic Books, 1995); D. Island & P. Letellier, *Men Who Beat the Men Who Love Them* (New York: Haworth Press, 1991); A. Holtzworth-Munroe & G. L. Stuart, "Typologies of Male Batterers," *Psychological Bull.* 116 (1994): 476.

63. 310 N.W.2d at 64. In United States v. Powers, 59 F.3d 1460 (4th Cir. 1995), the court, citing *Daubert*, excluded testimony that the defendant lacked the profile of a pedophile. See D. G. Saunders, "A Typology of Men Who Batter: Three Types Derived from Cluster Analysis," *Amer. J. Orthopsychiat.* 62 (1992): 264.

64. G. O. Gabbard, "Psychodynamic Approaches to Physician Sexual Misconduct," in J. D. Bloom, C. C. Nadelson, & M. T. Notman (eds.), *Physician Sexual Misconduct* (Washington, D.C.: American Psychiatric Press, 1999); R. I. Simon, *Clinical Psychiatry and the Law* (Washington, D.C.: American Psychiatric Press, 2d ed. 1992).

65. See S. B. Bisbing, L. M. Jorgenson, & P. K. Sutherland, *Sexual Abuse by Professionals: A Legal Guide* (Charlottesville: Michie, 1995), p. 263.

66. Federal Rules of Evidence, Rule 404(a).

67. Federal Rules of Evidence, Rules 404(b), 406.

68. Federal Rules of Evidence, Rule 404(a)(2). The prosecutor may not offer character evidence of the victim unless the accused does so first. In the trial of the four police officers who killed Amadou Diallo, the prosecution was criticized for "failing to humanize the victim"

(J. Abramson, "A Story the Jury Never Heard," *New York Times*, Feb. 26, 2000 p. 31), but the prosecution is precluded from initiating character evidence about the victim. The state's accusation does not depend on whether the victim is a saint or a sinner. Unless the defendant brings it up, evidence offered by the prosecution of the victim's character is irrelevant. A person is entitled to the protection of the law regardless of his character, but when the defendant raises the issue, it is to establish self-defense. S. Gillers, "A Weak Case, but a Brave Prosecution," *New York Times*, Mar. 1, 2000, p. 31. Moreover, prosecutorial argument that invites the jurors to put themselves in the shoes of the victim is considered improper. State v. Bashire, 606 N.W.2d 449 (Minn. App. 2000).

69. Quoted in M. Ivins, "Wyoming Jury Frees Law Official in Killings," *New York Times*, Dec. 1, 1979, p. 10.

70. R. Alsop, "The Dead Are Psychoanalyzed at Murder Trials; Technique Aids Suspects Pleading Self-Defense," *Wall Street Journal*, July 23, 1980, p. 40.

71. Until fairly recently, the character of a victim was admissible on behalf of the defendant in one type of case other than that of self-defense—forcible rape. It was held that where the defendant had alleged consent as a defense, the consenting character of the victim could be shown to make consent more likely. In the 1970s, a "shield law" was enacted in virtually every jurisdiction to exclude evidence of a victim's sexual behavior in sex offense cases. Federal Rules of Evidence, Rule 412. See generally, G. P. Fletcher, "Convicting the Victim," *New York Times*, Feb. 7, 1994, p. 11; K. Johnson, "Goetz Lawyer Tries Tough Legal Tactic by Attacking Victims," *New York Times*, May 1, 1987, p. 12.

72. M. Ivins, "Wyoming Jury Frees Law Official in Killing," *New York Times*, Dec. 1, 1979, p. 10.

73. W. Gaylin, *The Killing of Bonnie Garland* (New York: Simon & Schuster, 1982). Writing about the trial of John Sweeney for the murder of his daughter Dominique Dunne, Dominick Dunne writes:

> From the beginning we had been warned that the defense would slander Dominique. It is part of the defense premise that the victim is responsible for the crime. As Dr. Willard Gaylin says in his book *The Killing of Bonnie Garland*, Bonnie Garland's killer, Richard Herrin, murdered Bonnie all over again in the courtroom. It is always the murder victim who is placed on trial. John Sweeney, who claimed to love Dominique, and whose defense was that this was a crime of passion, slandered her in court as viciously and cruelly as he had strangled her. It was agonizing for us to listen to him, led on by [his attorney], besmirch Dominique's name. His violent past remained sacrosanct and inviolate, but her name was allowed to be trampled upon and kicked, with unsubstantiated charges, by the man who killed her.

D. Dunne, *Justice* (New York: Crown, 2001), p. 26.

74. K. Johnson, "Private Talks at the Chambers Trial," *New York Times*, Feb. 15, 1988, p. 15.

75. E. Hardwick, "The Menendez Show," *New York Review of Books*, Feb. 17, 1994, p. 14.

76. See A. E. Taslitz, "Abuse Excuses and the Logic and Politics of Expert Relevance," *Hastings L. Rev.* 49 (1998): 1039.

77. 493 S.E.2d 770 (N.C. App. 1997).

78. By amendment to Rule 404(a)(1) of the Federal Rules of Evidence, effective December 1, 2000, it is provided that when the accused attacks the character of an alleged victim, the door is opened to an attack on the same character trait of the accused. Prior to the amendment, the government could not introduce negative character evidence as to the accused unless the accused had introduced evidence of good character. Thus, in United States v. Fountain, 768 F.2d 790 (7th Cir. 1985), where the accused offered proof of self-defense, this permitted proof of the alleged victim's character trait for peacefulness, but it did not permit proof of the accused's character trait for violence. Under the amendment, the accused cannot attack the alleged victim's character and yet remain shielded from the disclosure of equally relevant evidence concerning the same character trait of the accused. The amendment is designed to permit a more balanced presentation of character evidence when an accused chooses to attack the character of the alleged victim.

7

Elusive Evidence: Syndromes, Body Language, and Dreams

Syndromes, body language, and dreams are known as *elusive evidence* (some say all psychological evidence is elusive by its very nature). These types of evidence—syndromes, body language, and dreams—are discussed in this chapter.

Syndrome Evidence

Syndrome evidence in courts of law is nontraditional.[1] The search for evidence, particularly in child abuse cases, has led to a new species of medical evidence: the *syndrome* diagnosis. Law professor Christopher Slobogin observes: "Probably the single biggest change in the nature of psychiatric testimony over the past 25 years has been the advent of 'syndrome testimony.' A quarter century ago forensic experts rarely spoke of syndromes in criminal court. Today, this type of testimony abounds."[2]

This type of evidence, designed to establish the cause of a trauma, apparently originated historically in radiology and clinical observation. John Caffey, the father of pediatric radiology, who spent twenty years trying to fit the bony abnormalities seen on x-rays of children into known syndromes, noted abnormalities that must be associated with child abuse as they were not seen in any known disease.[3] In

1962, Dr. C. Henry Kempe drew the attention of the medical profession to a set of presenting symptoms for which he coined the term "battered child syndrome."[4]

The term *syndrome* is well known in the medical community as being "a running together," a *sundromos* in the Greek, or, as the *Oxford English Dictionary* puts it, "a concurrence of several symptoms in a disease." Normally a syndrome is regarded as being identifiable when a collection of symptoms occurs together so often that they provide a recognizable clinical entity. There is controversy, however, over the admissibility of syndrome evidence in criminal or tort cases to establish either that a particular traumatic event or stressor actually occurred or to explain the behavior of the victim. In a child abuse case a psychiatrist or psychologist is presented to testify that the child exhibits the general characteristics of a sexually abused child and that, by implication, the child was sexually abused.[5] (Experts use the term *rape trauma syndrome* in the case of a young girl as well as in the case of an adult woman, and they tend to use the term *sexually abused child syndrome* in the case of a child of tender years or when the offender is a family member).[6] Because the defense in these cases is usually that the abuse did not occur and that the child is making it up, the testimony is designed to bolster the credibility of the child.[7]

Proponents of syndrome evidence argue that it is probative and logical. After all, what could seem more sensible than to look for patterns? Writing about syndrome identification, psychiatrists Randall Marshall, Robert Spitzer, and Michael Liebowitz have this to say:

> Because the etiology of most mental disorders is largely unknown, psychiatric research remains particularly dependent on the principles and process of syndrome identification. Identification of syndrome criteria with acceptable reliability can then facilitate investigation of syndrome validity with methodologies such as factor and cluster analysis, laboratory study, studies of comorbidity and distinction from other disorders, follow-up, family studies, and treatment response. Official recognition of a clinical syndrome can also greatly stimulate scientific interest, as illustrated by the surge of research in posttraumatic stress disorder (PTSD) since its recognition in DSM-III in 1980. Finally, diagnoses serve the crucial clinical objectives of identifying individuals in need of treatment and guiding treatment selection.[8]

In medical diagnosis, of course, the symptoms of an individual are compared with a pattern and a conclusion is drawn about etiology. As Jimmy Durante once put it, "If something looks like a duck, walks like a duck, and quacks like a duck, it must be a duck." Some courts call it "the duck test." Its application should be cautious, however, when it is based only on symptoms. Dr. Albert Drukteinis puts it thus:

> Medical conditions, generally, can be defined on different levels, depending on structural pathology, etiology, deviation from some physiological norm, observable signs or symptom presentation. As definitions move from more objective criteria of identifiable and measurable pathology to symptom presentation only, they change from disease to syndrome. Therefore, a syndrome is more likely to include arbitrary or subjective criteria, and to lie in a more gray area of certainty. However, by using the

term "syndrome," a word which has its roots in medicine, the symptom pattern described gains medical legitimacy.[9]

Certain assumptions about psychological evidence to ascertain a stressor are particularly questionable. One is the assumption that a certain post-traumatic stress syndrome is the pathway of a particular kind of stressor. In actuality, a wide variety of stressors may result in the trauma. Second is the assumption that victims of a particular stressor react in the same manner. In actuality, the impact of a stressor depends upon the interaction between predisposition and environmental influence. One person may break down; another may be stoic. In short, not all victims react with the same characteristics, and many persons with these characteristics have not been abused but instead may be suffering from something else, or they may be malingering or acting hysterically.[10]

Freud's patients recalled their trauma "with all the feelings that belong to the original experience."[11] In 1895 and 1896, Freud, in listening to his women patients, felt that something dreadful and violent lay in their past. The psychiatrists before Freud who had heard seduction stories believed their patients to be hysterical liars and dismissed their memories as fantasy. Freud believed that his patients were reporting the actuality. However, some nine years later he publicly retracted his theory about the etiology of hysteria. His patients, he now said in an about-face, had been deceiving themselves and him: "I was at last obliged to recognize that these scenes of seduction had never taken place, and that they were only fantasies that my patients had made up."[12] Other therapists, however, find that the incest fantasies of their patients are based on a history of incest.[13] *Revival of memory* therapists link problems of depression, eating disorders, and multiple personality disorder to childhood sexual abuse.[14]

So out of a concern for relevance comes the legal question: Does the victim's clinically observed emotional trauma support the allegation about the stressor? In the usual tort or criminal case, an act is not in dispute—say, an automobile accident—but rather causation and damages are in dispute. In a turnaround, in cases involving syndrome evidence, symptoms are offered as evidence that a certain act occurred, but is trauma stressor-specific? Is there something peculiar about the trauma suffered by a victim of a tort or crime that is different from the trauma suffered as a result of other stressors, such as a hurricane or an automobile accident? Are subcategories of post-traumatic stress disorder warranted—such as sexually abused child syndrome, rape trauma syndrome, battered spouse, battered elderly, or incest trauma?[15] These terms have developed to encompass the recurrent pattern of certain victims. Should they be elevated to the level of diagnostic nomenclature? Should they simply all be called PTSD? They are not listed as separate syndromes in the American Psychiatric Association's *Diagnostic and Statistical Manual of Mental Disorders*, the state of the art, but who knows, perhaps some day they will be.

A number of appellate decisions have been rendered on syndrome evidence. For some purposes, some appellate courts have recognized a number of categories of PTSD and have allowed testimony on them.[16] In rulings followed by many other courts, the California Supreme Court has admitted testimony on the battered child syndrome to prove child abuse but has excluded the rape trauma syndrome to prove that a rape had occurred. In 1984, in *People v. Bledsoe*,[17] the California Supreme Court made an attempt at explanation, saying that expert testimony concerning the battered child syndrome is admissible because that concept was devised for the purpose of determining whether a child's injuries were intentionally inflicted.

Dr. Kempe's formulation of the syndrome, however, was based on physical evidence. Put another way, the physical injuries sustained by the child do not form any injury pattern normally sustained by children in day-to-day activities. The battered child syndrome indicated that the injuries suffered by the child were not the result of accident. Following Dr. Kempe's formulation, courts in various jurisdictions allowed an expert medical witness to express an opinion that a child exhibits the battered child syndrome. In these cases the expert is permitted to give an opinion as to the cause of a particular injury, either on the basis of the expert's deduction from the appearance of the injury itself or from the syndrome.

Sexual child abuse, on the other hand, often leaves no physical injuries on which a diagnosis of battered child syndrome could be based. And what about an alleged rape? Should a rape counselor or other mental health professional be permitted to testify to an individual's postincident emotional trauma—a constellation of symptoms experienced by the victims of sexual assault, or rape trauma syndrome—in order to prove that a rape in fact occurred (or a sexual abuse syndrome to prove that molestations occurred)? In a rape case, it is argued that the complainant would not suffer the symptoms if she had consented to the sexual act.[18] (Consent is no defense, of course, in cases of sexual abuse involving children. In these cases, the issue is whether it occurred or whether the accused is the perpetrator.)

In *Bledsoe*, the California Supreme Court noted that the rape trauma syndrome is a fundamentally different concept than the battered child syndrome because "[the rape trauma syndrome] was not devised to determine the truth or accuracy of a particular past event." Rather, the court said, it is "a therapeutic tool" used to treat victims by counselors who consciously "avoid judging the credibility of their clients."[19] That distinction has been widely but not always followed.[20] Actually, any of the PTSDs are treatable without regard to the nature of the stressor or even whether a stressor actually occurred. (The rape crisis centers could be crisis centers for all people in emotional distress.)

While courts have more often rejected than accepted rape trauma syndrome in establishing the stressor, they have allowed evidence of a child sexual abuse syndrome to show that a child was sexually abused. As a result of the concern about child abuse, in the trial of accused child molesters, many courts in recent years, as we have just noted, have allowed mental health professionals to testify that the psychological problems of a child are evidence that abuse has in fact occurred.[21] Other courts draw a distinction without a difference, saying that an expert may testify that the particular behavior of the child was characteristic of, or consistent with, the behavior pattern of child sexual abuse victims generally, but the expert may not testify about whether the victim's allegations are truthful or whether sexual abuse did occur.[22]

In *State v. Kim*,[23] a child psychiatrist was allowed to present the following testimony on trauma, over objection:

Q: Based upon your experience, Dr. Mann, have you had an opportunity—in the past—to assess the credibility of reported rape cases by children involving family members?
A: Yes.
Q: Approximately how many times have you done this?

A: I would say about 70 times.

Q: And, as a result of your interviews and examinations of these witnesses, have you arrived at conclusions with respect to the truthfulness of these reported rape cases involving family members?

A: Yes.

Q: Upon what do you base your conclusions as to the credibility of such claims?

A: There are several factors. One is the consistency of the account of the alleged sexual abuse. There are some common emotional reactions we frequently find in victims, which consist of a fear about safety, fear of future sexual abuse, feelings of depression or anxiety, embarrassment to have the alleged happenings known to peers or other people around them, a negative view of sex, some doubts that one parent might be strong enough to prevent further sexual abuse.

Q: Now, as a result of your experience and training in this area, did you come to the conclusion as to the truthfulness of the rape case reported by [the complainant]?

A: Yes, I found her account to be believable.

Q: Now, in arriving at that conclusion, what factors did you consider?

A: Many of the factors I listed before. I found [the complainant's] account quite consistent. She was very much preoccupied with a fear about safety, which took on some almost phobic dimensions, telling me that she locked herself in her room and shut the windows when she was alone out of fear that the accused might come back and she might be re-abused. She was quite depressed, showed a negative attitude to sex and seemed somewhat naive in sexual matters, which made it very unlikely that she would have fantasized acts in that specific manner. Also a sense of fairness, I think, made it unlikely that she would make up a story just to get back at somebody.

In *Townsend v. State*,[24] the prosecution's expert witness opined that a child had been sexually abused on the basis of PTSD criteria as follows:

Q: As a result of your working with Sheila, what was your diagnosis of her?

A: Posttraumatic stress disorder as a result of sexual abuse.

Q: Now, I am sure this jury is like I am, do not understand the post-traumatic stress disorder.

A: Very simply stated, it is a disorder which is a function of being exposed to a traumatic or series of traumatic incidents.

Q: What are the characterizations of that disorder that you observed in Sheila?

A: In Sheila the observation of the anxiety, the fearfulness that was going to be the outcome. She's talked about the fearfulness of other kids hearing about what happened and how they are going to react to her. There are episodes when things—one of the things you see in post-trauma, there could be brushes with violence which are precipitated with minimal precipitation. There were also indications of that.

Q: Is this post-trauma stress disorder something that you have observed in other children in the 120 some cases that you worked on other children that have been sexually assaulted as Sheila had?

A: Yes.

In proving the rape of an adult, however, most courts, like the California Supreme Court in *Bledsoe,* have concluded that rape trauma syndrome does not meet the standard of general acceptance in the scientific community.[25] The court emphasized, however, that while such testimony is not admissible for the purpose of proving that a rape occurred, it may be admissible for other purposes, such as explaining to the jury certain ·popular myths concerning rape victims. It may be used to explain a delay in reporting. Likewise, in battered spouse cases, prosecutors call mental health professionals as expert witnesses to explain the individual's failure to make a timely report for fear of reprisal, fear of being blamed, and fear of terminating the relationship.[26]

Quite frequently the prosecutor seeks to introduce evidence to explain behavior unique to victims of sexual assault in order to enhance the credibility of its witnesses. Some child or adult victims of sexual assault, for example, may fear retaliation and may delay reporting the crime for a longer period than the victims of other crimes. Others may delay out of shame; still others may recant their earlier allegations. The *child sexual abuse accommodation syndrome* (developed by Dr. Roland Summit) has as its premise that children do not lie about sexual abuse, but change their stories for other reasons.[27]

Promptness in the report of a crime tends to be taken as evidence of reliability. It is regarded as an indication that the accusation is not a concoction. Indeed, the law of evidence regards spontaneity of a statement as an indicium of trustworthiness and makes an exception for it in the rule against hearsay.[28] How can a prosecutor deal with a delay in reporting, or with a recanting of the story? In *Bledsoe,* the court said: "[I]n such a context expert testimony on rape trauma syndrome may play a particularly useful role by disabusing the jury of some widely held misconceptions about rape and rape victims, so that it may evaluate the evidence free of the constraints of popular myths."[29] Thus, in another case, in Washington, a worker at a "sexual assault center" was allowed to testify that in over 50 percent of sexual abuse cases involving children there is a delay in reporting.[30]

Syndromes are multiplying. In the 1970s, there was much publicity about a disorder called the Stockholm Syndrome. The presenting symptom of this affliction affected hostages who showed signs of sympathy for the captors who had terrorized them. This condition was offered as an explanation for Patty Hearst's taking part alongside her former captors in a bank robbery. Not much is heard now about the Stockholm Syndrome, but we hear a lot about many others. London's *Spectator* reported that the prince and princess of Wales were both suffering slighted-spouse syndrome, the symptoms of which "are a loss of any dignity and a craving to tell the world one's own side of the story."[31] The Montana Supreme Court upheld an award of $240,000 in damages to a Beaverhead county farmer because the state's nearby highway construction was stressful to his pigs. A veterinarian gave expert testimony about porcine stress syndrome.[32] After a few days in Jerusalem, the Holy City, apparently normal pilgrims imagine they are biblical figures. The Holy City derangement is labeled Jerusalem Syndrome.[33] Then, too, turn-of-the-century jubilees caused the premillennium stress syndrome.[34]

In *Werner v. State,*[35] Judge Marvin Teague of the Texas Court of Criminal Appeals described the proliferation in this way: "Today, we have the following labels: 'The Battered Wife Syndrome'; 'The Battered Child Syndrome'; 'The Battered Husband Syndrome'; 'The Battered Patient Syndrome'; 'The Familial Child Sexual

Abuse Syndrome'; 'The Rape Trauma Syndrome'; 'The Battle Fatigue Syndrome'; 'The Vietnam Post-Traumatic Stress Syndrome'; 'The Policeman's Syndrome'; 'The Whiplash Syndrome'; 'The Low-Back Syndrome'; 'The Lover's Syndrome'; 'The Love Fear Syndrome'; 'The Organic Delusional Syndrome'; and 'The Holocaust Syndrome.' Tomorrow, there will probably be additions to the list, such as 'The Appellate Court Judge Syndrome.'"

Werner involved the admissibility of evidence on the Holocaust Syndrome, offered in support of a plea of self-defense (just as evidence of battered spouse is offered to establish a lower threshold for self-defense). The syndrome is one exhibited by children of survivors of the Holocaust who grew up hearing the stories from their parents of how entire Jewish families perished, without resisting, in the concentration camps during World War II. These children have formed a firm determination that if their lives are ever threatened, they will immediately resist forcibly and not permit injustice to be foisted upon them. This mind-set makes them vulnerable to precipitous use of deadly force in what they believe is self-defense when confronted with assaultive behavior.

In this case, a psychiatrist would have testified (if allowed) that the defendant showed "some" of the characteristics of the syndrome associated with children of survivors of Nazi concentration camps. He would also have testified "that one does not need to be thinking of an event for another event in one's life to have an effect, a subconscious effect on him." The State objected to the proffered testimony on the ground of relevancy; that is, if self-defense is urged, the test to be applied is "the standard of an ordinary and prudent person in the defendant's position at the time of the offense." The majority of the Texas Court of Criminal Appeals, sitting en banc agreed; but Judge Teague, while mocking the proliferating phenomenon of syndrome evidence, argued in dissent that the Holocaust Syndrome should be given the same deference as the battered spouse syndrome, or other syndrome, that is allowed to explain the effects of abuse on the condition of a defendant's mind.

It remains a controversial issue whether syndrome evidence should be admissible as evidence to establish that a specific stressor has in fact occurred. Because symptoms of a psychological nature are not stressor specific, the duck test is of questionable value. These symptoms do not imply etiology. With few exceptions, the American Psychiatric Association's *Diagnostic and Statistical Manual of Mental Disorders* does not set out the etiology of the disorders.[36] A wide variety of stressors may give rise to a given symptom, which may also be attributable to normal developmental variations.[37] During a therapy session, the poet Anne Sexton asked, "Do I make up a trauma to go with my symptoms?"[38]

As we have noted, a number of courts have allowed evidence of PTSD to explain the behavior of the victim in delaying a report or in recanting, while they have been divided on allowing it to establish the nature of a stressor or whether any stressor in fact occurred. To disallow syndrome evidence to directly prove an occurrence but to allow it to indirectly prove an occurrence by proving the complainant's credibility is to draw a distinction without a difference.[39] In either case the aim, in the last analysis, is to establish the occurrence of a stressor, either directly or through the truthfulness of the complainant. Explaining the delay in reporting by syndrome evidence is to enhance the credibility of the complaining witness and thereby, in effect, to establish the stressor. It is yet another loophole in the bar on credibility testimony.[40]

Body Language

Judges and juries have long made inferences based on body language—specific instructions by judges to juries advise them of the propriety of making decisions based on body language. *Body language* refers to the messages that people's bodies send out through their gestures, postures, or facial expressions. Increasingly, people are paying attention to it. Systematic research in *kinesics*, or the study of body language, however, began only with the publication in 1952 of Professor Ray Birdwhistell's *Introduction to Kinesics*.[41] Since then there have been numerous books and courses on how to understand body language. Julius Fast's book *Body Language*, published in 1970, remains the most popular.[42]

Charles Darwin was the first to wonder about the heritability of human facial expressions and body postures. To confirm his suspicion that all men and women use the same gestures and poses to express basic human emotions, he sent a query to colleagues in remote areas of the Americas, Africa, Asia, and Australia. Among his questions, he asked, "When a man is indignant or defiant does he frown, hold his body and head erect, square his shoulders and clench his fists?"[43] From around the world the reply was "yes" to his queries, and he became convinced that joy, sorrow, happiness, surprise, fear, and many other human feelings were expressed in panhuman gestural patterns inherited from a common evolutionary past.

The science of kinesics has systematized what people actually have long sensed—that they communicate not only with words but also with their bodies. Indeed, the Latin *gerere*, from which the word *gesture* comes, means "to show oneself." From the earliest time to the present, examples of body language have been recorded. They abound in the Bible: "A naughty person, a wicked man, walketh with a forward mouth, he winketh with his eyes, he speaketh with his feet, he teacheth with his fingers."[44] In Shakespeare's *Julius Caesar:* "Yon Cassius hath a lean and hungry look. He thinks too much; such men are dangerous."[45] In another place, Shakespeare wrote, "In thy face, I see the map of honor, truth, and loyalty."[46]

Charles Maurice de Talleyrand observed that a diplomat is given a tongue in order to hide his true thoughts. One may be deceived by verbal language, it being under the control of consciousness, but not, we are told, by the involuntary language of the body. The body never lies. "If you know what to look for," said Freud, "no mortal can keep a secret." Freud wrote: "He that has eyes to see and ears to hear may convince himself that no mortal can keep a secret. If his lips are silent, he chatters with his fingertips; betrayal oozes out of him at every pore."[47]

The theme is repeated time and again. James van Fleet, a consultant in business management and human relations, writes: "Nonverbal communication is freer from deception than verbal language. We find it easier to lie with words than with our bodies. . . . A person doesn't have to say a word to let you know what he's thinking or how he feels. His hands, eyes, mouth, and body can give away how he really feels inside."[48] Consider a woman who says she loves her husband but who is constantly pulling her wedding ring on and off; someone who says that he is glad to see you but who perspires seeing you.[49]

Psychiatrists and other medical practitioners must pay attention to *somatization*, or conversion of a mental condition into a physical disorder. The term *somatoform* derives from the Greek *soma*, meaning "body." Individuals with somatoform disorders are often said to *somatize*—that is, to experience emotional conflict or distress in the form of physical ailment. Freud's patient Dora lost her voice when the man she loved went away on a business trip. There was no neurological explanation for her aphonia. Freud concluded, "When the man she loved was away she gave up speaking; speech had lost its value since she could not speak to *him*."[50] The idea of a psychological impulse or conflict being expressed through physical symptoms became a key psychoanalytic explanation of conversion.[51]

Dr. George Sheehan, in *Running and Being*, put it this way: "Who I am is no mystery. There is no need to tap my phone or open my mail. No necessity to submit me to psychoanalysis. No call to investigate my credit rating. Nothing to be gained by invading my privacy. There is, in fact, no privacy to invade. Because like all human beings, I have no privacy. Who I am is visible for all to see. My body tells all. Tells my character, my temperament, my personality. My body tells my strength and weaknesses, tells what I can and can't do."[52]

Gerry Spence, the famed trial lawyer, says that he keeps a sharp eye on body language. He writes: "Body language is words heard with the eyes. Bodies reflect fear, boredom, interest, repulsion, openness, attraction, caring, hatred. Bodies will speak to us, if we will carefully listen with our eyes. And the easiest way to discover what the body language of another is telling us is for us to mimic the *other* and then ask ourselves how *we* are *feeling* when we take on the *other's* body positions."[53]

Fortune tellers read their clients' gestures as carefully as their palms. Airport security officers monitor the luggage check-in for people whose gestures make them suspicious. A tilt of the head, a crossing or uncrossing of the legs, even the buttoning or unbuttoning of a jacket, can speak pages about what a person is thinking or feeling about his or her immediate surroundings and situation. By watching the way soldiers march, it is possible to know their country. Ervin Litkei, composer of patriotic marches, observed that "when Americans are marching, you can feel the lightness. They don't have heavy steps like the Germans or Russians."[54]

The history of demeanor evidence from Roman to modern times is recounted by Judge Jerome Frank of the Second Circuit Court of Appeals in *NLRB v. Dinion Coil Co.*[55] In *Dinion Coil*, Judge Frank cites authorities who tell us that the fourteenth-century Postglossators—who, as judges or advocates, "had their eyes fixed upon the practical administration of the law"—maintained that:

> [T]he indispensable requisite for the judge to form his opinion on the trustworthiness of witness was that they appeared before him personally. . . . The personal impressions made upon the judge by the witnesses, their way of answering questions, their reactions and behavior in Court, were the only means of ascertaining whether their statements were trustworthy or not. . . . It was thought necessary, therefore, that the judge . . . should put on record in the files any specific reactions, e.g., that the witness stammered, hesitated in replying to a specific question, or showed fear during the interrogation.[56]

Judge Frank, we may note, taught evidence at the Yale Law School. In his book *Courts on Trial*, Judge Frank wrote:

> All of us know that, in everyday life, the way a man behaves when he tells a story—his intonations, his fidgeting, or composure, his yawns, the use of his eyes, his air of candor or of evasiveness—may furnish valuable clues

to his reliability. Such clues are by no means impeccable guides, but they are often immensely helpful.[57]

An attorney who attended a seminar on body language by Gerald Nierenberg and Henry Calero explained the benefits he had derived from consciously considering nonverbal communication. He said in the course of an office visit his client crossed his arms and legs "in a defensive position" and proceeded to spend the next hour admonishing him. Noticing the nonverbal implications of the client's gestures, he let his client talk it out of his system. Only after this did the lawyer offer professional advice on how to handle the difficult situation the client found himself in. The attorney stated that had he not attended the seminar he would have not given his client a chance to be receptive to him, since he would not have read his client's needs and would probably have attempted immediately to give him unheeded advice.[58]

One of the best-attended seminars at an annual meeting of car salespeople was on body language. "A car salesman," the instructor said, "can improve his chances of clinching a deal if he learns to read the subtle truths of body language." The sales pitch "must be adjusted to the mental peculiarities betrayed by a person's eye movements and, perhaps sealing the deal with a bond-creating touch of the shoulder."[59] And HMOs are sending physicians to workshops where they can learn body language to exude empathy while nimbly juggling patients.[60] Will it, however, be seen as phony?

In trials the law of evidence has been liberalized to allow opinion testimony by lay witnesses and they may give an opinion based on their interpretation of body language.[61] Moreover, jurors are instructed by the court that they may consider demeanor of a witness in assessing credibility.[62] A premise of several legal rules is that the opportunity of a trier of fact to view the demeanor of a witness is of great value to the trier in deciding whether to believe the witness's testimony.[63] Many judges prohibit jurors from taking notes out of concern that they will overlook informative nonverbal cues. Witnesses who appear anxious tend not to be believed.[64] The trial judge in a case that went to the U.S. Supreme Court told the jury that "wiping one's hands while testifying was almost always an indication of lying."[65]

On the basis of demeanor, the jury may decline to accept a witness's testimony though uncontradicted.[66] The importance of nonverbal elements in the assessment of witness credibility has often been noted by the courts. As one court said, "Juries and trial courts, quite often, properly give more weight to the demeanor of witnesses than to the substance of their statements in the determination of truth."[67]As another court said, "In determining the weight to be attached to the testimony of a witness it is proper to consider his appearance, general bearing, conduct on the stand, demeanor, manner of testifying, such as candor or frankness, or the clearness of his statements, and even the intonation of his voice."[68] The policy of appellate courts not to reverse a finding of fact by a trial court reflects a belief that the trier of fact is best able to assess credibility and make a more trustworthy judgment than would the appellate judges who have only a trial transcript before them. In his book *Grand Inquests*, Chief Justice William Rehnquist said about the assessment of a witness:

> First, a preliminary word of caution, familiar to lawyers and judges but perhaps not to others. All we have available to us today is the transcript

... of what each witness said. While we may assume that the report is accurate, a mere record of questions and answers tells us nothing about what the courts call the "demeanor" of the witness—the expression on his face, his attitude, his intonation, and similar things. ... It is the difference between reading a letter from someone and talking to the person face-to-face; the words used in the conversation may be the same as the ones used in the letter, but because one is able to see the person with whom one is conversing, the conversation may give an entirely different impression from the letter.[69]

In the investigation of the assassination of President Kennedy, the Warren Commission interviewed Dean Andrews, a New Orleans attorney, who had once said that Lee Harvey Oswald called him to represent him. Andrews's testimony appears at length in the commission's report, and it has been carefully studied by researchers into the assassination, and taken seriously (including by Oliver Stone in his film *JFK*). But anyone acquainted with Dean Andrews would know that he was a jokester (he died a few years ago). He was my classmate at the Tulane Law School, and he entertained us all with his antics. What is on paper often has to be taken with a grain of salt, but unfortunately it is not.[70]

Because of the importance of demeanor evidence, and the right of cross-examination, the Constitution and the hearsay rule provide for the right to confront witnesses. In the examination of a witness, trial lawyers are well advised, as Judge Frank suggested, to "watch every expression on the witness's face, every movement of his hands."[71] Louis Nizer, the celebrated lawyer, said that psychological insights are more effective in obtaining the truth than chemical or other tests provided by science. In a chapter titled "How to Tell a Liar" in his book *Reflections without Mirrors,* Nizer wrote that "nervous gestures such as scissoring the legs or shifting in the seat whenever a particular subject matter is raised is [a] distress signal sent out by the witness."[72] He concluded: "There is an imponderable over-all test of a witness's honesty. Does he look and sound truthful? It is a kind of summation of all the emanations which make him believable. It is his face, voice, directness, and above all his sincerity. That is why credibility has no relationship to education and culture. ... Character is a letter of credit written on the face."[73]

The polygraph (otherwise known as the "lie detector") measures physiological responses to questions that are interpreted to reveal whether the individual is telling the truth.[74] Not long ago Amir Lieberman and Tamir Segal of a software firm in Israel developed a lie detector on a disk, called Truster. The person whose probity is to be checked speaks into a computer microphone and the voice is tested for honesty. They found that when a person lies, the frequency of the vibrations of his voice changes (pathological liars whose minds do not separate between truth and lies are exceptions).[75] As everyone knows, Pinocchio's nose gave him away. His nose increased in length whenever he told a fabrication.[76]

Before the advent of the polygraph, phrenology held sway. It was launched as a science by the Viennese physician Franz Joseph Gall (1758–1828). Phrenologists believed bumps on the head and the shape of the head held the key to personality. Intrigued by phrenology, Mark Twain visited the offices of Lorenzo N. Fowler, a famous "practical phrenologist," in London in 1873, and found on tables all about the room, marble-white busts, hairless, every inch of the skull occupied by a shallow bump, and every bump labeled with its imposing name.[77] The *American Phrenological Journal and Miscellany* remained in publication until 1911.

Today, phrenology's failings are indeed obvious, but in our modern dismissal of it, its tremendous impact on nineteenth-century society can easily be forgotten. The brain has not been regarded throughout history as the seat of human thought. The main contribution of phrenology to contemporary psychology was that it focused attention on the brain, not the heart, liver, gallbladder, or spleen, as the seat of all thought and emotion (today's phrenology is brain imaging).[78]

Bessel van der Kolk, psychiatrist at Boston University, claims that memory of childhood abuse is stored in the hips, elbows, and toes.[79] In the 1970s, Alexander Lowen, the founder of *bioenergetic analysis,* had people beating and screaming into their pillows and practicing "deep" crying. Lowen saw the body as the repository of psychological or characterological problems and read the tensions in the facial muscles, the long skeletal muscles, and the joints as clues to the patient's problems.[80]

In the trial of the pirate Tardy, his bumps of combativeness and acquisitiveness were adjudged larger than his bump of veneration, and in a pamphlet, Professor A. E. Frew Mulley set out a phrenological delineation of the character of the man who killed President James Garfield in 1881, Charles Guiteau. His lawyers urged the insanity defense and brought in a number of neurologists to testify that he suffered from moral insanity. They invoked the theories of Cesare Lombroso, the Italian criminologist, and portrayed Guiteau as a classic example of the criminal degenerate. Lombroso's theory that criminal propensities could be ascertained by the width between the eyes and other such measurements is, like phrenology, now regarded with ridicule, but assuredly, as one commentator put it, a shopkeeper who fails to be alert to the facial features of his customers would soon go out of business.[81]

Profiling or stereotyping, true or not, has long been with us as a mode of thinking, and will always be with us. In the 1890s, it was commonplace to hear the shape of the nose associated with qualities of character. Various commentators noted that "it is certain that the shape of the nose is generally regarded not alone from an aesthetic point of view, but that to many minds it conveys an idea of weakness or strength of character, and also of social status. Certain types of nose are 'better bred' than others, and, other things being equal, a man with a 'good nose' is more likely to gain immediate respect than one with a 'vulgar' nose."[82]

The nose may be a symbolic displacement upward of the only human organ that varies in size depending on state of mind. The symbolic linkage can be traced to ancient times.[83] Then what about measuring what is below the waist? Is it revealing? As every male knows, what is below the waist governs what is above it. As a measure of truth-telling, Pinocchio's nose was a displacement upward and a phallic symbol. In *People v. John W.,*[84] a California case, the defense offered expert testimony that the defendant was not a sexual deviant on the basis of a clinical interview, an MMPI, and a penile plethysmograph examination. The expert's opinion that the defendant was not a sexual deviant was predicated largely on defendant's response to the plethysmograph. The trial judge rejected the expert testimony, and the court of appeals affirmed. The court held that the penile plethysmograph was a novel scientific technique, and that defendant had not established its general acceptance in the relevant scientific community.[85] In joking

A FREE LECTURE!

PHRENOLOGY!

DELIVERED BY WILLIAM CARROLL

January 5, 1860

Each lecture will close with the public examination of the heads of two individuals chosen by the audience.

Examinations daily at his room, with verbal or written descriptions of character.

From O. S. and L. N. Fowler TO THE PUBLIC

This is to certify that the bearer, William Carroll, has taken a full course of lessons calculated to prepare him for teaching and practicing the science of Phrenology, Physiology, and Anatomy. That he is also still farther prepared for this profession by an ardent love of the sciences and by excellent natural capabilities for that purpose; to a clear mind and good talents for learning, he adds good speaking capabilities and a phrenological organization adapting him to make an excellent examiner and lecturer. Our friends and the public may rely on obtaining from him a correct, reliable and thorough delineation of their characters. To these natural gifts he adds a lofty, noble, aspiring ambition; a good moral and strictly conscientious tone; good taste, and an organism which will wear well and improve with age. Nature has done more for him than for most persons. We commend him to the public patronage and confidence.

Subscriptions received for the
Phrenological and Water Cure Journals, and Life Illustrated

The Examination of Heads

12½ cents
children half-price
a reduction made for families and schools
November 15, 1853

Figure 7.1 *Announcement of Lecture on Phrenology*

about body language, Mae West quipped, "Is that a gun in your pocket, or are you just happy to see me?"

In his book *Telling Lies,* Paul Ekman sets out a checklist of thirty-eight clues to spot a liar. He is a psychologist at the University of California who has spent over thirty years studying nonverbal communications in cultures around the world. He confirmed Darwin's conviction that the same basic facial postures are used by various peoples around the world. Some twenty years ago he began studying signs of deceit. As part of his research, he discovered that each human emotion—joy, grief, surprise, anger, relief, and so on—is represented by the activation of a unique combination of facial muscles. He found that most people do not activate all of the facial muscles when they are lying that should be involved in genuine emotion.[86]

Another well-known expert on reading people is Jo-Ellan Dimitrius, who is employed by large law firms to help select jurors who will be sympathetic to their clients. Her reputation for being able to read people is such that she has been nicknamed "The Seer." She helped select the jury that acquitted the four police officers charged with beating Rodney King in Los Angeles, and perhaps most famously of all, she was part of the so-called dream team that picked the jury that acquitted O. J. Simpson. She has now turned to advising individuals on how to spot when people are deceiving them, particularly in intimate relationships.[87] Both Paul Ekman and Jo-Ellan Dimitrius have spoken at annual meetings of the American Academy of Psychiatry and Law. Dimitrius told her audience that studies of jurors revealed that 75 percent of jurors thought demeanor and personality of the expert (as opposed to credentials, publishing, etc.) impressed them the most.[88]

Sometimes it is easy even for a person unskilled in kinesics to make a valid interpretation of body language. As an example, imagine a woman walks into a man's office, unbuttons her dress, sits down with her body relaxed, legs spread apart, and smiles. Who doesn't know what she's saying by her gestures? Time and again, men interpret a woman's tight blouse as an invitation to sex. Legislation has been enacted, however, that excludes evidence of a woman's attire in a case of sexual harassment or rape. In testimony before the Senate Labor Committee on sexual harassment in the workplace, Phyllis Schlafly said: "When a woman walks across the room, she speaks with a universal body language that most men intuitively understand. Men hardly ever ask sexual favors of women from whom the certain answer is no."[89]

In a 1967 Clint Eastwood spaghetti western, *The Good, the Bad, and the Ugly*, Eastwood is facing four gunslingers intent on killing him. He survives without a scratch. After the dust settles, a bystander asks him, "How'd ya know which one 'ould draw first?" He replies, "The guy on the right had nervous eyes, so I figured he was too scared. The two in the middle were slightly behind the other two. They wouldn't have had clear shots. The guy on the left kept twichin' his fingers. I knew he'd be the first to draw."

At other times it may be more difficult or confusing, as, for example, when a certain judge grimaced at lawyers appearing before him, causing them considerable alarm. They did not know that the judge had suffered from the result of a stroke that left him with gestural scars. In an address at a bar association meeting, prominent trial lawyer Theodore I. Koskoff had the following advice about jury behavior:

> If the members of the jury are sitting on the edge of the chair, they're trying to hear what you're saying, or they're paying attention to what you're trying to say. If they're sitting relaxed, it may not mean much one way or the other. Maybe they've already made up their minds. Or, it may mean that they feel comfortable with you. If they're fidgeting, either they have hemorrhoids, or they're trying to grasp something or other. You can't overevaluate that kind of response, because that sort of response can be caused by many different things. But you should pay attention to it. They're telling you something. And sometimes it's the most reliable form of communication because it's not conscious.[90]

Seeking election, George Bush said "read my lips" about not raising taxes, but what were his lips really saying? Laura Rosetree of New York, who years ago became interested in reading faces, read Bush's lips: "I'm not going to be a bleeding heart." She says that every facial feature from eyebrows to chin dimples can betray how people think, behave, and handle life's challenges. She wrote the 285-page book, *I Can Read Your Face.*[91]

Needing to attend to the needs of their growing infants, women have developed a keener sense of intuition than men. They also rely on heightened awareness of their environment for protection because they tend to be physically weaker than men. "It is generally admitted," wrote Darwin, "that with woman the powers of intuition . . . are more strongly marked than in man."[92] Tests show that, on average, women read emotions, context, and all sorts of peripheral nonverbal information more effectively than men. Women absorb cues from a wider range of visual, aural, tactile, and olfactory senses simultaneously.[93]

Psychiatric evaluation, we know, depends upon inferences made from derivatives: speech, nonverbal communication, actions, behaviors.[94] In a child custody case, the inferences were dramatically put to the test in a trial.[95] In this case, the husband one day came home early from work to discover his wife in bed not with a man but with another woman. They were both lying there, naked. The wife claimed that they were just resting. (The other woman, when the husband came into the room, jumped under the bed, had a nervous breakdown, was hospitalized, and was unavailable as a witness.)

To counter the husband's eyeball testimony, the wife's attorney decided to have her undergo psychiatric and psychological testing. The doctor as expert witness was put on the stand, and on direct examination, he testified categorically that the wife was not a lesbian. The doctor was a recognized Gestalt therapist—the chief tenet of the Gestalt approach is that the analysis of parts, however thorough, cannot provide an understanding of the whole: It is necessary to look at the whole. Here is, in part, the cross-examination of the doctor:

Q: Do you believe everything that [the wife] said was the truth?

A: I have no reason to believe that it was not the truth. See, the way I determine the truth, when I listen to someone, I note discrepancies between what someone says with his words and what someone says with the rest of his body, with his tone of voice, with his physiological responses, with his facial movements—with everything that goes on.

Q: You mean you are sort of a walking polygraph?

A: Everyone is, if they are willing to pay attention to the messages that are put out. There is no such thing as telling a lie, when someone is really listening.

Q: How do you mean there is no such thing as telling a lie, doctor?

A: Well, what I mean by that is if you listen to what someone says with their words, and you also pay attention to the other messages that are communicated by the rest of the body, you will be able to appreciate the fact that you can check out what one portion of the body says by what the other portion of the body says, so that it's impossible for somebody to tell a lie and get away with it, if the respondent is willing to pay attention.

Q: You mean I talk with my feet?

A: You may be talking with your feet, you may be talking with your eyebrows, you may be talking with your forehead.

Q: Well, what did my foot say?

A: I could infer what it was saying, but you would have to verify that for me.

Q: What did it say?

A: When?

Q: Just then.

A: Could you tell me what it was saying?

Q: You heard the communication. I just wonder what it said.

A: Okay, this foot?

Q: My left foot.

A: Your left foot said to me, "I am feeling some discomfort and I want some relief, and I will raise myself, and I will put myself back down." That is what your left foot said.

Q: It said all that to me?

A: Yes.

Q: It said all that to me?

A: Yes.

Q: What did it say to you?

A: That is what it told me.

Q: It told you that it was tired?

A: That's right.

Q: What did my right foot say?

A: I don't know. It didn't move. It didn't say anything.

Q: It has to move to say something?

A: That is correct. You have to put the whole picture together.

The end result was that the father was awarded custody—even though his most valuable witness, the cross-examiner's left foot, was never sworn in.

Evidence of flight from a scene of a crime provides a basis for a search and is admissible at trial as relevant to show a consciousness of guilt. On countless occasions, the courts have ruled that flight immediately or shortly after the commission or accusation of a crime is relevant evidence of guilt. Analytically, the courts say, flight is an admission of guilt.[96] There's a saying, "The guilty flee where no man pursueth." Romeo slew Juliet's cousin and took flight. Running away from anything—be it an adult running from the scene of a homicide or a child running from an apple tree in a neighbor's yard—is automatically associated by all humans with a guilty state of mind. Of course, there may be other reasons for the running, maybe to catch a bus, but in Detroit, where there are few buses, that would hardly be a credible explanation.[97]

About to be arrested for the murders of Nicole Brown Simpson and Ronald Goldman, O. J. Simpson slipped away, and then there was a chase. On *Larry King Live*, Gerald Uelman, a member of the defense team, in answer to the question, "How do you explain the chase?" said, "Simpson was going through a lot of psychological pain. His wife was killed." Who believed that explanation? Vincent Bugliosi, former Los Angeles prosecutor, chastised the prosecution team for not introducing the evidence of the chase at trial. It was, he said, powerful incriminating evidence against Simpson. He described the prosecution as "the most incompetent criminal prosecution I have ever seen. By far."[98]

Analogous to flight, evidence of a suicide attempt by the accused has been held to be admissible as tending to show a consciousness of guilt, and it has been allowed to go to the jury to be considered together with all the other germane facts and circumstances of the case in establishing the guilt or innocence of the accused.[99] In *Tug Raven v. Trexler*,[100] a witness's testimony at a Coast Guard hearing investigating a tug boat disaster was "entitled to little weight" in view of his subsequent suicide, which "was circumstantial proof of a guilty conscience [and] must be deemed a weighty factor in diminishing the credibility of [his] exculpatory testimony." Moreover, lack of remorse following a killing or wounding may be relevant in establishing intent or a diagnosis of sociopathy.[101]

And what does a wink of the eye mean? That issue arose in a Pennsylvania case, *Commonwealth v. Holden*,[102] where the defendant was convicted of murder. At the time of his arrest, he was taken by the police to the home of one Ralph Jones who had been with the defendant for several hours prior to the killing. The prosecutor asked Jones at trial if, at the time he was being quizzed by the police in defendant's presence, the defendant did anything that was unusual. Jones replied that he sort of winked at him. The prosecutor then asked Jones what the defendant meant and Jones replied, "I think he was trying to get me to make an alibi for him to cover up some of his actions."

An objection to the evidence was overruled and the jury was thus informed that the defendant endeavored to have Jones frame an alibi for him. The Pennsylvania Supreme Court affirmed the conviction, but gave no attention to the point raised by Justice Musmanno in a dissenting opinion. Justice Musmanno wrote:

> It will be noted that the stupendous and compendious wink not only solicited the fabrication of a spurious alibi but specified that it was to cover up some of his actions. One movement of the eyelid conveyed a message of 21 words. Not even the most abbreviated Morse code could say so much with such little expenditure of muscular and mechanical power.

Justice Musmanno went on to say,

> If a witness is to be allowed to state what he believes a wink said, why should he not be allowed to interpret a cough? Or a sneeze? Or a grunt? Or a hiccough? Why should he indeed not be empowered to testify as to what is passing through an accused's brain? Why not permit mind readers to read a defendant's mind, and thus eliminate the jury system completely because who knows better than the defendant himself whether or not he committed the crime of which he stands accused?"

Could it be that Ralph Jones had taken a course in kinesics?

A hypothesis in neuropsychology holds that a negative hedonic state, such as stress, tends to increase a subject's eye-blink frequency and that a positive hedonic state, such as contentment or pleasure, tends to decrease eye-blink frequency. This hedonia hypothesis adds a new dimension to then Secretary of State Dean Rusk's statement to ABC newsman John Scali during the 1962 Cuban missile crisis: "Remember, when you report this, that, eyeball to eyeball, they blinked first."[103]

Dreams as Evidence

Dreams as evidence is problematical and controversial—Freud was responsible for reviving the idea that dreams were worth taking seriously. A longtime friend of O. J.

Simpson testified at his murder trial that O. J. told him—just hours after the murders—that he had had "lots of dreams" about killing Nicole. The prosecutors said the dreams show Simpson had a "fatal obsession" that finally led him to stab her and her friend Ronald Goldman to death. Was Simpson's "dream" really an admission couched as a dream? Or, if actually a dream, should it have been admissible as evidence of guilt?[104] Marcia Clark, the chief prosecutor in the Simpson case, reminded the court, "I think Walt Disney said it best in 'Sleeping Beauty.' A dream is a wish your heart makes." Judge Lance Ito admitted the evidence over defense's objection.[105]

The significance and meaning of dreams have intrigued people of all cultures and at all times. According to the Bible, young Joseph had a gift of dream interpretation. Throughout history, dreams have been used to discern the past and also to predict the future.[106] Dreams have meaning—they are not random events, disconnected from the thoughts, feelings, and preoccupations of the day. The "landscape of the night" is connected to the "landscape of the day," as one researcher put it.[107] "To dream," wrote Shakespeare in *Hamlet*, "perchance to speak the truth."

Dreams or fantasies are important communications to ourselves from ourselves. They express our hopes, our unease, our fears, and anxieties. Dreams or fantasies let people imagine doing things they would never do when awake; they safely dispel anger and frustration. Then there are dreams induced by trauma; dreaming is a way of dealing with the trauma.

In post-traumatic stress disorder, the traumatic event is often reexperienced by recurrent distressing dreams about the event. In evaluating an alleged injury, dreams may indicate whether an individual is malingering or suffering a traumatic neurosis. Children may have frightening posttraumatic dreams without recognizable content. Small children are vulnerable and easily scared; they dream of frightening monsters that chase and attack them.[108]

Various types of intrusive recall have been identified in PTSD. Posttraumatic nightmares, as contrasted with lifelong nightmares unrelated to trauma, are almost always accompanied by considerable body movement. Nightmares experienced after trauma usually include variations on the theme of the traumatic event. Survivors of natural disasters, victims of accidents and crimes, and combat veterans relive those terrifying events again and again in their dreams. When the image of a crisis is especially intense, it takes time to absorb it.[109]

Dreams or fantasies may furnish other kinds of clues as well. In interviewing a criminal defendant, the forensic expert inquires about dreams and fantasies. They may indicate that the defendant was expecting an assault and was acting in self-defense. A murder victim's fear has been used to prove the perpetrator's identity (at least in investigation). The hearsay statement of fear by a murder victim is admissible and relevant to prove or explain subsequent acts of the decedent.[110]

Studies abound on dreams and personality. The book on the personality of a child molester by Alan Bell and Calvin Hall documents the importance of dreams in understanding personality development.[111] Wayne Myers describes the secret longings, fantasies, and prejudices of therapists and how these affect their patients.[112] Robert L. van Castle explores the role that dreams have played in politics, art, religion, and psychology.[113]

Therapists, in evaluating whether a patient is dangerous, consider dreams and fantasies; therapists in many states are obliged to warn persons threatened by their patients.[114] In an incident at the Anderson Valley Water District, an employee informed the human resources department that several employees in one of the departments had talked of having lurid dreams about the department supervisor. In the dreams, they envisioned themselves committing violent acts against the supervisor. Management met several times, over a period of weeks, trying to decide how to respond to the report. They consulted a forensic psychiatrist, Stephen Baldridge, who thought the situation was indeed serious, although he stopped short of recommending termination of any employee. The managers considered a variety of options, such as counseling and suspensions, but finally decided on discharge of the employees. The union filed a grievance on behalf of the discharged employees. At the hearing, the union presented its own mental health professional, Dr. Walter Jones, who testified that having nightmares did not indicate a potential for violence. In a lengthy decision, the arbitrator held the discharge letter unacceptably ambiguous, because it "does not clearly state whether the grievants are being discharged for having dreams about killing" the supervisor, "making threats on his life, or something else." He ruled that employees could be discharged for making threats but that a dream is not tantamount to a threat. A dream, he said, is an "involuntary process over which the grievants have no control."[115]

The University of Michigan took action against Jake Baker, a student who posted a rape-torture fantasy on the Internet. The university said it was obliged to evaluate the safety of the woman named in the fantasy. At the hearing, a psychiatrist and psychologist both testified on behalf of the student that he was not a danger to himself or others. In an interview, Robert Ressler, a retired FBI (Federal Bureau of Investigation) agent and coauthor of *Sexual Homicide: Patterns and Motives*, said that while not everyone who has such fantasies becomes dangerous, "every serial killer starts with fantasizing. If it is becoming a preoccupation, a night-and-day fixation and really turning him on," he said, "that is a sign of real trouble."[116]

"Just thinking about it doesn't do the trick anymore," Jake Baker reportedly wrote in one e-mail message. "I need to do it." He was charged with the federal crime of transporting threatening material across state lines. The magistrate said that although Baker never physically approached or spoke with the woman named in the posting, it suggested that he was "disturbed" and "dangerous," "a ticking time bomb waiting to go off." His mother acknowledged that her son was angry but insisted, "He didn't *do* anything, he wrote fantasy." She might have added that he saw it many times in films.[117]

One evidence casebook asks (without answering) whether the "testimony" of Iago would be admissible against Cassio or Desdemona. In Shakespeare's *Othello*, Iago says, "In sleep I heard him [Cassio] say, 'Sweet Desdemona, Let us be way, let us hide our loves.'"[118] The question also appeared on a state bar examination.

What's the answer? Might dreams be compared to excited utterances and slips of the tongue, which are admissible in evidence? Although statements made in the course of a sodium amytal interview are not admissible, they may provide leads for investigation or they may be used in plea bargaining.

The admission of the evidence in the Simpson trial and the arrest of Jake Baker caused a Detroit newspaper columnist to wonder whether she should worry about her dreams. She wrote that by day she is a peacemaker, a compromiser, but at night she is a tempest, a monster, and sometimes a murdered. She wrote:

What if I decide to write down my dreams on Internet, where I can freely explore their nuances and deeper meanings with others interested in dream interpretations? Could I be arrested, like the student at the University of Michigan, for the sins of my unconscious mind? What if, God forbid, something accidentally happens to a loved one, only a few days after I confide my dark underbelly to a friend? Will I find myself on trial trying to defend myself against my own nightmares, like O. J. Simpson?

Hold me responsible for what I do. Jail me, punish me, ostracize me for my dastardly deeds. My actions are within my control. But where I go at night in my sleep is the quiet business of my unconscious mind. I should not be held responsible for my dreams.[119]

Dreams, of course, do not warrant an arrest, but they are significant. Recurrent dreams seem often to be statements about unresolved problems. Dreams are so closely related to our waking lives that we can use them to help us recognize and work out inner conflicts. The Talmud teaches, "A dream that has not been explained is like a letter that has not been read." Freud believed that so many mental operations, and the most consequential ones at that, are unconscious. His desire to understand the complexities of his own sexual constitution prompted him to begin to explore dreams systematically as a means of coming to grips with the unconscious. It was the royal road to knowledge of the mind. The dreams of his patient Sergei Pankejeff, a.k.a. the "Wolf Man," came to symbolize for Freud the latent homosexuality of Pankejeff. Indeed, all of Freud's case histories revolve around the dreams of his patients. Of course, as Freud cautioned, interpretations of dreams without self-disclosure are worthless, although at times Freud said it was unnecessary to have the associations of the patient to interpret the dream (a knife in a dream always represents a penis). Carl Jung believed in the universality of symbols in dreams.

In his autobiography, Art Buchwald relates that he never saw his mother, although she lived until he was in his thirties. She was in a mental hospital; as a child, he was not permitted to visit her, and when he grew up, he didn't want to. He preferred the mother he had invented to the one he would find in the hospital. The denial was a very heavy burden to carry around. When he grew up and was in analysis, discussions about his mother took up quite a bit of time. One of the reasons for this, he says, was that his mother turned up in so many dreams—watching him, following him, but never saying anything. He might escape her in the daytime, but not when he slept.[120]

In April 1991, almost a year after Harvard psychiatrist Margaret Bean-Bayog terminated with her patient, Harvard medical school student Paul Lozano, he died, at age twenty-eight, of a self-inflicted cocaine overdose. It made national headlines. An affirmative action student from a Mexican-American El Paso family, Lozano had a woeful academic background and a history of drug abuse and a number of suicide attempts. He was admitted several times to psychiatric hospitals. Therapy supposedly would sustain him at Harvard. Was he beyond therapy, or was the therapy inappropriate? According to reports, Bean-Bayog utilized "regressive and restitutive" therapy. She regressed him to the age of three and urged him to call her "Mom." She instructed him (including by notes and tape), "I'm your Mom, and I love you, and you love me very, very much." She saw him three to five times a week over a four-year span. In her records, she (naively) noted her sexual fantasies about him, such as "I'm going to miss so many things about you . . . phenomenal sex and being so appreciated." She claims these were nothing more than fantasies, her private way of examining her sexual feelings and bringing them under control. Surreptitiously, Lozano took her office records. Shortly following his death, his family came upon them. A lawsuit was filed accusing her of malpractice that resulted in the death of their son. The records were damming. Bean-Bayog gave up her medical license and settled with the Lozano family for the $1 million coverage of her insurance policy.[121]

The issue of the admissibility of dreams has been raised in a number of cases; most notably in recent years, the O. J. Simpson case. The usual ruling is that the evidence is not admissible as direct evidence (though it may be a factor in an expert opinion).[122] In 1861 in California, in apparently the first American case on the subject, a witness for the prosecution testified about the sleep talk of the defendant. The defendant was convicted of murder, and appealed. In a short opinion, the appellate court reversed, saying: "It is difficult to see upon what principle this evidence was admitted, and we are of the opinion that the objection to it should have been sustained. If the defendant was asleep, the inference is that he was not conscious of what he was saying, and words spoken by him in that condition constituted no evidence of guilt."[123]

In a civil action in Vermont for injuries from a dog bite, testimony from the father of the plaintiff that the boy had cried out, "Take him off," during his sleep was ruled inadmissible. The court said, "Words spoken while in sleep are not evidence of a fact or condition of mind. They proceed from an unconscious and irresponsible condition; they have little or no meaning; they are as likely to refer to unreal facts or conditions as to things real; they are wholly unreliable."[124]

In a New York case, the defendant was charged with murder and arson. The evidence against the defendant consisted almost entirely of his incriminating statements. Over objection, the accused's girlfriend was permitted to testify that on the morning of the victim's death by stabbing, the accused talked in his sleep about blood spurting and how he cleaned a knife, statements he did not recall after he had awakened. The appellate court said, "The circumstances in which the statements were purportedly made, in defendant's sleep, severely detract from their reliability, and in view of the prejudicial nature of the statements, it was error to admit them."[125]

In an Oregon case, a seven-year-old claimed that on three occasions her stepfather, whom she called "Daddy," inserted his finger in her "pee-pee." A medical examination provided no support for her assertions of sexual abuse. According to the foster parent, the child had cried out in her sleep, "Daddy, get off me. Daddy, stop, leave me alone." The stepfather was convicted of sexual abuse, but on appeal, a reversal resulted from the reviewing court's disapproval of the admission of the child's sleep talk. The use of the word "Daddy" did not necessarily refer to her stepfather, the court said.[126]

In an unreported child custody case, it was argued that the husband should not have any form of visitation rights, based upon inferences drawn from his dream diary, in which a number of sex dreams were recorded. The husband, a scientist, had kept a diary of his dreams for nearly six years, and during this time had recorded the details of nearly a thousand dreams. This diary was confiscated by his wife, who proceeded to check carefully the dreams for material that she thought might be incriminating if presented in court. She found a few dreams in which the husband had incestuous relations with some of their young daughters. The wife contended that those dreams proved her husband was an unfit father who would try to turn his incestuous dreams into reality if allowed future visits with the daughters. She therefore insisted that her husband be denied any visitation. A psychiatrist on behalf of the husband testified that while there were 7 dreams involving incest, approximately 130 involved sexual relationships with adult females; since this was nearly twenty times the number of incestuous dreams, it seemed as if the dreamer's main sexual interests were clearly of an adult heterosexual type. The judge ruled that the dream diary did not constitute sufficient evidence to deny visitation.[127]

In a case long ago, the West Virginia Supreme Court said it was questionable whether the accused was asleep or awake when the "exclamation escaped from her." The court said that it was proper to put it to the jury to decide whether the defendant was awake or asleep when the "ejaculation" was made and to make an intelligent estimate of its weight. The court analogized a statement made in sleep to an involuntary statement. Involuntary statements, when not coerced by law-enforcement officials, are admissible, however, depending upon their trustworthiness.[128]

In a Georgia case, Willie Calvin Sutton was convicted by a jury on circumstantial evidence of the murders of his two apparently illegitimate infant daughters and for setting fire to his home to conceal the crimes. He appealed, contending that the trial court erred in admitting testimony of a witness who overheard his incriminating statements. The evidence was conflicting as to whether the defendant was conscious or unconscious when he made the statements. Consciousness again was made the determining factor. Affirming the conviction, the Georgia Supreme Court said, "[The matter of consciousness is] within the province of the jury to decide. The statements were relevant and material to the issues before the court."[129]

In a Minnesota case, Raymond Posten was convicted of first-degree criminal sexual conduct. The Minnesota Supreme Court ruled that the admission of testimony relating the sleep talk of a six-year-old complainant concerning her fear of the defendant attacking her again, was not abuse of discretion by the trial court, given that the testimony was not the only evidence against the defendant and was used primarily for corroborative purposes.[130]

To be sure, a dream is heavily symbolic, but the dream message can be interpreted by the events of the day and associations to the dream. Dream analysts practice a broad, free-association-type interpretation. Dreams have to be interpreted in context, involving the events of the day and the individual's associations to the dream. Dreams and fantasies are informative, but it is not possible to fairly discern their meaning in the legal arena. For that reason, excluding them as evidence is warranted, and not for the reason that they occur involuntarily or in a state of unconsciousness.

It is also to be noted that under rape shield laws, evidence of the past sexual behavior of an alleged victim in sex offense cases is limited. The notes of the Advisory Committee of the Federal Rules of Evidence states that the excluded evidence includes evidence of "activities of the mind, such as fantasies or dreams."[131]

The Simpson case has generated discussion of the admissibility of dreams as evidence, but, one might ask, why accept O. J.'s characterization of his statement to his longtime friend as a report of a dream? Was it actually a dream, or was it a confession? Quite likely, following the crime, O. J. felt inner pressure to confess in order to relieve his conscience, so he told a friend that he dreamed he killed Nicole.

Notes

1. D. McCord, "Syndromes, Profiles and Other Mental Exotica: A New Approach to the Admissibility of Nontraditional Psychological Evidence in Criminal Cases," *Ore. L. Rev.* 66 (1987): 19.

2. C. Slobogin, "Psychiatric Evidence in Criminal Trials: A 25-Year Retrospective," in L. E. Frost & R. J. Bonnie (eds.), *The Evolution of Mental Health Law* (Washington, D.C.: American Psychological Association, 2000), p. 246.

3. J. Caffey, "Pediatric X-Ray Diagnosis," in *Yearbook* (Chicago: Medical Publishers, 7th ed. 1978), p. 1335; J. Caffey, "The Parent-Infant Traumatic Stress Syndrome," *Am. J. Radiology* 114 (1972): 218.

4. C. H. Kempe, F. N. Silverman, B. F. Steele, W. Droegemueller, & H. J. Silver, "The Battered Child Syndrome," *J. Am. Med. Assn.* 181 (1962): 17.

5. See, e.g., United States v. Whitted, 11 F.3d 782 (8th Cir. 1993); State v. Cates, 632 N.W.2d 28 (S.D. 2001); People v. James, 451 N.W.2d 611 (Mich. App. 1990). Under an exception to the hearsay rule, a treating physician or forensic examiner may testify as to what the child said about the incident and also about the identity of the offender. Rule 803(4), Federal Rules of Evidence; United States v. Iron Shell, 633 F.2d 77 (8th Cir. 1981); United States v. Renville, 779 F.2d 430 (8th Cir. 1985); State v. Robinson, 153 Ariz. 191, 735 P.2d 801 (1987); People v. Meeboer, 439 Mich. 310 484 N.W.2d 621 (1992).

6. See, e.g., People v. Bledsoe, 36 Cal.3d 236, 203 Cal. Rptr. 450, 681 P.2d 291 (1984); State v. McCoy, 400 N.W.2d 807 (Minn. App. 1987).

7. R. J. Roe, "Expert Testimony in Child Sexual Abuse Cases," *U. Miami L. Rev.* 40 (1985): 97.

8. R. D. Marshall, R. Spitzer, & M. R. Liebowitz, "Review and Critique of the New DSM-IV Diagnosis of Acute Stress Disorder," *Am. J. Psychiatry* 156 (1999): 1677.

9. A. M. Drukteinis, "Overlapping Somatoform Syndromes in Personal Injury Litigation," presented at the annual meeting of the American College of Forensic Psychiatry in Newport Beach, Cal., Mar. 30, 2000.

10. See P. R. McHugh, "How Psychiatry Lost Its Way," *Commentary,* Dec. 1999, p. 32; Note, "Unreliability of Expert Testimony on Typical Characteristics of Sexual Abuse Victims," *Georgetown L.J.* 74 (1980): 429.

11. D. W. Abse, "Hysteria," in S. Arieti (ed.), *American Handbook of Psychiatry* (New York: Basic Books, 1959), vol. 1, p. 272.

12. See J. M. Masson, "Freud and the Seduction Theory," *Atlantic,* Feb. 1984, p. 33. See also D. P. Spence, *Narrative Truth and Historical Truth: Meaning and Interpretation in Psychoanalysis* (New York: Norton, 1982).

13. Reported by Dr. Bertram Karon of Michigan State University in an address on delusions presented at a meeting of the Detroit Psychoanalytic Society, Apr. 11, 1987, in Ann Arbor.

14. See W. M. Grove and R. C. Barden, "Protecting the Integrity of the Legal System: The Admissibility of Testimony from Mental Health Experts under *Daubert/Kumho* Analyses," *Psychology, Public Policy, and Law* 5 (1999): 224.

15. For a discussion, see D. W. Shuman, "The Diagnostic and Statistical Manual of Mental Disorders in the Courts," *Bull. Am. Acad. Psychiatry & Law* 17 (1989): 25.

16. Evidence of rape trauma syndrome was allowed in State v. Marks, 231 Kan. 645, 647 P.2d 1292 (1982), but was rejected in State v. Saldana, 324 N.W.2d 227 (Minn. 1982). See Annot., "Admissibility, at Criminal Prosecution, of Expert Testimony on Rape Trauma Syndrome," 42 A.L.R.4th 879 (1985).

17. 36 Cal.3d 236, 203 Cal. Rptr. 4:50, 681 P.2d 291 (1984).

18. In United States v. Wesson, 779 F.2d 1443 (9th Cir. 1986), the Ninth Circuit allowed a doctor's testimony that the alleged rape victim's injuries were not consistent with consensual intercourse to "aid the jury in determining the credibility of the alleged victim's claim that the intercourse was nonconsensual." 779 F.2d at 1444. Similarly, in Henson v. State, 535 N.E.2d 1189 (Ind. 1989), the Indiana Supreme Court held that "fundamental fairness" required that the defense be allowed to present rape trauma syndrome evidence to show that the victim's behavior was inconsistent with that of a rape victim. See also United States v. Rivera, 43 F.3d 1291 (9th Cir. 1995); State v. Wilkerson, 295 N.C. 559, 247 S.E.2d 905 (1978);

People v. Whitfield, 425 Mich. 116, 388 N.W.2d 206 (1986). See P. A. Petretic-Jackson & S. Tobin, "The Rape Trauma Syndrome: Symptoms, Stages, and Hidden Victims," in T. L. Jackson (ed.), *Acquaintance Rape: Assessment, Treatment, and Prevention* (Sarasota, Fla.: Professional Resource Press, 1996), pp. 93–143. See the discussion on profile evidence in chapter 6, on propensity and other acts evidence.

19. The *Bledsoe* case involved a 28-year-old offender and a 14-year-old victim. People v. Bledsoe, 36 Cal.3d 236, 203 Cal. Rptr. 450, 681 P.2d 291 (1984).

20. In Spencer v. General Electric Co., 688 F.Supp. 1072 (E.D.Va. 1988); Commonwealth v. Zamarripa, 379 Pa. Super. 20, 549 A.2d 980 (Pa. Super. Ct. 1988). There are decisions to the contrary. See, e.g., State v. Allewalt, 308 Md. 89, 517 A.2d 741 (1986). See T. M. Massaro, "Experts, Psychology, Credibility and Rape: The Rape Trauma Syndrome Issue and Its Implications for Expert Psychological Testimony," *Minn. L. Rev.* 69 (1985): 395.

21. People v. Lukity, 596 N.W.2d 607 (Mich. 1999); State v. McCoy, 400 N.W.2d 807 (Minn. App. 1987); see also supra note 5.

22. In Oliver v. State of Texas, 2000 WL 1389677, a Texas appellate court held that an expert may not testify that a person's recitation of events is or is not the product of fantasy or manipulation, because such evidence is, in effect, particularized testimony concerning the person's credibility, but the court said, however, that an expert may testify about both the common traits or symptoms of child sexual abuse syndrome and whether the victim exhibits these traits. See also People v. Beckley, 434 Mich. 691, 456 N.W.2d 391 (1990); In re Brimer, 191 Mich. App. 401, 478 N.W.2d 689 (1991). The rule applies to child protective proceedings as well as to criminal prosecution.

23. 64 Hawaii 598, 645 P.2d 1130 (1982).

24. 734 P.2d 705 (Nev. 1987).

25. See chapter 3, on *Frye* and *Daubert*, for a discussion of standards for expert testimony.

26. See Ibn-Tamas v. United States, 407 A.2d 626 (D.C. 1979); Commonwealth v. Craig, 783 S.W.2d 387 (Ky. 1990). In State v. Kinney, 762 A.2d 833 (Vt. 2000), the court held that expert testimony of rape trauma syndrome is admissible to assist the jury in evaluating the evidence, and frequently to respond to defense claims that the victim's behavior after the alleged rape was inconsistent with the claim that the rape occurred. See D. McCord, "The Admissibility of Expert Testimony Regarding Rape Trauma Syndrome in Rape Prosecutions," *Bost. Coll. L. Rev.* 26 (1985): 1143. For discussion of the battered woman syndrome, see L. Walker, *The Battered Woman Syndrome* (New York: Springer, 1984). The prominent Australian barrister Ian Freckelton argues against the role of syndrome evidence in the legal system and questions whether battered woman syndrome and rape trauma syndrome merit the status that they have been accorded by some courts. I. Freckelton, "Contemporary Comment: When Plight Makes Right—The Forensic Abuse Syndrome," *Criminal L. J.* 18 (1994): 29. See also A. L. Hyams, "Expert Psychiatric Evidence in Sexual Misconduct Cases before State Medical Boards," *Am. J. Law & Med.* 17 (1992): 171.

27. R. C. Summit, "The Child Sexual Abuse Accommodation Syndrome," *Child Abuse & Neglect* 7 (1983): 177; see S. J. Ceci & H. Hembrooke (eds.), *Expert Witnesses in Child Abuse Cases* (Washington, D.C.: American Psychological Association, 1998); see also T. G. Gutheil & P. K. Sutherland, "Forensic Assessment, Witness Credibility and the Search for Truth through Expert Testimony in the Courtroom," *J. Psychiatry & Law* 27 (1999): 289.

28. Federal Rules of Evidence, Rule 803(2).

29. 681 P.2d at 298.

30. State v. Petrich, 101 Wash.2d 566, 683 P.2d 173 (1984).

31. Oct. 22, 1994, p. 36.

32. State of Montana v. Howery, 204 Mont. 417, 664 P.2d 1387 (1983).

33. D. Sontag, "On Millennium's Heels, One for Jews," *New York Times,* Dec. 31, 1999, p. 3; E. Umansky, "Jerusalem Syndrome and Other 'Narcissistic Delusions,'" *Forward,* June 4, 1999, p. 18.

34. R. D. Rosen, "Millencholy," *New York Times,* Dec. 29, 1999, p. 25.

35. 711 S.W.2d 639 (Tex. Cr. App. 1986).

36. For example, the most common childhood diagnosis—attention-deficit hyperactivity disorder—describes behavior without in any way explaining its origin. The medication Ritalin is commonly given to treat the symptoms. For a critique, see P. R. Breggin, *Reclaiming*

Our Children (New York: Perseus Books, 2000); R. DeGrandpre, *Ritalin Nation* (New York: W. W. Norton, 1999); L. H. Hiller, "Running on Ritalin," *Doubletake*, Fall 1998, p. 46.

37. In United States v. Charley, 176 F.3d 1265 (10th Cir. 1999), the Tenth Circuit ruled that a mental health counselor's opinion that the child's symptoms were more consistent with symptoms of children who have been sexually abused than with the symptoms of children who witness physical abuse of their mother was erroneously admitted, the court held, citing Kumho Tire Co. v. Carmichael, 119 S. Ct. 1167 (1999), because no sufficient foundation was laid for this kind of expert's analysis, and no reliability inquiry was undertaken. 176 F.3d at 1281. See chapter 3, on *Daubert*.

38. D. W. Middlebrook, *Anne Sexton: A Biography* (New York: Houghton Mifflin, 1991), p. xv.

39. In State v. Hall, 330 N.C. 808, 412 S.E.2d 883 (1991), evidence that a victim's symptoms are consistent with those of the typical sexual or physical abuse victim was held admissible, but only to aid the jury in assessing the complainant's credibility.

40. Hypothetical: In a prosecution for rape, the complainant testified that on a certain day she was at the Orange Blossom Bar where she met the defendant, a former boyfriend. She alleged that when the bar closed, she went to her automobile in the parking lot, and the defendant followed, took out a knife, and forced her to drive to her apartment, where he raped her. Some time later, she again visited the Orange Blossom Bar. By way of defense, defense counsel sought to introduce the testimony of an expert that he had "worked with patients who had suffered post-traumatic stress syndrome, including patients with rape in their backgrounds," and that in his opinion a person who had been raped would be unlikely to revisit the place where the incident had occurred. Should the court exclude the testimony? It likely would be allowed. P. Reidenger, "Private Nightmares," *ABAJ*, May 1990, p. 92; see also the discussion on postact behavior in the section of this chapter on body language.

In Commonwealth v. Rather, 37 Mass. App. Ct. 140, 638 N.E.2d 915 (1994), the Massachusetts Court of Appeals held that it was reversible error for the expert psychologist to testify about the "pattern of disclosure of child sexual abuse victims," saying that, given the circumstances in the case, "the jury could reasonably have concluded that the [expert] witness had implicitly rendered an opinion as to the general truthfulness of the victims." The court cited as support a prior holding that "while the proposed testimony fell short of rendering an opinion on the credibility of the . . . [victims] before the court, we see little difference in the final result. It would be unrealistic to allow this type of . . . testimony and then expect the jurors to ignore it when evaluating the credibility of the complaining [witness]." 37 Mass. App. Ct. at 149. In general, see C. Bleil, "Evidence of Syndromes: No Need for a 'Better Mousetrap,'" *S. Texas L. Rev.* 32 (1990): 37.

41. R. L. Birdwhistell, *Introduction to Kinesics* (Louisville, Ky.: University of Louisville Press, 1952). See also by R. L. Birdwhistell, *Kinesics and Context* (Philadelphia: University of Pennsylvania Press, 1970).

42. J. Fast, *Body Language* (Philadelphia: Evans, 1970). See also J. Fast, *Body Language in the Workplace* (New York: Penguin, 1991).

43. C. Darwin, *The Expression of the Emotions in Man and Animals* (1872; Chicago: University of Chicago Press, 1965).

44. Prov. 6:12, 13.

45. Act 1, scene 2.

46. *Henry the Sixth, Part II*, act 3, scene 1.

47. P. Gay (ed.), *The Freud Reader* (New York: W. W. Norton, 1989).

48. J. K. van Fleet, *The Complete Guide to Verbal Manipulation* (Paramus, N.J.: Prentice Hall, 1984), pp. 139, 142.

49. For the famous portrait of the physician Paul-Ferdinand Gachet, Vincent van Gogh seated his subject with his head resting on his hand, in the traditional pose of melancholy. He drew Gachet's melancholy pose from a portrait by Eugene Delacroix of the sixteenth-century Italian epic poet Torquato Tasso after he had been unjustly incarcerated for insanity. From the Delacroix, van Gogh also borrowed the painting's mood of desolation. Van Gogh had gone to see Gachet in the hope that he could provide a cure for van Gogh's illness, but was disappointed. The portrait spoke to van Gogh's understanding of his illness and his fears of the unresolved consequences of the doctor's failure to address his illness. In painting the portrait, van Gogh reversed the roles of patient and doctor. In a letter to the artist Paul

Gauguin, van Gogh explained his intent. "I have a portrait of Dr. Gachet," he wrote, "with the heartbroken expression of our time." About two weeks later, van Gogh committed suicide. The portrait, as it turned out, revealed his intention. C. Saltzman, *Portrait of Dr. Gachet: The Story of a Van Gogh Masterpiece* (New York: Viking, 1998).

50. S. Freud, *Standard Edition*, vol. 7, p. 40.

51. Time and again, therapists proclaim to be decoders not only of dreams but also of physical symptoms. Karl Abraham, a loyal member of Freud's inner circle, noted that facial tics, for example, resembled grimaces and therefore had "obvious hostile significance." Smith Ely Jelliffe, a prominent American analyst, explained in a 1917 textbook why an elderly woman with schizophrenia continually pounded one hand with her other fist. "It was discovered that in her earlier days she had been jilted by a shoemaker. This peculiar action could be seen, in the light of this knowledge, as but the movements of the shoemaker pounding at his last." The German psychoanalyst George Groddeck wrote in 1923: "Whoever breaks an arm has either sinned or wished to commit a sin with that arm, perhaps murder, perhaps theft or masturbation; whoever grows blind desires no more to see, has sinned with his eyes or wishes to sin with them; whoever gets hoarse has a secret and dares not tell it aloud." Groddeck was a self-described "wild analyst." See E. Dolnick, *Madness on the Couch: Blaming the Victim in the Heyday of Psychoanalysis* (New York: Simon & Schuster, 1998).

52. G. Sheehan, *Running and Being* (New York: Simon & Schuster, 1978), p. 32.

53. G. Spence, *How to Argue and Win Every Time* (New York: St. Martin's Press, 1995), p. 72.

54. A. Kozinn, "Ervin Litkei, 78, Composer of Many Patriotic Marches" (obituary), *New York Times*, Feb. 16, 2000, p. 23.

55. 201 F.2d 484, 487–90 (2d Cir. 1952). The Advisory Committee to the Federal Rules of Evidence stated: "The demeanor of the witness traditionally has been believed to furnish trier and opponent with valuable clues." Introductory Note on Article VIII on Hearsay in the Federal Rules of Evidence. In Pate v. Robinson, 383 U.S. 275 (1966), the U.S. Supreme Court stated that a defendant's "demeanor at trial might be relevant to the ultimate decision as to his sanity." 383 U.S. at 386. In Drope v. Missouri, 420 U.S. 162 (1975), the Supreme Court explained, "The import of our decision in *Pate v. Robinson* is that evidence of a defendant's irrational behavior, his demeanor at trial, and any prior medical opinion on competence to stand trial are all relevant in determining whether further inquiry is required [in regard competency to stand trial], but that even one of these factors standing alone may, in some circumstances, be sufficient." 420 U.S. at 180. See H. S. Sahm, "Demeanor Evidence: Elusive and Intangible Imponderables," *ABAJ* 47 (1961): 580.

56. 201 F.2d at 488.

57. J. Frank, *Courts on Trial* (Princeton, N.J.: Princeton University Press, 1949), p. 21. However, in Dyer v. MacDougall, 201 F.2d 265 (2d Cir. 1952), the court held that demeanor cannot solely be the basis for a summary judgment because it cannot be reviewed. Demeanor does not appear in the printed record on appeal. In this case the plaintiff brought an action for a slander that he alleged had been uttered by the defendant in the presence of four persons. They filed affidavits saying that they had heard no such utterance. The plaintiff attempted to avoid being thrown out of court by saying that he should be allowed to call the four witnesses, since they might be so unconvincing on the stand that the jury would not believe their denials of having heard the slander. The plaintiff had no other evidence to offer. Would the poor showing of the witnesses denying the plaintiff's unsupported allegation be sufficient evidence for a jury to find for the plaintiff? If so, the courts would lose all control over juries. Anyone could get his case to the jury by calling for the other side to deny it in court. J. R. Waltz & R. C. Park, *Evidence: Cases and Materials* (Westbury, N.Y.: Foundation Press, 9th ed. 2000), p. 737.

58. G. I. Nierenberg & H. H Calero, *How to Read a Person Like a Book* (New York: Hawthorne Books, 1971). It is reported that business communication in Japan differs from that in many other parts of the world in that Japanese managers have a keen ability to use nonverbal communication. S. Frank, "Learn to Exploit the Power of Silence," *Financial Times*, Aug. 31, 2001, p. 12.

59. Quoted in J. V. Higgins, "Body Language Is a New Way to 'Talk' with Customers," *Detroit News*, Mar. 3, 1982, p. F-1.

60. M. Chase, "HMOs Send Doctors to School to Polish Bedside Manners," *Wall Street Journal,* Apr. 13, 1998, p. B-1.

61. Federal Rules of Evidence, Rule 701.

62. Michigan Standard Jury Instruction 2d 4.01. In Instruction 3.6, the jury is told: "In deciding which you believe, you should rely on your own common sense and everyday experience. . . . There is no fixed set of rules for judging whether you believe a witness, but it may help you to think about . . . [h]ow did the witness look and act while testifying." In Powell v. St. John Hosp., 614 N.W.2d 666 (Mich. App. 2000), it was unsuccessfully argued that because a witness's bias against the defendant was evident from his demeanor, the jury did not need to know the origin of that bias.

63. For a critical view of demeanor evidence, see O. G. Wellborn, "Demeanor," *Cornell L. Rev.* 76 (1991): 1075.

64. A study by David Shaffer, a University of Georgia psychology professor, finds that when the evidence against a defendant is weak, jurors base their decision whether to convict largely on how composed the defendant appears. According to the study, jurors are more than five times as likely to convict if a defendant is nervous on the stand and the case against him is weak. Jurors assume that a witness who is nervous must be lying. V. Cope, "Study Finds Jurors Suspicious of Nervous Defendants," *Trial,* Oct. 1989. p. 101. In NLRB v. Universal Camera Corp., 190 F.2d 429, 430 (2d Cir. 1951), Judge Learned Hand wrote, "[O]n the issue of veracity the bearing and delivery of a witness will usually be the dominating factors, when the words alone leave any rational choice."

65. This was held to be an improper comment on the evidence in Quercia v. United States, 289 U.S. 466 (1932). The jury (without the assistance of the judge) is to interpret the body language of witnesses. The Supreme Court said,

> In the instant case, the trial judge did not analyze the evidence; he added to it, and he based his instruction upon his own addition. Dealing with a mere mannerism of the accused in giving his testimony, the judge put his own experience, with all the weight that could be attached to it, in the scale against the accused. . . . [T]he error was not cured by the statement of the trial judge that his opinion of the evidence was not binding on the jury and that if they did not agree with it they should find the defendant not guilty. His definite and concrete assertion of fact, which he had made with all the persuasiveness of judicial utterance, as to the basis of his opinion, was not withdrawn. His characterization of the manner and testimony of the accused was of a sort most likely to remain firmly lodged in the memory of the jury and to excite a prejudice which would preclude a fair and dispassionate consideration of the evidence.

286 U.S. at 471–72.

66. Borough of Nanty-Glo v. American Surety Co., 309 Pa. 236, 163 Atl. 523 (1932). Psychologist Saul M. Kassin observes that deception is often accompanied by fidgety movements of the hands and feet and restless shifts of posture. When people lie, especially when they are highly motivated to do so, he notes, there is also a rise in their voice pitch and an increased number of speech hesitations. He also notes that liars are betrayed by movement of the lower body, so jurors could be instructed to consider these cues as well, but ironically, the witness's body is often hidden from view—by the witness stand. S. M. Kassin, "The American Jury: Handicapped in the Pursuit of Justice, " *Ohio St. L.J.* 51 (1990): 687. What about deposition testimony and the surrogate witness? Since a witness's demeanor is considered relevant, jurors take a different view of the testimony when a deposition is read by a surrogate. The jurors must make judgments of credibility without ever seeing the actual witness. Hence, surrogate witnesses pave the way for abuse. Deposition readers are not supposed to embellish their performances. Id. at 690.

67. Indianapolis Railway v. Williams, 115 Ind. App. 383, 59 N.E.2d 586 (1945).

68. In re Gaston's Estate, 361 Pa. 105, 62 A.2d 904 (1949).

69. W. H. Rehnquist, *Grand Inquests* (New York: Morrow, 1992).

70. Yet, when it was proposed that Monica Lewinsky be put on the stand in an impeachment trial so as to let senators look her in the eye, some psychologists said that it would be

a chancy way to judge someone's credibility. To spot liars through their demeanor, they said, you might just as well flip a coin. "People do better at lie detection if they can't see the face," said Brandeis University psychology professor Leslie Zebrowitz, "people can control their face." Quoted in L. Asseo, "Experts: Testimony Won't Catch Witness Lies" (Associated Press news release), Feb. 4, 1999.

71. J. B. Carey, "Meeting the Alibi Defense," in *Trial Techniques* (Houston: National College of District Attorneys, 2d ed. 1978), p. 309.

72. L. Nizer, *Reflections without Mirrors* (New York: Doubleday, 1978), p. 242.

73. Ibid., p. 243.

74. In United States v. Ridling, 350 F.Supp. 90 (E.D.Mich. 1972), Judge Joiner in a lengthy opinion endorsed the lie detector (Judge Joiner is a former teacher of evidence).

75. J. Siegel, "You Shall Know the Truth," *Jerusalem Post*, Jan. 31, 1998, p. 29.

76. Pinocchio asks, "And how can you possibly know that I have told a lie?" He is told, "Lies, my dear boy, are found out immediately, because they are of two sorts. There are lies that have short legs, and lies that have long noses. Your lie, as it happens, is one of those that has a long nose." C. Collodi, *Pinocchio* (New York: M. A. Donohue, 1900 & 1920; San Francisco: Chronicle Books, 2001). See also C. Collodi, *Pinocchio,* trans. C. D. Chiesa (New York: Macmillan, 1969), p. 128. Benedetto Croce said, "The wood out of which Pinocchio is carved is humanity itself." B. Croce, *The Philosophy of Giambattista Vico* (Piscataway, N.Y.: Transaction, 2001).

77. D. J. Lopez, "Snaring the Fowler: Mark Twain Debunks Phrenology," *Skeptical Inquirer* 26 (Jan./Feb. 2002): 33. See also C. Neider (ed.), *The Autobiography of Mark Twain* (New York: Harper, 1959); M. B. Stern, *Heads and Headlines: The Phrenological Fowlers* (Norman, Okla.: University of Oklahoma Press, 1971).

78. The spleen was considered the organ of mirth and laughter, or alternatively, of melancholy and despair. The stomach was the seat of the human soul. See S. B. Nuland, *The Mysteries Within* (New York: Simon & Schuster, 2000); M. Morese, "Facing a Bumpy History," *Smithsonian,* Oct. 1997, p. 24. Still today, we speak of the heart or the gut as the repository of the faculty of intuition, and we speak of the influence of the media on the hearts of our children. See, e.g., R. C. Garza, "How Could a 6-Year-Old Kill?" (ltr.), *New York Times,* Mar. 5, 2000, p. WK-18.

79. For a critique, see M. A. Churchill, "Junk Science Invades Psychiatry," *Detroit News,* Jan. 7, 2000, p. 8.

80. A. Lowen, *The Language of the Body* (New York: Collier, 1958).

81. T. Dalrymple, "My Face or Yours?" *Spectator,* May 22, 1999, p. 12. Tattoos have long been associated with antisocial personality. See A. Favazza, *Bodies under Siege: Self-Mutilation in Culture and Psychiatry* (Baltimore: Johns Hopkins University Press, 1987); G. Newman, "The Implications of Tattooing in Prisoners," *J. Clin. Psychiatry* 43 (1982): 231.

82. A. C. Haddon, *The Study of Man* (New York: G. P. Putnam's Sons, 1898), p. 69. See also S. L. Gilman, *Making the Body Beautiful* (Princeton, N.J.: Princeton University Press, 1999).

83. M. Hollender, "The Nose and Sex," *Med. Aspects Human Sexuality,* Dec. 1972, p. 84. Seeing the nose as an analogy for genitalia, Freud believed that a nose job would provide a cure for sexual dysfunction. He arranged for the Viennese surgeon Wilhelm Fleiss to operate on the nose of one of his patients. In Nikolai Gogol's story "The Nose," assessor Kovalev lost his nose, and it ran amok. The devil decided to make fun of him. There is much of the implausible about the story, but then, too, are there not incongruities everywhere? Lorena Bobbitt, with a filleting knife, severed two-thirds of her husband's penis, and she aroused the anxiety of men worldwide. It was a cut felt 'round the world. R. Slovenko, "Bibbity Bobbity Boo," *J. Psychiatry & Law* 21 (1993): 545.

84. 185 Cal. App.3d 801, 229 Cal. Rptr. 783 (1986).

85. J. G. Barker & R. J. Howell, "The Plethysmograph: A Review of Recent Literature," *Bull. Am. Acad. Psychiatry & Law* 20 (1992): 113; see T. W. Campbell, "Sexual Predator Evaluations and Phrenology: Considering Issues of Evidentiary Reliability," *Behav. Sci. & Law* 18 (2000): 111.

86. P. Ekman, *Telling Lies* (New York: Norton, 1992).

87. J. E. Dimitrius & M. Mazzarella, *Reading People* (New York: Ballantine, 1999).

88. N. S. Kaye, "Reading the Expert Witness from the Perspective of a Juror," *Am. Acad. of Psychiatry & Law Newsletter,* Jan. 2000, p. 7.

89. Quoted in M. Royko, "Is a Woman of Class Safe from a Pass?" *Detroit Free Press,* May 3, 1981, p. B-3.

90. T. I. Koskoff, "The Language of Persuasion," in J. G. Koeltl (ed.), *The Litigation Manual: A Primer for Trial Lawyers* (Chicago: American Bar Association, 2d ed. 1989), p. 309.

91. L. Rosetree, *I Can Read Your Face* (Silver Spring, Md.: Aha! Experiences, 1988).

92. C. Darwin, *The Descent of Man, and Selection in Relation to Sex* (1871; Princeton, N.J.: Princeton University Press, 1981).

93. H. Fisher, *Anatomy of Love* (New York: Simon & Schuster, 1992).

94. See J. P. Spiegel & P. Machotka, *Messages of the Body* (New York: Free Press, 1974). The Alabama statutes on the transfer of a minor from juvenile court to a criminal court expressly lists the juvenile's demeanor as a factor to be considered. Ala. Code, sec. 12–15–34(d)(4) (1998 supp.).

95. Civil Action No. 42926, Superior Court for the County of Cobb, State of Georgia (1965).

96. United States v. Ballard, 423 F.2d 127 (5th Cir. 1970). The U.S. Supreme Court ruled that flight at the mere sight of a police officer could often, in the context of other factors, be suspicious enough to justify the police in conducting a stop-and-frisk search. L. Greenhouse, "Flight Can Justify Search by Police, High Court Rules," *New York Times,* Jan. 13, 2000, p. 1. Immigration guards at the Canadian border at Port Angeles, Washington, prompted by Ahmed Ressam's anxiety, searched his car and found one hundred pounds of explosives and sophisticated timing devices. N. C. Livingstone, "Border Security Isn't Enough to Stop Terrorists," *Wall Street Journal,* Dec. 23, 1999, p. 18.

97. The U.S. Supreme Court urged caution in inferences made from evidence of flight in Hickory v. United States, 160 U.S. 408 (1895).

98. See R. Slovenko, "Flight from the Scene," *J. Psychiatry & Law* 24 (1996): 617.

99. See, e.g., R. Cohen, "A German Suicide is Tied to Scandal," *New York Times,* Jan. 21, 2000, p. 1; G. Tett, "Two Japanese Financial Officials Commit Suicide: Pair Faced Questioning over Bribery Allegations," *Financial Times,* Jan. 30, 1998, p. 12.

100. 419 F.2d 536 (4th Cir. 1969).

101. See People v. Paquette, 543 N.W.2d 342 (Mich. App. 1995); S. E. Sunby, "The Capital Jury Absolution: The Intersection of Trial Strategy, Remorse, and the Death Penalty," *Cornell L. Rev.* 83 (1998): 1557. Of course, an accused person who did not commit the crime would not show remorse, there being no reason to show remorse, but the lack of remorse is often interpreted to indicate a guilty mind, as depicted in Errol Morris's documentary *The Thin Blue Line.* The documentary, released in 1989, is about the conviction and imprisonment of Randall Adams for the killing of a Dallas policeman.

Body language indicating remorse avoids the self-incrimination of a verbal declaration of remorse. The state may be able to use any incriminating statements in future proceedings against the defendant. For example, should the defendant prevail on appeal and receive a new trial, an admission made at sentencing may come back to haunt him. In effect, by making a verbal declaration, a defendant faces a choice between a reduced sentence and the exercise of the constitutional right under the Fifth Amendment that states, in pertinent part, that "no person shall . . . be compelled in any criminal case to be a witness against himself." See People v. Wesley, 428 Mich. 708, 411 N.W.2d 159 (1987); State v. Sachs, 526 So.2d 48 (Fla. 1988).

102. 390 Pa. 221, 134 A.2d 868 (1957).

103. E. K. Lindley (ed.), *The Winds of Freedom: Selections from the Speeches and Statements of Secretary of State Dean Rusk* (Boston: Beacon Press, 1963).

104. In 1980 Steven Linscott told police a shocking story about seeing a man attack and kill someone. He said it was just a dream, but it was a dream that occurred the same night a neighbor was murdered. To the police, this was not vision nor coincidence—this was a confession. He was convicted and sentenced to prison. DNA tests made him a free man some twelve years later. He writes about it in a book, *Maximum Security* (Wheaton, Ill.: Crossway Books, 1994). See J. E. Starrs, "Perchance to Dream!" *Scientific Sleuthing Rev.* 15 (Winter 1991): 1; S. Cohen, "Illinois Man's Bad Dream Became a Legal Nightmare, and Long Prison Term" (Associated Press news release), *Detroit News,* Sept. 18, 1994, p. A-10.

105. K. B. Noble, "Tale of Simpson's Dreams Stirs Uproar," *New York Times,* Feb. 2, 1995, p. 13; "Simpson Defense Grills Witness Harshly," *New York Times,* Feb. 3, 1995, p. B-14.

106. Pharaoh, awakened from disturbing dreams, searched for an interpreter. When his magicians and wise men failed him, Pharaoh's chief cupbearer, who spent time in prison with Joseph, recalled Joseph's past success as a dream interpreter. In prison, the cupbearer says, he and a baker told Joseph their dreams, "and as interpreted to us, so it was." Pharaoh accepted the recommendation. Gen. 41:13. A rabbinic view of dream interpretation is that the interpreter's message may alter reality. That is to say, Joseph did not simply discover the future meaning in dreams, he may have influenced the future. Berakhot 56a.

107. P. Evans (ed.), *Landscapes of the Night* (New York: Viking, 1983). Illustrations of the impact of dreams on daily life are as extensive as life itself. The famous singer and songwriter Gordon Summer, better known by the name Sting, revealed how his songs reflected the influence of the psychologist Carl Jung. He underwent Jungian analysis, or dream analysis. He wrote down what he dreamed and took it for analysis. He was encouraged to interpret his dreams and also to use them creatively, so he composed music based on what happened in his dreams. Specific examples of songs composed in this way were "The Dream of the Blue Turtle" and one of his biggest hits, "Every Breath You Take."

108. See E. Sharpe, *Dream Analysis* (London: Hogarth, 1951); H. Bloom & G. A. Awad, "Unconscious Fantasies: From the Couch to the Court," *Bull Am. Acad. Psych. & Law* 19 (1991): 119; S. de Saussure, "Dreams and Dreaming in Relation to Trauma in Childhood," *Int'l. J. Psychoanalysis* 63 (1982): 167; M. Horowitz et al., "Signs and Symptoms of Post Traumatic Stress Disorder," *Arch. Gen. Psychiatry* 37 (1980): 85; M. Kramer, "The Role of Dreaming in Post Traumatic Stress Disorder," *Sleep Res.* (supp.), 22 (1999): 253; M. Lansky, "Nightmares of a Hospitalized Rape Victim," *Bull. Menninger Clinic* 59 (1995): 4; L. J. Saul & E. Sheppard, "An Attempt to Quantify Emotional Forces Using Manifest Dreams," *J. Am. Psychoanal. Assn.* 4 (1956): 486; L. Terr, "Life Attitudes, Dreams and Psychic Trauma in a Group of 'Normal' Children," *J. Am. Acad. Child Psychiatry* 22 (1983): 221.

109. See C. B. Scrignar, *Post-Traumatic Stress Disorder* (New Orleans: Bruno Press, 3d ed. 1996); R. I. Simon (ed.), *Post Traumatic Stress Disorder in Litigation* (Washington, D.C.: American Psychiatric Association, 2d ed. 2002). Renee Fredrickson, a revival of memory therapist, claims that there are dreams with a set of symbols that point to the existence of a buried memory of sexual abuse. Snakes or other phallic symbols, she claims, are often references to abuse involving someone's penis. R. Fredrickson, *Repressed Memories: A Journey to Recovery from Sexual Abuse* (New York: Simon & Schuster, 1992). Dreams that "vividly portrayed an inner world of fear and vulnerability" are described in M. L. Glucksman, "Psychodynamics and Neurobiology: An Integrated Approach," *J. Am. Acad. Psychoanalysis* 23 (1995): 179. The patient associated snakes in his dreams with his brothers and others who could humiliate and reject. Id. at 187.

110. State v. Charo, 156 Ariz. 561, 754 P.2d 288 (1988).

111. Calvin Hall, a dream researcher, analyzed 1,368 of an individual's dreams over three years—the first time a person's dreams were used to analyze personality without recourse to other information. He knew nothing of the individual except his age and sex. The dreams, written on paper bags and laundry lists by the individual himself over a three-year period, were analyzed with an objective method of content analysis that compared the frequency or recurring elements in the person's dreams with those of an appropriate norm group. The analysis provided a study of a child molester. A. P. Bell & C. S. Hall, *The Personality of a Child Molester: An Analysis of Dreams* (Chicago: Aldine/Atherton, 1971). See also C. S. Hall & V. J. Nordby, *The Individual and His Dreams* (New York: New American Library, 1972).

112. *Shrink Dream: Tales of the Hidden Side of Psychiatry* (New York: Simon & Schuster, 1992).

113. *Our Dreaming Mind* (New York: Ballantine Books, 1994).

114. Transcript, Viviano v. Stewart, Civil District Court, Parish of Orleans, No. 87–12555 (Nov. 25, 1991), on appeal, 645 So.2d 1301 (La. App. 1994), 1995 La. Lexis 604 (La. S. Ct. 1995).

115. Reported in R. V. Denenberg & M. Braverman, *The Violence-Prone Workplace* (Ithaca, N.Y.: Cornell University Press, 1999), p. 69.

116. T. Lam, M. George, & W. Gerdes, "Internet Fantasist Kept in Jail," *Detroit Free Press*, Feb. 11, 1995, p. 3.

117. Ibid.

118. Act 3, scene 3.

119. D. Cooper, "When Dark Dreams Come to Light," *Metro Times* (Detroit), Feb. 15, 1995, p. 8.

120. A. Buchwald, *Leaving Home: A Memoir* (New York: Ballantine Books, 1993).

121. See G. S. Chafetz & M. E. Chafetz, *Obsession: The Bizarre Relationship between a Prominent Harvard Psychiatrist and Her Suicidal Patient* (New York: Crown, 1994); E. McNamara, *Breakdown: Sex, Suicide, and the Harvard Psychiatrist* (New York: Simon & Schuster, 1994).

122. See Annot., "Admissibility of Evidence Concerning Words Spoken While Declarant Was Asleep or Unconscious," 14 A.L.R.4th 802 (1982).

123. People v. Robinson, 19 Cal. 40 (1861).

124. Plummer v. Ricker, 71 Vt. 114, 41 Atl. 1045 (1898).

125. People v. Knatz, 76 App. Div.2d 889, 428 N.W.2d 709 (1980); reported in D. Bird, "New Trial Ordered Because of Dream," *New York Times,* June 17, 1980, p. B-20.

126. State v. Presley, 814 P.2d 550 (Ore. 1991). In a Massachusetts case, the Massachusetts Supreme Judicial Court reversed a criminal conviction that had been based in part on words uttered by the alleged victim in her sleep. Citing cases from Idaho and Oregon in which sleep talk was rejected, and a case from Minnesota in which its admission was upheld, the Massachusetts court commented that there is no uniformity among the states with respect to the admissibility of sleep talk, either in outcome or analytical approach. Commonwealth v. Almeida, 433 Mass. 717, 746 N.E.2d 139 (2000). In an Idaho case, a child's outcries during a nightmare implicating the father in sex abuse was excluded on grounds of Rule 403 of the Rules of Evidence, which provides, "Although relevant, evidence may be excluded if its probative value is substantially outweighed by the danger of unfair prejudice, confusion of the issues, or misleading the jury, or by considerations of undue delay, waste of time, or needless presentation of cumulative evidence." State v. Zimmerman, 121 Idaho 971, 829 P.2d 861 (1992).

127. Personal communication from Calvin S. Hall.

128. State v. Morgan, 35 W. Va. 260, 13 S.E.2d 815 (1891).

129. Sutton v. State, 237 Ga. 418, 228 S.E.2d 815 (1976).

130. The evidence was admitted under the "residual exception" to the hearsay rule. State v. Posten, 302 N.W.2d 638, 14 A.L.R.4th 793 (Minn. 1981).

131. The notes of the Advisory Committee to Rule 412 quote C. A. Wright & K. W. Graham's *Federal Practice and Procedure* (St. Paul, Minn.: West, 1980), vol. 23, sec. 5384, p. 548, which states: "While there may be some doubt under statutes that require 'conduct,' it would seem that the language of Rule 412 is broad enough to encompass the behavior of the mind. From a policy perspective, it is difficult to imagine a greater intrusion on the privacy of the victim than an inquiry into her sexual fantasies."

PART III

Criminal Cases

8

Competency to Stand Trial and Other Competencies

The issue of an accused's competency to stand trial, otherwise known as *triability*, has become one of high visibility, and it has become one of the more controversial issues in criminal law. As a consequence, the use of the plea of incompetent to stand trial is subject to greater scrutiny than ever before. While it has not received the publicity of the insanity plea, at least a hundred defendants are determined to be incompetent to stand trial for each defendant found not guilty by reason of insanity. An estimated twenty-five thousand triability evaluations are carried out annually, with about half of the evaluees found incompetent to stand trial and hospitalized in a forensic setting.[1]

The standard for determining triability is often confused with but is distinct from the insanity defense. The issue of triability focuses on competency for trial (it is forward-looking) while, in contrast, the insanity defense focuses on the defendant's mental condition at the time of the offense (it is backward-looking). Incompetency to stand trial abates the action and is procedural in effect, while insanity is substantive and renders the defendant not guilty. In law, unlike psychiatry or medicine, a term is context-defined—it depends on the legal issue. Thus, the term *insanity* or *competency* is variously defined in law to test, for example, competency to commit crime, to stand trial, or to make a will.

For the validity of the criminal process, a defendant must be competent at every stage of the proceeding, including having competency to be executed. In this chapter, in reverse order, following the discussion on competency to stand trial, we discuss competency to plead and competency to confess. The question whether the defendant was competent to confess is likely to be raised prior to trial, at a suppression hearing.

The rule on triability, or competency to stand trial, originated in cases of physical disability. Thus, the trial of an accused who had a heart attack or appendicitis would be postponed until such time as he would be physically able to be present. Subsequently, the notion developed that a person so disoriented or removed from reality that he could not properly participate and aid in a meaningful defense ought not to be put to trial. Simply put, the rule says, "A case is to be put off until the accused is able to stand trial"; that is to say, a continuance of the trial. The rule is designed (1) to safeguard the accuracy of the adjudication, (2) to allow the defendant to protect himself in the proceeding in order to have a fair trial, and (3) to preserve the dignity and integrity of the legal process. As frequently happens, however, rules take on new purpose in the process of application.

Triability has been used for legal maneuvering by both sides in criminal trials. The plea brings flexibility to the administration of the criminal law. The defense may use it to lay a foundation for the introduction of mitigating circumstances or to avoid the difficult and usually unsuccessful trial based on a claim of insanity.[2] The prosecution might raise the question of triability to preclude pretrial release or to obtain a lengthy commitment of the accused, especially when the case is weak on the merits or is controversial.[3]

In either event, the demonstrated effect of raising the plea has been to delay or interrupt the trial process. Although indefinite or prolonged delay is theoretically no longer permissible, the plea continues to be used for that purpose, and increasingly as a device to procure an otherwise unobtainable psychiatric examination for consideration in plea bargaining or sentencing. Thus psychiatric evaluation remains a part of the process and, sometimes, the very reason for the triability plea.

The earliest statute in English law dealing with competency to stand trial was passed in the thirty-third year of the reign of Henry VIII (1542), entitled "An act for due process to be had in high treasons, in cases of lunacy or madness."[4] It complains about malingering:

> In as muche as sometyme some personnes beinge accused of hyghe treasons, have after they have benne examined before kinges majesties counsayle, confessed theyr offences of hyghe treason, and yet never the lesse after the doynge of theyr treasons, and examinations and confessions therof, as afore saide, haue fallen to madnes or lunacye, wherby the condygne punishemente of theyr treasons, were they never soo notable and detestable, hath been deferred spared and delayed, and whether their madnes or lunacy by them outwardly shewed, were of trouth or falsely contrived and counterfayted, it is thinge almost impossible certainly to judge or try. Be it therefore enacted by authoritie of tis present parliament, to avoide al sinister counterfeit and false practices and ymaginations that may be used for excuse of punishment of high treasons, in suche cases where they be done or committed by any person or persons of good perfect and hole memory at the time of suche their offences. . . .

The statute then goes to prescribe trial in absentia for such cases, without regard for the mental condition of the accused. Upon the death of Henry VIII, this statute was repealed.

Since the mid-seventeenth century, the common-law rule has been that one cannot be required to plead to an indictment or stand trial when so disordered as to be incapable of putting forth a rational defense. For triability, the rule required presence of mind as well as presence of body. The accused must have the ability to cooperate with counsel in his own defense (a communicative ability) and the ability to understand the proceedings against him (a cognitive ability). Much depends on the complexity of the case. The issue can be raised at any time.

The Test of Triability

Virtually every court opinion nowadays on competency to stand trial quotes the standard of competency set forth in the 1960 U.S. Supreme Court two-paragraph per curiam opinion in *Dusky v. United States*,[5] which established the test of whether the defendant "has sufficient present ability to consult with his lawyer with a reasonable degree of rational understanding—and whether he has a rational as well as factual understanding of the proceedings against him." The Court said that it is not enough (as was the case previously) for the trial judge to find simply that the defendant is oriented to time and place and has some recollection of events. To apply the *Dusky* standard adequately, "the court must thoroughly acquaint itself with the defendant's mental condition."[6]

The test is generally considered to represent a constitutional principle binding on the various states. In any event, state rules regarding competency are generally consistent with the *Dusky* test. It appears to be widely recognized that *Dusky* establishes a minimal constitutional standard on competency. In 1975, in *Drope v. Missouri*,[7] the Supreme Court stated that it is a violation of due process to require a person to stand trial while incompetent, but the Court once again declined to spell out the precise meaning of "incompetent." The logical inference is that, although the test of incompetency is vague, the states may not abolish the rule of incompetency to stand trial, even though such action has been recommended.[8]

Some jurisdictions have attempted, with varying success, to spell out with more particularity the test for triability. Extensive criteria, for example, have been adopted by statute in New Jersey.[9] These specific criteria include:

(1) That the defendant has the mental capacity to appreciate his presence in relation to time, place and things; (2) that his elementary mental processes are such that he comprehends: (a) that he is in a court of justice charged with a criminal offense; (b) that there is a judge on the bench; (c) that there is a prosecutor present who will try to convict him of a criminal charge; (d) that he has a lawyer who will undertake to defend him against that charge; (e) that he will be expected to tell to the best of his mental ability the facts surrounding him at the time and place when the alleged violation was committed if he chooses to testify and that he understands the right not to testify; (f) that there is or may be a jury present to pass upon evidence adduced as to guilt or innocence of such charge

or, that if he should choose to enter into a plea negotiation or to plead guilty, that he comprehends the consequences of a guilty plea and that he be able knowingly, intelligently, and voluntarily to waive those rights that are waived upon such entry of a guilty plea and (g) that he has the ability to participate in an adequate presentation of his defense.

Florida adopted, slightly paraphrased, a list of thirteen "qualifiable clinical criteria" for assessing competence that were formulated by the Laboratory of Community Psychiatry at Harvard University.[10] Still another list of twenty similar yet somewhat different criteria was proposed in Nebraska.[11] Arizona has directed examining experts to file with the court reports addressing seven specific matters.[12]

Insofar as the compilation of numerous specific findings may lead to an overall picture of the defendant's mental state, such criteria can significantly aid the expert and the court in reaching a determination of competence, but insofar as each separate finding is mandated to support a finding of competence, the list becomes counterproductive, substituting particularized judgments on superficial aspects of the defendant's mental state for the more important ultimate conclusion of competence. The Supreme Court in *Dusky* and in *Drope* established a minimum standard, understandably and necessarily imprecise, in order to permit individual judges to evaluate each case in the light of the individual defendant's level of functioning in relation to the complexity of that case.

Prosecutors have often raised the issue of competency, but in many cases, the prosecutor and defendant have a joint commitment to the success of the motion. When initiated by the prosecutor, the process is often labeled "preventive detention." When raised by the defense, it is called "medical immunity" from trial. The prosecutor is allowed to raise the motion on the ground that the state has a responsibility to seek justice and to protect society. A defendant may not block an inquiry into competence. In a number of well-known cases in England in the latter part of the nineteenth century the prosecutor was allowed to raise the issue of fitness to proceed, a practice subsequently confirmed in the United States by the Supreme Court.[13]

Indeed, incompetency, however defined, may not be waived, even with the consent of the court. The trial court itself is obliged to raise the issue and to convene a hearing on the question at any time during proceedings when the evidence before the court raises a bona fide doubt as to the defendant's competence. In the leading case of *Pate v. Robinson*,[14] setting the precedent firmly, the undisputed facts were that the defendant, Robinson, had committed shocking acts of violence. He killed his wife and infant son. He also attempted suicide. Given "the uncontradicted testimony of Robinson's history of pronounced irrational behavior," the Supreme Court said that the trial court could not dispense with a hearing on competency, even though the defendant appeared alert and rational at trial.

Time Limit on Confinement

In 1972, in a much-discussed case, *Jackson v. Indiana*,[15] the U.S. Supreme Court set out a time limit on confinement for pretrial commitment for incompetency to stand trial, though it did not specify an exact period. Prior to this decision, the pretrial commitment procedure was widely used as a method for final disposition of a defendant's case. Commitment for incompetency was tantamount to confinement for life, especially when the accused was permanently retarded.

In this case, Theon Jackson, a 27-year-old "mentally defective deaf mute" who could not read, write, or communicate intelligently, had been charged in 1968 with robbery. The testimony at the competency hearing indicated that Jackson's condition precluded his comprehension of the nature of the charges against him or his effective participation in his own defense. The prognosis was "dim" that he would ever develop the necessary communicative skills. Nevertheless, following the usual practice, the state court, finding Jackson incompetent, ordered him committed until such time as he could be certified by the health department as "sane" and possessing "comprehension sufficient to understand the proceedings and make his defense."

The Supreme Court ruled that such prolonged commitment violates the due process clause of the Fourteenth Amendment. It stated that a person committed on account of incapacity to proceed to trial cannot be held more than the "reasonable period of time necessary to determine whether there is a substantial probability that he will attain that capacity in the foreseeable future." The Court further stated:

> If it is determined that this is not the case, then the State must either institute the customary civil commitment proceeding that would be required to commit indefinitely any other citizen or release the defendant. Furthermore, even if it is determined that the defendant probably soon will be able to stand trial, his continued commitment must be justified by progress toward that goal.[16]

In oft-quoted language, the Court said, "At the least, due process requires that the nature and duration of commitment bear some reasonable relation to the purpose for which the individual is committed." Inasmuch as Jackson was committed because he was incompetent to stand trial, the Court concluded that the purpose of such commitment must be to make the defendant competent. The Court in *Jackson* did not address the issue of the disposition of the criminal charge in the case of one for whom restoration of competency was not a foreseeable possibility. It stated only that if such a defendant was to be further confined, the confinement would have to be based on the criteria for civil commitment applicable in that jurisdiction.[17]

Following *Jackson*, various states either by judicial decision or legislation have limited the term of commitment to either a "reasonable period"; or a term of twelve, fifteen, or eighteen months; or not to exceed a maximum sentence for the offense charged. Some say that having a maximum period encourages malingering. It is to be noted, however, that the *Jackson* limitation on confinement is not faithfully followed in all places. Approximately half of the states have not implemented *Jackson*. Who is there to seek out the inmate and represent him? Not infrequently, no one wants the inmate out on the streets. Unlike the case of physical disability, the mentally disabled defendant is not, as a matter of prevailing practice, released on bail or on recognizance while awaiting trial, on the ground that the mentally ill are dangerous or a nuisance.[18] A number of states now provide for release on bail or on recognizance during the period of examination.[19]

Hearing and speech defects or illiteracy do not constitute mental illness, and thus are not grounds for commitment under civil commitment statutes. Moreover, in a civil commitment, the hospital has control over discharge; the courts are concerned about the discharge of certain individuals and do not want to leave disposition to the hospital. The triability issue is a way for the court to retain control over discharge. Before it became one of high visibility, the test of triability was not taken literally. The court, when calling on a psychiatrist for an opinion, did not really want to know whether the accused was capable of standing trial. The court itself could decide that by a few simple questions. What the court really wanted to know was whether the accused was likely to be dangerous or unduly bothersome in the community. In other words, labeling a person "incompetent to stand trial" signified that he was either dangerous or a nuisance and should be confined. That was then and remains to some extent today the hidden agenda.[20]

Before triability became an issue of high visibility, courts quite often failed to respond to communications from the hospital that the accused is able to stand trial. The hospital on its own initiative does not have the authority to return the accused to the local jailhouse whence he came nor to discharge the accused. The ploy in the use of triability to achieve detention was clearly demonstrated by the difficulties encountered by the hospital superintendent who would certify to the court that a defendant maintained on medication was competent to stand trial under a literal interpretation of the test. Just as an athlete may not use drugs to improve performance, an accused had to come to trial au naturel. Refusal to accept a defendant wanting to go to trial who was only synthetically competent strikingly indicated that the judge was concerned not with the defendant's capacity to undergo trial but with his ability to get along in the community without medication. In these cases the judge was concerned that the accused, an individual who has already shown himself—albeit allegedly—to be troublesome to the community, may not continue pharmacological treatment in the event of release and may again become a threat to society.

Modern advances in medication, science, and technology might be expected to affect the status of persons otherwise deemed incompetent. The competency rulings based on the use of psychotropic medication have been inconsistent, and they have also been one-sided. In the past, when the issue of competency was raised by the prosecutor or judge, it was usually held that a defendant had to be in a natural state, but, still today, a plea raised by the defendant that he should not be put to trial when on medication has been rarely successful.

The trend nowadays in trying minors as adults poses a triability issue, but trying minors as adults is not as new as it might appear. Before juvenile courts were established, minors were tried—and often sentenced—as adults. The courts applied common-law guidelines on criminal capacity. Those rules defined the age of adulthood for purposes of criminal responsibility as being seven years of age; the period between seven and fourteen was a zone of presumptive incapacity. The juvenile court system, which came into being at the turn of the twentieth century, had the aim of treating, rehabilitating, and protecting the young from exposure to the adult criminal system, but with the increase in violent crime committed by minors, approximately forty-five states have now passed laws to make it easier to prosecute minors as adults. In many cases the court is finding the juvenile incompetent to stand trial as an adult.

Stress of Trial

A problem is presented when the accused, though able to cooperate with counsel and understand the proceedings, alleges that the stress of trial (or nowadays the televising of the trial) will cause a physical or mental breakdown. In common law, the issue of incompetency could be raised not only as a bar to arraignment but also to trial, judgment, or execution. It is to be recalled that at this time in history, in the early 1800s, there were many capital offenses, some two hundred in number. The incompetency plea was allowed at any stage of the proceedings to undercut the penalty.

In various ways a witness or the accused who chooses to testify at trial is placed under stress; it is believed that stress aids in the ascertainment of truth. The idea that a witness breaks under heavy pressure or skillful cross-examination and finally tells the truth is depicted in countless tales. At one time in the United States, and still the practice in most other countries, the accused or witness had to stand while testifying (hence the term *witness stand*). The occasional physical strain of prolonged standing increased the anxiety. And, of course, he may be subjected to a vigorous cross-examination, which is regarded as one of the principal and most efficacious tests that the law has devised for the discovery of truth. The chapter titles in one book on cross-examination are illustrative of the practice: "Break Your Witness," "Step by Step Attack," "Witness on the Run," "The Kill," "Shock Treatment."[21]

What is the measure of competency to undergo the stress of trial? In a way, it is the type of question faced by many parents in deciding whether to push their child another step or to wait. At the wrong time, the ordeal will upset one's equilibrium. Given a particular stress, of whatever kind, anyone can break down. Can a given person's stress threshold be measured? Are stress and its effect predictable? Are the parameters known and fixed? In the case of the criminal defendant, is it the accusation, the pretrial wait, the trial, the decision, the sentence, or the lawyer's fee that will prove overwhelming? Will it make a difference whether the accused will take the stand to testify on his own behalf?

The televangelist Jim Baker, accused of siphoning millions of dollars from his PTL (Praise the Lord) ministry, crumpled to the floor of his lawyer's office and hid his head under a couch. He rolled into a fetal position and began to weep. The court suspended the trial and ordered Baker to the Federal Correctional Institution in Butner, North Carolina, for psychiatric evaluation, where it was reported that he was suffering from a Goyaesque hallucination in which "suddenly people took the form of frightening animals, which he felt were intent on destroying him, attacking him and hurting him." He was declared competent for trial, despite his panic attack and the trial was resumed.[22]

Right to Refuse Medication

Medication may alleviate anxiety, as we all know, but in a number of cases the defendant has urged a right not to be tried under medication. A defendant may claim that medication will make him appear glassy-eyed or drugged and that appearance would prejudice him in the eyes of the jury. Some defendants have argued that they have an absolute right not to be tried while under medication. In certain cases tranquilizing drugs may be necessary to control a defendant's disruptive behavior during trial.

Some defendants seeking trial immunity have argued for a right to appear in court with mental faculties unfettered. In allowing a defendant under medication to be tried, the New Mexico Supreme Court justified its decision in this way:

> There is no evidence that [tranquilizing drugs such as Thorazine] affected defendant's thought processes or the contents of defendant's thoughts; the affirmative evidence is that Thorazine allows the cognitive part of the brain to come back into play. The expert witnesses declined to call Thorazine a mind altering drug. Rather, Thorazine allows the mind to operate as it might were there not some organic or other type of illness affecting the mind.[23]

Another claim is that courtroom demeanor may be relevant to the theory of defense (insanity at the time of the crime), and demeanor is affected by medication. In *United States v. Charters*,[24] the Fourth Circuit observed, "The sanity of the defendant at the time he committed the crime is usually the primary issue in the trial of an 'incompetent' defendant made 'competent' through the administration of drugs. However, if the defendant is heavily medicated during the trial, the jury may get a false impression of the defendant's mental state at the time of the crime." The court in *Charters* also rejected the state's argument that forcible medication should be permitted on *parens patriae* grounds. The court stated, "The *parens patriae* interest cannot justify compelled medication until the need for an individual guardian or custodian has been determined, the guardian or custodian appointed, and the guardian or custodian has recommended that the medication be administered." Likewise, in a death penalty case in Washington, the defendant was given tranquilizers and at trial he appeared calm, collected, and somewhat lackadaisical as he related the details of the murder for which he was charged. The Washington Supreme Court reversed his conviction on the ground that there was reasonable possibility that his attitude and demeanor observed by the jury had substantially influenced their judgment.[25]

This view has wide support, especially among members of the legal profession, who by and large have a skewed impression of the effects of medication.[26] B. J. George, a prominent law professor and one-time law school dean, argued that in these cases medication should be barred as a matter of procedural due process. He wrote: "Due process can be denied by producing such a calming effect on a defendant that he or she cannot through conduct or mode of testifying demonstrate to a jury the irrationality or lack of control under pressure important to establish the insanity defense."[27] The courts hold that the defendant's demeanor, coupled with the content of his testimony, is sufficient to make the issue of his sanity a jury question even though he was the sole defense witness.[28]

In a case that reached the U.S. Supreme Court, David Riggins, while awaiting trial in a jail in Nevada on murder and robbery charges, complained about hearing voices and having trouble sleeping. After advising the prison psychiatrist that he had been successfully treated with the antipsychotic drug Mellaril in the past, the psychiatrist prescribed it for him. At the same time, through his lawyer, he asked for a determination of his competency to stand trial. Several months before his trial was to begin, he asked for a termination of his medication until the end of trial. He contended that continued medication would deny him due process because of the adverse effect the drugs would have on his demeanor and mental state during the trial, and would violate his right to show the jury his "true mental state" as part of the insanity defense he planned to raise.

The trial court denied the motion and he continued to receive medication each day through the completion of his trial. At trial, he testified on his own behalf in support of his insanity defense. The jury found him guilty and sentenced him to death. He appealed to the Nevada Supreme Court, claiming that the forced medication had interfered with his ability to assist in his defense and prejudicially affected his attitude, appearance, and demeanor at trial. The Nevada Supreme Court affirmed the conviction, holding that the denial of his request to terminate medication was not an abuse of discretion.[29] A dissent argued that forced antipsychotic medication should never be permitted solely to allow a defendant to be prosecuted.[30] In a decision in 1992, the U.S. Supreme Court reversed, finding that the trial court had failed to make findings sufficient to justify the administration of medication. The Supreme Court said that as a condition for forced medication, the state must show both an overriding justification and medical appropriateness. In this case, the Court said, the state failed to justify the "need" for the medication.[31] Arguably, however, the need for medication for therapeutic purposes is coextensive with the need for medication to render the individual competent to stand trial. Electroconvulsive therapy (ECT) is apparently not used to achieve triability (some argue that it causes memory loss).

In a Michigan case involving the shooting death of Dr. John Kemink, an otolaryngologist at the University of Michigan, it was undisputed that Chester Lee Posby, the defendant, shot and killed the doctor. The sole issue at trial was the defendant's sanity at the time of shooting. At the time of trial the defendant was on antipsychotic medication. Defense counsel requested discontinuance of the medication so that the jury could observe the defendant in an unmedicated state. Without the medication, defense counsel urged, the jury would get a truer picture of the defendant's mental condition. In other words, defense counsel wanted the jury to observe the defendant "as he was during the time of the shooting, in an unmedicated state." The psychiatrist who prescribed the medication testified that if the defendant were taken off it, he would in a matter of days again become delusional and disorganized and would not be competent to stand trial.

The trial court found an overriding state interest in maintaining the competency of the defendant that outweighs any right that he may have to be absent medication during the pendency of the trial. The state has a right, as does the defendant, the trial court said, to a speedy trial, and to grant the motion would be to restrict that right. The Court of Appeals overruled the trial court, saying that the request to be taken off antipsychotic medication implicates the defendant's right to present a defense. Citing the Supreme Court's decision in *Riggins*, the court noted that there was no evidence, and the trial court made no findings, with regard to whether the medication was essential for the sake of the defendant's own safety or the safety of others.

Taken off medication for a few days, the defendant could testify in an unmedicated state, and that, the court found, did not implicate the question of competency during trial. The defendant had already assisted in his defense and there would not have been any further adjournments needed, the court said, because the defendant would then be administered the medication immediately after testifying.[32]

Andrew Goldstein, an individual diagnosed as having schizophrenia who pushed a young woman in front of a subway train, was advised by his lawyers to go off his drugs in an effort to demonstrate to the jury the debilitating effects of his mental illness, but experts described the move as desperate and unethical.[33] In civil commitment proceedings, a few days before a scheduled hearing, psychiatrists often take the individual off medication to demonstrate to the judge his psychotic condition and thereby to convince the judge of the need of hospitalization. Taking the individual off medication for the hearing is considered preferable to having the person on the streets where he will possibly go off medication.

In lieu of taking the person off medication, what about allowing expert testimony to describe the effect of medication on demeanor? On this there is divided opinion. The Washington Court of Appeals said: "The ability to present expert testimony describing the effect of medication on the defendant is not an adequate substitute. At best, such testimony would serve only to mitigate the unfair prejudice which may accrue to the defendant as a consequence of his controlled outward appearance. It cannot compensate for the positive value to the defendant's case of his own demeanor in an unmedicated condition."[34] On the other hand, the New Mexico Supreme Court said: "The defense can introduce any prior unusual behavior of the defendant as evidence at the trial, and, in addition, can introduce at trial as evidence the fact that he [is] using [antipsychotic medication] and the effect that the drug medication has on the Defendant by expert testimony, unless the Court is persuaded to rule otherwise during trial proceedings."[35] The ABA Criminal Justice Mental Health Standards recommend allowing "either party . . . to introduce evidence regarding the treatment or habilitation and its effects" and to require the court to give appropriate instructions.[36]

A practical alternative may lie in allowing the defendant to present a videotape deposition of testimony given by him prior to trial in a medication-free state. In this way, the defendant could present probative evidence of his insanity through his manner and demeanor on the witness stand, thereby preserving his right to be tried while mentally competent and, at the same time, recognizing the state's interest in courtroom safety and order.

Would the defendant's demeanor on the witness stand while in an unmedicated state have approximated his mental state at the time of the shooting? The passage of time and circumstances and the treatment that he had received in the intervening time would attenuate its probative value. Actually, in the substantial time that elapses between offense and trial, no one, to a greater or lesser degree, is the same. One is not in the same emotional state—one integrates or disintegrates, and, if nothing else, one is older. In the murder trial of Nathaniel Abraham, the 13-year-old boy who was tried as an adult for a killing he had committed, the trial attorney sought to have the case dismissed, arguing that "the young person in front of the court today is not the same person as two years ago, and the jury will not be able to see what he was like then."[37]

The first rule of medicine is, "First do no harm." Is there a similar rule in the practice of law? Taking the individual off medication would be antitherapeutic—relapses cause brain damage—and to what end? Suppose the defendant testifies in an unmedicated state. What would be the likely outcome? Putting aside the empirical evidence that juries rarely return a verdict of not guilty by reason of insanity, the odds of an NGRI verdict are even less when the defendant at trial appears crazy. Ironically, the crazier a person appears to a jury, the more likely they would not return a verdict of NGRI. They would not want him out on the streets, an outcome generally believed to follow an NGRI verdict.

Amnesia

A claim made by a defendant of general inability to reconstruct the events of the period in question (when the claim is opposed by the state) has generally been held insufficient to establish denial of due process. As the Louisiana Supreme Court put it, amnesia does not make the defendant incapable of understanding the proceedings against him or of assisting in his defense, even if his emotional state impairs his recollection of the crime.[38] A general claim of being unable to remember events for the period in question is insufficient, the courts say, because if such a claim had to be accepted, almost every defendant could successfully assert such a defense.[39]

Were amnesia a basis for nontriability, how much amnesia would be required? How many accused remember everything? Other reasons militate against a ruling of nontriability. Amnesia is not mental illness, therefore commitment would not be possible. Then, too, defense lawyers do not want the accused to tell them about their complicity in the commission of a crime, as that would ethically preclude or inhibit their presentation of evidence. The Arizona Supreme Court said that it is a reproach to justice to try a person suffering from amnesia of an uncertain type and extent when it appears that reasonable continuance of the trial may provide the time needed to effectuate a limited or full recovery from the amnesic state. The court emphasized that each case must be considered on its own merits and that no absolutes may be justified without investigation.[40]

Generally, courts give little weight to amnesia in support of an incompetency plea. In *Wilson v. United States*,[41] the D.C. Circuit outlined in some detail the mechanism of *post facto* review of fairness. The court suggested that the trial judge should, before imposing sentence, make detailed findings, after taking any additional evidence deemed necessary concerning the effect of the amnesia on the fairness of the trial. The practical objection to the procedure outlined in *Wilson* is based on the possibility that a lengthy trial, carried to a verdict, would be a nullity.

Multiple Personality Disorder and Hypnosis

The individual diagnosed as multiple personality has posed perplexing problems. Multiples are often self-destructive and tend to emerge during periods of stress; a trial is a stressful event. A key dimension of the multiple personality disorder is amnesia, but as noted, the courts usually hold that amnesia alone is not sufficient grounds for a finding of incompetence to stand trial. But how can an attorney talk with a personality who comes and goes? Forensic experts muse: Which personality does one examine for competency? Does one examine all as they appear? And, if so, which one was involved in the offense?[42]

Since hypnosis is the primary tool utilized in the diagnosis of multiple personality, one must be concerned about the court rulings that individuals who have undergone hypnosis cannot be allowed to testify because of the impact of hypnosis on their testimony.[43] Most states hold that the testimony of a hypnotized witness is inadmissible, absent proof by clear and convincing evidence that the testimony being offered was based on facts recalled and related before hypnosis. In a Michigan case,[44] the prosecutor argued that hypnotically refreshed testimony of a complaining witness in a rape case should be admitted because the hypnosis was therapeutic in nature and not forensic or investigative. The purpose of the hypnosis was not specifically to refresh the victim's memory and, therefore, it was argued, was less suggestive. The Michigan Court of Appeals rejected this limitation, stating that the dangers associated with hypnotically induced testimony still existed. However, in the case of a defendant in a criminal case, the U.S. Supreme Court has ruled that the state may not bar his testimony, hypnotically enhanced or not. The defendant in a criminal case has a constitutional right to testify.[45]

Hearing Procedures

Some states provide for a jury hearing on the issue of triability, but such a hearing is not required on the theory that the question is procedural, that is, it is not a substantive one that involves guilt or innocence. Apart from the statutory requirement in a few states, no duty rests upon the court to impanel a jury on the issue, but the court must consider and determine it in a judicial manner.

In 1992, in *Medina v. California*,[46] the U.S. Supreme Court upheld a state statute that (1) put the burden of proving incompetency on the party asserting it, and (2) established a presumption of competency. In 1996, in *Cooper v. Oklahoma*,[47] the Court held unconstitutional a statute that placed the burden on the defendant to show incompetency by clear and convincing evidence. The Court held that under the constitutional guarantee of due process, a "preponderance of the evidence," the lowest evidentiary standard available, is all that can be required of a defendant to demonstrate incompetence. Under that relaxed test, a defendant must show only that he is more likely than not to be incompetent. The Court rejected a state argument that the higher burden of proof served the state's interest in efficiency and made it harder for malingerers to pretend to be mentally ill.

Who should assess the competency? Who is in the best position to assess it? The rules of evidence allow expert testimony when it will "assist" the court.[48] Does the court need help in assessing triability? If so, can expert psychological testimony provide this help? Might the assessment be left to defense counsel? After all, the defense attorney is not only in close and continuing communication with a client but also knows the extent to which defenses may turn on the client's ability to understand them and assist counsel in advancing them. The D.C. Court of Appeals once observed that because of this proximity to client and case, "counsel's first-hand evaluation of a defendant's ability to consult on his case and to understand the charges against him may be as valuable as expert psychiatric opinion on his competency."[49]

But can the defense attorney be relied on to make a trustworthy evaluation? That aside, important as counsel data may be bearing on client competency, they cannot be offered or demanded by a court if they rest on or are derived from confidential communications under the protective umbrella of the attorney-client privilege. Moreover, the attorney becoming a witness may strain the attorney-client relationship if a defendant observes defense counsel apparently testifying against the client's best interests as the client perceives them.[50]

Then why not leave the assessment to the judge or to another attorney? Why call for the assistance of mental health practitioners? The idea of assistance by mental health practitioners in this regard seems strange, but their evaluations are sought in an estimated 2 to 8 percent of felony cases.[51]

As we have noted, prosecutors, having the power to inject the issue of triability, have viewed the process as a mechanism to remove from society defendants against whom they might have a weak case or as a means of curbing anticipated violent behavior. In this respect, *nontriable* was a code word for "dangerous." What the court really wanted to know from the mental health professional was whether the accused was dangerous or an incorrigible nuisance. To say "incompetent" was another way of saying, "We should put him away." The process entailed automatic commitment, without right to pretrial release on bail (which was allowed a defendant suffering a physical disability such as a heart condition). It achieved preventive detention.[52]

Since 1972, when the Supreme Court in *Jackson* set out a durational limit for the length of commitment, that reason for engaging mental health professionals has disappeared, so what is the justification now for engaging the mental health professional? To ascertain whether the accused is suffering amnesia? That ascertainment is unnecessary, as courts give little or no weight to amnesia in support of an incompetency plea. To ascertain whether the accused is malingering? In general, the best way to detect malingering is by police investigation or surveillance of the accused. Psychiatric experts are surely not needed.

The original intent of the test of triability in mental cases was to excuse only flagrantly psychotic and mentally defective individuals. An unsophisticated layman or the custodial officer is able to apply the test; a commonsense point of view is all that is needed for a literal application of the test. Surely, in a literal application of the test, there would be no need for a diagnosis in depth or for Rorschach protocols. Assuredly, the sort of evaluation needed for measuring triability is not the same as that needed for treatment. Anything more subtle than what a custodial officer can detect ought not to be a basis to stay a trial, and, indeed, results in injustice and perversion of the criminal process. Moreover, the custodial officer, who has much experience with the criminal element and is able to observe the accused around the clock, is especially adept at detecting malingering.

It is not the suggestion here that the custodial officer or other jail attendants, who are especially adept at detecting malingering, should serve as the expert on an accused's fitness to stand trial. The point is that fitness to stand trial can be and ought to be measured by an ordinary view. Psychiatric examination does not further the inquiry. For a literal application of the test, the judge can by himself make as valid a decision as anyone on the basis of a few ordinary and simple questions put to the defendant.

It is said that a key issue in the determination of triability is whether the person is incompetent because of mental illness. Joseph T. Deters, prosecuting attorney in Cincinnati, has this to say:

> In order for there to be an issue of triability, the defendant must first, as a threshold issue, demonstrate a mental condition which affects his ability to understand the proceedings or aid in his defense. I am not sure whether the determination of whether a person has a mental condition is one which could be made without the aid of an expert. Once that prong is established, however, I agree that courts could rely on their own inquiry to determine the nature of the defendant's understanding. Having relied on the expert for the primary determination and not being fluent in the nature of mental conditions, however, it is no wonder that courts routinely

look to the expert to make their recommendation as to triability. Psychobabble is confusing to the jurist just as to other laymen in the field of psychiatry.[53]

But is diagnosis really relevant as to triability? If a defendant is capable of meeting the articulated requirements for competence, the presence or absence of mental illness is irrelevant. Legal criteria, not medical or psychological diagnostic categories, govern competency. Diagnosis is relevant only as to the question of potential restorability of competency with treatment. The possibility of restorability will be different in the case of psychotic depression than of dementia. Restorability is the question to be properly put to the mental health professional, not triability. Triability may be accomplished by education (particularly in the case of the low-I.Q. defendant), anxiety management, or medication for depression or psychosis.[54]

On-Site Examination

Studies indicate that a majority of mentally disordered defendants who are unfit can, with active treatment, attain fitness within a relatively short period of time, often less than ninety days. As a consequence, on-site examination is increasingly required, and this procedure prevents stowing the accused in some remote facility. On-site examination is also recommended as a less expensive procedure. Statutory changes in a number of states have made provisions for on-site examinations by a mental health team. Some states employ the principle of *least restrictive alternative* to the extent it is consistent with the defendant's pretrial release status. Like the defendant with a physical disability, the defendant with a mental disability may be placed in any appropriate public or private facility that agrees to accept him or with the Department of Mental Health on a "no decline" basis.

A Reevaluation of Triability

Should it really matter *why* the accused is unable to cooperate with counsel or to understand the proceedings against him or to endure the stress of trial? Is psychiatric diagnosis always necessary? What difference does it make whether the cause of the disability is organic or functional? In the case of a physical disorder (e.g., a heart condition), the accused may be able to assist counsel or understand the proceedings against him but be unable to withstand the stress of trial. On the other hand, in the case of mental disorder (whether organic or functional), the accused may not have the necessary communicative and cognitive ability to plead or go to trial. With it no longer being possible to use the triability issue to detain mentally disordered offenders indefinitely, the trend is away from the issue of the accused's mental condition.

A purely operational procedure would ask simply whether the person understands the charges and can assist counsel, or whether he can undergo trial or punishment. A clinical evaluation, however, follows from a mental illness interpretation of competency to stand trial. A number of courts in various states have ruled that evidence regarding triability may consist of lay observations as well as expert clinical testimony. The duty of the court to acquaint itself thoroughly with the defendant's mental condition may be satisfied by lay or clinical witnesses.[55]

The commentators who have urged abolition of the incompetency to stand trial plea (a theoretical proposal in view of the Supreme Court's decisions) question whether we are prisoners of the past, adhering to old rules in the face of wholly changed circumstances. Without the assistance of counsel, as was the case in early law, the defendant's physical and mental presence is essential if he is to use the right to cross-question witnesses and make a defense; but today, given the assistance of counsel, the defendant's presence would seem to be less important. (Actually, from a practical point of view, the crucial question is not the competency of the accused but rather the competency of the attorney.) In the course of upholding the trial court for excluding the defendant from the courtroom when his behavior was contumacious, Justice Hugo Black wrote in 1970 in *Illinois v. Allen*:[56]

> Although mindful that courts must indulge every reasonable presumption against the loss of constitutional rights . . . we explicitly hold today that a defendant can lose his right to be present at trial if, after he has been warned by the judge that he will be removed if he continues his disruptive behavior, he nevertheless insists on conducting himself in a manner so disorderly, disruptive, and disrespectful of the court that his trial cannot be carried on with him in the courtroom.

Is an exception to the prohibition against trials in absentia to be made only when the defendant has apparent control over his behavior? In factitious incompetency it may be said that if the defendant wants to be present, he has an easy choice: he can decide to behave, but such an option is not available to the person who is mentally "out of it." The Supreme Court in *Allen* ruled as it did in spite of the questionable mental competence of the defendant. In condoning trial in absentia, the Court may have implied that there are no longer any substantial societal interests underlying the defendant's ancient right to be present and that exceptions to the general prohibition against trials in absentia might be developed or expanded.

Competency to Plead

Should a distinction be drawn between competency to stand trial and competency to plead? The practical question is really not whether the accused is able to undergo trial, but rather whether he is fit to plead. In the vast majority of criminal cases, roughly 90 percent, there is no trial. The criminal convictions are entered by a guilty plea after plea bargaining. A trial, on the other hand, is open and public, and the state is put to its proof beyond a reasonable doubt. Theoretically, in plea bargaining or in the acceptance of a guilty plea, the plea must be entered voluntarily, with an understanding of the charge and consequences of the plea, and the judge must satisfy himself that a factual basis exists for the plea. But because the proceeding is clandestine, it might be suggested that only incompetency to plead ought not be waivable. The Court of Appeals for the Ninth Circuit, like a number of other courts, held that the competency of a defendant to waive counsel or plead guilty must be determined by a higher standard than for assessing competency for trial,[57] but the Supreme Court reversed this line of decisions.[58] The Court established a unitary standard for the determinations of competence to stand trial, competence to plead guilty, and competence to waive counsel. Holding a defendant incompetent to plead but competent to stand trial would result in forcing the defendant into a trial that the defendant would rather avoid to obtain a more favorable, negotiated sentence.[59]

In the past, serious difficulties arose when, on arraignment, the accused did not plead at all, or, in the ancient legal phrase, *remained mute*. As joinder of issue *(litis contestatio)* was essential, it made possible a legal maneuver by which the defendant would attempt to block the proceeding by not pleading. Prior to the nineteenth century this difficulty was harder to overcome, because at that time the accused was not entitled to legal representation in court if the charge was treason or felony. There was then no one to act on his behalf, and the court had no method of proceeding. When the court came to the conclusion that the accused remained obstinately mute, or *mute of malice*, he was subjected to a form of judicial torture to compel him to plead. Increasingly heavier weights were placed on his chest—he was literally pressed for his answer.

This *peine forte et dure* was abolished in England in 1772, and by an act of 1827, a plea of not guilty was entered wherever an accused person remained mute of malice. Prior to the beginning of the nineteenth century, it was not for the court to decide whether an accused who stood mute was mute of malice or mute by visitation of God. In this period, a jury was impaneled to try the issue. In such proceedings, witnesses were called to give evidence of the defendant's condition. If the accused was found unfit to plead, the judge would have no alternative but to order his detention.

Competency to Proceed *Pro Se*

The recent trials of Jack Kevorkian of "assisted suicide" fame and Colin Ferguson, who was charged with carrying out a massacre on the Long Island Railroad, were highly publicized cases where the defendant represented himself. They had "a fool for a client," as it is said whenever an individual represents himself. As they were deemed competent to stand trial, it followed that they had a right to represent themselves. Kevorkian no longer had the services of Geoffrey Feiger, who had defended him over the years, and he wanted no other attorney. Ferguson wanted no part of the "black rage" defense being prepared for him by his lawyers—basically a contention that he had been driven to murder by the effects of white racism. He insisted instead that he simply was not the killer. The trial was a spectacle (as was that of Kevorkian). "Obviously," said his one-time defense lawyer, "we should not allow an insane man to represent himself."[60]

Competency to Confess

What about a confession made to the police during an investigation? For the validity of a confession, must a suspect be competent to confess? What if the suspect is tricked by the police into confessing? Mentally incompetent individuals are especially vulnerable to trickery. The Supreme Court has held that the concept of *ordered liberty* (or "the sporting theory of justice") is fundamentally at odds with the use of overt coercion—such as physical torture and extreme psychological pressure—to extract a confession, but the Court has given wide leeway to police trickery. Lying meant to effectuate a search or seizure or fabrication in the interrogation context is routine practice. To induce a confession, the police may show fake sympathy for the suspect, or they might mislead the suspect into believing that only written statements are admissible. They might also tell the suspect that "whatever you say may be used *for* or against you in a court of law," though they are not likely to testify on behalf of the defendant in any subsequent prosecution.[61]

A confession is deemed admissible despite the fact that it was a product of command hallucinations caused by the defendant's mental illness. In *Colorado v. Connelly*,[62] the majority of the U.S. Supreme Court concluded that to consider such a confession "involuntary" as a constitutional matter, without some form of coercive police conduct, would unduly infringe upon the evidence laws of the states. In this case, the defendant told a psychiatrist that God's voice had told him to confess. There was internal, but not external, coercion. "Absent police conduct causally related to the confession," the majority said, a confession is "voluntary" under the due process clause.[63]

For there to be a constitutional violation, there must be not simply police "causation" but police "coercion." A subjective standard of voluntariness, taking into account all the defendant's weaknesses and infirmities, would make it exceedingly difficult to procure admissible confessions.[64] The standards of the ABA recommend, however, the use of expert testimony not on the admissibility (whether it was voluntary) but on the reliability or credibility of a mentally disabled defendant's statements.

To what extent, if any, may the manner of response, or silence, of an arrested person to a Miranda warning be used against him in a criminal prosecution? Recall that *Miranda* provides that after an individual is advised of his rights to an attorney and to remain silent, anything he says can be used against him. No less than the bar on the use of silence as an impeachment device, the use of silence as an admission by the defendant in the prosecutor's case-in-chief is prohibited. Under the Supreme Court's ruling in *Wainwright v. Greenfield*,[65] an expert or other witnesses for the state cannot testify about the way the accused reacted to the Miranda warning. To make it explicit, the Miranda warning might be revised to read as follows: "You have the right to remain silent, and anything you say can be used against you. If you choose to plead insanity, your silence or the way you behave will not be used against you." In this case a psychiatrist on behalf of the state expressed an opinion on the accused's sanity based in part on his post-Miranda warning behavior. It was deemed error.

Yet when a defendant elects to present an insanity defense, the critical question is the criminal responsibility of the accused at the time he committed the offense, and therefore, one might suggest, in determining sanity or lack thereof, the trier of fact should have access to all evidence reasonably bearing on the behavior of the accused at or near the time of the offense. But under the Supreme Court's ruling, the trier of fact may not be apprised of the defendant's post-Miranda warning behavior.

Conclusion

But the question still remains: What is to be done with the troublesome and possibly dangerous person who is unfit to stand trial? One should first ask whether he is indeed troublesome or dangerous and whether he would be responsive to treatment in a hospital setting. Moreover, how can he be kept under the control of the court? As a general principle of Anglo-American procedure, it is deemed irrelevant prior to determination of guilt for the court to inquire about what kind of person is before the bench. Apart from youthful offender laws that have a built-in provision for psychiatric evaluation, the only other way that the criminal law provides a means of getting this type of evaluation is when the accused pleads insanity at the time of offense. The presentence report that is possible following conviction often comes too late; the options open to the court at that time are more limited.

In contrast, courts in other countries allow great leeway in the testimony admitted as evidence. In these systems, the court seeks to find out as much as possible about the circumstances behind the acts that brought the accusation. For that, courts in the United States often turn to the incompetency issue. Under the guise of obtaining a triability evaluation, the court is able to obtain a psychiatric evaluation of the offender, and it wants the evaluation of the offender to be related to the need for institutionalization. Many defense attorneys, too, want a psychiatric report that they might use in litigation or as material for defense, and so they resort to the incompetency plea.

But now that the use of the incompetency plea to confine an individual is restricted, new questions have been posed. Should there be a moratorium on special buildings for the criminally insane? What shall be done with the troublesome and possibly dangerous person? What shall be done with the untried accused whose trial is impeded, or with the defendant who is found NGRI?

One way or another, when someone causes an outrage, society demands, and rightly so, that something be done. The Criminal Lunatics Act of 1800 in England provided for the detention in Broadmoor of both the untriable and the acquitted insane. In the United States, the indeterminate detention in facilities for the criminally insane and interminable delays of trial that marked the pre-*Jackson* period has pretty much ended.

Notes

1. D. L. Bacon, "Incompetency to Stand Trial: Commitment to an Inclusive Test," *So. Cal. L. Rev.* 42 (1969): 444; B. Winick, "Restructuring Competency to Stand Trial," *UCLA L. Rev.* 32 (1985): 921.

2. Should counsel for the defendant raise the issue of incompetency against the defendant's wishes? Would it be ineffective assistance of counsel? A split panel of the Tenth Circuit faced these questions in United States v. Boigegrain, 155 F.3d 1181 (10th Cir. 1998). The majority held that counsel was not ineffective, arguing that requiring an attorney to take the position requested by a possibly incompetent client disserves both the client and the truth-seeking process. The dissenting judge looked to the practice of counsel in commitment hearings in which the decision to oppose civil commitment is the client's. He argued that counsel was constitutionally ineffective and should have asked to withdraw from representing the defendant. The American Bar Association's *Criminal Justice Mental Health Standards* call for the defense attorney to move for an evaluation of competency whenever he "has a good faith doubt as to the defendant's competency," even over the defendant's objection. Standard 7–4.2.

3. Poet Ezra Pound, who spent World War II broadcasting for Mussolini, was found mentally unfit to face treason charges, and he spent thirteen years in the criminal ward of St. Elizabeths Hospital in Washington, D.C. Had he been tried, he would have insisted on testifying that America's entry into the war was a conspiracy between Roosevelt and the Jews. His long detention aroused the ire of the literary world here and abroad, and he was released in 1958. During his confinement he wrote his masterful Pisan Cantos. On the abuse of the triability plea, see T. S. Szasz, *Psychiatric Justice* (New York: Macmillan, 1965); S. Eizenstat, "Mental Competency to Stand Trial," *Harv. Civ. Rts. Civ. Lib. L. Rev.* 4 (1969): 379; C. Foote, "A Comment on Pre-Trial Commitment of Criminal Defendants," *U. Pa. L. Rev.* 108 (1960): 832.

4. 33 Henry VIII, ch. 20.

5. 362 U.S. 402 (1960).

6. United States v. Makris, 535 F.2d 899 at 907 (5th Cir. 1976).

7. 420 U.S. 170 (1975).

8. R. A. Burt & N. Morris, "A Proposal for the Abolition of the Incompetency Plea," *U. Chi. L. Rev.* 40 (1972): 66; A. L. Halpern, "Use and Misuse of Psychiatry in Competency Examination of Criminal Defendants," *Psychiatric Annals* 5 (1975): 123.

9. N.J.S. 2C: 4–4.

10. Florida Review Criminal Proceedings 3 (1980): 211. For a discussion of forensic assessment instruments, see T. Grisso, *Evaluating Competencies: Forensic Assessment Instruments* (New York: Plenum Press, 1986); R. Nicholson, "A Comparison of Instruments for Assessing Competency to Stand Trial," *Law & Human Behavior* 2 (1988): 313.

11. State v. Guatney, 207 Neb. 501, 299 N.W.2d 538 (1980).

12. D. Wexler et al., "The Administration of Psychiatric Justice: Theory and Practice in Arizona," *Ariz. L. Rev.* 13 (1971): 1–259. Professor Richard Bonnie suggests drawing a distinction between "competence to assist counsel" and "decisional competence." He writes: "Although the relevant psychological capacities may overlap, decision-making about defense strategy encompasses conceptual abilities, cognitive skills, and capacities for rational thinking that are not required for assisting counsel." R. J. Bonnie, "The Competence of Criminal Defendants: A Theoretical Reformulation," *Behav. Sci. & Law* 10 (1992): 291, 305.

13. Pate v. Robinson, 383 U.S. 375 (1966).

14. Ibid. See also Jermyn v. Horn, 266 F.3d 257 (3d Cir. 2001); McGregor v. Gibson, 248 F.3d 946 (10th Cir. 2001).

15. 406 U.S. 715 (1972).

16. 406 U.S. at 738.

17. The case of Donald Lang in Illinois paralleled that of Theon Jackson in Indiana. See D. Paull, *Fitness to Stand Trial* (Springfield, Ill.: Thomas, 1993); E. Tidyman, *Dummy* (Boston: Little, Brown, 1974).

18. See G. Morris & J. R. Meloy, "Out of Mind? Out of Sight: The Uncivil Commitment of Permanently Incompetent Criminal Defendants," *U.C. Davis L. Rev.* 27 (1993): 1.

19. Conn. Public Act No. 76–353 (1976). Professor Bruce Winick reports the "staggering costs" of competency evaluations. B. Winick, "Restructuring Competency to Stand Trial," *U.C.L.A. L. Rev.* 32 (1985): 921.

20. For a readable account of cases, see D. Woychuk, *Attorney for the Damned* (New York: Free Press, 1996).

21. In 1965, David O. Selznick, the Hollywood studio mogul who had produced *Gone with the Wind* and other major films, died while being questioned in a deposition for a case involving film distribution payments. Two years later, his son, L. Jeffrey Selznick, during a deposition in a case involving royalties from *Gone with the Wind*, said, "This is terrible," turned to his lawyer and collapsed into his arms, and died shortly thereafter.

22. M. Brower, "Unholy Roller Coaster," *People*, Sept. 18, 1989, p. 98. After months of a legal tug-of-war, Britain dropped extradition proceedings against General Augusto Pinochet, saying the 84-year-old former dictator was too ill to face charges of human rights violations during his 17-year rule. Jack Straw, the home secretary, said that his ability to understand the charges against him and to direct his defense had been seriously impaired by a series of strokes. "If so," wrote the *New York Times*, "justice would not be served by proceeding against an enfeebled and mentally incompetent defendant." Editorial, "Homecoming for General Pinochet," *New York Times*, Mar. 4, 2000, p. 30. But said the secretary general of the Family Members of the Disappeared, "Pinochet is in perfect shape, as anyone can see. All humanity should feel cheated by this sham." C. Krauss, "Pinochet Receives Hero's Welcome on Return to Chile," *New York Times*, Mar. 4, 2000, p. 3; P. Stephens, "Still Imprisoned by His Past," *Financial Times*, Mar. 3, 2000, p. 15.

23. State v. Jojola, 553 P.2d 1296, 1299 (N.M. 1976).

24. 829 F.2d 479 (1987), *rev'd*, 863 F.2d 302 (4th Cir. 1988).

25. The Washington Supreme Court said: "We do not intend to suggest that a new trial must be granted in every criminal case—or even in every capital case—where the appearance of the accused before the jury is marred by some mental, physical, or emotional impairment, regardless of the nature of the impairment, or the means by which it was brought about.

Each case of this type must be decided on its own facts." State v. Murphy, 56 Wash.2d 761, 355 P.2d 323 (1960).

26. See, e.g., L. C. Fentiman, "Whose Right Is It Anyway?: Rethinking Competency to Stand Trial in Light of the Synthetically Sane Insanity Defendant," *U. Miami L. Rev.* 40 (1986): 1109; S. Tomashefsky, "Antipsychotic Drugs and Fitness to Stand Trial: The Right of the Unfit Accused to Refuse Treatment," *U. Chi. L. Rev.* 52 (1985): 773.

27. B. J. George, "Emerging Constitutional Rights of the Mentally Ill," *Nat'l J. Criminal Defense* 2 (1976): 35.

28. People v. VanDiver, 140 Mich. App. 484, 364 N.W.2d 357 (1985).

29. Riggins v. State, 808 P.2d 535 (1991).

30. Ibid. at 541–43 (Springer, J., dissenting).

31. Riggins v. Nevada, 112 S. Ct. 2752 (1992). The court in *Riggins* did not specify what kind of premedication hearing would be required by due process. The Sixth Circuit has held that an administrative hearing before a psychiatrist was inadequate, because the issue of competency, involving as it does the questions of whether the defendant can aid counsel and how defendant will appear to the jury, is beyond the expertise of a medical professional. The court specified that the defendant's physicians must be present in person at the hearing, that the defendant must be allowed to present rebuttal testimony, the government's proposal of forced medication must be reviewed under the strict scrutiny standard, and the government must make its case by clear and convincing evidence. United States v. Brandon, 158 F.3d 947 (6th Cir. 1998).

32. People v. Posby, 574 N.W.2d 398 (Mich. App. 1997).

33. D. Rohde, "For Retrial, Subway Defendant Stops Taking His Medication," *New York Times*, Feb. 23, 2000, p. 21. That strategy was thwarted when Goldstein struck a social worker, and the judge ordered that he be offered his medication each day. He took the medication and did not take the stand. He was found guilty of second-degree murder. Jurors were apparently swayed by the prosecution's argument that he was calm and knew what he was doing when he grabbed the victim and threw her in front of a subway train. "He seemed to know what he was doing," one juror said after the trial. "He picked her and threw her. That was not a psychotic jerk, an involuntary movement." Though jurors said they all agreed he was mentally ill, they saw intent in the planning and execution of his act. J. E. Barnes, "Insanity Defense Fails for Man Who Threw Woman onto Track," *New York Times*, Mar. 23, 2000, p. 1.

34. State v. Maryott, 6 Wash. App. 96, 492 P.2d 239 (1971).

35. State v. Jojola, 553 P.2d 1296 (N.M. 1976).

36. Standard 7–4.14(b). In another approach, the New Hampshire Supreme Court permits the state to compel medication of an incompetent defendant initially, but "[i]f the defendant by his own voluntary choice, made while competent, becomes incompetent to stand trial because he withdraws from the medication, he may be deemed to have waived his right to be tried while competent. The trial court should however carefully examine the defendant on the record, while competent, to establish the following: that the defendant understands that if he is taken off the psychotropic medication he may become legally incompetent to stand trial; that he understands that he has a constitutional right not to be tried while legally incompetent; that the defendant voluntarily gives up this right by requesting that he be taken off the psychotropic medication; and that he understands that the trial will continue whatever his condition may be." State v. Hayes, 118 N.H. 458, 389 A.2d 1379 (1978).

37. B. Ballou, "Feiger Takes Over Murder Defense," *Detroit Free Press*, Oct. 20, 1999, p. 1.

38. State v. Pellerin, 286 So.2d 639 (La. 1973).

39. United States v. Atkins, 487 F.2d 257 (8th Cir. 1973).

40. State v. McClendon, 103 Ariz. 105, 437 P.2d 421 (1968); Comment, "Amnesia: A Case Study in the Limits of Particular Justice," *Yale L.J.* 71 (1961): 109.

41. 391 F.2d 460 (D.C. Cir. 1968).

42. R. Slovenko, "The Multiple Personality: A Challenge to Legal Concepts," *J. Psychiatry & Law* 17 (1989): 681.

43. B. Diamond, "Inherent Problems in the Use of Pretrial Hypnosis on a Prospective Witness," *Calif. L. Rev.* 68 (1980): 313.

44. People v. Reese, 149 Mich. App. 53 (1986).

45. Rock v. Arkansas, 483 U.S. 44 (1987).

46. 505 U.S. 437 (1992).

47. 517 U.S. 348 (1996).

48. Federal Rules of Evidence, Rule 702.

49. United States v. Davis, 511 F.2d 355, 360 (D.C. Cir. 1975).

50. American Bar Association Criminal Justice Mental Health Standards, Standard 7–4.8.

51. R. J. Bonnie, "The Competence of Criminal Defendants: A Theoretical Formulation," *Behav. Sci. & Law* 10 (1992): 291.

52. A. L. Halpern, supra note 8.

53. Personal communication.

54. See R. Roesch & S. L. Golding, "Treatment and Disposition of Defendants Found Incompetent to Stand Trial: A Review and a Proposal," *Int. J. Law & Psychiatry* 2 (1979): 349.

55. United States v. Makris, 535 F.2d 899 (5th Cir. 1976).

56. 307 U.S. 337 at 343 (1970).

57. Moran v. Warden, 972 F.2d 263 (9th Cir. 1992).

58. Godinez v. Moran, 113 S. Ct. 2680 (1993).

59. 113 S. Ct. at 2686. Richard Moran was executed in 1996 by lethal injection in Nevada.

60. J. Scott, "A Murder Trial, through the Looking Glass," *New York Times*, Feb. 4, 1995, p. 1. See A. R. Felthous, "The Right to Represent Oneself Incompetently: Competency to Waive Counsel and Conduct One's Own Defense before and after *Godinez*," *Mental & Physical Disability Law Rep.* 18 (1994): 105; M. L. Perlin, "'Dignity Was the First to Leave': *Godinez v. Moran*, Colin Ferguson and the Trial of Mentally Disabled Criminal Defendants," *Behav. Sci. & Law* 14 (1996): 61.

61. C. Slobogin, "Deceit, Pretext and Trickery: Investigative Lies by the Police," *Ore. L. Rev.* 76 (1997): 775.

62. 479 U.S. 157 (1986).

63. The American Psychological Association submitted an amicus curiae brief that stated: "Behavioral science does not use or rely upon the concepts of 'volition' or 'free will.' Accordingly, Dr. Metzner was not testifying as a scientist when he testified that respondent's command hallucinations impaired his 'volitional capacity.' Furthermore, even if Dr. Metzner only meant to testify that command hallucinations are, in a statistical sense, coercive, his testimony finds no support in the professional literature, and is contrary to clinical experience."

64. See J. D. Grano, *Confessions, Truth, and the Law* (Ann Arbor: University of Michigan Press, 1993).

65. 106 S. Ct. 634 (1986).

9
Criminal Responsibility

Criminal responsibility is based on two elements: *actus reus*, a wrongful act, and *mens rea*, a criminal intent. The state has the burden of establishing these elements by proof beyond a reasonable doubt. The accused is not obliged to present any evidence—the accused may be a spectator at his trial—but in the usual case the accused will try to negate evidence of *actus reus* or mens rea, or in the situation where the evidence by the prosecution satisfies these elements of the crime charged, the accused may claim an affirmative defense.

The concept of *criminal responsibility* goes beyond *not guilty by reason of insanity*, though the terms are often used synonymously. A number of defenses apart from not guilty by reason of insanity can negate criminal responsibility.

Affirmative Defenses

Justification and *excuse* are affirmative defenses—the terms are commonly used synonymously, as usually they both have the same effect: acquittal of the accused. Occasionally it may make a difference in result whether a particular defense is classified as a justification or as an excuse. While ordinarily either is a full defense to the charge, an excuse, such as provocation, is only mitigating. For an affirmative defense, the accused has the burden of persuasion but only by a preponderance of the evidence.

Justified conduct, strictly speaking, is conduct that is a good thing, or the right or sensible thing, or a permissible thing to do. On the other hand, an accused in asserting an excuse says, in essence, "I admit that I did something I should not have done, but I should not be held criminally accountable for my actions." Justification negates the social harm of an offense, whereas an excuse negates the moral blameworthiness of the actor for causing the harm.

Self-defense may justify killing, provided the reasonable person under the circumstances would have also responded with deadly force. Defendants who claim to have killed in self-defense must demonstrate that they believed the dangers they faced were lethal and imminent and that another reasonable person would have acted similarly. Provocation is a partial excuse, provided the accused's loss of control was reasonable. Provocation is what distinguishes intentional killings that are murder from those treated as the much less serious crime of manslaughter.

For the anxious or paranoid individual, just about every knock on the door is ominous, and time beyond count they reach for a gun, allegedly in self-defense. In claims of self-defense, duress, or provocation, the law examines these matters by a *reasonable person* standard—that is, what the reasonable person would have done under similar circumstances. In principle, in these cases, there is often no need for expert testimony, because judges and jurors are able to assess reasonableness, justification, provocation, and such.[1] However, there may be situations, such as that of the battered spouse, in which the trier of fact would find it of assistance to have a psychodynamic explanation to assess reasonableness or provocation.[2]

The *Actus Reus* Element of a Crime

Actus reus, we have noted, is one of the two elements of a crime, and the state must establish them by proof beyond a reasonable doubt. Under the concept of *actus reus*, within the meaning of the criminal law, *act* is "voluntary action." Thus, the convulsive movement of an epileptic person is not an act, nor is the reflex movement of a person suddenly stung by a bee.[3] It may be argued that medication was at least partially responsible for an uncharacteristic homicidal surge. It may be said that one can always find, or not find, a voluntary act on which to predicate criminal liability depending on how narrowly or broadly one frames the time period during which one looks. Thus, falling asleep at the wheel may be considered involuntary but not if it is considered that the person earlier could have chosen not to have driven at the time. Likewise, the epileptic seizure might have been avoided by medication.

The American Law Institute's Model Penal Code sets out the voluntary-act requirement for criminal responsibility, and it gives examples of involuntary acts.[4] The examples are illustrative, not exhaustive, leaving to the court a case-by-case development of the voluntary-act requirement. It states:

(1) A person is not guilty of an offense unless his liability is based on conduct which includes a voluntary act or the omission to perform an act of which he is physically capable.
(2) The following are not voluntary acts with the meaning of this section:
(a) a reflex or convulsion;

(b) a bodily movement during unconsciousness or sleep;

(c) conduct during hypnosis or resulting from hypnotic suggestion;

(d) a bodily movement that otherwise is not a product of the effort or determination of the actor, either conscious or habitual.[5]

In ordinary affairs a child who vomits on another is not punished for it, since the vomiting was an involuntary act, otherwise stated, not his fault. This sense of justice pervades the law; thus, one who urinates on the street violating an ordinance may get, to negate evidence of an unlawful offense, a doctor's note that he has bladder trouble. In common parlance, the formula is, "I couldn't help it" or "I didn't know what I was doing."[6]

Cases involving automatism or unconsciousness from sleepwalking or similar dissociative states are sometimes regarded as involving no action, and at other times they are characterized as instances of no intent, or at other times as predicated on a mental disorder, resulting in postacquittal requirements (i.e., civil commitment) found with an insanity acquittal. Types of automatism are delineated as: sleep automatism, epileptoid automatism, alcohol and drug automatism, hypoglycemic automatism, and psychogenic automatism. In practice, a claim of automatism has typically required providing a cause for it.[7]

At times, it is claimed that an act was involuntary on account of a command hallucination. Forensic psychologist J. Reid Meloy opines, "Most individuals with auditory hallucinations will resist those that command activity, but hallucinations of a persecutory nature may precipitate such autonomic arousal and be perceived as so imminently threatening that affective violence results."[8]

Some may hear a command from God or Satan. Obeying Satan is one thing, but obeying God is quite another, one might say. No biblical narrative is more dramatic than God's command to Abraham that he sacrifice his son Isaac.[9] Should obeying God make a difference in the halls of justice? Michael Abrahm, who broke into the home of George Harrison, the former Beatle, and stabbed him ten times, was found not guilty by reason of insanity because he believed himself to be St. Michael the Archangel, instructed by God to kill the "alien from Hell." He was convinced that Harrison was one of the phantom menaces predicted by Nostradamus. Needless to say, Harrison was outraged by the insanity verdict.[10]

The leading case on a command from God dates from 1915, *People v. Schmidt.*[11] The defendant, Hans Schmidt, was accused of killing and dismembering a woman and throwing her remains into the Hudson River. Claiming that God had commanded the killing "as a sacrifice and atonement," he pleaded insanity. The opinion of the court was written by Judge Benjamin Cardozo, one of the country's most renowned judges. He wrote: "[T]here are times and circumstances in which the word 'wrong' . . . ought not to be limited to a legal wrong." In particular, if a person has "an insane delusion that God has appeared to [the accused] and ordained the commission of a crime, we think it cannot be said of the offender that he knows that act to be wrong."[12]

The Model Penal Code comments on this situation, "A madman [who believes that God has commanded him] is plainly beyond reach of the restraining influence of law; he needs restraint but condemnation is entirely meaningless and ineffective."[13] A few years ago, in a New York case, Muthanna Shamma was held NGRI on child sex abuse charges, by virtue of a claim that he committed the abuse because an angel told him to do it, and he was hospitalized.[14]

During the mid-nineteenth century and earlier, American asylum superintendents frequently made the diagnosis of "religious insanity." Benjamin Rush in 1812 noted that 10 percent of individuals came to mental hospitals because of religious feelings causing unbearable guilt. Religious melancholy frequently resulted in suicide or homicide. Not long ago, in Uganda, five thousand people were killed in what was called the "movement for the restoration of the 10 commandments." Religious insanity is an ideologically distinct mental illness. It is always debatable whether an individual is mentally ill or exuberantly religious.[15]

Judge Cardozo's language in *Schmidt* may appear to warrant an insanity acquittal of a mentally ill person who, though knowing his act was legally wrong, felt morally justified in committing it. Judge Cardozo expressed caution:

> It is not enough that he has views of right and wrong at variance with those that find expression in the law. The variance must have its origin in some disease of the mind. The anarchist is not at liberty to break the law because he reasons that all government is wrong. The devotee of a religious cult that enjoins polygamy or human sacrifice as a duty is not thereby relieved from responsibility before the law.[16]

According to the Washington Supreme Court, "If wrong meant moral wrong judged by the individual's own conscience, this would seriously undermine the criminal law, for it would allow one who violated the law to be excused from criminal responsibility solely because, in his own conscience, his act was not morally wrong."[17] However, the court also created a "deific decree" exception to the general rule that *wrong* means "legal wrong," thus allowing a defense like that in *Schmidt*. The court, nonetheless, upheld the homicide conviction of a person who had been hospitalized on several occasions with a diagnosis of paranoia. He contended that he followed the Moscovite faith and that Moscovites believe it is their duty to kill an unfaithful wife. The court said that "[t]his is not the same as acting under a deific command." Citing *Schmidt*, the court said, "It is akin to the devotee of a religious cult that enjoins human sacrifice as a duty and is not thereby relieved from responsibility before the law. [The accused's] personal 'Moscovite' beliefs are not equivalent to a deific decree and do not relieve him from responsibility for his acts."[18]

A number of theorists suggest that duress or necessity (as well as self-defense) constitute not merely an affirmative defense but go to the presence of *actus reus*, that is, whether the act was voluntary. An accused is permitted a defense of duress if, due to human threats, he acts in an unlawful way; an accused is permitted a defense of necessity if, due to natural events, he has no alternative but to act in an unlawful way. Both defenses are similar to self-defense, which is the necessary use of reasonable force to protect oneself, as measured by a reasonable person standard, except that in self-defense, the accused uses force against the source of the threat, whereas in duress and necessity, harms are usually inflicted on nonthreatening and innocent persons. Daniel Goldhagen, impatient with what he calls "the paradigm of external compulsion," aims to show in his book *Hitler's Willing Executioners* that the crimes of the Holocaust were carried out by people obeying their own consciences, not blindly or fearfully obeying orders.[19]

At common law, we may note, if a wife committed a crime in the presence of her husband, the law presumed that he coerced her misbehavior and the crime was attributed to him (and so the husband had the right to chastise his wife). A new excuse from criminal responsibility, an excuse that in practice applies only to women, is self-defense based on the so-called battered woman syndrome (BWS) that is invoked when a woman kills her abusive male partner. The syndrome posits that the battered woman is too dysfunctional to leave the abusive man long before resorting to homicide. The acceptability of the evidence is due to the surge in consciousness about spousal abuse, irrespective of the law's definition of exculpatory or excusing conditions (the law of self-defense requires imminence, necessity, and proportionality). In the majority of states, evidence of battered woman syndrome is allowed in support of self-defense, or in other states, in support of an insanity defense.[20]

What about recent genetic research that indicates that some persons are endowed with a gene for impulsivity and aggression? Then, too, tests have shown that in the brains of people diagnosed as schizophrenic there is less activity in the prefrontal cortex, the part of the brain that governs thought and higher mental function. Psychiatrists say that individuals in the throes of an acute episode of schizophrenia often have associated with it impulsivity and aggression. Should defense attorneys ask for routine genetic or neurological testing of their clients?[21]

Though biological, sociological, and psychological determinism have had an influence on the criminal justice system, they have not made an appreciable inroad in its method of assessing responsibility. Genetic factors may be considered in mitigation after guilt has been assessed, but there is considerable evidence to suggest that individuals with genetic liability factors are less likely to learn from experience and more likely to commit further crimes.[22] Of course, to answer the question, "What made Hitler?" looking at his baby pictures, the epitome of wide-eyed innocence, it would be fanciful to attribute his implacable hatred of the Jews to genes.[23]

The perception that people are subject to forces beyond the individual's control would swallow any rule of responsibility. The test of criminal responsibility is delimiting. Most criminal offenders have poor control over their impulses or think poorly, so if that were an excuse, prisons would be empty. Over the years, however, a number of so-called sympathy defenses have been raised, sometimes successful, such as the adopted child syndrome, where the defense claims that the trauma of adoption, a fear of abandonment, and feelings of powerlessness and rejection produced a psychotic rage that causes sufferers to strike out, often at the adoptive parents.[24]

Impact of Mental Disorder on Mens Rea or *Actus Reus*

Mental disorder may prevent the formation of a required mens rea or *actus reus*, the elements of a crime that the state must establish by proof beyond a reasonable doubt, or it may establish a complete or partial excusing condition. Mental disorder defenses are raised when it is obvious that the accused committed the crime.

The controversy in criminal law on responsibility involving mental disorder reduces to this: Under what banner will evidence of mental disorder be presented, if at all, and what will be the consequences? Under a plea of not guilty (rather than a plea of not guilty by reason of insanity), will an expert be allowed to testify that the defendant did not intend the consequences of his act or did not voluntarily act?

The courts have held that due process is not offended by a rule that without pleading NGRI, a defendant cannot rebut evidence of intent (that the defendant actually lacked intent or lacked the capacity to form intent) by presentation of psychiatric testimony.[25] In this line of cases, in *United States v. Esch*,[26] the Tenth

Circuit held that, in the absence of any claim of mental disease or defect, the trial judge may exclude expert opinion as to the accused's capacity to form the requisite intent. Moreover, the court said, generalized testimony about the influence of personality traits is excludable as within the common knowledge and experience of lay jurors.

To put it another way, experts may speak on abnormality but not on normality. The reasons generally adduced for this is that the testimony is not helpful and that the role of the judge and jury must not be usurped by experts unnecessarily testifying on matters within ordinary knowledge. The English Court of Appeal has said:

> We all know that both men and women who are deeply in love can, and sometimes do, have outbursts of blind rage when discovering unexpected wantonness on the part of their loved ones: the wife taken in adultery is the classical example of the application of the defense of "provocation"; and when death or serious injury results, profound grief usually follows. Jurors do not need psychiatrists to tell them how ordinary folk who are not suffering from any mental illness are likely to react to the stresses and strains of life.[27]

Thus, under this view, psychiatric evidence that an individual is not violent but is susceptible to provocation in the ordinary way is not admissible. An expert witness may not be an expert on the ordinary man—this is the exclusive province of the jury. The jury is held not to be in need of assistance from expert testimony on the accused's ability to form the intent to commit the crime so long as the accused does not fall into the abnormal category. The law has the presumption that, absent evidence of insanity, we are all alike. Unless one pleads insanity, he is to be judged on the assumption that he has the same capacity as everyone to judge whether an action is right or wrong, reasonable or unreasonable.

What Is the Insanity Defense?

The insanity plea is another way of saying that an essential element of the offense is lacking. In terms of substantive criminal law, the insanity defense is not an affirmative defense, or excuse, as some commentators would have us believe, but, rather, failure of proof of one of the two fundamental elements of criminal responsibility. As an evidentiary matter, testimony on mental illness goes to the credibility of a defendant's claim that the consequences of his act were not intentional or that the act was not voluntary. A textbook illustration of this point is the man who strangles his wife believing that he is merely squeezing a lemon; his defense is that he lacked the intent to kill another human being. Evidence of mental illness gives credibility to his defense. Likewise, a defense of uncontrollable or involuntary behavior is substantiated by evidence of insanity.

Evidence of insanity is actually a form of character evidence although it is not formally considered as such in the law of evidence. The Federal Rules of Evidence and state codes deal only with the use of character evidence where the identity of the offender is in doubt; the accused is allowed to introduce evidence relating to a pertinent character trait that would suggest that he is not the type of person who would commit the type of crime charged, but character evidence might create a reasonable doubt not only as to identity but also as to *actus reus* and mens rea, and courts have long allowed its use for those purposes as well.

Though the insanity defense is a negation of an essential element of the crime alleged, cases and procedural law have progressed over the years in such a way as to make the insanity defense appear to be a separate defense, as some theorists maintain. Under this view, the insanity defense operates as a special or so-called affirmative defense, not a *failure of proof* defense, which means insanity is an "excuse."

At one time, the legal system called upon the accused either to plead guilty or not guilty at his arraignment, and under a not guilty plea he could present any evidence at trial, including that of insanity, to negate *actus reus* and mens rea. Trials in criminal law were trials by surprise, because of the absence of pretrial discovery. When the defense offered lay or expert witnesses on insanity at trial, the prosecutor would have to ask for a continuance of the trial to get expert testimony in rebuttal, in order to carry its burden of proving *actus reus* and mens rea.

Development as a Practical Matter of the Insanity Defense

The plea of not guilty by reason of insanity (NGRI), or the insanity defense as it is commonly known, serves three purposes:

1. It informs the prosecutor that psychiatric testimony will be forthcoming at trial. It provides an opportunity for the prosecutor to obtain an evaluation of the accused prior to trial, thereby avoiding a continuance at trial to obtain the evaluation. Efficiency dictates that the use of insanity evidence be pleaded before trial.[28] Accordingly, as a rule, psychiatric testimony on *actus reus* or mens rea is not allowed unless NGRI was entered as a plea at arraignment.
2. It channels the psychiatric testimony according to the terms of the test of criminal responsibility.
3. Most importantly, it results in a commitment rather than an acquittal under a not guilty plea that discharges the defendant. While theoretically an acquittal, an NGRI verdict results in a commitment.

What would happen in regard to these three purposes with the abolition of the insanity defense? Firstly, it would make trials *less*, not more, streamlined and bring back the surprise trial system. Secondly, it would provide less control over psychiatric evidence and would exacerbate the jury's problem of deciding about mental illness. Ironically, it likely would increase the importance of the psychiatrist's role in that determination. Thirdly, the commitment of the individual would be achieved in other ways. The several states that have supposedly abolished the insanity defense have turned more to detaining the accused as incompetent to stand trial.[29] As often happens, when the law is reformed in one area, it is deformed in another.

The Conceptual Center of Law and Psychiatry

The interplay of law and psychiatry has found most expression in the area of criminal responsibility. The consequence of this focus has been to make it the conceptual center of law and psychiatry. The annual Isaac Ray award lectures, begun in 1952 under the auspices of the American Psychiatric Association, have dealt mainly with criminal responsibility. The trials of John Hinckley Jr., the would-be assassin of President Reagan, and Jeffrey Dahmer, the Milwaukee anthropophagite, have in recent years again spotlighted the function and significance of the plea not guilty by reason of insanity, which at times has made the psychiatrist himself and his theories seem frivolous.

For centuries, it has been considered unjust to label a person as criminal or blameworthy unless his unlawful act was performed with a guilty mind (mens rea). Professor Alan Dershowitz has written:

> No matter how the law reads, it is a deeply entrenched human feeling that those who are grossly disturbed—whether they are called "madmen," "lunatics," "insane," or "mentally ill"—should not be punished like ordinary criminals. This feeling, which is as old as recorded history, is unlikely to be rooted out by new legislation.[30]

In the place of an eye for an eye, a tooth for a tooth, the Greeks allowed an excuse, the first time, in the case of Orestes, who was "driven" to kill his mother in order to avenge his father. Reduced states of competency vary in terms of their power to excuse. The law on criminal intent, as Justice Holmes once said, takes account of incapacities only when the weakness is marked, such as "infancy and madness."[31] Otherwise expressed, one is held accountable in criminal law only when one is competent to commit crime. The formulation of the rule theoretically determines the function of the court, the function of the jury, the instructions of the judge to the jury, and the scope of the evidence. Various tests have been formulated to determine when a person is sufficiently demented or defective as not to be held accountable for his acts.

In 1256 the English judge Henry de Bracton formulated what came to be known as the "wild beast" test. He asserted that an insane person should not be held morally accountable, since he was not far removed from a "beast." He wrote, "Such (mad)-men are not greatly removed from beasts for they lack reasoning." It was approved as a test during the next five centuries, to be finally dogmatized by Judge Tracy in 1724 at the trial of Edward Arnold. Thirty-six years later the wild beast test was abandoned in favor of the defendant's capacity to distinguish between right and wrong—the precursor of the *M'Naghten* test.[32]

The *M'Naghten* Test

Today, criminal responsibility is determined in England and in many jurisdictions in the United States according to the rule formulated in 1843 following the trial in England of a Scotsman by the name of Daniel M'Naghten. In this well-known case, M'Naghten (a paranoid schizophrenic, if labeled today) felt persecuted by the Tories, who were then in power. He decided to take action against them by killing Sir Robert Peel, the prime minister. He kept a watch on Peel's house, and when he saw a man come out, he shot Edward Drummond in the mistaken belief that he was shooting Peel. A defense of self-defense would be unavailing, as the perceived threat was not imminent and the perception of the threat was not that of a reasonable person. Instead, the jury, as instructed, found the defendant not guilty on the ground of insanity. He premeditated, but the premises of his thinking were bizarre. The acquittal was the beginning rather than the end of this celebrated case.[33]

Although acquitted of crime, M'Naghten was certified as being of unsound mind and detained in a lunatic asylum, where he spent his remaining twenty-two years. The verdict of not guilty on the ground of insanity, however, created a furor, and within a few days after the trial, the case was debated in the House of Lords. It was speculated that M'Naghten, a Scotsman, was a political assassin. The times were turbulent. Shortly before, Queen Victoria had been the target of an attempted assassination by an assailant who was also found not guilty by reason of insanity. On learning of the M'Naghten acquittal, she summoned the House of Lords to an extraordinary session. They were instructed to clarify and tighten the concept of criminal responsibility. They came forth with the so-called *M'Naghten* rules. These rules are extensive, but the pronouncement of greatest import provides:

> The jurors ought to be told in all cases that every man is presumed to be sane and to possess a sufficient degree of reason to be responsible for his crimes, until the contrary can be proved to their satisfaction; and that, to establish a defense on the ground of insanity, it must be clearly proved, that, at the time of the committing of the act, the party accused was labouring under such a defect of reason, from disease of the mind, as not to know the nature and quality of the act he was doing or, if he did know it, that he did not know he was doing what was wrong.

M'Naghten himself probably would not have been exculpated under the legal definition of insanity laid down in the test that bears his name. In a literal application of the *M'Naghten* rule, two (and probably only two) classes of lawbreakers would be exempted from punishment. For example, in the case of homicide: (1) the person thought that the gun with which he shot somebody was not a deadly weapon but a water pistol and was therefore unaware of the fact that it would kill (he did not "know the nature and quality of the act he was doing"); or (2) a person labored under the delusion that he was physically attacked and acted in legitimate self-defense ("he did not know he was doing what was wrong"). The question to be asked under the *M'Naghten* rule is not whether the lawbreaker knew the difference between right and wrong in general. Rather, the question is whether in the particular matter he "[knew] he was doing what was wrong," that is, whether he was under such a delusion that he thought he acted in legitimate self-defense.[34]

The *M'Naghten* rule has been criticized mainly because it concerns itself with cognition or intellectual understanding and makes no reference to emotion or control. A person, although not laboring under a defect of reason, may be incapable of controlling his behavior. The judges formulating the *M'Naghten* rule were aware that crime, like all human conduct, has multiple etiology, but they decided upon a narrow exculpatory provision. Under the *M'Naghten* rule as formulated, a person is not exempted from criminal responsibility because his capacity for self-control is affected by pathology. He is exempted when, laboring under a defect of reason from disease of the mind, he lacks moral judgment.

For years, the *M'Naghten* rule has been given lip service. Psychiatric testimony has been freely admitted in establishing "disease of the mind" and in interpreting the word *know* in the phrase "know he was doing what was wrong." *To know* includes more than simply knowledge that something is wrong; it includes, the courts say, a reasonably adequate grasp of the implications of the act. The interpretation of "premeditation," like that of "voluntary action," depends on how narrowly or broadly one frames the time period—some courts look at the few minutes before the commission of the act, others a longer period.[35]

The *Durham* Test

Notwithstanding the broad scope being given the *M'Naghten* rule, Judge David Bazelon of the Court of Appeals for the District of Columbia in 1954 in *Durham v. United States* ruled that the trial had not been adequate because the expert witness had not been permitted to present his full testimony. In the place of the *M'Naghten* rule, Judge Bazelon, looking at the New Hampshire law, formulated a *disease-defect-product* test, which provides: "An accused is not criminally responsible if his unlawful act was the product of mental disease or mental defect."[36] Unlike the *M'Naghten* rule, the *Durham* rule does not inquire about the impact of mental disease or defect on cognition.

In *Durham,* Judge Bazelon expressly stated that the purpose of the rule is to open the inquiry to the widest possible scope of medical or psychiatric testimony. He sought to remove the shackles, although theoretical, of the *M'Naghten* rule. In formulating his opinion, he relied heavily on the advice of leading forensic psychiatrists. The decision was widely heralded. Dr. Karl Menninger at the time described it as "more revolutionary in its total effect than the Supreme Court decision regarding segregation."[37] Forensic psychiatrists Lawrence Z. Freedman, Manfred Guttmacher, and Winfred Overholser together published a statement recommending its wide adoption, saying, "The *Durham* decision permits free communication of psychiatric information."[38] Dr. Gregory Zilboorg called it "a step toward enlightened justice."[39] The American Psychiatric Association awarded Judge Bazelon a certificate of commendation proclaiming that "he has removed massive barriers between the psychiatric and legal professions and opened pathways wherein together they may search for better ways of reconciling human values with social safety."[40]

As it turned out, however, the *Durham* rule resulted in confusion and a plethora of appeals. In cases where the rule was employed, judges and jurors alike were mired in confusion over the terms *disease, defect,* and *product.* With the exception of Maine, and a modification of it in New Mexico, the rule did not spread beyond the District of Columbia. In 1961, after a few years of the rule's application, Judge Bazelon's colleague on the U.S. Court of Appeals for the District of Columbia Circuit, Judge Warren Burger, later Supreme Court chief justice, angrily stated:

> Not being judicially defined, these terms "mental disease or defect" mean in any given case whatever the expert witnesses say they mean. We know also that psychiatrists are in disagreement on what is a "mental disease," and even whether there exists such a definable and classifiable condition. . . . [N]o rule of law can possibly be sound or workable which is dependent upon the terms of another discipline whose members are in profound disagreement about what those terms mean.[41]

The sweeping use of the terms *mental disease* or *defect* was only part of the problem. The product test brought in all the controversies of psychic determinism versus free will. What does "product" mean? Is every criminal act related to mental disorder? Is anyone accountable for his acts? Judge Holtzoff, district judge in the District of Columbia, observed: "It is not inconceivable that perhaps the so-called *Durham* formula would not have been adopted if it had been foreseen at the time that it would lead to the exculpation of sociopaths or psychopaths from criminal liability."[42] Judge Bazelon, too, became disillusioned; in 1964, he said, "The frequent failure to adequately explain and support expert psychiatric opinion threatens the administration of the insanity defense in the District of Columbia."[43] In 1967, in an apparent act of desperation, Judge Bazelon took the unusual step of writing a set of instructions, to accompany all orders requiring mental examinations, advising psychiatric witnesses as to how they should function.[44] Dr. Menninger, having once expressed great optimism about the possibilities of the *Durham* decision, recanted in his 1968 book *The Crime of Punishment*.[45]

The ALI Test

The American Law Institute's Model Penal Code, prepared during the years 1952 to 1962, recommended a combination of the right-wrong test and an updated version of "irresistible impulse":

(1) A person is not responsible for criminal conduct if at the time of such conduct as a result of mental disease or defect he lacks substantial capacity either to appreciate the criminality (wrongfulness) of his conduct or to conform his conduct to the requirements of the law,

(2) As used in this article, the terms "mental disease or defect" do not include an abnormality manifested only by repeated criminal or otherwise antisocial conduct.

Subsection 1 of the ALI test has two prongs that may be affected by mental disease or defect: (1) cognition or (2) control. Of the cognition prong, whereas *M'Naghten* spoke in terms of whether the defendant did or did not know, the ALI test refers to a lack of "substantial capacity" to "appreciate." The use of the word *appreciate* is designed to allow testimony about the defendant's emotional and affective attitude about the crime. The second prong excuses those whose mental disease or defect causes a loss of control over their actions at the time of the offense. A number of states that operate under the *M'Naghten* rule have extended the ground of the insanity plea through an addition known as *irresistible impulse*, popularly characterized as "the policeman at the elbow" test, under which an offender will be found insane only if he would have committed the offense in the presence of an officer. The defendant may have known what he was doing and known that it was wrong, but nevertheless may have been unable to resist an overwhelming impulse to commit the crime. This test is included as the second prong in subsection 1 of the ALI standard. The irresistible impulse test, when originally formulated in 1886 read: "Though conscious of [the nature of the act he is committing] and able to distinguish between right and wrong and know that the act is wrong, yet his will [that is,] the governing power of his mind, has been otherwise so completely destroyed that his actions are not subject to it, but are beyond his control."[46]

The formulation in subsection 2 of the ALI standard is designed specifically to include persons diagnosed as psychopathic, or having antisocial personality, within the scope of criminal responsibility. In a cartoon, the artist Honoré Daumier depicted an arrested man slouched despondently against the wall of his prison cell. "What really bothers me," he says, "is that I've been accused of twelve robberies." His lawyer is unmoved and replies, "So much the better. I will plead monomania." The cartoon was drawn at a time when a disease entity of "monomania" was identified by a French physician who treated the insane.[47] The ALI rejects as an abnormality that which is manifested only by repeated criminal or otherwise antisocial conduct.[48]

Rejection of *Durham*

Then, in 1972, some eighteen years after its adoption of the *Durham* rule, the U.S. Court of Appeals for the District of Columbia took the occasion to discard it in *United States v. Brawner*.[49] In this case, the American Psychiatric Association, American Psychological Association, American Civil Liberties Union, National District Attorneys Association, National Legal Aid and Defender Association, and the Georgetown Legal Intern Project filed briefs as amici curiae on such issues as the adoption of the ALI test for criminal responsibility and the possibility of the complete abolition of the insanity defense. The case was argued twice. In its amicus brief, the American Psychiatric Association suggested the rejection of the *Durham* test and endorsed instead the ALI standard. The amicus brief further suggested that if the court were to reject the ALI test, then the abolition of the insanity defense would be an alternative acceptable to the psychiatric profession. It stated that it would favor, with appropriate safeguards, abolishing the insanity defense, but it recognized that the abolition of the defense would have to be accomplished by constitutional amendment. The court, all nine members sitting en banc, including Judge Bazelon, unanimously decided in a 143-page opinion to throw out its *Durham* rule and adopt in its place the ALI standard.

In a year of deliberation of the case, the court considered and rejected the alternatives of abolishing the insanity defense entirely or of adopting a standard allowing the jury to decide sanity based simply on the question of whether the accused "can justly be held responsible." The court said that it rejected the abolition of the insanity defense because such an action should come from the legislative branch of government, not the judicial. (The Supreme Court on a number of occasions has indicated that where an insanity defense is raised, the failure to afford a defendant a fair and impartial hearing on the question is a denial of due process of law.) It said that it rejected allowing juries to decide sanity based on their own judgment, because such a procedure "would place too heavy a burden on the jury." In general, the court reasoned that the *Durham* rule did not work because of the latitude it gives expert witnesses to make value judgments in front of the jury. The "value judgments" referred to come in the form of medical or psychiatric testimony.

Acceptance of the ALI Test

The ALI test of criminal responsibility rapidly became accepted throughout the country. Over the following two decades, a majority of the states adopted the first paragraph, and many of these also adopted the second.[50] Of the eleven federal jurisdictions, all but one (the First Circuit, which has jurisdiction over federal cases in Maine, Massachusetts, and New Hampshire) used it. Volitional impairment, or the irresistible impulse concept, however, raised the difficult question: How can an impulse that was truly irresistible be differentiated from one that simply was not resisted? The psychiatric expert would invariably be asked the policeman-at-the-elbow question on cross-examination. "Would the defendant have committed this act if a policeman were standing next to him at the time?" An effective answer may be, "Your guess is as good as mine." Jack Ruby fatally shot Lee Harvey Oswald before a television audience right inside Dallas police headquarters. There is less likelihood that a defense of irresistible impulse will stand up when there is evidence of premeditation and planning, as they tend to demonstrate well-reasoned behavior or reasoned intent.

The Impact of the *Hinckley* Trial

In 1982, a District of Columbia jury shocked the nation by finding the would-be assassin of President Ronald Reagan, John W. Hinckley Jr., not guilty by reason of insanity.[51] The news ignited swift reactions from coast to coast. The verdict engendered countless editorials calling on lawmakers to abandon or modify the law. Television and radio call-in shows were swamped. The jurors were ridiculed in the media, and they were summoned before Congress to explain their decision, ostensibly to obtain information on any needed changes in the law. All in all, it dampened NGRI verdicts.[52]

In the aftermath of the trial, President Reagan submitted a bill to Congress to limit the scope of the insanity plea, which was followed by another bill submitted by Senator Strom Thurmond.[53] When submitting his bill, Senator Thurmond said, "We in the Senate would be shirking our duty to protect law-abiding citizens if we fail to take the time of this Congress to reform the insanity defense." More than forty bills were introduced in Congress to abolish or reform the defense.[54] Responding to the outcry, the American Bar Association and the American Psychiatric Association issued statements calling for a change in the law.[55]

The APA urged that insanity acquittals be granted only for impaired cognition (not for impaired control) resulting from mental disorders of the severity (if not always of the quality) of psychoses, and not for personality disorders or antisocial personalities. The APA's suggested standard was that the defendant be "unable to appreciate the wrongfulness of his conduct" because of "severely abnormal mental conditions that grossly and demonstrably impair a person's perception or understanding of reality." Likewise, the ABA recommended that insanity acquittals be granted only for impaired cognition (not for impaired control) as a result of a substantial process of functional or organic impairment, a recommendation adopted in federal law and the law of a number of states. Professor Stephen Morse, prominent scholar in law and psychology, proposed a "craziness test":

> A defendant is not guilty by reason of insanity if, at the time of the offense, the defendant was so extremely crazy and the craziness so substantially affected the criminal behavior that the defendant does not deserve to be punished.[56]

The insanity defense has always been controversial, but in the past, the controversy was mainly concerned with the formulation of the test to determine criminal insanity. Now there was intense controversy whether there should be any insanity defense at all. The *Hinckley* case quickened the debate in the United States, but the defense, for one reason or another, has been under attack for a long time. There was, for example, a great uproar following the *M'Naghten* trial in 1843 in England, and Queen Victoria sought a tightening of the defense. Professor Wei-hofen began his book published in 1933, *Insanity as a Defense in Criminal Law*, with the statement, "Probably no branch of the criminal law has been the subject of so much criticism and controversy as the defense of insanity."[57]

During the late 1970s, before the *Hinckley* verdict, twenty-four states passed laws tightening the test for determining insanity, and a few states enacted a guilty but mentally ill (GBMI) verdict.[58] President Nixon, like President Reagan, also attempted to abolish the insanity defense for federal crimes.[59] Advocates of reformation or abolition of the insanity defense argue that reform will bring many benefits, including streamlined trials, heightened law and order, and a return to jury decisions on the culpability of criminals without a battle of expert witnesses.[60] With the *Hinckley* decision receding from memory, the urge to change the insanity defense or adopt GBMI has waned.

To determine criminal responsibility, the issue is not simply whether the accused did or did not cause injury or harm, but whether he acted voluntarily and intended to cause the harm as well, knowing it was wrong. Professor Herbert Wechsler, an esteemed authority on criminal law, addressed an audience with the following example: "Suppose your elderly father, in an advanced arteriosclerotic state, is taken to the hospital and while there experiences a tantrum or delusion and knocks over a lamp, resulting in the death of an attendant. Would you be satisfied with a legal system in which he could be indicted and convicted of a homicidal crime? We would not."[61] Justice Holmes put it this way: "[A] law which punished conduct which would not be blameworthy in the average member of the community would be too severe for the community to bear. . . . Even a dog distinguishes between being stumbled over and being kicked."[62] Thus, long before Freud or the advent of psychiatry, the law has required a determination of blameworthiness in the ordinary moral sense, and has acquitted defendants who acted without moral culpability.[63]

Who Pleads Insanity?

As the defendant by pleading insanity admits causing the injury, attention is focused not on whether he committed the offense but on the history of the defendant to ascertain the intent or controllability of his conduct.[64] The accused is allowed to paint a more complete picture of his character and the interaction between his character and his conduct. According to John Wigmore, the leading authority on the law of evidence, when insanity is in issue "any and all conduct of the person is admissible in evidence."[65] Thus, once the defendant has raised the insanity defense, evidence of prior arrests, conviction, and antisocial conduct is admissible, a result not ordinarily permitted because it could unfairly prejudice the jury as to whether the defendant is guilty in a specific instance. As a consequence, in the majority of cases, a defendant with a criminal history does not raise the defense out of concern that his background will be brought to the attention of the jury and will tend to guarantee conviction, rather than acquittal.[66]

Usually, the defense is urged on behalf of those who have committed one episodic act of violence; the accused is a theretofore law-abiding citizen who explodes, often in a domestic dispute.[67] He himself may call the police and confess to committing the act, and he may call his lawyer, who is more likely to be a specialist in negligence, workers' compensation, or real estate than in criminal law. The criticism that the defense is used extensively by dangerous criminals, who thereby escape punishment, has no basis in fact.

Nevertheless, in quite a number of cases, the prosecutor charges the individual who was psychotic at the time of the offense with murder, and then declines to plea bargain. He is mindful of public opinion, and prefers to let judge or jury make the appropriate response to the charge. The evidence against the accused causing the harm is usually overwhelming, but his state of mind warrants a charge of manslaughter rather than first-degree murder.[68] A plea of insanity may prompt a lesser, more appropriate verdict. Studies report that 89 percent of insanity acquittees are schizophrenic, and that as a group they are less likely to recidivate than felons as a group or the two groups are about the same in the rate of recidivism.[69]

By classifying a person as either mad *or* bad, as the law would have it, the insanity defense tries to sort out the respective roles of the penal and hospital systems. It provides a way to determine, with the flexibility necessary in judging human minds, the difference between troubled and troublesome individuals and their dispositions. In many cases, as psychiatrists would say, an individual may be mad *and* bad, but in any event, criminal condemnation or imprisonment of a mentally ill person would be considered an affront to the moral sense of the community. In the judgment of many, for example, a mother suffering from a psychosis who kills her infant belongs not in prison but in a hospital. Our collective conscience, it is often said, does not allow punishment when the individual is not morally culpable.[70]

Frequency of the NGRI Plea

While the literature on criminal insanity is vast, the defense comes up only infrequently in trials (but more often in plea bargaining). In a lifetime of practice in forensic psychiatry, the practitioner may be involved in only a few trials involving a plea of insanity. In cases that go to trial, the insanity plea is a last-ditch defense. At best, it is estimated, insanity is raised in only 1 or 2 percent of the cases that go to trial (95 percent of criminal cases are plea-bargained), although at least 30 percent of the prison population (at the time of the crime as well as during imprisonment) have psychiatric problems sufficient to justify psychiatric intervention. Of that 1 or 2 percent of cases that go to trial, only about 10 percent end in an NGRI verdict, mostly involving crimes against property.[71] Cases like *Hinckley* go to trial because the victim, the offender, or the nature of the crime is extraordinary. The trials become media show cases because the individuals are well-known or the crimes so bizarre or atrocious as to make for good copy. And they invariably involve the presentation of conflicting psychiatric evidence.

The statistic that the insanity plea is involved in only 1 or 2 percent of cases that go to trial is misleading as to the varied uses of the plea. While evidence of insanity may not result in a verdict of NGRI, it may result in a conviction of a crime less than that charged, and in that sense, it is a victory for the defense. In nonserious cases, the prosecutor will often stipulate to an NGRI plea.[72] In some parts of the country, where civil commitment standards are stringent, individuals are charged with a minor offense (vagrancy or disturbing the peace) and under an NGRI plea are institutionalized, at least for a short period of time. Ironically, while now used frequently in misdemeanor cases, the plea in former times was mainly used in capital cases to avoid the death penalty. Every felony, of which there were many, carried the death penalty.

As a result of the California legislation enacted in 1994, known as the "Three-Strikes and You're Out Law," there has been a resurgence of the NGRI plea in order to avoid the lengthy penalty under that law. A person convicted of a third felony after two prior serious felonies will under the Three-Strikes law typically receive a sentence of no less than twenty-five years to life. Prior to Three-Strikes, it was uncommon to see criminal defendants malingering symptoms of mental illness in any but the most serious of felony cases, typically murder and rape. Subsequent to the adoption of the Three-Strikes law, malingering is seen by individuals charged with anything from murder and rape all the way down to petty theft (typically petty theft with a prior felony), presumably since any new felony conviction of a person with two prior strikes against them will result in a twenty-five-year to life sentence. Quite often, the prosecutor and defendant enter into an NGRI plea bargain.[73]

There is an old saying that statistics are like a bikini—what they reveal is interesting but what they conceal is vital. And that is the way it is with the statistics on the insanity defense. Most of the research report acquittal data, not plea data, and approximately 95 percent of cases are plea bargained. Plea data is difficult to obtain. As a consequence, it is problematical to determine how often the defense is utilized and how it fares in various jurisdictions.[74]

Burden of Proof

A factor almost as controversial and problematic as the test used to legally define insanity is the assignment of the burden of proof.[75] The allocation of the burden of proof on insanity is important, since psychiatric evidence is usually not sufficiently clear-cut to prove or disprove insanity beyond a reasonable doubt. The burden of proof may be understood as composed of three parts: the burden of pleading, the burden of production or going forward with the evidence, and the burden of persuasion.[76] The burden of production only requires that evidence be introduced to place a fact at issue in a trial, while the burden of persuasion requires that enough evidence be introduced to persuade the judge or jury of the actual existence of the fact.

In a criminal trial, the prosecution has the burden of proving the essential elements of the crime charged. The prosecution's burden of proof does not extend to proving the sanity of every defendant; instead the law presumes that defendants are sane at the time the alleged offenses are committed. It would be too time-consuming to offer evidence of sanity in every case. However, defendants may challenge this presumption of sanity by pleading NGRI. The *M'Naghten* rule states that jurors are to be told in all cases that every man is to be presumed to be sane and to possess a sufficient degree of reason to be responsible for his crimes, until the contrary is proved to their satisfaction.[77]

Once the defendant's mental condition becomes an issue, the burden of persuasion becomes important. By virtue of the presumption of sanity, the onus is placed on the accused to come forward with evidence of insanity. Under any test of criminal responsibility, it is usually sufficient to have "some evidence" of insanity in order to put the matter into controversy. There is, as noted, a distinction between "going forward with the evidence" (which may shift during the course of the trial) and a "burden of persuasion." It is problematic whether the prosecutor or the court has the authority or duty to impose an insanity defense on an apparently mentally disabled defendant.[78]

Two views are extant as to who must carry the burden of persuasion. About half of the state jurisdictions place the burden of persuasion on the prosecutor to disprove the elements of the defendant's insanity defense beyond a reasonable doubt. The other states, the federal courts, and the District of Columbia label insanity an affirmative defense, on which the defendant has the burden of persuasion by "clear and convincing evidence."[79] Following Hinckley's trial, the law was changed for the federal courts and within a number of states to place the burden of persuasion on the defendant, making it more difficult for the defendant to achieve an NGRI verdict. (Some states place the burden of persuasion on the defendant by a "preponderance of the evidence.")

The courts and legislatures have based their allocation of the burden of proof of sanity or insanity on their perceptions of the relationship between sanity and *actus reus* or mens rea. Those courts that place the burden of persuasion on the prosecution view sanity as necessary to the formulation of the requisite culpable mental state or voluntariness of the conduct, and hence as an essential element of the crime. Those that place the burden on the defendant do not perceive a necessary relationship between sanity and *actus reus* or mens rea, or they simply want to make it harder for a defendant to be found NGRI.

After the *Hinckley* trial, the American Bar Association recommended that the prosecution bear the burden of disproving the defendant's claim of insanity beyond a reasonable doubt in jurisdictions utilizing any test for insanity that focused solely on whether the defendant, as a result of mental disease or defect, was unable to know, understand, or appreciate the wrongfulness of his conduct. The ABA recommended that, in jurisdictions utilizing the ALI Model Penal Code test for insanity, the defendant bear the burden of proving a claim of insanity by a preponderance of the evidence.

The control prong of the insanity test raised the difficult question, according to a post-*Hinckley* statement of the American Psychiatric Association, of how can the psychiatrist differentiate between an impulse that was truly irresistible and one that simply was not resisted?[80] There is less likelihood that a defense of irresistible impulse will stand up when there is evidence of premeditation and planning, which tend to demonstrate well-reasoned behavior or reasoned intent. The serial killer claims an urge that he could not resist.

No matter which test of criminal responsibility is applied, the psychiatrist's testimony must describe the offender's state of mind at the time of the commission of the offense. It is necessary to project back from the time of examination to the time of the offense. The validity of an opinion on the defendant's mental condition at some given moment in the past—weeks or months prior to the examination— is invariably challenged on cross-examination. Information obtained from acquaintances and those who had custody of the defendant (jailers) following the crime is helpful.

In arriving at his opinion, the expert is often expected to have made or have had carried out the full battery of psychological tests (Rorschach, Thematic Apperception Test, Bender Gestalt, Minnesota Multiphasic Personality Inventory), and physiological tests (x-ray examination, physical examination, electroencephalogram, and neurological examination). Failure to apprise oneself of certain facts or test results or failure to use available examination techniques makes the expert vulnerable for the question, "Would that change your opinion, doctor?" Another attack on adequacy of examination involves questioning the amount of time that the expert spent with the accused.

Postact Behavior

Flight from the scene, attempts to avoid detection, and the circumstances of the apprehension of the accused are all relevant to the psychiatric examination.[81] If the defendant after the crime said that he was sorry that he did it or showed regret or remorse, the prosecutor may argue that this is an indication that he knew he had committed a wrongful act. In one case, the prosecutor proceeded this way in cross-examining the defense psychiatrist:[82]

> Q: So I ask you, sir, in your opinion . . . was he or did he indicate in any way that he was sorry that he killed this girl?
> A: He did not say he was sorry he had killed this girl and he was expecting the electric chair.
> Q: Doctor, can't you answer that question Yes or No?
> A: I can only answer it on the basis of what I observed. I observed that . . .
> Q: What is your opinion, doctor? Was he or was he not sorry that he killed the girl?
> A: My opinion was that he regretted killing the girl but somehow felt it was in the cards, that something like this was going to happen in his life and that he had no control over it, and this is the way it was going to be, he was going to get the chair and here it comes.
> Q: So your answer is, doctor, that in your opinion from your examination of him he was sorry that he killed the girl. That is true, isn't it?
> A: I would say he was sorry but felt there was nothing he could do about it.
> Q: Doctor, are you trying to hedge on the answer?
> A: I am trying to give you an accurate answer as to what I felt was going on in this man's mind.

Ironically, remorse and lack of remorse have both been used to indicate culpability or the lack thereof. In *United States v. McRae*,[83] the accused killed his wife by shooting her through the head with his deer rifle at point-blank range. That he did so was admitted; his defense was that the shooting was not intentional but accidental. His testimony at trial dwelt on his grief and his intense devotion to his wife, all in an attempt to cast his wife's death as accidental. He was allowed to introduce medical testimony of his hospitalization during a two-week period following the killing for "grief syndrome."

In the trial of O. J. Simpson, the prosecution sought to prove guilt (apart from other evidence) by the fact that he did not ask how Nicole Simpson was killed. In Albert Camus's novel *The Stranger*, the prosecution "proved" that the accused killed a stranger because he did not show proper grief at his own mother's funeral. The prosecutor found the reaction of the accused to be relevant and concluded with the statement, "I accuse the prisoner of behaving at his mother's funeral in a way that showed he was already a criminal at heart."[84]

Jury Decision Making

How do juries actually decide whether the accused is legally insane? Do the various formulations of criminal responsibility make a difference? To answer this question, Rita James Simon reported on a controlled experiment, introducing three variations into the record. The first variation was designed to test whether it makes any difference which criteria of mental incapacity—*M'Naghten, Durham,* or neither—a court directs the jury to apply. It was found that a jury instructed under the *M'Naghten* test is more likely to convict than is a jury instructed under *Durham;* whereas an uninstructed jury is likely to return the same verdict as a *Durham* jury. The second variation in the record was designed to test the effect were the jury to hear a considerably more elaborate evaluation of the accused's illness than is ordinarily given by psychiatrists in a case involving mental incapacity. No difference in the verdicts was found. The third variation was designed to determine whether verdicts would vary when there was an instruction that a verdict of not guilty on grounds of mental incapacity would necessarily result in commitment of the accused to a psychiatric hospital. Again, the variation was found to result in no difference.[85] Ironically, in the operation of the law, the crazier the accused, the more likely the jury will return a verdict of guilty, rather than NGRI. They want the crazy locked up.

Consequences of NGRI Verdict

Judges in many states, at the request of the defendant, instruct the jury on the consequences of an NGRI verdict. Otherwise, thinking that an insanity acquittee goes free, jurors would not likely return an NGRI verdict.[86] If and when an accused is found insane, he is exculpated, but nonetheless his freedom is curtailed. He has been shown to be either a person who does not know what he is doing or one who cannot control his conduct, which has resulted in serious harm to another. In the same manner as did the House of Lords following the *M'Naghten* decision, Congress and the various states have enacted legislation providing for commitment of any person who is acquitted on grounds of insanity. Commitment is made to a unit for the criminally insane, subject to release only upon a judicial finding that he "has recovered his sanity and will not in the reasonable future be dangerous to himself or others."[87] Regarding the entire procedure, Menninger aptly said: "Millions of dollars are spent annually to determine who has [responsibility] or hasn't it. If one is found to have it, he is locked up; if he is found not to have it, he is also locked up."[88]

In a turgid essay, penned about 1870, Mark Twain ridiculed the insanity defense, saying that rank criminal offenders were resorting to its use to escape the reach of the law, and he called for a law against the practice. The essay is titled, "A New Crime—Legislation Needed," the new crime being the use of the insanity defense. Mark Twain was perhaps unaware that the procedure was a device to temper the use of the death penalty, and he also presumed that these offenders were released. He apparently was not mindful of the fact that offenders acquitted on the plea of insanity are confined in a criminally insane unit of a mental hospital or penal institution. They do not walk out of the courthouse, free men.

As the insanity acquittee is not a free man, the prosecution urged the jury in the trial of James Hadfield in 1800 to return what was, at that time, a novel verdict, and it did: "We find the prisoner is Not Guilty; he being under the influence of insanity at the time the act was committed." He was detained for the rest of his forty years. Under the Insanity Bill of 1800, the court was empowered to order persons acquitted on account of insanity to be kept in strict custody, "in such place and such manner as the court may decide, during the King's pleasure."

It is preferable to be sent to the criminal unit of a mental hospital (with the possibility of release) than to be executed; but when the choice is between prison or a criminally insane unit, the option is for prison. The prison is less stigmatizing and is a more comfortable facility than the criminally insane unit, and the term of confinement is fixed, usually for a shorter period of time, but in recent years the law on disposition of an NGRI acquittee has changed, as we shall discuss.

When facts of the commission of the offense are undeniable—consider, for example, Jack Ruby's slaying of Lee Harvey Oswald or Arthur Bremer's shooting of Governor George Wallace—the defense of insanity, a subjective element, is the only tactic that a defense attorney has available to furnish judge or jury with a reason to acquit, or to return a verdict of a crime less than that charged. Hence, a defense attorney is obliged to argue the apparently fanciful, as was argued in the Bremer case, "This kid is pure schizophrenic . . . the kid's old lady is to blame for his mental disorders."[89]

Disposition of NGRI Acquittee

Without commitment as a consequence of an NGRI acquittal, the insanity defense would likely be considered unnecessary in the administration of the criminal law. The problem today is really not with the insanity defense per se, but with hospital release of the defendant. Until recently, an NGRI verdict was almost always followed by automatic commitment to a mental hospital (actually a jail) for a long period, often for life. However, beginning in the 1970s, a number of jurisdictions in the United States began to require that the person be released if found either no longer mentally ill or dangerous or in need of care or treatment, just as in the case of civil commitment.[90] As a result of this change in the law, the American public began to look askance at a system that regarded people who have already committed dangerous acts as largely equivalent to people who have not.

The issue, then, is whether NGRI and civil commitment proceedings on admission and discharge must be identical. An acquittal by reason of insanity is an explicit finding that the defendant suffered from a mental disability at the time of the offense, but it is not dispositive of the question of the defendant's mental condition at the time of acquittal. The verdict refers to the time of the act, but it is reasonable to presume that the mental illness continues up to the time of commitment. Automatic commitment of insanity acquittees for evaluation satisfies due process because it represents "a judicious weighing of the public's right to be protected from possibly dangerous mentally ill persons against the individual defendant's right to be protected against unjustified commitment."[91]

The controversial issue, however, is not so much over initial commitment but over discharge. Drug therapy may (quickly) remove the symptoms of mental illness without necessarily assuring that the individual is not dangerous. As far as the hospital is concerned, there is nothing more to treat, if ever there was anything to treat, and it feels justified in discharging the individual. The situation also occurs where the individual is mentally ill but not treatable. Questions arise: Should the hospital be used as a place of confinement? May the acquittee be transferred to a nonhospital facility? Who should have control over discharge? What, if any, conditions on release may be imposed? An individual who has been found NGRI in the case of a violent crime and is quickly discharged stirs up anxiety in the community.[92]

Taking NGRI acquittees as a fair and proper category, the burden of proof and the criteria for their commitment and discharge may be different than that in the case of the civilly committed patient.[93] The hospital and its staff generally prefer not to have control over discharge of the insanity acquittee, as they do over the civilly committed patient, as they do not enjoy immunity from suit; they prefer that control over discharge of the insanity acquittee be in the hands of the court, but that all too often results in an overcrowded hospital.[94]

In a 5–4 decision in *Jones v. United States*,[95] the Supreme Court in 1983 said that an insanity acquittee should be released only when "he has regained his sanity or is no longer a danger to himself or society." It does not matter, the Court said, how long the maximum jail term would have been if the defendant had been convicted. The *Jones* case involved a man who had been in a mental hospital over seven years. He was charged with trying to shoplift a coat from a department store, a misdemeanor that carries a maximum sentence of one year in jail. He pleaded not guilty by reason of insanity, and was committed to St. Elizabeths. He argued that once the maximum criminal sentence had expired, he was entitled as a matter of constitutional due process either to release from the mental hospital or to the relatively more favored legal status of a person who is under an order of civil, rather than criminal, commitment. Writing for the majority, Justice Powell said that imprisonment and commitment to a mental hospital serve two different purposes. The purpose of criminal commitment to a mental hospital, he said, is not punishment but treatment of a mentally ill person and protection of society "from his potential dangerousness." The continued confinement of such a person, Justice Powell said, "rests on his continuing illness and dangerousness." He added: "There simply is no necessary correlation between severity of the offense and length of time necessary for recovery. The length of the acquittee's hypothetical criminal sentence therefore is irrelevant to the purpose of his commitment."[96]

Guilty but Mentally Ill Verdict

Among the various proposals for change, the most fashionable suggestion has been the verdict of guilty but mentally ill. This alternative verdict was adopted in Michigan in 1975 and then in a number of other states.[97] Whenever the defendant pleads a defense of insanity, the jury may instead find him GBMI.[98] Proponents claimed a need for this new kind of verdict because the term *guilty* expresses the objective truth that the defendant committed the crime, while the term *mentally ill* expresses the subjective truth about the defendant, that he is sick. The GBMI verdict gives the jury the opportunity "of agreeing that the defendant is mentally ill, yet holding him criminally responsible."[99] Supposedly, GBMI avoids the either-or approach of guilty or not guilty by providing a middle ground.

Michigan's enactment of the GBMI verdict was a reaction to a decision in 1974 by the Michigan Supreme Court in *People v. McQuillan*.[100] In a decision followed by a number of other states, the Michigan Supreme Court held that after an initial period of sixty days, during which the insanity acquittee was to be evaluated, further confinement had to conform with the procedures and standards of the civil commitment process.[101] The case gave rise to the perception that there were too many NGRI's in the state, and they were not being kept in detention. Within a year of the decision, sixty-four persons who had been found NGRI were released, and within another year, two of the sixty-four had committed violent crimes—Ronald Manlen raped two women, and John McGee killed his wife. Public outrage moved the Michigan legislature to adopt promptly the new verdict of GBMI.[102]

The GBMI verdict was clearly designed as an anti-NGRI verdict. It accomplishes its goal by muddying the water. It appears to be a compromise verdict. In fact, it has exactly the same consequences as a guilty verdict—detention in the penal system or the death penalty. It is a second guilty verdict. The GBMI verdict hoodwinks the jury in the decisional process. Given two guilty verdict options (guilty or GBMI), the odds are increased that a jury will return a guilty verdict, in one form or other, rather than one of not guilty by reason of insanity. Juries think that GBMI is a compromise or middle ground because it sounds exculpatory—"guilty but mentally ill." It would sound more condemnatory if it said "guilty and mentally ill." The verdict is not a middle ground but can be described as a misleading distinction without a difference: it is another guilty verdict. The guilty but mentally ill verdict could just as well be "guilty but cirrhotic" or "guilty but flat feet." The defendant is found guilty, convicted, and imprisoned. He will get special attention if he needs it, as will any other prisoner.

Nor have trial courts in Michigan allowed defense counsel to offer evidence on the consequences of a GBMI verdict. Moreover, while the state is usually not allowed to invoke a plea of NGRI, the Michigan trial courts have allowed the prosecutor, in final argument, to tell the jury that they should find the defendant guilty but mentally ill where the defendant pleads NGRI and the evidence points to insanity.[103] Thus, the jury may believe they are helping the defendant by finding him GBMI rather than just guilty, unaware that the same consequences await him as any convicted person.

The GBMI verdict is not only misleading at trial but also in the plea-bargaining process. The plea is illusory because there is a false promise that the jurisdiction can ensure the outcome of what is allegedly the purpose of the GBMI verdict, namely treatment for those individuals who are found guilty and who are mentally ill.[104]

The GBMI verdict has clearly reduced the number of NGRI pleas (as distinguished from NGRI verdicts). Given a GBMI option, defense lawyers tend to prefer entering a not guilty plea rather than a plea of NGRI. With a not guilty plea, there is only one chance of being found guilty (a guilty verdict) but with an NGRI plea, there are two chances of being found guilty (guilty and GBMI). Thus, as the American Psychiatric Association stated, the GBMI verdict amounts to a disguised abolition of NGRI and gives juries an "easy way out" to avoid grappling with difficult issues of guilt, innocence, and insanity.[105]

Conclusion

The defense of insanity is a defense of last resort—it is not a popular defense with defendants, their counsel, or with juries. Insanity is raised in few trials, usually by a person without a criminal record who commits one episodic act of violence. Few of these trials end in acquittal, but evidence produced under the defense may diminish the verdict of guilt for a lesser crime, such as reducing murder to manslaughter. The specter of an insanity defense also affects the plea-bargaining process (over 90 percent of all felony dispositions) in a way generally favorable to the defense.

Contrary to popular belief, the test of criminal responsibility is a constraint on psychiatric evidence regarding *actus reus* or mens rea, and a verdict of NGRI provides some control over an acquittee. A not guilty plea, on the other hand, has only the limitation of relevancy. The *Hinckley* trial gave the impetus to "guilty but mentally ill" legislation, which in turn has resulted in not guilty pleas replacing NGRI pleas. In any event, following the uproar over the *Hinckley* verdict, jurors have become more reluctant to return an NGRI verdict.

The administration of the law is not a mechanical operation; it needs avenues for the exercise of discretion. The insanity plea is an excuse for behavior, the policy question being the extent to which an excuse will be tolerated. In law school courses on criminal law and procedure, emphasis is on rights of suspects and not on rights of victims. Individuals apparently tend to identify more with the offender than with the offended. It may be said that the law on criminal responsibility stems out of our fear of being accused or held accountable for something we may have done or imagined, even though beyond our reason or control. St. Augustine expressed thanks that he was not responsible for his dreams, which caused him embarrassment.

The insanity defense provides society with a vehicle for debating the meaning of criminal responsibility. As law professor George Fletcher put it,

> [T]he issue of insanity requires us to probe our premises for blaming and punishing. In posing the question whether a particular person is responsible for a criminal act, we are forced to resolve our doubts about whether anyone is ever responsible for criminal conduct. And if some are responsible and some are not, how do we distinguish between them? Is it a matter for the experts or is it a question of common sense? If it is for experts, why do they persistently disagree; if it is a matter of common sense, why is the issue so difficult to resolve?[106]

The questions do not lend themselves to simple answers, and that is because NGRI is used for various purposes. For that reason, statistics on the frequency or success of the plea of NGRI are less than satisfying. They do not illuminate the various uses of the plea. The plea is like a crystal ball—turn the sphere a little, and it casts a whole new light. At a time when the death penalty was possible for nearly all crimes, NGRI was used to circumvent that penalty. Nowadays the plea is frequently urged in order to bring about a conviction on a crime less than that charged. In that sense, the plea is successful, though it does not result in an acquittal on the basis of insanity. And, as we have noted, it is frequently used in plea bargaining. Unheard of in past times, the plea is used in cases of minor offenses (disturbing the peace or vagrancy) in order to obtain medical treatment for individuals who otherwise might have been civilly committed but for the difficulties in obtaining a civil commitment. Then, too, as a recent phenomenon, the plea is used to circumvent heavy criminal penalties under the Three-Strikes law. In short, like any excuse, the plea of NGRI provides some flexibility in the administration of the law.

Notes

1. See A. Buchanan, *Psychiatric Aspect of Justification, Excuse and Mitigation* (Philadelphia: Jessica Kingsley, 2000); G. F. Fletcher, *A Crime of Self-Defense: Bernhard Goetz and the*

Law on Trial (New York: Free Press, 1988); J. Dressler, "Justifications and Excuses: A Brief Review of the Concepts and the Literature," *Wayne L. Rev.* 33 (1987): 1155.

2. In controversial decisions, psychiatric testimony has been allowed to explain to the court (judge or jury) that constant or unpredictable abuse gradually leads individuals to develop a condition known as *learned helplessness*, which makes them feel that they have no control over the situation and are powerless to stop the abuse. As a consequence, the threshold in acting in self-defense is lowered. Given a scenario in which a woman has killed her abusive spouse, a lay jury or perhaps even a judge would generally make the assumption that a woman who was being abused could just get up and leave. Expert testimony regarding the concept of learned helplessness as part of the battered spouse syndrome would assist the court, as it would be out of the range of knowledge of the ordinary layperson. In a number of the cases where women have been prosecuted for killing their abusive partners, they have sought exculpation by asserting the defense of self-defense (even when the spouse was asleep when killed), and they have sought to introduce evidence of battered woman syndrome. See United States v. Brown, 891 F.Supp. 1501 (D.Kan. 1995); A. M. Dershowitz, *The Abuse Excuse* (Boston: Little, Brown, 1994); J. Dressler, *Understanding Criminal Law* (New York: Matthew Bender, 3d ed. 2001); K. J. Weiss, "Psychiatric Testimony and the 'Reasonable Person' Standard," *J. Am. Acad. Psychiatry & Law* 27 (1999): 580. See also B. C. Trowbridge, "Self Defense as a Mental Defense," *Am J. For. Psychology* 19 (2001): 63.

3. For an old sleepwalking case, see Fain v. Commonwealth, 78 Ky. 183, 39 Am. Rep. 213 (1879). For an epilepsy case, see People v. Freeman, 61 Cal. App.2d 110, 142 P.2d 435 (1943). See B. Hamer & A. Payne, "Sleep Automatism: Clinical Study in Forensic Nursing," *Perspectives Psychiatric Care* 29 (1993): 7; P. J. J. van Rensburg, C. A. Gagiano, & T. Verschoor, "Possible Reasons Why Certain Epileptics Commit Unlawful Acts during or Directly after Seizures," *Med. & Law* 13 (1994): 373.

4. Model Penal Code, sec. 2.01. See also Cal. Penal Code, sec. 26; Ill. Ann. Stat., sec. 4–1; N.J. Stat. Ann., sec. 2C: 2–1.

5. See J. P. McCutcheon, "Involuntary Conduct and the Criminal Law," *Int. J. Law & Psychiatry* 21 (1998): 305; S. J. Morse, "Culpability and Control," *U. Pa. L. Rev.* 142 (1994): 1587; K. W. Saunders, "Voluntary Acts and the Criminal Law: Justifying Culpability Based on the Existence of Volition," *U. Pitt. L. Rev.* 49 (1988): 443. See also M. S. Moore, *Act and Crime* (Oxford: Clarendon Press, 1993); M. Kelman, "Interpretive Construction in the Substantive Criminal Law," *Stan. L. Rev.* 33 (1981): 591.

6. In a number of cases it has been claimed that medication (such as Prozac or Halcion) prescribed for the treatment of mental illness had a disinhibiting effect resulting in an explosion of aggression. The defense, analogous to involuntary intoxication, claims that the medication side effects were unknown previously to the patient. State v. DeAngelo, 2000 Lexis 493 (Conn. Super. Ct. Feb. 24, 2000); Garza v. State, 829 S.W.2d 291 (Tex. App. 1992). See J. Cornwell, *The Power to Harm* (New York: Viking, 1996); J. Glenmullen, *Prozac Backlash* (New York: Simon & Schuster, 2001); R. Slovenko, *Psychiatry and Criminal Culpability* (New York: Wiley, 1995); M. L. Harris, "Problems with Prozac: A Defective Product Responsible for Criminal Behavior?" *J. Contemp. Legal Issues* 10 (1999): 359; C. M. Vale, "The Rise and Fall of Prozac: Products Liability Cases and 'The Prozac Defense' in Criminal Litigation," *St. Louis U. Pub. L. Rev.* 12 (1993): 525; P. B. Herbert, "Not Guilty by Reason of Prozac," *Newsletter of Am. Acad. Psychiatry & Law*, Apr. 2000, p. 16.

7. F. McAuley & J. P. McCutcheon, *Criminal Liability* (Dublin: Sweet & Maxwell, 2000), pp. 148–76; E. M. Coles, "Scientific Support for the Legal Concept of Automatism," *Psychiatry Psychology & Law* 7 (2000): 33; M. Corrado, "Automatism and the Theory of Action," *Emory L. J.* 39 (1990): 1191; P. Fenwick, "Automatism, Medicine, and the Law," *Psychological Medicine Monograph* (1990); S. J. Morse, "Craziness and Criminal Responsibility," *Behav. Sci. & Law* 17 (1999): 147. Psychologist E. Michael Coles writes, "The law, operating on the premise that only human beings can commit crimes, logically concludes that, since a crime cannot be committed by a machine, a crime cannot be committed by a person who is functioning like a machine." E. M. Coles, "Scientific Support for the Legal Concept of Automatism," *Psychiatry, Psychology & Law* 7 (2000): 33.

8. J. R. Meloy, *The Psychopathic Mind* (Northvale, N.J.: Jason Aronson, 1988), p. 194. See also J. Junginger, "Predicting Compliance with Command Hallucinations," *Am. J. Psychiatry* 147 (1990): 245; J. Junginger, "Command Hallucinations and the Prediction of Dangerous-

ness," *Psychiatric Services* 46 (1995): 911; M. E. Kasper, R. Rogers, & P. A. Adams, "Dangerousness and Command Hallucinations: An Investigation of Psychotic Inpatients," *Bull. Am. Acad. Psychiat. & Law* 24 (1996): 219; J. S. Thompson, G. L. Stuart. & C. E. Holden, "Command Hallucinations and Legal Insanity," *Forensic Reports* 5 (1992): 29.

9. See A. M. Dershowitz, *The Genesis of Justice* (New York: Time Warner, 2000), p. 103.

10. N. Bunyan & D. Bamber, "George Harrison Wins Concession to Victims," *Weekly Telegraph*, Nov. 22–28, 2000, p. 3. In Bass v. Aetna Ins. Co., 370 So.2d 511 (La. 1979), the Louisiana Supreme Court declined to allow application of the "Act of God" defense in a personal injury suit brought by one worshiper against another on allegations that the defendant ran into the plaintiff while the plaintiff was in the aisle of a church praying. The defendant contended that he was "trotting under the Spirit of the Lord" when the accident occurred. The court said, "If [the defendant's] defense is that he was not in control of his actions, it can be compared to voluntary intoxication, which will not exonerate one from delictual responsibility." 370 So.2d at 513.

11. 216 N.Y. 324, 110 N.E. 945 (1915). See G. H. Morris & A. Haroun, "'God Told Me to Kill': Religion or Delusion?" *San Diego L. Rev.* 38 (2001): 973.

12. 110 N.E. at 949. The State of New York having the *M'Naghten* test, Judge Cardozo was obliged to base the decision on impairment of cognition rather than on control.

13. ALI Model Penal Code, sec. 4.01, Comments, 46 (Tent. Draft No. 4, 1955).

14. D. Margolick, "Madness as an Excuse: Two Similar Arguments in the Same Court, with Starkly Different Results," *New York Times*, Jan. 28, 1994, p. B-11. In Davis v. State, 595 N.W.2d 520 (Minn. 1999), the expert on behalf of the defense testified that the defendant acted pursuant to command hallucinations that did not allow for choice. He based his opinion on the defendant's history of unprovoked assaults, his discontinuing his medication, his "bizarre" description of the evening's events, the fact that the defendant's actions served no purpose, and the fact that the defendant did not attempt to hide his involvement in the crime by changing his clothes. On cross-examination, the expert acknowledged explaining the legal insanity standards to the defendant during their first interview, creating a concern about the defendant tailoring descriptions of his symptoms to match the standard. On this record, the trial court found that the defendant should not be excused from criminal responsibility by reason of mental illness. See P. S. Appelbaum, P. C. Robbins, & J. Monahan, "Violence and Delusions: Data from the MacArthur Violence Risk Assessment Study," *Am. J. Psychiatry* 157 (2000): 566.

15. See R. Numbers, *The Disappointed* (Nashville: University of Tennessee Press, 1993).

16. 110 N.E. at 950. Years later, in describing the case at the New York Academy of Medicine, Cardozo identified the defendant as a priest who had been sexually intimate with the victim. He mentioned neither of those facts in his opinion, although they were relevant to judging the credibility of the defendant's claim that he had acted under God's command. A. L. Kaufman, *Cardozo* (Cambridge: Harvard University Press, 1998), pp. 383–95.

17. State v. Crenshaw, 98 Wash.2d 789, 659 P.2d 488 (1983). Invariably, perpetrators of harm believe in the moral justification of their actions, though they may know it is legally wrong. Even self-professed Satanists do not do evil for evil's sake, as they believe that Lucifer *deserves* to be God. Andrea Yates explained that killing her five children was her last chance to protect them from the fires of hell. Irrationality is turned into rationality. See R. F. Baumeister, *Evil: Inside Human Violence and Cruelty* (New York: W. H. Freeman, 1997); see also P. R. McHugh, "A Psychiatrist Looks at Terrorism," *Weekly Standard*, Dec. 10, 2001, p. 21.

18. 659 P.2d at 494. In State v. Cameron, 674 P.2d 650 (Wash. 1983), a defendant who believed his act was commanded by God was ruled insane. In McElroy v. State, 242 S.W. 883 (Tenn. 1922), the defendant was ruled sane based on similar facts. In Utah, in legal proceedings that lasted over fifteen years, Ronald Lafferty, who claimed that he got directions from God to kill four people, was convicted. At arraignment, he questioned the court about whether it could deal with spiritual matters. After the court told him that he was in a temporal court, not a spiritual one, he declined to enter a plea, and the court entered a not guilty plea. He was ruled competent to stand trial notwithstanding reports of psychiatrists that he was not competent. Lafferty v. Cook, 949 F.2d 1546 (10th Cir. 1991). It might be argued that Lafferty's belief in divine revelations and spirits was so bizarre that it was not within the legitimate protections of the First Amendment. See Thomas v. Review Bd.

of the Ind. Employment Sec. Div., 450 U.S. 707 (1981). The court, however, took judicial notice of the fact that belief in divine revelation and personal spiritual experiences are part of the doctrine of the Mormon religion, of which Lafferty had at one time been a member. State v. Lafferty, 776 P.2d 631 (Utah 1989). Notwithstanding, he was convicted and sentenced to death, and he lost in an appeal to the U.S. Supreme Court. Lafferty v. Utah, 2001 U.S. Lexis 10338 (Nov. 13, 2001).

19. D. J. Goldhagen, *Hitler's Willing Executioners: Ordinary Germans and the Holocaust* (New York: Knopf, 1996). Adolf Eichmann, who was convicted of crimes against the Jewish people and crimes against humanity, argued, "I did not want to kill; . . . my guilt is only in my obedience, my dutiful service in time of war, my loyalty to the oath, to the flag." The judge, in his sentencing statement, responded: "Even if we were to find that the defendant acted out of blind obedience, as he claims, we would still say that a man who participated in crimes of these dimensions, over years, must suffer the greatest punishment known to the law, and no order can mitigate this punishment. But we have found that the defendant acted out of internal identification with the orders given them, and with a great desire to achieve the criminal object, and it makes no difference, in our opinion, in imposing punishment for such horrifying crimes, how this identification and this desire were born or whether they were the product of ideological education given the defendant by the regime that appointed him, as the defense counsel claims." T. Segev, *The Seventh Million* (New York: Henry Holt, 1991), p. 357. Unlike the excuse of those Nazis who had "only obeyed orders," Albert Speer's explanation was hypnosis. Asked at Nuremberg how he could live with himself, he answered that his interrogator understood "nothing of life in a dictatorship, nothing of the ever-present fear that went with it," and, most importantly, "nothing about the charisma of a man like Adolf Hitler." J. Fest, *Speer: The Final Verdict* (London: Weidenfeld, 2001). See also J. E. Fest, *The Face of the Third Reich* (New York: Da Capo Press, 1999), p. 198.

20. For example, in Marley v. Indiana, 729 N.E.2d 1011 (Ind. App. 2000), the court ruled that a murder defendant could introduce evidence of battered woman's syndrome only in support of an insanity defense. Because PTSD is a recognized mental disorder, the court said, evidence of BWS is admissible only under an insanity plea. See also State v. LeCompte, 371 So.2d 239 (La. 1979). BWS was first articulated by psychologist Lenore Walker, who posited a theory of "learned helplessness" to explain why a woman might not leave a battering relationship. The theory analogizes to Martin Seligman's work with laboratory dogs that he subjected to repeated electric shocks over which the dogs had no control. When the dogs were later placed in a position from which they could escape, they failed even to try to flee. Walker argued that battered women similarly learn to believe that they are helpless to flee, even when that belief may later prove to be wrong. Furthermore, the battered woman perceives herself to be trapped in a cycle of violence from which there is no escape. The woman seeks to defend herself at the only time that she thinks possible—before the next, inevitable attack. See A. M. Coughlin, "Excusing Women," *Cal. L. Rev.* 82 (1994): 1; A. E. Taslitz, "What Feminism Has to Offer Evidence Law," *Sw. U. L. Rev.* 28 (1999): 171.

21. G. B. Palermo, "The Future of Criminology and the Law in the Light of New Research," *Int. J. Offender Therapy & Comparative Criminology* 43 (1999): 259. Unusual plasma androgen levels are said to "overinfluence" sexual offenders. R. Rada, "Plasma Androgens and the Sex Offender," *Bull. Am. Acad. Psychiatry & Law* 8 (1980): 456. It has also been claimed that women, just prior to or during early menstruation, may be prone to uncontrollable impulses resulting in violence. J. M. Abplanalp, "Premenstrual Syndrome," *Behav. Sci. & Law* 3 (1985): 103.

Genetics is not just a science, it is the ideology of our age. The Human Genome Project—the multibillion-dollar international attempt to map the human genome (the distribution of genes on chromosomes) to find where each gene lies and ultimately what each does—has been criticized as the ultimate reductionist project. To describe it as such is a way of saying that we are reducible to our genes or to biology. "It's genetic," is offered as an excuse or the answer for every possible issue. B. K. Rothman, *The Book of Life* (Boston: Beacon Press, 2001). Grossly exaggerated claims are made regarding the impact of genes on behaviors and lifestyles. As S. P. Rose observed, "Genes, it is said, are responsible for such diverse features of human conduct as sexual orientation; poor behavior in school; alcoholism; drug addiction; violence; risk-taking; criminal, antisocial, and impulsive behavior; political antiauthoritarianism; religiosity; tendency to mid-life divorce; and even compulsive shopping."

S. P. Rose, "Neurogenetic Determinism and the New Euphenics; Clinical Review," *British Med. J.* 317 (1998): 1707. The tendency to focus on genetics as a causal explanation for behaviors at the expense of other factors is called "genetic myopia." For a critique of a simple biological explanation of behavior, see R. Sapolsky, *The Trouble with Testosterone* (New York: Scribner, 1997).

22. S. H. Dinwiddie, "Genetics, Antisocial Personality, and Criminal Responsibility," *Bull. Am. Acad. Psychiatry & Law* 24 (1996): 95.

23. The cover of Ron Rosenbaum's book *Explaining Hitler: The Search for the Origins of His Evil* (New York: Random House, 2000), features a picture of a cuddly infant Adolf Hitler, a distasteful provocation, but designed to jolt readers out of assumptions about him. Placing blame on genes is often a topic of jest, as illustrated in a cartoon in the *Washington Post* (Oct. 19, 2001) by Mike Twohy that depicts a judge saying to a defendant, "I find your criminal gene guilty of expressing itself." In People v. Yukl, 83 Misc.2d 364, 372 N.Y.S.2d 313 (1975), the New York Supreme Court held that a genetic imbalance theory of crime causation has not been sufficiently established and accepted so as to warrant admission of evidence with regard to XYY syndrome as part of the defense of insanity. See also R. Rada, "Plasma Androgens and the Sex Offender," *Bull. Am. Acad. Psychiatry & Law* 8 (1980): 456.

24. The leading sympathy defenses, or abuse excuses, are set out in A. M. Dershowitz, *The Abuse Excuse and Other Cop-outs, Sob Stories, and Evasions of Responsibility* (Boston: Little, Brown, 1994); S. Estrich, *Getting Away with Murder* (Cambridge: Harvard University Press, 1998). See also P. J. Falk, "Novel Theories of Criminal Defense Based upon the Toxicity of Social Environment: Urban Psychosis, Television Intoxication, and Black Rage," *N. Car. L. Rev.* 74 (1996): 731; A. E. Taslitz, "Abuse Excuses and the Logic and Politics of Expert Relevance," *Hastings L. J.* 49 (1998): 1039.

25. The insanity plea, given the special plea of NGRI, is the route when evidence of mental illness affecting criminal responsibility is to be offered at trial. United States v. Westcott, 83 F.3d 1354 (11th Cir. 1996); People v. Carpenter, 464 Mich. 223, 627 N.W.2d 276 (2001); State v. Dalton, 98 Wis.2d 725, 298 N.W.2d 298 (1980); Annot., 16 A.L.R.4th 654. The doctrine of diminished capacity, where recognized, allows the introduction of psychiatric testimony on mental state without an NGRI plea. See R. Slovenko, *Psychiatry and Criminal Culpability* (New York: Wiley, 1995); R. P. Bryant & C. B. Hume, "Diminished Capacity—Recent Decisions and an Analytical Approach," *Vand. L. Rev.* 30 (1977): 213, 217.

26. 832 F.2d 531 (10th Cir. 1987).

27. Regina v. Byrne, (1960) 3 All E. R. 1, 4. In R. v. Turner, [1975] Q.B. 834, C.A., the court again set out the proposition that the loss of self-control that is essential to a successful plea of provocation is something regarded by the law as "falling within the realm of the ordinary juryman's experience." In R. v. Emery, [1993] 14 Cr. App. 394, the application of the rule appeared to have been relaxed so as to permit expert testimony relating to a condition that, although not a mental disorder, "is complex and is not known by the public at large." The court noted that the condition of dependent helplessness to which the evidence related "is complex and is not known by the public at large. Accordingly we are quite satisfied that it was appropriate for the learned judge to decide that this evidence should be allowed." The court commented further that "the question for the doctors was whether a woman of reasonable firmness with the characteristics of [the defendant], if abused in the manner which she said, would have had her will crushed so that she could not have protected the child." 14 Cr. App. R.(S.) at pp. 397–98. See R. D. Mackay & A. M. Colman, "Equivocal Rulings on Expert Psychological and Psychiatric Evidence: Turning a Muddle into a Nonsense," *Crim. L. R.* 1996: 88. Can provocation result in temporary insanity, thereby opening the door to psychiatric testimony? In a New Jersey case involving Agustin Garcia, who was charged with killing his former girlfriend, his lawyers argued that the shock of suddenly learning that his longtime girlfriend was marrying someone else induced a temporary mental illness known as acute adjustment disorder, which they said rendered him unable to control himself. The lawyers sought a manslaughter conviction. He was convicted of murder. "Jury Convicts Killer in Wedding-Day Murder," *New York Times*, Oct. 23, 2001, p. 20. See J. Dressler, "Rethinking Heat of Passion: A Defense in Search of a Rationale," *Crim. L. & Criminology* 73 (1982): 421; E. Y. Drogin, "To the Brink of Insanity: 'Extreme Emotional Disturbance' in Kentucky Law," *N. Ky. L. Rev.* 26 (1999): 99.

28. Michigan law, e.g., provides that a defendant who offers an insanity defense must

give notice to the court not less than thirty days before the date for the trial of the case or at such other time as the court directs. M.C.L., sec. 768.20a(1).

29. The several states (Idaho, Kansas, Montana, Nevada, Utah) that have sought to abolish the insanity defense typically allow expert testimony "on the issues of *mens rea* where any state of mind is an element of the offense." See Idaho Code, sec. 46–14–214 (1999); Nev. Rev. Stat. Ann., sec. 174.035 (1997); Utah Code Ann., sec. 76–2–305 (1999). In Montana v. Cowan, 861 P.2d 884 (1993), the Montana court upheld such abolition, noting that the state law allowed evidence with respect to the defendant's mental state on competency to stand trial, proof of his state of mind, and sentencing. The Nevada Supreme Court ruled that the state's restriction on the use of the insanity defense was unconstitutional. Nevada v. Finger, 27 P.3d 66 (2001). See B. E. Elkins, "Idaho's Repeal of the Insanity Defense: What Are We Trying to Prove?" *Idaho L. Rev.* 31 (1994): 153. As the other states, Kansas replaced the insanity defense with a mens rea definition of criminal responsibility. The legislation provides that it is a defense to prosecution of any criminal offense that "the defendant, as a result of mental illness or defect, lacked the mental state required as an element of the offense charged. Mental disease or defect is not otherwise a defense." Kan. Stat. Ann., sec. 22–3220 (1995).

30. A. Dershowitz, "Abolishing the Insanity Defense," *Crim. L. Bull.* 9 (1973): 434.

31. M. Lerner (ed.), *The Mind and Faith of Justice Holmes* (New York: Random House, 1943), p. 51.

32. A. M. Platt & B. L. Diamond, "The Origins and Development of the 'Wild Beast' Concept of Mental Illness and Its Relation to Theories of Criminal Responsibility," *J. History of Behavioral Sciences* 1 (1965): 365.

33. Daniel M'Naghten's Case, 10 Clark & Fin. 200, 8 Eng. Rep. 718 (1843). There is no agreement on the spelling of the defendant's name. It is variously spelled M'Naghten, M'Naughton, McNaughtan, McNaughten, McNaughton, and Mhicneachdain. The original report of the trial spelled it M'Naughton. The most common spelling—M'Naghten—is probably least likely to be correct. A photograph of his signature seems to read "McNaughtun," which prompted Justice Frankfurter to ask, "To what extent is a lunatic's spelling of his own name to be deemed an authority?" B. L. Diamond, "On the Spelling of Daniel M'Naghten's Name," *Ohio State L.J.* 25 (1964): 84.

34. Suppose someone who believes he is Christ attacks someone he identifies as the Devil. Delusional misidentification (as when an individual believes his spouse has been replaced by an imposter who threatens to harm him) is often seen in individuals with schizophrenia, schizoaffective disorder, or a psychotic disorder due to a general medical condition. Psychotic thinking plays a substantial if not significant role in the genesis of aggression in those who have dementia. Aggression arises from viewing the misidentified person as untrustworthy, evil, or threatening. J. A. Silva, G. B. Leong, R. Weinstock, & M. Ruiz-Sweeney, "Delusional Misidentification and Aggression in Alzheimer's Disease," *J. Forensic Sci.* 46 (2001): 581.

35. See M. H. Pauley, "Murder by Premeditation," *Am. Crim. L. Rev.* 36 (1999): 145.

36. Durham v. United States, 214 F.2d 862 (D.C. Cir. 1954).

37. K. A. Menninger, Introduction to D. L. Bazelon, "The Awesome Decision," *Saturday Evening Post*, Jan. 23, 1960, p. 32; quoted in R. Arens, *Make Mad the Guilty* (Springfield, Ill.: Thomas, 1969), p. vii.

38. See L. Z. Freedman (ed.), *By Reason of Insanity: Essays on Psychiatry and the Law* (Wilmington, Del.: Scholarly Resources, 1983).

39. G. Zilboorg, "The Role of the Psychiatrist as an Expert Witness in Criminal Court," *Bull. New York Acad. Med.* 32 (1956): 196.

40. See R. Slovenko, "Should Psychiatrists Honor Bazelon or Burger?" *J. Psychiatry & Law* 20 (1992): 635.

41. Blocker v. United States, 288 F.2d 853, at 859, 860 (D.C. Cir. 1961).

42. O'Beirne v. Overholser, 193 F.Supp. 652, at 660 (D.C. 1961).

43. Rollerson v. United States, 343 F.2d 269, at 271 (D.C. Cir. 1964).

44. Appendix, Washington v. United States, 390 F.2d 444, at 457 (D.C. Cir. 1967).

45. K. A. Menninger, *The Crime of Punishment* (New York: Viking, 1968). Slovenko assisted in the writing of the book.

46. A legal response to the criticism that the *M'Naghten* test failed to consider the defendant's ability to control his behavior came in the form of a supplementary test known as

the *irresistible impulse* rule. Parsons v. State, 81 Ala. 577, 2 So. 854 (1886). See also State v. Pike, 49 N.H. 399 (1897). The test met resistance in the legal community because it was believed that impulsivity could easily be feigned and that the test would lead to numerous invalid insanity acquittals. Impulse-control disorders include intermittent explosive disorder, kleptomania, pyromania, and pathological gambling. They are listed in the *DSM*. See J. M. Oldham, E. Hollander, & A. E. Skodol (eds.), *Impulsivity and Compulsivity* (Washington, D.C.: American Psychiatric Press, 1996). See chapter 11, on diminished capacity.

47. J. Goldstein, "Professional Knowledge and Professional Self-Interest: The Rise and Fall of Monomania in 19th-Century France," *Int. J. Law & Psychiatry* 21 (1998): 385.

48. On the psychopath (also known as sociopath), see chapter 10, on the mental disability requirement in the insanity defense. Some years ago the term *psychopathic personality* was discarded in a revision of the *DSM* nomenclature, and *personality disorders* was chosen as the appellation, and under it, there is a listing for Antisocial Personality Disorder. *DSM*, sec. 301.7 states: "The essential feature of Antisocial Personality Disorder is a pervasive pattern of disregard for, and violation of, the rights of others that begins in childhood or early adolescence and continues into adulthood. This pattern has also been referred to as psychopathy, sociopathy, or dyssocial personality disorder." Few who are familiar with the subject would disagree with the definition given by McCord and McCord: "The psychopath is an asocial, aggressive, highly impulsive person, who feels little or no guilt and is unable to form lasting bonds of affection with other human beings," W. McCord & J. McCord, *Psychopathy and Delinquency* (New York: Grune & Stratton, 1944). See also H. M. Cleckley, "Psychopathic States," in S. Arieti (ed.), *American Handbook of Psychiatry* (New York: Basic Books, 1959), vol. 1, pp. 567–88.

49. 471 F.2d 969 (D.C. Cir. 1972); noted in *N.Y.U. L. Rev.* 47 (1972): 962.

50. For an extensive discussion of the test, see People v. Martin, 386 Mich. 407, 192 N.W.2d 215 (1971).

51. United States v. Hinckley, 525 F.Supp. 1342 (D.D.C.), *op. clarified reconsideration denied,* 529 F.Supp. 520 (D.D.C.), *aff'd,* 672 F.2d 115 (D.C. Cir. 1982); S. Taylor, "Jury Finds Hinckley Not Guilty, Accepting His Defense of Insanity," *New York Times,* June 22, 1982, p. 1.

52. "Hinckley Bombshell End of Insanity Pleas?" *U.S. News & World Rep.,* July 5, 1982, p. 12.

53. S. 2902; S. 2903, 97th Cong., 2d Sess., 128 Cong. Rec. 511392–96; 511404–08 (Sept. 14, 1982).

54. For a summary of the bills introduced in Congress, see *Mental Disability L. Rep.* 6 (1982): 340. See R. J. Bonnie, J. C. Jeffries, & P. W. Low, *The Trial of John W. Hinckley, Jr.: A Case Study in the Insanity Defense* (New York: Foundation Press, 2d ed. 2000).

55. "The Insanity Defense: ABA and APA Proposals for Change," *Mental Disability L. Rep.* 7 (1983): 136; "American Psychiatric Association Statement on the Insanity Defense," *Am. J. Psychiatry* 140 (1983): 681.

56. S. J. Morse, "Excusing the Crazy: The Insanity Defense Reconsidered," *S. Cal. L. Rev.* 58 (1985): 777.

57. Professor Weihofen went on to say: "It is charged that the rules of law governing insanity as a defense to crime are vague and confused; that in so far as these rules are clear, they are clearly unsound, in that they are based upon notions of mental disorder discredited by modern science; and that the procedural machinery for trying cases where this defense is raised is inefficient and blundering in its results." H. Weihofen, *Insanity as a Defense in Criminal Law* (New York: Commonwealth Fund, 1933), p. 1. See also H. Weihofen, *Mental Disorder as a Criminal Defense* (Buffalo, N.Y.: Dennis, 1954).

58. See N. Morris, *Madness and the Criminal Law* (Chicago: University of Chicago Press, 1982).

59. In 1972, President Nixon proposed that the insanity defense be abolished for federal crimes but Congress never acted on his legislation. See A. Dershowitz, "Abolishing the Insanity Defense," *Crim. L. Bull.* 9 (1973): 434.

60. Dr. Abraham L. Halpern, a president of the American Academy of Psychiatry and Law, has worked continuously since the mid-1960s for the abolition of the insanity defense, asserting that it makes a mockery of the criminal justice system and frequently results in the misuse and abuse of psychiatry. Among his writings on the issue, see "The Insanity Defense: A Juridical Anachronism," *Psychiat. Ann.* 7 (1977): 398; "The Fiction of Legal Insanity and the

Misuse of Psychiatry," *J. Leg. Med.* 2 (1980): 18; "The Politics of the Insanity Defense," *Am. J. For. Psychiatry* 14 (1993): 1. See also J. Goldstein & J. Katz, "'Abolish the Insanity Defense'—Why Not?" *Yale L. J.* 72 (1963): 853. Professor Christopher Slobogin argues that abolishing the insanity defense has three potential practical benefits: It would improve the public's image of the criminal justice system; it may reduce the stigma associated with mental illness; and it should facilitate treatment of those with mental problems. C. Slobogin, "An End to Insanity: Recasting the Role of Mental Disability in Criminal Cases," *Va. L. Rev.* 86 (2000): 1199.

61. See Panel Discussion, "Insanity as a Defense," 37 F.R.D. 365 (1964). Criminal law does recognize some acts of omission as criminal acts, such as a parent's intentionally omitting to feed his child, or an epileptic person's intentionally driving without taking medicine to prevent a seizure.

62. See O. W. Holmes, *The Common Law* (Boston: Little, Brown, Howe ed. 1963), p. 42.

63. The American Psychiatric Association urged that the insanity defense be retained in some form because it rests upon the fundamental premise of the criminal law, namely, that people should be punished only if they are morally responsible for wrongful deeds. The 27,000-member association was stimulated to take a stand on the defense because of public and legislative outrage over the acquittal of Hinckley. In making the statement, the APA made no judgment as to whether the *Hinckley* verdict was proper or whether other standards and procedures would have resulted in a different verdict. See "Psychiatric Group Urges Stiffer Rules for Insanity Plea," *New York Times,* Jan. 20, 1983, p. 18.

64. Shifting the focus of attention from the deed to the biography of the defendant is criticized as a perversion of justice. See generally W. Gaylin, *The Killing of Bonnie Garland: A Question of Justice* (New York: Simon & Schuster, 1982); P. Meyer, *The Yale Murder* (New York: Harper & Row, 1982).

65. J. Wigmore, *Evidence* (Boston: Little, Brown, 1940), vol. 2, sec. 228 (emphasis omitted). See also People v. Martin, 386 Mich. 407, 192 N.W.2d 215 (1971).

66. Professor Don Linhorst of the St. Louis University School of Social Service reports that in a dataset of 1,066 Missouri insanity acquittees, 25.7 percent had a felony conviction prior to the insanity acquittal. The dataset did not contain information on the type of crime or the number of prior felony arrests or convictions. The dataset included only insanity acquittees, not defendants who may have pled insanity but were unsuccessful. See D. M. Linhorst, "The Unconditional Release of Mentally Ill Offenders from Indefinite Commitment: A Study of Missouri Insanity Acquittees," *J. Am. Acad. Psychiatry & Law* 27 (1999): 563.

67. See E. Tanay, *The Murderers* (Indianapolis: Bobbs-Merrill, 1976).

68. Compare this situation to that of a career criminal. In the latter case, the evidence as to the identity of the offender is often circumstantial. Often plea bargaining occurs because of weak evidence, and the defendant receives a relatively light sentence. Especially in large urban areas, there is trading as to the charge or sentence. Indeed, it may be suggested that evidence of mental illness or defect would not be necessary in many cases if there were more appropriate charging by the district attorney or the grand jury.

69. See S. B. Silver, M. I. Cohen, & M. K. Spodak, "Follow-up after Release of Insanity Acquittees, Mentally Disordered Offenders, and Convicted Felons," *Bull. Am. Acad. Psychiatry & Law* 17 (1989): 387.

70. Whatever the test, Judge Bazelon observed that juries will continue to make moral judgments under the fundamental precept that "[o]ur collective conscience does not allow punishment where it cannot impose blame." Durham v. United States, 214 F.2d 862, 876 (D.C. Cir. 1954).

71. The report (1949–1953) of the Royal Commission on Capital Punishment records a higher number. It noted that of 99,463 persons charged with felony crimes in a five-year period, 19.8 percent of the 374 charged with murder were acquitted by reason of insanity. London: Her Majesty's Stationery Office. See J. Gunn & P. J. Taylor, *Forensic Psychiatry* (Oxford: Butterworth-Heinemann, 1993); C. Cirincione, H. Steadman, & M. McGreevy, "Rates of Insanity Acquittals and the Factors Associated with Successful Insanity Pleas," *Bull. Am. Acad. Psychiatry & Law* 25 (1995): 399; J. Janofsky, M. Vandewalle, & J. Rappeport, "Defendants Pleading Insanity: An Analysis of Outcome," *Bull. Am. Acad. Psychiatry & Law* 17 (1989) 203; R. A. Pasewark, "Insanity Plea: A Review of the Research Literature," *J. Psychiatry & Law* 9 (1981): 14; H. Steadman et al., "Factors Associated with a Successful Insanity Defense," *Am. J. Psychiatry* 140 (1983): 401. In New York State there were 1 or 2 successful insanity cases per

year between 1958 and 1965, and approximately 9 cases per year between April 1, 1965, and August 30, 1971. Insanity acquittals rose to an average of 48 cases per year for the period 1971 to 1976 inclusive, and, after holding steady for the next four years, again rose to 124 cases in the year after the Insanity Defense Reform Act of 1980 went into effect. A. L. Halpern, "Elimination of the Exculpatory Insanity Rule," *Psychiatric Clinics of North America* 6 (Dec. 1983): 611. See also M. A. McGreevy, H. J. Steadman, & L. A. Callahan, "The Negligible Effects of California's 1982 Reform of the Insanity Defense Test," *Am. J. Psychiatry* 148 (1991): 744, where it is reported that 51 percent of the 1,300 individuals in a six-year period who entered an insanity plea were acquitted. See also E. Silver, C. Cirincione and H. J. Steadman, "Demythologizing Inaccurate Perceptions of the Insanity Defense," *Law & Human Behavior* 18 (1994): 63.

72. Plea bargaining accounts for the vast majority of the disposition of criminal cases, be it by a plea of guilty to a lesser charge or by a plea of NGRI. Since 1980, the percentage of cases decided by trial has decreased almost two-thirds, while the percentage of cases resolved by plea has been increased proportionately. From 1980 to 1999, the frequency of federal jury trials fell from nearly 16 percent of all adjudications to just a bit more than 4 percent. In 1980, one defendant went to trial for every four who pled guilty. By 1999, that ratio fell to one in twenty. Many individuals charged with crime are afraid to assert their right to a jury trial because of mandatory sentencing laws and sentencing guidelines. Prosecutors control sentences by controlling charges. The same problem is evident in state courts, too. I. H. Schwartz, "Consequences of the Disappearing Criminal Jury Trial," *Champion* 25 (Nov. 2001): 7.

Peter Plummer, a current Assistant Michigan Attorney General and former Assistant Prosecuting Attorney for Marquette County, Michigan, who has over thirty years of experience prosecuting various criminal offenses, commented, "Of thousands of felony and misdemeanor cases that I had, only three to six of them were actual true trials using the insanity defense. There were a lot of attempts to use the defense but either the defense counsel or defendant would opt out if my plea offer was good enough." Personal communication, Nov. 5, 2000. Time and again, when a mother kills her child, an insanity plea is accepted, as in the case of a Bay City, Michigan, woman who choked, hit, and stabbed her 10-year-old daughter. The 41-year-old mother claimed that voices in her head drove her to commit the acts. After struggling with her daughter, she disrobed, jumped from the second-story window of the duplex, and walked nude down the street until police found her. "The voices told her to get out of the house and not take anything with her," the judge told the press. "Judge Agrees with Mother's Insanity Plea" (Associated Press news release), *Detroit Legal News*, Nov. 13, 2001, p. 1.

73. H. B. Terrell, "Malingering Since Three-Strikes in California," *Forensic Examiner*, May/June 1999, p.22. Some states require a mental health hearing before accepting a plea based on insanity. Rennich-Craig v. Russell, 609 N.W.2d 123 (S.D. 2000). In a 2–1 ruling, the Ninth U.S. Circuit Court of Appeals threw out a shoplifter's fifty-year sentence under California's Three-Strikes habitual offender law as grossly disproportionate to the gravity of the offense and the culpability of the offender. Had the defendant's prior convictions not made him subject to the Three-Strikes law, he would have faced six months at most. Andrade v. Attorney General, 2001 U.S. App. Lexis 23720 (9th Cir. 2001). The ruling did not invalidate the law, but its application in a particular case. The ruling has unleashed a wave of appeals from many other prisoners who received comparable sentences in similar circumstances. The decision could wind its way to the U.S. Supreme Court, which, many observers say, has been looking for the right case to address Three-Strikes laws. The law was passed after the high-profile murder of Polly Klaas, a Petaluma, California, girl who was abducted and murdered by a convicted child molester. Amid public concerns about rising crime, former governor Pete Wilson made the law's passage a centerpiece of his reelection agenda. Forty states since then have adopted similar measures.

74. A few studies explore the extent to which the insanity defense was used in a jury trial, bench trial, or plea agreement, but they acknowledge the lack of information. See J. Petrila, "The Insanity Defense and Other Mental Health Dispositions in Missouri," *Int'l J. Psychiatry & Law* 5 (1982): 81; C. E. Boehnert, "Characteristics of Successful and Unsuccessful Insanity Pleas," *Law & Human Behavior* 13 (1989): 31.

75. In Maine, a criminal defendant charged with murder has the burden of proving by a preponderance of the evidence that he acted in the heat of passion or sudden impulse in

order to reduce the charge of homicide to manslaughter. The United States Supreme Court ruled that this burden did not comport with the due process requirement that the prosecution must prove every fact necessary to constitute the crime charged beyond a reasonable doubt. Mullaney v. Wilbur, 421 U.S. 684 (1975). However, two years later the Supreme Court upheld a New York law making "extreme emotional disturbance" for reducing a crime from murder to manslaughter an affirmative defense. Patterson v. New York, 421 U.S. 197 (1977). The defense of extreme emotional disturbance is but a slightly modified version of the defense of provocation, for which many states had long placed the burden of proof upon the defendant.

76. See E. W. Cleary, "Presuming and Pleading: An Essay on Juristic Immaturity," *Ariz. State L.J.* 1979: 115; J. McNaughton, "Burden of Production of Evidence: A Function of a Burden of Persuasion," *Harv. L. Rev.* 68 (1955): 1382.

77. See M'Naghten's Case, 8 Eng. Rep. 718 (1843).

78. Theodore Kaczynski, also known as "the Unabomber," did not want to be considered mentally ill. See A. Chase, "Harvard and the Making of the Unabomber," *Atlantic Monthly,* June 2000, p. 41; W. Glaberson, "Judge Orders Unabomber Suspect to Cooperate in Psychiatric Tests," *New York Times,* Jan. 10, 1998, p. 1; G. Witkin, "What Does It Take to Be Crazy?" *U.S. News & World Report,* Jan. 12, 1998, p. 7. The appellate courts are divided on the question of the court's authority or duty to impose an insanity defense on a mentally disabled defendant. The court in Frendak v. United States, 408 A.2d 364 (D.C. App. 1979), took note of conflicting holdings in various jurisdictions. A defendant may prefer confinement in prison rather than in a mental institution, or may wish to avoid the stigma associated with mental disorder. At the same time, the state has a duty to see that justice is served. In Whalen v. United States, 346 F.2d 812 (D.C. Cir. 1965), the D.C. Circuit permitted assertion of the defense over the defendant's objection on the ground that it would be morally repugnant to convict a person who was insane at the time of the offense. Given that a conviction is put in jeopardy by a failure by the defense to raise the insanity defense when warranted would seem to justify interposing it. The state, too, is entitled to a fair trial. See also People v. Redmond, 94 Cal. Rptr. 542 (Calif. App. 1971); Frendak v. United States, 408 A.2d 364 (D.C. App. 1979). In United States v. Marble, 940 F.2d 1543 (D.C. Cir. 1991), the D.C. Circuit overturned *Whalen* on the theory that Congress by the Insanity Defense Reform Act of 1984 made the insanity plea the prerogative of the defense. By recent legislation, Canada allows the insanity plea to be raised only by the defendant.

In Alvord v. Wainwright, 469 U.S. 956 (1984), the U.S. Supreme Court said that counsel has a duty to investigate his client's case and make a minimal effort to persuade him to plead insanity when it is his "only plausible defense." Defense counsel's failure to discover facts supporting a potential insanity defense is deemed to constitute ineffective assistance of counsel and a basis for reversal of a conviction. United States *ex rel.* Rivera v. Franzen, 594 F.Supp. 198 (N.D.Ill. 1984), on appeal, 794 F.2d 314 (7th Cir. 1986). How much weight should be given to the question of whether the defendant's articulated reason to refuse to enter an insanity plea is a rational one? Can a trial judge or defense counsel ever say that a defendant's claim of factual innocence or self-defense is "irrational"? In State v. Khan, 417 A.2d 585 (N.J. App. 1980), the defendant claimed that he killed in self-defense, but the psychiatric evidence strongly indicated that he acted under a paranoiac delusion. The insanity defense was interposed, but both issues were submitted to the jury—insanity and self-defense—with instructions that if the jury finds the defendant not insane at the time the homicide was committed, then the trial would proceed on the general issue of defendant's guilt or innocence of the crime charged, including the issue of self-defense.

Yale law professor Mirjan Damaska writes in his book *Evidence Law Adrift* (New Haven: Yale University Press, 1997), p. 115:

> If criminal law exempts from punishment legally insane individuals or persons who acted under duress, the facts underlying insanity or duress should be established— whenever their existence appears probable—as part of the court's duty. And the court should proceed to inquire into these facts even against the wishes of the accused: If the individual's interests were controlling, the criminal sanction could be misapplied from the relevant (that is, systemic) point of view.

It is argued that the major reason for permitting the imposition of the insanity defense on unwilling defendants is a policy preference for preserving the dignity of the law over the rights of individual competent defendants. See, e.g., R. D. Miller, J. Olin, D. Johnson, J. Doidge, D. Iverson, & E. Fantone, "Forcing the Insanity Defense on Unwilling Defendants: Best Interests and the Dignity of the Law," *J. Psychiatry & Law* 24 (1996): 487. On the other hand, in the article "The Imposition of the Insanity Defense on an Unwilling Defendant," *Ohio St. L.J.* 41 (1980): 637, Anne Singer argues the unconstitutionality and impracticability of imposing the insanity defense on uncooperative defendants.

79. See Rivera v. Delaware, 429 U.S. 877 (1976); R. I. Allen, "The Restoration of *In re Winship*: A Comment on Burdens of Persuasion in Criminal Cases after *Patterson v. New York*," *Mich. L. Rev.* 76 (1977): 30.

80. Professor Joseph Goldstein of the Yale Law School suggested at a meeting of the American Psychoanalytic Association that people who are caught up in a riot may be regarded as lacking the capacity to control their behavior, for the individual who is lost in the anonymity of a crowd bent on mischief may be said to have lost any normal ability to hold his impulses in check. Gang rape is discussed in G. Geis, "Group Sexual Assaults," *Med. Aspects Human Sexual.*, May 1971, p. 101.

81. For research-based guidelines for interview-based assessments, see R. Rogers & D. W. Shuman, *Conducting Insanity Evaluations* (Washington, D.C.: American Psychiatric Press, 2d ed. 2000).

82. McGuire v. Almy, 297 Mass. 323, 8 N.E.2d 760 (1937).

83. 593 F.2d 700 (5th Cir. 1979).

84. A. Camus, *The Stranger*, trans. M. Ward (1946; New York: Vintage, 1988), p. 64. See T. Lutz, *Crying: The Natural and Cultural History of Tears* (New York: W. W. Norton, 1999). See the discussion on body language in chapter 7.

85. Another study using five mock cases and different instructions (the wild beast test, *M'Naghten*, *M'Naghten* plus irresistible impulse, *Durham*, and the ALI test) found no overall significant differences among the instructions in outcome. N. Finkel et al., "Insanity Defenses: From the Juror's Perspective," *Law & Psychol. Rev.* 9 (1985): 77. The American Bar Association concluded that the difference in outcome in jurisdictions with a test which included a volitional prong and those that did not might be significant. ABA, *Criminal Justice Mental Health Standards*, Commentary to Standard 7–6.1 (1989).

86. See B. R. Schwartz, "Should Juries Be Informed of the Consequences of the Insanity Verdict?" *J. Psychiatry & Law* 8 (1980): 167. In Fulghum v. Ford, 850 F.2d 1529 (11th Cir. 1988), posttrial interviews of jurors revealed that they thought the defendant was insane but feared that a NGRI verdict would be "less effective" in removing him from society. A verdict cannot be overturned, however, by posttrial jury statements describing even serious errors or misunderstandings on points of law or the proper basis of decision. Rule 606(b), Federal Rules of Evidence.

87. See Jones v. United States, 463 U.S. 354 (1983); D. Herman, "Automatic Commitment and Release of Insanity Acquittees: Constitutional Dimensions," *Rutgers L.J.* 14 (1983): 667; J. Ellis, "The Consequences of the Insanity Defense: Proposals to Reform Post-Acquittal Commitment Law," *Cath. U. L. Rev.* 35 (1986): 961.

88. K. A. Menninger, *The Human Mind* (New York: Knopf, 3d ed. 1961), pp. 7–8.

89. See A. R. Matthews, *Mental Disability and the Criminal Law* (Chicago: American Bar Association, 1970).

90. See G. H. Morris, "Dealing Responsibly with the Criminally Irresponsible," *Ariz. St. L.J.* 1982: 855; A. A. Stone, "Psychiatric Abuse and Legal Reform," *Int. J. Law & Psychiatry* 5 (1982): 9; B. Kirschner, "Constitutional Standards for Release of the Civilly Committed and Not Guilty by Reason of Insanity: A Strict Scrutiny Analysis," *Ariz. L. Rev.* 20 (1978): 233; J. R. German & A. C. Singer, "Punishing the Not Guilty: Hospitalization of Persons Acquitted by Reason of Insanity," *Rutgers L. Rev.* 29 (1976): 1011; Comment," "Commitment Following an Insanity Acquittal," *Harv. L. Rev.* 94 (1981): 605.

91. People v. McQuillan, 392 Mich. 511, 528, 221 N.W.2d 569, 576 (1974). See also People v. Chavez, 629 P.2d 1040 (Colo. 1981); In re Lewis, 402 A.2d 1115 (Del. 1979); In re Jones, 228 Kan. 90, 612 P.2d 1211 (1980); Chase v. Kearns, 278 A.2d 132 (Me. 1971). "A finding of not guilty because of insanity shall be prima facie evidence that the acquitted person is presently dangerous to the person's self or others or property of others." Kan. Stat. Ann., sec. 22–3428(1) (1981).

92. See J. Gunn, "An English Psychiatrist Looks at Dangerousness," *Bull. Am. Acad. Psychiatry & Law* 10 (1982): 143.

93. The Fifth Circuit ruled that the presumption of continuing insanity that Georgia applied to insanity acquittees but not to persons civilly committed amounts to a denial of equal protection of the law, but that the provision requiring judicial approval for release of acquittees charged with crimes evidencing dangerousness was constitutional. See Benham v. Edwards, 678 F.2d 511 (5th Cir. 1982); Bolton v. Harris, 395 F.2d 642, 652 (D.C. Cir. 1968); State v. Simants, 330 N.W.2d 910 (Neb. 1983). See also W. J. Ingber, "Rules for an Exceptional Class: The Commitment and Release of Persons Acquitted of Violent Offenses by Reason of Insanity," *N.Y.U. L. Rev.* 57 (1982): 281. An insanity acquittee may be under enforced medical supervision. In re Rosenfield, 157 F.Supp. 18 (D.D.C. 1957).

94. The American Psychiatric Association urged tightened procedures to protect the public against premature release of potentially dangerous individuals. At the same time, the association said it was "quite skeptical" about procedures in many states requiring periodic psychiatric reassessments of whether an individual is still dangerous. Dr. Loren Roth, chairman of the group that drafted the APA's position paper, explained that psychiatrists "have great difficulty in predicting dangerous behavior" and that the best indicator of future violence is a past record of violence, not a psychiatric diagnosis. The association urged that decisions on whether to release such persons be made not solely on the basis of psychiatric testimony but by a broader group, perhaps similar to a parole board. No release should occur, the association said, unless the individual can be given carefully supervised outpatient treatment to protect himself and the public from harm. American Psychiatric Association, "Statement on the Insanity Defense," *Am. J. Psychiatry* 140 (1983): 681. In Oregon, a program begun in 1980 under the aegis of a multidisciplinary Psychiatric Security Review Board makes all decisions relating to confinement, release, and reconfinement of the insanity acquittee. See R. Rogers, "1981 Oregon Legislation Relating to the Insanity Defense and the Psychiatric Security Review Board," *Bull. Am. Acad. Psychiatry & Law* 10 (1982): 155; J. L. Bloom & J. D. Bloom, "Disposition of Insanity Defense Cases in Oregon," *Bull. Am. Acad. Psychiatry & Law* 9 (1981): 93. This model did not sweep the country, as the various states are generally reluctant to establish new boards, and indeed, in these days of tight budgets, the states are eliminating many of their existing boards. Other states, particularly those with only a handful of insanity acquittees, like Connecticut, would not make the expenditures necessary for this purpose.

95. 463 U.S. 354 (1983).

96. One recent study found that 85 percent of insanity acquittees were still under commitment five years after acquittal and 76 percent ten years after acquittal. D. M. Linhorst, "The Unconditional Release of Mentally Ill Offenders from Indefinite Commitment: A Study of Missouri Insanity Acquittees," *J. Am. Acad. Psychiatry & Law* 27 (1999): 563. Justice Powell said in *Jones* that "important differences" between those under civil commitment for mental illness and those who are committed following an insanity defense justify a refusal to apply the same standard of proof to both categories.

Patti Davis, President Reagan's daughter, notes the irony in the insanity defense:

> Initially, prosecutors claim the defendant isn't insane, he's accountable for his actions and should be punished. The defendant claims his mind is so ravaged by mental illness he can't be held responsible. Then the roles reverse. Once the defendant, now the patient, has been in a mental institution for a while, the claim is: I'm fine; I've been treated; I'm no longer a danger to society. The government then says no, he's too unstable, too ill. Keep him locked up.

P. Davis, "Don't Let Hinckley Roam Free," *Time,* Apr. 17, 2000, p. 34.

97. See S. L. Sherman, "Guilty But Mentally Ill: A Retreat From the Insanity Defense," *Am. J. L. & Med.* 7 (1981): 237; C. Slobogin, "The Guilty but Mentally Ill Verdict: An Idea Whose Time Should Not Have Come," *Geo. Wash. L. Rev.* 53 (1985): 494.

98. In Nevada, unlike in other states, GBMI is a special plea. In Arizona, NGRI was abolished, replaced by GBMI, and this has resulted in longer prison sentences.

99. See C. Nesson, "A Needed Verdict: Guilty but Insane," *New York Times,* July 1, 1982, p. 19, arguing that the "alternative verdict of 'guilty but mentally ill' should be adopted more widely to deal with the John Hinckleys of this world, the partly crazies, who deserve neither to be absolved of responsibility nor to be treated just like ordinary criminals." See also S. Taylor, "Too Much Justice," *Harper's,* Sept. 1982, 56, 65.

100. 392 Mich. 511, 221 N.W.2d 569 (1974).

101. Ibid.

102. See Mich. Comp. Laws Ann., sec. 678.36 (West 1982); Mich. Stat. Ann., sec. 28: 1059 (Callaghan 1978). See also G. A. Smith & J. A. Hall, "Evaluating Michigan's Guilty but Mentally Ill Verdict: An Empirical Study," *U. Mich. J. L. Ref.* 16 (1982): 77; G. D. Mesritz, "Guilty but Mentally Ill: An Historical and Constitutional Analysis," *J. Urb. L.* 53 (1976): 471. According to a study of the effects of the *McQuillan* case in Michigan, out of 223 defendants found not guilty by reason of insanity over a five-year period, 124 were released, following a sixty-day assessment period, as noncommittable according to the civil standards. Almost half of the remaining acquittees had been released within five years of acquittal, after an average of nine and a half months of postevaluation hospitalization. This represented a substantial decrease in periods of confinement from the rate during the pre-*McQuillan* years. See M. L. Criss & D. R. Racine, "Impact of Change in Legal Standard for Those Adjudicated Not Guilty by Reason of Insanity," *Bull. Am. Acad. Psychiatry & Law* 8 (1982): 261.

103. See J. Swickard, "New Insanity Verdict on Trial," *Detroit Free Press*, Jan. 31, 1983, p. 3; R. Slovenko, "The Case against 'Guilty but Ill'," *Detroit News*, Jan. 31, 1983, p. 11; J. Swickard, "Gunman Guilty but Mentally Ill in Buhl Attack," *Detroit Free Press*, Feb. 5, 1983, p. 1. Although obviously psychotic, John E. du Pont of the du Pont fortune was found GBMI, not NGRI, in the fatal shooting of David Schultz, a wrestling coach at du Pont's farm. The killing of Schultz was the culminating event in a series of incidents in du Pont's behavior that were bizarre in the extreme. His paranoia resulting in an overriding penchant for security knew no limits. He had excavators dig and dig again on his property so as to allay his fear that people in underground tunnels on his property constituted a threat to his well-being. His imaginary enemies were everywhere, no rock was too small to hide them. Defense counsel failed in trying to convince the U.S. Supreme Court to review the quirky nature of a GBMI verdict. He was sentenced to thirteen to thirty years confinement. Commonwealth v. du Pont, 730 A.2d 970 (Pa. Super. 1999). A number of books have been written about du Pont. See, e.g., C. Turkington, *No Holds Barred: The Strange Life of John E. du Pont* (Kansas City, Mo.: Turner, 1996); B. Ordine & R. Vigoda, *Fatal Match* (New York: Avon Books, 1998).

104. Transfers of mentally ill prisoners are rarely accomplished. In Maxwell v. McBryde, 12 Ariz. App. 269, 469 P.2d 835 (1970), Maxwell sought to be transferred from the Arizona State Prison to the Arizona State Hospital because he perceived he was mentally ill and in need of treatment. The prison resisted the transfer, taking the view that Maxwell would be better off in the prison (although there were no psychiatrists or psychologists on the prison staff) because the recovery rate at the hospital was poor. Furthermore, the hospital had requested that "criminally insane inmates" not be sent there. The court held that it was not for the prison physician, superintendent, or even the court to determine where the prisoner is to be treated, nor are the wishes of the hospital staff of the state hospital dispositive against the clear legislative mandate. The court required that the inmate proceed by bringing a special action against prison officials to compel them to commence a transfer proceeding. 469 P.2d at 837. See also Special Project, "The Administration of Psychiatric Justice: Theory and Practice in Arizona," *Ariz. L. Rev.* 13 (1972): 1, 174–80; A. Brooks, *Law, Psychiatry and the Mental Health System* (Boston: Little, Brown, 1973), p. 411.

105. The American Bar Association also opposed the enactment of statutes which supplant or supplement the NGRI verdict with an alternative verdict of GBMI. See S. J. Brakel & J. L. Cavanaugh, "Crime, Psychiatry and the Insanity Defense: A Report on Some Recent Reforms the United States," *Australian & New Zealand J. Psychiatry* 30 (1996): 134.

106. G. Fletcher, *Rethinking Criminal Law* (Boston: Little, Brown, 1978), p. 835.

10

The Mental Disability Requirement in the Insanity Defense

The threshold requirement in an insanity defense is "mental disease or defect."[1] Questions arise: What constitutes a mental disease or defect? Who are those whose mental disease or defect indicate they are free of moral blame? Should the law turn to psychiatry for a list of mental disorders having that quality? Is the question, on the other hand, an ethical or legal one, the answer to which is beyond psychiatry? The definition of mental disease or defect has given difficulty because of the simultaneous need to have the concept governed by legal concepts of responsibility and blame, and also to have links to medical criteria of mental disorder. To be sure, the definition of mental illness in criminal law is not the same as for purposes of insurance or treatment. The definition of mental illness is contextual.[2]

Mental disease or defect (mental illness in current terminology) is a threshold requirement not only in an insanity defense but runs throughout the law as a phenomenon that may have legal effects. A mental disease or defect may render a person incompetent to stand trial, may justify involuntary hospitalization or commitment as a sex offender, or may nullify a will or a contract. In each situation, there are two considerations: (1) Was the person mentally ill? and (2) If so, was the illness such as to satisfy the legal criteria as to consequences?

The various rules do not identify the mental disorders that constitute mental disease or defect. They identify only the specific effects that must result as a consequence of the disorder. Thus, under the *M'Naghten* test "it must be clearly proved that at the time of the committing of the act, the party accused was laboring under such a defect of reason, from disease of the mind as not to know the nature and quality of the act he was doing, or if he did know it that he did not know he was doing wrong."[3] The American Law Institute's Model Code provides: "A person is not responsible for criminal conduct if at the time of such conduct as a result of mental disease or defect he lacks substantial capacity either to appreciate the criminality [wrongfulness] of his conduct or to conform his conduct to the requirements of the law."[4]

Quite frequently, the two parts of the test of legal insanity are not clearly delineated, and they are often conflated. The widely used *Black's Law Dictionary* describes *legal insanity* in this way:

> The term is a social and legal term rather then a medical one, and indicates a condition which renders the affected person unfit to enjoy liberty of action because of the unreliability of his behavior with concomitant danger to himself and others. The term is more or less synonymous with mental illness or psychosis. In law, the term is used to denote that degree of mental illness which negates the individual's legal responsibility or capacity.[5]

Another illustration of the failure to clearly delineate the two parts of the test is the observation by New Jersey Chief Justice Weintraub:

> [T]he hard question under any concept of legal insanity is, What constitutes a "disease"? . . . The postulate is that some wrongdoers are sick while other are bad,[6] and that it is against good morals to stigmatize the sick. Who then are the sick whose illness shows they are free of moral blame? We cannot turn to the psychiatrist for a list of illnesses which have that quality because, for all his insight into the dynamics of behavior, he has not solved the riddle of blame. The question remains an ethical one, the answer to which lies beyond scientific truth. . . . [T]he traditional charge . . . to the jury does not attempt to say what is meant by "disease," and [there is a] rather universal reluctance to assay a definition. . . . We have described the problem, not to resolve it, but simply to reveal the room for disputation.[7]

Much was made of the contradictory and confusing expert testimony that was presented in the case of John Hinckley Jr., the would-be assassin of President Reagan.[8] The Federal Rules of Evidence (and their counterparts in state statutes) were amended to limit psychiatric testimony to presenting and explaining a diagnosis, such as whether the defendant had a mental disease or defect and what the characteristics of such a disease or defect, if any, may have been. In other words, psychiatric testimony would be limited to the first part of the test of legal insanity.[9]

Assertions that the Definition Should Come from the Medical Profession

From time to time there are claims made by leading authorities that the definition of mental disease or defect should come from the medical profession and not from either legislators or judges. In England, trial judges sometimes give the jury photocopied pages of a relevant part from a psychiatric text to study during their deliberations. Henry Weihofen, a prominent professor of law and psychiatry, wrote:

> [T]he existence of mental illness, like physical illness, is a medical question. This implies that just as in cases where the issue is the existence or non-existence of tuberculosis or a bone fracture, the law should look to factual evidence, and especially, where the fact is not easily apparent, to expert evidence. On its face, it would seem as absurd for the law to attempt its own definitions of mental illness as it would to define for itself what constitutes a physical ailment.[10]

Likewise, renowned forensic psychiatrist Bernard Diamond argued that the definition of mental illness ought not to differ in the legal context from that which has been accepted in the clinical context, that is to say, the definition of mental illness in the first part of the test. He wrote:

> I believe it is wrong to concede any threshold definition of mental illness other than that determined by scientific and clinical knowledge. . . [T]he diagnosis of mental illness is strictly a clinical matter to be determined in all instances by clinical criteria and definitions. But the point at which society determines a mentally ill person to be sufficiently disabled to warrant invoking a *parens patriae* intervention is a social and legal decision whose threshold can be much higher than that required to establish a diagnosis of mental illness. Similarly, it is not up to the law to establish the threshold for the existence of mental illness in a criminal defendant. But it is up to the law to determine the particular forms and degree of psychopathology it will recognize as exculpatory.[11]

Isaac Ray, the most influential American writer on forensic psychiatry in the nineteenth century, noted that legislators and jurists have only indicated some of the most obvious divisions of mental illness, without undertaking systematic classification to its various forms.[12] Judge Charles Doe of the New Hampshire Supreme Court in his correspondence with Dr. Ray replied that the law never wanted to restrict the insanity defense to particular forms of illness. On the bench, Judge Doe refused to grant judicial sanction to controversial medicolegal tests and definitions of mental illness or legal insanity. Instead, he would tell the jury that mental illness defies definition and that no test is applicable to every case. The jury, he said, must decide the case on its individual merits. If they believed from the lay and expert testimony that the act in question was the result of mental illness, the verdict must be not guilty by reason of insanity. In 1869, in *State v. Pike*,[13] Judge Doe told the jury that there was no single rigid test of "mental disease"; rather, "all symptoms and all tests of mental disease are purely matters of fact," grist for the jury's mill.[14]

Judge Doe felt that the law should abandon "old exploded medical theories" and embrace "facts established in the progress of scientific knowledge."[15]

Judge Warren Burger, when sitting on the U.S. Court of Appeals for the District of Columbia, lamented the lack of a definition of mental disease or defect. In a concurring opinion in 1961, he noted that the critical threshold issue is whether the defendant has a mental disease or defect and he said, "Not being judicially defined, these terms mean in any given case whatever the expert witnesses say they mean."[16]

A definition or holding of mental disease or defect in the test of criminal responsibility that differs from that in the law on commitment of the insanity acquittee may result in no confinement of the defendant, and as a result the public safety may be put at risk.[17] Take, for example, the prosecution in Illinois of Jearl Wood, who severely wounded a foreman at the plant where he was working. Expert testimony at trial was that the incident grew out of Wood's traumatic Vietnam experience. The jury found him not guilty by reason of insanity, and in a separate commitment hearing after the trial, a psychiatrist for the Illinois Department of Mental Health confirmed the PTSD diagnosis but felt that it did not warrant confinement in the mental health system. He "slipped through the cracks" of the two systems, as it was put.[18]

A Legal Definition

In 1962 in *McDonald v. United States*,[19] the D.C. Court of Appeals suggested a legal definition of mental disease or defect and was unwilling to leave the definition to science only. The court said:

> Our purpose now is to make it very clear that neither the court nor the jury is bound by *ad hoc* definitions or conclusions as to what experts state is a disease or defect. What psychiatrists may consider a "mental disease or defect" for clinical purposes, where their concern is treatment, may or may not be the same as mental disease of defect for the jury's purpose in determining criminal responsibility. Consequently, for that purpose the jury should be told that a mental disease or defect includes any abnormal condition of the mind which substantially affects mental or emotional processes and substantially impairs behavior controls.[20]

The guideline was considered necessary in order to implement the product test under *Durham,* which was then the test of criminal responsibility in the District of Columbia. The guideline was not helpful, as it remained necessary to have expert testimony as to an "abnormal condition of the mind which substantially affects mental or emotional processes and substantially impairs behavior controls." The issue became whether certain psychiatric diagnoses are ipso facto to be taken as an abnormal condition of the mind.

The *DSM* Definition

In the diagnosis of psychological disorders, as everyone knows, use is made of the American Psychiatric Association's compendium of mental disorders, the *Diag-*

nostic and Statistical Manual of Mental Disorders (DSM), now in a fourth edition.[21] As the history of the *DSM*s would reveal, defining mental disorders has been not only conceptually difficult but also politically controversial. Though the *DSM* is a compendium of disorders, it was not until *DSM-III* that, for the first time, a definition of mental disorder itself was offered. There has been no rigorous debate about whether the definition of mental disorder is conceptually adequate or even whether it is used systematically to decide what is pathological and belongs in the compendium.[22] In the last three editions of the *DSM*, the following definition of mental disorder is provided:

> In DSM-IV, each of the mental disorders is conceptualized as a clinically significant behavioral or psychological syndrome or pattern that occurs in an individual and that is associated with present distress (a painful symptom) or disability (impairment in one or more important areas of functioning) or with a significantly increased risk of suffering death, pain, disability, or an important loss of freedom. In addition, this syndrome or pattern must not be merely an expectable and culturally sanctioned response to a particular event, for example, the death of a loved one. Whatever its original cause, it must currently be considered a manifestation of a behavioral, psychological, or biological dysfunction in the individual. Neither deviant behavior (e.g., political, religious, or sexual) nor conflicts that are primarily between the individual and society are mental disorders unless the deviance or conflict is a symptom of a dysfunction in the individual, as described above.[23]

Critique of the *DSM* Categories

Until the late 1960s the widespread belief as promoted by Dr. Karl A. Menninger, renowned as doyen of American psychiatry, was that all mental illness was essentially the same in quality, although differing quantitatively in external appearance. It was a unitary and gradational theory of mental disorder (not one of discrete entities). Menninger railed against diagnostic categories.[24]

The scope of the *DSM*s has changed, but their formulation of discrete entities has remained unchanged. *DSM-I*, published in 1952, and *DSM-II*, published in 1968, were small booklets. *DSM-III*, which emerged in 1980, ran to five hundred pages and identified 182 disorders. *DSM-IV*, in some nine hundred pages, lists over three hundred mental disorders. In the introduction to *DSM-IV* it is noted:

> "[A]lthough this manual provides a classification of mental disorders, it must be admitted that no definition adequately specifies precise boundaries for the concept of 'mental disorder.' The concept of mental disorder, like many other concepts in medicine and science, lacks a consistent operational definition that covers all situations. . . . In *DSM-IV*, there is no assumption that each category of mental disorder is a completely discrete entity with absolute boundaries dividing it from other mental disorders or from no mental disorder. There is also no assumption that all individuals described as having the same mental disorder are alike in all important ways."[25]

Moreover, none of the various psychiatric diagnoses set out in the *DSM* of necessity entail impairment of cognition or control, although it is sometimes argued at trial. In *Hinckley*, the trial judge instructed the jury as follows about the diagnostic labeling:

> You have heard the evidence of psychiatrists and a psychologist who testified as [expert witnesses]. An expert in a particular field, as I indicated, is permitted to give his opinion in evidence, and in this connection you are instructed that you are not bound by medical labels, definitions, or conclusions as to what is or is not a mental disease or defect. What psychiatrists and psychologists may or may not consider a mental disease or defect for clinical purposes where their concern is treatment may or may not be the same as mental disease or defect for the purposes of determining criminal responsibility. Whether the defendant had a mental disease or defect must be determined by you under the explanation of those terms as it was given to you by the court.[26]

The Effect of a Definition in Law

Given a definition by decisional or statutory law, the term becomes a mixed question of law and fact. Rules setting out specific standards or requiring special types of proof narrow the expert's and jury's role. Given a legal definition, the trial judge may exclude evidence on certain mental illness, eliminating it from the concern of the jury. The expert or jury is not then left with unbridled discretion in determining what is mental illness. Thus, for example, under the definition in *McDonald*, evidence of anxiety disorder or personality defect would be excluded since it is not an "abnormal condition of the mind which substantially affects mental or emotional processes and substantially impairs behavior controls," and the court would frame instructions to the jury on the basis of the definition.

A number of jurisdictions have adopted a legal test of mental illness either by adopting the *McDonald* formulation or by using the definition of mental illness that is codified in the state's mental health code on civil commitment. Mental illness is there defined, very much as in *McDonald*, as a "substantial disorder of thought or mood which significantly impairs judgment, behavior, capacity to recognize reality, or ability to cope with the ordinary demands of life."[27] The contention has been made, when the definition of mental illness is taken from the mental health code, that only a degree of mental illness sufficient to justify involuntary civil commitment satisfies the threshold question of mental illness in the test of criminal responsibility; the definition, in essence, is that of psychosis, an umbrella term covering a range of mental disorders that are set out in *DSM*.

Though using the definition in the mental health code as above quoted, Michigan courts, however, have held that the definition of mental illness in the test of criminal responsibility is not limited to psychosis. In one case, the Michigan Court of Appeals objected to the "incorrect and excessively narrow" definitions given by the prosecution's expert, and it also objected to the expert's use of "imprecise" and "excessively colloquial" words such as "bananas" or "out in left field."[28] A jurisdiction providing a definition of mental illness that is of the level allowing civil commitment is Georgia. Georgia's legislation provides:

"Mentally ill" means having a disorder of thought or mood which signifi-cantly impairs judgment, behavior, capacity to recognize reality, or ability to cope with the ordinary demands of life, or having a state of significantly subaverage general intellectual functioning existing concurrently with de-fects of adaptive behavior which originates in the developmental period. The term "mentally ill" shall not include a mental state manifested only by repeated unlawful or antisocial conduct.[29]

In *Stewart v. United States*,[30] the D.C. Circuit Court of Appeals said that, as a question of fact, the jury alone has the right to determine which types and degrees of mental abnormality fall within the meaning of "disease or defect"; the trial judge is not to decide factual issues. The trial judge charged the jury that a psychopath "is not insane within the meaning of the law" and, in defining a psychopath for the jury, the judge stated that a psychopath, among other things, is a person of "low intelligence." The trial court's instruction to the jury was as follows:

Now, have in mind, ladies and gentlemen, that the law does not recognize as insanity a mental disorder unless it is a real mental disease. There are many people who are psychopathic to one degree or another; they are maladjusted; emotionally unstable; resentful, for one reason or another, of society; of low intelligence; indifference [*sic*] toward the rights of others, and so on. That is a psychopath. He is not insane within the meaning of the law; he is simply an abnormal, maladjusted person, or subnormal, as the case may be; he is a misfit; he does not care about others; indifferent to them, and so on. You must distinguish in your mind between that kind of mental disorder, because it obviously is a mental disorder, and a real mental disease.

The man who is in this court, as a defendant in a criminal case, time and time again, is an extreme example of what I am talking about. There is something wrong with his mind or he would not do it in the first place, but it does not follow that he is insane.[31]

The appellate court reversed the conviction because the instruction was de-fective. It said:

[I]n defining a psychopath for the jury, the [trial] court stated, among other things, that a psychopath is a person "of low intelligence." The undisputed testimony showed that appellant was a person of low intelligence, but the only definition of a psychopath offered by a psychiatric expert came from a Government witness who testified that a psychopath is "usually of su-perior intelligence." Thus, the court invaded the combined functions of the expert witness and the jury by assertions which had the effect of treat-ing factual issues as though they had already been settled by either the testimony or the law. Clearly this was error. It was the jury's function to determine from all the evidence, including the expert testimony, not only whether appellant suffered from an abnormal mental condition, but also whether the nature and extent of any condition from which it found him to be suffering was such as to relieve him of criminal responsibility under the standards then prevailing.[32]

The Exclusion in the ALI Test of Criminal Responsibility

Those jurisdictions that follow the ALI test of criminal responsibility exclude, by definition, the psychopath (also called sociopath) or antisocial personality from mental disease or defect. In a caveat paragraph, the ALI test excludes as a disability "an abnormality manifested only by repeated criminal or otherwise anti-social conduct."[33] The California Supreme Court gave the following rationale for the exception:

> [T]he assertion of the insanity defense by recidivists with no apparent sign of mental illness except their penchant for criminal behavior would burden the legal system, bring the insanity defense into disrepute, and imperil the ability of persons with definite mental illness to assert that defense. . . . To classify persons with "antisocial personality" as insane would put in the mental institutions persons for whom there is currently no suitable treatment, and who would be a constant danger to the staff and other inmates. Mental hospitals are not designed for this kind of person; prisons are.[34]

The psychiatrists, three in number, who participated in the drafting of the ALI test of criminal responsibility emphatically opposed the caveat paragraph. They maintained that it is not the business of the law to decide what is or is not a mental disease. Dr. Diamond concurred:

> They were quite right; it is no more within the province of the law to define mental illness than it is within the province of medicine to define exculpatory insanity. . . . The definitions of mental illness and the criteria for diagnosis should be determined solely by scientific and clinical standards, and the law should not encroach on scientific territory by creating its own definitions of mental illness and its own threshold levels.[35]

In accord, the Third Circuit had the following to say about the exception:

> Our study has . . . revealed two very persuasive reasons why this court should not hold that evidence of psychopathy is insufficient, as a matter of law, to put sanity or mental illness in issue. First, it is clear that as the majority of experts use the term, a psychopath is very distinguishable from one who merely demonstrates recurrent criminal behavior. . . . [From our survey], it can be seen that in many cases the adjective "psychopathic" will be applied by experts to persons who are very ill indeed.
> Our second reason for not holding that psychopaths are 'sane' as a matter of law is based on the vagaries of the term itself. In each individual case all the pertinent symptoms of the accused should be put before the court and jury and the accused's criminal responsibility should be developed from the totality of his symptoms. . . . The criminal law is not con-

cerned with . . . classifications but with the fundamental issue of criminal responsibility.[36]

In the celebrated *Scissors* murder trial in South Africa, expert testimony averred that psychopathy should be considered like the grading of a hotel—Grade I at one end to Grade V at the other, since psychopathy is not a matter of either-or. There may be, according to the testimony, "half-way psychopathy" or there may be dual diagnosis. Other testimony in the *Scissors* case averred that the accused had "psychopathic tendencies" or "latent psychopathy" that would come out when "pinched."[37]

In what came to be known as the "weekend flip-flop case," a St. Elizabeths psychiatrist on Friday afternoon testified that the defendant, diagnosed as a psychopath, was not suffering from a mental disease. The following Monday morning the St. Elizabeths staff decided to classify psychopathic personality as a mental disease. Returning to the stand Monday afternoon, the psychiatrist changed his testimony and declared that the defendant was suffering from a mental disease.[38] The ALI thereupon excluded psychopathy from the definition of mental disease or defect. The ALI Model Code, as we have noted, does not undertake a general definition of mental disease or defect.

Some courts faced with statutory adoption of the ALI's second paragraph have been unwilling to conclude that antisocial personality disorder is thereby barred as a basis for the insanity defense. Chief Judge John Biggs Jr. of the Third Circuit observed that (1) psychopaths are not defined solely by a propensity to commit antisocial behavior and (2) denying the insanity defense to those with the psychopath label would impermissibly base the defense on categories rather than on individual traits.[39]

Put another way, the ALI's second paragraph may be taken to refer to what is known in discourse on psychodynamics as *ego-syntonic*, that is, aspects of a person's behavior, thoughts, and attitudes that are viewed by the self as acceptable and consistent with the total personality, as contrasted to *ego-dystonic*, that is, aspects of a person's behavior, thoughts, and attitudes that are viewed by the self as repugnant or inconsistent with the total personality.

Exclusion of Other Personality Disorders

A number of jurisdictions have considered excluding other personality disorders as well as excluding psychopathy. Oregon legislation excludes from the insanity defense persons suffering "solely a personality disorder."[40] In their casebook on criminal law, Professors Sanford H. Kadish and Stephen J. Schulhofer posit the following without giving an answer:

> Suppose that psychiatric examination indicates that the defendant, because of "explosive personality disorder," lacks the capacity to "appreciate" the wrongfulness of his aggressive, violent reactions. Does he qualify for the insanity defense? Should the answer depend on whether the psychiatric profession classifies this abnormality as a "personality disorder" rather than as a psychosis? Consider whether the *McDonald* definition helps resolve the difficulties. The defendant's situation presumably is "ab-

normal," but is it a "condition of the mind" within the meaning of *McDon-ald*? Is this a legal or a medical question? Apart from the *McDonald* for-mulation, what is the "right" result in a case like this one?[41]

Connecticut has provided by legislation that pathological gambling cannot form the basis for an insanity defense.[42] Yet elsewhere the disorder is not excluded. In *United States v. Shorter*,[43] Judge Harold Greene of the U.S. District Court of the District of Columbia held that pathological gambling disorder had achieved general acceptance by mental health professionals and could be recognized as a disorder, but in this case, the court ruled, a causal link between that disorder and tax evasion or failure to pay taxes was not established.[44] In recognizing pathological gambling as a disorder, Judge Greene wrote:

> The experts presented by both the government and the defense appear to agree, with varying degrees of certainty, that pathological gambling is a recognized disorder. In this regard, the Court finds persuasive the inclu-sion of pathological gambling in the 1980 edition of the American Psy-chiatric Association Diagnostic and Statistical Manual of Mental Disorders (hereinafter DSM-III). The fact that pathological gambling was not in-cluded in the Manual prior to 1980 indicates that the disorder has only recently been recognized by the mental health community. . . . Neverthe-less, despite its relatively recent appearance in DSM-III, the Court con-cludes that the disorder has achieved general acceptance by mental health professionals, and that accordingly it may be "recognized" as a disorder by the courts.[45]

Various other jurisdictions contribute a smattering of their own exclusions. Arizona by statute excludes "temporary conditions arising from the pressure of circumstances."[46] California excludes "adjustment disorders" and "seizure disor-ders."[47] Colorado excludes "passion growing out of anger, revenge, hatred, or other motives."[48] Arizona also includes passion growing out of jealousy.[49] New Mexico states that "[T]he mental disease must extend over a considerable period of time, as distinguished from a momentary condition arising under the pressure of cir-cumstances."[50]

The various states exclude voluntary intoxication from alcohol or drugs. Okla-homa legislation provides: "No act committed by a person while in a state of vol-untary intoxication shall be deemed less criminal by reason of his having been in such a condition."[51] The usual rule in the various states is that intoxication or use of drugs (which itself is a crime) may mitigate responsibility for a crime, for example, reducing murder to manslaughter by virtue of negating the required mens rea.

The Result of Exclusion by Category

Exclusion by category puts emphasis on whether an individual falls within or with-out the category. It obliges the expert to put the defendant in a diagnostic category, and it results in a battle of categories as occurred, for example, in the *Hinckley* trial. The expert is invariably asked at trial, "What kind of mental disorder?" though the test of criminal responsibility, as Judge Doe noted, does not link the concept of mental disease or defect to any diagnostic entity. The test itself does not require the expert to set out a specific diagnosis or disorder or even to say whether the disorder is functional or organic.[52]

The psychiatric categories themselves are often impugned by the way some have been included or excluded from the manual. At trial, on cross-examination by the prosecution, the expert is often asked whether the categories are decided by vote. The 1973 convention of the American Psychiatric Association was punctuated by protests from the gay community, and under pressure the members voted to delete homosexuality from the manual but left a new diagnosis—sexual orientation disturbance.[53]

Limitation of Defense to Serious Mental Illness

In the wake of the *Hinckley* trial, the American Psychiatric Association recommended that mental disorders potentially leading to exculpation must be "serious" (like in the early common-law wild beast test). The APA urged that insanity acquittals be granted only for impaired cognition (and not for impaired control) resulting from mental disorders of the severity (if not always of the quality) of psychoses, and not for personality disorders or antisocial personalities. It stated, "[T]he terms mental disease or mental retardation include only those severely abnormal mental conditions that grossly and demonstrably impair a person's perception or understanding of reality and that are not attributable primarily to the voluntary ingestion of alcohol or other psychoactive substances."[54]

Likewise, following the *Hinckley* trial, the American Bar Association emphasized that mental disease must be attributable to a substantial process of functional or organic impairment, rather than to defects of character or strong passion. Were it otherwise, the ABA noted, the defense would have no threshold at all; every abnormal defendant—and every normal defendant who became abnormally impassioned—could be said to have a mental disease. The ABA also emphasized, however, that the substantial process of functional or organic impairment need not be a chronic or enduring one, and an acute psychotic break is a mental disease even in the absence of an underlying psychotic disorder.

The ABA's *Criminal Justice Mental Health Standards* recommend that mental disease or defect in the test of criminal responsibility refer to either "impairments of mind, whether enduring or transitory" or "mental retardation, which substantially affected the mental or emotional processes of the defendant at the time of the alleged offense." In hearings on the standard, representatives of the American Academy of Psychiatry and the Law urged a clarification of "impairments of mind."[55]

In the aftermath of the *Hinckley* trial, a federal statute was adopted in 1984 that provides:

> It is an affirmative defense to a prosecution under any federal statute that, at the time of the commission of the acts constituting the offense, the defendant as a result of a *severe* mental disease or defect, was unable to appreciate the nature and quality or the wrongfulness of his acts. Mental disease or defect does not otherwise constitute a defense. (emphasis added)[56]

According to the House Committee, the word *serious* was included "to emphasize that nonpsychotic behavior disorders or neuroses such as an 'inadequate personality,' 'immature personality,' or a pattern of 'antisocial tendencies' do not constitute the defense."[57]

Under the various state laws on the test of criminal responsibility, with some exceptions, mental illness is not equated with psychotic disorders. Other diagnostic categories or explanations like post-traumatic stress disorder or multiple personality disorder have been allowed as evidence to negate or diminish criminal responsibility.[58] Individuals who have obsessive compulsive disorder are not psychotic—they recognize their obsessive thoughts as excessive or unreasonable; cognition is not impaired. Like Lady Macbeth they may be unable to control their behavior. As the leading law commentator Glanville Williams long ago noted, a mental disorder, though not severe, could deprive the accused of intention or control of what he was doing.[59] While these disorders may not qualify for an insanity defense, they may result in a not guilty verdict on the ground that mens rea or *actus reus* was lacking.[60] From the viewpoint of the defendant, an acquittal is preferable to a verdict of not guilty by reason of insanity, but in many jurisdictions psychiatric evidence is admissible on cognition or control only when an insanity defense is urged.[61]

The *DSM* Caveat on the Use of the *DSM*

In its various revisions, the *DSM* has always included a statement cautioning against legal applications of the diagnoses set out in the manual. The purpose of diagnosis for the clinician is treatment and research, not accountability. The *DSM-III-R* and the current *DSM-IV* carry the caveat:

> The purpose of [the *DSM*] is to provide clear descriptions of diagnostic categories in order to enable clinicians and investigators to diagnose, communicate about, study, and treat the various mental disorders. It is to be understood that inclusion here, for clinical and research purposes, of a diagnostic category such as Pathological Gambling or Pedophilia does not imply that the condition meets legal or other nonmedical criteria for what constitutes mental disease, mental disorder, or mental disability. The clinical and scientific considerations involved in categorization of these conditions as mental disorders may not be wholly relevant to legal judgments, for example, that take into account such issues as individual responsibility, disability determination, and competency.[62]

Psychologist Stanley Brodsky, a frequent expert witness, points to the ambiguity of the caveat. He writes:

> When the phrase "such as Pathological Gambling or Pedophilia" is used, the reader is unclear how broad the reach of such diagnoses may be. In the same sense, the phrase "may not be wholly relevant" does not mean the same as irrelevant. Rather, the phrase describes an extensive range from almost wholly relevant to legal judgments down to partially relevant and all the way to irrelevant. The term *may be* is equally mushy. The more important part of the caution is the warning against wholesale application of diagnostic concepts to legal conclusions.[63]

The *DSM-IV* has an additional caveat on its use in forensic settings. It warns that these diagnoses should not be applied mechanistically by nonclinicians. It distinguishes the definition of mental disorder for legal purposes. It states:

> When the DSM-IV categories, criteria, and textual descriptions are employed for forensic purposes, there are significant risks that diagnostic information will be misused or misunderstood. These dangers arise because of the imperfect fit between the question of ultimate concern to the law and the information contained in a clinical diagnosis. In most situations, the clinical diagnosis of a DSM-IV mental disorder is not sufficient to establish the existence for legal purposes of a "mental disorder," "mental disability," "mental disease," or "mental defect." In determining whether an individual meets a specified legal standard (e.g., for competence, criminal responsibility, or disability) additional information is usually required beyond that contained in the DSM-IV diagnosis. This might include information about the individual's functional impairments, and how these impairments affect the particular abilities in question. It is precisely because impairments, abilities, and disabilities vary widely within each diagnostic category that assignment of a particular diagnosis does not imply a specific level of impairment or disability.[64]

The disclaimer notwithstanding, the *DSM* is used in assessing accountability, as it is state of the art, but the law is not limited to it in defining mental illness.

Interpreting the *DSM* Caveat to Justify Legislative Disregard of the *DSM*

In the decision upholding the Washington "Sexually Violent Predator" law, the State Supreme Court turned the *DSM* caveat on its head.[65] The petitioner in the case argued that the term "mental abnormality" found in the statute is not a true mental illness because it is a term coined by the legislature rather than the psychiatric and psychological community. The court said, "Over the years, the law has developed many specialized terms to describe mental health concepts. . . . The *DSM* explicitly recognizes . . . that the scientific categorization of a mental disorder may not be 'wholly relevant to legal judgments.'"[66] The court went on to quote the legislature that took a rather dim view of the *DSM*:

> Although 'mental abnormality' is not in the [DSM], . . . [i]n using the concept of mental abnormality, the legislature has invoked a more generalized terminology that can cover a much larger variety of disorders. Some, such as paraphilias, are covered in the *DSM-III-R;* others are not. The fact that pathologically driven rape, for example, is not yet listed in the *DSM-III-R* does not invalidate such a diagnosis. The DSM is, after all, an evolving and imperfect document. Nor is it sacrosanct. Furthermore, it is in some areas a political document whose diagnoses are based, in some cases, on what the American Psychiatric Association leaders consider to be practical realities.[67]

In 1997 in a 5–4 decision the U.S. Supreme Court upheld the Kansas Sexually Violent Predator Act, which established civil commitment procedures for individuals with a "mental abnormality" or a "personality disorder" who were likely to engage in "predatory acts of sexual violence."[68] The U.S. Supreme Court reversed the Kansas Supreme Court, which had held that substantive due process was violated because the definition of "mental abnormality" did not satisfy what is perceived to be the definition of mental illness required in a context of involuntary civil commitment.

Justice Thomas, writing the opinion of the Court, acknowledged that in addition to dangerousness, "some additional factor" that was causally linked to the dangerous behavior is constitutionally required. However, he wrote, substantive due process does not require that this condition be a mental disorder recognized by treatment professionals: "Not only do psychiatrists disagree widely and frequently on what constitutes mental illness . . . but the Court itself has used a variety of expressions to describe the mental condition of those properly subject to civil commitment."[69] The term mental illness does not carry "talismanic significance." He also said, "[W]e have traditionally left legislators the task of defining terms of a medical nature that have legal significance."[70] Except for Justice Ginsburg, the dissenters agreed with the majority that states have broad authority to define legal mental illness and that the statute's use of "mental abnormality" satisfies substantive due process.[71]

Conclusion

In sum, we may say, the definition of mental disability (or the other commonly used terms) is a matter of public policy. Beyond the existence or nonexistence of mental illness, the answer depends upon our concept of justice, our penal policy, the institutional facilities we have available, and other considerations. From the legal standpoint the differences are marked between prison inmates and insanity acquittees, but there are few to none clinically. On any day, almost two hundred thousand people in prison—more than one in ten of the total (a rate four times that in the general population)—are known to have schizophrenia, manic depression, or major depression, the three most severe mental illnesses.[72]

Notes

1. The terms *mental disease, mental defect, mental disorder, mental illness,* and *abnormal condition of the mind* are used interchangeably by courts and commentators. Historically, mental disease referred to mental illness and mental defect to mental retardation, but further definition was usually imprecise. In the various tests of criminal responsibility it seems to have gone unnoticed that there is in the wording a reduction of the mental to the physical. The threshold requirement in the test of criminal responsibility—on account of mental disease or defect—implies an underlying physical malfunction. It replaced the earlier idea of demon possession as the cause of aberrant behavior. Law professor Jules Gerard has argued that the qualifying illness in the insanity defense should stem from a physical malfunction as that would fit the basic policy of the law of refusing to recognize self-induced malfunctions. J. Gerard, "The Usefulness of the Medical Model to the Legal System," in A. Brooks & B. Winick (eds.), "Current Issues in Mental Disability Law," *Rutgers L. Rev.* 39 (1987): 135.

2. For the definition of mental illness for purposes of insurance, see Phillips v. Lincoln National Life Ins. Co., 978 F.2d 302 (7th Cir. 1992).

3. M'Naghten Case, 10 Clark & Fin. 200, 8 Eng. Rep. 718 (1843). See chapter 9.

4. ALI Model Penal Code, sec. 4.01 (Tent. Draft No. 4, 1955).

5. H. C. Black, *Black's Law Dictionary* (St. Paul, Minn.: West, 6th ed. 1990), p. 794.

6. Actually, it may be argued, there are four types of individuals: non–mentally ill good persons, non–mentally ill bad persons, mentally ill good persons, and mentally ill bad persons. Press accounts suggested that Theodore Kaczynski belongs in the last category. A. L. Halpern, "Kaczynski Could Be Both 'Sick' and 'Evil'" (ltr.), *Gannett Newspapers*, Jan. 10, 1998, p. 10. In law, however, it is said that mental illness absolves badness or undercuts free will.

7. State v. Guido, 40 N.J. 191, 191 A.2d 45 (1963).

8. In their book, *Breaking Points* (Grand Rapids, Mich.: Chosen Books, 1985) the senior Hinckleys summarized the key testimony of the principal doctors, all of whom had examined John at length: "Doctor [David] Bear, with the prestige of Harvard Medical School behind him, had concluded: 'It is a psychiatric fact that Mr. Hinckley was psychotic.' Dr. [Park] Dietz, equally of Harvard Medical School, had testified: 'Mr. Hinckley has not been psychotic at any time.'" See R. J. Bonnie, J. C. Jeffries, & P. W. Low (eds.), *A Case Study in the Insanity Defense* (New York: Foundation Press, 2d ed. 2000), p. 38. While conceding Hinckley's abnormality, Dr. Dietz insisted that he was never out of touch with reality—the hallmark of psychosis. Dr. Sally Johnson, a government psychiatrist, diagnosed that Hinckley was affected with only a relatively mild "personality disorder." Dr. William T. Carpenter Jr. testified that the defendant had the slowly developing, devastating illness then called "process schizophrenia," with a notoriously poor prognosis. See J. W. Clarke, *On Being Mad or Merely Angry* (Princeton: Princeton University Press, 1990).

9. Rule 704, Federal Rules of Evidence, as amended on Oct. 12, 1984; H.R. Report 98–1030, 98th Cong., 2d Sess., p. 230. The provision states: "No expert witness testifying with respect to the mental state or condition of a defendant in a criminal case may state an opinion or inference as to whether the defendant did or did not have the mental state or condition constituting an element of the crime charged or of a defense thereto. Such ultimate issues are matter for the trier of fact alone."

Under Rule 704(b) the courts have held that expert testimony is admissible concerning the *typical* effect of the defendant's mental condition. In United States v. Davis, 835 F.2d 274 (11th Cir. 1988), the defendant, who attempted to establish an insanity defense based on a multiple personality disorder, objected to the testimony of a government expert that such a disorder does not in itself indicate that a person does not understand what he is doing. The court upheld the admission of this testimony since it "did not include an opinion as to the defendant's capacity to conform his conduct to the law at the time of the robbery." Similarly, in United States v. Thigpen, 4 F.3d 1573 (11th Cir. 1993), the court allowed the expert to testify about the *general* effect of a schizophrenic disorder on a person's ability to appreciate the nature or wrongfulness of his actions. In United States v. Manley, 893 F.2d 1221 (11th Cir. 1990), expert defense opinion testimony was excluded where counsel inquired as to a hypothetical person's mental capacity with all of the defendant's pertinent characteristics. The court said that while Rule 704(b) does not bar "an explanation of the disease and its typical effect on a person's mental state," "a thinly veiled hypothetical" may not be used to circumvent the rule. See R. Slovenko, *Psychiatry and Criminal Culpability* (New York: Wiley, 1995), pp. 136–47.

10. "The Definition of Mental Illness," *Ohio State L.J.* 21 (1960): 1, 4.

11. "Reasonable Medical Certainty, Diagnostic Thresholds, and Definitions of Mental Illness in the Legal Context," *Bull. Am. Acad. Psychiatry & Law* 13 (1985): 121; reprinted in J. M. Quen (ed.), *The Psychiatrist in the Courtroom: Selected Papers of Bernard L. Diamond, M.D.* (Hillsdale, N.J.: Analytic Press, 1994), p. 217.

12. I. Ray, *A Treatise on the Medical Jurisprudence of Insanity* (Cambridge: Harvard University Press, 1962), p. 15. Original work published in 1838.

13. 49 N.H. 399 (1870).

14. Ibid. at 402.

15. Ibid. at 435, 438.

16. Blocker v. United States, 288 F.2d 853, 859 (Burger, C. J., concurring) (D.C. Cir. 1961).

17. The disposition of the insanity acquittee is discussed in R. Slovenko, *Psychiatry and Criminal Culpability* (New York: Wiley, 1995), pp. 170–93.

18. C. P. Erlinder, "Paying the Price for Vietnam: Post-Traumatic Stress Disorder and Criminal Behavior," *B.C.L. Rev.* 25 (1984): 305.

19. 312 F.2d 847 (D.C. Cir. 1962).

20. Ibid. at 851.

21. *Diagnostic and Statistical Manual of Mental Disorders* (Washington, D.C.: American Psychiatric Association, 4th ed. 1994).

22. H. Kutchins & S. A. Kirk, *Making Us Crazy: DSM: The Psychiatric Bible and the Creation of Mental Disorders* (New York: Free Press, 1997), p. 30.

23. *DSM-IV*, pp. xxi–xxii.

24. K. A. Menninger, *The Vital Balance* (New York: Viking, 1963).

25. *DSM-IV*, pp. xxi–xxii.

26. United States v. Hinckley, 525 F.Supp. 1342 (D.C.C. 1981), *op. clarified, reconsideration denied*, 529 F.Supp. 520 (D.C.C. 1982), *aff'd*, 672 F.2d 115 (D.C. Cir. 1982).

27. E.g., Mich. Comp. Laws, sec. 768.21a; see S. J. Brakel & R. S. Rock (eds.), *The Mentally Disabled and the Law* (Chicago: American Bar Foundation, 1971); R. S. Rock, M. A. Jacobson, & R. M. Janopaul, *Hospitalization and Discharge of the Mentally Ill* (Chicago: University of Chicago Press, 1968). See volume 2, chapter 1, on civil commitment.

28. People v. Doan, 141 Mich. App. 209, 366 N.W.2d 593 (1985); see P. E. Bennett, "The Meaning of 'Mental Illness' under the Michigan Mental Health Code," *Cooley L. Rev.* 4 (1986): 1.

29. Ga. Crim. Proc. Law, sec. 27–1503(a)(2).

30. 214 F.2d 879 (D.C. Cir. 1954).

31. Ibid. at 881.

32. Ibid. at 882.

33. ALI Model Penal Code, sec. 4.01 (explanatory note) (1985). The full ALI test is now being used in less than twenty states, down from its peak of more than twenty-five states in the early 1980s. States with a statutory ALI exclusion include Alaska, Arizona, Arkansas, Colorado, Connecticut, Delaware, Illinois, Kentucky, Maine, Maryland, New Mexico, North Dakota, Oregon, South Carolina, South Dakota, Texas, Vermont, and Wisconsin.

See P. A. Fairall & P. W. Johnston, "Antisocial Personality Disorder (APD) and the Insanity Defense," *Crim. L. J.* 11 (1987): 78; S. M. Reichlin, J. D. Bloom, & M. H. Williams, "Excluding Personality Disorders from the Insanity Defense—A Follow-up Study," *Bull. Am. Acad. Psychiatry & Law* 21 (1993): 91. See, in general, D. W. Black, *Bad Boys, Bad Men: Confronting Anti-social Personality Disorder* (New York: Oxford University Press, 1999); H. Cleckley, *The Mask of Sanity* (Augusta, Ga.: E. S. Cleckley, 5th ed. 1988; previous eds. by C. V. Mosby); R. D. Hare, *Without Conscience: The Disturbing World of the Psychopaths among Us* (New York: Guilford, 1999); J. R. Meloy, *The Psychopathic Mind* (Northvale, N.J.: Jason Aronson, 1988); W. H. Reid, D. Dorr, J. Walker, & J. Bonner, *Unmasking the Psychopath* (New York: Norton, 1986); R. I. Simon, *Bad Men Do What Good Men Dream* (Washington, D.C.: American Psychiatric Press, 1996); S. Yochelson & S. E. Samenow, *The Criminal Personality* (New York: Jason Aronson, vol. 1, 1976, vol. 2, 1977).

Psychopathy is characterized by a lack of inner conflict about the violation of social norms and bonds, the antisocial pursuit of power, and pathological thrill seeking, but it does not stand apart from a social structure that promotes and maintains it. "Never give a sucker an even break" is a certain degree of normalized psychopathy. In *The People of the Lie* (New York: Simon & Schuster, 1983), M. Scott Peck points out that people lacking a conscience are invariably boring, yet many people are enchanted with their often charming outer personality. Ted Bundy, the brutal killer, was portrayed as a handsome, intelligent young man, and he lured women with his charm, but within, he was empty. See R. K. Ressler & T. Shachtman, *Whoever Fights Monsters* (New York: St. Martin's, 1992).

Albert Einstein and Sigmund Freud, in an extraordinary correspondence, explored the topic of human violence. Einstein's letter concluded that "man has in him the need to hate and destroy." In his reply, Freud agreed "unreservedly," adding that human instincts could be divided into two categories: "those which seek to preserve and unite, and those which seek to destroy and kill." He wrote that the phenomenon of life evolves from their "acting together and against each other." Supporting the opinions of Einstein and Freud is the fact that violence and homicide occur in all cultures. Then again, one might say, frustration leading to violence prevails everywhere. See R. Chessick, "The Death Instinct Revisited," *J. Am. Acad. Psychoanalysis* 20 (1992): 3. The Einstein and Freud quotations appear in their published correspondence titled *Why War?* See P. Gay, *Freud: A Life for Our Time* (New York: W. W. Norton, 1988), p. 448.

Erik Hill, a Michigan State University freshman, was a poster boy for bad behavior during a rampage following a basketball game. It cost him $4,500, thirty-five days in jail, and a chance to graduate from the university. It was worth it, he boasted, "I had the greatest time of my life." J. S. Cohen & R. French, "Unrepentant Rioter Says He Had Time of His Life," *Detroit News*, Mar. 5, 2000, p. 10.

Psychopathic behavior is encouraged in wartime. During the civil war, Sherman's army had great fun destroying Atlanta, but they gave the rationale that they were saving the Union and freeing the slaves. See B. Catton, *The Civil War* (Boston: Houghton Mifflin, 1960); V. D. Hanson, *The Soul of Battle* (New York: Free Press, 1999). Numerous accounts have described the joy in killing. In the book *A Rumor of War* (New York: Henry Holt, 1997), Philip Caputo reports on his service in Vietnam that killing produced an emotion that verged on rapture. It was, he writes, a relief from the dullness of suburban life (pp. 4–5); "murder was fun" (p. 36); "ordinary people" became psychopaths. See also J. Bourke, *An Intimate History of Killing* (New York: Basic Books, 1999). See also J. Conroy, *Unspeakable Acts, Ordinary People: The Dynamics of Torture* (New York: Knopf, 2000).

34. People v. Fields, 35 Cal.3d 329, 370–72, 197 Cal. Rptr. 803, 830–31, 673 P.2d 680, 707–8 (1983).

35. Supra note 11. Dr. George E. Vaillant suggests that when the psychiatrist is protected from therapeutic frustration, when control is established, and flight is not possible, the "stigmata of psychopathy" disappear. He writes, "[I]n the eyes of most psychiatrists the outpatient sociopath may appear incorrigible, inhuman, unfeeling, guiltless, and unable to learn from experience; and yet in a prison hospital, the sociopath is fully human. . . . Cleckley's psychopath, immortalized in the *Mask of Sanity,* is a mythical beast." G. E. Vaillant, "Sociopathy as a Human Process," *Arch. Gen. Psychiatry* 32 (1975): 178.

Research has shown that individuals with antisocial personality disorder evince problems of depression or anxiety disorders as well as the abuse of alcohol or other drugs. See M. Zimmerman & W. Coryell, "DSM-III Personality Disorder Diagnoses in a Non-patient Sample," *Arch. Gen. Psychiatry* 46 (1989): 682. The late Richard L. Jenkins, who had a long-standing interest in the classification of delinquent behavior, strongly believed that degree of socialization was important in determining an individual's ultimate outcome. See F. A. Henn, R. Bardwell, & R. L. Jenkins, "Juvenile Delinquents Revisited: Adult Criminal Activity," *Arch. Gen. Psychiatry* 37 (1980): 1160.

36. United States v. Currens, 290 F.2d 751, 774 n. 32 (3d Cir. 1961).

37. B. Bennett, *Was Justice Done?: The Scissors Murder* (Cape Town, South Africa: Timmins, 1975); R. Slovenko, "'The Psychopath': Labeling in South Africa," *Crime, Punishment & Correction* (South Africa) 5 (1976): 9.

38. In re Rosenfield, 157 F.Supp. 18 (D.D.C. 1957). See also United States v. Brawner, 471 F.2d 969, 978 (D.C. Cir. 1972).

39. United States v. Currens, 290 F.2d 751, 774 n. 32 (3d Cir. 1961).

40. Ore. Stat., sec. 161.295 (1997). See S. M. Reichlin, J. D. Bloom, & M. H. Williams, "Excluding Personality Disorders from the Insanity Defense—A Follow-up Study," *Bull. Am. Acad. Psychiatry & Law* 21 (1993): 91; S. E. Reynolds, "Battle of the Experts Revisited: 1983 Oregon Legislation on the Insanity Defense," *Williamette L. Rev.* 20 (1984): 303.

The crime writer Ann Rule says: "The thin line between psychosis and personality disorder is a challenge for anyone involved in the justice system. I do believe that people who are frankly psychotic, people who truly don't know the difference between right and wrong at the time of the crime should not be sentenced to prison. With personality disorders which do not constitute mental illness under M'Naghten, I don't believe that people who suffer from anti-social personality disorder, histrionic personality disorder, narcissistic disorder, should be allowed to receive lesser sentences. It's possible that borderline personality disorder patients might qualify. My problem with giving any of these people a lesser sentence is that I believe they do know the difference between right and wrong; it simply does not matter to them because they view themselves as above the law and in a different class from other defendants." Personal communication (Dec. 19, 1999). Among Ann Rule's many books is *A Rage to Kill* (New York: Pocket Books, 1999).

41. S. H. Kadish & S. J. Schulhofer, *Criminal Law and Its Process: Cases and Materials* (Boston: Little, Brown, 6th ed. 1995), p. 976.

42. Conn. Gen. Stat., sec. 339–13 (1999). See R. J. Bonnie, "Compulsive Gambling and the Insanity Defense," *Newsletter Am. Acad. Psychiatry & Law* 9 (1984): 5.

43. 618 F.Supp. 255 (D.C. 1985). For a discussion of the pathological gamblihg disorder as well as other disorders, see S. J. Brakel & A. D. Brooks, *Law and Psychiatry in the Criminal Justice System* (Buffalo, N.Y.: Wm. S. Hein, 2001).

44. The defense contended that a pathological gambler is compelled by the internal mental pressures inherent in his disease to expend substantially all of his available funds for gambling, rather than for paying tax liabilities, and that this compulsion negates the element of willfulness required to convict for tax evasion or willful failure to pay. On this score, Judge Green said:

> The impressions gleaned from the testimony of defendant's experts is that the impact of pathological gambling disorder on the volitional faculties is, at best, unclear even among those mental health professionals specializing in the treatment of the disorder. It is, however, the broader community of psychologists and psychiatrists to which the court must turn in assessing the reliability of expert testimony and as to them clarity is not lacking. Each of the government's witnesses—three forensic psychiatrists and one forensic psychologist—categorically rejected the claim the pathological gamblers are unable to choose between gambling and paying taxes. Of greatest significance to the present case is Dr. Abraham L. Halpern's testimony that the "vast majority" of psychiatrists reject the proposition that pathological gamblers are unable to choose between gambling and paying taxes. Dr. Halpern, whom the Court has found to be an exceptionally well-qualified and persuasive witness, testified that pathological gamblers retain the ability to make conscious decisions about their financial expenditures.

Ibid. at 260.

45. 618 F.Supp. at 258.

46. Ariz. Rev. Stat. Anno., sec. 13–502A.

47. Cal. Penal Code, sec. 25.5.

48. Colo. Rev. Stat., sec. 16.8.101(1).

49. Ariz. Rev. Stat., sec. 13–502A. The relationship of impulsivity to psychiatric disorders is discussed in F. G. Moeller, E. S. Barratt, D. M. Dougherty, J. M Schmitz, & A. C. Swann, "Psychiatric Aspects of Impulsivity," *Am. J. Psychiatry* 158 (2001): 1793.

50. New Mexico Uniform Jury Instruction 14–5102.

51. Okla. Stat. Anno. 21–152.

52. The Seventh Circuit in United States v. Buchbinder, 796 F.2d 910 (7th Cir. 1986), noted that the expert is not required to specify the "exact mental disease" from which the accused suffers.

53. The controversy over the inclusion or exclusion of various categories is discussed, among other places, in P. J. Caplan, *They Say You're Crazy: How the World's Most Powerful Psychiatrists Decide Who's Normal* (Reading, Mass.: Addison Wesley, 1995); H. Kutchins & S. A. Kirk, *Making Us Crazy: DSM: The Psychiatric Bible and the Creation of Mental Disorders* (New York: Free Press, 1997); P. Wyden, *Conquering Schizophrenia* (New York: Knopf, 1998).

54. American Psychiatric Association, Statement on the Insanity Defense, *Am. J. Psychiatry* 140 (1983): 6.

55. American Bar Association, *Criminal Justice Mental Health Standards*, sec. 7–6.1 (Washington, D.C.: American Bar Association, 1983).

56. 18 U.S.C., sec. 17.49.

57. H.R. Rep. No. 98–1030, 98th Cong., 2d Sess. 229 (1984). At trial, under the doctrine of judicial notice, a jury may be instructed, but is not required (in a criminal case), to accept as conclusive any fact that may be judicially noticed. Judicial notice, which takes the place of actual proof, may be taken when the fact is generally known or "capable of accurate and ready determination by resort to sources whose accuracy cannot reasonably be questioned." Rule 201(g), Federal Rules of Evidence. The rules of evidence do not regulate in any way the process of noticing what are known as *legislative facts*. So-called legislative facts—in contrast to what are known as *adjudicative facts*—are not subject to the limitations of Rule 201(g) or other strictures on judicial notice. Adjudicative facts are those concerning the immediate parties—who did what, where, when, how, and with what motive or intent. Legislative facts,

on the other hand, are those that have relevance to legal reasoning and the lawmaking process, whether in the formulation of a legal principle or ruling by a judge or court. What serious mental illness is may be said to be a legislative fact, whereas whether the accused has it would be an adjudicative fact. In Powell v. Texas, 392 U.S. 514 (1968), the U.S. Supreme Court resorted to various extrarecord facts to determine the prevailing view of the medical profession concerning whether alcoholism is a disease.

58. Consider, for example, evidence of the following that has been allowed under an insanity plea. The evidence usually fails to result in an NGRI verdict, but it may bring about a verdict on a crime less than that charged by the state.

Erotomania. In a Michigan case, defense counsel was allowed to claim under a plea of insanity that Gerald Atkins (like Hinckley) was in a state of delusional erotomania when he went on a rampage through the Ford Wixom plant in 1996 killing the department manager and wounding three others, viewing the Ford plant and those in it as barriers in his unrequited love for a plant worker. It took a while to seat a jury—at least fifteen prospective jurors were excused after saying they did not believe in the insanity defense. J. A. McClear, "Jury Seated in Wixom Plant Slaying Trial," *Detroit News*, Apr. 1, 1988, p. C-4. Atkins was found guilty of first-degree murder. L. L. Brasier & H. McDiarmid, "Gunman Guilty in Fatal Rampage: Jury Doesn't Buy Insanity Defense in Ford Plant Shooting," *Detroit Free Press*, Apr. 21, 1998, p. 1. Erotomania is often called "delusional disorder, paranoid type" and is listed in *DSM-IV* as a subtype of delusional disorder. Hinckley made the bizarre claim that he tried to assassinate President Reagan so that he and Jodie Foster could move into the White House. Of the various diagnoses given Hinckley, erotomania was not one of them.

Television intoxication. The incessant barrage of violence in the media deeply influences the behavior of people. In a Florida case, Zamora v. State, 361 So.2d 776 (Fla. App. 1978), the defendant was allowed to argue insanity based on "involuntary subliminal television intoxication," which produced a lessened appreciation of the wrongfulness of killing. At trial the argument failed. Ronny Zamora, age fifteen at the time of the crime, was nicknamed "TV Guide," as he closely followed and copied what he saw on television. Ellis Rubin, the defense attorney, argued that Zamora was under the influence of television when he killed a neighbor. Rubin also urged "Internet intoxication" in representing an eighteen-year-old accused of threatening a Columbine High School student online. See E. Rubin & D. Matera, "*Get Me Ellis Rubin!" The Life, Times, and Cases of a Maverick Lawyer* (New York: St. Martin's Press, 1989), pp. 41–65. See also J. A. Meerloo, "Television Addiction and Reactive Apathy," *J. Nervous & Mental Disabilities* 120 (1954): 290.

Post-traumatic stress disorder. The lead case on PTSD in an insanity defense involved Charles Heads, a Vietnam veteran. At his first trial, despite a plea of insanity, he was convicted of first-degree murder. His conviction was overturned on unrelated grounds and his case was set for retrial. Between the trials, the APA issued the third edition of *DSM*, which recognized PTSD as a mental disorder. At Heads's second trial, he again asserted the insanity defense. He was found NGRI. His attorney, Jack Wellborn, said, "The insanity defense at [the] first trial never got off the ground because neither of the psychiatrists who had examined the defendant had found evidence of any recognized mental disorder." *DSM-III* made it possible to argue PTSD as a mental disorder. Reliance on PTSD as insanity also allowed the defense to introduce evidence usually not admissible: a film about Vietnam, extensive testimony by Vietnam veterans describing the war, and considerable testimony about Heads's childhood. J. Wellborn, "The Vietnam Connection: Charles Heads' Verdict," *Crim. Defense* 9 (1982): 7. In another Louisiana case, State v. Sharp, 418 So.2d 1344 (1982), the defendant claimed he was suffering from PTSD at the time of a homicide as a result of his Vietnam experience, and as a consequence he was unable to distinguish right from wrong. The court held that the defendant failed to prove his insanity. See also J. A. Silva, D. V. Derecho, G. B. Leong, R. Weinstock, & M. M. Ferrari, "A Classification of Psychological Factors Leading to Violent Behavior in Posttraumatic Stress Disorder," *J. Forensic Sci.* 46 (2001): 309.

The use of PTSD under an insanity defense in inner-city criminal cases is examined by L. Weintraub, "Inner-City Post-Traumatic Stress Disorder," *J. Psychiatry & Law* 25 (1997): 249. The author outlines how the legal system has applied PTSD under an insanity defense and explores the policy implications of the defense. She concludes that although many inner-city defendants can meet the medical and psychological criteria of PTSD, the legal system should not encourage the defense. See also R. Slovenko, "Legal Aspects of Post-Traumatic Stress Disorder," *Psychiatric Clinics of North America* 17 (1994): 439. In sentencing, evidence of PTSD may qualify as a mental disorder that can support a reduced sentence. United States v. Cantu, 12 F.3d 1506 (9th Cir. 1993). See L. F. Sparr & R. K. Pitman, "Forensic Assessment of Traumatized Adults," in P. A. Saigh & J. D. Bremner (eds.), *Posttraumatic Stress Disorder: A Comprehensive Text* (Boston: Allyn & Bacon, 1999), pp. 284–308.

Battered spouse syndrome. A variation of PTSD is the battered spouse syndrome. In cases involving a battered spouse who has killed, evidence is usually offered of battered spouse syndrome to support a claim of self-defense, but sometimes the defense finds it useful to present as an alternative theory that the battered spouse was not guilty by reason of insanity. Trial courts often admit battered spouse evidence for that purpose, see, e.g., People v. Gindorf, 512 N.E.2d 770, 773 (Ill. App. 1987); A. S. Berkman, "The State of Michigan versus a Battered Wife: A Case Study," *Bull. Menninger Clinic* 44 (1980): 603; but many of the appellate decisions assume that battered spouse syndrome is not a mental disease for purposes of the insanity defense, e.g., Bechtel v. State, 840 P.2d 1, 7 (Okla. Cr. App. 1992); State v. Myers, 570 A.2d 1260, 1266 (N.J. Super. 1990). See A. Browne, K. R. Williams, & D. G. Dutton, "Homicide between Intimate Partners—A 20-Year Review," in M. D. Smith & M. A. Zahn (eds.), *Homicide: A Sourcebook of Social Research* (Thousand Oaks, Cal.: Sage, 1999). See also C. Coffee, "A Trend Emerges: A State Survey on the Admissibility of Expert Testimony Concerning the Battered Woman Syndrome," *J. Fam L.* 25 (1986–87): 373; H. Levitt, "Battered Women: Syndrome versus Self-Defense," *Am. J. Forensic Psychol.* 90 (1991): 29; R. Schuller & N. Vidmar, "Battered Woman Syndrome Evidence in the Courtroom: A Review of the Literature," *Law & Hum. Behav.* 16 (1992): 273; S. Steinmetz, "The Battered Husband Syndrome," *Victimology* 2 (1977–78): 499; J. Walus-Wigle & J. R. Meloy, "Battered Woman Syndrome as a Criminal Defense," *J. Psychiatry & Law* 16 (1988): 389.

Multiple personality disorder. The multiple personality disorder may qualify for an insanity defense. See United States v. Denny-Shaffer, 2 F.3d 999 (10th Cir. 1993); R. Slovenko, "The Multiple Personality: A Challenge to Legal Concepts," *J. Psychiatry & Law* 17 (1989): 681. In the book *Jekyll on Trial: Multiple Personality and Criminal Law* (New York: New York University Press, 1997), law professor E. R. Saks with psychologist Stephen H. Behnke argue that most multiples should be held nonresponsible. See also S. H. Behnke, "Assessing the Criminal Responsibility of Individuals with Multiple Personality Disorder: Legal Cases, Legal Theory," *J. Am. Acad. Psychiatry & Law* 25 (1997): 391. In grabbling with the phenomenon of multiple personality, Saks and others make a category mistake to the effect that there are *actually* different personalities involved, not one person with the subjective sense of multiplicity. Dr. Richard Kluft, a psychoanalyst who has been a pioneer in diagnosing dissociation, reportedly had a high-functioning woman in classical analysis whose treatment had gone on for several years. Suddenly she jumped up, pointed at the couch, and announced, *"She* may believe in this analysis crap, but *I don't!"* At this point Kluft replied, "Back on the couch. You're in analysis, too." Reported in N. McWilliams, *Psychoanalytic Diagnosis* (New York: Guilford Press, 1994), p. 326. In *DSM-IV* "multiple personality disorder" is renamed "dissociative identity disorder" (DID). On Broadway or in Hollywood, DID is considered not a disorder but a talent. Peter Sellers once said revealingly, "If you ask me to play myself, I will not know what to do. I do not know who or what I am." D. Shiach, *The Movies* (London: Hermes House, 2001), p. 181.

On these and others mental disorders, see R. Slovenko, *Psychiatry and Criminal Culpability* (New York: Wiley, 1995), ch. 4. On postpartum depression (PPD), see "'I Killed My Children': What Made Andrea Yates Snap?" *Newsweek,* July 2, 2001, pp. 20–29. See B. Bursten, *Beyond Psychiatric Expertise* (Springfield, Ill.: Thomas, 1984).

59. Quoted in N. Walker, "McNaghten's Innings: A Century and a Half Not Out," *J. For. Psychiatry* 4 (1993): 207.

60. See W. LaFave & A. Scott, *Criminal Law* (St. Paul, Minn.: West, 1986), p. 312; R. Slovenko, *Psychiatry and Criminal Culpability* (New York: Wiley, 1995), ch. 2.

61. R. Slovenko, *Psychiatry and Criminal Culpability* (New York: Wiley, 1995), pp. 43, 112. Under the Federal Rules of Criminal Procedure, Rule 12.2, and comparable state rules,

the defendant must file written notice of an intent to rely on a defense of insanity. The defendant must also file written notice of intent "to introduce expert testimony relating to a mental disease or defect or any other mental condition of the defendant bearing upon the issue of guilt." Any report of an expert relating to that expert's testimony is discoverable by the government under Rule 16(b)(1)(B).

62. *DSM-IV*, p. xxvii.

63. *Testifying in Court* (Washington, D.C.: American Psychological Association, 1991), p. 70.

64. *DSM-IV*, p. xxiii.

65. In re Young, 122 Wash.2d 1, 857 P.2d 989 (1993), citing the caveat in *DSM-III-R*, p. xxix.

66. 857 P.2d at 1001–2 n. 5.

67. Ibid. at 1001.

68. Kansas v. Hendricks, 521 U.S. 346 (1997).

69. Ibid. at 359.

70. Ibid.

71. Ibid. at 373 (Breyer, J., dissenting).

72. See S. P. M. Harrington, "New Bedlam: Jails—Not Psychiatric Hospitals—Now Care for the Indigent Mentally Ill," *Humanist*, May/June 1999, p. 9; P. A. Streeter, "Incarceration of the Mentally Ill: Treatment or Warehousing?" *Michigan Bar J.* 77 (Feb. 1998): 166; F. Butterfield, "Prisons Replace Hospitals for the Nation's Mentally Ill," *New York Times*, Mar. 5, 1998, p. 1.

11

Diminished Capacity

The defense of diminished capacity, in one form or another, has been adopted in about one-third of the states, mainly in cases in which the defendant is charged with first-degree murder, although in theory it applies to all crimes involving specific intent as an essential element of the prosecution's proof. Judge or jury could always render a verdict of any cognate lesser offense under the charged crime, but it is perplexing what evidence is admissible or what is convincing to bring about a lesser verdict. In the 1920s, in the trial of Leopold and Loeb, who were accused of kidnapping and murder, Clarence Darrow made then-novel use of psychiatric testimony to avoid the death penalty.

The states that have not adopted the diminished capacity defense hold that evidence of mental capacity to negate criminal intent is all or nothing. These jurisdictions contend that to permit the defense of diminished capacity would, in effect, sneak in the insanity defense without labeling it as such, and without complying with the requirements or consequences of the insanity defense. As one court put it, "The purpose of requiring notice of intent to claim the defense of insanity is to protect the public and avoid unfair surprise to the prosecution at trial. . . . [It] is also designed to protect the integrity of the evidence regarding an insanity defense."[1]

Just what is *diminished capacity*? Nearly every commentary on diminished capacity (or diminished responsibility) begins with a statement that the subject is confusing. Law professor Stephen Morse aptly described diminished capacity as undiminished confusion.[2] Is diminished capacity simply a negation of an element of a crime—mens rea or volition—on which a defendant has a constitutional right to present trustworthy evidence, or is it a unique defense? Is it a defense fully covered by other concepts, hence that ought to be exorcised for the sake of clarity, as Occam's razor would dictate?

Mental state is the principal device used to measure culpability. Diminished capacity addresses whether there was specific intent at the time of the crime. The insanity defense acts as a complete defense to criminal guilt, whereas diminished capacity acts as a partial defense. It means that the intent necessary for a cognate lesser offense, one that requires only a general intent, was present. The evidence of diminished capacity, though not quite meeting the standard for not guilty by reason of insanity, may warrant a verdict of manslaughter instead of murder.[3]

As those charged with crime are reluctant to plead insanity as a defense, the doctrine of diminished capacity provides an avenue for psychiatric testimony in a criminal trial. Without it, the role of the psychiatrist as an expert in a criminal trial is much diminished.

In some jurisdictions, the defense of diminished capacity is available, if at all, only when the defendant's mental impairment leaves him unable or incapable to form the specific intent needed to commit the crime. In this vein, psychiatric testimony on mens rea must be couched in terms of the defendant's capacity to form a specific intent to commit the crime.[4] In legislation enacted in 1981, California provides that evidence of mental illness "shall not be admitted to show or negate the *capacity* to form any mental state," but is admissible solely on "the issue of whether or not the accused *actually formed* a required specific intent, premeditated, deliberated, or harbored malice aforethought, when a specific intent crime is charged" (emphasis added); it is called "diminished actuality."[5] It is problematical how a forensic examiner without testifying on capacity can be of assistance to the jury in determining whether the accused "actually formed" a specific intent. Most formulations of the diminished capacity doctrine allow psychiatric testimony to show either that the defendant was not capable of premeditating or deliberating, or in fact did not premeditate or deliberate.[6]

There is another doctrine sometimes called *partial mens rea* or *diminished responsibility*, which permits the fact finder to consider mitigating evidence of cognitive or volitional impairment that neither negates mens rea nor volition under the test of insanity. This variant is also sometimes called *diminished capacity*, which causes confusion by giving the term another meaning.[7] In establishing partial mens rea or diminished responsibility, as we shall later discuss, the issue is raised whether impulsivity or situational stress may be a consideration.[8] It is often said that diminished responsibility might involve either cognitive or volitional impairment, whereas the diminished capacity doctrine only concerns cognitive impairment.

Following the 1981 legislation, the California Court of Appeals in 1990 said in *People v. Saille:*[9]

> The special defense of diminished capacity, allowing the defendant to show he is less responsible for his actions, has been abolished. Our state has returned to the "strict *mens rea*" approach, only allowing the defendant to show that the requisite mental state was not actually formed due

to a mental disorder, thus refuting the prosecution's proof of an element of the offense.[10]

Diminished capacity or diminished responsibility has also been used in sentencing, where in individualized justice various factors are taken into consideration.[11] However, new federal sentencing guidelines and mandatory minimum sentences, and their counterparts in the various states, give a lesser role to the concepts of diminished capacity in the posttrial phase of a prosecution. The new guidelines focus on the nature of the act, with less attention to the psychological makeup of the actor. The exercise of discretion in considering the actor's mental state or capacity now occurs mainly in the pretrial and trial stages of prosecution. As a result, those matters that used to be considered only as factors in sentencing are now introduced in the trial stage in regard to the elements of the crime (mens rea or *actus reus*).[12]

Years ago, as we have noted, the various states of the United States provided that a defendant wishing to offer evidence of insanity had to enter a special plea, not guilty by reason of insanity. No longer would evidence of insanity be admissible under a not guilty plea. The special plea would avoid surprise and the need for a continuance to allow the prosecutor an opportunity to obtain an examination of the defendant. Similar concerns have arisen in diminished capacity cases. Evidence of diminished capacity does not call for a special plea, but beginning in the 1970s the courts began to rule that notice of the claim must be given the prosecutor in advance of trial.[13] As in the case of a NGRI plea, a forensic examination of the accused is obtained, and the medical or psychotherapy testimonial privilege is waived, allowing access to records.[14]

Also, as in the case of insanity, diminished capacity opens the door to evidence of the accused's criminal and employment record; in effect, the traditional rules of evidence are abandoned.[15] On the other hand, when a defense of self-defense or provocation is asserted, the door is not open to evidence of the defendant's history, as those defenses are based on what is expected of a reasonable person. A claim of diminished capacity, however, does not result in an acquittal but rather a conviction of a crime lesser than the charged offense and, unlike the case of NGRI, a claim of diminished capacity does not result in automatic commitment to a hospital.

Still different rules apply to a claim of intoxication (or use of drugs) at the time of the offense. In law, intoxication is not mental disorder or diminished capacity, hence evidence of it (by lay or expert testimony) can be offered to negate specific intent under a not guilty plea without prior notice, and it calls for an instruction on that effect.[16] Evidence of intoxication, as it is not deemed a mental disorder, does not require a plea of NGRI.[17] Indeed, the California Supreme Court ruled that the legislature by virtue of its repeal in 1981 of the diminished capacity doctrine did not thereby eliminate the viability of a jury instruction regarding the effect of intoxication on the defendant's state of mind at the time of the offense.[18] The California Penal Code, like that of many states, provides that evidence of voluntary intoxication is admissible "on the issue of whether or not the defendant actually formed a required specific intent, premeditated, deliberated, or harbored malice aforethought, when a specific intent crime is charged."[19] There is a split of authority as to whether intoxication can serve as a defense to rape, with some courts holding that because rape is a "general intent" crime, no amount of intoxication can negate the crime.[20] Intoxication is listed as a mitigating circumstance in the imposition of the death penalty.[21]

A defendant has a right to present any relevant evidence on mens rea, it being an essential or fundamental element of a crime. The question is, what type of evidence will be received, and under what banner (or concept) will the evidence be offered? Should the criminal law allow evidence of mental abnormality that does not go to establish legal insanity?

In *Fisher v. United States*,[22] the U.S. Supreme Court held that restricting mental disorder evidence to an insanity defense is constitutional. Subsequently, citing *Fisher*, the Seventh Circuit said, "A state is not constitutionally compelled to recognize the doctrine of diminished capacity," and hence, when the defendant does not plead insanity, "a state may exclude expert testimony offered for the purpose of establishing that a criminal defendant lacked the capacity to form a specific intent."[23] Courts have recognized that some defendants, who are acquitted for lack of mens rea based on mental disorder without pleading NGRI, cannot be released without endangering public safety.[24]

In recent years there has been considerable discussion on the interrelationship between automatism and insanity, with courts distinguishing between sane automatism and insane automatism. A claim of automatism asserts a loss of conscious control over one's bodily movements. Sane automatism may be deemed a complete or affirmative defense to a criminal charge, separate and apart from the defense of insanity.[25] Should psychiatric testimony on that or another type of mental condition be allowed only in the case of a plea of NGRI? Many jurisdictions so hold.[26] Somnambulism (sleepwalking) and epilepsy have been held to constitute mental illness, thus falling under the insanity defense.[27] An automatist defendant may be just as dangerous as an insane one, thus justifying treating certain automatist cases as cases of insanity.

The courts vacillate on what constitutes mental illness or mental defect, which in turn calls for a plea of NGRI in order to introduce evidence of it.[28] As we noted, under the doctrine of diminished capacity, where recognized, psychiatric testimony relevant to mens rea may be admitted into evidence without an insanity plea, and at the same time, in order for a defendant to successfully present a diminished capacity defense, under the prevailing view of that defense, the jury must find that the defendant was mentally ill.[29]

A number of state and lower federal courts have held that the doctrine of diminished capacity is constitutionally mandated, quoting the U.S. Supreme Court in another context, "[F]ew rights are more fundamental than that of an accused to present witnesses in his own defense."[30] Failure to raise a diminished capacity defense, where recognized, may constitute ineffective assistance of counsel, calling for a reversal of a conviction.[31] Moreover, under this view, a trial court's exclusion of diminished capacity evidence would be deemed a miscarriage of justice.[32]

In a dissent in *Fisher*, where the Supreme Court held that limiting mental disorder evidence to an insanity defense is constitutional, Justice Frank Murphy said, "There is no absolute or clear-cut dichotomous division of the inhabitants of this world into the sane and the insane," and quoting Professor Henry Weihofen, said, "Between the two extremes of 'sanity' and 'insanity' lies every shade of disordered or deficient mental condition, grading imperceptibly one into another, . . ." and he said, "More precisely, there are persons who, while not totally insane, possess such low mental powers as to be incapable of the deliberation and premeditation requisite to statutory first degree murder."[33]

The defense of diminished capacity relates only to the *specific intent* element of a crime; diminished capacity is not a defense to a *general intent* crime. Under the common law, courts developed a number of mens rea terms to describe various levels of culpability, such as "willful and wanton," "with a depraved heart," "with malice aforethought," and "with premeditation and deliberation." These various mental states have been subsumed under the traditional terminology of specific intent and general intent.[34] The late Dr. Karl Menninger, dean of American psychiatry and student of the criminal law, said that he did not understand any of these terms.[35] But who does? They are more colorful than definitional.

The American Law Institute's Model Penal Code sets out four levels of mens rea—purposeful, knowing, reckless, and negligent. It rejects the traditional terminology of specific intent and general intent—specific intent refers to purpose and knowledge, while general intent can be analogized to recklessness and negligence.[36] Specific intent is said to refer to an offender's subjective purpose or belief, while general intent is often determined by objective rather than subjective standards.[37]

Be that as it may, the categorization of mental states remains bewildering. No coherent rationale for designating some crimes as one type or another has been formulated, and the doctrine of specific intent developed more as a matter of expediency than as a logical outgrowth of legal theory. The late Dr. Bernard Diamond, leader in forensic psychiatry, wrote, "The differences between general and specific intent can be very confusing and unclear with certain crimes despite the fact that most serious consequences to the defendant hinge upon the distinction."[38]

As commonly defined, specific intent refers to a particular state of mind necessary to satisfy an element of an offense. For example, the intent necessary for first-degree (premeditated) murder includes a specific intent to kill. Without specific intent but with general intent, murder is reduced to manslaughter. Sometimes specific intent means an intent to do something beyond that which is done (e.g., assault with intent to commit rape). General intent is usually employed by the courts to explain criminal liability when a defendant did not intend to bring about a particular result. Negligent homicide requires only that the defendant negligently causes another's death. In sum and substance, whether a crime involves specific or general intent depends essentially on the definition of the crime.

Bank robbery, for example, is a general intent crime because Congress said so. Under legislation, Congress chose to distinguish between taking by force and violence (with no specific type of intent other than knowledge) and taking "with intent to steal."[39] In the first case, the manner of taking is the wrong being punished whereas in the latter example the wrongful purpose is targeted. Congress apparently intended to cast a broader net for persons wielding guns and threatening people's lives than someone who would break into an automated teller machine (ATM). On the other hand, there could be situations in which someone takes money by mistake, so it is important to go the extra step of proving the criminal intent with respect to larceny. Commenting on *United States v. Gonyea*,[40] a bank robbery case, Saul Green, then U.S. Attorney for the Eastern District of Michigan, observed:

> With bank robbery the evil intent is manifest by the act itself—threatening the lives of others. The effect of this in the law of diminished capacity has

proven to be important. If someone wishes to put forth a mental defense to a general intent crime, such as bank robbery, they will have to do it by bearing the burden of establishing an insanity defense as required by 18 U.S.C. §17. Mr. Gonyea unsuccessfully attempted to sidestep this evidentiary burden by using "diminished capacity" as a defense. Essentially the psychiatrist said Mr. Gonyea hated being poor and could not resist attempting to get rich by robbing banks, which apparently had something to do with him serving in Vietnam. In any event, in order to use diminished capacity as a defense it must negate *mens rea* (as distinguished from an insanity defense that excuses the crime). Thus in the case of a general intent bank robbery, the defendant would have to establish that the act itself was somehow involuntary like a seizure—a virtually impossible burden.[41]

Apart from situations where the statute specifically spells out whether the crime is a specific or general intent crime, the distinction may be problematical. Federal District Court Judge Avern Cohn says, "Simply put, my criterion for determining whether a crime is a general intent crime as opposed to a specific intent crime is akin to Justice Stewart's criteria for obscenity: 'I know it when I see it.'"[42] By interpreting the crime as one of general intent, the court closes the door on psychiatric testimony. In any event, as a practical matter, categories of intent avoid the all-or-nothing outcome of not guilty or guilty of the charged crime. It makes possible a range of verdicts, and hence discretion in verdict and sentence. Without this flexibility, for example, the intoxicated individual could readily be absolved of any guilt.

Nowadays, as a result of rulings that a commitment of an insanity acquittee is to be based on the criteria of civil commitment, there is an increasing tendency to have several charges in mental-disordered offender cases, so that acquittal (by reason of NGRI) on one charge and a verdict of guilty of another charge (not requiring specific intent) can result in imprisonment after release from the hospital.[43]

Another move to circumvent an NGRI verdict, or a verdict based on diminished capacity, has been the adoption by a number of states of a guilty but mentally ill verdict. Some call GBMI another form of diminished capacity, as it gets away from the all-or-nothing approach of the insanity defense. Some call it a compromise verdict, and juries seem to consider it as such. Theoretically, it is supposed to provide psychiatric care, but as a practical matter, as we have noted in chapter 9, the consequence is the same as a guilty verdict. GBMI is not a special plea (like not guilty or NGRI), but a verdict that can be returned whenever a plea of NGRI is entered. The jury is not informed of the consequences that follow a GBMI verdict.[44]

Diminished Responsibility

Some courts and commentators have expressed the concern that a rule premised on partial mens rea or diminished responsibility would open a wide door to unstructured psychiatric or other testimony in a broad array of cases, including situational stress or impulsivity. A parade of pathologies or impulsive behavior pass through the criminal courtrooms on any given day. Some jurisdictions restrict diminished capacity testimony to cognitive impairment as a result of mental illness, just as is done under the *M'Naghten* test of criminal responsibility, and exclude evidence on control, whatever the reason for the impairment.[45] Individuals who are manic are often severely impaired in their capacity to control behavior, while their cognitive impairment is less striking.[46] (Following the *Hinckley* trial, the federal government and a number of states joined those that exclude a volitional prong from the test of criminal responsibility.)

Always testifying for the defense, Dr. Bernard Diamond believed that something could always be said on behalf of the defendant.[47] Indeed, from a psychodynamic point of view, absolutely everything that one does is in the service of reparation, in order to achieve homeostasis. When Thomas McIlvane, a fired letter carrier, exploded with gunfire at the post office in Royal Oak, Michigan, a psychologist said, "I'm not trying to dismiss or discount what he's done, but people don't do things like that because they want to. It's because they don't think they have any other choice."[48]

A person thrown into disequilibrium must do something to reestablish that vital balance or, as it is sometimes expressed, "to stay on one's rocker."[49] In that sense, all thinking and behavior can be explained psychologically as a form of self-defense. Indeed, the adjustive techniques used by the mind are called *defense mechanisms*.[50] And so it is said that the victim is "the cornerstone of the offender's psychic economy."[51] The Paramount Pictures 1991 film *Juice*, directed by Ernest Dickerson, treats the theme of African-American teenagers on the street who can be acknowledged as men and get respect only through committing crime. Thus, the battle of the experts is really a battle over the merit of an excusing condition.[52]

In a memoriam to Dr. Bernard Diamond, Professor Jerome Skolnick of the University of California Law School had this to say:

> Bernard [Diamond] . . . perceived the "all-or-none" conceptualization of the insanity defense as central to the difficulties of introducing psychiatric knowledge into the law. At the same time, he perceived a key to resolving these difficulties in the ancient doctrine of *mens rea*. . . . [He] forged the idea of diminished responsibility of the mentally ill—which came in law to be called the doctrine of diminished capacity—out of the implications of a criminal law system that embraces the notion of moral blameworthiness in its determination of guilt. The idea of diminished responsibility can perhaps best be stated as a question: If it is proper to find a psychotic murderer not guilty by reason of insanity, that is, to excuse him entirely from moral blameworthiness because of his mental disorder, isn't it equally appropriate to diminish his criminal liability if he is not psychotic but nevertheless suffers from a lesser mental disease or defect?
>
> Bernard Diamond would have answered that question with a ringing affirmative. He argued that there were innumerable degrees of *mens rea*. And if there were, an "infinitely graduated" spectrum of legal responsibility was implied—corresponding to our contemporary understanding of the psychological reality of human beings.
>
> [F]or all his accomplishments, he will best be remembered for his work in psychiatry and the law, particularly for his development of the diminished capacity defense. Not only was Bernard the principal architect of the diminished capacity defense, but he was also its chief exponent in the courtroom. . . .
>
> Largely because of Bernard's courtroom victories and scholarly writings, there was a sharp increase in the use of psychiatric testimony in

murder trials in California during the 1960s. Eventually, however, such defenses began to fall out of favor. In part, one can point to a rise in crime from the mid-sixties which led to increasing punitiveness on the part of the sentencing system. It moved from indeterminate sentencing stressing rehabilitation to a determinate system emphasizing punishment as its goal. Since the practical result of diminished capacity was to reduce the penalty for murder, the public began to look askance at that defense.[53]

The legislation enacted in 1981 in California was designed specifically to nullify the judicial developments advocated by Dr. Diamond.[54] The legislature also enacted, however, a provision permitting evidence of mental disease or defect if it is offered to show the absence of specific intent.[55] Professor Morse won over Dr. Diamond.

Over and over the question continues to arise: Must diminished capacity be linked to a mental disease or defect? Is the mental disease or defect predicate in the insanity context applicable or necessary to diminished capacity? Is a diminished capacity argument foreclosed when there is no mental disease or defect analogous to that required for the insanity defense? Dr. Diamond opened his essay "Social and Cultural Factors as a Diminished Capacity Defense in Criminal Law" with challenging observations of such questions:

> Mental illness, as a defense in criminal law, has traditionally been closely linked to the medical model of psychological deviance. Without exception, every definition of criminal insanity starts with or includes the phrase "mental disease or defect." Although not every degree or kind of mental disease or defect is exculpating, a psychiatric diagnosis of some type is a necessary, if not sufficient, requirement for such a defense in the criminal trial. Social and cultural factors may be relevant evidence, but only insofar as they are material as causation or provocation of the psychiatric condition. The logic of such a restriction is not as clear as formerly when the medical model of mental illness was accepted unquestionably.[56]

Accepting the historical reality of the close association of the insanity defense with the medical model of deviance, should the same hold for the diminished capacity or diminished responsibility defense? The question of whether cultural difference may be taken into account as diminished capacity or diminished responsibility has arisen in a number of cases involving recent immigrants to the United States. One wonders how much the United States will bend its rules to accommodate the new wave of immigrants. In a multicultural society there is increased demand to explain why people do what they do.[57] To this end, may an anthropologist be used as an expert witness to provide the court with a cultural context for making a determination about the defendant's state of mind?

This issue was raised in *People v. Poddar*.[58] In this case, Prosenjit Poddar, a member of the Harijan ("untouchable") caste from India, was charged with the murder of Tanya Tarasoff, who he felt had rejected him. In the much publicized tort case, *Tarasoff v. Regents of the University of California*,[59] Tarasoff's parents sued the university, claiming that the therapist who had treated Poddar was negligent in failing to avert the homicide. In the criminal case, defense counsel offered the testimony of an anthropologist who had lived more than twenty years in India and who had studied adjustment difficulties of Indian students who had come to American universities. According to the offer of proof, the expert would testify to cultural stresses that affected the adjustment of the defendant in shifting from the simple culture in which he had lived to the sophisticated milieu of an American university. More particularly, the expert would testify that the cultural strain for Indians becomes acute in relationships between men and women because the usual marriage in India is arranged for the parties. Altogether, the anthropological testimony would give evidence of diminished capacity.

The trial judge ruled that the witness was not qualified to testify on the direct consequences of cultural stresses on the defendant, but the judge offered to allow the witness to testify to facts relevant to cross-cultural difficulties, and then to allow counsel to ask hypothetical questions of psychiatric experts using factual data supplied by the anthropologist. The defense counsel declined, stating that he wished to use the anthropologist as an independent expert witness on the issue of diminished capacity so that the jury could draw inferences from this testimony itself and not as filtered through the testimony of psychiatrists. The court of appeals held that the evidence was properly excluded in the form in which it was offered.[60]

A ruling more restrictive than that in *Poddar* occurred in *Chase v. United States*,[61] where a plea of NGRI was entered. The court completely barred an anthropologist from testifying, on the ground that the proffered testimony was not evidence of insanity (and as to insanity the witness would not likely have qualified as an expert).[62] On the other hand, in a New York case involving Dong Lu Chen, a Chinese man who beat his wife to death with a hammer after she admitted to an affair, a city judge gave him five years of probation for manslaughter after a cultural anthropologist testified that traditional Chinese values regarding adultery and loss of manhood made him violent.[63]

What should happen, law professor Doriane Coleman asks, in a case against a defendant accused of mutilating a girl's genitals by performing a circumcision on her, a custom prevalent in some countries but generally abhorred by Americans? "Do we want to say that we want to be so sensitive to essentially create a new criminal code?" she said. "Are we treating little girls from Africa differently than we're treating little girls from the United States? We could someday see balkanization of the criminal justice system, and we really have to ask whether we should go there."[64]

Not only foreign cultures but subcultures within the United States as well have been said to influence a criminal defendant's state of mind. People are said to be brainwashed by the environment in which they live. The Palestinian Authority, for example, inculcates two things into its population, starting with the children: a hatred of Jews and a love of death. Impressionable young people are taught that sacrificing their lives in the struggle against the infidels is the most noble of all goals. Victor Hugo observed that if a soul is left in darkness, sins will be committed, and, he argued, the guilty one is not he who commits the sin, but he who causes the darkness.[65] The author Phyllis Chesler depicts Aileen Wournos, the killer of seven men in what were known as the "I-75 slayings," as a victim of her own life of prostitution and years of abuse.[66]

The "subculture of poverty" or the "ghetto defense" has been the prototype for this kind of argument.[67] In these cases the jury is aware of the cultural or social background of the accused. The issue in the cases is the instruction to the jury. The best-known case is the 1972 decision from the District of Columbia, *United*

States v. Alexander & Murdock.[68] In this case, Gordon Alexander and Benjamin Murdock, both black men, in a hamburger place exchanged glares with a group of five white male Marine lieutenants and a woman. Alexander verbally challenged the Marines, one of whom responded with a racial epithet. Alexander and Murdock then drew guns and began shooting, killing two Marines and wounding another Marine and the woman. Alexander was found guilty of assault with a dangerous weapon. Murdock raised the insanity defense and was somewhat successful; he was convicted of second-degree murder rather than first-degree murder as charged.

On appeal Murdock claimed that the instructions given by the trial judge unfairly prejudiced his claim to a NGRI verdict. The instructions included the statement: "We are not concerned with a question of whether or not a man had a rotten social background. We are concerned with the question of his criminal responsibility. That is to say, whether he had an abnormal condition of the mind that affected his emotional and behavioral processes at the time of the offense." The appellate court found no error in that ruling, relying primarily on its prior decisions where it had rejected the doctrine of diminished responsibility in seemingly broad terms. The opinion provoked a lengthy dissent by Judge David Bazelon, which has been the subject of extensive commentary.[69]

Were Alexander and Murdock like actors on a stage with their roles set out for them? Should society, the media, or the gun manufacturer share or take the blame? In the never-ending discussion of free will and criminal responsibility, many answer affirmatively. In yet another opinion in the Murdock case, Judge Carl McGowan commented:

> The tragic and senseless events giving rise to these appeals are a recurring by-product of a society which, unable as yet to eliminate explosive racial tensions, appears equally paralyzed to deny easy access to guns. Cultural infantilism of this kind inevitably exacts a high price, which in this instance was paid by the two young officers who were killed. The ultimate responsibility for their deaths reaches far beyond these appellants.
>
> As courts, however, we administer a system of justice which is limited in its reach. We deal only with those formally accused under laws which define criminal accountability narrowly. Our function on these appeals is to determine whether appellants had a fair opportunity to defend themselves, and were tried and sentenced according to law.[70]

On the same day of the decision in *United States v. Alexander & Murdock,*[71] the same court heard arguments in the case of *United States v. Brawner.*[72] In a decision issued some ten weeks later, Judge Leventhal wrote in the course of a lengthy and scholarly opinion:

> [T]he latitude for salient evidence of *e.g.,* social and cultural factors pertinent to an abnormal condition of the mind significantly affecting capacity and controls does not mean that such factors may be taken as establishing a separate defense for persons whose mental condition is such that blame can be imposed. We have rejected a broad "injustice" approach that would have opened the door to expositions of *e.g.,* cultural deprivation, unrelated to any abnormal condition of the mind. . . . Determinists

may contend that every man's fate is ultimately sealed by his genes and environment, over which he has no control. Our jurisprudence, however, while not oblivious to deterministic components, ultimately rests on a premise of freedom of will. This is not to be viewed as an exercise in philosophic discourse, but as a governmental fusion of ethics and necessity, which takes into account that a system of rewards and punishments is itself part of the environment that influences and shapes human conduct. Our recognition of an insanity defense for those who lack the essential, threshold free will possessed by those in the normal range is not to be twisted, directly or indirectly, into a device for exculpation of those without an abnormal condition of the mind.

Finally, we have not accepted suggestions to adopt a rule that disentangles the insanity defense from a medical model, and announces a standard exculpating anyone whose capacity for control is insubstantial, for whatever cause or reason. There may be logic in these submissions, but we are not sufficiently certain of the nature, range and implications of the conduct involved to attempt an all-embracing unified field theory. The applicable rule can be discerned as the cases arise in regard to other conditions—somnambulism or other automatisms; blackouts due, *e.g.* to overdose of insulin; drug addiction. Whether these somatic conditions should be governed by a rule comparable to that herein set forth for mental disease would require, at a minimum, a judicial determination, which takes medical opinion into account, finding convincing evidence of an ascertainable condition characterized by "a broad consensus that free will does not exist."[73]

Judge Bazelon, concurring in part and dissenting in part, said: "Perhaps the decision rests on an unstated assumption that change is futile because we lack enough information about human behavior to make possible a meaningful use of the defense, or because we are unwilling or unable to act upon the information that is already at hand."[74] He suggested that a "rotten social background" excuse would spur society to provide effective assistance to the poor. He puts in doubt society's right to punish offenders.

Over a half-century ago, in 1946, a like issue was before the U.S. Supreme Court in *Fisher v. United States*, where the Court held it constitutional to limit mental disorder evidence to an insanity defense.[75] Fisher, a black janitor in a library in Washington, D.C., killed the librarian, Catherine Reardon, who had complained to supervisors about his care of the premises. According to Fisher's account, one morning when they were alone in the library, Reardon scolded him and called him a "black nigger," whereupon he became angry and struck her. When she ran away screaming, Fisher grabbed a piece of wood, ran after her, and struck her on the head with it. He then seized her by the throat and choked her until she was silent. A few minutes later, she screamed again and he stuck her in the throat with his pocketknife, killing her.

The defense tried to show that the killing was not deliberate and premeditated, and was therefore, at worst, only second-degree murder. Although evidence of Fisher's "aggressive psychopathic tendencies, low emotional response and borderline mental deficiency" was introduced, the trial court declined to instruct the jury that they could consider the personality of the defendant in determining whether he was guilty of murder in the first or second degree. Under instructions defining accepted tests of insanity, malice, deliberation, and premeditation, the jury found him guilty of murder with deliberate and premeditated malice. The D.C. Court of Appeals affirmed, saying:

> Modern psychiatry has given us much scientific information which disturbs the former certainty of our judgments of individual responsibility and moral guilt. It has revolutionized the methods of treatment and rehabilitation of prisoners. But the principal place for the application of such a therapeutic point of view where the court exercises discretion in the amount of the sentence and in the treatment of criminals is in our penal institutions. In the determination of guilt age-old conceptions of individual moral responsibility cannot be abandoned without creating a laxity of enforcement that undermines the whole administration of criminal law.[76]

The Supreme Court granted certiorari. The sole error urged by the petitioner was the trial judge's refusal of an instruction permitting the jury to weigh evidence of mental deficiencies—admittedly short of complete insanity under accepted tests—in determining whether the accused was able to, and did, premeditate and deliberate. In a 5–3 decision, the Supreme Court upheld the trial judge's refusal to give the requested instruction. The Court recognized that "[t]he jury might not have reached the result it did if the theory of partial responsibility for his acts which the petitioner urges had been submitted."[77] But under the case law of the District of Columbia,[78] the Court found that the accused was not entitled to an instruction on this theory, and declined to force the District of Columbia to adopt it.[79]

In *Commonwealth v. Terry*,[80] Benjamin Terry, a prison inmate, killed a prison guard, with a baseball bat he had hidden in his trousers, when he was returning to the cell block from the prison yard and the guard gave him a slight push. This contact allegedly reminded him of a prior altercation with the guard. At trial, the defense argued that Terry should be convicted only of second-degree murder, not premeditated, first-degree murder. A psychologist testified that Terry suffered from a "dyssocial personality with paranoid hysterical and explosive features and organic brain syndrome with epileptic seizures." The psychologist also testified:

> It's my opinion that the resentment and rage that he felt brought him to the point where he did make a decision and that decision was that he would protect himself and not let himself be beaten again. So that he decided to protect himself, and if somebody hurt him, he would hurt them.
>
> However, what I believe happened at that moment, then, within that context, is that when the guard grabbed him, he went into a rage; it was immediate, it was reactive, it was based on an emotional response. He didn't stop and deliberate and think and form the intent. He reacted.[81]

The Pennsylvania Supreme Court, upholding Terry's conviction and death sentence, found this testimony irrelevant to the diminished capacity issue, because it "directly advances impulsive rage as negating premeditation." According to past caselaw in Pennsylvania, "only 'mental disorders affecting cognitive functions necessary to form specific intent' are admissible."[82]

Those who put forward a psychosocial portrait have emphasized that extraneous social factors are as much the cause of crime as any evil and harmful desires on the part of the offender.[83] Dr. Ezra Griffith, an African-American psychiatrist at the Yale University Department of Psychiatry and a past president of the American Academy of Psychiatry and Law, says that African-American forensic psychiatrists are likely to be troubled by an ethics framework that ignores the special struggles linked to the matter of race.[84] The existential situation leads to an excuse or rationalization, however, with the result of much crime and little punishment.[85]

In his presidential address to the American Psychiatric Association, Dr. Alan Stone confessed that he has felt so guilty over his testimony in a military trial that he vowed never to testify again. A black sergeant, facing court-martial for stealing government property, was sent to Dr. Stone, then an army psychiatrist, to determine whether his behavior had been driven by kleptomaniacal impulses. After an examination, Stone "concluded that the sergeant did not have kleptomania or any other mental disorder that should excuse him from responsibility," and so testified. A sentence of five years at hard labor was imposed. In the course of evaluation, Dr. Stone made the discovery that the roots of the sergeant's crime lay not in kleptomania, but in his bitterness over the fate of a black man in a discriminatory society. In Dr. Stone's words, "[H]e stole with a sense of entitlement and reparation in protest of the racist world that had deprived him of his hopes." Though testimony about the social origins of the sergeant's actions would not have been exculpatory as a matter of law, Dr. Stone is of the opinion that it might have induced leniency in sentencing, and he blames himself for omitting it.[86]

The trend away from recognition or acceptance of a diminished capacity defense as suggested by Dr. Diamond implies that the doctrine may be a dying concept. Not quite. In the pretrial stage, the diminished capacity concept (whether or not called that) influences prosecutorial discretion and thus plays a role in the charge brought against the defendant. At trial, the defense is infrequently used. It has been important more for its symbolism than for its numbers.[87] It is like the insanity defense, always a last-ditch argument. It involves evidence of mental disorder, and defense counsel can never be sure whether the evidence will work against or in favor of the accused.

What of the future? Will excuses for behavior have greater or lesser appeal? Will there be an increase in jury nullification (as occurs frequently in the District of Columbia, where juries decline to convict in drug-related offenses), or will there be a decline? The rise in crime prompted the abandonment of Dr. Diamond's opening the door to psychiatric testimony. When crime is escalating, there is less interest and less focus on the psychodynamics underlying the behavior of the accused.

Notes

1. People v. Wallace, 408 N.W.2d 87, 89 (Mich. App. 1987). In 2001 the Michigan Supreme Court did away with the diminished capacity defense, notwithstanding acknowledging it on several occasions in the past. The court decided not to allow a defendant to introduce evidence of mental abnormalities short of legal insanity to avoid or reduce criminal responsibility. People v. Carpenter, 464 Mich. 223, 627 N.W.2d 276 (2001).

2. S. Morse, "Undiminished Confusion in Diminished Capacity," *J. Crim. L. & Criminology* 75 (1984): 1.

3. Experiments have shown the power of situations to influence people's behavior, sometimes even overriding individual personality traits and the dictates of personal con-

science. The popular TV show *Survivor* demonstrated the power of circumstances to determine behavior. See E. Goode, "Hey, What If Contestants Give Each Other Shocks?" *New York Times*, Aug. 27, 2000, p. WK-3.

4. Once the defendant introduces evidence of diminished capacity, the prosecution must produce evidence that the defendant did not suffer from diminished capacity.

5. For example, in United States v. Bright, 517 F.2d 584 (2d Cir. 1975), the court said that diminished capacity testimony should address *only* the capacity of the defendant to harbor the required mental state, not whether the defendant actually had that mental state. See also Simpson v. State, 269 Ind. 495, 381 N.E.2d 1229 (1978); State v. Craig, 82 Wash.2d 777, 514 P.2d 151 (1973).

6. Cal. Penal Code, sec. 28(a). See C. R. Clark, "Specific Intent and Diminished Capacity," in A. K. Hess & I. B. Weiner (eds.), *Handbook of Forensic Psychology* (New York: Wiley, 1999), p. 350.

7. American Law Institute Model Penal Code, sec. 4.01(1); see State v. Talbebet, 590 N.W.2d 732 (Iowa App. 1999).

8. See P. Arenella, "The Diminished Capacity and Diminished Responsibility Defenses: Two Children of a Doomed Marriage," *Colum. L. Rev.* 77 (1977): 827. Chief Judge Breitel of the New York Court of Appeals in People v. Patterson, 39 N.Y.2d 288, 347 N.E.2d 898 (1976), saw as a mark of an advanced criminology "[the enlarging of] the ameliorative defenses based on the nature of the offender and the conditions which produce some degree of excuse for his conduct."

9. 270 Cal. Rptr. 502, 508, 221 Cal. App.3d 280 (1990).

10. The California Supreme Court affirmed in a much-awaited decision, People v. Saille, 54 Cal.3d 1103 (1991). *Saille* was the lead case in a group of cases coming before the California Supreme Court relating to the effect of mental disease, defect, or disorder, or voluntary intoxication on the formation of malice aforethought.

11. United States v. Cantu, 12 F.3d 1506 (9th Cir. 1993). In England a "hen-pecked" husband who battered his wife to death with a hammer was sentenced to only six years' imprisonment after a judge told him that the dead woman's behavior "was calculated to impact on your mind." M. Weaver, "Six Years for Man Who Killed Nagging Wife," *Weekly Telegraph*, No. 432 (Nov. 1999), p. 6.

12. P. S. Bamberger (ed.), *Practice under the New Federal Sentencing Guidelines* (Englewood Cliffs, N.J.: Prentice Hall, 2 vols., 2d ed., 1992 supp.). The American Bar Association's Criminal Justice Mental Health Standards recommend that in all cases "[e]vidence of mental illness or mental retardation should be considered as a possible mitigating factor in sentencing a convicted offender." American Bar Association, *Criminal Justice Mental Health Standards*, 7–9.3 (1984 supp.). In capital cases, the Supreme Court has held that mental condition cannot be excluded from consideration as a mitigating circumstance. Eddings v. Oklahoma, 455 U.S. 104, 116 (1982). However, as a practical matter, evidence of mental illness, while intended to be a mitigating circumstance, is often taken by juries as aggravating.

13. See, e.g., People v. Mangiapane, 85 Mich. App. 379 (1978).

14. M. E. Phelan, "The Pitfalls of Preventing a Diminished Capacity Defense," *Criminal Justice* 5 (1990): 8.

15. "Where insanity is relied upon as a defense, every act of the accused's life which throws some light on such issue is relevant thereto. . . . The issue of insanity gives much latitude, both to the defendant and the State, for the introduction of evidence of defendant's acts, declarations and conduct, prior and subsequent to the alleged crime, subject to the limitation that the acts, declarations and conduct inquired about must have a tendency to shed light on the accused's state of mind when the act for which he is being tried was committed." Nichols v. State, 276 Ala. 209, 160 So.2d 619, 621 (1964).

16. In People v. Guillet, 342 Mich. 1, 69 N.W.2d 140 (Mich. 1955), the defendant accompanied a woman to a tavern, where they drank, then they went to his house, where they continued to drink. He made indecent advances, which she repulsed, only to be knocked down by the defendant, who continued, in the words of the Michigan Supreme Court, "his attempt to commit rape." The jury convicted the defendant of assault with intent to rape. The Michigan Supreme Court reversed the conviction because the judge had failed to tell the jury that intoxication is a defense to a specific intent crime—here, assault *with intent* to rape.

17. In Hopt v. Utah, 104 U.S. 631 (1881), the U.S. Supreme Court, after stating the fa-

miliar rule that voluntary intoxication is no excuse for crime, said: "[W]hen a statute establishing different degrees of murder requires deliberate premeditation in order to constitute murder in the first degree, the question of whether the accused is in such a condition of mind, by reason of drunkenness or otherwise, as to be capable of deliberate premeditation, necessarily becomes a material subject of consideration by the jury." 104 U.S. at 634. See also Bishop v. United States, 107 F.2d 297 (D.C. App. 1939); Heideman v. United States, 259 F.2d 943 (D.C. App. 1958).

18. People v. Ramirez, 50 Cal.3d 1158, 270 Cal. Rptr. 286, 791 P.2d 965 (1990); In re Cordero, 46 Cal.3d 161, 259 Cal. Rptr. 342, 756 P.2d 1370 (1988).

19. Cal. Penal Code, sec. 22(b)

20. E.g., Walden v. S., 178 Tenn. 71, 156 S.W.2d 385 (1941); but see S. v. Evenson, 237 Iowa 1214, 24 N.W.2d 762 (1946).

21. State v. Reeves, 476 N.W.2d 829 (Neb. 1991).

22. 328 U.S. 463 (1946).

23. Meunch v. Israel, 715 F.2d at 1144–45 (7th Cir. 1983), *cert. denied,* 467 U.S. 1228 (1984). See H. M. Huckabee, "Evidence of Mental Disorder on Mens Rea: Constitutionality of Drawing the Line at the Insanity Defense," *Pepperdine L. Rev.* 16 (1989): 573.

24. In State v. Wilcox, 70 Ohio St.2d 182, 436 N.E.2d 523 (1982), the Ohio Supreme Court noted: "The principal effect of the diminished capacity defense is to enable mentally ill offenders to receive shorter and more certain sentences than they would receive if they were adjudged insane. Having satisfied ourselves that Ohio's test for criminal responsibility adequately safeguards the rights of the insane, we are disinclined to adopt an alternative defense that could swallow up the insanity defense and its attendant commitment provisions." 70 Ohio St.2d at 186.

25. In State v. Cadell, 287 N.C. 266, 215 S.E.2d 348 (1975), Chief Justice Sharp, concurring in result and dissenting in part, wrote, at 215 S.E.2d at 366:

> [I]f a person is actually unconscious when he does an act which would otherwise be criminal, the absence of consciousness not only excludes the existence of any specific mental state, but also excludes the possibility of a voluntary act without which there can be no criminal liability. Unconsciousness, therefore, can never be an affirmative defense, which imposes the burden of proof upon the defendant, because the State has the burden of proving the essential elements of the offense charged, and "a voluntary act is an absolute requirement for criminal liability." Lafave and Scott, Criminal Law 181 (1972). Although the defense of unconsciousness "is sometimes explained on the ground that such a person could not have the requisite mental state for commission of the crime, the better rationale is that the individual has not engaged in a voluntary act." *Id.* at 337.

In discussing the relationship between the defenses of automatism and insanity, Justice Sharp noted that the defendant acquitted by reason of insanity could be detained in a hospital where he was not a continuing danger to the public, whereas one acquitted on the ground of unconsciousness was unconditionally released. He noted the judicial tendency to characterize instances in which the condition of unconsciousness is likely to recur as insanity rather than automatism so that the defendant may be committed. 215 S.E.2d at 369. See B. McSherry, "Getting Away with Murder? Dissociative States and Criminal Responsibility," *Int. J. Law & Psychiatry* 21 (1998): 163.

26. Apparently fourteen states and the District of Columbia take this position: Arizona, Delaware, Florida, Georgia, Indiana, Louisiana, Maryland, Minnesota, North Carolina, Ohio, Oklahoma, Virginia, Wisconsin, and Wyoming. In Johnson v. State, 292 Md. 405, 439 A.2d 542 (1982), the Maryland Court of Appeals explained:

> [T]he introduction of expert psychiatric testimony concerning the defendant's mental aberrations when the basic sanity of the accused is not at issue conflicts with the governing principle of the criminal law that all legally sane individuals are equally capable of forming and possessing the same types and degrees of intent. Consequently, an individual determined to be "sane" within the traditional constructs of the criminal law is held accountable for his action, regardless of his particular disabilities, weaknesses, poverty, religious beliefs, social deprivation or edu-

cational background. The most that it is proper to do with such information is to weigh it during sentencing. . . . [B]ecause the legislature, reflecting community morals, has, by its definition of criminal insanity already determined which states of mental disorder ought to relieve one from criminal responsibility, this court is without authority to impose our views in this regard even if they differed.

See H. M. Huckabee, "Avoiding the Insanity Defense Strait Jacket: The *Mens Rea* Route," *Pepperdine L.Rev.* 15 (1987): 1.

27. Tibbs v. C., 128 S.W. 871 (Ky. 1910) (somnambulism); P. v. Higgins, 186 N.Y.S.2d 623, 5 N.Y.2d 607, 159 N.E.2d 179 (1959) (epilepsy).

28. Query: What about a claim that a sexual advance triggered a violent so-called homosexual panic? Provocation may not be claimed as a defense, as the behavior is not deemed reasonable. In using provocation as a defense, the personal history of the defendant is not allowed in assessing whether his response was reasonable. Does homosexual panic constitute mental illness, calling for a plea of NGRI, which would allow evidence of mental illness? Does it constitute diminished capacity? The answer is debatable. See the discussion in chapter 19, on homosexuality.

Query: What about multiple personality disorder (also known as *dissociative identity disorder*)? Sidney Sheldon's novel *Tell Me Your Dreams* (New York: Morrow, 1998) is about a multiple personality charged with committing a series of brutal murders. Sheldon claims that 1 percent of the population has multiple personality disorder and that up to 20 percent of all patients in psychiatric hospitals have it (p. 15). In State v. Moore, 113 N.J. 239, 550 A.2d 117 (1988), where the defendant was charged with murder and entered a plea of NGRI, the New Jersey Supreme Court ruled that evidence of multiple personality disorder obliged the trial judge to instruct the jury that it may return a verdict of manslaughter. The appellate court ruled failure to charge diminished capacity was reversible error despite the fact that defendant did not request such an instruction. The court said: "In the instant case, where defendant did in fact present an insanity defense, the record persuades us that sufficient competent evidence was adduced at trial to support a charge of diminished capacity. As part of her insanity defense, defendant offered evidence that would permit a jury to decide whether she suffered from a condition that diminished her capacity to form the knowing or purposeful mental state required to convict her of murder."

Query: What about battered spouse syndrome? Originally, in cases of women accused of murdering their spouses or boyfriends who had abused them, the plea was NGRI. The battered spouse syndrome was regarded analogous to a post-traumatic stress disorder, but feminists soon regarded NGRI as a stigma, and it resulted in commitment, so the defense shifted to self-defense. Expert testimony is allowed to explain the lower threshold of self-defense as a result of the abuse. State v. Kelly, 97 N.J. 178, 478 A.2d 364 (1984); see A. M. Coughlin, "Excusing Women," *Cal. L. Rev.* 82 (1994): 1; V. M. Mather, "The Skeleton in the Closet: The Battered Woman Syndrome, Self-Defense, and Expert Testimony," *Mercer L. Rev.* 39 (1988): 545. England's Treason Act of 1351 made it a crime of petty treason for a wife to kill her husband, because he was her sovereign lord.

See R. Slovenko, *Psychiatry and Criminal Culpability* (New York: Wiley, 1995), pp. 67–117.

29. T. H. D. Lewin, "Psychiatric Evidence in Criminal Cases for Purposes Other than the Defense of Insanity," *Syracuse L. Rev.* 26 (1975): 1051. In a decision rendered at a time when the doctrine of diminished capacity was allowed in Michigan, the Michigan Supreme Court said that "mental illness" in diminished capacity may be simply "mental disturbance." See People v. Pickens, 446 Mich. 298, 521 N.W.2d 797 (1994). In People v. Carpenter, supra note 1, the Michigan Supreme Court in 2001 did away with diminished capacity.

30. Hughes v. Mathews, 576 F.2d 1250 (7th Cir. 1978), quoting Chambers v. Mississippi, 410 U.S. 284 (1973). However, in Muench v. Israel, 715 F.2d 1124 (7th Cir. 1983), the Seventh Circuit rejected a habeas corpus petition based on similar facts, stating: "[I]n Hughes we were not seeking to constitutionalize the law of evidence nor to impose a diminished responsibility doctrine on Wisconsin. . . . A theory that the Supreme Court has twice refused to impose upon the state of California, albeit in summary decisions, . . . is not one that this lower federal court will impose on the state of Wisconsin as a matter of federal constitutional due process." In Commonwealth v. Walczack, 468 Pa. 210, 360 A.2d 914, 920 (1976), the Pennsylvania Supreme Court held that, under the Pennsylvania constitution, due process requires the admission of psychiatric testimony that is relevant to mens rea. The court stated: "It is incon-

sistent with fundamental principles of American jurisprudence to preclude an accused from offering relevant and competent evidence to dispute the charge against him."

In Commonwealth v. McCusker, 448 Pa. 382, 292 A.2d 286 (1972), a murder prosecution where the defendant did not plead NGRI, the Pennsylvania Supreme Court in a change of its law allowed psychiatric evidence for the purpose of determining whether the defendant acted in the heat of passion. The court said, "Upon reflection and further consideration we now conclude that psychiatric evidence, coming as it does from a 'recognized and important branch of modern medicine,' should be admissible at trial for the purpose of determining whether a defendant acted in the heat of passion." 292 A.2d at 289.

In coming to the same conclusion, the American Law Institute's Model Penal Code, sec. 4.02(1), provides: "Evidence that the defendant suffered from a mental disease or defect is admissible whenever it is relevant to prove that the defendant did not have a state of mind that is an element of the crime." In comments to the provision, the drafters stated: "If states of mind such as deliberation or premeditation are accorded legal significance, psychiatric evidence should be admissible when relevant to prove or disprove their existence to the same extent as any other evidence." Comments to sec. 4.02, 193 (Tent. Draft No. 4, 1955).

More recently, finding that "logical relevance" so requires and "is probably constitutionally required," the American Bar Association has recommended a similar rule. Project of the American Bar Association (1986, 1989), Standard 7-6.2. The commentary states that expert testimony on mental condition "should be admissible on a *mens rea* issue even if a defendant has not pleaded a specific mental non-responsibility [insanity] defense, as long as it is relevant to a determination of guilt, innocence, or level of culpability." American Bar Association, *Criminal Justice Mental Health Standards*, 2: 121 (2d ed. ch. 7, 1986 supp.).

31. Commonwealth v. Legg, 711 A.2d 430 (Pa. 1998). In this case the defendant, shortly before she killed her husband, had been hospitalized for depression and suicidal and homicidal tendencies. See also People v. Lloyd, 590 N.W.2d 738 (Mich. 1999); State v. Thomas, 590 N.W.2d 755 (Minn. 1999).

32. In People v. Henderson, 60 Cal.2d 432, 35 Cal. Rptr. 77, 386 P.2d 677 (1963), the defendant testified that he had no intention to kill the deceased and that the act was done while he was in a dreamlike state. Two psychiatrists testified in corroboration of this explanation of the killing. The California Supreme Court held that the trial court erred in failing to give any instruction that would tell the jury for what purpose they could consider the evidence of that defense.

33. Fisher v. United States, 328 U.S. at 492, quoting H. Weihofen, "Partial Insanity and Criminal Intent," *Ill. L. Rev.* 24 (1930): 505, 508.

34. The term *malice* in law does not mean evil, enmity, anger, hatred, or the like; it is a term of art. John Hinckley apparently had nothing personally against President Reagan but would be said to have acted with malice in shooting the president. The California legislation of 1981 provides that malice includes no mental element other than an intent to kill. Cal. Penal Code, sec. 188. Under Maine's statute, malice is implied from "any deliberate, cruel act committed by one person against another suddenly or without a considerable provocation." Mullaney v. Wilbur, 421 U.S. 684 (1975).

35. Personal communication (1964).

36. See G. B. Melton, J. Petrila, N. G. Poythress, & C. Slobogin, *Psychological Evaluations for the Courts* (New York: Guilford Press, 1987), p. 127.

37. Evidence concerning subjective mental state would not be logically relevant in cases involving general intent crimes, because culpability would turn not on what a defendant actually perceived, believed, or intended but on what an ordinary person in the same situation would or should have perceived, believed, or intended. In the great majority of cases, however, evidence concerning a defendant's abnormal mental condition as it relates to mens rea will, if believed, reduce the grade of the offense.

38. B. J. Diamond, "Social and Cultural Factors and a Diminished Capacity Defense in Criminal Law," *Bull. Am. Acad. Psychiatry & Law* 6 (1978): 195, 199.

39. The statutory scheme is set out in 18 U.S.C., sec. 2113.

40. 140 F.3d 649 (6th Cir. 1998).

41. Personal communication (Sept. 28, 1998).

42. Personal communication (Mar. 16, 1999). Justice Stewart's comment appears in Jacobellis v. Ohio, 378 U.S. 184, 197 (1964). See E. Jaeger, "Obscenity and the Reasonable Person: Will He 'Know It When He Sees It?'" *Boston College L. Rev.* 30 (1989): 823.

43. In People v. Massip, 229 Cal. App.3d 1400 (1990), the defendant claimed that she was suffering from depression—commonly known as "baby blues"—that caused her to commit the crime. She claimed that she had heard voices telling her that her child was in pain and to put him out of his misery. She then placed the child under a tire, drove over him, and put him in a trash can. At the trial, she pleaded not guilty by reason of insanity, but a jury found her sane and convicted her of second-degree murder. She then asked for a retrial, but in a ruling that surprised attorneys on both sides, the trial judge reduced the verdict to voluntary manslaughter and also found the defendant not guilty by reason of insanity. See R. D. Miller, J. Olin, E. M. Ball, D. S. Johnson, J. B. Reynolds, & J. Covey, "Dual Commitments to Forensic Hospitals and Prisons: Rational Disposition or Political Compromise?" *J. Psychiatry & Law* 27 (1999): 157.

44. R. Slovenko, *Psychiatry and Criminal Culpability* (New York; Wiley, 1995).

45. United States v. Pohlot, 827 F.2d 889 (3d Cir. 1987); Commonwealth v. Terry, 513 Pa. 381, 521 A.2d 398 (1987).

46. It has been suggested that the court inquiry apply current scientific knowledge of the nature of impulsive aggression. See D. O. Lewis, *Guilty by Reason of Insanity* (New York: Ballantine, 1998); E. S. Barratt & L. Slaughter, "Defining , Measuring, and Predicting Impulsive Aggression: A Heuristic Model," *Behav. Sci. & Law* 16 (1988): 285; E. S. Barratt, M. S. Stanford, L. Dowdy, M. J. Liebman, & T. A. Kent, "Impulsive and Premeditated Aggression: A Factor Analysis of Self-Reported Acts," *Psychiatric Research* 86 (1999): 163; E. S. Barratt, M. S. Stanford, T. A. Kent, & A. Felthous, "Neuropsychological and Cognitive Psychological Substrates of Impulsive Aggression," *Biol. Psychiatry* 41 (1997): 1045; M. A. Pauley, "Murder by Premeditation," *Am. Crim. L. Rev.* 36 (1999): 145.

47. Personal communication (1978).

48. A. Wilson & W. W. Keebler, "The Blinking Light May Signal a Shock: Answering Machine Delivers News Coldly," *Detroit Free Press*, Nov. 18, 1991, p. E-1.

49. The principle of homeostasis can be extended to describe the total biological, psychological, and social behavior of the organism as it seeks to maintain a state of equilibrium. Dr. Karl Menninger states: "Increasing dysfunction, increasing dyscontrol, increasing dysorganization can be identified empirically in a series of hierarchical levels, each one reflecting a stage of greater impairment of control and organization." Deviant behaviors or psychiatric symptoms are thus looked upon as devices employed by the organism to deal with emergencies, disturbed equilibrium, and threatened dyscontrol. K. Menninger, *The Vital Balance* (New York: Viking, 1963), p. 80. See also S. Halleck, *Psychiatry and the Dilemmas of Crime* (New York: Harper & Row, 1967); M. J. Horowitz (ed.), *Hysterical Personality* (New York: Aronson, 1977).

50. A. Freud, *The Ego and the Mechanisms of Defense* (New York: International Universities Press, 1946).

51. State v. Herrin, Westchester Cy., N.Y., June 9, 1978; discussed in W. Gaylin, *Killing of Bonnie Garland: A Question of Justice* (New York: Simon & Schuster, 1982); P. Meyer, *The Yale Murder* (New York: Harper & Row, 1982). In People v. Gorshen, 51 Cal.2d 716, 336 P.2d (1959), Dr. Bernard Diamond testified that Gorshen's rage was a desperate attempt to ward off the imminent and total disintegration of his personality that would occur through regression into a schizophrenic relapse.

52. B. L. Diamond, "Social and Cultural Factors as a Diminished Capacity Defense in Criminal Law," *Bull. Am. Acad. Psychiatry & Law* 6 (1978): 195.

53. J. H. Skolnick, "Dr. Bernard L. Diamond," *Calif. L. Rev.* 78 (1990): 1433.

54. Cal. Penal Code, secs. 188, 189.

55. Cal. Penal Code, sec. 28.

56. *Bull. Am. Acad. Psychiatry & Law* 6 (1978): 195.

57. Zein Isa, a Palestinian-born grocer who brought his family to the United States in 1985, stabbed his sixteen-year-old daughter, Tina Isa, to death while her mother, Maria Isa, held her down. They called her a "she-devil" because she took a job and went out with a boy. The murder may defy understanding, reflecting as it does cultural and generational conflicts that seem utterly alien to most Americans. At the parents' trial, defense witness Nicolas Gavrielides, a State University of New York anthropology professor who was born and raised in Jerusalem, testified that the way Tina lived had offended her father's sense of honor. The parents were convicted of first-degree murder. "Die, My Daughter, Die!" *People*, Jan. 20, 1992, p. 71.

58. The California Supreme Court's decision in People v. Poddar appears at 10 Cal.3d 750, 111 Cal. Rptr. 910, 518 P.2d 342 (1974); discussed in W. J. Winslade & J. W. Ross, *The Insanity Defense* (New York: Scribner, 1983).

59. 118 Cal. Rptr. 129, 529 P.2d 553 (1974), *vacated,* 17 Cal.3d 425, 131 Cal. Rptr. 14, 551 P.2d 334 (1976). See the discussion of the case in volume 2, chapter 11, on the duty of therapists to third parties.

60. The decision of the Court of Appeals in People v. Poddar appears at 26 Cal. App.3d 230, 103 Cal. Rptr. 84 (1972). The court said:

> Diminished capacity is a mental infirmity. To the extent that it is to be evaluated by experts, the experts should be those qualified in the mental sciences. The effect, therefore, of such matters as cultural stress should be assessed by experts in the fields of psychiatry and psychology, and ultimately by the jury with the assistance of the testimony of such experts. We need not consider whether it would have been proper to exclude the anthropologist's testimony completely, because the court was willing . . . to allow the testimony as furnishing material for the opinions of the psychiatrists. It is desirable to give direction and control to the presentation of expert testimony of such delicate matters as the capacity of a person to deliberate or to entertain malice. To allow independent testimony on sociological, ethnic or like influences, not as reviewed by experts in psychological sciences, but as directly presented to the jury, would be to open the door to a vast amount of argument from various sources, the result of which would often be distraction of the jury and the removing of their deliberation from the essential element of the mental capacity of the accused.

Even without the expert testimony, the jury found Poddar guilty not of first-degree but of second-degree murder. One might ponder: Would the verdict have been any different—more severe or less severe—if the expert had testified? More often than not, juries are swayed more by the facts of the case than by expert opinions. Defense counsel objected to the exclusion of the expert testimony; as is the practice, to safeguard an appeal, defense counsel raises any and every possible error of the trial court.

61. 468 F.2d 141 (7th Cir. 1972).

62. The case concerned the acts of Frederick Chase and several others, who on May 25, 1969, broke into a Selective Service office, removed draft records, and burned them to protest the Vietnam War. They were tried on charges of destroying government property. Several of the defendants pleaded NGRI, claiming that by reason of mental illness they could not distinguish between right and wrong when they vandalized the Selective Service office. They were convicted. Among the issues on appeal was whether the trial judge had improperly excluded evidence supporting this claim. The Seventh Circuit explained why it did not find the exclusion improper (468 F.2d at 148–49):

> There is virtually nothing in the record to suggest that any of the defendants was suffering from any legally cognizable mental illness on May 24 or May 25, 1969, or that they did not fully understand that their conduct was "wrong" as measured by the standards prescribed by society. Their evidence of "insanity" merely tended to prove that their moral judgment as to whether certain conduct—specifically their own deliberate violations of law—was "right" or "wrong" was at odds with the judgment expressed by society at large. Under the standards for determining criminal responsibility . . . this defense was manifestly frivolous. . . . The trial judge properly excluded certain evidence which . . . would have provided no support for the claim that these defendants could not comprehend the criminal character of their conduct. Thus, an anthropologist was not allowed to testify that the defendants believed their conduct might be considered sane in one culture and insane in another. . . .
>
> The judge's evidentiary rulings were well within the scope of his discretion. We find absolutely no merit in the contention that these four dedicated intellectuals were not given an adequate opportunity to present their defense of "insanity."

63. Noted in J. Gibeaut, "Troubling Translations: Cultural Defense Tactic Raises Issue of Fairness," *ABAJ* 85 (Oct. 1999): 93.

64. Ibid. Many countries have laws that reduce or even eliminate sentences for those who kill in defense of family honor. Worldwide, thousands of times each year, a woman is killed by her father or brothers for acts that are seen as besmirching the family's honor, including committing adultery, defying a parental order to marry, being seen in public with a man, or becoming the victim of a rape. Editorial, "Honor Killings," *New York Times*, Nov. 12, 2000, p. WK-14.

65. V. Hugo, *The Miserables*, trans. C. E. Wilbour (New York: Random House, 1992).

66. Quoted in M. Reynolds, "'Good Girl' to Be Tried in Serial Slaying" (Reuters news release), *Detroit Free Press*, Jan. 11, 1992, p. 4.

67. As proof that the accused committed the crime, however, evidence of poverty or unemployment is generally not admissible because its probative value is deemed outweighed by unfair prejudice and discrimination. The argument that "poverty causes crime" cannot be used as evidence *against* an accused. People v. Stanton, 296 N.W.2d 70 (Mich. App. 1980).

68. 471 F.2d 923 (D.C. Cir. 1972).

69. Judge Bazelon said (471 F.2d at 926):

> The thrust of Murdock's defense was that the environment in which he was raised— his "rotten social background"—conditioned him to respond to certain stimuli in a manner most of us would consider flagrantly inappropriate. Because of his early conditioning, he argued, he was denied any meaningful choice when the racial insult triggered the explosion in the restaurant. He asked the jury to conclude that his "rotten social background," and the resulting impairment of mental or emotional processes and behavior controls, ruled his violent reaction in the same manner that the behavior of a paranoid schizophrenic may be ruled by his "mental condition." Whether this impairment amounted to an "abnormal condition of the mind" is, in my opinion, at best an academic question. But the consequences we predicate on the answer may be very meaningful indeed.

70. 471 F.2d at 965.

71. April 21, 1972.

72. 471 F.2d 969 (D.C. App. 1972).

73. 471 F.2d at 995.

74. 471 F.2d at 1012.

75. 328 U.S. 463 (1946).

76. 149 F.2d 28 at 29 (D.C. App. 1945).

77. 328 U.S. at 470.

78. United State v. Lee, 4 Mackey 489 (Sup. Ct. D.C. 1886).

79. The majority stated, "We express no opinion upon whether the theory for which petitioner contends should or should not be made the law of the District of Columbia. Such a radical departure from common law concepts is more properly a subject for the exercise of legislative power or at least for the discretion of the courts of the District." 328 U.S. at 476. In a dissenting opinion, Justice Frankfurter wrote:

> This case has been much beclouded by laymen's ventures into psychiatry. We are not now called upon to decide whether the antiquated tests set down more than a hundred years ago regarding mental responsibility for crime are still controlling or whether courts should choose from among the conflicting proposals of scientific specialists. This is not the occasion to decide whether the only alternative is between law which reflects the most advanced scientific tests and law remaining a leaden-footed laggard. The case turns on a much simpler and wholly conventional issue. For the real question, as I see it, is whether in view of the act of Congress defining murder in the first degree for prosecutions in the District and in light of the particular circumstances of this case, the trial court properly sent the case to the jury. That is a very different question from whether the court's charge was unimpeachable as an abstract statement of law. For Fisher is not the name of a theoretical problem. We are not here dealing with an abstract man who killed an abstract woman under abstract circumstances and received an abstract trial on

abstract issues. . . . The preoccupation at the trial, in the treatment of the conviction by the court below and by the arguments at the bar of this Court, was with alluring problems of psychiatry. Throughout this melancholy affair the insistence was on claims of Fisher's mental deficiencies and the law's duty to take into consideration the skeptical views of modern psychiatry regarding the historic legal tests for insanity. I cannot but believe that this has diverted attention from the more obvious and conventional but controlling inquiry regarding the absence or presence of the requisite premeditation, under the circumstances of this case.

That the charge requested by the defendant and denied did not go to this issue of premeditation unambiguously but in an awkward and oblique way did not lessen the responsibility of the trial judge to bring this issue—it was the crucial issue— sharply and vividly to the jury's mind. If their minds had been so focused, the jury might well have found that the successive steps that culminated in Miss Reardon's death could not properly be judged in isolation. They might well have found a sequence of events that constituted a single, unbroken response to a provocation in which no forethought, no reflection whatever, entered. A deed may be gruesome and not be premeditated. Concededly there was no motive for the killing prior to the inciting "you black nigger." The tone in which these words were uttered evidently pulled the trigger of Fisher's emotions, and under adequate instructions the jury might have found that what these words conveyed to Fisher's ears unhinged his self-control. While there may well have been murder, deliberate premeditation, for which alone Congress has provided the death sentence, may have been wanting. . . . I do not believe that the facts warrant a finding of premeditation. But, in any event, the justification for finding first-degree murder premeditation was so tenuous that the jury ought not to have been left to founder and flounder within the dark emptiness of legal jargon. The instructions to the jury on the vital issue of premeditation consisted of threadbare generalities, a jumble of empty abstractions equally suitable for any other charge of murder with none of the elements that are distinctive about this case, mingled with talk about mental disease. What the jury got was devoid of clear guidance and illumination. Inadequate direction to a jury may be as fatal as misdirection.

The case is discussed in H. Weihofen & W. Overholser, "Mental Disorder Affecting the Degree of a Crime," *Yale L.J.* 56 (1947): 959; H. L. Taylor, "Partial Insanity as Affecting the Degree of Crime—A Commentary on *Fisher v. United States*," *Calif. L. Rev.* 34 (1946): 625; Note, *Colum. L. Rev.* 46 (1946): 1005.

80. 513 Pa. 381, 521 A.2d 398 (1987), cited supra note 45.

81. *Diminished responsibility* is often distinguished from *diminished capacity* in that the former might involve either cognitive or volitional impairment, whereas the diminished capacity doctrine contemplates only evidence of cognitive dysfunction relevant to the capacity to form intent. In *Terry,* the Pennsylvania Supreme Court found testimony of impulsivity irrelevant to the diminished capacity issue, because it "directly advances impulsive rage as negating premeditation." 521 A.2d at 405.

82. 521 A.2d at 404.

83. R. Harris, *Murders and Madness* (Oxford: Clarendon Press, 1989).

84. E. E. H. Griffith, "Ethics in Forensic Psychiatry: A Cultural Response to Stone and Appelbaum," *J. Am. Acad. Psychiatry & Law* 26 (1998): 171. In the 2000 film *Boesman & Lena* set in South Africa during the days of apartheid, Boesman, a black man, is angry, bitter, and ready for violence at the slightest provocation. Defense attorneys for Colin Ferguson, who massacred passengers on the Long Island Railroad, wanted to enter a black rage defense on his behalf. Paul Harris, an attorney with the Center for Guerrilla Law in San Francisco, pioneered the modern version of the black rage defense when in 1971 he successfully defended a young black man charged with armed bank robbery. See P. Harris, *Black Rage Confronts the Law* (New York: New York University Press, 1997); see also A. E. Taslitz, "Abuse Excuse and the Logic and Politics of Expert Relevance," *Hastings L.J.* 49 (1998): 1039. Of course, as we know, juries can return a verdict contrary to the law—they do not have to give a reason for their decision. Returning a verdict contrary to the law is known as *jury nullification.* See R. Slovenko, "Jury Nullification," *J. Psychiatry & Law* 22 (1993): 545.

85. For a criticism, see S. Estrich, *Getting Away with Murder: How Politics Is Destroying the Criminal Justice System* (Cambridge: Harvard University Press, 1998); J. Q. Wilson, *Moral Judgment: Does the Abuse Excuse Threaten Our Legal System?* (New York: Basic Books, 1997); R. Slovenko, "Crime Revisited," *J. Psychiatry & Law* 18 (1990): 485; L. Weintraub, "Inner-City Post-Traumatic Stress Disorder," *J.Psychiatry & Law* 25 (1997): 249; B. Frank, "Race and Crime: Let's Talk Sense" (op-ed.), *New York Times*, Jan. 13, 1992, p. 15.

86. A. A. Stone, "Presidential Address: Conceptual Ambiguity and Morality in Modern Psychiatry," *Am. J. Psychiatry* 137 (1980): 887.

87. Steven Kaplan, a prosecuting attorney in Macomb County, Michigan, claims that "diminished capacity is like the Libertarian Party—it's interesting but it has little role to play." Personal communication (Oct. 15, 1999). Kaplan's position is debatable. Diminished capacity allows psychiatric testimony on mental state without an NGRI plea and commitment. In any event, the Michigan Supreme Court in 2001 did away with the defense in the state. See supra note 1.

12

Juvenile Justice

Under ancient biblical codes, the minor and the mental defective were not punished, because "their acts are without purpose." In Roman law, a minor under the age of seven was not held criminally responsible (an age that coincides with psychological development). In the early stages of the common law, infancy apparently was not a defense, but children were usually pardoned for their offenses. By the fourteenth century, it was established that a child under seven as a matter of law was not criminally responsible, and it was presumed that a child over seven lacked the capacity to commit a crime (evidence of capacity could overcome the presumption). By the seventeenth century, fourteen became the age of full responsibility.[1] Many states enacted statutes specifically directed at youthful behavior, which prohibited, for example, playing ball on public ways or sledding on the Sabbath. Other laws covering children specifically were similar to a Massachusetts statute of 1646:

> If any child[ren] above sixteen years old and of sufficient understanding shall curse or smite their natural father or mother, they shall be put to death, unless it can be sufficiently testified that the parents have been very unchristianly negligent in the education of such children, or so provoked

them by extreme and cruel correction that they have been forced there-unto to preserve themselves from death or maiming. . . .

If a man have a stubborn or rebellious son of sufficient years of un-derstanding, viz. sixteen, which will not obey the voice of his father or the voice his mother, and that when they have chastened him will not harken unto them, then shall his father and mother, being his natural parents, lay hold on him and bring him to the magistrates assembled in Court, and testify to them by sufficient evidence that this their son is stubborn and rebellious and will not obey their voice and chastisement, but lives in sundry notorious crimes. Such a son shall be put to death.[2]

A common crime during the nineteenth century by children was flight from the service of a master to whom they were apprentices. These offenses were dealt with severely.

Prior to the 1900s, juveniles in violation of the laws were brought to the adult criminal courts. Not only were they tried as adults, but they were sent to adult prisons as well. In 1851, Michigan prison inspectors complained the courts had committed five or six boys to the state prison—"one of whom is only 11 years of age."[3] In the late nineteenth century, according to a history of reform schools in the state, Michigan Governor Andrew Parsons insisted that juveniles be treated "not as men of understanding and hardened in iniquity, but [be trained]."[4]

Starting in the early nineteenth century, juries began injecting compassion into the law by refusing to convict children, even though the evidence clearly indicated their guilt. Reformers seized on this wave of jury nullification and created reform schools, which became homes for children convicted of crimes or found to be vagrants or ungovernable. These schools flourished for several decades until some were revealed to be little more than sweatshops for children.

In 1871 the reform school in Chicago burned in the city's great fire, and many of its charges ended up in the city jails. A year later, Chicago social leaders Lucy Flower, Adelaide Groves, and Julia Lathrop toured those jails and were appalled to find "quite small boys confined in the same quarters with murderers, anarchists and hardened criminals." These women, who believed that children were innately good and that the state had a moral duty to correct and save wayward youth, began lobbying for a separate children's court to handle cases involving children. Their efforts resulted in the Illinois legislature enacting a law to establish such a court.[5] On July 3, 1899, Cook County Juvenile Judge Richard Tuthill heard the nation's first juvenile court case, involving an eleven-year-old boy who was accused of larceny. The new court system was unique in four ways: (1) it was rehabilitative rather than punitive, (2) its records were confidential, (3) it did not place juveniles in adult facilities, and (4) it allowed informal procedures in court, preferring to act "as a wise parent" with a "wayward child," as Judge Julian Mack, one of the original juvenile court jurists put it.[6] By 1935, nearly all states enacted legislation establish-ing juvenile courts.

Waiver to Criminal Court

In subsequent years, with the increase in juvenile crime, the legislatures of all fifty states passed laws allowing or requiring transfer of juveniles, usually over the age of fourteen or fifteen, to the regular criminal courts. In order to transfer, or waive, juvenile court jurisdiction, certain criteria such as age, nature of the crime, and prior record have to be met. The waiver was usually for acts that would constitute a felony if committed by an adult.[7]

In 1966, in *Kent v. United States*,[8] the U.S. Supreme Court dealt with the issue of waiver of juvenile court jurisdiction to a court of general criminal jurisdiction. It did not, as was urged, strike down waiver of juveniles to criminal court. In the course of its opinion, Justice Fortas, who wrote the opinion for the Court, commented, "There is much evidence that some juvenile courts lack the personnel, facilities, and techniques to perform adequately as representatives of the state in a *parens patriae* capacity, at least with respect to children charged with law violations." The court was emphatic, however, that the waiver of jurisdiction was a "critically important" action to the juvenile because there are special rights and immunities that accrue from juvenile court handling: He is shielded from publicity. He may be confined, but, with rare exceptions, he may not be jailed along with adults. He may be detained, but only until he is twenty-one years of age. The child is protected against consequences of adult conviction, such as the loss of civil rights, the use of adjudication against him in subsequent proceedings, and disqualification for public employment.

A felony conviction, on the other hand, whether or not there is imprisonment, is a lifelong handicap, but there is the possibility of expunging at least one conviction from a record. As a consequence, trial as an adult has a number of protections not available in a juvenile proceeding, in particular, the applicability of the full panoply of the rules of evidence, the defense of not guilty by reason of insanity, and the unanimity of a jury of twelve. In 1967, in the case of *In re Gault*,[9] the U.S. Supreme Court legalized the juvenile court in considerable measure by establishing that juveniles were owed at least those elements of the due process essential to fundamental fairness (e.g., the right to counsel, written and timely notice of the charges, and the privilege against self-incrimination). In *Gault*, Justice Fortas described juvenile courts as "kangaroo courts" characterized by arbitrariness, ineffectiveness, and the appearance of injustice.[10]

In its 1966 opinion in *Kent*, the U.S. Supreme Court appended eight criteria for waiver, but none specifically called for expert testimony on the prospects for rehabilitation: (1) the seriousness of the alleged offense to the community and whether the protection of the community requires waiver; (2) whether the alleged offense was committed in an aggressive, violent, premeditated, or willful manner; (3) whether the offense was committed against persons or against property; (4) the prosecutive merit of the complaint; that is, whether there is evidence upon which a grand jury may be expected to return an indictment; (5) the desirability of trial and disposition of the entire event in one court with the juvenile associates in the alleged offense, who will be charged with the crime; (6) the sophistication of the juvenile; (7) the record and previous history of the juvenile in context to the previous findings of the court; and (8) the prospects for adequate protection of the public and the likelihood of rehabilitation of the juvenile by use of procedures, services, and facilities currently available to the juvenile court. The court held that juveniles facing waiver are entitled to representation by counsel, access to social service records, and a written statement of the reasons for waiver.

In a second *Kent* case, the juvenile again appealed the juvenile court's waiver of jurisdiction to criminal court, arguing that he was incompetent to be sent over to the criminal court because he was schizophrenic.[11] Writing the opinion of the

U.S. Court of Appeals for the District of Columbia, in 1968, Judge David Bazelon stated that it is implicit in the juvenile court scheme that no criminal punishment is to be the rule—and adult criminal punishment is to be the exception, which must be governed by the particular factors of individual cases. On the facts of the *Kent* case, waiver was deemed inappropriate; allowing insanity to justify waiver, it was said, is not in accord with the prevailing philosophy of the juvenile court. Judge Bazelon wrote: "Since waiver was not necessary for the protection of society and not conducive to [appellant's] rehabilitation, its exercise in this case violated the social welfare philosophy of the Juvenile Court Act. Of course, this philosophy does not forbid all waivers. We only decide here that it does forbid waivers of a seriously ill juvenile."[12] Judge Warren Burger, later chief justice of the Supreme Court, vigorously dissented, saying that Kent, if waived, would have in the criminal court all the rights in relation to his alleged psychiatric problems that he would have in the juvenile court.[13]

Waiver hearings (also known as *amenability* or *transfer hearings*) are designed to address the issue of: the juvenile offender's fit in juvenile court, a determination that rests on the minor's amenability to rehabilitation via those programs, services, and facilities accessible through juvenile court.[14] In 1992, in *Mikulovsky v. State of Wisconsin*,[15] the Wisconsin Supreme Court held that it is not mandatory for a juvenile court to hear expert testimony on a minor's rehabilitative prospects before transferring jurisdiction to adult court. The court apparently followed all the *Kent* criteria on waiver, the objection being that the court failed to hear certain testimony concerning one aspect, to wit, the psychologist's and social worker's opinions as to rehabilitation.

All states have established mechanisms whereby some juveniles may be prosecuted within the criminal justice system. These mechanisms, while having different names among the states, fall into three general categories according to who makes the transfer decision: (1) judicial waiver, (2) statutory exclusion, and (3) concurrent jurisdiction; the decision makers are, respectively, the juvenile court judge, the legislature, and the prosecutor. In judicial waivers, a hearing is held in juvenile court, typically in response to the prosecutor's request that the juvenile court judge waive the juvenile court's jurisdiction over the matter and transfer the juvenile to criminal court for trial in the adult system. Most state statutes limit juvenile waiver by age and offense criteria and by "lack of amenability to treatment" criteria. Judicial waiver provisions vary in the degree of flexibility that allow the court in decision making. Regardless of the degree of flexibility accorded to the court, the waiver process must adhere to certain constitutional principles of fairness, as set out by the Supreme Court in *Kent*.

In a growing number of states, legislatures have statutorily excluded certain young offenders from juvenile court jurisdiction based on age or offense criteria. Some states have defined the upper age of juvenile court jurisdiction as fifteen or sixteen and thus have excluded large number of youth under age eighteen from the juvenile court system. Many states also exclude certain individuals charged with serious offenses from juvenile court jurisdiction.

Under concurrent jurisdiction, state statutes give prosecutors the discretion to file certain cases in either juvenile or criminal court because original jurisdiction is shared by both courts. State concurrent jurisdiction provisions, like other transfer provisions, typically are limited by age and offense criteria. Prosecutorial transfer, unlike judicial waiver, is not subject to judicial review and is not required to meet the due process requirements set out in *Kent*. According to some state appellate courts, prosecutorial transfer is an executive function equivalent to routine charging decisions. Nearly all states rely on a combination of transfer provisions to move juveniles to the criminal system. Moreover, the Sexually Violent Predator laws that have been enacted in some eighteen states have been used to commit young men whose sex offenses were as juveniles.

What about the death penalty? In 1998, the U.S. Supreme Court ruled that the states may not execute anyone who was younger than sixteen at the time of the crime.[16] The 5–3 decision was followed a year later by a ruling allowing execution of those who were between sixteen and eighteen at the time of the crime.[17]

Responding to the sharp rise in juvenile crimes, at least forty-four states since 1992 have adopted new juvenile justice laws that allow more youngsters to be tried as adults. According to the Office of Juvenile Justice, juveniles in 1980 were the offenders in 8 percent of all homicides in the United States. By 1994, that number had doubled to 16 percent. Between 1988 and 1994, the arrest rate for males aged ten to seventeen for violent crimes rose 60 percent. Florida today prosecutes more juveniles as adults than any other state. In the last ten years, the number of teen-agers doing time in adult prisons in the United States has more than doubled. The suicide rate of juveniles in prison is appalling.[18]

Transfer research in the 1970s and 1980s found that, contrary to conventional wisdom, transfers (1) were not necessarily violent offenders, (2) did not necessarily receive harsher sanctions in criminal court that they would have received in juvenile court, (3) were not necessarily incarcerated, and (4) if incarcerated, did not necessarily receive longer sentences than their juvenile court counterparts. Research in the 1990s that compared the recidivism outcomes of transfers and of youth retained in the juvenile system found that transfers were more likely to recidivate within two years. After a six-year follow-up period, there was no difference between the groups in the proporation of offenders who recidivated, although the transferred youth who reoffended did so more quickly and more often, on average, than delinquents handled in juvenile court who reoffended.[19]

Juvenile Reform Legislation and the Trial of Nathaniel Abraham

The paradigm of developments nationwide was the enactment of juvenile reform legislation in 1996 in Michigan and the trial of Nathaniel Abraham. Under the legislation the prosecutor is given the discretion to charge a minor of any age as an adult for certain serious crimes. For those under fourteen, the trial is held not in an adult court (as widely reported), but in family court, and this is significant because the family court has experience with juvenile offenders and rehabilitation services. The most significant aspect of the law is that the sentencing judge has broad sentencing discretion. Upon conviction, the judge may impose a prison sentence not exceeding a similar sentence for an adult. At the other end of the sentencing spectrum, the judge may simply say to the offender, "You are free to go." Most important, the law provides for a *blended sentence*, under which the judge can sentence the defendant to a juvenile rehabilitation program with a review every year until age twenty-one. At or before age twenty-one, the judge makes a decision after hearing from professionals, such as psychiatrists and other treatment specialists who have been dealing with the defendant. If the professionals advise the judge that the defendant has not been rehabilitated and poses a significant danger to the public if released, the judge may continue the sentence into the adult prison system.

The law thus gives prosecutors the ability to protect the public from dangerous offenders, while giving judges flexibility to fashion sentences that fit the nature of the crime and the rehabilitative attitude of the juvenile in question. It allows the court to maintain control over the individual at the end of the age of minority, which was not possible under the prior juvenile laws. That is the rationale of the new law—to protect society from an individual who remains dangerous irrespective of the happenstance of reaching age twenty-one. No longer would an individual "age out of the system."

A number of years ago Michigan and other states mandated that juveniles seventeen or older be tried automatically as an adult (many other states and the federal government require that a defendant be at least eighteen to be automatically considered an adult). In 1923 the Michigan legislature had provided that a probate court judge, who had jurisdiction at the time over juveniles, could waive jurisdiction of those who had attained the age of fifteen and were charged with a felony to a court of general criminal jurisdiction,[20] and by an amendment in 1996, the age was lowered to fourteen.[21] For the fourteen through seventeen age group waiver is discretionary. In the law adopted in 1996, Michigan also allowed prosecutors, without court approval, to try any youth as an adult, no matter how young, but those under fourteen would be tried in family court. State Senator William van Regenmorter, the key force behind the tougher juvenile-offender law in Michigan, said, "I don't think these youngsters are beyond redemption, but whether they are rehabilitable or not is secondary in those rare cases to the incredible danger they pose for all the rest."[22]

The prosecution of Nathaniel Abraham under this law attracted global attention. The photos of the youngster on the front pages of newspapers—his wide-eyed naïveté and his apparent obliviousness to the magnitude of the harm he had done—made it seem nothing short of medieval to entertain the notion of imprisoning him for life. The law that was enacted in 1996 was not intended for youngsters as young as Abraham, who was charged under it when he was eleven, but rather for older adolescents who under the prior law would have been released at age twenty-one, reformed or not. In the decision to try Abraham as an adult, the prosecutor cited the boy's numerous run-ins with the police. By age eleven he was a veteran of contacts with police—twenty-two times, for incidents including arson, thefts, and attacks on older boys with a metal pipe.

In the trial of a minor as an adult, what of competency to confess, competency to stand trial, and criminal responsibility? With police wanting to question Nathaniel Abraham, his mother signed a form waiving his Miranda rights—the right to remain silent and to have an attorney present during questioning. The boy signed, too, and confessed, although defense attorneys later argued that he could not have understood the Miranda warning.[23] If his mother had not been present, he conceivably could have claimed a "Mama Miranda" warning, a right to see his mother. In Michigan, in an appellate opinion in *People v. Givans*,[24] the factors are set forth that a court should consider in deciding whether a statement from a juvenile was properly taken, including a requirement that the offender's parent or guardian be present. Abraham's mother was at his side the entire time he was advised of his rights.

There was a lengthy legal battle to exclude Abraham's confession on the ground that he did not understand Miranda. In Oakland County Family Court, Judge Eugene Arthur Moore, a veteran juvenile court judge, threw out the confession but was reversed on appeal.[25] The Michigan Court of Appeals ruled the confession admissible, the Michigan Supreme Court denied an appeal, and U.S. Supreme Court Justice John Paul Stevens denied an emergency request to hear the matter. Judge Moore said he had considered the evaluations of two psychologists who pegged Abraham's learning and emotional ability at age six to eight. "I'm satisfied he did not know the meaning of the statements," Judge Moore had declared, "or understand the consequence of what he said."

In ruling the confession admissible, the Michigan Court of Appeals said, "We find it a matter of great significance that defendant's mother was present and participated in the entire Miranda-waiver process. Parents normally have the duty and authority to act in furtherance of both the physical and legal needs of their minor children. This responsibility includes deciding whether the minor will undergo medical treatment, deciding what school the minor will attend, signing contracts for or on behalf of the minor, and assisting the minor in deciding whether to waive *Miranda* rights."[26] Of course, a defense attorney always advises a suspect to say nothing to the police, thus cutting off any confession.

What of competency to stand trial? In a footnote, the Michigan Court of Appeals commented, "[N]ot at issue before this court is whether defendant should be tried as an adult or a juvenile. Although the prospect of trying a person of defendant's age for first-degree murder as an adult invites great controversy, we express no opinion regarding this aspect of the case." [27]

Nationwide, prosecutors seek *restoration training* of the minor, and that involves role-playing as well as other training. A number of psychiatrists and psychologists maintain, however, that any minor under the age of thirteen is not competent to stand trial, given the minor's undeveloped mental and cognitive skills and decision-making ability.[28] One must view critically, however, the proposition that juveniles under age thirteen, one and all, do not have the capacity of triability.[29] Apparently out of bias against the criminal prosecution of minors, a number of psychiatrists and psychologists have taken an expanded view of the test of competency to stand trial, almost requiring the accused to have the knowledge of an attorney. In any event, seeing numerous trials on television, youngsters are well versed with the process.

During the two years awaiting trial, while the appeals were taking place, Abraham was held at Children's Village, a secure juvenile detention facility. Daniel Bagdale, who initially alone defended Abraham, before Geoffrey Feiger entered the scene, filed an unsuccessful motion that sought to dismiss the case "based on the fact that the young person in front of the court today is not the same person as two years ago, and the jury will not be able to see what he was like then." When Abraham committed the crime, in 1997, he was small, but two years later, at age thirteen, he had grown considerably. He was less of a sympathetic figure. The trial had been delayed because of the appeals regarding competency to confess and competency to stand trial. The argument was reminiscent of that made in cases of accused persons who plead insanity and are on medication at the time of trial. There it is claimed that their demeanor is not like that at the time of the offense and would mislead the jury.[30]

What of the criteria for triability set out by the U.S. Supreme Court in *Dusky v. United States?*[31] In numerous studies, psychiatrists and psychologists have done empirical studies on *competency* in various contexts, but their practical utility at law is problematical. Competency is not independent of the facts of the particular case, and the concept is often used at law as a ploy to reach a desired result. For whatever it may be worth, among the most extensively researched issues in recent decades has been that of competency to stand trial. Psychometric measures of triability have attempted to translate the criteria in *Dusky* that the accused must have a "sufficient present ability to consult with his lawyer with a reasonable degree of rational understanding" and have a "rational as well as factual understanding of the proceedings against him," into psychological and behavioral "functions" or "competency abilities."[32] Not surprisingly, as in other cases, the studies were of no moment in deciding Abraham's triability.

Judge Moore rejected the argument that Abraham was too young to be triable as an adult. Two independent psychological examinations concluded that he had the mental capacity to aid in his defense, but during the trial he looked quizzically at his attorneys. Every day he asked them, "When can I go home?" During the course of the trial he read *Action* comic books and drew pictures of Superman on a yellow legal pad. A trial judge is supposedly obliged to raise the issue of triability *sua sponte* at any time during the proceedings when a "bona fide doubt" appears as to the defendant's competency.[33] Nationwide, more often than not, when a minor aged fourteen to sixteen is bound over to the criminal court, they are returned to the juvenile court on the ground of incompetency to stand trial.

In an interview on *60 Minutes*,[34] under questioning by correspondent Ed Bradley, Abraham appeared to understand little of the legal process swirling around him. When asked if he understands that the prosecution has to prove its case beyond a reasonable doubt, his answer was "not really." When Bradley asked what he thinks the term means, he said, "She has to prove me guilty with a big explanation," referring to the assistant prosecutor who was trying the case. The judge's job, he added, is "just to sit there."

Under the 1996 law, Abraham was tried in family court, though tried as an adult; he was not transferred to criminal court, as is done in the case of minors over age fourteen. Abraham would not have found a judge more sympathetic to him than Judge Moore. Even with a conviction, the judge could have done anything he wanted, including returning Abraham home. Hence, the triability issue had less significance than in a trial in a criminal court.

At the trial six mental health professionals gave expert testimony on Abraham's criminal responsibility, with only two of them having interviewed him. The defense experts, five of them, all concluded that he did not have the mental ability to concoct a murder plot. "He's not very smart. He is operating on the level of a six-year-old. He has no ability to control his impulses," said child psychiatrist Thomas Gaultiere, who reviewed Abraham's medical record. Dr. Margaret Stack, a psychologist with the Michigan State Forensic Center, who examined Abraham, said, "His level of understanding is at a very, very primitive level. Nate does not have the capacity to carry out a plan." Michael Abramsky, a psychologist who frequently serves as an expert, testified that children at age eleven are still developing a moral code and that Abraham could not have understood the consequences of his actions. Abraham, he said, was a frightened child raising himself on the streets who began acting aggressively as a means of survival. Psychiatrist Gerald Shiener told the jurors that eleven-year-old children lack the mental capacity to form the intent necessary to plan and carry out first-degree murder. "A child that age," he said, "can't understand the full effects of what a weapon might do, and the consequences." He said that his review of the test and assessments of Abraham show the boy was functioning on the intellectual and emotional level of a six- to eight-year-old when he was eleven.

In cross-examination, the prosecutor pointed out that Abraham appeared to be able to plan; he talked about the shooting beforehand, he obtained bullets, he loaded the gun, and he shot it. For the prosecution, psychologist Lynne Schwartz, who examined Abraham in 1998, testified, "He knew what bullets were for. He did load a gun. He did shoot. The best way to gauge whether someone has the capacity to do something is look at what they do." The defense contended that the killing was a freak accident, that Abraham was shooting at a clump of trees and the bullet ricocheted and killed the victim.

The tactic of defense lawyers in criminal cases is, more often than not, to put the jury in a fog, as was done in the O. J. Simpson case, where the jury was utterly bewildered by the DNA evidence. The defense attorneys and experts blew a lot of smoke. After all, the state has to prove its case beyond a reasonable doubt, and the fog would create a doubt. Invariably, closing arguments by the defense in criminal cases are like those in a dog-bite case where defense counsel argued: (1) the defendant's dog didn't bite the plaintiff, (2) the plaintiff provoked the dog into biting him, and (3) the defendant didn't own the dog.

In the *Abraham* case the defense attorney, Geoffrey Feiger, contended in closing argument that Abraham did not intend or was not capable of intending to kill; and, for the first time, he slipped in the contention that the bullet did not come from Abraham's gun (ballistic experts at trial without challenge established that it did come from his gun). He would thus give a rationale to the jury to acquit or bring in a lesser verdict than first-degree murder. His two-and-half-hour closing argument was mainly an exhortation for nullification, and that has been the type of argument made by defense counsel in subsequent cases involving minors as criminal defendants.[35] The state, on the other hand, is precluded from making a "civic duty argument."[36]

The judge instructed the jury, "If prosecutors failed to prove intent, or you feel he suffers from diminished capacity, then you must find him not guilty of first-degree murder." The charge against Abraham was in the first degree, with intent to kill. The jury was advised that they could consider the lesser crime of second-degree murder, which carries up to life in prison, or negligent use of a firearm causing death, which carries up to two years in prison. As Feiger would have it, the judge did not instruct on lesser crimes of manslaughter or negligent homicide. Feiger went all-or-nothing—that is to say, the jury was either to convict Abraham of an intentional crime or return a not guilty verdict—thinking that the jury would not find him guilty of an intentional crime.[37]

During the course of deliberation the jury questioned the judge about elements needed to convict or acquit Abraham of second-degree murder. A conviction for second-degree murder requires that a defendant must have intended a high risk of death or great bodily harm. In a note sent to the judge, they asked, "Does 'intended to cause high risk of death/harm' imply that the defendant knew the consequences of his actions?" The judge told them to rely on his instructions to them regarding the law. Empirical studies have found that instructed jurors have no better grasp of the law than uninstructed jurors.[38] Judges adhere to their boilerplate instructions, for they may be reversed by what is said in an untested or informal instruction. The jury returned a verdict of second-degree murder.

Posttrial Discussion of the *Abraham* Case

The *Abraham* case began as a cause célèbre about the prosecution of minors as adults, but with the conviction it became a racist cause célèbre. Many said the law is used to single out blacks. A study, *The Color of Justice* by the Justice Policy Institute, reports that in California, where the study was done, minority youths are more than twice as likely as their white counterparts to be transferred out of the juvenile court system and tried as adults, and once transferred to the adult system, they were 18.4 times more likely to be jailed than were young white offenders. The report presumes racism but does not mention amenability to rehabilitation.[39] Among blacks nationally, 69 percent of births are to unwed mothers, more than double that among whites. Detroit, with a predominantly black population, ranks number one in births to unmarried parents among the nation's fifty largest cities.[40]

In posttrial interviews, the jurors said that they struggled in separating their emotions and the law. It was, they said, a gut-wrenching experience. They deliberated seventeen hours on four separate days. A few members of the jury spoke briefly about their deliberations. Of the testimony of the five psychologists and psychiatrists who said that Nathaniel Abraham was not smart enough, old enough, or cunning enough to murder somebody, the jurors said that they took the expert testimony into consideration, but they mostly relied on their experiences dealing with eleven-year-olds, the age Abraham was when he carried out the killing. "We gave Nathaniel every benefit of the doubt," said the jury foreman. "We came to the conclusion that someone that age can form intent, though we had doubts that the actual intent was to kill. We came to the conclusion that the gun doesn't raise up automatically. There was an intentional action." Another juror said, "He had a gun, loaded it and shot. Then there was a confession." The jury dropped the first-degree murder charge, finding insufficient premeditation. Another juror said that they were unaware of Abraham's history of run-ins with the police.

Sentencing of Nathaniel Abraham

The day of sentencing was marked by hundreds of protesters, including Rev. Al Sharpton and others from New York, who circled the courthouse chanting "Free Nathaniel" and "No Justice, No Peace," as African drums played in the background. They were relieved by the sentence. Judge Moore did not sentence Abraham to prison nor did he impose a blended sentence as requested by the prosecution. Instead, he not only ignored but criticized Michigan's law adopted in 1996 allowing youngsters under fourteen to be charged as adults. He sent Abraham to a juvenile facility where he will remain as under the prior law until he reaches the age of twenty-one, at which time he will be freed regardless of whether he has been rehabilitated.

In a twenty-minute speech, the judge called Abraham a symbol of society's failures and called for national and local juvenile justice reform. He called the case a wake-up call that our children are in trouble. "The safety net of a delayed sentence removes too much of the urgency," he said. "We can't continue to see incarceration as a long-term solution." The judge exhorted state officials to improve the state's system for handling juvenile offenders. "I urge the Legislature," the judge said, "to lean toward improving the resources and programs within the juvenile system rather than diverting more youth into an already failed adult system."[41]

How should the law handle minors who kill or who are hardened sociopaths? Should juvenile court judges, not prosecutors, decide whether minors charged with serious crimes be charged as adults or minors? Should there be multiple sentencing of minors, that is, at age eighteen or twenty-one the minor would appear in court for resentencing, at which time the judge would hear evidence about any rehabilitation? Would this rolling sentencing provide an incentive to the minor to improve his life behind bars? Such a system, it is argued, would hold minors responsible for their acts while recognizing that they are minors.[42]

The Lesson of the *Abraham* Case

A dysfunctional family in a dysfunctional environment is likely to produce dysfunctional children. So it was in the case of Nathaniel Abraham. His world was one of neglect, unheeded pleas, and a neighborhood where he could roam the streets alone at night, with no one intervening; where adult eyes turned the other way; and where the scene was one of addicts and hookers. A victim of a dysfunctional family in a dysfunctional environment, he became a menace. Children from dysfunctional families usually have some hope when they are exposed to functional adults outside their immediate family, but when these are absent, the situation is bleak. That is the lesson of the *Abraham* case.[43]

Psychiatric Services for Minors

National studies show that only an estimated one in five children with mental problems receive treatment, for reasons ranging from lack of services to parental neglect. It is estimated that as few as 5 percent of children with serious mental problems—or one in twenty—receive psychiatric help. For the economically disadvantaged, the situation is dire. The number of Medicaid-eligible children needing mental health services that actually receives them varies among the states, depending on the difficulty that psychiatrists have in coping with the state's Medicaid program.[44] They say the technicalities cause so much trouble for them that they cannot hope to accept Medicaid patients and keep their practices solvent. Nationwide, hospital beds for children and adolescents with psychiatric disorders continue to be cut. Some hospitals have discontinued hospital treatment altogether.[45]

Notes

1. In the case of State v. Doherty, 2 Overt. Tenn. Rep. 79 (1806), Mary Doherty, a youngster of twelve or thirteen years, was prosecuted for the murder of her father. Under the law of Tennessee at the time, if a person under fourteen does an act, such as that charged in the indictment, the presumption of law is that the person cannot discern between right and wrong. Under seven, the individual as a matter of law is deemed incapable of committing a crime. The jury in this case, after deliberation of a few hours, returned a verdict of not guilty. While in jail awaiting trial and during the trial the accused spoke only a few monosyllables. A note appended to the original report of the case indicates that on the day after her trial she was observed near the court quite animated and smiling at the judges in a way that indicated her pleasure with what turned out to be deception.

2. III Mass. Records 101.

3. F. B. McCarthy & J. G. Carr (eds.), *Juvenile Law and Its Processes* (Indianapolis: Bobbs-Merrill, 1980), p. 1.

4. Ibid. See also S. Fox, "Juvenile Justice Reform: An Historical Perspective," *Stan. L. Rev.* 22 (1970): 1187.

5. C. Wetzstein, "Kids' Court Centennial," *Insight*, Oct. 4–11, 1999, p. 30.

6. P. W. Tappan, *Juvenile Delinquency* (New York: McGraw-Hill, 1949), p. 167.

7. A collection of seventy-eight appellate decisions in juvenile law that span the range of juvenile opinion in this field during the twentieth century appears in J. C. Watkins, *Selected Cases on Juvenile Justice in the Twentieth Century* (Levinston, N.Y.: Mellen Press, 1999). In *The Juvenile Court & The Progressives* (Champaign: University of Illinois Press, 2000), Victoria Getis examines the Cook County Juvenile Court and describes the court's intrinsic flaws and the source of its debilitation in our own time.

8. 383 U.S. 541 (1966).

9. 387 U.S. 1 (1967).

10. 387 U.S. at 18, 19, 26, 28.

11. 401 F.2d 408 (D.C. Cir. 1968).

12. 401 F.2d at 412. Insanity as a defense in a juvenile court proceeding was reviewed in a New Jersey case, which held that a juvenile could be adjudicated a delinquent even though insane. The court noted the distinction between a juvenile case and an indictable offense; the focus in a juvenile proceeding is not upon the commission of the act itself but upon the consequences of it. In drawing this distinction, the court noted that an adjudication of delinquency brought about the protective and rehabilitative interests of the court. In re State of Interest of H.C., 106 N.J. Super. 583, 256 A.2d 322 (1969). A number of states, however, have found the right to assert an insanity defense to be an essential of "due process and fair treatment" that must be provided to a juvenile charged with delinquency. See Chatman v. Virginia, 518 S.E.2d 847 (Va. App. 1999); Louisiana v. Causey, 363 So.2d 472 (La. 1978); In re M.G.S., 72 Cal. Rptr. 808 (Cal. App. 1968).

13. 401 F.2d at 414. See T. Grisso, "Juvenile Offenders and Mental Illness," *Psychiatry, Psychology & Law* 6 (1999): 143.

14. B. H. Gross, "The Fitness of Juvenile Court," *J. Forensic Sci.* 44 (1999): 1199; C. Slobogin, "Treating Kids Right: Deconstructing and Reconstructing the Amenability to Treatment Concept," *J. Contemp. Legal Issues* 10 (1999): 299.

15. 196 N.W.2d 748 (Wis. 1972).

16. Thompson v. Oklahoma, 487 U.S. 815 (1988).

17. Stanford v. Kentucky, 492 U.S. 361 (1989). A ten-year-old black child was hanged in Louisiana in 1855, and a Cherokee Indian child of the same age was hanged in Arkansas in 1885. See V. L. Streib, "Death Penalty for Children: The American Experience with Capital Punishment for Crimes Committed While under Age Eighteen," *Okla. L. Rev.* 36 (1983): 613; cited in Thompson v. Oklahoma, 487 U.S. at 828 n. 27.

18. M. Talbot, "The Maximum Security Adolescent," *New York Times Magazine*, Sept. 10, 2000, p. 41.

19. Report, *Juvenile Transfers to Criminal Court in the 1990's: Lessons Learned from Four Studies*" (Washington, D.C.: U.S. Department of Justice, 2000). In the book *Cries Unheard* (New York: Henry Holt, 1998), Gitta Sereny reports on the change in the law in England and focuses on the case of Mary Bell, who in 1968, at age eleven, was tried and convicted of murdering two small boys in Newcastle Upon Tyne. From ages eleven to sixteen, she was confined in a secure unit (a locked educational establishment for a small number of youngsters held for serious offenses), and at age sixteen as required under the law she was sent to a maximum-security women's prison, where she remained until she was twenty-three.

20. Mich. Pub. Acts 1923, No. 105, sec. 6, amending Act 325 of Laws of 1907 that had a cut-off age of seventeen.

21. Mich. Pub. Act 409 (1996).

22. Quoted in L. L. Brasier, "Guilty at 13: What's Ahead for Abraham?" *Detroit Free Press*, Nov. 17, 1999, p. 1.

23. Researchers in the 1980s said that adolescents did about as well as adults in hypothetical decision-making situations, but that view has changed. Psychologist Thomas Grisso's research on Miranda waivers showed significant differences. While adolescents may reason well cognitively, they also seem to make choices that adults would view as bad choices. So

the question arises, do youths arrive at their decisions differently? The hypothetical theory now being studied is that about the age of thirteen to fourteen, there are no dramatic differences in capacity to understand information and reason between adolescents and adults, but psychosocial factors are more likely to be different. For example, compared to adults, youths do not give as much weight to long-range consequences, they are more accepting of risk, and they are more influenced by peers. T. Grisso & R. G. Schwartz, *Youth on Trial: A Developmental Perspective on Juvenile Justice* (Chicago: University of Chicago Press, 2000); M. N. Norko, "Guttmacher Lecture," *Newsletter of Am. Acad. Psychiatry & Law* 25 (Sept. 2000): 1.

24. 227 Mich. App. 113, 575 N.W.2d 84 (1997).

25. People v. Abraham, 234 Mich. App. 640 (1999).

26. 234 Mich. App. at 651.

27. 234 Mich. App. at 654 n. 9. In In re Carey, 615 N.W.2d 742 (Mich. App. 2000), the Michigan Court of Appeals urged that the state supreme court promulgate rules of procedure for juvenile competency determinations or that the legislature to enact any statutory provisions it deems necessary. 615 N.W.2d at 748 n. 4.

28. See T. Grisso, *Forensic Evaluation of Juveniles* (Sarasota, Fla.: Professional Resource Press, 1998); see also D. Cooper, "Juveniles Understanding of Trial-Related Information: Are They Competent Defendants?" *Behav. Sci. & Law* 15 (1997): 167; V. L. Cowden & G. R. McKee, "Competency to Stand Trial in Juvenile Delinquency Proceedings: Cognitive Maturity and the Attorney-Client Relationship," *J. Family Law* 33 (1994–95): 631; T. Grisso, "Competence of Adolescents as Trial Defendants," *Psych., Pub. Pol'y & L.* 3 (1997): 3; E. S. Scott, N. D. Repucci, & J. Woolard, "Evaluating Adolescent Decision Making in a Legal Context," *Law & Human Behavior* 19 (1995): 221.

29. Richard III at age thirteen was King of England—he read prodigiously. The media frequently interviews minors on worldly affairs. In the Russian magazine *Ogonek* (May 2001, p. 3), six youngsters of ages seven to twelve were asked the question, "What must be done in order to improve the country?" They gave informed and interesting answers. In *St. Petersburg Times* (May 22, 2001, p. 15), an eleventh grade student in Moscow wrote an informed op-ed article on trying to make sense of the chaos in the world today. Centuries ago, although minors under the age of seven were not held responsible under the common law, they were regarded as miniature adults. In the tenth century, artists were unable to depict a child except as an adult on a smaller scale. See Philippe Ariès, *Centuries of Childhood* (New York: Random House, 1962).

30. Riggins v. Nevada, 112 S. Ct. 2752 (1992); State v. Jojola, 553 P.2d 1296 (N.M. 1976); see B. J. Winick, "Psychotropic Medication in the Criminal Trial Process: The Constitutional and Therapeutic Implications of Riggins vs. Nevada," *N.Y. Law School J. Human Rights* 10 (1993): 637.

31. 362 U.S. 402 (1960).

32. On a juvenile's competency to stand trial, see R. Barnum & T. Grisso, "Competence to Stand Trial in Juvenile Court in Massachusetts: Issues of Therapeutic Jurisprudence," *New Eng. J. Crim. & Civil Confinement*," 20 (1994): 321; T. Grisso, "Dealing with Juveniles' Competence to Stand Trial: What We Need to Know," *Quinnipac L. Rev.* 18 (1999): 371; G. R. McKee, "Competency to Stand Trial in Preadjudicatory Juveniles and Adults," *J. Am. Acad. Psychiatry & Law* 26 (1998): 88. In 1999 Arkansas enacted legislation that provides that juveniles are to be evaluated according to "age-appropriate" standards, not by the traditional standards used to assess competency of adults. Ark. Code Ann., sec. 9–27–502 (1999). In Golden v. State, 341 Ark. 963, 21 S.W.3d 801 (2000), the Arkansas Supreme Court held that juveniles have a due process right to have their competency determined prior to adjudication. The Arizona legislature enacted legislation that provides that developmental immaturity can be used as grounds for finding a juvenile incompetent to participate in juvenile proceedings or to be transferred to criminal court. Ariz. Rev. Stat. Ann., sec. 8–291 (2000).

33. Pate v. Robinson, 383 U.S. 375 (1966).

34. Nov. 7, 1999.

35. Such were also the arguments, for example, in the trial of Nathaniel Brazill, a fourteen-year-old boy who beat a six-year-old playmate to death. D. Canedy, "Boy Who Killed Teacher is Found Guilty of Murder," *New York Times*, May 17, 2001, p. 12.

36. See R. Slovenko, "Jury Nullification," *J. Psychiatry & Law* 22 (1994): 165. For a contemporary critique of nullification, see G. Willis, *A Necessary Evil: A History of American Distrust of Government* (New York: Simon & Schuster, 1999).

37. That tactic was also used and backfired in the widely publicized case of Jean Harris, who was given a fifteen-year-to-life sentence for killing Dr. Herman Tarnower. J. Harris, *Stories from Prison* (New York: Scribners, 1988).

38. M. J. Saks, "What Do Jury Experiments Tell Us about How Juries (Should) Make Decisions?" *So. Cal. Interdisc. L.J.* 6 (1997): 1.

39. M. Males & D. Macallair, *The Color of Justice: An Analysis of Juvenile Adult Court Transfer in California* (San Francisco: Justice Policy Institute, 2000); T. Lewin, "Racial Discrepancy Found in Trying of Youths," *New York Times*, Feb. 3, 2000, p. 14.

40. B. Johnson, "Detroit's Single Families Define the Real State of the City," *Detroit News*, Feb. 4, 2000, p. 10.

41. Quoted in K. Bradsher, "Boy Who Killed Gets 7 Years; Judge Says Law Is Too Harsh," *New York Times*, Jan. 14, 2000, p. 1.

42. See P. T. Murphy, "Convicted at 14," *New York Times*, May 17, 2001, p. 23.

43. See, in general: D. F. Flannery & C. R. Huff (eds.), *Youth Violence: Prevention, Intervention, and Social Policy* (Washington, D.C.: American Psychiatric Press, 1999); J. C. Howell et al. (eds.), *Sourcebook on Serious, Violent, and Chronic Juvenile Offenders* (Thousand Oaks, Cal.: Sage, 1995); R. Loeber & D. P. Farrington (eds.), *Serious and Violent Juvenile Offenders: Risk Factors and Successful Interventions* (Thousand Oaks, Cal.: Sage, 1998); M. Sugar (ed.), *Responding to Adolescent Needs* (New York: Spectrum, 1980); J. Winterdyk (ed.), *Juvenile Justice Systems: International Perspectives* (Toronto: Canadian Scholars' Press, 1997); C. L. Scott, "Juvenile Violence," *Psychiatric Clin. North America* 22, no. 1 (1999): 71. Dr. Renatus Hartogs described Lee Harvey Oswald, at age thirteen, when he saw him at a detention home for New York City's juvenile delinquents, as being potentially explosive and suggested that he receive psychiatric treatment so that his inner violence —what might be called his silent rage—would not later erupt and cause harm. The recommendation was not carried out. As a young adult, following sojourns in the Soviet Union, he assassinated President Kennedy. R. Hartogs & L. Freeman, *The Two Assassins* (New York: Crowell, 1965).

44. Abuses in billing for private psychiatric hospitalization for minors is discussed in J. Sharkey, *Bedlam: Greed, Profiteering, and Fraud in a Mental Health System Gone Crazy* (New York: St. Martin's Press, 1994).

45. In eleven London boroughs the police are setting up a secret database of children as young as three who they fear might grow up to become criminals. Youngsters who behave badly or commit trivial misdemeanors will be put on the confidential register so that they can be monitored and supervised throughout childhood. Liberty, the organization that campaigns for civil liberties, expressed concern about the plan. D. Bamber, "Naughty Children to Be Registered as Potential Criminals," *Sunday Telegraph*, Nov. 25, 2001, p. 4.

13
Alcoholism

Alcohol has been used medicinally and in religious ceremonies for thousands of years, and it also has a long history of recreational use. According to the Old Testament, Noah "drank of the wine, and was drunken."[1] The Old Testament condemns drunkenness, but not alcohol. The Book of Proverbs proclaims, "Give strong drink unto him that is ready to perish, and wine unto those that be of heavy hearts. Let him drink, and forget his poverty, and remember his misery no more."[2] Gintaras Patacka, the popular Lithuanian writer who was hospitalized in psychiatric institutions on numerous occasions, often in relation to alcoholic episodes, wrote in one of his poems: "Alcohol is my god, it gives me power, stirs up my frozen blood, gives my lips song."[3] Moderation was recommended by no less an authority than Genghis Khan: "A soldier must not get drunk oftener than once a week. It would, of course, be better if he did not get drunk at all, but one should not expect the impossible."[4] The total prohibition declared in 1919 in Amendment 18 of the U.S. Constitution of the manufacture, sale, or transportation of intoxicating liquors lasted until 1933, by which time the bootlegger Al Capone ruled Chicago and Joseph P. Kennedy, father of a murdered-president-to-be, was a millionaire.

Alcohol (or drugs) has a variety of effects on people—some become amorous or sentimental, others simply sleepy, and some become violent. The use of alcohol may be related to criminal behavior, our focus in this chapter, in several ways.

1. The condition of being intoxicated in public may result in a charge of public drunkenness, vagrancy, disorderly conduct, or disturbing the peace. Of approximately six million arrests each year in the United States, fully one-third are for drunkenness.[5]

2. The release of impulses caused by the use of alcohol may result in a wide variety of crimes, including violence, sexual misconduct, robbery, burglary, forgery, and traffic violations. The intoxication may so impair the individual's judgment that he is unable to plan his behavior rationally or to appreciate its consequences. In some cases, termed *acute pathologic alcoholic intoxication*, the individual may be so sensitive to relatively small amounts of alcohol that just two ounces of whiskey or a can of beer may precipitate impulsive aggressive behavior. Mental illness and the use of alcohol especially portend dangerousness.

3. Prolonged intoxication may produce a brain syndrome characterized by a degree of confusion sufficient to lead to drastic misinterpretation of reality. An individual who has such a condition may engage in assaults or other types of antisocial behavior. Severe acute intoxication may also result in hallucinosis and delirium tremens accompanied by a high degree of disorganized behavior or amnesia. Thus the defendant's capacity to stand trial may be put in issue, resulting in pretrial commitment to the criminally insane unit of a mental hospital. Also, chronic alcoholism is a basis for suspension of a driver's license.

4. Prolonged use of alcohol may decrease the individual's capacity for effective participation in noncriminal activities. Although not intoxicated at the time an offense was committed, the individual may have been so incapacitated by the chronic use of alcohol that he was unemployable and could do little else than commit crime. In such a case, however, the use of alcohol is not deemed to be the proximate cause of the crime.[6]

Processing of Cases

The way of the law in dealing with alcoholism or alcohol-precipitated crimes (or with drug addiction or drug-precipitate crimes) has been a matter of much controversy. The criminalization or the hospitalization of the alcoholic (or drug addict) equally evoke controversy.

In an effort to do away with the punitive or moralistic approach, Alcoholics Anonymous (AA) termed alcoholism an illness, and the National Council on Alcoholism said, "Alcoholism is a disease." While the American Medical Association, the American College of Physicians, and the American Psychiatric Association also accept the concept of alcoholism as disease, Alcoholics Anonymous and the National Council emphasize, however, that alcoholism is not a mental disease or illness. Alcoholics do not wish to be confined in mental hospitals with "crazy people," and many feel that psychiatrists cannot do anything for them. They call alcoholism an "addiction" rather than a "disease" (alcohol is a narcotic depressant, and it is addictive— highly addictive to some individuals, more habit forming than addictive to others). William G. Wilson (1895–1971), known as "Bill W," developed the twelve-step program of group psychotherapy for the treatment of alcoholism (Alcoholics Anonymous), and it evolved during the 1960s and 1970s to cover a wide range of addictive or assumed addictive behaviors (including food-related disorders, codependency, and tobacco addiction, as well as the impact of addictive behavior on family members (through Al-Anon).[7]

The narcotic addict, the psychopath, and most alcoholics, however, are often said to lack motivation for treatment. As Dr. Sandor Rado, one of Freud's colleagues, put it: "Why should one give up the pleasures obtained from drink or drugs for the pains of reality? It takes maturity."[8] The alcoholic in Mary Chase's *Harvey* had a congenial companion in a huge, imaginary white rabbit, and he was not about to give that up for harsh reality. The alcoholic's game allegedly is to find a caregiver or a group like Alcoholics Anonymous to attend to him.[9]

The alcoholic's lack of motivation, though, may result from his intuitive judgment that therapists are not motivated in treating alcoholics. The counter-transference disposition of the therapist requires nice patients, mature patients, patients who beg for treatment. The alcoholic, the narcotic addict, and the psychopath do not usually meet these requirements.

It is generally difficult for the alcoholic to gain hospital admission, either voluntary or involuntary. At the behest of hospital superintendents, many states have deleted "drunkenness" or "substance abuse disorder" from commitment laws, and in those states alcoholism or substance abuse, of itself, is not a ground for commitment. Often hospital commitment can be accomplished only through the use of a cover diagnosis. As one psychiatrist has quipped, if the person says, "I am nervous, therefore I drink," he will be admitted, but if he says, "I drink, therefore I am nervous," he will not be admitted.

The mental care and treatment laws of many states provide that a person may be admitted to a state mental hospital as a voluntary patient if there are available accommodations and he believes he is in need of care or treatment and if the head of the hospital concurs. The law in a number of jurisdictions also provides that a peace officer may take into custody without a warrant any person whom he reasonably believes to be mentally ill and may injure himself or others if allowed to remain at liberty. The peace officer may take the individual to a state hospital instead of jail. Hospital superintendents often refuse admission to alcoholics, however, because they would soon fill up the hospital.

From all reports, it would appear that the endeavors of the prison system, particularly in regard to the alcoholic and drug addict, are Sisyphusian. Sisyphus for all eternity was doomed by the gods to roll a rock up a steep mountain slope, where, just before reaching the top, the rock would slip away and roll down again to the bottom, where Sisyphus was fated always to begin anew. So, too, the alcoholic is arrested, sent to jail for a short period, dried up and cleaned up, and then returned to the streets, where he is soon arrested again.

Deployment of police on the street and at the station house, the commitment of jail space and facilities, the time expended by judges, court administrators, and courtrooms: all these constitute an enormous burden and drain on a justice system already overtaxed by felony cases. The cost in public funds of maintaining this ineffective and wasteful process has reached astronomical proportions. The marchers in a revolving-door process continue to parade up to the judge's bench.

The marchers in a revolving-door process parade up to the hospital door as well. And the suicide rate of recovered alcoholics is five times greater than that of the general population.

The Crime of Public Drunkenness

Virtually every jurisdiction makes public drunkenness a crime. The Washington, D.C. Area Council on Alcoholism for years has decried the nationwide revolving-door policy as accomplishing nothing. Notwithstanding the inadequacy of treatment programs, the council took the position that it is essential to obtain a legal declaration that chronic alcoholics should be regarded as sick persons rather than as criminals. Hence, the council, backed by the National Capital Area Civil Liberties Union, made a test case of *Easter v. District of Columbia.*[10]

DeWitt Easter, a chronic alcoholic, had been arrested more than seventy times in the course of his fifty-nine years. Shunting Easter in and out of jail had obviously done him no good but had cost taxpayers thousands of dollars. Outpatient treatment at the D.C. Alcoholic Rehabilitation Center likewise had been ineffective. Council attorneys entered a plea of not guilty to the charge of public intoxication. The basis of the plea was that Easter's chronic addiction to alcohol resulted in a lack of self-control. The defense contended that Easter was a sick man and had simply exhibited in public the symptoms of his illness. It was argued that Easter had no control over his drunkenness and that he had not willfully violated the law. The trial court, however, ruled that Easter's act was voluntary and found him guilty, imposing a ninety-day suspended sentence. On appeal, the D.C. Court of Appeals acknowledged that facilities for treatment of alcoholics were inadequate but agreed with the trial court that since Easter had appeared drunk in public voluntarily he should be punished accordingly.[11] The decision was in accord with a long line of cases that hold an alcoholic responsible for public drunkenness because he started drinking voluntarily.

Seeking to establish a new precedent, the U.S. Court of Appeals for the District of Columbia granted leave to appeal. Here, attorneys for Easter successfully contended that punishment for his sickness constituted "cruel and unusual punishment" in violation of the Eighth Amendment. The criminal law is supposed to punish the doing of an act, not status or a state of being. Yet when an individual is arrested for drunkenness or vagrancy, it may be said that he is charged because of his status.

The court held that when expert medical and psychiatric evidence establishes that a defendant is a chronic alcoholic who has lost control over his use of alcoholic beverages, chronic alcoholism is a defense to a charge of public intoxication.[12] In its ruling, the court said that a judge may commit a chronic alcoholic for medical treatment but not for punishment. The court emphasized that its ruling does not absolve the voluntarily intoxicated person of criminal acts committed under the influence of alcohol. Thus, under this ruling, casually drunken people found in public places can still be prosecuted under anti-intoxication statutes. In a separate concurring opinion, Judge McGowan wrote: "The community will not tolerate uncontrolled drunkenness in public places and will insist that the police act to remove it as before. The power of the police in this respect is, in my view, unaffected by today's ruling."[13]

At about the same time the Court of Appeals for the Fourth Circuit entertained a case involving Joe Driver, who had been arrested 203 times during his lifetime for public drunkenness. This court also ruled that the conviction of a chronic alcoholic for public intoxication violates the prohibition against cruel and unusual punishment.[14] It was said:

The alcoholic's presence in public is not his act. It may be likened to the movement of an imbecile, or a person in a delirium. The upshot of our decision is that the state cannot stamp an unpretending chronic alcoholic as a criminal if his drunken public display is involuntary as a result of disease. However, nothing we have said precludes appropriate detention of him for treatment and rehabilitation so long as he is not marked a criminal.

The Supreme Court decision four years earlier, in 1962, in *Robinson v. California*,[15] provided the inspiration for these challenges to the public drunkenness statutes. In *Robinson*, the Court struck down a California statute that made it a criminal offense to use, be under the influence of, or "be addicted to the use of narcotics."[16] The facts showed that the accused was not under the influence of narcotics at the time of his arrest and did not manifest withdrawal symptoms thereafter. Justice Stewart, speaking for the majority, and Justice Douglas, concurring, referred to addiction as an illness. Justice Douglas said:

> If addicts can be punished for their addiction, then the insane can also be punished for their insanity. Each has a disease and each must be treated as a sick person. . . . This prosecution has no relationship to the curing of an illness. Indeed, it cannot, for the prosecution is aimed at penalizing an illness, rather than with providing medical care for it. We would forget the teachings of the Eighth Amendment if we allowed sickness to be made a crime and permitted sick people to be punished for being sick. This age of enlightenment cannot tolerate such barbarous action.[17]

The Supreme Court in *Robinson* noted that mental illness, leprosy, and venereal diseases, all of which were at one time thought to be problems of morality and therefore criminal, could not now constitutionally be made criminal offenses. The Court reasoned that narcotic addiction is in the same category as those other diseases and held the California statute unconstitutional.[18] In the course of holding it violative of the cruel and unusual punishment clause of the Constitution to punish a person criminally for the illness of addiction, the Court in *Robinson* suggested it would be constitutionally proper to confine addicts involuntarily for the express purpose of treatment. The dictum was heralded as the coming of the therapeutic state.

The Court's invalidation of the crime of addiction indicates that it is possible and necessary to separate the defendant's acts from his status. Does someone who is publicly drunk manifest behavior that is punishable by the very fact that he is drunk in public? In 1968, the Supreme Court was asked in *Powell v. Texas*,[19] to apply the *Robinson* doctrine to prohibit a state from punishing a chronic alcoholic for public drunkenness.[20] Unable to agree on the rationale of *Robinson*, the Court, in a 5–4 decision, held that a showing of alcoholism alone is not a sufficient defense. Five justices, however, were prepared to strike down such a conviction where the defendant could show that he appeared in public not by his own volition but under a compulsion that was part of his chronic alcoholic condition.

Leroy Powell had been convicted of being in a state of intoxication in a public place. In affirming the conviction, Justice Marshall, speaking for the majority, said that one could not "conclude, on the state of this record or on the current state of medical knowledge, that chronic alcoholics in general, and Leroy Powell in particular, suffer from such an irresistible compulsion to drink and to get drunk in public that they are utterly unable to control their performance of either or both of these acts and thus cannot be deterred at all from public intoxication." Moreover, he said, *Robinson* stands only for the proposition that an individual cannot be punished for mere status but must engage in some behavior or commit some act before criminal sanctions can be invoked against him. The Texas statute, he said, met this requirement because its sanctions were directed at socially offensive behavior. He wrote:

> *Robinson* so viewed brings this Court but a very small way into the substantive criminal law. And unless *Robinson* is so viewed it is difficult to see any limiting principle that would serve to prevent this Court from becoming, under the aegis of the cruel and unusual punishment clause, the ultimate arbiter of the standards of criminal responsibility, in diverse areas of the criminal law, throughout the country.
>
> It is suggested in dissent that *Robinson* stands for the "simple" but "subtle" principle that "criminal penalties may not be inflicted upon a person for being in a condition he is powerless to change." . . . In that view, appellant's "condition" of public intoxication was "occasioned by a compulsion symptomatic of the disease" of chronic alcoholism. . . . Whatever may be the merits of such a doctrine of criminal responsibility, it surely cannot be said to follow from *Robinson*. The entire thrust of *Robinson*'s interpretation of the cruel and unusual punishment clause is that criminal penalties may be inflicted only if the accused has committed some act, has engaged in some behavior, which society has an interest in preventing, or perhaps in historical common law terms has committed some actus reus. It thus does not deal with the question of whether certain conduct cannot constitutionally be punished because it is, in some sense, "involuntary" or "occasioned by a compulsion."[21]

As Justice Marshall wrote, the conclusion to be drawn from *Powell* and *Robinson* is that the federal Constitution goes only "a very small way into the substantive criminal law." The concept of a voluntary act is left to the states, and while there is some disagreement, the requirement of a voluntary act for criminal responsibility has usually not been taken to preclude prosecution for alcohol or drug use, even by individuals who might be considered as addicted by their use.

It is significant to observe that Justice Marshall took note of the unavailability of treatment methods or facilities for the alcoholic and said, in effect, that it is better to use the penal process for a limited time than to impose the same de facto conditions for an indefinite period. Therapeutic commitment not being very effective, Justice Marshall was ready to backtrack on it.[22]

In a concurring opinion, Justice White suggested that punishment of a chronic alcoholic for public intoxication might constitute punishment for the underlying condition of chronic alcoholism and therefore be unconstitutional where "it was not feasible for him to have made arrangements to prevent his being in public when drunk." That is, a homeless alcoholic would not be accountable for being drunk in public. Since Powell had made no showing that he was unable to stay off the streets on the night in question and had a home to which he could go, Justice White concurred in affirmance of the conviction.[23]

Under present practice, police in many jurisdictions do not charge the drunken person with drunkenness but rather with vagrancy or disorderly conduct. The Supreme Court ruled unconstitutional in 1972 a vague Jacksonville, Florida, vagrancy ordinance as being a status crime. Vagrancy laws typically define what they purport to proscribe so vaguely and indefinitely that criminalization of status and not conduct is the result. Replacement of the charge of drunkenness or vagrancy by that of disorderly conduct gained in use.

In large cities such as New York, the police sweep drunken people off the street and enter a charge of drunkenness because requirements of proof are less onerous. These people are often brought before the judge en masse—ten to twenty at a time. To establish a crime of disorderly conduct, on the other hand, the prosecutor must present certain definite evidence (type and place of disturbance). But as a practical matter police work is not increased inasmuch as defendants invariably plead guilty to either charge, so there is no trial and no need for an offer of proof. In the typical drunk arrest the defendant is almost never represented by counsel, and as a consequence the procedures are usually perfunctory.

Alcohol-Precipitated Crimes

The decisions in *Easter, Driver,* and *Powell* relate to the crime of drunkenness involving a chronic alcoholic and do not apply directly to alcohol-precipitated crimes. In such crimes as robbery and murder, alcohol may sometimes be a precipitating or contributing factor, but unlike the defense of insanity, the defense of drunkenness usually does not result in exculpation of the offender. An offender is not allowed to set up his own "wickedness" as a defense. Lord Coke in 1603 observed that those who voluntarily deprive themselves of their reason, such as "drunkards," should not be heard to claim insanity as a defense in a civil or criminal action.

A distinction is made, however, between the criminal conduct of a chronic alcoholic and that of a person in an acute state of intoxication. At one time insanity was referred to as wickedness. Similarly, chronic alcoholism and drug addiction have been considered to be products of bad-life conduct calling for punitive response. This view has changed through the magic of the ontological characterization of alcoholism as a disease. Thus, chronic alcoholism may result in *settled insanity,* and thus provide a defense. When a person engages in criminal conduct while under the periodic affect of alcohol, however, the prevailing view is that the act is a product of willful self-inflicted incapacity, and the intoxication is disregarded at law. If intoxication were an excuse, it is said, a person wishing to commit a crime could simply get drunk and then with impunity perform the forbidden act.[24]

The law reflects the common viewpoint. To take an example of noncriminal behavior: a woman who drinks and as a result regresses psychologically at such times may allow men to fondle her. In such a case, her husband is justified in reproaching her. If she does not abstain, he is justified in leaving her. On the other hand, if a woman allows others to fondle her because of a chronic condition such as low intelligence, it is generally considered that the husband is not justified in reproaching or leaving her. It is thought that he ought to impose nonpunitive controls or safeguards. On the same principle, punitive responsibility is imposed when an individual, before becoming intoxicated, foresaw his own potential for criminality. One who is aware of becoming dangerous when intoxicated is culpable on an ordinary principle of recklessness: To foresee is to forestall.[25] Involuntary intoxication is a defense, but "involuntary intoxication," the courts say, is "a most unusual condition."[26]

To raise the issue of criminal responsibility, that is, not guilty by reason of insanity, it must appear from the evidence that the accused, at the time of the alleged criminal act, had some mental disease or defect. An addiction to alcohol or narcotics, standing alone, is not deemed a mental disease or defect as a matter of law.

Proof of mental disease or defect does not depend upon psychiatric labels or medical classifications and terms, although testimony of an expert in those terms may raise the issue for jury determination. The defendant's mental condition may be shown by observation and opinions of lay witnesses as well as by experts. Lay testimony describing significantly bizarre, abnormal conduct also could be sufficient to raise the issue, but this must be "more than a scintilla of evidence." In *Heard v. United States*,[27] the U.S. Court of Appeals for the District of Columbia said:

> A mere showing of [alcohol or] narcotics addiction, without more, does not constitute "some evidence of" mental disease or "insanity" so as to raise the issue of criminal responsibility. Some mentally ill persons are addicts and some addicts are mentally ill; the two conditions can coincide but we give no more credence to the notion that all addicts are mentally ill, than to the converse that all mentally ill persons are addicts. To so hold would make every addict's case an insanity case.

In *Robinson*, the U.S. Supreme Court did not consider narcotics addiction to be a mental illness in the criminal responsibility (*M'Naghten* or ALI) context. Its holding was merely that the addiction status may not be punished as a crime. The court in the *Heard* case, which involved the criminal-responsibility issue, found that "a mere showing of narcotics addiction, without more, does not constitute 'some evidence of' mental disease," and consequently the mental issue was withheld from the jury. Hence, as the cases demonstrate, narcotic or alcohol addiction is not equated with mental disease as a matter of law.[28]

General Intent versus Specific Intent Crimes

Taking a general intent versus specific intent approach, the courts, on a crime-by-crime basis, have distinguished which crimes do and which do not permit the required mens rea to be questioned by evidence of the defendant's toxic condition. While, out of policy, voluntary intoxication or substance abuse is not considered a mental disease or defect under NGRI, nor a defense under a not guilty plea in a crime of general intent, it may result in a diminished verdict or sentence, or in a finding of guilty but mentally ill.[29]

Defense to Disbarment

Lawyers facing charges leading to disbarment are allowed to introduce mental illness and substance abuse conditions as mitigating factors. These conditions can lead to a reduction in the penalties in many cases, such as suspension in lieu of disbarment if they are held to be the root cause of the misconduct. Psychiatric testimony has been a prominent factor in many of these decisions. While these cases are classified as civil proceedings, the psychiatric defense aspects can be very similar to an insanity plea.[30]

Americans with Disabilities Act

Alcoholism and drug addiction are difficult issues under the Americans with Disabilities Act (ADA). Congress recognized that employers must have the opportunity to ensure that their workplaces remain safe and efficient. Therefore, the ADA expressly states that employers may prohibit the use of alcohol or illegal drugs in the workplace and may require that employees not be under the influence of alcohol or drugs while working.[31] Moreover, an alcoholic or illegal drug user may be held to the same job qualifications, and the same standards of job performance and behavior as all other employees, even if their poor performance or behavior is related to their alcoholism or drug use.[32] The ADA also permits drug testing in the workplace.[33]

The ADA does not protect *current* drug use, be it on or off the job. Consequently, employers do not violate the ADA when they refuse to hire an applicant, or discipline or fire employees currently using illegal drugs, when they act on the basis of that use. Current drug use is not limited to use on the day of the employment action, but may be based on drug use in the weeks and months prior to discharge.[34] The Equal Employment Opportunity Commission (EEOC) guidelines make clear that current use means the use of drugs that has "occurred recently enough to indicate that the individual is actively engaged in such conduct."[35]

On the other hand, the ADA protects *past* drug use as a disability. Employers have a duty to accommodate employees if the employees are rehabilitated or in a rehabilitation program, currently do not use illegal drugs, and can perform the essential functions of the job held or desired. The accommodation may be to provide additional sick leave or vacation time to attend rehabilitation programs, or to provide a flexible work schedule.[36]

Drunken Driving

During the past decade or two, with the proliferation of automobiles, there has been much concern and publicity about drunken driving. As a result, legislation has been enacted that relates to driving and alcohol use. State statutes or the *Tarasoff* duty to report may require reporting by physicians of patients with conditions that may affect their ability to drive an automobile. State psychiatric hospitals have a duty to identify and report impaired drivers.[37] Legislation mandates alcohol therapy for any person who has a prior conviction for driving under the influence of alcohol.[38]

Will it make any more than a whit of difference in the carnage on the highways? What difference would it make even if every driver was sober as a judge? It is estimated that only one out of one hundred thousand intoxicated drivers are involved in an accident, so how dangerous is it to drive while under the influence? What about causation? What does *alcohol-related* mean in statistics on "alcohol-related crashes"? Judy Snow of the Michigan state police informed me, "We acknowledge that cause is a hard thing to determine, so we report what we call alcohol-involved accidents. This only states that alcohol was present to a degree that it *could* contribute to the accident."[39]

One can only be struck by the variation in reporting. The medical examiner in St. Louis County, Minnesota, claimed that drinking is a factor in 80 to 90 percent of traffic fatalities. The medical examiner in Nueces County, Texas, claimed 90 to 100 percent of traffic fatalities are alcohol related. A study in Atlanta claimed 30 percent of the fatalities are due to alcohol and 50 percent to failure to wear a seatbelt. The Michigan AAA (American Automobile Association) said 44 percent of the deaths are alcohol related.

Of course, alcohol dulls areas of the brain that enable people to make sensible decisions, it slows reaction time by interfering with reflexes and coordination, and it causes drowsiness and loss of alertness and concentration—but those conditions may result from a host of other factors, such as driver habits, boredom, overeating, and medication. There are great similarities in the properties of alcohol and the benzodiazepine group of drugs that are widely used as medication. Not sleeping enough can have the same results as drinking too much.

A generation ago it was uncouth to eat or drink while walking on the sidewalk or while driving or riding in a car. Now, fast food and a beverage are standard equipment for almost every driver. Today's car is used for eating, drinking, dressing, talking on the telephone, and other activities. Not only do we have overwhelming distractions when we are driving today, but relying on the judgment of others is pretty risky, even when they are sober, considering the mentality and attitude of many of them.

Road construction, icy or wet roadways, vehicle construction, and density of traffic are all highly contributing factors to the casualty toll. Wearing a seatbelt in a chicken box going seventy miles per hour provides about as much protection as wearing a jockstrap for warmth in wintertime. In his book *Drink: A Social History of America*, Andrew Barr writes, "[V]ested interests conspire to exaggerate the number of deaths and injuries caused by drinking drivers and to play down other causes of traffic accidents. This is a conspiracy in which the public appears content to participate."[40]

The vast majority of accidents involve going off the road, tiredness, falling asleep, irritability, and a host of other things having little or nothing to do with alcohol or seatbelts. In Israel twice as many people have died in automobile accidents as have been killed in all of the nation's wars. In Israel, where most people do not drink very much, the blame is put on the sun. (Alcohol is so insignificant in Israel that there is no legal barrier to the presence of young people in bars.)

To be sure, alcohol and the failure to wear a seatbelt play a role in the motor death toll, but by focusing on them, attention is distracted from the fact that fatalities are part and parcel of the automobile way of life. The more cars on the road, the more likelihood there is of an accident. MADD (Mothers Against Drunk Driving) ought to be just MAD (Mothers Against Driving). The psychiatrist Joost Meerloo called the automobile way of life a form of mass suicide.[41]

The Crusade of Carrie Nation

There was also a women's movement in the nineteenth century to prevent drinking. In the 1840s groups of married women formed associations to demand that their husbands pledge themselves to abstain from alcoholic drinks, on pain of withdrawal of conjugal favors. Then, too, old-line Anglo-Saxons did not like the drinking habits of their newer and poorer Irish and German immigrants, not to mention the later immigrants from eastern and southern Europe. Female campaigners could not vote for prohibitory legislation because they were not enfranchised, so they resorted to extralegal methods.

The most famous attacks on saloons were carried out by Carrie Nation in Kansas at the beginning of the twentieth century, with the aid of a hatchet. Carrie Nation was fired by the mission of ridding the world of "demon rum," and was convinced that without alcohol, America would be a better place. Her foes were the numerous saloons that flourished in Kansas despite the fact that the state was declared dry back in 1880, four decades before prohibition was imposed on the rest of the United States. However, the law in Kansas was on the books only to satisfy pious preachers, while all others could drink with the authorities' tacit approval. Bringing her to justice meant admitting that, regardless of the law, saloons operated freely. Since everyone made believe that there were no saloons, they were unwilling to destroy the pretense. This allowed her to go on smashing her way across the state with total impunity, which she relished to the full.

Across the country, women took to smashing up the saloons because, according to an article at the time, "For years and years, and weary, suffering years, multiplied into decades, have the women of America waited to see the traffic destroyed which annually sends 60,000 of their sons, brothers, fathers and husbands into the drunkard's grave."[42] The alternative to smashing up the saloons was for women to agitate to be given the right to vote so that they could legislate to prevent men from drinking. The length of time it took for the prohibitionist movement to achieve its ends—a period of sixty-nine years between the introduction of state prohibition in Maine in 1851 and the imposition of national prohibition in 1920—can partly be explained by the amount of time and energy expended on obtaining for women the right to vote. It was no coincidence that national prohibition and female suffrage were both introduced in the same year, 1920 (as the Eighteenth and Nineteenth Amendments to the Constitution respectively). As any schoolchild knows, prohibition did not work out quite as planned. Franklin D. Roosevelt poured cocktails to celebrate the end of abstention in 1933.[43]

New Pathways

How might the law go beyond its present role and confront the alcoholic with the problem of his alcoholism in a forceful way? Is there room for improvement in the administration of the law? Possibly the law can learn something from industry. Insurance companies, recognizing that alcoholism and accidents go hand in glove, strive to develop treatment programs in industry. In the best industrial programs the individual is not allowed to get away with his alcoholism. He is encouraged to do something about it, and he is threatened by loss of his job. The coercion is strong, but it is not "quit drinking or you're fired." A strategy of constructive confrontation involves intervening on the basis of inadequate job performance rather than condemning deviant behavior. Under this strategy, management offers to help at no jeopardy to the person's job. The employee is told, "Look, your drinking is hurting your work and you're going to have to shape up. But we're not going to punish you for trying to do something about your problem." The job is used as a lever to alter the behavior.[44] Man's work is probably the most important thing in his life, and its threatened loss may persuade him to undertake psychiatric treatment seriously. A man's wife, like his work, is important to him, but while she may threaten to leave him unless he stops drinking, all too often she really wants him to remain an alcoholic. Without his drinking, they may have nothing to talk about and nothing to keep him dependent on her.[45]

What threat can the law employ? What is effective in dealing with the alcoholic professional person may be ineffective with the alcoholic derelict, and the municipal courts deal mainly with the latter group. For the most part, judges are no more successful than a man's wife in encouraging the alcoholic to seek treatment or otherwise modify his behavior.

Alcoholism is a multisided problem and, therefore, responsibility does not lie with one agency or discipline alone. Effective motivation lies within an interested and emotionally involved individual, but awakening of motivation may derive from different sources: the individual, the group, the community, or the state.[46]

Alcoholics Anonymous advises judges: "Don't sentence the alcoholic to AA. It won't work. It is wise to give the alcoholic a choice. Ask him whether he prefers to do his time—whatever you are used to giving him: thirty days, sixty days, ninety days—or whether he would like to talk to a member of Alcoholics Anonymous. By giving him a choice, you allow him to make a decision, and since it is his decision, he will be a lot more cooperative and a lot more willing to try."[47] So the court must *ask* the alcoholic to request treatment. This type of asking must be phrased so that one cannot decline, although the semblance of choice must remain. The judge must be silver-tongued.

Alcohol is a handy drug that is used by many in an attempt to deal with an emotional need. In the usual case, the use of alcohol is not to satisfy thirst or to aid the digestive process. It is a coping mechanism, a means of dealing with anxiety, tension, fear, grief, depression, frustration, and inhibition. In driving a motor vehicle, one may need "one for the road," so horrendous has driving become. Thus, the problem of alcoholism cannot be dealt with in isolation by one discipline. It is a human problem, traversing many disciplines, including medicine, sociology, religion, law, psychiatry, and public health.[48] As expressed by Justice Brennan of the Michigan Supreme Court:

> If there is in the law a "revolving door" there is also a "revolving door" in medicine. In the book "Alcoholics Anonymous" is a case history of a man who was committed both voluntarily and involuntarily to Bellevue Hospital 35 times without success. His case is not rare. The truth is that there is no simple cure for alcoholism which falls within the confines of a single discipline. . . . The criminal law dispenses the power of governmental sovereignty. It is the ultimate coercive force in society. The fact that alcoholism cannot be cured by this coercive force alone is no reason for the law to abdicate its obligation to protect society from that public and disorderly drunkenness which disrupts our domestic tranquility and offends against public safety and the common good.[49]

Although statistics indicate a correlation between crime and the use of alcohol (as well as drugs), this is not to say that such use causes crime or vice versa. Rather one must consider that both stem out of a common matrix. One should not assume, however, that alcohol (or drug) use has no influence whatever on the criminal behavior of those who demonstrate marked tendencies toward alcohol (or drug) abuse and the commission of various crimes. The use of alcohol (or drugs) provides reinforcement that may either enhance or diminish the possibility of an eventual criminal outcome. When a crime, or indeed any act, occurs, it is the culmination of a series of interactions, including such factors as age, sex, race, economic status, location, and availability of weapons. The overwhelming majority of homicides (80 percent) are committed not by criminals but by persons who become enraged at a time when a weapon, usually a handgun, is available. The number of handguns in circulation is, thus, a critical factor in the extent of homicide. The position of the moon, on the other hand, would seem to have little to do with the incidence of crime.

The general rule, as discussed, is that mental disease or defect as defined in law will exculpate an offender, but drunkenness will not. Voluntary intoxication or temporary insanity resulting from intoxication is not a defense. Mental disease caused by long-term excessive drinking, however, will exculpate to the same degree as any psychosis having a different origin. The courts do not probe for the cause of settled insanity.

In regard to minor offenders, the extent that treatment will be a consideration lies with those who believe in rehabilitation. Toward this goal, the Congress established an Institute on Alcohol Abuse and Alcoholism within the Department of Health, Education, and Welfare. Some states have changed their laws to provide for health treatment, and some have repealed the legal sanctions against alcoholism.[50] The National Conference of Commissioners on Uniform State Laws recommended the following provisions: First, a person appearing to be incapacitated by alcohol must be taken into protective custody (which is not technically an arrest) by the police or a special emergency service patrol and is to be taken to a public-health facility for emergency treatment. Second, if the subject has inflicted physical harm on another or may do so, he may be committed for emergency treatment for up to five days on the certificate of an independent physician. Third, commitment is made by a court with the period of treatment being thirty days, and extensions for a maximum of seven months.[51]

Notes

1. Gen. 9:21.
2. Prov. 31:6.
3. Quoted in *Republica* (Lithuania), July 20, 2001, p. 7.
4. See A. Barr, *Drink: A Social History of America* (New York: Carroll & Graf, 1999).
5. In some states private as well as public drunkenness is a crime, although the charge is usually made only against the lower-class derelict. For example, Kansas law provided: "If any person shall be drunk in any highway, street, or in any public place or building, or if any person shall be drunk in his own house, or in any private building or place, disturbing his family or others, he shall be deemed guilty of a misdemeanor, and upon conviction thereof shall be fined in any sum not exceeding one hundred dollars ($100.00), or by imprisonment in the county jail for a period not exceeding thirty (30) days." Kan. Stat. 21–2129 (repealed 1949).
6. When mental illness is the result of long and continued intoxication or substance abuse, it affects responsibility in the same way as mental illness produced by other causes. Lack of responsibility can be shown by settled mental illness without regard to the chain of causation. Professor Monrad Paulsen observed: "To give the genesis of mental disorder a legal effect is to put upon the processes of litigation an impossible task. If the full exculpatory

effect of mental disease were not denied to those illnesses which are related to unwise choices of life, many cases other than those of the alcoholics would be involved." M. Paulsen, "Intoxication as a Defense to Crime," *U. Ill. L. For.* 1961: 1. See also H. Fingarette, "How an Alcoholism Defense Works under the ALI Insanity Test," *Int'l J. Law & Psychiatry* 2 (1979): 299. As one court put it, "Insanity resulting from long-term voluntary alcohol abuse is a valid defense even though the defendant may also have been intoxicated [at] the time of the offense." People v. Chapman, 418 N.W.2d 658, 659 (Mich. App. 1987). See S. Halleck, *Psychiatry and the Dilemmas of Crime* (New York: Harper & Row, 1967); M. C. Slough, "Some Legal By-Products of Intoxication," *Kan. L. Rev.* 3 (1955): 181.

7. Bill W, *Twelve Steps and Twelve Traditions* (New York: Alcoholics Anonymous, 1953). See also R. Thomsen, *Bill W* (New York: Harper & Row, 1975); H. M. Trice & W. J. Staudenmeier, "A Sociocultural History of Alcoholics Anonymous," *Recent Developments in Alcoholism* 7 (1989): 11. To be sure, the variations of addictive behavior are beyond count inasmuch as any type of behavior that is exaggerated may be deemed pathological or an addiction. A "workaholic," the coinage of a minister, Wayne E. Oates, is someone who is often compulsive, driven, restless, and positively addicted to a calling. Oates's concept was that work can become an addiction akin to alcoholism. He wrote, "The work addict drops out of the human community." W. E. Oates, *Confessions of a Workaholic: The Facts about Work Addiction* (Nashville: Abingdon Press, 1971; reprinted, Cleveland: World, 1972). See also id., *Workaholics: Make Laziness Work for You* (New York: Doubleday, 1978). A "sportsaholic" is someone who lives life *through* sports *for* sports. See K. Quick, *Not Now, Honey, I'm Watching the Game* (New York: Simon & Schuster, 1997). Racism is called an addiction in J. E. Dobbins & J. H. Skillings, "Racism as a Clinical Syndrome," *Am. J. Orthopsychiatry* 70 (2000): 14.

8. S. Rado, "The Psychoanalysis of Pharmacothymia (Drug Addiction)," *Psa. Q.* 2 (1933): 1.

9. E. Berne, *Games People Play* (New York: Grove Press, 1964). The longing for mothering and home, something to make up for an earlier inadequate home, is echoed in the famous words of one alcoholic, Stephen Foster: "We will sing one song for my old Kentucky home, For my old Kentucky home far away."

10. 209 A.2d 625 (D.C. App. 1965).

11. Ibid.

12. Easter v. District of Columbia, 361 F.2d 50 (D.C. Cir. 1966).

13. Ibid. at 60.

14. Driver v. Hinnant, 356 F.2d 761 (4th Cir. 1966).

15. 370 U.S. 660 (1962).

16. Ibid. at 665.

17. Ibid. at 674, 678.

18. The majority of the Court at that time probably reflected on Samuel Butler's biting satire, *Erewhon*, in which the sick were punished for being sick. In *Erewhon*, a person having pulmonary consumption was sentenced to "imprisonment, with hard labor, for the rest of [his] miserable existence," and the judge reproached him in his oral opinion: "You may say that it is not your fault. . . . I answer that whether your being in a consumption is your fault or not, it is a fault in you, and it is my duty to see that against such faults as this the commonwealth shall be protected. You may say that it is your misfortune to be criminal; I answer that it is your crime to be unfortunate." S. Butler, *Erewhon* (New York: Modern Library, 1927).

19. 392 U.S. 514 (1968).

20. *Powell* was not the Court's first opportunity to consider the question. In Budd v. California, 385 U.S. 909 (1966), the Court denied certiorari to a petition presenting substantially the same questions raised by Powell.

21. 392 U.S. at 533.

22. 392 U.S. at 529–30.

23. Ibid. at 550–51 n. 2. A critique of the involuntariness and disease concepts in this context appears in H. Fingarette, "The Perils of *Powell:* In Search of a Factual Foundation for the 'Disease Concept of Alcoholism,'" *Harv. L. Rev.* 83 (1970): 793. See also People v. Hoy, 380 Mich. 597, 158 N.W.2d 436 (1968).

24. In the early eighteenth century, Lord Chief Justice Matthew Hale said that a person who commits a crime while drunk "shall have no privilege by this voluntary contracted madness, but shall have the same judgment as if he were in his right senses." M. Hale, *The History of the Pleas of the Crown* (London: Nutt & Gosling, 1st ed. 1736; London: Professional Books,

1972), p. 32. In 1868 the Michigan Supreme Court said: "A man who voluntarily puts himself in condition to have no control of his actions, must be held to intend the consequences. The safety of the community requires this rule. Intoxication is so easily counterfeited, and when real it is so often resorted to as a means of nerving the person up to the commission of some desperate act, and is withal so inexcusable in itself, that the law has never recognized it as an excuse for crime." People v. Garbutt, 17 Mich. 9, 16, 97 Am. Dec. 162 (1868).

Some states have codified the common-law rule on intoxication. The provision does not bar someone who is both mentally ill and intoxicated from making a case for legal insanity, but it does make it more difficult. Michigan's statute states: "A person who is under the influence of voluntarily consumed or injected alcohol or controlled substances at the time of his alleged offense shall not thereby be deemed to have been legally insane." Mich. Comp. Laws Ann., sec. 768.21a(2). Connecticut's statute provides: "It shall not be a defense under this section if such disease or defect was proximately caused by the voluntary ingestion, inhalation or injection of intoxicating liquor or any drug or substance, or any combination thereof, unless such drug was prescribed for the defendant by a licensed practitioner . . . and was used in accordance with the directions of such prescription." Conn. Gen. Stat. Ann., sec. 53a-13 (1999).

25. See J. Hall, *General Principles of Criminal Law* (Indianapolis: Bobbs-Merrill, 1960).

26. City of Minneapolis v. Altimus, 306 Minn. 462, 238 N.W.2d 851, 858 (1976). Involuntary intoxication may be raised as a temporary insanity defense. People v. Wilkins, 184 Mich. App. 443, 459 N.W.2d 57 (1990). There are two situations where the madness induced by intoxication would not be contracted voluntarily and therefore, would have exculpatory significance. Hale said, supra note 24 at p. 134:

> [First,] if a person by the unskillfulness of his physician, or by the contrivance of his enemies, eat or drink such a thing as causeth such a temporary or permanent phrenzy, . . . this puts him into the same condition, in reference to crimes, as any other phrenzy, and equally excuseth him. [Second,] although the *simplex* phrenzy occasioned immediately by drunkenness excuse not in criminals, yet if by one or more such practices, an *habitual* or fixed phrenzy be caused, though this madness was contracted by the vice and will of the party, yet this habitual and fixed phrenzy thereby caused puts the man into the same condition in relation to crimes, as if the same were contracted involuntarily at first.

Each of these two propositions now represents prevailing law in the United States. The courts have held that defendant is entitled to an instruction on the effects, say, of the drug Halcion on preexisting mental condition. The voluntary intoxication instruction is not applicable when the drug is prescribed as a treatment. People v. Turner, 680 P.2d 1290 (Colo. App. 1983); People v. Caulley, 197 Mich. App. 177, 494 N.W.2d 853 (1992). Compare Garza v. State, 829 S.W.2d 291 (Tex. App. 1992) (failure to instruct on involuntary intoxication caused by Prozac was not error where there was no evidence that the defendant consumed Prozac and that he was in the 1 percent of the population for which Prozac is believed to cause violent behavior). Compare also Blaylock v. State, 600 So.2d 1250 (Fla. App. 1992). In a case in England, Zoe O'Shea, charged with armed robbery, claimed that pills she was taking for bulimia turned her into a Jekyll and Hyde character. The judge described the case as "wholly exceptional" and placed her on probation for two years. M. Harper, "Diet Pills Turned Me into an Armed Robber," *Evening Standard*, Mar. 29, 1993, p. 15.

As steroids are being used to build muscle mass and strength, the question arises whether unexpected side effects of the steroids are a basis for an insanity defense, as are drugs secretly slipped into someone's drink, causing the person to lose control, or whether the ingestion of steroids will be regarded as voluntary intoxication—not an excuse for criminal conduct, but perhaps evidence of a lack of premeditation. The question has arisen in a number of cases. In a murder case in Florida (which follows the *M'Naghten* rule), the jury rejected the defense. In this case, the victim's body, battered and naked, was found suspended between two poles in a field, with his hands tied to one pole and his feet to the other. "Defense in Slaying Case Cites Steroid Addiction" (Associated Press news release), *New York Times*, May 30, 1988, p. 20. However, in a Maryland case, the trial judge, in a trial without jury, ruled that the defendant "had met his burden of proof by a preponderance of the evidence, that he was . . . suffering from an organic personality syndrome caused by the toxic levels of anabolic steroids taken to enhance his ability to win a bodybuilding contest and that this disorder substantially impaired his ability to appreciate the criminality of his acts and to conform his conduct to the requirements of the law" (Maryland follows the ALI test of criminal responsibility). Noted in C. C. Kleinmann, "Forensic Issues Arising from the Use of Anabolic Steroids," *Psychiat. Annals* 20 (Apr. 1990): 219. The charges in the Maryland case were arson and burglary, not murder as in the Florida case. As a practical matter, whatever the test of criminal responsibility—whether the restrictive test in Florida or the broader ALI test— the more serious the crime, the more difficult it is to procure exoneration.

In an unusual federal murder case, a defense of insanity based on the long-term effects of environmental toxins was successful. In this case, Navajo tribesman Terrence Frank admitted he shot and killed two people and seriously wounded two others in a dispute on an Arizona reservation. The defense successfully argued that Frank had brain damage caused by radiation from the uranium surrounding his home, where American Indian labor and crudely cut mines provided half of all uranium. Uranium-related brain damage, coupled with the effects of alcohol the defendant drank that day, made him temporally insane at the time of the shootings. Dr. Fred Rosenthal, a San Francisco psychiatrist and a former scientific adviser to the United Nations on the effects of atomic radiation, testified, "I'm not saying that radiation or brain damage always leads to murder, but if you have somebody who's not functioning well . . . and you add to that intoxication, then things like this can happen." C. A. Lucus, "Toxin Defense Successful," *National Law J.*, May 1, 1989, p. 7.

27. 348 F.2d 43 (D.C. 1964).

28. *Heard* has been followed in subsequent decisions, e.g., Bailey v. United States, 386 F.2d 1 (5th Cir. 1967). Judge Wright, dissenting in *Heard*, contended that longstanding drug addiction with adequate exposition of cause and effect, is "some evidence" of mental illness sufficient to take the mental issue to the jury.

In State v. Martin, 591 N.W.2d 481 (Minn. 1999), the defense gave notice to the state of its intention to claim mental illness or mental deficiency, relying upon a psychiatric report that stated in part:

> Based on the history and my examination I concluded that at the time of the alleged offense with reasonable medical certainty, [defendant] was highly intoxicated to the point where he blacked out and had lost control of his mental faculties to the point where he was incapable of mustering any criminal intent or of being mentally competent to understand the nature or quality of any behavior or to appreciate right from wrong.

The claim was rejected. The trial court stated: "[Defendant has] never been diagnosed as mentally ill, nor has he ever been diagnosed or treated suffering from any mental deficiency. Everything that has been submitted goes to the effects of his use of alcohol, and again, how that affected him before, during, and after the incident occurred." The trial court also rejected a defense of involuntary intoxication, stating:

> The [defendant] has never maintained that he was laboring under the effects of involuntary intoxication again before, during or after this offense occurred, and so what we have plainly and simply is a circumstance where the defense has raised the issues surrounding voluntary intoxication and has also referenced possible blackout that may have occurred during that intoxication.

In accord with precedent, the Minnesota Supreme Court agreed with the trial court that the facts alleged by the defense only rise to the level of voluntary intoxication and cannot be the basis of a claim of mental illness or mental deficiency. 591 N.W.2d at 485.

In 1855 the Ohio Supreme Court ruled that delirium tremens was a form of legal insanity but that intoxication was not. In Maconnehey v. Ohio, 5 Ohio (Critchfield) Reports 69 (1855), the court explained that the reason delirium tremens excuses responsibility but intoxication does not is that delirium tremens is always shunned rather than courted by the patient and is not voluntarily assumed. E. R. Pinta, *A History of Psychiatry at the Ohio State University 1847–1993* (Columbus: Ohio State University Department of Psychiatry, 1994), p. 22; H. Silving, "Intoxicants and Criminal Conduct," in *Essays in Mental Incapacity and Criminal Conduct* (Springfield, Ill.: Thomas, 1967), p. 214.

29. See State v. Doppler, 590 N.W.2d 627 (Minn. 1999); State v. Aguilar, 325 N.W.2d 100 (Iowa 1982); People v. Culp, 310 N.W.2d 421 (Mich. App. 1981); People v. Davis, 301 N.W.2d 871 (Mich. App. 1980); State v. Soldier, 299 N.W.2d 568 (S.D. 1980).

30. See Attorney Grievance Commission v. White, 614 A.2d 955 (Md. 1992).

31. 42 USCA, sec. 12114(c)(1), (2).

32. 42 USCA, sec. 12114(d).

33. 42 USCA, sec. 12114(a).

34. Collings v. Longview Fibre, 63 F.3d 838 (9th Cir. 1995).

35. 29 CFR, sec. 1630, App. 1630.3.

36. 42 USCA, sec. 12114(b). See T. D. Colbridge, "Defining Disability under the Americans with Disabilities Act," *FBI Law Enforcement Bull.*, Oct. 2000, p. 28.

37. Mich. Comp. Laws 257. 625b(5) (1999). Under Michigan's Mental Health Code, addiction is not a basis for civil commitment.

38. S. L. Godard & J. D. Bloom, "Driving, Mental Illness, and the Duty to Protect," in J. C. Beck (ed.), *Confidentiality versus the Duty to Protect: Foreseeable Harm in the Practice of Psychiatry* (Washington, D.C.: American Psychiatric Press, 1990), pp. 191–204. Drunken drivers often abuse drugs besides alcohol, and not a few of them have other kinds of psychological problems, too. In short, if drunken drivers are to be screened, they should be screened for other psychiatric disorders as well. S. Lapham et al., "Prevalence of Psychiatric Disorders among Persons Convicted of Driving While Impaired," *Arch. Gen. Psychiatry* 58 (2001): 943. In an editorial accompanying the report by Lapham, Dr. George Woody said, "Detecting various psychological problems in drunken drivers would benefit not just them but the public." G. Woody, "More Reasons to Buckle Your Belt" (commentary), *Arch. Gen. Psychiatry* 58 (2001): 950. In an interview, Woody noted that the effect of major depression on driving ability or of post-traumatic stress disorder on driving ability has not been studied very well. He added that the same applies to antisocial personality disorder, although one might speculate that the impulsiveness associated with antisocial personality disorder might be associated with more aggressive driving. J. Arehart-Treichel, "Drunken Drivers Often Have Multiple Psychiatric Problems," *Psychiatric News*, Nov. 16, 2001, p. 17. See also R. Slovenko, "Desocialization by Automobile" (editorial), *Int'l J. Offender Therapy & Comp. Criminology* 45 (2001): 535.

39. One of the most commonly enforced exclusions in an insurance policy for accidental death claims involves alcohol and drugs. The interpretation of the exclusion depends on the state of occurrence. Under California law, alcohol exclusion clauses require the insurance company to show that the death of the insured was "in consequence of" the influence of alcohol. In other words, the influence of alcohol must be the proximate cause of death for the exclusionary provision to be effective. Olson v. Am. Bankers Ins. Co., 30 Cal. App.4th 816 (Cal. App. 1994). However, in Georgia, courts have held that the alcohol exclusion does not require that the intoxication cause the accident, injury, or loss. Therefore, the exclusion applies without a causation requirement. Jefferson Pilot Life Ins. Co. v. Clark, 202 Ga. App. 385, 414 S.E.2d 521 (1991).

40. Supra note 4, p. 292.

41. J. A. M. Meerloo, *Suicide and Mass Suicide* (New York: Dutton, 1968).

42. Quoted in A. Barr, supra note 4, p. 148.

43. Ibid. at p. 149.

44. This is the central theme of the book *The Alcoholics* (London: Lion Books, 1953) by Jim Thompson, the popular crime-noir novelist.

45. This was well depicted in the play and film (MGM, 1954) *Brigadoon*, where two friends wandering through an enchanted wood pause to rest, and the following conversation ensues:

JEFF: Maybe we took the high road instead of the low road. (Takes a flask from his inside pocket.) Would you like a drink?

TOMMY: No, thanks.

JEFF: Good. That leaves more for me. (He unscrews the top.)

TOMMY: Didn't you tell me you were going to cut down on that stuff?

JEFF: Yes, I did. But I'm a terrible liar. Besides, it doesn't pay. I remember one time I was going with a wonderful girl and she used to plead with me and plead with me to give it up. So one day I did. Then we discovered we had nothing more to talk about so we broke up.

A. Lerner & F. Loewe, *Brigadoon* (New York: Coward-McCann, 1947). (Copyright 1947, Alan Jay Lerner.)

On the other hand, a spouse may be an indispensable support, as illustrated in Clifford Odet's prize-winning play (New York: Viking Press, 1951) and film (Paramount, 1954), *The Country Girl*, in which the wife of an actor buoys him up from backsliding into alcoholism and failure. Thus, a spouse may be a factor the effect of which is very difficult to predict.

46. K. S. Ditman & G. G. Crawford, "The Use of Court Probation in the Management of the Alcohol Addict," *Am. J. Psychiatry* 122 (1966): 757.

47. M. Reed, "The Function of Alcoholics Anonymous," in *Processing the Alcoholic Defendant: Report of Proceedings of the Rocky Mountain Regional Conference of Municipal Judges* (Washington, D.C.: U.S. Dept. of Health, Education, and Welfare, 1959).

48. See A. Barr, supra note 4; D. Jersild, *Happy Hours: Alcohol in a Woman's Life* (New York: HarperCollins, 2001); C. G. Schoenfeld, "Alcohol, Alcoholism, and the Law: A Psychoanalytically Oriented Analysis," *J. Psychiatry & Law* 12 (1984): 67.

49. People v. Hoy, 380 Mich. 597, 158 N.W.2d 436, 444–45 (1968).

50. Massachusetts law provides that "any person who is incapacitated in a public place may be assisted by a police officer with or without his consent to his residence, to a facility or to a police station." If treatment at a facility is not available, an incapacitated person may be held in protective custody at a police station until he is no longer incapacitated or for a period of not longer than twelve hours, whichever is shorter. Mass. Ann. Laws, ch. 111B, sec. 8 (1999). See K. A. Menninger, *Whatever Became of Sin?* (New York: Hawthorn Books, 1973).

51. See F. P. Grad, A. L. Goldberg, & B. A. Shapiro, *Alcoholism and the Law* (Dobbs Ferry, N.Y.: Oceana, 1971).

14

Drug
Addiction

As in many countries, the use of drugs in the United States is widespread. The high incidence of addiction to drugs is indicative of personal as well as societal tragedies. Nearly every segment of society—sports, entertainment, the military, transportation, executive offices, assembly lines—has been affected by substance abuse.

The fundamental mechanism by which commonly abused drugs affect behavior—the way they impair conscience and performance by their specific effects on the brain—is not widely understood by the public. The drugs are appealing because they relieve tension or temporarily produce a pleasant effect of alertness that may enhance performance, but their long-term effects not only harm the user but pose danger for all of society. In the mythological tale of Daedalus and Icarus, getting "high" was the cause of Icarus's downfall and death, though it was construed as a pleasant experience.

According to United Nations estimates, Americans are spending almost $60 billion on illegal drugs a year, mainly on the "soft" drug, marijuana, and its "hard" counterparts, cocaine and heroin. The war on drugs is fought with strict penalties. There are 450,000 Americans behind bars for drug offenses, eight times the number in 1980 (Europe, with a larger population, jails fewer people for all offenses). In 1980, the federal government spent around $5 billion on drug control; federal, state, and local spending in 1999 exceeded $40 billion, which included greatly expanded programs of crop eradication, border patrolling, and sting operations. About a third of the federal government's drug-control spending goes toward drug education or drug treatment.

A number of jurisdictions have established "therapeutic drug courts," the first in Miami in 1989, and now there are some seven hundred across the United States. While they now only hear about 1 percent of the country's drug cases, policy experts predict that the treatment-based courts will grow to handle most of the nation's nonviolent drug users. The concept is called "therapeutic jurisprudence." The program calls for counseling, including the attendance at twelve-step programs and urine tests three times a week. Offenders who fail the program are sentenced to the usual prison term for the crime that initially brought them to court; offenders must plead guilty to the charges against them to begin the program. The sentence is suspended during their participation, and the charges are dropped upon the offender successfully completing the program.[1]

Almost without exception, therapists find that treatment without coercion (be it by criminal sanction, family, employer, or licensing board) is not likely to be successful, and the treatment must be longer than a few months. Deep in denial, addicts usually do not enter treatment unless coerced, and left to their own devices, they do not stay long in treatment.[2] As when training a dog, positive and negative reinforcements are necessary for change. If drug use were legal, like alcohol use, the number of drug addicts would likely reach the number of alcoholics, to the detriment of the individual and to society. William J. Bennett, cochairman of the Partnership for a Drug-Free America, says, "What we were doing in the 1980s and early 1990s—worked. It can work again."[3]

The Drug User

From the time of the apple in the Garden of Eden, people have been ingesting all sorts of things to deal with anxiety and despair, to buttress courage, to escape, or to change their feelings. Some people turn to cigarettes, others to alcohol, and still others to cocaine or Prozac.[4] The reasons addicts give for using illicit drugs sound much like the reasons some psychiatrists give for prescribing psychotropic drugs. "It makes them feel better," or, "They can't function without it." Both reasons deal with symptoms, not the cause of the distress. The bane of the illicit drugs is addiction, and it takes hold quickly.[5]

Drug use may also be an attention-getting maneuver, just as an attempt at suicide may be motivated by a desire for attention. The user will become a subject of concern to family members, police, guidance counselors, welfare workers, social workers, psychiatrists, psychologists, and community agencies. In short, the wheel that squeaks the loudest gets the most grease.[6]

Still others say that in a crazy world, drug use is a sane strategy. Transform the self, since it is hopeless to revolutionize society, proclaimed the Beatles in their song "Revolution"—"Well, you say you want to change institutions / Well, you better change your minds instead." Put another way, when you don't like the world the way it is and you can't change it, then drugs are a convenient way of at least changing it in your mind.

Blacks make up 17 percent of cocaine users but 88 percent of those convicted on crack-cocaine charges. Casual drug use is down, but the population of hard-core addicts (responsible for most drug-related crime) has held steady near five million. Dirty needles result in the spread of HIV.

Many from the drug culture say that the prelude to drug use is a feeling of despair or boredom, which is considered the devil's most powerful weapon. To potential users, life is unexciting, lacking in action, and providing no real involvement, no commitment, no source of meaning. Many youngsters are plagued by a sense of timelessness, boredom, and lassitude. Sociologists call this loss of interest *alienation;* much has been written about it. Experimental drug experiences also appear attractive as a means of warding off adolescent sexual wishes and relieving the isolation and depressive bleakness of the moment. The novelist Walter Kirn claims that in rural America, the culture of drugs is one of the few that youngsters can call their own. He writes,

> [R]ural America is poor America, and that country poor is different from city poor—different in a way that makes kids desperate for a psychedelic change of scenery. . . . When I was growing up we found ways of making ourselves feel as though we existed. Me, I liked the drama of the drug thing. . . . [A friend] wanted to exist, in the worst way. He was like me, a fool for inner cinema, a restless Huck Finn on a methamphetamine raft. . . . If the government experts really want to know why so many country kids, as I was once, light so many joints and snort so many lines, I can tell them. Boredom and freedom.[7]

While some persons take drugs (or alcohol) to help them function and to conform to social expectations, others take them out of refusal or inability to conform to social expectations. In recent decades, drugs (along with ever-changing hair and dress trends) have also been used to define an antiestablishment culture. Young people were not clamoring for admission into the adult world; instead they were rejecting it. Drug use is, for many, the rite of passage out of the square world into a subculture. The isolation and loneliness of the style of life of the square world evoke anguish and despair, which so many people seek to escape by drugs. Other users provide companionship, and as people need friendship and a sense of belonging, the subculture's drug use becomes a style of life. Happiness, says Charlie Brown, is being one of the gang.

Drug use may be likened to a disease in that the idea of use is contagious and spreads, affecting many. It is also described as an infection, an irresistible craving, as a simple result of the body's altered physiology. Arrests of persons under eighteen for drug-law violations have increased nearly twentyfold since the early 1990s, and the arrest rate for females under eighteen is up 2,330 percent. It is estimated that nearly half the high school students in New York City are more than occasional users of some psychoactive drug. Delinquency rates are higher for youths selling drugs than for those using them.

Drug Testing and Education Programs

Proposals for drug testing often meet with the response that it invades privacy, but that response fails to consider the right of the public to be protected against the dangers inflicted by those who use drugs, notably the hard drugs.

The law on drug testing is murky. Historically, the Fourth Amendment was

325

viewed as requiring "some quantum of individualized suspicion" for a search or seizure to be constitutional, but more recently the U.S. Supreme Court has ruled that a search unsupported by probable cause can be constitutional "when special needs, beyond the normal need for law enforcement, make the warrant and probable-cause requirement impracticable."[8] In 1995 the Supreme Court ruled in an Oregon case that random drug tests for student athletes do not violate the Constitution's Fourth Amendment protection against unreasonable searches.[9] By choosing to "go out for the team," the Court noted, school athletes voluntarily subject themselves to a degree of regulation even higher than that imposed on students generally.[10]

In October 1998, the Supreme Court let an Indiana school district continue conducting random drug testing for all students participating in extracurricular activities,[11] but in March 1999, the Court refused to let another Indiana school district require all high school students suspended for disciplinary reasons to undergo drug testing before they were reinstated. Without comment, the Court let stand a ruling that struck down the requirement as a violation of students' privacy rights.[12] As the Court's action was not a decision it set no precedent, but its denial of review confused the already murky law on student drug testing.[13] In June 1988, the Colorado Supreme Court held a school district's policy requiring suspicionless drug testing of students participating in extracurricular activities (in this case the school's marching band) was unconstitutional.[14] Most recently, in opening its 1999–2000 term, the Supreme Court let school officials require drug testing of everyone offered a teaching job.[15]

Since the 1980s drug testing in the workplace has been a controversial issue. In the Reagan administration's war on drugs, government agencies led the way in instituting drug testing programs for their workforces. These were challenged as a violation of the Fourth Amendment's prohibition against unreasonable search and seizure.[16] In 1989, the Supreme Court upheld postaccident drug testing of railroad workers and testing of Customs Service personnel involved in drug interdiction efforts.[17] Since then, drug testing programs affecting government workers in public safety jobs, like pilots, train engineers, or police officers, have generally been upheld, whereas blanket testing of administrative or clerical workers has not.[18] As the first state to do so, Michigan in 1999 enacted legislation requiring drug testing and treatment as a condition for obtaining welfare benefits—it was enjoined as unconstitutional.[19]

In the private sector, where employees are not protected by the Fourth Amendment, drug testing has become widely accepted, particularly in the preemployment context. According to the American Management Association, over 90 percent of large companies now test their employees for drugs.[20] The Americans with Disabilities Act of 1990, which prohibits job discrimination against a qualified individual because of a disability, provides that a preemployment medical examination can be required only after a conditional offer of employment has been made. The ADA also requires that any preemployment physical or mental examinations be job related.[21]

About half of the states have instituted compulsory drug education programs in their public schools. Publicity, however, is a double-edged sword; it may serve to educate, but it may also stimulate or escalate an activity. In a study of the relationship between drug education and drug use, a research group at the University of Michigan found that high school students who were exposed to a drug education program sharply increased experimentation with drugs. According to the research team, the increased knowledge about drugs gained by the students in drug education classes led to loss of the fears that had deterred drug use.[22] Dr. Joseph Adelson, professor of psychology at the University of Michigan, argues, however, that there is little reason to believe that youngsters are quite that resistant to their elders' importunings—if they were, we would not see so few of them now smoking cigarettes.[23]

Advisory board members of the National Organization for the Reform of Marijuana Laws say that there has been miseducation, not education, on drug use. They claim that since the 1930s the dangers of marijuana have been grossly exaggerated, and as people discover that fact from experience, warnings about heroin, amphetamines, methaqualone, and barbiturates are ignored. Moreover, overdramatization by the media, in its insatiable demand to fill its space and time slots, has made drug use seem glamorous, contributing to its increased use. The euphoric highs attributed to drugs by rock, rave, rap, and other pop music artists have glorified and romanticized their use.

All this is exploited for profit. Says a character in Mario Puzo's *The Godfather*, "There is more money potential in narcotics than in any other business."[24] History shows that the underworld always makes a tremendous profit by supplying what convention may condemn and the law prohibit but which nevertheless the people crave. The true cost of a pound of opium, for example, is about $12, but when it reaches the streets, it brings as much as $12,000. As long as there is such fantastic profit to be made in drug traffic, the narcotics laws tend to be self-defeating.

The Criminal Law Reaction to Drug Use

There are those who argue that laws on drug use serve no purpose other than to make illicit drug traffic a highly lucrative business. There is much cynicism, particularly among youth, about the validity of many of the restrictions and penalties imposed by federal and state drug laws and the value of treatment programs. The debate over ways to control drug addiction (or alcoholism) is put as an either-or matter, from strict police enforcement to sympathetic medical treatment. The famed billionaire financier George Soros (among many others) claims that the drug war cannot be won, and he argues that the war on drugs is doing more harm to society than drug abuse itself. He suggests de-emphasizing the criminal aspect of drug use but accompanied by more social opprobrium for the drug culture. Education and social disapproval of cigarette smoking, he notes, have been much more successful than the war on drugs.[25] There are campaigns urging juries to say not guilty in drug cases—to nullify the law—just as jurors in early nineteenth-century America routinely refused to enforce the Alien and Sedition Act, they widely rejected the Fugitive Slave Act in the mid-nineteenth century, and they refused to enforce alcohol prohibition in the early twentieth century.[26]

Society is frequently willing to repress a relatively small group whose behavior is viewed as threatening to the overall culture, particularly when the group in question has little social, economic, or political influence. Mao Tse-tung, determined to revitalize China, reportedly had sixty thousand pushers executed during his first year in power and another forty thousand the following year. In the 1996 documentary film *The Battle of Algiers*, there is a scene in which Algerian revolutionaries shoot and kill a fellow Algerian because he is dealing dope to other Algerians.

The death penalty so used is one way to stop drug traffic, but when threatening behavior becomes widespread, especially among influential members of society, isolation of the offender no longer appears to be a feasible solution to the problem. The effectiveness of criminal sanctions against the user must then be evaluated not only in terms of deterrence success but also in terms of costs of the policy to the individual and society. There come times when the cost of seeking to attain an objective promises to exceed the value that could accrue from its attainment.[27]

Academics and practitioners alike have addressed the legal consequences of the war on drugs: a perceived threat to civil liberties protected by the Fourth Amendment and other constitutional provisions, the imposition of stiff mandatory sentences, the racial inequities in the sentencing for crack and powder cocaine under federal law, the use of racial profiling, the lack of due process in the civil forfeiture process, and many more issues. The high social and financial costs of the war on drugs have also prompted calls for legalization of drugs by some political and judicial figures. In recent years there has been a loosening or eliminating of mandatory minimum sentences for drug crimes (Connecticut, Indiana, Louisiana), but there are increases in authorized penalties elsewhere. Following September 11, 2001, as a necessary by-product of limitation of resources, funds earmarked by the Congress for the war on drugs are increasingly being used for the war on terrorism.

Official Drug Policy

Since early in the twentieth century, drug-control policy in the United States has been premised on the judgment that drug abuse is an evil to be suppressed by the application of criminal enforcement and penal sanctions. Any intent to heal or rehabilitate has been viewed as secondary to the deterrence function, and attempts to justify these measures in terms of rehabilitation of the individual have led to largely irrelevant debates on the feasibility of protecting the individual from himself and the efficacy of medical-versus-criminal modes for dealing with the behavior. The old dope fiend is now called "drug abuser," but the approach to drug addiction remains essentially unchanged.

A report by the Group for the Advancement of Psychiatry, *Drug Misuse: A Psychiatric View of a Modern Dilemma*,[28] urged the United States to redirect its attack against drug misuse. The report suggested that drug abuse be handled through drug treatment and education programs, not through the current widespread practice of treating drug addiction and misuse as a criminal offense. The report recommended that drug misusers whose only crime is possession should be regarded as troubled persons instead of criminals, law-enforcement activities should be directed primarily toward the illegal manufacture and distribution of dangerous drugs, and physicians should review their use of mood- and behavior-altering drugs to ensure the appropriate use of such psychoactive drugs.

The drug-misuse problem, according to the GAP report, "has reached the point where many persons are in chemically ecstatic nightmares, where all societies are in turmoil as some of their brightest minds decay and their crime rates soar." Statistics, the study indicates, show that heroin addiction continues to rise, that indiscriminate use of dangerous drugs among youth may be creating a drug subculture, and that physicians may be contributing to drug misuse by overprescribing mood-affecting drugs. The report pointed out that no effective programs have been launched against the problem of overuse of medically prescribed psychoactive drugs, and little effort, in terms of human resources and money, is going into drug treatment and education programs directed against the more serious drug problems.

While pointing out the failure of the law-enforcement approach to drug addiction, the report makes no mention of drug treatment efforts that have been attempted. In 1919, outpatient clinics were established by local health departments but were soon closed because of the violent local reaction. Forty special clinics were established throughout the United States in 1923 but were closed the same year, an action supported by most state and local authorities and by the House of Delegates of the American Medical Association. At the time, maintenance facilities for alcohol (called "saloons") or for drugs met strong reaction. With no clinical assistance or support, addicts turned to the underworld for drugs. This was followed by an increased demand for new laws and for their enforcement.

Confronted with the failure of the outpatient clinics, the U.S. Public Health Service, in 1935, opened a hospital exclusively for drug addicts in Lexington, Kentucky, and another in 1938, in Fort Worth, Texas. In 1965, some thirty years later, Dr. George Vaillant completed a thorough follow-up study of one hundred New York addicts who had been admitted to Lexington. It was discovered that within twelve years of discharge, 90 percent of this group had returned to the use of drugs and 90 percent had been given prison terms. Ninety-six percent of all voluntary admissions returned to the use of drugs within one year of discharge. The Lexington hospital was later placed under the auspices of the National Institute of Mental Health for the study and research of drug addiction and related problems; the Fort Worth hospital was turned over to the Federal Bureau of Prisons as a correctional institution, the majority of the population consisting of convicted drug abusers.

Persuaded that the lack of success of the two Public Health Service Hospitals was due to geographical separation from the community, which precluded a flexible and continuous treatment program, the Congress enacted, in 1966, the Narcotic Addict Rehabilitation Act, commonly referred to as NARA. The program differs from the Lexington–Fort Worth treatment concept in that it provides for aftercare facilities in the community. The act, as amended in 1968, provided appropriations for the establishment of outpatient services for individuals released from the Public Health Service Hospitals and for assistance to states and municipalities to develop treatment programs and facilities. In addition, the act provided for grants and jointly financed cooperative arrangements to be made to programs in the states and localities.

Arguments by the proponents of policy modification are often based on comparison. For example, it is said that marijuana is less harmful to the individual or to society than is alcohol. "If ingesting alcohol is a constitutional right, is ingesting opium, or heroin, or barbiturates, or anything else, not such a right?" The logic is similar to that employed in the argument over the Vietnam War, where one mentioned the death toll in Southeast Asia and another adduced the annual traffic death figures, assuming that the comparison solves all problems and closes the discussion. Indeed, if such comparisons are to be made, one might say that of all the harms resulting from activity prohibited by the criminal code, those caused by alcoholism and drug addiction are indeed minuscule compared to those done by the automobile. (Each year in the United States about 45,000 persons are killed in automobile accidents, another 4,600,000 are injured or maimed, and the property loss is in the billions of dollars, not to mention the ecological disaster.)

Since the particular hazards of use differ for each, it makes no sense to compare the harmfulness of the various drugs. The potential harm to the individual from any psychoactive drug depends on the intensity, frequency, and duration of use. One may compare, insofar as the individual is concerned, only the harmfulness of specific effects. Is heroin less harmful than alcohol because, unlike alcohol, it directly causes no physical injury, or is heroin more harmful than alcohol because its use is more incapacitating in a behavioral sense? The secretary of health, education, and welfare in a report to Congress, "Marihuana and Health," concluded that assessment of the relative dangers of particular drugs is meaningful only when possible benefits of the drugs are weighed against the comparative scope of their use and their relative impact on society.

History of Drug Misuse

The Civil War introduced the problem of drug addiction to the United States, which is now the leading consumer of legal and illegal drugs. With the discovery of the hypodermic syringe, many soldiers were given morphine injections to alleviate pain from wounds. It was thought that injecting morphine and other derivatives of opium under the skin would not stimulate the so-called opium appetite as did oral administration. This belief proved erroneous. By the end of the Civil War, in 1865, it was estimated that about 60,000 persons in the United States were addicted to the use of morphine by means of self-administered hypodermic injections. There are said to be now at least 500,000 narcotic addicts in the United States, or about 0.25 percent of the population. Just as the countries producing the crude drug had become extensive opium consumers, so the countries manufacturing the morphine and other alkaloids became heavy consumers.

In 1898, a further impetus was given to the use of opium with the discovery of heroin; the name derives from its allegedly heroic quality. Claims were made that it was free from habit-forming properties and was useful in the treatment of opium addiction. Medical literature for the next ten or twelve years advocated this use of heroin. It was not until about 1910 that the medical profession began to realize that heroin was more dangerous than morphine or other opium derivatives in addiction-forming properties.

During the nineteenth century morphine or heroin addiction was called "the American disease" and was said to be as American as apple pie. During this period any person could purchase drugs at any drugstore. It may not be a coincidence that in the United States a pharmacy or apothecary shop came to be known as a *drugstore*. (A *drugstore cowboy* is one who loafs around drugstores.) There were literally hundreds of commercial preparations openly available that contained opium, laudanum, morphine, and so on. Cough syrups containing considerable laudanum were recommended for crying children and for older women. Some of the most popular soda pops had cocaine in them. So-called soothing syrups and various tonics, which were nothing more than narcotic preparations, were used by women in menopause. Diarrhea cordials depended on opium for what little virtue they possessed.

During the last twenty years of the nineteenth century, the law entered the field first with municipal ordinances and later state statutes. By 1912, all but one state and most cities had laws governing the prescription and sale of opiates, although in practice these laws were not rigorously enforced. The peak of the patent-medicine industry in the United States was reached just prior to the passage by Congress of the Pure Food and Drugs Act in 1906. The decline of this industry was further affected in 1914 with the passage of the Harrison Narcotic Act. The pharmaceutical industry, now prosperous, through its extensive advertising suggests that any psychic discomfort can be overcome simply by taking a tranquilizer or antidepressant.

The prevailing law on drug misuse has been developed in the areas of narcotics, dangerous drugs, and marijuana. It is to be noted that the law contains no definition of these terms. A large volume of literature provides a pharmacological or psychological classification of substances in terms of their effect on the natural organism, but legislation and international treaties refer to specific drugs and substances; they do not attempt to make a broad definitional classification. The categories of narcotic substances and dangerous drugs are: opium and its derivatives morphine and heroin, produced from the poppy seed; cocaine, produced from the coca bush; Cannabis sativa, or Indian hemp, known as hashish, marijuana, bhang, and other names, depending on geographic location; and other psychotropic substances, which are chemically manufactured. The Congress has enacted more than fifty laws relating to drug misuse.[29]

The ubiquity of the use of marijuana is reflected by its numerous aliases or nicknames—weed, grass, Mary Jane, reefer, muggles, pot, tea. Charged with battling the growing influx of heroin and opium, Harry Anslinger, America's first drug czar, appointed in 1930 to run the newly created Federal Bureau of Narcotics, began to focus instead on marijuana, which had only begun to find its way across the border from Mexico (brought in by Mexican laborers) in the early part of the century. "Alien Weed Makes Men into Killers" read a headline in the *El Paso Times*,[30] and a 1920s' silent film *High on the Range* showed an innocent cowboy turning into a homicidal maniac after just one puff of what the intertitle ominously called "a new kind of cigarette." Anslinger aspired to be toward drugs what J. Edgar Hoover was toward crime, and he claimed, "If you smoke marijuana, you will go insane"; "If you smoke it, you will become a heroin addict"; "If you smoke it, you will kill people"; "If you smoke it, you will become an unmotivated, dysfunctional loser."[31] He managed to bury the 1944 LaGuardia Committee Report, commissioned by the mayor of New York, that reported that "the sociological, psychological, and medical ills commonly attributed to marijuana have been found to be exaggerated."[32] In 1972, the National Commission on Marihuana and Drug Abuse, put together by President Richard Nixon, also returned a finding that marijuana ought to be decriminalized.[33] Not only did Nixon condemn the report, he created a new superagency, the Drug Enforcement Administration (DEA), to further combat the drug. It was claimed that Red China was upping production in "a Communist plot to dope up America."[34] While, like any narcotic, marijuana has its dangers, regarding it as "the most dangerous drug in America"[35] has proved to be a counterproductive—not to mention extremely costly—proposition. By intensely criminalizing the substance, by pushing for laws mandating harsh minimum sentences, the antimarijuana forces have helped create a multibillion-dollar, not terribly effective war on drugs and a society that puts more people behind bars than almost any on earth. Several states have passed legislation allowing medicinal use of marijuana, though they go in the face of federal drug laws.[36]

Methadone

Methadone, an addictive synthetic drug, is now approved for use in the management of established heroin dependence, but physician-induced dependence upon methadone could be a cause for tort action. In the controversy over the use of methadone as a substitutive agent in the treatment of opiate dependence, it is said to be as useful as shifting from scotch to bourbon.

The distinction between drug use and drug abuse is a matter of degree. A drug, like any instrument, is not inherently good or bad; its value depends on its use. Methadone acts on the central nervous system, eliminating craving and withdrawal symptoms. In effect, one addictive drug is substituted for another but with apparent advantage to both the user and society. The user is assured a constant supply of the drug in accurate dosage and is enabled to work, or complete his education, and to stay out of jail. Society is spared the serious crimes that physical dependence upon an opiate often prompts a user to commit in order to support his habit.

Methadone treatment has generally been confined to an institutional setting where a knowledgeable staff and ancillary services are available. In this setting, the drug is given in orange juice each morning to the heroin-dependent patient, and its effect is closely observed. Urine tests are taken daily for the presence of heroin or other drugs, and those patients not faithfully following the regimen are dismissed. Most important, candidates for the program are carefully screened, and only those are admitted who have a documented history of abuse of one or more opiate drugs (the duration of which is to be stated), with confirmed history of one or more failures of withdrawal treatment, and evidence of current abuse of opiates.

Because inadequate public funding has made it impossible for public institutions to meet the enormous need, the individual practitioners have entered the field. Psychiatrists, internists, and general practitioners have sought to fill this gap between need and service. However, the individual practitioner does not have the time, and often not the training, to determine whether an opiate user has a well-established physical dependence. He is also more likely to issue methadone by prescription on a weekly basis and without supervising compliance with the program.

The iatrogenic induction of methadone dependence, where no real physical dependence upon opiates previously existed, represents a very real problem. The American Medical Association and the National Academy of Sciences condemn the administration of narcotic drugs on an enduring basis, except for patients with intractable pain associated with an incurable disease or where withdrawal would jeopardize the life of an aged or infirm addict. The use of these drugs for a short term to ease the vicissitudes of withdrawal is accepted.

Judicial Processing of Cases

The social and psychological characteristics of the addict distinguish him from the traditional criminal. Most crimes associated with drug addiction involve violations of federal or state laws on use or possession as well as thefts, burglaries, and robberies committed in order to obtain funds to purchase drugs. The addict's physical needs differ little from those of the diabetic, except that the diabetic will eventually die without insulin while the addict will suffer extreme physiological discomfort without drugs. In the case of drug-precipitated crimes, though prompted by a physiological compulsion that demands satisfaction, the addict is usually declared criminally responsible. A rare exception to this general rule may be made when the offense was committed in a psychotic state, as for example morphine delirium or cocaine psychosis.[37] Stealing by a drug addict to buy drugs to satisfy his craving may be said, psychiatrically speaking, to be a function of his disease, but the law in this area does not entertain the defense of not guilty by reason of insanity. In *United States v. Lyons,*[38] the Fifth Circuit held that iatrogenic narcotics addiction alone may constitute a mental disease or defect sufficient to support the defense of insanity in a criminal prosecution.

Alcohol and drug use are associated. Ninety-two percent of offenders on the day of family violence reported or tested positive for alcohol or psychoactive drug use. Whether labeled a disease or not, addicts clearly have changes in their nervous system from the drug use that affects their volition in regard to seeking the drugs. In any event, there is some component of will in the drug-seeking behavior of addicts, and we continue, as we must, to hold people accountable for their actions.

It is to be recalled that the law does not make addiction per se a crime. When Lawrence Robinson was arrested and convicted under a unique California statute that made addiction illegal, the U.S. Supreme Court reversed the conviction.[39] Drawing an analogy, not necessarily valid psychiatrically, between the status of addiction and such other conditions as leprosy and venereal disease, the Court said that holding one criminally responsible for a status or condition constitutes cruel and unusual punishment in violation of the Constitution. The police officer who arrested Robinson did not catch him in the act of using or possessing narcotics but saw discolorations, scabs, and needle marks on his arms. The principle of the case, long a foundation of the law, bars criminal responsibility for being an alcoholic, exhibitionist, homosexual, prostitute, vagrant, or the like; but it does not preclude responsibility for doing or manifesting the status. Thus, the state can criminally punish an addict or anyone else for the use, possession, concealment, and purchase of drugs, or for being under the influence of drugs. One year after *Robinson*, a report was filed by a presidential advisory commission recommending that there be civil commitment to treatment facilities rather than criminal prosecution for drug addicts, a recommendation that resulted in the passage three years later, in 1966, of the aforementioned Narcotic Addict Rehabilitation Act and the adoption of a similar law in several states.

In the use and possession cases, the accused usually claims that the police illegally obtained the evidence, and if a motion to suppress the evidence is successful, the matter is ended. In crimes involving drug use, prostitution, and gambling, there are generally no victims to complain of their injuries. As a result, it becomes necessary for the police to devise ways of searching out the offenders. The judge can readily say that the police obtained the evidence illegally or entrapped the defendant (that is, the methods used by the police are "repugnant to fair play and justice"). In cases dealing with marijuana offenses, large numbers of middle-class youth have become involved in its use, and judicial decisions have given increasing weight to the consequences of the criminal-law process on the individual. Faced with the alternative of a felony conviction or acquittal, a significant number of judges tend to throw out the case on a ruling of evidence.[40]

If the motion to suppress the evidence is overruled, and if on chemical analysis the seized drug proves to be within the prohibited class, the defendant has little option but to plead guilty. The cases as presented in court are thus quite cut and dried. Under most state and federal statutes, in order to obtain a conviction, it is necessary to show both a knowledge of the thing possessed and an intent to possess it. Since such knowledge is seldom susceptible of direct proof, a presumption of guilt is inferred from the fact of possession.

Such considerations as the fact that the accused is seeing a psychiatrist may be urged to persuade a district attorney not to prosecute or may be used to persuade a judge to suspend sentence and grant probation. Apart from such pretrial or posttrial considerations, however, psychiatric evidence plays a small role in the disposition of these cases. Extrajudicially, however, the medical profession has played a role in assessing individual and social consequences of various policies with regard to the control of drugs and in the operation of treatment centers, which has influenced the administration of the law.[41]

Legal control and medical programs are often intertwined, though public officials change year by year in considering drug use mainly a medical problem, then a social one, then a criminal one. Treatment as well as prevention programs do not receive enthusiastic support because of the lack of evidence of accomplishment. The record to date is dismal, but in the last analysis it is indicative of the great need of a large number of people to get stoned out of their minds. Women in pregnancy often are unaware (or do not care) about the harm that results to the fetus by their use of drugs. To protect the fetus, the attempt has been made to civilly commit drug-dependent women for the period of their pregnancy.[42] More frequently, they are kept in jail during their pregnancy.[43]

There is memory of an earlier time when aspirin for most people seemed medicine enough against the world they lived in. Gone is the spirit reflected in the old refrain in "Home on the Range": "Where seldom is heard a discouraging word / And the skies are not cloudy all day." Historically the extensive use of drugs has occurred during the decline of a society, not during its golden period. While it may be debated whether the heavy use of drugs is a cause or a symptom of social decay, or both, the deterioration of both individuals and society as a whole is apparent to all, except possibly to the user.

Notes

1. The results to date are mixed. Wake County, North Carolina, which started a program in 1996 for drug addicts to get court-supervised treatment instead of going to prison, reports that its first twenty-five graduates later committed crimes at least as often as those who went to prison and received treatment. The drug courts in the county cost taxpayers about $337,000 a year. A. Weigl, "Drug Court Gets Shaky Start," *News & Observer*, Dec. 18, 2000, p. 1. On the other hand, Arizona, the first state to begin treating all its nonviolent drug offenders instead of locking them up, estimates that it saved more than $2.5 million in the program's first fiscal year of operation. Editorial, "Drug Treatment Gets a Boost," *New York Times*, Dec. 13, 1999, p. 36. A 1999 report by the Arizona Supreme Court found that 77 percent of offenders stayed off drugs during the year following their arrest. M. Roosevelt, "Patients, Not Prisoners," *Time*, May 7, 2001, p. 46. See generally L. B. Erlich, *A Textbook of Forensic Addiction Medicine and Psychiatry* (Springfield, Ill.: Thomas, 2001).

2. Dr. Sally Satel, a psychiatrist at Yale University, writes, "As a psychiatrist who treats addicts I have learned that legal sanctions—either imposed or threatened—may provide the leverage needed to keep them alive by keeping them in treatment. Voluntary help is often not enough." She adds, "Addicts would be better off if more of them were arrested and forced to enroll in treatment programs. . . . [This is] the essence of humane therapy." S. L. Satel, "For Addicts, Force Is the Best Medicine," *Wall Street Journal*, Jan. 7, 1998, p. 6. See also S. L.

Satel, *Drug Treatment: The Case for Coercion* (Washington, D.C.: American Enterprise Institute, 1999). Dr. Thomas Szasz calls it "therapeutic tyranny" and likens it to the tyranny in Nazi Germany. He ignores the burden put on society as well as on the self by those who act irresponsibly. Those who are familiar with any of Szasz's many writings during the past forty years are not surprised by his contention. See T. Szasz, *Pharmacracy: Medicine and Politics in America* (Westport, Conn.: Praeger, 2001).

3. W. J. Bennett, "The Drug War Worked Once. It Can Again," *Wall Street Journal*, May 15, 2001, p. 26.

4. See D. T. Courtwright, *Forces of Habit* (Cambridge: Harvard University Press, 2001). Steven Soderbergh's film *Traffic* (2001) hammers home the idea that user demand is the true force behind the drug problem. Ernest Jones in a chapter called "The Cocaine Episode" in his biography of Freud reports that Freud was deeply into coke in the mid-1880s. Elated by the drug, Jones reports, Freud used it freely, recommended it to everybody, and made it out to be the universal remedy. Evidence of overdose and addiction began to accumulate, however, and when the discovery of cocaine's only legitimate medical function—local anesthetic in eye surgery, still the only one—was made in 1887 by Carl Koller, Freud supposedly dropped using it. Some people, though, wonder whether Freud's use of cocaine was just an "episode." See W. Kendrick, "Not Just Another Oedipal Drama," in Joy Press (ed.), *War of the Words* (New York: Three Rivers Press, 2001), pp. 137–65.

The drug kingpin Inzio Tulippa in Mario Puzo's novel *Omerta* (New York: Ballantine Books, 2000) defends the selling of drugs: "Drugs were the salvation of the human spirit, the refuge of those damned to despair by poverty and mental illness. They were the salve for the lovesick, for the lost souls in our spiritually deprived world. After all, if you no longer believed in God, society, your own worth, what were you supposed to do? Kill yourself? Drugs kept people alive in a realm of dreams and hope. All that was needed was a little moderation" (p. 115). "And what about tobacco and alcohol? They did much more damage" (p. 120).

5. A lawsuit was instituted contending that the manufacturer of the popular antidepressant Paxil concealed evidence that the drug can be addictive. The lawsuit was filed on behalf of thirty-five people from across the country who said they suffered symptoms ranging from electric-like shocks to suicidal thoughts after discontinuing use of the drug. The lawsuit claimed that the pharmaceutical company concealed the possibility of physical and psychological withdrawal symptoms from the drug. It alleged fraud, deceit, negligence, and breach of warranty. The suit failed. "Lawsuit Claims Paxil Is Addictive" (Associated Press news release), *Detroit News*, Aug. 2001, p. 6.

6. E. Berne, *Games People Play* (New York: Grove Press, 1964). In a My Turn article in *Newsweek*, writer Joan France said to hell with her spoiled-rotten son, who wanted to get her involved in a drug-rehabilitation program.

7. W. Kirn, "Crack Country," *New York Times Magazine*, Feb. 13, 2000, p. 15. For a history of opium and its effects over the last four thousand years, during which it has always been both a blessing and a curse, see M. Booth, *Opium: A History* (New York: St. Martin's Press, 1996).

8. Griffin v. Wisconsin, 483 U.S. 868 (1987); see United States v. Martinez-Fuerte, 428 U.S. 543 (1976).

9. Vernonia School District v. Acton, 515 U.S. 646 (1995). Likewise, the California Supreme Court found that the NCAA's (National Collegiate Athletic Association) drug testing program did not violate the athlete's state constitutional right to privacy. The court held that the NCAA's interest in health and safety outweighed the diminished privacy expectations of the athletes. Hill v. NCAA, 865 P.2d 633 (Cal. 1994).

10. 515 U.S. at 655.

11. "High Court Allows Drug Tests in School" (Associated Press news release), *Detroit News*, Oct. 6, 1998.

12. Anderson Community School Corp. v. Willis, 526 U.S. 1019 (1999); on appeal from 158 F.2d 415 (7th Cir. 1998).

13. See D. Hawkins, "Trial by Vial: More Schools Give Urine Tests for Drugs—but at What Cost?" *U.S. News & World Report*, May 31, 1999, p. 70.

14. Trinidad Sch. Dist. No. 1 v. Lopez, 963 P.2d 1095 (Colo. 1998).

15. In opening its 1999–2000 term the Supreme Court declined, without comment, to hear a challenge to a policy of the school board in Knoxville of requiring all newly hired

teachers, and those transferring from one teaching position to another, to submit to a drug test. The trial judge threw out the suspicionless testing requirement after finding that there was no documented evidence of a drug abuse problem among teachers and that teaching is not heavily regulated for safety reasons. The Sixth Circuit reversed that ruling, saying that even without evidence of a drug problem among teachers, drug testing is justified by the "unique role" teachers play in school children's lives. Teachers and principals are "front-line observers in providing for a safe school environment," the appeals court said. "Simple common sense and experience with life" would indicate that children could be at risk from teachers with drug problems. 158 F.3d 361 (6th Cir. 1998). In their Supreme Court appeal, the teachers argued that this justification was inadequate, and noted that they were not challenging the right of the school board to test any teacher about whom a suspicion had been raised. Knox County Education Association v. Knox County Board of Education, No. 98–1799 (1999).

16. In determining whether a search is reasonable, the courts apply a balancing test. The leading case is Schmerber v. California, 384 U.S. 757 (1966) (blood test).

17. The first of the two 1989 U.S. Supreme Court cases that dealt with drug testing is Skinner v. Railway Labor Executives' Assn., 489 U.S. 602 (1989). The Court applied the *special needs* exception that was created in New Jersey v. T.L.O., 469 U.S. 325 (1985). In relying on *T.L.O.*, the Court in *Skinner* held that if there are "special needs" as set forth in *T.L.O.*, suspicion of wrongdoing prior to a search is not required and the "search may be reasonable despite the absence of such suspicion." 489 U.S. at 624. In the second of the two 1989 U.S. Supreme Court cases involving drug testing, Nat'l Treasury Employees Union v. Von Raab, 489 U.S. 656 (1989), the Court held that drug tests were reasonable for employees carrying firearms and involved in drug interdiction. The Court held that "employees who are directly involved in the interdiction of illegal drugs or who are required to carry firearms in the line of duty likewise have a diminished expectation of privacy in respect to the intrusions occasioned by a urine test." 489 U.S. at 672.

18. Examples of cases prohibiting drug testing of administrative or clerical workers include Am. Fed. of Govt. Employees v. Cheney, 754 F.Supp. 1409 (N.D. Cal. 1990, *aff'd*, 944 F.2d 503 (9th Cir. 1991) (court denied blanket drug testing of pathologists and dental hygienists); Transp. Inst. v. U.S. Coast Guard, 727 F.Supp. 648 (D.C. Cir. 1989) (court denied drug testing of civilian Coast Guard cooks, mess staff, and cleaners); Nat. Fed. of Fed. Employees v. Cheney, 884 F.2d 603 (D.C. Cir. 1989) (court held that the Army cannot test civilian laboratory workers but it can test employees who occupy positions in the aviation, police, or guard departments); Taylor v. O'Grady, 888 F.2d 1189 (7th Cir. 1989) (court upheld the drug testing of gun-carrying prison guards but did not permit the testing of administrative personnel).

19. Marchwinski v. Howard, 113 F.Supp.2d 1134 (E.D. Mich. 2000). The statute was criticized in an editorial "Drug Tests" in the *Detroit Free Press,* Oct. 1, 1999, p. 12, which stated: "Unlike people who agree to undergo testing for employment, people who turn to the government for help during the hard times can't choose another human services agency. The government's the only game in town. . . . Poor people who have substance abuse problems should be encouraged to get treatment voluntarily without their children. Forcing people who have fallen on hard times to give up their privacy rights in exchange for temporary assistance—especially under a policy based on myth—is an insult. It's also bad government." A New York proposal is discussed in N. Bernstein, "Welfare Officials to Search Records of Drug Treatment," *New York Times,* Sept. 25, 1999, p. 14. The ACLU challenged the practice as an invasion of privacy, not on the ground that people on welfare need drugs more than others to escape their reality.

20. American Management Association, 1995 Survey: Workplace Drug Testing and Drug Abuse Policies. See R. Coulson, *Alcohol, Drugs, and Arbitration: An Analysis of Fifty-Nine Arbitration Cases* (New York: American Arbitration Association, 1988).

21. 42 U.S.C. 12112.

22. Research indicates that drug prevention programs in the main have no impact on alcohol or drug use. The U.S. Department of Education says that DARE (Drug Abuse Resistance Education) is not on its list of programs whose effectiveness is proven. Experts warn of a cozy relationship between prevention program creators and evaluators and those who stand to profit by selling programs. J. Upton, "DARE Doesn't Work," *Detroit News,* Feb. 27, 2000, p. 1.

23. J. Adelson, "Drugs and Youth," *Commentary,* May 1989, p. 24.

24. M. Puzo, *The Godfather* (New York: Random House, 1969).

25. G. Soros, "The Drug War Cannot Be Won: It's Time to Just Say No to Self-Destructive Prohibition," *Washington Post*, Feb. 2, 1997, p. C-1. See also T. S. Szasz, *Ceremonial Chemistry* (New York: Doubleday, 1974); J. W. Shenk, "America's Altered States," *Harper's*, May 1999, p. 38; "Beyond Legalization: New Ideas for Ending the War on Drugs" (special issue), *Nation*, Sept. 20, 1999. The Dutch liberalization program is criticized in L. Collins, "Holland's Half-Baked Drug Experiment," *Foreign Affairs*, May/June 1999, p. 82.

26. "Just Say Not Guilty?" (advertisement), *Nation*, May 8, 2000, p. 24.

27. Culture conflicts and group struggles were vital factors in the course of the temperance and prohibition movement in the United States. Organized labor was hostile to prohibition up to the final adoption of the Eighteenth Amendment, but business interests, persuaded that sobriety among their employees was conducive to their efficiency, supported the dry forces. A considerable number of cases relating to the Eighteenth Amendment and its enforcement came before the Supreme Court, where its validity was challenged and sustained. Licensing of manufacturers of alcohol and alcoholic preparations for medicinal and industrial use as well as investigation and reporting of violations of the prohibition law were made duties of the commissioner of internal revenue, although taxation and revenue were not the purpose of the law. During the twelve and a half years of the life of the National Prohibition Act, popularly known as the Volstead Act, federal prohibition officers arrested more than 750,000 persons, of whom more than 500,000 were convicted. The courts, faced with congestion and intolerable delays, resorted to "bargain days," on which persons charged with violating the prohibition law could plead guilty, dispense with trial, and be assessed a fine. With the collapse in 1930 and 1931 of the period of prosperity, the public began to fear the power of the racketeers, and opinion rapidly developed in opposition to the amendment and the Volstead Act. The Democratic party adopted, in the presidential campaign of 1932, a platform openly advocating repeal of the Eighteenth Amendment. On December 5, 1933, national prohibition was terminated. There is now a legitimate, large, profitable, and flourishing industry built on liquor in the United States, and the same future is likely for marijuana. See "Drug Addiction," *Encyc. Brit.* 7 (1965): 702; *Encyc. Soc. Sci.* 3 (1931): 242; "Narcotics," *Encyc. Brit.* 16 (1965): 32.

28. Group for the Advancement of Psychiatry Committee on Mental Health Services, *Drug Misuse: A Psychiatric View of a Modern Dilemma* (New York: Scribner, 1971).

29. M. R. Sonnenreich, R. L. Bogomolny, & R. J. Graham, *Handbook of Federal Narcotic and Dangerous Drug Laws* (Washington, D.C.: U.S. Govt. Ptg. Off., 1969). A First Amendment exercise-of-religion argument has been made to delimit in a minor way the application of the drug laws. In a much-publicized case, the California Supreme Court ruled that Navajo Indians using peyote in accordance with the dictates of their native church, although in violation of the Health and Safety Code, were using peyote in a bona fide "pursuit of religious faith." People v. Woody, 40 Cal. Rptr. 69, 394 P.2d 814 (1964). Thereafter, Dr. Timothy Leary contended that the First Amendment protected his use of marijuana as an integral part of the exercise of religion. The Court of Appeals for the Fifth Circuit said that there was no evidence to show that the use of marijuana is a formal requisite of the practice of Hinduism, the religion which Leary professed to follow. Leary v. United States, 383 F.2d 851 (5th Cir. 1967), *reversed on evidentiary grounds*, 395 U.S. 6 (1969).

30. See D. F. Musto, *The American Disease: Origins of Narcotics Control* (New York: Oxford University Press, 1987).

31. See E. R. Bloomquist, *Marijuana: The Second Trip* (Beverly Hills: Glencoe Press, 1971); W. B. Eldridge, *Narcotics and the Law* (Chicago: University of Chicago Press, 1967); J. Kaplan, *Marijuana: The New Prohibition* (New York: World, 1970).

32. See M. K. Sanders, "Addicts and Zealots: The Chaotic War against Drug Abuse," *Harper's*, June 1970, p. 71.

33. House Committee on Interstate and Foreign Commerce, *Drug Use in America: Problem in Perspective* (Second report of the National Commission on Marihuana and Drug Abuse), 93d Cong., 1st sess., 1973, H. Doc. 50210.

34. See R. Nixon, *Beyond Peace* (New York: Random House, 1994), p. 228.

35. K. K. Skinner, A. Anderson, & M. Anderson (eds.), *Reagan, in His Own Hand* (New York: Free Press, 2001), *American Law in the 20th Century* (New Haven: Yale University Press, 2002), p. 106.

36. California and then some seven other states by legislation allow the medical use of marijuana, but federal authorities have threatened physicians with loss of license for writing prescriptions under the Federal Controlled Substance Act. The common-law defense of "necessity" is not recognized under the act. Years ago, in Webb v. United States, 249 U.S. 96 (1919), the U.S. Supreme Court held that a physician who prescribed morphine for addicts who needed a fix, and a druggist who filled the prescriptions, violated the Harrison Narcotic Drug Act of 1914. The decision put an end to the career of so-called dope doctors, who made a living by prescribing drugs. L. M. Friedman, *American Law in the 20th Century* (New Haven: Yale University Press, 2002), p. 106. See S. H. Verhovek, "What Is the Matter with Mary Jane?" *New York Times*, Oct. 15, 2000, p. WK-3; see generally R. Bonnie, *The Marihuana Conviction: A History of Marihuana Prohibition in the United States* (Charlottesville: University Press of Virginia, 1974). The fact that a physician prescribes a drug does not prevent it from being abused. Typically, marijuana is used in conjunction with alcohol or other drugs. It is now reported that marijuana poses the risk of accidents due to the effects of impaired short-term memory, concentration, perception, and motor skills. In some people, marijuana increases blood pressure. Chronic use of the drug can cause psychological changes such as anxiety, depression, and apathy, with such behavioral changes as decline in school or work performance. The drug also has serious side effects on pregnancies such as birth defects. "An Overview of Substance Abuse," *Newsletter of Michigan Psychiatric Society* 32 (Sept./Oct. 2000): 1.

37. The Court of Appeals in Brown v. United States, 331 F.2d 822 (D.C. Cir. 1964), observing that "narcotic addiction is an illness," ruled that insanity based upon drug addiction was a question of fact for the jury and remanded the case for a new trial. See also State v. Cook, 273 N.C. 377, 160 S.E.2d 49 (1968). See A. K. Dolan, "The Impact of Methadone Maintenance on Civil and Criminal Liability," *S. Cal. L. Rev.* 46 (1973): 713.

38. 731 F.2d 243 (5th Cir. 1984).

39. Robinson v. California, 370 U.S. 660 (1962). See R. C. Boldt, "The Construction of Responsibility in the Criminal Law," *U. Pa. L. Rev.* 140 (1992): 2245.

40. There is racial equality in drug use: blacks represent 13 percent of the total population and 15 percent of all drug users; whites represent 71 percent of the population and 72 percent of all drug users—but there is racial inequality in arrest, conviction, and imprisonment: blacks represent 45 percent of all drug arrests and receive 74 percent of all prison sentences for drug possession. National Household Survey on Drug Abuse, *Preliminary Results from the National Household Survey on Drug Abuse* (Rockville, Md.: Dept. of Health and Human Services, 1998); E. Luna, "The Prohibition Apocalypse," *DePaul L. Rev.* 46 (1997): 483.

41. J. Kaplan, "The Role of the Law in Drug Control," *Duke L.J.* 1971: 1065; B. L. Segal, "New Frontiers in the Defense of Drug Cases," *Contemp. Drug* 1 (1971): 49; "Prosecution and Defense of a Drug Case: A Panel," *Contemp. Drug* 1 (1972): 97.

42. P. H. Soloff, S. Jewell, & L. H. Roth, "Civil Commitment and the Rights of the Unborn," *Am. J. Psychiatry* 136 (1979): 114. Under the doctrine of *parens patriae,* the courts have also compelled a Jehovah's Witness to submit to blood transfusion to protect the life of an unborn child. See, e.g., Raleigh Fitkin-Paul Morgan Memorial Hosp. v. Anderson, 42 N.J. 421, 201 A.2d 537 (1964).

43. The U.S. Supreme Court, with three justices dissenting, ruled that a public hospital may not test pregnant patients for drug use and tell police who tested positive. The Court held that (1) urine tests were "searches" within the meaning of the Fourth Amendment, and (2) tests, and reporting of positive test results to police, were unreasonable searches absent patients' consent, in view of the policy's law-enforcement purpose. Ferguson v. City of Charleston, 121 S. Ct. 1281 (2001). It is to be noted that the Court did not preclude the use of all medical test results in criminal prosecutions. When the testing is done by private hospitals, not acting at governmental direction, or for primarily medical purposes, or pursuant to an exigent need (such as drawing blood from someone when there is a reasonable belief that their use of alcohol contributed to a motor vehicle collision), or pursuant to the patient's voluntary consent, the test results may be used by law enforcement for criminal prosecution in compliance with the Fourth Amendment.

15

Imposition of and Carrying Out the Death Penalty

The psychiatrist may be involved in one or two stages in the death penalty process: (1) imposition of the death penalty, and (2) carrying out the death penalty. The criminal law has three concepts of incapacity (insanity), each pertinent to a different stage; the capacity to stand trial, the capacity to commit crime, and the capacity to be executed under a death warrant.

In a recent ten-year period about 22,000 criminal homicides were recorded annually in the United States. Of these, over the ten-year period, about 4,000 cases were egregious enough to qualify for the death penalty, and about 250 over the ten-year period actually resulted in a death sentence. However, over the ten-year period only 22 people, on average, were executed annually. The number of executions increased to 98 in 1999, the highest number since the U.S. Supreme Court reinstated the death penalty in 1976, but still a small fraction of the 3,700 who sit on death rows nationwide. Far more death row inmates die of natural causes than are executed. In effect, the process in the United States caters to both proponents of the death penalty (by its imposition) and the abolitionists (by rarely carrying it out). Although juries imposed the death penalty more and more frequently in the 1980s and 1990s, the number of people executed in the United States in any given year has yet to exceed the number killed by lightning, as one commentator put it.[1]

Imposition of the Death Penalty

On the imposition of the death penalty, the Supreme Court in 1972 rendered highly publicized death penalty opinions in which it ruled 5–4 that the death penalty in the form it then had was unconstitutional.[2] While no unifying reason supported the decision, the net result, with each justice writing his own opinion (243 pages in all), was that the death penalty, as imposed within the discretion of juries, violates the Eighth Amendment, not because it is inherently intolerable, but because it is applied so rarely, "so wantonly and freakishly," that it serves no valid purpose and now constitutes cruel and unusual punishment. Only two justices—Justices Brennan and Marshall—ruled the death penalty unconstitutional per se. The dissenting justices felt that the majority had gone beyond judicial jurisdiction and trespassed upon the prerogatives of the legislature.

Thus capital punishment in the form it then had was rendered cruel and unusual by operation of what was intended to be, at the time of its introduction, an ameliorative feature of the criminal justice system—the jury's discretion to impose a lesser sentence than death. The Court, finding no reason to believe that the death sentence was imposed with "informed selectivity," concluded that it was imposed in a way that arbitrarily and capriciously discriminated against minorities and the poor.

Chief Justice Warren Burger then touched on changes that would have to be made to allow the use of the death penalty in compliance with the result of the case. The Court implied that capital punishment would be sanctioned if the penalty is uniformly and consistently applied. It was thought that legislative enactment of mandatory death sentences would seemingly provide an answer.

Following the Supreme Court's decision in 1972 that the death penalty it had under consideration was unconstitutional because of the discriminatory nature in its application, a number of states enacted statutes making the death sentence mandatory for all who committed a designated type of offense. Although their ostensible aim was to avoid discrimination against minority peoples, such statutes did not survive the scrutiny of the Supreme Court. In 1976, in *Woodson v. North Carolina*, the Supreme Court ruled that it is cruel and unusual punishment to mandate the death penalty for all who commit certain crimes.[3] Two years later, in 1978, in *Lockett v. Ohio*,[4] Chief Justice Burger wrote:

> In capital cases the fundamental respect for humanity underlying the Eighth Amendment requires consideration of the character and record of the individual offender and the circumstances of the particular offense as a constitutionally indispensable part of inflicting the penalty of death.[5]

According to that line of decisions, a death penalty statute is deemed valid if in each case the appropriateness of capital punishment can be ascertained in the light of aggravating or mitigating factors. Under the approved statutes, after a defendant has been found guilty, the court must conduct a hearing and consider, among other things, the mental status of the defendant. Since then, one prime question asked of the expert witness is whether the person is likely to be more violent and dangerous to fellow prisoners and to others than any of the other prisoners who are currently incarcerated.

In a 1983 opinion of the Supreme Court, *Barefoot v. Estelle*,[6] there was a challenge to the use of psychiatrists in capital sentencing hearings. In the sentencing phase of the bifurcated trial (the defendant had been found guilty of murder of a policeman), the prosecution introduced the testimony of two psychiatrists in order to establish the aggravating circumstances allowing imposition of the death penalty. The psychiatrists who testified had not examined the defendant (he declined to be interviewed); their testimony was based on information in a lengthy hypothetical question posed to them on the stand by the prosecutor. Nonetheless, they agreed on a diagnosis of the defendant as a sociopath, and agreed "within reasonable medical certainty" that he would commit future acts of violence. One of the psychiatrists claimed that the certainty of this prediction was "one hundred percent and absolute."[7] Errol Morris's 1988 documentary film *The Thin Blue Line* ridiculed the psychiatrist James Grigson, also known as "Dr. Death."[8]

The defendant's challenge to Dr. Grigson's testimony was supported by an amicus curiae brief filed by the American Psychiatric Association that argued that psychiatric predictions of future dangerousness ought to be excluded as a matter of law because the empirical data consistently indicate a large margin of error. Justice White, writing for five members of the six-person majority, evidently feared that excluding psychiatric testimony on dangerousness might lead to challenges in a variety of cases (including civil commitment). Thus, he wrote, "The suggestion that no psychiatrist's testimony may be presented with respect to a defendant's future dangerousness is somewhat like asking us to disinvent the wheel." He went on to say, "We are unconvinced . . . that the adversary process cannot be trusted to sort out the reliable from the unreliable evidence."[9]

Future dangerousness involves prediction, and hence it is always problematical—a bit of crystal-ball gazing. In a decision handed down in 2000, *Saldano v. Texas*,[10] the Supreme Court vacated a death sentence issued by a Texas court to an Argentine man convicted of a murder committed during a robbery. Under Texas law, the jury deciding on a sentence of death is to consider whether the defendant presents "a continuing threat to society," and in this case, Walter Quijano, a clinical psychologist who testified as the prosecution's expert witness, told the jurors they could take into account the fact that Hispanics were "over represented" in prison compared to their population and might therefore be considered dangerous. In statistical terms, ethnicity or gender is correlated—not causative—with dangerousness, but that may not be mentioned by the expert (though ethnicity or gender is apparent to the jury). Ruling that ethnicity had been improperly injected into the sentencing process, the Supreme Court held that the sentencing hearing had violated the defendant's rights to equal protection and due process, and therefore vacated the sentence for a new hearing "in which race is not considered." In an earlier case, in 1986, *Skipper v. South Carolina*, a majority of the Supreme Court said that the defendant's behavior in jail between the time of his arrest and trial is indicative of future behavior, and hence good behavior during that time should be considered as a mitigating factor in the sentencing consideration.[11] In 1992, the Supreme Court ruled that the defendant has a right to inform the jury that because of earlier criminal convictions, he would be ineligible for parole if he were sentenced to life in prison rather than death.[12]

In *Lockett* in 1978, the Supreme Court said that in a capital case the accused is entitled under the Eighth and Fourteenth Amendments to present, in all but the rarest kind of capital case, "any aspect of [his] character or records, and any circumstances of the offense that [he] proffers as a basis for a sentence less than death."[13] A statute that restricts mitigating factors is unconstitutional, Chief Justice Burger wrote, because it "creates the risk that the death penalty will be imposed in spite of actions which may call for a less severe penalty." However, Justice Burger noted that "nothing in this opinion limits the traditional authority of a court to exclude, as irrelevant, evidence not bearing on the defendant's character, prior record, or the circumstances of [his] offense."[14] Put another way, for relevancy, the extenuating circumstances must have a causal nexus to the crime. Justice Burger also noted that no opinion is expressed as to whether the need to deter certain kinds of homicide would justify a mandatory death sentence, as, for example, when a prisoner—or escapee—under a life sentence is found guilty of murder.[15]

Commentators have argued that the defendant should be permitted to offer any evidence that might persuade the jury not to impose a death sentence, including evidence calling into question the morality or efficacy of the death penalty or describing the process of execution.[16] The Georgia Supreme Court allowed testimony from the defendant's grandfather that he did not want his grandson executed for killing his parents.[17] In Oklahoma, the statute permits the defendant to present evidence of any mitigating circumstance. In *Eddings v. Oklahoma*, the U.S. Supreme Court reversed a death sentence because the sentencing court declined to consider that evidence of "a difficult family history and of emotional disturbance" may constitute relevant mitigating evidence. Evidence was presented that the defendant had an antisocial personality.[18]

It is bewildering what is considered as an aggravating or mitigating circumstance. Shortly after *Eddings*, the Alabama Supreme Court, in a similar case, stated, "[E]vidence was presented that the defendant had an antisocial personality. Here, the defendant's mental or emotional disturbance must be considered as relevant mitigating evidence."[19] In *State v. Caldwell*,[20] the South Carolina Supreme Court held that evidence of antisocial personality that made it difficult for the defendant to obey laws warrants an instruction on the statutory mitigating factor of mental disorder. In this case, a psychiatrist testified for the defense that after his examination of the defendant, his opinion was that he had an "antisocial personality which is synonymous with a psychopathic personality." He described the condition as one in which an individual is not constrained by societal norms and therefore is likely to obey rules of his own. The psychiatrist also stated that if given the opportunity, the defendant could repeat the act and kill again. In reaching his diagnosis, the psychiatrist used a list of criteria suggesting that the disorder begins early in life. The South Carolina Supreme Court concluded, "Because this evidence raised the inference that [the defendant] was suffering from a mental disorder at the time the murder was committed, the trial judge erred in failing to instruct the statutory mitigating circumstances."[21] In other cases, as in *Barefoot v. Estelle*, sociopathy is considered an aggravating circumstance.[22]

The new death penalty laws did not create a new ethical dilemma for psychiatrists, as sometimes alleged. Actually, as fanciful as the courtroom testimony may seem, it is the same type of testimony that is presented in reports and testimony in all types of cases affecting the verdict or sentence, and it has a long history of use in death penalty cases, both in the imposition and in the execution of the penalty. Clarence Darrow decided that the best chance of saving Richard Loeb and Nathan Leopold from execution was to plead them guilty to first-degree murder and then to introduce psychiatric testimony in the form of a plea for mitigation of sentence.

The post-1970s death penalty in the United States bears a striking resemblance to South African law enacted in 1935, which provided that the death penalty may be avoided when there are extenuating circumstances. No definition of extenuating circumstances was given in the law, but they are recognized to be facts associated with a crime that diminish morally, although not legally, the degree of the prisoner's guilt. Among the more important circumstances that were considered in South Africa were mental condition, provocation and other emotional disturbances, intoxication, belief in witchcraft, compulsion, absence of premeditation, youth, political and social and other not ignoble motives, minor degree of participation, repentance and endeavors to assist the victim before *actus reus* is complete, and consent by the victim. Usually, the presence of extenuating circumstances can be determined on the basis of the evidence given before the verdict, but on occasion, it was stated, it may be desirable for the prosecutor and the defense to present evidence and arguments before the sentence is passed, because the question arises only after the verdict. The onus of proof of such extenuating circumstances rests on the accused. Likewise, the post-1970s American statutes allow psychiatric testimony to determine whether the death penalty should be imposed. With the demise of apartheid, South Africa abolished the death penalty, as have most other countries.[23]

The typical contemporary capital sentencing statute in the United States sets out a list of both aggravating and mitigating factors, much as did the South African statute. The prosecution must establish, usually by proof beyond a reasonable doubt, at least one of the aggravating factors. The statutes do not inform the fact finder how to balance the aggravating and mitigating circumstances. These aggravating and mitigating factors call for the participation of psychiatrists or psychologists. Almost without exception, offenders charged with a capital offense have a similar history: they grew up in fractured families marked by drugs, alcohol, violence, and mental illness. Psychiatrist Dorothy Lewis and colleagues studied fourteen death row inmates who had committed particularly heinous crimes and found that all but one had a history of severe and sometimes bizarre abuse.[24]

Supreme Court Justices Blackmun, Scalia, and Thomas have noted that the mandate of unlimited mitigating circumstances has resulted in an arbitrary system. Today's sentencing scheme is also arbitrary because of undefined aggravating factors, unlimited nonstatutory aggravating factors, and *victim impact* evidence.[25] Phrases such as "relishing of the murder," "gratuitous violence," and "senselessness of the murder" are open to broad interpretation.[26] The courts also have upheld the use of "lack of remorse" as a nonstatutory aggravating circumstance.[27] Another use of nonstatutory aggravating circumstances is the admission of victim impact statements.[28] The Supreme Court outlawed capital punishment in 1972 because states were arbitrarily imposing it, but the imposition of the death penalty under the new laws is no less arbitrary.

About two-thirds of state capital sentencing statutes expressly incorporate one or more of the mitigating factors listed in the American Law Institute's Model Penal Code, to wit, (1) whether the defendant was suffering from "extreme mental or emotional disturbance" at the time of the offense, (2) whether "the capacity of the defendant to appreciate the criminality of his conduct or to conform his conduct to the requirements of law was impaired as a result of mental disease or defect or intoxication," and (3) whether "the murder was committed under circumstances which the defendant believed to provide a moral justification or extenuation of his conduct."[29] Of the thirty-eight states that permit capital punishment, eighteen now have laws that prohibit execution of mentally retarded individuals.[30] Twenty-three of the thirty-eight states permit the execution of youthful, or juvenile, offenders. From 1976, the time the Supreme Court lifted the ban on the death penalty, until the end of 2001, seventeen men have been executed for crimes they committed while they were minors (nine of those were in Texas). When, if ever, the penalty is actually carried out, however, they are much older (e.g., Gerald Mitchell was age thirty-three when executed on October 23, 2001, for a murder he committed at the age of seventeen on June 4, 1985).

While mental illness is listed as a mitigating factor in sentencing, and mental illness at the time of execution is a basis for a stay of execution, jurors concede (in posttrial interviews) that they consider it an aggravating factor. At trial, jurors are not obliged—indeed, are not permitted—to explain the basis for their verdicts. Studies find a strong correlation between the unsuccessful assertion of an insanity defense and a death sentence. Indeed, a failed insanity defense is one of the most accurate predictors of who will receive the death penalty. Unless the mental illness can be disconnected from dangerousness, defense counsel is best advised not to argue mental illness. Based on interviews with 187 jurors who served on fifty-three capital cases, Professor Stephen Garvey found that jurors were "more likely to have found the defendant frightening to be near" when the killing was the "work of a madman" or the defendant was "vicious like a mad animal."[31]

In a Georgia case trial counsel was aware that the defendant, William Lipham, had been institutionalized in mental hospitals, children's homes, and treatment centers and that his records noted several behavioral problems, anxiety disorders, head injuries, and a possible learning disability. The mitigation defense consisted of turning over the 2,500 pages of records to the jury and asking it to look for mitigating evidence itself. The Georgia Supreme Court held that this presentation of mitigating evidence without a mental health expert to evaluate it—along with the expectation that the jury would read all 2,500 pages and understand them without guidance—was unreasonable and constituted ineffective assistance of counsel. This deficiency, the court said, was prejudicial because without it Lipham might not have been sentenced to death.[32]

Jurors are instructed that to impose the death sentence they must unanimously agree that the specified aggravating factors have been established beyond a reasonable doubt. Proof of an adverse impact on the victim's family (by victim impact testimony) has been held not to relieve the prosecution of its burden to prove beyond a reasonable doubt at least one aggravating circumstance that has been alleged.[33] An extensive study involving interviews with hundreds of people who have served as jurors in death penalty cases revealed that jurors often misunderstand what will happen to the defendant if they decide not to impose the death penalty, believe that their decision is merely advisory, or misunderstand which factors can and cannot be considered, what level of proof is required, and what degree of concurrence is required for aggravating and mitigating factors.[34]

Professor William Bowers and colleagues found that 48.3 percent of 864 capital jurors surveyed, drawn from seven states, had predetermined life or death by the conclusion of the guilt phase of the trial, with 28.6 percent electing death and 19.7 life (51.7 percent were undecided).[35] Professor Marla Sandys stated "the data reveal quite dramatically that . . . the majority of jurors reach their decisions about guilt and punishment at the same time."[36] The finding may not be surprising given that prospective jurors who are opposed to the death penalty are disqualified from serving on the jury. The Supreme Court has held that the Constitution does not prohibit the states from "death-qualifying juries" in capital cases.[37]

Carrying Out the Death Penalty

Although there may seem to be some novelty in the use of psychiatric testimony to determine whether the death penalty should be imposed, psychiatric testimony has been used for decades to determine the executionability of a person condemned to death. In the first situation, the psychiatrist may be called as a witness to testify whether the death penalty ought to be imposed; in the latter situation, the psychiatrist may be called to testify whether it ought to be carried out.

Execution of the death sentence can be avoided in several ways. After the trial stage is completed in a capital case, as in other cases, the court machinery continues to operate for some time. The jury's decision is blocked by further litigation and seemingly endless hearings. Legal delays took up fourteen years in the case of John Wayne Gacy, who killed thirty-three young men, though he confessed to the killings and his guilt was never in doubt. He had 523 separate appeals, none of them based on a claim of innocence.

Appeals are made at all levels of the state courts as well as the federal courts. In capital cases, it is said, the courts must be emphatically sure: "No man shall be executed while there is the slightest doubt either as to his guilt or as to the legality of the process by which his guilt was determined." Appellate courts carefully scan the transcript; error is uncovered and deemed prejudicial that would have been overlooked in noncapital cases. Due to the gravity of the sentence and the obligation of the state to ensure fairness, various jurisdictions impose restrictions on the right of a prisoner to forego appeals (the prisoner must have "sufficient rational ability" to waive appeals).

The courts are not commended, however, but bitterly criticized for their scrutiny of capital cases. We hear it said, "The whole procedure is insane." "The lengthy procedure is the enduring shame of American judicial procedure." These criticisms are commonplace because the basis of appeal or writ of habeas corpus is recognized as often frivolous. Time and again, a new dodge will appear, a writ will be taken, and years will pass. Any argument is useful. For example, when a black offender was sentenced to death, the objection of jury discrimination was regularly urged, even when the trial was eminently fair and the black defendant in fact would not have wanted blacks sitting on the jury. In one case in California, not especially unusual, there were eight trials, costing the state over $500,000.

When court procedures are finally exhausted, when review is no longer pending, the fate of the prisoner passes into the hands of the executive branch of the government, which, under the United States system, is charged with executing the orders of the judiciary. It has been generally assumed that the jury's decision imposing the death penalty is carried out—at least following appeals. But what actually has happened at this stage?

In many jurisdictions, the governor has to order the execution, and he often avoids the decision as long as possible. Reprieves are commonplace. The governor could, definitively, avoid the execution by pardon or by commutation of the death sentence to a prison term. Governors often hesitate to intervene in this way, however, because they feel they would be usurping the power of the court. Twelve jurors—not the governor—listen at the trial. Interposition often occurs in another way.

The warden (or sheriff) having custody of the prisoner plays a principal role in the implementation of the penalty. The execution of the penalty depends very much on the attitude of the warden toward the penalty and whether he will attest to the incompetency or insanity of the condemned person. The issue of competency to be executed becomes relevant when the date of execution has been set.

In 1986, in *Ford v. Wainwright,*[38] the Supreme Court in a plurality opinion ruled that the Constitution precludes a state from executing people who have temporarily or permanently become incompetent or insane, but even before 1986 the rule had been well established, either by statute or common law, although the logic behind the rule is vague. In the words of one jurist, "Whatever the reason of the law is, it is plain the law is so." One might argue that if anyone is to be executed it should be the criminally insane, but it would go against the sporting theory of justice. One judge, dissenting against the rule, said: "Is it not an inverted humanitarianism that deplores as barbarous the capital punishment of those who have become insane after trial and conviction but accepts the capital punishment of sane men?" Alvin Ford died a natural death in 1991 while on death row.

In *Ford v. Wainwright* the plurality did not set forth what standard was applicable in the determination of incompetence or insanity. Justice Poweli, the swing vote in the opinion, proposed a standard when he stated in his concurrence that, "I would hold that the Eighth Amendment forbids the execution only of those who are unaware of the punishment they are about to suffer and why they are to suffer it." Justice Powell was a voice of one, yet the standard he posited has been embraced by some courts as the constitutional minimum. He discussed in his concurrence the rationale behind the Eighth Amendment prohibition of executing the insane:

> [T]oday as at common law, one of the death penalty's critical justifications, its retributive force, depends on the defendant's awareness of the penalty's existence and purpose. Thus, it remains true that executions of the insane both impose a uniquely cruel penalty and are inconsistent with one of the chief purposes of executions generally. . . . A number of States have more rigorous standards, but none disputes the need to require that those who are executed know the fact of their impending execution and the reason for it.

Justice Powell then addressed the states with more rigorous standards in a footnote of his concurring opinion:

> [A] number of States have remained faithful to Blackstone's view that a *defendant cannot be executed unless he is able to assist in his own defense.* . . . Modern case authority on this question is sparse, and while some older cases favor the Blackstone view, those cases largely antedate the recent expansion of both the right to counsel and the availability of federal and state collateral review. . . . Under these circumstances, I find no sound basis for constitutionalizing the broader definition of insanity, with its requirement that the defendant be able to assist in his own de-

fense. States are obviously free to adopt a more expansive view of sanity in this context than the one the Eight Amendment imposes as a constitutional minimum. (Emphasis added)

This "more expansive" view is recommended in the American Bar Association Criminal Justice Mental Health Standards. There is a significant common-law background for the requirement that a defendant be able to assist in his defense, even after conviction.

Explanations for the exemption rule, as found in the literature, are various. It is said: "If the defendant is sane he might argue some reason not previously considered why the sentence should not be carried out." This theory offers the condemned man a last chance to prove his innocence. Yet the same logic would suffice to postpone, perhaps indefinitely, the execution of a sane man, for time for intelligent reflection may disclose new reasons for a stay of execution of the sane as well. Another common explanation is that killing an insane person does not have the same moral quality as killing a sane person. The moral basis underlying the forensic responsibility rule at the time of the deed is carried over until the time of execution, although the person was found legally sane and responsible at the time of the deed. A third defense of the rule involves the conception of the self. God would not, on the Great Day, make a person answer for that of which he remembered nothing: he is not the same person. The law likewise says that a man is not subject to execution for crime when he is not the same person forensically now that he was then (but, as Heraclitus long ago explained, all is flux). Finally, some insist that the rule is based on the lack of retributory satisfaction derived by society in executing an insane person. A related belief is that a person should not be put to death while insane because in that condition he is unable to make his peace with God. To a modern audience, this argument is hardly convincing, and the condemned man himself often rejects spiritual solace in his final hours and looks instead to a good last meal.

Whatever the underlying reasons, however illogical they may be, the rule has been perpetuated, either by statute or judicial decision, in every state having the death penalty. However, the procedure by which the rule is implemented is slipshod. At common law the prisoner was brought before a judge who either decided the question of insanity himself or at his discretion impaneled a jury to assist him. But most states in practice, if not in law, entrusted the initial decision to the warden. The condemned person may file a petition for postconviction relief.

The Supreme Court in 1950, in *Solesbee v. Balkom*,[39] said that postponement of execution because of postconviction insanity bears a close affinity not to trial but to reprieves of sentences, which is an executive power, and "seldom, if ever, has this power of executive clemency been subjected to review by the courts." In *Solesbee* the Court found that Georgia had not violated due process in constituting its governor an "apt and special tribunal" for determining, in ex parte proceedings, the sanity of a condemned man at the time of execution. (In federal and military cases, Abraham Lincoln was apparently the first president to intercede in an execution on account of supervening insanity.)

Inquiries have been held entirely behind closed doors without any opportunity for submission of facts on behalf of the person whose sanity is to be determined. It was long recognized that due process does not require that a condemned man who asserts supervening insanity be given a full judicial proceeding to adjudicate

his claim. In 1897, in *Nobles v. Georgia*,[40] the Supreme Court said that if such proceedings were required "it would be wholly at the will of a convict to suffer any
punishment whatever, for the necessity of his doing so would depend solely upon
his fecundity in making suggestion after suggestion of insanity, to be followed by
trial upon trial."

In *Solesbee*, the Supreme Court, noting that the governor in deciding on execution had the aid of specifically trained physicians, went on to say:

> It is true that governors and physicians might make errors of judgment.
> But the search for truth in this field is always beset by difficulties that may
> beget error. Even judicial determination of sanity might be wrong. . . . We
> cannot say that it offends due process to leave the question of a convicted
> person's sanity to the solemn responsibility of a state's highest executive
> with authority to invoke the aid of the most skillful class of experts on the
> crucial questions involved.[41]

In this case, the condemned man lost out, but if the governor decides in his favor,
a fortiori, no one is interested or has standing to complain to the courts.

The power of the governor was often delegated to agencies such as pardon
and parole boards. In 1958, in *Caritativo v. California*,[42] the Court, extending its
decision in *Solesbee*, upheld a procedure whereby the initiation of proceedings to
determine the sanity of a condemned man in his custody is made by the warden
in his sole judgment. If the warden "has good reason to believe" that a condemned
man has become insane, he must so advise the judge or district attorney of the
judicial district where the convict was sentenced, and an investigation may be
ordered. On some occasions the convicted prisoner is so hated by the correctional
officials that they obfuscate evidence of mental disorder.[43]

Justice Harlan in *Caritativo*, said: "Surely it is not inappropriate for [the state]
to lodge this grave responsibility in the hands of the warden, the official who beyond all others had had the most intimate relations with, and best opportunity to
observe, the prisoner." But Justice Frankfurter, joined by Justices Brennan and
Douglas, strongly dissented:

> Now it appears that [the determination of the sanity of a man condemned
> to death], upon which depends the fearful question of life or death, may
> . . . be made on the mere say-so of the warden of a state prison, according
> to such procedure as he chooses to pursue, and more particularly without
> any right on the part of a man awaiting death who claims that insanity
> has supervened to have his case put to the warden. There can hardly be
> a comparable situation under our constitutional scheme of things in
> which an interest so great, that an insane man not be executed, is given
> such flimsy procedural protection and where one asserting a claim is de-
> nied the rudimentary right of having his side submitted to the one who
> sits in judgment.[44]

In its 1986 decision in the aforementioned case of *Ford v. Wainwright*,[45] the
Supreme Court found Florida's procedure, which relied on the governor's assessment of clinical reports, as unconstitutional, on three grounds: (1) it provided no
opportunity for the condemned individual or his counsel to be heard; (2) it did not

permit challenge of the state-employed mental health professionals' findings on the competency issue; and (3) it left the final decision as to competency to the executive rather than the judicial branch. Although thus ruling Florida's statute unconstitutional, the Court did not explicitly establish a right to counsel at competency proceedings, nor did it require that the condemned individual have a formal opportunity to cross-examine opposing experts or be provided funds for an independent expert.[46] Justice Marshall, who wrote the Court's opinion, suggested that Florida might create a competency procedure similar to that used in the competency-to-stand-trial or civil-commitment contexts, but the majority did not agree on this point, with several members cautioning against requiring, as a constitutional ruling, a full-blown "sanity trial."[47]

In a subsequent case involving Thomas Provenzano, who was sentenced to death in Florida for murdering a court bailiff, the Florida Supreme Court declared that the state's failure to provide exculpatory information from a mental evaluation did not create reversible error, given the trial counsel's ability to obtain this information from other sources.[48] Six years later, the Florida Supreme Court remanded for a hearing on his competency for execution.[49] A month later, the Florida Supreme Court found that the trial court had abused its discretion for (1) not continuing a hearing so that Provenzano could present psychologist Patricia Fleming, (2) declaring that Fleming was not an expert because she lacked a Ph.D., and (3) refusing to allow Provenzano to cross-examine a state expert.[50] The trial court thereupon held proceedings at which Fleming and other witnesses for both Provenzano and the state gave testimony, and after which defense counsel stated on the record that everything he could offer on Provenzano's behalf had been presented. The trial court determined that Provenzano was competent for execution. The Florida Supreme Court affirmed. Despite his delusions that he was Jesus Christ, Provenzano understood the details of his trial and his conviction, that he is to be executed, and the reasons why. The Florida Supreme Court considered the case "troubling" given Provenzano's apparent mental health problems, even though his exaggeration of his symptoms and malingering made determining the exact nature of his condition difficult. However, the Florida Supreme Court, citing the U.S. Supreme Court's decision in *Ford v. Wainwright*, held that the Eighth Amendment requires only that a defendant have an awareness of what penalty they are being given and why they have received it.[51]

The Trauma of Death Row

A person under a death sentence is sentenced to death; he is not sentenced to prison. He is placed under the custody of the warden. He is not part of the prison population. He is placed in a separate cell.[52] In the United States, where legal maneuvers in capital cases usually take several years, the prisoner during this time sits in isolation on death row.[53] Earlier, during the trial stage, which rarely takes less than a year, he sat in jail, without opportunity for release on bail, and usually without therapy. Following conviction, death even more preys on his mind. In the words of one prisoner: "The days are so long. There is nothing to pass the time. Nothing to keep your mind occupied. I feel like I don't even exist. I'm here and I'm not here. I have headaches. I just want to scream."[54]

Wait long enough and chances are that the prisoner will hallucinate (or he will die a natural death). More likely than not, he will deteriorate. Psychiatrists point out that offenders are usually people who release tension by acting out, by using muscle, and they become very anxious when locked up. Without any activity, they tend to break down and become psychotic. Capital offenders are likely to be unstable anyway, but solitary confinement does much to break down the sanity of the most normal of men, as the experiments of Donald O. Hebb and others on sensory deprivation have vividly demonstrated. Governor Earl Long once remarked in my presence, "Who in hell wouldn't go mad?" (Louisiana at the time of the remark had not carried out an execution in over ten years.)[55] Tranquilizers are the order of the day.

The condemned man who does not become genuinely psychotic will find it expedient to malinger. He jumps up and down. He seldom does anything correctly. He makes absurd statements. When shown a watch reading 2:30, he may say the time is 6 o'clock. When shown a fifty-cent piece, he may call it a dollar bill. Such symptoms are popularly called the "nonsense syndrome," and, in psychiatry, the *Ganser syndrome*. The condemned man learns, either through the grapevine or from the subtle advice of his attorney, that under the law insanity precludes execution. As a last-ditch measure he may act upon this information. The condemned man is entitled to the information, just as a businessman has a right to advice on loopholes in the tax laws.

The following conversation, which I tape recorded in June 1964, illustrates the contrivance put on in the prison to affect transfer to the hospital:

> EXAMINER AT HOSPITAL: Tell me what happened at the penitentiary to make them send you to the hospital.
> PATIENT (formerly prisoner): Nothing.
> EXAMINER: Huh?
> PATIENT: My lawyer came and got me.
> EXAMINER: Your lawyer came and got you? Are you afraid of dying?
> PATIENT: [No answer.]
> EXAMINER: Did your lawyer tell you what to do to get out of there?
> PATIENT: No.
> EXAMINER: Looks to me like a good lawyer would have told you how to act. He didn't tell you how to act?
> PATIENT: [Inaudible mumbles.]
> EXAMINER: I didn't understand you. He told you to act crazy?
> PATIENT: Uh-hum.
> EXAMINER: What did he say?
> PATIENT: He kept telling me . . . [Inaudible].
> EXAMINER: The last time he came up, what did he do?
> PATIENT: He asked if I ever had an epileptic fit.
> EXAMINER: What did you tell him?
> PATIENT: I told him no.
> EXAMINER: What did he say then?
> PATIENT: He said that an epileptic fit was the last straw. [In the lingo, an epileptic fit is the way of a crazy man.]
> EXAMINER: He told you this?
> PATIENT: Yes.
> EXAMINER: Did he tell you how to act?
> PATIENT: No, he didn't want to incriminate himself.

EXAMINER: He told you that he did not want to incriminate himself?
PATIENT: That's right.
EXAMINER: So he didn't tell you how to act. But he got his point across to you?
PATIENT: [Inaudible.]
EXAMINER: Huh? How did you know how to act when he told you about epileptic fits?
PATIENT: I just knew.

Sporadic malingering is difficult to prove, especially when the motivation to fake is great. In the prison setting, however, as Justice Harlan noted, the individual may be observed on a 24-hour basis; over this period of time it is difficult to keep up a simulated psychosis. Prison personnel can usually spot an inmate whose bizarre behavior is an act. They know "he's not a real psycho." The problem becomes more difficult when an unstable person begins to fake mental illness, and then, like a man running downhill, finds he cannot stop.

Happily for the condemned man, prison officials in most states have usually closed their eyes to the simulation. Who wants to pull the switch? The condemned man's keepers get to know him, and they develop some feeling for him. As they dislike executing anyone, they have tended to accept feigned craziness as genuine. So, ostensibly for observation or treatment, the condemned man has been referred to a prison psychiatrist or transferred to the security area of a mental hospital (the criminally insane section), where he usually has lived out the rest of his days, often as a trusty.

One easily believes what one wishes to believe. Wardens and psychiatrists, perhaps for different reasons, can readily find a symptom of madness. There is always evidence available, however episodic, to warrant a stay of execution. The Supreme Court has conceded that "the search for truth in this field is always beset by difficulties that may beget error." The law has long recognized that people may have lucid intervals and nonlucid intervals. Psychiatrists use labels such as *dissociative states* and *three-day schizophrenia*. We are disintegrated when we wake up in the morning and when we are asleep. We "pull ourselves together." We all have "crazy spells." We question at times the judgment of our best friends and colleagues, and at such times we call them crazy. It is not possible to have a touch of pregnancy, but it is possible to have a touch of psychosis; the latter is not an all-or-none condition. Part of one's personality may be affected by a psychotic process, but the remnants of the ego may function properly. Given the type of person who commits a capital crime, mental and emotional aberrations of marked degree are readily in evidence. There is also the syndrome in which the prisoner thinks he is malingering, and the warden or psychiatrist knows the prisoner thinks so but justifiably considers him crazy nonetheless.

There is a direct corollary between the number and the location of executions. The carrying out of the death penalty has depended to a marked degree on whether the chair is moved around from jailhouse to jailhouse or whether all condemned persons are sent to a centralized place—the state penitentiary—for execution. Since the 1970s many states have enacted legislation providing that executions are to be carried out at the state penitentiary rather than at the various county jails. Legislators, able to see problems in both ideological and financial terms, realize that it is expensive and cumbersome to transport the chair from jail to jail.

351

When execution of the death penalty is to take place in the local or county jail, it is more likely to be carried out. For one reason, the condemned man, when in the state penitentiary, far removed from the scene of the crime, is more likely to be forgotten by an enraged community than if he remained in close proximity to the scene of the crime. For another, the warden of a penitentiary is in a position very different from that of the sheriff of a local jailhouse. The warden is practically a feudal lord, and his attitude is likely to be every bit as imperious. He feels the inherent power of his position, and he is usually willing to exercise the broad discretion to postpone invested in him by law.

In former times it was customary for an execution to take place as near as possible to the scene of the crime. A nearby tree was selected or a gallows was erected in a large open space in the town. By the 1930s, with a few exceptions, public executions disappeared from the American scene. Citizens organized to prohibit public executions because, as reports in newspapers of the time disclose, "the crowds often assumed the characteristics of a mob and often indulged in the wildest and most unrestrained orgies."[56] The executions incited widespread agitation, brawling, drunkenness, and crime. Many good citizens got carried away in the heat and violence of the moment and participated in some dreadful acts. So executions were first moved from outdoors to inside the local jailhouse, and then gradually, as noted, from the local jailhouse to the state penitentiary. But what happened there?

The population of the state penitentiary is large, and ordinarily the atmosphere there is tense. It becomes volatile whenever there is an execution. The macabre event provokes brawling and violence among the convicts, as it formerly did on the outside among the citizenry. The warden is motivated to defer the execution not only because he has some feelings for the condemned man but also because he values his job. All administrators want things to run smoothly. Unpleasant publicity is the bane of officialdom, and riots make ugly headlines.

But headlines of a different nature may exert influence on the warden in the other direction. The more publicity attending the trial, the more famous or notorious the criminal, the more likely the execution. In such cases, the warden rarely "has good reason to believe" that the prisoner has become insane, and he finds it expedient not to initiate an investigation. Fredric Wertham, psychiatrist and writer, was denied permission to see Ethel Rosenberg when she was at Sing Sing; but in earlier interviews her attorney reported her as in despair, without lipstick or makeup, her hair uncombed, not caring how she looked.[57] In Kansas, a young man, Lee Andrews, was sentenced to death for the murder of his parents. He was a university student and spent his time in his cell reading books. He did not act crazy. In addition, prominent citizens intervened asking executive clemency, much to the annoyance of the governor. The case was headlined in the papers. As a result, widespread attention focused on Andrews, and he was executed. California regularly executes its condemned men (following a protracted and expensive judicial process), but even outside California, Caryl Chessman probably would have been executed. The eyes of the world were upon him. Ironically, he protested too much. He made too much noise, and he protested via book-writing—the mark of a rational man.

In *Caritativo*, it was held proper for the state to condition a condemned man's right to a sanity investigation upon a preliminary determination by the warden that "good reason exists for the belief that the convict has become insane." More often than not, the various reasons underlying the rule of competency to be executed merge or fade away into the simple statement, "you're not supposed to execute someone who doesn't know what's happening." Theoretically, mental illness, of itself, is not sufficient to bring into operation the rule of suspension of execution. *Mental illness* as a legal concept is not identical with the medical concept of the term. It may be that a person who does not know what is happening is mentally ill, but mental illness alone is not the test. Indeed, a person may be mentally well but nonetheless may not know what is happening, for example, a person of very low intelligence.

Actually, the test on executionability is void of meaning. It would not even exempt the blithering idiot. In several recent rulings the Supreme Court made no reference to the reasons for the rule but simply said, in dictum, that it is unlawful to execute a prisoner who has become incompetent or insane after his conviction. Theory notwithstanding, medical status of itself thus serves as a haven from legal action.

Although in *Caritativo* the Supreme Court specifically stated that wardens are not obliged to obtain a psychiatric examination of the condemned man, they have as a general practice delegated the responsibility to a prison psychiatrist, or, with the authorization of the trial court, have transferred the prisoner to the security treatment area of a mental hospital for examination and treatment. In this way, the warden guarantees a responsible and good-faith determination, and he is usually satisfied with the result. The trial court invariably will postpone execution, without a date, when it receives a psychiatric report stating that the condemned man does not realize he is to be executed for the crime he has committed.[58]

To review, the jury—a group so large that individual responsibility is lost—relieves the judge of the death penalty decision at the trial. The judge then transfers the condemned man to the warden, who is able to delegate the responsibility to the psychiatrist. Thus, in the end, the decision on execution of the death penalty is essentially left to one individual—the psychiatrist. He is given a nonmedical—and absurd—responsibility. He is asked to report back to the warden when the prisoner is ready to be electrocuted.

Professor Albert Ehrenzweig of the University of California Law School compared the procedure to a game of ping-pong, but this is hardly an apt comparison.[59] The psychiatrist knows that the warden does not want him to make a return play. He rarely reports that his patient, regardless of his mental status, is "ready to be electrocuted," although, as a matter of fact, in this age of tranquilizing drugs a man could readily be shaped up for execution. The ethical guideline of the American Academy of Psychiatry and the Law calling for "honesty and striving for objectivity" in an evaluation tends to fall by the wayside.

While death may be postponed for the condemned man while in the security treatment unit, his stay there does not always encourage forgetfulness of his sentence. With inadequate facilities, attendants, and security protection, mental hospitals find discipline a stiff problem in these units. Consequently, prisoners transferred from the penitentiary to the hospital are warned that misbehavior will result in their being sent back "to fry." The capital penalty abolitionist may take note that, here, recalcitrant persons already condemned to death can be deterred by the threat of execution. Every now and then, the hospital director, to show he means business, returns an unruly inmate to the penitentiary—and to his death. This accounts for many of the executions in states where, according to statistics, they occur sporadically.

Another punitive practice in the security treatment unit of many hospitals involves the conversion of electroconvulsive therapy from a therapy to a threat. In ordinary psychiatric practice, ECT is the somatic therapy of choice in cases of depression. Its potential as a punishment, however, is obvious: a little electricity cures, but it hurts, and too much kills. Furthermore, for a man facing the electric chair, the psychological implications in the threat of being "buzzed" can well be imagined.

None of these unpleasant procedures for controlling the condemned man in the hospital's security area, however, seem half as bizarre on a close look as authority's reason for putting him there. The psychiatrist is asked to treat the prisoner (patient). To what end? Why, so that he may be electrocuted! This goal of therapy is, indeed, a curious footnote to the Hippocratic oath. Little wonder that the psychiatrist, with a prisoner on his hands who has been brought out of his psychotic state by ECT or drugs, fails to report that the man is ready to be electrocuted. The psychiatrist knows that such a statement from him is tantamount to an endorsement of the death penalty, so he is likely to play it cool and do nothing or to use delaying tactics. Ordinarily, he is not in sympathy with the death penalty; but, in any event, he feels that the decision is not for him to make. "Who is fit to be executed?" is a moral, not a scientific, inquiry.

Society cannot fairly blame the psychiatrist for taking the law into his own hands. As Dr. Menninger said, "Most psychiatrists dislike very much being called in when somebody wants to know if the accused is well enough so that his head may be chopped off. I don't think the psychiatrist is very interested in acting as assistant to the executioner."[60] Clearly, psychiatrists share the understandable human trait of being reluctant to push a person down the road to death. Moreover, they are doctors whose training and credo aim to preserve life, not to hasten its ending. Their attitude toward the condemned man as patient is readily explained. For over a decade Dr. Alfred Freedman and Dr. Abraham Halpern sought to establish an ethical rule that would prohibit physician participation in legally authorized executions.[61]

Litigation has raised the question of forcibly medicating a condemned person in order to render him competent to be executed. In *Perry v. Louisiana,*[62] the trial court, after sentencing Perry to death but finding him incompetent to be executed unless maintained on medication, ordered that he be forcibly medicated to ensure his competence. After exhausting state court remedies, Perry sought relief from the U.S. Supreme Court. It remanded the case for reconsideration in light of its decision in 1990 that allowed forcible medication of penitentiary inmates only when considered "medically appropriate."[63] On remand, the Louisiana Supreme Court ruled it impermissible to forcibly medicate individuals to render them competent to be executed.[64] Since then Louisiana, Maryland, and South Carolina provide for the commutation of a death sentence to life imprisonment without parole when the individual is found incompetent to be executed. They now do not ask psychiatrists to medicate a death row inmate so as to render him rational enough to be put to death.[65]

The question arises whether a physician's decision to treat an ill individual should be dependent on what lies ahead for the individual. Should a physician who is a pacifist decline to treat an ill individual who plans to enter the military service? Should a physician who has a negative view of homosexuality decline to treat an ill individual who will continue to engage in homosexual activity? Should a physician decline to treat an ill individual on death row only when the date of execution has been set? In any event, the odds are against the actual carrying out of the death penalty.[66]

But what about the law—the law of the land—that shall prevail? How do we explain this reluctance, this dalliance and indecision that has marked the course of the law all along the way from death sentence to death row? Although the ultimate punishment issue has evoked national debate for at least a century and a half, it is clear that by a cumbersome and slipshod method, the penalty was in effect nearly eliminated long before the Supreme Court's decision in 1972 voiding jury discrimination in sentencing. After the penalty was reinstated in 1976, it took twelve years to carry out one hundred executions. Now there are calls to expedite the process. No member of the Court adheres to the view long held by the late Justices Thurgood Marshall and William J. Brennan Jr. that the death penalty is an affront to a civilized society, let alone the position adopted by Justice Harry A. Blackmun at the end of his career that the "machinery of death," as he called it, was simply not as fair in practice as the Court had deemed it to be in theory by upholding new state death penalty laws in 1976 and permitting the states to resume executions.[67]

Opponents of the death penalty once made broad calls for abolition by arguing that executing people was immoral. Now, while that argument is still made, opponents are focusing their attacks on questions of fairness, racial bias, and guilt or innocence.[68] In years past, and still today, the capacity-to-stand-execution procedure, via the executive department, in many cases achieved the functional abolition of the death penalty. The repugnance felt for the death penalty emerged cloaked as a rational medical decision. Perhaps this was not a chance achievement.

Notes

1. D. Frum, "The Justice Americans Demand," *New York Times*, Feb. 4, 2000, p. 27. Most of the executions are carried out in a few states. The number of executions from 1976 until the end of 1999 are as follows: Texas, 206; Virginia, 75; Florida, 44; Missouri, 41; Louisiana, 25; Georgia, 23; South Carolina, 24; Arkansas and Oklahoma, 21; Alabama, 20; Arizona, 10; North Carolina, 15; Illinois, 12; Delaware, 10; Nevada, 8; California and Indiana, 7; Utah, 6; Mississippi, 4; Nebraska, Washington, Maryland, and Pennsylvania, 3; Montana, and Kentucky, 2; Ohio, Wyoming, Colorado, and Idaho, 1.

The Babylonian Code of Hammurabi (c. 1750 B.C.) provided death as a penalty for twenty-five different offenses, including corruption by government officials, theft, and the fraudulent sale of beer. Under the Old Testament, death was deemed the appropriate punishment for various offenses, including murder, adultery, blasphemy, homosexuality, bestiality, sorcery, witchcraft, and cursing a parent. During the reign of Henry II (1154–1189), English law first recognized that crime was more than a personal affair between the victim and the criminal. By 1500, English law recognized eight major capital offenses: treason, petty treason (killing of husband by the wife), murder, larceny, robbery, burglary, rape, and arson. Various kings greatly expanded the list of capital offenses, and the reign of Henry VIII was especially bloody. During his thirty years as king, 72,000 subjects were put to death, an average of 2,000 subjects per year. Shortly after 1800, England recognized more than two hundred capital crimes, ranging from crimes against person and property to crimes against the public peace. R. Coyne & L. Entzeroth (eds.), *Capital Punishment and the Judicial Process* (Durham, N.C.: Carolina Academic Press, 1994).

2. The court ruled in three cases, all involving black defendants, one of them for a robbery-murder, and two for rape. Furman v. Georgia, 408 U.S. 238 (1972). The death penalty is on the statute books of all states except fourteen—Alaska, Hawaii, Iowa, Maine, Massachusetts, Michigan, Minnesota, New Mexico, North Dakota, Oregon, Rhode Island, Vermont, West Virginia, and Wisconsin. The history of the abolitionist movement is related in M. Meltsner, *Cruel and Unusual: The Supreme Court and Capital Punishment* (New York: Random House, 1973).

3. 428 U.S. 280 (1976). Following the invalidation of North Carolina's mandatory death penalty, James Woodson was resentenced to life in prison. In 1991, he was paroled from prison, and in 1993, he completed his sentence and was discharged from parole. In December 2000, he was a minister at a church in North Carolina.

4. 438 U.S. 586 (1978).

5. 438 U.S. at 604. As a result of the Supreme Court's decision, Sandra Lockett's death sentence was reduced to life imprisonment, and in 2000, she was paroled from prison.

6. 463 U.S. 880 (1983).

7. See P. Appelbaum, "Hypotheticals, Psychiatric Testimony, and the Death Sentence," *Bull. Am. Acad. Psychiatry & Law* 12 (1984): 169; R. Slovenko, "Psychiatric Opinion without Examination," *J. Psychiatry & Law* 28 (2000): 103. Thomas Barefoot was executed by lethal injection in Texas in 1984.

8. A Texas magazine article tagged Grigson with the "Dr. Death" label because of his frequent testimony for the state against defendants in capital murder trials. Invariably called as a state's witness, Grigson testifies during the punishment phase of trials, when the jury must determine whether a defendant convicted of capital murder will get a life sentence or be executed. The CBS news program *Sixty Minutes* wanted to film the testimony of Grigson in a capital murder trial but was refused. E. Kingshott, "Judge Objects to TV Filming of 'Dr. Death,'" *The News* (San Antonio), Jan. 10, 1980, p. 1. By and large, psychiatrists who testify in capital cases are criticized by psychiatrists who are opposed to the death penalty (the vast majority of psychiatrists), whether or not the psychiatrist testifies on the basis of an examination and not simply on the basis of a hypothetical. See F. D. Master, "Alvaro Calambro: Competency to be Executed," *Am. J. Forensic Psychiatry* 20 (1999): 17.

9. 463 U.S. at 896. Trial judges have continued to appoint Dr. Grigson to evaluate the defendant for the imposition of the death penalty or for competency to be executed. See, e.g., Caldwell v. Johnson, 226 F.3d 367 (5th Cir. 2000); Bennett v. State, 766 S.W.2d 227 (Tex. Cr. App. 1989). In a lengthy dissent in *Bennett*, Judge Teague criticized the appointment of Dr. Grigson, or "Dr. Death." He suggested that whenever Dr. Grigson is appointed, the defendant should stop what he is then doing and commence writing out his last will and testament—because he will in all probability soon be ordered by the trial judge to suffer a premature death. 766 S.W.2d at 232.

10. 120 S. Ct. 2214 (2000). On remand to the Texas Court of Criminal Appeals, the court questioned the authority of the attorney general to confess error in the U.S. Supreme Court and to seek a new sentencing trial. As of December 2001, the issue had not been resolved.

11. 76 U.S. 1 (1986). Ronald Skipper waived his right to jury resentencing, and was resentenced by a newly assigned judge, to life in prison with the possibility of parole. He was denied parole in 2000.

12. Simmons v. South Carolina, 512 U.S. 154 (1992). In Ramdass v. Angelone, 120 S. Ct. 2113 (2000), the Court ruled that the defendant was not entitled to the instruction because his prior convictions had not become final, making him nominally eligible for parole in twenty-five years. Jonathan Simmons waived jury resentencing and was resentenced by a newly assigned judge to life in prison without possibility of parole. Bobby Ramdass was executed in 2000 by lethal injection in Virginia.

13. 438 U.S. at 604.

14. 438 U.S. at 605.

15. Ibid.

16. R. J. Bonnie, A. M. Coughlin, J. C. Jeffries, & P. W. Low, *Criminal Law* (Westbury, N.Y.: Foundation Press, 1997), p. 725; B. S. Ledewitz, "The Requirement of Death: Mandatory Language in Pennsylvania Death Penalty Statute," *Duq. L. Rev.* 21 (1982): 103.

17. Romine v. State, 251 Ga. 208, 305 S.E.2d 93 (1983). In Payne v. Tennessee, 501 U.S. 808 (1991), the Supreme Court, overruling two of its earlier decisions, held that the Eighth Amendment erects no per se bar prohibiting a capital sentencing jury from considering victim impact evidence. It said, "A state may legitimately conclude that evidence about the victim and about the impact of the murder on the victim's family is relevant to the jury's decision as to whether or not the death penalty should be imposed." 501 U.S. at 827.

18. 455 U.S. 104 (1982). On remand, after hearing additional evidence, the trial judge again sentenced Monty Eddings to death. In 1984, the Oklahoma Court of Criminal Appeals modified the sentence to life imprisonment because state law did not authorize the remand of a death judgment imposed by a jury for resentencing before a different jury and equal protection required that the same rule apply when the sentence was imposed by a judge. Eddings v. State, 688 P.2d 342 (Okla. Crim. App. 1984).

19. Clisby v. State, 456 So.2d 99 (Ala. Crim. App. 1983).

20. 388 S.E.2d 816 (S.C. 1990).

21. 388 S.E.2d at 823.

22. See C. M. Sevilla, "Anti-Social Personality Disorder: Justification for the Death Penalty?" *J. Contemp. Legal Issues* 10 (1999): 247.

23. All fifteen members of the European Union (EU) have done away with the death penalty, and the EU now has an official policy of promoting its abolition throughout the world. The United Nations (UN) Commission on Human Rights in Geneva for several years in a row has passed resolutions calling for its restriction and eventual abolition. See R. Hood, *The Death Penalty: A Worldwide Perspective* (New York: Oxford University Press, 1996). With spiraling crime in South Africa, surveys show that the vast majority of the population want the death penalty (and vigilante groups put offenders to death). M. Mathabane, "South Africa's Lost Generation," *New York Times*, June 4, 1999, p. 29. Hundreds of people protest outside the courts demanding the death sentence for men who rape young children. Rape support groups have called for the death penalty. Some 21,000 cases of child rape were reported to the police in 2000 in South Africa, most committed by relatives of the victims. According to myth, sex with a virgin will protect a man against AIDS or even cure him of it. "Protesters Demand Execution of Rapists" (news release), *Detroit Free Press*, Nov. 24, 2001, p. 9. Alexander Solzhenitsyn, the famous Russian writer and winner of the Nobel Prize for literature, maintains that Russia can put an end to terrorism only by abolishing the moratorium on the capital punishment in the country. (Unlike the suicide bombers in the Middle East, the Chechen terrorists value their own lives.) Solzhenitsyn says, "There are times when the state needs capital punishment in order to save society. That is the way the question stands in Russia today." He recalled how the father of writer Vladimir Nabokov tried for twenty years to abolish capital punishment in Russia, but when the country was deluged by "all the filthy abomination of the 1917 February revolution" and was engulfed by a wave of unpunished crimes, Nabokov's father admitted to his Duma deputy colleagues that he had erred and that it would be possible to check the rampage of violence only by carrying out death sentences. Solzhenitsyn is convinced that those in Europe who dictate to Russia to abolish capital punishment had never experienced such severe trials that Russia went through. "A Nobel Prize Winner Speaks Out" (Reuters news release), Apr. 29, 2001.

24. D. O. Lewis et al., "Characteristics of Juveniles Condemned to Death," *Am. J. Psychiatry* 145 (1988): 588.

25. Should the court allow a victim's close relatives to testify at sentencing that they forgive the defendant? The court in Greene v. State, 343 Ark. 526, 37 S.W.3d 579 (2001), answered in the negative. The testimony was not relevant as mitigating evidence because it did not speak to the character or deeds of the defendant. Neither was it relevant as victim impact evidence:

> We conclude that penalty recommendations from family members of the victim are not relevant as victim-impact evidence. Certainly, the penalty recommendation from Edna Burnett that Greene proposes would not counteract mitigating evidence or show the human cost of the murder on the victim's family. But in addition, if this court permitted forgiveness and penalty recommendations as victim-impact evidence, then it stands to reason that it must also allow any evidence of nonforgiveness by the victim's family and any recommendation of a harsher sentence such

as death. We cannot condone either brand of testimony as both would interfere with and be irrelevant to a jury's decision on punishment. Indeed, such testimony would have the potential of reducing a trial to "a contest of irrelevant opinions."

Utah's death penalty statute allows evidence of any relevant aggravating or mitigating circumstances. Section 76–3-207 (2) of the Utah Code states, in pertinent part, "In [capital felony] sentencing proceedings, evidence may be presented as to any matter the court deems relevant to sentence, including . . . the defendant's character, background, [and] history." State v. Lafferty, 749 P.2d 1239 (Utah 1988). Arizona's statutory scheme makes a death sentence possible only after the trial judge finds at least one aggravating factor. Walton v. Arizona, 497 U.S. 639 (1990). Childhood circumstances must be shown in Pennsylvania. Jermyn v. Horn, 266 F.3d 257 (3d Cir. 2001). See, in general, J. L. Kirchmeier, "Aggravating and Mitigating Factors: The Paradox of Today's Arbitrary and Mandatory Capital Punishment Scheme," *Wm. & Mary Bill of Rights J.* 6 (1998): 345; see also R. Burt, "Disorder in the Court," *Mich. L. Rev.* 85 (1987): 1741; P. Crocker, "Concepts of Culpability and Deathworthiness: Differentiating Between Guilt and Punishment in Death Penalty Cases," *Fordham L. Rev.* 66 (1997): 21; K. B. Dekleva, "Psychiatric Expertise in the Sentencing Phase of Capital Murder Cases," *J. Am. Acad. Psychiatry & Law* 29 (2001): 58; C. Steiker & J. Steiker, "Let God Sort Them Out?: Refining the Individualization Requirement in Capital Sentencing," *Yale L.J.* 102 (1992): 835.

Casebooks have been developed for use in courses in law school on the death penalty. R. Coyne & L. Entzeroth, *Capital Punishment and the Judicial Process* (Durham, N.C.: Carolina Academic Press, 1994); N. Rivkind & S. F. Shatz, *Cases and Materials on the Death Penalty* (St. Paul, Minn.: West, 2001). See the symposia on the death penalty in *Behav. Sci. & Law* 5 (1987): 381–494; *Thomas M. Cooley L. Rev.* 13 (1996): 753–1012. See also V. L. Streib (ed.), *A Capital Punishment Anthology* (Cincinnati: Anderson, 1993).

26. The Arizona Supreme Court explained the state's "especially heinous, cruel or depraved" aggravating factor: (1) whether the killer relished the murder; (2) whether the killer inflicted gratuitous violence on the victim beyond that necessary to kill; (3) whether the killer needlessly mutilated the victim; (4) whether the crime was senseless; and (5) whether the victim was helpless." State v. Detrich, 932 P.2d 1328, 1339 (Ariz. 1997). In State v. Martinez-Villareal, 702 P.2d 670, 680 (Ariz. 1985), the Arizona Supreme Court found "depravity" based upon the defendant's bragging that the killing showed his "machismo," but in State v. Graham, 660 P.2d 460, 463 (Ariz. 1983), it found no "depravity" in the defendant bragging that the victim "squealed like a rabbit." Dr. Michael Welner is engaged in developing a "depravity scale"; the project was discussed at the 2001 annual meeting in New Orleans of the American Psychiatric Association. See M. Welner, "A Depravity Scale for Today's Courts," *Forensic Echo,* May 1998, p. 4.

27. United States v. Ngyyen, 928 F.Supp. 1525, 1541–42 (D.Kan. 1996).

28. Payne v. Tennessee, 490 U.S. 805 (1989).

29. American Law Institute, Model Penal Code 210.6(4). In Zant v. Stephens, 462 U.S. 862 (1983), the Supreme Court said that it would be constitutionally impermissible to give aggravating effect to factors such as "race, religion or political affiliation or . . . conduct that actually should militate in favor of a lessor penalty, such as perhaps the defendant's mental illness." 462 U.S. at 885.

30. See D. L. Rumley, "A License to Kill: The Categorical Exemption of the Mentally Retarded from the Death Penalty," *St. Mary's L.J.* 24 (1993): 1299. In Penry v. Lynaugh, 492 U.S. 302 (1989), involving a mentally retarded man, Johnny Paul Penry, the U.S. Supreme Court said "it is not cruel and unusual punishment, in violation of the Eighth Amendment, to execute the mentally retarded, so long as [the jury] can consider and give effect to mitigating evidence of mental retardation in imposing sentence." The Court ordered a new trial for Penry, and at his second trial, he was again sentenced to death. He was sentenced to die for the 1979 rape and murder of a 22-year-old woman who was decorating her new home at the time he forced his way in and attacked her. After twenty years on death row, as he was about to be executed, the Court granted a stay of execution. Penry's lawyers contended that in the second trial, the jury was not given clear instructions to evaluate his mental maturity. Prosecutors do not deny that Penry has a low IQ, but they claimed he is not nearly so limited as he is portrayed. In a 6–3 decision, the Court overturned the death sentence on the ground that the jurors did not get clear instructions about how to weigh the defendant's mental abilities against the severity of the crime. Penry v. Johnson, 531 U.S. 1003 (2001).

One day before the justices heard arguments in Penry's case, they raised the stakes much higher by agreeing to hear a separate North Carolina case that asks the same question *Penry* did over a decade ago: Does executing mentally retarded individuals violate the Eighth Amendment prohibition of cruel and unusual punishment? The new case involved Ernest McCarver, an inmate with an IQ of 67, but shortly after the Supreme Court agreed to hear the case, North Carolina rendered it moot by enacting legislation, made retroactive, barring the execution of people who are mentally retarded. As a substitute, the Supreme Court accepted a case brought on behalf of Daryl Atkins, a retarded man on Virginia's death row. Atkins, whose IQ was tested before trial at 59, was convicted in 1996 of killing a truck driver in a carjacking and robbery. Of course, a declaration that the retarded must be spared makes irrelevant the issue of proper death penalty jury instructions.

Connecticut and Florida say that an individual is retarded if his IQ is more than two standard deviations below the average (which would make it roughly 70 or lower), coupled with "deficits in adaptive behavior" manifested between birth and age eighteen. For a critique, see J. Q. Wilson, "Executing the Retarded," *National Review,* July 23, 2001, p. 37. One would assume that a mentally retarded individual who meets the test of competency to stand trial would also be competent to be executed. See chapter 8, on competency to stand trial.

31. S. P. Garvey, "The Emotional Economy of Capital Sentencing," *N. Y. U. L. Rev.* 75 (2000): 26; see also W. J. Bowers, M. Sandys, & B. Steiner, "Foreclosing Impartiality in Capital Sentencing: Jurors' Predispositions, Attitudes and Premature Decision-Making," *Cornell L. Rev.* 83 (1998): 1476; S. P. Garvey, "Aggravation and Mitigation in Capital Cases: What Do Jurors Think?" *Colum. L. Rev.* 98 (1998): 1538; G. Goodpaster, "The Trial for Life: Effective Assistance of Counsel in Death Penalty Cases," *N. Y. U. L. Rev.* 58 (1983): 299; J. S. Liebman & M. J. Shepard, "Guiding Capital Sentencing Discretion beyond the 'Boiler Plate': Mental Disorder as a Mitigating Factor," *Geo. L.J.* 66 (1978): 757; C. Slobogin, "Mental Illness and the Death Penalty," *Calif. Crim. L. Rev.* 1 (2000): 3, reprinted in *MPDLR* 24 (July/Aug. 2000): 667; L. T. White, "The Mental Illness Defense in the Capital Penalty Hearing," *Behav. Sci. & Law* 5 (1987): 419.

32. Turpin v. Lipham, 1998 WL 804430 (Ga. 1998); Cargle v. State, 909 P.2d 806 (Okla. Cr. App. 1995).

33. Cargle v. State, 909 P.2d 806 (Okla. Cr. App. 1995). In Payne v. Tennessee, 501 U.S. 808 (1991), the U.S. Supreme Court reasoned that "[v]ictim impact evidence is simply another form or method of informing the sentencing authority about the specific harm caused by the crime in question, evidence of a general type long considered by sentencing authorities." The Court emphasized that the state has a legitimate interest in countering the defendant's mitigating evidence by showing that the victim also is an individual and "a unique loss to society." 501 U.S. at 825. The Court concluded that it was "now of the view that a State may properly conclude that for the jury to assess meaningfully the defendant's moral culpability and blameworthiness, it should have before it at the sentencing phase evidence of the specific harm caused by the defendant." 501 U.S. at 825.

34. W. J. Bowers, "The Capital Jury Project: Rationale, Design, and Preview of Early Findings," *Ind. L.J.* 70 (1995): 1043; see also W. J. Bowers, "The Capital Jury: Is It Tilted Toward Death?" *Judicature* 79 (1996): 220. In Weeks v. Angelone, 120 S. Ct. 727 (2000), the U.S. Supreme Court ruled that the trial judge is not obliged to clear up the jury's confusion over the sentencing instruction. The jurors sent the judge a question: If they found [the defendant's] crime to be "outrageously or wantonly vile," or that he was likely to commit other violent acts, was it their "duty" to sentence him to death? Under Virginia law, one such "aggravating circumstance" must be present for a jury to impose the death sentence. The judge referred the jurors to a passage in his written instructions that told them they could impose a death sentence or opt for life imprisonment if they found that death was "not justified." Defense counsel argued that the judge's answer unfairly handicapped their client, because it did not clearly point out that they could consider mitigating evidence such as the defendant's remorse. Justice John Paul Stevens, author of the dissenting opinion, agreed, saying that there was a "virtual certainty" that the jury was confused, as well as "no reason to believe" the judge's answer had resolved the confusion.

35. W. J. Bowers et al., "Foreclosed Impartiality in Capital Sentencing: Jurors' Predispositions, Guilt-Trial Experience, and Premature Decision Making," *Cornell L. Rev.* 83 (1998): 1476.

36. M. Sandys, "Cross-Overs—Capital Jurors Who Change Their Minds about the Punishment: A Litmus Test for Sentencing Guidelines," *Ind. L.J.* 70 (1995): 1183.

37. Out of context, the term *death qualify* might be taken to mean "to qualify (someone) for the punishment of death." A. H. Soukhanov, *Word Watch* (New York: Henry Holt, 1995), p. 183. With a charge of a capital crime, prosecutors may initially seek the death penalty, thereby getting a "death qualified" jury, one more likely to convict than a non-death qualified jury, and then at the conclusion of the trial, they may not ask for imposition of the death penalty. It happens not infrequently. In the trial of Andrea Yates, charged with drowning her five children, defense counsel claimed that the prosecutor sought the death penalty in bad faith as a ploy to ensure a conviction. "Death Penalty Bid for Mom Denounced" (news release), *Detroit Free Press*, Dec. 3, 2001, p. 9.

38. 477 U.S. 399 (1986).

39. 339 U.S. 9 (1950).

40. 168 U.S. 398 (1897).

41. 339 U.S. at 12–13.

42. 357 U.S. 549 (1958).

43. New evidence regarding a prisoner's mental competence or whether a warden acted in bad faith in not disclosing the new evidence does not constitute grounds for a federal court to alter or amend its judgment upholding a state court's finding that the prisoner is competent when the state court is not first given an opportunity to consider the evidence. Franklin v. Francis, 306 F.Supp. 1009 (S.D. Ohio 1999).

44. 357 U.S. at 552–53.

45. Supra note 38.

46. G. B. Melton, J. Petrila, N. G. Poythress, & C. Slobogin, *Psychological Evaluation for the Courts* (New York: Guilford, 2d ed. 1997), p. 182.

47. The standards of the American Bar Association, taking an intermediate position, recommend that the indigent condemned be entitled to an independent evaluation of competency, that the condemned be represented by counsel at the competency hearing, and that the burden be on the condemned to show incompetence by a preponderance of the evidence. Commentary to *Criminal Justice Mental Health Standards*, standard 7–5.2 (1984). In Singleton v. State, 313 S.C. 75, 437 S.E.2d 53 (1993), the South Carolina Supreme Court set out the following procedure:

> [T]he defendant or his/her guardian may apply for subsequent Post Conviction Relief [PCR] on the basis of competency. . . . At the evidentiary hearing, the applicant, through competent evidence or expert testimony, must show by a preponderance of the evidence that he or she lacks the requisite competency for execution. If the PCR court finds the applicant incompetent in accordance with the standard [set out in the ABA Criminal Justice Mental Health Standards], then the appropriate remedy is to issue a temporary stay of execution pending a mandatory review by this Court.
>
> Once the defendant is found incompetent and the stay of execution is affirmed by this Court, the burden necessarily shifts to the State to move for a hearing upon the defendant's return to competency. At this subsequent hearing, the State must show by a preponderance of the evidence that the defendant is competent to be executed. If the State establishes competency, then the PCR court may lift the previous stay of execution subject to the review of this Court.

48. 616 So.2d 428 (Fla. 1993).

49. 751 So.2d 37 (Fla. 1999).

50. 751 So.2d 597 (Fla. 1999).

51. Provenzano v. Florida, 2000 WL 674703 (Fla. 2000). A dissent stated that Provenzano's delusion that he was going to die because he was Jesus Christ indicated that his mental illness had put him out of touch with reality and made him unfit for execution, as he did not know the real reason he was being put to death.

52. Missouri now houses its death row inmates among the general population, but this is not the norm. See E. H. Mallett, "Death Row Defense," *Champion*, Aug./Sept. 2000, p. 3. In Texas, the condemned now live in a new high-security unit about fifty miles away from the Huntsville Unit of the Texas Department of Criminal Justice, in Livingston.

53. In the novel *The Green Mile* (New York: Simon & Schuster, 1996), Stephen King notes similarity between death row and the nursing home (p. 250).

54. Upon imposing the death sentence on Thomas J. Koskovich, a 21-year-old, Judge Reginal Stanton of New Jersey Superior Court set a deadline of five years for the state to carry out the execution, and if the state has not carried it out by then, the judge ordered that the sentence automatically be changed to life in prison. In a statement read in the courtroom, he criticized the nation's courts for delays in executions. "The process has become unacceptably cruel to defendants," he said, "who spend long years under sentence of death while the judicial system conducts seemingly interminable proceedings which remind many observers of a cruelly whimsical cat toying with a mouse." R. Hanley, "Judge Orders Death Penalty with a Five-Year Deadline," *New York Times*, May 8, 1999, p. 17. Centuries ago, the judge in his sentence directed execution to be performed on the next day. W. Blackstone, *Commentaries* 397. See J. L. Gallemore & J. H. Panton, "Inmate Responses to Lengthy Death Row Confinement," *Am. J. Psychiatry* 129 (1972): 167.

How did the Jewish population of Europe react once it began to dawn upon them that the Germans had decided to murder them? Yehuda Bauer, a prominent scholar of Holocaust studies, writes: "Psychologically, Jewish responses to knowledge of impending destruction were no different from similar responses of other groups. Russian or Polish peasants on the point of execution by German troops, French resistance fighters caught and sentenced to death, Serb villagers confronting Croat or German murderers—people facing inescapable destruction behave in much the same way. The range of reactions extends from numbed fear and hysterical crying to heroic defiance." Y. Bauer, *Rethinking the Holocaust* (New Haven: Yale University Press, 2001), p. 26. The depiction in Truman Capote's *In Cold Blood* of inmates awaiting death is noted in chapter 21, on post-traumatic stress disorder.

55. For prisoners executed between 1977 and 1997, the average elapsed time on death row was 111 months from the last sentencing date. U.S. Department of Justice, Bureau of Justice Statistics Bulletin, "Capital Punishment," 1997, p. 12. Supreme Court Justice Clarence Thomas has argued that "[i]t is incongruous to arm capital defendants with an arsenal of 'constitutional' claims with which they may delay their executions, and simultaneously to complain when executions are inevitably delayed." Knight v. Florida, 120 S. Ct. 459 (1999).

56. L. M. Friedman, *Crime and Punishment in American History* (New York: Basic Books, 1993), p. 168. See also id., *American Law in the 20th Century* (New Haven: Yale University Press, 2002), pp. 217–23.

57. See S. Roberts, *The Brother: The Untold Story of Atomic Spy David Greenglass and How He Sent His Sister, Ethel Rosenberg, to the Electric Chair* (New York: Random House, 2001).

58. See M. L. Radelet, *Executing the Mentally Ill* (Thousand Oaks, Cal.: Sage, 1993); K. Heilbrun et al., "The Debate in Treating Individuals Incompetent for Execution," *Am. J. Psychiatry* 149 (1992): 596; K. Heilbrun, "Assessment of Competency for Execution? The Guide of Mental Health Professionals," *Bull. Am. Acad. Psychiatry & Law* 16 (1988): 205; D. Mossman, "Assessing and Restoring Competency to be Executed: Legal Contours and Implications for Assessment," *Crim. Justice & Behavior* 18 (1991): 164; G. B. Leong, J. A. Silva, R. Weinstock, & L. Ganzini, "Survey of Forensic Psychiatrists on Evaluation and Treatment of Prisoners on Death Row," *J. Am. Acad. Psychiatry & Law* 28 (2000): 427; D. H. Wallace, "The Need to Commute the Death Sentence: Competency for Execution and Ethical Dilemmas for Mental Health Professionals," *J. Law & Psychiatry* 15 (1992): 317; B. Ward, "Competency for Execution: Problems in Law and Psychiatry," *Fla. St. U. L. Rev.* 14 (1986): 35.

59. A. Ehrenzweig, "A Psychoanalysis of the Insanity Plea—Clues to the Problems of Criminal Responsibility and Insanity in the Death Cell," *Yale L.J.* 73 (1964): 425.

60. D. Goleman, "Proud to Be a Bleeding Heart," *Psychology Today*, June 1978, p. 80. See also L. Freeman (ed.), *Karl Menninger, M.D.: Sparks* (New York: Crowell, 1973), p. 244.

61. See A. M. Freedman & A. L. Halpern, "The Psychiatrist's Dilemma: A Conflict of Roles in Legal Executions," *Australian & New Zealand J. Psychiatry* 33 (1999): 629; A. M. Freedman & A. L. Halpern, "The Erosion of Ethics and Morality in Medicine: Physician Participation in Legal Executions in the United States," *N. Y. Law School L. Rev.* 41 (1996): 169; J. C. Schoenholtz, A. M. Freedman, & A. L. Halpern, "The 'Legal' Abuse of Physicians in Deaths in the United States: The Erosion of Ethics and Morality in Medicine," *Wayne L. Rev.* 42 (1996): 1505; see also M. A. Norko, "Reflections on Halpern's Call," *Am. Acad. Psychiatry & Law Newsletter*, Apr. 2000, p. 3. As a result of their efforts, the American Medical Association adopted a pro-

hibition again participation by a physician in an execution, even "attending or observing an execution" or pronouncing death of the prisoner, let alone administering a lethal substance. See S. L. Halleck, "Psychiatry and the Death Penalty: A View from the Front Lines," in L. E. Frost & R. J. Bonnie (eds.), *The Evolution of Mental Health Law* (Washington, D.C.: American Psychological Association, 2001), p. 181.

62. 498 U.S. 38 (1990) (per curiam).

63. In Washington v. Harper, 494 U.S. 210 (1990), the U.S. Supreme Court upheld the constitutionality of involuntary medication for mentally ill prisoners who pose a danger to themselves or others provided such treatment is in their medical interest.

64. State v. Perry, 610 So.2d 746 (La. 1992). See D. Mossman, "Denouement of an Execution Competency Case: Is *Perry* Pyrrhic?" *Bull. Am. Acad. Psychiatry & Law* 23 (1995): 269.

65. See Md. Ann. Code art. 27, sec. 75A(d)(3); Perry v. Louisiana, 610 So.2d 746 (La. 1992); Singleton v. State, 313 S.C. 75, 437 S.E.2d 53 (1993). See also Singleton v. Norris, 267 F.3d 859 (8th Cir. 2001). See M. L. Radelet & G. W. Barnard, "Treating Those Found Incompetent for Execution: Ethical Chaos with Only One Solution," *Bull. Am. Acad. Psychiatry & Law* 16 (1988): 297.

66. Dr. Robert D. Miller presents the results of a national survey of attorneys general inquiring about procedures for the determination of competency to be executed and treatment of incompetent condemned prisoners, and discusses the ethical issues involved. R. D. Miller, "Evaluation of and Treatment to Competency to be Executed: A National Survey and an Analysis," *J. Psychiatry & Law* 16 (1988): 67.

67. Callins v. Collins, 114 S. Ct. 1127 (1994).

68. J. Yardley, "Of All Places: Texas Wavering on Death Penalty," *New York Times,* Aug. 19, 2001, p. WK-4. For years it has been said that IQ and other mental test scores are not really valid, when it comes to determining one's "real" ability to do academic work, but when it comes to the death penalty, it is argued that one with a low IQ does not know that killing is wrong. T. Sowell, "Why Did IQ Scores Become Valid? To Avoid Execution" (syndicated column), *Detroit News,* Mar. 3, 2002, p. 16.

16

Sentencing and the Psychiatric Forensic Center

"**L**et the punishment fit the crime" is a phrase we learned from the popular operetta *The Mikado* by Gilbert and Sullivan and that has become a cliché; at one time this concept was the byword of major penal reform. Proponents of this principle in England sought to limit the application of the death penalty, which was exacted for over 160 offenses, on the ground that such a harsh penalty did not fit all these offenses. Nowadays, both federal and state criminal statutes are rife with *enhanced penalty* provisions that expose a defendant to increased punishment based upon issues that are not elements of the crime but that are instead considered "sentencing factors." (The term *factor* refers to an issue relevant for sentencing purposes only, and *element* refers to an issue that the government must prove beyond a reasonable doubt to obtain a conviction.)

The sentencing factors are adjudicated in a proceeding that follows the determination of guilt of the elements, and they may alter the minimum and maximum sentence range. The rules of evidence often do not apply, and hearsay may be admitted. The government's burden is to prove the issue only by a preponderance of the evidence. There is no right to cross-examine witnesses or a right to a jury.[1]

The Act and the Actor

Reformers of the criminal law over the years have advocated an individualized approach in which the punishment fit the criminal, not simply the crime. Themis, the ancient Greek goddess of justice and equity, was once depicted with large, wide-open eyes, but in the late nineteenth century, she was blindfolded, emphasizing the objectivity or anonymity with which justice is meted out. Emphasis on the act was an important political achievement, assuring equality before the law. A criminal act was to be adjudged and punished the same, at least that was the hope, whether committed by a prince or a pauper. Reformers would have Themis remove her blindfold and look at the actor as well as the act, at least at the sentencing stage—not at whether the actor is a prince or pauper but at the psychodynamics of the actor's behavior.

Criminal justice is meted out in a hierarchy that includes police, prosecutors, judges, and juries. They are motivated and constrained in different ways.[2] Initially, in some measure, the police officer (the court of first instance) considers the act and the actor. For one way, the classification of self-defense or justifiable homicide is based on police investigation.[3] For another way, at least in the case of a minor offense, the police officer may take a disturbed individual to a mental hospital rather than to jail; or after booking at the jail, may transfer the individual to a hospital.[4] In the wake of several jail deaths (mainly due to drug overdose), Detroit Chief of Police Benny Napoleon issued a public statement: "If someone comes in suffering from withdrawal, complaining that he is ill, that person should be taken to the hospital and treated by a physician. There is absolutely no question about it. Anyone who did not do that is clearly in violation of department policy."[5]

In a recent development, in at least four states, mentally ill persons accused of committing nonviolent crimes are being dealt with in special mental health courts—and the concept could spread nationwide under a proposed federal law. Under this development, criminal court judges can refer people charged with misdemeanors to these mental health courts. There, a judge and an in-house psychiatric social worker confer and can refer the defendant to a community-based mental health treatment center instead of jail, if necessary. This development is largely a response to the high rate of mental illness in jails and prisons already overcrowded with violent or recidivistic offenders. In another development, drug courts and other programs have been established in a number of jurisdictions aimed at reducing prison costs by diverting nonviolent drug users into serious drug treatment programs.[6]

By and large, however, following booking at the jailhouse, a criminal offender become a faceless number in the various stages of the criminal process. The offender is prosecuted, tried, and processed depending upon the type of offense committed. Offenses are generally divided into four classes: class one (e.g., murder, rape), punishable by death or life imprisonment; class two (e.g., armed robbery, burglary), punishable by imprisonment at hard labor; class three (e.g., theft over $100, pandering, crime against nature), punishable by imprisonment with or without hard labor; and class four (e.g., simple battery, prostitution), punishable by fine or imprisonment.

In medicine, the physician considers the medical history of the patient. In law, on the other hand, evidence at trial of the defendant's prior acts is as a rule inadmissible to prove guilt, as the defendant is not obliged to defend his life history. As a general proposition, with certain exceptions, a defendant's prior difficulties with the law, such as specific prior criminal acts or bad reputation, cannot be used by the prosecutor at trial even though such facts might tend to prove a defendant's propensity to commit the crime for which he is on trial. Speaking on the inadmissibility of evidence of bad character to establish a probability of guilt, the U.S. Supreme Court stated:

> Not that the law invests the defendant with a presumption of good character . . . but it simply closes the whole matter of character, disposition, and reputation on the prosecution's case-in-chief. The state may not show defendant's prior trouble with the law, specific criminal acts, or ill name among his neighbors, even though such facts might logically be persuasive that he is by propensity a probable perpetrator of the crime. The inquiry is not rejected because character is irrelevant; on the contrary, it is said to weigh too much with the jury and to so overpersuade them as to prejudge one with a bad general record and deny him a fair opportunity to defend against a particular charge. The overriding policy of excluding such evidence, despite its admitted probative value, is the practical experience that its disallowance tends to prevent confusion of issues, unfair surprise, and undue prejudice.[7]

The criminal law's approach of looking to the act rather than to the actor, if literally applied, is mechanical. The law of the act and that of the actor are compromised by a dual-track approach, that is, by proceeding on the basis of the act (elements of the crime), at the trial level and on the basis of the actor (sentencing factors) at the sentencing and postsentencing levels. Regarding the sentence determination, the Supreme Court observed that "it is surely true that a trial judge generally has wide discretion," and "before making that determination, a judge may appropriately conduct an inquiry broad in scope, largely unlimited either as to the kind of information he may consider, or the source from which it may come."[8]

A concern is that explanation turns into exculpation. *Tout comprendre, c'est tout pardonner.* Many fear that understanding leads to sympathy for offenders and even to condoning their acts. Claude Lanzmann, who produced *Shoah*, a nine-hour documentary on the Holocaust, said any attempt to explain Hitler's motivation immediately relieves him of guilt. In ten years of research, Ron Rosenbaum read what the Hitler theorists had been saying, and agreed with Lansmann.[9] He wrote that explaining Hitler is "obscenely immoral" for "any attempt to understand Hitler inevitably degenerates into an exercise in empathy with him. To understand all is to forgive all, and . . . even the first steps down the slippery slope to understanding are impermissible."[10]

In the case of Hitler, some historians look for a Jewish catalyst. Hitler's father was illegitimate, and there are suggestions that his serving-girl grandmother had been impregnated by the son of the wealthy Jewish household where she had been working. Others find another explanation for Hitler's behavior. One of the most bizarre is what British historian Alan Bullock calls the "one-ball business," that Hitler had only one testicle and that crazed him enough to murder the Jews. A corollary to this theory is that a billy goat bit off one of his testicles. Rosenbaum says, "That's an interesting instance of the way theories about Hitler serve other agendas. I think the guy who advanced that theory in a way wanted to exculpate the German political culture from responsibility for Hitler by saying it was this horrible, ridiculous, bizarre accident and had nothing to do with the health of the political culture."[11]

Individualization of Disposition

Toward the end of the nineteenth century, legislatures began to announce that the basic purpose of the criminal law was correction or rehabilitation rather than punishment. It was an endorsement of various declarations. The Declaration of Principles adopted by the first congress of the American Prison Association in 1870 said, "[T]reatment is directed to the criminal rather than to the crime, [hence] its great object should be his moral regeneration . . . not the infliction of vindictive suffering." The declaration called for classification of criminals "based on character"; for the indeterminate sentence under which the offender would be released as soon as the "moral cure" had been effected and "satisfactory proof of reformation" obtained; for "preventive institutions for the reception and treatment of children not yet criminal but in danger of becoming so"; for education as a "vital force in the reformation of fallen men and women"; and for prisons of a moderate size, preferably designed to house no more than three hundred inmates.

The Wickersham Commission, appointed by President Hoover in 1931, stated in its report:

> We conclude that the present prison system is antiquated and inefficient. It does not reform the criminal. It fails to protect society. There is reason to believe that it contributes to the increase of crime by hardening the prisoner. We are convinced that a new type of penal institution must be developed, one that is new in spirit, in method, and in objective. The Commission recommends: individual treatment . . . indeterminate sentence . . . education in the broadest sense . . . skillful and sympathetic supervision of the prisoner on parole. . . .[12]

Two committees, one representing the American Bar Association and the other the American Psychiatric Association, met in 1929 to draft a position statement that advocated the following:

1. That there be available to every criminal and juvenile court a psychiatric service to assist the court in the disposition of offenders.
2. That no criminal be sentenced for any felony in any case in which the judge has any discretion as to the sentence until there be filed as a part of the record a psychiatric report.
3. That there be a psychiatric service available to each penal and correctional institution.
4. That there be a psychiatric report on every prisoner convicted of a felony before he is released.
5. That there be established in every state a complete system of transfer and parole and that there be no decision for or against any parole or any transfer from one institution to another without a psychiatric report.

Thereafter, representatives of the APA and the ABA met with members of the American Medical Association, and the same recommendations were unanimously endorsed by the latter group. Thus, official bodies of psychiatrists, physicians, and lawyers of the United States were in agreement on these principles, although in practice they have been largely ignored.

Under the law the prosecutor is not entitled to interview or examine the accused but must make out its case on the basis of evidence presented by others. The proposals of the ABA and APA of 1929 would not tamper with this traditional limitation on the prosecutor. Generally, it is only when a plea of insanity, incompetency to stand trial, or a sex offense is at issue that a commission is appointed by the court to examine the defendant. The goal of the recommended principles was to make psychiatric services available to the court or institution in other instances as well.

Whether all lawbreakers should be dealt with in the same way, depending only on their offense, or whether physical and mental conditions should be given relevance are questions that must be agreed upon initially if such proposals are to become meaningful. Should a man who has a peptic ulcer be dealt with differently from a man not so afflicted? Should a woman who is manifestly depressed be handled differently from a woman who presents no visible signs of depression? Should a stupid individual be dealt with differently from an openly hostile one? Traditionally the law gives relevance only to minority and insanity (as defined by the test of criminal responsibility) in personalizing an offense.

On the one hand, it is argued that individualization of disposition would result in a weakening of the rule of law. The basic meaning of law, it is said, is holding everyone responsible to the same rules. The law, through its representatives, it is argued, has no business concerning itself with the whole person but only with that person's unlawful acts. When the whole person is considered, irrelevant factors or arbitrariness are more apt to enter the picture. If the whole person is to be considered, what will be looked for? The street gang in the 1961 film version of *West Side Story* pleaded, "Gee, Officer Krupke, deep down inside there is good!"

In a 1971 report, "Struggle for Justice: A Report on Crime and Punishment in America," the American Friends Service Committee contended that the basic principle underlying the rule of law has been lost in recent decades as the shifting focus of the criminal system from the act to the individual gave rise to the practice of varying criminal sanctions according to individual characteristics. There being no sound scientific or moral basis for such variations, the report strongly recommended a return to the principle of uniform application of penal sanctions. It was felt that society should have a limited set of rules stating which types of behavior are not permissible, that these rules should apply to absolutely everybody, and that they should be enforced with absolute consistency. The report would replace the Department of Corrections, which it considers a euphemism, by a Department of Punishment. The recommendation was that all treatment be made voluntary. (Hegel contended that a criminal does not receive his due honor unless the concept and measure of his punishment are derived from his own act and still less does he receive it if he is treated either as a harmful animal who has to be made harmless or with a view to deterring or reforming him.)

It is not clear how much change was actually proposed in the report, since the committee saw no alternatives to prisons, that second offenses should be punished with increased severity, and that the chief features of indeterminacy—such as good time, though subject to judicial appeal—be retained. Its argument in favor of "uniformly distributing punishment according to what the act calls for" (whatever that means) failed to address the fact that de jure equality usually results in de facto inequality. Does not discrimination have merit when individualization is done on a rational rather than arbitrary basis? If discretion were to play no role in the judicial process, then machines could replace judge or jury.

An individual commits a heinous act. Should he be sent to a hospital or to prison? Is he ill or bad, or both? Is he able to control his hostile urges? Should he be afforded counseling or supervision? Should he be given medication? Should consideration be given to the impact of a sentence on the family members of the victim or the offender? The psychiatric evaluation of offenders is premised on a philosophy of individualized processing. The prominent forensic psychiatrist Seymour Halleck said, "The major contribution of American psychiatry to the criminal law has been the development of theories of behavior that emphasize the individual."[13]

In the illustrations that follow, should the individual have been left alone, processed through the criminal law, or sent to a hospital? In these cases focus was placed on the offense rather than on the offender, consequently they were handled through the process of the criminal law:

1. Frank Stroud killed his mother, and then proceeded to have sexual relations with her dead body. He was charged with first-degree murder.
2. Ethel Bailey, a middle-aged woman, was charged with aggravated arson. She set fire to the mattress in her rented house "to destroy the evil spirits" and sat there with her 4-year-old son until the firemen arrived.
3. Charlotta Gavin, age 30, killed her 13-week-old daughter under a viaduct on an interstate highway, then disrobed and walked naked down the highway. She was charged with first-degree premeditated murder. At the arraignment she politely acknowledged the murder charge and corrected the judge's pronunciation of her daughter's name.[14]
4. Jim Wilson, charged with burglary, had been involved in two similar incidents before in which he broke into a home and would simply stand over a bed occupied by a woman. At the time of the incident he was seeing a psychiatrist who reported that he had been working with him and that he seemed to be doing fine. He had a job and reportedly was getting along well with his wife and children. His lawyer, attempting to have the charge dismissed, argued that a man who enters a house and looks down at a woman in bed and has done so on three occasions is a sick man and not a burglar. Labeling a man a criminal, when in reality he is sick and can be cured, he added, is a disservice to society—the man who is labeled a criminal has difficulty obtaining work and supporting a family and the repercussions are catastrophic. The district attorney, however, mindful of adverse publicity in the press, refused to dismiss the case at that point. He might have refused the charge initially, however, upon an assurance that Wilson would be put in a hospital.
5. Hedy Lamarr, the sultry actress of the 1940s who was widely regarded as the sexiest woman in the world, allegedly shoplifted about $86 worth of goods. At the time she was carrying $14,000 in royalty checks in her pocketbook. She said, at the time of her arrest, "I am willing to pay for these

things. Other stores let me do it."[15] At the trial Hedy Lamarr's son testified that she had been distressed the day she was arrested because, among other things, "she was not as beautiful as she had been." A psychiatrist testified that he did not think she could have formulated the intent to deprive the store of the property as she was under emotional stress.[16]

The elderly present special problems in the criminal law process. There are inmates who become elderly in prison, and there are those who commit crime when elderly. In the latter situation, age itself is not a defense to a crime, unlike the case of a minor, but there may be mental illness or diminished capacity. In both the case of the elderly inmate and the elderly criminal, there are problems of administration. It costs three times as much to house an elderly prisoner than others. Health care in prisons is based on acute care, not chronic care. With parole a vanishing concept, efficiency and cost may trump retributive concerns in punishment. The Three-Strikes laws adopted in some twenty-two states result in more elderly in prison. The laws differ as to the crimes that come under them and the discretion given to the prosecutor in enforcing them.

A judge once remarked that the primary function of the court is not to determine guilt or innocence—that would be too easy a task—but rather to decide what should be done with the defendant. Lawyers experienced in the practice of criminal law commonly say that no less than 98 percent of defendants who come before the courts are in fact guilty. Perhaps the cases just described were properly dealt with, perhaps not. In any event the decisions were not made after full exploration. These cases all occurred over fifty years after the establishment of the first adult court psychiatric clinic.

The Forensic Center

The concept of a court clinic or forensic center had its origin in 1909 when William Healy began his pioneer work in Cook County Juvenile Court in Chicago.[17] This led to the establishment of the Psychopathic Laboratory, the first adult court psychiatric clinic, in the same city in 1914. At first, the idea spread quickly, and in the early 1920s clinics were established either informally or by legislative act in a number of cities. However, the trend lagged during the war and postwar years.

The organization and operation of today's clinics or forensic centers are by no means uniform. The variety represents, to some degree, the different philosophies of the legal and psychiatric professions as to the method whereby such service should be integrated into the administration of the criminal law.[18] The operation of clinics or forensic centers can be subsumed in either one or more of the following categories:

1. To conduct pretrial examinations to determine either the fitness of the defendant to stand trial or the legal responsibility of the defendant for the crime committed
2. To carry out treatment and restoration of functions
3. To conduct presentence examinations and prepare a report that the judge may use to determine the proper sentence or treatment for the offender
4. To conduct postsentence examinations that may be for either of two purposes: preparation of a psychiatric history and recommendations for the

treatment of the offender at the institution or penitentiary, to whichever he is sent; or recommendations as to the proper course of therapy to be followed, if needed, when the offender is placed on probation

Each of these operations, which may be carried out by a court-appointed examiner as well as by a clinic, has its advantages and disadvantages. An important if not crucial issue is the matter of financing an adequate evaluation. Quite often, psychiatrists who are court-appointed do skimpy evaluations, light on data and heavy on conclusions, because the courts are unwilling or unable to pay for adequate assessments and some psychiatrists are inclined to abbreviate their procedures proportional to their compensation.

In the case of a pretrial examination, an evaluation may serve to keep the offender out of the criminal law process when that would serve no useful function. There is a practice of dismissing a charge if the accused will go to a psychiatrist for treatment, and if the psychiatrist will indicate that the accused is not a threat to himself or to others. Pretrial examination, however, is mainly performed with a view toward its use at trial.

Through the efforts of Dr. Vernon L. Briggs, a law was passed in 1921 in Massachusetts that required that every defendant charged with a felony be given a psychiatric examination prior to his trial and that the evidence be made available at the trial. Kentucky and Michigan subsequently enacted statutes comparable to the Briggs Law. Unfortunately in such a system, there is a tendency for the examinations to be made perfunctorily and in a disinterested fashion. Moreover, psychiatrists are often reluctant to participate in pretrial examinations because they will likely become involved as witnesses at trial, and they know that court appearances are time-consuming and cross-examinations often humiliating.

An example of a posttrial operation was the Kansas State Reception and Diagnostic Center, located near the Menninger Foundation in Topeka and drawing upon its resources. Established in 1961 with Dr. Karl A. Menninger as its motivating force, its purpose was "to provide a thorough and scientific examination and study of all felony offenders of the male sex sentenced by the courts . . . to state penal institutions so that each such offender may be assigned to a state penal institution having the type of security (maximum, medium, or minimum) and programs of education, employment, or treatment designed to accomplish a maximum of rehabilitation for such offender."[19] In order to implement the purpose of the center, which was concerned only with postsentence evaluation, Kansas enacted a law giving the trial judge the unusual authority to modify a sentence after its imposition, so as to take account of the center's report.[20] The trial judge could modify a sentence within 120 days after its imposition to grant probation. Since the court could reduce but not increase the original sentence following the center's report, there was a tendency in initial sentencing to impose the maximum. The prisoner, who was sent to the center for a maximum 60-day period of evaluation, usually tried to con the examiner, putting on convincing acts of subservience. The cost of operation was approximately five times per inmate more costly than prison, a fact that some legislators found difficult to justify. The center was closed in 1997, as were other state institutions during the 1990s.

A postsentence examination often comes too late. By that time the offender has already been evaluated by the police, the district attorney, and the judge or jury. In effect, examination by the clinic is a fourth evaluation, and therefore it should come as no surprise that most of the recommendations made at this time suggest that the offender be kept in custody. Moreover, the type of person referred by the judge is usually one who is an annoyance to him (e.g., he may refer only bad-check writers). Initiation of the psychiatric examination is thus left to a person who is generally unfamiliar with the symptoms of mental disorders. Finally, it should be noted that recommendations that are made for the purpose of treatment of the offender in some penitentiary or institution are often impractical. If the examining psychiatrist is unfamiliar with the institution to which the individual will be sent, he is not in a position to make recommendations that can be realistically carried out.

A psychiatric court clinic's mode of operation is affected, at least in part, by its origin. For example, a clinic established as a result of community reaction to the occurrence of sexual crimes is likely to focus on such cases. A clinic created in large measure due to demands from a committee on probation is likely to work through the probation department rather than directly with the court. The Detroit clinic, as might be expected, originally showed a special interest in traffic offenders. The Center for Forensic Psychiatry in Ypsilanti, Michigan, essentially carries out evaluations on competency to stand trial and criminal responsibility.

The Medical Office of the Circuit Court of Baltimore goes back to the time of Dr. John Oliver, who was an ordained priest and a professor of psychiatry and history at the Johns Hopkins School of Medicine. Around 1918 one of the lower court judges asked him to sit on the bench with him and express his ideas. Dr. Oliver then moved to the Supreme Bench, the circuit court, or general trial court. He used to examine defendants for mental retardation and also evaluate defendants in nonsupport cases. When blood typing became possible the office arranged for that in paternity cases. Then, in 1932, Dr. Manfred Guttmacher was appointed medical officer, and slowly the staff was enlarged. He expanded the clinic work from nonsupport and paternity cases to include more presentence recommendations in criminal cases.

When Dr. Guttmacher died in 1966, Dr. Jonas Rappeport, one of the founders of the American Academy of Psychiatry and Law and for many years its executive director, succeeded him in 1967. At that time the office consisted of a chief medical officer, two assistant medical officers, an administrator, a social worker, and a psychologist. There was also a separate staff for juveniles under the chief medical officer. Dr. Rappeport ran the office until July 1992, by which time the staff included another staff medical officer, psychologist, and two social workers, and it developed an accredited forensic psychiatry fellowship program, a field placement program for psychological interns, and a field placement for graduate social work students. Furthermore, all residents from the programs at Johns Hopkins and the University of Maryland psychiatric residency programs rotated through this service. Dr. Thomas Ogelsby was appointed chief medical officer upon Dr. Rappeport's retirement.[21]

At the Chester Mental Health Center in Illinois, individuals are referred to the state security/forensic hospital *after* having been found unfit to stand trial, *after* having been found NGRI, or from other state hospitals if too aggressive and dangerous to be safely managed in less restrictive settings. The emphasis is on treatment and restoration of function. Forensic issues addressed include primarily restoration of fitness, restoration of sanity, civil commitment, and court-ordered medication. Though a maximum security hospital, security measures are relatively unimposing: security officers wear civilian clothes, containment fences have fine netting rather than sharp barbs, key pads and proximity badges have almost entirely replaced lock and key for main points of entry and egress. Treatment programs take place in pleasant, nicely furnished settings.[22]

The makeup of the staff at the various centers or clinics differ according to its purpose, but generally, they are staffed by a combination of psychiatrists, psychologists, and oftentimes social workers and correctional officers. These staff members, with differing viewpoints on the system of criminal justice, must work together as a team so that proper recommendations may be made to the court. At most centers (or clinics), the staff is employed on a part-time basis. Because the centers are publicly funded, adequate salaries are generally not available for full-time employment of competent personnel. This disadvantage is offset, in part, by the fact that a staff psychiatrist who works at the clinic on a part-time basis, while also engaging in general psychiatric work, has been found to have a better perspective while performing his work at the center.

The actual work performed depends not only on the chief purpose of the clinic but also on the workload and the available personnel. In many centers only a small proportion of cases get an exhaustive workup. The center's function is often to weed out the grossly abnormal, that is, the psychotic and the mentally defective patients. The center's report generally estimates the patient's intelligence, describes any physical pathology present, and contains a personality evaluation. In many centers the report will also contain a summary and recommendations as to the disposition to be made of the patient. Reports submitted to the court tend to be verbose, and as a consequence the judge often reads only the concluding paragraph (Churchill during World War II limited all bureau reports made to him to one page). Treatment is not the primary function of most centers. Those established more recently, however, often provide for talking or drug therapy while the offender is on probation, if the court finds this to be the best disposition to be made in a particular case.[23]

A different type of organization was the forensic psychiatric clinic established at Temple University, which operated from 1965 to 1967, when it ran out of funds. At the earliest possible stage of a legal problem consultation was made available to indigents and their attorneys without fee. The reports were kept confidential by furnishing them to counsel, which brought them under the protection of the attorney-client privilege rather than under the much more limited physician-patient privilege. The services of the Temple clinic were unique, coining into operation at the earliest phase of the legal problem while the situation was still fluid and open. It was also unique in that its services were available for civil as well as criminal cases.[24] In the past, civil cases have been ignored, for the most part, in the operation of court clinics. Individuals, however, often present themselves to legal agencies with ostensible legal problems that mask or hide serious emotional problems. It may be merely happenstance that a person seeks a legal rather than a medical remedy.[25]

The Isaac Ray Center in Chicago is not a public agency but a nonprofit corporation dedicated to the forensic application of the behavioral sciences. It was founded in 1978 with the signing of a contract with the State of Illinois to evaluate and treat offenders found not guilty by reason of insanity, a population with whom no one else seemed to want to deal. Now, under a contract with Cook County, it provides mental health services at the local jail, which in effect has become the largest single repository in the state for individuals with psychiatric problems. And on a case-by-case basis it deals with a host of other problems in which mental health and criminal behavior are intertwined: workplace violence, sexual violence, psychological fitness of local and national law enforcement officials, and even the problems of victims of and witnesses to traumatizing criminal events. In addition, the center has a commitment to research and education, as evidenced by the publication of many studies on matters as diverse as the identification and treatment of sex offenders and recidivism among individuals released from mental institutions, as well as basic texts on mental health and law for the interdisciplinary audience. Each year it trains a contingent of postdoctoral fellows, residents, and even J.D. candidates (via its affiliation with a law school) in the basic forensic issues, tactics, and ethics.

A forensic psychiatric clinic that has a university affiliation such as at Case Western University and University of Virginia can play an important role in the education of medical students, law students, and probation officers. The affiliation also serves to overcome the difficulty of obtaining well-trained and competent psychiatrists. The teaching program in forensic psychiatry at the University of Virginia was begun in 1969 by the School of Medicine, initially oriented toward the training of psychiatric residents, and later, drawing upon an interdisciplinary faculty, it began to offer academic credit to selected law students.[26]

Affiliation with a university tends to overcome many obstacles facing court clinics, in particular, the difficulty in attracting highly trained and scarce professional personnel because a public agency may be unable to pay adequate salaries. Quite often, psychiatrists working in court clinics are unlicensed, poorly trained, and do not speak English as their first language. It is particularly difficult to obtain competent psychiatrists to work in clinics that do not provide treatment. A further drawback is that psychiatrists who work exclusively in diagnostic and advisory clinics seem to lose their touch. In the court-clinic setting, a somewhat stereotyped image of the patient may emerge and cause a psychiatrist to lose perspective of his work.

The Sentencing Crisis

In litigation over a cow the court is told everything about the cow, but in litigation involving people the court is told very little about the people. In many jurisdictions computer technology has not been applied to police statistics, criminal identification, and crime records, and not even this information is available to deal with crime generally or with the offender in particular. As a result of lack of information, sentencing became chaotic, with judges by their own account regularly handing out sentences they considered either too lenient or too harsh. Studies found the following: (1) allowance by courts and prosecutors, unable to handle their caseloads, of a great deal of plea-bargaining, in which a defendant is offered a reduced charge and a light sentence in return for a guilty plea; (2) a loss of faith in the prison system by some judges, which results in their refusal to send all but the most dangerous defendants to prison, and in cases where they do send a man to prison, they said, they do so unwillingly, believing they are creating an even worse criminal; and (3) a belief by some judges who said they knowingly give light sentences because sentences, whether light or harsh, do nothing to cut down crime.

The sentencing crisis highlighted sentence disparities, that is, similar defendants charged with similar crimes getting vastly different sentences, reflecting differences in the defendant's finances, race, geography, and the judge's personality. To many observers, sentences were arbitrary. Some blamed unfair sentences on the discretionary sentencing power invested in judges.

The new federal sentencing guidelines and mandatory minimum sentences, and their counterparts in many states, give a lesser role to evaluation in the posttrial phase of a criminal proceeding. The guidelines focus on the nature of the offense, with little attention to the nature of the actor. The exercise of discretion in considering the actor's mental state or capacity now occurs almost entirely in the pretrial and trial stages of prosecution.

The sentencing guidelines are a complicated table of forty-three levels that defendants move up or down based on various factors in a crime, such as the use of a weapon or the amount of money stolen. A judge is permitted to depart from the guidelines when prosecutors say the defendant has cooperated or when the judge finds there are other significant factors not adequately considered by the U.S. Sentencing Commission. To some extent, there can be a downward departure in sentencing on the basis of "significantly reduced mental capacity."[27] One study found that judges, prosecutors, and defense lawyers all cooperate to circumvent the guidelines by fudging the actual facts of a crime.[28]

In general, a problem is more readily diagnosed than cured. Thus, the link is easy to establish between crime and slum-bred poverty, broken homes, rootlessness, availability of firearms, drugs, and limited police resources, but it is another matter to do something about them.

Notes

1. See S. N. Herman, "The Tail That Wagged the Dog: Bifurcated Fact-Finding under the Federal Sentencing Guidelines and the Limits of Due Process," *S. Cal. L. Rev.* 66 (1992): 289; Comment, "Awaiting the Mikado: Limiting Legislative Discretion to Define Criminal Elements and Sentencing Factors," *Harv. L. Rev.* 112 (1999): 1349. See also the symposia on sentencing in *Behav. Sci. & Law* 7 (1989): 1–137; *Cooley L. Rev.* 16 (1999): 1–160.

2. See J. Schrag & S. Scotchmer, "Crime and Prejudice: The Use of Character Evidence in Criminal Trials," *J. Law, Economics & Organization* 10 (1994): 319.

3. As defined by the FBI Uniform Crime Reporting Program, murder is the "willful killing of one human being by another." Deaths by "justifiable or excusable" homicides are excluded from the homicide tally and placed in a separate category. Cities with high murder rates may be tempted to reclassify some homicides into an excluded category in an attempt to demonstrate a declining homicide rate. Editorial, "Homicides in Detroit," *Detroit Legal News,* Sept. 15, 1999, p. 10.

4. Some thirty years ago Dr. Lloyd Rowland, director of the Louisiana Association for Mental Health, developed a program and published brochures instructing police on the handling of the mentally ill but it has been forgotten. There is little instruction in police academies on the handling of the mentally ill and there is little inclination to take a disturbed individual to a hospital rather than to a jail. The fatal shooting of a mentally disturbed man in Brooklyn, Gidone Busch, raised concerns again about the use of excessive force by New York City police officers. S. Sachs, "Man Shot by Police Was on a Troubled Quest," *New York Times,* Sept. 2, 1999, p. 1.

5. A. Mullen, "Death in the Lockup," *Detroit Metro Times,* Sept. 15, 1999, p. 14. See also T. M. Green, "Police as Frontline Mental Health Workers: The Decision to Arrest or Refer to Mental Health Agencies," *Int. J. Law & Psychiatry* 20 (1997): 469; see also M. Klein, "Law Enforcement's Response to People with Mental Illness," *FBI Law Enforcement Bull.* 71 (Feb. 2002): 11.

6. Editorial, "Drug Treatment Gets a Boost," *New York Times*, Dec. 13, 1999, p. 36.

7. Michelson v. United States, 335 U.S. 469 (1948).

8. United States v. Tucker, 92 S. Ct. 589, 591 (1972).

9. Lanzmann's *Shoah* is discussed in I. Clendinnen, *Reading the Holocaust* (New York: Cambridge University Press, 1999); R. Rosenbaum, *Explaining Hitler: The Search for the Origins of His Evil* (New York: Random House, 1998).

10. R. Rosenbaum, supra note 9, p. xv.

11. Ibid., pp. 140–49. See also H. Schoeck & J. W. Wiggins (eds.), *Psychiatry and Responsibility* (New York: Van Nostrand, 1962).

12. See. M. Guttmacher, "The Status of Adult Psychiatric Clinics," *Nat. Prob. & Parole Assn. J.* 1 (1957): 97. again, years later, former president Richard Nixon wrote: "For decades, social reformers viewed prisons primarily as places to save souls, raise up the downtrodden, and transform inmates' lives for the better. This conception, embodied in the euphemism 'houses of correction,' has not worked. Rehabilitation, for the most part, has been a failure. As long ago as 1975 one landmark study of more than two hundred attempts to measure the effects of rehabilitation programs concluded that these efforts had no 'appreciable effect on recidivism.' According to U.C.L.A. professor James Q. Wilson, 'It did not seem to matter what form of treatment in the correctional system was attempted. Indeed, some forms of treatment . . . actually produced an increase in the rate of recidivism.'" R. Nixon, *Beyond Peace* (New York: Random House, 1994), p. 230.

13. S. Halleck, "American Psychiatry and the Criminal: A Historical Review," *Am. J. Psychiatry*, supplement to March 1965 issue. See also id., *The Mentally Disordered Offender* (Washington, D.C.: American Psychiatric Press, 1987); K. A. Menninger, *The Crime of Punishment* (New York: Viking, 1968).

14. The judge found Charlotta Gavin not guilty by reason of insanity. "Judge Finds Woman Discovered Nude with Dead Baby as Mentally Ill" (Associated Press news release), *Detroit Legal News*, Dec. 19, 2000, p. 1. Some jurisdictions have an infanticide statute that would distinguish the case from murder. In jurisdictions without an infanticide statute (as in Michigan where the Gavin case occurred), the accused tends to plead insanity. In the prevailing view, prosecutors charge what the facts may warrant, leaving it to the defense to assert any defense or mitigating circumstances. The local newspaper, upon reporting the murder charge filed against Gavin, was deluged with calls and letters expressing dismay. Personal communication of Dec. 21, 2000, by Ben Schmitt, reporter at the *Detroit Free Press*. The insanity defense makes possible a verdict more acceptable to the public than murder or a verdict of not guilty. See M. Jackson, *New-Born Child Murder* (Manchester: Manchester University Press, 1996); C. E. Holden, A. S. Burland, & C. A. Lemmen, "Insanity and Filicide: Women Who Murder Their Children" in E. P. Benedek (ed.), *Emerging Issues in Forensic Psychiatry: From the Clinic to the Courthouse* (San Francisco: Jossey-Bass, 1996), pp. 25–34; P. J. Resnick, "Child Murder by Parents: A Psychiatric Review of Filicide," *Am. J. Psychiatry* 126 (1969): 325.

15. Commenting on the case, Harry Golden wrote in the *Carolina Israelite*, Jan.–Feb. 1966, p. 13:

> Whoever arrested Hedy Lamarr was a particularly conscienceless and/or stupid store detective. . . . I have discovered that in this one particular area, psychiatry works wonders. Of course, we are not discussing thieves who make off with thousands of dollars of merchandise, or those who deal in stolen goods. This is a police matter and not a case for a psychiatrist. Any store detective who doesn't recognize Hedy Lamarr and know she has this problem, and further know she is good for the merchandise, ought to be hawking peanuts.

16. Hedy Lamarr was acquitted. Associated Press news release, Apr. 23 & 26, 1966. See also R. Severo, "Hedy Lamarr, Sultry Star Who Reigned in Hollywood of 30's and 40's, Dies at 86," *New York Times*, Jan. 20, 2000, p. 16. In Arthur Hailey's account of the auto industry one of the principal characters—a lonely, bored wife of an executive—shoplifts for the zest of it. Usually in such cases, if apprehended, the well-heeled make good the price and no criminal record is made. A. Hailey, *Wheels* (New York: Doubleday, 1971).

17. H. L. Witmer, *Psychiatric Clinics for Children* (New York: Commonwealth Fund, 1940).

18. M. S. Guttmacher, "Adult Psychiatric Court Clinics," in R. Slovenko (ed.), *Crime, Law and Corrections* (Springfield, Ill.: Thomas, 1966), p. 479; see also S. Seligsohn, "Psychiatric Court Clinics," *Temp. L.Q.* 29 (1956): 347. Michigan's Wayne County Prosecutor Mike Duggan in 2001 began a pretrial diversion program for defendants who may be mentally ill. If an examination by a prosecutor-appointed psychiatrist finds mental illness, the case may be moved from the criminal justice system to the mental health system. The practice has yet to be evaluated. F. Girard, "Promising Athlete Accused of Murder," *Detroit News*, Dec. 28, 2001, p. 1.

19. Kansas Stat. Ann. 76–24ao3. See K. Targownik, "The Kansas State Reception and Diagnostic Center—Procedurally and Clinically," *Washburn L.J.* 6 (1967): 285; Comment, "The Kansas State Reception and Diagnostic Center: An Empirical Study," *Kan. L. Rev.* 19: (1971): 821. For a discussion of Dr. Menninger's role in the establishment of the center, see K. A. Menninger, *The Crime of Punishment* (New York: Viking, 1968); D. Goleman, "Proud to Be a Bleeding Heart," *Psychology Today*, June 1978, p. 80.

20. Kansas Stat. Ann. 62–2239.

21. Communication from Dr. Jonas Rappeport (Oct. 4, 1999).

22. Communication from Dr. Alan Felthous (Oct. 3, 1999).

23. B. O'Connell, "Court Clinics: The American Experience," *Med. Sci. & Law* 4 (1964): 266. The city court system of Baltimore and the University of Maryland Medical School established a special offenders clinic offering psychotherapy and supervision for nonviolent sexual offenders and impulsively violent individuals. The program designers cited the need for such a facility in the face of the high recidivism rate for these offenders, whose problems have been so-called treated with fines, imprisonment, or extended probation.

24. R. L. Sadoff, S. Polsky, & M. S. Heller, "The Forensic Psychiatry Clinic: Model for a New Approach," *Am. J. Psychiatry* 123 (1968): 1402.

25. H. C. Modlin, "Sick or Bad?" *Washburn L.J.* 6 (1967): 307.

26. B. Hoffman, R. Showlater, & C. Whitebread, "A Forensic Psychiatry Clinic in Evolution," *J. Psychiatry & Law* 2 (1974): 423.

27. See, e.g., United States v. Cantu, 12 F.3d 1506 (9th Cir. 1993) (reduced sentence on account of diminished capacity due to post-traumatic stress disorder).

28. Reported in J. M. Moses, "Many Judges Skirt Sentencing Guidelines," *Wall Street Journal*, May 7, 1993, p. B-12. In the last decade, specialists have begun marketing their services as experts in sentence mitigation. They are lawyers, criminologists, or former corrections officials known as "postconviction specialists." Federal guidelines generally require that a defendant who pleads not guilty before a jury and is subsequently convicted is required to serve time. Defense lawyers, however, have some influence over where their clients serve prison time. Typically, they present the judge with an elaborate profile of the criminal to be sentenced, including details like the person's record of community service, illnesses, or special needs that might bear on where the time will be served. A. Kuczynski, "For the Elite, Easing the Way to Prison," *New York Times*, Dec. 9, 2001, sec. 9, p. 1.

By statute, a sentencing court must order full or partial restitution (there is a presumption that the defendant can make restitution and can make it immediately). Mich. Comp. Laws 780.766(2). The judge can order the defendant to pay the cost of psychological and medical treatment for members of the victim's family that has been incurred as a result of the offense. Mich. Comp. Laws 780.766(4)(d). A restitution order remains effective until it is satisfied. Mich. Comp. Laws 780.766(13).

On drug sentences, Michigan law states that a court may depart from the minimum term of imprisonment "if the court finds on the record that there are substantial and compelling reasons to do so." Mich. Comp. Laws 333.7401(4). Substantial and compelling reasons are ones that are objective and verifiable factors. In order to justify a departure, these factors "should keenly and irresistibly grab our attention and we should recognize them as being of considerable worth in deciding the length of sentence." People v. Fields, 448 Mich. 58 (1995). The following have been identified by the court in *Fields* as a nonexclusive list of such factors: the existence of mitigating circumstances, the defendant's prior record, the defendant's age, the defendant's work history, and postarrest factors (e.g., cooperation with law enforcement officials).

17

Right of the Indigent Accused to Psychiatric Assistance

The U.S. Supreme Court in 1985 declared the right of an indigent defendant to psychiatric assistance. The decision, *Ake v. Oklahoma*,[1] was hailed as a landmark in forensic psychiatry, but even before it, thirty-four states had enacted legislation providing psychiatric assistance to indigent defendants, and courts in eight other states had made similar pronouncements.[2] *Ake*'s contribution was that it made the assistance of a psychiatrist a constitutional right binding on the states as well as on the federal government. *Ake* gave the right to the assistance of a psychiatrist a constitutional underpinning, namely, that of due process.[3]

In this case Glen Burton Ake was accused of capital murder. At his arraignment he displayed such bizarre behavior that the judge, on his own initiative, ordered an examination to decide Ake's competency to stand trial. The examining psychiatrist concluded that he was a paranoid schizophrenic and at times delusional. Based on this report, the court committed him to a state hospital, where he was found incompetent to stand trial. Six weeks later, he was found to have regained his competency and the case was scheduled for trial.

Prior to trial his attorney indicated he would raise the defense of insanity, and requested psychiatric assistance, because Ake was indigent. The request was denied. At trial there was no expert testimony for either side on his sanity at the time of the offense. The Oklahoma Court of Criminal Appeals affirmed his conviction, holding that the state had no obligation to provide psychiatric services to indigents even in capital cases.[4]

The U.S. Supreme Court reversed the conviction. Due process, the Court said, requires that the indigent accused be equipped with the "basic tools" to ensure "a proper functioning of the adversary process."[5] To that end, a psychiatric expert is necessary, the Court said, considering "the pivotal role that psychiatry has come to play in criminal proceedings."[6] The Court elaborated:

> In this role, psychiatrists gather facts, through professional examination, interviews, and elsewhere, that they will share with the judge and jury; they analyze the information gathered and from it draw plausible conclusions about the defendant's mental condition, and about the effects of any disorder on behavior; and they offer opinions about how the defendant's mental condition might have affected his behavior at the time in question. They know the probative questions to ask of the opposing party's psychiatrists and how to interpret their answers.[7]

The Court concluded:

> We therefore hold that when a defendant demonstrates to the trial judge that his sanity at the time of the offense is to be a significant factor at trial, the State must, at a minimum, assure the defendant access to a competent psychiatrist who will conduct an appropriate examination and assist in evaluation, preparation, and presentation of the defense. That is not to say, of course, that the indigent defendant has a constitutional right to choose a psychiatrist of his personal liking or to receive funds to hire his own. Our concern is that the indigent defendant have access to a competent psychiatrist for the purpose we have discussed, and as in the case of the provision of counsel we leave to the state the decision on how to implement this right.[8]

In the years since 1985, state courts have construed *Ake* with widely varying results (and his name has been given various pronunciations). The following questions have arisen: (1) What are the boundaries of the indigent criminal defendant's constitutional right to expert assistance? (2) Is the *Ake* doctrine limited to capital cases? (3) Does Ake apply in the appointment of a psychiatrist in contexts other than the insanity defense? (4) Is the expert to be a "friend of the court" or a partisan expert? (5) What is the necessary showing in order to obtain an expert? (6) Can a failure to provide an expert be deemed "harmless error"? (7) Will an appellate court look at the competency of the expert assistance?

Boundaries of the Right to Expert Assistance

The Supreme Court limited its holding by specifying that the defendant is not entitled to a psychiatrist of his choice, and it left implementation of the right to a psychiatrist to the states, as in the case of the provision of counsel, where the states are free to arrange a public defender program, to appoint counsel, or to permit the indigent to choose counsel at state expense.[9]

In cases on the appointment of counsel, the Court has divided on the issue of whether procedural due process or equal protection provides the appropriate framework for analysis. It is thought that use of equal protection analysis in indigent access cases opens floodgates that would prove unmanageable.[10] "Considerations of cost," as constitutional law professor Laurence Tribe has put it, "may play a role in deciding exactly what level of protection a right should receive."[11] The courts have made it clear that indigent defendants are not entitled to state or federal resources to duplicate the defense services (expert or otherwise) that a wealthier person can obtain.[12]

It is estimated that 85 percent of all U.S. felony defendants cannot afford to hire their own lawyer;[13] and of these cases only a small percentage raise the insanity defense. From 1992 through 1994, a total of 216 charges were made in Milwaukee for first-degree intentional homicide; 10 of those defendants raised the insanity defense; none were successful.[14] In 1979 in Wyoming, out of 21,012 felony defendants only 102, less than .5 percent, pleaded insanity, and just 1 person was actually found NGRI.[15] During the 1990s, however, as a result of the deinstitutionalization of mental hospitals, the insanity plea has been frequently entered in cases concerning the mentally ill who have been apprehended for minor offenses.[16] In these cases NGRI is often plea bargained. Would more appointment of experts result in more NGRIs? Quite possibly, for in this era of deinstitutionalization, jails have replaced mental hospitals; the population of the mentally ill has been shifted in large measure from the hospital to the jails.

How have the states implemented the right to the assistance of a psychiatrist? Public defenders across the country differ on the impact that *Ake* has had on the states—some say no impact, others say some impact.[17] That divergence of opinion is explainable. One explanation is that, as noted, some forty-two states even before *Ake* provided psychiatric assistance; another is that, then as now, implementation depends on funding, and that varies around the country. Public defenders say, "We have to fight hard to persuade a judge to authorize funds for experts."

Approximately twenty-five states have a statewide defender system, and they have a budget, more or less, for obtaining experts. In other states public defenders do not have a budget allocation for experts.[18] Attorneys have a tradition of working pro bono, but that is not true of experts. And for a fee of $150 or $200, provided by the court, experts are not willing to face the public humiliation called cross-examination. Still other experts feel compromised working with overly taxed and poorly funded public defenders.

In death penalty cases, however, there is greater scrutiny on appeal and more resources are put into prosecution and defense. The Arizona Supreme Court ordered the resentencing of a capital murder defendant who had been improperly deprived of expert assistance because the lower court would not authorize more than $1,000.[19] Though the Supreme Court in *Ake* said that the defendant is entitled to only one expert, various states in capital cases have allowed two experts, one to serve as a consultant in preparing the case and another to testify at trial.

Contexts Other Than Capital Offenses

The widely shared belief is that the death penalty is qualitatively different from other forms of punishment, and on the basis of this belief, safeguards have been established in capital cases that have no application to noncapital cases. The majority opinion in *Ake* did not explicitly address this question, but Chief Justice

Burger in a concurring opinion claimed that "nothing in the Court's opinion reaches non-capital cases,"[20] and in a dissenting opinion, Justice Rehnquist urged that any right to psychiatric assistance be limited to capital cases.[21] In view of these comments, some courts have held that *Ake* does not reach noncapital cases or they have indicated uncertainty.[22] The prevailing view, however, is that it applies to noncapital crimes. The controversy is reminiscent of the contention made at one time that the right to the appointment of counsel applies only in capital cases.

Contexts Other Than an Insanity Defense

Does *Ake* apply, for example, to a rape case where insanity is not an issue? The Sixth Circuit held that a psychiatrist need not be provided to a capital murder defendant who raised a diminished capacity defense, it being outside the context of an insanity defense.[23] The Tenth Circuit, however, held that a trial court violated due process by denying state-funded psychiatric assistance to a defendant who had not yet pleaded insanity, but who could have made a threshold showing that his sanity would be significant to his defense.[24] Later, the Tenth Circuit also held that the state had to fund a psychiatric expert to assist in legitimate defense preparation.[25]

Experts Other Than Psychiatrists

The Court in *Ake* did not address the question of whether the right to expert assistance extends to experts other than psychiatrists, but the logic of the decision would apply, and it is applied, to provide other kinds of experts.[26] In its only other post-*Ake* case where the issue has arisen, the Supreme Court declined to consider the defendant's argument that he should have been granted an investigator, a fingerprint expert, and a ballistics expert, on the ground that he had failed to make a sufficient showing of need for them.[27] Senator Carl Levin of Michigan and Senator Orrin Hatch of Utah have sponsored bills to make DNA testing available to all defendants in capital cases. The reality, though, is that DNA evidence rarely assists a criminal defendant. DNA evidence, where it exists, does not sow doubt; it inserts certainty, and it is the kind of proof that helps the prosecution prove its case beyond a reasonable doubt.

The Expert's Proper Role

Is the expert to be a neutral (a friend of the court), a partisan expert, or a defense consultant? (Justice Rehnquist used the term *defense consultant*.[28]) The Ethical Guidelines of the American Academy of Psychiatry and the Law initially expected forensic psychiatrists to be impartial and objective but now call for adherence to "the principles of honesty and striving for objectivity."[29] The late Dr. Bernard L. Diamond in an address at the 1988 annual meeting of AAPL stated:

> [The] idealized image of the expert who is impartial, detached [and] scientifically objective . . . is an illusion. Few are deceived by such a posture, but many experts still claim . . . [that they give] evidence without prejudice, bias, or advocacy, beholden to neither side, retaining their purity and detachment. . . . For thirty years I have persistently tried to deflate such a

notion and expose the hidden biases and phony status behind the idea of the impartial expert. Until recently, I have never had much success, but now that the United States Supreme Court, in *Ake v. Oklahoma*, has endorsed such advocacy and adversarial roles for the psychiatric expert, perhaps my colleagues will also see the light.[30]

For the majority, Justice Marshall in *Ake* wrote that once the necessary showing is made, "the state must, at a minimum, assure the defendant access to a competent psychiatrist who will conduct an appropriate examination and assist in evaluation, preparation, and presentation of the defense."[31] For one to carry out all of these functions, however, may compromise the credibility of the expert as a witness, but only one expert is provided under *Ake*. Justice Marshall stated the tasks of the psychiatrist as follows: "[T]o conduct a professional examination on issues relevant to the defense, to help determine whether the insanity defense is viable, to present testimony, and to assist in preparing the cross-examination of a State's psychiatric witnesses."[32]

The Court reasoned that psychiatry is not "an exact science" and therefore it is important that the jury hear "the psychiatrists for each party" to equip it to make as informed a decision as possible.[33] The court singled out the conflicting testimony of psychiatrists though professionals in all fields present, no less, conflicting testimony (as witness the expert testimony in the highly publicized O. J. Simpson trial as to whether the physical evidence was tainted). The Court stated:

> Psychiatry is not . . . an exact science, and psychiatrists disagree widely and frequently on what constitutes mental illness, on the appropriate diagnosis to be attached to given behavior and symptoms, on cure and treatment, and on likelihood of future dangerousness. Perhaps because there often is no single, accurate psychiatric conclusion on legal insanity in a given case, juries remain the primary factfinders on this issue, and they must resolve differences in opinion within the psychiatric profession on the basis of the evidence offered by each party.[34]

According to *Ake*, evaluation by a neutral court psychiatrist does not satisfy due process. Justice Rehnquist, dissenting in *Ake*, recognized that the majority had virtually held that access to a defense expert is required. A year earlier then–D.C. Circuit Judge Scalia stated:

> [T]he mere availability of cross-examination of . . . [psychiatric] experts is [not] sufficient to provide the necessary balance in the criminal process. That would perhaps be so if psychiatry were as exact a science as physics, so that, assuming the . . . psychiatrist precisely described the data . . . , the error of his analysis could be demonstrated. It is, however, far from that. Ordinarily the only effective rebuttal of psychiatric opinion testimony is contradictory opinion testimony.[35]

Since *Ake*, the Tenth Circuit has ruled that the defendant is entitled to "his own competent psychiatric expert."[36] The Tenth Circuit has said that an expert who shares "a duty to the accused and a duty to the public interest" is burdened by "an inescapable conflict of interest."[37] In another decision, quoting *Ake*, the

Tenth Circuit held that assistance from merely a "neutral" state expert is constitutionally insufficient.[38] The Texas Court of Criminal Appeals has held that neutrality is not enough, and that even if the defense psychiatrist does not see a viable insanity defense, he should still perform partisan tasks.[39]

Under an insanity plea the defendant has the burden of going forward with evidence of insanity in view of the presumption of sanity, and in many jurisdictions the defendant also has the burden of persuasion. Lay witnesses may testify on insanity, but they are confined to their observations on insanity at the time of seeing the defendant, and they may not give a diagnosis or opinion; on the other hand, experts are permitted to give an opinion and to project the time of the offense. The defense as a practical matter needs expert testimony to establish insanity or to assist the defense in the cross-examination of the state's expert witnesses. The presentation and communication skills of an expert in an insanity case are more important than in other cases because of the prejudice against the insanity defense; juries are biased against it.

Turning to the sentencing phase in a capital proceeding, where aggravating and mitigating circumstances are considered, the Supreme Court in *Ake* held that the state must provide the defendant with "access to a psychiatric examination on relevant issues, to the testimony of the psychiatrist, and to assistance in preparation at the sentencing phase."[40] Justice Marshall divided the *Ake* analysis to address separately the guilt and sentencing phases of the trial.[41]

Obtaining the Appointment of a Psychiatrist

The Court limited its holding to cases where "a defendant demonstrates to the judge that his sanity at the time of the offense is to be a significant factor at trial."[42] The Court noted, "A defendant's mental condition is not necessarily at issue in every criminal proceeding . . . and it is unlikely that psychiatric assistance . . . would be of probable value in cases where it is not."[43] It is only when or after an insanity plea has been entered that it is clear that mental condition will be at issue.[44]

According to the decision in *Ake*, the standard for determining when a defendant is entitled to the assistance of a psychiatrist is "when the mental state of the defendant is seriously in question." A general request for expert assistance is not adequate; that is, some degree of specificity and particularity must be shown to enable a court to determine the reasonableness of the necessity for expert assistance.[45] Here is a representation by a public defender:

> We need a psychiatrist for the guilt and penalty phases of this case since there is a duty to explore all possible defenses. In this case we have to explore: the defense of insanity, intoxication, and extreme emotional disturbance; whether the mental state of the client was intentional or wanton. We must have the ability to investigate and present statutory and non-statutory mitigating factors, including: whether our client was emotionally or mentally disturbed; mental difficulties less than insanity; his personality type; his possibilities for rehabilitation; the influence of his family and others on who he is and his actions; why he is involved with drugs and what effect drugs had on him; who the client is and why he acts as he does; the influence of his being adopted; his father's death; [etc.].[46]

The American Bar Association Criminal Justice Mental Health Standards provides that "the court should grant the defense motion as a matter of course unless the court determines that the motion has no foundation."[47] In a post-*Ake* case, the Georgia Supreme Court suggested that the trial court, at the defendant's request, appoint a psychiatrist or other mental health expert "to examine the defendant in order to determine whether his sanity is likely to be a significant factor in his defense."[48] Such a procedure, a variation of catch-22, requires an expert to ascertain whether an expert will be needed.

A matter of controversy is whether the hearing to obtain the appointment of a psychiatrist should be ex parte or whether the prosecutor is entitled to be present at the hearing. The defense is reluctant to disclose strategy to the prosecution, and it also claims the confidentiality of the attorney-client relationship. For these reasons, the hearing has been allowed ex parte.[49]

Failure to Provide an Expert and Harmless Error

In reviewing an allegation of an *Ake* violation, may an appellate court engage in *harmless error* analysis? Ordinarily, constitutional violations demand a rule of automatic reversal. In wanting to grant certiorari in *State of Arizona v. Vickers*,[50] Justice Marshall, who wrote the *Ake* opinion, argued for automatic reversal for *Ake* violations, not a surprising position given his long-held opposition to the death penalty; it would be another weapon in the armamentarium to undercut the death penalty.

In this case the Arizona Supreme Court affirmed the death sentence of a defendant who claimed his constitutional rights had been violated when the trial court refused to provide additional medical tests to assist him in preparing an insanity defense. He sought to establish that he suffered from temporal lobe epilepsy, and he argued that further tests conducted at an out-of-state facility were necessary to prove the disorder. The Arizona Supreme Court said that the defendant had failed to demonstrate that the benefits of additional testing and the risk of an erroneous deprivation of his constitutional rights outweighed the cost of the additional medical procedures. It went on to say that there was "no indication . . . that further testing would have helped defendant prove his insanity defense."[51] To Justice Marshall, however, the Arizona Supreme Court inappropriately engaged in harmless error analysis. Dissenting from the denial of certiorari, Justice Marshall wrote:

> [T]he Arizona high court maintained that further testing was of "questionable value" to petitioner's insanity defense and that the risk of an erroneous judgment was minimal because three state experts testified that Vickers was not insane at the time of the offense. This reasoning wrongly subjects *Ake* claims to harmless-error analysis. In *Ake*, we did not endeavor to determine whether the petitioner's case had been prejudiced by the lack of a psychiatrist.[52]

In *United States v. Smith*,[53] the Second Circuit held that the trial court's failure to appoint a psychiatrist to bolster a defendant's duress claim in a noncapital case is harmless error, but the court was careful to note, however, that in applying the harmless error rule it was not judging the propriety of harmless error analysis for an indigent criminal defendant claiming insanity as a defense. In an article in the *Virginia Law Review*,[54] it is argued that *Ake* violations, by their very nature, so impair the judicial process that justice demands a rule of automatic reversal. Logically, when there has been a showing that psychiatric assistance is reasonably necessary, then obviously it is not harmless error to deny the assistance, but it is difficult to show that the trial court was in error in saying that psychiatric assistance was not reasonably necessary.

Competency of the Expert Assistance

The Supreme Court in *Ake* ruled that the defendant is entitled to competent psychiatric assistance. When *Ake* is applicable, the Georgia Supreme Court noted that it specifically requires a psychiatrist; hence, the Georgia Supreme Court ruled that providing the defense with access to a mental health expert other than a psychiatrist would not satisfy the guideline.[55] The majority, concurring, and dissenting opinions in *Ake* taken together use the words *psychiatric* and *psychiatrist* more than sixty times; no reference to specific experts other than psychiatrists is made. The Georgia Supreme Court said that psychologists or other mental health professionals, while they do not satisfy the guideline at trial, may be used to make the requisite initial showing that *Ake* is applicable.[56]

Appellate courts will review whether failure to appoint a psychiatrist violated the *Ake* guideline, but they will not review the competency of the assistance provided by the psychiatrist. The appointment of an expert is designed to carry out the "effective assistance of counsel," but the courts will not explore the effectiveness of the expert's assistance though it may affect the assistance of counsel. The Seventh Circuit said it was reluctant to open up this type of *Ake* claim to a battle of the experts in a "competence" review. The Seventh Circuit said,

> Every aspect of a criminal case which involves the testimony of experts could conceivably be subject to such a review—a never-ending process. . . . A conclusion to the contrary would require this court and other federal courts to engage in a form of "psychiatric medical malpractice" review as part-and-parcel of its collateral review of state court judgments. The ultimate result would be a never-ending battle of psychiatrists appointed as experts for the sole purpose of discrediting a prior psychiatrist's diagnosis. We do not believe this was the intent of the Court in *Ake* when it held that indigent defendants who raise a defense of insanity are entitled to psychiatric assistance in the preparation of their defense.[57]

And the Seventh Circuit noted, "As was pointed out by the [Supreme] Court in *Ake,* the fact that due process requires that a competent psychiatrist be appointed does not mean that the indigent defendant has a constitutional right to select a psychiatrist of his personal liking or one who will testify in his favor."[58] The state is not required, as the Fourth Circuit said, to finance a defendant's "shopping excursion for a favorable expert."[59] And the Fifth Circuit said, *Ake* does not guarantee access to a psychiatrist "who will reach only biased or favorable conclusions."[60]

The Ninth Circuit said, "Allowing such battles of psychiatric opinions during successive collateral challenges to a death sentence would place federal courts in a psycho-legal quagmire resulting in the total abuse of the habeas process."[61] In that case, the prosecutor argued that permitting a challenge to the psychiatric assistance would open up a Pandora's box. "The courts will sink in a morass of post-trial challenges to the effectiveness of the psychiatric assistance provided," it said. "Psychiatrists are notoriously apt to differ from each other. A defendant will always be able to get a second psychiatrist to say his first psychiatrist performed incompetently."[62]

While the courts will not explore the effectiveness of the assistance provided by a psychiatrist, they will look at ineffective assistance of counsel. It is actually the most common contention urged on appeal.[63] In *Hill v. Lockhart*,[64] the claim of ineffective assistance of counsel was that the defense counsel failed to investigate and present the defendant's extensive history of mental illness, which could have been used at trial to support his insanity defense during the guilt phase and his offer of mitigating circumstances during the penalty phase. At the time of his arrest, he had been hospitalized for psychiatric evaluation at least four times, and he had been placed on a psychiatric ward while in prison at least four times. This evidence was not presented. Quoting the American Bar Association's Project on Standards for Criminal Justice, the Eighth Circuit said, "It is the duty of the lawyer to . . . explore all avenues leading to facts relevant to . . . degree of guilt."[65]

Another allegation often made is a claim of newly discovered evidence. As a general principle, newly discovered evidence that would have provided a defense to the charged crimes and special circumstances, as well as essential mitigatory evidence at the penalty hearing, warrants federal habeas corpus relief if it would "probably produce an acquittal." However, it is a matter of controversy whether the evidence is new evidence or would probably produce an acquittal, or whether it would probably result in a penalty other than death. Newly discovered evidence that the defendant had brain damage or a delusional disorder is highly suspect.[66] The appeal lawyer for Sylvester Adams, who was executed in South Carolina, argued unsuccessfully that the jury was not told that Adams was mildly retarded or that he had a mental illness that could cause him to burst into a rage.[67]

Conclusion

The publicity about conflicting psychiatric testimony has led to two results: (1) the need for a partisan expert, and (2) a bar on an appeal challenging the competency of the psychiatric assistance. Because psychiatry is not "an exact science," said the Supreme Court in *Ake*, juries remain the "primary factfinders," and, the Court suggested, it is important that the jury hear "the psychiatrists for each party" to equip it to make as informed a decision as possible.[68]

To many, Justice Marshall's observations in *Ake* on the importance of the role of the psychiatrist sounds fanciful. Studies show that jurors perceive expert psychiatric testimony as a useful, but not determinate, factor when reaching their verdict.[69]

Notes

1. 470 U.S. 68 (1985).
2. 470 U.S. at 78. Other avenues have also been open to an indigent defendant. Congress had enacted a "statutory remedy for discovering, treating and diagnosing of persons found

to be mentally ill and unable to stand trial"; that remedy has been used by both the defense and the prosecution as a means to determine the mental condition of the defendant at the time of the offense. 18 U.S.C., secs. 4244–4248 (1982). Rule 28 of the Federal Rules of Criminal Procedure allowed the court to appoint an expert, either agreed upon by the parties or one of its own selection, who would be required to advise both parties of his findings and could be called by either party to testify. Rule 706 of the Federal Rules of Evidence, adopted in 1975, authorizes the court appointment of expert witnesses, and with the exception of nine states, the various states adopted a version of the rule. The Advisory Committee Note accompanying the rule seems to mandate that judges appoint experts more liberally than they did at common law, but that has not happened. The advocates of party selection of expert witnesses triumphed. E. J. Imwinkelried, "Court Appointment of Expert Witnesses in the United States: A Failed Experiment," *Medicine & Law* 8 (1989): 601.

3. K. T. Smith, "The Indigent Defendant's Right to Psychiatric Assistance," *No. Car. Central L.J.* 17 (1986): 208; J. M. West, "Expert Services and the Indigent Criminal Defendant: The Constitutional Mandate of *Ake v. Oklahoma*," *Mich. L. Rev.* 84 (1986): 1326.

4. Ake v. State, 663 P.2d 1, 6 (Okla. Crim. App. 1983).

5. 470 U.S. at 77.

6. 470 U.S. at 79.

7. 470 U.S. at 80.

8. 470 U.S. at 83. At his retrial in 1996, Ake was convicted and was sentenced to two terms of life imprisonment plus two terms of two hundred years. His convictions were affirmed. Ake v. State, 778 P.2d 460 (Okla. 1989).

9. 470 U.S. at 83.

10. See Griffin v. Illinois, 351 U.S. 12, 34–36 (1963) (Harlan, J., dissenting).

11. *American Constitutional Law* (Westbury, N.Y.: Foundation Press, 2d ed. 1988), p. 715.

12. Ross v. Moffitt, 417 U.S. 600 at 612 (1974). In Williams v. Collins, 16 F.3d 626 (5th Cir. 1994), the court dismissively noted it is "well settled" that a state is not required "to pay for the same assistance that a wealthier defendant might buy." 16 F.3d at 637.

13. "Harper's Index," *Harper's*, Sept. 1995, p. 9.

14. G. B. Palermo et al., "Trial by Jury: A Pilot Study of Juror Perception of Mental Health Professional Testimony in NGRI Pleas for First Degree Intentional Homicide," *Med. & Law* 15 (1996): 17; G. Melton, J. Petrila, N. Poythress, & C. Slobogin, *Psychological Evaluation for the Courts* (New York: Guilford Press, 1978).

15. R. Slovenko, *Psychiatry and Criminal Culpability* (New York: Wiley, 1995).

16. J. Conklin, *Criminology* (New York: Macmillan, 4th ed. 1992); G. B. Palermo & R. Knudten, "The Insanity Plea in the Case of a Serial Killer," *Int'l J. Offender Therapy & Comparative Criminology* 38 (1994): 3; L. E. McCutcheon, "Not Guilty by Reason of Insanity: Getting It Right or Perpetuating the Myths?" *Psychological Reports* 73 (1994): 764.

17. Personal communications.

18. See M. P. Goodman, "The Right to a Partisan Psychiatric Expert: Might Indigency Preclude Insanity?" *N.Y.U. L. Rev.* 61 (1986): 703; N. Hollander & L. M. Baldwin, "Expert Testimony in Criminal Trials: Creative Uses, Creative Attacks," *Champion*, Dec. 1991, p. 7; E. C. Monahan, "Obtaining Funds for Experts in Indigent Cases," *Champion*, Aug. 1989, p. 10.

19. State of Arizona v. Eastlack, 883 P.2d 999 (Ariz. 1994).

20. 470 U.S. at 87.

21. Ibid.

22. Isam v. State, 488 So.2d 12 (Ala. Crim. App. 1986) ("*Ake* does not reach noncapital cases"); expressing uncertainty: Williams v. Newsome, 254 Ga. 714, 334 S.E.2d 171 (1985); Satterwhite v. State, 697 S.W.2d 503 (Tex. Crim. App. 1985). See J. W. West, "Expert Services and the Indigent Criminal Defendant: The Constitutional Mandate of *Ake v. Oklahoma*," *Mich. L. Rev.* 84 (1986): 1326.

23. Kordenbrock v. Scroggy, 919 F.2d 1091 (6th Cir. 1990). The Washington Court of Appeals held that *Ake* applies to a claim of diminished capacity. State v. Paulsen, 726 P.2d 1036 (Wash. App. 1986).

24. Liles v. Saffle, 945 F.2d 333 (10th Cir. 1991), *cert. denied,* Saffle v. Liles, 502 U.S. 1066 (1992).

25. Dunn v. Roberts, 963 F.2d 308 (10th Cir. 1992).

26. See Washington v. State, 800 P.2d 252 (Okla. Crim. App. 1990); F. W. Bennett, "Toward Eliminating Bargain Basement Justice: Providing Indigent Defendants with Expert Services and an Adequate Defense," *Law & Contemp. Prob.* 58 (1995): 95.

27. Caldwell v. Mississippi, 105 S. Ct. 2633 (1985).

28. 470 U.S. at 87.

29. See S. Rachlin, "From Impartial Expert to Adversary in the Wake of Ake," *Bull. Am. Acad. Psychiatry & Law* 16 (1988): 25; C. R. Showalter & W. L. Fitch, "Objectivity and Advocacy in Forensic Psychiatry after *Ake v. Oklahoma*," *J. Psychiatry & Law* 15 (1987): 177.

30. "The Image and Role of the Forensic Psychiatrist," presented in San Francisco on Oct. 10, 1988; published as "The Forensic Psychiatrist: Consultant versus Activist in Legal Doctrine," *Bull. Am. Acad. Psychiatry & Law* 20 (1992): 119. See also B. Diamond & D. Louisell, "The Psychiatrist as an Expert Witness: Some Ruminations and Speculations," *Mich. L. Rev.* 63 (1965): 1335; B. L. Diamond, "The Fallacy of the Impartial Expert," *Archives of Criminal Psychodynamics* 3 (1959): 221; "The Psychiatrist as Advocate," *J. Psychiatry & Law* 1 (1973): 5. Dr. Diamond's papers are collected in J. M. Quen (ed.), *The Psychiatrist in the Courtroom: Selected Papers of Bernard L. Diamond, M.D.* (Hillsdale, N.J.: Analytic Press, 1994).

31. 470 U.S. at 83. In Martin v. Wainwright, 770 F.2d 918 (11th Cir. 1985), the court held that access to a competent psychiatrist does not necessarily mean a psychiatrist who will reach conclusions favorable to the defendant. See M. P. Goodman, "The Right to a Partisan Psychiatric Expert: Might Indigency Preclude Insanity?" *N.Y.U.L. Rev.* 61 (1986): 703.

32. 470 U.S. at 82. See the discussion in P. S. Appelbaum, "In the Wake of *Ake:* The Ethics of Expert Testimony in an Advocate's World," *Bull. Am. Acad. Psychiatry & Law* 15 (1987): 15.

33. 470 U.S. at 81.

34. Ibid.

35. United States v. Byers, 740 F.2d 1104 (D.C. Cir. 1984).

36. Smith v. McCormick, 914 F.2d 1153, 1159 (9th Cir. 1990).

37. Marshall v. United States, 423 F.2d 1315, 1319 (10th Cir. 1970).

38. United States v. Crews, 781 F.2d 826, 834 (10th Cir. 1986).

39. DeFreece v. State, 848 S.W.2d 150 (Tex. Cr. App. 1993), *cert. denied,* 114 S. Ct. 284 (1993).

40. 470 U.S. at 83–84. In Tuggle v. Thompson, 854 F.Supp. 229 (W.D. Va. 1994), a federal court overturned a state's conviction of a capital murder defendant who had been denied the assistance of an independent psychiatric expert during sentencing. The prosecution argued that the sentence should stand based on the jury's finding of "vileness," which independently supported the sentence.

41. 470 U.S. at 83.

42. Ibid.

43. 470 U.S. at 82.

44. If "a reasonable attorney would pursue an insanity defense," then funds for a psychiatrist must be forthcoming. Guither v. United States, 391 A.2d 1364 (D.C. App. 1978). See also State v. Gambrell, 347 S.E.2d 390 (N.C. 1986).

45. There is controversy as to what constitutes a clear showing that mental condition will be a significant factor at trial. In Cartwright v. Maynard, 802 F.2d 1203 (10th Cir. 1986), the court held that the defendant did not establish the need of a psychiatric expert to establish his defense of unconsciousness. In Volson v. Blackburn, 794 F.2d 173 (5th Cir. 1986), the court held that the defendant's allegation that he did not know the difference between right and wrong was insufficient to demonstrate that sanity would be a significant factor at trial. See also State v. Hamilton, 448 So.2d 1007 (Fla. 1984); Commonwealth v. Lockley, 408 N.E.2d 834 (Mass. 1980).

46. E. C. Monahan, supra note 18.

47. 7–3.3(a) (1984).

48. Lindsey v. State, 254 Ga. 444, 330 S.E.2d 563 (1985).

49. Washington v. State, 800 P.2d 252 (Okla. Crim. App. 1990) (interpreting *Ake* as mandating that the evidentiary hearing to determine defendant's need for expert services be held ex parte); D. H. Lee, "In the Wake of *Ake v. Oklahoma:* An Indigent Criminal Defendant's Lack of Ex Parte Access to Expert Services," *N.Y.U. L. Rev.* 67 (1992): 154. For a discussion of

an incorrect determination of indigency, see R. J. Wilson, "Disclose or Not: The Client Who Falsely Obtains Appointed Counsel," in R. J. Uphoff (ed.), *Ethical Problems Facing the Criminal Defense Lawyer* (Chicago: American Bar Assn., 1995), ch. 12.

50. 768 P.2d 1177 (Ariz. 1989), *cert. denied,* 497 U.S. 1033 (1990).

51. 768 P.2d at 1182.

52. State v. Vickers, 497 U.S. 1033, 1037 (1990).

53. 987 F.2d 888 (2d Cir.), *cert. denied,* 114 S. Ct. 209 (1993).

54. M. J. Lorenger, "*Ake v. Oklahoma* and Harmless Error: The Case for a Per Se Rule of Reversal," *Va. L. Rev.* 81 (1995): 521; see Tuggle v. Thompson, 854 F.2d 1229 (W.D. Va. 1994).

55. Lindsey v. State, 254 Ga. 444, 330 S.E.2d 563 (1985).

56. Lindsey v. State, 330 S.E.2d at 566–67.

57. Silagy v. Peters, 905 F.2d 986, 1013 (7th Cir. 1990).

58. 905 F.2d 986 at 1013.

59. Williams v. Martin, 618 F.2d 1021 (4th Cir. 1980).

60. Granviel v. Lynaugh, 881 F.2d 185, 192 (5th Cir. 1989).

61. Harris v. Vasquez, 949 F.2d 1497, 1518 (9th Cir. 1990).

62. 949 F.2d at 1531.

63. See J. Podgers, "The Blame Game: Criminal Defendants Try to Reverse Convictions by Claiming Ineffective Counsel," *ABAJ*, Sept. 1995, p. 44. It is sometimes alleged that defense counsel was sleeping at trial and the appellate court says, "Sleeping counsel is equivalent to no counsel at all" (but it provides a basis for appeal, and it may be the only basis for appeal). See B. Herbert, "The Death Factory," *New York Times*, Oct. 2, 2000, p. 31; R. Slovenko, "Sleeping-Lawyer Trick" (ltr.), *New York Times*, Nov. 8, 2000, p. 22.

64. 28 F.2d 832 (8th Cir. 1994).

65. 28 F.2d at 842.

66. United States v. McCarthy, 54 F.3d 51 (2d Cir. 1995) (delusional disorder); Harris v. Vasquez, 949 F.2d 1497, 1523 (9th Cir. 1990) (brain damage). In Harvey v. Horan, 2002 WL 86874 (4th Cir.), the court of appeals noted that if persons convicted of crimes are to be entitled to avail themselves of advances in technology (such as DNA evidence) to challenge a conviction, such entitlement should be accomplished by state or federal legislative action, or by state courts acting under their own constitutions, rather than by a federal court as a matter of constitutional right.

67. "South Carolina Executes Man for Killing Neighbor in Robbery" (Associated Press news release), *New York Times*, Aug. 19, 1995, p. 8.

68. 470 U.S. at 81.

69. G. B. Palermo et al., supra note 14.

PART IV
Sexual
Deviation

18

Sex
Offender
Legislation

Over the years society has been particularly concerned about sex offenses, due to the frequency of this type of offending and the anxiety it generates. Prior to the enactment of the current sexual predator laws more than one-half the states during the period from 1930 through 1970 enacted umbrella-type legislation to deal with sex offenders. The legislation—known as the *sexual psychopath statute*—operated in a legal system that already provided criminal sanctions for the same conduct independent of this statute. In addition, civil commitment procedures in all states are applicable to mentally ill persons who might constitute a danger to themselves or others or who are in need of care or treatment.

The Early Sexual Psychopath Legislation

The early sexual psychopath legislation usually provided for the indeterminate commitment of the so-called sexual psychopath. There was, however, no uniformity in the definition of *sexual psychopath* or circumstances that called for initiation of the special proceedings. Generally, however, the term *sexual psychopath* was defined as "one lacking the power to control his sexual impulses or having criminal propensities toward the commission of sex offenses."[1] Such a definition involved a prediction or prognosis as well as a diagnosis or description of the current situation.

The statutes reflected the therapeutic optimism of the time. The feeling was that psychiatry could identify and treat potentially dangerous sex offenders. The American Bar Association Criminal Justice Mental Health Standards noted the assumptions underlying this special dispositional legislation:

> (1) There is a specific mental disability called sexual psychopathy; (2) persons suffering from such a disability are more likely to commit serious crimes, especially dangerous sex offences, than other criminals; (3) such persons are easily identified by mental health professionals; (4) the dangerousness of these offenders can be predicted by mental health professionals; (5) treatment is available for the condition; and (6) large numbers of persons afflicted with the designated disabilities can be cured.

The statutes divided into preconviction and postconviction types. The postconviction type apply only to those convicted of sexual crimes; the preconviction type included persons charged with the commission of a specific sexual offense and applied also to those accused of being sexual psychopaths. Here the law took the position of dealing with status or being rather than actual doing. It is allegedly an attempt to bridge a legal lag by legislative enactment. But was it a legal advance? How helpful was it? The late Dr. Philip Roche in his Isaac Ray Award lecture said, "The pursuit of demons disguised as sexual psychopaths affords a glimpse of a 16th-century approach to mental illness."[2]

A law based on being rather than doing tends to defer to psychiatry or psychology, but what are the standards to be used as a measuring device? One might assume that sexual psychopaths or deviates have much in common and form a distinct class. Such homogeneity, however, assuredly does not exist. The terms *sexual psychopath* or *deviate* do not adequately define any legal entity any more than does the term *offender*, which covers the waterfront. Sexual psychopathy is not a distinct psychiatric category of neurosis or psychosis. Among the deviates, representing the gamut of mental disorders, are neurotics, schizophrenics, schizoid personalities, alcoholics, persons with chronic brain damage, or mentally retarded individuals. It is like the grouping of the jaundices, which brings together strange bedfellows. All that those in the grouping share is a single trait, one that psychiatrists must consider as a symptom.

The American Psychiatric Association's *Diagnostic and Statistical Manual of Mental Disorders* has a category called *paraphilias,* under the section entitled "Sexual Dysfunction": "exhibitionism, fetishism, frotteurism, pedophilia, sexual masochism, sexual sadism, transvestic fetishism, voyeurism, and not otherwise specified."[3] The essential features of a paraphilia are sexual interests directed primarily toward objects other than people of the opposite sex, sexual acts not usually associated with coitus, or coitus performed under bizarre circumstances, as in necrophilia, pedophilia, sexual sadism, and fetishism. Even though many find their practices distasteful, they remain unable to substitute normal sexual behavior for them.

The label *sexual psychopath* is frequently called into question. There is disagreement as to whether it is a form of mental illness, a form of evil, or a form of fiction.[4] The Group for the Advancement of Psychiatry stated that the term *sexual psychopath* is not a psychiatric diagnosis and has no precise clinical meaning.[5] From a psychiatric point of view the term is meaningful only descriptively, not psychodynamically. Consequently, the enforcement of the law resulted in a roundup of the vagrant and nuisance type of offender and failed to reach the dangerous, aggressive offender. The late Judge Ploscowe commented, "The sex-psychopath laws fail miserably in this vital task."[6]

The sexual psychopath legislation was not implemented with staff and facilities for treatment, one of the major purposes of the legislation. The justification for deprivation of liberty under the legislation was treatment, but since treatment was lacking, the process failed to measure up to the standard set out in 1966 by the Court of Appeals for the District of Columbia in *Rouse v. Cameron,* which stated: "Had appellant been found criminally responsible he could have been confined four years and the end is not in sight. Since this difference rests solely on the need for treatment, a failure to supply treatment may raise a question of due process of law."[7]

On the day *Rouse* was decided, the same court ruled in *Millard v. Cameron:* "In *Rouse v. Cameron* . . . [we] held that the petitioner was entitled to relief upon showing that he was not receiving reasonably suitable and adequate treatment. Lack of such treatment, we said, could not be justified by lack of staff facilities. We think the same principles apply to a person involuntarily committed to a public hospital as a sexual psychopath."[8] A New York court refused to commit a sex offender to a "one day to life" sentence unless it could be "reasonably certain that treatment will be given."[9] The court noted that confinement was based on the expectation of improvement resulting from treatment, which would be impossible because the psychiatric clinic at the institution had been closed down.

Actually the term *treatment* is a holdover from medical training and social usage, and is here misleading because of its medical connotations. The sex offender and some other mentally ill persons are not sick or diseased (unless by *disease* we mean dis-ease, lack of ease or discomfort).[10] Abjuring the language of clinical medicine as prejudicial and confusing, Freud too saw health and disease not as clinical entities but as forms of self-expression. The ego, Freud said, will "deform itself" to avoid disruptive anxiety.[11]

Special institutions such as Atascadero State Hospital in California was established to implement the state's sexual psychopath statute. California, Michigan, and Wisconsin made the most use of their statutes. What was the news about them? To say the least, they did not work out. Indeed, a consensus described these institutions as a hoax.

A special institution is theoretically justified only when there is a homogeneity within the group and when a particular institution can offer a special service for that group. Neither criterion was met. Supposedly, the special proceeding was adopted to detain the dangerous, aggressive offender, but the person usually confined was the mentally defective individual or the impoverished farm boy bewildered by city life. The proceeding was designed to offer treatment, but whatever that was supposed to constitute, it assuredly was not available. One court said, "If [hospitals] are to be no more than pens into which we are to sweep that which is offensive to 'normal society,' let us be honest and denominate them as such."[12]

The special proceeding served only to stigmatize. The inmate labeled a sexual psychopath lived up to the role and in the institution he himself often placed a sign around his neck, such as, "I am a masturbator," "I am a peeping-tom." His self-esteem, low before, became even more abysmal. His troubles with the opposite sex multiplied. Imagine, if you will, his problem when later seeking female companionship. Surely a woman would not want to associate with a sexual psychopath, and surely no employer would likely hire one.

Thus sexual psychopath legislation did little more than detain some persons who were regarded as freaks, stigmatize them, and render them forever social outcasts. Nevertheless, it was suggested that the concept of sex crime in sexual psychopath legislation be broadened to include any criminal act in which some type of sexual satisfaction is the motivating force. Some persons with sexual conflicts may obtain sexual stimulation by committing arson, by stealing women's undergarments, or by plunging a knife into a woman's back. A boy with a fetish for motorcycles may steal them to get "sexual" satisfaction out of driving away at high speed. Offenses such as arson, shoplifting (kleptomania), burglary, and murder often have sexually motivating aspects. Breaking and entering by the adolescent is often equated with breaking and entering of the forbidden area of the female (rape). Dr. Karl Menninger observed: "Sexual impulses are frequently involved in compulsive behavior. . . . Sexual elements are often transparent in fire-setting, kleptomania, addictive gambling, reckless car driving, and various kinds of physical violence. Sometimes, rather than being merely transparently present, the sexual factor is barely conspicuous."[13]

In such cases, however, because the victim has not been sexually assaulted and there has been no use of the sex organs, it could only be inferred that the act might have some sexual significance. The courts that operated on the basis of such inference were soon mired in problems, because practically any activity, at some level, could be labeled sexual in nature. As a rule, under the criminal law generally, motivation (as distinguished from intent) is not an element of a crime. Hate crime legislation that has been proposed would also be mired in ascertaining motivation.

On the other hand, behavior that involves the sexual organs, and which may involve some sexual gratification or overt expression of sexual activity, is not necessarily motivated initially by a desire for sexual satisfaction. The late Dr. Bernard Glueck cited an example of the older man who feels grossly inadequate in his adjustment with other adults, but who does feel relatively comfortable and happy when he is with children. Glueck stated:

> Very often this individual may find himself in a situation that initially has no sexual motivation but is entirely motivated by a desire for some sort of interpersonal satisfaction. However, in the course of his contact with children, or when the control and judgment faculties are weakened by alcohol, sexual excitement and arousal may develop as an additional pattern, frequently viewed by the individual as an unwanted complication, with the result that some type of prohibited sexual act occurs.[14]

There may be nonsexual motivations in sexual offenses as well as sexual motivations in nonsexual offenses. Hatred and inadequacy more than sexual motivation predominates in most acts of rape. Generally speaking, a rapist might be said to be acting out hostile or destructive rather than sexual impulses. To twist Lord Acton's phrase: powerlessness corrupts, and absolute powerlessness corrupts absolutely. One who is impotent to cope with a situation tends to choose the most primitive way—violence. Even the term *rape* has the nonsexual meaning of pillaging and destroying. Indeed, it is not uncommon for librarians to place *The Rape of Nanking* in the section of the library on sex offenses.

Sexual psychopath legislation was open to the oft-heard criticism that the law looks only at a symptom. Sexual difficulties are, after all, symptoms of personality and relating problems. Sex, being a human-relating experience (potentially the closest one of all), nearly always reflects personality problems. These problems are also reflected in other behavior. The symptom of deviant sexual behavior prompted sexual psychopath legislation; but interpreting all behavior as sexual in origin in order to overcome the shortcomings and limitations of other statutes was not the way to deal with people who have severe problems relating to others. The sorry experience in those states that enacted sexual psychopath legislation and established special institutions furnishes ample evidence of the shortcomings of this approach. Michigan's Goodrich Act of 1939, the first sexual psychopath legislation in the country, was enacted to allay public hysteria resulting from the brutal sex crimes committed by an offender by the name of Goodrich.[15] A futile endeavor, it was repealed in 1968.[16] In 1960, twenty-six states and the District of Columbia had some form of sexual psychopath legislation;[17] in 1992, it was half that number.[18] They were called a "failed experiment." Brakel, Parry, and Weiner explained in their book *The Mentally Disabled and the Law:*

> Growing awareness that there is no specific group of individuals who can be labeled sexual psychopaths by acceptable medical standards and that there are no proven treatments for such offenders has led such professional groups as the Group for the Advancement of Psychiatry, the President's Commission on Mental Health, and, most recently, the American Bar Association Committee on Criminal Justice Mental Health Standards to urge that these laws be repealed.[19]

When repealing its sex offender statute in 1981 the California legislature declared: "In repealing the mentally disordered sex offender commitment statute, the Legislature recognizes and declares that the commission of sex offenses is not itself the product of mental disease."[20]

New Sexually Violent Predator Legislation

With the demise of indeterminate sentencing generally, the 1990s witnessed a renewed interest in sex offender commitment. Starting with Washington in 1990, at least seventeen other states have enacted laws for the commitment of "sexually violent predators," to wit: persons (1) convicted of a sexually violent offense, (2) about to be released from confinement, and (3) found to be suffering from "a mental abnormality or personality disorder which makes the person likely to engage in predatory acts of sexual violence."[21] The laws were sparked by cases like Earl Shriner's rape and sexual mutilation of a six-year-old boy in Washington, and the killings of Megan Kanka in New Jersey and Polly Klaas in California.[22]

The new laws are different from the early sexual psychopath statutes and from ordinary civil commitment laws in several important respects. First, they do not require a medically recognized serious mental disorder. Second, they do not require any allegation or proof of recent criminal wrongdoing. Third, they require sex offenders to serve their full prison term prior to commitment. Fourth, no bona fide treatment program need be in place. The new legislation has no great hopes for treatment, as earlier legislation did, and much more emphasizes incapacitation.[23]

The new legislation, known as the Sexually Violent Predator law, establishes civil commitment procedures for individuals with "mental abnormality" or "personality disorder" who were likely to engage in "predatory acts of sexual violence."[24] In using the concept of *mental abnormality*, the legislation invokes terminology that can cover a variety of disorders. In challenging Washington's SVP statute, the state's psychiatric association said in an amicus brief, "Sexual predation in and of itself does not define a mental illness. It defines criminal conduct." Be that as it may, the Washington Supreme Court, in 1993, upheld its SVP statute against constitutional challenge, saying:

> The fact that pathologically driven rape, for example, is not yet listed in the [DSM] does not invalidate such a diagnosis. The DSM is, after all, an evolving and imperfect document, nor is it sacrosanct. Furthermore, it is in some areas a political document whose diagnoses are based, in some cases, on what American Psychiatric Association leaders consider to be practical realities. What is critical for our purposes is that psychiatric and psychological clinicians who testify in good faith as to mental abnormality are able to identify sexual pathologies that are as real and meaningful as other pathologies already listed in the DSM.[25]

The court turned the disclaimer in the *DSM*—that it is intended for clinical purposes, not for purposes of the law—on its head. The court said, "Over the years, the law has developed many specialized terms to describe mental health concepts. . . . The DSM explicitly recognizes . . . that the scientific categorization of a mental disorder may not be 'wholly relevant to legal judgments.'"[26]

In 1994 the Minnesota Supreme Court upheld its statute but limited its scope to those who exhibit (1) an habitual course of misconduct in sexual matters, (2) "an utter lack of power to control sexual impulses," in addition to (3) proof that the person will attack or otherwise injure others.[27]

In 1996 the Kansas Supreme Court ruled its statute, almost identical to the Washington statute, as unconstitutional.[28] The Kansas Supreme Court held that the statute violated substantive due process because the definition of *mental abnormality* did not satisfy what is perceived to be the definition of *mental illness* required in the context of involuntary civil commitment. The court did not address double jeopardy or ex post facto issues. The court noted that the laws targeted individuals who could not be committed under the general civil commitment law.

In 1997 in a 5–4 decision in *Kansas v. Hendricks,*[29] the U.S. Supreme Court upheld the Kansas statute. The majority opinion, written by Justice Clarence Thomas, held that the act does not violate the double jeopardy or ex post facto prohibitions. Justice Thomas acknowledged that in addition to dangerousness, "some additional factor" that was causally linked to the dangerous behavior is constitutionally required. However, he wrote, substantive due process does not require that this condition be a mental disorder recognized by treatment professionals: "Not only do psychiatrists disagree widely and frequently on what constitutes mental illness . . . but the Court itself has used a variety of expressions to describe the mental condition of those properly subject to civil commitment." He also said, "[W]e have traditionally left to legislators the task of defining terms of a medical nature that have legal significance." Because the Kansas statute requires proof that individuals suffer from a volitional impairment rendering them dangerous beyond their control, he concluded, the statute does not allow commitment of individuals based solely on dangerousness.[30]

The majority also concluded that the law was civil in nature rather than punitive in purpose or effect, and thus it did not violate either double jeopardy or ex post facto prohibitions. Except for Justice Ginsburg, the dissenters agreed with the majority that states have broad authority to define legal mental illness and that the statute's use of "mental abnormality" satisfies substantive due process. However, the dissenters concluded that the statute was essentially punitive in nature rather than civil, thus violating both double jeopardy and ex post facto prohibitions. Under the laws offenders are committed after they have served virtually their entire criminal sentence. Under the earlier sexual psychopath legislation the prosecutor had to choose between conviction in the criminal system or commitment in the civil system.

The Court suggested in dicta that treatability is not a constitutionally required element for commitment, although treatment may be required if the state considers the individual amenable to treatment. The Court observed that the state may be obliged to provide treatment that is available for disorders that are treatable. Moreover, the state can defer such treatment until after the offender had served his full prison term. Justice Thomas wrote, "[U]nder the appropriate circumstances and when accompanied by proper procedure, incapacitation may be a legitimate end of the civil law. . . . We have never held that the Constitution prevents a State from civilly detaining those for whom no treatment is available, but who nevertheless pose a danger to others."[31] In a concurring opinion, Justice Anthony Kennedy, who was the swing vote, said, "If the object or purpose of the . . . law had been to provide treatment but the treatment provisions were adopted as a sham or mere pretext, [this would amount to] an indication of the forbidden purpose to punish."

In 1999, acting on a petition for a writ of habeas corpus from Andre Brigham Young, a convicted rapist who has been held under an SVP law for nine years following his release from prison, the U.S. Court of Appeals for the Ninth Circuit held that he was entitled to a chance to prove his contentions that he was not receiving treatment and that conditions at the state's Special Commitment Center were equivalent to prison or worse. The Ninth Circuit found that if the actual conditions of the offender's confinement appeared to be punitive rather than therapeutic, the extra time could raise double jeopardy and new-penalty problems despite the "civil" designation.[32] In an 8–1 decision the Supreme Court overturned the Ninth Circuit's ruling, all but ruling out the prospect that additional confinement could ever be challenged in federal court as double jeopardy.[33] In *Hendricks*, the Court had said that the additional confinement was neither double jeopardy nor an imposition of a new penalty for an old offense.

In *Young*, the majority opinion left important questions unanswered, as Justice O'Connor acknowledged in observing, "We have not squarely addressed the relevance of conditions of confinement to a first instance determination" of whether a statute could properly be called civil in nature. Justices Scalia and Souter, while joining Justice O'Connor's opinion, wrote separately to say that in their view, whether a statute was civil or criminal depended completely on the intent of the legislature. If a civil statute was administered in an unduly punitive way, these two justices said, the remedy was not to invoke the double jeopardy clause but to sue the administrators in state court. Justice Stevens, the sole dissenter, urged, "If conditions of confinement are such that a detainee has been punished twice in violation of the double jeopardy clause, it is irrelevant that the scheme has been previously labeled as civil without full knowledge of the effects of the statute."

Some years ago, in 1988, the American Psychiatric Association's Council of Psychiatry and Law said that the continued hospitalization of non–mentally ill personality-disordered persons who have recovered from their mental illness in a maximum security hospital following acquittal of crime by reason of insanity, is justified on the grounds that "[t]hose who suffer from personality disorders may also benefit from the special management available only in a psychiatric institution where sensitive, comprehensive, unique and imaginative treatment programs can often be developed to assist them in overcoming their destructive behavior."[34]

Of the eighteen sexual predator laws that have been enacted, the treatment setting in seven states is a hospital, while in the other states it is a segregated unit within a correctional facility, or a correctional facility devoted exclusively to sexual predators. In all eighteen states, the agencies responsible for providing treatment are the state health services, mental health, or social services departments. The ambiguous issue, however, is whether the states must invest sufficient resources in treatment to reach a minimum standard of intervention that could be expected to effect change and whether the costs will come out of the diminishing mental health budget.

In amici briefs, the American Psychiatric Association as well as its district branches, taking a different position than it did in 1988, and the American Civil Liberties Union argued against these laws because sex offenders do not necessarily have a mental illness, no curative treatment is yet available for their behavior, and, consequently, lifetime preventive detention is likely. They also argued that mental health professionals cannot predict future behavior accurately, so some individuals would be committed who would not commit other crimes and others would be set free who will.[35] First behavior, of all evidence, is the best predictor of future behavior. It is argued that sex offenders would be better dealt with by the criminal justice system, with stiffer criminal sentences for repeat sex offenders.[36]

It may be said that criminal activity ought to be examined with a view to appropriate disposition, but sexual offender legislation is a woefully awkward and misleading way to achieve it. Such legislation is, moreover, an expensive way of achieving social control over a relatively small number of offenders. Sooner or later, it will be realized that the costs in implementing the SVP laws are so exorbitant that they will be abandoned or repealed.

The sorry experience under the earlier sexual psychopath legislation should be a lesson that this approach ought not to be followed. Better approaches are indeterminate sentencing of all offenders or heavier sentences for repeat violent sex offenders. A number of states have recently enacted lifetime sentences for repeat offenders who commit violent crimes, including sex offenses. A state commission in Michigan in 1999 recommended longer terms for violent offenders. Under this approach the need for special sexual psychopath legislation is diminished, but the hypothesis that increased sentences will improve public safety is untested. Suggestions to the contrary have included the possibility that repeat sex offenders may be more likely to kill their victims to avoid discovery as the severity of the sentence increases.

From all reports, psychotherapy serves little, if at all, in changing the behavior of sex offenders. What they learn in psychotherapy is the jargon of psychotherapy. They learn the phrases that will get them past the assessment of being an incorrigible—that they have "recognized the causes" of their behavior, and "seen the offense from the victim's point of view." Evidence is thin, however, that they learn to control their behavior, or that they are telling the truth when they say those fine phrases.

What about castration, surgical or chemical? Texas not long ago enacted legislation allowing surgical castration of repeat sex offenders. The law makes it voluntary, and those who agree must also agree to take part in a study of sexual behavior after the operation that eliminates testosterone, which is blamed for male sexual aggression. To date, the legislation has not been applied out of concern that it may lead to litigation on the basis that consent under the circumstances is not voluntarily given.[37]

The Michigan Court of Appeals overturned a trial judge's sentence of Depo-Provera treatment as a condition of probation, finding the condition punitive, unlawful, and coercive, as well as virtually impossible to perform with "informed consent."[38] Further, the court said that "Depo-Provera treatment fails as a lawful condition of probation because it has not gained acceptance in the medical community as a safe and reliable medical procedure."[39] In Germany, where surgical castration is practiced, the recidivist rate is said to have dropped from the 80 percent range to 3 percent. Chemical castration (by medication), as opposed to surgical castration, has side effects, including diabetes and heart problems.[40]

Castration of whatever type—if it works—may be considered more humane than confinement. The offender is not only free after his sentence is served but is also freed from the uncontrollable impulses that drive him to violate the freedom of others.[41] Yet a word of caution: Castration may reduce recidivism among offenders who commit a sex crime out of sexual urges, but many sex crimes are carried out as a way to assert power or to express rage or hostility. For these offenders, castration is no remedy.[42]

Around the turn of the twentieth century, in 1913, California enacted legislation calling for "asexualization" of individuals who had committed two sex crimes, or three serious crimes of any sort, and any convict who gave "evidence" in the prison that "he is a moral and sexual pervert."[43] Eventually about half the states had some sort of eugenics statute. Washington state required all state institutions to report those under their care who were "feeble-minded, insane, epileptic," as well as "habitual criminals, moral degenerates and sexual perverts," whose "offspring," because of the inheritance of "inferior or anti-social traits," would likely become "a social menace or wards of the state."[44] These were then candidates for sterilization.[45] Many believed that crime was biological destiny. As late as the 1930s, in the science of criminal anthropology, it was reported that criminals had "relatively shorter and broader faces. . . . The nose is relatively shorter and broader . . . ears with less roll of the helix or rim," along with "stunted growth and inferior development."[46]

Sex Offender Registration Laws

All fifty states and the federal government have enacted some type of sex offender registration law since 1994, when young Megan Kanka was beaten, raped, and murdered by a convicted sexual offender who lived near her family's New Jersey home. Compliance with the federal law is one of seventeen requirements for states to receive a federal grant that pays for crime prevention and victim's assistance programs. For a grant, states must require sex offenders to register their names and addresses with local authorities for life. The states must require sex offenders who work or attend school in a different state to register with both states.

Whatever the federal law, registration schemes vary from state to state. The following categories have been conceptualized: (1) self-identification model, (2) police discretion model, and (3) police book model. The self-identification model requires the offender to identify himself to the community and the police. The police discretion model provides law-enforcement agencies with the discretion over whether to release information to the community about convicted sex offenders. In this model, the community is not notified about all offenders but rather those who are considered dangerous. The police book model allows members of the community to obtain information law enforcement upon their request. The statutes focus on sexual assaults, including forcible rape and sexual abuse of children, but several statutes also target promoters of child pornography and child prostitution. Lesser crimes such as indecent exposure or public indecency are enumerated in some of the statutes. A number of states focus their registration statutes exclusively on offenders against children while others focus on habitual sex offenders.[47]

In some states, sexual offenders are currently required to register only for a limited length of time and can ask a court to terminate the registration order. These or other states are at risk of losing grant money if the federal government determines their sex offender registration laws are too weak. Michigan has had a sex registry since 1995 and made it public in 1999. There are now 27,583 offenders on the list, with 1,799 of them tried in juvenile courts. The listing in Michigan stays on the registry for a period of twenty-five years; Wyoming for ten years. Failure to register is a felony. Juveniles convicted of a sex crime (those tried in juvenile courts as well as juveniles tried as adults) are listed on the registry.[48]

Some states, to track the whereabouts of discharged offenders, have gone beyond maintaining sex offender registries. They post the information, along with photographs and details of crimes, on Web pages accessible to anyone with a computer and modem. Proponents of the trend, including many state officials, say expanding community notification to the Internet is a valuable and relatively simple way to disseminate information. Critics say online registries, while popular with the public, are a quick fix to a complex issue, and they could stigmatize and victimize marginal offenders and could ultimately produce more sex crimes than they prevent. As notification laws become ubiquitous, so have incidents in which ex-offenders have been harassed by neighbors, evicted by landlords, fired from new jobs, or beaten by revenge-minded mobs.[49]

To Sum Up

As each new legal experiment is introduced, perhaps it would be to everyone's advantage if it were tested in the manner of a true experiment, with information gathered about its effectiveness in enhancing community safety and fairness. From such an information base, the next legal steps might have more chance of achieving both. Although the efficacy of sex offender treatment remains inconclusive, its current empirical status may have less to do with its therapeutic soundness than it does the manner in which treatment is employed or structured within the criminal justice system.[50]

Notes

1. E.g., Minn. Stat. Ann., sec. 526.09 (1947). See D. E. J. MacNamara & E. Sagarin, *Sex, Crime, and the Law* (New York: Free Press, 1977); R. Slovenko (ed.), *Sexual Behavior and the Law* (Springfield, Ill.: Thomas, 1965).

2. P. Q. Roche, *The Criminal Mind* (New York: Farrar, Straus & Cudahy, 1958), p. 25.

3. *DSM-IV*, p. 522.

4. S. L. Halleck, *Psychiatry and the Dilemmas of Crime* (New York: Harper & Row, 1967), p. 99.

5. Group for the Advancement of Psychiatry, *Psychiatry and Sex Psychopath Legislation: The 30's to the 80's* (Washington, D.C.: American Psychiatric Assn., 1977), p. 840.

6. M. Ploscowe, *Sex and the Law* (New York: Ace Books, 1962).

7. 373 F.2d 451, 453 (D.C. Cir. 1966).

8. 373 F.2d 468, 472 (D.C. Cir. 1966).

9. People v. Jackson, 20 App. Div.2d 170, 245 N.Y.S.2d 534 (1963).

10. T. S. Szasz, *The Myth of Mental Illness* (New York: Harper & Row, 1961).

11. See *Standard Edition of the Complete Works of Sigmund Freud* (London: Hogarth Press, 1953), 2: 1, 6; 7: 51, 75, 170, 235; 16: 274; 18: 29.

12. Whitree v. State, 56 Misc.2d 693, 711, 290 N.Y.S.2d 486, 504 (1968).

13. K. Menninger, *The Vital Balance* (New York: Viking, 1963), p. 191. In a study of Adolf Hitler, *The Psychopathic God: Adolf Hitler* (New York: Basic Books, 1977), the historian Robert Waite suggests that Hitler's use of the extended stiff-arm salute was a substitute for his sexual shortcomings. Indeed, Hitler often boasted that his ability to hold his arm stiff was proof of his masculine power. Likewise, Hitler's lifelong preoccupation with constructing buildings reflected, in Professor Waite's view, behavior designed to quell anxiety about physical defects by making other kinds of structures whole. For all these pent-up fixations, Waite believed, Hitler's rabid anti-Semitism was, for him, a safety valve. In Jews (and to a lesser extent minorities such as gay men and lesbians), Hitler found a convenient receptacle for the "displacement and projection" of all that he most feared and loathed about himself.

14. B. Glueck, "An Evaluation of the Homosexual Offender," *Minn. L. Rev.* 41 (1957): 187.

15. The Michigan statute provided: "Any person . . . suffering from a mental disorder and [who] is not feeble-minded, which mental disorder is coupled with criminal propensities to the commission of sex offenses, is hereby declared to be a criminal sexual psychopathic person." Mich. Stat. Ann., secs. 780.501–509.

16. Repealed by Public Act No. 143 (1968).

17. J. F. Grabowski, "The Illinois Sexually Dangerous Persons Act: An Examination of a Statute in Need of Change," *So. Ill. U. L. J.* 12 (1988): 437, 454 n. 106.

18. Colorado, Connecticut, District of Columbia, Illinois, Massachusetts, Minnesota, Nebraska, New Jersey, Oregon, Tennessee, Utah, Virginia, and Washington.

19. S. J. Brakel, J. Parry, & B. Weiner, *The Mentally Disabled and the Law* (Chicago: American Bar Association, 3d ed. 1985).

20. Cal. Welf. & Inst. Code, secs. 6300–6330, *repealed by* 1981 Cal. Stat., ch. 928.

21. See. R. Wettstein, "A Psychiatric Perspective on Washington's Sexually Violent Predators Statute," *U. Puget Sound Law Rev.* 15 (1992): 597; R. Sherman, "Psychiatric Gulags or Wise Safekeeping?" *Nat'l L.J.*, Sept. 5, 1994, pp. 1, 24.

22. The new laws are widely known as "Megan's Law," named after Megan Kanka, a seven-year-old girl who was raped and murdered by a pedophile who had become a neighbor without the knowledge of Megan's parents.

23. A review of the six assessment procedures used for assessing the recidivism of previously convicted sexual offenders appears in T. W. Campbell, "Sexual Predator Evaluations and Phrenology: Considering Issues of Evidentiary Reliability," *Behav. Sci. & Law* 118 (2000): 111, which argues that these instruments amount to experimental procedures and, therefore, they cannot support expert testimony in a legal proceeding. See also T. W. Campbell, "Assessing Sexual Offender Recidivism Risk: Static-Risk Variables Alone?" *Am. J. For. Psychology* 19 (2001): 15. See B. J. Winick & J. Q. LaFond (eds.), Symposium, "Sex Offenders: Scientific, Legal, and Policy Perspectives," *Psych., Pub. Pol'y & Law* 4 (Mar./June 1988): nos. 1 & 2; A. Brooks, "The Constitutionality and Morality of Civilly Committing Violent Sexual Predators," *U. Puget Sound L. Rev.* 15 (1992): 709; A. Horwitz, "Sexual Psychopath Legislation: Is There Anywhere to Go but Backwards?" *U. Pitt. L. Rev.* 57 (1995): 35; E. S. Janus, "Sex Offender Commitments: Debunking the Official Narrative and Revealing the Rules-in-Use," *Stanford L. & Policy Rev.* 8 (1997): 71; J. Q. LaFond, "Washington's Sexually Violent Predator Law: A Deliberate Misuse of the Therapeutic State for Social Control," *U. Puget Sound L. Rev.* 15 (1992): 655; S. J. Schulhofer, "Two Systems of Social Protection: Comments on the Civil-Criminal Distinction, with Particular Reference to Sexually Violent Predator Laws," *J. Contemp. Legal Issues* 8 (1996): 69; R. M. Wettstein, "A Psychiatric Perspective on Washington's Sexually Violent Predator Statute," *U. Puget Sound L. Rev.* 15 (1992): 597; H. V. Zonana & M. A. Norko, "Sexual Predators," *Psychiatric Clin. North America* 22 (1999): 109; H. V. Zonana, "The Civil Commitment of Sex Offenders," *Science* 278 (Nov. 14, 1998): 1248.

24. See the symposia on sex offender laws in *Behavioral Science & Law* 18 (2000): nos. 1–3. See also G. B. Palermo & M. A. Farkas, *The Dilemma of the Sexual Offender* (Springfield, Ill.: Thomas, 2001); G. Palermo, "A Dynamic Formulation of Sex Offender Behavior and Its Therapeutic Relevance," *Forensic Psychology Practice*, Feb. 2002 (in press). It may be noted that the laws on sex do not cover promiscuity, as violence or lack of consent is not involved. In the inner cities of the United States it is not uncommon to encounter males who have as many as ten, fifteen, or twenty children (by different women) and see none of them; many of these fathers are in prison. Generally speaking, the behavior is no longer considered sinful and is even supported by welfare. Uniquely, the Wisconsin Supreme Court affirmed a ban preventing a father of nine who owed child support from having more children unless he proves he will support all his offspring. It was a condition of probation, which the court said is reasonably related to the goal of rehabilitation, and is narrowly tailored to serve the compelling state interest in requiring parents to support their children. State v. Oakley, 2001 WI 123, 2001 Wisc. Lexis 1597 (2001). See D. D. Hansen, "The American Invention of Child Support: Dependency and Punishment in Early American Child Support Law, *Yale L.J.* 108 (1999): 1123.

25. In re Young, 122 Wash.2d 1, 857 P.2d 989 (1993).

26. 857 P.2d at 1001.

27. In re Linehan, 518 N.W.2d 609 (Minn. 1994). See also Hince v. O'Keefe, 632 N.W.2d 577 (Minn. 2001). In the Italian comedy film *The Monster*, the psychiatrist is lampooned in his effort to evaluate Loris (Robert Benigni), who is suspected of being a "sex fiend."

28. In re Hendricks, 259 Kan. 246, 912 P.2d 129 (1996), ruling on Kan. Stat. Ann., sec. 59–29a01 *et seq.*

29. 117 S. Ct. 2072 (1997).

30. 117 S. Ct. at 2080. In 2001, the Supreme Court again reviewed the Kansas law, this time on whether states must prove that offenders cannot control their behavior in order to confine them indefinitely as sexual predators. The case involved Michael Crane, who went to prison in 1994 for sexually assaulting a video store clerk and exposing himself to a tanning salon attendant in Kansas City. When he was about to be paroled in 1998, prosecutors went to court to have him committed to a state hospital. The jury agreed to have him committed, following narrow guidelines issued by the judge. He was placed on conditional release after having completed the state's treatment program. The Kansas Supreme Court ordered a new trial, saying that the jury that found him likely to commit another similar crime should also have found him unable to control his behavior. In the 1997 case, child molester Leroy Hendricks had admitted he "can't control the urge." In *Crane*, in argument before the U.S. Supreme Court, the state contended that the control requirement is too broad, because almost all sexual offenders possess at least some control over their actions. During argument, the

justices pressed the attorneys to say specifically how far the Court should go in setting a standard for the proof that states must offer. The Court ruled that it is not necessary for the state to establish "total" or "complete" lack of control. Kansas v. Crane, 122 S. Ct. 867 (2002). Dissenting, Justice Scalia said, "I suspect that the reason the Court avoids any elaboration is that elaboration which passes the laught test is impossible." 122 S. Ct. at 876.

31. 117 S. Ct. at 2084.

32. Young v. Weston, 898 F.Supp. 744 (W.D.Wash. 1995). In Sharp v. Weston, 233 F.3d 1166 (9th Cir. 2000), the Ninth Circuit held that persons committed as sexually violent predators have a Fourteenth Amendment right to mental health treatment that gives them a realistic opportunity to be cured and released. The court acknowledged that although the state enjoys wide latitude in developing treatment programs, the courts may take action when there is substantial departure from accepted professional judgment or no exercise of professional judgment at all. The court noted that under Youngberg v. Romeo, 457 U.S. 307 (1982), the decisions made by professionals are presumptively valid but not conclusive. In Pool v. McKune, 987 P.2d 1073 (Kan. 1999), the question was raised whether convicted sex offenders serving a criminal sentence have a right to privacy under the Fourth Amendment that would preclude required plethysmograph testing in a Sexual Abuse Treatment Program, a prison-based eighteen-month rehabilitation program for sex offenders. The Kansas Supreme Court held that neither the scope of the intrusion, the manner in which the test is conducted, nor the place in which it is conducted outweighs the penological interest in rehabilitating sex offenders.

Innovations in dealing with sex offenders have often tested constitutional boundaries. In another Kansas case, *McKune v. Lile*, the U.S. Supreme Court has been called upon to decide whether a state violates a convicted sex offender's right against compelled self-incrimination by taking away prison privileges if the inmate refuses to accept responsibility for any previously undisclosed crimes as part of a therapy program. Presumably, by accepting responsibility for past crimes, it would indicate remorse and hence a therapeutic gain. The Kansas program uses a polygraph examination to test the completeness and accuracy of an inmate's disclosures. There is no immunity from prosecution for previously undisclosed crimes, although in the years of the program's existence, no inmate has been prosecuted for a confession given in the course of treatment. The case began in 1994 when the inmate, Robert Lile, serving a life sentence for rape and approaching his parole date, refused to participate in the Sexual Abuse Treatment Program, and as a result he was reduced to the lowest level of the prison's classification system and ordered transferred to a maximum-security prison. L. Greenhouse, "Inmates' Self-Incrimination Debated at Supreme Court," *New York Times*, Nov. 29, 2001, p. 24.

33. Seling v. Young, 531 U.S. 250 (2001). See E. S. Janus, "Sex Predator Commitment Laws: Constitutional but Unwise," *Psychiatric Annals*, June 2000, p. 411.

34. Council of Psychiatry and Law, American Psychiatric Association, "Final Report of the Subcommittee to Review the Insanity Defense" (1988), p. 3.

35. There is a continuing debate about whether predictions of dangerousness are accurate enough to support deprivation of liberty. Should risk assessment, which is based on group behavior, be sufficient to establish that a particular individual will be dangerous in the future? For the most part, courts have rejected this argument based largely on public safety concerns. E. S. Janus & P. E. Meehl, "Assessing the Legal Standard for Predictions of Dangerousness in Sex Offender Commitment Proceedings," *Psych., Pub. Pol'y & Law* 3 (1997): 33. The New Jersey Court of Appeals has ruled that the state met its burden of establishing that under the *Frye* standard, actuarial tools for predicting sex offenders' risk of committing future acts of sexual violence are generally accepted by the scientific community and, thus, are admissible as scientific evidence in SVP commitment proceedings. In re Commitment of R.S., 773 A.2d 72 (N.J. Super. Ct. App. Div. 2001). For a critique, see T. W. Campbell, "Sexual Predator Evaluations and Phrenology: Considering Issues of Evidentiary Reliability," *Behav. Sci. & Law* 18 (2000): 111.

See D. Boerner, "Confronting Violence: In the Act and in the World," *U. Puget Sound L. Rev.* 15 (1992): 525; A. D. Brooks, "The Constitutionality and Morality of Civilly Committing Violent Sexual Predators," id. 15 (1992): 709, 1992; G. Gelb, "Washington's Sexually Violent Predator Law: The Need to Bar Unreliable Psychiatric Predictions of Dangerousness from Civil Commitment Proceedings," *UCLA L. Rev.* 39 (1991): 213.

36. B. Bodine, "Washington's New Violent Sexual Predator Commitment System: An Unconstitutional Law and an Unwise Policy Choice," *U. Puget Sound L. Rev.* 14 (1990): 105; see also S. J. Brakel & J. L. Cavanaugh, "Of Psychopaths and Pendulums: Legal and Psychiatric Treatment of Sex Offenders in the United States," *New Mex. L. Rev.* 30 (2000): 69.

37. California initiated legislation requiring certain convicted sex offenders as a condition of probation to submit to treatment with the progesterone agent medroxyprogesterone acetate. A number of other states have done the same. The bills do not clearly define what is meant by *chemical castration* other than to list the medication(s) that may be used. See R. D. Miller, "Forced Administration of Sex-Drive Reducing Medications to Sex Offenders: Treatment or Punishment?" *Psych., Pub. Pol'y & Law* 4 (1998): 175. The South African government is considering chemical castration for repeat sex offenders. The South African constitution prohibits "cruel and inhuman" punishment, but Inkatha Freedom Party Member of Parliament (MP) Suzanne Vos pointed out that "it is used in the United States to punish repeat offenders." R. Brnad, "Castration Meted for Repeat Rapists," *Cape Times,* Oct. 25, 1999, p. 3.

38. People v. Gauntlett, 134 Mich. App. 737, at 751 (1984).

39. 134 Mich. App. at 750.

40. During the seventeenth and eighteenth centuries, for some two hundred years, young males were retained as mellifluous sopranos by surgical castration. The cause is attributed to the prohibition against women singing in church or appearing onstage. With the invention of Italian opera, a popular style of entertainment, singers with women's voices were required. Until the late eighteenth century, Italian opera and castrati were indistinguishable concepts. And 70 percent of male opera singers were castrati.

Moreover, throughout history, eunuchs were created for various purposes. They often served in harems, where the frustrated women could not be supervised by genitally intact men. In the Byzantine and Ottoman empires, they also filled top administrative and military posts, controlling finances and the destinies of entire peoples. Unlike uncastrated men, who had families of their own, eunuchs could be trusted not to intrigue on behalf of the sons they would never have. E. Abbott, *A History of Celibacy* (New York: Scribner, 2000).

41. See G. G. Abel & C. Osborn, "Stopping Sexual Violence," *Psychiatric Ann.* 22 (1992): 301; J. V. Becker, M. S. Kaplan, & R. Kavoussi, "Measuring the Effectiveness of Treatment for the Aggressive Adolescent Sexual Offender," *Ann. N. Y. Acad. Sci.* 528 (1988): 215; F. S. Berlin & C. F. Meinecke, "Treatment of Sex Offenders with Antiandrogenic Medication: Conceptualization, Review of Treatment Modalities, and Preliminary Findings," *Am. J. Psychiatry* 138 (1981): 601; J. M. W. Bradford & D. McLean, "Sexual Offenders, Violence and Testosterone: A Clinical Study," *Can. J. Psychiatry* 1984: 335, T. A. Kiersch, "Treatment of Sex Offenders with Depo-Provera," *Bull. Am. Acad. Psychiatry & Law* 18 (1990): 179.

42. Randy Thornhill, an evolutionary biologist, and Craig T. Palmer, an evolutionary anthropologist, contend that rape is primarily a crime of sex, not violence and power as a generation of social scientists and feminist scholars have argued. R. Thornhill & C. T. Palmer, *A Natural History of Rape: Biological Bases of Sexual Coercion* (Boston: MIT Press, 2000), excerpted in "When Men Rape," *Science,* Jan./Feb. 2000, p. 30; critically reviewed in E. Goode, "What Provokes a Rapist to Rape?" *New York Times,* Jan. 15, 2000, p. 21.

43. Laws Cal. 1913, ch. 720, p. 109. An amendment to the penal code in 1923 authorized a judge to order an "operation . . . for the prevention of procreation" to be performed on men found guilty of "carnal abuse of a female person under the age of ten years."

44. Laws Wash. 1921, p. 162.

45. The Nazis relied on these laws to justify ethnic cleansing. See R. N. Proctor, *Racial Hygiene: Medicine under the Nazis* (Cambridge: Harvard University Press, 1988). Statistics on schizophrenia and heredity were compiled by Ernst Rudin, a pioneer in psychiatric genetics and a prominent figure in Nazi Germany. He served on Hitler's Task Force of Heredity Experts, headed by Heinrich Himmler, which formulated the 1933 laws mandating sterilization for those who were retarded, schizophrenic, or epileptic, among other conditions. He praised Hitler for his "decisive path-breaking step toward making racial hygiene a fact among the German people . . . and inhibiting the propagation of the congenitally ill and inferior." R. J. Lifton, *The Nazi Doctors* (New York: Basic Books, 1986).

46. See L. M. Friedman, *American Law in the 20th Century* (New Haven: Yale University Press, 2002), pp. 108–9.

47. A. R. Bedarf, "Examining Sex Offender Community Notification Laws," *Calif. L. Rev.* 83 (1995): 885.

48. The reason many juvenile records are expunged at adulthood is to give nonviolent offenders the chance to learn from mistakes and start afresh, but that is not reflected when discretion cannot be exercised concerning the sex offender registry. The lengthy registration period in some states (twenty-five years in Michigan) prompts recommendations for separate rules for teen offenders. Editorial, "Sex List," *Detroit Free Press*, Nov. 20, 2001, p. 5.

49. P. Zielbauer, "Sex Offender Registries on Web Draw Both Praise and Criticism," *New York Times*, May 22, 2000, p. 18. In England, following the murder of eight-year-old Sarah Payne, a campaign began to enact a version of Megan's Law, called Sarah's Law. Rupert Murdoch's newspaper *News of the World* carried on a "name and shame" campaign that resulted in vigilante attacks against suspected pedophiles and the deaths of innocent people, and it was discontinued. E. Vulliamy & N. P. Walsh, "The Paedophile Panic," *Observer*, Aug. 6, 2000, p. 14; A. Gillan, "Paper Relents over Drive to Shame," *Guardian*, Aug. 5, 2000, p. 1. Canada allows anyone who fears on reasonable grounds that some person will commit a sex offense of a minor under the age of fourteen to file a charge before a provincial court judge. Canada Criminal Code sec. 810.1; discussed in *National Post*, Oct. 21, 2000, p. 9.

50. W. Edwards & C. Hensley, "Restructuring Sex Offender Sentencing: A Therapeutic Jurisprudence Approach to the Criminal Justice Process," *Int'l J. Offender Therapy & Comp. Crim.* 45 (2001): 646.

19

Homosexuality: From Condemnation to Celebration

The history of homosexuality has been one of condemnation punctuated by intervals of celebration. For nearly two thousand years homosexuality has been viewed as evidence of moral weakness, criminality, or pathology. These have been the perspectives, in turn, of religion, law, and medicine. Until recently, homosexuality was seen not as the mark of a distinctive, oppressed minority group, but rather as an individual and very personal problem. The development of a homosexual lobby, if you will, had its genesis in 1969 after a riot erupted outside a bar on Christopher Street in New York's Greenwich Village. Homophiles began to mobilize for the first time and soon became a major political and economic force. Taking a cue from the civil rights and feminist movements, the struggle for homosexual rights emerged from obscurity.

In 1985 the Gay and Lesbian Alliance Against Defamation was founded, and in 1987 (the year coincidentally that Rock Hudson died of AIDS), its representatives persuaded the *New York Times* to change its editorial policy and use the word *gay* instead of *homosexual*.[1] The term *gay*, signifying celebration, became common currency. At rallies there were the chants: "Gay is good. Gay is proud. Gay is natural. Gay is normal." "Say it loud, we're gay and proud." "2–4–6–8, gay is just as good as straight." The Gay and Lesbian Alliance Against Defamation is known by its acronym, GLAAD.[2] "Gay pride will rank as one of the great inventions of the 20th century," proclaimed Deb Price, an avowed gay who writes a weekly syndicated column about homosexuality.[3] At the same time, the AIDS epidemic has ravaged the gay (and drug-user) community—it is called another holocaust.[4]

Homosexuality, and society's mainly adverse reaction to it, has a history as long as civilization itself. The people of ancient Sodom proudly proclaimed their homosexuality, but were condemned by the prophet Isaiah, who deemed homosexuality as akin to bestiality.[5] Leviticus 18:22 defined homosexuality as a crime—in biblical language, an "abomination." Leviticus 20:13 went much further: "If a man lies with a man sexually as with a woman, they have performed an abomination; they shall surely be put to death." The first commandment in the Bible, in Genesis 9:1, is "be fruitful and multiply."

Homosexuality, however, seems to have flourished in ancient Greece. Greek homosexual love in the fourth century was both passionate and physical. Plato and his friends were overt homosexuals. As far as Plato was concerned, romantic passion was only possible between men and boys. Plato's love for Dion was a model for many ideas about romantic love until the medieval period. The homosexual relationship was cast in the same mold as the modern-day romantic love between men and women.

It would, however, be a mistake to consider homosexual love as the rule in ancient Greece. Although Solon granted homosexuals civil rights, homosexuality was not condoned by the common populace, and its practitioners were mocked in Aristophanes' plays. The usual justification for homosexuality in Greece was that women were not fit companions for Athenian intellectuals. By and large, women were relegated to a life of obscurity and illiteracy, and were considered boring. There were some sophisticated women, however, such as the poet Sappho, who ran a school for women on the island of Lesbos (from which the term *lesbian* is derived). But such women were the exception rather than the rule. Demosthenes voiced the typical attitude: "Courtesans we keep for pleasure, concubines for daily [sexual] attendance on our persons, and wives to bear us legitimate children and to be our housekeepers."[6]

Toward the end of the seventeenth century, religious disapprobation of homosexuality became reinforced by state condemnation, as the sin became a crime. Some penal codes retained the religious abhorrence of homosexuality, describing it as a crime not merely against society, but "against nature."[7] Legal codes in the American colonies set death as the penalty for sodomy, and in several instances courts directed the execution of men found guilty of this act.[8] Although most states abolished the death penalty for sodomy by 1825, all but two (Kansas and Utah) in the mid-twentieth century still classified it as a felony.[9] Only murder, kidnapping, and rape carried heavier sentences. Although few men and almost no women were punished under such laws, the statutes imposed the stigma of criminality.

The most famous prosecution resulted in the conviction in 1895 of Oscar Wilde, England's celebrated playwright and now a gay icon. Although homosexuality was a criminal offense, Wilde had made little effort to conceal his relations with younger men, particularly Lord Alfred Douglas. Douglas's father, the Marquess of Queensberry, hounded Wilde relentlessly, finally sending him a note calling him a "Sodomite." Wilde sued for libel, a fatal mistake. In the course of the trial his private affairs were mercilessly exposed, and he lost the case. He was then prosecuted for committing indecent acts, convicted, and sentenced to two years at hard labor.[10] He emerged from the degradation of prison a broken and penniless man, and he went to Paris, where he died soon thereafter, at age forty-six, his health ruined by imprisonment. He died a sad and lonely death, desperately poor and largely abandoned by those he thought his friends. His family changed their surname to Holland to escape the opprobrium surrounding their name.

By the twentieth century, prosecution for homosexual activity had grown increasingly rare. Generally speaking, prosecutions for sodomy in the twentieth century, even where outlawed, were limited to those involving either gross indiscretion[11] or forceful action.[12] Prosecuting officials and courts seemed to read "notoriety" or "brutality" into the sodomy statutes as essential elements of the offense. The issue in these cases, then, was not really one of homosexuality versus heterosexuality, but rather of the gross violation of social amenities. Writings on the law of homosexuality, as a rule, omit any reference to notoriety or violence and, as a result, they misrepresent the state of enforcement of the law.[13]

The decline in the criminalization of homosexuality was a reflection of the increasing medicalization of it. As early as the nineteenth century, homosexuality began to be discussed as an illness or disease. It was argued that homosexuals were not so much sinners or criminals as they were mentally ill. In the 1880s and 1890s, doctors debated whether homosexuality was a vice indulged in by weak-willed, depraved individuals, an acquired form of insanity, or a congenital defect that indicated evolutionary degeneracy. By the early twentieth century many were saying that homosexuality was hereditary in origin. The advent of Freudian theory in the 1920s, however, changed both the medical explanations and societal perceptions of homosexuality. The Freudian legacy was to focus on early childhood and unresolved Oedipal conflicts. The emphasis shifted from a concern with genetics to psychic conflict. Freud's biographical reconstruction of the life of Leonardo da Vinci suggested that the combination of an absent father and a dominant mother was central in the development of male homosexuality. In contrast, Dr. Irving Bieber and his colleagues in 1962 published data on approximately one hundred homosexual males in psychoanalytically oriented therapy, which found an abusive father to be the common denominator.[14]

Events surrounding World War II abetted the perception of homosexual behavior as illness. The federal government ordered psychiatric screening of inductees during World War II, leading to an increase in visibility and enhanced prestige for psychiatry. Homosexuals were deemed medically unfit for service. Americans, by and large, came to view sexual behavior not as moral or immoral, but as sick or healthy, with homosexuality falling into the sick category.[15]

In 1948, Alfred Kinsey and his associates entered the scene. In their much-publicized work, they demonstrated that homosexual and heterosexual responsiveness in human beings is not always found in clearly differentiated patterns. They showed that these levels of responsiveness are spread across a continuum that ranges from exclusive heterosexual reactivity to exclusive homosexual reactivity, with various gradations in between. Kinsey suggested a seven-point scale for this continuum based on both overt experience and inner psychological reactions. His study painted a picture of the sexuality of ordinary Americans that was startling. Nothing had challenged the conventional wisdom about homosexuality as much as his finding that fifty percent of males admitted erotic responses to their own sex.[16] Kinsey's work gave an added push at an important time to the emergence of the modern urban homosexual subculture.

Shortly after the war, however, when communism replaced Nazism as a threat to the country, or so it was perceived, President Truman established a loyalty program for federal employees, and in 1950, the Senate produced a report, *The Employment of Homosexuals and Other Sex Perverts in Government.*[17] Some members of congress argued that "sex perverts" imperiled national security on the grounds that they were particularly vulnerable to blackmail.[18] Kinsey's research caused such commotion that he was denounced as a communist and his research funds were withdrawn.[19]

During the 1960s, the portrayals of homosexual life multiplied in literature and in the mass media. With the growing volume of such material came a new way of seeing the homosexual lifestyle. A significant number of persons began to view homosexuals not as isolated, aberrant individuals, but as members of a group. The militancy of homosexual activists allowed the movement to exploit the sexual permissiveness that characterized American culture in the 1960s. The national debate about sexual matters that was sparked by the Kinsey reports cleared away the residue of proscriptions on sexual discourse that was the legacy of Victorianism. Popular attitudes remained hostile, however, and for the overwhelming majority of homosexual men and women a retreat to a secret life was preferable to the stigma that openness would bring.

Homosexuals found that they still had to deal with the sickness label, which has wider application than the criminal label. While relatively few homosexuals have been convicted of any "crime against nature"—the vast majority of homosexuals have as spotless a record as heterosexuals—they all fell under the *mental disorder* label of the American Psychiatric Association's *Diagnostic and Statistical Manual of Mental Disorders.* The first edition of the manual, published in 1952, classified homosexuality as a sexual deviation.[20] The general category within which the sexual deviations appeared was Sociopathic Personality Disturbance, a designation referring to individuals who are ill primarily in terms of society's reaction to them because they fail to conform to the prevailing cultural milieu.[21] In *DSM-II,* the second edition of the manual published in 1968, homosexuality was also classified as a sexual deviation, but sexual deviations were now categorized under Personality Disorders, a group distinguished by deeply ingrained maladaptive patterns of behavior perceptibly different in quality from psychotic and neurotic symptoms.[22]

The sickness label backfired on homosexuals. As sickness, it applied broadly, whereas the original label applied only to those who were charged with "crime against nature." Government and many private employers justified employment discrimination and other policies against all homosexuals by referring to *DSM.* "Homosexuals are sick," they said, and they were able to point to a respected authority. So, in the early 1970s, homosexuals argued that much of the prejudice confronting them was a product of psychiatric stigmatization. As a consequence, various homosexual activist groups, supported by some psychiatrists, urged that homosexuality should not be considered a form of mental illness. They demonstrated at the annual meetings of the American Psychiatric Association, disrupted meetings, and stormed the speaker platforms.

In 1973, the APA board of trustees voted unanimously (with two abstentions) to eliminate the general category of homosexuality from *DSM* and to replace it with a category called "sexual orientation disturbance." This designation would apply only to *ego-dystonic* homosexuality, that is, that of homosexuals who are either subjectively distressed by or in conflict with their sexual orientation. The APA's

Task Force on Nomenclature had recommended that homosexuality be regarded as "a normal variant of human sexuality," but in order to obtain passage, the board of trustees changed the wording of the task force that homosexuality "by itself does not constitute a psychiatric disorder" to "does not necessarily constitute a disorder."[23] In 1974, APA members voted by ballot to ratify the trustees' decision. The vote was 5,854 (58 percent) for the trustees' position, 3,810 (37.8 percent) against, and 367 abstentions. About half of the membership did not vote. One bemused observer labeled it the single greatest cure in the history of psychiatry.

Under the circumstances, the conclusion is inescapable that the vote was made under compulsion. Dr. Ronald Bayer summarized the events as follows:

> The entire process, from the first confrontations organized by gay demonstrators at psychiatric conventions to the referendum demanded by orthodox psychiatrists, seemed to violate the most basic expectations about how questions of science should be resolved. Instead of being engaged in a sober consideration of data, psychiatrists were swept up in political controversy. The American Psychiatric Association had fallen victim to the disorder of a tumultuous era, when disruptive conflicts threatened to politicize every aspect of American social life. A furious egalitarianism that challenged every instance of authority had compelled psychiatric experts to negotiate the pathological status of homosexuality with homosexuals themselves. The result was not a conclusion based on an approximation of the scientific truth as dictated by reason, but was instead an action demanded by the ideological temper of the times.[24]

Dr. Jon K. Meyer commented,

> At the moment, homosexuality is perhaps the most difficult subject in psychiatry to address. Few conditions affecting the psyche and behavior have been so intensely scrutinized, debated, and politicized. Conceptualization of homosexuality—as a life-style, a preference, an illness, a sociopolitical movement, a biological predisposition—is marked by a fundamental lack of consensus.[25]

Homosexuals hailed the change in the APA nomenclature in *DSM-III* as an "instant cure."[26] Shortly after the APA vote, the federal government in 1975 eliminated the ban on employment of homosexuals.[27] Then, too, the Americans with Disabilities Act of 1990 specifically provides that homosexuality and bisexuality are not impairments and as such cannot constitute disabilities.[28] Homosexuals have grown as an organized political power, notably in San Francisco, where an estimated 40 percent of single men and women are homosexual. Bill Clinton was elected president with considerable support from African-American, gay, and female voters.

The end of the twentieth century was marked by unprecedented state-level changes in the law on homosexuality. Today, ironically, homosexuality is constitutionally protected in the United States, but prayer is not. In the year 1999 in state after state, gay rights legislation advanced further and faster than ever before— thanks to the growing number of openly gay lawmakers, the diligence of statewide gay groups, and the emerging national consensus that gay people should be treated with respect.[29] New Hampshire, among other states, repealed its ban on gay adoptive and foster parents. Missouri voted to expand its hate crimes law to protect gays. California passed a domestic partnership bill that gives unmarried partners—gay or heterosexual—vital benefits, including hospitalization and inheritance rights.[30] The Vermont Supreme Court, on the basis of a 200-year-old clause of the state constitution that government should be "instituted for the common benefit, protection and security of the people, nation or community," ordered the state to guarantee the same protections and benefits to homosexual couples that it does to married heterosexuals.[31] Since 1990, Canada, Denmark, France, Greenland, Hungary, Iceland, the Netherlands, Norway, and Sweden have created one form or another of domestic-partnership arrangements for the benefit of homosexuals.

The publicity about homosexuality is now pervasive and well-nigh inescapable. Homosexuality has gone from condemnation to celebration. It is openly displayed and discussed. It is portrayed on stage and screen and in many publications. Not only offbeat publishers but mainline publishers and university presses (notably Duke University Press and University of Wisconsin Press) have long lists of books on homosexuality. Guide books on city life include the homosexual scene. Gay study courses are now offered at a number of leading universities in the United States. Tens of thousands of homosexual men and women march in annual Christopher Street Liberation Day parades in major cities. The Victorians would be dismayed.

Recognition of Various Homosexual Rights

Before the 1960s, homosexuals generally feared to speak out about their sexual orientation or to organize groups to secure their legal rights. The few organized groups that did exist used names designed to conceal their homosexual nature so that prospective members would feel less uncomfortable about joining them. Beginning in the 1960s, when the issue came before the courts, it was held rather consistently that advocacy of homosexual rights, even in a state that penalizes private, adult, consensual sodomy, is not advocacy of or incitement to imminent lawless action and is, therefore, protected speech.[32] Thus, government may not prevent homosexuals from speaking or participating in the forum of ideas solely because of the content of their speech absent some compelling state interest.[33]

At many universities, homosexual-student service organizations have received university recognition and the benefit of school-run facilities enjoyed by other recognized groups. It has been held that a state-run university may not constitutionally reject a student organization whose fundamental purpose is to provide a forum for the discussion of homosexuality. That the presence of such a group may make homosexual behavior more prevalent on campus is not enough, the courts say, to justify a prior restraint on the students' constitutional rights to freedom of association.[34]

A more controversial area concerns the First Amendment rights of homosexual teachers in public schools.[35] It is generally recognized that an adverse employment action is permissible if the controversial speech either falls outside First Amendment protection or implicates the employee's fitness to perform his or her assigned duties. In *National Gay Task Force v. Board of Education*,[36] the Tenth Circuit Court of Appeals held unconstitutional an Oklahoma statute that permitted public schools to fire teachers for "advocating, soliciting, imposing, encouraging or promoting public or private homosexual activity in a manner that creates a substantial risk that such conduct will come to the attention of school children or school employees."[37] The U.S. Supreme Court, in a 4–4 decision with no written opinion, upheld the Tenth Circuit's ruling.[38] That part of the Tenth Circuit's ruling that upheld another part of the Oklahoma statute under which a teacher could be dismissed for public homosexual activity was not appealed and was not before the Supreme Court.[39] The Supreme Court's decision, because it was a tie vote, does not serve as a precedent for other cases, but it is final in the six states (Colorado, Kansas, New Mexico, Utah, Wyoming, and Oklahoma) within the Tenth Circuit. There are, however, no similar cases pending, as Oklahoma had the only such law in the nation. The chief counsel for the National Gay Task Force commented that despite the absence of a formal opinion, the Supreme Court's ruling was "a benchmark of the progress of the gay rights movement."[40] Be that as it may, given the growing concern over the protection of schoolchildren, the case aroused considerable public controversy and ended in a split vote. Discrimination against homosexual teachers will no doubt continue; surveys of public opinion indicate that the majority of people favor excluding homosexuals from the teaching profession.[41]

The arguments involving homosexual teachers are akin to the child custody or visitation cases where homosexuality (implicitly or expressly) often raises a presumption of unfitness or improper influence. Some courts have allowed homosexuals to have custody or visitation only if they limit their behavior in certain ways.[42] Most children of homosexuals are ashamed of their parent's homosexuality, just as they are ashamed of other aberrations. Although some research shows that most children of homosexuals become heterosexual adults, this is not accomplished without a price.[43]

Homosexuals have also battled for acceptance in the media. In general, in the absence of any state action, the choice of material that goes into a newspaper is left solely to the editor's discretion. Much less so today than previously, many newspapers reject advertisements that are deemed offensive or not fit for family consumption. In one case a homosexual-students' rights organization sought to require publication of a proposed organizational meeting in the student-run campus newspaper. The court refused to compel publication of the advertisement because no state action was found where the university officials exercised no control over what was published and the editor was elected by the students.[44]

In the broadcasting media, the Federal Communications Commission compels every broadcast licensee to ascertain the "problems, needs and interests" of its community and to design informational programming to meet these needs. Such needs are determined through polling the public and interviewing representative leaders of significant groups within the community.[45] Homosexual rights leaders contend that, given the number of homosexuals in the general population (estimates range from 5 percent to 10 percent of males, and from 2 percent to 5 percent of females), they are not properly represented on television. These concerns for a right of access to the media are still in conflict with the discretionary powers of corporate broadcasters.

Today there are homosexual tabloids given away free in just about every city, and the pages are filled with advertisements directed at the homosexual community. A Gay Financial Network sells financial services products that recognize the distinct needs of the gay and lesbian community. It publishes a top-fifty list of powerful and gay-friendly corporations. The gay and lesbian community is estimated to have over $800 billion in assets; 65 percent of gay men and lesbians have completed college, and they are not necessarily raising families so their disposable income is greater. The organizing of gays has made it good business to appeal to the homosexual market.[46]

Homosexual organizations have had difficulty in attaining the ultimate symbol of acceptance: tax-exempt status. In general, the Internal Revenue Service (IRS) has denied the applications of homosexual organizations seeking tax-exempt status. Under the Internal Revenue Code, in order to enjoy tax-exempt and tax-deductible status, an organization must generally be operated for one or more of the following purposes: religious, charitable, scientific, public safety, literary, or educational, or for the prevention of cruelty to children or animals. Such organizations are prohibited from carrying on propaganda or attempting to influence legislation. Any such group engaged in "advocacy" of a position must present a "full and fair exposition of the issues" in order to maintain the exemption.[47]

A ruling by the Internal Revenue Service sets out a standard for when a nonprofit homosexual rights organization meets the educational organization standards, to wit, a group that is formed to educate the public about homosexuality in order to foster an understanding and tolerance of homosexuals and their problems, and qualifies for an exemption under section 501(c)(3) of the Internal Revenue Code.[48] This ruling suggests that a somewhat elaborate factual basis must be demonstrated concerning the organization's educational activities before the tax-exempt status will be granted. Moreover, the ruling emphasizes that groups that advocate or seek to convince people that they should or should not become homosexuals will not be granted tax-exempt status.[49]

With public opinion polls showing Americans becoming more accepting of gays in the workplace, the military may be one of the last major areas of gay intolerance remaining in society. When President Clinton tried to lift the ban on gay service members in 1993, he faced a near-rebellion from the joint chiefs of staff and resounding defeat in Congress. "Don't ask, don't tell" was the compromise that was designed to permit gays to serve without fear of harassment or expulsion as long as they kept their orientation to themselves.[50] Anthropologist Lionel Tiger postulates that the military recruiting crisis is due to the presence of homosexuals and women in the military—it is no longer macho to be in the military.[51]

Is Homosexuality Contagious?

Restrictions on teachers, media access, and other publicity about homosexuality are rooted in the idea that homosexuality is contagious, and should be contained. Are such fears warranted? Is homosexuality contagious? In a sense, yes. All people are capable of homosexual behavior, though not all have the motivation for it. An individual's personality or behavior is formed, or deformed, by surrounding societal norms and pressures. For example, in the days of the Soviet Union, threats persuaded youngsters to switch to the right hand for important tasks such as writing. In many societies, left-handers, like homosexuals, have been considered somewhat odd, deceitful, or even evil. As a result, there are few left-handers in such societies. When it is all right to be left-handed, there are more left-handers. In the same sense, when it is not considered queer to be homosexual, their population increases. When the barriers are down, more people go over to "the other side," as homosexuality is called in some countries. People are tri-sexual: they will try anything. Indeed, the mere description of a condition can make it contagious, be it homosexuality or acrotomophilia (a sexual attraction to amputees).[52]

Jean O'Leary, co–executive director of the National Gay Task Force, conceded that the antihomosexual forces are probably quite right in one respect: "If children understand that one can be a happy and functioning homosexual, perhaps with a beloved teacher as an example, there will be more homosexuals."[53] In a case where homosexuals sought recognition as a student organization on campus, it was argued that formal recognition by the university would tend to "perpetuate" or "expand" homosexual behavior and cause latent homosexuals to become overt homosexuals.[54]

In marked contrast to the United States and other Western countries, there were few overt homosexuals in the Soviet Union. In every society some things are assumed to be good, and other things are assumed to be bad. In this system of images, the homosexual in the Soviet Union was perceived as evil incarnate. That country uniformly enforced the law against homosexuality with a heavy hand (five years in a Gulag prison camp).[55] Actually, though, it is the stigma associated with homosexuality, far more than the criminal penalty itself, that deterred homosexuality. It was an utter disgrace to be homosexual in the Soviet Union. It was such a dirty word that no one wanted even to hear it mentioned.[56]

What causes a person to be gay, straight, or bisexual? Homosexual activity is sometimes explained as "compulsive activity," that is, activity that is beyond free choice. Others claim that it is the outcome of a deliberate choice motivated by curiosity, opportunity, or caring for another person of the same sex. Quite often, homosexuality is based more on dependency than on sexuality.[57] Some say that physiological factors, such as sex hormone levels, are at the root of homosexuality. Still others claim that homosexuality begins in the home. In either event, it is asserted that sexual orientation is established at a young age, by three or four, before children enter school. In any case, the propensity is aided or averted by the social matrix. The more negative the stigma associated with certain behavior, the less likely people are to engage in such behavior.[58]

Homophobia

Having been identifiably homosexual for twenty years or more, Michael Lassell spent a good deal of time and energy attempting to root out exactly what it is about homosexuals that some heterosexuals hate so much. Unable to figure it out, he instead in a book sets out twenty-five reasons to hate heterosexuals.[59] He and other homosexuals are celebrating, but homosexuality remains, in the judgment of many, the worst fate that could befall a person. In a study of children of the superrich, Dr. Roy R. Grinker Jr. found his patients to be bland, bored, and relatively uninvolved; in essence, he found them emotional zombies. Yet one father, whose daughter at the age of thirty had not one single friend or activity, responded to Dr. Grinker's findings, "Thank God, she's not a lesbian."[60] That, for him, would have been the real tragedy.

Even the use of the word *gay* by homosexuals to identify themselves is an irritant to others. "It saddens me as a word-lover that, within a period of 30 years, the fine old Anglo-Saxon word 'gay' has changed its meaning completely," writes "Philologos" in the *Forward*.[61] "'Gay,' used to be one of the most agreeable words in the language," the historian Arthur Schlesinger Jr. observed. "Its appropriation by a notably morose group is an act of piracy."[62] Such is the anxiety provoked by homosexuality that when homosexuals took the word to brighten their image, it dropped from general usage in its other senses. *Gay* as a description of an emotional state has become practically archaic. The chances of being misunderstood, or at the least of provoking amused smiles, are too great to risk using it that way. The new *Encarta World English Dictionary* now gives the primary definition of the word as "homosexual" and reserves "full of light-heartedness and merriment" for its secondary sense, but who would use it in that sense? The result is an impoverishment of the language.

Very few people, if any, would now describe a light-hearted evening as "a very gay time." In New England, the Adam Smith Fish Company, owners of the vessel *Gay Wind*, filed notice with the U.S. Coast Guard that they wanted to rename it. A group of citizens in Knoxville petitioned the city to change the name of its main thoroughfare, Gay Street. If that was unsuccessful, said the group, it would try to persuade homosexuals to give up describing themselves as *gay*. More than half of the residents of Gay Drive in West Seneca, New York, petitioned for a street name change, and their street became Fawn Trail. Baltimore retains Gay as the name of one of its main streets.

After reading an editorial on the Knoxville street question in the *Montgomery Advertiser*, Benjamin Smith Gay wrote a letter to the editor, "Having lived more than 73 years, bearing my name 'GAY,' I am deeply wounded by the fact that a group of divergents now call themselves Gays," he wrote. "I have not instituted litigation, but when such groups defile one's name, it is justified." When the British ambassador to Ireland was assassinated, his friend Sir Christopeher Soames, in a spontaneous radio tribute, said, "He was a gay person. . . ." Officials of the BBC were stunned and dropped the word when the tribute was rebroadcast. Other expressions used in the homosexual culture have also dropped out of general currency. When is the last time someone said, "I feel like a queen?" And now that *outing* is used to refer to the public exposure by gays of other gays who hitherto had kept their homosexuality private, the word *outing* is rarely used in its "trip to the countryside" sense.

Public policy concerning homosexuals has changed in recent years, to be sure, but the feelings of contempt and hostility continue to run deep and are still reflected in many of the laws and attitudes of contemporary society. Dr. Laura Schlessinger, talk radio's top-rated host, calls gays "deviants" who "undermine civilization." Not long ago the *New York Times* quoted Harvey Mansfield, a popular professor of government at Harvard, as declaring that homosexuality would undermine civilization if it was made respectable.[63] Critics call such statements irrational, given that in this day of overpopulation, unlike at the time of Moses, birth control is laudable, and homosexuals through history have made major contributions to the arts and sciences by sublimating their urge for creativity in those directions.

Still others object to the homosexual not out of fear for the threat to their sense of identity but out of impatience with the hostile and paranoid trends of these often "angry young men." Every group, every society, is concerned about its cohesiveness and does what it can to protect itself; sometimes the dangers are illusory, sometimes not. Behavior that overtly violates established modes and customs is a vehicle for unconscious aggressive impulses; the public display of homosexuality may involve destructive or self-destructive behavior. The psychic pain of homosexuality is dramatically portrayed in the film *Gods and Monsters* (1999), which depicts the life of James Whale, director of the famous Frankenstein movies. To deal with the existential pathos, many homosexuals commit suicide, or they drink quite heavily, and they often make a public nuisance of themselves. The late Dr. Karl A. Menninger, renowned as dean of American psychiatry, wrote:

> [T]he fact remains that as we see homosexuality clinically and officially it nearly always betrays its essentially aggressive nature. What passes for love under such circumstances is largely counterfeit. . . . No amount of euphemism and romanticism can disguise this. . . . This aggression is often thinly contained. Not only does it overflow in jealous rages or sadistic exploitations, but in backlashes at the despised and despising "normal" environment. Embittered individuals betray these feelings in various subtle or not so subtle ways.[64]

It may be said that a reaction is setting in to the celebration of homosexuality, just as two thousand years ago when the biblical injunction followed an earlier celebration. The noisy coming out of the closet may enhance self-esteem, but it is again provoking a backlash.[65] Truman Capote, who never had any qualms about his homosexuality, suggested a back-to-the-closet movement. But gays maintain that the celebration of homosexuality brought about the political, legal, and social gains the homosexual community has made, although meeting resistance, and they are unlikely to be reversed.

Homosexuality—at one time a sin, a crime, and a sickness—may one day be more tolerated and accepted by the heterosexual majority, though likely never wholeheartedly approved of nor afforded the status of heterosexuality. The centuries-old condemnation of homosexuality is not simply a by-product of the taboo in the Judeo-Christian religion. In non-Judeo-Christian countries, too, it is considered a shameful aberration, even in India, where people are quite at ease regarding androgynous qualities. In China, homosexuality has long been regarded as a transgression, as illustrated in Chen Kaige's film *Farewell My Concubine* (1993), which has widely been shown and reviewed in the United States.

In India, homosexuality is generally regarded as a shameful aberration, and it is also known to be fairly common in fact but condoned only if practiced in secret.[66] Psychoanalyst Bertram Schaffner on visits to India says that he was cautious whenever he raised the question of homosexuality, since he knew it to be a distasteful, controversial subject for Indians, but the men he was interviewing frequently raised the issue on their own. One even said to Dr. Schaffner, "There is no homosexuality in India, because two men cannot produce a child." Dr. Schaffner observed,

> As an analyst, I presume that conscious and unconscious conflicts around sexual orientation must inevitably arise for some Indian men. Perhaps the religious injunction to family formation and parenthood is a powerful factor in suppressing potential homosexual behavior. Indian men are able to carry simultaneous masculine and feminine identifications without worrying that this is pathological, or that this will automatically lead to homosexuality. Because Indians regard it as normal to have both masculine

and feminine attributes, in contrast to the Western insistence on two totally distinct gender identities, and "having to be real boys or real girls," androgyny must lead to gender disturbance.[67]

Homosexual Panic

The alleged ringleader in the beating death of college student Matthew Shepard in Wyoming sought to invoke a *homosexual panic* (now called *gay panic*) defense, claiming that he snapped after a sexual advance from Shepard. Then in Michigan Jonathan Schmitz claimed that he was humiliated by Scott Amedure, who said on a television taping that he had a crush on Schmitz. He went and got a gun and shot and killed Amedure. These highly publicized cases were just two of the many over the years where in criminal cases the defendant asserts he was provoked by some act or words of the homosexual victim.

Is there any merit at all to claims of gay panic? Is evidence of it warranted in a criminal trial? It does not constitute mental illness under an insanity defense, and it does not allow a defense of self-defense or provocation, as those defenses are based on the behavior expected of a "reasonable person." Those defenses are exculpatory.[68] But what about diminished capacity or diminished responsibility in jurisdictions that recognize that doctrine? The doctrine is recognized in Michigan (in the case of mental illness) but not in Wyoming. In diminished capacity or diminished responsibility jurisdictions evidence of impulsive behavior is admissible to reduce a crime from one requiring specific intent (first-degree murder) to one of general intent (second-degree murder or manslaughter). Schmitz was convicted of second-degree murder. And in all jurisdictions various factors about the defendant may be considered in sentencing.

Indeed, in certain individuals, the perceived threat of a homosexual assault may cause anxiety, rage, and fear and may lead to violent acts to ward off the humiliation to masculine pride.[69] Dr. Charles Socarides, clinical professor of psychiatry at New York's Albert Einstein School of Medicine, observed, "The person perceives [the threat of a homosexual assault] as not only physical injury, but a total destruction of one's identity and personality. The panic is an emergency reaction to the threat of shame, embarrassment and humiliation of the worst kind: destruction of self."[70]

Homosexual panic was first described in 1920 by Dr. Edward Kempf on the basis of a study of seventeen individuals who exhibited the panic. Just seeing a homosexual, much less being approached sexually, was found to cause anxiety, sometimes panic, in individuals precariously balanced. A defense of a fragile ego is called *psychological defensiveness*. Some can simply walk away from a sexual advance, but others are stirred beyond control. Shepard's attackers were trying to kill something more than Shepard, something that threatened their equilibrium.

The homosexual reminds us of our struggle for identity, and how tenuous that hold is. The mixed-up identity of the homosexual used to be noted by the sobriquet "tutti-fruitti," later shortened to "fruit." The homosexual's perceived mixed-up identity stirs anxiety, to a greater or lesser degree, and the anxiety is compounded by the culture. Challenging a person's sexuality is usually more disruptive to one's equilibrium than religious or racial insults. That is the reason for homophobia, though there are other reasons as well for bias against gays.[71]

An intriguing incident underscoring the centrality of belief in one's identity is contained in M. Rokeach's book *The Three Christs of Ypsilanti*.[72] Rokeach was a psychologist at Ypsilanti State Hospital at the time of the writing of the book. One evening Rokeach, to put a stop to a quarrel between his two young daughters, addressed each by the other's name. The quarrel was immediately forgotten in the delight of what the girls interpreted as a new game. Shortly thereafter, however, the younger daughter became somewhat uncertain about whether they still were playing and asked for reassurance, "Daddy, this is a game isn't it?" "No," he replied, "it's for real." They played on a bit longer, but soon both girls became disturbed and apprehensive. Then they pleaded with their father to stop, which he did.

In this incident, which took less than ten minutes, the father violated his children's belief in their own identities. For the first time in their lives, something had led them to experience serious doubts about a fact they had previously taken for granted, and this sent both of them into a panic reaction. The stimulus that evoked it seemed on the surface trivial enough—it involved nothing more than changing a single word, their name—but this word represented the most succinct summary of many beliefs, all of which together make up one's sense of identity. To have challenged "who I am" is upsetting.

Gay activists charge that the gay panic defense is designed to use antigay prejudice to win sympathy for defendants. The strategy is simple—the crime victim is the criminal, the defendant is his victim. "All that matters is that you create a foothold, doctrinally, for lawyers to tell the stories about virtuous outlaws and vicious victims," it is said.[73] The introduction of evidence of gay panic, or the attempt to introduce it, has become increasingly popular in murder trials, a fact alarming to gay activists. "What's going on here," says Evan Wolfson, staff attorney for Lambda Legal Defense and Educational Fund, "is people relying on or playing to a jury's recoil and horror at the thought of homosexual sex, so much so that they stop seeing the victim as a human and, rather, see the victim as a predator."[74] The gay community seeks to exclude all evidence of the victim's homosexuality or the offender's alleged gay panic, yet ironically, they seek the passage of so-called hate laws that would draw attention to the homosexuality of the victim.[75]

In his book *Rough News, Daring Views*,[76] the late Jim Kepner reports on cases, notably during the 1950s, when the theory of homosexual panic was resorted to as a defense. In the 1980s, it was urged by a defendant in a Louisiana murder trial, who claimed that when the victim touched his leg, it unleashed his "excessive hostility toward and fear of homosexuals." It was urged as a defense in Minneapolis in 1988 by a defendant who claimed his "revulsion from the deceased's homosexual advances elicited a heat-of-passion response." In 1989 in Pennsylvania, a defendant who shot two women who were strangers to him in a campground, reloading his .22-caliber rifle eight times, claimed his "personal abhorrence of lesbians and his surreptitious observation of two women making love" provoked homosexual panic. The defenses in all of these cases proved unsuccessful, but in Toronto, in 1992, a nineteen-year-old was acquitted of fatally stabbing his boss, claiming he was both in fear for his life and operating out of homosexual panic.[77]

In a 1989 California case, *People v. Huie*,[78] the defendant, charged with murder, claimed that the victim had made a sexual advance toward him, and sought to introduce evidence that the alleged advance triggered a violent "pseudohomosexual panic." The trial court excluded the defense. On appeal, defense counsel argued that his experts were not going to testify "that the defendant at the time of this alleged incident was suffering from any mental disease or disorder, defect or ill-ness," but that they were going to address events in his childhood that constituted a "compelling trauma" ostensibly relevant to the formation of the necessary crim-inal intent. He contended that the expert testimony would show that the defendant "actually lacked the mental state necessary to support the charged offense of mur-der" as a result of childhood events that bore "directly upon his state of mind at the time of the incident." But because the California Penal Code excluded evidence of mental condition except where it reveals a mental disease, defect, or disorder, the trial court's exclusion of the evidence was upheld.

Reparative Therapy

Psychiatrist Richard Isay, an avowed homosexual, claims that it would be mal-practice to convert a homosexual patient into a heterosexual person, as "it would create psychopathology."[79] Others are of the same view. "Reparative therapy raises serious ethical concerns for those who practice it and for the psychiatric profession as a whole," writes psychiatrist Jack Drescher.[80] Freud believed (and many of his early disciples agreed with him) that the object of psychoanalysis should not be the "cure" of homosexuality (which he thought was impossible anyway) but rather, as he said in a letter to an American mother distressed by the homosexuality of her son, to help the homosexual find harmony, peace of mind, and full efficiency.[81] In *Three Essays,* Freud declared that heterosexual intercourse with a loved partner was the ultimate sexual goal.[82]

In 2000, the board of trustees of the American Psychiatric Association agreed to strengthen and expand the APA's 1998 position statement on reparative, or con-version, therapies. The amended statement is designed to clarify many of the re-lated issues for both the general public and professionals. The statement reiterates the APA's position that homosexuality is not a mental illness and emphasizes that to classify it as such stems from no scientific evidence but rather "from efforts to discredit growing social acceptance of homosexuality as a normal variant of human sexuality." Moral and political issues have obscured science, the statement cau-tioned. The amended statement strengthened the APA's stance that "there are no scientifically rigorous outcome studies to determine either the actual efficacy or harm of 'reparative' treatments." What literature does exist on the topic "consists of anecdotal reports of individuals who have claimed to change and then later recanted those claims," the statement noted, and "actively stigmatizes homosex-uality."

The statement emphasized that the risks of undergoing therapies aimed at changing sexual orientation are not inconsequential and can include "depression, anxiety, and self-destructive behavior, since therapist alignment with societal prej-udices against homosexuality may reinforce self-hatred already experienced by the patient." These conversion therapies inevitably fail to inform the patient that he or she "might achieve happiness and satisfying interpersonal relationships as a gay man or lesbian," the statement noted.

The statement added a warning to therapists against influencing the course of therapy "either coercively or through subtle influence." Because of an absence of evidence of efficacy after forty years of studies on the topic, the statement rec-ommended that "ethical practitioners refrain from attempts to change individuals' sexual orientation, keeping in mind the medical dictum to 'First, do no harm.'"[83]

Moreover, it is argued, the claim that homosexuality can be "cured" or "repaired" repathologizes homosexuality.[84] According to some psychiatrists, there is evidence that attempts to change sexual orientation through reparative therapy frequently lead to emotional distress, depression, and suicidality.[85]

In support of reparative therapy, a number of former homosexuals who claimed to have converted to heterosexuality as a result of psychotherapy protested at the May 1999 annual meeting of the American Psychiatric Association, urging the association to reintroduce homosexuality in its manual of mental disorders, saying that it would promote treatment and would caution against the gay lifestyle. The organization NARTH (National Association for Research and Therapy of Homosexuality) maintains that homosexuality is a treatable developmental disorder. The organization, founded in 1992 by Drs. Charles Socarides, Benjamin Kaufman, and Joseph Nicolosi, has grown to over nine hundred mental health professionals and concerned lay people. Gay groups have disrupted conventions or pressured hotels into canceling meetings of NARTH and also of the Rev. Louis Sheldon's Traditional Values Coalition. Gay groups also campaigned to cancel Dr. Laura Schlessinger's TV show.[86]

At the May 2000 annual meeting of the APA in Chicago, a panel that planned to discuss whether sexual preference can be changed through therapy was cancelled after two psychiatrists withdrew, saying that the subject was too politically charged for a scientific meeting. The cancellation sparked a protest by a group of self-described former homosexuals who say reorientation therapy can work. They carried placards, "Gays and Lesbians can change . . . It's Possible!"[87]

Then, at the May 2001 annual meeting of the APA in New Orleans, Dr. Robert Spitzer, who had spearheaded the move in 1973 to remove homosexuality from the *DSM*, stated that "some people can change from gay to straight, and we ought to acknowledge that." He was prompted to undertake a study on witnessing the demonstrators at the 1999 meeting who claimed to have shifted from gay to straight. The study was met with a barrage of media publicity as well as critiques. Based on telephone interviews with two hundred men and women who had undergone help to change their sexual orientation, Spitzer said 66 percent of the men and 44 percent of the women had maintained "good heterosexual functioning." Spitzer conceded that the subjects were "unusually religious" and were not necessarily representative of most gays in the United States.[88] It was not noted but it has long been assumed that, among men, the insertor (one taking the male position) in the sexual encounter is more likely to be a better candidate than the insertee for reparative therapy. In undertaking reparative or conversion therapy, pressure from family or society does not vitiate the "voluntary" requirement for an informed consent, but information about the risks of treatment is problematical.

Prior to 1974, clinicians who were behaviorally oriented conducted research to change sexual orientation utilizing deconditioning methods with motivated homosexual patients. Preliminary results indicated some success but were not conclusive. Following the 1974 APA administrative decision, research in this area virtually ceased. Nonscientific professional and personal attitudes, political concerns, and fear of censure on ethical grounds quashed scientific inquiry and research. Instead emotionalism and polemical discussions center on whether it is right to offer strongly motivated homosexual patients an opportunity to change their sexual orientation rather than whether it is possible or beneficial.

Creatures of every species have a drive to reproduce—that is the usual course

421

of nature, and when the sex drive is diverted from its natural object onto something else, precluding the possibility of procreation, this suggests a "biological error," or so says Laura Schlessinger, who holds a doctorate in physiology. Whether it should be considered a sin, whether it should be considered a mental illness, and whether it is amenable to change remain controversial.

Notes

1. While acknowledging this preference, the reader should note that the term *homosexual* will be used throughout this text to avoid the cumbersome repetition of the phrase "gay male and lesbian."

2. The struggle to build a gay rights movement in the United States is depicted in D. Clendinen & A. Nagourney, *Out for Good* (New York: Simon & Schuster, 1999).

3. Price writes: "The 20th century brought the gradual dawning of the realization that there's nothing wrong with being gay, that you can't fix what ain't broken. And with that realization came the understanding that what needed fixing was and is society's prejudice. Gay people began coming out the closet—first in a courageous trickle, now in a courageous torrent—to challenge the myths and lies that have triggered beatings, lobotomies, castration, excommunication, firings, murders, ostracism, hatred and self-hatred." D. Price, "Gay Pride Transforms 20th Century," *Detroit News,* Dec. 20, 1999, p. 13. Deb Price's column was (and is) unique in a family newspaper and began in the *Detroit News,* a once conservative paper until taken over by Gannett. See also J. Murdoch & D. Price, *Courting Justice: Gay Men and Lesbians v. The Supreme Court* (New York: Basic Books, 2001).

No longer unique are Pride Scholarship funds created at universities for gay and lesbian students (also available to bisexual and transgendered students). J. S. Cohen, "Gay Scholarship Set Up at MSU," *Detroit News,* Feb. 4, 2000, p. C-1. At one time so-called pink money from the gay community to support a political candidate was viewed as radioactive. When Michael Dukakis ran for president, he refused an offer from gay leaders to raise $1 million for his campaign. Now, however, gay money has come out of the closet in support of political candidates.

4. Dr. Ehrenstein, *Open Secret* (New York: Harper Collins, 2000), p. 50. See also K. Mason "Walk This Way," *Out,* Sept. 1993, p. 1.

5. Isa. 3:9.

6. See R. Brain, *Friends and Lovers* (New York: Basic Books, 1976), pp. 65–67.

7. See J. Marmor (ed.), *Homosexual Behavior: A Modern Reappraisal* (New York: Basic Books, 1980); R. Slovenko, "A Panoramic View: Sexual Behavior and the Law," in R. Slovenko (ed.), *Sexual Behavior and the Law* (Springfield, Ill.: Thomas, 1965), p. 81. For example, Oklahoma's statute provides: "Every person who is guilty of the detestable and abominable crime against nature, committed with mankind or with a beast, is punishable by imprisonment in the penitentiary for a period not more than twenty (20) years." Okla. Stat. Ann., tit. 21, sec. 886 (West 2000). The United States Supreme Court upheld a similar Florida statute against a constitutional challenge of being void for vagueness, saying, in effect, that the meaning of the term "crime against nature" is commonly known. Wainwright v. Stone, 414 U.S. 21 (1973).

8. An English statute of 1533 made "buggery" punishable by death. 25 Henry VIII, ch. 6. The "crime against nature" statutes had their origin in this statute and in early Christian writings.

9. See R. Slovenko, supra note 7, at p. 81.

10. Noel Pemberton Billing, a demagogic Tory MP of the extreme right, said of Oscar Wilde, "I think he had a diabolical influence on everyone he met. I think he is the greatest force of evil that has appeared in Europe during the last 350 years. He was the agent of the devil in every possible way. He was a man whose sole object in life was to attack and to sneer at virtue, and to undermine it in every way by every possible means, sexually and otherwise." C. Hitchens, "Lord Trouble," *N.Y. Review of Books,* Sept. 21, 2000, p. 26. See also B. Belford, *Oscar Wilde: A Certain Genius* (New York: Random House, 2000); A. Rowse, *Homosexuals in History: A Study of Ambivalence in Society, Literature and the Arts* (New York: Macmillan, 1977), pp. 164–69.

11. See State v. Mortimer, 105 Ariz. 472, 467 P.2d 60 (1970). At the present time in England, the organization Outrage! is pressing for the legalization of gay sex in saunas, public lavatories, and "cruising areas." It succeeded in obtaining legislation lowering the age of consent for male homosexuals from eighteen to sixteen, bringing the age of consent into line with the law for heterosexuals. Tony Blair, the prime minister, seeks to repeal legislation that bans local authorities from promoting homosexuality in schools. G. Jones, "Legalize Gay Sex in Public Lavatories, Says Outrage," *Weekly Telegraph*, Mar. 2000, no. 447, p. 8.

12. See State v. Trejo, 83 N.M. 511, 494 P.2d 173 (Ct. App. 1972). At the present time, of the eighteen states that still have sodomy laws on the books, five apply to same-sex-only, while thirteen and the military apply to everyone, straight or gay. With the U.S. Supreme Court declining to rule these laws unconstitutional, the focus has shifted to state legislatures and courts. During the 1990s, eight states repealed their sodomy laws, and others are on the verge of doing so.

13. See generally E. Boggan, M. Haft, C. Lister, J. Rupp, & T. Stoddard, *An ACLU Handbook: The Rights of Gay People* (New York: Avon Books, rev. ed. 1983); W. Barnett, *Sexual Freedom and the Constitution* (Albuquerque: University of New Mexico Press, 1973). For example, a discussion of cases involving gay people dancing together in public places may fail to note evidence that the parties were engaged in intimate fondling while on the dance floor, behavior which would have been illegal for heterosexuals as well. For an omission of this type, see *ACLU Handbook*, p. 78 (discussing Becker v. New York State Liquor Auth., 21 N.Y.2d 289, 234 N.E.2d 443, 287 N.Y.S.2d 400 (1967)).

14. I. Bieber et al., *Homosexuality* (New York: Basic Books, 1962).

15. It is reported that the sexual psychopath law was applied to "the passing of bad checks by a suspected homosexual," and that California's Atascadero State Hospital was known as "Dachau for Queers," and that in the 1960s the *New York Times* referred to homosexuals in Times Square as "promenading perverts." W. N. Eskridge, *Gaylaw: Challenging the Apartheid of the Closet* (Cambridge: Harvard University Press, 1999); reviewed in R. A. Posner, "Ask, Tell," *New Republic*, Oct. 11, 1999, p. 52.

16. A. Kinsey, W. Pomeroy, & C. Martin, *Sexual Behavior in the Human Male* (Philadelphia: W. B. Saunders, 1948).

17. In June 1950, the Senate bowed to mounting pressure and authorized an investigation into the employment of homosexuals and "other moral perverts" in government. In its December 1950 report the senators remarked that even one "sex pervert in a government agency tends to have a corrosive influence upon his fellow employees. These perverts will frequently attempt to entice normal individuals to engage in perverted practices. . . . One homosexual can pollute a Government office." S. Rep. No. 241, 81st Cong., 2d Sess. 3–5 (1950).

18. See S. Doc. No. 64, 85th Cong., 1st Sess. 239 (1957); Department of Defense Directive No. 5220 (1966); Note, "Government-Created Employment Disabilities of the Homosexual," *Harv. L. Rev.* 82 (1969): 1738, 1749; Note, "Security Clearance for Homosexuals," *Stan. L. Rev.* 25 (1973): 403.

19. *Star-Ledger* (Newark, N.J.), Jan. 20, 1985, at 45, col. 1.

20. American Psychiatric Association, *Diagnostic and Statistical Manual: Mental Disorders* (Washington, D.C.: Author, 1st ed. 1952), pp. 38–39.

21. Ibid. at p. 38.

22. American Psychiatric Association, *Diagnostic and Statistical Manual of Mental Disorders* (Washington, D.C.: Author, 2d ed. 1968).

23. The APA vote on homosexuality is widely mocked, but the APA sought to appease by coming up with a compromise. It decided not to include homosexuality among the paraphilias (sexual deviations) but wanting to legitimize the treatment of homosexuality, it created a category called *ego-dystonic homosexuality*, which covers those homosexuals for whom their sexual orientation is a persistent concern. American Psychiatric Association, *Diagnostic and Statistical Manual of Mental Disorders* (Washington, D.C.: Author, 3d ed. 1980). Individuals who are chronically distressed by their homosexuality can receive a diagnosis of ego-dystonic homosexuality under the rubric of Sexual Disorder Not Otherwise Specified. *DSM-IV*, sec. 302.9. To be consistent, however, none of the paraphilias should be considered a mental disorder when ego-syntonic. According to this logic, there would be no mental disorder in the case of a necrophiliac who is not distressed by it. "Distress" is not a factor in the *DSM*'s paraphilias; why is it a factor in homosexuality? The debate continues. See Group for

the Advancement of Psychiatry, *Homosexuality and the Mental Health Professions* (Mahwah, N.J.: Analytic Press, 2000).

24. R. Bayer, *Homosexuality and American Psychiatry, The Politics of Diagnosis* (New York: Basic Books, 1981), p. 3. See also R. Bayer & R. Spitzer, "Edited Correspondence on the Status of Homosexuality in DSM III," *J. Hist. Behav. Sc.* 18 (1982): 32.

25. J. K. Meyer, "Ego-Dystonic Homosexuality," in H. I. Kaplan & B. J. Sadock (eds.), *Comprehensive Textbook of Psychiatry* (Baltimore: Williams E. Wilkins, 4th ed. 1985), p. 1056. Dr. Harold Voth of the Menninger Foundation wrote, "It is my firm belief that the APA's position on homosexuality is doing enormous harm to our society. Furthermore, nowhere in *DSM-III* is a condition disqualified as a mental disorder if it is ego-syntonic. This provision makes us look like fools." H. Voth, Ltr., *Psychiatric News*, Mar. 18, 1983, p. 2. Dr. Stanley Lesse, editor of the *American Journal of Psychotherapy*, wrote in an editorial:

> The pronouncement of the Board (of the American Psychiatric Association) was in response to the lobbying techniques of organized homosexual groups.... The APA pronouncement will spew confusion in psychiatry and the allied professions not merely in terms of homosexuality but, as we have implied, in relation to other psychologic problems. We predict lobbying by many groups representing a variety of psychiatric ailments, and we very likely can predict additional ambivalent but destructive pronouncements. The APA through its Board of Trustees is also guilty of a broad social disservice.
>
> We previously expressed the view in [an] editorial that discrimination against homosexuals in business and in government should in most instances be eliminated as speedily as possible just as all legal restrictions on sexual acts between consenting adults should be eliminated. This would correct a grievous sociolegal injustice. However, the recent pronouncement by the APA Board of Trustees is not binding upon serious, thinking psychiatrists, psychotherapists, and social scientists who find its viewpoint an illogical step backwards into clinical confusion and denial.

S. Lesse, "To Be or Not to Be an Illness: That Is the Question of the Status of Homosexuality," *Am. J. Psychotherapy* 18 (1974): 1.

26. See R. Restak, "Psychiatry in America," *Wilson Q.* 7 (1983): 95, 119.

27. 42 U.S.C., sec. 12211(a).

28. In response to the decision in Society for Individual Rights, Inc. v. Hampton, 63 F.R.D. 399 (N.D.Cal. 1973), *aff'd*, 528 F.2d 905 (9th Cir. 1975), the Civil Service Commission issued a bulletin in December 1973, prohibiting those engaged in suitability evaluations from making a determination of unsuitability based solely on homosexual status or admission of homosexual acts. The Civil Service Regulations were amended in 1975 to reflect the Hampton opinion by deleting the word *immoral* from the list of reasons which may disqualify an applicant for a federal government position. See 5 C.F.R., sec. 731.202; Federal Personnel Manual Supplement 731–33 App. 2.

29. Also in 1999, in an event making headlines, President Clinton over Republican objections appointed James Hormel, a San Francisco philanthropist and heir to a meat-packing fortune, as ambassador to Luxembourg, making him the nation's first openly gay envoy. On the same day Hillary Clinton participated in a private fund-raising dinner in New York for gay men and lesbians sponsored by the Democratic National Committee. The Senate majority leader, Trent Lott of Mississippi, who sought to block the appointment of Hormel, said homosexuals are sinners, like alcoholics or kleptomaniacs. K. Q. Seelye, "Clinton Appoints Gay Man as Ambassador as Congress Is Away," *New York Times*, June 5, 1999, p. 26. By and large, politicians now campaigning for office seek the support and donations of gays. See A. Sullivan, "Not a Straight Story," *New York Times Magazine*, Dec. 12, 1999, p. 64.

30. California law (eff. Jan. 1, 2002) allows partners who register with the Secretary of State the ability to make medical decisions for incapacitated partners, sue for wrongful death, adopt a partner's child, will property to a partner, use sick leave to care for a partner or a partner's children, be exempt from state income tax on a partner's health benefits, leave a job to relocate with a partner without losing unemployment benefits, or file for disability benefits on behalf of a seriously ill or incapacitated partner.

In a recent ruling, the Massachusetts Supreme Judicial Court held that gays who help their partners raise a child have visitation rights after the couples break up. The court ruled in the case of a lesbian who helped her partner raise her son, saying the woman was de facto a parent of the child. "It is to be expected that children of nontraditional families, like other children, form parent relationships with both parents, whether those parents are legal or de facto," Justice Ruther Adrams wrote for the four-member majority. The court acknowledged that the best interests standard is "somewhat amorphous." Gay and lesbian parents can adopt in Massachusetts, which would make them legal parents, but in the case considered by the court, the nonbiological parent had not adopted the child. Justice Charles Fried, in a strongly worded dissent, said allowing visitation "was wholly without warrant in statute, precedent or any known principle." He also charged that the court was taking an unwarranted step toward endorsing same-sex marriages, calling the decision "judicial lawmaking." E.N.O. v. L.M.M., SJC-07878, June 29, 1999.

31. Baker v. State, 744 A.2d 864 (Vt. 1999).

32. See *ACLU Handbook,* supra note 13, p. 9.

33. See Pickering v. Board of Educ., 391 U.S. 563 (1968).

34. See Gay Student Servs. v. Texas A & M Univ., 737 F.2d 1317 (5th Cir. 1984), *appeal dismissed,* 471 U.S. 1001 (1985); Gay Lib v. University of Missouri, 558 F.2d 848 (8th Cir. 1977), *cert. denied,* 434 U.S. 1080 (1978); Gay Alliance of Students v. Matthews, 544 F.2d 162 (4th Cir. 1976); Gay Students Org. v. Bonner, 509 F.2d 652 (1st Cir. 1974).

35. See, e.g., Acanfora v. Board of Educ., 359 F.Supp. 843 (D.Md. 1973), *aff'd on other grounds,* 491 F.2d 498 (4th Cir.), *cert. denied,* 419 U.S. 836 (1974). Acanfora was transferred from his teaching position to an administrative position when school officials discovered he was a homosexual. The district court held that Acanfora was wrongfully transferred, but denied relief because of his subsequent publicizing of the incident in the media. Id. at 499. The Fourth Circuit, however, held that Acanfora's speech was protected by the First Amendment, but nonetheless affirmed the court's holding because Acanfora had purposefully withheld information concerning his activities in a homosexual organization in his employment application. Id. at 504.

In response to the ruling of the U.S. Supreme court on curbing sexual harassment by public school students, gay writer Deb Price wrote in a syndicated column, "Students must be taught that there's nothing wrong with being gay." *Detroit News,* June 1, 1999, p. 11. In reply, a letter writer said ("Immoral Lessons" (ltr.), *Detroit News,* June 8, 1999, p. 8):

> How could teachers possibly teach this when they know that the homosexual lifestyle is extremely dangerous, even deadly, rather than normal and desirable? Statistics show clearly that the median age of death for homosexuals is more than 30 years less than that of married men in the United States. How could teachers possibly teach this if they are convinced that the Bible clearly teaches that homosexuality is morally wrong and not what God intends for individuals or society? Let's do all we can to keep our schools free of sexual harassment. But let's not allow homosexual activists to infiltrate schools with programs designed to indoctrinate children to accept and engage in homosexual behavior.

36. 729 F.2d 1270 (10th Cir. 1984), *aff'd mem. by an equally divided court,* 470 U.S. 903 (1985).

37. Okla. Stat., tit. 70, sec. 6–103–15(A)(2) (1972) (repealed 1990). The Oklahoma statute was partly inspired by the antihomosexual activist, and former Miss Oklahoma, Anita Bryant. Bryant had spoken before the Oklahoma legislature in 1978, denouncing homosexual teachers and claiming that as role models, homosexual teachers led young people into homosexuality. *New York Times,* Mar. 27, 1985, p. 9.

38. Board of Education v. National Gay Task Force, 470 U.S. 903 (1985).

39. National Gay Task Force v. Board of Education, 729 F.2d at 1273.

40. *New York Times,* Mar. 27, 1985, p. 9 (quoting Leonard Graff).

41. J. Dressler, "Gay Teachers: A Disesteemed Minority in an Overly Esteemed Profession," *Rut. Cam. L.J.* 9 (1978): 399, 402 n. 7.

42. See, e.g., Nadler v. Superior Court, 255 Cal. App.2d 523, 63 Cal. Rptr. 352 (1967) (court ordered that another adult be present during a lesbian mother's visitation). See generally B. F. Armanno, "The Lesbian Mother: Her Right to Child Custody," *Golden Gate L. Rev.* 4 (1973): 1; B. S. Harris, "Lesbian Mother Child Custody: Legal and Psychiatric Aspects," *Bull. Am. Acad. Psychaitry & Law* 5 (1977): 75; M. Riley, "The Avowed Lesbian Mother and Her Right to Child

Custody: A Constitutional Challenge That Can No Longer Be Denied," *San Diego L. Rev.* 12 (1975): 799.

43. See C. Chase (ed.), *Queer 13: Lesbian and Gay Writers Recall Seventh Grade* (New York: Weisbach Books, 1998).

44. The causative influence of parents may be outweighed by broader exposure to the values that society accords to sex roles. See W. Gadpaille, "Sexual Identity Problems in Children and Adolescents," in H. Leif (ed.), *Sexual Problems in Medical Practice* (Chicago: American Medical Assn., 1981), p. 243. See generally R. Stoller, *Sex and Gender: On the Development of Masculinity and Femininity* (New York: Science House, 1968).

45. See T. I. Emerson, "Legal Foundations of the Right to Know," *Wash. U.L.Q.* 1976: 1, 10–11.

46. A. Michaels, "Finances of Gays and Lesbians Prove to Be a Profitable Niche," *Financial Times*, Dec. 3, 1999, p. 8.

47. See Big Mama Rag v. United States, 631 F.2d 1030, 1036 (D.C. Cir. 1980). *Big Mama Rag*, a radical feminist newspaper that the IRS viewed as promoting lesbianism, was denied tax-exempt status by the IRS on the grounds that it did not qualify as "educational" within the IRS guidelines. The court reversed the IRS's denial of tax-exempt status, holding that the definition of *education* was too vague and gave the IRS too much discretion.

48. Rev. Rul. 78-305, 1978-2 C.B. 172.

49. Ibid. at 173.

50. See J. E. Halley, *Don't: A Reader's Guide to the Military's Anti-Gay Policy* (Durham, N.C.: Duke University Press, 1999); C. Moskos, "Don't Knock 'Don't Ask, Don't Tell,'" *Wall Street Journal*, Dec. 16, 1999, p. 22; E. Schmitt, "How Is This Strategy Working? Don't Ask," *New York Times*, Dec. 19, 1999, sec. 4, p. 1.

51. Personal communication (Oct. 12, 1999). The venerable Judge Richard Posner of the Seventh Circuit Court of Appeals argues that the practical fact that homophobia exists in the military is a compelling reason to exclude gay people. L. MacFarquhar, "The Bench Burner," *New Yorker*, Dec. 10, 2001, p. 78. It is noted that of the four services, only the Marines have not experienced recruiting problems. It is the only branch of the military that has stood fast against the social culture on its military culture. It has refused to gender-integrate training or bow to the will of a politically correct agenda. See S. Gutmann, *"The Kinder, Gentler Military: Can America's Gender-Neutral Fighting Force Still Win Wars?"* (New York: Scribner, 2000), reviewed in F. Fukuyama, "GI Jane," *Commentary*, Feb. 2000, p. 56; C. Stewart & D. Forsmark, "Alienating Soldiers May Be Source of Military Recruiting Crisis," *Detroit News*, Dec. 9, 1999, p. 16.

52. See C. Elliot, "A New Way to Be Mad," *Atlantic Monthly*, Dec. 2000, p. 72.

53. *New York Post*, June 10, 1977, p. 29.

54. Gay Lib. v. University of Missouri, 558 F.2d 848, 851 n.7 (8th Cir. 1977).

55. The distinguished German historian Lothar Machtan claims that Adolf Hitler was homosexual, an assertion that is hardly new, but his book has attracted attention. L. Machtan, *The Hidden Hitler* (New York: Basic Books, 2001); excerpted in "The Gay Dictator," *Sunday Telegraph*, Oct. 7, 2001, p. 1. In a critical review, Dr. Walter Reich, a lecturer in psychiatry at Yale and former director of the U.S. Holocaust Memorial Museum, argues that Hitler's sexuality does not explain his crimes against humanity. W. Reich, "All the Führer's Men," *New York Times Book Review*, Dec. 16, 2001, p. 6. In the secret wartime report on Hitler, Dr. Walter C. Langer wrote, "The belief that Hitler is homosexual has probably arisen because he does show so many feminine characteristics. . . . It does seem that Hitler feels much more at ease with homosexuals than with normal persons, but this may be because they are all fundamentally social outcasts and consequently have a community of interests that tends to make them think and feel more less alike. In this connection it is interesting to note that homosexuals, too, frequently regard themselves as a special form of creation or as chosen ones whose destiny it is to initiate a new order." W. C. Langer, *The Mind of Adolph Hitler: The Secret Wartime Report* (New York: Basic Books, 1972), p. 174. Yet homosexuals were persecuted. The documentary film *Paragraph 175* relates the horror of the Nazi purge of homosexuals from the life of Germany. The German penal code enacted in 1871 provided, "An unnatural sex act committed between persons of male sex or by humans with animals is punishable by imprisonment; the loss of civil rights may also be imposed." This provision, expanded by the Nazis, remained law in West and East Germany until nearly the end of the

1960s. During the years of the Weimar Republic, between the end of World War I and the rise of Hitler, the law was rarely enforced, and the Berlin of the 1920s was called "a homosexual Eden." The film *Paragraph 175* is reviewed in L. van Gelder, "Condemned by the Nazis, but Not for Religion," *New York Times*, Sept. 13, 2000, p. B-5.

56. See L. Essig, *Queer in Russia* (Durham, N.C.: Duke University Press, 1999).

57. L. Ovesey, *Homosexuality and Pseudohomosexuality* (New York: Science House, 1969).

58. The belief that homosexuality is a matter of choice leads to negative attitudes toward gays and lesbians, while conversely, the belief that it is not a matter of choice leads to favorable attitudes. See S. LeVay, *Queer Science* (Cambridge: MIT Press, 1996).

59. *The Hard Way* (New York: Masquerade Books, 1995).

60. Address by Dr. Roy Grinker, 130th annual meeting of the American Psychiatric Association (May 3, 1977).

61. Philologos, "On Language: Purist or Permissive?" *Forward*, Oct. 15, 1999, p. 12.

62. Actually, in the nineteenth century, the word *gay* was applied to female licentiousness, from whence it may have gravitated toward its homosexual use. In the nineteenth century the "gay life" was prostitution, to "gay it" was to go with prostitutes, a "gay house" was a brothel where prostitutes known as "gay ladies" or "gay girls" could be found. R. W. Holder, *The Faber Dictionary of Euphemisms* (London: Faber & Faber, 1987). In the eighteenth century, the term was often used to refer to a man who was a habitual womanizer, as "he's a real gay Lothario," an expression in Nicholas Rowe's *The Fair Penitent* (1703). Nowadays, of course, *gay* almost always means "homosexual."

63. L. Richardson, "The Mentor Conservatives Turn to for Inspiration," *New York Times*, Oct. 16, 1999, p. 17.

64. K. A. Menninger, *The Vital Balance* (New York: Viking Press, 1963), p. 197.

65. See R. Brookhiser, "The Gay Moment," *National Review*, July 26, 1999, p. 42.

66. See W. D. O'Flaherty, *Women, Androgynes, and Other Mythical Beasts* (Chicago: University of Chicago Press, 1980), p. 88.

67. B. Schaffner, "Androgyny in Indian Culture: Psychoanalytic Implications," address at annual meeting of the American Academy of Psychoanalysis on January 8, 2000, in New York.

68. See J. Dressler, "When 'Heterosexual' Men Kill 'Homosexual' Men: Reflections on Provocation Law, Sexual Advances, and the 'Reasonable Man' Standard," *J. Crim. L. & Criminology* 85 (1995): 726; R. B. Mison, "Homophobia in Manslaughter: The Homosexual Advance as Insufficient Provocation," *Cal. L. Rev.* 80 (1992): 133.

69. The illustrations of the anxiety provoked by homosexuality are without limit. Lee Iacocca, formerly chairman of Chrysler and earlier with Ford, writes in his autobiography that Henry Ford ordered him to get rid of a certain executive because he was a "fag," "his pants are too tight," "he's a queer," "he's got an effeminate bearing." L. Iacocca, *Iacocca: An Autobiography* (New York: Bantam Books, 1984), pp. 98–99. In football, men dress up as gladiators, and their touching behinds is permissible, but men embracing or walking hand in hand raises eyebrows. M. Slade, "Displaying Affection in Public," *New York Times*, Dec. 17, 1984, p. 14.

Indeed, just calling someone a homosexual may draw gunfire. See "Remark about 'Gays' May Have Led to 4 Slayings" (Associated Press news release), *New York Times*, Dec. 19, 1984, p. 17. Killers of gays are unusually conflicted about their own sexual impulses, and the research documented in the PBS "Frontline: Assault on Gay America" (Feb. 15, 2000) is persuasive. Interviewed in prison, where they are serving life sentences for the 1999 murder of Billy Jack Gaither, a resident of a small town in Alabama, Steven Mullins and Charles Butler Jr. made it clear Gaither never touched them, but his sin, they said, was to "disrespect" them by assuming they would welcome gay sex.

A few years ago a man killed two coworkers and wounded four others because he thought that they were accusing him of being homosexual. He killed himself shortly after the rampage. There was no evidence that the victims even broached homosexual themes, suggesting the possibility that the assailant was delusional regarding his homosexual preoccupation. J. A. Silva, G. B. Leong, & R. Weinstock, "Homicidal Violence in an Ambulatory Public Job Setting: The Role of Delusional Thinking," *Am. J. For. Psychiatry* 21 (2000): 57; M. Gold & J. Cox, "Gunman Felt Mocked, Police Say Shooting Worker Yelled, 'I Am Not Gay!' During Rampage, According to Officials," *Los Angeles Times*, June 7, 1997, p. 1.

Lawsuits for defamation arising out of an imputation of homosexuality are legion. See, e.g., Nowark v. Maguire, 22 A.D.2d 901, 255 N.Y.S.2d 318 (1964); Buck v. Savage, 323 S.W.2d 363 (Tex. Civ. App. 1959); Hayes v. Smith, 832 P.2d 1022 (Colo. App. 1991). Nowadays, in trials in Texas, when asked on cross-examination about his expulsion from the American Psychiatric Association on account of his testimony in death penalty cases, Dr. James Grigson retorts, "And that's the very same organization that does not consider homosexuality to be a mental disorder." By that retort, his credibility seems to be enhanced among the jurors.

70. C. W. Socarides, *The Overt Homosexual* (New York: Grune & Stratton, 1968). Dr. Cecil Mynatt Jr., a state psychiatrist, recanted his testimony against Gerardo Valdez, sentenced to die for a 1989 killing. The psychiatrist said in an affidavit filed with an appeal that new information convinced him that Valdez was temporarily insane when he shot his victim. He said homosexual panic brought on paranoia in Valdez at the time of the shooting. J. Thomas, "Help for Mexican on Death Row," *New York Times*, Aug. 24, 2001, p. 12.

71. See R. M. Baird & S. E. Rosenbaum (eds.), *Hatred, Bigotry, and Prejudice* (Amherst, N.Y.: Prometheus Books, 1999); E. Young-Bruehl, *The Anatomy of Prejudice* (Cambridge: Harvard University Press, 1996), pp. 137–59; R. Slovenko, "Sexual Deviation: Response to an Adaptational Crisis," *U. Colo. L. Rev.* 40 (1968): 222.

72. M. Rokeach, *The Three Christs of Ypsilanti: A Psychological Study* (New York: Knopf, 1964).

73. D. Osborne, "Homosexual Panic," *Lesbian & Gay New York News*, Nov. 4, 1999, p. 4. See also C. Patton, " 'Gay Panic': A Specious Defense" (ltr.), *New York Times*, Nov. 4, 1999, p. 26.

74. Quoted in M. R. Keenan, " 'Homosexual Panic' Claims Put Gay Activists on the Defensive," *Detroit News*, Apr. 27, 1993, p. C-7.

75. Hate crime legislation sets out punishment based on motive rather than intention. Normally, the prosecutor has to prove the defendant acted with mens rea—that, for example, he acted intentionally, maliciously, or recklessly. In contrast, to prosecute a hate crime, the prosecutor must also prove *why* the defendant intended to harm. The problem of figuring out why is a can of worms. What if a mugger chooses to victimize disabled people not because of hate but because they are less likely to fight back? See R. Dooling, "Good Politics, Bad Law," *New York Times*, July 26, 1998, sec. 7, p. 22. Dooling is a lawyer whose most recent novel, *Brain Storm*, dramatizes a hate crime trial. See also F. M. Lawrence, *Punishing Hate: Bias Crimes under American Law* (Cambridge: Harvard University Press, 1999).

76. New York: Harrington Park Press, 1998.

77. See R. Slovenko, *Psychiatry and Criminal Culpability* (New York: Wiley, 1995), pp. 111–14.

78. San Francisco Super. C., No. 125603, Court of Appeals, 1st App., div. 5, No. A042962, 1989.

79. See R. A. Isay, *Becoming Gay: The Journey to Self-Acceptance* (New York: Pantheon, 1996); see also R. A. Isay, "Remove Gender Identity Disorder in DSM," *Psychiatric News*, Nov. 21, 1997, p. 9. For a reply, see H. M. Voth, "Dr. Isay's Proposal" (ltr.), *Psychiatric News*, Feb. 6, 1998, p. 14.

80. J. Drescher, "Reparative or Destructive?" *Clinical Psychiatric News*, Mar. 1998, p. 12. See also "APA Maintains Reparative Therapy Not Effective," *Psychiatric News*, Jan. 15, 1999, p. 1. Protests over reparative therapy appear in L. Faderman, *Odd Girls and Twilight Lovers* (New York: Columbia University Press, 1991), pp. 134–38. The 978-page book published in 1996 by the American Psychiatric Press, *Textbook of Homosexuality and Mental Health*, edited by Robert P. Cabaj and Terry S. Stein, starts from the belief that homosexuality is a normal variation of human sexuality and not mental illness. See also B. J. Cohler & R. M. Galatzer-Levy, *The Course of Gay and Lesbian Lives* (Chicago: University of Chicago Press, 2000); J. Drescher, *Psychoanalytic Therapy and the Gay Man* (Mahwah, N.J.: Analytic Press, 1998); T. Domenici & R. C. Lesser (eds.), *Disorienting Sexuality* (New York: Routledge, 1995).

81. Freud's therapeutic pessimism as well as his acknowledgment that many homosexuals, though arrested in their development, could derive pleasure from both love and work provides the context in which he wrote his compassionate and now famous "Letter to an American Mother" of 1935. He wrote:

> I gather from your letter that your son is a homosexual. I am most impressed by the fact that you do not mention this term yourself in your information about him.

May I question you, why you avoid it? Homosexuality is assuredly no advantage, but it is nothing to be ashamed of, no vice, no degradation, it cannot be classified as an illness; we consider it to be a variation of the sexual function produced by a certain arrest of sexual development. Many highly respectable individuals of ancient and modern times have been homosexuals, several of the greatest men among them (Plato, Michelangelo, Leonardo da Vinci, etc.). It is a great injustice to persecute homosexuality as a crime, and cruelty too. If you do not believe me, read the books of Havelock Ellis.

By asking me if I can help, you mean, I suppose, if I can abolish homosexuality and make normal heterosexuality take its place. The answer is, in a general way, we cannot promise to achieve it. In a certain number of cases we succeed in developing the blighted germs of heterosexual tendencies which are present in every homosexual, in the majority of cases it is no more possible. It is a question of the quality and the age of the individual. The result of treatment cannot be predicted.

What analysis can do for your son runs in a different line. If he is unhappy, neurotic, torn by conflicts, inhibited in his social life, analysis may bring him harmony, peace of mind, full efficiency whether he remains a homosexual or gets changed.

E. Jones, *The Life and Work of Sigmund Freud, The Last Phase: 1919–1930* (New York: Basic Books, 1957), vol. 3. See also P. Friedman, "Sexual Deviations," in S. Arieti (ed.), *American Handbook of Psychiatry* (New York: Basic Books, 1959), vol. 1, ch. 29, pp. 606–7.

In his first major work with regard to sexuality, "Three Essays on the Theory of Sexuality" (1905), Freud dismantled the connection between the sexual instinct and the object or aim. Hence, if there is no natural object and no natural aim to the instinct, then deviations from genital intercourse cannot be called perverse. But Freud defused this argument by using a Darwinian evolutionary model of psychosexual development that organized all human activity in relation to the survival of the species. By defining "normal" sexuality as procreative, sexuality was essentialized and homosexuality was pathologized. *Standard Edition* (London: Hogarth, 1953), vol. 7, pp. 123–245.

82. See W. Gaylin, *Talk Is Not Enough: How Psychotherapy Really Works* (New York: Little, Brown, 2000); adapted in "Nondirective Counseling or Advice?: Psychotherapy as Value Laden," *Hastings Center Report*, May–June 2000, p. 31.

83. "APA Stakes Out Positions on Controversial Therapies," *Psychiatric News*, Apr. 21, 2000, p. 45.

84. M. Kirby, "Psychiatry, Psychology, Law and Homosexuality: Uncomfortable Bedfellows," *Psychiatry, Psychology & Law* 7 (2000): 139.

85. See, e.g., D. W. Hicks, "Homosexuality" (ltr.), *Psychiatric News*, July 20, 2001, p.22.

86. J. Leo, "Watch What You Say," *U.S. News & World Report*, Mar. 20, 2000, p. 18.

87. P. Gorner, "Analysts Drop Gay Therapy Discussion," *Chicago Tribune*, May 18, 2000, p. 1.

88. E. Goode, "Scientist Says Study Shows Gay Change Is Possible," *New York Times*, May 9, 2001, p. 15.

PART V
Civil
Cases

20
Tort Liability of the Mentally Incompetent and Their Caretakers

The liability of the mentally ill has become a more frequent legal issue due to the increasing numbers of mentally ill in the community and limited community support systems, as well as the increase in litigation generally. The possibility of a lethal situation is now increased by the widespread use of guns or motor vehicles. The vast majority of tort claims for death or injury involve motor vehicle accidents.

Elements of a Tort

A *tort* is a civil or private wrong, based on the general principle that every act of a man that causes damage to legally protected interest of another obliges him, if at fault, to repair it. The key concepts in this principle are: *act, damage, causation,* and *fault.* Etymologically speaking, the word *tort* is derived from the Latin *tortus,* meaning "twisted" or "wrested aside." The metaphor is apparent: a tort is conduct that is twisted or crooked. The word *tort* is used in English as a general synonym for "wrong." Law Professor Leon Green described tort law as the "general law for the adjustment of the hurts that result from everyday activities of people."[1]

Tort law is said to have three major goals: (1) to deter harm-causing behavior, (2) to provide compensation to victims, and (3) to provide fairness or justice between the parties. Some scholars and courts have emphasized one goal to the near exclusion of the others. Some focus on the compensation goal, emphasizing the "social insurance" role of tort judgments. Others, by contrast, have emphasized deterrence as the primary goal of tort law, with compensation of the victim merely a detail, at least from an economic standpoint. But, by and large, courts, practitioners, and scholars routinely have recognized deterrence, compensation, and fairness all as proper goals of the tort system. All would agree that the right of citizens to bring suit for private wrongs, reinforced by widespread knowledge of that right, provides an important outlet for conflict that otherwise would break out into violence. An interesting recognition of this point appears in a federal district judge's comment that recent libel law has restricted the ability of public figures to collect damages to the point that they might have to "resort to fisticuffs or dueling" to get satisfaction.[2]

Act. The beginning point of tort liability is an act, or behavior. A person is not liable for his mere thoughts or for a failure to act (when there is no duty to act). An act is an essential element for liability. In tort as well as in criminal law, *act* is defined as a volitional movement or an "external manifestation of the actor's will." Thus, as the American Law Institute's *Restatement of Torts* illustrates, "a contraction of a person's muscles that is purely a reaction to some outside force, such as a knee jerk or the blinking of the eyelids in defense against an approaching missile, or the convulsive movements of an epileptic, are not acts of that person. So, too, movements of the body during sleep when the will is in abeyance are not acts." And so, too, if *A* pushes *B* against *C*, knocking *C* down and breaking his arm, *B* is not liable, since his act was not volitional.[3]

The definition of an *act* as "a voluntary bodily movement," favored in legal theory since John Austin, generates the problem of defining *voluntary*.[4] W. C. Fields, it may be recalled, quipped that his wife drove him to drink. There is general agreement that mental incapacity can compromise voluntariness. The factors that generally influence a clinician's assessment of voluntariness are the nature of the individual's experiential symptoms, the hypothesized causes of those symptoms, and the manner in which they are treated.[5] Acts performed under hypnosis are open to question as to whether they are involuntary. Hypnosis experts claim that it is impossible to make a subject perform an act "which he felt morally unable to do."[6]

As a general principle, one who is stricken by paralysis, has an epileptic seizure, is overcome by poisonous gas, or has lost consciousness under like circumstances is not held liable for what he does or fails to do. Violent behavior following a seizure may stem from an epileptic individual's misinterpretation of well-meant attempts by bystanders to protect him against the consequences of his confused conduct— and is usually characterized by a clouded consciousness, paranoid ideas, and hallucinations.[7]

Of automatism under the law it is said: "[I]f a person in a condition of complete automatism inflicted grievous injury, that would not be actionable."[8] The case for no liability rests largely upon the proposition that the defendant has done no act at all and thus cannot have committed any tort, intentional or otherwise. The result is consistent with the moral basis of tort liability but not with protecting innocent people from the aggression of others.

George Orwell in an essay, "Such, Such Were the Joys," wrote that in his boarding school days, bed-wetting was looked on as a disgusting crime that the child committed on purpose and for which the proper cure was a beating. Night after night he prayed fervently, "Please God, do not let me wet my bed! Oh, please God, do not let me wet my bed!"[9] In law, the bed-wetting would not be considered an "act," there being no volition or consciousness about it.

Damage. The concept of *damage* does not include injury to every known human interest but only to a legally protected interest. For example, alienation of affections or mental sufferings in various jurisdictions is not such an interest. In law, the terms *hurt, harm, injury,* and *damage* are used synonymously to refer to an invasion of a legally protected interest. The term *damages* (pl.) is also used to refer to the liability or compensation that the defendant tortfeasor must pay to repair the wrong.

Damages are generally divided into two categories under the law: special damages and general damages. Special damages are future and past medical expenses—hospital and custodial care, therapeutic costs—as well as the loss of earning capacity, for life. General damages are for past and future pain and suffering that the individual is going to experience, for life, and for past and future loss of ability to carry on and enjoy life's activities. Many states have placed caps on damages for pain and suffering. "How can you set damages?" The typical response is: "It's awfully difficult to determine. Law is not an exact science."

Causation. In order for there to be liability under the law of torts, there must be a causal relation or nexus between conduct and hurt. The famous ditty in *Poor Richard's Almanac* may be recalled:

> For want of a nail the shoe is lost,
> for want of a shoe the horse is lost,
> for want of a horse the rider is lost.
> For want of a rider the message is lost,
> for want of a message the battle is lost—
> the war is lost—the fatherland is lost.

As the theory called "sensitive dependence on initial conditions" (chaos, for short) would have it, tiny actions can have enormous unforeseeable consequences. In the culture of popular science, the idea is known as "the butterfly effect." Sometimes big changes follow from small events, and sometimes these changes can happen very quickly. A single sick person can start an epidemic of the flu, a few fare-beaters and graffiti can fuel a subway crime wave, or a satisfied customer can fill the empty tables of a new restaurant.[10] When the effect seems far out of proportion to the cause, it is not deemed a proximate cause in law. The horseman who had failed to inspect the hooves on his mare was a link in the causal chain that led to the loss of the fatherland, but it would not be deemed the *proximate cause* required in law. And, of course, correlation is not causation (a joke making the rounds is that the four states that carry out the death penalty by electrocution also happen to have stellar college football teams).

The defendant's act or omission (when there is a duty to act) must be a substantial factor in bringing about the harm. The law is concerned with proximate cause, also called *legal cause,* that takes a pragmatic view, and not with the "first cause" of philosophy or "field theory" of science. As Judge Andrews put it:

> We cannot trace the effect of an act to the end, if end there is. Again, however, we may trace it part of the way. A murder at Serajevo may be the necessary antecedent to an assassination in London twenty years hence. An overturned lantern may burn all Chicago. We may follow the fire from the shed to the last building. We rightly say the fire started by the lantern caused its destruction. This would be cause, but not the proximate cause. What we do mean by the word *proximate* is that because of convenience, public policy, or a rough sense of justice, the law arbitrarily declines to trace a series of events beyond a certain point. This is not logic. It is practical politics.[11]

Fault. Another key element of a tort is *fault,* either based on intent or negligence. The term *intent* denotes the actor's desire to cause the consequences of his act, or his belief that such consequences are substantially certain to result. *Intent* in the law of torts is limited, wherever it is used, to the consequences of the act rather than to the act itself. Thus, as illustrated in the ALI's *Restatement of Torts,* one who fires a gun in the middle of the desert and hits someone who is there without his knowledge does not intend that result.[12] A delusional interpretation of reality does not excuse tort liability.

Intent, for the purposes of determining civil liability, unlike criminal liability, does not presuppose a value judgment or moral culpability. The actor need not know that what he was doing was wrong. Thus, an individual who intends to affect a chattel in a manner inconsistent with another's right of control, though acting in good faith, and under a mistake, is liable for a "conversion."[13] Irrespective of good motives, the abducting and deprogramming of a member of a religious cult is a "battery" and "false imprisonment."[14]

In tort law it is usually irrelevant that an actor intended no harm, or perhaps even intended benefit, to his victim. It requires only that the actor have substantial certainty that a battery or other invasion of a legally protected interest will result. The intent required for the tort of battery, for example, is the intent to cause contact, and if it turns out to be harmful or offensive, there is damage, and that fulfills the requirements of the tort. A requirement of harm or offense would make this tort inapplicable to many situations in which it might otherwise be applied, such as practical jokes, mistaken identity, or medical treatment.[15] Some courts state that a desire to harm is necessary,[16] but that is not the usual requirement. A surgeon who performs an operation does not desire to do harm—indeed, he desires to help—but without the defense of consent, liability would be for a battery.[17]

Negligence is not defined in terms of state of mind but as "conduct which falls below the standard of care established by law for the protection of others against unreasonable risk of harm."[18] A person either must act with the care and skill expected of a reasonable, careful, and prudent person under the circumstances or bear responsibility for the resulting damage. The test is not whether the individual had acted according to the best of his own judgment.[19]

The *Restatement of Torts* sets out the general rule: "Unless the actor is a child, his insanity or other mental deficiency does not relieve the actor from liability for conduct which does not conform to the standard of a reasonable man under like circumstances."[20] The *Restatement* gives an example:

> *A*, who is insane, believes that he is Napoleon Bonaparte, and that *B*, his nurse, who confines him in his room, is an agent of the Duke of Wellington, who is endeavoring to prevent his arrival on the field of Waterloo in time to win the battle. Seeking to escape, he breaks off the leg of a chair, attacks *B* with it and fractures her skull. *A* is subject to liability to *B* for battery.[21]

Liability without Fault

Liability without fault (intent or negligence), otherwise known as *strict liability*, was the foundation of tort law until the latter half of the nineteenth century. The principal action was strict liability for trespass, not surprising in a society in which the chief source of wealth was land. A concomitant of the industrial revolution was the concept, urged by entrepreneurs, that there should be no liability without fault. The entrepreneur was held liable to workers only if he were deemed at fault, which happened rarely indeed because risks or hazards involved in carrying on an activity in itself do not constitute fault. There is also reason to believe that the courts found the defense of contributory negligence, along with the concepts of fault and proximate cause, to be a convenient instrument of control over the jury whereby the liabilities of developing industry were kept within bounds.

Today, in the employer-employee relationship, workers' compensation laws provide that an employee is entitled to compensation for injuries arising in the course and scope of employment, irrespective of any fault, but payment is limited to a fixed schedule. Under no-fault automobile insurance plans, adopted widely, a motorist's insurance company covers his medical and auto damage expenses no matter what caused the accident. In other situations the foundation of tort liability is fault, except in the situations of ultrahazardous activity or products liability, where the principle of strict liability applies.

The Plaintiff's Contributory Negligence

The important public policy that innocent victims be compensated is one reason that mental illness has not been allowed to vitiate tort liability. The central conflict in tort law is whether liability should be based upon the moral fault of the defendant and his responsibility for that fault, or whether the focus should be on compensation for the victim.[22] These considerations, however, are not applicable to the issue of a plaintiff's contributory negligence, that is, conduct contributing as a legal cause to the harm that the plaintiff has suffered because it falls below the standard to which he is required to conform for his own protection. The issue of psychiatric status of the plaintiff in a tort suit tends to be of greater importance than in the case of a defendant.

The traditional common-law rule denies recovery to a plaintiff who is contributorily negligent, whatever the negligence of the defendant.[23] In most states the doctrine of contributory negligence has been replaced by comparative negligence, under which the negligent plaintiff is not completely barred from compensation, but it is reduced by the percentage of his fault.

The courts, while employing an objective standard-of-conduct test for defendant's negligence, tend to employ a subjective standard for the plaintiff's contributory or comparative negligence. The *Restatement* says that the policy factors that disallow insanity of an actor from excusing conduct, which would otherwise be negligence on the part of a defendant, do not have the same force as applied to the plaintiff's contributory or comparative negligence. The subjective standard allows an "insane" plaintiff's behavior to be measured in relation to his actual competency, which would tend not to defeat his claim.[24] Psychiatric testimony would be material to establish lack of competency.[25] In response to intentional wrongdoing, it is inconsequential to say that the plaintiff was negligent in failing to avoid harm. Thus, if *A* intends to strike *B*, it is no defense to say that *B* was negligent in failing to avoid the blow.

What about a hypersensitive or idiosyncratic plaintiff? The defendant's knowledge of the plaintiff's special susceptibilities to emotional distress is relevant to the determination of whether a cause of action for intentional infliction of emotional distress is available. In one notorious case the plaintiff, an eccentric elderly woman, believed that a pot of gold was buried in her backyard and was constantly digging for it. Fully aware of her frailties, the defendant buried a pot with other contents where she would dig it up. When she did so, he had her escorted by a procession in triumph to the city hall, where she opened the pot under circumstances of extreme public humiliation. She suffered mental distress, which further unsettled her and contributed to her early death. In the form of a judgment, her heirs got a "pot of gold."[26]

Privileges of a Defendant

The privileges or defenses of a defendant (consent, self-defense, defense of others, defense of property, necessity) depend upon the reasonable belief that a fact exists, not a subjective belief. A defendant, believing that the plaintiff is reaching into his pocket for a gun, attacks the plaintiff to defend himself; the plaintiff was actually reaching for his handkerchief. The issue is whether the defendant had reasonable grounds to fear an immediate attack by the plaintiff.[27]

Mental Disability as a Defense

Mental incompetence may be shown under the law to modify contractual obligations, testamentary capacity, and criminal responsibility, but "lunatics usually have been held liable for their torts."[28] The courts almost invariably impose liability on mentally disordered defendants as if they had no such disorder.[29] At least five states have statutorily codified the principle.[30]

This general rule is applied in cases of both negligence and intentional torts. In cases of negligence, an individual is expected to comply with the objective *reasonable person* standard. The rule is also applied with respect to intentional torts, but there is some authority holding an insane person may not have the mental capacity to form the specific intent for certain intentional torts such as malicious prosecution, misrepresentation, and defamation.[31] In *C. T. W. v. B. C. G.*,[32] the defendant sexually abused his stepgrandchildren. He sought to defend against tort liability on the ground that the sexual abuse was the result of a "pedophilic disorder." The court rejected the argument that the defendant should be held only to the standard of "an ordinary prudent person with the mental illness of pedophilia."

Justifications of the general rule that the insane are liable for their torts include the following: (1) the fairness of holding that "where one of two innocent persons must suffer a loss, it should be borne by the one who occasioned it," (2) the encouragement of custodians or caretakers to be vigilant over the care of insane persons, (3) the difficulty of identifying actual mental illness by those feigning insanity to avoid liability for harmful acts, and (4) the complications and difficulties of introducing insanity defenses as used in the criminal law into tort doctrine.[33]

As the verdict in criminal cases of not guilty by reason of insanity does not have a counterpart of not liable by reason of insanity in tort cases, a person may be found NGRI in a criminal case but nonetheless may be liable in a tort case.[34] The courts do not inquire in tort cases as they do in criminal cases whether, in the matter at hand, the defendant was able to distinguish right from wrong.[35]

By and large, the decisions adhere to the line set out in 1937 by the Massachusetts Supreme Judicial Court in *McGuire v. Almy*.[36] In this case, the plaintiff, a registered nurse, was employed to take care of the defendant, who was insane. The defendant was "ugly, violent and dangerous" and injured the plaintiff. The Massachusetts Supreme Judicial Court, reversing the trial court, held for the plaintiff. Of the liability of insane persons, it said: "[T]he law will not inquire . . . into [a defendant's] peculiar mental condition with a view to excusing him if it should appear that delusion or other consequence of his affliction has caused him to entertain that intent or that a normal person would not have entertained it."

The insane person is deemed capable of having an intent to bring about a specific result, even though the intent is induced by a delusion; and his act is deemed voluntary, even though he may be diagnosed as having pyromania or kleptomania.[37] For battery resulting in death or wrongful death, the courts on many occasions have held a defendant civilly liable, notwithstanding an earlier acquittal of the criminal charge on account of insanity. The insane have been held liable for trespass to land and conversion of goods. They have been held liable for setting fire to buildings. Imbecility or mental defectiveness is taken into account as a defense only if it has reached an extreme stage.

The traditional rule was again reaffirmed in 1988 by the Connecticut Supreme Court in *Polmatier v. Russ*.[38] In this case the defendant shot and killed his father-in-law. The defendant told a police officer that his father-in-law was a heavy drinker and he wanted to make his father-in-law suffer for his bad habits. He also told the police officer that he was a supreme being and had the power to rule the destiny of the world and could make his bed fly out of the window. To a psychiatrist, he stated that he believed that his father-in-law was a spy for the Red Chinese and that he believed his father-in-law was not only going to kill him, but going to harm his infant child. The psychiatrist testified at both the criminal and civil proceedings, saying that, at the time of the homicide, the defendant had "a severe case of paranoid schizophrenia" that involved delusions of persecution, grandeur, influence, and reference, and he also had auditory hallucinations. He did not suggest during his testimony that the defendant may be malingering. He concluded that the defendant could not form a rational choice but that he could make "a schizophrenic or crazy choice." He was absolved of criminal liability by reason of insanity, but in the civil action he was found liable.[39]

Commentators trace the majority rule back to the dictum of a seventeenth-century English case when strict liability was generally the rule. In *Weaver v. Ward*,[40] the English court said, "[I]f a lunatic kills a man this shall not be a felony, because felony must be done *animo felonico* [with felonious intent]. Yet in trespass which tends only to give damages according to a hurt or loss, it is not so." The majority rule is not, however, without criticism.[41] Professor Bohlen in an article published in 1924 stated:

> [W]here a liability, like that for the impairment of the physical condition of another's body or property, is imposed upon persons capable of fault only if they have been guilty of fault, immaturity of age or mental deficiency, which destroys the capacity for fault, should preclude the possibility of liability. . . . But so long as it is accepted as a general principle that liability for injuries to certain interests are to be imposed only upon those guilty of fault in causing them, it should be applied consistently and no liability should be imposed upon those for any reason incapable of fault.[42]

Similar views have more recently been expressed by other commentators.[43] One of them characterizes the tort standard as "almost facially unfathomable."[44] Given the "conventional wisdom" that the mentally ill or mentally retarded constitute a "grave threat to society," it should not be surprising, says Professor James Ellis, that "such an atmosphere would foster a rule that refused to absolve such persons from compensating victims for the damage they caused."[45] The criticisms, however, have had little impact on the jurisprudence.

The traditional civil law, in contrast to the common law, holds that a mentally unsound person "cannot commit a fault."[46] The German Civil Code excludes civil responsibility for one who is unable to exercise free will, except where he brought on temporary disability by use of alcohol or similar means.[47] On the other hand, some civil law codes impose liability in at least some cases. The Civil Code of Mexico provides that the incompetent person is liable unless some other person, such as a guardian, is liable.[48]

The most oft-cited U.S. case on standard of care, *Williams v. Hays*,[49] involved a sea captain who had been on duty continuously for three days during a storm. During the calm weather following the storm he permitted his vessel to drift on a shoal and be destroyed. The evidence tended to show that he refused to consider the seriousness of the situation, staggered about the vessel, made irresponsive answers to questions, and appeared to be dazed, drunk, or insane. The day of the wreck he twice refused the assistance of tugboats offering to tow the disabled vessel. He sought to invoke temporary insanity as a defense. The New York Court of Appeals declared the insanity of the defendant furnished no defense—his acts must be measured by the same standard as that applied to the action of a sane person—but at the same time the court, contrary to the majority rule, sent the case back for a new trial because evidence had been refused tending to show that the defendant became mentally incompetent by reason of his extreme efforts to save the brig, which, if proved, the court thought would furnish an excuse. The suit was discontinued—a practical victory for the defendant. In light of the decision it was uncertain how far an insane person would be held responsible for his acts or omissions.[50]

Under American law, the acts of an epileptic person or a person seized with temporary unconsciousness—conditions regarded as involuntary or accidental—

are distinguished from the acts of an insane person. Thus, a motorist who suddenly loses control of his car because of a heart attack, a stroke, a fainting spell, or an epileptic seizure is not liable unless he knew, or should have known, that he was likely to become ill, in which case he is negligent in driving the car at all.[51]

There is some analogy between a motorist's going berserk at the wheel and a ship captain's going insane during a voyage; the ship captain case has been cited in a number of automobile cases.[52] In a society where nearly everyone drives an automobile, it will not be surprising to find mental illness among drivers. Michael Douglas in the 1992 film *Falling Down* cracks up on a freeway and goes on a rampage.[53] Barbara Bush, the wife of President George Bush, wrote in her memoirs that she was so deeply depressed in the mid-1970s that she sometimes stopped her car on the highway shoulders for fear that she might deliberately crash the vehicle into a tree or an oncoming auto.[54] State statutes require physicians to report patients with conditions that may affect their ability to drive, and under these statutes, physicians may be held responsible for vehicle accidents caused by their patients.[55] In nonserious cases, no-fault automobile insurance resolves the matter.

Obtaining mental health care does not reduce tort law's expectations of the defendant. Indeed, it may actually increase its expectations of the defendant. Insight gained through diagnosis or treatment may increase the defendant's awareness of the risks that he poses and require him to act with reference to that increased knowledge.[56] An individual may be deemed negligent for failing to seek professional help.[57]

In rare cases where the court has judged that the individual could not foresee an attack of mental illness that played a role in causing injury, the illness is treated somewhat like a physical illness. In this situation, the attack of mental illness is viewed like a heart attack or an attack of epilepsy, for example, when it occurs while driving. An individual who knew he was subject to epileptic attacks and drove anyway would be liable. Psychiatric testimony may delineate the manner in which mental illness played a role in the accident and provide information as to the possibility that the attack was sudden and unanticipated.[58]

In an oft-cited Wisconsin case, *Breunig v. American Family Ins. Co.*,[59] a psychiatrist testified that the defendant, an insured motorist, believed God took hold of the steering wheel and directed her car. She saw a truck coming and stepped on the gas in order to become airborne. She believed she could fly like Wonder Woman. To her surprise she was not airborne before striking the truck, but she was airborne after the impact. There was evidence that she had been delusional. The appellate court, finding that the defendant had knowledge of her condition, upheld a verdict for the plaintiff. It is only a sudden, first-time breakdown that excuses. The court said that if a situation arises in which the defendant is suddenly overcome without forewarning by a disabling mental disorder, liability will not be imposed.[60] Of course, psychiatrists may say that mental illness compromises cognition, and hence an insane person may not actually know about his condition or have the ability to make a rational decision.

In a Colorado case, *Johnson v. Lombotte*,[61] the defendant was under observation by court order and was being treated for "chronic schizophrenic state of paranoid type." On the day in question, she escaped from the hospital and found an automobile with its motor running a few blocks from the hospital. She drove off, having little or no control of the car, and soon collided with the plaintiff. Later, she was adjudged mentally incompetent and committed to a state hospital. As in *Breu-*

nig, the Colorado Supreme Court said that this was not a case of sudden mental seizure with no forewarning. The court said, "The defendant knew she was being treated for a mental disorder and hence would not have come under the nonliability rule [in cases of sudden attack]."[62]

Liability of Caretakers

Apart from the liability of insane persons, there may be a question of liability of those responsible for their custody and supervision. Even if a mentally ill person is said to lack the ability to form the intent to commit a tort, an action may lie against persons responsible for caring for the mentally ill person, based on negligent supervision.[63] According to circumstances, the plaintiff may sue the hospital, psychiatrist, or the parents or guardian who looks after the individual.[64] Since the 1980s there has been increasing litigation related to psychiatrists' failure to predict that patients will harm themselves or others and subsequent failure to do anything to prevent these harms. The majority of suits imposing liability on the psychiatrist or hospital involves the suicide of a patient in the inpatient setting. The burden of proving fault is on the plaintiff.[65]

Attacks on Caretakers

A number of recent cases have drawn another exception to the general rule that insane persons are liable for their torts. These are cases in which the insane person has been institutionalized and injures a caretaker. More that a hundred health care workers are killed annually during the course of their work, not to mention the number who are seriously injured. Earlier decisions, as we have noted, imposed liability, holding in favor of the caretaker,[66] but today, the courts tend to say in cases where the defendant is institutionally confined and the injured party is employed to care for or control him, that such imposition of responsibility would serve no purpose in cases involving defendants "with no control over [their] actions and [who are] thus innocent of any wrongdoing in the most basic sense of that term."[67] Even in the case of the killing of a caretaker, there is usually neither a civil nor a criminal proceeding (nor a funeral service like that given police officers).[68]

Insurers of the Mentally Ill

It is important to determine not only whether the mentally ill will be held liable in tort but also whether there is a source of compensation. Quite often, the mentally ill are indigent or have no insurance, so a lawsuit would be pointless (though civil commitment or a criminal proceeding may be appropriate). Generally speaking, in the majority of tort cases damages are not paid by the tortfeasor but by an insurer, especially in this day of broad coverage for general liability in family insurance policies. Unless the person being sued is cash rich, chances of collecting a judgment are small if he does not have liability insurance.

Most litigated cases of torts of the mentally ill involve coverage under their liability or other insurance policy. The standard liability policy language has undergone substantial changes over the last several years. Prior to 1966, liability policies generally stated that damage or injury would be covered by the policy only if it was "caused by an accident which occurs during the policy period." Any duty of the insurer to defend or indemnify the insured was restricted by this "accident" requirement, but due to the difficulties in construing the word *accident*—including conflicting opinions on whether the term was to be understood from the viewpoint of the insured or the victim—the National Bureau of Casualty Underwriters and the Mutual Insurance Rating Bureau rewrote the standard policy language in 1966. The revision provided coverage "for damage . . . caused by an occurrence," and defined *occurrence* as "an accident . . . which results, during the policy period, in bodily injury or property damage neither expected nor intended from the standpoint of the insured."

The revision, defining *accident* from the standpoint of the insured, not the victim, is a position favorable to insurers since it denies coverage to insured who commit intentional torts. Two lines of cases, however, have developed in the interpretation of this provision. One line has adopted the view that the insured's subjective intent must be explored in determining coverage. If the insured did not have the specific subjective intent of causing harm to the plaintiff, his acts are deemed accidental, thus falling within the meaning of *occurrence.* The result is a decision in favor of coverage, thereby providing compensation for the victim. Psychiatric testimony is usually involved when a subjective approach is taken.[69] Another line of cases, taking a contrary approach, focuses on an objective analysis of the insured's actions. In so doing, the majority of these courts has found that the intent to inflict injury may be inferred as a matter of law when the insured's actions are of a reprehensible character (such as sexual molestation).[70] Under this objective analysis approach, a finding of no coverage is inevitably the result.[71]

The New Jersey Supreme Court in 1963 handed down a decision that quickly became the leading case concerning the effect of insanity on the operation of intentional-exclusionary clauses in insurance policies. In *Ruvolo v. American Casualty Co.*,[72] a physician, Anthony Ruvolo, shot and killed another physician with whom he had practiced medicine. At the time, Ruvolo had a personal liability insurance policy that provided that the insurer would pay all sums that Ruvolo "shall become legally obligated to pay as damages because of the death of any person resulting from [his] activities." The coverage was limited by an exclusionary clause providing that the policy did not apply to death "caused intentionally by or at the direction of the insured."

The victim's widow filed a wrongful death suit, which Ruvolo's insurer refused to defend on the ground that the death had been caused by Ruvolo's intentional act. The guardian of the insured then filed a declaratory judgment action against his insurer, seeking to establish that the policy afforded coverage. Relying upon the affidavits of psychiatrists that Ruvolo was insane at the time of the killing and lacked the capacity to form a rational intent, the trial court granted summary judgment for the plaintiff. The trial court held that an act performed under such circumstances could not be considered intentional.

On appeal, the New Jersey Supreme Court concluded that if an insured would have been excused from responsibility under the state's criminal standard (at the time the *M'Naghten* test), then the act was not intentional for the purposes of the insurance policy. The court also provided for a finding of volitional incapacity, like the capacity to conform conduct test used in the ALI criminal standard. The *Ruvolo* case has been followed in a number of other cases.[73]

Disputes over suicide arise in connection with two different types of insurance policies: life insurance policies that exclude benefits for suicide within a certain period of time, and accidental death policies or double-indemnity riders to life insurance policies.[74] In *Kennedy v. Washington National Ins. Co.*,[75] the insured died through autoerotic asphyxiation when he placed a rope around his neck to reduce the supply of oxygen to his brain to heighten the sexual pleasure during masturbation. In a dispute over a life insurance policy that included an additional accidental death benefit, the court held that the death was accidental within the meaning of the policy. The court held that the insured's death was not precluded from being accidental because he voluntarily exposed himself to a known high risk of death. Although the insured's act could be considered bizarre or unusual, the court held, there was no evidence that his death was highly probable, expected, or a natural result, since his conduct was solely for the purpose of seeking sexual gratification.

The issue of suicidal intent has been raised as an issue in insurance litigation to recover death benefits under a life insurance policy. Some life insurance policies have a provision precluding recovery of the full value of the policy if death results from "suicide, whether sane or insane." However, it may be argued that the insured did not understand the physical nature and consequences of the act, and, in such a case, the insurer may be held liable for the full amount of the policy.[76] The suicide exclusion has been held not to be applicable in cases of a compulsion or an irresistible impulse to kill oneself.[77] The courts find an irresistible impulse when the decedent acted in a sudden frenzy; on the other hand, the courts find control when a suicide note is written or poison is purchased.[78]

Summary

The general rule is that the mentally ill are responsible under tort law, a rule almost invariably applied to both torts of intention and of negligence (except when the victim is a caretaker). There is no counterpart of not liable by reason of insanity to the criminal law's not guilty by reason of insanity. However, as a general principle, the courts equate a sudden, unforeseeable mental incapacity with physical causes such as a sudden heart attack or stroke.

At the same time, while holding the mentally ill responsible under tort law, the courts tend to find coverage under an insurance policy. Holding the mentally ill liable in tort goes hand in glove with holdings of insurance coverage. Moreover, the courts frequently impose liability on psychiatrists and hospitals for negligent supervision or failure to warn or protect third parties.[79]

Notes

1. L. Green, "The Study and Teaching of Tort Law," *Tex. L. Rev.* 34 (1955): 1, 3.

2. Quoted in M. S. Shapo, *Tort and Injury Law* (New York: Lexis, 2000), p. 8.

3. *Restatement (Second) Torts*, sec. 2 (Washington, D.C.: American Law Institute, 1964).

4. See H. Morris (ed.), *Freedom and Responsibility* (Stanford: Stanford University Press, 1961), ch. 3.

5. S. L. Halleck, "Clinical Assessment of the Voluntariness of Behavior," *Bull. Am. Acad. Psychiatry & Law* 20 (1992): 221; id., "Which Patients Are Responsible for Their Illnesses?" *Am. J. Psychotherapy* 42 (1988): 338.

6. Quoted in F. L. Bailey, *The Defense Never Rests* (New York: Signet, 1971), p. 265. In United States v. Fishman, 743 F.Supp. 713 (N.D.Cal. 1990), where the defendant was charged with mail fraud, the court held that the theories of mental health professionals regarding

coercive persuasion practices of religious cults were not sufficiently established within the scientific community to be admissible as evidence of the defendant's theory that he was brainwashed by a religious cult. See J. T. Richardson, "Cult/Brainwashing Cases and Freedom of Religion," *J. Church & State* 31 (1989): 451.

7. Interictal aspects that are relevant to the form of epileptic automatism may be the person's natural tendencies, the same psychodynamic factors that determine the content of dreams, the person's social background of violence, and the contents of the person's thoughts immediately before a seizure. P. H. van Rensburg, C. A. Gagiano, & T. Verschoor, "Possible Reasons Why Certain Epileptics Commit Unlawful Acts during or Directly after Seizures," *Med. & Law* 13 (1994): 373. See Lobert v. Pack, 337 Pa. 103, 9 A.2d 365 (1939).

8. Morriss v. Marsden, [1952] 1 All E.R. 925 (Q.B.).

9. G. Orwell, *A Collection of Essays* (New York: Harcourt, Brace, 1950), p. 1.

10. M. Gladwell, *The Tipping Point: How Little Things Can Make a Big Difference* (Boston: Little, Brown, 2000).

11. Dissenting in Palsgraf v. Long Island R.R. Co., 248 N.Y. 339, 162 N.E. 99 (1928).

12. *Restatement (Second) Torts*, sec. 8A.

13. United States v. Freed, 401 U.S. 601, 607 (1971); Vosburg v. Putney, 80 Wis. 523, 50 N.W. 403 (1891).

14. Eilers v. Coy, 582 F.Supp. 1093 (D.Minn. 1984).

15. R. A. Epstein, "Intentional Harms," *J. of Legal Studies* 4 (1975): 391; O. M. Reynolds, "Tortious Battery: Is 'I Didn't Mean Any Harm' Relevant?" *Okla. L. Rev.* 37 (1984): 717.

16. See, e.g., Newman v. Christensen, 149 Neb. 471, 31 N.W.2d 417 (1948); Matheson v. Pearson, 619 P.2d 321 (Utah 1980); Gouger v. Hardtke, 482 N.W.2d 84 (Wis. 1992).

17. See Mohr v. Williams, 95 Minn. 261, 104 N.W. 12 (1905). In Clayton v. New Dreamland Roller Skating Rink, 14 N.J. Super. 390, 82 A.2d 458 (1951), *cert. denied*, 13 N.J. 527, 100 A.2d 567 (1953), the plaintiff fell at a skating rink and broke her arm. Over the protests of the plaintiff and her husband, the defendant's employees proceeded to manipulate the arm in an attempt to set it. They committed a battery.

18. *Restatement (Second) Torts*, sec. 282.

19. "[S]aying that the liability for negligence should be co-extensive with the judgment of each individual ... would be as variable as the length of the foot of each individual." Vaughan v. Menlove, 3 Bing. (N.C.) 467, 132 Eng. Rep. 490 (1837). See D. E. Seidelson, "Reasonable Expectations and Subjective Standards in Negligence Law: The Minor, the Mentally Impaired, and the Mentally Incompetent," *Geo. Wash. L. Rev.* 50 (1981): 17.

20. *Restatement (Second) Torts*, sec. 283B.

21. Ibid., sec. 895J, comment c.

22. Professor James, arguing for the latter position, wrote: "[I]f the standard of conduct is relaxed for defendants who cannot meet a normal standard, then the burden of accident loss resulting from the extra hazards created by society's most dangerous groups (*e.g.*, the young, the novice, the accident-prone) will be thrown on the innocent victims of substandard behavior. Such a conclusion shocks people who believe that the compensation of accident victims is a more important objective of modern tort law than a further refinement of the tort principle, and that compensation should prevail when the two objectives conflict." F. James, "The Qualities of the Reasonable Man in Negligence Cases," *Mo. L. Rev.* 16 (1951): 1, 2.

23. *Restatement (Second) Torts*, sec. 467.

24. Ibid., sec. 464. Allowance was made for the plaintiff's inability to exercise the judgment of a reasonable person in Seattle Elect. Co. v. Hovden, 190 Fed. 7 (9th Cir. 1911); Dassinger v. Kuhn, 87 N.W.2d 720 (N.D. 1958). The case of Wright v. Tate, 208 Va. 291, 156 S.E.2d 562 (1967), seems to stand alone in declining to make any allowance for the plaintiff's mental disability and holding him to the standard of the ordinary reasonable person. The court said, "If the rule were otherwise, there would be a different standard for each level of intelligence, resulting in confusion and uncertainty in the law." See W. Seavey, "Negligence—Subjective or Objective?" *Harv. L. Rev.* 41 (1927): 1; Note, "Standard of Care Required of Persons under Physical Disability," *N. Car. L. Rev.* 34 (1955): 142.

25. In Lynch v. Rosenthal, 396 S.W.2d 272 (Mo. 1965), a child psychologist testified on behalf of the plaintiff, a "low moron," who got his hand caught in the defendant's corn picker. The psychologist's testimony dealt with the understanding of the plaintiff. In this case the

court used a subjective test, rather than the average reasonable person test, in determining whether the plaintiff was contributorily negligent.

26. Nickerson v. Hodges, 146 La. 735, 84 So. 37 (1920). In a criminal case a jury convicted a man of assaulting a woman he rendered helpless by saying the word *sex*. The woman, age thirty-nine, had conversion hysteria that allegedly caused her to faint at the sound of sex-related words. He took advantage of her condition. S. McLaughlin, "Man, 42, Convicted in 'Sex' Word Assault," *Denver Times* (Reuters), Mar. 12, 1994, p. B-7.

27. See, e.g., Keep v. Quallman, 68 Wis. 451, 32 N.W. 233 (1887).

28. McGuire v. Almy, 297 Mass. 323, 8 N.E.2d 760 (1937).

29. See G. Alexander & T. Szasz, "Mental Illness as an Excuse for Civil Wrongs," *Notre Dame Law.* 43 (1967): 24; W. Curran, "Tort Liability of the Mentally Ill and Mentally Deficient," *Ohio St. L.J.* 21 (1960): 52; H. J. F. Korrell, "The Liability of Mentally Disabled Tort Defendants," *Law & Psych. Rev.* 19 (1995): 1; S. Morse, "Psychiatric Responsibility and Tort Liability," *J. For. Sci.* 12 (1967): 305; R. Sadoff, "Tortious Liabilty of the Insane: A Psychiatric Evaluation," *Pa. Bar Assn. Q.* 39 (1967): 73; H. L. Silverman & B. Seidler, "Psychological Evaluation of the Law of Torts," *A.B.A.J.* 47 (1961): 180; K. G. Anderson, "Insanity as a Defense to the Civil Fraud Penalty," *Duke L.J.* 1963: 428; R. M. Augue, "The Liability of Insane Persons in Tort Actions," *Dick. L. Rev.* 60 (1956): 211.

See also W. G. H. Cook, "Mental Deficiency in Relation to Tort," *Colum. L. Rev.* 21 (1921): 333; A. A. Ehrenzweig, "A Psychoanalysis of Negligence," *Nw. U.L. Rev.* 47 (1953): 855; L. H. Eldredge, "Tort Liability of an Insane Person," *Pa. Bar Assn. Q.* 26 (1955): 176; W. B. Hornblower, "Insanity and the Law of Negligence," *Col. L. Rev.* 5 (1905): 278; S. I. Splane, "Tort Liability of the Mentally Ill in Negligence Actions," *Yale L.J.* 93 (1983): 153; E. C. E. Todd, "Insanity as a Defence in a Civil Action of Assault and Battery," *Modern L. Rev.* 15 (1952): 486; id., "The Liability of Lunatics in the Law of Tort," *Austl. L.J.* 26 (1952): 299; G. B. Weisiger, "Tort Liability of Minors and Incompetents," *U. Ill. L.F.* 1951: 277; W. J. Wilkinson, "Mental Incompetency as a Defense to Tort Liability," *Rocky Mt. L. Rev.* 17 (1944): 38.

30. See Cal. Civ. Code, sec. 41 (West 1990); Mont. Code Ann., sec. 27-1-711 (1989); N.D. Cent. Code, sec. 14-10-03 (1981); Okla. Stat. Ann., tit. 15, secs. 25, 26 (West 1972); S.D. Laws Ann., sec. 27A-2-4 (1976).

31. In Barylski v. Paul, 38 Mich. App. 614, 196 N.W.2d 868 (1972), the court suggested that insanity might be a defense in cases in which the tort required a specific intent such as the malice requirement in malicious prosecution, but not in the ordinary battery case.

32. 809 S.W.2d 788 (Tex. App. 1991).

33. These grounds are critically examined in J. Ellis, "Tort Responsibility of Mentally Disabled Persons," *Am. B. Found. Res. J.* 1981: 1079, 1083.

34. M. Yancey, "Hinckley May Have to Pay Reagan Guards He Wounded" (Associated Press news release), *Detroit Free Press*, Aug. 15, 1992, p. 6.

35. The ALI's *Restatement of Torts*, sec. 283, originally took no position as to the standard to be applied to an insane person in negligence cases, but this was changed in *Restatement (Second) Torts*, sec. 283B, to state that the mentally ill are to be held in all respects to the standard of the reasonable person who is sane. This is not consistent with the rule on children, but children form a readily discernible category.

Some oft-cited cases may be noted. In Ward v. Conatser, 63 Tenn. 64 (1874), the defendant, who claimed insanity as a defense to a civil suit, shot and permanently injured the plaintiff. The court charged the jury that "insanity cannot be looked to as a justification of the shooting." In Central Ga. Ry. v. Hall, 124 Ga. 322, 52 S.E. 679 (1905), the court held that mental illness is not a defense to a tort action even when the defendant has been formally adjudged incompetent or committed to a mental hospital.

In an old but well-known Kansas case, Seals v. Snow, 123 Kan. 88, 254 P. 348 (1927), the widow of Arthur Seals brought a civil action against Martin Snow to recover damages for the death of her husband. The evidence indicated that Snow was insane when he shot Seals and was unable to distinguish right from wrong. The verdict nonetheless was for the plaintiff.

Another homicide case applying the majority rule is McIntyre v. Sholty, 121 Ill. 660, 13 N.E. 239 (1887), where liability was imposed on an insane person's estate for the wrongful killing of the plaintiff's wife. As in *McGuire*, the court reasoned: "There is, to be sure, an appearance of hardship in compelling one to respond for that when he is unable to avoid for want of the control of reason. But the question of liability in these cases is one of public policy."

In Mullen v. Bruce, 168 Cal. App.2d 494, 335 P.2d 945 (1959), the defendant, a patient under treatment for delirium tremens resulting from alcoholism, injured the plaintiff, her special-duty nurse, who was trying to prevent the defendant from leaving; the court imposed liability. In Williams v. Kearbey, 132 Kan. App.2d 564, 775 P.2d 670 (1989), the defendant, a junior high school student, shot and injured two people at his school. The jury found that the defendant was insane at the time of the shootings, and because of this fact, the defendant argued that he should not be held civilly liable. The court, following the majority rule, said that a defendant's insanity does not establish a defense to liability. That rule, the court said, reflected a policy decision "to impose liability on an insane person rather than leaving the loss on the innocent victim."

36. 297 Mass. 323, 8 N.E.2d 760 (1937). The court echoed the oft-quoted statement of Justice Oliver W. Holmes: "If, for instance, a man is born hasty and awkward, is always hurting himself or his neighbors, no doubt his congenital defects will be allowed for in the courts of Heaven, but his slips are no less troublesome to his neighbors than if they sprang from guilty neglect. His neighbors accordingly require him, at his peril, to come up to their standard, and the courts which they establish decline to take his personal equation into account." O. W. Holmes, *The Common Law* (Boston: Little, Brown, 1881), p. 108.

37. Note, "Liability of the Insane Defendant," *Cornell L.Q.* 34 (1948): 274. See also S. L. Halleck, "Which Patients Are Responsible for Their Illnesses?" *Am. J. Psychiatry* 42 (1988): 338.

38. 206 Conn. 229, 537 A.2d 468 (1988).

39. An earlier Connecticut case declined to follow the majority point of view. Fitzgerald v. Lawhorn, 29 Conn. Supp. 511, 294 A.2d 338 (Com. Pl. 1972).

40. 80 Eng. Rep. 284 (1616).

41. Bolen v. Howard, 452 S.W.2d 401 (Ky. 1970) (questioning doctrine).

42. F. Bohlen, "Liability in Tort of Infants and Insane Persons," *Mich. L. Rev.* 23 (1924): 9, 31–32.

43. R. M. Ague, "The Liability of Insane Persons in Tort Actions," *Dick. L. Rev.* 60 (1956): 211; W. G. H. Cook, "Mental Deficiency in Relation to Tort," *Colum. L. Rev.* 21 (1921): 333; W. J. Curran, "Tort Liability for the Mentally Ill and Mentally Deficient," *Ohio St. L.J.* 21 (1960): 52; J. W. Ellis, "Tort Responsibility of Mentally Disabled Persons," *Am. Bar. Found. Res. J.* 1981: 1079; W. J. Wilkinson, "Mental Incompetency as a Defense to Tort Liability," *Rocky Mtn. L. Rev.* 17 (1944): 38.

Defending the imposition of tort liability on mentally disordered defendants: G. J. Alexander & T. S. Szasz, "Mental Illness as an Excuse for Civil Wrongs," *Notre Dame Law.* 43 (1967): 24; S. I. Splane, "Tort Liability of the Mentally Ill in Negligence Actions," *Yale L.J.* 93 (1983): 153.

44. D. E. Seidelson, "Reasonable Expectations and Subjective Standards in Negligence Law: The Minor, the Mentally Impaired, and the Mentally Incompetent," *Geo. Wash. L. Rev.* 50 (1981): 17.

45. J. Ellis, "Tort Responsibility and the Mentally Disabled," *Am. Bar. Found. Res. J.* 1981: 1079.

46. In a 1934 Louisiana case, Yancey v. Maestri, 150 So. 509 (La. App. 1934), no longer followed in the state, an insane person seriously wounded the plaintiff, who was held to have no cause of action since by Roman and Spanish law alike "an insane person or lunatic or madman" is not responsible for his tort, it being considered an "inevitable accident." Judge Higgins wrote, "The common law considers the effect of the insane person's act, while the civil law regards the cause of it."

47. German Civil Code, sec. 827.

48. Codigo Civil para el Distrito Federal, sec. 1911.

49. 143 N.Y. 442, 38 N.E. 449 (1894), qualified in 157 N.Y. 541, 52 N.E. 589 (1899); discussed in W. J. Wilkinson, "Mental Incompetency as a Defense to Tort Liability," *Rocky Mt. L. Rev.* 17 (1944): 38.

50. Note, "Insane Persons—Tort Liability," *Minn. L. Rev.* 22 (1938): 853.

51. In Cohen v. Petty, 62 App. D.C. 187, 65 F.2d 820 (1933), the plaintiff, a passenger in defendant's car, alleged that the defendant was at fault in driving his automobile, operating it at an excessive rate of speed, and losing control of it. The car ran off the road and plaintiff was injured in the accident. Defendant claimed he fainted, had never fainted before, was in

good health, and had no indication that he might faint. All of a sudden, as the plaintiff acknowledged, he exclaimed, "Oh, I feel sick." His head fell back and his hand left the wheel. On the day in question he was not feeling bad until the moment before the illness and the fainting occurred. The trial court directed a verdict in favor of the defendant and the appellate court affirmed that verdict, finding the plaintiff had failed to show any fault on the part of the defendant. See J. B. Craig, "Heart Attacks as a Defense Negligence Action," *Clev.-Mar. L. Rev.* 12 (1963): 59. But see Sauers v. Sack, 34 Ga. App. 748, 131 S.E. 98 (1921), where an epileptic seizure was viewed as similar to insanity and the defendant was held liable. In this case the defendant was shown to be accustomed to having epileptic or other similar attacks.

52. See, e.g., Sfroza v. Green Bus Lines, 150 Misc. 180, 268 N.Y. Supp. 446 (1934).

53. See M. Arnold, "Driven Mad," *Jerusalem Post*, Oct. 8, 1999, p. 16; A. Martin, "Driving Ourselves Crazy," *Detroit Free Press Magazine*, Aug. 9, 1992, p. 7.

54. B. Bush, *A Memoir* (New York: Scribners, 1994).

55. S. L. Godard & J. D. Bloom, "Driving, Mental Illness, and the Duty to Protect," in J. C. Beck (ed.), *Confidentiality versus the Duty to Protect: Foreseeable Harm in the Practice of Psychiatry* (Washington, D.C.: American Psychiatric Press, 1990), pp. 191–204.

56. See G. H. Morris, "Requiring Sound Judgments of Unsound Minds: Tort Liability and the Limits of Therapeutic Jurisprudence," *SMU L. Rev.* 47 (1994): 1837; D. W. Shuman, "Therapeutic Jurisprudence and Tort Law: A Limited Subjective Standard of Care," *SMU L. Rev.* 46 (1992): 409.

57. In C. T. W. v. B. C. G., supra note 32, a pedophile was held negligent for failing to seek professional help and not avoiding situations where he would be alone with children.

58. In Kuhn v. Zabotsky, 9 Ohio St.2d 129, 224 N.E.2d 137 (1967), a psychiatrist, called by the defense, testified that the defendant was mentally ill and that he was suffering from a psychotic depression reaction, but the psychiatrist did not testify that the defendant had (for the first time) blacked out at the time of the accident. Verdict was for the plaintiff. See S. L. Halleck, *Law in the Practice of Psychiatry* (New York: Plenum, 1980), p. 275.

59. 45 Wis.2d 536, 173 N.W.2d 619 (1970).

60. Twenty-four years later, in 1994, a Wisconsin appellate court said that *Breunig* compelled a conclusion that an individual with a *permanent* mental disability that prevents the individual from controlling or appreciating his conduct cannot be held liable in negligence. In this case, the patient suffered Alzheimer's disease. The court said that to the extent that it prevented him from appreciating or controlling his actions, he could not be held liable in negligence. The patient attacked a member of a health center's staff. Gould v. American Family Mut. Ins. Co., 523 N.W.2d 295 (Wis. App. 1994). Some law professors suggest that Alzheimer's disease be regarded as a physical condition, with the standard of care then being "the reasonable person with Alzheimer's." See Memorial Hosp. v. Scott, 261 Ind. 27, 300 N.E.2d 50 (1973) (multiple sclerosis); *Prosser & Keeton on the Law of Torts* (St. Paul, Minn.: West, 5th ed. 1984), p. 175.

61. 147 Colo. 203, 363 P.2d 165 (1961).

62. In a Canadian case, the court found no negligence when a truck driver was overcome by a sudden insane delusion that his truck was being operated by the remote control of his employer and, as a result, he was in fact helpless to avert a collision. The truck driver had syphilis of the brain. He sat transfixed at the wheel, powerless to do anything about the collision that ensued. Buckley & Toronto Transp. Comm'n v. Smith Transport, 1946 Ont. Rep. 798, 4 Dom. L. Rep. 721 (1946).

63. See Rausch v. McVeigh, 105 Misc.2d 163, 431 N.Y.S.2d 887 (1980) (cause of action for negligent supervision against parents of 22-year-old autistic son who attacked his therapist). To encourage individuals to take on the role of guardian, laws in various states provide that a guardian is not liable to third person for acts of the ward. For example, Michigan law provides: "[A] guardian of a legally incapacitated person is responsible for the care, custody, and control of the ward, but is not liable to third persons by reason of that responsibility for acts of the ward." M.L.D., sec. 700.455 (1). The circumstance of a person being under guardianship as insane does not take away his legal capacity to be sued. Ingersoll v. Harrison, 48 Mich. 234, 12 N.W. 179 (1882). Not only are guardians not held responsible for the acts of their wards, abuses by guardians of their wards are widespread, and the guardians are rarely held responsible. Nowadays, with families split apart, lawyers and corporations are often named guardian for a number of people, and they are paid a fee for their service. W.

Wendland-Bowyer, "Who's Watching the Guardians?" (3-part series), *Detroit Free Press*, May 24–26, 2000, p. 1.

64. See Tarasoff v. Regents of University of California, 17 Cal.3d 425, 551 P.2d 334, 131 Cal. Rptr. 14 (1976); T. E. Gammon & J. K. Hulston, "The Duty of Mental Health Care Providers to Restrain Their Patients or Warn Third Parties," *Mo. L. Rev.* 60 (1995): 1995; R. I. Simon, "Psychiatrists' Duties in Discharging Sicker and Potentially Violent Inpatients in the Managed Care Era," *Psychiatric Services* 49 (Jan. 1998): 62.

65. R. I. Simon, *Clinical Psychiatry and the Law* (Washington, D.C.: American Psychiatric Press, 2d ed. 1992), p. 274.

66. See McGuire v. Almy, 297 Mass. 323, 8 N.E.2d 760 (1937); Van Vooren v. Cook, 273 App. Div. 88, 75 N.Y.S.2d 362 (1947); Mullen v. Bruce, (68 Cal. App.2d 494, 335 P.2d 945 (1959).

67. Anicet v. Gant, 580 So.2d 273 (Fla. Dist. App. 1991); see also Gould v. American Family Mut. Ins. Co., 523 N.W. 295 (Wis. App. 1994); Mujica v. Turner, 582 So.2d 24 (Fla. Dist. App. 1991); Van Vooren v. Cook, 273 App. Div. 88, 75 N.Y.S.2d 362 (1947). In Herrle v. Estate of Marshall, 45 Cal. App.4th 1761, 53 Cal. Rptr.2d 713 (1996), it was held that a nurse's aide assumed the risk of attack by a patient suffering from Alzheimer's disease. As a consequence of the decision, a dissenter argued that caretakers would be well-advised to use greater force on the patient to avoid injury to themselves. Workers' compensation would provide compensation for employees injured in the course of their employment. See also Creasy v. Rusk, 730 N.E.2d 659 (Ind. 2000).

68. R. Slovenko, *Psychiatry and Criminal Culpability* (New York: Wiley, 1995); S. K. Hoge & T. G. Gutheil, "The Prosecution of Psychiatric Patients for Assaults on Staff: A Preliminary Empirical Study," *Hosp. & Community Psychiatry* 38 (1987): 44; S. Rachlin, "The Prosecution of Violent Psychiatric Inpatients: One Respectable Intervention," *Bull. Am. Acad. Psychiatry & Law* 22 (1994): 239.

69. See State Farm Fire & Cas. Co. v. Wicka, 474 N.W.2d 324 (Minn. 1991); D. E. Seidelson, "Reasonable Expectations and Subjective Standards in Negligence Law: The Minor, The Mentally Impaired, and the Mentally Incompetent," *Geo. Wash. L. Rev.* 50 (1981): 17.

70. I. N. Perr, "Liability of the Mentally Ill and Their Insurers in Negligence and Other Civil Actions," *Am. J. Psychiatry* 142 (1985): 1414; C. A. Salton, "Mental Incapacity and Liability Insurance Exclusionary Clauses: The Effect of Insanity upon Intent," *Cal. L. Rev.* 78 (1990): 1027; R. I. Simon, "You Only Die Once—But Did You Intend It?: Psychiatric Assessment of Suicide Intent in Insurance Litigation," *Tort & Ins. L.J.* 25 (1990): 650; Note, "Insanity, Intent, and Homeowner's Liability," *La. L. Rev.* 40 (1979): 258.

71. The Washington Court of Appeals in Public Employees Mut. Ins. Co. v. Rash, 48 Wash App. 701, 740 P.2d 370 (1987), held that an insurer is not liable to pay a claim under a homeowner's policy for the insured's sexual assault on a minor in light of the exclusion from policy coverage of injuries caused by insured that are expected or intended. The court said that the insured's subjective intent or incapability of forming intent is irrelevant in determining whether damage caused by the insured is covered by the policy. See also Germantown Ins. Co. v. Martin, 407 Pa. Super. 326, 595 A.2d 1172 (1992).

72. 39 N.J. 490, 189 A.2d 204 (1963).

73. See George v. Stone, 260 So.2d 259 (Fla. App. 1972); Rosa v. Liberty Mutual Ins. Co., 243 F.Supp. 407 (D.Conn. 1965); Congregation of Rodef Sholom v. American Motorists Ins. Co., 91 Cal. App.3d 690, 154 Cal. Rptr. 348 (1979); Nationwide Mutual Fire Ins. Co. v. Turner, 29 Ohio App.3d 73, 503 N.E.2d 212 (1986).

74. It was questioned whether Freddie Prinze, the TV star, actually meant to kill himself. Despite the uncontested fact that he shot himself in the presence of a witness, his family and managers tried to prove in court that it was not legally suicide. They had hoped to obtain the $550,000 in insurance—the only big item in Prinze's estate—that two insurance companies refused to pay because of a suicide clause. The family's lawyers pressed two lines of attack, both based on the fact that intent is a key element in suicide. One was that for months before his death, he had been scaring friends by pretending to shoot himself, keeping the safety catch on his gun; he may have tried it the last time unaware the catch was off. An alternate argument was that use of a depressant drug had rendered him incapable of willing his own death. See G. Schuman, "Suicide and the Life Insurance Contract: Was the Insured Sane or Insane? That Is the Question—Or Is It?" *Tort & Ins. L.J.* 28 (1993): 745.

The courts are divided on their willingness to admit psychological autopsy evidence. At one extreme, a federal court held that a psychological autopsy offered as evidence in a suit over life insurance proceeds was "pure speculation," which did "nothing to assist the trier of fact in the least" in determining whether the deceased had been murdered or committed suicide. Foster v. Globe Life & Acc. Ins. Co., 808 F.Supp. 1281 (N.D.Miss. 1992). At the other end of the spectrum is the decision of a Florida appellate court affirming a child abuse conviction of a woman whose seventeen-year-old daughter had committed suicide. Its ruling was based in part on a psychological autopsy that found the mother's mistreatment of her daughter, whom she had forced to work as a stripteaser, to be a "substantial contributing factor" in the daughter's decision to kill herself. Jackson v. State, 553 So.2d 719 (Fla. App. 1989). See M. Hansen, "Suicidal Missions," *ABAJ*, Mar. 2000, p. 28.

75. 136 Wis.2d 425, 401 N.W.2d 842, 62 A.L.R.4th 815 (1987).

76. Reviewing a suicide exclusion clause, the U.S. Supreme Court in Mutual Life Ins. Co. v. Terry, 15 Wall. 580, 21 L. Ed. 236 (1873), said: "If the death is caused by the voluntary act of the insured, he knowing and intending that his death shall be result of his act but when his reasoning faculties are so far impaired that he is not able to understand the moral character, the general nature, consequences and effect of the act he is about to commit, or when he is impelled thereto by an insane impulse, which he has not the power to resist, such death is not within the contemplation of the parties to the contract and the insurer is liable." See also Searle v. Allstate Life Ins. Co., 38 Cal.3d 425, 212 Cal. Rptr. 466, 696 P.2d 1308 (1985).

77. Fuller v. Preis, 35 N.Y.2d 425, 322 N.E.2d 263, 363 N.Y.S.2d 568 (1974).

78. See Brown v. American Steel & Wire Co., 43 Ind. App. 560, 88 N.E. 80 (1909). For a review of the cases, see Grant v. F.P. Lathrop Constr. Co., 81 Cal. App.3d 796, 146 Cal. Rptr. 45 (1978).

79. The concept of *accident* is disappearing, with blame placed on the alleged wrongdoing, the victim, or a third party. In early 2001 the *British Medical Journal* decided to ban the use of the word *accident*. The *Journal of Accident and Emergency Medicine* also dropped the word and changed its name to *Emergency Medicine Journal*. Ronald Davis, North American editor of the *British Medical Journal*, and Barry Pless, editor of the journal *Injury Prevention*, wrote in a joint editorial, "An accident is often understood to be unpredictable—a chance occurrence or an 'act of God' and therefore unavoidable. However, most injuries and their precipitating events are predictable and preventable. That is why the BMJ has decided to ban the word." Medical sociologists have argued for years about whether the use of the *a* word prejudices public thinking away from prevention and towards fatalistic explanations. Most explanations in contemporary society involve networks of causality without appeal to change. T. Barlow, "You Better Believe It—It's Just an Accident," *Financial Times*, Nov. 3–4, 2001, p. II.

21
Post-traumatic Stress Disorder

The term *post-traumatic stress disorder* refers to a psychogenic disorder following a psychic injury with or without physical injury. It is also known by many other names: *traumatic neurosis, neurosis following trauma, neurosis following accident, terror neurosis (schreckneurose), acute neurotic reaction, triggered neurosis, postaccident anxiety syndrome, post-traumatic hysteria, hysterical paralysis, social neurosis, personal injury neurosis, industrial neurosis, accident neurosis, occupational neurosis, litigation neurosis, justice neurosis, compensation neurosis, compensationitis, desire neurosis, unconscious malingering, retirement neurosis, pension neurosis, fate neurosis,* and *secondary gain neurosis.*

Commonly, these terms refer to a disorder developing from an injury caused by another person, which is complicated by factors in compensation and litigation, but compensation is not an essential element in the etiology of the neurosis. The term *traumatic neurosis* came into use during World War II, a successor to the old term *shell shock,* and more recently, *post-traumatic stress disorder* has come into use.[1] In the military situation, other labels include: *war neurosis, combat fatigue, combat neurosis, battle stress,* and *stress reaction.* In some measure, the use of a particular descriptive label reflects a particular attitude toward the phenomenon. The terms *malingering* and *goof-off* are commonly used to refer to conscious deception.

Otto Rank, a prominent member of Freud's early coterie, in a book *The Trauma of Birth* makes the event of birth itself the crucial fact of life and interprets later psychosexual crises of childhood as variations on the theme of the terror of the issue from the womb and the wish to return to embryonic bliss. From this premise he reinterprets many of the common Freudian concepts. The painful experience of birth leaves all of us with a measure of "primal anxiety." The universal desire to forget this pain Rank calls "primal repression." Therapy would take nine months, the time period of gestation.[2]

Actually, there is nothing new about PTSD except its name. Willa Cather once observed that if you give the people a new word, they think they have a new fact. It has long been known that traumatic events can produce serious emotional reactions. In the 1666 diary of Samuel Pepys, six months after he survived the Great Fire of London, he wrote, "It is strange to think how to this very day I cannot sleep a night without great terrors of the fire; and this very night could not sleep to almost two in the morning through great terrors of the fire."[3] In 1871, when Chicago went up in flames, many people came down with PTSD. Veterans of combat in World War I suffered from "shell shock"; many veterans of World War II had "battle fatigue." Soon the term *traumatic neurosis* came into wide professional but not official usage, which lasted until 1980 when the term was officially replaced by *post-traumatic stress disorder*. The attack on September 11, 2001, of the World Trade Center made it an everyday term.

In 1980, with the publication of *DSM-II*, PTSD entered the psychiatric nomenclature as a listing under the heading of Anxiety Disorders. (*DSM-II* had eliminated gross stress reactions, including combat stress, and replaced them with "(transient) adjustment reaction of adult life.")[4] In *DSM-IV*, of 1994, the minimum duration of symptoms of PTSD must be one month. The symptoms include free-floating anxiety, muscular tension, irritability, impaired concentration, repetitive nightmares reproducing the traumatic incident, and social withdrawal. *DSM-IV* introduced a new diagnosis, *acute stress disorder*, when the symptoms occur within four weeks of the traumatic event and the symptoms last only for two days to a month. It might be considered a brief PTSD or a normal response to trauma. It is listed among anxiety disorders, to manifest its association with PTSD.

Although one or another term referring to a psychogenic disorder following a psychic injury has been used and respected in scientific literature throughout the world, none appear as a nosological entity in the *DSM* until 1980. Some psychiatrists did not and still do not agree that PTSD is an entity. Some see it as a complex of symptoms or scars, not as a disorder. They view most cases as indistinguishable from derivatives of anxiety—hysterical-conversion type, hysterical dissociative type, phobic, obsessive-compulsive—depression, depersonalization, or hypochondriasis. Other psychiatrists, however, see it as a distinct category of mental disorder that develops in individuals as a result of a specific psychic insult.

A psychiatric diagnostic category is not essential to a cause of action in law, but the listing of stress reactions in the *DSM* has tended to give the claim more legitimacy. Forensic psychiatrists promoted the listing of PTSD in the *DSM*. With the inclusion of PTSD, attorneys on behalf of victims of trauma have increasingly used that formulation in civil as well as in criminal cases. As expert witnesses, psychiatrists embrace PTSD to explain the psychological sequelae of trauma in personal injury cases as well as to formulate opinions regarding criminal responsibility. *DSM-IV* also describes a condition called "post-traumatic stress disorder, delayed type," where the symptoms do not appear until at least six months after the trauma.

In 1980 the Veterans Administration (VA) had authorized compensation and other benefits for PTSD, delayed type. It was the first time since World War I that the Department of Veterans Benefits could consider disorders to be service-connected when the symptoms appeared long after military discharge. The result was a surge of admission to VA hospitals (providing care otherwise not available). The veterans presented themselves to examiners fully aware of the checklist of the diagnostic features of the disorder. PTSD became a political diagnosis.[5]

For a diagnosis of PTSD, the *DSM-III* specified a stressor that is "outside the range of usual human experience" that would be markedly distressing to almost anyone.[6] The manual gave examples of "common experiences" that do not qualify for PTSD—"simple bereavement, chronic illness, business losses, or marital conflict." Researchers, however, found patients who met symptom criteria for PTSD without meeting the stressor criterion. Dr. Bonnie Green, who served on the advisory committee for the PTSD diagnosis for *DSM-III-R* and on the *DSM-IV* PSTD advisory committee, reports that the most debate regarding this diagnosis centered on the definition of the stressor criterion and also on whether there should be additional diagnoses that reflect responses to traumatic events.[7] *DSM-IV* omits the phrase "outside the range of usual human experience," but like *DSM-III-R*, it requires "an event or events that involved actual or threatened death or serious injury, or a threat to the physical integrity of self or others."

PTSD is taken as the prototypical environmentally caused disorder, as it allegedly only arises in the aftermath of an environmental insult—the *DSM* suggests that the symptoms of PTSD emerge from an event or events. In a review of the world literature on response to trauma, however, it was concluded that "toxic events are not reliably powerful in yielding a chronic, event-focused clinical disorder such as PTSD."[8] Indeed, with the exception of events like the Holocaust, most people, it was reported, do not respond to toxic events with persistent symptoms that would rise to the level of a diagnosable disorder like PTSD. Individuals who do are characterized by preexisting factors such as long-standing personality traits of emotionality and personal vulnerability, suggesting that their preevent factors contribute more to serious distress disorders than the toxic event.[9]

In any event, in tort litigation, PTSD is a favored diagnosis in cases of emotional distress because it is alleged to be incident specific. The diagnosis tends to rule out other factors important to the determination of causation (vulnerability and resilience). Thus, plaintiffs can argue that all of their psychological problems issue from the alleged traumatic event and not from myriad other sources encountered in life. A diagnosis of depression, on the other hand, opens the issue of causation to many factors other than the stated cause of action. Dr. Alan A. Stone, a past president of the American Psychiatric Association, puts it this way:

> By giving diagnostic credence and specificity to the concept of psychic harm, PTSD has become the lightning rod for a wide variety of claims of stress-related psychopathology in the civil arena. Unlike the diagnostic concept of neurosis, which emphasizes a complex etiology, PTSD posits a straightforward causal relationship that plaintiffs' lawyers welcome. Beyond its significance as an apparent solution to the legal problem of causation, PTSD's greatest importance is that it seems to make matters sci-

entific and objective that the court once considered too subjective for legal resolution.[10]

The diagnostic category is now entrenched in the jurisprudence and also in ordinary language. In *Trial* magazine, it was written: "No diagnosis in the history of American psychiatry has had a more dramatic and pervasive impact on law and social justice than post-traumatic stress disorder."[11] Seeing the mayhem in the 1998 film *Saving Private Ryan*, a movie-goer said, "[It] was not a movie; it was an ordeal. I told my husband that I thought I was going to have post-traumatic stress syndrome and wondered if I could sue somebody."[12]

At trial, psychiatric testimony is offered on the issues of causation and damage. The legal claim of a person who seeks compensation for PTSD may fall into one of the following categories: a tort action for personal injury allegedly inflicted by the fault (intentional or negligent) of the defendant; a workers' compensation claim for disability allegedly due to an accidental injury received in the course and scope of employment; or a claim under a life-, health-, or accident-insurance policy.

There is only limited legal redress for the infliction of mental pain and anguish. It has seemed quixotic (at least to members of the legal community) for the law to attempt to secure an emotional or mental state, hence the courts afforded legal redress only in the more outrageous types of cases. Wholly aside from the question of how far the law should go in protecting emotional or mental nondisturbance, difficult evidentiary questions are presented of causation and assessment of harm.

To be sure, recovery for emotional distress has long been recognized as an additional or parasitic element of damages in a tort action. Thus, where the actor's tortious conduct results in the invasion of another's legally protected interest, as where it inflicts bodily harm, the ensuing emotional distress may be taken into account in determining the damages recoverable. As a general principle, however, freedom from mental and emotional disturbance has received only limited independent recognition as a legally protected interest.[13]

In a variety of situations where the disturbance is grievous, for instance, in actions for assault, defamation, false imprisonment, invasion of privacy, and malicious prosecution, the law has afforded protection. Gradually, the general proposition developed that one who, without just cause or excuse and beyond all bounds of decency, purposely inflicts mental distress of a serious nature is subject to liability. Thus, a joker who tells a woman that her son has been mutilated in an accident would be liable for her ensuing mental anguish. The tort is called "intentional infliction of mental distress."

In cases of negligence resulting in fright, shock, or other mental suffering, the various jurisdictions have required proof of physical impact or injury. Over the years the law has been concerned about a flood of litigation or fraudulent claims if compensation were awarded in cases of negligence causing mental distress without accompanying physical impact or injury. As a New York court in 1896 said:

> If the right of recovery [for mental distress in negligence cases without physical impact or injury] should be one established, it would naturally result in a flood of litigation in cases where the injury complained of may be easily feigned without detection, and where the damages must rest upon mere conjecture or speculation. The difficulty which often exists in cases of alleged physical injury, in determining whether they exist, and if

so, whether they were caused by the negligent act of the defendant, would not only be greatly increased, but a wide field would be opened for fictitious or speculative claims. To establish such a doctrine would be contrary to principles of public policy.[14]

Likewise, at about the same time, an English court said:

According to the evidence of the female plaintiff her fright was caused by seeing the train approaching, and thinking they were going to be killed. Damages arising from mere sudden terror unaccompanied by an actual physical injury, but occasioning a nervous or mental shock, cannot under such circumstances, their Lordships think, be considered a consequence which, in the ordinary course of things, would flow from the negligence of the gate-keeper. If it were held that they can, it appears to their Lordships that it would be extending the liability for negligence much beyond what that liability has hitherto been held to be. Not only in such a case as the present, but in every case where an accident caused by negligence had given a person a serious nervous shock, there might be a claim for damages on account of mental injury. The difficulty which now often exists in cases of alleged physical injuries of determining whether they were caused by the negligent act would be greatly increased, and a wide field opened for imaginary claims.[15]

The theory is that impact or injury affords a guarantee of causal connection and genuineness of harm. But the theory was mocked in a famous Georgia circus case, "impact" being found where one of the performing horses defecated on a spectator's lap, to her great humiliation.[16]

The most frequently cited public policy factors a court will consider when deciding whether liability should not attach to damages caused by a defendant's negligence are: (1) the injury is too remote from the negligence, (2) the injury is wholly out of proportion to the defendant's culpability, (3) in retrospect it appears extraordinary that the negligence would have brought about the harm, (4) allowing recovery places an unreasonable burden on the defendant, (5) allowing recovery is too likely to open the way for fraudulent claims, (6) allowing recovery will enter a field having no sensible or just stopping point.

Wholly aside from the questions of how far the law should go in protecting against emotional disturbance, there are difficult evidentiary questions of (1) fault, (2) causation, and (3) assessment of damages. The vulnerability of the victim is considered differently in each of these various elements that together constitute a tort.

Fault

For fault, the risk reasonably to be perceived determines the duty of care. Foreseeability is the traditional test. Thus, a greater duty of care is imposed on a motorist when he sees a handicapped person or child crossing the street. When the vulnerability of a person is not reasonably apparent, the fair assumption is that he is an ordinary individual. Negligence is failing to observe the care expected of a reasonable person in like circumstances.

What about a duty of care to those who witness or learn about the event (e.g., parents who learn of injury to their child)? (The term *bystander* is used to describe a person who sees or learns of the event.) The *DSM* recognizes that a person who witnesses an event that threatens the physical integrity of others may suffer PTSD. In law in 1968 a trend began to allow an action for mental distress for bystanders witnessing negligent as well as intentional injury. That year, in the famous case of *Dillon v. Legg*,[17] the California Supreme Court ruled in favor of a mother who saw her infant daughter killed when hit by a car. It set out standards for a bystander action: a close relationship to the person injured, close proximity to the scene, and "sensory and contemporaneous observation" of the accident. The bystander cases in California culminated in the decision in 1989 in *Thing v. La Chusa*,[18] where the California Supreme Court circumscribed the class of bystanders to whom a defendant owes a duty to avoid negligently inflicting emotional distress. In *Thing*, the guidelines in *Dillon* became precise rules. The court set out the limits as follows:

> In the absence of physical injury or impact to the plaintiff himself, damages for emotional distress should be recoverable only if the plaintiff: (1) is closely related to the injury victim, (2) is present at the scene of the injury-producing event at the time it occurs and is then aware that it is causing injury to the victim and, (3) as a result suffers emotional distress beyond that which would be anticipated in a disinterested witness.

Under *Thing*, regardless of foreseeable and actual emotional harm to the plaintiff, the plaintiff would be denied recovery unless actually present and a witness to the injury or threat to a close relation. In *Thing*, a mother who heard her son had been struck by a car, and who rushed to the scene to find her son bloody and apparently dead, had no cause of action for her own distress because she had not been within the zone of danger and had not actually witnessed the injury.[19]

A number of jurisdictions have loosened the requirement that the plaintiff has to be at the scene of the alleged act that caused the mental suffering. In the *Dillon* case, the distressed mother was outside the "zone of danger"—there was no possibility that the mother would be hit by the car that killed her daughter, but she was at the scene. In 1980, the Supreme Judicial Court of Massachusetts allowed a wife and children to sue for mental distress arising out of seeing their injured husband/father at a hospital hours after an accident allegedly caused by the defendant.[20] The Ohio Supreme Court in 1983 suggested a standard of "serious and reasonably foreseeable" that a bystander would sustain emotional injury.[21]

In the famous Buffalo Creek disaster, where a dam broke due to the alleged negligence of the defendant, there was a settlement of claims brought by a number of plaintiffs who suffered emotional distress though they witnessed no one caught up in the flood. They were miles away when the water broke through the dam; they heard the news. The 20-to-30-foot tidal wave of rampaging water and sludge, sometimes traveling at speeds up to thirty miles per hour, devastated Buffalo Creek's sixteen small communities.[22]

Causation

For causation, the law looks for proximate cause. There is no litmus test for determining proximity, and there may be more than one proximate cause. Some courts use the foreseeability test in determining causation, but usually the courts say it is a question of the objective evidence. For causation, there is the well-known expression, "the tortfeasor must take his victim as he finds him," so that peculiar vulnerability to harm does not excuse. However, it may be argued, sometimes successfully, that the straw that broke the camel's back is not a proximate cause.

The so-called delayed PTSD may be the result of a cumulation of events resulting in a crisis. (In law, the statute of limitations begins when the injury is "made known.") The proximate cause may arguably be either the earlier or a later event. The term *proximate* has connotations of nearness in time, but that is not its meaning in law. *Legal cause* or *responsible cause* are more appropriate terms, but those terms also leave much room for vagaries in decision making. In a number of cases, the courts have said that the determination of proximate cause is the province of judges not juries but more often than not, it is a decision left to the jury.

In days gone by, when the term *traumatic neurosis* was used, psychiatrists distinguished between a "true traumatic neurosis," where a healthy individual suffers emotional distress as a result of an overwhelming stress, and a "triggered neurosis," where a vulnerable individual decompensates as a result of stress that would be quite inconsequential to a healthy individual. For the law, however, the distinction is one without a difference. The argument may prevail, however, that in the case of a triggered neurosis, a triggering event is not a proximate cause.

Trauma, of course, as we have noted, is a relative concept—stimulus in relation to the coping ability of an individual. An individual's response to an injury event may be influenced by preexisting vulnerabilities that facilitate the development and maintenance of symptoms. A prior history of major depression is identified as a significant risk factor for developing PTSD.[23] When a stressor is within the range of common experience, the evidence tends to support a finding that it is not a proximate cause. Also, when a stressor is not outside the range of common experience, suspicion of malingering arises.

The difference in the legal and medical concept of causation results from the differences in the basic problems and exigencies of the two disciplines. In the law of torts, it is said that the tortfeasor is not entitled to complain that his victim was not a perfect specimen. Likewise, in the field of workers' compensation, the employer takes his employee as he finds him. In legal contemplation, if an injury operates on an existing bodily condition or predisposition and produces a further injurious result, that result is deemed caused by the injury.

A number of survivors of Nazi concentration camps who subsequently suffered serious psychiatric disorders were denied compensation because certain psychiatric experts appointed by the German Consulate declined to acknowledge a causal connection between the victims' experiences and later mental disorders. In a parallel to Otto Rank's birth trauma theory, these psychiatrists adhered to a theory of constitutional etiology or childhood neurosis that, coupled with their general approach, made it unlikely that they would recommend compensation for the victims.[24]

Theories pointing to distal causes call to mind the argument that if the injured person had never been born, the injury would not have happened. Therefore, the courts ask whether the wrongful act was the proximate cause. Lord Chancellor Francis Bacon's maxim was: *In jure non remota, sed proxima, spectatur* [In law, not the remote cause, but the nearest one, is looked to]. Testimony of the medical expert witness usually ends up thus:

Q. From everything that you know about this case, Doctor, do you feel there is a causal relationship between the explosion of July 4, and the symptoms that she has shown that you have reported [sudden loss of weight, inability to perform ordinary household duties, extreme nervousness and irritability]?

A. Yes, the trauma was the triggering point for breaking the balance in her. So to speak, the trauma threw her off her rocker.

Q. Trauma?

A. Any trauma. It may be emotional trauma or physical trauma. In this case it was the explosive sound that she heard and the fears that were aroused by it.

Legal, or proximate, cause may be illustrated by the once-upon-a-time story of the camel that carried loads across the desert for its master. This camel had a weaker back than other camels, but because his master had never loaded him too heavily he had been able to do his job well and was his master's favorite. At the beginning of one trip the camel was loaded as usual, but while the master's back was turned a prankster put a straw atop the load. The weight of this straw was just enough to break the camel's back. The prankster's act being the legal cause of the camel's broken back, he is liable to the camel's master for all damages that the master suffers. Thus, the law is interested more in the straw that broke the camel's back than in all the straws already piled on his back.

Consider also the example of a fifty-year-old man who has been walking all his life on the brink of a precipice. He has walked close to the brink, but he has kept his footing. Along comes someone who gives this man a push—not much of a push but just enough to make him lose his balance and plunge over the edge. It may not have been enough of a push to make a different person lose his balance. But for the purpose of legal causation it is enough to show that but for the push the man could have kept on walking, even if for only one more step. The person who gave the push must pay for all injuries resulting from the plunge.[25] Thus, the court says, "If a man is negligently run over or otherwise negligently injured in his body, it is no answer to the sufferer's claim for damages that he would have suffered less injury, or no injury at all, if he had not had an unusually thin skull or an unusually weak heart."[26]

Law professors like to discuss the case of *Steinhauser v. Hertz Corp.*[27] In this case, the plaintiff, a fourteen-year-old girl, was riding as a passenger in a car with her parents when it was struck by another vehicle. The occupants did not suffer any bodily injuries. Within minutes after the accident, the plaintiff began to behave in a bizarre manner. After a series of hospitalizations, she was diagnosed as suffering from a "schizophrenic reaction—acute—undifferentiated." Prior to the accident she had a "'prepsychotic' personality" and displayed a predisposition to abnormal behavior. Nevertheless, there was testimony that, had it not been for the accident, she might have been able to lead a normal life and that the accident was the precipitating cause of her psychosis. The trial court did not allow plaintiff's counsel to elicit testimony as to whether the accident could have been an aggravating cause of her condition. In reversing a verdict of no cause of action, the U.S. Court of Appeals for the Second Circuit stated that the evidence made clear that plaintiff had some degree of pathology that was activated into schizophrenia by the emotional trauma connected with the accident and that she was entitled to have that issue fairly weighed by a jury.

Assessment of Damages

Let us assume the accident was a proximate cause in bringing about the disability. When assessing the amount of damages, the functioning of the plaintiff before and after the defendant's act is compared. The question is: What could the person do before the accident that he could not do afterward? At trial the testimony on before and after would detail specific instances of change: outgoing versus withdrawn, loving versus indifferent, mild-mannered versus abusive, reliable versus erratic, and clean versus slovenly. The before-and-after testimony would dwell on difference in personality, character traits, and behavior, with the behavior change constituting the better proof since it is more objective and more understandable by the jury. By and large, attorneys prefer before-and-after testimony by lay witnesses to psychological testing. Malingering is always a concern in cases alleging emotional distress, but psychological testing indicating malingering may indicate malingering on the tests rather than in the world outside the testing room.

Damages are not measured in the abstract, for example, by the "value of an eye," as the value of an eye is different for a one-eyed person than it is for a person with normal eyesight. A one-eyed person may be functioning quite well prior to injury, but upon losing the remaining eye he would be totally visually incapacitated. However, there may be factors that tend to diminish the value of the interest impaired by the defendant's tort. Thus, in a claim for wrongful death, the value of the deceased's life is assessed in light of relevant factors bearing on its prospective duration, including any disease likely to reduce it.[28]

There is a distinction to be drawn between the issue of negligence and the extent of liability. In seeking to avoid negligent conduct, as we have noted, the reasonable person must consider the effect of his conduct upon ordinary people, and, generally speaking, may disregard the possibility of encountering exceptionally sensitive people—to require that one guard against exceptional sensitivity would impose an undue restraint upon conduct. Once it is held, however, that the defendant has been negligent toward the plaintiff, that is, he should have foreseen injury to an ordinary person or because he knew of the peculiar sensitivities of the plaintiff, he is liable for the consequences or injuries resulting from the plaintiff's special sensitivity.[29] An extreme illustration is the case where a milk vendor knowingly left a milk bottle with a chipped top on a customer's doorstep. The customer, without contributory negligence on her part, cut her hand in taking it in, for which the vendor was clearly liable. Unfortunately, the customer suffered from an unusual blood condition that caused blood poisoning and subsequent death. Because a breach of a duty of care to an ordinary person was established, the court imposed liability for the consequential death.[30]

This principle is also applicable where the plaintiff is peculiarly susceptible to nervous shock or neurosis, provided the initial breach of duty owed to him is established. If any injury to a legally protected interest of the plaintiff could be reasonably foreseen, the defendant is liable for all the consequences resulting from his wrongful act.[31] Some courts, however, impose liability only for such damage as could have been foreseen, rather than for all damages that actually resulted. In such cases, the average reasonable person's foresight, rather than the plaintiff's injury, is the measure of recovery.

In many situations more than one person may be legally responsible for a given injury. Frequently, concurrent liability results not from any planned action but from quite independent conduct by two or more tortfeasors resulting in one individual injury to the plaintiff. The acts are said to have concurred or coalesced in causing the injury, as where two negligent motorists collide and hurt a pedestrian or passenger. The acts may be successive in a time sense, though concurrent in their causative effect, as where one person spills gasoline, which later catches fire when a burning match is tossed on it. Neither cause is by itself sufficient without the other to result in the injury; but it makes no difference if each alone is sufficient, as in the case of two merging fires, either of which could have caused the entire damage. In all these cases, the plaintiff, of course, is allowed but one satisfaction of his loss (he is entitled to reparation, not a bonus); but this does not preclude his seeking a judgment against one or all.

There are cases where it may be feasible to allocate the damages, attributing different injuries to separate causes. For example, if A and B strike C, one injuring his arm, the other his leg, A and B may be held liable for the particular injury that each caused. A similar result may be reached when pollution of a stream can be attributed to several factories in proportion to the volume of discharge. More typical cases, however, are those where the defendant's tortious conduct contributed, together with other responsible causes, to an injury that is not divisible. Often enough, the defendant's share of responsibility may be no greater, perhaps much smaller, than that of other cooperating causes. But if the defendant's conduct is altogether trivial in causal potency, neither necessary nor sufficient to produce the injury because the other coexisting causal factors would by themselves have sufficed, it may fairly be dismissed entirely from consideration. Thus, a person would not be held responsible for having thrown a match that caused a raging fire that subsequently destroyed the plaintiff's home. Proximate cause, which the law requires, must be a substantial factor. If the defendant's act, however, is not trivial in causal potency and if the damages are not divisible, he is liable to the plaintiff for the entire in jury and is left to seek contribution from the other tortfeasors.[32]

Critique of the Testimony

In general, testimony concerning emotional disturbance tends to provoke either hostility or ridicule. On the one hand, psychiatric testimony may seem arbitrary, as in the case where psychiatrists failed to make recommendations in favor of concentration-camp victims. The testimony in any case must overcome the preconceptions that everyone has about psychological disorders. On the other hand, psychiatric testimony may seem fanciful, bringing into disrepute both law and psychiatry. However accurate these charges may be, there is the important consideration that psychiatric testimony tends to arouse feelings of severe anxiety about one's own mental condition. It may provoke reaction or anxiety in judge or jury—indeed, in anyone—a situation that is handled by denial, laughter, or ridicule.[33]

Overload may break a leg, or it may overwhelm the central nervous system. Credibility of psychiatric testimony on PTSD is enhanced by discussion of the syndrome. The constellation of key symptoms, essential or near-essential, include free-floating anxiety, varying from mild apprehensiveness to panic ("something is about to happen"); irritability and belligerency; muscular tension ("I just can't seem to relax"); easy fatigability; impaired concentration and memory; insomnia; repetitive frightening dreams (directly or symbolically reproducing the traumatic incident); sexual inhibition or disinterest; and social withdrawal ("peace and quiet at any price").

Often the information must come from the spouse or other family member, since the person with the disabilities labeled traumatic neurosis is often verbally unproductive, unimaginative, and a poor observer of his own feelings and behavior. He is usually the type of person who uses his body to express his feelings and thinks in concrete terms. He tends to think of injury only in physicalistic terms.

For most people, peacetime conditions are less traumatic than those of wartime. But for others, wartime provides a solace. Billy the Kid and his friends always slept better after a good fight with Indians. The routine of peacetime activities was traumatic for Lawrence of Arabia, the maverick British Army officer who became a hero when he led the Arabs against the Turks in World War I. In the words of Winston Churchill, when he unveiled a memorial to Lawrence at Oxford:

> Lawrence was one of those beings whose pace of life was faster and more intense than what is normal. Just as an aeroplane only flies by its speed and pressure against the air; so he flew best and easiest in the hurricane. He was not in complete harmony with the normal. The fury of the Great War raised the pitch of life to the Lawrence standard. The multitudes were swept forward till their pace was the same as his. In this heroic period he found himself in perfect relation both to men and events.[34]

Adjustment in any given situation depends upon the interaction of an individual's particular makeup with his environment. Every individual has certain emotional strengths and weaknesses. Symptoms of breakdown develop when stresses, internal or external, bear upon the individual's specific emotional vulnerabilities. Hence, no event, itself, can be described as traumatic. The response to the event may be creative. One-third of the Air Force's Vietnam POWs reported benefits from their POW experience—reprioritized life goals, new view of family importance, and so on. Only when the event has a noxious influence, a disorganizing effect on the organism, is the event called traumatic. Preconditions to the nature of the response are constitutional factors, past experience, and the psychic state at the time of the particular stimulus.[35]

The trauma of slavery or persecution is not a sudden assault against ego integrity or dignity. It is a social condition that gradually molds and forms the person. There is no clear-cut point of beginning and ending. While Philip Roth's Portnoy complained about the Jewish mother's "smothering love," others point out the traumatizing effect of segregated or slum conditions. A "Black Manifesto" demands that whites pay "reparations due us as people who have been exploited and degraded, brutalized, killed and persecuted";[36] Professor Boris Bittker of Yale years ago offered justification in law for the proposition in his book *The Case for Black Reparation*.[37] A Broadway production performed in 2001 about African Americans suffering PTSD carried the playful but very serious title, *Post-Traumatic Slave Syndrome*. Then, too, there is so-called post-therapy stress disorder that follows psychotherapy (as in the case of the revival of memory of child abuse).

Trauma involves not just what occurs externally but the dovetailing of external events and inner psychic organization. What may be traumatic to one person need not be to all others, nor need it adversely affect the same person at a different time. Two passengers in a car accident, for example, while sharing the same experience, may develop different symptoms. Although they are exposed to presumably the same stress experience, the type and extent of psychopathology that develops will be specific for each individual. The sight of human genitalia may result in impairment of some people's eyesight; to others, it is a pleasure.

Not every intruding stimulus is a traumatic one. The common assumption is that the only real ones are the big ones. It is not the particular content of an experience, however, but as Freud in 1933 stated, "The essence of a traumatic situation is an experience of helplessness on the part of the ego in the face of accumulation of excitation, whether of external or internal origin."[38]

The movie director Richard Brooks in filming Truman Capote's *In Cold Blood* was intrigued that death-row prisoners are not overwhelmed with anxiety as they go to their execution. Discussing this phenomenon at a staff conference at the Menninger Foundation, the group (including this author) concluded that people are less likely to be overwhelmed by anxiety when they have had an opportunity to prepare psychologically for the event. Thus, a motorist unexpectedly bumped from the rear, though with relatively slight impact, may suffer greater emotional distress than he would in a case of a major frontal collision that was foreseen, though only seconds in advance. Likewise, a shipwreck that is expected results in far less traumatic consequences than one that comes as a surprise. An earthquake is usually traumatic because it is sudden and unpredictable, whereas people pre-warned about a fire or a tornado may experience less emotional distress. When there is notice, people can prepare psychologically and hence are less helpless. One who has traumatic neurosis has repetitive dreams about the event so that he can relive and master it, very much like a child at play or the re-creation of a traumatic event.

What emerges, then, is a picture of trauma as stimuli over which the person has no control. Overwhelmed by stimuli, the individual seeks seclusion, which accounts for his withdrawal, and through the mechanism of denial the experience is minimized. Because he feels helpless, it is important that families, physicians, lawyers, compensation-board members—all who have any contact with him—do everything they can to foster those factors that emphasize his independence, strength, and capacity for self-sufficiency. His image of himself as an active and effective person should be maintained to the highest possible degree.

Rare is the individual who can function well without the emotional support of sweetheart, spouse, or parent. "What should I find to hold onto without you?"[39] Winston Churchill wrote to his wife from the trenches in World War I. Much of lovemaking—fondling and petting—represents a regression. When a deteriorating home life becomes unbearable, often the individual somehow manages to be injured in order to obtain emotional comfort. In need of comfort, a person may become as helpless as a baby; by an accident he may find himself helped and supported just like one. Injury provides an unembarrassing way to be cared for and loved in a childlike, protected fashion, a need present in everyone. The individual seeks such comfort at his job as well as at home. Workers' compensation, received while debilitated from injury, is often viewed as a dole made up by fellow workers. A *dole* is, according to the *American Heritage Dictionary*, "a charitable dispensation of goods, especially money, food or clothing." The injured individual may feel, "I never knew before that I had such good friends." Companies with a liberal and supportive policy find that employees quickly return to work following an injury.

Malingering

Litigation problems tend to discourage recovery and promote malingering. An attempt at social reinvolvement may be detrimental to a legal cause of action in tort or workers' compensation. The courts regard with suspicion a claim that is made in the face of a speedy return to work or low medical bills. As one court expressed it, "In view of his ability to return to work this seems quite a quick recovery for a person who sued for $193,000 for disability."

The significant increase of personal-injury litigation and workers' compensation suits in recent years is indicative of a burgeoning claims consciousness of the public. This phenomenon is due to various factors, including the notoriety accorded successful litigants and their advocates, the paternalistic role of modern-day government, and to some extent, the factor of malingering. With the increased number of claims, it is not surprising that allegations and insinuations of malingering are made ever more frequently.

The widely accepted definition of *malingering* is the "conscious simulation or exaggeration of injury, illness or disability." The difference between hysteria (or conversion hysteria) and malingering is said to be only one of degree: malingering is the conscious imitation of illness, whereas hysteria is its unconscious simulation. In malingering, there is deliberate and persistent planning; the conscious mind is a participant in the simulated disorder. Dr. Thomas Szasz says, "The significant issue here is knowing the rules of the game. A person who knows nothing about the rules of the sickness game cannot malinger."[40]

Malingering is defined in *DSM-IV* as "the intentional production of false or grossly exaggerated physical or psychological symptoms, motivated by external incentives, such as evading military duty, avoiding work, obtaining financial compensation, avoiding criminal prosecution or obtaining drugs."[41] *Pure malingering* is the conscious exaggeration of existing symptoms or the fraudulent allegation that prior genuine symptoms are still present. *False imputation* is the ascribing of actual symptoms to a cause consciously recognized as having no relationship to the symptoms. Surveys of forensic specialists generated estimates of malingering between 7.4 percent for nonforensic settings and 17.4 percent for forensic settings.[42]

The courts distinguish "compensation neurosis" from "conscious malingering." Although it is a general principle of law that a claimant has a duty to minimize his damages, an unconscious desire for compensation is not a bar to legal recovery. "'Compensationitis,' curable only by application of a 'greenback poultice,' may constitute a disability compensable under the law." This is the sardonic view as expressed by many courts; and physicians also say, "A good application of 'green poultice' is the best cure known for many injuries."[43]

A plaintiff's lawyer, anticipating the issue of malingering, may decide as a tactical matter to raise the issue himself and deflate it. To do this he examines the psychiatrist testifying on behalf of the plaintiff as follows:

> Q. Now, Doctor, when you examined the patient, did you believe that his complaints were imaginary?

A. When you say imaginary, if you mean they didn't exist, no, they were real. That is, to him they were real. It appeared to me that he was suffering from certain symptoms and as far as he was concerned they existed.

Q. Do you mean, Doctor, that these symptoms, even though unsupported by any physical evidence, were present for no reason at all?

A. No, there is a reason for the symptoms but it is my opinion that the patient is not conscious of these reasons. Therefore, the symptoms became real to him.

Q. Why does the patient exhibit these symptoms?

A. Because he stands to gain a resolution of some unconscious emotional conflict.

Q. Then, Doctor, do you believe that the patient is conscious or aware of the fact that he is demonstrating physical symptoms without physical evidence to support these symptoms? In other words, Doctor, is the patient consciously motivated, say for instance, by an expectant monetary award, to demonstrate these symptoms you have described?

A. I am of the opinion based on this patient's history, the symptoms I personally observed and from my experience, that this man was not consciously motivated to display these symptoms. The only gain, as some might call it, that he derived from these symptoms was on an unconscious level, and this was somehow an attempt to resolve his inner problems. Also, a person who is malingering usually displays a different set of symptoms than this patient. Most often we see physical symptoms such as paralysis of a limb or a marked limp. The symptoms this patient displayed were of a psychological nature, extreme anxiety, loss of motivation, dependency, and despondency. I doubt whether this patient had the sophistication to consciously demonstrate these symptoms and expect to gain anything of value.

The possibility of litigation appears to be a significant factor in determining whether pain and perpetuating disability will be exaggerated, be it workers' compensation cases, tort claims, evasion of duty cases, or criminal cases. Years ago, on the extent and detection of malingering, Philadelphia attorney Frederick Lipman said:

We do not know how frequent malingering is. We do not know what causes malingering. We are not sure of the differential diagnosis of malingering and neurosis. We do not know to what extent a physician's bias affects his diagnosis. The literature in this area is sparse and generally lacks an objective basis. Both the legal and medical professions need more scientific studies to help provide the answer to these and many other unsolved questions.[44]

It appears that medical specialists in fields of the most objective empirical orientation (e.g., neurosurgery), tend to see malingering as being much more prevalent than do those in the most subjective specialty, psychiatry. Perhaps the reason for this disparity lies in the psychiatrist's greater appreciation of the unconscious factors surrounding complaints of injury, an appreciation that seems to militate against a diagnosis of malingering.[45]

The diagnostic tools most useful in detecting malingering are careful physical examination of the claimant and study of the claimant's social and clinical history. The physician's clinical experience and knowledge of illness patterns play an important role in the making of a diagnosis. The diagnostic tools favored by a physician will depend to a large extent on his field of specialization and will vary with the illness or injury to be diagnosed. Some physicians feel that psychological testing is an invaluable aid in the detection of malingering, even if the allegedly injured person has been tested before and realizes the purpose of the tests. Others feel that such tests are rarely conclusive when the subject is knowledgeable or sophisticated.

Warning signs to detect PTSD malingering include: (1) an excessively idealistic premorbid view of life and functioning; (2) antisocial personality, with criminal history, and job and financial irresponsibility; (3) poor work record; (4) prior claims of incapacitating injuries; (5) claims of impairment in work but not in recreation; (6) evasiveness; (7) inconsistency in symptom presentation; and (8) repetitive, unvarying dreams. Malingering in which the individual is completely fabricating symptoms with no evidence whatsoever of a causal event is much more rare than partial malingering, which involves the exaggerating of legitimate, existing symptoms or the claim that symptoms are still present when in fact they are not. There is also the phenomenon of false imputation, in which an individual consciously ascribes symptoms to a cause that he knows is unrelated.[46]

In evaluating the genuineness of alleged PTSD, the clinician considers the reasonableness of the relationship between the reported symptoms and the stressor, the time elapsed between the stressor and development of symptoms, and the relationship between current symptoms and psychiatric problems before the stressor. Dr. Phillip Resnick, noted authority on the detection of malingering, points out that malingering individuals may know which symptoms to report but may be unable to give convincing descriptions or examples from their personal life, or they exaggerate the severity of the stressor. Malingerers are likely to concentrate on telling about reliving the trauma, whereas individuals genuinely suffering PTSD focus more on the phenomenon of psychic numbing. In true posttraumatic dreams, the typical pattern is a few dreams that reenact the traumatic event, followed by nightmares that are variations on the traumatic theme, in which other elements of the individual's daily life are incorporated into their dreams. Malingerers may claim repetitive dreams that exactly re-create the trauma night after night without variation.[47]

What about the person with hypochondria, who fervently believes in the reality of his complaints although they cannot be objectively substantiated? That phenomenon too is sometimes called "unconscious malingering."[48] Apart from the constellation of common symptoms of PTSD, some yardsticks have been suggested that differentiate between the malingerer and the hypochondriac or neurotic individual. The malingerer is generally unwilling to submit to medical examinations unless he can see material rewards for doing so, because he has no pains or disability to be cured by treatment, whereas the neurotic patient not only searches for treatment due to his discomfort but is faithful in taking medication and in following any regimen prescribed. A malingerer will often carry on his normal social life, finding pleasure in activities that do not relate to the alleged injury, whereas the neurotic person usually is unable to maintain the capacity for either work or pleasure and shows general evidence of increased tension and introversion. The malingerer's history will usually reveal that he has been a social misfit for years.

Another yardstick is the manner in which the claim is made. One who tenaciously pursues a claim is unlikely to be very much in depression, an indication of traumatic neurosis. A depressed person would not be much interested in a claim or much of anything else. The content of dreams and the way that the dreams are reported furnish an important clue in detecting malingering. Freud spoke of the dream as "the royal road to the unconscious."[49]

Diagnosis is the Sherlock Holmes dimension of medicine. Indeed, it was a physician—Sir Arthur Conan Doyle—who created the character of that master sleuth, modeled after his former teacher Dr. Joseph Bell. Sherlock Holmes said he deduced his conclusions, but actually he made inferences, and the inferential process is always open to doubt. Only an accountant is entitled to say, "It's as simple as adding two and two." However, the detective may be more helpful than the physician or psychiatrist (although dressed in a London Fog coat or smoking a pipe) in obtaining evidence to identify malingering. Surveillance by private detective agencies is producing evidence (such as movies) that is frequently used in court to establish malingering. One film of the complainant's activities may disprove or rebut a wealth of medical testimony and expert opinion.

At one time an expert medical witness was not allowed to express an opinion as to whether a litigant was or was not malingering. The jury was considered as qualified as the witness to form an opinion on that subject. Otherwise put, a diagnosis of malingering very much reflects a moral judgment: it may tell us more about the observer than about the observed.[50]

Notes

1. Peter Marin has written that for the Vietnam veteran "post traumatic stress disorder" was in many respects but a euphemism for the torment the veterans experienced in returning to a country that would not let them repent, and would not repent itself. "For in making the guilt his alone, or in making it sound as if it were his alone," Marin wrote, the Vietnam veteran was deprived "of precisely the kind of community and good company that make it possible for people to see themselves clearly," P. Marin, "Living in Moral Pain," in W. Capps (ed.), *The Vietnam Reader* (New York: Routledge, 1991), pp. 43, 48. See B. Shephard, *A War of Nerves: Soldiers and Psychiatrists in the Twentieth Century* (Cambridge: Harvard University Press, 2001).

2. O. Rank, *The Trauma of Birth* (New York: Basic Books, 1952). Jane Goodall, renowned as "the Einstein of behavioral sciences," begins her autobiography with the observation that the first breath she drew abled her to "yell about the pain and indignity of [her] forced expulsion from the womb." J. Goodall, *Reason for Hope* (New York: Warner Books, 1999), p. 1. The type of delivery (e.g., by caesarean section) apparently has an impact on personality development. Personal communication by Dr. Emanuel Tanay (Jan. 12, 2002).

3. R. J. Daly, "Samuel Pepys and Posttraumatic Stress Disorder," *Brit. J. Psychiatry* 143 (1983): 64.

4. *DSM-II*, sec. 307.3.

5. The Veterans Health Administration hospital system consists of 173 hospitals, 771 clinics, and 206 readjustment counseling centers. In this $20 billion system, the largest number of doctors are psychiatrists. In fact, the VA is the single largest provider of mental health services in the country, serving more than 650,000 patients a year. M. Szegedy-Maszak, "The War of Emotions," *U.S. News & World Report*, Dec. 17, 2001, pp. 46–48. In a book Vietnam veteran B. G. Burkett and a colleague have provided embarrassing examples of veterans deceiving mental health professionals (or the latter acquiesce in the deception). They attacked the very foundation of the VA's understanding of PTSD, the National Readjustment Study, costing $9 million to complete, that concluded that when lifetime prevalence was added to current PTSD, more than half of male veterans and nearly half of the female veterans had

experienced clinically stress-reaction symptoms. B. G. Burkett & G. Whitley, *Stolen Valor* (Dallas: Verity Press, 1998). In an article in 1983, psychiatrist Landy Sparr and psychologist Loren Pankratz were apparently the first to describe the imitators of PTSD. They described five men who said they had been traumatized in the Vietnam War; three said they were former prisoners of war. In fact, none had been prisoners of war, four had never been in Vietnam, and two had never even been in the military. L. Sparr & L. D. Pankratz, "Factitious Posttraumatic Stress Disorder," *Am. J. Psychiatry* 140 (1983): 1016.

6. *DSM-III*, sec. 307.3.

7. B. L. Green, "Recent Research Findings on the Diagnosis of Posttraumatic Stress Disorder: Prevalence, Course, Comorbidity, and Risk," in R. I. Simon (ed.), *Posttraumatic Stress Disorder in Litigation* (Washington, D.C.: American Psychiatric Press, 1995), pp. 13–29.

8. M. Bowman, *Individual Differences in Posttraumatic Response* (Mahwah, N.J.: Erlbaum, 1997).

9. L. D. Pankratz, "Posttraumatic Stress Disorder," *False Memory Syndrome Foundation Newsletter*, Nov./Dec. 2001, pp. 8–9. In the aftermath of the September 11, 2001, attack on the World Trade Center, Terry Keane, director of the National Center for Post Traumatic Stress Disorder in Boston, estimated that 20 to 30 percent of the people who escaped the burning towers and victims' relatives will suffer from PTSD. S. Kugler, "Trade Center Survivors Still Must Deal with Post-Traumatic Stress Disorders" (Associated Press news release), *Detroit News*, Dec. 17, 2001, p. 9. Still, it is said, "PTSD is a diagnosis that is given when the psychiatrist does not know what is going on." Comment by Dr. Sander J. Breiner at conference of the Michigan Society for Psychoanalytic Psychology on Dec. 9, 2001, in Southfield, Michigan.

10. A. A. Stone, "Post-Traumatic Stress Disorder and the Law: Critical Review of the New Frontier," *Bull. Am. Acad. Psychiatry & Law* 21 (1993): 23, 29–30.

11. M. J. Pangia, "Post-Traumatic Stress Disorder: Litigation Strategies," *Trial*, Sept. 2000, p. 18.

12. Quoted in T. King, "Just Walk Out," *Wall Street Journal*, Nov. 24, 2000, p. W-1. From Christmas shopping people suffer "post-traumatic mall syndrome." M. Alvear, "The Christmas That Comes to the Door," *New York Times*, Dec. 25, 2000, p. 21.

13. See D. Mendelson, *The Interfaces of Medicine and Law: The History of the Liability for Negligently Caused Psychiatric Injury (Nervous Shock)* (Brookfield, Vt.: Ashgate, 1998).

14. Mitchell v. Rochester Railway Co., 151 N.Y. 107, 45 N.E. 354 (1896).

15. Victoria Railways Commissioners v. Coultas, 13 App. Cas. 222 (P.C. 1888).

16. "[T]he plaintiff was an unmarried white lady, and . . . while in attendance as a guest of the defendant at a circus performance given by the defendant for the defendant's guests . . . a horse, which was going through a dancing performance immediately in front of where the plaintiff was sitting, [ridden] by the defendant's servant . . . [was] caused to back toward the plaintiff, and while in this situation the horse evacuated his bowels into her lap. . . . [T]his occurred in full view of many people, some of whom were the defendant's employees, and all of whom laughed at the occurrence, [so] that as a result thereof the plaintiff was caused much embarrassment, mortification, and mental pain and suffering, to her damage in a certain amount. . . . [T]he damage alleged was due entirely to the defendant's negligence and without any fault on the part of the plaintiff." Christy Bros. Circus v. Turnage, 38 Ga. App. 581, 144 S.E. 680 (1928).

17. 68 Cal.2d 728, 441 P.2d 912, 69 Cal. Rptr. 72 (1968).

18. 48 Cal.3d 644, 257 Cal. Rptr. 865, 771 P.2d 814 (1989).

19. In an Alaska case, Kelley v. Kohua Sales & Supply, 56 Hawaii 204, 532 P.2d 673 (1975), the plaintiff, located in California, suffered a heart attack after being informed about the death of her daughter and granddaughter in an automobile accident that occurred in Hawaii. The court denied the plaintiff's claim because she was not located "a reasonable distance from the scene."

20. Ferriter v. Daniel O'Connell's Sons, 381 Mass. 507, 413 N.E.2d 690 (1980).

21. Paugh v. Hanks, 6 Ohio St.3d 72, 451 N.E.2d 759 (1983).

22. G. M. Stern, *The Buffalo Creek Disaster* (New York: Random House, 1976).

23. S. H. Putnam, J. H. Ricker, S. R. Ross, & J. E. Kurtz, "Considering Premorbid Functioning" in J. J. Sweet (ed.), *Forensic Neuropsychology* (Lisse: Swets & Zeitlinger, 1999), pp. 39–81.

24. The emotional aftereffects of the Holocaust on those of its victims who survived took

time to reveal themselves. Immediately after the war, everyone had wanted to forget and to get on with building new lives. In the late 1950s, however, physicians in Scandinavia began to study the Holocaust survivor population there and found that many of its members were having problems. The issue of compensation began to arise. The West German government offered reparations to camp victims, but only if a causal link could be established between their current ill-health and the traumatic experiences they had undergone. A number of German experts then testified in the German courts that it was common knowledge that all psychic traumata, of whatever degree or duration, lose their effects when the psychologically traumatizing event ceases to operate.

In response, psychiatrists outside Germany, notably Jewish psychoanalysts, sought to prove that the effects of that experience were prolonged. In 1961, after seeing some eight hundred people, Dr. William Niederland, a psychoanalyst in New York, coined the phrase "survivor syndrome." He contended that massive psychic trauma caused "irreversible changes" in the personality. The survivors, he found, suffered from depression, anxiety, and nightmares. An Israeli psychiatrist, Shamai Davidson, believed that "the somewhat stereo-typed diagnostic construct" of the survivor syndrome was both too sweeping and too pessimistic. He said, "Each survivor is unique in the individual nature and meaning of his experiences and responses to the shared events in the same situation often had entirely different meanings for different survivors." See W. G. Niederland, "The Problem of the Survivor," *J. Hillside Hosp.* 10 (1961): 233.

Chaim Shatan was struck by the resemblance between the emotional aftereffects of extensive Vietnam combat experience, the "homecoming syndromes" of prisoners of war, and the "survivor syndromes" of living concentration inmates. For Dr. Robert Lifton, Hiroshima was "the main encounter," which he described in his 1968 book *Death in Life: Survivors of Hiroshima* (New York: Random House). See H. Krystal (ed.), *Massive Psychic Trauma* (New York: International Universities Press, 1968); B. Shephard, *A War of Nerves* (Cambridge: Harvard University Press, 2001); K. R. Eissler, "Perverted Psychiatry?" *Am. J. Psychiatry* 123 (1967): 1352.

25. The example is taken with modification from the opinion of Chief Justice Bernstein of the Arizona Supreme Court in Tatman v. Provincial Homes, 94 Ariz. 165, 382 P.2d 573 (1963).

26. This was the observation in a case where the defendant negligently drove a two-horse van into a tavern and frightened a pregnant woman so badly that she suffered a nervous shock and, as a consequence, a miscarriage. The court held the defendant responsible for this damage. Dulieu v. White & Sons [1901] 2 K.B. 669. In Marzolf v. Gilgore, 933 F.Supp. 1021 (D.Kansas 1996), the patient who had been given phenothiazine-class drugs for over fourteen years was held to have a cause of action against the physician who prescribed the drug for the final six months of the long drug-taking period. The early prescription "primed" the patient for the later complications. The final doses, rather than those of the prior thirteen and a half years, may be deemed the cause-in-law of the patient's tardive dyskinesia (TD). Summary judgment for the physician was denied as the facts created a question for the jury. Thus, under this view, a physician coming on the scene late in the treatment of the patient may be held to have caused a disability (tardive dyskinesia) although his prescribed dosage was on the low side. See H. L. A. Hart & T. Honore, *Causation in the Law* (Oxford: Clarendon Press, 2d ed. 1995).

27. 421 F.2d 1169 (2d Cir. 1970).

28. Value is an estimate of worth at the time and place of the wrong. Hence, an existing disease or a prior accident that reduces the plaintiff's life expectancy limits accordingly the value of his life in an action for wrongful death. Consider the case of a person who has a fatal illness, such as cancer, which will inevitably shorten his life, and he is negligently killed. The value of his life is measured by his anticipated future earnings, along with other factors. The fact that his disease was certain to get worse is taken into account.

29. Under workers' compensation laws, fault of the employer is not an essential element to the cause of action; compensation is made for accidental injury arising out of and in the course of employment. The issues in workers' compensation cases are the meanings of the terms "accidental injury" and "arising out of and in the course of employment." In a notable workers' compensation case, an employee dropped a piece of machinery from a scaffolding and imagined that he had fatally injured a coworker. It worried him, and he died within three weeks of the incident. The court held that a worker or his family is entitled to payment even

though there was no physical injury or catastrophic event that precipitated the mental anguish. Klein v. Darling Co., 217 Mich. 485, 187 N.W. 400 (1921).

See also Carter v. General Motors Co., 361 Mich. 577, 106 N.W.2d 105 (1961), where psychiatric testimony established that constant emotional pressures of the job were the cause of an employee's disability. Like Charlie Chaplin in the 1936 film *Modern Times,* the assembly-line process overwhelmed Carter. In this much-publicized decision, the Michigan Supreme Court ruled that psychiatric disability is as much compensable under workers' compensation law as physical injury. Holding employers responsible for psychiatric disabilities, however, may make them hesitant to hire people like Carter. The law on workers' compensation is only one mechanism of carrying out the social philosophy of taking care of people who cannot take care of themselves. Alternatives are the guaranteed minimum annual wage and pension plans. Generally, in workers' compensation cases, it is held that nervous or mental breakdown produced solely by the stress or boredom of employment does not constitute an accidental injury within the meaning of the statute. See "Work, Stress, and Disability in the New Millennium" (special issue), *Int. J. Law & Psychiatry* 22 (1999): 417–616.

Under Michigan's legislation, as revised, "mental disabilities shall be compensable when arising out of *actual* events of employment, not unfounded perceptions thereof" (emphasis added). Mich. Comp. Laws, sec. 418.310(2). In addition to requiring "actual events," the amended legislation went further by requiring a definite connection between the events and the disability, to the extent that mental impairments would "be compensable if contributed to or aggravated or accelerated by the employment in a *significant manner* (emphasis added). Id. at sec. 418.401(2)(b). Under the legislation, a claimant must prove a significant factual causal connection between the actual events of employment and the mental disability. This requires a consideration of the totality of the evidence and circumstances, including employment and nonemployment factors, and the degree to which each might contribute to the alleged condition. Predisposition to mental illness does not preclude a successful compensation claim, and so even ordinary events of employment and normal daily stresses could affect one's mental health. Gardner v. Van Buren Public Schools, 445 Mich. 23, 517 N.W.2d 1 (1994). As with so many other elements of workers' compensation claims, the meaning of *significant manner* is subject to interpretation. It is to be noted that the arguments for both employer and employee are presented to the magistrate or referee, who (we hope) has a great deal of experience in sorting out the facts and ascribing appropriate significance to them, with relatively few cases going on appeal to the courts. With experience in adjudicating claims comes a tendency toward comparing claimants. One may say that when a prior claim was allowed or denied, the claimant with a similar profile would receive a similar decision. It reflects the adjudicator's way of thinking and maintaining consistency in applying the legislation.

Workers' compensation is not the only remedy for a person injured in the course of employment. If it can be established that the injury was caused intentionally by the employer or by gross negligence, relief in tort may also be available against the employer, as well as an action against a third party who may have been responsible for the injury. Mental injury caused by termination from employment is not compensable. Robinson v. Chrysler Corp., 139 Mich. App. 449, 363 N.W.2d 4 (1984); Calovecchi v. Michigan, 461 Mich. 616, 611 N.W.2d 300 (2000).

Other special compensation programs—for childhood vaccine injuries, black lung, nuclear accidents, and to some extent, automobile accidents—have been established. They have been designed to reduce the disparities in awards and the time and expense of litigation so characteristic of the tort system. In response to the catastrophe of September 11, 2001, Congress provided at least $11 billion in compensation funds. From time to time it has been recommended that a compensation program like that in New Zealand be established in all types of injury. P. H. Schuck, "Equity for All Victims," *New York Times,* Dec. 19, 2001, p. 33.

30. Koehler v. Waukesha Milk Co., 190 Wis. 52, 208 N.W. 901 (1926), discussed in G. Williams, "The Risk Principle," *L.Q. Rev.* 77 (1961): 179.

31. Battalia v. New York, 10 N.Y.2d 237, 176 N.E.2d 729 (1961) (plaintiff was badly frightened when the belt on a ski lift was not locked properly); Slay v. Hempstead, 206 So.2d 718 (La. App. 1968) (woman during menopause period suffered traumatic neurosis after her car was struck in the rear). A number of suits have been brought seeking recovery of damages for emotional distress resulting from racial, ethnic, or religious abuse or discrimination in violation of civil rights legislation. Annot., 40 A.L.R.3d 1290.

32. One court expressed it thus:

[I]f there is competent testimony, adduced either by plaintiff or defendant, that the injuries are factually and medically separable, and that the liability for all such injuries and damages, or parts thereof, may be allocated with reasonable certainty to the impacts in turn, the jury will be instructed accordingly and mere difficulty in so doing will not relieve the triers of the fact of this responsibility. This merely follows the general rule that "where the independent concurring acts have caused distinct and separate injuries to the plaintiff, or where some reasonable means of apportioning the damages is evident, the courts generally will not hold the tortfeasors jointly and severally liable."

But if, on the other hand, the triers of the facts . . . decide that they cannot make a division of injuries, we have, by their own finding, nothing more or less than an indivisible injury, and the precedents as to indivisible injuries will control. They were well summarized in Cooley on Torts in these words: "Where the negligence of two or more persons concurs in producing a single indivisible injury, then such persons are jointly and severally liable, although there was no common duty, common design, or concerted action."

Maddux v. Donaldson, 362 Mich. 425, 108 N.W.2d 33 (1961). See also Duma v. Janni, 26 Mich. App. 445, 182 N.W.2d 596 (1971).

33. Extensive nationwide publicity was given a case involving the crash of a runaway San Francisco cable car that allegedly led to "promiscuity and unnatural sex drives." Newspaper headlines included "Crash Stimulated Sex Drive" and "Oversexed Woman Blames Cable Car Crash." The woman contended that the crash brought on a sexual need that led to affairs with more than one hundred men. Psychiatric testimony supporting the complaint maintained that the accident unlocked memories of her strict disciplinarian father. News reports, *Detroit Free Press*, Apr. 3, 1970, p. 8; *Detroit News*, Apr. 3, 1970, p. 12.

34. Churchill's address appears as the introduction to *The Home Letters of T. E. Lawrence and His Brothers* (New York: Macmillan, 1954), p. xiii. A letter written by T. E. Lawrence months before his death reveals that he was so unhappy with the prospect of leaving the RAF (Royal Air Force) that he considered suicide. The correspondence gives support to those who were not convinced that his death in a motorcycle crash three months later was an accident. He ended the letter with the line: "Alas and alas, why must good things end and one grow old? I don't want to grow old . . . ever." C. Edwardes, "Lawrence of Arabia Wrote Letter Contemplating Suicide," *Sunday Telegraph*, Nov. 18, 2001, p. 13. Another notable example is Vladimir Mayakovsky, whose powerful poetry could not have been sustained under any circumstances except that of the Russian Revolution. With the deceleration of the revolution, he cropped his hair, Samson-like, and his strength slowly drained; finally he committed suicide. W. Woroszylski, *The Life of Mayakovsky* (London: Gollancz, 1971).

35. See G. Mendelson, *Psychiatric Aspects of Personal Injury Claims* (Springfield, Ill.: Thomas, 1988); C. B. Scrignar, *Post-Traumatic Stress Disorder* (New Orleans: Bruno Press, 3d ed. 1996); R. I. Simon (ed.), *Posttraumatic Stress Disorder in Litigation: Guidelines for Forensic Assessment* (Washington, D.C.: American Psychiatric Press, 2d ed. 2002).

36. See R. Robinson, *The Debt: What America Owes to Blacks* (New York: Dutton, 2000).

37. For more recent discussion, see R. Robinson, *The Debt: What America Owes to Blacks* (New York: Dutton, 2000). Needless to say, the claim for reparations is highly controversial. Suppose an individual about to board the Titanic was unlawfully arrested and as a consequence he was not on the ship when it sank. Would he not have been grateful for the detention? The African-American professor of economics Walter Williams has frequently said that today's black Americans have benefited immensely from the suffering of their ancestors— they have been saved from the horrors of Africa. See K. B. Richburg, *Out of America: A Black Man Confronts Africa* (New York: Basic Books, 1997). Black and Arab involvement in slavery is deeper and of far more duration than that of the United States. Slavery (of which human sacrifice was an important component) has the most solid history within Africa itself and therefore the most logical reparations measure ought to come from Africa. Twenty times more Americans have ancestors who went to war to end slavery than ancestors who owned slaves. See D. Horowitz, *Uncivil Wars: The Controversy over Reparations for Slavery* (San Francisco:

Encounter Books, 2002); J. McWhorter, "Against Reparations," *New Republic,* July 23, 2001, p. 32. See also D. D'Souza, *What's So Great about America* (New York: Regnery, 2002).

38. See A. Kardiner, "Traumatic Neuroses of War," in S. Arieti (ed.), *American Handbook of Psychiatry* (New York: Basic Books, 1959), vol. 1, p. 245.

39. See Introduction to *The Home Letters of T. E. Lawrence and His Brothers,* supra note 34.

40. T. S. Szasz, *The Myth of Mental Illness* (New York: Harper & Row, 1974), p. 236.

41. *DSM-IV,* p. 683, sec. V65.2.

42. B. E. McGuire, "The Assessment of Malingering in Traumatic Stress Claimants," *Psychiatry, Psychology & Law* 6 (1999): 163. A number of studies have been published on the use of neuroimaging of PTSD. See, e.g., J. D. Bremmer, "Neuroimaging of Posttraumatic Stress Disorder," *Psychiatric Annals* 28 (1998): 445. Its use as evidence at trial, however, is questionable (by analogy to the inadmissibility of the lie detector). See D. T. Lykken, *A Tremor in the Blood: Uses and Abuses of the Lie Detector* (New York: Plenum, 1998).

43. See, e.g., Miller v. U.S. Fidelity & Guaranty Co., 99 So.2d 511 (La. App. 1957).

44. F. D. Lipman, "Malingering in Personal Injury Cases," *Temp. L.Q.* 35 (1962): 141, 162.

45. Dr. Karl Menninger pointed out the personality deformity of the malingerer thus: "[He] does not himself believe that he is ill but tries to persuade others that he is, and they discover, they think, that he is not ill. But the sum of all this, in the opinion of myself and my perverse-minded colleagues, is precisely that he is ill, in spite of what others think. No healthy person, no healthy-minded person, would go to such extremes and take such devious and painful routes for minor gains that the invalid status brings to the malingerer." K. Menninger, *The Vital Balance* (New York: Viking Press, 1963), p. 208.

46. See T. M. Keane, "Guidelines for the Forensic Psychological Assessment of Posttraumatic Stress Disorder Claimants," in R. I. Simon (ed.), *Posttraumatic Stress Disorder in Litigation* (Washington, D.C.: American Psychiatric Press, 1995); P. J. Resnick, "Malingering of Posttraumatic Disorders," in R. Rogers (ed.), *Clinical Assessment of Malingering and Deception* (New York: Guilford Press, 2d ed. 1997); J. D. Bremmer, "Neuroimaging of Posttraumatic Stress Disorder," *Psychiatric Annals* 28 (1998): 445; R. D. Miller, "The Use of Placebo Trial as Part of a Forensic Assessment," *J. Psychiatry & Law* 16 (1988): 217; J. W. Schutte & G. A. Barrientos, "Uses and Abuses of PTSD," *Trial Lawyer* 21 (1998): 394; S. D. Wiley, "Deception and Detection in Psychiatric Diagnosis," *Psychiatric Clinics of North America* 21 (1998): 869.

47. P. J. Resnick, "The Detection of Malingered Mental Illness," *Behavioral Sci. & Law* 2 (1984): 21.

48. See T. S. Szasz, *The Myth of Mental Illness* (New York: Hoeber-Harper, 1961). On the screen Woody Allen, of course, is the undisputed master of hypochondria. He transforms every headache into a sign of a terminal illness. In the 2001 film *Bandits,* Billy Bob Thornton takes Woody Allen one step further in playing a compulsively anxious criminal. He becomes so preoccupied with his fictional tumor that he actually collapses. He is well-versed in the intimate details of every ailment from tinnitus to partial paralysis. The film is reviewed in J. McCartney, "Criminal Capers," *Sunday Telegraph,* Dec. 2, 2001, p. 7.

49. See chapter 7, on dreams as evidence.

50. Guidelines for a psychiatric medicolegal report are set out in B. Hoffman, "How to Write a Psychiatric Report for Litigation Following a Personal Injury," *Am. J. Psychiatry* 143 (1986): 164; G. Mendelson, "Writing a Psychiatric Medico-Legal Report," *Australian Forensic Psychiatric Bull.* 16 (Nov. 1999): 5. The role of PTSD as the basis of a finding of not guilty by reason of insanity or diminished capacity is discussed in chapter 9, on criminal responsibility.

22

Duty to Minimize Damages

There's a saying in the law of torts: "A plaintiff may not let the meter run." In other words, there is a duty to mitigate damages, sometimes called the doctrine of *avoidable consequences.* The rule does not allow damages that the plaintiff could have avoided by reasonable conduct following the wrong committed by the defendant. The rule has an application in the law of contracts as well as in tort law.[1] In criminal law, as we shall note, the doctrine of avoidable consequences may play a role in measuring the degree of the offense.

In the law of torts the rule on avoidable consequences is distinguished from the defense of *contributory negligence,* which is unreasonable conduct on the part of the plaintiff that contributes to the happening of the injury in the first place. Under a well-established principle of tort law, the plaintiff's contributory negligence that bars recovery must *concur* with the defendant's, whereas the relevant conduct of the plaintiff under the doctrine of avoidable consequences *follows* the defendant's. Both the doctrine of contributory negligence and the doctrine of avoidable consequences, however, rest upon the same fundamental policy of making recovery of damages depend upon the plaintiff's proper care for the protection of his own interests, and both require of the plaintiff only the standard of the reasonable person under the circumstances.

Another problem is presented when the plaintiff's conduct *prior* to the accident is found to have played no part in bringing about the accident, but to have aggravated the ensuing damages. The courts have apportioned the damages, holding that the plaintiff's recovery should be reduced to the extent that they have been aggravated by his own antecedent negligence. In a failure to wear a seat belt, some jurisdictions by statute provide for a certain reduction of damages.[2] In the case of insurance against vandalism or theft, insurance policies may require that the insured protect and secure the premises, otherwise the insurer provides no coverage for the loss.

The rule on contributory negligence—or as supplanted by comparative negligence—is a fault apportionment rule, while the rule of avoidable consequences is a causal apportionment rule. The distinction is important because if the plaintiff's fault in failing to avoid injury is counted as comparative fault in a modified comparative fault jurisdiction, it might add up to more than 50 percent and thus might bar the plaintiff's claim.[3] If not counted as comparative fault, but as a failure to mitigate damages, the plaintiff's fault then would only bar damages that could be traced to that failure.

In recent years some courts have ruled that with the advent of comparative fault, as a replacement of contributory negligence that bars recovery entirely, no separate avoidable consequences rules are required. Under these rulings, comparative fault analysis is used, both as to preinjury fault of the plaintiff and postinjury failure to minimize damages.[4] In such jurisdictions, the instruction to the jury is as follows: "If you find that plaintiff failed to mitigate damages, you will include this as part of plaintiff's fault in your comparison of fault."[5] That may be logical when the plaintiff suffers a single indivisible injury, but not when the plaintiff's postinjury negligence causes some separate item of harm.

The avoidable consequence rule reduces damages for discrete identifiable items of loss caused by the plaintiff's fault. Thus, if the plaintiff, after injury, unreasonably refuses to accept medical attention for a foot injury, and as a result ultimately suffers amputation of the foot that otherwise would have healed, then the avoidable consequences rule would deny recovery for loss of the foot but would not affect other damages.

Although mitigation of damages is not among the common affirmative defenses listed in court rules, it is recognized as such.[6] The defense is waived if not raised in the defendant's first responsive pleading or by an amended pleading. The defendant also has the burden of proving the plaintiff's failure to mitigate damages. A typical jury instruction states:

> A person has a duty to use ordinary care to minimize his or her damages after *(he or she/ his or her property)* has been *(injured/damaged)*. It is for you to decide whether plaintiff failed to use such ordinary care and, if so, whether any damage resulted from such failure. You must not compensate the plaintiff for any portion of *(his/her)* damages which resulted from *(his/ her)* failure to use such care.[7]

The rest of this chapter provides an overview of what has been or has not been required to mitigate damages. First and foremost, the duty to minimize damages may include a duty to seek and follow medical treatment, including surgery, that does not involve danger to life or extraordinary suffering. There must be a showing that treatment would in fact have mitigated the damages.[8] The refusal to undergo surgery is not considered arbitrary and unreasonable when the claimant has a sincere, deep-seated fear of it.[9] The refusal is also not considered unreasonable when the claimant is backed up by a physician's opinion that rebuts the medical recommendation submitted by the defendant.[10]

The duty to mitigate damages applies with equal force in medical malpractice cases. Under this principle, as generally followed, a patient's failure to follow a physician's directions subsequent to the physician's negligent treatment does not relieve against the primary liability but serves to mitigate the damages.[11] Thus, a patient's neglect of his health following his physician's negligent treatment does not bar all recovery but may be a reason for reducing damages. In a case where a dentist was negligent, the patient terminated treatment and delayed securing the services of another dentist. A contributory negligence instruction was disallowed, but the jury was permitted to consider the plaintiff's delay as a factor in determining damages.[12] Similarly, a patient's failure to follow a physician's directions subsequent to the physician's negligent treatment "could only serve to mitigate the damages . . . but not to relieve against the primary liability."[13]

Following an injury an individual may become so despondent that he commits suicide. The question arises: Is the original tortfeasor (or employer, in a workers' compensation case) responsible for the death? Could it have been avoided by psychiatric care? Was it an "intervening cause"? In older cases, courts as a matter of law found that suicide breaks the chain of causation.[14] However, in more recent cases, the question is often left to the jury.[15] In *Fuller v. Preis*,[16] the decedent, a doctor, committed suicide some seven months after an automobile accident from which he suffered head injury and experienced many seizures. The theory for recovery of damages was that the automobile crash caused the suicide. The jury found that the doctor was unable to control an "irresistible impulse" to destroy himself as a result of the accident. Most courts find an irresistible impulse only when the decedent acted in a sudden frenzy.[17]

A plaintiff who suffers disfigurement is not obliged to undergo plastic surgery, even if the refusal is for no other reason than that he is wary of anesthesia. Plastic surgery is considered to be a high-benefit procedure but also high risk in areas of the body where there is limited blood flow. It's not low risk/high benefit that is usually the justification of a requirement to minimize damages. There are perceived as well as known risks even in cosmetic surgery. It is common knowledge that Michael Jackson, the pop star, was hideously disfigured and visibly scarred as a result of it.

In workers' compensation cases alleging permanent serious disfigurement, the defense often alleges that the reason the disfigurement is permanent or serious is because the claimant has not bothered to see a physician about having it reduced. The Louisiana Court of Appeals said, "The plaintiff must eventually determine for himself whether he will retain the permanent disfigurement or submit to an operation for its correction."[18]

A constitutional issue arises when a patient has a religious belief about treatment. Christian Scientists and many Pentecostal groups teach that all physical maladies may be cured spiritually. Jehovah's Witnesses generally accept medical care, but they believe it is a sin to accept blood transfusion even in a life-and-death situation. The Book of Acts (chapter 5) directs the faithful to "abstain from blood," an admonition the church interprets to proscribe transfusions.[19] A reduction in a tort judgment for failure to mitigate may constitute an undue interference with religious freedom.[20] In an oft-cited case, *Lange v. Hoyt,*[21] the Connecticut Supreme Court applied a reasonable person standard, but instructed the jury to regard the plaintiff's Christian Science beliefs as a relevant factor in its assessment of mitigation efforts. In *Williams v. Bright,*[22] a New York court said that a jury's determination that a Jehovah's Witness's rejection of blood transfusion in surgery as "unreasonable" is an improper judgment as to the soundness of their religion. If a religious-based refusal of medical treatment is permitted, an accompanying issue may be whether all religions, faiths, and equivalent belief systems should be treated similarly.

In criminal cases, what would have been a battery often turns into negligent homicide or murder because of lack of medical care, as may occur when Jehovah's Witnesses refuse blood transfusions.[23] In an English case, *R. v. Blaue,*[24] the refusal of the deceased, for religious reasons, to accept a blood transfusion that would have saved her life did not relieve her assailant of causal responsibility. In this case it was reasonable to conclude that the act of stabbing was an operative cause of her death and the real issue was whether her subsequent conduct was sufficient to break the chain of causation. The court made reference to the *thin skull* rule: "It has long been the policy of the law that those who use violence on other people must take their victims as they find them. This, in our judgment, means the whole man, not just the physical man."[25]

The reference to the thin skull rule was probably unnecessary to the decision and its extension to psychological conditions questionable. The more problematic cases are those where the conduct of the victim after the assault is under scrutiny. In *R. v. Roberts,*[26] it was stated that such conduct does not break the chain of causation unless it is "daft," that is, it is not an objectively foreseeable consequence of the accused's act nor is it within the range of responses that might be expected. There might well be convincing policy reasons for considering conduct inspired by religious convictions not to be daft.[27]

In all cases, the availability of emergency medical services is an important factor in homicide or aggravated battery rates. A victim who is near a hospital gets care, another, who is far away, dies. The intent and behavior of the actor may be the same, but the consequences are often fortuitous.[28] Studies indicate that the differential distribution of medical resources is partially responsible for variation in criminally induced lethality rates.[29] Time and again, in various cases, expert testimony is offered that prompt medical treatment could have saved the victim's life.[30]

In *People v. Webb,*[31] a Michigan case, the deceased had consumed a large quantity of alcohol and got into an argument with the defendant at a bar. The defendant struck the deceased repeatedly in the face, and kicked him in the ribs after he had fallen to the floor. Injured and bleeding from the mouth, he went home, at which time his wife called paramedics, but he refused treatment. After the paramedics left he finally agreed he should go to the hospital, but he died moments after the paramedics returned. The medical examiner testified that had he accepted medical treatment promptly, a relatively easy procedure might have prevented the death. The Michigan Court of Appeals, in reversing a dismissal, held that the victim's knowing and voluntary refusal to seek immediate medical treatment was not as a matter of law a supervening cause of death; the issue of causation, the court said, should have gone to the jury.[32]

An accused may be exculpated of a homicide charge if the medical treatment provided the victim was "grossly negligent." In the case of a victim with a nonfatal wound who received medical treatment deemed grossly negligent, it is said that the treatment breaks the causal link to the resulting death, and this may exculpate the accused from guilt of a homicide. Merely negligent medical treatment, on the other hand, is deemed a foreseeable event, and does not suffice.[33] In the trial of Bernhard Goetz, who gunned down four young men he believed were about to mug him on a New York subway train, the prosecutor sought to blame Goetz for one of the victim's subsequent brain damage, while the defense attorney argued strenuously that it was the result of medical malpractice no one could have foreseen.[34]

As has been stated, in the law of torts there is an old axiom that a defendant must take a plaintiff as he finds him and hence may be held liable in damages for aggravation of a preexisting illness.[35] To put it differently, the defendant cannot complain that the plaintiff was not a healthy victim, but he may complain that the plaintiff did not take such preaccident precautions as wearing a seat belt. Furthermore, after the accident, the plaintiff may be obliged to change his style of life in order to mitigate damages. Questions arise: Must the plaintiff stop smoking, stop drinking, or lose weight in order to mitigate the extent of his injury? His style of life may give him comfort. In a case of an overweight plaintiff who suffered a serious back injury in a collision, the Louisiana Supreme Court said that the plaintiff had an affirmative responsibility to make every reasonable effort to follow medical advice to lose weight in order to mitigate damages—losing weight would have alleviated the stress on her back.[36] In another case, the Minnesota Supreme Court ruled that the plaintiff, a disabled employee, had "an obligation to cooperate with his doctor's directions to achieve weight reduction and thereby improve his condition to the point where employment in another field, possibly after retraining, would be feasible."[37]

What about medical treatment that takes the form of exercise? Is there an element of risk? Whether or not there has been an unreasonable refusal to exercise depends on the possibility of pain in connection with the exertion, the age of the plaintiff, and the probability of benefit from it.[38]

A plaintiff's failure to obtain treatment may be excused when the failure is a result of the injury itself. In *Botek v. Mine Safety Appliance Corp.*,[39] the plaintiff suffered a post-traumatic stress disorder that was exacerbated by his failure to initiate treatment at an early date. In cases of PTSD, treatment soon after the event usually results in recovery. Experts testified that with counseling and drug therapy, the plaintiff could have achieved a satisfactory result in three to six months. Instead, by the time the trial began, the plaintiff had endured the effects of the emotional disorder for more than seven years. He explained that he had made no effort to obtain treatment because he suffered from depression as a result of the incident and was not motivated to seek treatment. The court ruled that where a claimant's rejection of treatment is part of his emotional injuries, he may obtain damages in spite of the failure to receive treatment.[40]

The reasonableness of avoiding treatment can be an issue in cases where a psychotherapist has engaged in "undue familiarity" with a patient. As a result of the undue familiarity, there may be reluctance of the patient to see another therapist. "I have lost all faith in therapists," say patients. One psychiatrist cites the case of a sexually exploited female psychiatric patient who suffered immeasurably as a result of the abuse by her therapist. He writes, "The effects of the affair were disastrous at the time of its occurrence and proved to be a serious complication for subsequent treatment. As a consequence her illness was aggravated . . . and a deep mistrust formed toward subsequent psychiatrists and psychoanalysts."[41] Similarly, a study of sixteen female patients of a gynecologist who conducted internal examinations in a sexually abusive manner reported that they developed an aversion to gynecological health care after their experience.[42]

An injured party may have a duty to obtain vocational retraining as part of the duty to mitigate damages. The use of vocational rehabilitation is appropriate in cases where the plaintiff claims to have suffered a loss of work capacity because of injury. Since many public agencies provide rehabilitation services to the disabled, the defense can argue that the individual has not fulfilled his obligation to mitigate his damages by obtaining these services. Vocational rehabilitation expert testimony is helpful in proving that the plaintiff has not mitigated his damages.

It is a matter of fact for the jury to determine whether a reasonable person under the circumstances should have sought vocational retraining as a part of the duty to mitigate damages, just as it is a matter of fact for the jury to determine whether a reasonable person under the circumstances should have undergone medical treatment in order to mitigate damages. Because the determination is a question of fact for the jury, not a matter of law, it is reversible error on the part of a trial judge to instruct a jury that an injured party has a specific duty to obtain vocational training as part of the duty to mitigate damages.[43]

By the way, disability income insurance policies, depending upon the policy, may not require training for another occupation in the event of inability to continue in one's field.[44] Thus, one young lawyer who felt harried working in a law office—she called it "a meat grinder"—as attested by her psychiatrist is now spending her days gardening at home and collecting disability income insurance. Under her policy she need not undertake training in a different field.[45] In response to the new stresses of medical practice, many physicians have retired early or have filed for disability insurance and given up their practices.[46]

In a workers' compensation case, a psychiatrist who treated the claimant recommended that he submit to a sodium amytal interview, which would make him drowsy and less resistant and more amenable to suggestion. The purpose would be to overcome, by suggestion, the "psychoneurosis conversion hysteria which was superimposed on a minor foot injury." The psychiatrist stated that if the treatment were successful a cure could be affected in two or three sessions. The claimant refused to take the treatment on the advice of his personal physician, who stated that he did not believe the psychiatric treatment alone would effect a cure. No doctor testified that the treatment might be harmful, or that the claimant's resistance would make the treatment completely ineffectual. The court found, on appeal, that the claimant's refusal to submit to the proposed treatment was unreasonable.[47]

What about electroconvulsive therapy, or electroshock therapy as it is also known? Nowadays it is safe and effective—it is low risk/high benefit—but in the public image it is high risk/low benefit, and stigmatizing. Its very name is alarming. A claimant's refusal to submit to ECT is not deemed unreasonable.[48]

In the case of psychiatric treatment, a plaintiff who declines treatment often says: "I don't want to be seen by a psychiatrist." "I hate psychiatrists." "I don't want their medication." Is it a reasonable refusal in view of the side effects?[49] Does the plaintiff have a phobia about psychiatrists? What about the stigma surrounding psychiatric care? Even ex-convicts rank above former mental patients in societal acceptance.[50]

What about the mitigation of damages in cases where a pharmacist negligently supplies a tranquilizer rather than birth control pills called for by the prescription, as happened in *Troppi v. Scarf*?[51] The defense suggested that parents who seek to recover for the birth of an unwanted child are under a duty to mitigate damages by placing the child for adoption (or obtaining an abortion). If the child is "unwanted," the defendant asked, why should they object to placing the child up for adoption (or aborting), thereby reducing the financial burden on defendant for his maintenance?[52] The court replied:

> [T]o impose such a duty upon the injured plaintiff is to ignore the very real difference which our law recognizes between the avoidance of conception and the disposition of the human organism after conception. This most obvious distinction is illustrated by the constitutional protection afforded the right to use contraceptives, while abortion is still a felony in most jurisdictions [no longer]. At the moment of conception, an entirely different set of legal obligations is imposed upon the parents. A living child almost universally gives rise to emotional and spiritual bonds which few parents can bring themselves to break.[53]

A defendant is not likely to raise a failure to mitigate damages when the plaintiff could not afford treatment. The plaintiff would respond, "I didn't have the money for treatment. I couldn't afford it. That's why I went to a lawyer." The jury would likely be moved by sympathy. And as a matter of law a claimant may be excused from mitigating damages when lacking sufficient financial resources to do so.[54] In cases where liability is not at issue, and the only question is that of damages, a defendant might cover the expenses of treatment at the outset when injury occurs in order to minimize the damages. It is a common practice in employer-employee and carrier-passenger relationships.[55]

Since the late 1980s dispatching teams of counselors (known as "grief workers") has become commonplace on the occurrence of a traumatic event.[56] Now, shortly after the police, paramedics, and television crews arrive on the scene, grief counselors arrive. The theory of grief work is to work it through and find closure as soon as possible. Early intervention is reputedly the key to recovery following trauma. Psychiatrist Sally Satel cautions, however, that this is not always successful. She writes: "An emphasis on experiencing psychic pain can make some people feel even more vulnerable and out of control. Forced ventilation makes little sense for those whose ordinary copying style is to remain calm, maybe too calm for some people's taste, and spring into purposeful activity."[57] Then, too, communities have long had rituals for coming to terms with calamity.[58] Quite often, when grief workers arrive at the scene of a disaster, they find that survivors do not seek counseling, and the grief workers, feeling unwanted, become depressed and provide therapy for each other.

Notes

1. See M. B. Kelly, "Living with the Avoidable Consequences Doctrine in Contract Remedies," *San Diego L. Rev.* 33 (1996): 175; for an application in the employment context, see R. Fraser, "The Unavoidable Doctrine of Avoidable Consequences," *Fla. Bar J.* 54 (1980): 369.
2. Michigan's statute provides: "Failure to wear a safety belt in violation of this section

may be considered evidence of negligence and may reduce the recovery for damages arising out of the ownership, maintenance, or operation of a motor vehicle. However, such negligence shall not reduce the recovery for damages by more than 5%." MCL 257.710e(h)(5). See Lowe v. Estate Motors, 428 Mich. 439 (1987); Comment, "Apportionment of Damages in the 'Second Collision' Case," *Va. L. Rev.* 63 (1977): 475. Sometimes the wearing of a seat belt may aggravate the ensuing damages, as happened when Carlos Morales shoved a woman out of his truck and unwittingly dragged her through city streets for nine miles as she was tangled in the seat belt. "Homicide Charge for Man in Truck-Dragging Death" (Associated Press news release), *New York Times*, Nov. 26, 1998, p. 25. See S. S. Cacciatore, "How to Beat the 'Seat Belt Defense,'" *Law. Alert* 5 (Mar. 24, 1986): 174.

3. About a dozen jurisdictions (e.g., Florida, California, New York, Michigan, and Arizona) and several federal statutes (e.g., FELA, Jones Act) have adopted the pure comparative negligence approach. In those jurisdictions, the plaintiff's recovery is reduced by the percentage of fault attributable to the plaintiff. About a dozen jurisdictions (e.g., Georgia, Arkansas, Colorado, Tennessee, and Nebraska) have adopted a modified form of comparative negligence in which the plaintiff's recovery is reduced by the percentage of fault attributable to the plaintiff as long as the plaintiff's fault is "not as great as" the defendant's. If the plaintiff's fault is equal to or greater than the defendant's, the plaintiff is completely barred from recovery. See McIntyre v. Balentine, 833 S.W.2d 52, 56 & n. 5 (Tenn. 1992). About twenty jurisdictions (e.g., Wisconsin, Connecticut, Pennsylvania, Ohio, and Illinois) have adopted a modified form of comparative negligence in which the plaintiff's recovery is reduced by the percentage of fault attributable to the plaintiff as long as the plaintiff's fault is "not greater than" the fault of the defendant's. If the plaintiff's fault is greater than the defendant's, the plaintiff is completely barred from recovery. See McIntyre v. Balentine, 833 S.W.2d 52, 56 & n. 6 (Tenn. 1992); A. S. Brown & W. L. Gold, "Litigating Comparative Fault and Avoidable Consequences Issues," *New Jersey L.J.* 144 (1986): 10.

4. See Coker v. Abell-Howe Co., 491 N.W.2d 143, 148–49 (Iowa 1992).

5. In Ort v. Klinger, 496 N.W.2d 265 (Iowa App. 1992), that jury instruction was proffered by the defendant, but the trial court did not give it. The Iowa Court of Appeals said that the version that the trial court gave was sufficient. The trial court gave the following instruction in the place of the defendant's proposal: "If by slight expense and inconvenience a person exercising ordinary care could have thus reduced the consequences of her injury, and failed to do so, she can not recover for any damage that might have been avoided." 496 N.W.2d at 268.

6. In Stump v. Norfolk Shipbuilding & Dry Dock Corp., 187 Va. 932, 48 S.E.2d 209 (1948), a workers' compensation case, an employee refused medication for infected abrasion of skin; the ultimate loss of leg was held not compensable. In Skidmore v. Drumon Fine Foods, 119 So.2d 523 (La. App. 1960), a claimant with persistent pain following amputation of a finger was required to submit to simple, minor surgery or lose his compensation. See Michigan Court Rules 2.111(f)(3)(a) (not listing failure to mitigate as affirmative defense).

7. Michigan Standard Jury Instruction 53.05.

8. See Miller v. Eichhorn, 426 N.W.2d 641, 643 (Iowa App. 1988).

9. In Small v. Combustion Engineering, 209 Mont. 387, 681 P.2d 1081 (1984), a manic-depressive claimant refused knee surgery out of fear of detrimental consequences; refusal was held not unreasonable because of mental disorder. See American Asbestos Textile Corp. v. Ryder, 281 A.2d 53, 56 (N.H. 1971); Zimmerman v. Ausland, 266 Ore. 427, 433–35, 513 P.2d 1167, 1170–71 (1973); see E. Kelly, "Refusal of Surgery in Mitigation of Damages," *Clev.-Mar. L. Rev.* 10 (1961): 421; Annot., "Duty of Injured Person to Submit to Surgery to Minimize Tort Damages," 62 A.L.R.3d (1975). The states differ in their approach as to whether the reasonableness of a refusal of treatment be examined objectively or subjectively. See Genuardi Supermarkets v. WCAB, 674 A.2d 1194 (Pa. 1996); Schwab Construction v. McCarter, 25 Va. App. 104, 486 S.E.2d 562 (1997); Johnson v. Jones, 123 N.C. App. 219, 472 S.E.2d 587 (1996); Dorris v. Mississippi Regional Housing Authority, 695 So.2d 567 (Miss. 1997).

10. In McAuley v. London Transport Executive, [1957] 2 Lloyds Reports 500, the claimant sustained injuries to his hand, severing the ulnar nerve at the wrist. He refused an operation. The defendant's physician advised that it would give him a 90 percent chance of recovering the gross motor movements to the outer fingers of his damaged hand, and even some chance (35 percent) of the return of some fine movements to the same fingers. The trial judge held

that his refusal was unjustified in the circumstances, and attributed most of his disability to the refusal, rather than to the accident itself. The judge's decision was upheld on appeal. The appellate court ruled that a plaintiff should not disregard the advice of a physician though acting on behalf of the defendants; that the plaintiff was not advised by any doctor not to have the operation; and that, therefore, his refusal was unreasonable. The court said, "[T]he plaintiff, as a reasonable person, ought either to accept that advice, or else go to his own doctor and say: 'Doctor, this is what I have been advised by Mr. So-and-So, the surgeon at Such-and-Such a hospital; what do you think about it?' Of course, the plaintiff here never did any such thing."

11. See Lawrence v. Wirth, 309 S.E.2d 315, 317–18 (Va. 1983); Jenkins v. Charleston Gen. Hosp. & Training School, 90 W. Va. 230, 243–44, 110 S.E. 560, 565–66 (1922); Beadle v. Paine, 46 Ore. 424, 431–32, 80 Pac. 903, 906 (1905); H. L. Hirsh, "When a Patient Contributes to His Medical Malpractice Relatively," *Medicine & Law* 4 (1985): 229.

12. Sanderson v. Moline, 7 Wash. App. 439, 499 P.2d 1281 (1972).

13. Beadle v. Paine, 46 Or. 424, 421, 80 Pac. 903, 906 (1905).

14. See Scheffer v. Railroad Co., 105 U.S. 249, 252 (1881).

15. See Stafford v. Neurological Med. Inc., 811 F.2d 470, 473–74 (8th Cir. 1987) (allowing jury to decide whether suicide was an "irresistible impulse").

16. 35 N.Y.2d 425, 322 N.E.2d 263, 363 N.Y.S.2d 568 (1974).

17. For a good review of the cases on this issue, see Grant v. F.P. Lathrop Constr. Co., 81 Cal. App.3d 790, 146 Cal. Rptr. 45 (1978). In Food Distributors v. Estate of Ball, 24 Va. App. 692, 485 S.E.2d 155 (1997), the court provides a review of the varying approaches taken by the states in the work-related suicide cases. See volume 2, chapter 10, on suicide.

18. Wilson v. Yellow Cab Co. of Shreveport, 64 So.2d 463 (La. App. 1953).

19. Jehovah's Witnesses do, however, allow a treatment called *auto transfusion,* in which a "cell saver" is used to remove and filter blood before returning it to the patient.

20. See generally, J. Pomeroy, "Reason, Religion, and Avoidable Consequences: When Faith and the Duty to Mitigate Collide," *N.Y.U.L. Rev.* 67 (1992): 1111; Comment, "Medical Care, Freedom of Religion, and Mitigation of Damages," *Yale L.J.* 87 (1978): 1466. In Mann v. Algee, 924 F.2d 568 (5th Cir. 1991), a wrongful death action, the defense contended that the decedent would have lived had she accepted a blood transfusion, and it attacked the sincerity and reasonableness of the decedent's religious beliefs. Over a strong dissent by Judge Rubin, the Fifth Circuit upheld a verdict in favor of the defense.

21. 159 Atl. 575 (Conn. 1932).

22. 1995 WL 619381 (N.Y. Sup.).

23. Time and again a negligent motorist who hits a Jehovah's Witness is convicted of vehicular manslaughter even though a blood transfusion could have prevented the death. In these cases the defense argues to no avail that the defendant is responsible for the injury, not for the death, but the courts rule that the car accident was a proximate cause of the death. See State of Louisiana v. Baker, 1998 La. App. Lexis 2966; L. Gorov, "Fatality Case in Calif. Melds Religion, Law," *Boston Globe,* Dec. 12, 1998, p. 1.

24. [1975] 1 W. L. R. 1411.

25. [1975] 1 W. L. R. 1415.

26. [1971] 56 Cr. App. R. 95.

27. See F. McAuley & J. P. McCutheon, *Criminal Liability* (Dublin: Round Hall Sweet & Maxwell, 2000), pp. 255–56.

28. For a wide-ranging commentary, see N. Rescher, *Luck* (New York: Farrar Straus Giroux, 1995). The U.S. homicide rate is lower than it might otherwise be because of advanced medical therapies available in the United States, which render many attempted homicides unsuccessful. J. Moore, "Trouble in Paradise" (ltr.), *Sciences,* Sept./Oct. 1988, p. 10. The condition of the victim prior to the injury is also a factor in the outcome. The seat belt defense has been disallowed in criminal negligent homicide cases. See B. D. Fisher & J. H. Fisher, "Use of the Safety Belt Defense in Michigan Negligent Homicide Cases," *Mich. Bar J.,* 68 (Feb. 1989): 144. Insurance policies exclude coverage for bodily injuries expected or intended by the insured. In Aetna Cas. & Surety Co. v. Sprague, 163 Mich. App. 650 (1987), the insured unsuccessfully argued that it was his negligence in failing to take his medication and pursue psychiatric treatment that was the proximate cause of the victim's death. In a criminal trial the insured had been found guilty but mentally ill. The

Michigan Court of Appeals said that "the complaint is a transparent attempt to trigger insurance coverage by characterizing allegations of tortious conduct under the guise of 'negligent' activity." 163 Mich. App. at 654.

29. See W. G. Doerner & J. C. Speir, "Stitch and Sew: The Impact of Medical Resources upon Criminally Induced Lethality," *Criminology* 24 (1986): 319.

30. "Shaun Gates, 4, could have survived the beating that killed him if he had been taken to the hospital," a pediatrician testified in the trial of Southgate housewife "Robin Ryan." Quoted in P. Ross, "Doctor Says Shaun Could Have Lived," *Detroit News*, Mar. 13, 1986, p. B-6. "Three-year-old Dominic Mileto bled internally for possibly three hours and might have survived a severe beating if he had gotten medical attention, an assistant Wayne County medical examiner testified." News report, "Pathologist Says Beaten Boy Could Have Been Saved," *Detroit News*, Apr. 27, 1988, p. B-5.

31. 163 Mich. App. 462 (1987).

32. See 163 Mich. App. at 465, where the court noted that the defendant takes his victim as he finds him, and a severely drunken victim may reasonably be expected to refuse treatment.

33. People v. Robinson, 107 Mich. App. 417, 420, 309 N.W.2d 624, 626 (1981).

34. See G. P. Fletcher, *A Crime of Self-Defense: Bernhard Goetz and the Law on Trial* (New York: Free Press, 1988).

35. The *eggshell skull* doctrine, also known as the thin skull doctrine, holds that a tortfeasor is liable for injuries even when those injuries are heightened by an unforeseeable, preexisting physical condition of the victim. An English court first articulated the rule in Dulieu v. White & Sons, 2 K.B. 669 (1901), stating: "If a man is negligently run over or otherwise negligently injured in his body, it is no answer to the sufferer's claim for damages that he would have suffered less injury, or no injury at all, if he had not had an unusually thin skull or an unusually weak heart." 2 K.B. at 679. The rule has been applied to cases of preexisting psychological incapacity—the thin psyche—as well as to explicitly physical conditions. As an English court put it, "There is no difference in principle between an egg-shell skull and an egg-shell personality." Malcolm v. Broadhurst, 3 All E.R. 508, 511 (Q.B. 1970). In Steinhauser v. Hertz Corp., 421 F.2d 1169 (2d Cir. 1970), the U.S. Court of Appeals for the Second Circuit held that a fourteen-year-old girl predisposed toward schizophrenia could potentially recover damages for the full-blown psychosis that a car accident allegedly precipitated.

36. Aisole v. Dean, 574 So.2d 1248, 1254 (La. 1991).

37. Fenton v. Murphy Motor Freight Lines, 297 N.W.2d 294, 296 (Minn. 1980).

38. See Brown v. Premier Mfg. Cp., 77 Mich. App. 573, 579 (1977); Blair v. Eblen, 461 S.W.2d 370, 372 (Ky. 1970). See also Sanderson v. Secrest Pipe Coating Co., 465 S.W.2d 65 (Ky. 1971) (failure to follow a course of exercise); Byrd v. WCAB, 81 Pa. 325, 473 A.2d 723 (1984) (claimant canceled eight of twelve physical therapy sessions and suffered second jury because of failure to complete therapy; held unreasonable).

39. 611 A.2d 1174 (Pa. 1992).

40. 611 A.2d at 1176–77.

41. H. Voth, "Love Affair Between Doctor and Patient," *Am. J. Psychotherapy* 26 (1974): 394.

42. A. Burgess, "Physician Sexual Misconduct and Patients' Responses," *Am. J. Psychiatry* 138 (1981): 1335.

43. See Garceau v. Bunnell, 434 N.W.2d 794, 797 (Wis. App. 1988).

44. The current State Farm disability income policy provides: "During the first twenty-four months of Total Disability, Total Disability means complete incapacity, as the result of injury or sickness, of the insured to engage in his/her occupation and which requires the regular care of a licensed physician other than the insured. After the insured has been disabled for twenty-four months, Total Disability means the complete inability to engage in any occupation for which the insured is or becomes reasonably fitted by education, training, or experience."

45. Communication from Dr. Victor Bloom of Grosse Pointe, Michigan (Dec. 4, 1998).

46. J. P. Lassierer, "Doctor Discontent" (editorial), *New England J. Med.* 339 (Nov. 19, 1998): 1543.

47. Commonwealth, Dept. of Highways v. Lindon, 380 S.W.2d 247 (Ky. 1964).

48. In Dohmann v. Richard, 282 So.2d 789 (La. App. 1973), the Louisiana Court of Appeals said (282 So.2d at 793–94):

> [W]e are [here] dealing with what is perhaps the most misunderstood field of medicine, i.e., treatment of the mind. Plaintiff is not being asked to have a fractured bone placed in a cast, a hernia repaired, or any other conventional form of surgery. Instead it is proposed that he subject himself to electro-shock, a form of treatment designed to work a charge in his personality. Furthermore we bear in mind that our society has not progressed to a point in which it accepts mental illnesses, and particularly the drastic treatment thereof by such measures as shock therapy, with the same tolerance that it now regards physical surgery or treatment. Accordingly we cannot disregard the effect that such treatment, given the present attitudes of our society, is likely to have on plaintiff's future relations with peers. In so stating we do not intend to in any way demean the value of such treatments or to question the effectiveness with which they are generally credited with the medical profession, but refer only to the attitudes held toward them by public at large. . . . [T]he treatment is of undoubted value and benefit in many cases and may very well be so in the case at bar. However, we are not prepared to hold at this time that psychiatric therapy of this sort falls within the spirit, or the letter, of that line of jurisprudence which requires injured persons to mitigate their damages. Accordingly . . . we are unable to hold that the plaintiff's refusal to submit to electroshock therapy is unreasonable.

49. The courts often point to the negative side effects of psychotropic medication. See B. J. Winick, *The Right to Refuse Mental Health Treatment* (Washington, D.C.: American Psychological Association, 1997).

50. In Vitek v. Jones, 445 U.S. 480 (1980), the U.S. Supreme Court noted the "stigmatizing consequences" of a transfer from prison to a mental hospital. See P. J. Fink & A. Tasman (eds.), *Stigma and Mental Illness* (Washington, D.C.: American Psychiatric Press, 1992); R. Slovenko, *Psychotherapy and Confidentiality* (Springfield, Ill.: Thomas, 1998), pp. 503–20. See R. E. T. Corp. v. Frank Paxton Co., 329 N.W.2d 416, 422 (Iowa 1983); Zimmerman v. Ausland, 266 Or. 427, 433, 513 P.2d 1167, 1170 (1973).

51. 187 N.W.2d 511 (Mich. App. 1971).

52. See S. D. Sayre, "Abortion or Adoption: A Rational Application of the Avoidable Consequences Rule to the Computation of Wrongful Conception Damages," *West. State U. L. Rev.* 12 (1985): 781.

53. 187 N.W.2d at 519.

54. See R. E. T. Corp. v. Frank Paxton Co., 329 N.W.2d 416, 422 (Iowa 1983).

55. See Klein Indust. Salvage v. Dept of Industry, Labor & Human Relations, 259 N.W.2d 124 (Wis. 1977)—"we have said that a claimant cannot be said to have unreasonably refused treatment if none was offered by the employer." 259 N.W.2d at 126.

56. When a kennel full of pets caught on fire, killing many of them, before rushing to the scene the veterinarian telephoned a psychologist, who in turn rounded up three other psychologists to provide counseling for the pet owners. Counseling sessions were arranged at a nearby church and were led by a psychologist whose speciality is pet loss support. He noted that owners whose pets die in accidents experience the same emotions others feel at the loss of a relative. "It's important to remember," he said, "it's not the object that you attach affection to, it's the intensity of the emotion." C. Christoff, "Trauma Greets Pet Owners at Burned Kennel," *Detroit News*, Nov. 27, 1999, p. 1. In Israel families are informed of the death of a combatant in the military by a counselor (not by letter, as in the United States).

57. In response to the events of September 11, 2001, New York City Police Commissioner Bernard Kerik, apparently concerned about how his 55,000-member force was holding up, announced mandatory mental health counseling for every member of the New York Police Department. The purpose was to stave off the development of PTSD. A similar program was implemented following the 1995 bombing of the Alfred P. Murrah Federal Building in Oklahoma City, after which nearly 9,000 participated in some form of mental health counseling. A number of rescue workers committed suicide after the bombing in Oklahoma City. K. P. O'Meara, "The Grief Police" (cover story), *Insight*, Jan. 28, 2002, p. 10. In the days of World War II, soldiers who had succumbed to shell shock (in modern jargon, PTSD) were returned

to duty within two to five days by a kind of therapy (hypnosis), but there is apparently no current evidence that psychological debriefing is a useful treatment for the prevention of PTSD after traumatic incidents. The evidence indicates not only that this is not happening, but it also indicates that debriefing may actually prolong the process of recovery. Why? It has been suggested that debriefing "medicalises" normal distress by generating in an individual the expectation of a pathological response. An exposure that is brief, such as in debriefing, may exacerbate, rather than ameliorate, distress. A. C. MacFarlane, "The Longitudinal Course of Posttraumatic Morbidity: The Range of Outcomes and Their Predictors," *J. Nerv. Ment. Dis.* 176 (1988): 30; B. Raphael, L. Meldrum, & A. C. MacFarlane, "Does Debriefing after Psychological Trauma Work?" *BMJ* 310 (1995): 1479. Debriefing of jurors who have been exposed to photographs of mutilated victims is recommended in S. M. Kaplan & C. Winget, "The Occupational Hazards of Jury Duty," *Bull. Am. Acad. Psychiatry & Law* 20 (1992): 325.

Pointing out what in other cultures might seem obvious, Dr. Satel writes, "Most people, in fact, are quite resilient and don't need registered experts to deal with anguish. Are our priests and rabbis not up to the task? Are our families' instincts to comfort not keen enough?" S. L. Satel, "An Overabundance of Counseling?" *New York Times,* Apr. 23, 1999, p. 25; see also "A Surfeit of Disaster: When Horror Strikes, Does Counseling Help?" *Economist,* May 8, 1999, p. 21. In another critique, Dr. Thomas Szasz writes, "PTSD is now routinely *imputed* to people, especially to children helpless to reject the label. . . . Adults, too, are treated as if they could not manage their own grief unassisted by helpers they do not seek. A plane crashes. Relatives and friends of the victims are met by 'grief counselors.' What in the past Americans would have considered ugly meddling, they now accept as medically sound mental health care." T. Szasz, *Pharmacracy: Medicine and Politics in America* (Westport, Conn.: Praeger, 2001), pp. 150–51. In times of sadness and mourning, pets provide comfort and support. At Ground Zero at the demolished World Trade Center some psychiatrists and chaplains made use of animal-assisted therapy (AAT) dogs, finding that when people began to open up to dogs, it became their opening to help. A famous psychiatrist approached one grieving woman who was lying down at Pier 94 with an AAT dog and began to offer assistance. Her reply: "No thank you, I'm in very good hands with this dog." S. Dale, "Comfort Dogs," *Dog World,* Feb. 2002, p. 48.

58. See R. A. Haig, *The Anatomy of Grief* (Springfield, Ill.: Thomas, 1990). Thomas Lynch, a funeral director, observes that TV reporters have become our virtual therapists, trumping "grief facilitators," by dressing public interest and passing curiosity in the needful garb of bereavement. T. Lynch, "Grief, Real and Imagined," *New York Times,* Oct. 30, 1999, p. 27.

23
Child
Custody

With the advent of divorce and the demise of the father as master of the children, disputes over child custody arise. The courts are now asked to determine which of the competing parties is entitled to be named custodian of the child. These disputes divide into three types: parent versus parent, parent versus nonparent, and nonparent versus nonparent. Increasingly, the psychiatrist is asked to provide data and opinion to assist the court in reaching or justifying its decision. The task of the psychiatrist is to uncover and offer testimony relevant to which party should be given custody or visitation.

Approximately one in two marriages in the United States ends in divorce, affecting about one million children per year. Approximately 10 percent of divorces involve custody litigation. Divorce cases are generally uncontested and raise no custody problem, a fact that is remarkable given that a petition must be filed to obtain a divorce, thereby putting the parties in the judicial system, and the process is often prolonged and exacerbates the ire of the parties. By and large, businesses negotiate or mediate a dispute without filing a lawsuit, but for marital conflicts it is necessary to enter the judicial process. Few states promote mediation, and lawyers quite often find it in their interest not to mediate. In any event, litigation (filing a petition for divorce) is necessary and occurs before any mediation of a marital conflict.

Usually a father contests custody only when they consider the mother grossly unfit or he feels very hostile toward her. Fathers as a rule recognize that mothers can render better care and that the children usually wish to be with the mother, and consequently they do not request child custody or possession of the family home in the divorce action. The mother is literally the housekeeper. It is observable among the human and animal species that it is generally the mother who cares for and protects the young. And, of course, as fathers may recognize, a custody dispute is apt to be a futile endeavor. Surveys of sample cases indicate that maternal custody is awarded in 85 to 95 percent of the cases.[1]

Worldwide, rituals and songs express love and affection for mother, and rarely if ever is father mentioned. Russia is Mother Russia (Germans salute the Fatherland). A popular song in Russia (and translated into other languages) says:

> May there always be sun,
> May there always be sky,
> May there always be momma,
> May there always be me.

In gatherings in Georgia in the Caucasus, where Stalin was born, there is first a toast to mother, then a toast to Stalin.

In recent years, with the changing role of the mother in modern society, a number of decisions, albeit few in number, have emerged awarding custody to the father. Members of FARCE (Fathers' Awareness of Rights and Custody Equality) have picketed at the Capitol. Yet, following divorce, the contact of fathers with their children drops off at a staggering rate. Only one-sixth of all children see their fathers as often as once a week after a divorce, and close to one-half do not see them at all. Ten years after a divorce, fathers are entirely absent from the lives of almost two-thirds of these children. About 30 percent of children are now born to unwed parents. While children of divorce typically have a tie with their fathers that is severed, most children born to unwed mothers never develop this tie at all.[2]

Historical Right of Fathers

In an earlier day, when divorce was exceptional, the fundamental principle of the law was that the father possessed the paramount right to the custody and control of his minor children. The husband and wife were deemed to be one, and that one was the husband. In family and commercial matters, as Sir William Blackstone (1723–1780), author of *Commentaries on the Laws of England* (1765–1769), said, "a mother as such is entitled to no power but only to reverence and respect." The mother's right to custody of her children was recognized only upon the death of the father and, unlike his right, hers was not considered a natural right. The issue of custodianship, when it arose, usually involved a relative or other third person who sought custody of the child to prevent parental neglect or abuse. The courts invariably held for the natural parent, on the theory that the child was the property of the father. (There was then no Society for the Prevention of Cruelty to Children.) The concept that a child's custody was a property or natural right of the father is illustrated by Mark Twain's description of Huck's drunken, vagrant father who occasionally came home to exercise his rights over him.

The judge and the widow went to law to get the court to take me away from him and let one of them be my guardian; but it was a new judge that had just come, and he didn't know the old man; so he said courts mustn't interfere and separate families if they could help it; said he'd druther not take a child away from its father. So Judge Thatcher and the widow had to quit on the business.

That pleased the old man till he couldn't rest. He said he'd cowhide me till I was black and blue if I didn't raise some money for him. I borrowed three dollars from Judge Thatcher, and pop took it and got drunk, and went a-blowing around and cussing and whooping and carrying on; and he kept it up all over town, with a tin pan, till most midnight, then they jailed him and next day they had him before court, and jailed him again for a week. But he said he was satisfied; said he was boss of his son, and he'd make it warm for him.[3]

Best Interests of the Child

King Solomon anticipated the modern *best interests of the child* standard by awarding a child to the woman who would give up the child rather than to the woman who would have the child cut in two if she could not get her selfish way. Solomon did not have to determine who the biological mother was. The guiding rule now followed by the courts in child custody disputes is the best interests of the child. With the emancipation of women, and with divorces becoming more frequent, a parental rights doctrine could hardly resolve custody disputes between parents. The courts came to say, beginning with Justice Cardozo's classic decision in 1925 in *Finlay v. Finlay*,[4] that the prime consideration in child custody disputes is the best interests of the child. Upon examination of the decisions purporting to employ this rule, however, it is seen that the best interests of the child will coincide with a parental rights decision. In effect, courts employ the semantics of the best interests test to achieve a parental rights decision, with the mother usually obtaining custody. Similarly, in disputes between parents and third parties, the child's best interest is usually interpreted to mean custody by a natural parent. The parental rights and best interests doctrines are, in effect, opposite sides of the same coin. The fusion of the doctrines results from the generally justifiable view that custody by a natural parent, particularly the mother, is in the best interests of the child.

The phrase *best interests of the child* is magnanimous, but what criteria or evidence do the courts use in reaching such a decision? Cases in which courts spell out their reasoning are very few in number, resulting in criticism reminiscent of Plato's castigation of the poets who would say so many fine-sounding things yet could not, under questioning, tell precisely what they meant. The best interests doctrine is invoked as though it were a magic formula by which the court, in Solomon-like fashion, would achieve the proper solution in each case. At any rate, the doctrine serves to avoid awarding custody to an abusive or drug-addicted parent.

The task of the courts was simple under the parental rights doctrine. The best interests doctrine does open channels of inquiry, but the results usually turn out to be the same. Custody decisions contain amorphous platitudes, but there is a simple rule of thumb that generally governs the cases: custody goes to the mother.

Assumptions in Deciding Custody

There are certain other assumptions in deciding custody arrangements, however, than just the basic supposition that the mother makes the better custodian, at least for young children: (1) certain types of behavior are so detrimental to a child's welfare that they disqualify a parent as a custodian, (2) the parents' wishes and the child's wishes should be taken into consideration, and (3) the noncustodial parent has no duties in terms of the child's welfare except the payment of support.

Fitness of the party has been the criterion most frequently cited by the court in determining the best interests of a child. This attribute generally refers to the moral climate provided by the party. As one court put it, "As employed by our courts in custody cases the word 'fit' connotes moral rectitude."[5] Sexual indiscretion known to the children is the most common basis for finding a parent unfit. A separated wife is not required to live in monastic seclusion, but a "calculated and continued public course of misconduct" is regarded as detrimental to the interest and welfare of the children.[6]

In the view of many psychiatrists and other professionals, however, a parent's sexual conventionality or unconventionality has little to do with his or her capacity to function effectively as a parent. They agree that involving the child in such unconventionality is harmful, but there are many women who function effectively as mothers notwithstanding one or more shifts of sexual partners. They do not believe, as do a majority of judges, that the legality of such sexual relationships should be a test of fitness.

Emotional Instability of a Parent

It is within the moral rectitude category that the issue of emotional instability of a parent is raised when evidenced by alcoholism, drug addiction, promiscuity, incest, exhibitionism, or other criminal behavior. Marital fault may be a factor bearing upon the best interests issue. Apart from the aforementioned specific types of evidence, the possibility of emotional harm to a child caused by a mentally disturbed parent is rarely considered in the courtroom. Parental psychosis unattended by such evidence is not sufficient to warrant change of custody, although it is estimated that 15 percent of children who have a severely mentally disordered parent will themselves become psychotic, and 40 to 50 percent will develop socially deviant behavior. It is held, though, that a parent who is adjudged incompetent or is a patient in a mental hospital is not a fit custodian.[7]

By and large, the law on custody reaches a result remarkably similar to that advocated by the late Dr. D. W. Winnicott, prominent English child psychiatrist. In a paper dealing with the effects of psychotic parents on the emotional development of the child, Winnicott said:

> Parental psychosis does not produce childhood psychosis. Aetiology is not as simple as all that. Psychosis is not directly transmitted like dark hair or haemophilia, nor is it passed on to a baby by the nursing mother in her milk. It is not a disease. . . . [P]sychiatric patients . . . are people who are casualties in the human struggle for development, for adaptation, and for living. . . . Parents with [schizoid characteristics] fail in many subtle ways in their handling of their infants (except insofar as they hand over their

children to others, being aware of their own deficiency). . . . [I]n my practice I have always recognized the existence of a type of case in which it is essential to get a child away from a parent, especially a parent who is psychotic or severely neurotic. . . . [O]ne [must keep] in mind always the stage of development of the infant at the time of the operation of a traumatic factor. The infant may be almost entirely dependent, merged in with the mother, or may be ordinarily dependent and gradually gaining independence, or the child may have already become to some extent independent. . . . I for one do not want legal power to take children from parents except where cruelty or gross neglect awakens society's conscience. Nevertheless, I do know that decisions to take children from psychotic parents have to be made. Each case needs very careful examination, or in other words, highly skilled casework.[8]

Allegations of Child Abuse

By recent legislation, California specifically states that a court-ordered child custody evaluation shall include history of child abuse, domestic violence, substance abuse, and psychiatric illness, and psychological and social functioning.[9] To affect the outcome in a dispute over custody or visitation, allegations of child abuse are made that are often false. In a large sample of nine thousand families involved in custodial visitation disputes, Thoennes and Tjaden found that the rate of reporting was six times greater than that observed in a national incidence study.[10] Ceci and Bruck concluded that studies generally indicate that approximately one-third of all such allegations made in this context are likely false and that as many as 50 percent or more of such reports in this context are erroneous claims. They further concluded that false reports from preschool children, due to their limited language and nascent symbolizing capacity, and, moreover, due to their similar cognitive limitations in terms of distinguishing reality from fantasy, are significantly more "suggestible" and, hence, less competent at accurately reporting actual occurrences of sexual behavior on the part of their caretakers.[11]

Preference of Child

Most jurisdictions, either by statute or decision, allow the judge to consider the child's preference, giving due weight to his age and maturity. Some state statutes set out the age at which to allow choice. Adolescents often want an advocate to express their desire and viewpoint. The judge often interviews the child or adolescent privately (contrary to the general principle of open proceedings), in an attempt to insure that neither party is exerting influence upon his choice.

The preference of children is often influenced by what is colloquially called "brainwashing," or what Dr. Richard Gardner refers to as "parental alienation syndrome." Judges are now being asked to decide if children who do not wish to be with or visit their father or mother suffer from clinical alienation or if they are simply expressing a reasonable desire to avoid contact. A few years ago in Michigan two psychiatrists—Dr. Savitri Bhama and Dr. Rajendra Bhama—were engaged in a prolonged and bitter custody fight over their two young children, almost depleting their assets in legal fees. The mother claimed that her husband alienated the young children from her, hence their desire to be with him, and she sued for intentional infliction of mental distress as well as a change of custody to her. The court found that the father's conduct was "outrageous." The children were returned to the mother, and the suit for intentional infliction of mental distress was allowed.[12]

Psychiatrists question the wisdom of asking a child to make a choice or, for that matter, involving him to any extent in custody proceedings. Discussing cases involving eight-, eleven-, and fourteen-year-olds, they point out that forcing the child to choose the parent with whom he wishes to live is the equivalent to his saying that one parent is good and the other bad, or that one loves him while the other does not.[13] The child often avoids such a predicament by stating that it makes no difference with whom he lives. Conversely, some children may have definite opinions that may be against their own best interests.[14] As a practical matter, custody is awarded in accordance with the preference of adolescents, otherwise they would likely make the custodian's life miserable.

The child, unable to be with both parents together, may perhaps wish to have his time divided equally between his parents, but awards that alternate custody are not usually made. Alternating custody, while legally possible, was not done even in the day of the parental rights doctrine. The best interests of the child thus prevailed in this respect even when the expressed doctrine was parental rights. Stability in environment and central authority are desiderata in child rearing, but there is something of a trend toward shared custody, so as to maintain a link with the father.

However, an agreement between the parties may provide that the child will be six months, for example, with the father and six months with the mother, with a change of schools twice a year. Parents and attorneys will sometimes agree to such schedules in order to hurdle the first step—the divorce and settlement—expecting to return to court at a later time. Often, such schedules are then altered in a suit brought by the mother. For the welfare of the child, judges would do well to refuse to accept an agreement that divides the child in such a way between the parents. Moreover, it is usually recommended that siblings not be split up, the custody of some going to the father and others to the mother.[15]

Visitation

The award of custody to one parent is partially counterbalanced by the grant of visitation rights to the other. The noncustodial parent has a right of visitation (also known as "parenting time") as a matter of course, which is forbidden only in the case of gross unfitness or failure to pay child support. The noncustodial parent is usually obliged to make support payments, which is considered as a special kind of debt that the courts can enforce through the criminal law or as a civil contempt order. Psychiatric testimony may be used in the determination of visitation rights as well as custody.[16]

Nowadays, varied and complicated family structures have arisen because of divorce, decisions not to marry, single-parent families, remarriages and stepfamilies, parents who abandon their children to temporary caretakers, and children being raised by third parties because parents are deemed unfit. Given that situation, the state of Washington enacted a law specifying that "any person may petition the court for visitation rights at any time." Under that law, the court could grant such rights if they "served the best interest of the child." The Washington

Supreme Court and the U.S. Supreme Court both ruled, however, that the statute was too broad and gave too little deference to the wishes of the parent. The U.S. Supreme Court ruled that these cases should be decided on a case-by-case basis.[17]

Then, too, nowadays people move about often, and when a custodian parent moves to another area, the noncustodial parent's visitation is curtailed as a practical matter as a result of the distance, and the child is uprooted from the old environment. In dealing with a removal petition, the courts frequently rely on the test articulated by the New Jersey Supreme Court in *D'Onofrio v. D'Onofrio*:[18]

(1) It should consider the prospective advantages of the move in terms of its likely capacity for improving the general quality of life for both the custodial parent and the children.

(2) It must evaluate the integrity of the motives of the custodial parent in seeking the move in order to determine whether the removal is inspired primarily by the desire to defeat or frustrate visitation by the noncustodial parent, and whether the custodial parent is likely to comply with substitute visitation orders when she is no longer subject to the jurisdiction of the courts of this State.

(3) It must likewise take into account the integrity of the noncustodial parent's motives in resisting the removal and consider the extent to which, if at all, the opposition is intended to secure a financial advantage in respect of continuing support obligations.

(4) Finally, the court must be satisfied that there will be a realistic opportunity for visitation in lieu of the weekly pattern which can provide an adequate basis for preserving and fostering the parental relationship with the noncustodial parent if removal is allowed.

The *D'Onofrio* test focuses on what is in the best interests of the new family unit, that is, custodial parent and child, and not what is in the best interests of the child, the latter having been decided in the earlier custody hearings (though implicitly the best interests of the child come into consideration under the test). The *D'Onofrio* test recognizes the increasingly legitimate mobility of today's society.[19]

Change of Custody

A custody order is not settled for all time but may be relitigated. The doctrine of *res judicata*—a matter settled by judgment—does not apply in custody cases. A custody struggle may mean it's just trial, trial again. In order to obtain a modification of a decree, however, there must be a clear showing of a significant change of circumstances since the time of the prior custody award. The remarriage of the parents, changing employment circumstances, the capacities of the parents, and the actual needs of the child constitute a change of circumstances that may warrant changing the child's custody.[20] It must then be shown that the new circumstances require a change of custody in order to promote the best interests of the child. In cases involving welfare assistance, there may be the testimony of a caseworker, who has the right to make home visits. A home visitation without a search warrant has been held not to constitute an "unreasonable search" within the meaning of the Fourth Amendment, on the ground that the home visit is not a criminal investigation.

All too frequently, a claim of changed circumstances represents simply another round in an ongoing battle, with the child as pawn. Some interspousal warfare may be described as "cruel and unusual punishment." Medea acted out her murderous rage on her children to retaliate against Jason. Holy deadlock does not end with the divorce. One vindictive tactic may be moving to another locale. Considerable wardship work of the courts contains an international flavor, and as the number of binational marriages increases, the number of "kidnappings" outside the country is bound to increase. The 1961 Hague Convention says that disputes over the custody of a child should be handled by the country of the child's "habitual residence," although that may not be in the child's best interests.

Severance of Parental Rights and Adoption

Many cases are presented in which the child has been, for a considerable time, in actual custody of a relative or foster parents who could adopt him. An adoption proceeding places the child in the permanent custody of the adoptive party, who must first satisfy the court as to eligibility, and has the effect of a final decree. It often occurs that after the remarriage of one of the parents, the stepparent seeks to adopt the child. Although adoption is beneficial to the child and would give him a sense of security, it is generally only in cases of abandonment or desertion by the natural parent that the court allows the stepparent to adopt the child. Otherwise, the desire of the natural parent guides the court in permitting adoption.

An order terminating the rights of parents must be justified by conditions that have produced serious, substantial, and continuous damage to the health and welfare of the child. Additionally, there must be evidence that termination will be truly in the best interests of the child. Severance of parental rights is a serious act, affecting not only the rights of parents but also the rights of children.[21] Yet, unless parental ties are fully severed in appropriate cases, many children would reach adulthood in a succession of foster homes or institutions—temporary placements that become a permanent way of life. Thousands of children live in that interim status of temporary placement, without roots, without family. Often forgotten by their parents and frequently separated from siblings, they are children without identification with a family unit and without opportunity to form lasting family loyalties. Freeing children from grossly neglectful or abusive parents so that new, constructive, parental relationships may be established with adoptive parents seems a logical measure.[22]

The problem of parental abuse or neglect, whether or not the parents are divorced, raises a basic question as to the rights, duties, and obligations of the community. There is widespread protest over the lack of good, publicly funded child care centers. While not protecting the well-being of children in that way, every state, beginning first in 1963, has enacted legislation requiring a physician to report cases of child (physical) abuse, with failure to report constituting a criminal offense. The legislation grants immunity from civil and criminal liability to those who report the abuse. How much right should public officials have in intervening in the parent-child relationship? Out of some deep sense as to the scope of state power, the legislation is limited to physical abuse, as that involves concrete or tangible evidence. In the case of parental psychosis, although ignored by courts of ordinary jurisdiction in deciding custody, the juvenile court may find emotional neglect of the child and remove him from the home.

The concept of child neglect in law, like the concept of mental illness in psychiatry, is built upon limited data and focuses narrowly on the parent or child, apart from the social context in which they live. Like a flashlight in a dark room, investigation of only the individual is narrow in its illumination. Sometimes the light on even that limited area is weak. In an article dealing with family law and the challenge it presents to psychiatry, the late Dr. Andrew S. Watson criticized psychiatry for offering opinions not supported by statistical evidence. Many questions put to psychiatrists by lawyers involve predictions, and, he said, psychiatrists present ambiguous conclusions drawn from shadowy observational data. He wrote: "Because of the lack of such basic information in this and most other family-law areas, when efforts are made by psychiatrists or social workers to alter custody of a child by means of court procedure, they are quite incapable of responding to the judge's request for some kind of evidence to justify the change."[23]

Besides lacking scientific validity, the opinions of mental health professionals concerning dispositions have often been based on data irrelevant to the legal questions in dispute. Psychologist Thomas Grisso has observed:

> Custody cases involving divorced or divorcing parents rarely involve questions of parental fitness, but rather the choice between two parents, neither of whom [is] summarily inadequate [as a parent]. . . . Mental health professionals do not have reason to be proud of their performance in this area of forensic assessment. Too often we still evaluate the parent but not the child, a practice that makes no sense when the child's own, individual needs are the basis for the legal decision. Too often we continue to rely on the assessment instruments and methods that were designed to address *clinical* questions, questions of psychiatric diagnosis, when clinical questions bear only secondarily upon the real issues in many child custody cases. Psychiatric interviews, Rorschachs, and MMPIs might have a role to play in child custody assessments. But these tools were *not* designed to assess parents' relationships to children . . . [or their] childrearing attitudes and capacities, and *these* are often the central questions in child custody cases.[24]

Even if the best interests test were in reality to replace the parental rights approach, there is the hard problem of determining what the best interests of the child require. Upon the death of the custodial parent, the surviving parent is frequently pitted against a third person. There is fear, albeit infrequently articulated, that application of the best interests doctrine as the real test for custody determination might result in a further undermining of the family. While there is psychological basis for the traditional recognition of the right to custody in the natural parent, there may be times when the importance of the physical relationship is outweighed by other considerations, as in the case where there has been a long, affectionate relationship in a stable environment with another party.

No one can forget Charlie Chaplin's 1921 film *The Kid*, when the mother of the illegitimate child, now suddenly rich, wanted to reclaim her baby from the tramp who had loved and cared for it. In a much-publicized case, which came to be known as the Baby Lenore case, Olga Scarpetta gave up her out-of-wedlock child, Lenore, for adoption, although she was of a wealthy family. After the child was placed through a public agency with New York lawyer Nick DeMartino and his wife, the mother changed her mind and, in a successful fight through the New York courts, obtained an order returning the child. (An adoption through an agency is usually anonymous.) The adoptive parents immediately moved to Florida, where the court fight began anew. The New York courts had ruled that the mother's prompt change of mind encouraged it to follow the general rule that a child is better off with its natural mother, especially if she is capable of rearing the child. But the Florida court, noting that the child was now more than two years old, said more damage would be done if Lenore were returned to the mother. The mother then asked the Supreme Court to review the case because of the contradictory rulings of the courts in two states, but she was turned down in a routine order that made no comment on the issues. The adoptive parents then, in 1972, proceeded to complete the legal adoption procedure in Florida.

Another case rejecting the natural parent and attracting national attention occurred in Iowa. Hal Painter placed his seven-year-old son, Mark, with the Bannisters, the maternal grandparents, after the death of the boy's mother and sister in an automobile accident. He had placed Mark first with his own foster parents, who were living in a trailer, and he rented a room in a house where no children were allowed. A request by the foster mother that he pay board for the child precipitated his call to the Bannisters. Four years later, having remarried, he sought custody. Custody, however, was ordered continued with the grandparents, despite the usual presumption that a parent is entitled to custody.[25]

The psychological report submitted to the court indicated that the child's previous relationship with his father was unclear and that he had established a sound relationship with the grandfather that if disrupted could result in emotional damage to the child. Obscuring the report, however, the court commented unfavorably on the father's occupation, freelance photography, and the relative merits of a rural, church-oriented upbringing versus a "more interesting Bohemian life." The decision, allowing another to take the place of a natural parent, provoked a storm of protest.[26]

Guidelines for Determining Custody

Troubled by the criticism resulting from the *Painter* case, Dr. Richard Jenkins at that time came to the defense of the best interests doctrine. As director of the Department of Child Psychiatry at the University of Iowa, Dr. Jenkins daily witnessed the emotional and physical battering of children by parents. Sensitive to their plight, he formulated a position statement on child custody for the American Orthopsychiatric Association, of which he was an active member, that determinations of custody should be based on the best interests of the child. It was adopted unanimously by the association's Committee on Law and Mental Health (including Slovenko) and approved unanimously by the board, the majority of the Resolutions Committee, and the membership. It reads:

> The American Orthopsychiatric Association supports the view that the determining consideration in child-custody cases should be the welfare of the child. Children are not property and should not be regarded as possessions. The rights of a parent to the custody of his child are dependent upon his assuming parental responsibility and functioning as a parent. While there is a strong initial presumption that the custody of a child

should rest with his natural parent, the law has long recognized that this presumption may be set aside if the parent is unfit for or fails to assume parental responsibilities.

The Association believes that the presumption in favor of the parent should rest upon the actual existence of a deep bond of mutual attachment between child and parent, such as normally grows out of a parent-child and child-parent relationship. Where such a bond exists, it outweighs all consideration of what advantages a foster home may have to offer because of wealth, education, or social position. Within the range of lawful behavior it is more important than any value judgment about the family atmosphere. On the other hand, when the natural parent has not functioned as a parent or has been so ineffectual in that functioning that no such mutual bond exists, and when a mutual bond has developed between the child and a foster parent, such a developed relationship is, in the judgment of this Association, also worthy of great respect in the determination of child custody.

In terms of future mental health of our population, the welfare of the child, not the welfare nor interests of the parent nor of the foster parent, should be the determining consideration. The Association will study such issues as the kinds of criteria and evidence which should be useful in deciding what may be in the best interest of the child.[27]

The Committee on Law and Mental Health initially reserved adoption of the statement, not because of the best interests principle, which it fully affirmed, but because the committee felt that the real issue was the difficulty in determining what the child's best interests were and in setting out the issues to be considered in reaching that determination. Since the 1980s several organizations have published standards and guidelines for evaluating child custody disputes, including the American Psychiatric Association Task Force on Clinical Assessment in Child Custody (1981), the American Psychological Association (1994), and the American Association of Family and Conciliation Courts (1994). The standards of the American Psychiatric Association and the American Psychological Association provide reference sections that list guidelines from other organizations.

The Uniform Marriage and Divorce Act, which has been adopted in many states, sets out a rather indeterminate approach as to the factors to be considered in a custody dispute. It provides:

The court shall determine custody in accordance with the best interest of the child. The court shall consider all relevant factors including:
  (1) the wishes of the child's parent or parents as to his custody;
  (2) the wishes of the child as to his custodian;
  (3) the interaction and interrelationship of the child with his parent or parents, his siblings, and any other person who may significantly affect the child's best interest;
  (4) the child's adjustment to his home, school, and community; and
  (5) the mental and physical health of all individuals involved.
The court shall not consider conduct of a proposed custodian that does not affect his relationship to the child.[28]

Trial courts thus are given broad discretion in making child custody awards. The trial court's decision regarding custody will not be upset on appeal "absent a showing of an abuse of discretion or manifest injustice." However, to ensure the court acted within its broad discretion, "the facts and reasons for the court's decision must be set forth fully in appropriate findings and conclusions." The findings must be sufficiently detailed "to ensure that the trial court's discretionary determination was rationally based." "Specificity of findings is particularly important in custody determinations. This is so because the issues involved are highly fact sensitive."[29] In making a custody determination, the trial court is required to "at least consider all statutorily mandated factors," although it "need not make specific findings on each of the factors, as long as determination is based on substantial evidence relating to factors and set forth explicitly in findings."[30] Religion may at times be a factor in determining the child's custody or education.[31]

Michigan's Child Custody Act of 1970 was the first statute to set out criteria of best interests of the child. It defines *best interests of the child* as the sum total of designated factors to be considered, evaluated, and determined by the court, which include:

(a) The love, affection, and other emotional ties existing between the competing parties and the child.

(b) The capacity and disposition of competing parties to give the child love, affection, and guidance, and continuation of the educating and raising of the child in its religion or creed, if any.

(c) The capacity and disposition of competing parties to provide the child with food, clothing, medical care, or other remedial care recognized and permitted under the laws of this state in lieu of medical care, and other material needs.

(d) The length of time the child has lived in a stable, satisfactory environment and desirability of maintaining continuity.

(e) The permanence, as a family unit, of the existing or proposed custodial home.

(f) The moral fitness of the competing parties.

(g) The home, school, and community record of the child.

(h) The mental and physical health of the competing parties.

(i) The reasonable preference of the child, if the court deems the child to be of sufficient age to express preference.

(j) Any other factor considered by the court to be relevant to a particular child-custody dispute.[32]

These are sweeping, elastic terms that may say much and at the same time say nothing. Another section of the act provides that there is a rebuttable presumption that the best interests of the child require that he should remain in the custody of a natural parent as against the claim of a third party. It provides:

When the dispute is between the parents, between agencies, or between third persons, the best interests of the child shall control. When the dispute is between the parent or parents and an agency or a third person, it is presumed that the best interests of the child are served by awarding custody to the parent or parents unless the contrary is established by clear and convincing evidence.[33]

Significant questions are: To whom does the child turn when hurt or in trouble? In whom does the child confide? For whom does the child behave better and why? Winnicott suggested an ordinary-good-parent concept—to wit, it is possible to be a good-enough parent, and that should give one full legal right to custody without the necessity of determining the psychologically best parent by some complicated formula drawn out by behavioral scientists.

Types of Custodial Arrangements

Some unusual custodial arrangements are split custody, joint custody, and custody with one other than a parent. Split custody, separating the siblings, is not favored by the courts; however, joint custody, which places custody equally with both parents, was popular a few years ago. Some custody experts criticized joint custody; others endorsed it. Under joint custody, either spouse as during the marriage may give consent for the medical or other care of the child.[34] Unless the animosity of the parties precludes a joint custody arrangement, it is the one alternative that attempts to use a living pattern and visitation schedule that most approximates the natural family situation. Those who get along ignore whatever the court may have ordered and make their own arrangements. Those who cannot get along have little choice but to turn to the more traditional and unnatural system, which grants sole custody to one parent and sets out in detail each parent's rights and privileges regarding the children's living arrangements and visitation. When reasonable visitation is unworkable, the court may render an order such as the following:

> The [mother] shall have custody of the minor children of the parties, and the [father] shall have the right of visitation with the children every Wednesday night from 7:00 P.M. to 9:30 P.M. of the first and third weeks and the first and third weekends from 6:00 P.M. of Friday afternoon to 6:00 P.M. on Sunday afternoon. The [mother] shall have the children on the second, fourth, and fifth weekends. During those weeks the [father] shall have the children from 7:00 P.M. to 9:30 P.M. on Tuesday and Thursday nights. In the event either cannot exercise visitation, they are to notify the other party as soon as practical, but at least an hour before the visitation was to occur.

Under prevailing practice, the noncustodial parent is given access or visitation rights, although, as with joint custody, they may be attacked as perpetuating a relationship that is not in the best interests of the child. Visitation, like custody, is theoretically made in the interest of the child. If there is strong evidence that visitation is creating discord or tension, the court may be persuaded to curtail or bar it entirely. The right of visitation is not linked to the payment of child support. In their book *Beyond the Best Interests of the Child*,[35] Joseph Goldstein, Anna Freud, and Albert Solnit suggested that when a decision has been made on placement with one parent, there should be no court-required visitation with the other parent. In those situations in which a court order is necessary for the visitation, they say, the visitation is more likely to be unfavorable to the child's development. They believe the court to be too blunt an instrument to rule on the vagaries of child rearing. Most lawyers would argue, however, that a rule leaving the control of visitation to the custodial parent would all too often result in the termination of visitation; even more, they say, the children would be the victims of a continuing feud between the parents. The courts say that the proposal, which would deny the non-custodial parent a legally enforceable right of visitation, represents such a shift in policy that the question of whether it should be adopted should be left to the legislatures. No state has adopted the proposal.

Battle of Experts

No less than in cases of criminal responsibility, a battle of the experts takes place in custody disputes as to what is in the best interests of the child. The controversy on the merits of joint custody is one illustration. Contradictory views are also expressed in cases inquiring whether a homosexual parent should be denied custody or visitation rights. Thus, in one case in which a lesbian mother and her estranged husband battled for custody of their minor daughters, one child psychologist advised the court that the children should remain with the mother, provided her lover move out of the house. A psychiatrist, calling homosexuality a character disorder, recommended that the children be placed in the custody of their father. Another psychologist said the mother's lover should remain in the house if the children were to stay there. In the past, homosexuality was an automatic impediment to gaining custody, and in some parts of the country, it still is.[36]

Decision making in custody disputes is dependent on expert testimony, particularly that of a court-appointed expert. The court cannot rely on the testimony of neighbors or friends, as each side would round up those biased in its favor and the inquiry would not be advanced. There are varying opinions, however, on the scope of the expert testimony.

Some say that mental health professionals should not specifically name the best parent for the child; others say that they should limit themselves to pointing out the person's adequacies or inadequacies as a parent. The court, however, usually expects the expert in such a case to express an opinion on the ultimate issue. In rendering an opinion that one party is more fit than the other to be named custodian, the expert should interview both parties. The expert usually says that both are adequate but that one is more fit than the other to be named custodian. As the report is seen by the parties, the expert would be well advised not to say that the parents look older than their stated ages.

Although the adversary system may serve well in criminal proceedings, it is arguably not the best system in family conflicts. Although the introduction of no-fault laws has removed the divorce decision from an adversary proceeding, the conflict over property, alimony, custody, and visitation is still dealt with in the traditional adversarial manner. The issue of fault and the focus of the dispute have been shifted from divorce to that of property and custody, and there the parties fight, and they fight over everything—the horse, the saddle, and the manure. When the client has a deep pocket, some lawyers let the meter run—they make motions that have marginal or no relevance or usefulness but that add to billable hours.

It has been suggested that a system requiring attempts at mediation or arbitration initially and then allowing for adversary resolution when the more conciliatory methods break down would avoid much psychological trauma and result in significant savings as well. Moreover, with court dockets increasing with respect to family breakups, there is a need to look to other ways to handle the issues. Local courts and private organizations in a number of states have marital mediation services in operation.

The child custody dispute is by its nature unsuited to the procedural and evidentiary restrictions of the adversary system. The proceeding is unique, since its purpose is not to determine the rights of the parties but the best interests of the child. Therefore, while the hearsay rule and the right to confrontation provide needed protection in an adversary proceeding, it is argued that they are inappropriate in child custody hearings. The decision that a judge is called upon to make in a custody dispute is more closely analogous to the sentencing stage of a criminal trial than to a determination on the merits, and therefore, it is said, the judge should be given comparable discretion to rely on confidential reports of experts.

Custody Investigation and Reports

Recognizing that "custodial questions have sociological implication," the courts are mindful that "common-law adversary proceedings and social jurisprudence are not entirely harmonious" and that "some reconciliation between them is necessary."[37] This has consequences concerning consent to an investigation and consent to the admissibility and confidentiality of the report.

Statutes in a number of states deal specifically with custody investigation and custody reports. Michigan law provides that the court may utilize the community resources in behavioral sciences and other professions in the investigation and study of custody disputes and consider their recommendations for the resolution of the disputes. Florida authorizes a court investigation in any child custody case and provides that the court may consider the report that it obtains unrestricted by the technical rules of evidence. Virginia makes a report admissible even though not authorized by or disclosed to the parties. In the absence of a governing statute, consent of the parties is essential if ordinary rules of evidence and right to cross-examination are to be dispensed with. The general rule is that on factual questions, a court may not consider material that is unknown to the parties. Therefore, the parties are entitled to a copy of the custody report in ample time before the trial and may subject investigators to cross-examination regardless of consent to the investigation.

It is generally agreed that the court may order an independent investigation. Many states have enacted counterparts to Rule 35 of the Federal Rules of Civil Procedure, which provides that where the "mental or physical condition of a party is in controversy," the court may, upon motion and for good cause shown, order that party to submit to a mental examination by a qualified physician. In any event, obtaining the consent of the parties to allow an investigation is not a major obstacle. There is really no free choice in the matter, as consent is given to avoid prejudice. To illustrate, in one case the trial judge stated that in light of the evidence presented, neither spouse should be awarded custody and requested the parties to consent to an independent investigation. When the plaintiff refused, the judge awarded custody to the defendant.[38]

In a number of jurisdictions, the court often suggests that the parties consult a psychiatrist. The "two hats" syndrome arises when the court order asks the expert to provide therapy as well as an evaluation, or the court sometimes says to do an extended evaluation. Wearing two hats—therapist and forensic evaluator—poses ethical questions, including the issue of confidentiality expected in therapy. It complicates both the therapy and the evaluation.[39]

In cases where the parties consult a psychiatrist to resolve their dispute, they usually accept the recommendation made by the psychiatrist. A result of the psychiatric consultation is that the fight over custody is often displaced to fighting over something like the automobile. However, it is not easy for the parties to locate a psychiatrist who will counsel with them, for many psychiatrists are reluctant to get involved in custody matters. In the event that the matter is not resolved and the dispute goes to trial, the expert often serves as an expert for both sides, the fee divided between the parties. The court hearing is usually very brief, and argument usually has little to do with the best interests of the child or who will be the best parent. As a practical matter, lawyers take few objections or appeals, due in part to the fact that too many lawyers regard divorce and child custody cases as garbage cases and do not prepare the case properly. A brief hearing, though, may be preferable to an inappropriate hearing. A court fight may deepen the animosity between the parties and may alienate children called upon to testify.

When both parties recognize that neither is fit and fear that the court will remove the child, they may try to circumvent such a ruling by not contesting custody. The tactic is usually successful. In some cases, commitment to a training school would have been in the best interests of the child. The appointment of an attorney to represent the child as guardian in hearings where custody is disputed or where there is a cause for concern for the child's well-being has been used in a number of family courts. He has the resources of the family court's staff of social workers to make a custody investigation and evaluation. The no-fault divorce law usually provides for the appointment of an attorney to represent the children in the divorce action, but thus far the provision has not been used to any great extent.[40]

In lieu of the formulation of new rules appropriate to the nature of child custody proceedings, Dr. Lawrence S. Kubie offered a proposal that would oust the court of jurisdiction altogether. Under his proposal, parents upon divorce would agree to joint legal custody of their children and joint resolution of all custodial issues. In case of an impasse, a committee consisting of specialists (psychiatrists or educators) selected by the parties in advance would have the power to make a binding determination.[41] Such an agreement could be useful, despite the fact that courts have complete authority to determine what is in the best interests of the children and that agreements between the parents are not binding upon the court insofar as they relate to children. Such an agreement may well have the effect of causing both parents to submit these questions to a committee, however, rather than resorting to court action. Arbitration agreements respecting custody have been upheld.[42] Apart from the Kubie proposal, the development of the family court offers a way to avoid the uncomfortable atmosphere and procedures of traditional courts.

In child custody litigation, the options available to the judge, to be sure, are limited. *Fit custodian* is a relative term. Both contestants may be fit, although not ideal, but all too often the question is: Which of the contestants is the least unfit?

Changing Social Conditions

One consequence of changing social conditions is that more men, even in cases of illegitimacy, are asking for custody and more judges are granting it. The old order changeth, *o tempora, o mores.* There is a reevaluation of the assumption that the mother is always the better parent.[43] Moreover, while for years husbands have run away from home lives, now there is a new runaway: the wife. No accurate statistics exist, but around the country, interviews with marriage counselors, psychiatrists, detective agencies, and women's liberation groups confirm the growth of the phenomenon called the *dropout wife,* the woman who abandons her family and all responsibility to them.[44]

The no-fault divorce law is also a factor contributing to the rise in child custody litigation. Under the old fault-grounds law, a husband wanting out of marriage would be inclined to take a settlement in terms of support and child custody. This bargaining usually occurred where proof of misconduct was lacking but one or both parties was through with the marriage. Under the no-fault law, the husband, knowing he will get out of the marriage no matter what, is less inclined to agree in advance to the wife's demands on child custody and property matters.[45]

Comment

Recent years have seen changes that may well make it necessary to think through the problem of child custody again. Few families are families any longer in the old sense. At one time, when divorce was a rarity, the family was an extended one (grandparents, uncles, aunts, cousins) all living together or nearby in a stable community. Today, the family has been reduced to a nuclear one with only two adults; when there is a divorce, which is commonplace, it is reduced to one, placing an enormous burden on the person bringing up the children.

In an industrialized society, the family is no longer the production labor unit it was in the peasant or artisan family, for example. Its economic function is limited to the organization of everyday activities. With a decreased economic function, the family has been dispersed, and, thus reduced in size, it has not been able to manage adequately other traditional functions. At the same time there has not been a corresponding development of community services to fill the void.

The economy and social structure place a premium on mobility, and the split parents often find themselves in strange and different environments, usually unaided by nursery schools or other facilities for children. While there has been much talk of family assistance, proposed legislation on child development, day care, and education has to date usually been vetoed. Despite a generalized cultural piety about family life, as Daniel P. Moynihan said years ago, the U.S. Government has been marked by a lack of social policies in support of the family as an institution.[46] Some young people see communes as the way out of their isolation and as a way of obtaining assistance in rearing their children.

With the nationwide incidence of divorce approaching one divorce for every two marriages, one out of six children has experienced the divorce of his parents. Alvin Toffler, author of *Future Shock,* predicted a subtle but very significant shift to much more temporary marital arrangements and intensification of the present pattern of divorce and remarriage to the point where it will be accepted that marriages are not for life. "I'm not endorsing it," said Toffler, "but I think it's likely to be the case."[47]

The noted British historian Professor Arnold Toynbee in numerous publications expressed the view that nations rise or fall in relation to the moral unity of the family and the moral purpose of the state, and he saw a decline in both. On the whole he was pessimistic, but he hoped that an ethical reformation would come out of the spiritual needs of the contemporary world.

Notes

1. In Nefzger v. Nefzger, 595 N.W.2d 583 (N.D. 1999), the North Dakota Supreme Court held that the wife's continued alcohol use, her three extramarital affairs, and her twenty-year history of marijuana use did not render her unfit for custody, as she was said to be the primary caretaker of the parties' three children.

2. R. Weissbourd, "Distancing Dad," *American Prospect*, Dec. 6, 1999, p. 32.

3. M. Twain, *The Adventures of Huckleberry Finn* (Indianapolis: Bobbs-Merrill, 1967), p. 34; noted in the excellent article by Carroll Leavell, "Custody Disputes and the Proposed Model Act," *Ga. L. Rev.* 2 (1968): 162.

4. 240 N.Y. 429, 148 N.E. 624 (1925).

5. State *ex rel.* Tuttle v. Hanson, 274 Wis. 423, 80 N.W.2d 387 (1957).

6. Shrout v. Shrout, 224 Ore. 521, 356 P.2d 935 (1960) (mother who had her children bring beer to her while she was in the bedroom with her lover held unfit); cf. Fulco v. Fulco, 254 So.2d 603 (La. 1971) (mother not deprived of custody for having boyfriend stay overnight on at least one occasion and for making at least two weekend out-of-town trips with the boyfriend).

7. Annot., "Mental Health of Contesting Parents as Factor in Award of Child Custody," 74 A.L.R.2d 1068 (1960).

8. D. W. Winnicott, *The Family and Individual Development* (London: Tavistock, 1965), p. 69.

9. California Rules of Court, Rule 1257.3 (1999).

10. N. Thoennes & P. Tjaden, "The Extent, Nature and Validity of Sexual Abuse Allegations in Custody/Visitation Disputes," *Child Abuse & Neglect* 14 (1990): 151.

11. S. J. Ceci & M. Bruck, *Jeopardy in the Courtroom: A Scientific Analysis of Children's Synthesis* (Washington, D.C.: American Psychological Association, 1995).

12. Bhama v. Bhama, 169 Mich. App. 73, 425 N.W.2d 733 (1988). Many of the cases referred for custody evaluation involve parents who deliberately attempt to alienate their children from the other parent. In some cases the alienating parent may have a legitimate reason to be concerned about the target parent. Sometimes this target parent is marginal—he may be an alcohol or drug abuser, or he may be inconsistent about keeping promises and appointments to see the children. The majority of cases—at least the ones that result in legal action—involve a deliberate attempt to remove the child from contact with the target parent for reasons that address the needs of the parent doing the alienating rather than those of the child. The motivation for this alienation is usually either the convenience of the alienating parent or a desire to use the children to inflict revenge on a hated ex-spouse. It is not uncommon for the alienating parent to make false allegations of abuse. In such cases, even if they fail to convince the court that there has been abuse, they will have curtailed contact between the child and the other parent long enough to complete the alienation process. If the court suspends parenting time or changes custody pending the outcome of the investigation, it may well provide sufficient time to complete this alienation process. M. G. Brock, "Parental Alienation," *Detroit Legal News*, Jan. 16, 2002, p. 3.

13. K. E. Alexander & S. Sichel, "The Child's Preference in Disputed Custody Cases," *Conn. Fam. Lawyer* 6 (1991): 45; J. E. Schowalter, "Views on the Role of the Child's Preference in Custody Litigation," *Conn. Bar J.* 53 (1979): 298; J. M. Suarez, "The Role of the Child's Choice in Custody Proceedings," *Case & Comment*, July–Aug. 1968, p. 46.

14. In a study, youngsters were asked whether they would rather their parents either

spent more time at home or earned more money. A mere 20 percent said they would like to see a bit more of their mother and father; 60 percent said they would settle for the cash option instead. L. Kellaway, "Working Hard on a Guilt Trip," *Financial Times*, Dec. 20, 1999, p. 12.

15. Annot., "'Split,' 'Divided' or 'Alternate' Custody of Children," 92 A.L.R.2d 695.

16. Bowler v. Bowler, 355 Mich. 686, 96 N.W.2d 129 (1959) (mother diagnosed as "schizophrenic, paranoid type, chronic, active" and, according to testifying psychiatrists, should have been in a mental institution, denied visitation as well as custody); In re Two Minor Children, 53 Del. 565, 173 A.2d 876 (1961) (mother who had deserted family and lived openly with her lover denied visitation rights notwithstanding expert testimony that she had now become emotionally stable and had a sincere desire to see the children). See also Annot., "Right of Putative Father to Visit Illegitimate Child," 15 A.L.R.3d 887.

17. In re Custody of Sara Smith, 137 Wash.2d 1, 969 P.2d 21 (1998); Troxel v. Granville, 120 S. Ct. 2054 (2000). In this case grandparents (parents of the children's father, who had committed suicide) petitioned to obtain greater visitation rights. The children's mother did not seek to deny visitation, but did not wish to grant as much as the grandparents wanted. Justice Sandra Day O'Connor, writing the Court's plurality opinion, took care not to disparage the important role of grandparents. She observed that the rise of single-parent households, in which 28 percent of children are being raised, is making grandparents more important. Judge O'Connor noted that the trial court went so far as to put the burden on the mother to show why expanded visitation was *not* appropriate. The U.S. Supreme Court said the due process clauses of the Fifth and Fourteenth Amendments to the U.S. Constitution have long been held to create "heightened protection against government interference with certain fundamental rights and liberty interests." The Court held that custodial parents may determine the extent and conditions of grandparent visitation. Ordinarily, however, family law issues, such as visitation and custody, are left to the states, not the federal courts. In a dissent, Justice Antonin Scalia noted that there is no discussion of parental rights in the Constitution.

18. 144 N.J. Super. 200, 365 A.2d 27 (1976), *aff'd*, 144 N.J. Super. 352, 365 A.2d 716 (1976); cited in Henry v. Henry, 119 Mich. App. 319, 326 N.W.2d 497 (1982).

19. The American Academy of Matrimonial Lawyers sets out the following factors in its proposed Model Relocation Act:

(1) The nature, quality, extent of involvement, and duration of the child's relationship with the person proposing to relocate and with the nonrelocating person, siblings, and other significant persons in the child's life; (2) the age, developmental stage, needs of the child, and the likely impact the relocation will have on the child's physical, educational, and emotional development, taking into consideration any special needs of the child; (3) the feasibility of preserving the relationship between the non-relocating person and the child through suitable [visitation] arrangements, considering the logistics and financial circumstances of the parties; (4) the child's preference, taking into consideration the age and maturity of the child; (5) whether there is an established pattern of conduct of the person seeking the relocation, either to promote or thwart the relationship of the child and the non-relocating person; (6) whether the relocation of the child will enhance the general quality of life for both the custodial party seeking the relocation and the child, including but not limited to, financial or emotional benefit or educational opportunity; (7) the reasons of each person for seeking or opposing the relocation; and (8) any other factor affecting the best interest of the child.

In a comment it is stated:

Unfortunately, while the list of factors is comprehensive, it does little to resolve the dilemma so often presented in litigation. If the contestants are two competent, caring parents who have had a healthy post-divorce relationship with the child, the competing interests are properly labeled 'compelling and irreconcilable.' The child's custodian may have a compelling interest to move with the child, the non-custodial person may have a compelling competing interest in maintaining the relationship with the child, which may be significantly undermined by the move. The child has a compelling interest in stability—both in the stability of remaining with the custodian and with maintaining frequent contact with the noncustodial parent. In sum, even a perfect list of factors, when applied to decide such a contest, will not resolve the dilemma, i.e., relocation often is a problem seemingly incapable of a satisfactory solution.

See C. S. Bruch & J. M. Bowemaster, "The Relocation of Children and Custodial Parents: Public Policy, Past and Present," *Fam. L.Q.* 30 (1996): 245; J. S. Wallerstein & T. J. Tanke, "To Move or Not to Move: Psychological and Legal Considerations in the Relocation of Children Following Divorce," *Fam. L.Q.* 30 (1996): 305.

20. Prevatt v. Penney, 138 So.2d 537 (Fla. App. 1962).

21. See F. J. Dyer, *Psychological Consultation in Parental Rights Cases* (Washington, D.C.: American Psychiatric Press, 1999).

22. The best interests doctrine notwithstanding, the guiding maxim adhered to by the courts is that blood is thicker than water. In a contest between a natural parent and a foster parent, the former is generally awarded custody. Parental rights may not be terminated solely on the ground that the child would be better off in another home. S.K.L. v. Smith, 480 S.W.2d 119 (Mo. 1972). See H. H. Foster, "Adoption and Child Custody: Best Interests of the Child?" *Buffalo L. Rev.* 22 (1972): 11.

23. A. S. Watson, "Family Law and Its Challenge for Psychiatry," *J. Family L.* 2 (1962): 71. See P. C. Ellsworth & R. J. Levy, "Legislative Reform of Child Custody Adjudication: An Effort to Rely on Social Science Data in Formulating Legal Policies," *Law & Soc. Rev.* 4 (1969): 167.

24. T. Grisso, "Forensic Assessment in Juvenile and Family Cases: The State of the Art" (address at the Summer Institute on Mental Health Law, University of Nebraska–Lincoln, June 1, 1984). The American Psychological Association has published guidelines for child custody evaluations published in *American Psychologist* 49 (1994): 677. See also R. H. Woody, *Child Custody: Practice Standards, Ethical Issues, and Legal Safeguards for Mental Health Professionals* (Sarasota, Fla.: Professional Resource Press, 2000).

25. Painter v. Bannister, 258 Iowa 1390, 140 N.W.2d 152, *cert. denied,* 385 U.S. 949 (1966).

26. See, e.g., *Life,* Mar. 4, 1966, p. 101; *McCall's,* May 1966, p. 96; *New Yorker,* Apr. 2, 1966, p. 35. The case was also extensively commented upon in the law reviews, e.g., W. H. Poteat, "Iowa Supreme Court v. Wild Oats," *Maine L. Rev.* 18 (1966): 173. The father himself wrote a book, *Mark, I Love You.* Subsequently, during the boy's annual summer visit to California, the father decided to hold onto him, and to appeal to a California court. The grandparents agreed to leave the decision to the boy, who chose to stay with his father and stepmother. At this time the grandfather was in poor health, a matter that presumably influenced Mark's decision. The grandparents made no appearance in the California court action awarding custody to the father. Superior Court, County of Santa Cruz, Aug. 28, 1968.

More recently, in an interstate court battle that sparked another national debate about the rights of children in adoption cases and changed laws in several states, Dan and Cara Schmidt, an Iowa couple, won the battle to regain custody of their daughter, once known as Baby Jessica. Dan Schmidt, 48, and Cara Clausen, 37, of Iowa joined forces in 1991 to regain custody of their infant daughter, whom Clausen, while unmarried, had put up for adoption. Clausen changed her mind about the adoption and informed Schmidt he was the father. They married and they went to court in the month after the girl's birth to get her back. Robby and Jan DeBoer of Michigan were awarded temporary custody of the infant they named Jessica and began adoption proceedings. The DeBoers were portrayed almost universally as the child's best hope for a safe, stable childhood. The DeBoers lived in Ann Arbor and were more affluent and better educated than the Schmidts, who lived in a trailer in rural Iowa. The DeBoers ignored the Schmidts' pleas for the return of the infant when she was only a month old, and stubbornly defended their dubious claim until the reparation at court order when she was two. The Schmidts won custody in 1993 after the U.S. Supreme Court upheld the orders of Michigan and Iowa courts that they had legal rights to the child. The resolution of the custody battle took two and a half years and was played out in emotional court battles and TV interviews. The nation debated whether the child belonged with her biological parents or in the DeBoers' home. The DeBoers were not able to adopt the infant, and the Iowa Supreme Court ordered her return to the Schmidts in 1992. In 1999, six years after winning the bitter battle for custody, the Schmidts divorced. M. George, "Iowa Couple in Custody Battle to Split," *Detroit Free Press,* Oct. 7, 1999, p. B-2.

27. Newsletter, American Orthopsychiatric Association, May 21, 1968, p. 8. It was approved by a mail vote of the membership of 517 yes to 17 no, or 97 percent approval.

28. Uniform Marriage and Divorce Act, sec. 402, 9A U.L.A. 561 (1987).

29. The quotations are from cases cited in Sukin v. Sukin, 842 P.2d 922 (Utah App. 1992).

30. Brown v. Brown, 600 N.W.2d 869 (N.D. 1999); In re Marriage of Converse, 826 P.2d 937 (Mont. 1992); Sukin v. Sukin, 842 P.2d 922 (Utah App. 1992).

31. Religious pressures may adversely affect interspousal disputes, including those over child custody. The judgments of the battling parents may be affected by religious beliefs and may possibly affect the future of their fought-over children. In Aldous v. Aldous, 99 S.D.2d 197, 473 N.Y.S.2d 60 (1984), the court noted that religion can be considered as a factor in determining custody but it cannot be the only factor—it can be taken into account as one of the factors determining the best interests of the child. When a child has developed religious beliefs, particularly over a long period of time, courts will consider them. In Grayman v. Hession, 84 A.D.2d 111, 446 N.Y.S.2d 505 (1982), the court ordered the custodial parent, a nonobservant Catholic, to enroll the child in Hebrew school because the custodial parent had agreed to the child's receiving religious training in the Jewish religion since the child's birth. During visitation, the courts have usually allowed a demonstration of the noncustodial parent's faith, but do not always permit further exposure of the child to the religion's doctrine and activities, because it could lead to conflict and strain. Matter of SEI v. JWW, 143 Misc.2d 455, 541 N.Y.S.2d 675 (1989). In a decision arousing the ire of the Jewish Orthodox community, an Italian court took child custody away from Tali Pikan-Rosenberg after she became religiously observant and married an Orthodox Jew. Jewish leaders charged that the Italian court's characterization of Orthodox Judaism as a cult was shocking and that it set a dangerous precedent. News report, "Italian Custody Case Attracts Attention of Jewish Bigs," *Forward*, Dec. 10, 1999, p. 7. The ruling was vacated by an appeals court. "Italian Court Rules on Custody," *Forward*, Jan. 7, 2000, p. 13.

32. Mich. Comp. Laws Ann., sec. 722.23 (Supp. 1972).

33. Ibid. at sec. 722.25.

34. Noncustodial parents can take a child for emergency medical care, just as anyone can take a child for the treatment of an emergency. The authorization of routine medical care is an area of confusion, however, but the common medical practice is to treat children at the request of noncustodial parents. See W. Bernet, "The Noncustodial Parent and Medical Treatment," *Bull. Am. Acad. Psychiatry & Law* 21 (1993): 357.

35. J. Goldstein, A. Freud, & A. J. Solnit, *Beyond the Best Interests of the Child* (New York: Free Press, 1973).

36. Tennessee apparently has never adjudicated custody to a homosexual parent. In Rhode Island and Virginia a homosexual parent has only a slim chance of being awarded custody. During the 1980s in New Hampshire a homosexual was barred from being a foster or adoptive parent (David Souter, now on the Supreme Court, voted in favor of the law). Hutchens and Kirkpatrick stress the importance of educating the court about social science research in this area. D. J. Hutchens & M. J. Kirkpatrick, "Lesbian Mothers/Gay Fathers," in D. H. Schetky & E. P. Benedek (eds.), *Emerging Issues in Child Psychiatry and the Law* (New York: Brunner/Mazel, 1985). A number of studies find no detriment to children having lesbian mothers. D. J. Kleber, R. J. Howell, & A. L. Tibbits-Kleber, "The Impact of Parental Homosexuality in Child Custody Cases: A Review of the Literature," *Bull. Am. Acad. Psychiatry & Law* 14 (1986): 81. Others find that children of homosexual fathers may be distressed by their father's gay identity. F. W. Bozett, "Gay Fathers," in F. W. Bosert (ed.), *Gay and Lesbian Parents* (New York: Praeger, 1987). In England a male homosexual couple was granted the right to be named as the legal parents of surrogate twin babies. S. Pook, "Babies Can Have Two Gay Fathers, Judge Rules," *Weekly Telegraph*, no. 431 (1999), p. 3.

37. Kesseler v. Kesseler, 10 N.Y.2d 445, 180 N.E.2d 402 (1962).

38. Withrow v. Withrow, 212 La. 427, 31 So.2d 849 (1947); Comment, "Use of Extra-Record Information in Custody Cases," *U. Chi. L. Rev.* 24 (1957): 349.

39. W. Bernet, "The Therapist's Role in Child Custody Disputes," *J. Am. Acad. Child Psychiatry* 22 (1983): 180.

40. R. W. Hansen, "Guardians Ad Litem in Divorce and Custody Cases: Protection of the Child's Interests," *J. Family L.* 4 (1964): 181. Professor Levy argued, however, that if the guardian *ad litem* is to serve his function properly, he may feel compelled to make the proceeding

more contentious (and so more traumatic) than it would have been without him; and, Levy said, if there is any area of universal agreement about custody adjudication, it is that adversary procedures do more harm than good. See R. J. Levy, "Treatment of Child Custody Problems in the Family Code," in Proceedings of the Institute on the Family Code Project, Southern Methodist University, mimeo., 1967.

41. L. S. Kubie, "Provisions for the Care of Children of Divorced Parents: A New Legal Instrument," *Yale L.J.* 73 (1964): 1197.

42. Sheets v. Sheets, 22 App. Div.2d 176, 254 N.Y.S.2d 320 (1964); Note, "Committee Decision of Child Custody Disputes and the Judicial Test of 'Best Interest,'" *Yale L.J.* 73 (1964): 1201.

43. In a case in New York, Family Court Judge Richard C. Delin commented, "The cliché that 'a young child is better off with its mother' has no automatic status in law—nor in human nature—and will be increasingly challenged in a world of working women." In this case, following divorce the mother entered into a relationship with a man that might have "terminated at the whim of either," while the father had remarried a "suitable person." In transferring custody to the father, Judge Delin cited what he called the "low moral standards" of the mother and further ordered regarding visitation that the young girl not set foot in her mother's residence or be allowed "in the presence of the paramour" with whom the mother was "cohabiting." (The mother was a university graduate and a social worker.) The marriage contract impresses the court as an intention to establish a long-term relationship, which is in the best interest of the child. The question is asked: "How much will a judge's view of the child's 'best interest' be dated by his own image of how children should be brought up, or of how a woman should play the role of mother?" *New York Times*, Feb. 23, 1972, p. 44.

44. *Life*, Mar. 17, 1972, p. 34.

45. Under the old law, both parties often arrived at an accommodation as to property settlement, alimony, support, and custody, which was presented to the court for approval. One party then withdrew from the lawsuit, permitting the judge to grant the divorce without an actual contested trial. Under no-fault, however, parties anticipating that they will receive their divorce are often unwilling to make concessions—particularly on property settlements—and the case goes to trial. "In my personal opinion," said Michigan County Circuit Judge Michael L. Stacey, "no-fault typifies the occasional legislation that produces results contrary to what was actually desired. My own experience has been that I am trying many more contested divorce trials. And since there are more trials, attorneys trying these cases have to charge for the additional time spent in court and, in those cases at least, the divorce costs are increased." Quoted in "Advisory Contact," *Detroit News*, Apr. 30, 1972, p. B-1. On challenges to psychological evidence in custody cases, see M. J. Ackerman & A. W. Kane, *Psychological Experts in Divorce Actions* (New York: Aspen, 3d ed. 2001).

46. D. P. Moynihan, "Income by Right," *New Yorker*, Jan. 13, 20, 27, 1973; reprinted in his book *The Politics of a Guaranteed Income* (New York: Random House, 1973). See also J. Q. Wilson, *The Marriage Problem: How Our Culture Has Weakened Families* (New York: HarperCollins, 2002); E. Scott, "Rational Decisionmaking about Marriage and Divorce," *Va. L. Rev.* 76 (1990): 9.

47. A. Toffler, *Future Shock* (New York: Random House, 1970).

24

Contractual Capacity

Countless legal decisions and commentaries point out that consent, the essence of a contract, must be freely and fully given in order to bind the party. According to theory, the "lunatic," though capable of holding property, is, strictly speaking, incapable of any legal act because he has no capacity for willing.

In both Roman and early English common law, there could be no agreement if a party were incapable of understanding. Roman law provided that "an insane person cannot contract any business whatever, because he does not understand what he is doing."[1] Early English common law said that contracts are based on a meeting of minds, and if a party lacked sufficient mind, there could be no such meeting. Over a century ago, voiding a power of attorney given by one confined in a lunatic asylum, the U.S. Supreme Court said: "The fundamental idea of a contract is that it requires the assent of two minds, but a lunatic, or a person *non compos mentis* has nothing which the law recognizes as a mind, and it would seem, therefore, upon principle, that he cannot make a contract which may have any efficacy as such."[2] The Court noted that just as the lunatic is not amenable to the criminal laws, because "he is incapable of discriminating between that which is right and that which is wrong," he also may not be held to the provisions of that which purports to be a contract.

Historically, the principal categories of persons having no capacity or limited capacity to contract were married women, infants, and lunatics. Statutes some-times authorize, as in cases of lunacy, the appointment of guardians for habitual drunkards, narcotic addicts, spendthrifts, older persons, or convicts. Even without the appointment of a guardian, civil powers of convicts may be suspended in whole or in part during imprisonment, and Native American Indians are for some pur-poses treated as wards of the U.S. government.

Lunacy and infancy have usually been equated with regard to contractual ca-pacity. As one court put it, "Infancy and lunacy are disabilities similar in their effect on the contracts of parties, and we see no good reason why a different role should be applied to the contracts of persons *non compos mentis* from that applied in the case of infants."[3] However, one's contractual capacity, where there has been no ruling of incompetency and thus no appointment of a guardian, is a question of fact depending upon the transaction, whereas the contractual incapacity of any minor is a matter of law. Thus, a minor by operation of law is not bound by a purchase of a car. The decisions of minors, who are denied the right to make many decisions for themselves, are made for them by their parents and their schools; as an additional protection, courts are permitted to override parental decisions that do not appear to be in the minor's interests.[4] At the turn of the twentieth century married women came to have contractual capacity, and while a husband may com-plain about his wife's purchases or other dealings, he can now do little or nothing about it.

In the Middle Ages, when commerce was in its formative stage, the doctrine of incapacity did not substantially affect trade, because guilds rather than individ-uals were the trading units. However, with the development of commerce, it was soon recognized that a strict application of the doctrine would prove inimicable. Consequently, the meeting-of-the-minds theory was replaced in large measure by the objective theory of contractual obligation, which merely requires a manifes-tation of assent. Several statutes, including the Uniform Sales Act, the Uniform Negotiable Instruments Law, and the Uniform Commercial Code have been adopted with a view toward securing transactions. For example, every holder of a negotiable instrument is deemed prima facie a holder in due course, and defenses such as fraud, duress, and mistake are not available against a holder in due course.

The outcome of a controversy thus turns very much upon the question whether the transaction involved is a commercial mercantile act. Unlike Anglo-American legal tradition, many civil law countries long ago had two separate codes of law—a commercial code or code of commerce to govern what is called *commercial trans-actions* (e.g., wholesale purchase of wine) and the civil code to govern what is called *consumer transactions* (e.g., purchase of a bottle of wine). In addition to different applicable laws, separate courts often have been established to handle the two different classes of cases. One example is the commercial court in France, where two of the three judges are merchants, and a special class of lawyers, called *agréés*, handles the cases.

The morality of business differs markedly from that of sports, which, tradi-tionally a heroic concept, is associated with such moral ideals as fair play, mag-nanimity in victory, loyalty, and unselfish teamwork. God and sportsmaster are even merged in one image: "For when the One Great Scorer comes / To write against your name, / He marks—not that you won or lost— / But how you played the game."[5] The condemnation of shabby behavior, "It isn't cricket," is not used in the business world, where laissez faire prevails, a doctrine staunchly supported by the law during the nineteenth century.

In business, a number of studies have concluded that personality makes or breaks a man as an economic success. Sherlock Holmes describes the Gold King, the famous millionaire in *The Problem of Thor Bridge:* "If I were a sculptor and desired to idealize the successful man of affairs, iron of nerve and leathery of conscience, I should choose [him] as my model. His tall, gaunt, craggy figure had a suggestion of hunger and rapacity. An Abraham Lincoln keyed to base uses instead of high ones would give some idea of the man. His face might have been chiseled in granite, hard-set, craggy, remorseless, with deep lines upon it, the scars of many a crisis." The Gold King put it thus, "Business is a hard game, and the weak go to the wall. I played the game for all it was worth. I never squealed myself, and I never cared if the other fellow squealed."[6] The precept of W. C. Fields is famous: "Never give a sucker an even break." And he commented, "You can fool some of the people all of the time, and all of the people some of the time, and that's enough to make a good living."[7]

Increasing legal attention, however, is now being given to the quality of a product—the object of the transaction—overshadowing problems of the contracting party's capacity or of a vice of consent such as error, fraud, or duress. In ordinary transactions distributors and retailers and everyone else along the trail of sale exercise less discretion than in former times. Apart from the price usually being fixed, the real selling job is done by the manufacturer in mass media advertising. While not called duress or brainwashing, advertising increases demand and seduces the onlooker to become a customer. Indeed, the contracting seller and buyer now may be in contact but not in conversational touch. In large stores, the seller need not even look at the buyer but only at the article chosen for purchase, the buyer's money, and perhaps his hand. A store policy of liberal return or exchange—"The customer is always right"—renders moot contractual remedies based on contractual incapacity or vice of consent. Unless prohibited by law or sanitary regulations, or in special circumstances such as millinery, bathing suits, electric razors, and personal items, any merchandise will usually be accepted for credit, refund, or exchange. In large transactions, where the parties are usually artificial persons—that is, corporations and governmental agencies—rather than natural persons, the tendency of modern legislation is to restrict the assertion of the defense of ultra vires. Flea-market concepts of marketing are very much outdated in this age of technology and vast corporate enterprise.

Bargaining between natural persons not being relied upon to supply the terms of a contract, the quality of goods is determined more in light of social policy. Strict liability in tort and implied warranty in contract have ushered in a new era of consumer protection. The doctrine *caveat emptor* (let the buyer beware) is no longer a hallowed precept. A product now carries a warranty implied by law that it will perform its function in a way that one would reasonably expect; in addition, the manufacturer owes a duty to the public to use due care in the design and manufacturer of its product or be subject to tort liability. In the 1980s, an estimated 50,000 product-liability suits were filed, but they are now filed at the rate of 500,000 annually. While it is debatable whether this rash of lawsuits is actually resulting in improved products, they are increasingly successful in compensating injured persons.

Consumer Legislation

During the 1970s the various states enacted comprehensive consumer legislation. Although the legislation protects all consumers, special emphasis is placed on a consumer's mental condition. The legislation makes it an unfair trade practice to "[take] advantage of the consumer's inability reasonably to protect his interests by reason of disability, illiteracy, or inability to understand the language of an agreement presented by the other party to the transaction who knows or reasonably should know of the consumer's inability."[8] Merchants may argue that the mercantile world is too complex to screen out consumers meeting these criteria, but a consumer's appearance, actions, and verbal cues should trigger awareness to the possibility that the consumer is mentally deficient. The duty placed on the merchant is not as strict as it may appear, especially in light of the fact that the merchant has to meet only a "reasonable" standard.[9]

The civil law offers other protections. A bargain is not enforceable if either its formation or its performance is criminal, tortuous, or otherwise opposed to public policy. An agreement to commit a crime or tort against a third person is clearly an illegal bargain. An agreement that provides for a greater interest rate than is permitted by law is usurious and illegal, although in practice the prohibition seems to apply to very few transactions. The law on informed consent requires a degree of competence to consent to medical treatment or experimentation.[10] A lawyer who intentionally takes advantage of an elderly or other person with diminished mental capacity to obtain their signature on a document may face disbarment.[11]

Gambling

There is a conflict of authority as to the enforceability of an obligation arising out of a gambling transaction. (Playing the stock market is not considered gambling; the public-relations people at the New York Stock Exchange dispel the notion that buying stocks is gambling.) When gambling is against public policy and made unlawful, gambling wins or losses are not recoverable at law. In such jurisdictions, the gambling trade depends to a large extent on trust. English humorist Henry Cecil, who has done for the law what Richard Gordon has done for the medical profession, observed:

> Racing men rightly say that, whereas in ordinary transactions everything is normally written down, and often long and (to the laymen) unintelligible contracts are signed in transactions involving only quite small amounts, in the racing world many thousands of pounds are staked by word of mouth only, and the parties are entirely dependent upon one another's honesty. . . . The reason for it is simply that betting could not otherwise exist in this country. There are, of course, some defaulters and fraud is sometimes practiced. But the average bookmaker and punter, though not in the rest of their lives necessarily conspicuous for their reliability, are completely honest in their betting transactions.[12]

"Gaming" is the current euphemism for gambling. If it is deemed by the jurisdiction to be within public policy, an obligation of even a chronic gambler is legally enforceable, even though excessive gambling (or gaming) is a form of addiction and free will may be impaired. Fyodor Dostoyevsky in *The Gambler*, the most directly autobiographical of his novels, describes the compulsive gambling that gripped him.[13] The gambler may have an easy-come, easy-go attitude, and he and his family may eat beans while he plays in a crap game. Gambling may be the simplest expression of the desire to win money, however illogical, or it may be merely the desire to escape boredom. The gambling casino is sometimes the only place where those with low incomes feel that they are treated with respect and dignity. A character in the film *American Movie* says gambling is preferable to drugs or alcohol because you always lose with drugs or alcohol.[14]

In Dostoyevsky's time a gambling obligation typically arose not at a casino but at an informal get-together and cash was usually not put up front. The typical scenario now is a gambler with a credit card who gets money, time and again, from an ATM, usually near a casino, loses it, and then may try to declare bankruptcy. Not too long ago state-sanctioned casino gambling in the United States was limited to Nevada and Atlantic City, but today much of the country plays host to some type of gambling. First-generation Las Vegas belonged to Mafia-linked entrepreneurs (such as Bugsy Siegel), but the second was shaped by Wall Street financiers with access to capital markets. Many state legislators, city mayors, and state governors have pushed gambling as a means to stimulate local economies, but a social ramification is an increase in the number of people who fall prey to compulsive gambling.[15]

The courts have split on the dischargeability in bankruptcy of credit card debt incurred for gambling by a debtor to be wiped away, but certain debts are excepted from discharge for policy reasons. The Bankruptcy Code excepts any debt for money, property, services, or credit that was obtained by "false pretenses, a false representation, or actual fraud." Credit card companies have maintained that gambling debts should fall under the fraud exception to discharge, arguing that the debtor did not intend to repay the debt at the time it was incurred.[16]

Compulsive Spending

The law on bankruptcy offers a limited protection to another type of addict known as the compulsive spender. Economists view compulsive spending as good for the country—"shop until you drop!"—but psychiatrists may see it as a mental disorder. Inordinate buying (oniomania) is seen as a *forme fruste* of kleptomania. Abraham Lincoln's wife was a depressive who tried to forget her troubles by shopping on a monumental scale, once buying three hundred pairs of gloves in three months. The inclusion of compulsive shopping was discussed for *DSM-IV* but not adopted.[17] William Wordsworth, some two hundred years ago, wrote, "The world is too much with us; late and soon, / Getting and spending, we lay waste our powers."[18]

Marriage counselors and spouses at or near financial bankruptcy view compulsive spending as tragedy, comparable to alcoholism. The psychiatric explanations for compulsive spending are varied. One explanation is a need to buy love or objects denied in early life; other explanations list feelings of worthlessness, deprivation, and lack of self-esteem, the latter especially applicable to those who overspend on others in an attempt to be recognized. Easy credit and charge accounts allow the compulsive spender to spend his salary much in advance. While the bankruptcy law may limit his liability, his outlook is grim. Credit counseling centers, financed by business and lending institutions hoping to prevent the debtor from going into voluntary bankruptcy and extinguishing their claims entirely, have been established in various communities. Some courts have recently allowed recovery for emotional distress or its physical consequences caused by unfair attempts or harassment in collecting a debt. Midnight collection calls or breaking down a door to recoup merchandise sold is prohibited.

Effect of Mental Incapacity

Although limited in application, lunacy, mental illness, or mental incompetence may continue to present problems of contractual capacity. The view that a lunatic has no capacity to contract (making the transaction absolutely void) has given way to the doctrine that the contract is voidable, at the option of the incompetent person or his guardian, if at the time of the contract he did not understand, on account of mental illness or defect, the nature and consequences of the transaction.[19]

The test is twofold, as are other legal tests on mental capacity: (1) the person must have a mental illness or defect, and (2) the illness or defect must affect his understanding of the transaction to the degree stated. In addition to the *understanding* test, courts sometimes apply an *insane delusion* test. As there defined, an insane delusion is a belief in the reality of facts that do not exist and in which no rational person could believe, and the delusion is related to and motivates the contract. The test has been applied in such cases as the maker of a promissory note believing that unless he made the note he would be killed or imprisoned[20] and a husband, believing his wife was having an illicit affair, deeding his property to his son.[21]

It has been asserted, though, that mental incompetency has no effect on a contract unless other grounds of avoidance are present, such as fraud, undue influence, or gross inadequacy of consideration. Years ago Henry Weihofen, a prominent professor of law and psychiatry, summarized the law of competency to contract: "Was this transaction so foolish or irrational that it shows the person did not adequately understand what he was doing?"[22] Thus, the sale of a truckload of soap to an individual ostensibly needing only a bar may raise the issue of contractual capacity in the form of a vice of consent. The less sophisticated or competent, the more an individual is susceptible to fraud, duress, or error. It is commonly said that an informed consumer is the best protection against fraud or other vice of consent.

To some extent, agreement is an element in civil and criminal procedure as well as in the substantive law of contracts. In the Roman law of civil procedure, the *litis contestatio* entailed a formal contract between the parties agreeing as to the issue in litigation. The criminal law provides a preliminary proceeding known as the *arraignment* (colloquially known as the "arrangement"), in which the accused is called upon to answer to the indictment. His choice of answer is simple and limited: he may plead guilty, not guilty, or not guilty by reason of insanity. If he says, "Maybe I'm guilty and maybe I'm not," a not guilty plea is entered. At one time a refusal to plead—standing mute—deprived the court of capacity to hear the case, a logical result of the view that the court is an arbitrator entirely disinterested in the litigation. This, though, did not provide an escape for defendants. Pressure could be and literally was brought to bear. By placing increasingly heavier weights on his chest, an answer was forced out of him. Hence the common phrase, "to press someone for an answer." A brave and obstinate defendant might allow himself to be pressed to death, in order to avoid conviction and consequent forfeiture of his property to the crown, which would leave his family destitute. Today standing mute is considered the equivalent of pleading not guilty.[23]

Today, in criminal cases, the question of a defendant's ability to comprehend arises in the areas of plea bargaining, waiver of constitutional rights, and assisting counsel in preparation of defense. Ordinarily, a plea of guilty is the result of plea bargaining between prosecutor and defense counsel. The question of the defendant's ability to comprehend and voluntarily waive his constitutional rights usually centers, not on the plea-bargaining stage, but on the issue of whether the police at the time prior to interrogation had advised the defendant of his right to remain silent, that any statements made could be used as evidence against him, and that he has the right to the presence of an attorney, either retained or appointed. The defendant may elect to waive these rights, but such waiver has full force and effect only if made "voluntarily, knowingly, and intelligently."[24] Organic brain disorder, for example, may preclude comprehension of these rights. Thus, a psychiatrist may establish that the defendant is intellectually defective and does not have the "capability of understanding the intricacies of so-called rights."[25]

Is a woman with battered woman's syndrome capable of voluntarily entering into a property settlement agreement with her husband? Is her will constrained by her condition? Is she, in effect, incompetent? Experts say that a temporary interruption in the pattern of battering does not mean that she has recovered sufficiently to freely and voluntarily enter into a settlement agreement without an extended period of therapy. If she has an attorney at the time of making the agreement, the attorney may help to equalize the bargaining positions of the parties. At a court hearing, expert testimony that she was a battered woman may be used to repudiate the agreement.

Basically, the law of contracts, when affected by incapacity or mental illness, involves two conflicting policies. On the one hand is the objective view, which seeks to uphold the security of transactions and the reasonable expectations of the contracting parties. On the other hand is the policy of protecting mentally incompetent individuals from the consequences of their own acts and the acts of others. When one party knows of the incompetency of the other, the policy of securing reasonable expectations carries less weight.[26] Likewise, where a mentally incompetent person by contract obtains basic necessities, that is, shelter, clothes, food, and medical services, the policy of protecting him is less critical, for in such cases there is usually a fair trade.[27] Where necessities have been supplied to an incompetent person, or to a minor, the court raises an "implied contract" against the incompetent individual or his estate; the law in effect makes the contract for the parties.

There is a crucial proviso to the rule that a contract made by an incompetent or mentally ill person is voidable at his election. The court will declare rescission of the contract provided that the other party can be restored to status quo. If the parties cannot be returned to their previous positions, rescission will be denied provided that the other party was ignorant of the incompetence and the transaction was fair and reasonable. Otherwise, the rule might easily transform the incompetent person's shield to a sword. The incompetent party has the personal option to avoid or ratify, but the power of avoidance is conditioned on restoration of the benefits he has received. The burden of proving incompetence is upon the party alleging it, but once incompetence has been shown, the burden of proving lack of knowledge and fairness is upon the party asking that the transaction be enforced. The determination of the individual's mental status at the time of making the contract is made by inferences from historical data and from assessing the individual's current mental condition.

The courts have said that in order to convey land, the grantor must have sufficient mentality to understand and appreciate the nature and consequences of the conveyance upon his rights and interests. A plea of incapacity has usually been successful in upsetting a conveyance only where there is unconscionability or gross inadequacy of the consideration for the conveyance. (Louisiana by statute requires that there be a consideration in land contracts of at least one-half market value.) In one case where the consideration was adequate, the grantor was held capable of executing the deed notwithstanding testimony that at the time of conveyance he ate moldy food, did not bathe, could not carry on a coherent conversation, was jittery, and urinated on the streets of the town and in friends' homes in front of women.[28] The more improvident the transaction, the more likely a court is to find incapacity. The question asked by courts is: Was the transaction so foolish or irrational that it shows the person did not adequately understand what he was doing?[29]

Taking advantage or duping one obviously incompetent, even though an adult, may be a type of fraud that warrants invoking the protective policy of the law. Thus, an incompetent adult would, like the boy in "Jack and the Beanstalk" who sold his mother's cow for some beans, be allowed to recover the cow or its value if the beans turn out to be worthless and not magical. Strictly speaking, the word *fraud* means only "conscious misrepresentation"; but in a broad sense, as Williston said, "It is doubtless a fraud to enter into a contract with an insane person knowing his condition."[30] Thus, the question of a party's mental capacity provides the court with a means to control unfair bargains.

In a transgression of role boundary, therapists at times involve their patients in business deals. The traditional model of psychotherapy assumes a clear separation between the personal and professional roles of the therapist and patient as essential to proper and effective treatment. Sex between a therapist and patient has been exposed to the public eye, but there are other, less-publicized boundary violations. Some therapists ask patients to include them in business deals that patients have discussed during the course of therapy. Some therapists are made beneficiaries of large bequests in the patient's will.[31] In a much-publicized case, a psychiatrist used a stock tip obtained from a patient during the course of therapy to turn a large profit. The Securities and Exchange Commission learned from the patient of this transmission of insider information about a merger, and it charged the therapist with profiting illegally. The therapist neither admitted nor denied the charges but surrendered the profits and paid a fine of the same amount.[32]

Defects in judgment caused by brain damage or mental deficiency may preclude the understanding deemed necessary for contractual capacity. An insane delusion that motivates contractual action may call for legal protection when there is a substantial degree of divorcement from reality. Many older persons lose or change their judgment in matters of money, arousing the concern of family members who may seek the appointment of a guardian.[33]

A more difficult case is presented by the hypomanic person who, during the manic or expansive phase of the manic-depressive syndrome, engages in all sorts of ambitious schemes. In the hypomanic state he may accomplish great things because of his tremendous energy output and enthusiasm. (Some of the most effective fund-raisers are hypomanic.) A hypomanic individual may become wealthy in a short time on his ventures, but just as quickly his world may crumble.

During a manic period, relating to others is expanded. There may be a surge of entertainment, incurring great expense. Invitation lists are extended as if there were a need to pack the environment with people. Contacting is accelerated. Long-distance calls are made into all time zones. The telephone bill is many times normal. The telephone company, however, is scrupulously detached in these matters. As one observer put it, theirs is not to wonder why but only to collect.

Apart from psychogenic factors, there may be a pharmacological explanation for manic behavior. For example, alcohol tends to have an expansive effect on many people. The amphetamines, affecting the frontal lobe, tend to have this result. In the drug culture *amphetamine* is called "speed." Berton Roueche in a case study, *Ten Feet Tall*, describes the overreaching social behavior of a man experiencing a brief manic episode due to the side effects of cortisone treatment. In this case a New York schoolteacher was treated for periarteritis nodosa, a destructive inflammation of the arteries that was often fatal before the advent of adrenocorticotropic hormone (ACTH) and cortisone. After a prescription of cortisone that induced a manic-depressive reaction, the patient began to order costly clothing by telephone to avoid the "petty inconvenience" of walking from store to store. This was contrary to his usual behavior of shopping cautiously in endless searches to select his clothes.[34]

An investigation by the *New York Times* revealed that Dr. Max Jacobson (called Dr. Feelgood), a general practitioner in New York, over a period of years injected a concoction containing amphetamine into the veins of the country's most celebrated people.[35] Many of the VIPs seen by the doctor insisted—without always knowing what was in the injections—that he helped them achieve success. Most of them said that the shots gave them boundless energy and more productive and pleasurable lives.[36] Following the disclosure of Dr. Jacobson's practice, details of similar practices by other physicians emerged, as several former patients and other persons came forward with information.

The individual in a manic or expansive frame of mind has an understanding of his transactions, but his judgment may be grossly impaired, and he may not be able to control his behavior. As one commentator says: "If the understanding test of the law is inadequate, it is so mainly for cases where the person intellectually comprehends the nature and quality of his act but nevertheless lacks effective control of his actions."[37] With rare exception, though, the courts hold the manic-depressive individual to his contractual obligation, since he has the necessary cognitive ability required in law.

An illustrative case is *Beale v. Gibaud*,[38] in which an action was brought to enforce two promissory notes. The defendant had been moderate in his business transactions until, one year, he bought an automobile dealership. His wife said of him then, "He had an exaggerated idea of his business ability and his financial worth." His confidence led him to purchase a second business. After a few months in a sanatorium, followed by a seemingly normal period, he moved to Florida and began trading feverishly in real estate. It was during this period that the promissory notes in dispute were executed. Two psychiatrists testified on behalf of the defendant, declaring that he was suffering from a manic-depressive illness that had prompted his actions. It was claimed that he was suffering from "an exalted phase of manic-depressive insanity" that caused him to disregard "the impulse of inhibition that a man ordinarily uses in normal health in checking up his transactions," and he was "led by his rosy promise of great success in his transactions." The court found the evidence unconvincing, and, applying the understanding test, was persuaded by testimony on his comprehension of the terms of the contract, the rationality of his conduct, and the regularity of the business transacted.

In *Lovell v. Keller*,[39] in which a similar conclusion was reached, an action was brought to recover the purchase price of stock. The plaintiff, a guardian, claimed that her ward was insane at the time the contract was made. The contract was made and the stock delivered prior to the appointment of plaintiff as guardian of the person and property of the ward. At the trial the plaintiff testified, in substance, that her ward was extravagant. An eminent psychiatrist was thereupon called to substantiate the contention of the plaintiff that her ward "was at the time of said purported contract and has since remained incompetent to contract, by reason of lunacy." During the course of his testimony he testified, referring to the ward, that: "She was very much elated, she had a lack of sequels in her ideas, she had ideas which were incompatible with her financial state, she was doing a number of business transactions which seemed unwise. . . . She went into tantrums and was a very difficult person in her behavior." It was his belief that "she was suffering from a mild hypomania, that is, a mild mania. Many people have a rhythm of emotion in which they run into depressions which are apt to alternate with periods of elation. All the best work of the world is done by people in a state of elation, but at times it runs into a completely abnormal and pathological situation." The characteristics of hypomania were described as "overelation, lack of proportion, extravagance, violence of behavior." His testimony on direct examination continued further:

Q. Was she, in your opinion, at the time, capable of making a contract and knowing what she was doing?
A. She could make a contract, she would know perfectly well she was making a contract, if that is the whole of our question.
Q. My question is, whether she was capable in your opinion of making a contract and realizing the consequences of what she was doing in that connection?
A. Not realizing the consequences, she would know its nature perfectly but would not be capable of balancing the facts of the contract.

On cross-examination the attorney for the defendant brought out that the ward was capable of understanding the nature of the contract:

Q. Did I understand you to say, Doctor, that she would understand perfectly the nature of any contract she would not realize the full consequences of it?
A. I believe so.
Q. But she might, mightn't she?
A. I wouldn't trust her.
Q. What?
A. I wouldn't have trusted her.
Q. That is, you wouldn't like to have her transact your business for you?
A. No.
Q. That is about the size of it, isn't it?

A. Right.

Q. But she would know the nature of any contract she entered into?

A. She was quite able to read and understand what she was reading.

Q. And quite able to understand what it was about?

A. Perfectly.

Q. Perfectly?

A. But I believe incapable of judging and balancing wisely.

Q. Balancing wisely—whom do you know that balances them wisely, name me somebody?

A. As wisely—

Q. [continuing] That can know when they make a contract that they are going to profit by it?

A. As wisely as a normal person and as wisely as I think she would have judged had she been all—

Q. [interrupting] Had she not been afflicted with this elation and depression—but, by affliction with those periods of elation or depression, do you mean to say that she could not enter into a contract under which she might profit?

A. Well, she—

Q. [interrupting] Well, answer that, won't you?

A. Certainly, she might profit by it.

Q. She might?

A. Yes. . . .

Q. But you do know as a natural matter of fact person suffering in the manner that she suffered at that time could execute a contract and, while it might even be unwise, know what she was doing?

A. Yes. This lady's mind as against her intellectual faculties was clear enough, but she was really suffering in my opinion from an emotional insanity . . . the instrument in her mind was intact enough, she was being driven like a whirlwind by an abnormal emotional drive, and when the emotional drive is abnormal, the intellect does not work as it ordinarily does.

Upon redirect examination, the following questions were put to the witness, and he was allowed to answer without objection:

Q. Your opinions already expressed, Doctor, were founded upon your observation of the patient?

A. Certainly.

Q. Now, will you tell the jury based upon your entire observations, and having in mind the point [the defense attorney] has brought out, what your present opinion is as to her condition then, whether she was normal or abnormal?

A. I have no doubt whatever that she was abnormal.

Q. You have no doubt?

A. That she was suffering from acute mania.

Q. Was she competent or incompetent?

A. Financially?

Q. To manage her affairs?

A. Incompetent.

The evidence was held insufficient to warrant a holding of contractual incapacity. The court said that the evidence failed to show that the mind of the ward was so impaired at the time the contract was made that she was incapable of carrying on her affairs as would a reasonable and sensible woman.

These cases occurred in the 1930s, before the wide popularity of psychiatry. Then, in 1963, in apparently the first decision of its kind, a New York court in *Faber v. Sweet Style Mfg. Corp.*,[40] appraising a manic-depressive individual's capacity to enter into a binding contract, allowed him to rescind a transaction for the purchase of land. Testimony revealed that he had been seeing a psychiatrist because he was in a state of depression, that he ceased doing so and within three months had entered into numerous business ventures and embarked upon a buying spree. Previously frugal and cautious, he became expansive, began to drive at high speeds, to take his wife out to dinner, to be more active sexually, and to discuss his prowess with others. In this three-month period, he purchased three expensive cars for himself, his son, and his daughter; began to discuss converting his bathhouse and garage property into a twelve-story cooperative and put up a sign to that effect; and discussed the purchase of land for the erection of houses. Against the advice of his lawyer, he purchased the land in question for $41,000 and talked about erecting a 400-room hotel with marina and golf course. Finding him incompetent to enter into the contract because he "acted under the compulsion of a mental disease or disorder but for which the contract would not have been made," the court granted rescission. This motivational standard of incompetency had never before been applied in a contract case. When, as is generally the case, cognitive capacity is the sole criterion used, the manic person is held competent because manic-depressive psychosis affects motivation rather than ability to understand. The court gave as its reason for departing from traditional law that "the standards by which competence to contract is measured were, apparently, developed without relation to the effects of particular mental diseases or disorders and prior to recognition of manic-depressive psychosis as a distinct form of mental illness."

The *Faber* case never reached the appellate level, and its effect upon the continued validity of the cognitive test even in New York remained uncertain until the 1969 decision in *Ortelere v. Teachers Retirement Board.*[41] In this case, Mrs. Grace W. Ortelere, a teacher for over forty years in the New York City school system, suffered from a nervous breakdown and went on medical leave of absence. Prior to this, she selected one of the retirement options that made her husband the sole beneficiary of the unexhausted reserve in the pension fund. While still on medical leave and under psychiatric care, however, she wrote to the Retirement System indicating that she planned to retire and asked about the various options available to her. She then executed a retirement application opting for the highest monthly yield without any cash reserve payable to her beneficiary. Shortly thereafter she collapsed from an aneurysm and ten days later she died. Her husband instituted action to set aside the election of the high-yield option.

The evidence conclusively established that the deceased fully understood her acts, but according to the psychiatric testimony, she was unable to control her conduct. She was under psychiatric treatment for involutional psychosis, melancholia type, and also for cerebral arteriosclerosis. On appeal, the court held (4–3), citing *Faber*, that a contract may be voided if the party who executed it is laboring under a mental defect that prohibits him from acting in a reasonable manner and the other party has knowledge of the defect. The court restricted its holding by stating that relief would be granted only if two conditions existed: (1) the other party knew or was put on notice about the incompetent person's impairment, and (2) the illness that motivated the incompetent person's behavior was nothing less serious than medically classified psychosis.[42] In addition, the court implied that it would not allow avoidance if the other party had significantly changed its position in reliance on the contract. The dissent summarized its objections by concluding that the majority's standard would undermine the security of contracts, put excessive emphasis on psychiatric testimony, and encourage frivolous claims.

In *Shoals Ford v. Clardy*,[43] an Alabama case, the court set aside the purchase of a truck by an individual diagnosed as manic-depressive. The auto dealer was informed by the wife that her husband was in a manic phase and was not capable of making informed decisions about purchasing a vehicle. Nevertheless, the dealer continued to exert pressure on him to complete the purchase. The trial court charged the jury as follows:

> I . . . charge you that manic depression is a mental illness, but that is not to say that all manic-depressives may be classified as legally insane. Some are and some are not. In order to determine if a person is legally insane, you will have to determine whether or not [the individual] in this case, had sufficient capacity to understand in a reasonable manner the nature and effect of the act he was doing. Or put another way, that he had a reasonable perception or understanding of the nature and terms of the contract.

In addition to setting aside the purchase, the jury awarded punitive damages, finding that the defendant auto dealer had acted "wantonly" in coercing the completion of the transaction. The state supreme court affirmed.

Depression, at the low end of the manic-depressive syndrome, may also cloud judgment. I heard one lawyer, who for forty years swung between the highs and lows of manic-depression, put it thus: "I enjoyed the manic phases. I was a big shot, on top of the world. I spent not only my own money, but everybody else's I could get my hands on. I bought six suits at a time, a lot of stupid unnecessary things." But in between the highs, on plunges into depression, he dreaded getting out of bed and spent little time at the office. When in a state of depression, innumerable persons have altered their lives to their regret: sold their homes or businesses, quit their jobs, turned away from friends and family, undertaken divorces, even given their children up for adoption. Later, when they felt their old selves, they found their lives wrecked.

Dr. Manfred Guttmacher in his book *America's Last King* describes George III as manic-depressive and attributes the loss of the colonies to his condition.[44] According to the National Institute of Mental Health, 125,000 Americans are hospitalized each year with depression and another 200,000 are treated on an outpatient basis, while another 4 to 8 million go without help. Everyone has highs and lows in mood, and grief reaction to a serious loss is a normal part of living; but when the mood swing is exaggerated to the point of impairing function, or grief is prolonged for months at a time, psychiatry labels the condition as depression.

While the legal test applied in *Ortelere* is unique, its adoption has been encouraged by the *Restatement (Second) of Contracts*.[45] The test corresponds roughly to the two-pronged test of cognition or control of the American Law Institute test of criminal responsibility.[46] The court in *Ortelere* noted that the change it made regarding the law of contractual capacity paralleled those that have occurred in the law of criminal insanity. The traditional test of criminal insanity, like that of contractual incapacity, has been expressed in the pure cognitive terminology of the *M'Naghten* rule, which holds a person responsible for all actions, even if uncontrollable, as long as he was aware of what he was doing.

Does the person who does not understand what he is doing deserve more sympathy than the person who is unable to control his conduct? The latter type of incompetence presents a greater danger to the security of contracts because he is more difficult to discover. In *Ortelere*, the board of education was aware of the decedent's impairment, because of her nervous breakdown that necessitated a leave of absence. In most contracts, the parties are not likely to have known each other intimately enough to evaluate one another's mental health. Hence, situations where the new standard will benefit an incompetent individual will be few and far between.[47]

Competency and Multiple Personality

One of the most famous multiple personality cases took an interesting turn when Christine Costner Sizemore, whose life was the basis for the book (by psychiatrists C. H. Thigpen and H. M. Cleckley) and subsequent movie classic (starring Joanne Woodward) *The Three Faces of Eve*, challenged Twentieth Century Fox Film Corporation's claim that it held the motion-picture rights to her life story. Actress Sissy Spacek had wanted to coproduce and star in a movie based on a new book by Sizemore, *In Sickness and Health*, but negotiations bogged down when Fox claimed it held the rights to any movies about her. Fox claimed that it owned those rights since 1956, when one of Sizemore's personalities signed over to Fox, "forever," the film rights to "all versions of my life story heretofore published or hereafter published" for $7,000. Sizemore's attorney contended that the original contract proves that Fox knew Sizemore was still deranged—beneath her signature were typed three more names: Eve White, Eve Black, and Jane. (The three Eves were timid Eve White, flamboyant Eve Black, and practical Jane.) In the new book, Sizemore details her life in the years following her development into an "integrated personality"— after her real self was distilled from the competing personalities through therapy. She alleged that she was unduly influenced in 1956 into signing away the rights to her life story by her then psychiatrist and author C. H. Thigpen.[48] The case was settled.[49] Following the case, publishers were advised to obtain the consent of all the multiples for the publication of a book by a person with MPD.[50] But is the fact of several personalities, on the face of it, a sign of incompetency, as Sizemore's attorney claimed?

Effect of Mental Hospitalization

Hospitalization is indicative of contractual incapacity. The determination of competency of patients in mental hospitals, however, is complicated by the unsettled and confused relationship between commitment and legal competency. The Draft Act Governing Hospitalization of the Mentally Ill,[51] adopted in a number of states, specifically provides that every patient in a mental hospital shall retain his civil rights, including the right to contract, unless he has been adjudicated incompetent.

The court in *Wyatt v. Stickney,*[52] which, it will be recalled, set out minimum constitutional standards for the treatment of the mentally ill, stated that "no person shall be deemed incompetent to manage his affairs, to contract, to hold professional or occupational or vehicle operator's licenses, to marry and obtain a divorce, to register and vote, or to make a will solely by reason of his admission or commitment to the hospital." Be that as it may, the fact of past or present mental hospitalization will at least raise some doubt concerning competency and will red-flag every transaction of a mental patient, with the exception of petty-cash purchases.

Whether persons who are in need of mental hospitalization as well as those who are committed are necessarily incapable of managing their own affairs is a subject on which there is considerable controversy. Observations such as the following, which were presented at an American Psychiatric Association Mental Hospital Institute, are illustrative: "If they aren't competent to look after themselves outside the hospital, they are not competent to transact business. . . . The idea that a person is allowed to sell real estate while he is deprived of the right to walk the streets, I find difficult to comprehend."[53] Mental disabilities, however, are of such variety of kind and of degree that concluding one is incompetent from the fact of his hospitalization is without justification. Evidence is needed of incompetency, mental illness, or disability, as well as the causal connection between the incompetency and the disability.

In a proceeding for the appointment of a guardian for an allegedly incompetent individual, the superintendent of the hospital testified that the individual was of "unsound mind and might dissipate his estate or become the victim of designing persons." He stated that this individual had dementia praecox and that he had delusions of persecution and was convinced that his neighbors had joined in a conspiracy to fill his home with poison gas. The superintendent did not, however, testify to any facts in support of his opinion and admitted that he had not questioned the patient concerning the extent of his property, claims against the estate, and the like. The allegedly incompetent person testified in his own behalf and according to the court "demonstrated an intelligent grasp of his financial situation, recited detailed facts such as the mortgage arrangements related to his home, and convinced the court he was well familiar with the nature and extent of any property now or heretofore owned by him." In denying the petition, the court stated: "[T]he criterion is not the mental illness but rather the inability to manage property by reason of mental illness. Unless the mental illness produces or results in such inability to manage property, the court is not warranted in appointing the guardian for the estate of a mentally ill person."[54]

Responding to an "equal protection of the law" attack on a state statute that denied trial by jury to persons facing civil commitment but granted it in proceedings to appoint a guardian, a U.S. district court said:

It is true that both the class of persons subjected to involuntary commitment proceedings and the class of persons subjected to the appointment of a guardian may have mental problems. However, it is at that point that the similarity ends. The standards and purposes of the proceedings to commit someone who is mentally ill . . . are entirely different from the standards and purposes of the appointment of a guardian to one who is found incapable of handling his own affairs. . . .

Assuming arguendo that the classification involved did affect persons similarly situated, we are of the opinion that the difference in treatment is totally justified under the rational basis test. A finding that a person is not capable of handling his own affairs so as to require appointment of a guardian seems to us more susceptible to the practical wisdom of a jury than determining whether a person is mentally ill or an inebriate and dangerous to himself or others. The latter finding may not unreasonably have been thought by the legislature to be beyond the competency of a jury.[55]

Appointment of a Guardian or Conservator

Given the close identity between guardianship and civil commitment criteria, guardianship may be regarded as a less restrictive alternative to commitment. Until the 1970s, most states joined a competency proceeding to a commitment proceeding inasmuch as commitment usually meant commitment for life. In effect, the hospital was made guardian of the individual. Institutionalized persons were presumed incompetent at least until release and perhaps until a court "restored" them to competency. Today, as a result of short-term commitment, the various states specifically eliminate the presumption of incompetency for institutionalized persons. A number of states still grant hospital administrators some authority over a patient's financial affairs (e.g., disposition of social security benefits) and a few allow other restrictions that are necessary for the patient's medical welfare. In *Katz v. Superior Court*,[56] parents of members of the Unification Church obtained at the trial level an order of temporary conservatorship (guardianship) to allow their adult children to be deprogrammed, but the decision was overturned by the California appellate court in a ruling that quelled the growing use of conservatorship laws for such purposes around the country.

In *guardianship* a person is appointed by the court to exercise powers over the person of a minor or of a legally incapacitated person. A guardianship is established to provide continuing care and supervision of a proposed ward.[57] A *conservator*, on the other hand, is a person who exercises power over the estate of a minor or legally incapacitated person. The purpose of establishing a conservatorship is to manage the property and affairs of a person who, because of incompetency, mental illness, age or physical infirmity, or other reasons, cannot adequately manage them on his own. (Quite often, the term *guardian* is used to include conservatorship.)[58] They are both fiduciaries to their wards. They act directly on behalf of their wards, they are not agents of their wards.[59] Conservators may also be considered trustees because they exercise the same powers of property management for their wards that trustees exercise on behalf of their settlors and beneficiaries.

When a guardian is sought for a person with assets that may be at risk or need to be managed, a conservator should also be sought as a protection to the ward. The conservator manages and uses the assets for the ward's benefit, must account to the court, and must file a report (whereas a guardian does not). The guardian and the conservator may be the same person; the guardian or the ward might prefer to have another person exercise authority over the assets. The conservator may be an institution such as a bank or trust company. The factors to consider include the size and complexity of the estate, the inclinations and abilities of those available and willing to serve, and the needs of the ward.

Clear and convincing evidence must show that the adult "is impaired to the extent that the person lacks sufficient understanding or capacity to make or communicate informed decisions concerning his or her person."[60] The impairment might arise from mental illness, mental deficiency, physical illness or disability, chronic use of drugs, chronic intoxication, or other cause. To determine incapacity, the process of decision making is examined, not the outcome of the decision. Whether a decision is responsible or one with which others disagree or feel not to be in the individual's best interest is not the issue.

Any person interested in the proposed ward's welfare, including the proposed ward in his own behalf, may petition for a finding of incapacity and appointment of a guardian.[61] The petition for guardianship must contain specific facts about the person's condition and specific examples of his recent conduct that demonstrate the need for guardianship.[62] This serves two purposes: (1) it informs the person who is the subject of the petition of specific allegations so that he may prepare a defense, and (2) it can help identify and weed out spurious petitions.

The appointment of a conservator is often not considered necessary unless property of considerable value is involved and is in danger of dissipation. An individual's competence to manage his person or property is not in issue until challenged, usually by a family member who wishes to protect the family or the individual from the consequences of his disability or who wishes to protect the subject's property that may soon pass to the petitioner by the statute of descent and distribution.[63] Persons whose property interests require at least some management are increasing in number due to the development of pension plans, veterans' benefits, insurance policies, annuities, and social security.[64]

Important aspects of a diagnostic evaluation include the notion of *reversibility versus irreversibility*—whether the medical disorder is a potentially curable or reversible one or whether it is a progressive, irreversible process—as well as determining the extent of impairment. In older adults, the most common cause of progressive, irreversible cognitive impairment that may lead to mental incompetence is Alzheimer's disease. The second most common cause is multi-infarct dementia.[65]

After an individual has been formally adjudicated incompetent and a conservator has been appointed, the theory of the law is that the conservator is vested with control of the ward's property and that any contract entered into by the ward is entirely null and void. The ward is legally unable to write or endorse checks, sell property, or enter into business (but he may write a will). Historically, declaration of legal incompetency was an all-or-nothing situation, but now specific or limited guardianship may be ordered.[66]

The laws of the various states provide that a guardian or conservator should be sought and may be appointed for a *legally incapacitated adult.* This is defined as an adult whose judgment, by virtue of mental illness, deficiency, physical illness, or disability, is impaired to the extent that the person lacks sufficient understanding and capacity to make or communicate responsible decisions concerning his person.[67] A guardian or conservator of a legally incapacitated person has the same powers, rights, and duties respecting the incapacitated adult (ward) that a parent has respecting that parent's unemancipated minor child.[68]

A determination by a psychiatrist that a patient is or is not mentally competent does not necessarily answer the question of whether a patient is legally competent. Legal competency, as a practical matter, is arguably a less stringent standard. Formal medical opinion or evidence may not be necessary, but it may be desired by the court and helps ensure the success of a petition. To avoid any actual or apparent conflict of interest, a hospital employee or staff physician should not act as a temporary or permanent guardian, although the hospital or other health care provider may initiate guardianship proceedings. As a practical matter locating an outside individual willing to serve as a guardian is one of the most difficult tasks facing hospitals generally and discharge planners specifically. Some states have a *public guardian*, a publicly funded position to represent individuals without family or friends willing to act as a guardian. Even where a patient has a guardian, problems arise where the guardian is, for one reason or another, not properly carrying out his responsibilities, and court intervention may be desirable or necessary.

In most states there are few rules governing who can serve as a guardian or conservator. Frequently, a family member fills the role, but as families become more dispersed, the courts are increasingly appointing professional guardians. Many of them are lawyers, but most states require only that they be an adult and not a felon or ward themselves. Since the 1990s there has been a rise of guardianship companies, some caring for hundreds of wards at a time. There is no regulation, no licensing, no testing.[69] In Florida, which has a large elderly population and a history of frauds by guardians, the legislature in 1987 enacted a law requiring guardians to be bonded and under training and requiring credit and criminal background checks.[70]

Quite often operators of nursing homes are named as guardian, or in any event, quite frequently they authorize the so-called chemical straitjacketing of residents. Federal legislation has been enacted to guard against the practice.[71] An estimated 1.6 million people in the United States reside in nursing homes. The quality of care varies widely, as does the number of complaints filed. A coalition of advocates for elderly people has called for federal legislation to give patients the right to install a camera in their room and also in other locations, particularly the shower and dining room. Undoubtedly, the cameras would encourage more lawsuits against nursing homes, but that would empower victims and give the nursing home industry an incentive to halt abuses.[72]

What about termination of guardianship or conservatorship? In cases where the guardianship or conservatorship is dormant or where a considerable time has elapsed since the adjudication, the courts tend to hold that the fact of adjudication merely raises a rebuttable presumption of incompetency. A ward actually may have improved and the guardianship may have been allowed to lapse, but the parties neglected to return to court to have the guardianship formally terminated. The courts are usually willing to hear evidence that the ward at the time of the act had recovered sufficiently to be considered competent. Some severe mental illnesses rendering a person incompetent are treatable, and over a period of time the individual's competency may be restored. A psychiatrist may be used to help the patient be adjudicated competent and to regain decision-making power.

There being no central statewide registration of incompetent individuals, it is difficult for persons to ascertain whether those with whom they intend to transact business have been declared incompetent.

Impairment of Ability to Fulfill a Contract

What about an individual's ability to fulfill a contract when he becomes mentally ill after entering into the contract? On occasion psychiatrists have been asked to testify about an individual's ability to fulfill rather than to enter into a contract. Mental illness occurring after the time of the making of an agreement—at the time of performance—may excuse a failure to perform the obligations of the contract. The case may arise, for example, of an actor who, during the contract period of his services, suffers a severe depression. In such events, the mental or physical disability may excuse the obligations of both contracting parties, the actor's because of inability to perform and the employer's because of failure of consideration.

The longer the term of employment, the greater the possibility of encountering difficulties in fulfilling it. There are limitations, though, on the term period. The free-enterprise system would be circumvented were long-term contracts of employment enforced as a matter of course. The Code Napoleon, adopted in the aftermath of the French Revolution, limits the contractual period for personal services to one year, the original purpose of the provision being to preclude contracts that would have resulted in a return to serfdom or slavery. The Louisiana Civil Code, steeped in the French code, limits the period to a maximum of five years.[73] Free enterprise notwithstanding, one proviso everywhere in the United States is that skilled employees who have trade secrets may be barred from working for a competitor; they may leave their jobs only to engage in noncompetitive work or go unemployed.

Many of the early immigrants to America, where, they were told, "no white man acknowledged a master," bound themselves to service for a period of years after arriving in the land that supposedly flowed with milk and honey. The greater number of immigrants were bound to the captain of the ship for their passage to America. On arrival in the port of entry, merchants were on hand to purchase the services of the immigrants who contracted their labors for periods of several years. During that time they received no salary, only lodging, food, and clothing; their lot was a hard one.

In all jurisdictions, personal performance is discharged by any illness that makes it impossible or seriously injurious to health. The excuse makes allowances for the accidents and fragility of human life. A note from the doctor, which is obtained to excuse from school attendance, serves other excuses as well. (Football coaches, however, need no excuse; they apparently may quit at whim.) A number of companies have developed for their employees a compassionate-leave policy. An official of the American Society for Personnel Administration says, however, that the thought of paying for maternity time-off repels some employers. "To pay a woman a salary during that period, when maternity is a matter of her choice, grates a little bit." The Equal Employment Opportunity Commission states that pregnancy, miscarriage, abortion, childbirth, and recovery are "temporary disabilities and should be treated as such."[74] On the other hand, while mental or physical disability of an employee may excuse inadequate performance or nonperformance, it is increasingly serving less as a justification for the employer to send him away. Tenure and union practices and the developing concept of a right to a job are restrictions on the employer's rights to dismiss an employee. (The nation's president, though, begins his administration with the "resignations" of his appointments in hand.) Difficulties resulting from old age are generally avoided by mandatory retirement; the inflexibility of the rule, though, is subject to much criticism.

In socialist countries, the right to a job turned into a duty to work. One who did not work was regarded as a parasite. In Soviet ideology, work was seen not only as a material but also as a moral necessity. Checks and counterchecks and various types of stimuli urged the worker to produce more and more, faster and faster. At countless meetings speakers told about superb achievements. In the case of alleged inability to work, a certificate of one physician was obtained to excuse a brief absence and of a three-member panel for a long-term absence. During the days of the Soviet Union, it was quipped, "everyone has a job but no one works."

It may be concluded that while in theory the law of contracts has a role for psychiatry, practice shows that psychiatry has essentially influenced the law of contracts very little. The test of capacity to contract, with a few exceptional cases, has remained essentially the same for centuries. Supervening problems relating to performance are examined in terms of the traditional impossibility concept. Qualitative differences between mental disorders, as related to the type of transaction, and foreseeability of illness or disability are issues that remain relatively unexplored.

Notes

1. J. D. Calamari & J. M. Perillo, *The Law of Contracts* (St. Paul, Minn.: West, 4th ed. 1998), p. 7.
2. Dexter v. Hall, 82 U.S. 9 (1872).
3. Atwell v. Jenkins, 163 Mass. 362, 40 N.E. 178 (1895). A significant number of cases under the heading of "Contracts of Insane Persons" in law treatises do not deal with insanity, but with other forms of mental infirmity, such as senility, mental retardation, temporary delirium deriving from physical injuries, intoxication, and the side effects of medication. See J. D. Calamari & J. M. Perillo, *The Law of Contracts* (St. Paul, Minn.: West, 4th ed. 1998), pp. 206–303. See also M. Guttmacher & H. Weihofen, "Mental Incompetency," *Minn. L. Rev.* 36 (1952): 179; Comment, "Civil Insanity," *Cornell L. Q.* 44 (1958): 76.
4. In early times, the child worked, and the father as head of the family was entitled to his services or income in exchange for the duty of support, but there was not the role differentiation between minors and adults as found in contemporary society. The status of minority now means compulsory education until sixteen or older, and closure of the labor market, except as provided in occasional statutes designed to cover the child prodigy in sports or entertainment. Schooling for many young people now is a holding operation; attendance at school, on the other hand, was earlier regarded as a privilege. In medieval society, after the age of seven, children worked and played alongside adults. Education existed mainly in the form of the apprenticeship; schools were for those who wished to learn Latin (schoolboys made their own rules and came and went as they pleased). P. Ariès, *Centuries of Childhood* (New York: Knopf, 1962).

Child labor laws enacted in the industrial age, designed to protect young people from exploitation, today serve to deny them employment opportunities. They weave young people into a cocoon, isolating them from the world of jobs and trades. Summer or casual employment is also becoming increasingly difficult for minors to obtain. Among the obstacles, insurance companies selling workers' compensation advise their customers not to hire minors because of the high risk of accidents. A number of recent studies argue for an early competence model. In *Some Thoughts Concerning Education*, sec. 95, John Locke wrote on youthful irresponsibility, "The sooner you *treat him as a man*, the sooner he will begin to be one." See P. Adams et al., *Children's Rights: Toward the Liberation of the Child* (New York: Praeger, 1971); I. Illich, *Deschooling Society* (New York: Harper & Row, 1971); E. Reimer, *School Is Dead* (New York: Doubleday, 1971); G. Kaimowitz, "Legal Emancipation of Minors in Michigan," *Wayne L. Rev.* 19 (1972): 23.
5. G. Rice, in J. B. Simpson (compiler), *Simpson's Contemporary Quotations* (Houghton Mifflin, 1988).
6. A. C. Doyle, *The Problem of Thor Bridge* (New York: Lee Press, 1994).
7. S. Louvish, *Man on the Flying Trapeze: The Life and Times of W. C. Fields* (New York: W. W. Norton, 1997); S. Klawans, "The Enduring Charm of Buoyant Corruption," *New York Times*, Jan. 6, 2002, p. AR-28.
8. MCL, sec. 445.903(1)(x).

9. D. L. Perkins, "Unfair Trade Practices under the Michigan Consumer Protection Act: A Movement Toward Uniformity," *Detroit Coll. L. Rev.* 1977: 833, 855. Furnace scams are commonplace. Consumers are frequently frightened into believing that their lives are threatened if the furnace is not replaced. Fear is a great manipulator, and it is easy to terrify older people by planting the thought that they will be left to freeze or die of carbon monoxide poisoning. A supposed inspector will point to expansion joints and warn that there are cracks in the unit. A normal buildup of soot will be described as evidence that life-threatening carbon monoxide is creeping into the home. E. Shapiro, "When Temperatures Drop, Furnace Scams Heat Up," *Detroit Free Press*, Jan. 18, 1994, p. C-3.

10. In Zinermon v. Burch, 494 U.S. 113 (1990), the U.S. Supreme Court held that a voluntary admission must be based on "express and informed consent." The individual thought he was entering heaven. Given his condition, the Court concluded that the hospital knew or should have known that he was incapable of giving informed consent. He should have been given the procedural safeguards required for an involuntary commitment. See B. Winick, "Competency to Consent to Voluntary Hospitalization: A Therapeutic Jurisprudence Analysis of *Zinermon v. Burch*," *Int'l J. of Law & Psychiatry* 14 (1991): 169.

11. Committee on Professional Ethics v. Shepler, 519 N.W.2d 92 (Iowa 1994).

12. H. Cecil, *Daughters-in-Law* (Harmondsworth, Middlesex: Penguin, 1963).

13. In *The Gambler*, written in 1866, Dostoyevsky remarks that no other human activity provides so many and such strong emotions in so short a space of time: fevered hope, despair, elation, joy, misery, excitement, disappointment. British psychiatrist Theodore Dalrymple describes it as crack cocaine without the chemicals. T. Dalrymple, *Life at the Bottom: The Worldview That Makes the Underclass* (Chicago: Ivan R. Dee, 2001), p. 112.

14. The film, a Sony Classics release, is reviewed in T. Long, "'American Movie' Shows How a Nobody Became a Film Maker," *Detroit News*, Feb. 4, 2000, p. D-3; see also the review by Roger Ebert, *Chicago Sun-Times*, Jan. 21, 2000.

15. The casino industry is now listed on the stock exchange. Gambling licenses became the de facto national reparations program to compensate Native Americans for the theft of their homeland. By the mid-1990s, legal gambling had become nearly as ubiquitous on the U.S. landscape as factory-outlet shopping. Casino service jobs became the equivalent of the blue-collar assembly-line work of the mid-twentieth century. As a theosophical matter, many say, the casino presents proof of a wicked people who deserve to perish. Las Vegas is called "the place where America's spirit crawled off to die." J. H. Kunstler, *The City in Mind: Meditations on the Urban Condition* (New York: Free Press, 2001), p. 142. See also J. Tolson, "The Face of the Future?" *U.S. News & World Report*, June 11, 2001, p. 48.

16. See E. Drought, "Navigating Scylla and Charybdis: *In re Briese*, Gambling and Credit Card Debt Dischargeability," *Wis. L. Rev.* 1997: 1323. The psychodynamics of compulsive gambling is discussed in E. Bergler, *The Psychology of Gambling* (London: Hanison, 1958).

17. There are a number of national organizations with local affiliates or chapters that provide help for compulsive spenders: Debtors Anonymous, Overcomers Outreach, Shopaholics Limited. Carolyn Wesson's book *Women Who Shop Too Much* (New York: St. Martin's Press, 1990), a self-help guide, focuses on the problem of shopping and spending as well as in-depth steps to recovery for compulsive shoppers. It is estimated that one in seven people are hooked on buying items they will not use. See J. B. Twitchell, *Lead Us into Temptation: The Triumph of American Materialism* (New York: Columbia University Press, 1999); P. Underhill, *Why We Buy* (New York: Simon & Schuster, 1999); T. Serju, "Shopping Addiction Takes Effort to Cure," *Detroit News*, Aug. 14, 1995, p. F-6.

Solicitations for debt counseling are everywhere—radio spots, mail, e-mails, and television ads—all calling out to the fiscally unfit. "Are you in debt? Having trouble paying it off? We can help!" They promise ways to avoid bankruptcy, stave off credit collection calls, and minimize bills while paying down thousands of dollars in debts. Too good to be true? In some cases, it is, but some so-called nonprofit agencies bilk the consumer out of hundreds of dollars. Travis Plunkett, legislative director for Consumer Federation of America in Washington, D.C., says that the credit counseling industry is in turmoil. L. Yue, "Consumers Should Recognize Debt Counseling Is Business," *Detroit Free Press*, Dec. 29, 2001, p. 11.

18. W. Wordsworth, *The Complete Poetical Works* (London: Macmillan and Co., 1988; Bartleby.com, 1999).

19. H. C. Black, *A Treatise on the Rescission of Contracts and Cancellation of Written*

Instruments (Kansas City, Mo.: Vernon, 1929), vol. 2, sec. 262, p. 737; W. F. H. Cook, "Mental Deficiency and the English Law of Contracts," *Colum. L. Rev.* 21 (1921): 424. Protection is provided against deception in the criminal law as well as in the civil law. The criminal law makes it a crime to misappropriate or take anything of value either without the owner's consent or by means of fraudulent conduct, practices, or representations. In traditional criminal law, however, larceny did not follow from fraud, since a type of consent was secured. The current criminal codes usually set out a crime of theft that provides that a defrauder is guilty of theft if the transaction between the parties could be avoided because of fraud. See, e.g., La. Rev. Stat. 14:67(A).

A misrepresentation under which property or money was obtained is punishable even though it would not have deceived persons of ordinary prudence. It is only necessary that the misrepresentation actually deceive the victim. Admission of opinion evidence tending to disclose the victim's susceptibility to deception is within the trial court's discretion. State v. Armstrong, 203 N.W.2d 269 (Iowa 1972). Full-time consumer complaint desks have been instituted in many district attorney offices. In the median city, the desk averages between twenty and thirty calls a day. Complaints investigated have been mainly in reference to automobile dealers, home repair providers, insurance salesmen, job placement agencies, and real estate agencies.

20. Ellars v. Mossbarger, 9 Ill. App. 122 (1881).

21. Eubanks v. Eubanks, 360 Ill. 101, 195 N.E. 521 (1935).

22. Professor Weihofen wrote:

[A]lthough the courts formulate the issue in terms of subjective 'understanding,' they actually rely on more objective standards of behavior, because whether a person had a subjective state of mind can never be directly known; it can only be inferred from objective conduct. It is perhaps correct to say that the objective evidence upon which courts place most reliance is the 'normality' or 'abnormality' of the particular transaction in question. The essential question, as the courts seem to view it, is: Was this transaction so foolish or irrational that it shows the person did not adequately understand what he was doing? This factor is given so much weight that Professor Green called it 'the key to an inarticulate standard.' The dominant evidentiary factor 'is whether the court sees the particular transaction in its results as that which a reasonable man might have made.'

H. Weihofen, "Mental Incompetency to Contract or Convey," *So. Cal. L. Rev.* 39 (1966): 211, 225.

23. E. W. Puttkammer, *Administration of Criminal* (Chicago: University of Chicago Press, 1953), p. 164.

24. "Internal compulsion" does not invalidate a confession. In Colorado v. Connelly, 479 U.S. 157 (1986), the defendant approached a police officer, stating, without any prompting, that he had murdered someone and wanted to talk about it. He was immediately advised of his Miranda rights. He said he wished to confess because "his conscience had been bothering him." The next day he said "voices" had come to him. He "followed the directions of voices in confessing." The trial court and the state supreme court, affirming, said that an individual's capacity for "rational judgment and free choice may be overborne as much by certain forms of severe mental illness as by external pressure." People v. Connelly, 702 P.2d 722, 728 (Colo. 1985). Reversing the decision, the U.S. Supreme Court ruled that a confession is involuntary only when there is coercive police activity. 479 U.S. at 164.

25. People v. Stanis, 41 Mich. App. 565, 200 N.W.2d 473 (1972).

26. In Kendall v. Ewert, 259 U.S. 139 (1922), the transactor was a "common and habitual drunkard," of which the transactee had knowledge and caused the transactor to part with valuable mineral lands for the insignificant sum of $700.

27. Usually, necessities are considered to consist of those things reasonably necessary for the support, maintenance, and comfort of the incompetent person according to his status and condition in life. The term *necessities* thus includes food and clothing, as well as needed medical services and the costs of hospitalization in a mental institution. Chandler v. Prichard, 321 S.W.2d 891 (Tex. Civ. App. 1959) (medical services including nursing and other usual services rendered a person of unsound mind constitute necessities). But see Woolbert v. Lee Lumber Co., 151 Miss. 56, 117 So. 354 (1928) (house is not a necessity).

28. Fortenberry v. Herrington, 188 Miss. 735, 196 So. 232 (1940). An example of "unconscionability" upsetting a contract is illustrated by Weaver v. American Oil Co., 276 N.E.2d 144 (Ind. 1971), which held unconscionable a lease containing a clause that not only exculpated the lessor oil company from its liability from negligence but also compelled the lessee to indemnify the lessor for any damages or loss incurred as a result of its negligence. The litigation arose as a result of the oil company's employee spraying gasoline over the lessee, his assistant, and the leased premises, resulting in burns and injuries to each man. The Indiana Supreme Court ruled that the contract was unconscionable, as defined by the Uniform Commercial Code, pointing out that the lessee had left high school after only one and a half years and had spent his time, prior to leasing the service station, working at various skilled and unskilled labor-oriented jobs. "He was not one who should be expected to know the law or understand the meaning of technical terms. . . . There is nothing in the record to indicate that [the lessee] read the lease; that the agent asked [the lessee] to read it; or that the agent, in any manner, attempted to call [the lessee's] attention to the 'hold harmless' clause in the lease." Id. at 145.

The court observed that whenever one party drafts a contract and the other will not read it, the drafter makes an implied warranty to the other party that there is nothing hidden in the fine print that is either unconscionable or unusual. "The burden should be on the party submitting such 'a package' in printed form to show that the other party had knowledge of any unusual or unconscionable terms contained therein." The court emphasized that it did not mean "to say or infer [imply] that parties may not make contracts exculpating one of his negligence and providing for indemnification, but it must be done knowingly and willingly as in insurance contracts made for that very purpose."

29. Stratton v. Grant, 139 Cal. App.2d 814, 294 P.2d 500 (1956). From the original European settlers the North American Indians got beads and liquor for their land. Although not foolish or irrational, the Indians did not understand the nature of the contract. They did not have the notion that land could be bought and sold.

30. S. Williston, *A Treatise on the Law of Contracts* (New York: Baker, Voorhis, 1936), vol. 1, p. 741.

31. See J. H. Gold & J. C. Nemiah (eds.), *Beyond Transference: When the Therapist's Real Life Intrudes* (Washington, D.C.: American Psychiatric Press, 1993); R. I. Simon, "The Practice of Psychotherapy: Legal Liabilities of an 'Impossible' Profession," in R. I. Simon (ed.), *Review of Clinical Psychiatry and the Law* (Washington, D.C.: American Psychiatric Press, 1991), vol. 2, p. 25.

32. B. Northrup, "Psychotherapy Faces a Stubborn Problem: Abuses by Therapists," *Wall Street Journal*, Oct. 29, 1986, p. 1.

33. "Incompetency Resulting from Senile Dementia," *Am Jur. & Proof of Facts* 10 (1961): 385.

34. B. Roueche, *The Incurable Wound* (New York: Berkeley Books, 1958).

35. They included author Truman Capote, movie director Cecil B. DeMille, singer Eddie Fisher, President and Mrs. Jack Kennedy, playwright Alan Jay Lerner, Rep. Claude Pepper, movie director Otto Preminger, fashion designer Emilio Pucci, actor Anthony Quinn, and playwright Tennessee Williams.

36. The doctor reported that he gave President Jack Kennedy injections for the summit meeting with Premier Nikita Khrushchev. Movie director Cecil B. DeMille in his autobiography says that he took the doctor along to Egypt as his guest and personal physician during the filming of *The Ten Commandments*. Eddie Fisher often wined and dined the doctor in Hollywood and Las Vegas and, it is said, did not like to open an act without the doctor in the wings. But some of the patients complained of bad reactions and enslaving addictions to amphetamine. According to the Federal Bureau of Narcotics and Dangerous Drugs, which investigated the doctor at different times over almost five years, a review of the doctor's records showed that a substantial quantity of amphetamines that had been purchased could not be accounted for.

37. R. C. Allen, E. Z. Ferster, & H. Weihofen, *Mental Impairment and Legal Incompetency* (Englewood Cliffs, N.J.: Prentice-Hall, 1968), p. 266.

38. 15 F.Supp. 1020 (W.D. N.Y. 1936).

39. 146 Misc. 100, 261 N.Y.S. 557 (1933).

40. 40 Misc.2d 212, 242 N.Y.S.2d 763 (1963); noted in *N.Y.U. L. Rev.* 39 (1964): 356.

41. 25 N.Y.2d 196, 250 N.E.2d 460, 303 N.Y.S.2d 362 (1969); noted in *Brooklyn L. Rev.* 36 (1969): 145; *N.Y.U. L. Rev.* 45 (1970): 585; *Wayne L. Rev.* 16 (1970): 1188.

42. The court emphasized that "the system was, or should have been fully aware of Mrs. Ortelere's condition." The court emphasized the "special relationship" between a retirement system and its members. See also Keith v. New York State Teachers' Retirement System, 46 A.D.2d 938, 362 N.Y.S.2d 231 (1974). Many employers found their pension plans through professional insurers, who are not likely to know of an employee's psychosis. In Pentinen v. Retirement System, 60 A.D.2d 366, 401 N.Y.S.2d 587 (3d Dept. 1978), the court held that the widow of a state employee shown to have been suffering a psychosis could not withdraw her election to receive retirement benefits from the State Employees' Retirement System in the form of a life annuity because the incompetency was not known to the system; her grief was not, alone, enough to give the system notice of the incompetency.

43. 588 So.2d 879, 883 (Ala. 1991).

44. M. Guttmacher, *America's Last King* (New York: Scribner, 1941).

45. *Restatement (Second) of Contracts*, sec. 15, states a test of contractual capacity in terms of both cognition and volition. The Pennsylvania Supreme Court in McGovern v. Com., State Employees Retirement Board, 512 Pa. 377, 517 A.2d 523 (1986) specifically rejected sec. 15 and appeared to adhere to a cognitive test: "If the benefit contract is freely entered into with an understanding of its terms, the contract cannot be set aside."

46. See chapter 9, on criminal responsibility.

47. Rescission of contract because of alleged manic-depressive state was denied in Fingerhut v. Kralyn Enterprises, 71 Misc.2d 846, 337 N.Y.S.2d 394 (1971); the plaintiff failed to sustain his burden of proof that when he executed the contract he "did so solely as a result of serious mental illness, namely, psychosis."

Another case, which was settled without trial, involved a man, about fifty years of age, married, with four children, who suffered from manic-depressive periods. He was treated at Lafayette Clinic, Detroit, Michigan, in 1969 for depression. He was a partner in a fur business in a Detroit suburb, and the business was relatively successful. He was conscientious in his business endeavors but had difficulty during occasional states of depression. In 1972, he became hypomanic for five to six months. His symptoms included a decrease in sleep, rapid speech, extravagance, distractability, and a general feeling of well-being. During this period he made three trips to Las Vegas. On the first trip, he spent at gambling the money he had brought and then wrote a check payable to the casino for about $2,000. He repeated this pattern on the second trip, when he wrote a check for about $4,000. These two checks were paid upon presentation. On the third trip, the casino extended him credit after he had lost his cash reserve. After signing a document, he was given chips, totaling many times what he had spent on the previous trips.

Query: Should he be relieved of the responsibilities of fulfilling his contractual obligations, i.e., paying the debt? He understood the transaction in which he had engaged. He was not induced to enter into the transaction by any illegal undue influence, fraud, or overreaching. And the parties can be returned to the status quo, a usual prerequisite to void the contract of an incompetent person, only by payment of the money. But this requirement may be excused when one party is aware of the other's incapacity. Las Vegas thrives on people who are in a flamboyant and optimistic state of mind; it does its best to stimulate manic behavior. The illumination of the *Money Game* by Adam Smith is Keynes's observation that the investment game (the stock market) is intolerably boring save to those with a gambling instinct, while those with the instinct must pay to it "the appropriate toll." A. Smith, *Money Game* (New York: Random House, 1968).

A young man proposing marriage tells his girlfriend, "I want to give you all the things you've never had. I think I can get a bank loan." The bank, aware of the purpose of the loan, makes it. Was the transaction the result of mental illness or defect, and was the young man able to act in a reasonable manner in relation to the transaction? See B. D. Lewin, *The Psychoanalysis of Elation* (New York: Norton, 1950). To speak thoughtfully, Henry Thoreau said in *Walden*, we must be far enough apart so that "all animal heat and moisture may have a chance to evaporate." H. Thoreau, *Walden* (Houghton Mifflin, 1997). See E. T. Hall, *The Hidden Dimension* (New York: Doubleday, 1966). For the view that the right to make or enforce a contract should not be abridged by the label of mental illness, see G. J. Alexander & T. S. Szasz, "From Contract to Status via Psychiatry," *Santa Clara L. Rev.* 13 (1973): 537.

48. R. G. Blumenthal, "After All These Years, Here Is the Fourth Face of Eve: Plaintiff," *Wall Street Journal*, Feb. 1, 1989, p. B-1; N. J. Easton, "The Real 'Eve' Faces Court Battle over Biography," *Detroit News*, Feb. 13, 1989, p. B-3; D. Van Biema & M. Grant, "Three Faces of Eve Told Her Story, Now Chris Sizemore Is Battling a Major Studio over Movie Rights and Wrongs," *People*, Mar. 1989, p. 79.

49. "'Faces of Eve' Woman Settles Film Co. Lawsuit," *New York City Tribune*, June 21, 1990, p. 5. Robert K. Ressler, then director of the FBI's Forensic Behavioral Services, mused that the greatest difficulty in inviting Chris Sizemore to speak was that since she had three personalities, they would have to triple their regular honorarium. R. K. Ressler & T. Shachtman, *Whoever Fight Monsters* (New York: St. Martin's Press, 1992), p. 269.

50. *60 Minutes*, CBS, Oct. 22, 1989.

51. Public Health Service Pub. No. 51, 1952.

52. 344 F.Supp. 373, 387 (M.D.Ala. 1972).

53. D. Blain, *Better Care in Mental Hospitals* (Washington, D.C.: American Psychiatric Association, 1949), p. 43.

54. Streda Estate, 137 Legal Intel. No. 97, p. 1, col. 3 (Del. Cy. Orphans Ct. 1957); see J. Parry, S. J. Brakel, & B. Weiner, *The Mentally Disabled and the Law* (Chicago: American Bar Foundation, 3d ed. 1985).

55. French v. Blackburn, 428 F.Supp. 1351, 1361 (M.D. N.C. 1977), *aff'd*, 443 U.S. 901 (1979).

56. 73 Cal. App.3d 952, 141 Cal. Rptr. 234 (1977).

57. Ordinarily statutes set out the powers and duties of a guardian in a general way, and they are articulated more particularly in the court's order of appointment. Frequently, however, statutes specifically withhold certain powers, or require court approval before taking certain actions. Kansas Stat. Ann. 59-3018 provides in part:

(e) The general powers and duties of a guardian shall be to take charge of the person of the ward and to provide for the ward's care, treatment, habilitation, education, support and maintenance and to file an annual accounting. . . .

(g) A guardian shall not have the power:
(1) To place a ward in a facility or institution, other than a treatment facility, unless the placement of the ward has been approved by the court. . . .
(2) To place a ward in a treatment facility unless approved by the court, except that a ward shall not be placed in a state psychiatric hospital or state institution for the mentally retarded unless authorized by the court pursuant to K.S.A. 1986 Supp. 59-3018a.
(3) To consent, on behalf of a ward, to psychosurgery, removal of a bodily organ, or amputation of a limb unless the procedure is first approved by order of the court or is necessary, in an emergency situation, to preserve the life or prevent serious impairment of the physical health of the ward.
(4) To consent on behalf of the ward to the withholding of life-saving medical procedures, except in accordance with provisions of K.S.A. 65-28,101 to 65-28,109, inclusive, and amendments thereto.
(5) To consent on behalf of a ward to the performance of any experimental biomedical or behavioral procedure or to participation in any biomedical or behavioral experiment unless:
(A) It is intended to preserve the life or prevent serious impairment of the physical health of the ward; or
(B) it is intended to assist the ward to develop or regain that person's abilities and has been approved for that person by the court.
(6) To prohibit the marriage or divorce of a ward.
(7) To consent, on behalf of a ward, to the termination of the ward's parental rights.
(8) To consent, on behalf of a ward, to sterilization of the ward, unless the procedure is first approved by order of the court after a full due process hearing where the ward is represented by a guardian ad litem.

58. The American Bar Association's Senior Lawyers Division in 1997 published "Guardianship & Conservatorship: A Handbook for Lawyers," a guide to the issues surrounding

guardianship and conservatorship. The publication covers the steps necessary for filing a guardianship case, including how to obtain a medical evaluation alleging disability, what to do when multiple parties seek guardianship, how to prepare for trial, and the issues specific to guardianship of minors.

59. Banker's Trust Co. v. Russell, 263 Mich. 677, 249 N.W. 27 (1933).

60. Mich. Comp. Laws Ann., sec. 700.8(2).

61. Mich. Comp. Laws Ann., sec. 700.443.

62. Mich. Comp. Laws Ann., sec. 700.443(1).

63. See E. F. Dejowski, *Protecting Judgement-Impaired Adults* (Binghamton, N.Y.: Haworth Press, 1990); D. J. Sprehe, "Geriatric Psychiatry and the Law," in R. Rosner (ed.), *Principles and Practice of Forensic Psychiatry* (New York: Von Nostrand Reinhold, 1994) pp. 501–7; J. W. Fisher, "Legal Aspects of the Psychosocial Management of the Demented Patient," *Psychiatric Annals* 24 (1994): 197; W. C. Schmidt & R. Peters, "Legal Incompetents' Need for Guardians in Florida," *Bull. Am. Acad. Psychiatry & Law* 15 (1987): 69.

64. T. S. Szasz & G. J. Alexander, "Law, Property and Psychiatry," *Am. J. Orthopsychiatry* 42 (1972): 610; response: A. A. Stone, "Law, Property, and Liberty: A Polemic That Fails," *Am. J. Orthopsychiatry* 42 (1972): 627.

65. G. T. Grossberg, "Determining Mental Competence in Older Adults," *Psychiatric News*, Sept. 2, 1994, p. 13.

66. A guardian is sometimes called a *conservator, curator, committee, tutor,* or *fiduciary*. The guardian may have limited responsibilities or full control over all decisions. In some states a guardian makes personal decisions, such as whether to place the ward in a nursing home, and a conservator makes financial decisions.

67. See, e.g., Mich. Comp. Laws Ann., sec. 700.8(2).

68. Mich. Comp. Laws Ann., sec. 700.455.

69. A durable power of attorney for health care and other decisions can also be used if the individual becomes incapacitated. Standards in appointing a guardian are vague. Hearings typically take less than fifteen minutes. Supervision of guardians is poor. As a rule, guardians are supposed to notify the court of decisions made on behalf of a ward, and in some states they must get permission before making major expenditures or decisions. However, there is usually minimal oversight and a judge may give a guardian's report only a cursory glance.

70. D. Starkman, "Guardians May Need Someone to Watch Over Them," *Wall Street Journal*, May 8, 1998, p. B-1.

71. The legislation, known by its initials OBRA, enacted in 1987, calls for documentation to justify the use of antipsychotic medication.

72. See Debate, "Cameras in Nursing Homes," *USA Today*, Sept. 21, 1999, p. 18.

73. La. Civil Code, art. 167.

74. 29 CFR 1630 app.

25
Testamentary Capacity

Unlike contracts, testaments (otherwise called "wills") require judicial approval—they are admitted to probate. The word *will* originally referred only to bequests of land, while *testament* was reserved for bequests from one's personal effects, but today the words are used synonymously, or as in the expression "last will and testament" (the term "dead giveaway" is sometimes used colloquially).

In the event of a challenge of the capacity of the testator to write the will, the capacity must be determined postmortem, the testator being dead at the time of the controversy. Even the most careful lawyer seldom makes a video or tape recording of the execution of the will or calls in a psychiatrist to examine the testator at the time the will is executed, but even that type of evidence is not conclusive.[1]

"Where there is a will, there is a way to break it," it is said, but it occurs only in the exceptional case. Of all wills probated in the course of a year apparently not more than 3 percent are contested, and of these contests not more than 15 percent are successful. In view of that slight risk, such precautions as having psychiatrists present at the making of the will are not deemed appropriate. Wills are usually attested before two witnesses, but they are not essential witnesses at the probate of the will; they are present at the making of the will solely to give solemnity to the event.

Our concern is this: In what way is psychiatric evaluation of the testator, either at the time of the execution of the will or postmortem, of value to the court in assessing testamentary capacity? Often, the only ground available by which a disappointed heir can contest a decedent's will is an alleged lack of testamentary capacity at the time of the making of the will. To establish either capacity or incapacity, when capacity is challenged, psychiatric testimony is usually summoned.

The tactic usually resorted to when there are no other challenges to the will is to attack the capacity of the testator to make a will. In the inquiry it is asked: Was the testator aware that he was signing his will? Could the testator appraise the quantity and the quality of property? Did he understand who were his legal heirs? Inability to pass that test may be due to, among other things, senile dementia, mental enfeeblement, or delirium. The will, however, may have been made during a lucid interval. It is very difficult for a contestant to establish that the will was not made during a lucid interval.[2]

Eccentricities, unjustified prejudices, or peculiar beliefs or opinions do not of themselves establish lack of mental capacity, although they may be given consideration. The provisions of a will depend on the health, mental condition, and surroundings of the testator. A will rationally made out in a lawyer's office in the testator's prime of life may be thrown aside by the testator during the last days of illness or senility and replaced with a totally different will that is unfair and even ridiculous—unfair in the sense that relatives and lifelong companions and employees are dropped in favor of a new passing acquaintance. In a moment of the testator's senility, vindictiveness, anger, helplessness, or humor, the testament may take a dismaying turn.

According to theory, if an individual has testamentary capacity, freedom of testation allows his will to be as unjust and capricious as his desires may dictate. "One has the right to make an unjust will, an unreasonable will, or even a cruel will."[3] This freedom of testation is quite in contrast with prior history.

Real property (land), the principal source of wealth, was not in early history subject to testamentary disposition. All land was held on behalf of the lord, and it was laid down as a rule of law that land was not subject to a devise. A medieval feudal lord might occasionally permit his tenant to make a post-obit gift (as he might also acquiesce in an inter vivos alienation), but the devisee was obligated to pay the lord a heavy price to obtain possession. As obligations owed to the lord were ancillary to the possession of land, he was cautious about a change of tenants. Among the lord's rights was the *jus primae noctis* (right of the first night). A diversion of the land from the heirs to a stranger by devise would tend to weaken or undercut feudal obligations. Thus, in the case of realty, the common law evolved a strict rule of primogeniture, which may be called a principle of "first come, first served," whereby a tenant's land, on his death, would descend to his eldest son. Feudal society was a fixed society.

The ecclesiastical courts had sole jurisdiction over deathbed gifts of personal property (personalty) but were allowed no rights over realty. The church instilled the fear of a spiritual ban by refusing absolution to those who died intestate and thus encouraged testamentary dispositions of personalty. There was a close connection between the last will and the last confession, fostered by the church, which asserted the right to control and force gifts by will for pious purposes. In primitive times, the possessions of a deceased person went to whoever got there first and grabbed them. The family and others often hovered around like a flock of vultures.

Later in the course of history, clergymen called in to perform the last rites were asked to write down the wishes of the dying man. By the thirteenth century wills of personal property had developed from mere deathbed distributions into wills in the modern sense. Wills became *ambulatory*, that is, they included property acquired after as well as before the making of the will and were revocable at any time before the testator's death. The will was not required to be in any particular form.

With the passing of time, public interest increasingly demanded that land be freely alienable, and the claims of the lord had to give way. During the fifteenth and early part of the sixteenth centuries, it became a common practice of a tenant to convert property to a friend to hold it for use and benefit of the tenant or third party in order to avoid certain feudal incidents. After enactment of the Statute of Uses in 1535, legal title was vested in the party for whom the use of the land was created. A consequence of this statute was a loss of the power that had developed to transmit a use estate through wills. Shortly thereafter, in 1540, the enactment of the Statute of Wills allowed a limited power to devise land by an instrument in writing. Since then, there has been an almost unbroken policy in favor of freedom of testation. It is interesting to note that such testaments are designated as wills, indicating freedom of determination.[4]

The policy underlying the prohibition against the transfer of land, while strengthening the institution of feudalism, also protected the heir against dissipation of the inheritance by the ancestor. Along with the rule of free testation were developed means to avoid the so-called unnatural disposition. Some jurisdictions provided that a certain portion of the estate must go to children, who were called forced heirs. Most reliance was placed, though, on the concepts of testamentary capacity and undue influence. Life insurance, though, is not governed by testamentary concepts and may even circumvent forced heirs.

Criteria for Testamentary Capacity

The statutes of the various states usually provide that in order to be capable of making a will, the person must have a "sound and disposing mind and memory," leaving to the courts the determination of capacity in each case. Only Georgia by statute defined *testamentary capacity* and the effect of specific mental aberrations. Its statutory provisions begin by stating that "every person may make a will, unless laboring under some legal disability arising either from a want of capacity or a want of perfect liberty of action."[5] The subsequent sections stated:

> The amount of intellect necessary to constitute testamentary capacity is that which is necessary to enable the party to have a decided and rational desire as to the disposition of his property. His desire must be decided, as distinguished from the wavering, vacillating fancies of a distempered intellect. It must be rational, as distinguished from the ravings of a madman, the silly pratings of an idiot, the childish whims of imbecility, or the excited vagaries of a drunkard.
>
> Infants under 14 years of age are considered wanting in that discretion necessary to make a will.
>
> An insane person generally will not make a will. A lunatic may, during a lucid interval. A monomaniac may make a will, if the will is in no way the result of or connected with his monomania. In all such cases it must

appear that the will speaks the wishes of the testator, unbiased by the mental disease with which he is affected.

Eccentricity of habit or thought does not deprive a person of the power of making a will; old age and weakness of intellect resulting therefrom do not of [themselves] constitute incapacity. If that weakness amounts to imbecility, the testamentary capacity is gone.

In cases of doubt as to the extent of this weakness, the reasonable or unreasonable disposition of the [person's] estate should have much weight in the decision of the question.

Conviction of crime shall not deprive a person of the power of making a will.

A person deaf, dumb, and blind may make a will, provided both the interpreter and the scrivener are attesting witnesses thereto and are examined upon the petition for probate of the same. In such cases, strict scrutiny into the transaction should precede the admission of the paper to record.

The very nature of a will requires that it should be freely and voluntarily executed; hence, anything which destroys this freedom of volition invalidates a will, such as fraudulent practices upon testator's fears, affections, or sympathies, duress or any other influence, whereby the will of another is substituted for the wishes of the testator.

A will procured by misrepresentation or fraud of any kind, to the injury of the heirs at law, is void.[6]

These provisions of the Georgia law were taken from a very long opinion in an 1848 case in which the main authority cited was *Shelford on Lunacy*, written in 1833.[7] Interestingly enough, articles on testamentary capacity that have been written in recent years by psychiatrists or others offer essentially the same observations, with some change in terminology.

In the various jurisdictions, where the criteria are judge-made, the courts uniformly state that at the time the testator makes his will, he must be capable of knowing, without prompting, (1) the nature of the act he is making, (2) the nature and extent of his property, and (3) the natural objects of his bounty and their claims upon him. In deciding whether these criteria have been met in a particular case, the court is guided by the individual facts of the case, hence unlike in constitutional law, for example, the cases do not lend themselves to deep legal analysis.

While the specific requirements for mental capacity to make a will are minimal, the necessary capacity requires a greater mental competency than is required for marriage. A person may have insufficient capacity to make a will on the same day as the person has sufficient capacity to marry.[8] Thus an old man suffering from cerebral arteriosclerosis may be able to marry but not make a will. Marriage alone will give the surviving spouse a share of the senile spouse's estate, even though he has no capacity to devise it to her.[9]

1. *Nature of Act.* The testator must know he is executing a will. This does not mean that the testator comprehends the possible legal effects of the words he employs but that he realizes the import of the act. In usual practice the lawyer writes the will and reads it to the testator, who thereupon signs it. Most vengeful wills are written by the testator by hand, without benefit of

a lawyer, and are probably written in the heat of anger. A testator who was toxic, confused, or did not recognize anyone at the time of the writing very possibly did not appreciate the nature of the act he was performing. This requirement is of particular importance in the case of the deathbed will where the testator may not have consciousness of what he is signing.

2. *Nature and Extent of Property.* The omission by a testator from his will of important parts of his property might indicate such a lack of memory as to constitute testamentary incapacity. The capacity to dispose of an estate may depend upon its size and complexity.

3. *Natural Objects of Bounty.* The natural objects of the testator's bounty usually include his blood relatives but may include others as well. The old notion of bequeathing a child a penny anticipates a future effort to contest the will on grounds of testamentary capacity. A testator's failure to mention a child could be deemed lack of memory. According to this notion, the protection of the family afforded by the testamentary capacity limitation lies not so much in preventing the testator from pauperizing his family as in preventing his pauperizing them without first considering them. The testator mentions his child: "My child married without my consent. I consider her as though she was never born." Joan Crawford disinherited her children "for reasons known to them"; she left her fortune to charity. By noting their existence, she indicated that she was aware of the natural objects of her bounty, but she chose to disinherit them.

Failure to have knowledge of the elements—nature of act, knowledge of property, and natural objects of bounty—constitutes, in the usual rhetoric, lack of sound and disposing mind and memory. Sometimes, instead of using these three elements as the criteria of a sound mind, a court may say that the lack of knowledge must be the product of an unsound mind (whatever that is) in order for there to be testamentary incapacity. The mere fact of the testator having used drugs of the type that could influence the functioning of the mind would not necessarily deprive the testator of testamentary capacity or would not necessarily render him susceptible to undue influence.

The concept of *lucid interval* is used as a defense of a will that is contested when the testator is known to have been severely demented or mentally ill for some time. For instance, if the testator was schizophrenic, the court will probably find the will valid if written during a lucid period, but not if it was related to a delusion. To determine whether the will was written during a lucid or delusional period, the expert, in order to be persuasive, must interview people who had contact with the testator at the time of the writing of the will—say, neighbors or the clerk at the bank—and also other evidence, such as a diary.

Given the criteria for testamentary capacity, what type of questions may properly be asked of an expert concerning the capacity of a testator to make a will (or a grantor involving a deed)? The principle is that it is improper to ask an expert for an opinion of a party's mental capacity to make a will because the answer would constitute a legal conclusion or would not be helpful to the court. The issue of capacity to make a will is one for the jury. Moreover, a question phrased in those terms is improper because it assumes that the expert is aware of the legal standard of competence required to execute a will. Thus, it is improper to ask the expert: "Do you think the testator has sufficient mental capacity to declare his last will and testament and dispose of his property?"[10] In addition to expert testimony, the mental capacity of the testator is often addressed by having lay witnesses describe the testator's behavior at the time of signing of the will.[11]

By and large, the courts disallow answers to questions that involve a direct answer as to an individual's capacity to execute a will or a deed. Incorporating one or more phrases of the legal definition of *capacity* has resulted in a host of inconsistent decisions. As a rule, answers to questions phrased in terms of the legal definition of *testamentary capacity* are held to be admissible since such questions do not require the witness to base his conclusions on anything other than the question asked and his knowledge of the testator's mental condition.

Conditions Affecting Capacity

Several conditions are discussed in the cases in determining whether the testator was of unsound mind.

Organic Brain Damage. Brain injuries, syphilitic infection, chronic encephalitis, congenital brain anomalies, and epilepsy may render a testator incompetent to execute a will. Organic brain damage interferes with one's cognitive capacity. Wills of elderly people are most subject to challenge, usually on the basis of organic brain disease. Old age has traditionally prompted charges of senility from disgruntled heirs and would-be beneficiaries.[12] While senility is not purely a chronological fact, common infirmities of old age are Alzheimer's disease, senile psychosis or senile dementia, and cerebral arteriosclerosis. These syndromes are characterized by impairment of memory, symptoms of confusion and disorientation, and paranoid delusions. There may be fluctuating levels of consciousness or, as the courts put it, "lucid intervals" or "glimmers of reason" that may sustain capacity.

Bodily Infirmity or Disease. Any injury or disease, of sufficient severity, is capable of causing at least temporary derangement. Psychotic conditions frequently follow toxic conditions of the bloodstream, such as uremia. Severe infections, such as typhoid fever and pneumonia, may result in delirium. Testimony by the testator's physician about his bodily conditions is thus relevant on the issue of testamentary capacity.

Mental Deficiency. Mental deficiency may impair the testator's ability to know the natural objects of his bounty or to recall the nature and extent of his property. Illiteracy may be probative of mental deficiency.

Alcohol or Drug Condition. Hallucinations or paranoid delusions may result from alcohol or drug intoxication. Excessive use of alcohol or drugs over an extended duration may produce permanent degeneration of the brain. Psychological effects are also produced by drugs administered to alleviate pain in terminally ill patients. In all these cases, delusions may influence the provisions of a testament.

Psychological State of Mind. Belief in witchcraft, spiritual influences, religious fanaticism, or eccentricity do not in themselves render the testator incapable of executing a valid will.[13] W. C. Fields, who hated Christmas, used to say menacingly to his relatives, "Nobody who observes Christmas will be mentioned in my last testament."[14]

One of the many cases involving an eccentric testator is In re *Johnson's Estate*,[15] where the testator, who had never been married, willed her estate to the Humane Society for the care of cats and dogs. Her nephew, who was expressly left out of the will, claimed that the testator lacked testamentary capacity and that he was omitted from her will because she had an insane delusion and false belief that he was a worthless character and was trying to get her money and property. No medical testimony was given as to the mental condition of the testator. The evidence tendered to defeat the will indicated only that the testator lived and conducted herself in a rather eccentric and abnormal manner. In the later years of her life her principal interest appears to have been in dogs and cats, which were given free use of her home and premises.

In *Johnson*, the court, quoting authority, said: "An eccentric person may make a will, and eccentricity of conduct is not sufficient, of itself, to invalidate a will. Singularity should not be confounded with insanity, and eccentricities, bad manners, and grotesque conduct, generally, are not evidence of insanity, especially where they are normal to the testator." The court went on to rule that the testator did not have an insane delusion regarding the nephew. The testator's opinion that the nephew was a worthless person may have been erroneous, the court said, but it was not an insane delusion affecting her testamentary capacity.

Many people, especially as they grow older, lose patience with those around them. An incidental occurrence may take on larger proportions, until the testator concludes that the action had great significance. The testator may then retaliate by cutting the alleged offender out of his will. This situation may ultimately lead to a will contest based on the testator's capacity. The challenger claims the belief is an insane delusion, and attempts to void the will.

Insane Delusion. As a general rule, courts do not reform or invalidate wills because of mistake, whereas they do invalidate wills resulting from an insane delusion. Suppose, for example, that the testator falsely believes that her son has been killed and therefore executes a will leaving all her property to her daughter. In fact the son is alive. The testator is mistaken, not under an insane delusion, and therefore the daughter is entitled to the property.[16]

How is a delusion distinguished from a mistake? As commonly put, a delusion, unlike a mistake, is not susceptible to correction when the individual is told the truth; it is not subject to a reality check. One who is not delusional *possesses* an idea, while one who is delusional is *possessed by* an idea. Among those who have mental disorder, schizophrenics are most likely to be delusional. The *DSM*, drawing on the work of Karl Jaspers, defines a *delusion* as:

> a false personal belief based on an incorrect inference about external reality and firmly sustained, in spite of what almost everyone else believes, and in spite of what constitutes incontrovertible and obvious proof of evidence to the contrary. The belief is not one ordinarily accepted by other members of the person's culture or subculture.[17]

The law uses the term *insane delusion* (not simply *delusion*). The Michigan Supreme Court, citing earlier cases, provided the following definition:

An insane delusion exists when a person persistently believes supposed facts which have no real existence, and so believes such supposed facts against all evidence and probabilities and without any foundation or reason for the belief, and conducts himself as if such facts actually existed. . . . If there are any facts, however little evidential force they may possess, upon which the testator may in reason have based his belief, it will not be an insane delusion, though on a consideration of the facts themselves his belief may seem illogical and foundationless to the court; for a will, it is obvious, is not to be overturned merely because the testator has not reasoned correctly.[18]

This concept has been dubbed the *any facts* test, meaning that if there is any factual basis or reason for the alleged insane belief, there will be no finding of an insane delusion. The determination of falsity is easy when the delusion is clearly bizarre and arises from internal morbid processes, as in the case of the old childless woman who believed that her baby was being withheld from her in the hospital ward refrigerator. The determination is also easy when the interpretation on which the delusion is based is clearly autistic, as in the case of the man who mentioned that when he entered a public bathroom he saw a piece of soap on the basin and understood that it meant that he himself was a piece of soap.[19]

Once the presence of a delusion has been confirmed, the next evaluative step is the determination of the degree of influence of the delusion on the behavior, or, in other words, the measurement of the motivational capacity of the delusional idea. To what extent and in what way does the delusion affect the testator's perception of reality, judgment, and behavior in relation to the will? Proof of the existence of a delusion at the time of making the will does not ipso facto establish a causal relationship between the delusion and the content of the will. The question is whether the delusion distorted the testator's cognitive skills in relation to preparation of the will (as, e.g., a testator has the delusion that his wife seeks to poison him and so leaves her out of his will).[20] Only that part of the will caused by the insane delusion fails; if the entire will was caused by the insane delusion, the entire will fails. Insane delusion cases often involve some false belief about a member of the family.

Delusional thinking may destroy testamentary capacity when it causes a disposition different from that which it might reasonably be found that the testator otherwise would have made. Delusions of grandeur ("I own the world") or poverty ("I own nothing") may render the testator incapable of knowing the extent of his property for the purpose of making a valid will. A delusion of marital infidelity, especially prone to occur in the involutional and senile psychosis, may result in a will that seeks to disinherit the spouse or to disinherit the child, who is believed by the testator not to be his and thus not the natural object of his bounty.[21]

A review of decisions of insane delusion indicates that there must be a great deal of proof that the suspicions or belief of a testator are completely unfounded before they can be held to be an insane delusion. "The conception must be persistently adhered to against all evidence and reason."[22]

A Michigan case: it was alleged that the testator disinherited her son because she believed her daughter-in-law was immoral and that the latter's mother ran a house of ill-fame. The court said, "Contestant had the burden of proving that testatrix believed her statements, she had no reasonable information or evidence supporting them, and, but for such belief, she would not have disinherited him."[23]

A New Jersey case: the testator, a militant feminist, regarded men as a class with an insane hatred, and she left her male relatives out of her will. She looked forward to the day when women could bear children without the aid of men and all males would be put to death at birth. She never married. She once wrote: "My father was a corrupt, vicious, and unintelligent savage, a typical specimen of the majority of his sex. Blast his worm-stinking carcass and his whole damn breed." The court held that she lacked testamentary capacity.[24]

A Missouri case: the testator was so angry with her child that instead of seeing the child she saw a grotesque phantom and did not include her in her will. The jury upheld the will. A physician who treated the testator testified: "Well, if we are to be practical about this thing, I think she was of sound mind. . . . She seemingly had her faculties so far as conducting her business. She made no statements that would make me feel that she was of unsound mind."[25]

Vindictive disinheritance is not equated with insane delusion, though that is the contention when the will is challenged. Vindictive disinheritance is usually based on long-standing differences between parents and children, parental displeasure with the children's way of life, and accusation that the children have been disrespectful. It is possible to infer that writing a will gives parents one of their only opportunities for getting their animosity off their chest. Invariably, when rage motivates the provisions of a will, the will is used as a weapon to express hostility. One mother wrote in her will, "My only son, Roger, is not to have a penny from my estate. During his whole lifetime since he attained majority, he has been disobedient, ungrateful, and a constant source of anxiety, humiliation, and sorrow." A wealthy banker cut two family members from his will with a stinging codicil: "To my wife and her lover, I leave the knowledge I wasn't the fool she thought I was. To my son, I leave the pleasure of earning a living; for twenty-five years he thought the pleasure was mine."

Not infrequently, suicide notes have instructions for the disposition of property. The state of mind necessary to carry out a suicide is probably incompatible with a thoughtful consideration of one's circumstances. What is remembered tends to be only slights, disappointments, and grievances. Thus, it was written in a suicide note: "Don't let that rotten son of a bitch So-and-So get his hands on my car."[26]

Undue Influence

Undue influence, as that concept has come to be known, is the kind of influence that comes from the outside, as contrasted with motivations that originate within the testator's own mind, and that is applied unfairly with the intent of benefiting the person who exercised the influence. Questions arise most often when someone in constant attendance is made the beneficiary of a changed will. The psychiatrist is called upon to testify as to the susceptibility of the testator to undue influence. Undue influence is urged as a challenge to a will in cases where the testator has capacity to make a will. Where testamentary capacity is lacking, the issue of undue influence need not be broached.[27]

One of the extreme examples of undue influence or lack of testamentary capacity occurred in In re *Lande's Estate*.[28] In this case a doctor who was the sole beneficiary of his bachelor brother's will kept him in a private room under the influence of drugs such as morphine for some time prior to his death. He allowed no one else to see the testator during the last ten days of illness, when the will was made that excluded from inheritance another brother who was kept ignorant of the testator's illness. As shown by the record, the Minnesota Supreme Court said, an overdose of morphine is "destructive to the mental condition. It shatters reason and dethrones the will. The rascally doctor 'substituted his own will for that of the testator.'" The court ruled that the will was obtained by undue influence, and it could also have said that the testator lacked testamentary capacity.[29]

In the book *Undue Influence: The Epic Battle for the Johnson & Johnson Fortune,* David Margolick calls that will contest "the largest, costliest, most spectacular and most conspicuous in American history."[30] On one side was Barbara Plasecka Johnson, a farmer's daughter who had only $200 when she left Poland in 1967. On the other side were Mrs. Johnson's six grown stepchildren—the progeny of J. Seward Johnson, who lavished more attention on his prize Holsteins than on his unhappy family. The grand prize: the $402,824,971 that Johnson left behind when he died in 1983. His children wanted more than what they got; Mrs. Johnson was the principal beneficiary and had sworn not to give them "the dust off half a penny." The children claimed that Mrs. Johnson and her attorney had, in effect, brainwashed the dying Johnson. A last-minute settlement netted the children a larger sum as well as $10 million for their attorney.

When one is at death's doorstep, one may be particularly susceptible to the overreaching influence of others. The concept of *coveted result* includes obtaining for oneself or another a benefit such person would normally not receive. Bequests to physicians and ministers attending the patient during the terminal illness are suspect. The law places an evidentiary burden on a fiduciary who has been left a bequest to establish that no undue influence was exercised.[31]

Some eight factors have been identified as tending to establish undue influence: (1) whether the person accused of undue influence has made any fraudulent representations to the deceased; (2) whether the will was hastily executed; (3) whether such execution was concealed; (4) whether the person benefited was active in securing the drafting and execution of the will; (5) whether the will was consistent with prior declarations of the decedent; (6) whether the provisions were reasonable rather than unnatural in view of the decedent's attitudes, views, and family; (7) whether the decedent was susceptible to undue influence; and (8) whether there existed a confidential relationship between the decedent and the person allegedly exerting the undue influence.[32]

The transference that develops in the psychiatrist-patient relationship may constitute undue influence jeopardizing a bequest made by the patient to the psychiatrist or clinic. The law places the burden of proof on a fiduciary who is left a bequest to establish that no undue influence was exercised. In Louisiana, undue influence is not recognized as grounds for invalidating a will, but the principle of the doctrine is recognized, at least in part, by the limitation upon bequests to physicians and ministers attending the patient during the terminal illness. A presumption of undue influence arises "when there is a confidential relationship between the testator and a beneficiary who actively participates in preparation and execution of the will and unduly profits therefrom."[33]

Guardianship

An incompetency proceeding and the appointment of a guardian may be considered necessary when a member of the family is dissipating the family's assets. The guardianship process may be used when property is in danger of dissipation in the case of, say, aged, retarded, alcoholic, and psychotic individuals. The issue is whether the person is capable of managing his own affairs; however, a guardian appointed to take control over property of one deemed incompetent cannot make a will for the ward. An adjudication of insanity or the appointment of a guardian does not necessarily indicate a lack of mental capacity to make a will but it may give rise to a presumption of incompetence.[34]

The Unfairness Rationale

It is commonly said, "You cannot take it with you," but to whom do you leave it, under what conditions, and for what reason? To be remembered lovingly, or to get even posthumously? Testaments reveal emotions of love and gratitude, of spite and hate. Time and again, people have used their last bequests to redress wrongs committed by them in life, to gain revenge, and, most manipulative, to control events after they are gone.[35] Charles Atlas bequeathed part of his bodybuilding fortune to his son with the stipulation that he be baptized a Roman Catholic. Groucho Marx supposedly said, when asked if he intended to leave a large amount of money to his heirs, "Why should I, what did the future generation ever do for me?"[36]

W. C. Fields, who left an estate of $800,000 in 1946 (a large sum at the time), bequeathed only $10,000 to his wife (they were married in 1900 and estranged but never divorced) and $10,000 to his son. A heavy drinker, Fields recuperated in several sanatoriums. The wife and son contested the will and overrode many of the comedian's last wishes. In an attempt to deter any contest of the will, Fields included the following provision: "I wish to disinherit anyone who in any way tries to confuse or break this will or who contributes in any way to break this will." Fields's famous statement, "Never give a sucker an even break," turned out, in this instance, with Fields looking like the sucker, and his wife and son getting the break.[37]

The question is posed: "We are writing a will and want to leave all our money to our two children. One is very rich and the other lives almost hand to mouth. Do we divide equally or give the poorer one a greater proportion?" In the *New York Times*, the ethicist Randy Cohen responded:

> Why give the money to either of them? It's yours to enjoy as you choose; it is not their fortune to be held in trust. You're free to bequeath it to a home for incorrigible cats or squander it on riotous living. Parents are not obliged to enrich their adult children.
>
> Perhaps the most ethical approach is to ask how the money will do the most good, a question that leads some people to donate their savings to a cause they believe in rather than keep it in the family. Indeed, this might be asked at any point in one's life, not just when drawing up a will.[38]

In actual fact, the real basis of the testamentary incapacity or undue influence action is the alleged unfairness of a distribution that excludes close members of the

Figure 25.1 *Mother Goose & Grimm © 2001 by Grimmy, Inc. Distributed by Tribune Media Services. All rights reserved.*

family, but it is a legally unacceptable means of challenge and the claim is therefore based on incapacity or undue influence. There may be real cases of incapacity and undue influence, but more often than not these are artificial bases of the claims of contestants. Since the accumulation of an estate is the result of the efforts of the entire family, directly or indirectly, it is unfair economically to disinherit those members who have participated in what might be called a joint venture. Moreover, if helpless dependents will become public charges, disinheritage is unfair to the interests of society generally. A parent is under a duty to provide for the support and maintenance of his children during the period of their dependence.

The societal interest in testaments is unlike the sanctity of contracts. For example, an individual on the same day that he executed a will may have purchased stock or an automobile. If he later attempts to void the contract on the basis of contractual incapacity, the court will likely decide against him in the interest of commerce. On the other hand, if at the time of his death his will is contested on the ground of testamentary capacity, the court, in the interest of family maintenance, is unlikely to uphold the will if he has pauperized a helpless member of his family. The interest of commerce underlies the sanctity of contract; the interest of family maintenance underlies the societal interest in testaments. Testaments, unlike contracts, require passage in the courts as a matter of course.

The suggestion that decisions are usually based upon the unnaturalness or abnormality of the disposition rather than on the testator's understanding is also supported by the fact that the court examines the dispositive elements of the will by admitting the will in evidence in the contest. Strictly speaking, though, the terms of the will are irrelevant to the issue of mental competency. Since the lawyer usually prepares the will, it does not provide a sample of the testator's handwriting, except for the signature, which may be evidence of incompetence.[39]

An examination of the cases seems to reveal that, by and large, the validity of a will depends upon the extent it affords family protection. Societal notions of fairness usually seem to prevail, regardless of the evidence tending to prove the existence or lack thereof of testamentary capacity or undue influence.[40] The courts are more likely to overturn a will when close relatives are disinherited and left penniless than when a nondependent relative challenges the will. At one time or another Louisiana in its civil code and some other states limited the disposable portion of an estate in the event of children; also, a spouse as a matter of law is one-half owner of community property. In an article on the role of mental competency, law professor Leon Green stated: "It is submitted that in determining the issue of mental incompetency, more frequently than otherwise, courts are passing upon the abnormality of the transaction rather than on the ability of the alleged incompetent to understand the transaction."[41] Philadelphia lawyer Edwin Epstein put it this way:

> The attack on the testator's mental competency is often a mere litigative trapping which the contestants assume to give them a pretext for challenging the will, since the law presently provides no procedure by which they can argue the real basis of their claim—*i.e.,* that the will is unfair to them and they are unhappy with the provisions made for them in it. Although this economic dissatisfaction underlies almost every will contest, the contestants must artificially base their case on lack of capacity or on the other presently legally acceptable bases for challenge.[42]

The unfairness rationale may be shown by comparative cases in which the courts have given differing weight to evidence of testamentary incapacity.[43] The term *testamentary capacity* is a rubric to equalize distribution. In the Institutes of Justinian, that famous Roman emperor tells us that if a child is disinherited by a parent, he may impeach the will by "the pretext that the testator was of unsound mind at the time of the execution. This does not mean that he was really insane, but the will, though legally executed, bears no mark of that affection to which the child was entitled."[44]

Sometimes a will is executed during the relatively early years of the testator's life, when he is sound and hearty, and he may not have written another will, although subsequently there may have been significant family changes that would ordinarily dictate it. The testator in his later years may have been psychotic, but to upset the will, the doctrine of testamentary capacity is unavailing because the time of the making of the will is the determining one. The law here comes to the rescue of the family in a different way. Under the common law, and expressly by statute in a number of states, wills are held to be revoked by operation of law by certain changes in the domestic relations of the testator. Many states provide by statute that a subsequent marriage revokes a will, that a subsequent divorce implicitly revokes a testamentary gift to the wife, or that children born subsequent to the writing of the will are included within it.

The source of this doctrine of implied revocation is attributed to the Roman law. Cicero in his *De Oratore* wrote: "For who is it that would seek to inherit under this will which the father of the family made before his son was born? Nobody; because it is agreed that a will is broken through lack of knowledge."[45] The Louisiana Civil Code expressly provides that a testament is revoked by the later birth of a legitimate child or the subsequent adoption of a child by the testator. Usually a testamentary gift is made to a class, such as children or grandchildren, which would include members of the class who are born after the execution of the will or would exclude those who may predecease the testator.[46]

It is highly unlikely that a testament will be upset by a claim of a collateral or distant relative, irrespective of the testamentary capacity of the testator. As one judge caustically observed: "A man without parents, wife, or children, can scarcely be said to have natural objects of his bounty; and when he has been permitted to go through life attending to his own affairs, and taking good care of his estate, it is too late, after he has made his will and died, for collaterals to discover that for six or eight years his mind has been under a cloud, and that it passed into total eclipse just at the moment of their disappointment."[47]

The idea of testatorial absolutism must be taken with a grain of salt. There is a deep-seated aversion to the power of arbitrarily diverting the natural course of the devolution of property. Generally speaking, the interests of society in family maintenance are greater than its interests in the protection of the freedom of testation. In order for that preference to be given priority, it is necessary for a will contestant to allege, in effect, that the testator was crazy. Will contests based upon a testator's supposed lack of testamentary capacity are simply "litigatory trappings which the contestants assume."[48]

Notes

1. See In re Bottger's Estate, 14 Wash.2d 676, 129 P.2d 518 (1942); Note, "Psychiatric Assistance in the Determination of Testamentary Capacity," *Harv. L. Rev.* 66 (1953): 1116. In John Grisham's novel *The Testament* (New York: Doubleday, 1999), Troy Phelan, a thrice-married billionaire, is disgusted with his no-good offspring. Before committing suicide, he signs a surprise will (with psychiatrists present who can later attest to his competency) that leaves most of his fortune to an illegitimate daughter who is a missionary in Brazil.

2. See G. W. Beyer & W. R. Buckley, "Videotape and the Probate Process: The Nexus Grows," *Okla. L. Rev.* 42 (1989): 43. In In re Dokken, 604 N.W.2d 487 (S.D. 2000), the testator did not have contractual capacity, a guardian had been appointed, and when the testator failed to take medication, he had psychotic episodes that involved beating on and talking to trees and disposing of his clothing in the garbage. He was held to have testamentary capacity. The court said, "[I]t is not necessary that a person desiring to make a will should have sufficient capacity to make contracts and do business generally nor to engage in complex and intricate business matters. . . . The testator may lack mental capacity to such an extent that according to medical science he is not of sound mind and memory, and nevertheless retain the mental capacity to execute a will." 604 N.W.2d at 491.

3. In re Willits' Estate, 175 Cal. 173, 165 Pac. 537 (1970).

4. See W. J. Spaulding, "Testamentary Competency: Reconciling Doctrine with the Role of the Expert Witness," *Law & Human Behavior* 9 (1985): 113. In Russia, where feudalism lasted until 1862, Peter the Great in 1714 issued a decree on the law of inheritance which provided: (1) Immovables were not to be alienated but were to remain in the family. (2) Immovables were to pass from a testator to one of his sons, selected by the testator. Movables were to be divided by the testator as he wished among the remaining children. Failing sons, the same system was to be applied to daughters. In cases of intestacy, immovables were to go to the eldest son, failing whom, the eldest daughter, and movables were to be divided equally among the other children. (3) A child testator could leave his immovables to "any member of his family he pleased" and could dispose of his movables as he liked, either to relations or to strangers. In cases of intestacy where there were no children, the immovables went to the nearest relative and the movables were to be divided "in equal parts to whomsoever may be thought proper." Decree of March 3, 1714. In this way noble families would not be extinguished "but would continue to be illustrious and eminent," whereas the division of estate would lead to the ruin of noble families and turn them into simple countrymen "of which there are already numerous examples in the Russian people." V. Klyuchevsky, *Peter the Great* (New York: Vintage Books, 1958), p. 106.

5. Ga. Code Ann., tit. 113, sec. 201.

6. Ibid. at secs. 202–209.

7. In this case, the testator was about ninety years old, was rendered almost speechless

by age and the loss of his health, was bedridden, and on account of his bodily infirmities at least, if not mental, was rendered pretty much incapable of attending to and managing his ordinary business. The court said, "All attempts to draw the line between capacity and incapacity have ended where they began, namely: in nothing. All agree that there must be a sound and disposing mind and memory, but to define the precise quantum, *hoc opus, hic labor est.*" Potts v. House, 6 Ga. 324 (1848).

8. See Estate of Park, [1953] 2 All E.R. 408. In contrast, an oft-cited case in Scotland, *Blair v. Blair,* stands for the principle that a marriage (then indissoluble) could not be made by a person defective in their reason (though showing some little sense), while a revocable one like a last will and testament could. J. Erskine, *An Institute of the Law of Scotland* (Edinburgh: Bell & Bradfute, 5th ed. 1812), vol. 1, p. 158; R. Houston & U. Frith, *Autism in History: The Case of Hugh Blair of Borgue* (Oxford: Blackwell, 2000), p. 93.

9. Various states in the United States have legislation prohibiting persons without capacity from entering into contracts for marriage. Michigan law, for example, in relevant part states: "No insane person, idiot, . . . shall be capable of marriage." MCL 551.6. The statute is a means by which a marriage engineered by a predator could be voided after the death of the deceased person. The Michigan case of Almond v. Hudson, No. 99-918792 (Jan. 26, 2000) involved a paraplegic requiring 24-hour care who was the prey of a day care aide. Almond had been under full guardianship and adjudged incapacitated by a probate court. Against the guardian's explicit instructions, the day care aide took him out of his home to the clerk's office where she obtained a marriage license and marriage. Almond left a substantial estate to be distributed when he died. His mother (guardian) contested the marriage to the short-term day care giver. Since one of the parties to the alleged marriage was already deceased, the issue was whether the marriage, "a civil contract," was void ab initio. Because marriage is a civil contract like any other civil contract requiring capacity, a void contract for marriage is one that, in effect, was never formed. The statute was the basis for annulment of the marriage. See also Evasic v. Evasic, No. 215875 (Feb. 4, 1999). The Michigan senate recently passed Bill 0067 repealing MCL 551.6, and it also initiated Bill 0273, which would allow a court to grant a guardian power to consent to a ward's decision to marry only if it finds by clear and convincing evidence that the individual lacks capacity to marry and is unlikely to ever regain that legal capacity. If enacted, the only way to protect the vulnerable individual would be a ruling on testamentary or contractual capacity. B. Callahan, "Marriage Laws Discriminate against the Disabled" (ltr.), *Mich. Bar J.* 80 (June 2001): 10. In Hoffman v. Kohns, 385 So.2d 1064 (Fla. App. 1980), where a housekeeper married a senile man, a will made one day later was set aside, but the marriage was held valid.

10. It is sometimes allowed, however. In a New Mexico will contest, a psychiatrist, claiming that he was familiar with the standard of competency necessary to execute a will, was allowed to testify that the testator was probably competent at the time she signed the will. Lucero v. Lucero, 884 P.2d 527 (N.M. Applicant 1994). Allowing the psychiatrist to testify to the legal consequences of the testator's state of mind is criticized in L. A. Frolik, "Science, Common Sense, and the Determination of Mental Capacity," *Psychology, Public Policy, and Law* 5 (1999): 41. See Carr v. Radkey, 393 S.W.2d 806 (Tex. 1965).

11. The witnesses on behalf of a contestant to a will must offer testimony that the testator did not (1) understand the nature of his acts, (2) know the extent of his property, (3) understand the proposed disposition of it, or (4) know the natural objects of his bounty. In Nebraska Methodist Hosp. v. McCloud, 155 Neb. 500, 52 N.W.2d 325 (1952), the court noted that all of the witnesses for the contestant simply testified that in their opinion the testator was "not of sound mind" or "not really of sound mind," but not one question was asked, nor any answer of the witnesses, that intimated much less stated any standard of mental quality upon which testamentary incapacity could be predicated. Thus the issue of testamentary capacity became a question of law for the court. See also In re Estate of Ellis, 9 Neb. App. 598, 616 N.W.2d 59 (2000).

One of leading cases in the law of evidence on hearsay, Wright v. Tatham, 112 Eng. Rep. 488 (Exch. Ch. 1837), involved testamentary capacity. The case involved a contest over the will of John Marsden, an English gentleman who left his estate to his steward. Marsden's relative, Admital Tatham, contested the will, claiming that Marsden was mentally incompetent. In support of Marsden's competency, the steward offered into evidence several letters that had been found in Marsden's effects. All had been written to Marsden by third persons.

These letters were written in language suggesting that the writers believed Marsden to be mentally competent; otherwise they would not have written to him in the way that they did. The steward wanted the court to infer the writers' belief in Marsden's competence from the letters, and to infer from the belief that the fact believed was true. The Privy Council held them to be hearsay, holding that conduct, even when not intended as assertive, is hearsay when offered to show the actor's belief and hence the truth of the belief. In the United States, on the other hand, implied assertions are not classified as hearsay. See Federal Rules of Evidence, Rule 801.

12. See, e.g., In re Ver Vaecke's Estate, 327 Mich. 419 (1923) (property willed to house-keeper). People are living longer, and as a result there is a marked increase in late-life illnesses such as Alzheimer's and Parkinson's. In the course of the dementia, intellect and memory are devastated. See J. P. Rosenfeld, *The Legacy of Aging: Inheritance and Disheritance in Social Perspective* (Norwood, N.J.: Ablex, 1979); D. Shenk, *The Forgetting—Alzheimer's: Portrait of an Epidemic* (New York: Doubleday, 2001); W. F. Gorman, "Testamentary Capacity in Alzhei-mer's Disease," *Elder L.J.* 4 (1996): 225; M. Houts, "Alzheimer's Disease and Testamentary Capacity," *Trauma* 26 (1985): 2; D. C. Marson, "Loss of Competency in Alzheimer's Disease: Conceptual and Psychometric Approaches," *Int'l. J. Law & Psychiatry* 24 (2001): 267; J. P. Rosenfeld, "Bequests from Resident to Resident: Inheritance in a Retirement Community," *Gerontologist* 19 (1979): 594.

The Division of Neuropsychology of Henry Ford Hospital in Detroit recently developed a Testamentary Capacity Assessment Program to protect the rights of older adults to dis-tribute property by documenting and understanding their abilities and suggesting com-pensatory strategies when indicated. It provides a focused and concise evaluation of cog-nitive and emotional processes targeted at addressing the client's decision-making ability, awareness, and knowledge of personal assets. The evaluation includes an extensive, in-depth clinical interview including a battery of paper-and-pencil neuropsychological tests and functional measures and an assessment of depression and general mental health. It provides a detailed report with recommendations, if needed, and the staff is available if expert testimony is required.

13. Religious fanaticism marked the will of Joseph Lieberman's uncle, Bernard Manger, who left an estate of $40 million. He disinherited two of his four children because they had married people who were not born Jewish. As he grew older, Manger became more and more concerned that intermarriage was threatening the existence of the Jewish people. P. Kuntz & B. Davis, "A Beloved Uncle's Will Tests Diplomatic Skills of Joseph Lieberman," *Wall Street Journal*, Aug. 25, 2000, p. 1. Some courts hold that religious or other beliefs held too intensely can destroy testamentary capacity. Religious beliefs may become, on some level, insane de-lusions that render invalid will provisions affected by them. The question, of course, is how to determine whether a belief has become a delusion and, if so, whether the delusion caused the testator to make a challenged disposition. On this question, courts disagree. J. B. Baron, "Empathy, Subjectivity, and Testamentary Capacity," *San. Diego L. Rev.* 24 (1987) 1043.

14. S. Louvish, *Man on the Flying Trapeze: The Life and Times of W. C. Fields* (New York: W. W. Norton, 1997).

15. 308 Mich. 366, 13 N.W.2d 852 (1944).

16. See Bowerman v. Burris, 138 Tenn. 220, 197 S.W. 490 (1917). The Uniform Probate Code sec. 2-302(c)(1990) gives a child an intestate share where the testator mistakenly believes the child is dead. See J. Dukeminier & S. M. Johanson, *Wills, Trusts, and Estates* (Boston: Little, Brown, 5th ed. 1995).

17. See K. Jaspers, *General Psychopathology* (Manchester, Eng.: Manchester University Press, 1963), pp. 95–96.

18. In re Solomon's Estate, 334 Mich. 17, 53 N.W.2d 597 (1952).

19. This was an Israeli case. *Soap* is an Israeli slang term for "fool." See R. Mester, P. Toren, & N. Gonen, "The Delusion Based Will: The Question of Validity," *Med. & Law* 13 (1994): 555.

20. As it is said, a person possessed by a delusion can make a valid will unless the will was the "offspring of the delusion." The court in State v. Jones, 50 N.H. 369 (1871), said that a man "who labors under a delusion that his legs are made of glass, or that he is charged with controlling the motions of the planetary system, but is in other aspects sane," need not be deemed incapable of making a valid will. A man may believe he is the supreme ruler of

the universe, but if that delusion does not affect any provisions in his will, it is deemed to be a valid will. Fraser v. Jennison, 42 Mich. 206, 3 N.W. 882 (1880).

21. Tawney v. Long, 76 Pa. 106 (1874); see G. L. Usdin, "The Physician and Testamentary Capacity," *Am. J. Psychiatry* 114 (1957): 249.

22. Hooper v. Stokes, 107 Fla. 607, 145 So. 855 (1933). In this case the testator was shown to have addressed his son, the contestant, in humiliating terms, and at one time was said to have spoken of him in language too lecherous and indecent to quote. The probate judge revoked the probate of the will, and bottomed his opinion on the view that any father who would speak of his son in such an indecent and lewd manner was so unnatural as to be motivated by an insane delusion. The Florida Supreme Court reversed, saying that the probate judge misinterpreted the legal effect of the evidence as a whole. In In re Estate of Hodtum, 267 So.2d 686 (Fla. App. 1972), the testator left his estate to a Masonic lodge but then called his attorney to write a new will out of the belief that he had been kicked out of the Masons. The attorney, after ascertaining that the testator had no basis upon which to believe that he had been kicked out of the Masons, refused to draft a new will. Another attorney drew the will as directed. The court found that there was no evidence to establish any basis for the testator's belief of having been expelled from the Masons. Finding that the delusion had no basis in fact and was the cause of making the new will, which he would not have made but for the delusion, the court revoked the second will.

23. Jackson City Bank & Trust Co. v. Townley, 268 Mich. 340 (1934). In In re Rosa's Estate, 210 Mich. 628, 178 N.W. 23 (1920), a niece challenged the testator's will, saying it was the product of an insane delusion that the niece was an immoral woman. The testator left all of her estate to a nonrelative who handled her business and personal affairs; therefore, the will was also challenged on the ground of undue influence. In reviewing an appeal, the Michigan Supreme Court found it was reasonable for the jury to find the testator was experiencing an insane delusion, perhaps spurred on by the influence of the interested third-party beneficiary. See, in general, F. K. Hoops, D. S. Hoops, & F. H. Hoops, "Bringing and Defending a Will Contest in Michigan, *Det. C. L. Rev.* 1997: 815.

24. In re Strittmater's Estate, 53 A.2d 205 (N.J. 1947). Assuming this hatred of men was an insane delusion, did it cause the bequest? The court assumed it did. The testator devised her property to the National Women's Party. Some cousins, whom she saw very little in the last years of her life, contested the will on the ground of insanity. The court, probably out of male bias, assumed that her hatred of men was irrational. The case would likely today not be decided the same way. The testator did not cut off close relatives who supported her during her life.

25. Hardy v. Barbour, 304 S.W.2d 21 (Mo. 1957).

26. Suicide notes, of course, vary. They are categorized into five types: notes that blame someone, notes that deny that an obvious reason is the cause ("I did not kill myself because my wife left me"), notes that blame and deny ("My wife is to blame, but I did not kill myself because she left me"), notes that contain an insight ("Perhaps I gave her reason to leave me"), and notes that contain no explanation at all and have only instructions for the disposition of property. See A. Wilkinson, "Notes Left Behind," *New Yorker*, Feb. 15, 1999, p. 44.

27. A typical jury instruction on undue influence is as follows: "General influence, however strong or controlling, is not undue influence unless it is brought to bear directly upon the act of preparing the will and imposes another person's plans or desires upon the testator. If the will, as finally executed, expresses the free and voluntary plans and desires of the testator, the will is valid, regardless of the exercise or influence." The jury is also typically instructed: "Undue influence sufficient to invalidate a will is that which substitutes the plans or desires of another for those of the testator. The influence must be such as to control the mind of the testator in the making of his will, to overcome his power of resistance, and to result in his making a distribution of his property which he would not have made if he were left to act freely and according to his own plans and desires." See Ohio Jury Instructions, sec. 363.05.

28. 236 N.W. 705 (Minn. 1931).

29. See generally, D. J. Sharpe, "Medication as a Threat to Testamentary Capacity," *No. Car. L. Rev.* 35 (1957): 380.

30. New York: William Morrow, 1993. See also B. Goldsmith, *Johnson v. Johnson* (New York: Knopf, 1987).

31. See, e.g., Jahn v. Harmes, 249 N.W.2d 638 (Iowa 1977); Flemming v. Hall, 374 Mich. 278, 132 N.W.2d 35(1965); Totorean v. Samuels, 216 N.W.2d 429 (Mich. App. 1974); In re Estate of Garfield, 222 N.W.2d 369 (Neb. 1974).

32. Dr. Ben Bursten reports a case of the readiness of a testator to build a large and grotesque house and to pay outrageous bills when his newfound friends presented them to him. That attested to the testator's vulnerability, but even if the testator was vulnerable, the person left out of the will and challenging it on the ground of undue influence must prove the beneficiary actually exerted the undue influence. B. Bursten, *Psychiatry on Trial: Fact and Fantasy in the Courtroom* (Jefferson, N.C.: McFarland, 2001), p. 79. The elements of undue influence usually include a testator subject to or susceptible of undue influence, and opportunity to exercise undue influence, a disposition to exert undue influence, and a result appearing to be the effect of undue influence. Matter of Estate of Hogan, 708 P.2d 1018 (Mont. 1985). See J. D. Lewis, "Will Contests," *Arizona Attorney*, Mar. 21, 1990; D. J. Sprehe & A. L. Kerr, "Use of Legal Terms in Will Contests: Implications for Psychiatrists," *Bull. Am. Acad. Psychiatry & Law* 24 (1996): 255. See also L. A. Frolik, "The Strange Interplay of Testamentary Capacity and the Doctrine of Undue Influence: Are We Protecting Older Testators or Overriding Individual Preferences?" *Int'l. J. Law & Psychiatry* 24 (2001): 253. In a study of cults, Dr. Margaret Singer identifies six factors that make up the components for a person to exercise undue influence over another: isolation, creating a siege mentality, dependency, sense of powerlessness, sense of fear and vulnerability, and keeping the person in ignorance by manipulating the environment. M. T. Singer, "Undue Influence and Written Documents: Psychological Aspects," *Cultic Studies J.* 10 (1993): 19. Evidence that the party benefiting by a will made no attempt to keep others from seeing and conversing with the testator tends to show the absence of a disposition to exert undue influence. In re Estate of Ellis, 9 Neb. App. 598, 616 N.W.2d 59 (2000).

33. In re Estate of Madsen, 535 N.W.2d 888 (S.D. 1995).

34. Estate of Goddard, 164 Cal. App.2d 152, 330 P.2d 399 (1958); In re Cummins Estate, 271 Mich. 215, 259 N.W. 894 (1935); Higbee Will, 365 Pa. 381, 75 A.2d 599 (1950). One may have the mental capacity to sign a will but not the capacity to sign a contractual agreement. Thus, in Acacia v. Jago, 280 Mich. 360 (1937), the appointment of a guardian voided a contract signed by the ward for assignment of insurance proceeds.

Under the Estates and Protected Individuals Code (EPIC) adopted by the various states to provide uniformity on the law of wills, the minimum age requirement to execute a will is eighteen years of age. See J. Dukeminier & S. M. Johanson (eds.), *Wills, Trusts, and Estates* (Boston: Little, Brown, 5th ed. 1995). In a case years ago, In re Estate of Teel, 483 P.2d 603 (Ariz. App. 1971), the decedent was approximately fifty-four years of age when he executed his will, but he was developmentally disabled and possessed the mental capacity of a ten- to twelve-year-old. The court upheld the will, stating that the age requirement was to be interpreted in chronological/physical sense.

35. See N. Roth, *The Psychiatry of Writing a Will* (Springfield, Ill.: Thomas, 1989). An old Jewish tradition, fallen into disuse, is the *ethical will,* used to convey feelings to close ones. One illustration: "There's nothing more precious than time—use it wisely." Another: "For the sake of a father who took a wrong turn, take the right one." See R. Slovenko, "Deathbed Declarations," *J. Psychiatry & Law* 24 (1966): 469. For compilations of vindictive wills, see F. Thomas, *Last Will and Testament* (New York: St. Martin's, 1972); R. S. Menchin, *The Last Caprice* (New York: Simon & Schuster, 1963). On humorous wills, see F. L. Golden, *Laughter Is Legal* (New York: Pocket Books, 193); De Morgan, "Wills—Quaint, Curious and Otherwise," *Green Bag* 13 (1901): 567; J. M. Gest, "Some Jolly Testators," *Temp L.Q.* 8 (1934): 297; E. M. Million, "Humor in or of Wills," *Vand. L. Rev.* 11 (1958): 737.

36. S. Kanfer, *Groucho: The Life and Times of Julius Henry Marx* (New York: Knopf, 2000).

37. W. C. Fields's animosity toward small children and dogs is well known, as is his warning, "Never give a sucker an even break." He often played the loving (though crooked) guardian of some young person. S. Klawans, "The Enduring Charm of Buoyant Corruption," *New York Times,* Jan. 6, 2000, p. AR-28. For a discussion of his will, see H. E. Nass, *Wills of the Rich and Famous* (New York: Warner Books, 1991). The woman who stood by Fields for the final fifteen years of his life, and figured prominently in his will, was Carlotta Monti, who was at his bedside on Christmas Eve, 1946, as he fought a losing battle to retain consciousness. The battle over Fields's money was fought in the courts for four years. Under California's

community property laws, Fields's estranged wife claimed half of everything. In the end she settled for $65,000. Another of Fields's last wishes was ignored. Though he joked that he loathed children, he requested in his will the establishment of a "W. C. Fields College for orphan white boys and girls" and stipulated that "no religion of any sort is to be preached." Between the court squabbles and lawyers' fees, nothing ever came of the nondenominational, if racist, orphanage. C. Panati, *Browser's Book of Endings* (New York: Penguin, 1999), pp. 68–69.

38. R. Cohen, "Heir Unapparent," *New York Times Magazine*, Dec. 12, 1999, p. 58. The estate of another famous comedian—Groucho Marx—was embroiled in controversy over testamentary capacity. See S. Kanfer, *Groucho: The Life and Times of Julius Henry Marx* (New York: Knopf, 2000).

39. Before drafting a will, a lawyer does not have a duty to investigate the mental capacity of a client though he may appear rather bizarre. In Gonsalves v. Superior Court, 19 Cal. App.4th 1366, 24 Cal. Rptr.2d (1993), the lawyer-drafter was sued by the disinherited heir, charging that the lawyer should have known of the testator's alleged incompetence. The court held that a lawyer is not required to investigate the client's condition and may rely on his own judgment regarding capacity or lack thereof.

40. Likewise, in the case of life insurance, where policies usually include a suicide clause exempting payment, the clause is generally enforced only when there is clear and convincing evidence that the insured contemplated suicide when he took out the policy, a circumstance amounting to fraud. Workers' compensation laws also exclude payments to beneficiaries in the case of suicide, but benefits are usually awarded notwithstanding such evidence. Police reports tend to list a suicide as an accident or as a death by natural causes.

41. L. Green, "Proof of Mental Incompetency and The Unexpected Major Premise," *Yale L.J.* 53 (1944): 271.

42. E. M. Epstein, "Testamentary Capacity, Reasonableness and Family Maintenance: A Proposal for Meaningful Reform," *Temple L.Q.* 35 (1962): 231.

43. In Matter of Arnold's Estate, 16 Cal.2d 573, 107 P.2d 25 (1940), the evidence of psychosis was fairly extensive (loss of memory as a result of chronic alcoholism); but the case reflects the general hesitancy of courts to overturn a testamentary disposition where the testator has provided for the natural objects of his bounty. In Matter of Gilbert's Estate, 148 Cal. App.2d 761, 307 P.2d 395 (1957), the testator's will, which left her entire estate to educational institutions and charities, was contested by her cousins. (Charitable and religious organizations strive to develop good will—and good wills!) The court, in holding that the decedent was competent, minimized the extent and weight given to testimony that she was "very frantic looking, very wild looking." In cases where the disinherited contestant is a member of the testator's more immediate family, however, the courts are more impressed with this type of evidence. Thus, in Matter of Kirk's Estate, 161 Cal. App.2d 145, 326 P.2d 151 (1958), where the testator's two disinherited sons contested a will that left the major part of the estate to the testator's brother, sister-in-law, and grandchildren, the court held that the testator's psychosis with cerebral arteriosclerosis was such as to evidence clearly a lack of testamentary capacity. In Matter of Bourguin's Estate, 161 Cal. App.2d 289, 326 P.2d 604 (1958), the testator left the bulk of her estate to a Christian Science rest home in which she died. In so doing, she neglected her son. The court relied heavily on evidence of physical debility in finding a lack of testamentary capacity. The court in Matter of Alexander's Estate, 111 Cal. App. 1, 295 Pac. 53 (1931), is unusually candid in alluding to the fact that the reasonableness or unreasonableness of the provisions of the will is used in determining the question of testamentary capacity. The court in Hutchins v. Barlow, 221 Miss. 811, 74 So.2d 870 (1954), said that where it appears that a will is inconsistent with the duties of the testator in regard to his family, the proponents of the will must give a reasonable explanation thereof. See P. Ariès, "Wills and Tombs—The Rise of Modern Family Feeling," *New Society*, Sept. 25, 1969, p. 473.

44. H. J. Wolff, *Roman Law: An Historical Introduction* (Norman: University of Oklahoma Press, 1951), p. 147.

45. Ibid., p. 59.

46. E. Durfee, "Revocation of Wills by Subsequent Change in the Condition or Circumstances of the Testator," *Mich. L. Rev.* 40 (1942): 406; W. A. Graunke & J. H. Beuscher, "The Doctrine of Implied Revocation of Wills by Reason of Change in Domestic Relations of the

Testator," *Wis. L. Rev.* 5 (1930): 387; T. H. Leath, "Lapse, Abatement and Redemption," *No. Car. L. Rev.* 39 (1961): 313.

47. Stevenson's Executor v. Stevenson, 33 Pa. 469 (1859). Whether a will is unnatural depends upon the circumstances of each case. In re Estate of Velk, 192 N.W.2d 844 (Wis. 1972). It has been more acceptable for a wife to bequeath nothing to her husband than vice versa. One wife had a provision in her will, which was probated, that provided: "Whereas I have been a faithful, dutiful, and loving wife to my husband, and whereas he reciprocated my tender affections for him with acts of cruelty and indifference, and whereas he has failed to support and maintain me in that station of life which would have been possible and proper for him, I hereby limit my bequest to him to one dollar." Loetsch v. N.Y. City Omnibus Corp., 291 N.Y. 308, 32 N.E.2d 448 (1943).

48. E. M Epstein, supra note 42.